D0022503

NEURAL NETWORKS

A Comprehensive Foundation

Simon Haykin
McMaster University
Hamilton, Ontario, Canada

Macmillan College Publishing Company
New York
Maxwell Macmillan Canada
Toronto
Maxwell Macmillan International
New York Oxford Singapore Sydney

Editor: John Griffin
Production Supervisor: Margaret Comaskey
Production Manager: Lynn Pearlman
Cover Designer: Robert Freese
Illustrations: Academy ArtWorks

This book was set in Times Roman and Helvetica by Bi-Comp Inc., and printed and bound by Hamilton Printing Company. The cover was printed by Lehigh Press.

Copyright © 1994 by Macmillan College Publishing Company, Inc.

Printed in the United States of America

All rights reserved. No part of this book may be reproduced or transmitted in any form or by any means, electronic or mechanical, including photocopying, recording, or any information storage and retrieval system, without permission in writing from the publisher.

Macmillan College Publishing Company
866 Third Avenue, New York, New York 10022

Macmillan College Publishing Company is part
of the Maxwell Communication Group of Companies.

Maxwell Macmillan Canada, Inc.
1200 Eglinton Avenue East
Suite 200
Don Mills, Ontario M3C 3N1

Library of Congress Cataloging in Publication Data

Haykin, Simon
Neural networks / Simon Haykin.
p. cm.
Includes bibliographical references and index.
ISBN 0-02-352761-7
1. Neural networks (Computer science) I. Title.
QA76.87.H39 1994
006.3—dc20 93-28092
CIP

Printing: 1 2 3 4 5 6 7 8 Year: 4 5 6 7 8 9 0 1 2 3

To the countless researchers in neural networks
for their original contributions,

the many reviewers for their critical inputs,

my many graduate students for their keen interest,

and

my wife, Nancy, for her tolerance

Preface

Neural Networks, or artificial neural networks to be more precise, represent an emerging technology rooted in many disciplines. They are endowed with some unique attributes: universal approximation (input–output mapping), the ability to learn from and adapt to their environment, and the ability to invoke weak assumptions about the underlying physical phenomena responsible for the generation of the input data. This book, written from an engineering perspective, provides a detailed treatment of neural networks, supported with examples, computer-oriented experiments, and applications. The book is organized into 15 chapters and 4 appendixes.

Chapter 1 presents an overview of what neural networks are, followed by a description of models of a neuron (the basic element of a neural network) and the commonly used architectures of neural networks. Then the issue of knowledge representation inside a neural network is discussed. Historical notes are included to provide a source of motivation and inspiration to the reader.

Chapter 2 is devoted to the learning process that is fundamental to the operation of a neural network. The important learning algorithms (rules) and learning paradigms are delineated. Statistical aspects of the learning process are discussed, and the elements of a learning theory are presented.

Chapters 3 through 5 are devoted to simple forms of neural networks involving a single layer of neurons. Chapter 3 discusses the correlation matrix memory using a single layer of linear neurons. Chapter 4 discusses the elementary perceptron used as a linearly separable pattern classifier. Chapter 5 discusses the least-mean-square (LMS) algorithm involving a single linear neuron. The material presented in these three chapters paves the way for more sophisticated neural networks to follow.

Chapters 6 and 7 describe supervised multilayer feedforward networks. Chapter 6 is devoted to multilayer perceptrons trained with the back-propagation algorithm, which represents the workhorse of neural networks. The virtues and limitations of the back-propagation (BP) algorithm are discussed. Chapter 7 is devoted to radial-basis-function (RBF) networks with particular emphasis on regularization theory. These two approaches to the design of neural networks are complementary in that BP learning provides a global method for the design of a neural network, whereas RBF learning provides a local method.

Chapter 8 is devoted to recurrent networks rooted in statistical physics. In particular, three models are described, namely, the Hopfield network, the Boltzmann machine, and the mean-field-theory learning machine. These networks are radically different from those considered in Chapters 6 and 7 in that they make abundant use of feedback.

Chapters 9 through 11 constitute the next part of the book, devoted to self-organizing machines. The material presented in Chapter 9 focuses on Hebbian learning, with emphasis on principal components analysis. Chapter 10 describes a class of neural networks called self-organizing feature maps, which rely on the use of competitive learning. Chapter

11 is rooted in information theory, emphasizing the principle of maximum information preservation as a way of attaining self-organization, and related issues.

Chapter 12 describes a particular class of modular networks, involving the use of adaptive experts. The individual networks learn in a supervised way, whereas the expert (overseeing these networks) functions in a competitive mode.

Chapter 13 emphasizes the role of time as an essential dimension of learning. Specifically, we describe three models. The first one represents a natural extension of the multilayer perceptron, replacing the ordinary synaptic weights with finite-duration impulse response (FIR) filters. The second model is a recurrent structure with hidden neurons, which introduces time into the operation of the network by virtue of the built-in feedback. The third model extends the latter model by using a pipelined structure.

Chapter 14 discusses neurodynamics, with the neural network being viewed as a nonlinear dynamical system. The stability problem is given particular attention, with emphasis on the Liapunov function. The Hopfield network is revisited in light of the concepts introduced in this chapter. The Cohen–Grossberg theorem, representing a generalization of the Hopfield network, is discussed. Two other models, the brain-state-in-a-box model and recurrent back-propagation learning, are also discussed in detail.

Chapter 15 is devoted to very-large-scale-integrated (VLSI) circuit implementations of neural networks. VLSI technology has much to commend its use for building neural networks.

The book also includes four appendixes devoted to the pseudoinverse matrix memory, a general tool for a convergence analysis of stochastic approximation algorithms, a brief discussion of statistical thermodynamics, and the Fokker–Planck equation.

Each chapter of the book ends with a list of problems, some of which are of a challenging nature. A Solutions Manual, containing complete solutions to all these problems, can be obtained by writing to the publisher.

The book is written at a level suitable for use in a graduate course on neural networks in engineering, computer science, and physics. It is hoped that researchers in other disciplines such as psychology and the neurosciences will also find the book useful. The book should also appeal to newcomers and professional engineers wishing to learn about neural networks.

Acknowledgments

I am deeply indebted to the many reviewers who have given freely of their time to read through the book, in part or in full. In particular, I am most grateful to Dr. J.A. Anderson, Brown University, Dr. A.G. Barto, University of Massachusetts, Dr. T. Leen, Oregon Graduate School, Dr. F. Palmieri, University of Connecticut, and Dr. J. Shynk, University of California at Santa Barbara, for their critical inputs on many parts of the book. I wish to thank Dr. R. Linsker, IBM Research, Dr. D. Lowe and Dr. S.P. Luttrell, both of the Defence Research Agency, Malvern (UK), Dr. A.T. Russo, Bell Labs, Wippany, Dr. R. Sutton, GTE Laboratories, Dr. T. Sanger, MIT, Dr. E. Wan, Stanford University, Dr. J. Chadam, McMaster University, Dr. T. Luo, McMaster University, Dr. W.J. Freeman, University of California at Berkeley, Dr. J. Alspector, Bell Core, Dr. E. Säckinger, Bell Labs (Holmdell), Dr. D. Hammerstrom, Adaptive Solutions (Oregon), Dr. A. Andreou, The John Hopkins University, Dr. S. Becker, McMaster University, Dr. C. Peterson, University of Lund, Sweden, Dr. R. Jacobs, University of Rochester, Dr. M. Jordan, and Dr. G. Cybenko, Dartmouth College, Dr. J. Principe, University of Florida, Gainsville, and Dr. A. H. Gee, Cambridge University, for their highly valuable inputs on selected chapters of the book. I also had constructive inputs from Dr. V.N. Vapnik, Bell Labs, Dr. B. Mulgrew, University of Edinburgh, Dr. R.J. Williams, Northeastern University, Dr. T.H. Brown, Yale University, Dr. T. Poggio, MIT, Dr. J. Cowan, University of Chicago, Dr. S. Grossberg, Boston University, Dr. C. Mead, Cal Tech, Dr. M. Hirsh, University of California at Berkeley, Dr. J. Atick, Rockefeller University, Dr. S.V.B. Aiyer, IBM, and Dr. F.J. Pineda, The Johns Hopkins University, which are all appreciated.

I am indebted to my colleague Dr. R. Racine, Psychology Department, McMaster University, for critically reading the few parts of the book relating to neuroscience. His sketch of a neuron constituting Fig. 1 of Chapter 1 is deeply appreciated.

I am grateful to my graduate students Paul Yee, Don Hargreaves, Brian Delsey, and Richard Mann (presently at the University of Toronto) for reading the manuscript, in part or in full, and for making many helpful suggestions to improve the book.

I wish to thank S. Becker, B. Delsey, R. Dony, R. Jacobs, and P. Yee for reading the page proofs, and for making suggestions for last-minute improvements.

I am grateful to the following people and organizations for permission to reproduce certain figures in the book:

- R. Mann for Figs. 10.9, 10.12, P10.5, and P10.6
- Mehrdad Hazeghi and Ramesh Bharadwaj for Figs. 10.21 and 10.22
- C. Bachynsky for Figs. 8.7, 8.8, 8.9, and 8.10
- P. Yee for Figs. 6.11, 6.12, 6.13, 6.14, 6.15, 6.16, and 7.7
- E. Wan for Figs. 13.10 and 13.11

- L. Li for Fig. 13.16
- B. Delsey for Fig. 10.16
- C. Deng for Figs. 6.22, 6.23, and 6.24
- Morgan Kaufmann for Figs. 1.21 and 7.10
- The American Association for the Advancement of Science for Fig. 8.1
- *Annual Review of Neuroscience* for Fig. 10.2
- Springer-Verlag, Germany, for Figs. 14.7, 8.14, and 8.16
- John Hopfield for Figs. 8.1 and 14.12
- Pergamon Press Inc. for Figs. 9.10, 9.11, 9.12, and 15.8
- IEEE Publishing Services for Figs. 6.30, 6.31, 6.32, 6.33, 6.34, 6.35, 6.36, 9.5, 10.23, 15.6, and 15.7
- Oxford University Press for Fig. 10.1
- Carfax Publishing Co. for Fig. 8.20
- D.S. Broomhead for Fig. 7.9
- D.J. Amit for Fig. 8.15
- Ralph Linsker for Figs. 9.2 and 9.3
- Geoffrey Hinton for Fig. 13.2
- S.P. Luttrell for Fig. 10.26

I am grateful to Terry Sanger for his kind effort to supply the data needed to reproduce the images of Figs. 9.10 and 9.12.

I wish to thank Elaine Tooke, Peggy Findlay, and Ian Macdonald of the Science and Engineering Library at McMaster University for their kind help in checking the list of references.

I am most grateful to my editor, John Griffin, for his patience, understanding, and encouragement in the course of writing this book. It has been truly a pleasure to work with Margaret Comaskey of Macmillan in the production of the book; I am indebted to her for a meticulous effort.

Last, but by no means least, I am truly indebted to my secretary Lola Brooks, who has worked with me through so many different versions of the book during the last three years, and does it always with a smile and a pleasant sense of humor.

Contents

9 Self-Organizing Systems I: Hebbian Learning **352**

10 Self-Organizing Systems II: Competitive Learning **397**

Abbreviations and Symbols

Abbreviations

ADPCM	adaptive differential pulse-code modulation
ANNA	analog neural network arithmetic and logic
APEX	adaptive principal components extraction
AR	autoregressive
BM	Boltzmann machine
BP	back-propagation
b/s	bit per second
BSB	brain-state-in-a-box
cmm	correlation matrix memory
CMOS	complementary metal-oxide-silicon
CNAPS	connected network of adaptive processors
det	determinant
DSP	digital signal processor
erf	error function
erfc	complimentary error function
exp	exponential
FIR	finite-duration impulse response
GHA	generalized Hebbian algorithm
HMM	hidden Markov model
Hz	hertz
I_{max}	maximum mutual information
Infomax	maximum information preservation
LBG	Linde–Buzo–Gray
MDL	minimum-description length
ML	maximum likelihood
LFSR	linear feedback shift register
LMS	least-mean-square
ln	natural logarithm
log	ordinary logarithm
LVQ	learning vector quantization
max	maximum
MDAC	multiplexing digital-to-analog converter
MFT	mean-field theory
min	minimum
MLP	multilayer perceptron
$O(\cdot)$	order of

OBD	optimal brain damage
OBS	optimal brain surgeon
OCR	optical character recognition
PCA	principal components analysis
pim	pseudoinverse matrix memory
Prob$\{z = y\|\mathbf{x}\}$	probability that $z = y$, given the vector **x**
RBF	radial basis function
RISC	reduced instruction set computer
sgn(x)	signum function of x, equal to $+1$ for $x > 0$ and equal to -1 for $x < 0$
SIMD	single instruction stream–multiple data stream
SNR	signal-to-noise ratio
SOFM	self-organizing feature map
sup	supremum
tanh	hyperbolic tangent
TDNN	time-delay neural network
tr[**R**]	trace of matrix **R**
VC dimension	Vapnik–Chervononkis dimension
VLSI	very-large-scale integration
XOR	exclusive OR

Important Symbols

$\mathbf{a}^T\mathbf{b}$	inner product of vectors **a** and **b**
$\mathbf{a}\mathbf{b}^T$	outer product of vectors **a** and **b**
$\binom{l}{m}$	binomial coefficient
$A \cup B$	union of A and B
b_k	bias applied to neuron k
cos(**a**,**b**)	cosine of the angle between vectors **a** and **b**
E	energy function
E	statistical expectation operator
$\mathscr{E}_{\text{av}}$	average squared error
$\mathscr{E}(n)$	instantaneous value of the sum of squared errors
$\mathscr{E}_{\text{total}}$	total sum of error squares
$f(\mathbf{x},\mathbf{d})$	joint probability density function of vectors **x** and **d**
$f(\mathbf{x})$	probability density function of **x**
$f(\mathbf{d}\|\mathbf{x})$	probability density function of **d**, given **x**
$\mathscr{F}*$	subset (network) with the smallest minimum empirical risk
$\mathbf{H}^{-1}$	inverse of matrix **H**
$H_{P^+\|P^-}$	entropy of the probability distribution P_α^+ relative to the probability distribution P_α^-
i	square root of -1
$\mathbf{I}$	identity matrix
J	mean-square error
k_B	Boltzmann constant
n	discrete time
$p_{\beta\alpha}$	transition probability from state α to state β
P_c	average probability of correct classification

$\mathbf{P}^*$	adjoint of differential operator $\mathbf{P}$
P_e	average probability of error
$P(e\|\mathscr{C})$	conditional probability of error e given that the input is drawn from class $\mathscr{C}$
P_α^+	probability that the visible neurons of a Boltzmann machine are in state α, given that the network is in its clamped condition (i.e., positive phase)
P_α^-	probability that the visible neurons of a Boltzmann machine are in state α, given that the network is in its free-running condition (i.e., negative phase)
$\hat{r}_x(j,k;\, n)$	estimate of autocorrelation function of $x_j(n)$ and $x_k(n)$
$\hat{r}_{dx}(k;\, n)$	estimate of cross-correlation function of $d(n)$ and $x_k(n)$
$\mathbf{R}$	matrix quantity, signified by the use of bold-face uppercase letter
$\mathbf{R}$	correlation matrix of an input vector
$\langle s_j \rangle$	average of state s_j in a ''thermal'' sense
t	continous time
T	temperature
w_o	optimum value of synaptic weight vector
w_{kj}	synaptic weight of synapse j belonging to neuron k
$\mathbf{w}^*$	optimum weight vector
$\hat{x}$	estimate of x, signified by the use of a caret (hat)
$\|x\|$	absolute value (magnitude) of x
x^*	complex conjugate of x, signified by asterisk as superscript
$\mathbf{x}$	vector, signified by the use of boldface lower-case letter
$\\|\mathbf{x}\\|$	Euclidean norm (length) of vector $\mathbf{x}$
$\mathbf{x}^T$	transpose of vector $\mathbf{x}$, signified by the superscript T
z^{-1}	unit-delay operator
Z	partition function
$\delta_j(n)$	local gradient of neuron j at time n
Δw	small change applied to w
∇	gradient operator
∇^2	Laplacian operator
$\nabla_w J$	gradient of J with respect to w
$\nabla \cdot \mathbf{F}$	divergence of vector $\mathbf{F}$
η	learning-rate parameter
θ_k	threshold applied to neuron k (i.e., negative of bias)
λ	regularization parameter
λ_k	kth eigenvalue of a square matrix
$\varphi_k(\cdot)$	nonlinear activation function of neuron k
$\in$	symbol for ''belongs to''
$\cup$	symbol for ''union of''
$\cap$	symbol for ''intersection of''

CHAPTER 1

Introduction

1.1 What Is a Neural Network?

Work on artificial neural networks, commonly referred to as "neural networks," has been motivated right from its inception by the recognition that the brain computes in an entirely different way from the conventional digital computer. The struggle to understand the brain owes much to the pioneering work of Ramón y Cajál (1911), who introduced the idea of *neurons* as structural constituents of the brain. Typically, neurons are five to six orders of magnitude slower than silicon logic gates; events in a silicon chip happen in the nanosecond (10^{-9} s) range, whereas neural events happen in the millisecond (10^{-3} s) range. However, the brain makes up for the relatively slow rate of operation of a neuron by having a truly staggering number of neurons (nerve cells) with massive interconnections between them; it is estimated that there must be on the order of 10 billion neurons in the human cortex, and 60 trillion synapses or connections (Shepherd and Koch, 1990). The net result is that the brain is an enormously efficient structure. Specifically, the *energetic efficiency* of the brain is approximately 10^{-16} joules (J) per operation per second, whereas the corresponding value for the best computers in use *today* is about 10^{-6} joules per operation per second (Faggin, 1991).

The brain is a highly *complex, nonlinear, and parallel computer* (information-processing system). It has the capability of organizing neurons so as to perform certain computations (e.g., pattern recognition, perception, and motor control) many times faster than the fastest digital computer in existence today. Consider, for example, human *vision,* which is an information-processing task (Churchland and Sejnowski, 1992; Levine, 1985; Marr, 1982). It is the function of the visual system to provide a *representation* of the environment around us and, more important, to supply the information we need to *interact* with the environment. To be specific, the brain routinely accomplishes perceptual recognition tasks (e.g., recognizing a familiar face embedded in an unfamiliar scene) in something of the order of 100–200 ms, whereas tasks of much lesser complexity will take days on a huge conventional computer (Churchland, 1986).

For another example, consider the *sonar* of a bat. Sonar is an active echo-location system. In addition to providing information about how far away a target (e.g., a flying insect) is, a bat sonar conveys information about the relative velocity of the target, the size of the target, the size of various features of the target, and the azimuth and elevation of the target (Suga, 1990a, b). The complex neural computations needed to extract all this information from the target echo occur within a brain the size of a plum. Indeed, an echo-locating bat can pursue and capture its target with a facility and success rate that would be the envy of a radar or sonar engineer.

How, then, does a human brain or the brain of a bat do it? At birth, a brain has great structure and the ability to build up its own rules through what we usually refer to as "experience." Indeed, experience is built up over the years, with the most dramatic development (i.e., hard-wiring) of the human brain taking place in the first two years from birth; but the development continues well beyond that stage. During this early stage of development, about 1 million synapses are formed per second.

Synapses are elementary structural and functional units that mediate the interactions between neurons. The most common kind of synapse is a *chemical synapse,* which operates as follows. A presynaptic process liberates a *transmitter* substance that diffuses across the synaptic junction between neurons and then acts on a postsynaptic process. Thus a synapse converts a presynaptic electrical signal into a chemical signal and then back into a postsynaptic electrical signal (Shepherd and Koch, 1990). In electrical terminology, such an element is said to be a *nonreciprocal two-port device.* In traditional descriptions of neural organization, it is assumed that a synapse is a simple connection that can impose *excitation* or *inhibition,* but not both on the receptive neuron.

A developing neuron is synonymous with a plastic brain: *Plasticity* permits the developing nervous system to adapt to its surrounding environment (Churchland and Sejnowski, 1992; Eggermont, 1990). In an adult brain, plasticity may be accounted for by two mechanisms: the creation of new synaptic connections between neurons, and the modification of existing synapses. *Axons,* the transmission lines, and *dendrites,* the receptive zones, constitute two types of cell filaments that are distinguished on morphological grounds; an axon has a smoother surface, fewer branches, and greater length, whereas a dendrite (so called because of its resemblance to a tree) has an irregular surface and more branches (Freeman, 1975). Neurons come in a wide variety of shapes and sizes in different parts of the brain. Figure 1.1 illustrates the shape of a *pyramidal cell,* which is one of the most common types of cortical neurons. Like many other types of neurons, it receives most of its inputs through dendritic spines; see the segment of dendrite in the insert in Fig. 1.1 for detail. The pyramidal cell can receive 10,000 or more synaptic contacts and it can project onto thousands of target cells.

Just as plasticity appears to be essential to the functioning of neurons as information-processing units in the human brain, so it is with neural networks made up of artificial neurons. In its most general form, a *neural network* is a machine that is designed to *model* the way in which the brain performs a particular task or function of interest; the network is usually implemented using electronic components or simulated in software on a digital computer. Our interest in this book is confined largely to an important class of neural networks that perform useful computations through a process of *learning.* To achieve good performance, neural networks employ a massive interconnection of simple computing cells referred to as "neurons" or "processing units." We may thus offer the following definition of a neural network viewed as an adaptive machine[1]:

> *A neural network is a massively parallel distributed processor that has a natural propensity for storing experiential knowledge and making it available for use. It resembles the brain in two respects:*
>
> 1. *Knowledge is acquired by the network through a learning process.*
> 2. *Interneuron connection strengths known as synaptic weights are used to store the knowledge.*

The procedure used to perform the learning process is called a *learning algorithm,* the function of which is to modify the synaptic weights of the network in an orderly fashion so as to attain a desired design objective.

[1] This definition of a neural network is adapted from Aleksander and Morton (1990).

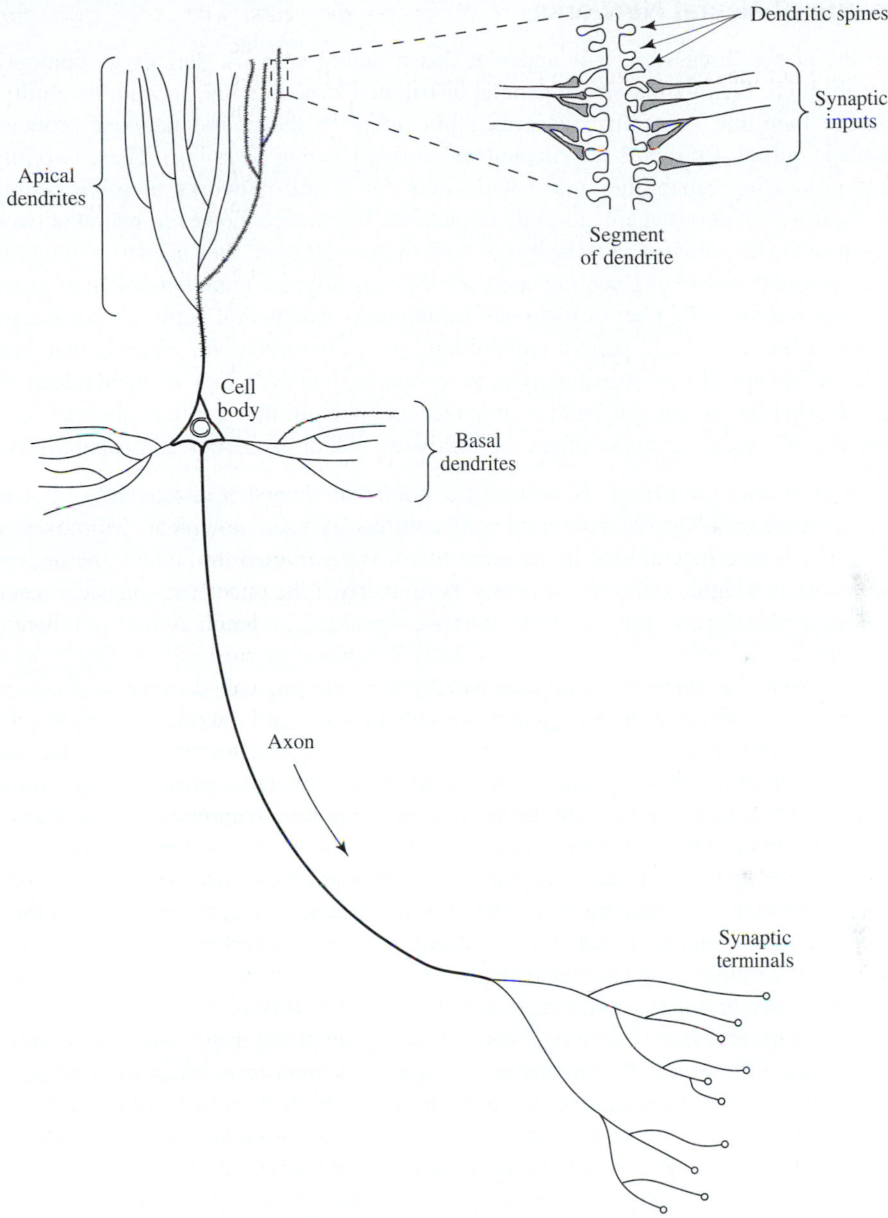

FIGURE 1.1 The pyramidal cell.

The modification of synaptic weights provides the traditional method for the design of neural networks. Such an approach is the closest to linear adaptive filter theory, which is already well established and successfully applied in such diverse fields as communications, control, radar, sonar, seismology, and biomedical engineering (Haykin, 1991; Widrow and Stearns, 1985). However, it is also possible for a neural network to modify its own topology, which is motivated by the fact that neurons in the human brain can die and that new synaptic connections can grow.

Neural networks are also referred to in the literature as *neurocomputers, connectionist networks, parallel distributed processors,* etc. Throughout the book we use the term ''neural networks''; occasionally, the term ''neurocomputer'' or ''connectionist network'' is used.

Benefits of Neural Networks

From the above discussion, it is apparent that a neural network derives its computing power through, first, its massively parallel distributed structure and, second, its ability to learn and therefore generalize; generalization refers to the neural network producing reasonable outputs for inputs not encountered during training (learning). These two information-processing capabilities make it possible for neural networks to solve complex (large-scale) problems that are currently intractable. In practice, however, neural networks cannot provide the solution working by themselves alone. Rather, they need to be integrated into a consistent system engineering approach. Specifically, a complex problem of interest is *decomposed* into a number of relatively simple tasks, and neural networks are assigned a subset of the tasks (e.g., pattern recognition, associative memory, control) that *match* their inherent capabilities. It is important to recognize, however, that we have a long way to go (if ever) before we can build a computer architecture that mimics a human brain.

The use of neural networks offers the following useful properties and capabilities:

1. *Nonlinearity.* A neuron is basically a nonlinear device. Consequently, a neural network, made up of an interconnection of neurons, is itself nonlinear. Moreover, the nonlinearity is of a special kind in the sense that it is distributed throughout the network. Nonlinearity is a highly important property, particularly if the underlying physical mechanism responsible for the generation of an input signal (e.g., speech signal) is inherently nonlinear.

2. *Input–Output Mapping.* A popular paradigm of learning called *supervised learning* involves the modification of the synaptic weights of a neural network by applying a set of labeled *training samples* or *task examples.* Each example consists of a unique *input signal* and the corresponding *desired response.* The network is presented an example picked at random from the set, and the synaptic weights (free parameters) of the network are modified so as to minimize the difference between the desired response and the actual response of the network produced by the input signal in accordance with an appropriate statistical criterion. The training of the network is repeated for many examples in the set until the network reaches a steady state, where there are no further significant changes in the synaptic weights; the previously applied training examples may be reapplied during the training session but in a different order. Thus the network learns from the examples by constructing an *input–output mapping* for the problem at hand. Such an approach brings to mind the study of *nonparametric statistical inference* which is a branch of statistics dealing with model-free estimation, or, from a biological viewpoint, *tabula rasa* learning (Geman et al., 1992). Consider, for example, a *pattern classification* task, where the requirement is to assign an input signal representing a physical object or event to one of several prespecified categories (classes). In a nonparametric approach to this problem, the requirement is to "estimate" arbitrary decision boundaries in the input signal space for the pattern-classification task using a set of examples, and to do so *without* invoking a probabilistic distribution model. A similar point of view is implicit in the supervised learning paradigm, which suggests a close analogy between the input–output mapping performed by a neural network and nonparametric statistical inference.

3. *Adaptivity.* Neural networks have a built-in capability to *adapt* their synaptic weights to changes in the surrounding environment. In particular, a neural network trained to operate in a specific environment can be easily *retrained* to deal with minor changes in the operating environmental conditions. Moreover, when it is operating in a *nonstationary* environment (i.e., one whose statistics change with time), a neural network can be designed to change its synaptic weights in real time. The natural architecture of a neural network for pattern classification, signal processing, and control applications, coupled with the adaptive capability of the network, make it an ideal tool for use in adaptive pattern classification, adaptive signal processing, and adaptive control. As a general rule, it may be said that the more adaptive we make a system in a properly designed fashion, assuming the adaptive system is stable, the more robust its performance will likely be when the system is required to operate in a nonstationary environment. It should be emphasized, however, that adaptivity does not always lead to robustness; indeed, it may do the very opposite. For example, an adaptive system with short time constants may change rapidly and therefore tend to respond to spurious disturbances, causing a drastic degradation in system performance. To realize the full benefits of adaptivity, the principal time constants of the system should be long enough for the system to ignore spurious disturbances and yet short enough to respond to meaningful changes in the environment; the problem described here is referred to as the *stability–plasticity dilema* (Grossberg, 1988). Adaptivity (or ''in situ'' training as it is sometimes referred to) is an open research topic.

4. *Evidential Response.* In the context of pattern classification, a neural network can be designed to provide information not only about which particular pattern to *select,* but also about the *confidence* in the decision made. This latter information may be used to reject ambiguous patterns, should they arise, and thereby improve the classification performance of the network.

5. *Contextual Information.* Knowledge is represented by the very structure and activation state of a neural network. Every neuron in the network is potentially affected by the global activity of all other neurons in the network. Consequently, contextual information is dealt with naturally by a neural network.

6. *Fault Tolerance.* A neural network, implemented in hardware form, has the potential to be inherently *fault tolerant* in the sense that its performance is degraded gracefully under adverse operating conditions (Bolt, 1992). For example, if a neuron or its connecting links are damaged, recall of a stored pattern is impaired in quality. However, owing to the distributed nature of information in the network, the damage has to be extensive before the overall response of the network is degraded seriously. Thus, in principle, a neural network exhibits a graceful degradation in performance rather than catastrophic failure.

7. *VLSI Implementability.* The massively parallel nature of a neural network makes it potentially fast for the computation of certain tasks. This same feature makes a neural network ideally suited for implementation using *very-large-scale-integrated* (VLSI) technology. The particular virtue of VLSI is that it provides a means of capturing truly complex behavior in a highly hierarchical fashion (Mead and Conway, 1980), which makes it possible to use a neural network as a tool for real-time applications involving pattern recognition, signal processing, and control.

8. *Uniformity of Analysis and Design.* Basically, neural networks enjoy *universality* as information processors. We say this in the sense that the same notation is used in all the domains involving the application of neural networks. This feature manifests itself in different ways:

- Neurons, in one form or another, represent an ingredient *common* to all neural networks.
- This commonality makes it possible to *share* theories and learning algorithms in different applications of neural networks.
- Modular networks can be built through a *seamless integration of modules.*

9. *Neurobiological Analogy.* The design of a neural network is motivated by analogy with the brain, which is a living proof that fault-tolerant parallel processing is not only physically possible but also fast and powerful. Neurobiologists look to (artificial) neural networks as a research tool for the interpretation of neurobiological phenomena. For example, neural networks have been used to provide insight on the development of premotor circuits in the oculomotor system (responsible for eye movements) and the manner in which they process signals (Robinson, 1992). On the other hand, engineers look to neurobiology for new ideas to solve problems more complex than those based on conventional hard-wired design techniques. Here, for example, we may mention the development of a model sonar receiver based on the bat (Simmons et al., 1992). The bat-inspired model consists of three stages: (1) a front end that mimics the inner ear of the bat in order to encode waveforms; (2) a subsystem of delay lines that computes echo delays; and (3) a subsystem that computes the spectrum of echoes, which is in turn used to estimate the time separation of echoes from multiple target glints. The motivation is to develop a new sonar receiver that is superior to one designed by conventional methods. The neurobiological analogy is also useful in another important way: It provides a hope and belief (and, to a certain extent, an existence proof) that physical understanding of neurobiological structures could indeed influence the art of electronics and thus VLSI (Andreou, 1992).

With inspiration from neurobiological analogy in mind, it seems appropriate that we take a brief look at the structural levels of organization in the brain, which we do in the next section.

1.2 Structural Levels of Organization in the Brain

The human nervous system may be viewed as a three-stage system, as depicted in the block diagram of Fig. 1.2 (Arbib, 1987). Central to the system is the *brain,* represented by the *neural (nerve) net* in Fig. 1.2, which continually receives information, perceives it, and makes appropriate decisions. Two sets of arrows are shown in Fig. 1.2. Those pointing from left to right indicate the *forward* transmission of information-bearing signals through the system. On the other hand, the arrows pointing from right to left signify the presence of *feedback* in the system. The *receptors* in Fig. 1.2 convert stimuli from the human body or the external environment into electrical impulses that convey information to the neural net (brain). The *effectors,* on the other hand, convert electrical impulses generated by the neural net into discernible responses as system outputs.

In the brain there are both small-scale and large-scale anatomical organizations, and different functions take place at lower and higher levels. Figure 1.3 shows a hierarchy of interwoven levels of organization that has emerged from the extensive work done on the analysis of local regions in the brain (Churchland and Sejnowski, 1992; Shepherd and Koch, 1990). Proceeding upward from *synapses* that represent the most fundamental level and that depend on molecules and ions for their action, we have neural microcircuits, dendritic trees, and then neurons. A *neural microcircuit* refers to an assembly of synapses organized into patterns of connectivity so as to produce a functional operation of interest. A neural microcircuit may be likened to a silicon chip made up of an assembly of transistors. The smallest size of microcircuits is measured in micrometers (μm), and their fastest speed of operation is measured in milliseconds. The neural microcircuits are grouped to form *dendritic subunits* within the *dendritic trees* of individual neurons. The whole *neuron,* about 100 μm in size, contains several dendritic subunits. At the next level of complexity, we have *local circuits* (about 1 mm in size) made up of neurons with similar

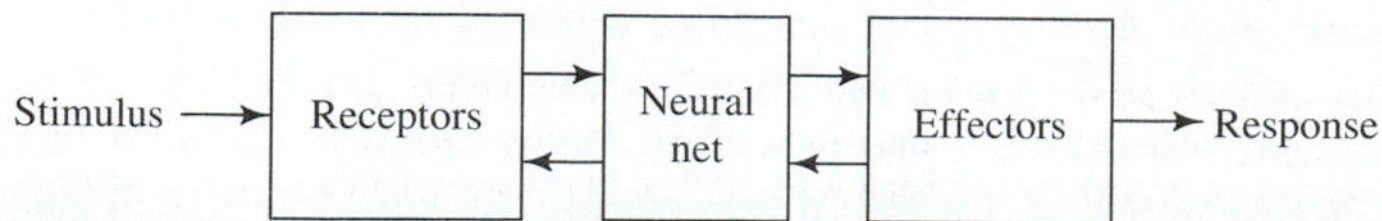

FIGURE 1.2 Block diagram representation of nervous system.

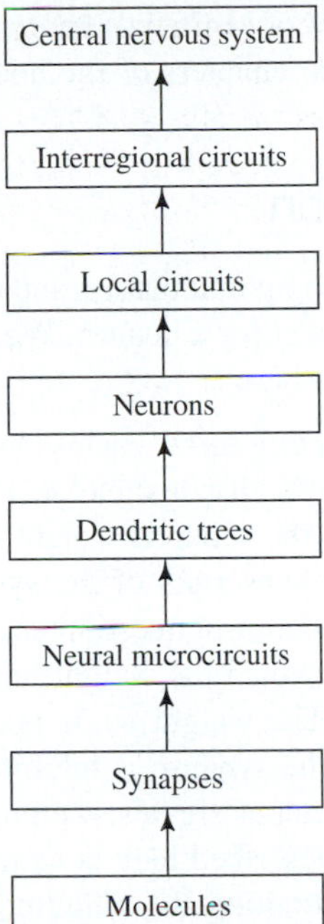

FIGURE 1.3 Structural organization of levels in the brain.

or different properties; these neural assemblies perform operations characteristic of a localized region in the brain. This is followed by *interregional circuits* made up of pathways, columns, and topographic maps, which involve multiple regions located in different parts of the brain. *Topographic maps* are organized to respond to incoming sensory information. These maps are often arranged in sheets, as in the superior colliculus, where the visual, auditory, and somatosensory maps are stacked in adjacent layers in such a way that stimuli from corresponding points in space lie above each other. Finally, the topographic maps, and other interregional circuits mediate specific types of behavior in the *central nervous system.*

It is important to recognize that the structural levels of organization described herein are a unique characteristic of the brain. They are nowhere to be found in a digital computer, and we are nowhere close to realizing them with artificial neural networks. Nevertheless, we are inching our way toward a hierarchy of computational levels similar to that described in Fig. 1.3. The artificial neurons we use to build our neural networks are truly primitive in comparison to those found in the brain. The neural networks we are presently able to design are just as primitive compared to the local circuits and the interregional circuits in the brain. What is really satisfying, however, is the remarkable progress that we have made on so many fronts during the past 10 years. With the neurobiological analogy as the source of inspiration, and the wealth of theoretical and technological tools that we are bringing together, it is for certain that in another 10 years our understanding of artificial neural networks will be much more sophisticated than it is today.

Our primary interest in this book is confined to the study of artificial neural networks from an engineering perspective,[2] to which we refer simply as neural networks. We begin

[2] For a complementary perspective on neural networks with emphasis on neural modeling, cognition, and neurophysiological considerations, see Anderson (1994). For a highly readable account of the computational aspects of the brain, see Churchland and Sejnowski (1992). For more detailed descriptions of neural mechanisms and the human brain, see Kandel and Schwartz (1991), Shepherd (1990a, b), Koch and Segev (1989), Kuffler et al. (1984), and Freeman (1975).

the study by describing the models of (artificial) neurons that form the basis of the neural networks considered in subsequent chapters of the book.

1.3 Models of a Neuron

A *neuron* is an information-processing unit that is fundamental to the operation of a neural network. Figure 1.4 shows the *model* for a neuron. We may identify three basic elements of the neuron model, as described here:

1. A set of *synapses* or *connecting links,* each of which is characterized by a *weight* or *strength* of its own. Specifically, a signal x_j at the input of synapse j connected to neuron k is multiplied by the synaptic weight w_{kj}. It is important to make a note of the manner in which the subscripts of the synaptic weight w_{kj} are written. The first subscript refers to the neuron in question and the second subscript refers to the input end of the synapse to which the weight refers; the reverse of this notation is also used in the literature. The weight w_{kj} is positive if the associated synapse is excitatory; it is negative if the synapse is inhibitory.
2. An *adder* for summing the input signals, weighted by the respective synapses of the neuron; the operations described here constitute a *linear combiner.*
3. An *activation function* for limiting the amplitude of the output of a neuron. The activation function is also referred to in the literature as a *squashing function* in that it squashes (limits) the permissible amplitude range of the output signal to some finite value. Typically, the normalized amplitude range of the output of a neuron is written as the closed unit interval [0,1] or alternatively [−1,1].

The model of a neuron shown in Fig. 1.4 also includes an externally applied *threshold* θ_k that has the effect of lowering the net input of the activation function. On the other hand, the net input of the activation function may be increased by employing a *bias* term rather than a threshold; the bias is the negative of the threshold.

In mathematical terms, we may describe a neuron k by writing the following pair of equations:

$$u_k = \sum_{j=1}^{p} w_{kj} x_j \tag{1.1}$$

and

$$y_k = \varphi(u_k - \theta_k) \tag{1.2}$$

where $x_1, x_2, \ldots, x_p$ are the input signals; $w_{k1}, w_{k2}, \ldots, w_{kp}$ are the synaptic weights of

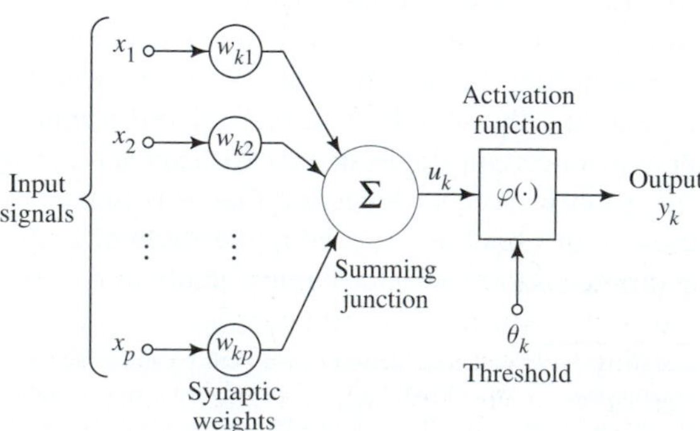

FIGURE 1.4 Nonlinear model of a neuron.

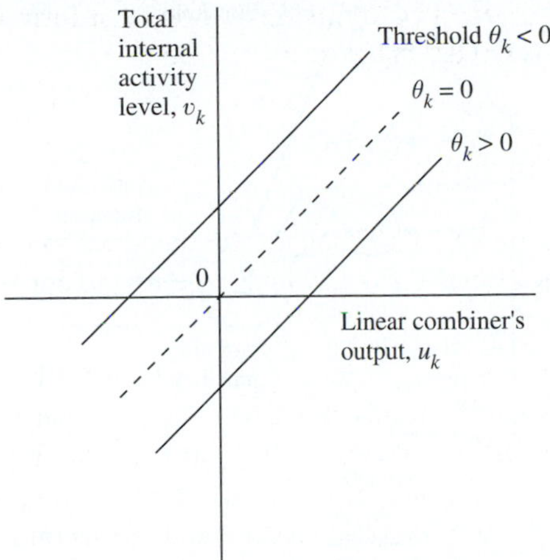

FIGURE 1.5 Affine transformation produced by the presence of a threshold.

neuron k; u_k is the *linear combiner output;* θ_k is the *threshold;* $\varphi(\cdot)$ is the *activation function;* and y_k is the output signal of the neuron. The use of threshold θ_k has the effect of applying an *affine transformation* to the output u_k of the linear combiner in the model of Fig. 1.4, as shown by

$$v_k = u_k - \theta_k \tag{1.3}$$

In particular, depending on whether the threshold θ_k is positive or negative, the relationship between the effective internal *activity level* or *activation potential* v_k of neuron k and the linear combiner output u_k is modified in the manner illustrated in Fig. 1.5. Note that as a result of this affine transformation, the graph of v_k versus u_k no longer passes through the origin.

The threshold θ_k is an external parameter of artificial neuron k. We may account for its presence as in Eq. (1.2). Equivalently, we may formulate the combination of Eqs. (1.1) and (1.2) as follows:

$$v_k = \sum_{j=0}^{p} w_{kj} x_j \tag{1.4}$$

and

$$y_k = \varphi(v_k) \tag{1.5}$$

In Eq. (1.4) we have added a new synapse, whose input is

$$x_0 = -1 \tag{1.6}$$

and whose weight is

$$w_{k0} = \theta_k \tag{1.7}$$

We may therefore reformulate the model of neuron k as in Fig. 1.6a. In this figure, the effect of the threshold is represented by doing two things: (1) adding a new input signal fixed at -1, and (2) adding a new synaptic weight equal to the threshold θ_k. Alternatively, we may model the neuron as in Fig. 1.6b, where the combination of fixed input $x_0 = +1$ and weight $w_{k0} = b_k$ accounts for the *bias* b_k. Although the models of Figs. 1.4 and 1.6 are different in appearance, they are mathematically equivalent.

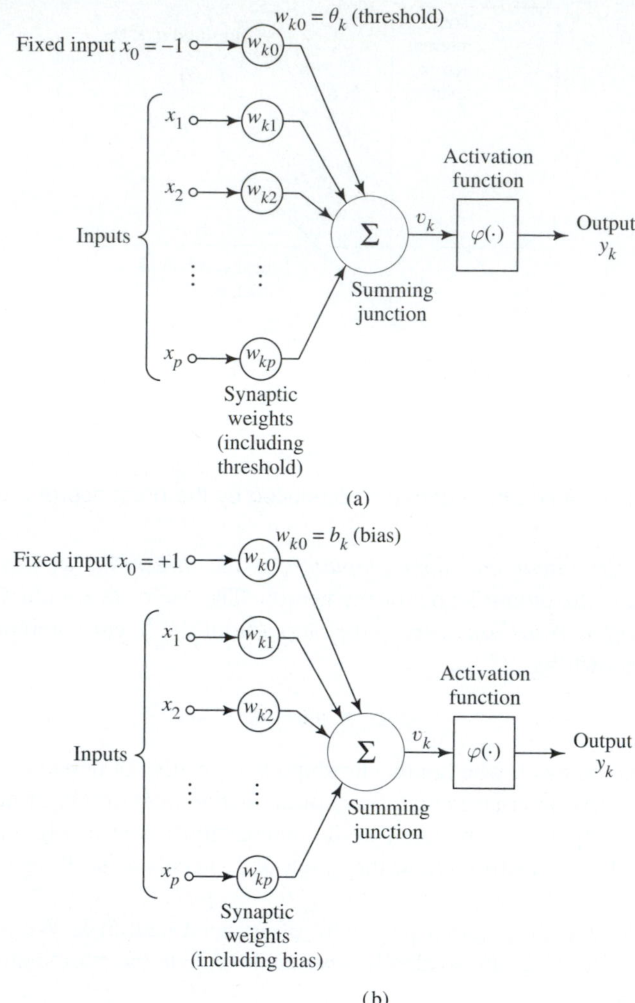

FIGURE 1.6 Two other nonlinear models of a neuron.

Types of Activation Function

The activation function, denoted by $\varphi(\cdot)$, defines the output of a neuron in terms of the activity level at its input. We may identify three basic types of activation functions:

1. *Threshold Function.* For this type of activation function, described in Fig. 1.7a, we have

$$\varphi(v) = \begin{cases} 1 & \text{if } v \geq 0 \\ 0 & \text{if } v < 0 \end{cases} \tag{1.8}$$

Correspondingly, the output of neuron k employing such a threshold function is expressed as

$$y_k = \begin{cases} 1 & \text{if } v_k \geq 0 \\ 0 & \text{if } v_k < 0 \end{cases} \tag{1.9}$$

where v_k is the internal activity level of the neuron; that is,

$$v_k = \sum_{j=1}^{p} w_{kj} x_j - \theta_k \tag{1.10}$$

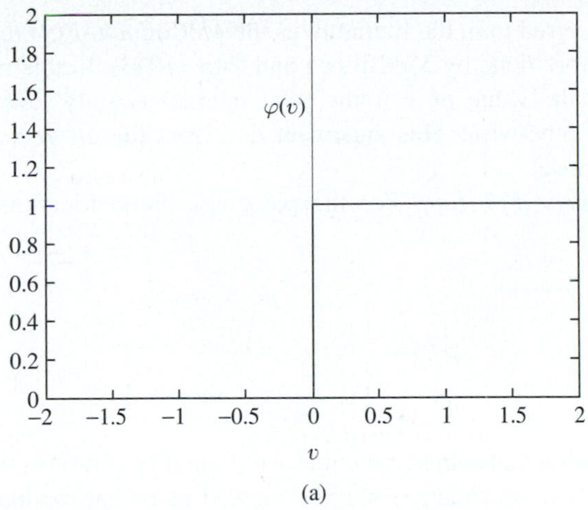

(a)

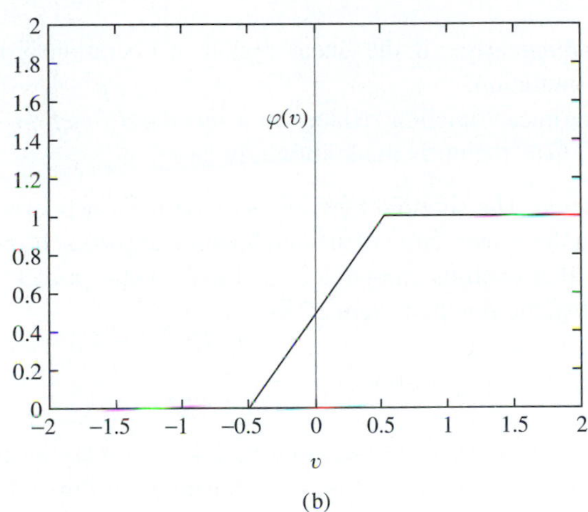

(b)

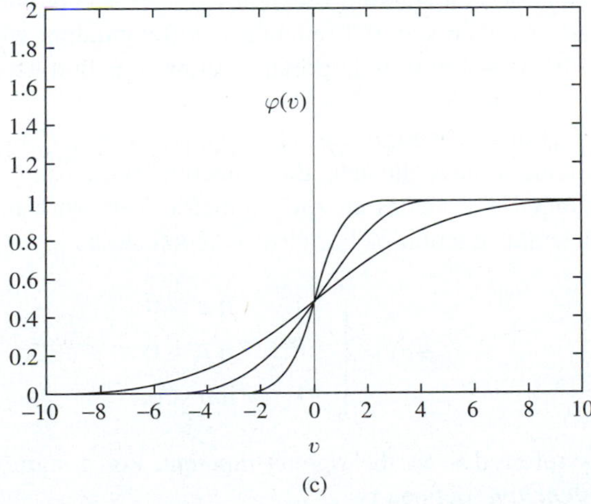

(c)

FIGURE 1.7 (a) Threshold function. (b) Piecewise-linear function. (c) Sigmoid function.

Such a neuron is referred to in the literature as the *McCulloch–Pitts model,* in recognition of the pioneering work done by McCulloch and Pitts (1943). In this model, the output of a neuron takes on the value of 1 if the total internal activity level of that neuron is nonnegative and 0 otherwise. This statement describes the *all-or-none property* of the McCulloch–Pitts model.

2. *Piecewise-Linear Function.* For the piecewise-linear function, described in Fig. 1.7b, we have

$$\varphi(v) = \begin{cases} 1, & v \geq \frac{1}{2} \\ v, & -\frac{1}{2} > v > -\frac{1}{2} \\ 0, & v \leq -\frac{1}{2} \end{cases} \tag{1.11}$$

where the amplification factor inside the linear region of operation is assumed to be unity. This form of an activation function may be viewed as an *approximation* to a nonlinear amplifier. The following two situations may be viewed as special forms of the piecewise-linear function:

1. A *linear combiner* arises if the linear region of operation is maintained without running into saturation.
2. The piecewise-linear function reduces to a *threshold function* if the amplification factor of the linear region is made infinitely large.

3. *Sigmoid Function.* The sigmoid function is by far the most common form of activation function used in the construction of artificial neural networks. It is defined as a strictly increasing function that exhibits smoothness and asymptotic properties. An example of the sigmoid is the *logistic function,* defined by

$$\varphi(v) = \frac{1}{1 + \exp(-av)} \tag{1.12}$$

where a is the *slope parameter* of the sigmoid function. By varying the parameter a, we obtain sigmoid functions of different slopes, as illustrated in Fig. 1.7c. In fact, the slope at the origin equals $a/4$. In the limit, as the slope parameter approaches infinity, the sigmoid function becomes simply a threshold function. Whereas a threshold function assumes the value of 0 or 1, a sigmoid function assumes a continuous range of values from 0 to 1. Note also that the sigmoid function is differentiable, whereas the threshold function is not. (Differentiability is an important feature of neural network theory, as will be described later in Chapter 6.)

The activation functions defined in Eqs. (1.8), (1.11), and (1.12) range from 0 to $+1$. It is sometimes desirable to have the activation function range from -1 to $+1$, in which case the activation function assumes an antisymmetric form with respect to the origin. Specifically, the threshold function of Eq. (1.8) is redefined as

$$\varphi(v) = \begin{cases} 1 & \text{if } v > 0 \\ 0 & \text{if } v = 0 \\ -1 & \text{if } v < 0 \end{cases} \tag{1.13}$$

which is commonly referred to as the *signum function.* For a sigmoid we may use the *hyperbolic tangent function,* defined by

$$\varphi(v) = \tanh\left(\frac{v}{2}\right) = \frac{1 - \exp(-v)}{1 + \exp(-v)} \tag{1.14}$$

Allowing an activation function of the sigmoid type to assume negative values as prescribed by Eq. (1.14) has analytic benefits (see Chapter 6). Moreover, it has neurophysiological evidence of an experimental nature (Eekman and Freeman, 1986), though rarely with the perfect antisymmetry about the origin that characterizes the hyperbolic tangent function.

1.4 Neural Networks Viewed as Directed Graphs

The *block diagram* of Fig. 1.4 or that of Fig. 1.6a provides a functional description of the various elements that constitute the model of an artificial neuron. We may simplify the appearance of the model by using the idea of signal-flow graphs without sacrificing any of the functional details of the model. Signal-flow graphs with a well-defined set of rules were originally developed by Mason (1953, 1956) for linear networks. The presence of nonlinearity in the model of a neuron, however, limits the scope of their application to neural networks. Nevertheless, signal-flow graphs do provide a neat method for the portrayal of the flow of signals in a neural network, which we pursue in this section.

A *signal-flow graph* is a network of directed *links* (*branches*) that are interconnected at certain points called *nodes.* A typical node j has an associated *node signal* x_j. A typical directed link originates at node j and terminates on node k; it has an associated *transfer function* or *transmittance* that specifies the manner in which the signal y_k at node k depends on the signal x_j at node j. The flow of signals in the various parts of the graph is dictated by three basic rules:

RULE 1. A signal flows along a link only in the direction defined by the arrow on the link.

Two different types of links may be distinguished:

(a) *Synaptic links,* governed by a *linear* input–output relation. Specifically, the node signal x_j is multiplied by the synaptic weight w_{kj} to produce the node signal y_k, as illustrated in Fig. 1.8a.

(b) *Activation links,* governed in general by a *nonlinear* input–output relation. This form of relationship is illustrated in Fig. 1.8b, where $\varphi(\cdot)$ is the nonlinear activation function.

RULE 2. A node signal equals the algebraic sum of all signals entering the pertinent node via the incoming links.

This second rule is illustrated in Fig. 1.8c for the case of *synaptic convergence* or *fan-in.*

RULE 3. The signal at a node is transmitted to each outgoing link originating from that node, with the transmission being entirely independent of the transfer functions of the outgoing links.

This third rule is illustrated in Fig. 1.8d for the case of *synaptic divergence* or *fan-out.*

For example, using these rules we may construct the signal-flow graph of Fig. 1.9 as the model of a neuron, corresponding to the block diagram of Fig. 1.6a. The representation shown in Fig. 1.9 is clearly simpler in appearance than that of Fig. 1.6a, yet it contains all the functional details depicted in the latter diagram. Note that in both figures the input

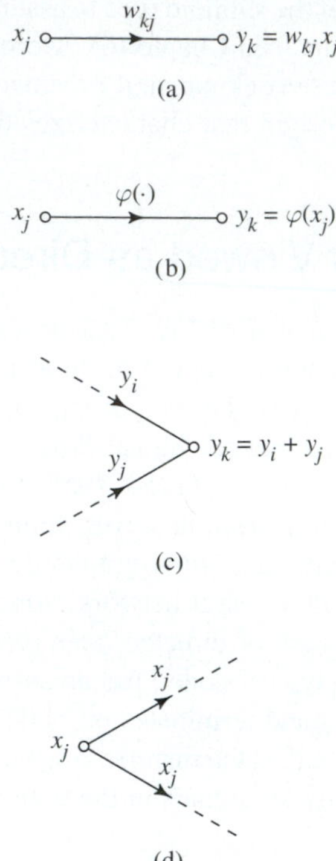

FIGURE 1.8 Illustrating basic rules for the construction of signal-flow graphs.

$x_0 = -1$ and the associated synaptic weight $w_{k0} = \theta_k$, where θ_k is the threshold applied to neuron *k*.

Indeed, based on the signal-flow graph of Fig. 1.9 as the model of a neuron, we may now offer the following mathematical definition of a neural network:

> *A neural network is a directed graph consisting of nodes with interconnecting synaptic and activation links, and which is characterized by four properties:*
>
> 1. *Each neuron is represented by a set of linear synaptic links, an externally applied threshold, and a nonlinear activation link. The threshold is represented by a synaptic link with an input signal fixed at a value of −1.*

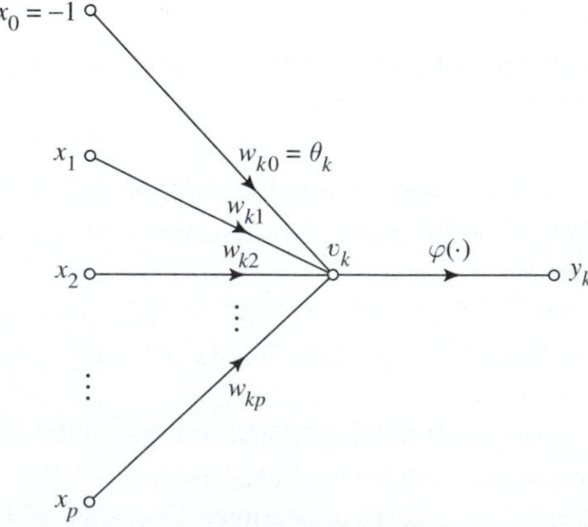

FIGURE 1.9 Signal-flow graph of a neuron.

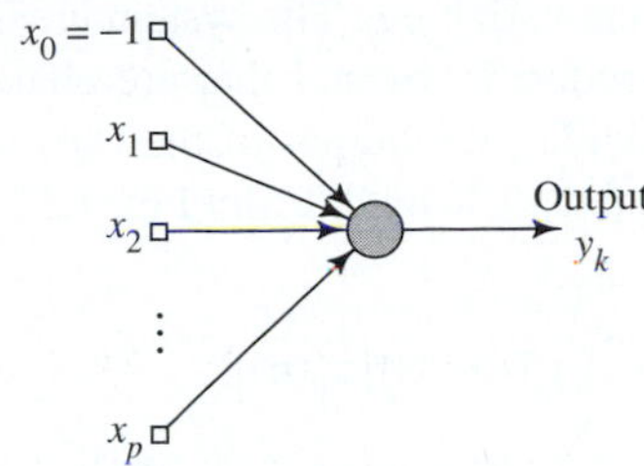

FIGURE 1.10 Architectural graph of a neuron.

2. *The synaptic links of a neuron weight their respective input signals.*
3. *The weighted sum of the input signals defines the total internal activity level of the neuron in question.*
4. *The activation link squashes the internal activity level of the neuron to produce an output that represents the state variable of the neuron.*

A directed graph so defined is *complete* in the sense that it describes not only the signal flow from neuron to neuron, but also the signal flow inside each neuron. When, however, the focus of attention is restricted to signal flow from neuron to neuron, we may use a reduced form of this graph by omitting the details of signal flow inside the individual neurons. Such a directed graph is said to be *partially complete.* It is characterized as follows:

1. *Source nodes* supply input signals to the graph.
2. Each neuron is represented by a single node called a *computation node.*
3. The *communication links* interconnecting the source and computation nodes of the graph carry no weight; they merely provide directions of signal flow in the graph.

A partially complete directed graph defined in this way is referred to as an *architectural graph* describing the layout of the neural network. It is illustrated in Fig. 1.10 for the simple case of a single neuron with p source nodes and a single node representing threshold. Note that the computation node representing the neuron is shown shaded, and the source node is shown as a small square. This convention is followed throughout the book. More elaborate examples of architectural layouts are presented in Section 1.6.

1.5 Feedback

Feedback is said to exist in a dynamic system whenever the output of an element in the system influences in part the input applied to that particular element, thereby giving rise to one or more closed paths for the transmission of signals around the system. Indeed, feedback occurs in almost every part of the nervous system of every animal (Freeman, 1975). Moreover, it plays a major role in the study of a special class of neural networks known as *recurrent networks.* Figure 1.11 shows the signal-flow graph of a *single-loop feedback system,* where the input signal $x_j(n)$, internal signal $x_j'(n)$, and output signal $y_k(n)$

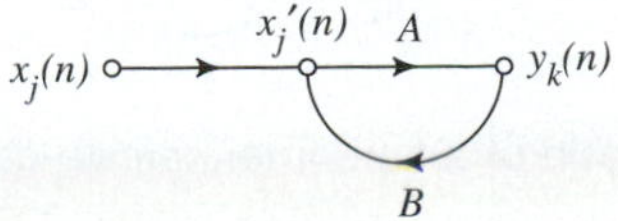

FIGURE 1.11 Signal-flow graph of a single-loop feedback system.

are functions of the discrete-time variable n. The system is assumed to be *linear,* consisting of a forward channel and a feedback channel that are characterized by the "operators" A and B, respectively. In particular, the output of the forward channel determines in part its own output through the feedback channel. From Fig. 1.11 we readily note the following input–output relationships:

$$y_k(n) = A[x_j'(n)] \tag{1.15}$$

$$x_j'(n) = x_j(n) + B[y_k(n)] \tag{1.16}$$

where the square brackets are included to emphasize that A and B act as operators. Eliminating $x_j'(n)$ between Eqs. (1.15) and (1.16), we get

$$y_k(n) = \frac{A}{1 - AB}[x_j(n)] \tag{1.17}$$

We refer to $A/(1 - AB)$ as the *closed-loop operator* of the system, and to AB as the *open-loop operator.* In general, the open-loop operator is noncommutative in that $BA \neq AB$. It is only when A or B is a scalar that we have $BA = AB$.

Consider, for example, the single-loop feedback system shown in Fig. 1.12, for which A is a fixed weight w, and B is a *unit-delay operator* z^{-1}, whose output is delayed with respect to the input by one time unit. We may then express the closed-loop operator of the system as

$$\begin{aligned}\frac{A}{1 - AB} &= \frac{w}{1 - wz^{-1}}\\ &= w(1 - wz^{-1})^{-1}\end{aligned} \tag{1.18}$$

Using the binomial expansion for $(1 - wz^{-1})^{-1}$, we may rewrite the closed-loop operator of the system as

$$\frac{A}{1 - AB} = w\sum_{l=0}^{\infty} w^l z^{-l} \tag{1.19}$$

Hence, substituting Eq. (1.19) in (1.17), we get

$$y_k(n) = w\sum_{l=0}^{\infty} w^l z^{-l}[x_j(n)] \tag{1.20}$$

where again we have included square brackets to emphasize the fact that z^{-1} is an operator. In particular, from the definition of z^{-1} we have

$$z^{-l}[x_j(n)] = x_j(n - l) \tag{1.21}$$

where $x_j(n - l)$ is a sample of the input signal delayed by l time units. Accordingly, we may express the output signal $y_k(n)$ as an infinite weighted summation of present and past

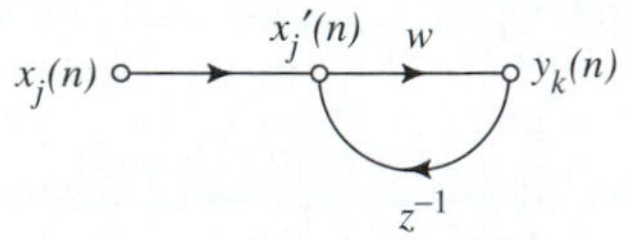

$x_j(n)$ $x_j'(n)$ w $y_k(n)$ z^{-1}

FIGURE 1.12 Signal-flow graph of a first-order, infinite-duration impulse response (IIR) filter.

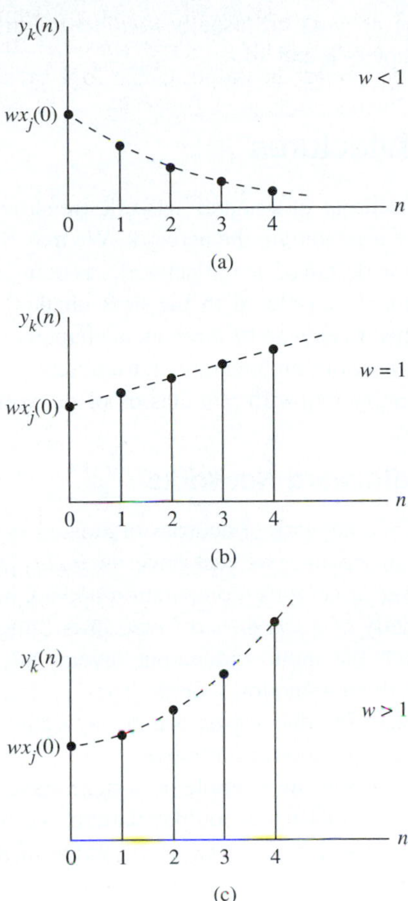

FIGURE 1.13 Time responses of Fig. 1.12 for three different values of forward weight *w*.

samples of the input signal $x_j(n)$, as shown by

$$y_k(n) = \sum_{l=0}^{\infty} w^{l+1} x_j(n - l) \tag{1.22}$$

We now see clearly that the dynamic behavior of the system is controlled by the weight w. In particular, we may distinguish two specific cases:

1. $|w| < 1$, for which the output signal $y_k(n)$ is exponentially *convergent;* that is, the system is *stable.* This is illustrated in Fig. 1.13a for a positive w.
2. $|w| \geq 1$, for which the output signal $y_k(n)$ is *divergent;* that is, the system is *unstable.* If $|w| = 1$ the divergence is linear as in Fig. 1.13b, and if $|w| > 1$ the divergence is exponential as in Fig. 1.13c.

The case of $|w| < 1$ is of particular interest: It corresponds to a system with *infinite memory* in the sense that the output of the system depends on samples of the input extending into the infinite past. Moreover, the memory is *fading* in that the influence of a past sample is reduced exponentially with time n.

The analysis of the dynamic behavior of neural networks involving the application of feedback is unfortunately complicated by virtue of the fact that the processing units used for the construction of the network are usually *nonlinear.* Further consideration of this issue is deferred until Chapters 8 and 14.

1.6 Network Architectures

The manner in which the neurons of a neural network are structured is intimately linked with the learning algorithm used to train the network. We may therefore speak of learning algorithms (rules) used in the design of neural networks as being *structured.* The classification of learning algorithms is considered in the next chapter, and the development of different learning algorithms is taken up in subsequent chapters of the book. In this section we focus our attention on network architectures (structures).

In general, we may identify four different classes of network architectures:

1. Single-Layer Feedforward Networks

A *layered* neural network is a network of neurons organized in the form of layers. In the simplest form of a layered network, we just have an *input layer* of source nodes that projects onto an *output layer* of neurons (computation nodes), but not vice versa. In other words, this network is strictly of a *feedforward* type. It is illustrated in Fig. 1.14 for the case of four nodes in both the input and output layers. Such a network is called a *single-layer network,* with the designation ''single layer'' referring to the output layer of computation nodes (neurons). In other words, we do not count the input layer of source nodes, because no computation is performed there.

A linear associative memory is an example of a single-layer neural network. In such an application, the network associates an output pattern (vector) with an input pattern (vector), and information is stored in the network by virtue of modifications made to the synaptic weights of the network.

2. Multilayer Feedforward Networks

The second class of a feedforward neural network distinguishes itself by the presence of one or more *hidden layers,* whose computation nodes are correspondingly called *hidden*

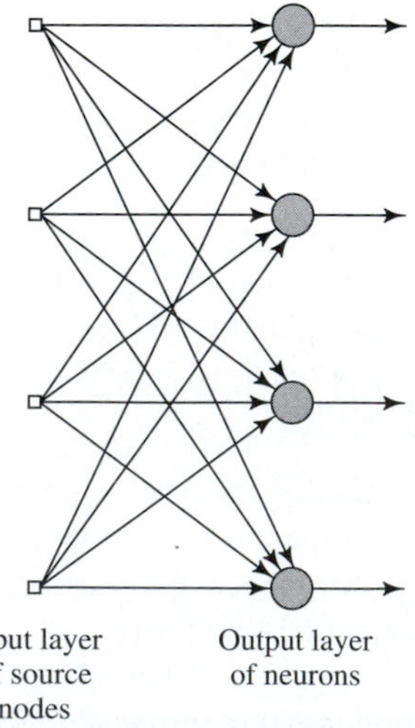

FIGURE 1.14 Feedforward network with a single layer of neurons.

neurons or *hidden units*. The function of the hidden neurons is to intervene between the external input and the network output. By adding one or more hidden layers, the network is enabled to extract higher-order statistics, for (in a rather loose sense) the network acquires a *global* perspective despite its local connectivity by virtue of the extra set of synaptic connections and the extra dimension of neural interactions (Churchland and Sejnowski, 1992). The ability of hidden neurons to extract higher-order statistics is particularly valuable when the size of the input layer is large.

The source nodes in the input layer of the network supply respective elements of the activation pattern (input vector), which constitute the input signals applied to the neurons (computation nodes) in the second layer (i.e., the first hidden layer). The output signals of the second layer are used as inputs to the third layer, and so on for the rest of the network. Typically, the neurons in each layer of the network have as their inputs the output signals of the preceding layer only. The set of output signals of the neurons in the output (final) layer of the network constitutes the overall response of the network to the activation pattern supplied by the source nodes in the input (first) layer. The architectural graph of Fig. 1.15 illustrates the layout of a multilayer feedforward neural network for the case of a single hidden layer. For brevity the network of Fig. 1.15 is referred to as a 10-4-2 network in that it has 10 source nodes, 4 hidden neurons, and 2 output neurons. As another example, a feedforward network with p source nodes, h_1 neurons in the first hidden layer, h_2 neurons in the second layer, and q neurons in the output layer, say, is referred to as a p-h_1-h_2-q network.

The neural network of Fig. 1.15 is said to be *fully connected* in the sense that every node in each layer of the network is connected to every other node in the adjacent forward layer. If, however, some of the communication links (synaptic connections) are missing from the network, we say that the network is *partially connected.* A form of partially connected multilayer feedforward network of particular interest is a locally connected network. An example of such a network with a single hidden layer is presented in Fig. 1.16. Each neuron in the hidden layer is connected to a local (partial) set of source nodes

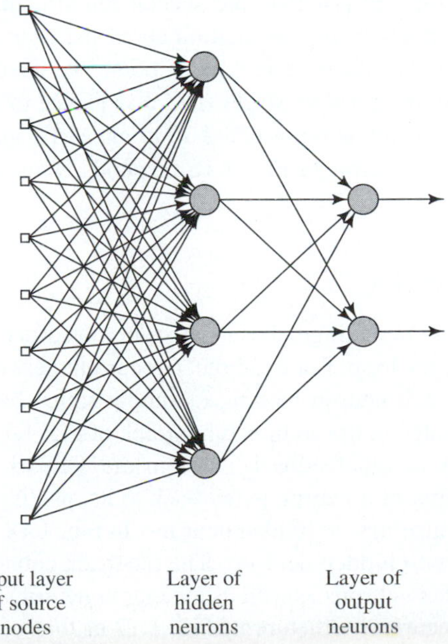

FIGURE 1.15 Fully connected feedforward network with one hidden layer and output layer.

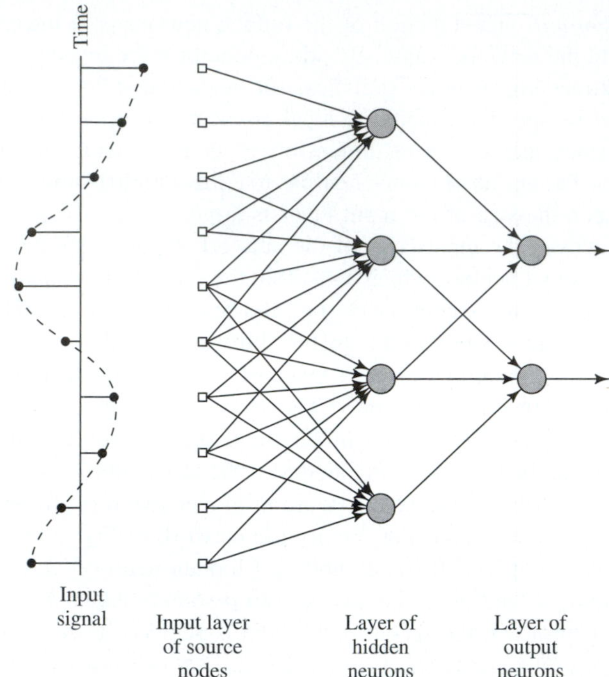

FIGURE 1.16 Partially connected feedforward network.

that lies in its immediate neighborhood; such a set of localized nodes feeding a neuron is said to constitute the *receptive field* of the neuron. Likewise, each neuron in the output layer is connected to a local set of hidden neurons. The network of Fig. 1.16 has the same number of source nodes, hidden neurons, and output neurons as that of Fig. 1.15. However, comparing these two networks, we see that the locally connected network of Fig. 1.16 has a *specialized* structure. In practice, the specialized structure built into the design of a connected network reflects *prior* information about the characteristics of the activation pattern being classified. To illustrate this latter point, we have included in Fig. 1.16 an activation pattern made up of a *time series* (i.e., a sequence of uniformly sampled values of time-varying signal), which is represented *all at once* as a spatial pattern over the input layer. Thus, each hidden neuron in Fig. 1.16 responds essentially to local variations of the source signal.

3. Recurrent Networks

A *recurrent neural network* distinguishes itself from a feedforward neural network in that it has at least one *feedback* loop. For example, a recurrent network may consist of a single layer of neurons with each neuron feeding its output signal back to the inputs of all the other neurons, as illustrated in the architectural graph of Fig. 1.17. In the structure depicted in this figure there are *no* self-feedback loops in the network; self-feedback refers to a situation where the output of a neuron is fed back to its own input. The recurrent network illustrated in Fig. 1.17 also has *no* hidden neurons. In Fig. 1.18 we illustrate another class of recurrent networks with hidden neurons. The feedback connections shown in Fig. 1.18 originate from the hidden neurons as well as the output neurons. The presence of feedback loops, be it as in the recurrent structure of Fig. 1.17 or that of Fig. 1.18, has a profound impact on the learning capability of the network, and on its performance. Moreover, the feedback loops involve the use of particular branches composed of *unit-delay elements*

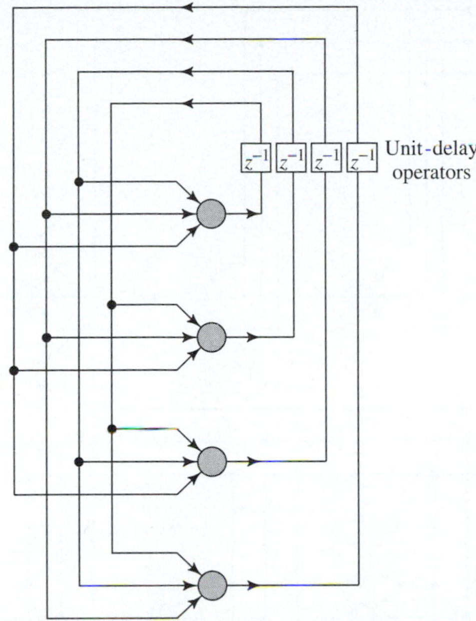

FIGURE 1.17 Recurrent network with no self-feedback loops and no hidden neurons.

(denoted by z^{-1}), which result in a nonlinear dynamical behavior by virtue of the nonlinear nature of the neurons. Nonlinear dynamics plays a key role in the storage function of a recurrent network, as we will see in Chapters 8 and 14.

4. Lattice Structures

A *lattice* consists of a one-dimensional, two-dimensional, or higher-dimensional array of neurons with a corresponding set of source nodes that supply the input signals to the array; the dimension of the lattice refers to the number of the dimensions of the space in

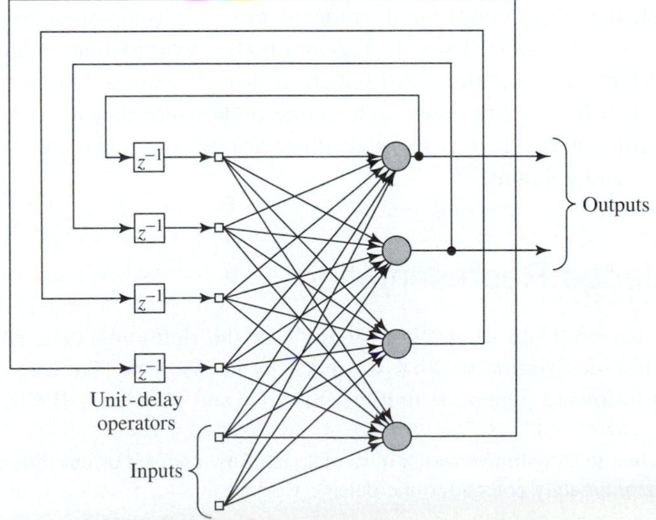

FIGURE 1.18 Recurrent network with hidden neurons.

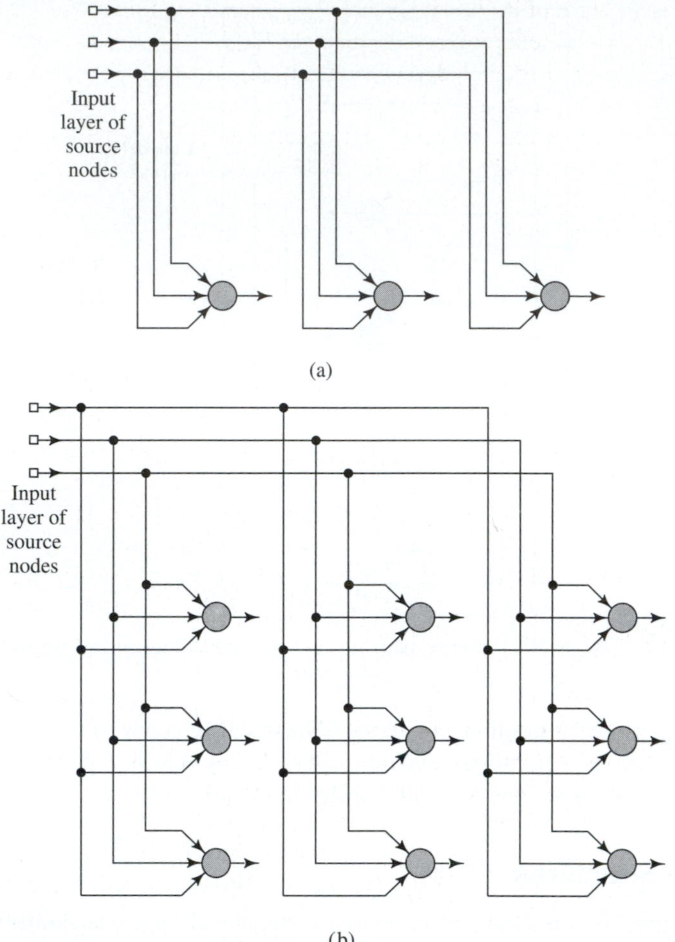

FIGURE 1.19 (a) One-dimensional lattice of 3 neurons. (b) Two-dimensional lattice of 3-by-3 neurons.

which the graph lies. The architectural graph of Fig. 1.19a depicts a one-dimensional lattice of 3 neurons fed from a layer of 3 source nodes, whereas the architectural graph of Fig. 1.19b depicts a two-dimensional lattice of 3-by-3 neurons fed from a layer of 3 source nodes. Note that in both cases each source node is connected to every neuron in the lattice. A lattice network is really a feedforward network with the output neurons arranged in rows and columns.

1.7 Knowledge Representation

In Section 1.1 we used the term ''knowledge'' in the definition of a neural network without an explicit description of what we mean by it. We now take care of this matter by offering the following generic definition (Fischler and Firschein, 1987):

> Knowledge refers to stored information or models used by a person or machine to interpret, predict, and appropriately respond to the outside world.

The primary characteristics of *knowledge representation* are twofold: (1) what information is actually made explicit; and (2) how the information is physically encoded for subsequent use. By the very nature of it, therefore, knowledge representation is goal directed. In real-world applications of intelligent machines, it can be said that a good solution depends on a good representation of knowledge (Woods, 1986; Amarel, 1968). So it is with neural networks, representing a special class of intelligent machines. Typically, however, the possible forms of representation from the inputs to internal network parameters are highly diverse, which tends to make the development of a satisfactory solution by means of a neural network a real design challenge.

A major task for a neural network is to learn a model of the world (environment) in which it is embedded and to maintain the model sufficiently consistent with the real world so as to achieve the specified goals of the application of interest. Knowledge of the world consists of two kinds of information:

1. The known world state, represented by facts about what is and what has been known; this form of knowledge is referred to as *prior information.*
2. Observations (measurements) of the world, obtained by means of sensors designed to probe the environment in which the neural network is supposed to operate. Ordinarily, these observations are inherently noisy, being subject to errors due to sensor noise and system imperfections. In any event, the observations so obtained provide the pool of information from which the examples used to train the neural network are drawn.

Each *example* consists of an input–output pair: an *input signal* and the corresponding *desired response* for the neural network. Thus, a set of examples represents knowledge about the environment of interest. Consider, for example, the *handwritten digit recognition problem,* in which the input consists of an image with black or white pixels, and with each image representing one of 10 digits that are well separated from the background. In this example, the desired response is defined by the ''identity'' of the particular digit whose image is presented to the network as the input signal. Typically, the set of examples used to train the network consists of a large variety of handwritten digits that are representative of a real-world situation. Given such a set of examples, the design of a neural network may proceed as follows:

- First, an appropriate architecture is selected for the neural network, with an input layer consisting of source nodes equal in number to the pixels of an input image, and an output layer consisting of 10 neurons (one for each digit). A subset of examples is then used to train the network by means of a suitable algorithm. This phase of the network design is called *learning.*
- Second, the recognition performance of the trained network is tested with data that has never been seen before. Specifically, an input image is presented to the network, but this time it is not told the identity of the digit to which that particular image belongs. The performance of the network is then assessed by comparing the digit recognition reported by the network with the actual identity of the digit in question. This second phase of the network operation is called *generalization,* a term borrowed from psychology.

Herein lies a fundamental difference between the design of a neural network and that of its classical information-processing counterpart (pattern classifier). In the latter case, we usually proceed by first formulating a mathematical model of environmental observations, validating the models with real data, and then building the design on the basis of the model. In contrast, the design of a neural network is based directly on real data, with the *data set being permitted to speak for itself.* Thus, the neural network not only provides an implicit model of the environment in which it is embedded, but also performs the information-processing function of interest.

The examples used to train a neural network may consist of both *positive* and *negative* examples. For instance, in a passive sonar detection problem, positive examples pertain to input training data that contain the target of interest (e.g., a submarine). Now, in a passive sonar environment, the possible presence of marine life in the test data is known to cause occasional false alarms. To alleviate this problem, negative examples (e.g., echos from marine life) are included in the training data to teach the network not to confuse marine life with the target.

In a neural network of specified architecture, knowledge representation of the surrounding environment is defined by the values taken on by the free parameters (i.e., synaptic weights and thresholds) of the network. The form of this knowledge representation constitutes the very design of the neural network, and therefore holds the key to its performance.

The subject of knowledge representation inside an artificial neural network is, however, very complicated. The subject becomes even more compounded when we have multiple sources of information activating the network, and these sources interact with each other. Our present understanding of this important subject is indeed the weakest link in what we know about artificial neural networks. Nevertheless, there are four rules for knowledge representation that are of a general common-sense nature (Anderson, 1988). The four rules are described in what follows.

RULE 1. Similar inputs from similar classes should usually produce similar representations inside the network, and should therefore be classified as belonging to the same category.

There are a plethora of measures for determining the ''similarity'' between inputs. A commonly used measure of similarity is based on the concept of Euclidian distance. To be specific, let $\mathbf{x}_i$ denote an N-by-1 real-valued vector

$$\mathbf{x}_i = [x_{i1}, x_{i2}, \ldots, x_{iN}]^T \tag{1.23}$$

all of whose elements are real; the superscript T denotes matrix *transposition.* The vector $\mathbf{x}_i$ defines a point in an N-dimensional space called *Euclidean space* and denoted by $\mathbb{R}^N$. The *Euclidean distance* between a pair of N-by-1 vectors $\mathbf{x}_i$ and $\mathbf{x}_j$ is defined by

$$\begin{aligned} d_{ij} &= \|\mathbf{x}_i - \mathbf{x}_j\| \\ &= \left[\sum_{n=1}^{N} (x_{in} - x_{jn})^2\right]^{1/2} \end{aligned} \tag{1.24}$$

where x_{in} and x_{jn} are the nth elements of the input vectors $\mathbf{x}_i$ and $\mathbf{x}_j$, respectively. Correspondingly, the similarity between the inputs represented by the vectors $\mathbf{x}_i$ and $\mathbf{x}_j$ is defined as the *reciprocal* of the Euclidean distance d_{ij}. The closer the individual elements of the input vectors $\mathbf{x}_i$ and $\mathbf{x}_j$ are to each other, the smaller will the Euclidean distance d_{ij} be, and the greater will therefore be the similarity between the vectors $\mathbf{x}_i$ and $\mathbf{x}_j$. Rule 1 states that if the vectors $\mathbf{x}_i$ and $\mathbf{x}_j$ are similar, then they should be assigned to the same category (class).

Another measure of similarity is based on the idea of a *dot product* or *inner product* that is also borrowed from matrix algebra. Given a pair of vectors $\mathbf{x}_i$ and $\mathbf{x}_j$ of the same dimension, their inner product is $\mathbf{x}_i^T\mathbf{x}_j$ written in expanded form as follows:

$$\mathbf{x}_i^T\mathbf{x}_j = \sum_{n=1}^{N} x_{in}x_{jn} \tag{1.25}$$

The inner product $\mathbf{x}_i^T\mathbf{x}_j$ divided by $\|\mathbf{x}_i\|\,\|\mathbf{x}_j\|$ is the cosine of the angle subtended between the vectors $\mathbf{x}_i$ and $\mathbf{x}_j$.

The two measures of similarity defined here are indeed intimately related to each other, as illustrated in Fig. 1.20. The Euclidean distance $\|\mathbf{x}_i - \mathbf{x}_j\|$ between the vectors $\mathbf{x}_i$ and $\mathbf{x}_j$ is portrayed as the length of the line joining the tips of these two vectors, and their inner product $\mathbf{x}_i^T\mathbf{x}_j$ is portrayed as the "projection" of the vector $\mathbf{x}_i$ onto the vector $\mathbf{x}_j$. Figure 1.20 shows clearly that the smaller the Euclidean distance $\|\mathbf{x}_i - \mathbf{x}_j\|$ and therefore the more similar the vectors $\mathbf{x}_i$ and $\mathbf{x}_j$ are, the larger will the inner product $\mathbf{x}_i^T\mathbf{x}_j$ be.

In signal processing terms, the inner product $\mathbf{x}_i^T\mathbf{x}_j$ may be viewed as a *cross-correlation function.* Recognizing that the inner product is a scalar, we may state that the more positive the inner product $\mathbf{x}_i^T\mathbf{x}_j$ is, the more similar (i.e., correlated) the vectors $\mathbf{x}_i$ and $\mathbf{x}_j$ are to each other. The cross-correlation function is ideally suited for echo location in radar and sonar systems. Specifically, by cross-correlating the echo from a target with a replica of the transmitted signal and finding the peak value of the resultant function, it is a straightforward matter to estimate the arrival time of the echo. This is the standard method for estimating the target's range (distance).

RULE 2. Items to be categorized as separate classes should be given widely different representations in the network.

The second rule is the exact opposite of Rule 1.

RULE 3. If a particular feature is important, then there should be a large number of neurons involved in the representation of that item in the network.

Consider, for example, a radar application involving the detection of a target (e.g., aircraft) in the presence of clutter (i.e., radar reflections from undesirable targets such as buildings, trees, and weather formations). According to the *Neyman-Pearson criterion,* the probability of detection (i.e., the probability of deciding that a target is present when it is) is maximized, subject to the constraint that the probability of false alarm (i.e., the probability of deciding that a target is present when it is not) does not exceed a prescribed value (Van Trees, 1968). In such an application, the actual presence of a target in the received signal represents an important feature of the input. Rule 3, in effect, states that there should be a large number of neurons involved in making the decision that a target is present when it actually is. By the same token, there should be a very large number of neurons involved in making the decision that the input consists of clutter only when it actually does. In both situations the large number of neurons assures a high degree of accuracy in decision making and tolerance with respect to faulty neurons.

RULE 4. Prior information and invariances should be built into the design of a neural network, thereby simplifying the network design by not having to learn them.

Rule 4 is particularly important because proper adherence to it results in a neural network with a *specialized (restricted) structure.* This is highly desirable for several

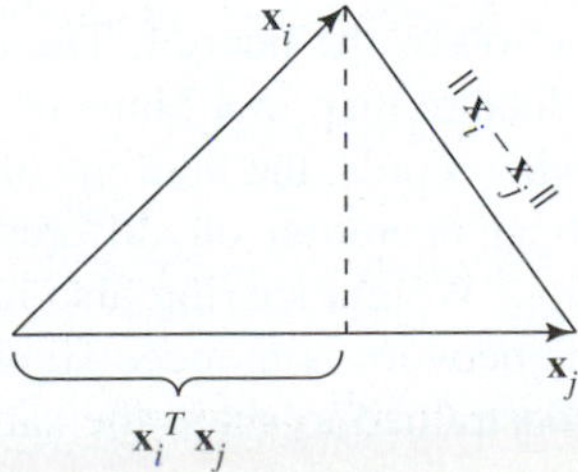

FIGURE 1.20 Illustrating the relationship between inner product and Euclidean distance as measures of similarity between patterns.

reasons (Russo, 1991):

1. Biological visual and auditory networks are known to be very specialized.
2. A neural network with specialized structure usually has a much smaller number of free parameters available for adjustment than a fully connected network. Consequently, the specialized network requires a smaller data set for training, learns faster, and often generalizes better.
3. The rate of information transmission through a specialized network (i.e., the network throughput) is accelerated.
4. The cost of building a specialized network is reduced by virtue of its smaller size, compared to its fully connected counterpart.

How to Build Prior Information into Neural Network Design

An important issue that has to be addressed, of course, is how to develop a specialized structure by building prior information into its design. Unfortunately, there are no well-defined rules yet for doing this; rather, we have some *ad-hoc* procedures that are known to yield useful results. To be specific, consider again the example involving the use of a multilayer feedforward network for *handwritten digit recognition* that is a relatively simple human task but not an easy machine vision task, and which has great practical value (LeCun et al., 1990a). The input consists of an image with black or white pixels, representing one of 10 digits that is well separated from the background. In this example, the prior information is that an image is *two-dimensional* and has a strong *local structure.* Thus, the network is specialized by constraining the synaptic connections in the first few layers of the network to be *local;* that is, the network is chosen to be locally connected. Additional specialization may be built into the network design by examining the use of a *feature detector,* which is to reduce the input data by extracting certain "features" that distinguish the image of one digit from that of another. In particular, if a feature detector is found to be useful in one part of the image, then it is also likely to be useful in other parts of the image. The reason for saying so is that the salient features of a distorted character may be displaced slightly from their position in a typical character. To solve this problem, the input image is scanned with a single neuron that has a local receptive field, and the synaptic weights of the neuron are stored in corresponding locations in a layer called a *feature map.* This operation is illustrated in Fig. 1.21. Let $\{w_{ji} \mid i = 0, 1, \ldots, p - 1\}$ denote the set of synaptic weights pertaining to neuron j. The *convolution* of the "kernel" represented by this set of synaptic weights and an input pixel denoted by $\{x(n)\}$ is defined by the sum

$$y_j(n) = \sum_{i=0}^{p-1} w_{ji} x(n - i) \tag{1.26}$$

where n denotes the nth sample of an input pixel; such a network is sometimes called a *convolutional network.* Thus, the overall operation performed in Fig. 1.21 is equivalent to the convolution of a small-size kernel (represented by the set of synaptic weights) of the neuron and the input image, which is then followed by soft-limiting (squashing) performed by the activation function of the neuron. The overall operation is performed in parallel by implementing the feature map in a plane of neurons whose weight vectors are constrained to be equal. In other words, the neurons of a feature map are constrained to perform the same mathematical operation on different parts of the image. Such a technique is called *weight sharing.*[3] Weight sharing also has a profitable side effect: The number of free parameters in the network is reduced significantly, since a large number of neurons in the network are constrained to share the same set of synaptic weights.

---

[3] It appears that the weight-sharing technique was originally described in Rumelhart et al. (1986b).

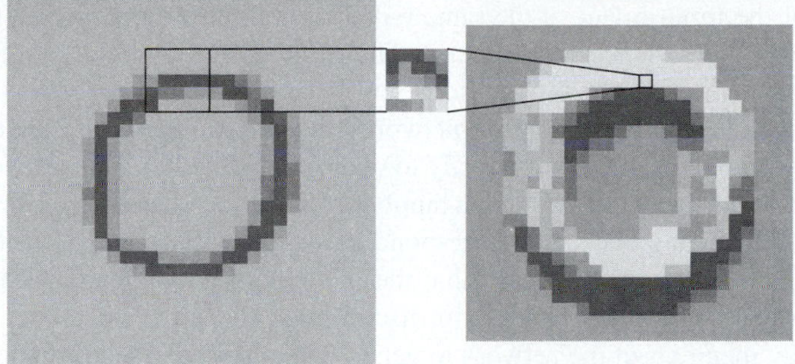

FIGURE 1.21 Input image (left), weight vector (center), and resulting feature map (right). The feature map is obtained by scanning the input image with a single neuron that has a local receptive field, as indicated. White represents −1, black represents +1. (From LeCun et al., 1990a, by permission of Morgan Kaufmann.)

In summary, prior information may be built into the design of a neural network by using a combination of two techniques: (1) *restricting the network architecture* through the use of local connections and (2) *constraining the choice of synaptic weights* by the use of weight sharing. Naturally, the manner in which these two techniques are exploited in practice is strongly influenced by the application of interest. In a more general context, the development of well-defined procedures for the use of prior information is an open problem. Prior information pertains to one part of Rule 4; the remaining part of the rule involves the issue of invariances, which is considered next.

How to Build Invariances into Neural Network Design

When an object of interest rotates, the image of the object as perceived by an observer usually changes in a corresponding way. In a coherent radar that provides amplitude as well as phase information about its surrounding environment, the echo from a moving target is shifted in frequency due to the Doppler effect that arises because of the radial motion of the target in relation to the radar. The utterance from a person may be spoken in a soft or loud voice, and yet again in a slow or quick manner. In order to build an object recognition system, a radar target recognition system, and a speech recognition system for dealing with these phenomena, respectively, the system must be capable of coping with a range of *transformations* of the observed signal (Barnard and Casasent, 1991). Accordingly, a primary requirement of pattern recognition is to design a classifier that is *invariant* to such transformations. In other words, a class estimate represented by an output of the classifier must not be affected by transformations of the observed signal applied to the classifier input.

There exist at least three techniques for rendering classifier-type neural networks invariant to transformations (Barnard and Casasent, 1991):

1. *Invariance by Structure.* Invariance may be imposed on a neural network by structuring its design appropriately. Specifically, synaptic connections between the neurons of the network are created such that transformed versions of the same input are forced to produce the same output. Consider, for example, the classification of an input image by a neural network that is required to be independent of in-plane rotations of the image about its center. We may impose rotational invariance on the network structure as follows. Let w_{ji} be the synaptic weight of neuron j connected to pixel i in the input image. If the condition $w_{ji} = w_{jk}$ is enforced for all pixels i and k that lie at equal distances from the center of the image, then the neural network is invariant to in-plane rotations. However, in order to maintain rotational invariance, the synaptic weight w_{ji} has to be duplicated for every pixel of the input image at the same radial distance from the origin. This points to a shortcoming of invariance by structure: The number of synaptic connections in the neural network becomes prohibitively large even for images of moderate size.

2. *Invariance by Training.* A neural network has a natural ability for pattern classification. This ability may be exploited directly to obtain transformation invariance as follows. The network is trained by presenting it a number of different examples of the same object, with the examples being chosen to correspond to different transformations (i.e., different aspect views) of the object. Provided that the number of examples is sufficiently large, and if the network is trained to learn to discriminate the different aspect views of the object, we may then expect the network to generalize correctly transformations other than those shown to it. However, from an engineering perspective, invariance by training has two disadvantages. First, when a neural network has been trained to recognize an object in an invariant fashion with respect to known transformations, it is not obvious that this training will also enable the network to recognize other objects of different classes invariantly. Second, the computational demand imposed on the network may be too severe to cope with, especially if the dimensionality of the feature space is high.

3. *Invariant Feature Space.* The third technique of creating an invariant classifier-type neural network is illustrated in Fig. 1.22. It rests on the premise that it may be possible to extract *features* that characterize the essential information content of an input data set, and which are invariant to transformations of the input. If such features are used, then the network as a classifier is relieved from the burden of having to delineate the range of transformations of an object with complicated decision boundaries. Indeed, the only differences that may arise between different instances of the same object are due to unavoidable factors such as noise and occlusion. The use of an invariant-feature space offers three distinct advantages: (1) The number of features applied to the network may be reduced to realistic levels; (2) the requirements imposed on network design are relaxed; and (3) invariance for all objects with respect to known transformations is assured (Barnard and Casasent, 1991); however, this approach requires prior knowledge of the problem.

In conclusion, the use of an invariant-feature space as described herein may offer the most suitable technique for neural classifiers.

To illustrate the idea of invariant-feature space, consider the example of a coherent radar system used for air surveillance, where the targets of interest include aircraft, weather systems, flocks of migrating birds, and ground objects. It is known that the radar echoes from these targets possess different spectral characteristics. Moreover, experimental studies have shown that such radar signals can be modeled fairly closely as an *autoregressive (AR) process* of moderate order (Haykin et al., 1991); an AR model is a special form of regressive model defined for complex-valued data by

$$x(n) = \sum_{i=1}^{M} a_i^* x(n-i) + e(n) \tag{1.27}$$

where the $\{a_i \mid i = 1, 2, \ldots, M\}$ are the *AR coefficients, M* is the *model order,* $x(n)$ is the *input,* and $e(n)$ is the *error* described as white noise. Basically, the AR model of Eq. (1.27) is represented by a *tapped-delay-line filter* as illustrated in Fig. 1.23a for $M = 2$. Equivalently, it may be represented by a *lattice filter* as shown in Fig. 1.23b, the coefficients

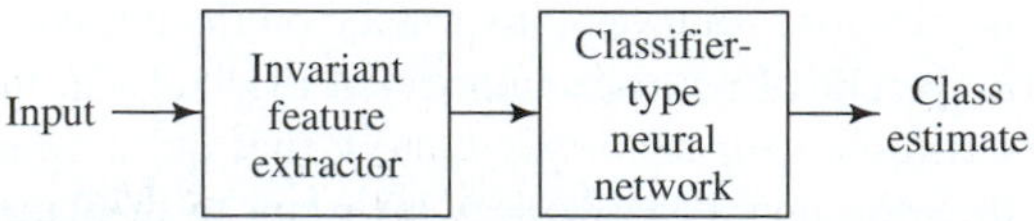

FIGURE 1.22 Block diagram of invariant feature-space type of system.

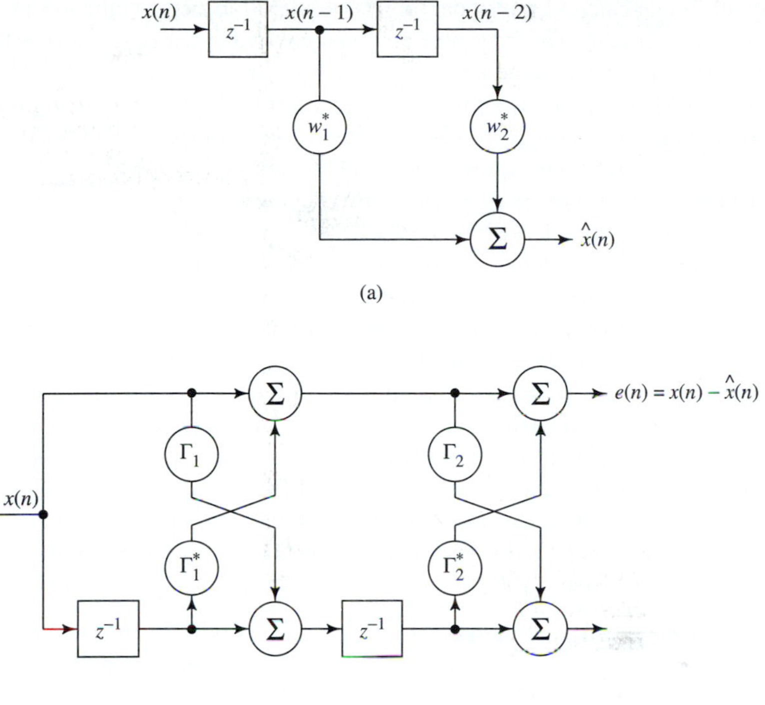

FIGURE 1.23 Autoregressive model of order 2: (a) tapped-delay-line model; (b) lattice filter model. (The asterisk denotes complex conjugation.)

of which are called *reflection coefficients* (Haykin et al., 1991). There is a one-to-one correspondence between the AR coefficients of the model in Fig. 1.23a and the reflection coefficients of that in Fig. 1.23b. The two models depicted in Fig. 1.23 assume that the input $x(n)$ is complex valued as in the case of a coherent radar, in which case the AR coefficients and the reflection coefficients are all complex valued; the asterisk in Fig. 1.23 signifies *complex conjugation.* For now, it suffices to say that the coherent radar data may be described by a set of *autoregressive coefficients,* or, equivalently, by a corresponding set of *reflection coefficients.* The latter set has a computational advantage in that efficient algorithms exist for their computation directly from the input data. The feature-extraction problem, however, is complicated by the fact that moving objects produce varying Doppler frequencies that depend on their radial velocities measured with respect to the radar, and that tend to obscure the spectral content of the reflection coefficients as feature discriminants. To overcome this difficulty, we must build *Doppler invariance* into the computation of the reflection coefficients. The phase angle of the first reflection coefficient turns out to be equal to the Doppler frequency of the radar signal. Accordingly, Doppler frequency *normalization* is applied to all coefficients so as to remove the mean Doppler shift. This is done by defining a new set of reflection coefficients $\{\rho'_m\}$ related to the set of reflection coefficients $\{\rho_m\}$ computed from the input data as follows:

$$\rho'_m = \rho_m e^{-jm\theta} \qquad m = 1, 2, \ldots, M \tag{1.28}$$

where θ is the phase angle of the first reflection coefficient and M is the order of the AR model. The operation described in Eq. (1.28) is referred to as *heterodyning.* A set of *Doppler-invariant radar features* is thus represented by the normalized reflection coefficients $\rho'_1, \rho'_2, \ldots, \rho'_M$, with ρ'_1 being the only real-valued coefficient in the set. As mentioned previously, the major categories of radar targets of interest in air surveillance are weather, birds, aircraft, and ground. The first three targets are moving, whereas the last one is not. The heterodyned spectral parameters of radar echoes from ground are known to have echoes similar in characteristic to those from aircraft. It is also known that a ground echo can be discriminated from an aircraft echo by virtue of its small Doppler shift. Accordingly, the radar classifier includes a postprocessor as in Fig. 1.24, which operates on the classified results (encoded labels) for the purpose of identifying the ground class (Haykin and Deng, 1991). Thus, the *preprocessor* in Fig. 1.24 takes care of Doppler shift-invariate feature extraction at the classifier input, whereas the *postprocessor* uses the stored Doppler signature to distinguish between aircraft and ground returns.

A much more fascinating example of knowledge representation in a neural network is found in the biological sonar system of echo-locating bats. Most bats use *frequency-modulated* (FM or ''chirp'') signals for the purposes of acoustic imaging; in an FM signal the instantaneous frequency of the signal varies with time. Specifically, the bat uses its mouth to broadcast short-duration FM sonar signals and uses its auditory system as the sonar receiver. Echoes from targets of interest are represented in the auditory system by the activity of neurons that are selective to different combinations of acoustic parameters. There are three principal neural dimensions of the bat's auditory representation (Simmons and Saillant, 1992; Simmons, 1991):

- *Echo frequency,* which is encoded by ''place'' originating in the frequency map of the cochlea; it is preserved throughout the entire auditory pathway as an orderly arrangement across certain neurons tuned to different frequencies.
- *Echo amplitude,* which is encoded by other neurons with different dynamic ranges; it is manifested both as amplitude tuning and as the number of discharges per stimulus.
- *Echo delay,* which is encoded through neural computations (based on cross-correlation) that produce delay-selective responses; it is manifested as target-range tuning.

The two principal characteristics of a target echo for image-forming purposes are *spectrum* for target shape, and *delay* for target range. The bat perceives ''shape'' in terms of the arrival time of echoes from different reflecting surfaces (glints) within the target. For this to occur, *frequency* information in the echo spectrum is converted into estimates of the *time* structure of the target. Experiments conducted by Simmons and co-workers on the big brown bat, *Eptesicus fuscus,* critically identify this conversion process as consisting of parallel time-domain and frequency-to-time-domain transforms whose converging outputs create the common delay or range axis of a perceived image of the target. It appears that the unity of the bat's perception is due to certain properties of the transforms themselves, despite the separate ways in which the auditory time representation of the echo delay and frequency representation of the echo spectrum are initially performed. Moreover, feature invariances are built into the sonar image-forming process so as to make it essentially independent of the motion of the target and the bat's own motion.

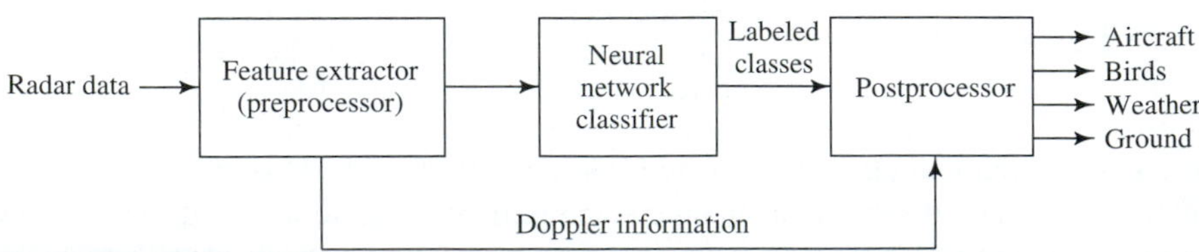

FIGURE 1.24 Doppler shift-invariant classifier of radar signals.

Returning to the main theme of this section, namely, that of knowledge representation in a neural network, the issue of knowledge representation is intimately related to that of network architecture described in Section 1.6. Unfortunately, there is no well-developed theory for optimizing the architecture of a neural network required to interact with an environment of interest, and for evaluating the way in which changes in the network architecture affect the representation of knowledge inside the network. Indeed, satisfactory answers to these issues are usually found through an exhaustive experimental study, with the designer of the neural network becoming an essential part of the structural learning loop.

1.8 Visualizing Processes in Neural Networks

An insightful method to overcome the weakness in our present understanding of knowledge representation inside a neural network is to resort to the experimental use of *visualization* of the learning process. By so doing we are merely recognizing the fact that representing information-bearing data by visual means is the essence of scientific visualization. Indeed, such an approach permits the human eye–brain system to perceive and infer visual information by pictorial means, thereby providing a highly efficient tool for the transfer of information between the neural-network simulator and the user. This is all the more so, given the enhanced facilities for the interactive manipulation of imaging and display processes that are presently available (Wejchert and Tesauro, 1991; Nielson and Shriver, 1990).

Yet it has to be said that the use of graphical display of the learning process experienced by a neural network has not received the attention it deserves. Nevertheless, we may make mention of the Hinton diagram described by Rumelhart and McClelland (1986) and the bond diagram proposed by Wejchert and Tesauro (1991).

The *Hinton diagram* involves drawing columns of squares, with each column representing the synaptic weights and threshold of a particular neuron in the network. The size of each square represents the magnitude of a certain synaptic weight; the color of the square, black or white, indicates the polarity of the weight, positive or negative, respectively. The various columns of squares are positioned in the diagram so as to maintain correspondence with the network architecture. Consider, for example, the simple, two-layer feedforward network of Fig. 1.25a. The Hinton diagram for this network is shown in Fig. 1.25b. Starting from the bottom of the diagram, the first column of squares represents the two weights and threshold of the top hidden neuron. The second column of squares represents the two weights and threshold of the bottom hidden neuron. Finally, the third column of squares represents the two weights and threshold of the output neuron. The top row of squares in the diagram represents the thresholds of the individual neurons.

A limitation of the Hinton diagram, however, is that it does not explicitly reveal the network topology in relation to the synaptic weight data. We usually find it highly informative to have a graphical representation that explicitly integrates synaptic weight values with network topology, for then we are able to see how the internal representation of synaptic weights relates to the particular problem the neural network is learning. Such an objective is met by the *bond diagram,* according to which the synaptic weights are displayed as "bonds" between the nodes of the network (Wejchert and Tesauro, 1991). In particular, the stronger a synaptic connection between two nodes is, the longer would the bond be. Figure 1.25c shows the bond diagram for the network of Fig. 1.25a. Figure 1.25c shows clearly that the bond diagram incorporates synaptic weight data with network topology. Note that a bond representing a synaptic weight extends from *both* nodes of the connection in question. Thus, looking at any node in the bond diagram, we immediately

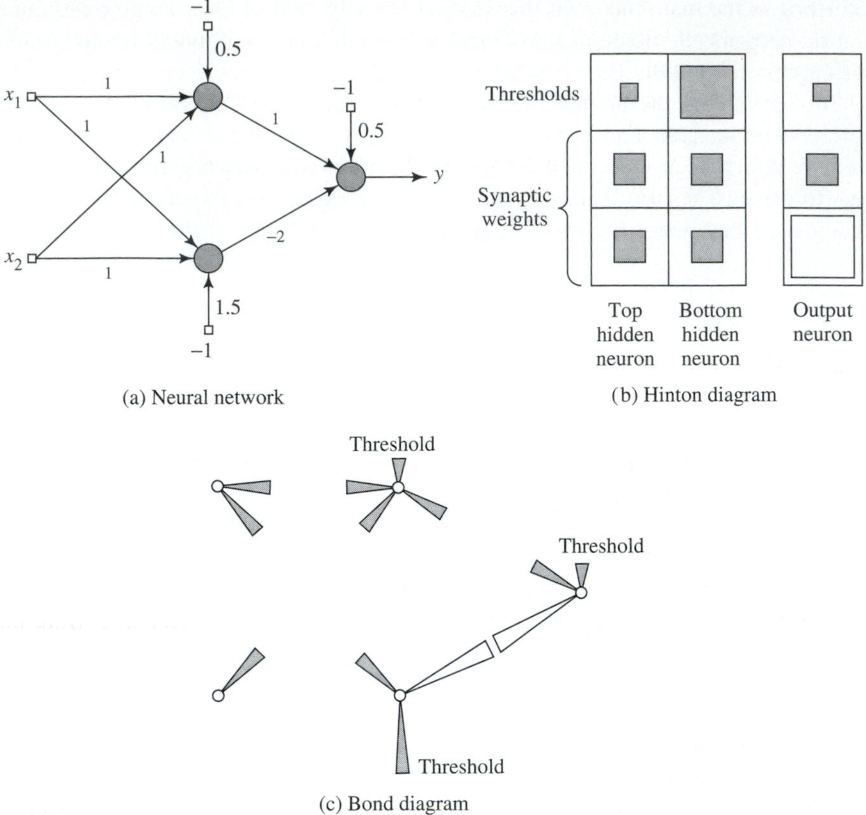

FIGURE 1.25 (a) Neural network. (b) Hinton diagram. (c) Bond diagram.

see the magnitude and polarity of the synaptic weights feeding into and out of that node. This form of a graphical display offers the following advantages over the Hinton diagram (Wejchert and Tesauro, 1991):

- A sense of direction is built into the bond diagram, since each bond in the display points to the node to which it is connected.
- The collection of synaptic weights represented by bonds forms a distinct pattern that may be readily perceived by the user, which makes it possible to infer global information from the bond diagram.

In summary, the bond diagram is a useful real-time visual tool for revealing how internal representations in a neural network are related to the function being performed by the network. It is also helpful in revealing insights about the dynamics of the learning process. Although the use of the bond diagram (or the Hinton diagram for that matter) represents an increase in software complexity, this is a small price to pay for the insight gained about the process of neural network learning.

1.9 Artificial Intelligence and Neural Networks

The aim of *artificial intelligence* (AI) is the development of paradigms or algorithms that require machines to perform tasks that apparently require *cognition* when performed by humans. This statement on AI is adapted from Sage (1990); note that this is not the only accepted definition of AI. Note also that in the statement we have purposely used the term "cognition" rather than "intelligence," so as to broaden the tasks tackled by AI to include perception and language as well as problem solving, conscious as well as unconscious processes (Memmi, 1989).

An AI system must be capable of doing three things: (1) store knowledge; (2) apply the knowledge stored to solve problems; and (3) acquire new knowledge through experience. An AI system has three key components: representation, reasoning, and learning (Sage, 1990), as depicted in Fig. 1.26.

1. *Representation.* The most distinctive feature of AI is probably the pervasive use of a language of *symbol* structures to represent both general knowledge about a problem domain of interest and specific knowledge about the solution to the problem. The symbols are usually formulated in familiar terms, which makes the symbolic representations of AI relatively easy to understand by a human user. Indeed, the clarity of symbolic AI makes it well suited for human–machine communication.

"Knowledge," as used by AI researchers, is just another term for data. It may be of a declarative or procedural kind. In a *declarative* representation, knowledge is represented as a static collection of facts, with a small set of general procedures used to manipulate the facts. A characteristic feature of declarative representations is that they appear to possess a meaning of their own in the eyes of the human user, independent of their use within the AI system. In a *procedural* representation, on the other hand, knowledge is embodied in an executable code that acts out the meaning of the knowledge. Both kinds of knowledge, declarative and procedural, are needed in most problem domains of interest.

2. *Reasoning.* In its most basic form, *reasoning* is the ability to solve problems. For a system to qualify as a reasoning system, it must satisfy certain conditions (Fischler and Firschein, 1987):

- The system must be able to express and solve a broad range of problems and problem types.
- The system must be able to make *explicit* any *implicit* information known to it.
- The system must have a *control* mechanism that determines which operations to apply to a particular problem, when a solution to the problem has been obtained, or when further work on the problem should be terminated.

Problem solving may be viewed as a *searching* problem. A common way to deal with "search" is to use *rules, data,* and *control* (Nilsson, 1980). The rules operate on the data, and the control operates on the rules. Consider, for example, the "traveling salesman problem," where the requirement is to find the shortest tour that goes from one city to another, with all the cities on the tour being visited only once. In this problem the data are made up of the set of possible tours and their costs in a weighted graph, the rules

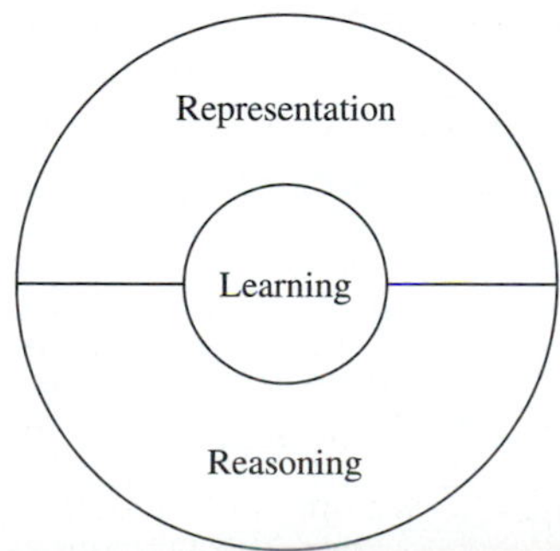

FIGURE 1.26 Illustrating the three key components of an AI system.

define the ways to proceed from city to city, and the control decides which rules to apply and when to apply them.

In many situations encountered in practice (e.g., medical diagnosis), the available knowledge is incomplete or inexact. In such situations, *probabilistic reasoning* procedures are used, thereby permitting AI systems to take the uncertainty of the problem into account.

3. *Learning.* In a simple model of machine *learning,* depicted in Fig. 1.27, the environment supplies some information to a *learning element,* the learning element then uses this information to make improvements in a *knowledge base,* and finally the *performance element* uses the knowledge base to perform its task. The kind of information supplied to the machine by the environment is usually imperfect, with the result that the learning element does not know in advance how to fill in missing details or ignore details that are unimportant. The machine therefore operates by guessing, and then receiving *feedback* from the performance element. The feedback mechanism enables the machine to evaluate its hypotheses and revise them if necessary.

Machine learning may involve two rather different kinds of information processing: inductive and deductive. In *inductive* information processing, general patterns and rules are determined from raw data and experience. In *deductive* information processing, on the other hand, general rules are used to determine specific facts. Similarity-based learning uses induction, whereas the proof of a theorem is a deduction from known axioms and other existing theorems. Explanation-based learning uses both induction and deduction.

The importance of knowledge bases and the difficulties experienced in learning have led to the development of various methods for augmenting knowledge bases. Specifically, if there are experts in a given field, it is usually easier to obtain the compiled experience of the experts than to try to duplicate and direct experience that gave rise to the expertise. This, indeed, is the idea behind *expert systems.*

Having familiarized ourselves with symbolic AI machines, how would we compare them to neural networks as cognitive models? For this comparison, we follow three subdivisions: level of explanation, style of processing, and representational structure (Memmi, 1989), as described next.

1. *Level of Explanation.* In classical AI, the emphasis is on building *symbolic representations* that are presumably so called because they stand for something. Typically, the representations are discrete and arbitrary: abstract properties, and not analog images. From the point of view of cognition, it is unquestionable that AI assumes the existence of mental representations, and it models cognition as the *sequential processing* of symbolic representations (Newell and Simon, 1972).

The assumptions made in neural networks as to what constitutes a satisfactory explanation of cognitive processes are entirely different from those in classical AI. The emphasis in neural networks is on the development of *parallel distributed processing* (PDP) *models.* These models assume that information processing takes place through the interaction of a large number of neurons, each of which sends excitatory and inhibitory signals to other neurons in the network (Rumelhart and McClelland, 1986). Moreover, neural networks place great emphasis on *neurobiological* explanation of cognitive phenomena.

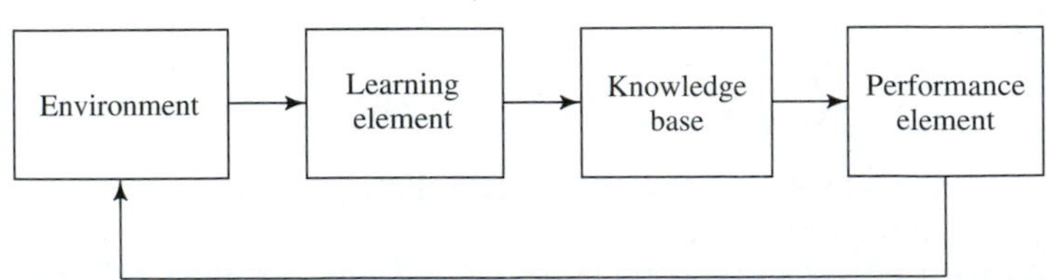

FIGURE 1.27 Simple model of machine learning.

2. *Processing Style.* In classical AI, the processing is *sequential,* as in typical computer programming. Even when there is no predetermined order (scanning the facts and rules of an expert system, for example), the operations are performed in a step-by-step manner. Most probably, the inspiration for sequential processing comes from the sequential nature of natural language and logical inference, as much as from the structure of the von Neumann machine. It should not be forgotten that classical AI was born shortly after the von Neumann machine, in the same intellectual era.

On the other hand, *parallel processing* is an outstanding feature of neural networks. Indeed, parallelism is not only conceptually essential to the processing of information in neural networks, but also the source of their flexibility. Moreover, parallelism may be massive (hundreds of thousands of neurons), which gives neural networks a remarkable *robustness.* With the computation spread over many neurons, it usually does not matter that much if the states of some neurons in the network deviate from their expected values. Noisy or incomplete inputs may still be recognized, a damaged network may still be able to function satisfactorily, and learning does not have to be perfect; performance of the network degrades gracefully within a certain range. The network is made even more robust by virtue of the "coarse coding" (Hinton, 1981), where each feature is spread over several neurons. Thus, parallel distributed processing approximates the flexibility of a continuous system, in sharp contrast with the rigidity and brittleness of discrete symbolic AI.

Another interesting corollary of parallelism is the automatic processing of contextual information. Knowledge is not represented by declarative expressions, but by the very structure and activation state of the neural network. The content necessary for a given problem is then nothing less than the whole neural network. Every neuron is potentially affected by the global activity of all other neurons in the network, with the result that context is dealt with automatically.

In short, sequential information processing favors classical AI, whereas parallel information processing favors neural networks. Nevertheless, symbolic AI systems can be implemented in parallel too. For example, the LISP language, which has become an important language used in AI, has been implemented on a massively parallel computer called the *connection machine* (Hillis, 1985). By the same token, there is no reason why a sequential process could not be implemented on a neural architecture; in fact, neural networks are simulated in software sequentially.

3. *Representational Structure.* With a language of thought pursued as a model for classical AI, we find that symbolic representations possess a *quasi-linguistic structure.* Like expressions of natural language, the expressions of classical AI are generally complex, built in a systematic fashion from simple symbols. Given a limited stock of symbols, meaningful new expressions may be composed by virtue of the *compositionality* of symbolic expressions and the analogy between syntactic structure and semantics.

The nature and structure of representations is, however, a crucial problem for neural networks. Indeed, this matter has been the subject of much debate in the literature between classical AI and neural network theorists. In the March 1988 Special Issue of the journal *Cognition,* Fodor and Pylyshyn make some potent criticisms about the computational adequacy of neural networks in dealing with cognition and linguistics. They argue that neural networks are on the wrong side of two basic issues in cognition: the nature of *mental representations,* and the nature of *mental processes.* According to Fodor and Pylyshyn, *for* classical AI theories but *not* neural networks:

- Mental representations characteristically exhibit a combinatorial constituent structure and a combinatorial semantics.
- Mental processes are characteristically sensitive to the combinatorial structure of the representations on which they operate.

In a neural network, representations are distributed. It does not, however, follow that whatever is distributed must have constituents, and being distributed is very different from having semantic or syntactic constituent structure (Fodor and Pylyshyn, 1988). Unfortunately, most of the neural network models proposed to date for distributed structure representations are rather *ad hoc;* they solve the problem for a particular class in a way that cannot be extended easily.

To sum up, we may describe symbolic AI as the formal manipulation of a language of algorithms and data representations in a *top-down* fashion. On the other hand, we may describe neural networks as parallel distributed processors with a natural learning capability, and which usually operate in a *bottom-up* fashion. For the implementation of cognitive tasks, it therefore appears that rather than seek solutions based on symbolic AI or neural networks alone, a more potentially useful approach would be to build *structured connectionist models* that incorporate both of them. By so doing, we are able to combine the desirable features of adaptivity, robustness, and uniformity offered by neural networks with the representation, inference, and universality that are inherent features of symbolic AI (Feldman, 1992). For such a hybrid system to be successful, however, it is important that we carefully evaluate the areas in which each method works best. Classical AI techniques are best suited for natural language processing, planning, or explicit reasoning, whereas neural networks are best suited for lower-level perceptual processes, pattern matching, and associative memories. Thus, by combining these two different methods within the same system, we may be able to compound the benefits of both classical AI and neural networks, and alleviate their individual shortcomings. An example of such a hybrid network architecture used for classification and probability estimation is described in Goodman et al. (1992).

1.10 Historical Notes

We conclude this introductory chapter on neural networks with some historical notes.[4]

The modern era of neural networks is said to have begun with the pioneering work of McCulloch and Pitts (1943). McCulloch was a psychiatrist and neuroanatomist by training; he had spent some 20 years thinking about the representation of an event in the nervous system. Pitts was a mathematical prodigy, who joined McCulloch in 1942. According to Rall (1990), the 1943 classic paper by McCulloch and Pitts arose within a neural modeling community that had been active at the University of Chicago for at least five years prior to 1943, under the leadership of Rashevsky.

In their paper, McCulloch and Pitts described a logical calculus of neural networks. This paper was widely read at the time, and still is. It is noteworthy that von Neumann used idealized switch-delay elements derived from the idealized neural elements of McCulloch and Pitts in the construction of the EDVAC (Electronic Discrete Variable Automatic Computer) that developed out of the ENIAC (Electronic Numerical Integrator and Computer) (Aspray and Burks, 1986). The ENIAC was the first general-purpose electronic computer, which was built at the Moore School of Electrical Engineering of the University of Pennsylvania during the period 1943 to 1946. The McCulloch–Pitts theory of formal neural networks featured prominently in the second of four lectures delivered by von Neumann at the University of Illinois in 1949.

[4] The historical notes presented here are largely (but not exclusively) based on the following sources: (1) the paper by Saarinen et al. (1992); (2) the chapter contribution by Rall (1990); (3) the paper by Widrow and Lehr (1990); (4) the papers by Cowan (1990) and Cowan and Sharp (1988); (5) the paper by Grossberg (1988c); (6) the two-volume book on neurocomputing (Anderson et al., 1990; Anderson and Rosenfeld, 1988); (7) the chapter contribution of Selfridge et al. (1988); (8) chap. 1 of the book by Arbib (1987); (9) the collection of papers of von Neumann on computing and computer theory (Aspray and Burks, 1986).

In 1948, Wiener's famous book *Cybernetics* was published, describing some important concepts for control, communications, and statistical signal processing. The second edition of the book was published in 1961, adding some new material on learning and self-organization. In Chapter II of both editions of the book, Wiener appeared to grasp the physical significance of statistical mechanics in the context of the subject matter, but it was left to Hopfield (more than 30 years later) to bring the linkage between statistical mechanics and learning systems to full fruition.

The next major development in neural networks came in 1949 with the publication of Hebb's book *The Organization of Behavior,* in which an explicit statement of a physiological learning rule for *synaptic modification* was presented for the first time. Specifically, Hebb proposed that the connectivity of the brain is continually changing as an organism learns differing functional tasks, and that *neural assemblies* are created by such changes. Hebb followed up an early suggestion by Ramón y Cajál and introduced his now famous *postulate of learning,* which states that the effectiveness of a variable synapse between two neurons is increased by the repeated activation of one neuron by the other across that synapse. Hebb's book was immensely influential among psychologists, but unfortunately it had little or no impact on the engineering community. It is also unfortunate that the concept of neural assemblies, which has more profound implications than Hebb's postulate of learning, has generally been ignored by the network modelers.

Hebb's book has been a source of inspiration for the development of computational models of *learning and adaptive systems.* The paper by Rochester, Holland, Habit, and Duda (1956) is perhaps the first attempt to use computer simulation to test a well-formulated neural theory based on Hebb's postulate of learning; the simulation results reported in that paper clearly showed that inhibition needed to be added for the theory actually to work. In that same year, Uttley (1956) demonstrated that a neural network with modifiable synapses may learn to classify simple sets of binary patterns into corresponding classes. Uttley introduced the so-called *leaky integrate and fire neuron,* which was later formally analyzed by Caianiello (1961). In later work, Uttley (1979) hypothesized that the effectiveness of a variable synapse in the nervous system depends on the statistical relationship between the fluctuating states on either side of that synapse, thereby linking up with Shannon's information theory.

In 1952, Ashby's book, *Design for a Brain: The Origin of Adaptive Behavior,* was published, which is just as fascinating to read today as it must have been then. The book was concerned with the basic notion that adaptive behavior is not inborn but rather learned, and that through learning the behavior of an animal (system) usually changes for the better. The book emphasized the dynamic aspects of the living organism as a machine and the related concept of stability.

In 1954, Minsky wrote a "neural network" doctorate thesis at Princeton University, which was entitled "Theory of Neural-Analog Reinforcement Systems and Its Application to the Brain-Model Problem." In 1961, an excellent early paper by Minsky on AI, entitled "Steps Toward Artificial Intelligence," was published; this latter paper contains a large section on what is now termed neural networks.

Also in 1954, the idea of a *nonlinear adaptive filter* was proposed by Gabor, one of the early pioneers of communication theory, and the inventor of holography. He went on to build such a machine with the aid of collaborators, the details of which are described in Gabor et al. (1960). Learning was accomplished by feeding samples of a stochastic process into the machine, together with the target function that the machine was expected to produce.

Another topic that was investigated in the 1950s is *associative memory,* work on which was initiated by Taylor (1956). This was followed by the introduction of the *learning matrix* by Steinbuch (1961); this matrix consists of a planar network of switches interposed between arrays of "sensory" receptors and "motor" effectors. In 1969, an elegant paper on nonholographic associative memory by Willshaw, Buneman, and Lonquet-Higgins was published. This paper presents two ingenious network models: a simple optical system realizing a correlation memory, and a closely related neural network suggested by the optical memory. Other significant contributions to the early development of associative memory include papers by Anderson (1972), Kohonen (1972), and Nakano (1972), who independently and in the same year introduced the idea of a *correlation matrix memory* based on the *outer product* learning rule.

An issue of particular concern in the context of neural networks is that of designing a reliable network with neurons that may be viewed as unreliable components. This important problem was solved by von Neumann (1956) using the idea of redundancy, which motivated Winograd and Cowan (1963) to suggest the use of a *distributed* redundant representation for neural networks. von Neumann was one of the great figures in science in the first half of the twentieth century. The *von Neumann architecture,* basic to the design of a digital computer, is named in his honor. In 1955, he was invited by Yale University to give the Silliman Lectures during 1956. He died in 1957, and the unfinished manuscript of the Silliman Lectures was published later as a book, *The Computer and the Brain* (1958). This book is interesting because it suggests what von Neumann might have done if he had lived; he had started to become aware of the profound differences between brains and computers.

Some 15 years after the publication of McCulloch and Pitt's classic paper, a new approach to the pattern-recognition problem was introduced by Rosenblatt (1958) in his work on the *perceptron.* The crowning achievement of Rosenblatt's work was the so-called *perceptron convergence theorem,* the first proof for which was outlined by Rosenblatt (1960b); proofs of the theorem also appeared in Novikoff (1963) and Singleton (1962), among others. In 1960, Widrow and Hoff introduced the *least mean-square (LMS) algorithm* and used it to formulate the *Adaline* (adaptive linear element). The difference between the perceptron and the Adaline lies in the training procedure. One of the earliest trainable layered neural networks with multiple adaptive elements was the Madaline (multiple-adaline) structure proposed by Widrow and his students (Widrow, 1962). In 1965, Nilsson's book, *Learning Machines,* was published, which is still the source for the best-written exposition of linearly separable patterns in hypersurfaces. During the classical period of the perceptron in the 1960s, it seemed as if neural networks could do anything. But then came the book by Minsky and Papert (1969), who used elegant mathematics to demonstrate that there are fundamental limits on what one-layer perceptrons can compute. In a brief section on multilayer perceptrons, they stated that there was no reason to suppose that any of the virtues of one-layer perceptrons carry over to the many-layered version.

An important problem encountered in the design of a multilayer perceptron is the *credit assignment problem* (i.e., the problem of assigning credit to hidden neurons in the network). The terminology ''credit assignment'' was first used by Minsky (1961), under the title ''Credit Assignment Problem for Reinforcement Learning Systems.'' By the late 1960s, most of the ideas and concepts necessary to solve the perceptron credit assignment problem were already formulated, as were many of the ideas underlying the recurrent (attractor neural) networks that are nowadays referred to as Hopfield networks. However, we had to wait until the 1980s for the solutions of these basic problems to emerge. According to Cowan (1990), there were three reasons for this lag of over 10 years:

- One reason was technological; there were no personal computers or workstations for experimentation. For example, when Gabor developed his nonlinear learning filter, it took his research team a further six years to build the filter with analog devices (Gabor, 1954; Gabor et al., 1960).

- The other reason was in part psychological, in part financial. The 1969 monograph by Minsky and Papert certainly did not encourage anyone to work on perceptrons, nor agencies to support the work on them.

- The analogy between neural networks and lattice spins was premature. The *spin-glass model* of Sherrington and Kirkpatrick was not invented until 1975.

Rightly or wrongly, these factors contributed in one way or another to the dampening of continued interest in neural networks in the 1970s. Many of the researchers, except for those in psychology and the neurosciences, deserted the field during that decade. Indeed, only a handful of the early pioneers maintained their commitment to neural networks. From a physics and engineering perspective, we may look back on the 1970s as a "decade of dormancy" for neural networks.

An important activity that did emerge in the 1970s was *self-organizing maps* using competitive learning. The computer simulation work done by von der Malsburg (1973) was perhaps the first to demonstrate self-organization. In 1976, Willshaw and von der Malsburg published the first paper on the formation of self-organizing maps, motivated by topologically ordered maps in the brain.

In the 1980s, major contributions to the theory and design of neural networks were made on several fronts, and with it there was a resurgence of interest in neural networks.

Grossberg (1980), building on his earlier work on competitive learning (Grossberg, 1972, 1976a, b), established a new principle of self-organization that combines bottom-up adaptive filtering and contrast enhancement in short-term memory with top-down template matching and stabilization of code learning. Given such a capability, and if the input pattern and learned feedback match, a dynamical state called *adaptive resonance* (i.e., amplification and prolongation of neural activity) takes place. This phenomenon provides the basis of a new class of neural networks known as *adaptive resonance theory* (ART).

In 1982, Hopfield used the idea of an energy function to formulate a new way of understanding the computation performed by recurrent networks with symmetric synaptic connections. Moreover, he established the isomorphism between such a recurrent network and an *Ising model* used in statistical physics. This analogy paved the way for a deluge of physical theory (and physicists) to enter neural modeling, thereby transforming the field of neural networks. This particular class of neural networks with feedback attracted a great deal of attention in the 1980s, and in the course of time it has come to be known as *Hopfield networks.* Although Hopfield networks may not be very realistic models for neurobiological systems, the principle they embody, namely, that of storing information in dynamically stable networks, is profound. The origin of this principle may in fact be traced back to pioneering work of many other investigators:

- Cragg and Tamperley (1954, 1955) made the observation that just as neurons can be "fired" (activated) or "not fired" (quiescent), so can atoms in a lattice have their spins pointing "up" or "down."

- Cowan (1967) introduced the "sigmoid" firing characteristic and the smooth firing condition for a neuron that was based on the logistic function.

- Grossberg (1967, 1968) introduced the *additive model* of a neuron, involving nonlinear difference-differential equations, and explored the use of the model as a basis for short-term memory.

- Amari (1972) independently introduced the additive model of a neuron, and used it to study the dynamic behavior of randomly connected neuronlike elements.

- Wilson and Cowan (1972) derived coupled nonlinear differential equations for the dynamics of spatially localized populations containing both excitatory and inhibitory model neurons.

- Little and Shaw (1975) described a *probabilistic model* of a neuron, either firing or not firing an action potential, and used the model to develop a theory of short-term memory; in the context of biological neurons, *action potential* refers to an electrical impulse sent down the axon when a neuron is fired.

- Anderson, Silverstein, Ritz, and Jones (1977) proposed the *brain-state-in-a-box (BSB) model,* consisting of a simple associative network coupled to a nonlinear dynamics.

It is therefore not surprising that the publication of Hopfield's paper in 1982 generated a great deal of controversy. Nevertheless, it is in Hopfield's 1982 paper that the principle of storing information in dynamically stable networks is first made explicit. In 1983, Cohen and Grossberg established a general principle for designing a *content-addressable memory* that includes the continuous-time version of the Hopfield network as a special case. A distinctive feature of an attractor neural network is the natural way in which *time,* an essential dimension of learning, manifests itself in the nonlinear dynamics of the network; in this context, the Cohen–Grossberg theorem is of profound importance.

Another important development in 1982 was the publication of Kohonen's paper on self-organizing maps (Kohonen, 1982a) using a one- or two-dimensional lattice structure, which was different in some respects from the earlier work by Willshaw and von der Malsburg. Kohonen's model appears to have received much more attention in the literature than the Willshaw–von der Malsburg model.

In 1983, Kirkpatrick, Galatt, and Vecchi described a new procedure called *simulated annealing,* for solving combinatorial optimization problems. Simulated annealing is rooted in statistical thermodynamics. It is based on a simple technique that was first used in computer simulation by Metropolis et al. (1953). The idea of simulated annealing was later exploited by Ackley, Hinton, and Sejnowski (1985) in the development of a stochastic learning algorithm that uses some nice properties of the Boltzmann distribution—hence the name *Boltzmann learning.*

A paper by Barto, Sutton, and Anderson on *reinforcement learning* was also published in 1983. Although they were not the first to use reinforcement learning (Minsky considered it in his 1954 Ph.D. thesis, for example), this paper has generated a great deal of interest in reinforcement learning and its application in control. Specifically, they demonstrated that a reinforcement learning system could learn to balance a broomstick (i.e., a pole mounted on a cart) in the absence of a helpful teacher. The system required only a failure signal that occurs when the pole falls past a critical angle from the vertical, or the cart reaches the end of a track.

In 1984, Braitenberg's book, *Vehicles: Experiments in Synthetic Psychology,* was published. Under the guise of science fiction, Braitenberg describes various machines with simple internal architecture, and which embody some important principles of goal-directed, self-organized performance. The properties of the machines and their behavior are inspired by facts about animal brains, in the study of which he was personally involved directly or indirectly over a span of 20 years.

In 1986 the development of the *back-propagation algorithm* was reported by Rumelhart, Hinton, and Williams (1986a). In that same year, the two-volume book, *Parallel Distributed Processing: Explorations in the Microstructures of Cognition,* by Rumelhart and McClelland, was published. This latter book has been a major influence in the use of back-propagation learning, which has emerged as the most popular learning algorithm for the training of multilayer perceptrons. In fact, back-propagation learning was discovered independently in two other places about the same time (Parker, 1985; LeCun, 1985). After the discovery of the back-propagation algorithm in the mid-1980s, it turned out that the algorithm had been described earlier by Werbos in his Ph.D. thesis at Harvard University in August 1974; Werbos's Ph.D. thesis was the first documented description of efficient reverse-mode gradient computation that was applied to general network models with neural networks arising as a special case. It is most unfortunate that Werbos's work remained almost unknown in the scientific community for over a decade.

In 1988 Linsker described a new principle for self-organization in a perceptual network (Linsker, 1988a). The principle is designed to preserve maximum information about input activity patterns, subject to such constraints as synaptic connections and synapse dynamic range. A similar suggestion had been made independently by several vision researchers. However, it was Linsker who used abstract concepts rooted in information theory (originated by Shannon in 1948) to formulate the *principle of maximum information preservation.*

Also in 1988, Broomhead and Lowe described a procedure for the design of layered feedforward networks using *radial basis functions* (RBF), which provide an alternative to multilayer perceptrons. The basic idea of the radial basis function goes back at least to the *method of potential functions* that was originally proposed by Bashkirov, Braverman, and Muchnik (1964), and the theoretical properties of which were developed by Aizerman, Braverman, and Rozonoer (1964a, b); a description of the method of potential functions is presented in the classic book, *Pattern Classification and Scene Analysis,* by Duda and Hart (1973). Nevertheless, the paper by Broomhead and Lowe has led to a great deal of research effort linking the design of neural networks to an important area in numerical analysis and also linear adaptive filters. In 1990, Poggio and Girosi (1990a) further enriched the theory of RBF networks by applying Tikhonov's regularization theory.

In 1989, Mead's book, *Analog VLSI and Neural Systems,* was published. This book provides an unusual mix of concepts drawn from neurobiology and VLSI technology. Above all, it includes chapters on silicon retina and silicon cochlea, written by Mead and co-workers, which are vivid examples of Mead's creative mind.

Perhaps more than any other publications, the 1982 paper by Hopfield and the 1986 two-volume book by Rumelhart and McLelland were the most influential publications responsible for the resurgence of interest in neural networks in the 1980s. Neural networks have certainly come a long way from the early days of McCulloch and Pitts. Indeed, they have established themselves as an interdisciplinary subject with deep roots in the neurosciences, psychology, mathematics, the physical sciences, and engineering. Needless to say, they are here to stay, and will continue to grow in theory, design, and applications.

PROBLEMS

1.1 An example of the sigmoid function is defined by

$$\varphi(v) = \frac{1}{1 + \exp(-av)}$$

whose limiting values are 0 and 1. Show that the derivative of $\varphi(v)$ with respect to v is given by

$$\begin{aligned}\varphi'(v) &= \frac{d\varphi}{dv} \\ &= a\varphi(v)[1 - \varphi(v)]\end{aligned}$$

What is the value of $\varphi'(v)$ at the origin?

1.2 Another form of the sigmoid function is defined by

$$\varphi(v) = \frac{1 - \exp(-av)}{1 + \exp(-av)}$$

$$= \tanh\left(\frac{av}{2}\right)$$

where tanh denotes a hyperbolic tangent. The limiting values of this second sigmoid function are -1 and $+1$. Show that the derivative of $\varphi(v)$ with respect to v is given by

$$\varphi'(v) = \frac{d\varphi}{dv}$$

$$= \frac{a}{2}[1 - \varphi^2(v)]$$

What is the value of $\varphi'(v)$ at the origin? Suppose that the slope parameter a is made infinitely large. What is the resulting form of $\varphi(v)$?

1.3 Consider the pseudolinear activation function $\varphi(v)$ shown in Fig. P1.3.
(a) Formulate $\varphi(v)$ as a function of v.
(b) What happens to $\varphi(v)$ if a is allowed to approach zero?

1.4 Repeat Problem 1.3 for the pseudolinear activation function $\varphi(v)$ shown in Fig. P1.4.

1.5 Develop a signal-flow graph of the neuron model shown in Fig. 1.4.

1.6 Compare the number of synaptic weights in the fully connected feedforward network of Fig. 1.15 with that of the partially connected feedforward network of Fig. 1.16.

1.7 A neuron j receives inputs from four other neurons whose activity levels are 10, -20, 4, and -2. The respective synaptic weights of neuron j are 0.8, 0.2, -1.0, and -0.9. Calculate the output of neuron j for the following two situations:
(a) The neuron is linear.
(b) The neuron is represented by a McCulloch–Pitts model.
Assume that the threshold applied to the neuron is zero.

1.8 Repeat Problem 1.7 for a neuron model based on the sigmoid function

$$\varphi(v) = \frac{1}{1 + \exp(-v)}$$

1.9 A fully connected feedforward network has 10 source nodes, 2 hidden layers, one with 4 neurons and the other with 3 neurons, and a single output neuron. Construct an architectural graph of this network.

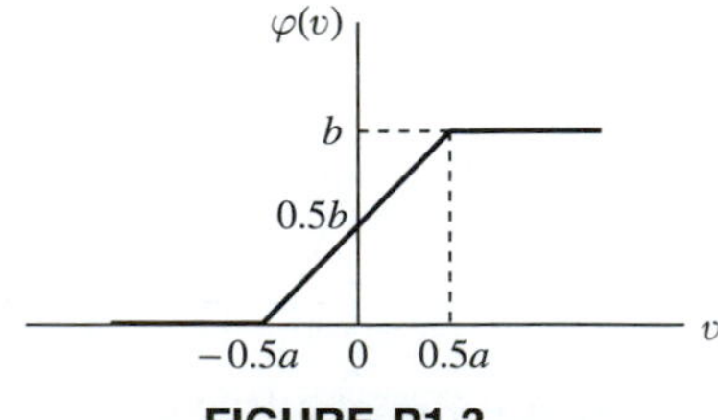

FIGURE P1.3

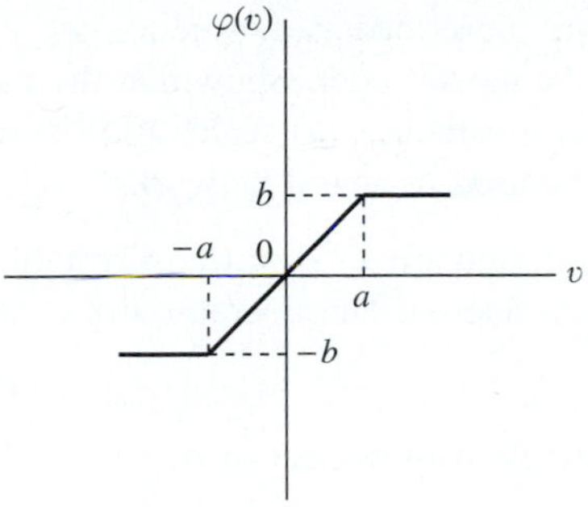

FIGURE P1.4

1.10 (a) Figure P1.10 shows the signal-flow graph of a 2-2-2-1 feedforward network. The function $\varphi(\cdot)$ denotes a logistic function. Write the input–output mapping defined by this network.

(b) The network described in Fig. P1.10 has no thresholds. Suppose that thresholds equal to $+1$ and -1 are applied to the top and bottom neurons of the first hidden layer, and thresholds equal to -1 and $+2$ are applied to the top and bottom neurons of the second hidden layer. Write the new form of the input–output mapping defined by the network.

1.11 Consider a multilayer feedforward network, all the neurons of which operate in their linear regions. Justify the statement that such a network is equivalent to a single-layer feedforward network.

1.12 Construct a fully recurrent network with 5 neurons, but with no self-feedback.

1.13 A recurrent network has 3 source nodes, 2 hidden neurons, and 4 output neurons. Construct an architectural graph that would be descriptive of such a network.

1.14 A lattice network uses a 4-by-4 array of neurons. Construct the architectural graph of such a network.

1.15 A useful form of preprocessing is based on the *autoregressive* (*AR*) *model* described by the difference equation (for real-valued data)

$$y(n) = w_1 y(n-1) + w_2 y(n-2) + \cdots + w_M y(n-M) + e(n)$$

where $y(n)$ is the model output; $e(n)$ is a sample drawn from a white-noise process

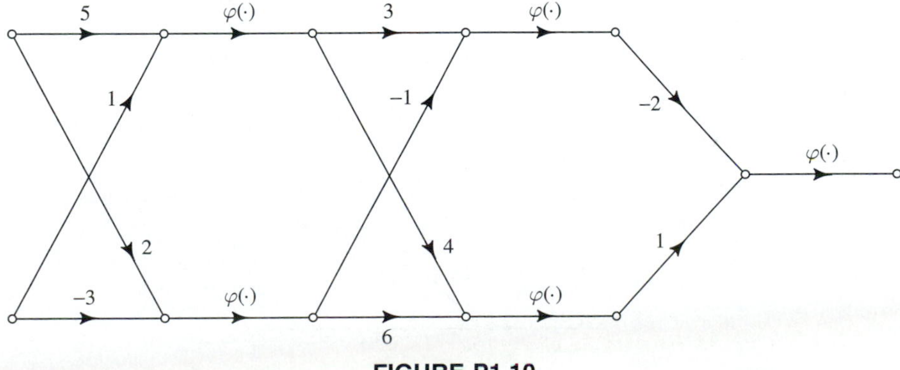

FIGURE P1.10

of zero mean and some prescribed variance; $w_1, w_2, \ldots, w_M$ are the AR model coefficients; and M is the model order. Show that the use of such a model provides two forms of geometric invariance: (a) scale, and (b) time translation. How could these two invariances be used in neural networks?

1.16 Let $\mathbf{x}$ be an input vector, and $\mathbf{s}(\alpha,\mathbf{x})$ be a transformation operator acting on $\mathbf{x}$ and depending on some parameter α. The operator $\mathbf{s}(\alpha,\mathbf{x})$ satisfies two requirements:

- $\mathbf{s}(0,\mathbf{x}) = \mathbf{x}$
- $\mathbf{s}(\alpha,\mathbf{x})$ is differentiable with respect to α.

The *tangent vector* is defined by the partial derivative $\partial\mathbf{s}(\alpha,\mathbf{x})/\partial\alpha$ (Simard et al., 1992).

Suppose that $\mathbf{x}$ represents an image, and α is a rotation parameter. How would you compute the tangent vector for the case when α is small? The tangent vector is locally invariant with respect to rotation of the original image; why?

1.17 **(a)** Construct Hinton diagrams for the multilayer feedforward network described in parts (a) and (b) of Problem 1.10.

(b) Construct the corresponding bond diagrams for this multilayer feedforward network.

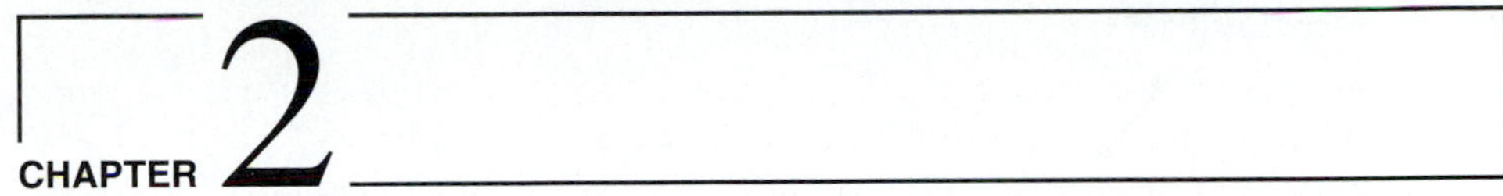

Learning Process

2.1 Introduction

Among the many interesting properties of a neural network, the property that is of primary significance is the ability of the network to *learn* from its environment, and to *improve* its performance through learning; the improvement in performance takes place over time in accordance with some prescribed measure. A neural network learns about its environment through an iterative process of adjustments applied to its synaptic weights and thresholds. Ideally, the network becomes more knowledgeable about its environment after each iteration of the learning process.

There are too many notions associated with ''learning'' to justify defining the term in a precise manner (Minsky, 1961). Moreover, the process of learning is a matter of viewpoint, which makes it all the more difficult to agree on a precise definition of the term (Natarajan, 1991). For example, learning viewed by a psychologist is quite different from learning in a classroom sense. Recognizing that our particular interest is in neural networks, we use a definition of learning that is adapted from Mendel and McClaren (1970).

We define learning in the context of neural networks as follows:

> *Learning is a process by which the free parameters of a neural network are adapted through a continuing process of stimulation by the environment in which the network is embedded. The type of learning is determined by the manner in which the parameter changes take place.*

This definition of the learning process implies the following sequence of events:

1. The neural network is *stimulated* by an environment.
2. The neural network *undergoes changes* as a result of this stimulation.
3. The neural network *responds in a new way* to the environment, because of the changes that have occurred in its internal structure.

To be specific, consider a pair of node signals x_j and v_k connected by a synaptic weight w_{kj}, as depicted in Fig. 2.1. Signal x_j represents the output of neuron j, and signal v_k represents the internal activity of neuron k. In the context of synaptic weight w_{kj}, the signals x_j and v_k are commonly referred to as *presynaptic* and *postsynaptic activities,* respectively. Let $w_{kj}(n)$ denote the value of the synaptic weight w_{kj} at time n. At time n an *adjustment* $\Delta w_{kj}(n)$ is applied to the synaptic weight $w_{kj}(n)$, yielding the updated value $w_{kj}(n + 1)$. We may thus write

$$w_{kj}(n + 1) = w_{kj}(n) + \Delta w_{kj}(n) \tag{2.1}$$

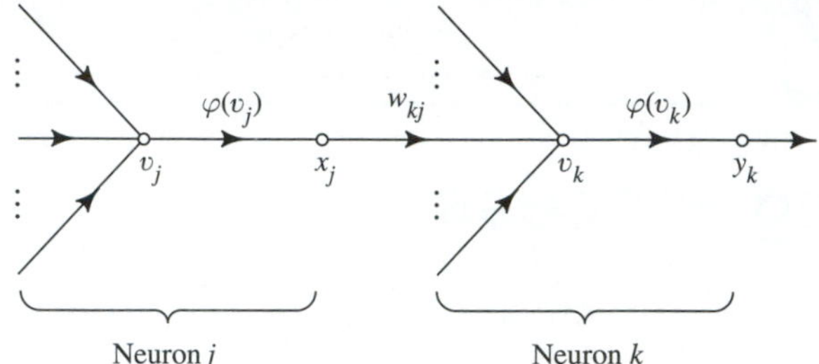

FIGURE 2.1 Signal-flow graph depicting a pair of neurons j and k embedded in a neural network; both neurons are assumed to have the same activation function $\varphi(\cdot)$.

where $w_{kj}(n)$ and $w_{kj}(n + 1)$ may be viewed as the *old* and *new* values of the synaptic weight w_{kj}, respectively. Equation (2.1) sums up the overall effect of events 1 and 2 implicit in the definition of the learning process presented above. In particular, the adjustment $\Delta w_{kj}(n)$ is computed as a result of stimulation by the environment (event 1), and the updated value $w_{kj}(n + 1)$ defines the change made in the network as a result of this stimulation (event 2). Event 3 takes place when the response of the new network, operating with the updated set of parameters $\{w_{kj}(n + 1)\}$, is reevaluated.

A prescribed set of well-defined rules for the solution of a learning problem is called a *learning algorithm.*[1] As one would expect, there is no unique learning algorithm for the design of neural networks. Rather, we have a "kit of tools" represented by a diverse variety of learning algorithms, each of which offers advantages of its own. Basically, learning algorithms differ from each other in the way in which the adjustment Δw_{kj} to the synaptic weight w_{kj} is formulated. Another factor to be considered is the manner in which a neural network (learning machine) relates to its environment. In this latter context, we speak of a *learning paradigm* referring to a *model* of the environment in which the neural network operates. We may thus offer the *taxonomy of learning* described in Fig. 2.2; the elements of this taxonomy are explained in the sequel.

Organization of the Chapter

The chapter is organized as follows. In Sections 2.2 through 2.5 we describe the four basic rules: *error-correction learning, Hebbian learning, competitive learning,* and *Boltzmann learning.* Error-correction learning is rooted in optimum filtering. In contrast, both Hebbian learning and competitive learning are inspired by neurobiological considerations. Boltzmann learning is different altogether in that it is based on ideas borrowed from thermodynamics and information theory. *Thorndike's law of effect,* included as one of the learning algorithms (rules) listed in Fig. 2.2, is discussed in Section 2.8 on reinforcement learning.

In Section 2.6 we consider the *credit-assignment problem,* which is basic to the learning process. Then in Sections 2.7 through 2.9 we consider the three basic classes of learning paradigms: *supervised learning, reinforcement learning,* and *self-organized* (*unsupervised*) *learning.* As its name implies, supervised learning is performed under the supervision of an external "teacher." Reinforcement learning involves the use of a "critic" that evolves through a trial-and-error process. Unsupervised learning is performed in a self-organized manner in that *no* external teacher or critic is required to instruct synaptic

[1] The word "algorithm" is derived from the name of the Persian mathematician Mohammed al-Kowârisimi, who lived during the ninth century and who is credited with developing the step-by-step rules for the addition, subtraction, multiplication, and division of ordinary decimal numbers. When the name was written in Latin, it became Algorismus, from which *algorithm* is but a small step (Harel, 1987).

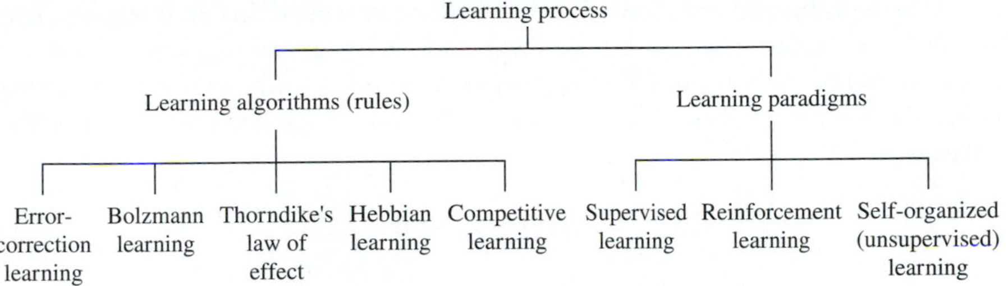

FIGURE 2.2 A taxonomy of the learning process.

changes in the network. At this point we are ready to consider a list of *learning tasks* in Section 2.10, followed by a discussion in Section 2.11 on the role of *time* in learning.

Next we consider some important theoretical issues. In Section 2.12 we consider the statistical nature of the learning process. Then in Section 2.13 we present some ideas on a mathematical theory of learning. Finally, in Section 2.14 we present a critique on the various issues discussed in the chapter.

2.2 Error-Correction Learning

Let $d_k(n)$ denote some *desired response* or *target response* for neuron k at time n. Let the corresponding value of the *actual response* of this neuron be denoted by $y_k(n)$. The response $y_k(n)$ is produced by a *stimulus* (vector) $\mathbf{x}(n)$ applied to the input of the network in which neuron k is embedded. The input vector $\mathbf{x}(n)$ and desired response $d_k(n)$ for neuron k constitute a particular *example* presented to the network at time n. It is assumed that this example and all other examples presented to the network are generated by an environment that is probabilistic in nature, but the underlying probability distribution is unknown.

Typically, the actual response $y_k(n)$ of neuron k is different from the desired response $d_k(n)$. Hence, we may define an *error signal* as the difference between the target response $d_k(n)$ and the actual response $y_k(n)$, as shown by

$$e_k(n) = d_k(n) - y_k(n) \tag{2.2}$$

The ultimate purpose of error-correction learning is to minimize a *cost function* based on the error signal $e_k(n)$, such that the actual response of each output neuron in the network approaches the target response for that neuron in some statistical sense. Indeed, once a cost function is selected, error-correction learning is strictly an optimization problem to which the usual tools may be brought to bear. A criterion commonly used for the cost function is the *mean-square-error criterion,* defined as the mean-square value of the *sum of squared errors:*

$$J = E\left[\frac{1}{2}\sum_k e_k^2(n)\right] \tag{2.3}$$

where E is the *statistical expectation operator,* and the summation is *over all the neurons in the output layer* of the network. The factor $\frac{1}{2}$ is used in Eq. (2.3) so as to simplify subsequent derivations resulting from the minimization of J with respect to free parameters of the network. Equation (2.3) assumes that the underlying processes are *wide-sense stationary.* Minimization of the cost function J with respect to the network parameters leads to the so-called *method of gradient descent* (Haykin, 1991; Widrow and Stearns,

1985). However, the difficulty with this optimization procedure is that it requires knowledge of the statistical characteristics of the underlying processes. We overcome this practical difficulty by settling for an *approximate* solution to the optimization problem. Specifically, we use the *instantaneous value* of the sum of squared errors as the criterion of interest:

$$\mathscr{E}(n) = \frac{1}{2}\sum_k e_k^2(n) \tag{2.4}$$

The network is then optimized by minimizing $\mathscr{E}(n)$ with respect to the synaptic weights of the network. Thus, according to the *error-correction learning rule* (or *delta rule,* as it is sometimes called), the adjustment $\Delta w_{kj}(n)$ made to the synaptic weight w_{kj} at time n is given by (Widrow and Hoff, 1960)

$$\Delta w_{kj}(n) = \eta e_k(n) x_j(n) \tag{2.5}$$

where η is a positive constant that determines the *rate of learning.* In other words, the adjustment made to a synaptic weight is proportional to the product of the error signal (measured with respect to some desired response at the output of that neuron) and the input signal of the synapse in question. Note that this input signal is the same as the output signal of the presynaptic neuron that feeds the neuron in question.

Error-correction learning relies on the error signal $e_k(n)$ to compute the correction $\Delta w_{kj}(n)$ applied to the synaptic weight $w_{kj}(n)$ of neuron k in accordance with Eq. (2.5). The error signal $e_k(n)$ is itself computed from Eq. (2.2). Finally, Eq. (2.1) is used to compute the updated (new) value $w_{kj}(n + 1)$ of the synaptic weight in question. These three equations are represented in the signal-flow graph of Fig. 2.3, which also includes a *storage* element represented by the *unit-delay operator* z^{-1}; that is,

$$z^{-1}[w_{kj}(n + 1)] = w_{kj}(n) \tag{2.6}$$

Figure 2.3 also includes representations of the defining equations

$$v_k(n) = \sum_j x_j(n) w_{kj}(n) \tag{2.7}$$

and

$$y_k(n) = \varphi(v_k(n)) \tag{2.8}$$

that pertain to the model of neuron k. Note also that the nodes in the signal-flow graph of Fig. 2.3 represent a "mixture" of signals and weights, which explains why the transfer function of the link connecting $w_{kj}(n)$ to $v_k(n)$ is represented by $x_j(n)$, and that of the link connecting $e_k(n)$ to $w_{kj}(n + 1)$ is $\eta x_j(n)$. Thus, the multiplication of $x_j(n)$ by $w_{kj}(n)$ results from the fact that $w_{kj}(n)$ acts as the input to the branch of transmittance $x_j(n)$. The links with no designations [i.e., the link from $w_{kj}(n)$ to $w_{kj}(n + 1)$, and the link from $d_k(n)$ to $e_k(n)$] are presumed to have unity for their transfer functions. This latter convention is followed throughout the book.

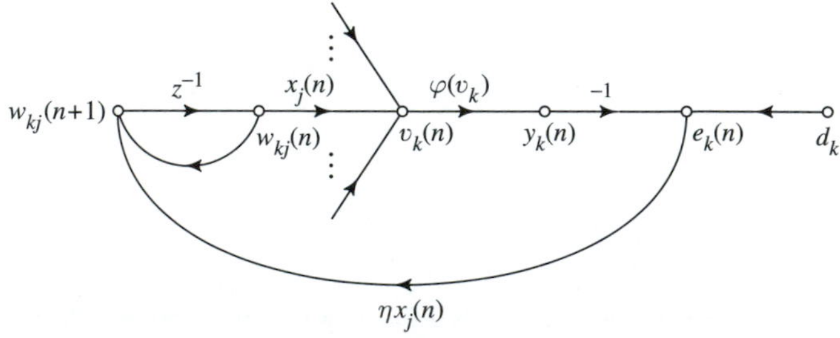

FIGURE 2.3 Signal-flow graph of error-correction learning.

Figure 2.3 clearly shows that error-correction learning behaves like a *closed feedback system.* Hence care has to be exercised in the choice of the value assigned to the learning-rate parameter η, so as to ensure *stability* of the error-correction learning process. Indeed, the learning-rate parameter η has a profound impact on the performance of error-correction learning in that it affects not only the rate of convergence of learning but also the convergence itself. If η is small, the learning process proceeds smoothly, but it may take a long time for the system to converge to a stable solution. If, on the other hand, η is large, the rate of learning is accelerated, but now there is a danger that the learning process may diverge and the system therefore becomes unstable.[2]

A plot of the cost function J versus the synaptic weights characterizing the neural network consists of a multidimensional surface referred to as an *error-performance surface* or simply *error surface.* Depending on the type of processing units used to construct the neural network, we may identify two distinct situations:

1. The neural network consists entirely of linear processing units, in which case the error surface is exactly a quadratic function of the weights in the network. That is, the error surface is bowl-shaped with a *unique* minimum point (barring the existence of a degenerate solution).
2. The neural network consists of nonlinear processing units, in which case the error surface has a *global minimum* (perhaps multiple global minima) as well as *local minima.*

In both cases, the objective of the error-correction learning algorithm is to start from an arbitrary point on the error surface (determined by the initial values assigned to the synaptic weights) and then move toward a global minimum, in a step-by-step fashion. In the first case this objective is indeed attainable. In the second case, on the other hand, it is not always attainable, because it is possible for the algorithm to get trapped at a local minimum of the error surface and therefore never be able to reach a global minimum.

2.3 Hebbian Learning

Hebb's postulate of learning is the oldest and most famous of all learning rules; it is named in honor of the neuropsychologist Hebb (1949). Quoting from Hebb's book, *The Organization of Behavior* (1949, p. 62):

> When an axon of cell A is near enough to excite a cell B and repeatedly or persistently takes part in firing it, some growth process or metabolic changes take place in one or both cells such that A's efficiency as one of the cells firing B, is increased.

Hebb proposed this change as a basis of associative learning (at the cellular level), which would result in an enduring modification in the activity pattern of a spatially distributed "assembly of nerve cells."

---

[2] To ensure stability we may use standard optimization criteria for choosing the learning-rate parameter η. According to one such criterion, we have

$$0 < \eta < \frac{2}{\lambda_{\max}(\mathbf{H}(\mathbf{w}))}$$

where $\mathbf{H}(\mathbf{w})$ is the *Hessian* of the cost function J evaluated at the current point $\mathbf{w}$ in weight space, and $\lambda_{\max}(\mathbf{H}(\mathbf{w}))$ is the largest eigenvalue of $\mathbf{H}(\mathbf{w})$. The Hessian $\mathbf{H}(\mathbf{w})$ is a symmetric matrix whose elements are defined by the second-order partial derivatives of the cost function J with respect to the elements of the weight vector $\mathbf{w}$. This stability condition is, however, impractical to compute, particularly if the Hessian is not known.

The above statement is made in a neurobiological context. We may expand and rephrase it as a two-part rule as follows (Stent, 1973; Changeux and Danchin, 1976):

1. *If two neurons on either side of a synapse (connection) are activated simultaneously (i.e., synchronously), then the strength of that synapse is selectively increased.*
2. *If two neurons on either side of a synapse are activated asynchronously, then that synapse is selectively weakened or eliminated.*

Such a synapse is called a *Hebbian synapse.*[3] (The original Hebb rule did not contain part 2.) More precisely, we define a Hebbian synapse as a synapse that uses a *time-dependent, highly local, and strongly interactive mechanism to increase synaptic efficiency as a function of the correlation between the presynaptic and postsynaptic activities.* From this definition we may deduce the following four key mechanisms (properties) that characterize a Hebbian synapse (Brown et al., 1990):

1. *Time-dependent mechanism.* This mechanism refers to the fact that the modifications in a Hebbian synapse depend on the exact time of occurrence of the presynaptic and postsynaptic activities.
2. *Local mechanism.* By its very nature, a synapse is the transmission site where information-bearing signals (representing ongoing activity in the presynaptic and postsynaptic units) are in *spatiotemporal* contiguity. This locally available information is used by a Hebbian synapse to produce a local synaptic modification that is input-specific. It is this local mechanism that enables a neural network made up of Hebbian synapses to perform unsupervised learning.
3. *Interactive mechanism.* Here we note that the occurrence of a change in a Hebbian synapse depends on activity levels on both sides of the synapse. That is, a Hebbian form of learning depends on a "true interaction" between presynaptic and postsynaptic activities in the sense that we cannot make a prediction from either one of these two activities by itself. Note also that this dependence or interaction may be deterministic or statistical in nature.
4. *Conjunctional* or *correlational mechanism.* One interpretation of Hebb's postulate of learning is that the condition for a change in synaptic efficiency is the conjunction of presynaptic and postsynaptic activities. Thus, according to this interpretation, the co-occurrence of presynaptic and postsynaptic activities (within a short interval of time) is sufficient to produce the synaptic modification. It is for this reason that a Hebbian synapse is sometimes referred to as a *conjunctional synapse.* For another interpretation of Hebb's postulate of learning, we may think of the interactive mechanism characterizing a Hebbian synapse in statistical terms. In particular, the correlation over time between presynaptic and postsynaptic activities is viewed as being responsible for a synaptic change. Accordingly, a Hebbian synapse is also referred to as a *correlational synapse.*

Synaptic Enhancement and Depression

The definition of a Hebbian synapse presented above does not exclude additional processes that may result in *synaptic depression* (i.e., weakening of a synapse connecting a pair of neurons). Indeed, we may generalize the concept of a Hebbian modification by recognizing that positively correlated activity produces synaptic strengthening, and that either uncorre-

[3] For a detailed review of Hebbian synapses, including a historical account, see Brown et al. (1990). For additional review material, see Constantine-Paton et al. (1990).

lated or negatively correlated activity produces synaptic weakening (Stent, 1973). Synaptic depression may also be of a noninteractive type. Specifically, the interactive condition for synaptic depression may simply be noncoincident presynaptic or postsynaptic activity.

We may go one step further by classifying synaptic modifications as *Hebbian, anti-Hebbian,* and *non-Hebbian* (Palm, 1982). According to this scheme, a Hebbian synapse increases its strength with positively correlated presynaptic and postsynaptic activities, and decreases its strength when these activities are either uncorrelated or negatively correlated. Conversely, an anti-Hebbian synapse[4] weakens positively correlated presynaptic and postsynaptic activities, and strengthens negatively correlated activities. In both Hebbian and anti-Hebbian synapses, however, the modification of synaptic efficiency relies on a mechanism that is time-dependent, highly local, and strongly interactive in nature. A non-Hebbian synapse, on the other hand, does not involve such a mechanism.

Mathematical Models of Hebbian Modifications

To formulate Hebb's postulate of learning in mathematical terms, consider again the situation depicted in Fig. 2.1. It shows a synaptic weight w_{kj} with presynaptic and postsynaptic activities denoted by x_j and y_k, respectively. According to Hebb's postulate, the adjustment applied to the synaptic weight w_{kj} at time n is expressed in the form

$$\Delta w_{kj}(n) = F(y_k(n), x_j(n)) \tag{2.9}$$

where $F(\cdot,\cdot)$ is a function of both postsynaptic and presynaptic activities. The activity terms $x_j(n)$ and $y_k(n)$ are often treated as dimensionless variables.

As a special case of Eq. (2.9), we may write

$$\Delta w_{kj}(n) = \eta y_k(n) x_j(n) \tag{2.10}$$

where η is a positive constant that determines the *rate of learning*. Equation (2.10) is the simplest rule for a change in the synaptic weight w_{kj}, expressed as a product of the incoming and outgoing signals. This rule clearly emphasizes the correlational nature of a Hebbian synapse. It is sometimes referred to as the *activity product rule*. The top curve of Fig. 2.4 shows a graphical representation of Eq. (2.10) with the change Δw_{kj} plotted versus the input x_j.

From this representation we see that the repeated application of the input signal (presynaptic activity) x_j leads to an *exponential growth* that finally drives the synaptic weight w_{kj} into saturation. To avoid such a situation from arising, we need to impose a limit on the growth of synaptic weights. One method for doing this is to introduce a nonlinear *forgetting factor* into the formula for the synaptic adjustment $\Delta w_{kj}(n)$ in Eq. (2.10). Specifically, we redefine $\Delta w_{kj}(n)$ as follows (Kohonen, 1988):

$$\Delta w_{kj}(n) = \eta y_k(n) x_j(n) - \alpha y_k(n) w_{kj}(n) \tag{2.11}$$

where α is a new positive constant and $w_{kj}(n)$ is the synaptic weight at time n. Equivalently, we may write

$$\Delta w_{kj}(n) = \alpha y_k(n)[c x_j(n) - w_{kj}(n)] \tag{2.12}$$

where c is equal to η/α. Equation (2.12) is sometimes referred to as a *generalized activity product rule*. This equation implies that for inputs for which $x_j(n) < w_{kj}(n)/c$, the modified synaptic weight $w_{kj}(n + 1)$ at time $n + 1$ will actually decrease by an amount proportional to the postsynaptic activity $y_k(n)$, as illustrated by the bottom curve in Fig. 2.4. On the

[4] The term anti-Hebbian is not used consistently in the literature. The interpretation given in the text corresponds to the terminology used in Palm (1982).

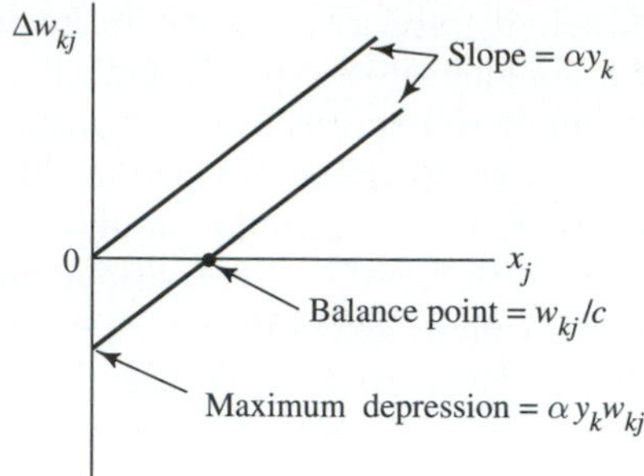

FIGURE 2.4 Illustrating Hebb's rule and its modification according to Eq. (2.12).

other hand, when $x_j(n) > w_{kj}(n)/c$, the modified synaptic weight $w_{kj}(n + 1)$ increases in proportion to $y_k(n)$. We thus see that the activity *balance point* for modifying the synaptic weight at time $n + 1$ is a variable, equal to w_{kj}/c, that is proportional to the value of w_{kj} at the time of presynaptic activation. The use of this approach eliminates the problem of runaway synaptic weight instability and results in a negatively accelerated synaptic modification curve.

Another way of formulating Hebb's postulate is in statistical terms in the sense that changes in synaptic weights are made proportional to the *covariance* between presynaptic and postsynaptic activities (Sejnowski, 1977a, b). Specifically, the change in synaptic weight w_{kj} at time n is written as

$$\begin{aligned}\Delta w_{kj}(n) &= \eta \operatorname{cov}[y_k(n), x_j(n)] \\ &= \eta E[(y_k(n) - \bar{y}_k)(x_j(n) - \bar{x}_j)]\end{aligned} \tag{2.13}$$

where η is a proportionality constant that determines the rate of learning; E is the statistical *expectation operator*; and $\bar{x}_j$ and $\bar{y}_k$ are the mean values of the presynaptic and postsynaptic activities, respectively. The latter pair of constants allows the synaptic weight w_{kj} to go up and down. Equation (2.13), as a bidirectional rule, is referred to as the *activity covariance rule*. According to this rule, on the average, the strength of a synapse should increase if the presynaptic and postsynaptic activities are positively correlated, decrease if they are negatively correlated, and remain unchanged if they are uncorrelated. Expanding terms in Eq. (2.13) and recognizing that the expectation of the sum of a number of terms is the same as the sum of their individual expectations, we may redefine the activity covariance rule as follows:

$$\Delta w_{kj}(n) = \eta\{E[y_k(n)x_j(n)] - \bar{y}_k\bar{x}_j\} \tag{2.14}$$

The first term in Eq. (2.14) has a form similar to the simple Hebbian rule of Eq. (2.10), except for the use of expectation. The second term may be viewed as a threshold that is proportional to the product of the mean values of the presynaptic and postsynaptic activities. The activity covariance rule, as described here, has been formulated using ensemble averages; a corresponding version of the rule may also be formulated using time averages.

Neurobiological Considerations

Hebb's postulate of learning has been a subject of intense experimental interest among neurophysiologists and neuropsychologists for many years. According to Kelso et al. (1986), a time-dependent, highly local, and strongly interactive mechanism is responsible for one form of *long-term potentiation* in the hippocampus; there is strong neuropsychological evidence indicating that the *hippocampus* plays a key role in certain aspects of learning or memory. Long-term potentiation (LTP) is a use-dependent and long-lasting increase in synaptic strength that may be induced by short periods of high-frequency activation of excitatory synapses in the hippocampus. The experiment showing that LTP in certain hippocampal synapses is Hebbian appears to have been replicated by other investigators, as reviewed by Brown et al. (1990).

However, physiological evidence reported by Granger et al. (1994) appears to show that the induction of synaptic LTP at some sites can be at variance with predictions based on Hebb's postulate of learning. For example, the degree of potentiation can depend on the temporal order in which synapses are stimulated (Larson and Lynch, 1989), previous potentiations do not always affect subsequent potentiations (Muller and Lynch, 1988), and correlated presynaptic and postsynaptic activities do not induce potentiation at some sites unless the depolarization exceeds the NMDA (*N*-methyl-D-aspartate) receptor channel voltage threshold (Artola and Singer, 1987). A non-Hebbian LTP induction rule is derived directly from these physiological results by Granger et al. (1993), from which the simple Hebbian learning rule emerges as a special case.

It is also of interest to note that, according to Hetherington and Shapiro (1993), the mechanisms proposed by Hebb for the formation of "nerve cell assemblies" are underconstrained and may not be sufficient to accomplish the formation. Cell assemblies are groups of interconnected neurons that become capable of self-sustaining, reverbatory activity through repeated activation. Using computer simulations, Hetherington and Shapiro have demonstrated that (1) an anti-Hebbian rule is needed to decrease the saturation of cell assembly activity, (2) a synaptic modification rule that decreases synaptic weights when postsynaptic activity occurs in the absence of presynaptic activity is necessary, but not sufficient, for stable assemblies, and (3) dendritic trees must be partitioned into independent regions of activation.

2.4 Competitive Learning

In *competitive learning,* as the name implies, the output neurons of a neural network compete among themselves for being the one to be active (fired). Thus, whereas in a neural network based on Hebbian learning several output neurons may be active simultaneously, in the case of competitive learning only a single output neuron is active at any one time. It is this feature that makes competitive learning highly suited to discover those statistically salient features that may be used to classify a set of input patterns.

The idea of competitive learning may be traced back to the early works of von der Malsburg (1973) on the self-organization of orientation sensitive nerve cells in the striate cortex, Fukushima (1975) on a self-organizing multilayer neural network known as the *cognitron,* Willshaw and von der Malsburg (1976) on the formation of patterned neural connections by self-organization, and Grossberg (1972, 1976a, b) on adaptive pattern classification. Also, there is substantial evidence for competitive learning playing an important role in the formation of topographic maps in the brain (Durbin et al., 1989), and recent experimental work by Ambros-Ingerson et al. (1990) provides further neurobiological justification for competitive learning.

There are three basic elements to a competitive learning rule (Rumelhart and Zipser, 1985):

- A set of neurons that are all the same except for some randomly distributed synaptic weights, and which therefore *respond differently* to a given set of input patterns.
- A *limit* imposed on the "strength" of each neuron.
- A mechanism that permits the neurons to *compete* for the right to respond to a given

subset of inputs, such that only *one* output neuron, or only one neuron per group, is active (i.e., "on") at a time. The neuron that wins the competition is called a *winner-takes-all neuron.*

Accordingly, the individual neurons of the network learn to specialize on sets of similar patterns, and thereby become *feature detectors.*

In the simplest form of competitive learning, the neural network has a single layer of output neurons, each of which is fully connected to the input nodes. The network may include *lateral connections* among the neurons, as indicated in Fig. 2.5. In the network architecture described herein, the lateral connections perform *lateral inhibition,* with each neuron tending to inhibit the neuron to which it is laterally connected. The rest of the synaptic connections in the network of Fig. 2.5 are excitatory.

For neuron j, say, to be the winning neuron, its net internal activity level v_j for a specified input pattern $\mathbf{x}$ must be the largest among all the neurons in the network. The output signal y_j of winning neuron j is set equal to one; the output signals of all the neurons that lose the competition are set equal to zero.

Let w_{ji} denote the synaptic weight connecting input node i to neuron j. Each neuron is allotted a *fixed* amount of synaptic weight (all synaptic weights are positive), which is distributed among its input nodes; that is, we have

$$\sum_i w_{ji} = 1 \qquad \text{for all } j \tag{2.15}$$

A neuron learns by shifting synaptic weights from its inactive to active input nodes. If a neuron does not respond to a particular input pattern, no learning takes place in that neuron. If a particular neuron wins the competition, then each input node of that neuron relinquishes some proportion of its synaptic weight, and the weight relinquished is then distributed equally among the active input nodes. According to the *standard competitive learning rule,* the change Δw_{ji} applied to synaptic weight w_{ji} is defined by

$$\Delta w_{ji} = \begin{cases} \eta(x_i - w_{ji}) & \text{if neuron } j \text{ wins the competition} \\ 0 & \text{if neuron } j \text{ loses the competition} \end{cases} \tag{2.16}$$

where η is the learning-rate parameter. This rule has the overall effect of moving the synaptic weight vector $\mathbf{w}_j$ of winning neuron j toward the input pattern $\mathbf{x}$.

To illustrate the essence of competitive learning, we may use the geometric analogy depicted in Fig. 2.6 (Rumelhart and Zipser, 1985). It is assumed that each input pattern $\mathbf{x}$ has some constant length, so that we may view it as a point on an N-dimensional unit

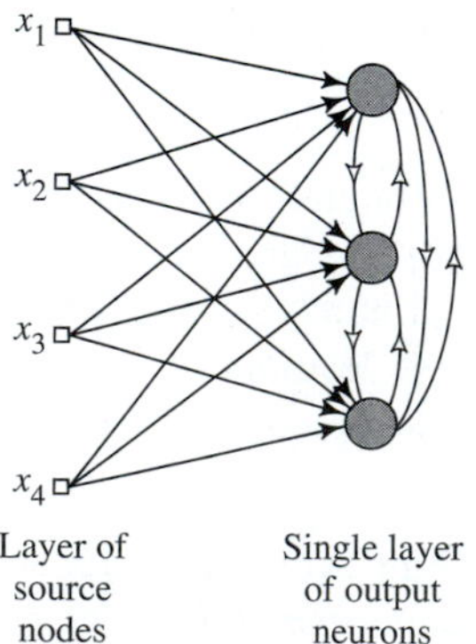

FIGURE 2.5 Architectural graph of a simple competitive learning network with feedforward (excitatory) connections from the source nodes to the neurons, and lateral (inhibitory) connections among the neurons; the lateral corrections are signified by open arrows.

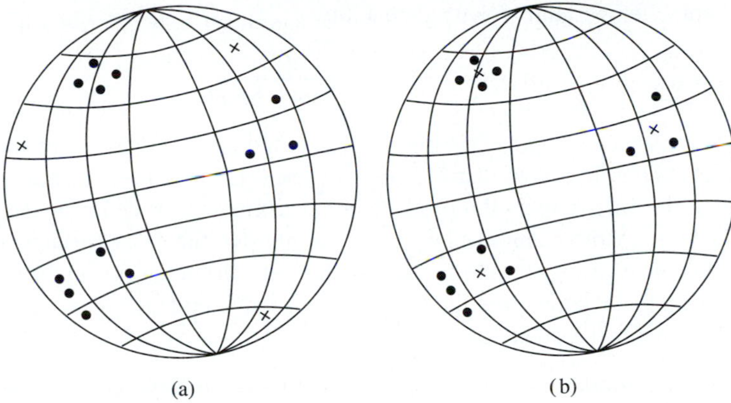

(a) (b)

FIGURE 2.6 Geometric interpretation of the competitive learning process. The dots represent the input vectors, and the crosses represent the synaptic weight vectors of three output neurons. (a) Initial state of the network. (b) Final state of the network.

sphere, where N is the number of input nodes; N also represents the dimension of each synaptic weight vector $\mathbf{w}_j$. It is further assumed that all neurons in the network are constrained to have the same Euclidean length (norm), as shown by

$$\sum_j w_{ji}^2 = 1 \qquad \text{for all } j \tag{2.17}$$

Thus, when the synaptic weights are properly scaled, they form a set of vectors that fall on the same N-dimensional unit sphere. In Fig. 2.6a we show three natural groupings (clusters) of the stimulus patterns represented by dots; this figure also includes a possible initial state of the network (represented by crosses) that may exist before learning. Figure 2.6b shows a typical final state of the network that results from the use of competitive learning. In particular, each of the output neurons has discovered a cluster of inputs by moving its synaptic weight vector to the center of gravity of the discovered cluster (Rumelhart and Zipser, 1985; Hertz et al., 1991).

2.5 Boltzmann Learning

The *Boltzmann learning rule,* named in honor of L. Boltzmann, is a stochastic learning algorithm derived from information-theoretic and thermodynamic considerations (Hinton and Sejnowski, 1986; Ackley et al., 1985). A formal derivation of the rule is presented in Chapter 8. Here we merely emphasize the essence of what Boltzmann learning is.

In a Boltzmann machine, the neurons constitute a recurrent structure, and they operate in a binary manner in that they are either in an "on" state denoted by $+1$ or in an "off" state denoted by -1. The machine is characterized by an *energy function E,* the value of which is determined by the particular states occupied by the individual neurons of the machine, as shown by

$$E = -\frac{1}{2}\sum_i \sum_{\substack{j \\ i \neq j}} w_{ji} s_j s_i \tag{2.18}$$

where s_i is the state of neuron i, and w_{ji} is the synaptic weight connecting neuron i to neuron j. The fact that $i \neq j$ means simply that none of the neurons in the machine has self-feedback. The machine operates by choosing a neuron at *random*—say, neuron j—at some step of the learning process, and flipping the state of neuron j from state s_j to state $-s_j$ at some temperature T with probability

$$W(s_j \rightarrow -s_j) = \frac{1}{1 + \exp(-\Delta E_j / T)} \tag{2.19}$$

where ΔE_j is the *energy change* (i.e., the change in the energy function of the machine) resulting from such a flip. Note that T is not a physical temperature, but rather a pseudo-temperature. If this rule is applied repeatedly, the machine will reach *thermal equilibrium.*

The neurons of a Boltzmann machine partition into two functional groups: *visible* and *hidden.* The visible neurons provide an interface between the network and the environment in which it operates, whereas the hidden neurons always operate freely. There are two modes of operation to be considered:

- *Clamped condition,* in which the visible neurons are all clamped onto specific states determined by the environment.
- *Free-running condition,* in which all the neurons (visible and hidden) are allowed to operate freely.

Let ρ_{ji}^{+} denote the *correlation* between the states of neurons i and j, *conditional* on the network being in its clamped condition. Let ρ_{ji}^{-} denote the *unconditional correlation* between the states of neurons i and j (i.e., the network operates in the free-running condition). Both correlations are averaged over all possible states of the machine when it is in thermal equilibrium. The correlations ρ_{ji}^{+} and ρ_{ji}^{-} are defined as follows,

$$\rho_{ji}^{+} = \sum_{\alpha} \sum_{\beta} P_{\alpha\beta}^{+} s_{j|\alpha\beta} s_{i|\alpha\beta} \tag{2.20}$$

$$\rho_{ji}^{-} = \sum_{\alpha} \sum_{\beta} P_{\alpha\beta}^{-} s_{j|\alpha\beta} s_{i|\alpha\beta} \tag{2.21}$$

where $s_{i|\alpha\beta}$ denotes the state of neuron i, given that the visible neurons of the machine are in state α and the hidden neurons are in state β. The factor $P_{\alpha\beta}^{+}$ is the conditional probability that the visible neurons are in state α and the hidden neurons are jointly in state β, given that the machine is in its clamped condition; and $P_{\alpha\beta}^{-}$ is the conditional probability that the visible neurons are in state α and the hidden neurons are jointly in state β, given that the machine is free-running. Then, according to the *Boltzmann learning rule,* the change Δw_{ji} applied to the synaptic weight w_{ji} from neuron i to neuron j is defined by (Hinton and Sejnowski, 1986)

$$\Delta w_{ji} = \eta(\rho_{ji}^{+} - \rho_{ji}^{-}), \qquad i \neq j \tag{2.22}$$

where η is a learning-rate parameter. Note that both ρ_{ji}^{+} and ρ_{ji}^{-} range in value from -1 to $+1$.

A distinctive feature of Boltzmann learning is that it uses only locally available observations under two operating conditions: clamped and free-running.

2.6 The Credit-Assignment Problem

When studying learning algorithms for distributed systems, it is useful to consider the notion of *credit assignment* (Minsky, 1961). Basically, the credit-assignment problem is the problem of assigning *credit* or *blame* for overall outcomes to each of the internal decisions made by a learning system and which contributed to those outcomes. In many cases of interest, the dependence of outcomes on internal decisions is mediated by a sequence of actions taken by the learning system. In other words, internal decisions affect which particular actions are taken, and then the actions, not the internal decisions, directly influence overall outcomes. In situations of this kind, we may decompose the credit-assignment problem into two subproblems (Sutton, 1984):

1. The assignment of credit for outcomes to actions. This is called the *temporal credit-assignment* problem in that it involves the instants of time *when* the actions that deserve credit were actually taken.
2. The assignment of credit for actions to internal decisions. This is called the *structural credit-assignment problem* in that it involves assigning credit to the *internal structures* of actions generated by the system.

The structural credit-assignment problem is relevant when, in the context of a multicomponent learning system, we have the problem of determining precisely which particular component of the system should have its behavior altered and by how much, in order to improve the overall system performance. On the other hand, the temporal credit-assignment problem is relevant when there are many actions taken by a learning system that result in certain outcomes, and the problem is to determine which of these actions were in actual fact responsible for the outcomes. The combined temporal and structural credit-assignment problem would have to be faced by any distributed learning system that attempts to improve its performance in situations involving temporally extended behavior (Williams, 1988).

The original complete name given to the credit-assignment problem by Minsky (1961) was "the basic credit-assignment problem for complex reinforcement learning systems." Nevertheless, the term "credit assignment" is equally applicable to other learning systems (Williams, 1988). In particular, it is in relation to the structural credit-assignment problem for learning tasks involving supervised multilayer networks that the term "hidden neurons" has arisen. Such a unit is simply one whose behavior is important to the correct operation of the network on a particular learning task, yet the precise nature of the unit's behavior is not defined directly by the task at hand. Thus, in order to solve the prescribed task, the network has to assign certain forms of behavior to its hidden neurons through the specification of supervised learning. Details of how the structural credit-assignment problem is solved in supervised multilayer networks are presented in Chapter 6. For now we need to elaborate on what we mean by supervised learning and reinforcement learning, which we do in the next two sections.

2.7 Supervised Learning

An essential ingredient of *supervised* or *active learning* is the availability of an external *teacher,* as indicated in the arrangement of Fig. 2.7. In conceptual terms, we may think of the teacher as having knowledge of the environment that is represented by a set of *input–output examples.* The environment is, however, *unknown* to the neural network of interest. Suppose now that the teacher and the neural network are both exposed to a training vector (i.e., example) drawn from the environment. By virtue of built-in knowledge, the teacher is able to provide the neural network with a *desired* or *target response* for that training vector. Indeed, the desired response represents the optimum action to be performed by the neural network. The network parameters are adjusted under the combined influence of the training vector and the error signal; the *error signal* is defined as the difference between the actual response of the network and the desired response. This adjustment is carried out iteratively in a step-by-step fashion with the aim of eventually making the neural network *emulate* the teacher; the emulation is presumed to be optimum in some statistical sense. In other words, knowledge of the environment available to the teacher is transferred to the neural network as fully as possible. When this condition is reached,

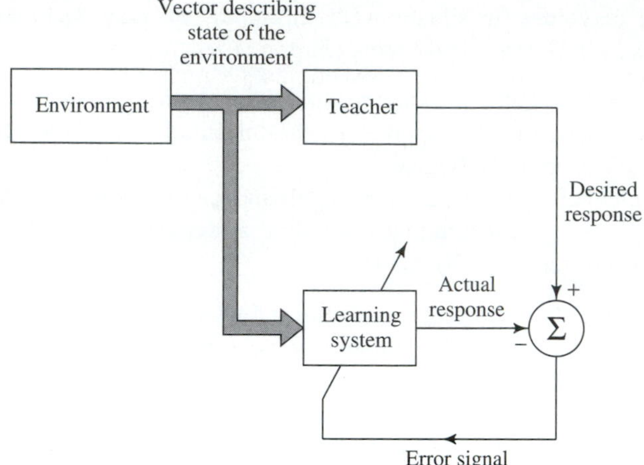

FIGURE 2.7 Block diagram of supervised learning.

we may then dispense with the teacher and let the neural network deal with the environment thereafter completely by itself (i.e., in an unsupervised fashion).

The form of supervised learning we have just described is indeed the error-correction learning discussed previously in Section 2.2. It is a closed-loop feedback system, but the unknown environment is not in the loop. As a performance measure for the system, we may think in terms of the mean-squared error (i.e., the expected value of the sum of squared errors) defined as a function of the free parameters of the system. This function may be visualized as a multidimensional *error-performance surface* or simply *error surface,* with the free parameters as coordinates. The true error surface is *averaged* over all possible input–output examples (Haykin, 1991). Any given operation of the system under the teacher's supervision is represented as a point on the error surface. For the system to improve performance over time and therefore learn from the teacher, the operating point has to move down successively toward a minimum point of the error surface; the minimum point may be a local minimum or a global minimum. A supervised learning system is able to do this by virtue of some useful information it has about the *gradient* of the error surface corresponding to the current behavior of the system. The gradient of an error surface at any point is a vector that points in the direction of *steepest descent.* In fact, in the case of supervised learning from examples, the system uses an *instantaneous estimate* of the gradient vector, with the example indices presumed to be those of time. The use of such an estimate results in a motion of the operating point on the error surface that is typically in the form of a "random walk." Nevertheless, given an algorithm designed to minimize the cost function of interest, and given an adequate set of input–output examples and enough time permitted to do the training, a supervised learning system is usually able to perform such tasks as pattern classification and function approximation satisfactorily.

Examples of supervised learning algorithms include the ubiquitous *least-mean-square* (*LMS*) *algorithm* (Widrow and Hoff, 1960) and its generalization known as the *back-propagation* (*BP*) *algorithm* (Werbos, 1974), considered in Chapters 5 and 6, respectively. The LMS algorithm involves a single neuron, whereas the back-propagation algorithm involves a multilayered interconnection of neurons. The back-propagation algorithm derives its name from the fact that error terms in the algorithm are back-propagated through the network, on a layer-by-layer basis. Naturally, the back-propagation algorithm is more powerful in application than the LMS algorithm. Indeed, the back-propagation algorithm includes the LMS algorithm as a special case.

Supervised learning can be performed in an off-line or on-line manner. In the *off-line* case, a separate computational facility is used to design the supervised learning system. Once the desired performance is accomplished, the design is "frozen," which means that the neural network operates in a *static* manner. On the other hand, in *on-line* learning the learning procedure is implemented solely within the system itself, not requiring a separate computational facility. In other words, learning is accomplished in *real time,* with the result that the neural network is *dynamic.* Naturally, the requirement of on-line learning places a more severe requirement on a supervised learning procedure than off-line learning.

A disadvantage of supervised learning, regardless of whether it is performed off-line or on-line, is the fact that without a teacher, a neural network cannot learn new strategies for particular situations that are not covered by the set of examples used to train the network. This limitation may be overcome by the use of reinforcement learning, described next.

2.8 Reinforcement Learning

Reinforcement learning is the on-line learning of an input–output mapping through a process of trial and error designed to maximize a scalar performance index called a *reinforcement signal.* It appears that the term "reinforcement learning" was coined by Minsky (1961) in his early studies of artificial intelligence, and then independently in control theory by Waltz and Fu (1965). However, the basic idea of "reinforcement" has its origins in experimental studies of animal learning in psychology (Hampson, 1990). In this context it is particularly illuminating to recall Thorndike's classical *law of effect* (Thorndike, 1911):

> Of several responses made to the same situation, those which are accompanied or closely followed by satisfaction to the animal will, other things being equal, be more firmly connected with the situation, so that, when it recurs, they will be more likely to recur; those which are accompanied or closely followed by discomfort to the animal will, other things being equal, have their connections with that situation weakened, so that, when it recurs, they will be less likely to occur. The greater the satisfaction or discomfort, the greater the strengthening or weakening of the bond.

Although it cannot be claimed that this principle provides a complete model of biological behavior, its simplicity and common-sense approach have made it an influential learning rule.

Indeed, we may rephrase Thorndike's law of effect to offer the following sensible definition of reinforcement learning (Sutton et al., 1991; Barto, 1992):

> *If an action taken by a learning system is followed by a satisfactory state of affairs, then the tendency of the system to produce that particular action is strengthened or reinforced. Otherwise, the tendency of the system to produce that action is weakened.*

The paradigm of reinforcement learning[5] can be of a nonassociative or associative type, as described here (Sutton, 1984):

---

[5] For overview treatment of reinforcement learning theory, see Barto (1985, 1990) and Williams (1988, 1992). For a qualitative review paper on reinforcement learning with emphasis on adaptive critic methods, see Barto (1992).

The May 1992 Special Issue of *Machine Learning* is devoted to theoretical and practical issues involved in reinforcement learning (Sutton, 1992a).

- *Nonassociative reinforcement learning,* in which the learning system has the task of selecting a single optimal action rather than to associate different actions with different stimuli. In such a learning problem the reinforcement is the *only* input that the learning system receives from its environment. Nonassociative reinforcement learning has been studied as function optimization under the umbrella of genetic algorithms (Holland, 1975, 1992), and as stochastic learning automata theory (Narendra and Thathachar, 1989).
- *Associative reinforcement learning,* in which the environment provides additional forms of information other than reinforcement, and in which a *mapping* in the form of a stimulus–action association must be learned. Associative reinforcement learning, which is closer to Thorndike's law of effect, is mostly represented by research in neural networks. In the context of application, it is naturally linked to optimal control theory (Werbos, 1989, 1992; Sutton et al., 1991; Watkins, 1989; Barto et al., 1990).

The primary focus in this section is on associative reinforcement learning.

Evaluation Function

Consider a learning system interacting with an environment described by a discrete-time dynamical process with a finite set of *states* X. At time step $n = 0, 1, 2, \ldots,$ the environment is in state $\mathbf{x}(n)$, where $\mathbf{x}(n) \in X$. After observing the environmental state $\mathbf{x}(n)$ at time step n, the learning system performs an *action* $\mathbf{a}(n)$, selected from a finite set of possible actions A that can depend on $\mathbf{x}(n)$. The action $\mathbf{a}(n)$ affects the environment, causing it to make a transition from state $\mathbf{x}(n)$ to a new state $\mathbf{y}$ in a manner independent of its past history, as explained more fully later. Let $p_{\mathbf{xy}}(\mathbf{a})$ denote the probability of this state transition, which depends on action $\mathbf{a}(n)$. After action $\mathbf{a}(n)$ is taken, the learning system receives *reinforcement* $r(n + 1)$, which is determined in some random manner depending on the state $\mathbf{x}(n)$ and action $\mathbf{a}(n)$. We assume that the sequence of events described herein is allowed to continue for an indefinite number of time steps.

The objective of reinforcement learning is to find a *policy* for selecting the sequence of actions that is optimal in some statistical sense. We restrict ourselves to a *stationary* policy that specifies actions based on the current state of the environment alone. More precisely, we assume that the probability that the environment makes a transition from state $\mathbf{x}(n)$ to $\mathbf{y}$ at time $n + 1$, given that it was previously in states $\mathbf{x}(0), \mathbf{x}(1), \ldots,$ and that the corresponding actions $\mathbf{a}(0), \mathbf{a}(1), \ldots,$ were taken, depends entirely on the current state $\mathbf{x}(n)$ and action $\mathbf{a}(n)$ as shown by

$$\begin{aligned}\text{Prob}\{\mathbf{x}(n+1) = \mathbf{y} | \mathbf{x}(0), \mathbf{a}(0); \mathbf{x}(1), \mathbf{a}(1); \ldots ; \mathbf{x}(n), \mathbf{a}(n)\} \\ = \text{Prob}\{\mathbf{x}(n+1) = \mathbf{y} | \mathbf{x}(n), \mathbf{a}(n)\}\end{aligned} \tag{2.23}$$

A sequence of states so defined is said to constitute a first-order *Markov chain* (Bertsekas, 1987) with transition probabilities $p_{\mathbf{xy}}(\mathbf{a})$. Assuming that the environment is initially in the state $\mathbf{x}(0) = \mathbf{x}$, a natural measure of the learning system's performance is the *evaluation function* defined as follows (Barto et al., 1990):

$$J(\mathbf{x}) = E\left[\sum_{k=0}^{\infty} \gamma^k r(k+1) | \mathbf{x}(0) = \mathbf{x}\right] \tag{2.24}$$

where the expectation operator E is taken with respect to the policy used to select actions by the learning system. The summation term inside the expectation in Eq. (2.24) is called the *cumulative discounted reinforcement.* The term $r(k + 1)$ is the reinforcement received from the environment after action $\mathbf{a}(k)$ is taken by the learning system; it can be positive (reward), negative (punishment), or zero. The factor γ is called the *discount-rate parameter,* whose value lies in the range $0 \leq \gamma < 1$. By adjusting γ, we are able to control the extent to which the learning system is concerned with long-term versus short-term consequences of actions. In particular, when $\gamma = 0$, the cumulative reinforcement in Eq. (2.24) reduces simply to the immediate reinforcement $r(1)$ due to the first action $\mathbf{a}(0)$. If, on the other hand, $\gamma = 1$, the cumulative reinforcement may not be finite in general; hence, the use of $\gamma = 1$ is avoided.

The basic idea behind reinforcement learning is to learn the evaluation function $J(\mathbf{x})$ so as to *predict* the cumulative discounted reinforcement to be received in the future. We next describe a particular realization of reinforcement that has been demonstrated to achieve this objective.

Adaptive Heuristic Critic

Figure 2.8 shows the block diagram of a reinforcement learning system first described in Barto et al. (1983) and Sutton (1984). The system is novel in that it uses a *critic* to convert the *primary reinforcement signal* received from the environment into a higher-quality reinforcement signal called the *heuristic reinforcement signal;* both of these reinforcement signals are scalars. The learning system itself consists of three components: *learning element, knowledge base,* and *performance element.* Such a division of responsibilities is commonly followed in artificial intelligence (see Section 1.9). The learning element is responsible for making all changes in the knowledge base. The performance element is responsible for selecting actions randomly on the basis of a distribution that is determined by the knowledge base and the particular environment in which the system is embedded. By virtue of inputs received from both the environment and the knowledge base, the performance element determines the *input-to-distribution-of-output-actions mapping.* The

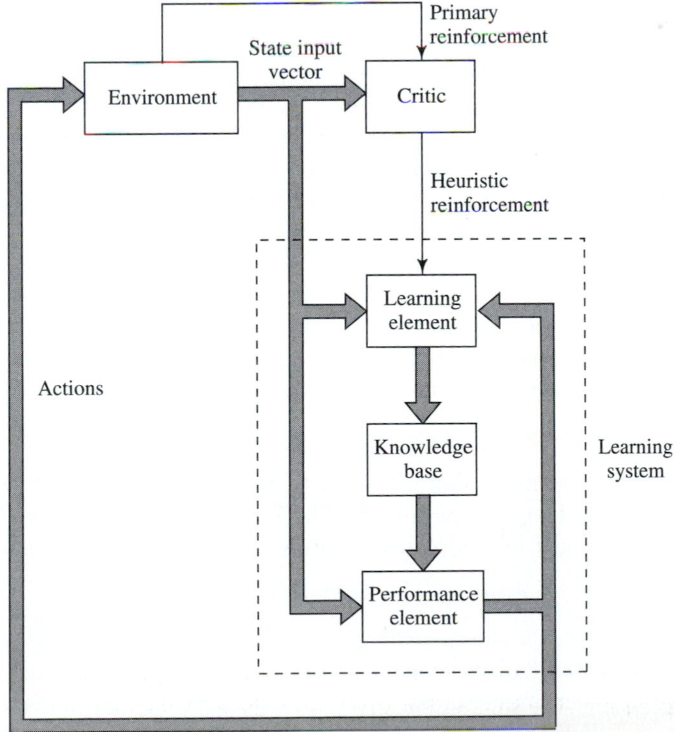

FIGURE 2.8 Block diagram of adaptive heuristic critic.

critic includes a *predictor* as a main subcomponent. With the state vector and primary reinforcement signal supplied by the environment as inputs, the predictor produces an estimate of the evaluation function $J(\mathbf{x})$ defined in Eq. (2.24). It is noteworthy that both the critic and the performance element lend themselves to implementation using neural networks.

The system is designed to learn under *delayed reinforcement,* which means that the learning system observes a temporal sequence of input state vectors (stimuli) that eventually result in the generation of the heuristic reinforcement signal. In delayed-reinforcement learning the goal of learning is to optimize the evaluation function $J(\mathbf{x})$ defined in Eq. (2.24) as the expectation of the cumulative reinforcement computed over a sequence of two or more time steps rather than simply the immediate reinforcement. It may turn out that certain actions that were taken earlier in a sequence of time steps are in fact the best determinants of overall system behavior. The function of the learning system is to *discover* such actions.

In practice, delayed-reinforcement learning is difficult to perform for two basic reasons:

- There is *no* teacher available to provide a target output (desired response) at each time step of the learning process.
- The temporal delay incurred in the generation of the primary reinforcement signal implies that the learning system must solve a *temporal credit-assignment problem.* By this we mean that the learning system must be able to assign credit and blame individually to each action in a sequence of time steps that led to the final outcome, when the primary reinforcement may only evaluate the outcome.

In spite of these difficulties, delayed-reinforcement learning has attracted a great deal of attention in the machine-learning community. In an intellectual sense, the notion that a learning system can interact with its environment and learn to perform a prescribed task solely on the basis of the outcomes of its experience resulting from interaction with the environment is very appealing indeed (Tesauro, 1992).

The predictor in the critic provides a mapping from the input state vector $\mathbf{x}(n)$ to a prediction of forthcoming reinforcement. Since the predictor adapts with time, the prediction so made is also time-varying. Let $\hat{J}_n(k)$ denote the *prediction of reinforcement forthcoming after time k* using the state input vector $\mathbf{x}(n)$ received at time n. Correspondingly, the heuristic reinforcement signal $\hat{r}(n+1)$ produced at the output of the critic at time $n+1$ is defined by (Sutton, 1984)

$$\hat{r}(n+1) = r(n+1) + \gamma \hat{J}_n(n+1) - \hat{J}_n(n) \tag{2.25}$$

where γ is the discount-rate parameter.

Learning in the performance element of the learning system takes place by adjusting each free parameter (synaptic weight) w_{ij} in accordance with the recursion (Sutton, 1984)

$$w_{ij}(n+1) = w_{ij}(n) + \eta \hat{r}(n+1)\bar{e}_{ij}(n) \tag{2.26}$$

where $\hat{r}(n+1)$ is the heuristic reinforcement signal at time $n+1$, and η is a positive constant called the *learning-rate parameter.* The $\bar{e}_{ij}(n)$ is an average parameter called an *eligibility trace,* computed in accordance with the first-order difference equation

$$\bar{e}_{ij}(n) = \lambda \bar{e}_{ij}(n-1) + (1-\lambda)e_{ij}(n) \tag{2.27}$$

for $n > 0$. The parameter λ is a *forgetting factor* that lies in the range $0 \leq \lambda \leq 1$. If λ is close to unity, then the credit assigned to an action decreases slowly as the time between it and primary reinforcement increases; if λ is close to zero, then credit decreases rapidly. The term e_{ij} is the *eligibility* of w_{ij}, defined as the product of two factors, one of which depends on the action selected and the other of which depends on the presence or absence

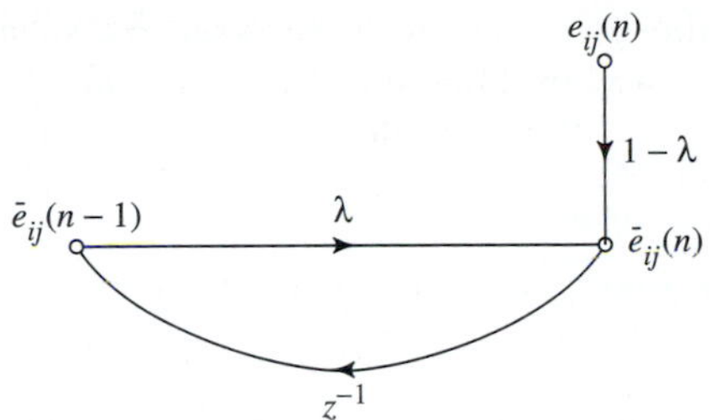

FIGURE 2.9 Signal-flow graph of Eq. (2.27).

of a stimulus. This product is called the eligibility of w_{ij} because it indicates the extent to which w_{ij} is "eligible" to undergo modification should reinforcement be received (Klopf, 1982). Equation (2.27) is a standard discrete-time linear recursive filter, as shown by the signal-flow graph of Fig. 2.9. Although it requires a single memory unit represented by the unit-delay operator z^{-1} in Fig. 2.9, it is basically equivalent to remembering all past behavior.

Equations (2.25), (2.26), and (2.27) constitute the *adaptive heuristic critic* (AHC) algorithm in its entirety, involving the eligibility $e_{ij}(n)$.

Temporal-Difference Methods

As mentioned previously, the critic includes a predictor as its main subcomponent. Specifically, it uses past experience to predict its future behavior, and thereby provides a solution to the temporal credit-assignment problem. Indeed, learning to predict is one of the most basic and prevalent tasks in learning. An important advantage of *prediction learning* is that it does *not* require a teacher for special supervision; rather, the training examples are taken directly from the temporal sequence of input state vectors itself.

In the conventional approach to prediction learning, adjustments to the parameters of the predictor are made on the basis of the error between the actual and predicted values. On the other hand, in a class of incremental learning procedures called *temporal-difference (TD) methods,* of which the AHC algorithm is an early version, parameter adjustments are made on the basis of the error or difference between temporally successive predictions (Sutton, 1988).[6] Accordingly, learning occurs in TD methods whenever there is a change in prediction over time. In Sutton (1988) it is argued that learning to predict by TD methods is both *more accurate and easier to compute* than by conventional methods.

In the *TD*(λ) *method,* adjustments to synaptic weights of the neural network constituting the predictor part of the critic in Fig. 2.8 take the following form (Sutton, 1988):

$$\mathbf{w}(n+1) = \mathbf{w}(n) + \eta\big(P(n+1) - P(n)\big) \sum_{k=1}^{n} \lambda^{n-k} \nabla_{\mathbf{w}} P(k) \tag{2.28}$$

where η is a learning-rate parameter [which need not be the same as that in Eq. (2.26)], $P(n)$ is the predictor's output produced in response to the input state vector $\mathbf{x}(n)$, and $\nabla_{\mathbf{w}}P(n)$ is the gradient vector of the prediction $P(n)$ with respect to the weight vector $\mathbf{w}$ at time n. Basically, Eq. (2.28) couples a temporal-difference method for temporal credit assignment to structural credit assignment via a gradient-descent method.

[6] Another algorithm that has attracted considerable attention is *Q-learning* (Watkins, 1989), which may be viewed as a generalization of TD methods. Whereas TD methods are designed to estimate the evaluation function of a given policy, Q-learning is designed to estimate the optimal evaluation function. Littman and Boyan (1993) describe a self-adjusting algorithm based on *Q*-learning that is able to discover a *routing policy* for a packet-switched communication network; the algorithm uses a simplified model of the network.

As before, the forgetting factor λ lies in the range $0 \leq \lambda \leq 1$. It provides a smooth heuristic interpolation between two limiting cases (Tesauro, 1992):

- Case $\lambda = 1$, corresponding to an explicit supervised pairing of the input state vector $\mathbf{x}(n)$ with an absolute final outcome.
- Case $\lambda = 0$, corresponding to an explicit pairing of $\mathbf{x}(n)$ with the next prediction $P(n + 1)$.

The earliest and best-known use of a temporal-difference method is found in Samuel's early studies of machine learning using the game of checkers (Samuel, 1959). Specifically, it was verified that a computer can be programmed to learn to play a game of checkers better than the person who wrote the program. This was achieved by programming the computer to learn from experience. Similar methods have been used by many other investigators. However, the first formal results in the theory of TD(λ) methods were presented by Sutton (1988). This approach to prediction learning was applied to solve the temporal credit-assignment problem in the adaptive heuristic critic (Sutton, 1984; Barto et al., 1983). In Tesauro (1992), the TD(λ) method is applied to learn the game of backgammon from the outcome of self-play. With zero knowledge built in at the start of learning (i.e., given only a "raw" description of the board state), the network is able to learn to play at a strong intermediate level. In a subsequent study (Tesauro, 1994), hand-crafted features are added to the network's input representation, enabling TD-gammon to play at a strong master level that is extremely close to the world's best human players.

Supervised Versus Reinforcement Learning

The performance measure used for a supervised learning system is defined in terms of a set of targets (i.e., desired responses) by means of a known error criterion (e.g., mean-square error). A supervised learning system may therefore be viewed as an *instructive* feedback system. In contrast, a reinforcement learning system addresses the problem of improving performance and therefore learning on the basis of *any* measure whose values can be supplied to the system. We may therefore view a reinforcement learning system as an *evaluative* feedback system.

To be more precise, in a supervised learning system the teacher provides *directed* information about how the system should change its behavior to improve performance. This information is of a local nature, defined by an instantaneous estimate of the gradient of the error surface at the current operating point, and which makes it possible for the system to provide a reasonable answer to the following key question: What is the direction along which the system should change its free parameters to achieve improvement in performance? In a reinforcement learning problem, on the other hand, there is *no* teacher to supply gradient information during learning. The only piece of available information is represented by the *reinforcement* received from the environment; the learning system has to do things and see what happens to get gradient information. Although the reinforcement is a scalar, whereas the gradient in supervised learning is a vector, the key point to note is that in reinforcement learning the information contained in reinforcement evaluates behavior but does not in itself indicate if improvement is possible or how the system should change its behavior (Barto, 1992).

To obtain information of a directional nature, a reinforcement learning system *probes* the environment through the combined use of *trial and error* and *delayed reward;* that is, the system engages in some form of *exploration,* searching for directional information on the basis of intrinsic properties of the environment. In so doing, however, a reinforcement learning system is slowed down in its operation, because a behavioral change made to obtain directional information is generally in conflict with the way in which the resulting directional information is exploited to change behavior for performance improvement. This phenomenon is known as the *conflict between identification and control* (Barto, 1992) or the *conflict between exploration and exploitation* (Thrun, 1992; Holland, 1975). Stated in another way, there is always a conflict between the following two factors (Barto, 1992):

- The desire to use knowledge already available about the relative merits of actions taken by the system
- The desire to acquire more knowledge about the consequences of actions so as to make better selections in the future

The best decision made in light of one factor is not always the best decision made according to the other. This kind of a conflicting situation is absent in supervised learning, as it is normally practiced.

2.9 Unsupervised Learning

In *unsupervised* or *self-organized* learning there is no external teacher or critic to oversee the learning process, as indicated in Fig. 2.10. In other words, there are no specific examples of the function to be learned by the network. Rather, provision is made for a *task-independent measure* of the quality of representation that the network is required to learn, and the free parameters of the network are optimized with respect to that measure. Once the network has become tuned to the statistical regularities of the input data, it develops the ability to form internal representations for encoding features of the input and thereby create new classes automatically (Becker, 1991).

To perform unsupervised learning, we may use a competitive learning rule. For example, we may use a neural network that consists of two layers, namely, an input layer and a competitive layer. The input layer receives the available data. The competitive layer consists of neurons that compete with each other (in a prescribed fashion) for the "opportunity" to respond to features contained in the input data. In its simplest form, the network operates in accordance with a "winner-takes-all" strategy. As described in Section 2.4, in such a strategy the neuron with the greatest total input "wins" the competition and turns on; all the other neurons then switch off.

Supervised Versus Unsupervised Learning

Among the algorithms used to perform supervised learning, the *back-propagation algorithm* has emerged as the most widely used and successful algorithm for the design of multilayer feedforward networks. There are two distinct phases to the operation of back-propagation learning: the forward phase and the backward phase. In the forward phase the input signals propagate through the network layer by layer, eventually producing some response at the output of the network. The actual response so produced is compared with a desired (target) response, generating error signals that are then propagated in a backward

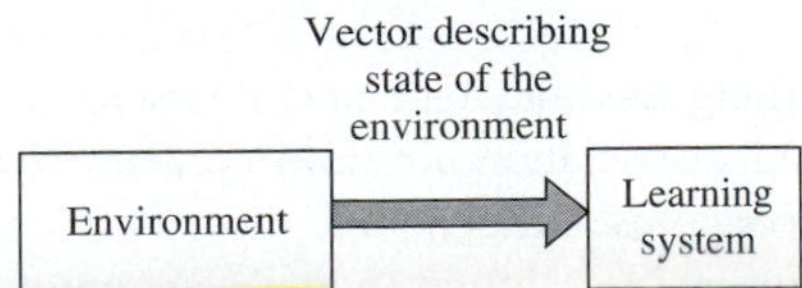

FIGURE 2.10 Block diagram of unsupervised learning.

direction through the network. In this backward phase of operation, the free parameters of the network are adjusted so as to minimize the sum of squared errors. Back-propagation learning has been applied successfully to solve some difficult problems such as speech recognition from text (Sejnowski and Rosenberg, 1987), handwritten-digit recognition (LeCun et al., 1990a), and adaptive control (Narendra and Parthasarathy, 1990). Unfortunately, back-propagation and other supervised learning algorithms may be limited by their poor *scaling* behavior. To understand this limitation, consider the example of a multilayer feedforward network consisting of L computation layers. The effect of a synaptic weight in the first layer on the output of the network depends on its interactions with approximately F_i^L other synaptic weights, where F_i is the *fan-in,* defined as the average number of incoming links of neurons in the network. Hence, as the size of the network increases (i.e., F_i or L or both increase), the network becomes more computationally intensive, and so the time required to train the network grows *exponentially* and the learning process becomes unacceptably slow.

One possible solution to the scaling problem described herein is to use an unsupervised learning procedure. In particular, if we are able to apply a self-organizing process in a sequential manner, one layer at a time, it is feasible to train deep networks in time that is *linear* in the number of layers. Moreover, with the ability of the self-organizing network to form internal representations that model the underlying structure of the input data in a more explicit or simple form, it is hoped that the transformed version of the sensory input would be easier to interpret, so that correct responses could be associated with the network's internal representations of the environment more quickly (Becker, 1991). In other words, the hybrid use of unsupervised and supervised learning procedures may provide a more acceptable solution than supervised learning alone, particularly if the size of the problem is large (Jacobs and Jordan, 1991; Nowlan and Hinton, 1991; deSa and Ballard, 1992).

2.10 Learning Tasks

The choice of a particular learning procedure is very much influenced by the learning task which a neural network is required to perform. In this context we may identify the following learning tasks that befit the use of neural networks in one form or another:

1. *Approximation.* Suppose that we are given a *nonlinear input–output mapping* described by the functional relationship

$$d = g(\mathbf{x}) \tag{2.29}$$

where the vector $\mathbf{x}$ is the input and the scalar d is the output. The function $g(\cdot)$ is assumed to be unknown. The requirement is to design a neural network that *approximates* the nonlinear function $g(\cdot)$, given a set of examples denoted by the input–output pairs $(\mathbf{x}_1,d_1)$, $(\mathbf{x}_2,d_2)$, . . . , $(\mathbf{x}_N,d_N)$. The approximation problem described here is a perfect candidate for supervised learning with $\mathbf{x}_i$ serving as the input vector and d_i serving the role of desired response, where $i = 1, 2, \ldots, N$. Indeed, we may turn the issue around and view supervised learning as an approximation problem. This particular approach to learning is considered in detail in Chapter 7.

2. *Association.* This learning task may take one of two forms, namely, *autoassociation* and *heteroassociation.* In autoassociation a neural network is required to *store* a set of patterns (vectors) by repeatedly presenting them to the network. Subsequently, the network is presented a partial description or distorted (noisy) version of an original pattern stored in it, and the task is to *retrieve* (*recall*) that particular pattern. Heteroassociation differs from autoassociation in that an arbitrary set of input patterns are *paired* with another arbitrary set of output patterns. Autoassociation involves the use of unsupervised learning, whereas the type of learning involved in heteroassociation is of a supervised nature.

3. *Pattern Classification.* In this learning task there is a fixed number of categories (classes) into which stimuli (activations) are to be classified. To resolve it, the neural network first undergoes a training session, during which the network is repeatedly presented a set of input patterns along with the category to which each particular pattern belongs. Then later on, a new pattern is presented to the network, which has not been seen before but which belongs to the same population of patterns used to train the network. Now the task for the neural network is to classify this new pattern correctly. Pattern classification as described here is a supervised learning problem. The advantage of using a neural network to perform pattern classification is that it can construct nonlinear decision boundaries between the different classes in a nonparametric fashion, and thereby offer a practical method for solving highly complex pattern classification problems. It should also be noted that there is an important role for unsupervised learning in pattern classification, especially when there is no *a priori* knowledge of the categories into which the stimulus patterns are to be classified. In this latter situation, unsupervised learning is used to perform the role of *adaptive feature extraction* or *clustering* prior to pattern classification.

4. *Prediction.* The issue of predicting is one of the most basic and pervasive learning tasks. It is a temporal signal-processing problem in that we are given a set of M past samples $x(n-1), x(n-1), \ldots, x(n-M)$ that are (usually) uniformly spaced in time, and the requirement is to *predict* the present sample $x(n)$. Prediction may be solved using error-correction learning in an unsupervised manner in the sense that the training examples are drawn directly from the time series itself. Specifically, the sample $x(n)$ serves the purpose of the desired response; hence, given the corresponding prediction $\hat{x}(n)$ produced by the network on the basis of the previous samples $x(n-1), x(n-2), \ldots, x(n-M)$, we may compute the *prediction error*

$$e(n) = x(n) - \hat{x}(n|n-1, \ldots, n-M) \tag{2.30}$$

and thus use error-correction learning to modify the free parameters of the network. Prediction may be viewed as a form of *model building* in the sense that the smaller we make the prediction error in a statistical sense, the better will the network serve as a physical model of the underlying stochastic process responsible for the generation of the time series. When this process is of a *nonlinear* nature, the use of a neural network provides a powerful method for solving the prediction problem by virtue of the nonlinear processing units built into its construction. The only exception to the use of nonlinear processing units, however, is the output unit of the network, which operates in its linear region. This provision makes it possible for the dynamic range of the predictor output to match that of the predictor input. Moreover, it is consistent with the assumption that the prediction error $e(n)$ is drawn from a white Gaussian noise process. The implication of such a model is that all the available information content of the input time series has been extracted by the predictor, with the result that the samples constituting the prediction error process are statistically independent, a condition that is satisfied by samples drawn from a white Gaussian noise process.

5. *Control.* The control of a process is another learning task that naturally befits the use of a neural network. This should not be surprising because, after all, the human brain is a computer (i.e., information processor), the outputs of which as a whole system are *actions.* Indeed, in the context of control, the brain is living proof that it is possible to build a generalized controller that takes full advantage of parallel distributed hardware, that can handle many thousands of actuators (muscle fibers) in parallel, that can handle nonlinearity and noise, and that can optimize over a long-range planning horizon (Werbos,

1992). The term *neurocontrol* has been coined by Werbos to refer to the class of controllers that involve the use of neural networks. To illustrate a particular form of neurocontrol, consider an unknown nonlinear dynamic system defined by

$$\text{Plant: } \{u(t), y(t)\} \tag{2.31}$$

where $u(t)$ is the control input and $y(t)$ is the resulting plant output. Suppose also that we have chosen a reference model defined by

$$\text{Reference model: } \{r(t), d(t)\} \tag{2.32}$$

where $r(t)$ is the reference input and $d(t)$ is the desired response. In *model reference adaptive control* (*MRAC*) the objective is to determine a bounded control input $u(t)$ for all continuous time $t \geq 0$ such that (Narendra and Annaswamy, 1989)

$$\lim_{t \to \infty} |d(t) - y(t)| = 0 \tag{2.33}$$

in which case the plant is made to follow a desired trajectory determined by the reference model. Parthasarathy and Narendra (1991) have shown that it is possible to design an adaptive controller using supervised neural networks so that the overall system is globally asymptotically stable. (The issue of global asymptotic stability is discussed in Chapter 14.) It is also of interest to note that the *adaptive heuristic critic* (Sutton, 1984; Barto et al., 1983), a type of reinforcement learning system described in Section 2.9, is a natural tool for neurocontrol. More advanced forms of neurocontrol are discussed by Werbos (1992).

6. *Beamforming.* Beamforming is a form of *spatial filtering,* the purpose of which is to locate a target signal embedded in a background of additive interference. In radar and sonar environments, the task of beamforming is usually complicated by two factors:

- The target signal of interest originates from an unknown direction.
- There is no *a priori* statistical information available on the interference.

To cope with a situation of this kind we have to resort to the use of an *adaptive beamformer* consisting of an array of antenna elements, designed to steer the main lobe of its spatial pattern (i.e., amplitude versus angle) automatically toward the target and also place nulls along the unknown directions of the interfering signals so as to cancel them out (Haykin, 1991; Widrow and Stearns, 1985). Such a function befits the use of a neural network, for which we have relevant cues from psychoacoustic studies of human auditory responses (Bregman, 1990) and studies of feature mapping in the cortical layers of auditory systems of echo-locating bats (Simmons and Saillant, 1992; Suga, 1990a). In particular, we ourselves are endowed with an auditory system (including a pair of ears) with an exceptional *attentional selectivity* that helps us deal with the *cocktail party effect,* for example, where in a crowded room we are able to focus on a conversation at a faraway corner of the room despite all the background noise around us. The echo-locating bat illuminates the surrounding environment by broadcasting short-duration frequency-modulated (FM) sonar signals, and then uses its auditory system (also including a pair of ears) to focus attention on its prey (e.g., a flying insect). Our pair of ears and that of a bat provide for some form of spatial filtering (interferometry, to be precise), which is then exploited by the auditory system to produce attentional selectivity. Indeed, this is why we need an array with two or more antenna elements to solve the adaptive beamforming problem. A beamformer that uses a neural network to enact adaptivity is called a *neurobeamformer,* which comes under the general heading of *attentional neurocomputers* (Hecht-Nielsen, 1990). The nature of the adaptive beamforming task described here requires that a neurobeamformer would have to operate essentially in an unsupervised manner. Speidel (1991) describes some neurobeamformers for sonar scene analysis, the formulations of which have been inspired by auditory system responses, and related work by von der Malsburg and Schneider (1986) on the application of a self-organized model for the segmentation of sound spectra.

The diversity of these six learning tasks discussed here is testimony to the *universality* of neural networks as information-processing systems. In a fundamental sense, these learning tasks are all problems of learning a *mapping* from (possibly noisy) examples of that mapping. Without the imposition of prior knowledge, each of the tasks is in fact *ill-posed* in the sense of nonuniqueness of possible solution mappings. One method of making the solution well-posed is to use regularization, the theory of which is described in Chapter 7.

2.11 Adaptation and Learning

Space is one fundamental dimension of the learning process; *time* is the other. The spatiotemporal nature of learning is exemplified by many of the learning tasks (e.g., control, beamforming) discussed in the previous section. Moreover, animals ranging from insects to humans have an inherent capacity to represent the temporal structure of experience. Such a representation makes it possible for an animal to adapt its behavior to the temporal structure of an event in its behavioral space (Gallistel, 1990).

When a neural network operates in a *stationary* environment (i.e., one with statistical characteristics that do not change with time), the essential statistics of the environment can in theory be *learned* by the network under the supervision of a teacher. In particular, the synaptic weights of the network can be computed by having the network undergo a training session with a set of data that is representative of the environment. Once the training process is completed, the synaptic weights of the network should capture the underlying statistical structure of the environment, which would justify "freezing" their values thereafter. Thus a *learning system* relies on *memory* to recall and exploit past experiences.

Frequently, however, the environment of interest is *nonstationary,* which means that the statistical parameters of the information-bearing signals generated by the environment vary with time. In situations of this kind, the traditional methods of supervised learning may prove to be inadequate, because the network is not equipped with the necessary means to *track* the statistical variations of the environment in which it operates. To overcome this shortcoming, the network has to be able continually to *adapt* its free parameters to variations in the incoming signals in a *real-time* fashion. Thus an *adaptive system* responds to every distinct input as a novel one. Given such a capability, it may be argued that, *when operating in a nonstationary environment, the more adaptive we make a system in a properly controlled fashion, the more likely it is that it would perform better.* We ourselves are living examples of what adaptive systems are able to accomplish in the face of continually changing conditions.

How, then, can a neural network adapt its behavior to the temporal structure of the incoming signals in its behavioral space? Figure 2.11 shows the conceptual arrangement of a single level of neural processing that may be used to provide for this adaptation (Mead, 1990). The box labeled "Model" operates as a *predictor* in the sense that it uses previous experience gained over the course of time to compute what is likely to happen. In particular, based on *past* values of the input signal denoted by the vector $\mathbf{x}(n-1)$ and network parameters computed at time $n-1$, the model provides an *estimate* $\hat{\mathbf{x}}(n)$ of the actual input vector $\mathbf{x}(n)$ at time n. Typically, the predicted value $\hat{\mathbf{x}}(n)$ (representing experience) is different from the actual value $\mathbf{x}(n)$ (representing expectation). The *comparator*

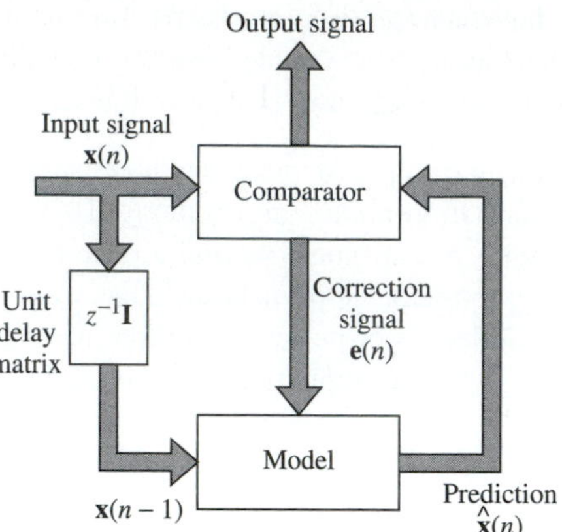

FIGURE 2.11 Block diagram of adaptive system.

in Fig. 2.11 then computes the difference between the actual value $\mathbf{x}(n)$ and the predicted value $\hat{\mathbf{x}}(n)$; in effect, $\mathbf{x}(n)$ performs the role of a desired response vector. This difference signal, denoted by the vector $\mathbf{e}(n)$, is called the *innovation* (Haykin, 1991; Kailath, 1968); it represents "new" information contained in the input signal $\mathbf{x}(n)$ at the time of computation. If the innovation $\mathbf{e}(n)$ is zero, no new information is produced in the sense that the model already knows what was about to happen, and therefore there is no need to change. If, on the other hand, the innovation $\mathbf{e}(n)$ is nonzero, the implication is that an unexpected event has occurred, and the system should try to track it.

The innovation is exploited in two ways:

1. The innovation $\mathbf{e}(n)$ supplies a *correction* signal applied to the model, causing it to adjust its free parameters and thereby learn what is happening in the surrounding environment. Learning in the system described in Fig. 2.11 is thus accomplished by means of the adaptation *feedback* from the comparator to the model. For example, in the case of an important class of adaptive filters, known as *Kalman filters,* tracking of statistical variations in the environment is accomplished in real time by updating an estimate of the "state vector" of the filter as follows (Kalman, 1960):

$$\begin{pmatrix}\text{Estimate of state}\\ \text{vector at time } n\end{pmatrix}$$

$$= \begin{pmatrix}\text{estimate of state}\\ \text{vector at time } n,\\ \text{given information}\\ \text{at previous time } n-1\end{pmatrix} + (\text{gain matrix}) \cdot \begin{pmatrix}\text{innovation,}\\ \text{based on new}\\ \text{information received}\\ \text{at time } n\end{pmatrix} \qquad (2.34)$$

   The product of the gain matrix and the innovation acts as a correction term for making changes in the synaptic weights of the network.

2. The innovation $\mathbf{e}(n)$ is available as *output* for transfer on up to the next level of neural processing for interpretation. By repeating this operation on a level-by-level basis, the information processed tends to be of progressively higher quality, because each neural level processes only the information that could not be processed at lower levels.

Mead (1990) describes an *adaptive silicon retina* based on the innovation scheme[7] of Fig. 2.11. For this application, the predictions made by the model are the simple assertions

[7] It is of interest to note that the innovation scheme of Fig. 2.11 also provides the basis for a popular waveform-encoding technique called *differential pulse-code modulation* (Jayant and Noll, 1984).

that the incoming image has no second-order spatial derivative and first-order temporal derivative. If the image does not conform to these predictions, the difference between the expectation and the experience of the model is sent upward to be processed at higher levels of the adaptive retina.

We may thus build temporal structure into the design of a neural network by having the network undergo *continual training* with *time-ordered examples;* according to this approach, a neural network is viewed as a *nonlinear adaptive filter* that represents a generalization of linear adaptive filters.[8] Alternatively, temporal structure can be "learned" by extending traditional methods of supervised learning. Examples of both approaches are described in Chapter 13 on temporal processing.

2.12 Statistical Nature of the Learning Process

The learning process experienced by a neural network is a *stochastic process;* the reason for stochasticity is rooted in the environment in which the network is embedded. In this section we focus on some statistical aspects of the process (White, 1989a, 1992). To begin with, we note that a neural network is merely one form in which empirical knowledge about a physical phenomenon (environment) of interest may be encoded. By "empirical" knowledge we mean a set of measurements that characterizes the phenomenon. To be more specific, consider the example of a phenomenon described by a vector $\mathbf{x}$ representing a set of *independent variables,* and a scalar d representing a *dependent variable.* The elements of the vector $\mathbf{x} \in \mathbb{R}^p$ may have different physical meaning. The assumption that the dependent variable is a scalar has been made merely to simplify the exposition without loss of generality. Suppose also that we have N measurements or *observations* of $\mathbf{x}$, denoted by $\mathbf{x}_1, \mathbf{x}_2, \ldots, \mathbf{x}_N$, and a corresponding set of observations of d, denoted by $d_1, d_2, \ldots, d_N$.

Ordinarily, we do *not* have knowledge of the exact functional relationship between $\mathbf{x}$ and d. We thus write

$$d = g(\mathbf{x}) + \epsilon \tag{2.35}$$

where $g(\mathbf{x})$ is some function of the argument vector $\mathbf{x}$, and ϵ is a random *expectational error* that represents our "ignorance" about the dependence of d on $\mathbf{x}$; Eq. (2.35) represents a generalization of Eq. (2.29). The statistical model described by Eq. (2.35) is called a *regressive model;* it is depicted in Fig. 2.12a. In this model the function $g(\mathbf{x})$ is defined

[8] The problem of designing an optimum linear filter that provides the theoretical framework for linear adaptive filters was first conceived by Kolmogorov (1942) and solved shortly afterward independently by Wiener (1949). On the other hand, a formal solution to the optimum nonlinear filtering problem is mathematically intractable. Nevertheless, in the 1950s a great deal of brilliant work was done by Zadeh (1953), Wiener and his collaborators (Wiener, 1958), and others that did much to clarify the nature of the problem.

Gabor was the first to conceive the idea of a nonlinear adaptive filter in 1954, and went on to build such a filter with the aid of collaborators (Gabor et al., 1960). Basically, Gabor proposed a shortcut through the mathematical difficulties of nonlinear adaptive filtering by constructing a filter that optimizes its response through learning. The output of the filter is expressed in the form

$$y(N) = \sum_{n=0}^{N} w_n x(n) + \sum_{n=0}^{N} \sum_{m=0}^{N} w_{n,m} x(n) x(m) + \cdots$$

where $x(0), x(1), \ldots, x(N)$ are samples of the filter input. (Nowadays, this polynomial is referred to as the *Gabor–Kolmogorov polynomial* or *Volterra series*.) The first term of the polynomial represents a linear filter characterized by a set of coefficients $\{w_n\}$. The second term characterized by a set of dyadic coefficients $\{w_{n,m}\}$ is nonlinear; this term contains the products of two samples of the filter input, and so on for the higher-order terms. The coefficients of the filter are adjusted via gradient descent to minimize the mean-square value of the difference between a target (desired) response $d(N)$ and the actual filter output $y(N)$.

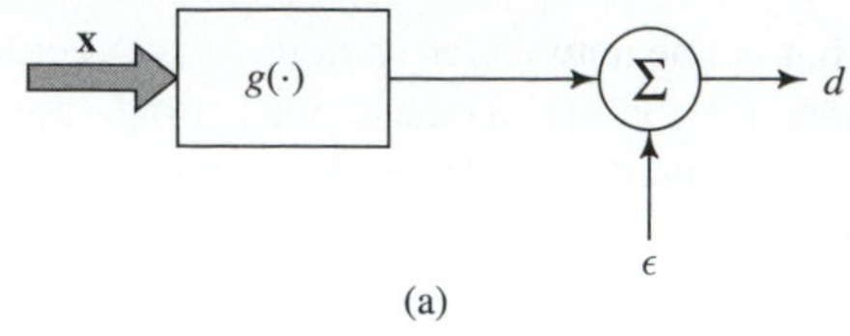

(a)

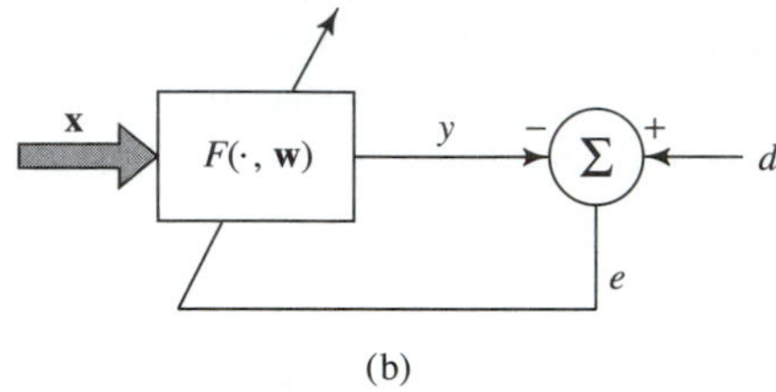

(b)

FIGURE 2.12 (a) Regressive model (mathematical). (b) Neural network model (physical).

by (White, 1989a)

$$g(\mathbf{x}) = E[d|\mathbf{x}] \tag{2.36}$$

where E is the statistical expectation operator. The *conditional expectation* $E[d|\mathbf{x}]$ defines the value of d that will be realized "on average," given a particular realization of $\mathbf{x}$. Whenever this conditional expectation exists, it can be represented solely as a function of $\mathbf{x}$. The model of Fig. 2.12a includes the case of an exact relationship between $\mathbf{x}$ and d as the special case in which $\epsilon = 0$ for all $\mathbf{x}$. In the general case of a probabilistic relationship between $\mathbf{x}$ and d, the expectational error ϵ is nonzero with nonzero probability.

The regressive model of Fig. 2.12a has two useful properties:

1. *The average value of the expectational error* ϵ, *given any realization of* $\mathbf{x}$, *is zero; that is,*

$$E[\epsilon|\mathbf{x}] = 0 \tag{2.37}$$

This property follows directly from Eqs. (2.35) and (2.36).

2. *The expectational error* ϵ *is uncorrelated with the function* $g(\mathbf{x})$; *that is,*

$$E[\epsilon g(\mathbf{x})] = 0 \tag{2.38}$$

This property is the well-known *principle of orthogonality;* it simply states that all the information available to us about $\mathbf{x}$ has been encoded into the regression function $g(\mathbf{x})$.

The regressive model of Fig. 2.12a is a "mathematical" model, the purpose of which is to use $\mathbf{x}$ in order to explain or predict d. A neural network provides a "physical" device for implementing this objective. It does so by encoding the empirical knowledge represented by the training data set $\{\mathbf{x}_i, d_i | i = 1, 2, \ldots, N\}$ into a set of synaptic weights. In this context, $\mathbf{x}_i$ represents the input vector and d_i represents the corresponding value of the desired response (target output). Let $\mathbf{w}$ denote the synaptic weight vector of the neural network selected to "approximate" the regressive model of Fig. 2.12a. Let the actual response of the network be defined by

$$y = F(\mathbf{x},\mathbf{w}) \tag{2.39}$$

The synaptic weight vector $\mathbf{w}$ of the network is adjusted in an iterative fashion in response to the error signal e, defined as the difference between the desired response d and the actual response y of the network; that is,

$$e = d - y \tag{2.40}$$

Figure 2.12b depicts the idea behind the adaptive procedure used to optimize the selection of the synaptic weight vector $\mathbf{w}$. The criterion for optimization is the minimization of the *mean-square value of the error signal,* as shown by

$$\begin{aligned} J(\mathbf{w}) &= \tfrac{1}{2}E[e^2] \\ &= \tfrac{1}{2}E[(d - y)^2] \\ &= \tfrac{1}{2}E[(d - F(\mathbf{x},\mathbf{w})^2] \end{aligned} \tag{2.41}$$

where the factor $\frac{1}{2}$ has been introduced so as to be consistent with earlier notation and that used in later chapters. The cost function defined here is based on ensemble averaging. The network is optimized by minimizing the cost function $J(\mathbf{w})$ with respect to $\mathbf{w}$. To do this minimization, we rewrite Eq. (2.41) in the form

$$\begin{aligned} J(\mathbf{w}) &= \tfrac{1}{2}E[(d - g(\mathbf{x}) + g(\mathbf{x}) - F(\mathbf{x},\mathbf{w}))^2] \\ &= \tfrac{1}{2}E[(d - g(\mathbf{x}))^2] + E[(d - g(x))(g(\mathbf{x}) - F(\mathbf{x},\mathbf{w}))] + \tfrac{1}{2}E[(g(\mathbf{x}) - F(\mathbf{x},\mathbf{w}))^2] \\ &= \tfrac{1}{2}E[(d - g(\mathbf{x}))^2] + \tfrac{1}{2}E[(g(\mathbf{x}) - F(\mathbf{x},\mathbf{w}))^2] \end{aligned} \tag{2.42}$$

The final equality in Eq. (2.42) holds, because of the following considerations:

1. The use of Eq. (2.35) yields the expectation of the cross-product term in the second line of Eq. (2.42) as

$$\begin{aligned} E[(d - g(\mathbf{x}))(g(\mathbf{x}) - F(\mathbf{x},\mathbf{w}))] &= E[\epsilon(g(\mathbf{x}) - F(\mathbf{x},\mathbf{w}))] \\ &= E[\epsilon g(\mathbf{x})] - E[\epsilon F(\mathbf{x},\mathbf{w})] \end{aligned} \tag{2.43}$$

2. The expectational error ϵ is uncorrelated with the function $g(\mathbf{x})$ in the regressive model of Fig. 2.12a as shown in Eq. (2.38).
3. The expectational error ϵ in the regressive model is naturally uncorrelated with the approximating function $F(\mathbf{x},\mathbf{w})$ realized by the neural network; that is,

$$E[\epsilon F(\mathbf{x},\mathbf{w})] = 0 \tag{2.44}$$

Noting that the first term of Eq. (2.42) is independent of $\mathbf{w}$, it follows therefore that the synaptic weight vector $\mathbf{w}_o$ that minimizes the cost function $J(\mathbf{w})$ will also minimize the multiple integral

$$E[(g(\mathbf{x}) - F(\mathbf{x},\mathbf{w}))^2] = \int_{\mathbb{R}^p} f(\mathbf{x})(g(\mathbf{x}) - F(\mathbf{x},\mathbf{w}))^2 \, d\mathbf{x} \tag{2.45}$$

where $\mathbf{x} \in \mathbb{R}^p$, and $f(\mathbf{x})$ is the probability density function of $\mathbf{x}$. In other words, $\mathbf{w}_o$ is a synaptic weight vector having the property that $F(\mathbf{x},\mathbf{w}_o)$ is a *mean-squared error minimizing approximation to the conditional expectation function* $g(\mathbf{x}) = E[d|\mathbf{x}]$. It is this aspect of the statistical nature of the learning process that becomes the focus of interest under the mean-squared error-measure performance (White, 1989a). Note also that, according to Eqs. (2.36) and (2.42), we have

$$J(\mathbf{w}) \geq \tfrac{1}{2} E[(d - E[d|\mathbf{x}])^2] \tag{2.46}$$

which states that, among all functions of $\mathbf{x}$, the regressive model is the *best* estimator of the desired response d given the input vector $\mathbf{x}$, "best" being defined in the mean-square sense.

The environment measure represented by the probability density function $f(\mathbf{x})$ plays a critical role in the determination of the optimum weight vector $\mathbf{w}_o$ of the neural network. A neural network optimized in this way will produce small errors (on average) for values of $\mathbf{x}$ that are most likely to occur at the cost of larger errors (on average) for values of $\mathbf{x}$ that are unlikely to occur. It follows that a neural network characterized by the synaptic weight vector $\mathbf{w}_o$ that minimizes Eq. (2.45) for a specified $f(\mathbf{x})$ will not give optimum performance in an operating environment characterized by a probability density function different from $f(\mathbf{x})$. This critical role holds in general, not just for the mean-squared error criterion (White, 1989a).

The Bias/Variance Dilemma

From our earlier discussion following Eq. (2.42), we note that the squared distance to the regression function, namely,

$$(g(\mathbf{x}) - F(\mathbf{x},\mathbf{w}))^2 = (E[d|\mathbf{x}] - F(\mathbf{x},\mathbf{w}))^2$$

represents a natural measure of the effectiveness of the function $F(\mathbf{x},\mathbf{w})$ as a predictor of d. We also note that in a neural network that learns under the supervision of a teacher, information contained in the training set

$$D = \{(\mathbf{x}_1,d_1), (\mathbf{x}_2,d_2), \dots, (\mathbf{x}_N,d_N)\} \tag{2.47}$$

is, in effect, transferred to a set of synaptic connections represented by the weight vector $\mathbf{w}$, as indicated by

$$D \rightarrow \mathbf{w} \tag{2.48}$$

Thus, to be explicit about dependence on the training set D, we rewrite the approximating function $F(\mathbf{x},\mathbf{w})$ as $F(\mathbf{x},D)$. Consider then the mean-squared error of the function $F(\mathbf{x},D)$ as an estimator of the regression function $g(\mathbf{x}) = E(d|\mathbf{x})$, which is defined by

$$E_D[(E[d|\mathbf{x}] - F(\mathbf{x},D))^2]$$

where the expectation operator E_D represents the average over all the patterns in the training set D. Proceeding in a manner similar to the derivation of Eq. (2.42), we may show that, for a given input vector $\mathbf{x}$ (Geman et al., 1992):

$$\begin{aligned}
E_D[(E[d|\mathbf{x}] &- F(\mathbf{x},D))^2] \\
&= E_D[(E[d|\mathbf{x}] - E_D[F(\mathbf{x},D)] + E_D[F(\mathbf{x},D)] - F(\mathbf{x},D))^2] \\
&= E_D[(E[d|\mathbf{x}] - E_D[F(\mathbf{x},D)])^2] + E_D[(E_D[F(\mathbf{x},D)] - F(\mathbf{x},D))^2] \\
&\quad + 2E_D[(E[d|\mathbf{x}] - E_D[F(\mathbf{x},D)])(E_D[F(\mathbf{x},D)] - F[\mathbf{x},D])] \\
&= (E[d|\mathbf{x}] - E_D[F(\mathbf{x},D)])^2 + E_D[(F(\mathbf{x},D) - E_D[F(\mathbf{x},D)])^2] \\
&\quad + 2(E[d|\mathbf{x}] - E_D[F(\mathbf{x},D)]) \cdot E_D[E_D[F(\mathbf{x},D)] - F(\mathbf{x},D)] \\
&= (E_D[F(\mathbf{x},D)] - E[d|\mathbf{x}])^2 + E_D[(F(\mathbf{x},D) - E_D[F(\mathbf{x},D)])^2]
\end{aligned} \tag{2.49}$$

where we have made use of the fact that the conditional mean $E[d|\mathbf{x}]$ has constant expectation with respect to the training set D, and then finally reduced the cross-product term to zero since

$$E_D[E_D[F(\mathbf{x},D)] - F(\mathbf{x},D)] = E_D[F(\mathbf{x},D)] - E_D[F(\mathbf{x},D)]$$
$$= 0 \tag{2.50}$$

We now make two observations:

1. The difference term $E_D[F(\mathbf{x},D)] - E[d|\mathbf{x}]$ represents the *bias* of the approximating function $F(\mathbf{x},D)$ measured with respect to the regression function $g(\mathbf{x}) = E[d|\mathbf{x}]$.
2. The ensemble-averaged term $E_D[(F(\mathbf{x},D) - E_D[F(\mathbf{x},D)])^2]$ represents the *variance* of the approximating function $F(\mathbf{x},D)$.

Accordingly, Eq. (2.49) states that the mean-square value of the estimation error between the regression function $g(\mathbf{x})$ and the approximating function $F(\mathbf{x},D)$ consists of the sum of two terms: bias squared and variance.

If, on the average, the approximating function $F(\mathbf{x},D)$ is different from the regression function $g(\mathbf{x})$, we say that $F(\mathbf{x},D)$ is a *biased estimator* of $g(\mathbf{x})$. On the other hand, if

$$E_D[F(\mathbf{x},D)] = g(\mathbf{x})$$

we say that $F(\mathbf{x},D)$ is an *unbiased estimator* of $g(\mathbf{x})$. Of course, an unbiased estimator may still have a large mean-square error if the variance is large. To achieve good performance, the bias and variance of the approximating function $F(\mathbf{x},D)$ would both have to be small.

In the case of a neural network that learns by example, and that does so with a training set of fixed size, we find that the price for achieving a small bias is large variance. It is only when the size of the training set is allowed to become infinitely large that we can hope to eliminate both bias and variance at the same time. We therefore have a "dilemma," and the consequence is prohibitively slow convergence (Geman et al., 1992). The bias/variance dilemma may be circumvented if we are willing to *purposely* introduce bias, which then makes it possible to eliminate the variance or reduce it significantly. Needless to say, we have to be sure that the bias built into the network design is in fact harmless for the problem at hand. The bias is said to be "harmless" in the sense that it will contribute significantly to mean-squared error only if we try to infer regressions that are not in the anticipated class. In essence, bias would need to be *designed* for each specific application of interest. A practical way of achieving such an objective is to use a *constrained* network architecture, which usually performs better than a general-purpose architecture. For example, the constraints and therefore the bias may take the form of prior knowledge built into the network design using (1) *weight sharing* where several synapses of the network are controlled by a single weight, or (2) *local receptive fields* assigned to individual neurons in the network, as demonstrated in the application of a multilayer perceptron to the optical character recognition problem (LeCun et al., 1990a).

2.13 Learning Theory

In this chapter we have described various aspects of the learning process, and in subsequent chapters of the book we shall build on the many ideas described herein. Unfortunately, however, we still lack a full understanding of *learning theory,* that is, the mathematical structure describing the underlying learning process. We need such a theory in order to formulate the fundamental principle on the basis of which we may search for solutions

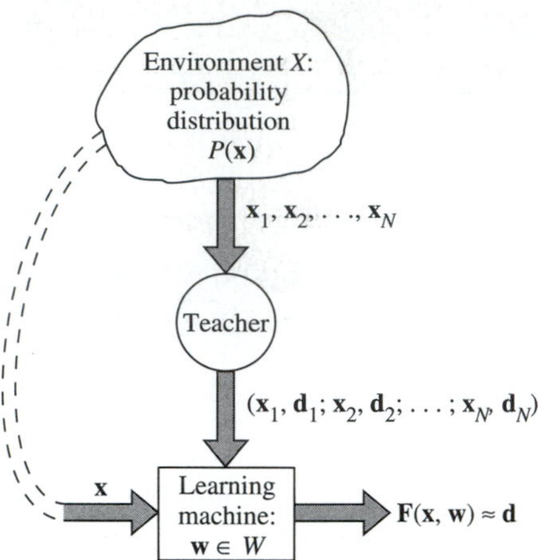

FIGURE 2.13 Model of the supervised learning process.

to specific learning tasks. In this section of the chapter, we briefly address the issues involved in this important subject in the context of supervised learning.

One model of supervised learning consists of three interrelated components, illustrated in Fig. 2.13 and abstracted in mathematical terms as follows (Vapnik, 1992):

- *Environment,* which supplies a vector $\mathbf{x}$ with a fixed but unknown probability distribution $P(\mathbf{x})$.
- *Teacher,* which provides a desired response (target output) vector $\mathbf{d}$ for every input vector $\mathbf{x}$, in accordance with a conditional probability distribution $P(\mathbf{d}|\mathbf{x})$ that is also fixed but unknown. The vectors $\mathbf{x}$ and $\mathbf{d}$ are related by an unknown function, as follows:

$$\mathbf{d} = \mathbf{g}(\mathbf{x}) \tag{2.51}$$

- *Learning machine* (algorithm), which is capable of implementing a set of input–output mapping functions described by

$$\mathbf{y} = \mathbf{F}(\mathbf{x},\mathbf{w}) \tag{2.52}$$

  where $\mathbf{y}$ is the actual output vector produced by the machine in response to the input vector $\mathbf{x}$, and $\mathbf{w}$ is a set of free parameters (synaptic weights) selected by the machine from the parameter (weight) space W.

The learning problem is that of selecting, from an *a priori* given set of input–output mappings, that particular function $\mathbf{F}(\mathbf{x},\mathbf{w})$ that approximates the desired response vector $\mathbf{d}$ supplied by the teacher in an optimum fashion, "optimum" being defined in some statistical sense. The selection is itself based on a set of N *independent, identically distributed* (i.i.d.) training examples:

$$(\mathbf{x}_1,\mathbf{d}_1), (\mathbf{x}_2,\mathbf{d}_2), \ldots, (\mathbf{x}_N,\mathbf{d}_N) \tag{2.53}$$

The feasibility of supervised learning depends on the key question[9]: Do the training examples defined by Eq. (2.53) contain sufficient information to construct a learning

[9] The problem posed here is referred to as the *sample complexity problem* in the machine-learning literature (Natarajan, 1991). There is a second question relevant in the framework of supervised learning: What is the worst-case computation time required to train a learning machine using a set of training examples of a given size? This is referred to as the *time (computational) complexity problem;* for its consideration, see Natarajan (1991).

machine capable of good generalization performance? The answer to this issue lies in the use of tools pioneered by Vapnik and Chervonenkis (1971), which we adopt in the sequel. Specifically, we proceed by viewing the supervised learning process as an *approximation problem,* which involves finding the function $\mathbf{F}(\mathbf{x},\mathbf{w})$ that is the "best" available approximation to the desired function $\mathbf{g}(\mathbf{x})$.

Let $L(\mathbf{d},\mathbf{F}(\mathbf{x},\mathbf{w}))$ represent a measure of the *loss* or *discrepancy* between the desired response vector $\mathbf{d}$ corresponding to an input vector $\mathbf{x}$ and the actual response $\mathbf{F}(\mathbf{x},\mathbf{w})$ produced by the learning machine. A popular definition for the loss $L(\mathbf{d};\mathbf{F}(\mathbf{x},\mathbf{w}))$ is the *quadratic loss function* defined as the squared Euclidean distance between the vector $\mathbf{d}$ and the approximation $\mathbf{F}(\mathbf{x},\mathbf{w})$, as shown by

$$L(\mathbf{d};\mathbf{F}(\mathbf{x},\mathbf{w})) = \|\mathbf{d} - \mathbf{F}(\mathbf{x},\mathbf{w})\|^2 \tag{2.54}$$

The validity of the learning theory presented here does not, however, depend on the form of the loss function. Accordingly, we develop the theory in its general form, without restricting it to any particular loss function.

The expected value of the loss is defined by the *risk functional* (Vapnik, 1992)

$$R(\mathbf{w}) = \int L(\mathbf{d};\mathbf{F}(\mathbf{x},\mathbf{w}))\, dP(\mathbf{x},\mathbf{d}) \tag{2.55}$$

where $P(\mathbf{x},\mathbf{d})$ is the joint probability distribution of the input vector $\mathbf{x}$ and the desired response vector $\mathbf{d}$, and the integral is taken in the *Riemann–Stieltjes sense.*[10] The goal of the learning process is to minimize the risk functional $R(\mathbf{w})$ over the class of functions $\mathbf{F}(\mathbf{x},\mathbf{w})$, $\mathbf{w} \in W$. However, the evaluation of the risk functional $R(\mathbf{w})$ is complicated by the fact that the joint probability distribution

$$P(\mathbf{x},\mathbf{d}) = P(\mathbf{d}|\mathbf{x})P(\mathbf{x}) \tag{2.56}$$

is unknown, where $P(\mathbf{d}|\mathbf{x})$ is the conditional probability distribution of $\mathbf{d}$ given $\mathbf{x}$, and $P(\mathbf{x})$ is the probability distribution of $\mathbf{x}$. The only information that we have to work with is contained in the training set. To overcome this mathematical difficulty, we use the inductive principle of empirical risk minimization (Vapnik, 1982). This principle does not require probability distribution estimation, and is perfectly suited to the philosophy of neural networks.

Principle of Empirical Risk Minimization

The basic idea of this method is to use the training set of independent examples described in Eq. (2.53) and the loss $\mathbf{F}(\mathbf{x},\mathbf{w})$ to construct the *empirical risk functional* (Vapnik, 1982)

$$R_{\text{emp}}(\mathbf{w}) = \frac{1}{N}\sum_{i=1}^{N} L(\mathbf{d}_i;\mathbf{F}(\mathbf{x}_i,\mathbf{w})) \tag{2.57}$$

which does not depend on the unknown probability distribution $P(\mathbf{x},\mathbf{d})$. Unlike the original risk functional $R(\mathbf{w})$, the empirical risk functional $R_{\text{emp}}(\mathbf{w})$ can in theory be minimized with respect to the weight vector $\mathbf{w}$. Let $\mathbf{w}_{\text{emp}}$ and $\mathbf{F}(\mathbf{x},\mathbf{w}_{\text{emp}})$ denote the weight vector and the corresponding mapping that minimize the empirical risk functional $R_{\text{emp}}(\mathbf{w})$ in Eq. (2.57). Similarly, let $\mathbf{w}_o$ and $\mathbf{F}(\mathbf{x},\mathbf{w}_o)$ denote the weight vector and the corresponding mapping that minimize the actual risk functional $R(\mathbf{w})$ in Eq. (2.55). Both $\mathbf{w}_{\text{emp}}$ and $\mathbf{w}_o$ belong to the weight space W. The problem we now have to consider is the condition

[10] The Riemann–Stieltjes integral (or simply the Stieltjes integral) of a function $f(x)$ with respect to another function $\alpha(x)$ is written as $\int f(x)\, d\alpha(x)$. The Riemann integral of $f(x)$ is a special case of the Riemann–Stieltjes integral with $\alpha(x) = x$. The Riemann–Stieltjes integral exists for every continuous function $f(x)$ if and only if $\alpha(x)$ is of bounded variation.

under which the approximate solution mapping $\mathbf{F}(\mathbf{x},\mathbf{w}_{\text{emp}})$ is "close" to the desired solution mapping $\mathbf{F}(\mathbf{x},\mathbf{w}_o)$ as measured by the mismatch between $R(\mathbf{w}_{\text{emp}})$ and $R(\mathbf{w}_o)$.

For each fixed $\mathbf{w} = \mathbf{w}^*$, the risk functional $R(\mathbf{w}^*)$ determines the *mathematical expectation* of a random variable defined by

$$Z_{\mathbf{w}^*} = L(\mathbf{d};\mathbf{F}(\mathbf{x},\mathbf{w}^*)) \tag{2.58}$$

In contrast, the empirical risk functional $R_{\text{emp}}(\mathbf{w}^*)$ is the *empirical* (*arithmetic*) *mean* of the random variable $Z_{\mathbf{w}^*}$. According to the classical theorems of probability theory, in sufficiently general cases we find that as the size N of the training set is made infinitely large, the empirical mean of the random variable $Z_{\mathbf{w}^*}$ converges to its expected value. This observation provides theoretical justification for the use of the empirical risk functional $R_{\text{emp}}(\mathbf{w})$ in place of the risk functional $R(\mathbf{w})$. It is important to note, however, that just because the empirical mean of $Z_{\mathbf{w}^*}$ converges to its expected value, there is no reason to expect that the weight vector $\mathbf{w}_{\text{emp}}$ that minimizes the empirical risk functional $R_{\text{emp}}(\mathbf{w})$ will also minimize the risk functional $R(\mathbf{w})$.

We may satisfy this requirement in an approximate fashion by proceeding as follows. If the empirical risk functional $R_{\text{emp}}(\mathbf{w})$ approximates the original risk functional $R(\mathbf{w})$ *uniformly* in $\mathbf{w}$ with some *precision* ε, then the minimum of $R_{\text{emp}}(\mathbf{w})$ deviates from the minimum of $R(\mathbf{w})$ by an amount not exceeding 2ε. Formally, this means that we must impose a stringent condition, such that for any $\mathbf{w} \in W$ and $\varepsilon > 0$, the probabilistic relation

$$\text{Prob}\left\{\sup_{\mathbf{w}} |R(\mathbf{w}) - R_{\text{emp}}(\mathbf{w})| > \varepsilon\right\} \to 0 \qquad \text{as } N \to \infty \tag{2.59}$$

holds (Vapnik, 1982); the symbol "sup" stands for "supremum of." When Eq. (2.59) is satisfied, we say that a *uniform convergence in the weight vector* $\mathbf{w}$ *of the empirical mean risk to its expected value occurs.* Equivalently, provided that for any prescribed precision ε we can assert the inequality

$$\text{Prob}\left\{\sup_{\mathbf{w}} |R(\mathbf{w}) - R_{\text{emp}}(\mathbf{w})| > \varepsilon\right\} < \alpha \tag{2.60}$$

for some $\alpha > 0$, then, as a consequence, the following inequality also holds:

$$\text{Prob}\{R(\mathbf{w}_{\text{emp}}) - R(\mathbf{w}_o) > 2\varepsilon\} < \alpha \tag{2.61}$$

In other words, if the condition (2.60) holds, then with probability at least $(1 - \alpha)$, the solution $\mathbf{F}(\mathbf{x},\mathbf{w}_{\text{emp}})$ that minimizes the empirical risk functional $R_{\text{emp}}(\mathbf{w})$ will give an actual risk $R(\mathbf{w}_{\text{emp}})$ that deviates from the true minimum possible actual risk $R(\mathbf{w}_o)$ by an amount not exceeding 2ε. Indeed, the condition (2.60) implies that with probability $(1 - \alpha)$ the following two inequalities are satisfied simultaneously (Vapnik, 1982):

$$R(\mathbf{w}_{\text{emp}}) - R_{\text{emp}}(\mathbf{w}_{\text{emp}}) < \varepsilon \tag{2.62}$$

$$R_{\text{emp}}(\mathbf{w}_o) - R(\mathbf{w}_o) < \varepsilon \tag{2.63}$$

Furthermore, since $\mathbf{w}_{\text{emp}}$ and $\mathbf{w}_o$ are the minimum points of $R_{\text{emp}}(\mathbf{w})$ and $R(\mathbf{w})$, respectively, it follows that

$$R_{\text{emp}}(\mathbf{w}_{\text{emp}}) \le R_{\text{emp}}(\mathbf{w}_o) \tag{2.64}$$

Thus, adding the inequalities (2.62) and (2.63), and then using (2.64), we may write (see Fig. 2.14)

$$R(\mathbf{w}_{\text{emp}}) - R(\mathbf{w}_o) < 2\varepsilon \tag{2.65}$$

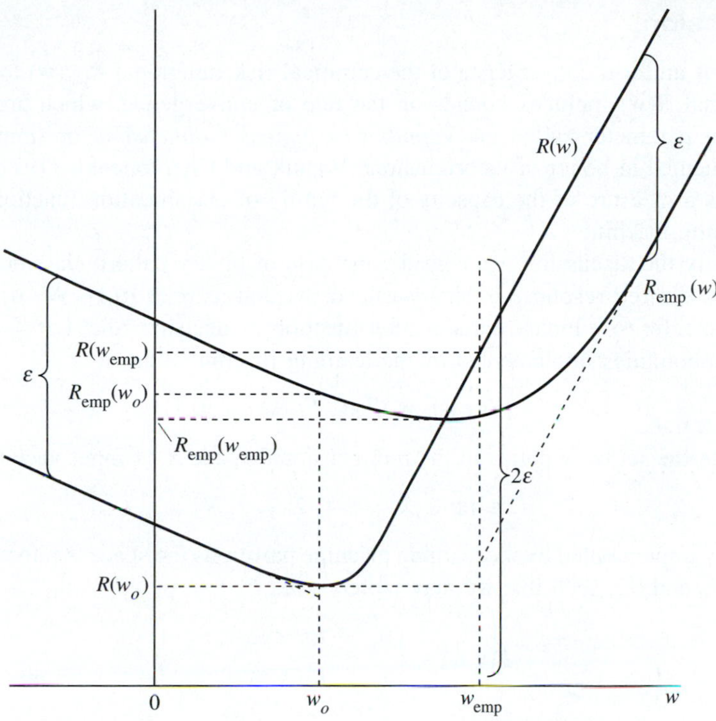

FIGURE 2.14 Illustrating the inequalities (2.62) to (2.65).

Also, since the inequalities (2.62) and (2.63) are both satisfied simultaneously with probability $(1 - \alpha)$, so is the inequality (2.65). Equivalently, we may state that with probability α the inequality

$$R(\mathbf{w}_{emp}) - R(\mathbf{w}_o) > 2\varepsilon$$

holds, which is a restatement of (2.61).

We are now ready to make a formal statement of the *principle of empirical risk minimization* (Vapnik, 1982, 1992):

In place of the risk functional $R(\mathbf{w})$, construct the empirical risk functional

$$R_{emp}(\mathbf{w}) = \frac{1}{N}\sum_{i=1}^{N} L(\mathbf{d}_i;\mathbf{F}(\mathbf{x}_i,\mathbf{w}))$$

on the basis of the set of i.i.d. training examples

$$(\mathbf{x}_i,\mathbf{d}_i), \qquad i = 1, 2, \ldots, N$$

Let $\mathbf{w}_{emp}$ denote the weight vector that minimizes the empirical risk functional $R_{emp}(\mathbf{w})$ over the weight space W. Then $R(\mathbf{w}_{emp})$ converges in probability to the minimum possible value of the actual risk $R(\mathbf{w})$, $\mathbf{w} \in W$, as the size N of the training set is made infinitely large, provided that the empirical risk functional $R_{emp}(\mathbf{w})$ converges uniformly to the actual risk functional $R(\mathbf{w})$. Uniform convergence is defined as

$$\text{Prob}\left\{\sup_{\mathbf{w}\in W}|R(\mathbf{w}) - R_{emp}(\mathbf{w})| > \varepsilon\right\} \rightarrow 0 \qquad \text{as } N \rightarrow \infty$$

This condition is a necessary and sufficient condition for the consistency of the principle of empirical risk minimization.

VC Dimension

The theory of uniform convergence of the empirical risk functional $R_{emp}(\mathbf{w})$ to the actual risk functional $R(\mathbf{w})$ includes bounds on the rate of convergence, which are based on an important parameter called the *Vapnik–Chervonenkis dimension,* or simply the *VC dimension,* named in honor of its originators, Vapnik and Chervonenkis (1971). The VC dimension is a measure of the capacity of the family of classification functions realized by the learning machine.

To simplify the discussion, we consider the case of binary pattern classification from here on. The desired response is binary-valued, written as $d \in \{0,1\}$. We use the term *dichotomy* to refer to a binary classification function or decision rule. Let $\mathcal{F}$ denote the family of dichotomies implemented by the learning machine, that is,

$$\mathcal{F} = \{F(\mathbf{x},\mathbf{w}): \mathbf{w} \in W, F: \mathbb{R}^p \rightarrow \{0,1\}\} \tag{2.66}$$

Let $\mathcal{S}$ denote the set of N points in the p-dimensional space X of input vectors; that is,

$$\mathcal{S} = \{\mathbf{x}_i \in X; i = 1, 2, \ldots, N\} \tag{2.67}$$

A dichotomy implemented by the learning machine partitions the space $\mathcal{S}$ into two disjoint subspaces $\mathcal{S}_0$ and $\mathcal{S}_1$, such that we may write

$$F(\mathbf{x},\mathbf{w}) = \begin{cases} 0 & \text{for } \mathbf{x} \in \mathcal{S}_0 \\ 1 & \text{for } \mathbf{x} \in \mathcal{S}_1 \end{cases} \tag{2.68}$$

Let $\Delta_{\mathcal{F}}(\mathcal{S})$ denote the number of distinct dichotomies implemented by the learning machine, and $\Delta_{\mathcal{F}}(l)$ denote the maximum of $\Delta_{\mathcal{F}}(\mathcal{S})$ over all $\mathcal{S}$ with $|\mathcal{S}| = l$, where $|\mathcal{S}|$ is the cardinality of $\mathcal{S}$; *cardinality* is a measure of the size of a set. For example, for a finite set $\mathcal{S}$, the cardinality $|\mathcal{S}|$ is simply the number of elements in $\mathcal{S}$. We say that $\mathcal{S}$ is *shattered* by $\mathcal{F}$ if $\Delta_{\mathcal{F}}(\mathcal{S}) = 2^{|\mathcal{S}|}$, that is, if all the dichotomies of $\mathcal{S}$ can be induced by functions in $\mathcal{F}$.

For example, let $X = \mathbb{R}^2$ be the real plane, and let $\mathcal{F}$ be the set of all rectangles with sides parallel to the coordinate axes of the plane. The set of four points shown as dots in Fig. 2.15 are shattered by $\mathcal{F}$. Specifically, we note that for any subset of these four points, there exists an axis-parallel rectangle that includes that particular subset of points and excludes the rest (Natarajan, 1991).

Returning to the general discussion delineated by the family of dichotomies in Eq. (2.66) and the corresponding set of points $\mathcal{S}$ in Eq. (2.67), we may formally define the VC dimension as follows (Blumer et al., 1989; Baum and Haussler, 1989; Vapnik and Chervonenkis, 1971):

The VC dimension of the family of dichotomies $\mathcal{F}$ is the maximum cardinality of any set of points $\mathcal{S}$ in the input space X that is shattered by $\mathcal{F}$.

In other words, the VC dimension of $\mathcal{F}$ is the largest N such that $\Delta_{\mathcal{F}}(N) = 2^N$. Stated in somewhat more familiar terms, the VC dimension of the set of classification functions $\{F(\mathbf{x},\mathbf{w}); \mathbf{w} \in W\}$ is the maximum number of training examples that can be learned by the machine without error for all possible binary labelings of the classification functions.

The VC dimension[11] is a purely combinatorial concept that has no connection with the geometric notion of dimension. In some cases the VC dimension is determined simply by the free parameters of a learning machine; in most practical situations, however, it is

[11] The VC dimension is closely related to the *separating capacity* of a surface encountered in pattern classification (Cover, 1965); this latter concept is discussed in Chapter 7.

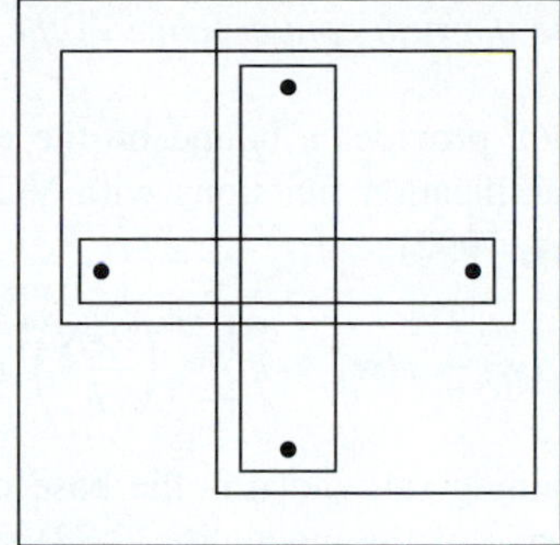

FIGURE 2.15 Illustrating the shattering process.

difficult to evaluate the VC dimension by analytic means. The point to note is that the VC dimension has emerged as an important parameter in modern learning theory (Blumer et al., 1989; Haussler, 1988). It features prominently in the bounds on the rate of uniform convergence, as described in the next subsection, where it is shown that a finite value for the VC dimension implies uniform convergence.

Rates of Uniform Convergence

In light of the notation introduced for binary pattern classification, in particular, with the desired response defined as $d \in \{0,1\}$, we find that in a corresponding way the loss function has only two values, as shown by

$$L(d;F(\mathbf{x},\mathbf{w})) = \begin{cases} 0 & \text{if } F(\mathbf{x},\mathbf{w}) = d \\ 1 & \text{otherwise} \end{cases} \tag{2.69}$$

Under these conditions, the risk functional $R(\mathbf{w})$ and the empirical risk functional $R_{\text{emp}}(\mathbf{w})$ defined in Eqs. (2.55) and (2.57), respectively, take on the following interpretations:

- The risk functional $R(\mathbf{w})$ is the *average probability of classification error* (i.e., error rate), denoted by $P(\mathbf{w})$.
- The empirical risk functional $R_{\text{emp}}(\mathbf{w})$ is the *training error* (i.e., frequency of errors made during the training session), denoted by $\nu(\mathbf{w})$.

Now, according to the *law of large numbers* (Gray and Davisson, 1986), the empirical frequency of occurrence of an event converges almost surely to the actual probability of that event as the number of trials (assumed to be independent and identically distributed) is made infinitely large. In the context of our study, this result means that for any weight vector $\mathbf{w}$ and precision $\varepsilon > 0$, the following condition holds (Vapnik, 1982):

$$\text{Prob}\{|P(\mathbf{w}) - \nu(\mathbf{w})| > \varepsilon\} \rightarrow 0 \quad \text{as } N \rightarrow \infty \tag{2.70}$$

where N is the size of the training set. Note, however, that the condition (2.70) does not imply that the classification rule (i.e., a particular weight vector $\mathbf{w}$) that minimizes the training error $\nu(\mathbf{w})$ will also minimize the average probability of classification error $P(\mathbf{w})$. For a training set of sufficiently large size N, the proximity between $\nu(\mathbf{w})$ and $P(\mathbf{w})$ follows from a stronger condition, which stipulates that the following condition holds for any $\varepsilon > 0$ (Vapnik, 1982):

$$\text{Prob}\left\{\sup_{\mathbf{w}} |P(\mathbf{w}) - \nu(\mathbf{w})| > \varepsilon\right\} \rightarrow 0 \quad \text{as } N \rightarrow \infty \tag{2.71}$$

In such a case we speak of *the uniform convergence of the frequency of training errors to their average probability.*

The notion of VC dimension provides a bound on the rate of uniform convergence. Specifically, for the set of classification functions with VC dimension h, the following inequality holds (Vapnik, 1982, 1992):

$$\text{Prob}\left\{\sup_{\mathbf{w}}|P(\mathbf{w}) - \nu(\mathbf{w})| > \varepsilon\right\} < \left(\frac{2eN}{h}\right)^h \exp(-\varepsilon^2 N) \tag{2.72}$$

where N is the size of the training set, and e is the base of the natural logarithm. We want to make the right-hand side of the inequality (2.72) small for large N, in order to achieve uniform convergence. The factor $\exp(-\varepsilon^2 N)$ is helpful in this regard, since it decays exponentially with increasing N. The remaining factor $(2eN/h)^h$ represents a *growth function* (Abu-Mostafa, 1989). Provided that this factor does *not* grow too fast, the right-hand side will go to zero as N goes to infinity. This requirement is indeed satisfied if the VC dimension h is finite. In other words, a finite VC dimension is a necessary and sufficient condition for uniform convergence. Note that if the input space X has finite cardinality, then any family of dichotomies $\mathcal{F}$ will obviously have finite VC dimension with respect to X, but the reverse is not necessarily true.

Let α denote the probability of the occurrence of the event

$$\sup_{\mathbf{w}}|P(\mathbf{w}) - \nu(\mathbf{w})| > \varepsilon$$

Then, with probability $1 - \alpha$, we may state that for all weight vectors $\mathbf{w} \in W$ the following inequality holds:

$$P(\mathbf{w}) < \nu(\mathbf{w}) + \varepsilon \tag{2.73}$$

Using the bound described in Eq. (2.72) and the definition for the probability α, we may thus set

$$\alpha = \left(\frac{2eN}{h}\right)^h \exp(-\varepsilon^2 N) \tag{2.74}$$

Let $\varepsilon_0(N,h,\alpha)$ denote the special value of ε that satisfies Eq. (2.74). Hence, we readily obtain the following important result (Vapnik, 1992):

$$\varepsilon_0(N,h,\alpha) = \sqrt{\frac{h}{N}\left[\ln\left(\frac{2N}{h}\right) + 1\right] - \frac{1}{N}\ln\alpha} \tag{2.75}$$

where ln denotes the natural logarithm. We refer to $\varepsilon_0(N,h,\alpha)$ as a *confidence interval,* the value of which depends on the size N of the training set, the VC dimension h, and the probability α.

The bound described in (2.72) with $\varepsilon = \varepsilon_0(N,h,\alpha)$ is achieved for the worst case $P(\mathbf{w}) = \frac{1}{2}$, but not, unfortunately, for small $P(\mathbf{w})$, which is the case of interest in practice. For small $P(\mathbf{w})$, a more useful bound is obtained by considering a modification of the inequality (2.72) as follows (Vapnik, 1982, 1992):

$$\text{Prob}\left\{\sup_{\mathbf{w}}\frac{|P(\mathbf{w}) - \nu(\mathbf{w})|}{\sqrt{P(\mathbf{w})}} > \varepsilon\right\} < \left(\frac{2eN}{h}\right)^h \exp\left(-\frac{\varepsilon^2 N}{4}\right) \tag{2.76}$$

In the literature, different results are reported for the bound in (2.76), depending on which particular form of inequality is used for its derivation. Nevertheless, they all have a similar form. In any event, from (2.76) it follows that with probability $1-\alpha$, and simultaneously for all $\mathbf{w} \in W$ (Vapnik, 1992),

$$P(\mathbf{w}) < \nu(\mathbf{w}) + \varepsilon_1(N,h,\alpha,\nu) \tag{2.77}$$

where $\varepsilon_1(N,h,\alpha,\nu)$ is a new confidence interval defined in terms of the former confidence interval $\varepsilon_0(N,h,\alpha)$ as follows (see Problem 2.16):

$$\varepsilon_1(N,h,\alpha,\nu) = 2\varepsilon_0^2(N,h,\alpha)\left(1 + \sqrt{1 + \frac{\nu(\mathbf{w})}{\varepsilon_0^2(N,h,\alpha)}}\right) \tag{2.78}$$

Note that this second confidence interval depends on the training error $\nu(\mathbf{w})$. For $\nu(\mathbf{w}) = 0$, it reduces to the special form

$$\varepsilon_1(N,h,\alpha,0) = 4\varepsilon_0^2(N,h,\alpha) \tag{2.79}$$

We may now summarize the two bounds we have derived for the rate of uniform convergence as follows:

1. In general, we have the following bound on the rate of uniform convergence:
$$P(\mathbf{w}) < \nu(\mathbf{w}) + \varepsilon_1(N,h,\alpha,\nu)$$
where $\varepsilon_1(N,h,\alpha,\nu)$ is as defined in Eq. (2.78).
2. For a small training error $\nu(\mathbf{w})$ close to zero, we have
$$P(\mathbf{w}) \lesssim \nu(\mathbf{w}) + 4\varepsilon_0^2(N,h,\alpha)$$
which provides a fairly precise bound for real-case learning.
3. For a large training error $\nu(\mathbf{w})$ close to unity, we have the bound
$$P(\mathbf{w}) \lesssim \nu(\mathbf{w}) + \varepsilon_0(N,h,\alpha)$$

Structural Risk Minimization

The *training error* is the frequency of errors made by a learning machine of some weight vector $\mathbf{w}$ during the training session. Similarly, the *generalization error* is defined as the frequency of errors made by the machine when it is tested with examples not seen before. Here it is assumed that the test data are drawn from the same population as the training data. Let these two errors be denoted by $\nu_{\text{train}}(\mathbf{w})$ and $\nu_{\text{gene}}(\mathbf{w})$, respectively. Note that $\nu_{\text{train}}(\mathbf{w})$ is the *same* as the $\nu(\mathbf{w})$ used in the previous subsection; we used $\nu(\mathbf{w})$ there to simplify the notation. Let h be the VC dimension of a family of classification functions $\{F(\mathbf{x},\mathbf{w}); \mathbf{w} \in W\}$ with respect to the input space X. Then, in light of the theory on the rates of uniform convergence, we may state that with probability $1 - \alpha$, for a number of training examples $N > h$, and simultaneously for all classification functions $F(\mathbf{x},\mathbf{w})$, the generalization error $\nu_{\text{gene}}(\mathbf{w})$ is lower than a *guaranteed risk* defined by the sum of a pair of competing terms (Guyon et al., 1992; Vapnik, 1992),

$$\nu_{\text{guarant}}(\mathbf{w}) = \nu_{\text{train}}(\mathbf{w}) + \varepsilon_1(N,h,\alpha,\nu_{\text{train}}) \tag{2.80}$$

where the confidence interval $\varepsilon_1(N,h,\alpha,\nu_{\text{train}})$ is itself defined by Eq. (2.78). For a fixed number of training examples N, the training error decreases monotonically as the capacity or VC dimension h is increased, whereas the confidence interval increases monotonically. Accordingly, both the guaranteed risk and the generalization error go through a minimum. These trends are illustrated in a generic way in Fig. 2.16. Before the minimum point is reached, the learning problem is *overdetermined* in the sense that the machine capacity h is too small for the amount of training detail. Beyond the minimum point, the learning

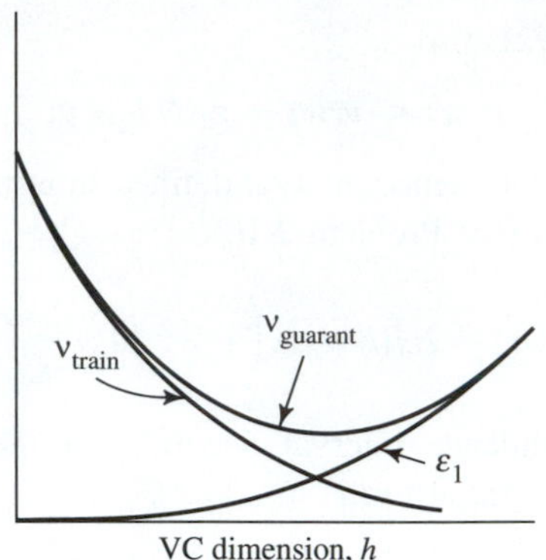

FIGURE 2.16 Illustrating the variations of ν_{train}, ε_1, and ν_{guarant} with the VC dimension h.

problem is *underdetermined* in the sense that the machine capacity is too large for the amount of training data. The challenge in solving the learning problem is to realize the best generalization performance by matching the machine capacity to the available amount of training data for the problem at hand. The *method of structural risk minimization* provides a systematic procedure for achieving this goal by controlling the VC dimension of the learning machine (Vapnik, 1992; Guyon et al., 1992).

Consider a family of binary pattern classifiers $\{F(\mathbf{x},\mathbf{w}); \mathbf{w} \in W\}$, and define a nested structure of n subsets

$$\mathcal{F}_k = \{F(\mathbf{x},\mathbf{w}); \mathbf{w} \in W_k\}, \qquad k = 1, 2, \ldots, n \tag{2.81}$$

such that we have

$$\mathcal{F}_1 \subset \mathcal{F}_2 \subset \cdots \subset \mathcal{F}_n \tag{2.82}$$

where the symbol $\subset$ signifies "is contained in." Correspondingly, the VC dimensions of the individual subsets satisfy the condition

$$h_1 < h_2 < \cdots < h_n \tag{2.83}$$

Then, the method of structural risk minimization proceeds as follows (Vapnik, 1992; Guyon et al., 1992):

- The empirical risk (i.e., training error) for each subset is minimized, and the particular subset $\mathcal{F}^*$ with the smallest minimum is selected.
- For the subset $\mathcal{F}^*$, the best compromise between the two competing terms of the guaranteed risk, namely, the training error and the confidence interval, is determined. The aim here is to find a network structure such that decreasing the VC dimension occurs at the expense of the smallest possible increase in training error.

We now mention three different examples of implementing the principle of structural risk minimization (Guyon et al., 1992; Vapnik, 1992).

1. *Control Through Varying Numbers of Hidden Neurons.* In this example the machine capacity is controlled by varying the number of hidden neurons. Specifically, a family of pattern classifiers is considered by having an ensemble of fully connected neural networks, with the number of hidden neurons in one of the hidden layers increasing monotonically.

2. *Control Through Weight Decay.* In this second example the neural network has a fixed architecture, and control of the capacity is exercised by varying the Euclidean norm of the weight vector **w**. Specifically, a choice of structure is introduced by considering a family of pattern classifiers defined by

$$\mathcal{F}_k = \{F(\mathbf{x},\mathbf{w});\ \|\mathbf{w}\| \le c_k\}, \qquad k = 1, 2, \ldots, n \tag{2.84}$$

where

$$\|\mathbf{w}\|^2 = \sum_j w_j^2$$

and

$$c_1 < c_2 < \cdots < c_n$$

The minimization of the empirical risk within the subset $\mathcal{F}_k$ of the structure is achieved by minimizing the augmented cost functional

$$R(\mathbf{w},\lambda_k) = \frac{1}{N}\sum_{i=1}^{N} L(d_i;\ F(\mathbf{x}_i,\mathbf{w})) + \lambda_k\|\mathbf{w}\|^2 \tag{2.85}$$

where the loss $L(d_i;\ F(\mathbf{x}_i,\mathbf{w}))$ is typically defined in terms of a quadratic cost function as in Eq. (2.54), and λ_k is a *regularization parameter,* so-called in recognition of the squared Euclidean norm $\|\mathbf{w}\|^2$ playing the role of a complexity *regularizer.* The sequence $c_1 < c_2 < \cdots < c_n$ is matched with a monotonically decreasing sequence of positive regularization parameters $\lambda_1 > \lambda_2 > \cdots > \lambda_n$. The minimization of the cost functional defined in Eq. (2.85) is equivalent to the *weight decay procedure.*

3. *Preprocessing.* Another effective method of reducing the capacity of a pattern classifier is to reduce the dimension of the input space, which has the effect of reducing the number of necessary weights (free parameters) in the classifier. Such a reduction is commonly accomplished by using a feature-extraction method known as *principal components analysis* (PCA). In PCA we perform an eigenanalysis on the correlation matrix of the training input vectors of dimension *p,* which are then approximated by a linear combination of the eigenvectors associated with the *m* largest eigenvalues, where $m \le p$. A structure is thus introduced by ranking the classifiers according to the reduced dimension *m.*

We shall have much more to say on these procedures in subsequent chapters. For now, it suffices to say that tuning the capacity of a pattern classifier to the available amount of training data through the method of structural risk minimization provides a powerful procedure for the design of neural networks.

2.14 Discussion

In this chapter we have discussed important issues relating to the many facets of the learning process in the context of neural networks. In so doing, we have laid down the foundations for much of the material to follow. The four learning rules, namely, *error-correction learning, Hebbian learning, competitive learning,* and *Boltzmann learning,* described in the early part of the chapter are indeed basic to the design of supervised and self-organized neural networks that go far beyond the reach of linear adaptive filters in both capability and universality.

A discussion of learning methods would be incomplete without mentioning the *Darwinian selective learning model* (Reeke et al., 1990; Edelman, 1987). *Selection* is a powerful biological principle with applications in both evolution and development. It is at the heart of the immune system (Edelman, 1973), which is the best-understood biological recognition system. The Darwinian selective learning model is based on the theory of neural group selection. It presupposes that the nervous system operates by a form of selection, akin to natural selection in evolution but taking place within the brain and during the lifetime of each animal. According to this theory, the basic operational units of the nervous system are not single neurons but rather local groups of strongly interconnected cells. The membership of neurons in a group is changed by alterations in the neurons' synaptic weights. Local competition and cooperation among cells are clearly necessary to produce local order in the network. A collection of neuronal groups is referred to as a *repertoire.* Groups in a repertoire respond best to overlapping but similar input patterns due to the random nature of neural growth. One or more neuronal groups in a repertoire respond to every input pattern, thereby ensuring some response to unexpected input patterns that may be important. Darwinian selective learning is different from the learning algorithms commonly used in neural network design in that it assumes that there are many subnetworks by design, and that only those with the desired response are selected during the training process.

In the study of supervised learning, as presented in this chapter, a key provision is a "teacher" capable of applying exact corrections to the network outputs when an error occurs as in error-correction learning, or "clamping" the free-running input and output units of the network to the environment as in Boltzmann learning. Neither of these models is possible in biological organisms, which have neither the exact reciprocal nervous connections needed for the back-propagation of error corrections nor the nervous means for the imposition of behavior from outside (Reeke et al., 1990). Nevertheless, supervised learning has established itself as a powerful paradigm for the design of artificial neural networks.

In contrast, self-organized (unsupervised) learning rules such as Hebbian learning and competitive learning are motivated by neurobiological considerations. However, to improve our understanding of self-organized learning, we also need to look at Shannon's *information theory* for relevant ideas. Here we should mention the *principle of maximum information preservation* (Linsker, 1988a, b), which provides the mathematical formalism for the processing of information in a self-organized neural network in a manner somewhat analogous to the transmission of information in a communication channel. The principle of maximum information preservation is discussed in detail in Chapter 11.

In this chapter we also described reinforcement learning, the theory of which is closely linked with optimal control theory and dynamic programming. *Dynamic programming,* originated by Bellman, provides an efficient mechanism for sequential-decision making. The mathematical basis of dynamic programming is the *principle of optimality* (Bertsekas, 1987; Bellman and Dreyfus, 1962; Bellman, 1957):

> *An optimal policy has the property that whatever the initial state and initial decision are, the remaining decisions must constitute an optimal policy with regard to the state resulting from the first decision.*

As used here, a "decision" is a choice of control at a particular time, and a "policy" is the entire control sequence or control function (Brogan, 1985). The role of dynamic programming in reinforcement learning is discussed by Watkins (1989), Watkins and Dayan (1992), and Werbos (1992).

We finally described the *principle of empirical risk minimization* as a mathematical basis of *supervised learning theory.* The *VC dimension,* originally formulated by Vapnik and Chervonenkis, is fundamental to the understanding of this new learning theory. The theory is certainly elegant in conceptual terms and yet so practical in terms of the performance measures used for its formulation. Although the presentation was made within the confines of the pattern-recognition paradigm, it is equally applicable to regression models (Vapnik, 1982). However, the theory is still in its early stages of development.

The VC dimension is closely related to the *probably approximately correct* (PAC) *learning model* originated by Valiant (1984). The salient feature of the PAC learning model is that it is distribution-free, producing a hypothesis that is a good approximation to the target (desired) function with high probability. The relationship between the PAC learning model and the VC dimension is discussed in Blumer et al. (1989) and Haussler (1988). The combination of these two concepts is also used by Baum and Haussler (1989) to study learning in multilayer feedforward networks. The results obtained by Baum and Haussler represent a worst-case sample complexity analysis of learning; the essence of these results is presented in Chapter 6.

PROBLEMS

2.1 The delta rule described in Eq. (2.5) and Hebb's rule described in Eq. (2.10) represent two different methods of learning. List the features that distinguish these two rules from each other.

2.2 The error-correction learning rule may be implemented by using inhibition to subtract the desired response (target value) from the output, and then applying the anti-Hebbian rule (Mitchison, 1989). Discuss this interpretation of error-correction learning.

2.3 Consider a group of people whose collective opinion on a topic of interest is defined as the weighted average of the individual opinions of its members. Suppose that if, over the course of time, the opinion of a member in the group tends to agree with the collective opinion of the group, then the opinion of that member is given more weight. If, on the other hand, the particular member consistently disagrees with the collective opinion of the group, then that member's opinion is given less weight. This form of weighting is equivalent to positive-feedback control, which has the effect of producing a consensus of opinion among the group (Linsker, 1988a).

Discuss the analogy between the situation described and Hebb's postulate of learning.

2.4 A generalized form of Hebb's rule is described by the relation

$$\Delta w_{kj}(n) = \alpha F(y_k(n))G(x_j(n)) - \beta w_{kj}(n)F(y_k(n))$$

where $x_j(n)$ and $y_k(n)$ are the presynaptic and postsynaptic signals, respectively; $F(\cdot)$ and $G(\cdot)$ are functions of their respective arguments; $\Delta w_{kj}(n)$ is the change produced in the synaptic weight w_{kj} at time n in response to the signals $x_j(n)$ and $y_k(n)$. Find (a) the balance point and (b) the maximum depression that are defined by this rule.

2.5 An input signal of unit amplitude is applied repeatedly to a synaptic connection whose initial value is also unity. Calculate the variation in the synaptic weight with time, using the following two rules:

(a) Simple form of Hebb's rule described in Eq. (2.10), assuming that the learning-rate parameter $\eta = 0.1$.

(b) Modified form of Hebb's rule described in Eq. (2.12) assuming that $\eta = 0.1$ and $c = 0.1$.

2.6 The Hebbian mechanism described by Eq. (2.10) involves the use of positive feedback. Justify the validity of this statement.

2.7 Figure P2.7 shows the block diagram of an *adaptive language-acquisition system* (Gorin, 1992). The synaptic connections in the neural network part of the system

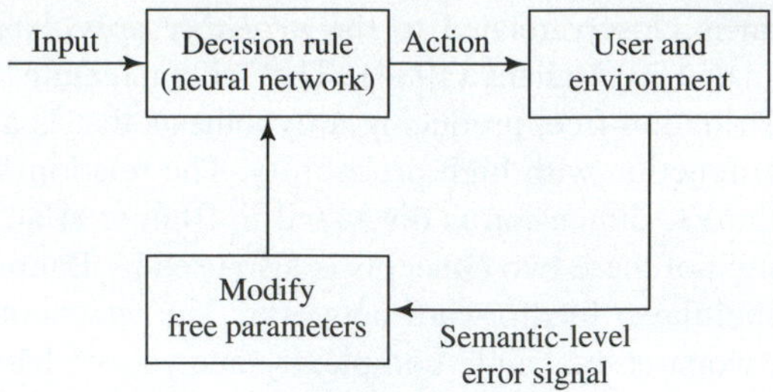

FIGURE P2.7

are strengthened or weakened, depending on feedback as to the appropriateness of the machine's response to input stimuli. This system may be viewed as an example of reinforcement learning. Rationalize the validity of this statement.

2.8 Unsupervised learning can be implemented in an off-line or on-line fashion. Discuss the physical implications of these two possibilities.

2.9 Formulate the expression for the output y_j of neuron j in the network of Fig. 2.5. You may assume the following:

$$x_i = i\text{th input signal}$$

$$w_{ji} = \text{synaptic weight form input } i \text{ to neuron } j$$

$$c_{kj} = \text{weight of lateral connection from neuron } k \text{ to neuron } j$$

$$v_j = \text{net activity level of neuron } j$$

$$y_j = \varphi(v_j)$$

What is the condition that would have to be satisfied for neuron j to be the winning neuron?

2.10 Repeat Problem 2.9, assuming that each output neuron includes self-feedback.

2.11 Consider the difficulties that a learning system would have to face in assigning credit for the outcome (win, loss, or draw) of a game of chess. Discuss the notions of temporal credit assignment and structural credit assignment in the context of this game.

2.12 A supervised learning task may be viewed as a reinforcement learning task by using as the reinforcement signal some measure of the closeness of the actual response of the system to the desired response. Discuss this relationship between supervised learning and reinforcement learning.

2.13 Figure P2.13 shows the block diagram of a linear prediction-error filter, where $\hat{x}(n)$ is the prediction made in response to the inputs $x(n-1), x(n-2), \ldots, x(n-p)$. Evaluate the variance of the filter output $e(n)$ Assume that $x(n)$ has zero mean.

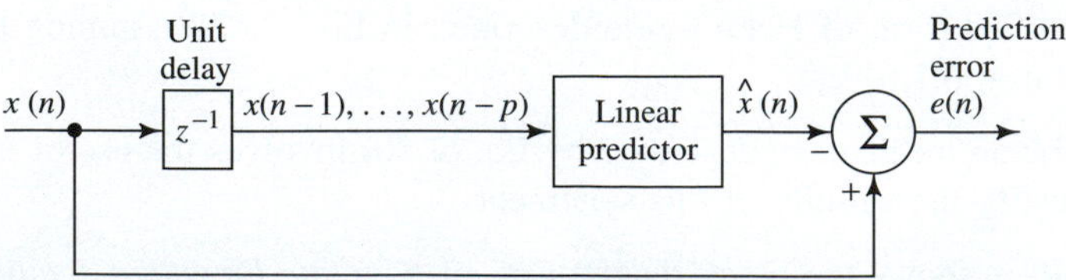

FIGURE P2.13

2.14 Consider a linear binary pattern classifier whose input vector **x** has dimension p. The first element of the vector **x** is constant and set to unity, so that the corresponding weight of the classifier introduces a bias. What is the VC dimension of the classifier with respect to the input space?

2.15 Consider the simple example of linear decision rules in a p-dimensional space X of input vectors **x**. What is the VC dimension with respect to the input space X?

Note. The reader may refer to Section 4.2 before solving Problems 2.14 and 2.15.

2.16 The inequality (2.76) defines a bound on the rate of uniform convergence, which is basic to the principle of empirical risk minimization.
(a) Justify the validity of Eq. (2.77), assuming that the inequality (2.76) holds.
(b) Derive Eq. (2.78) that defines the confidence interval ε_1.

CHAPTER 3

Correlation Matrix Memory

3.1 Introduction

In a neurobiological context, *memory* refers to the relatively enduring neural alterations induced by the interaction of an organism with its environment (Teyler, 1986). Without such a change, there can be no memory. Furthermore, for the memory to be useful, it must be accessible to the nervous system so as to influence future behavior. In the first place, however, an activity pattern must be stored in memory through a *learning process.* Indeed, memory and learning are intricately connected. When a particular activity pattern is learned, it is stored in the brain, from which it can be recalled later when required. Memory may be divided into "short-term" and "long-term" memory, depending on the retention time (Arbib, 1989). *Short-term memory* refers to a compilation of knowledge representing the "current" state of the environment. Any discrepancies between knowledge stored in short-term memory and a "new" state are used to update the short-term memory. *Long-term memory,* on the other hand, refers to knowledge stored for a long time or permanently.

In this chapter we study a brainlike distributed memory that operates by *association,* which is rather simple to understand and yet fundamental in its operation. Indeed, association has been known to be a prominent feature of human memory since Aristotle, and all models of cognition use association in one form or another as the basic operation (Anderson, 1985). For obvious reasons, this kind of memory is called *associative memory.*

A fundamental property of associative memory is that *it maps an output pattern of neural activity onto an input pattern of neural activity.* In particular, during the learning phase, a *key pattern* is presented as stimulus, and the memory transforms it into a *memorized* or *stored pattern.* The storage takes place through specific changes in the synaptic weights of the memory. During the retrieval or recall phase, the memory is presented with a stimulus that is a noisy version or an incomplete description of a key pattern originally associated with a stored pattern. Despite imperfections in the stimulus, the associative memory has the capability to recall the stored pattern correctly. Accordingly, associative memories are used in applications such as pattern recognition, to recover data when the available information is imprecise.

From this brief exposition of associative memory, we may identify the following characteristics of this kind of memory:

1. The memory is distributed.
2. Both the stimulus (key) pattern and the response (stored) pattern of an associative memory consist of data vectors.
3. Information is stored in memory by setting up a spatial pattern of neural activities across a large number of neurons.

4. Information contained in a stimulus not only determines its storage location in memory but also an address for its retrieval.
5. Despite the fact that the neurons do not represent reliable and low-noise computing cells, the memory exhibits a high degree of resistance to noise and damage of a diffusive kind.
6. There may be interactions between individual patterns stored in memory. (Otherwise, the memory would have to be exceptionally large for it to accommodate the storage of a large number of patterns in perfect isolation from each other.) There is therefore the distinct possibility of the memory making errors during the recall process.

Autoassociation Versus Heteroassociation

We may distinguish two basic types of association: autoassociation and heteroassociation. In an *autoassociative memory,* a key vector is associated with itself in memory—hence the name. Accordingly, the input and output signal (data) spaces have the same dimensionality. In a *heteroassociative memory,* on the other hand, arbitrary key vectors are associated (paired) with other arbitrary memorized vectors. The output space dimensionality may or may not equal the input space dimensionality. In both cases, however, a stored vector may be recalled (retrieved) from the memory by applying a stimulus that consists of a partial description (i.e., fraction) or noisy version of the key vector originally associated with a desired form of the stored vector. For example, the data stored in an autoassociative memory may represent the photograph of a person, but the stimulus may be composed from a noisy reproduction or a masked version of this photograph.

Linearity Versus Nonlinearity

An associative memory may also be classified as linear or nonlinear, depending on the model adopted for its neurons. In the *linear* case, the neurons act (to a first approximation) like a linear combiner. To be more specific, let the data vectors $\mathbf{a}$ and $\mathbf{b}$ denote the stimulus (input) and the response (output) of an associative memory, respectively. In a linear associative memory, the input–output relationship is described by

$$\mathbf{b} = \mathbf{M}\mathbf{a} \tag{3.1}$$

where $\mathbf{M}$ is called the *memory matrix.* The matrix $\mathbf{M}$ specifies the network connectivity of the associative memory. Figure 3.1 depicts a block-diagram representation of a linear associative memory. In a *nonlinear* associative memory, on the other hand, we have an input–output relationship of the form

$$\mathbf{b} = \varphi(\mathbf{M}; \mathbf{a})\mathbf{a} \tag{3.2}$$

where, in general, $\varphi(\cdot; \cdot)$ is a nonlinear function of the memory matrix and the input vector.

Organization of the Chapter

In this chapter we study the characterization of linear associative memory and methods for learning the storage matrix from pairs of associated patterns. The effects of noise

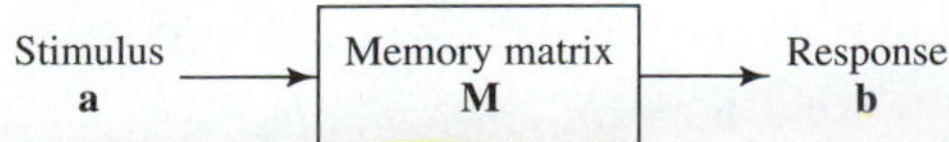

FIGURE 3.1 Block diagram of associative memory.

(distortion) on the quality of recall are also considered. Nonlinear associative memories are considered in subsequent chapters.

In Section 3.2 we discuss the idea of distributed memory mapping, which provides the basis for the study of linear associative memories. Then, in Section 3.3 we describe the outer product rule, which is a generalization of Hebb's postulate of learning, for the design of a special form of linear associative memory known as the correlation matrix memory. The recall properties of this type of memory are also discussed. Section 3.4 describes how an error-correction mechanism may be incorporated into the design of a correlation matrix memory, forcing it to associate perfectly. The chapter concludes with Section 3.5, presenting a comparison between the correlation matrix memory and another linear associative memory known as the pseudoinverse memory; the basic theory of this latter type of memory is presented in Appendix A at the end of the book.

3.2 Distributed Memory Mapping

In a *distributed memory,* the basic issue of interest is the simultaneous or near-simultaneous activities of many different neurons, which are the result of external or internal stimuli. The neural activities form a large spatial pattern inside the memory that contains information about the stimuli. The memory is therefore said to perform a distributed mapping that transforms an activity pattern in the input space into another activity pattern in the output space. We may illustrate some important properties of a distributed memory mapping by considering an idealized neural network that consists of two layers of neurons. Figure 3.2a illustrates the case of a network that may be regarded as a model component of a nervous system (Scofield and Cooper, 1985; Cooper, 1973). Each neuron in the input layer is connected to every one of the neurons in the output layer. The actual synaptic connections between the neurons are very complex and redundant. In the model of Fig. 3.2a, a single ideal junction is used to represent the integrated effect of all the synaptic contacts between the dendrites of a neuron in the input layer and the axon branches of a neuron in the output layer. In any event, the level of activity of a neuron in the input layer may affect the level of activity of every other neuron in the output layer.

The corresponding situation for an artificial neural network is depicted in Fig. 3.2b. Here we have an input layer of source nodes and an output layer of neurons acting as computation nodes. In this case, the synaptic weights of the network are included as integral parts of the neurons in the output layer. The connecting links between the two layers of the network are simply wires.

In the mathematical analysis to follow in this chapter, the neural networks in Figs. 3.2a and 3.2b are both assumed to be *linear.* The implication of this assumption is that each neuron acts as a linear combiner.

To proceed with the analysis, suppose that an activity pattern $\mathbf{a}_k$ occurs in the input layer of the network and that an activity pattern $\mathbf{b}_k$ occurs simultaneously in the output layer. The issue we wish to consider here is that of learning from the association between the patterns $\mathbf{a}_k$ and $\mathbf{b}_k$.

The patterns $\mathbf{a}_k$ and $\mathbf{b}_k$ are represented by vectors, written in their expanded forms as follows:

$$\mathbf{a}_k = [a_{k1}, a_{k2}, \ldots, a_{kp}]^T \tag{3.3}$$

and

$$\mathbf{b}_k = [b_{k1}, b_{k2}, \ldots, b_{kp}]^T \tag{3.4}$$

where the superscript T denotes *transposition.* For convenience of presentation, we have assumed that the input space dimensionality (i.e., the dimension of vector $\mathbf{a}_k$) and the

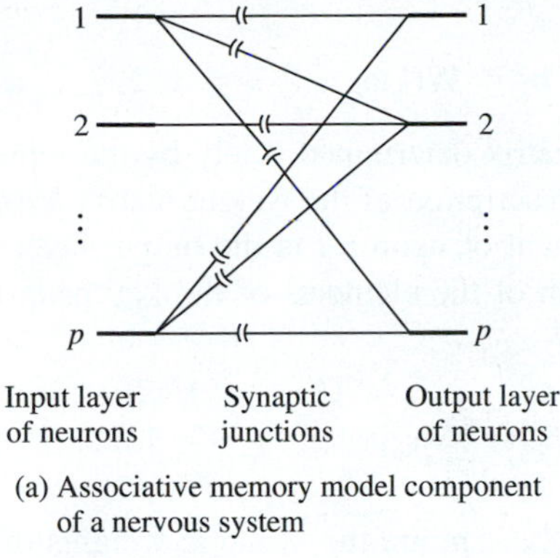

(a) Associative memory model component of a nervous system

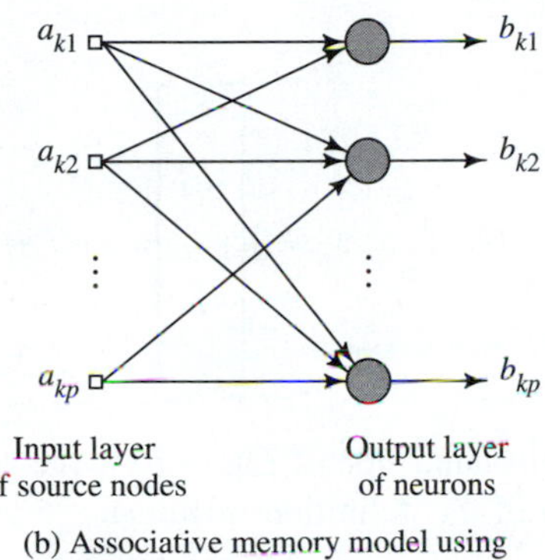

(b) Associative memory model using artificial neurons

FIGURE 3.2 (a) Associative memory model of a nervous system. (b) Associative memory model using artificial neurons.

output space dimensionality (i.e., the dimension of vector $\mathbf{b}_k$) are the same, equal to p. From here on, we will refer to p as *network dimensionality* or simply *dimensionality*. Note that p equals the number of source nodes in the input layer or neurons in the output layer. For a neural network with a large number of neurons, which is typically the case, the dimensionality p can therefore be large.

The elements of both $\mathbf{a}_k$ and $\mathbf{b}_k$ can assume positive and negative values. This is a valid proposition in an artificial neural network. It may also occur in a nervous system by considering the relevant physiological variable to be the difference between an actual activity level (e.g., firing rate of a neuron) and a nonzero spontaneous activity level.

For a specified dimensionality p, the neural network of Fig. 3.2a or 3.2b can associate a number of patterns—say, q. In general, the network can support a number of different associations up to a potential capacity of p. In reality, however, the capacity of the network to store different patterns (i.e., q) is less than the dimensionality p.

In any event, we may describe the different associations performed by the network by writing

$$\mathbf{a}_k \rightarrow \mathbf{b}_k, \qquad k = 1, 2, \ldots, q \tag{3.5}$$

The activity pattern $\mathbf{a}_k$ acts as a stimulus that not only determines the storage location of information in the stimulus $\mathbf{a}_k$, but also holds the key for its retrieval. Accordingly, $\mathbf{a}_k$ is referred to as a *key pattern,* and $\mathbf{b}_k$ is referred to as a *memorized pattern.*

With the networks of Fig. 3.2 assumed to be linear, the association of a key vector $\mathbf{a}_k$ with a memorized vector $\mathbf{b}_k$ described in symbolic form in Eq. (3.5) may be recast in matrix form as follows:

$$\mathbf{b}_k = \mathbf{W}(k)\mathbf{a}_k, \qquad k = 1, 2, \ldots, q \tag{3.6}$$

where $\mathbf{W}(k)$ is a weight matrix determined solely by the input–output pair $(\mathbf{a}_k, \mathbf{b}_k)$.

To develop a detailed description of the weight matrix $\mathbf{W}(k)$, consider Fig. 3.3, which shows a detailed arrangement of neuron i in the output layer. The output b_{ki} of neuron i due to the combined action of the elements of the key pattern $\mathbf{a}_k$ applied as stimulus to the input layer is given by

$$b_{ki} = \sum_{j=1}^{p} w_{ij}(k) a_{kj}, \qquad i = 1, 2, \ldots, q \tag{3.7}$$

where the $w_{ij}(k)$, $j = 1, 2, \ldots, p$, are the synaptic weights of neuron i corresponding to the kth pair of associated patterns. Using matrix notation, we may express b_{ki} in the equivalent form

$$b_{ki} = [w_{i1}(k), w_{i2}(k), \ldots, w_{ip}(k)] \begin{bmatrix} a_{k1} \\ a_{k2} \\ \vdots \\ a_{kp} \end{bmatrix}, \qquad i = 1, 2, \ldots, q \tag{3.8}$$

The column vector on the right-hand side of Eq. (3.8) is recognized as the key vector $\mathbf{a}_k$. Hence, substituting Eq. (3.8) in the definition of the stored vector $\mathbf{b}_k$ given in Eq. (3.4), we get

$$\begin{bmatrix} b_{k1} \\ b_{k2} \\ \vdots \\ b_{kp} \end{bmatrix} = \begin{bmatrix} w_{11}(k) & w_{12}(k) & \ldots & w_{1p}(k) \\ w_{21}(k) & w_{22}(k) & \ldots & w_{2p}(k) \\ \vdots & \vdots & \vdots & \vdots \\ w_{p1}(k) & w_{p2}(k) & \ldots & w_{pp}(k) \end{bmatrix} \begin{bmatrix} a_{k1} \\ a_{k2} \\ \vdots \\ a_{kp} \end{bmatrix} \tag{3.9}$$

Equation (3.9) is the expanded form of the matrix transformation or mapping described in Eq. (3.6). In particular, the p-by-p weight matrix $\mathbf{W}(k)$ is defined by

$$\mathbf{W}(k) = \begin{bmatrix} w_{11}(k) & w_{12}(k) & \ldots & w_{1p}(k) \\ w_{21}(k) & w_{22}(k) & \ldots & w_{2p}(k) \\ \vdots & \vdots & \vdots & \vdots \\ w_{p1}(k) & w_{p2}(k) & \ldots & w_{pp}(k) \end{bmatrix} \tag{3.10}$$

The individual presentations of the q pairs of associated patterns described in Eq. (3.5) produce corresponding values of the individual matrix, namely, $\mathbf{W}(1)$, $\mathbf{W}(2)$, $\ldots$, $\mathbf{W}(q)$. Recognizing that the pattern association $\mathbf{a}_k \rightarrow \mathbf{b}_k$ is represented by the weight matrix $\mathbf{W}(k)$, we may define a p-by-p *memory matrix* that describes the summation of the weight matrices for the entire set of pattern associations as follows:

$$\mathbf{M} = \sum_{k=1}^{q} \mathbf{W}(k) \tag{3.11}$$

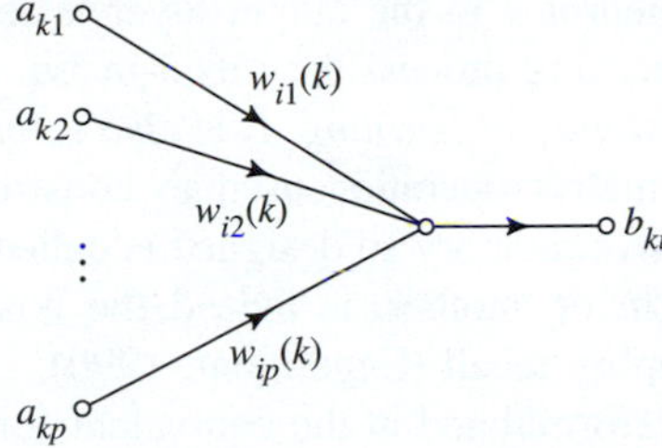

FIGURE 3.3 Signal-flow graph model of linear neuron.

The memory matrix **M** defines the overall connectivity between the input and output layers of the associative memory. In effect, it represents the *total experience* gained by the memory as a result of the presentations of q input–output patterns. Stated in another way, the memory matrix **M** contains a piece of every input–output pair of activity patterns presented to the memory.

The definition of the memory matrix given in Eq. (3.11) may be restructured in the form of a recursion, as shown by

$$\mathbf{M}_k = \mathbf{M}_{k-1} + \mathbf{W}(k), \qquad k = 1, 2, \ldots, q \tag{3.12}$$

where it is noted that the initial value $\mathbf{M}_0$ is zero (i.e., the synaptic weights in the memory are all initially zero), and the final value $\mathbf{M}_q$ is identically equal to **M** as defined in Eq. (3.11). According to the recursive formula of Eq. (3.12), the term $\mathbf{M}_{k-1}$ is the old value of the memory matrix resulting from $(k - 1)$ pattern associations, and $\mathbf{M}_k$ is the updated value in light of the increment $\mathbf{W}(k)$ produced by the kth association. Note, however, that when $\mathbf{W}(k)$ is added to $\mathbf{M}_{k-1}$, the increment $\mathbf{W}(k)$ loses its distinct identity among the mixture of contributions that form $\mathbf{M}_k$. But, in spite of the synaptic mixing of different associations, information about the stimuli may not have been lost, as demonstrated in the next section. Note also that as the number q of stored patterns increases, the influence of a new pattern on the memory as a whole is progressively reduced.

3.3 Correlation Matrix Memory

Suppose that the associative memory of Fig. 3.2b has learned the memory matrix **M** through the associations of key and memorized patterns described by $\mathbf{a}_k \rightarrow \mathbf{b}_k$, where $k = 1, 2, \ldots, q$. We may postulate $\hat{\mathbf{M}}$, denoting an *estimate* of the memory matrix **M** in terms of these patterns as follows (Anderson, 1972, 1983; Cooper, 1973):

$$\hat{\mathbf{M}} = \sum_{k=1}^{q} \mathbf{b}_k \mathbf{a}_k^T \tag{3.13}$$

The term $\mathbf{b}_k \mathbf{a}_k^T$ represents the *outer product* of the key pattern $\mathbf{a}_k$ and the memorized pattern $\mathbf{b}_k$. This outer product is an "estimate" of the weight matrix $\mathbf{W}(k)$ that maps the output pattern $\mathbf{b}_k$ onto the input pattern $\mathbf{a}_k$. Since the patterns $\mathbf{a}_k$ and $\mathbf{b}_k$ are both p-by-1 vectors by assumption, it follows that their outer product $\mathbf{b}_k \mathbf{a}_k^T$, and therefore the estimate $\hat{\mathbf{M}}$, is a p-by-p matrix. This dimensionality is in perfect agreement with that of the memory matrix **M** defined in Eq. (3.11). Note also that the format of the summation of the estimate $\hat{\mathbf{M}}$ bears a direct relation to that of the memory matrix defined in Eq. (3.11).

A typical term of the outer product $\mathbf{b}_k \mathbf{a}_k^T$ is written as $b_{ki}a_{kj}$, where a_{kj} is the output of source node j in the input layer, and b_{ki} is the output of neuron i in the output layer. In the context of synaptic weight $w_{ij}(k)$ for the kth association, source node j is recognized as a presynaptic node and neuron i in the output layer is recognized as a postsynaptic node. Hence, the "local" learning process described in Eq. (3.13) may be viewed as a *generalization of Hebb's postulate of learning.* It is also referred to as the *outer product rule,* in recognition of the matrix operation used to construct the memory matrix $\hat{\mathbf{M}}$. Correspondingly, an associative memory so designed is called a *correlation matrix memory.* Correlation, in one form or another, is indeed the basis of learning, association, pattern recognition, and memory recall (Eggermont, 1990).

Equation (3.13) may be reformulated in the equivalent form

$$\hat{\mathbf{M}} = [\mathbf{b}_1, \mathbf{b}_2, \ldots, \mathbf{b}_q]\begin{bmatrix}\mathbf{a}_1^T \\ \mathbf{a}_2^T \\ \vdots \\ \mathbf{a}_q^T\end{bmatrix}$$

$$= \mathbf{B}\mathbf{A}^T \tag{3.14}$$

where

$$\mathbf{A} = [\mathbf{a}_1, \mathbf{a}_2, \ldots, \mathbf{a}_q] \tag{3.15}$$

and

$$\mathbf{B} = [\mathbf{b}_1, \mathbf{b}_2, \ldots, \mathbf{b}_q] \tag{3.16}$$

The matrix $\mathbf{A}$ is a p-by-q matrix composed of the entire set of key patterns used in the learning process; it is called the *key matrix.* The matrix $\mathbf{B}$ is a p-by-q matrix composed of the corresponding set of memorized patterns; it is called the *memorized matrix.*

Equation (3.13) may also be restructured in the form of a recursion as follows:

$$\hat{\mathbf{M}}_k = \hat{\mathbf{M}}_{k-1} + \mathbf{b}_k\mathbf{a}_k^T, \qquad k = 1, 2, \ldots, q \tag{3.17}$$

A signal-flow graph representation of this recursion is depicted in Fig. 3.4. According to this signal-flow graph and the recursive formula of Eq. (3.17), the matrix $\hat{\mathbf{M}}_{k-1}$ represents an old estimate of the memory matrix; and $\hat{\mathbf{M}}_k$ represents its updated value in the light of a new association performed by the memory on the patterns $\mathbf{a}_k$ and $\mathbf{b}_k$. Comparing the recursion of Eq. (3.17) with that of Eq. (3.12), we see that the outer product $\mathbf{b}_k\mathbf{a}_k^T$ represents an estimate of the weight matrix $\mathbf{W}(k)$ corresponding to the kth association of key and memorized patterns, $\mathbf{a}_k$ and $\mathbf{b}_k$. Moreover, the recursion of Eq. (3.17) has an initial value $\hat{\mathbf{M}}_0$ equal to zero, and it yields a final value $\hat{\mathbf{M}}_q$ identically equal to $\hat{\mathbf{M}}$ as defined in Eq. (3.13).

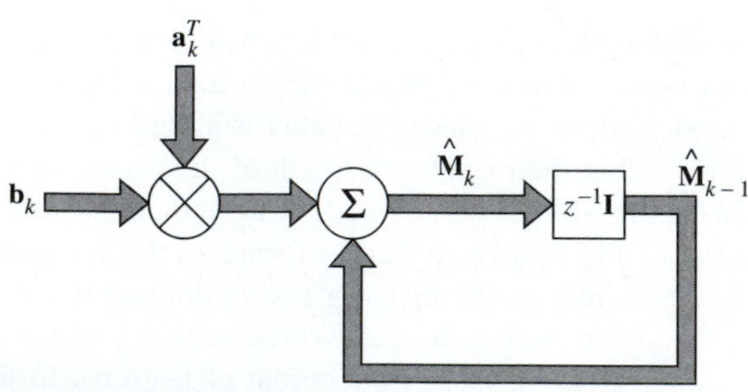

FIGURE 3.4 Signal-flow graph representation of Eq. (3.17).

Recall

The fundamental problem posed by the use of an associative memory is the address and recall of patterns stored in memory. To explain one aspect of this problem, let $\hat{\mathbf{M}}$ denote the memory matrix of an associative memory, which has been completely learned through its exposure to q pattern associations in accordance with Eq. (3.13). Let a key pattern $\mathbf{a}_j$ be picked at random and reapplied as *stimulus* to the memory, yielding the *response*

$$\mathbf{b} = \hat{\mathbf{M}}\mathbf{a}_j \tag{3.18}$$

Substituting Eq. (3.13) in (3.18), we get

$$\begin{aligned} \mathbf{b} &= \sum_{k=1}^{q} \mathbf{b}_k \mathbf{a}_k^T \mathbf{a}_j \\ &= \sum_{k=1}^{q} (\mathbf{a}_k^T \mathbf{a}_j)\mathbf{b}_k \end{aligned} \tag{3.19}$$

where, in the second line, it is recognized that $\mathbf{a}_k^T\mathbf{a}_j$ is a scalar equal to the *inner product* of the key vectors $\mathbf{a}_k$ and $\mathbf{a}_j$. Moreover, we may rewrite Eq. (3.19) as

$$\mathbf{b} = (\mathbf{a}_j^T \mathbf{a}_j)\mathbf{b}_j + \sum_{\substack{k=1 \\ k\neq j}}^{q} (\mathbf{a}_k^T \mathbf{a}_j)\mathbf{b}_k \tag{3.20}$$

Let each of the key patterns $\mathbf{a}_1, \mathbf{a}_2, \ldots, \mathbf{a}_q$ be normalized to have unit energy; that is,

$$\begin{aligned} E_k &= \sum_{l=1}^{p} a_{kl}^2 \\ &= \mathbf{a}_k^T \mathbf{a}_k \\ &= 1, \qquad k = 1, 2, \ldots, q \end{aligned} \tag{3.21}$$

Accordingly, we may simplify the response of the memory to the stimulus (key pattern) $\mathbf{a}_j$ as

$$\mathbf{b} = \mathbf{b}_j + \mathbf{v}_j \tag{3.22}$$

where

$$\mathbf{v}_j = \sum_{\substack{k=1 \\ k\neq j}}^{q} (\mathbf{a}_k^T \mathbf{a}_j)\mathbf{b}_k \tag{3.23}$$

The first term on the right-hand side of Eq. (3.22) represents the "desired" response $\mathbf{b}_j$; it may therefore be viewed as the "signal" component of the actual response $\mathbf{b}$. The second term $\mathbf{v}_j$ is a "noise vector" that arises because of the *crosstalk* between the key vector $\mathbf{a}_j$ and all the other key vectors stored in memory. Indeed, if the individual patterns are statistically independent, then from the central limit theorem of probability theory, we may conclude that the noise vector $\mathbf{v}_j$ is Gaussian-distributed. We thus see that Eq. (3.22) represents a classic *signal in Gaussian noise detection problem* (Van Trees, 1968). In a general setting, these noise considerations may severely limit the number of patterns that can be reliably stored in an associative memory.

In the context of a linear signal space, we may define the *cosine of the angle* between a pair of vectors $\mathbf{a}_j$ and $\mathbf{a}_k$ as the inner product of $\mathbf{a}_j$ and $\mathbf{a}_k$ divided by the product of their individual Euclidean *norms* or *lengths,* as shown by

$$\cos(\mathbf{a}_k, \mathbf{a}_j) = \frac{\mathbf{a}_k^T \mathbf{a}_j}{\|\mathbf{a}_k\| \|\mathbf{a}_j\|} \tag{3.24}$$

The symbol $\|\mathbf{a}_k\|$ signifies the norm of vector $\mathbf{a}_k$, defined as the square root of the energy of $\mathbf{a}_k$, as shown by

$$\begin{aligned}\|\mathbf{a}_k\| &= (\mathbf{a}_k^T\mathbf{a}_k)^{1/2} \\ &= E_k^{1/2}\end{aligned} \tag{3.25}$$

Returning to the situation at hand, we note that the key vectors are normalized to have unit energy in accordance with Eq. (3.21). We may therefore simplify the definition of Eq. (3.24) as

$$\cos(\mathbf{a}_k, \mathbf{a}_j) = \mathbf{a}_k^T\mathbf{a}_j \tag{3.26}$$

Correspondingly, we may redefine the noise vector of Eq. (3.23) as

$$\mathbf{v}_j = \sum_{\substack{k=1 \\ k\neq j}}^{N} \cos(\mathbf{a}_k, \mathbf{a}_j)\mathbf{b}_k \tag{3.27}$$

We now see that if the key vectors are *orthogonal* (i.e., perpendicular to each other in a Euclidean sense), then

$$\cos(\mathbf{a}_k, \mathbf{a}_j) = 0, \qquad k \neq j \tag{3.28}$$

and therefore the noise vector $\mathbf{v}_j$ is identically zero. In such a case, the response $\mathbf{b}$ equals $\mathbf{b}_j$. Accordingly, we may state that the *memory associates perfectly* if the key vectors form an *orthonormal set;* that is, they satisfy the following pair of conditions:

$$\mathbf{a}_k^T\mathbf{a}_j = \begin{cases} 1, & k = j \\ 0, & k \neq j \end{cases} \tag{3.29}$$

Suppose now that the key vectors do form an orthonormal set, as prescribed in Eq. (3.29). What is then the limit on the *storage capacity* of the associative memory? Stated another way, what is the largest number of patterns that can be reliably stored? The answer to this fundamental question lies in the rank of the memory matrix $\hat{\mathbf{M}}$. The *rank* of a matrix is defined as the number of independent columns (rows) of the matrix.[1] The memory matrix $\hat{\mathbf{M}}$ is a p-by-p matrix, where p is the dimensionality of the input space. Hence the rank of the memory matrix M is limited by the dimensionality p. We may thus formally state that the number of patterns that can be reliably stored can never exceed the input space dimensionality.

Practical Considerations

Given a set of key vectors that are linearly independent but nonorthonormal, we may use a *preprocessor* to transform them into an orthonormal set; the preprocessor is designed to perform a *Gram–Schmidt orthogonalization* on the key vectors prior to association. This form of transformation is linear, maintaining a one-to-one correspondence between the input (key) vectors $\mathbf{a}_1, \mathbf{a}_2, \ldots, \mathbf{a}_q$ and the resulting orthonormal vectors $\mathbf{c}_1, \mathbf{c}_2, \ldots, \mathbf{c}_q$, as indicated here:

$$\{\mathbf{a}_1, \mathbf{a}_2, \ldots, \mathbf{a}_k\} \rightleftharpoons \{\mathbf{c}_1, \mathbf{c}_2, \ldots, \mathbf{c}_k\}$$

where $\mathbf{c}_1 = \mathbf{a}_1$, and the remaining $\mathbf{c}_k$ are defined by (Strang, 1980)

$$\mathbf{c}_k = \mathbf{a}_k - \sum_{i=1}^{k-1} \left(\frac{\mathbf{c}_i^T\mathbf{a}_k}{\mathbf{c}_i^T\mathbf{c}_i}\right)\mathbf{c}_i, \qquad k = 2, 3, \ldots, q \tag{3.30}$$

[1] If r is the rank of a rectangular matrix of dimensions m by n, we then obviously have $r \leq \min(m,n)$.

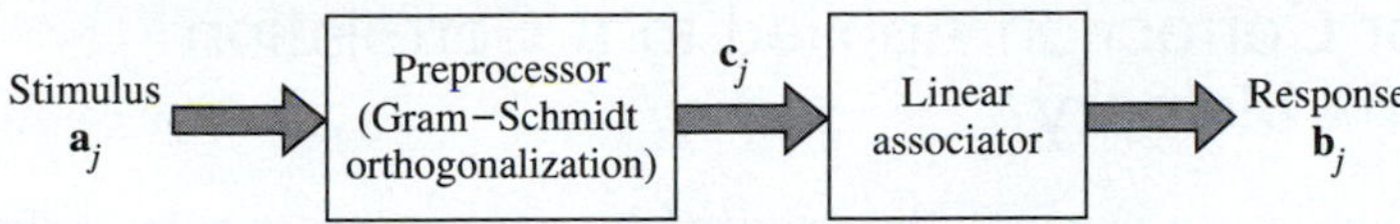

FIGURE 3.5 Extension of associative memory.

The associations are then performed on the pairs $(\mathbf{c}_k, \mathbf{b}_k)$, $k = 1, 2, \ldots, q$. The block diagram of Fig. 3.5 highlights the order in which the preprocessing and association are performed.

The orthogonality of key vectors may also be approximated using statistical considerations. Specifically, if the input space dimensionality p is large and the key vectors have statistically independent elements, then they will be close to orthogonality with respect to each other.[2]

Logic

In a real-life situation, we often find that the key patterns presented to an associative memory are not orthogonal nor are they highly separated from each other. Consequently, a correlation matrix memory characterized by the memory matrix of Eq. (3.13) may sometimes get confused and make errors. That is, the memory occasionally recognizes and associates patterns never seen or associated before.

To illustrate this property of an associative memory, consider a set of key patterns,

$$\{\mathbf{a}_{\text{key}}\}: \mathbf{a}_1, \mathbf{a}_2, \ldots, \mathbf{a}_q \tag{3.31}$$

and a corresponding set of memorized patterns,

$$\{\mathbf{b}_{\text{mem}}\}: \mathbf{b}_1, \mathbf{b}_2, \ldots, \mathbf{b}_q \tag{3.32}$$

To express the closeness of the key patterns in a linear signal space, we introduce the concept of *community*. In particular, we define the community of the set of patterns $\{\mathbf{a}_{\text{key}}\}$ as the lower bound of the inner products $\mathbf{a}_k^T\mathbf{a}_j$ of any two patterns $\mathbf{a}_j$ and $\mathbf{a}_k$ in the set. Let $\hat{\mathbf{M}}$ denote the memory matrix resulting from the training of the associative memory on a set of key patterns represented by $\{\mathbf{a}_{\text{key}}\}$ and a corresponding set of memorized patterns $\{\mathbf{b}_{\text{mem}}\}$ in accordance with Eq. (3.13). The response of the memory, $\mathbf{b}$, to a stimulus $\mathbf{a}_j$ selected from the set $\{\mathbf{a}_{\text{key}}\}$ is given by Eq. (3.20), where it is assumed that each pattern in the set $\{\mathbf{a}_{\text{key}}\}$ is a unit vector (i.e., a vector with unit energy). Let it be further assumed that

$$\mathbf{a}_k^T\mathbf{a}_j \geq \gamma \qquad \text{for } k \neq j \tag{3.33}$$

If the lower bound γ is large enough, the memory may fail to distinguish the response $\mathbf{b}$ from that of any other key pattern contained in the set $\{\mathbf{a}_{\text{key}}\}$. Indeed, if the key patterns in this set have the form

$$\mathbf{a}_j = \mathbf{a}_0 + \mathbf{v} \tag{3.34}$$

where $\mathbf{v}$ is a stochastic vector, then there is a real likelihood that the memory will recognize $\mathbf{a}_0$ and associate with it a vector $\mathbf{b}_0$ rather than any of the actual pattern pairs used to train it in the first place; $\mathbf{a}_0$ and $\mathbf{b}_0$ denote a pair of patterns never seen before. This phenomenon may be termed *animal logic,* which is not logic at all (Cooper, 1973).

---

[2] We say two random variables x and y are *statistically independent* if their joint probability density function satisfies the condition $f(x,y) = f(x)f(y)$, where $f(x)$ and $f(y)$ are the probability density functions of x and y, respectively.

3.4 Error Correction Applied to a Correlation Matrix Memory

The correlation matrix memory characterized by the memory matrix of Eq. (3.13) is simple to design. However, a major limitation of such a design is that the memory may commit too many errors, and the memory has no mechanism to correct for them. Specifically, given the memory matrix $\hat{\mathbf{M}}$ that has been learned from the associations $\mathbf{a}_k \rightarrow \mathbf{b}_k$ for $k = 1, 2, \ldots, q$ in accordance with Eq. (3.13), the actual response $\mathbf{b}$ produced when the key pattern $\mathbf{a}_j$ is presented to the memory may not be close enough (in a Euclidean sense) to the desired response $\mathbf{b}_j$ for the memory to associate perfectly. This shortcoming of the correlation matrix memory is inherited from the use of Hebb's postulate of learning that has no provision for feedback from the output to the input. As a remedy for it, we may incorporate an *error-correction mechanism* into the design of the memory, forcing it to associate perfectly (Anderson and Murphy, 1986; Anderson, 1983).

Suppose that we wish to construct a memory matrix $\hat{\mathbf{M}}$ that describes the synaptic weights of a neural network with two layers, as shown in Fig. 3.2a or 3.2b. We have two fundamental objectives in mind. First, the memory matrix $\hat{\mathbf{M}}$ learns the information represented by the associations of Eq. (3.5), reproduced here for convenience:

$$\mathbf{a}_k \rightarrow \mathbf{b}_k, \qquad k = 1, 2, \ldots, q \tag{3.35}$$

Second, the memory accurately reconstructs each one of these associations.

To proceed then with the development of the error-correction procedure, let $\hat{\mathbf{M}}(n)$ denote the memory matrix learned at iteration n. A key vector $\mathbf{a}_k$, selected at random, is applied to the memory at this time, yielding the "actual" response $\hat{\mathbf{M}}(n)\mathbf{a}_k$. Accordingly, we may define the *error vector:*

$$\mathbf{e}_k(n) = \mathbf{b}_k - \hat{\mathbf{M}}(n)\mathbf{a}_k \tag{3.36}$$

where $\mathbf{b}_k$ is the activity pattern to be associated with $\mathbf{a}_k$. We may view $\mathbf{b}_k$ as the "desired" response. The error vector $\mathbf{e}_k(n)$ is, in turn, used to compute an adjustment to the memory matrix at time n, which is constructed in accordance with the rule:

$$(\text{Adjustment}) = \begin{pmatrix} \text{learning-} \\ \text{rate} \\ \text{parameter} \end{pmatrix} \cdot (\text{error}) \cdot (\text{input}) \tag{3.37}$$

For the problem at hand, we may therefore write

$$\begin{aligned} \Delta\hat{\mathbf{M}}(n) &= \eta \mathbf{e}_k(n)\mathbf{a}_k^T \\ &= \eta[\mathbf{b}_k - \hat{\mathbf{M}}(n)\mathbf{a}_k]\mathbf{a}_k^T \end{aligned} \tag{3.38}$$

where η is a *learning-rate parameter,* the difference $\mathbf{b}_k - \hat{\mathbf{M}}(n)\mathbf{a}_k$ is the error, and $\mathbf{a}_k^T$ is the input. The adjustment $\Delta\hat{\mathbf{M}}(n)$ is used to increment the old value of the memory matrix, resulting in the updated value

$$\begin{aligned} \hat{\mathbf{M}}(n+1) &= \hat{\mathbf{M}}(n) + \Delta\hat{\mathbf{M}}(n) \\ &= \hat{\mathbf{M}}(n) + \eta[\mathbf{b}_k - \hat{\mathbf{M}}(n)\mathbf{a}_k]\mathbf{a}_k^T \end{aligned} \tag{3.39}$$

Ordinarily, a positive constant value is assigned to the learning-rate parameter η. This has the effect of building a *short-term memory* into the operation of the algorithm, because recent changes are recalled more accurately than changes in the remote past. Sometimes, however, the learning-rate parameter is *tapered* with respect to time, so as to approach zero when many associations are learned by the memory (Anderson and Murphy, 1986). To initialize the algorithm described in Eq. (3.39), we may set $\hat{\mathbf{M}}(0)$ equal to zero.

Figure 3.6 shows a signal-flow graph representation of the error-correction algorithm described in Eq. (3.39). The outer-feedback loop of this graph emphasizes the error-correction capability of the algorithm. However, the presence of this feedback loop also means that care has to be exercised in the selection of the learning-rate parameter η, so as to ensure stability of the feedback system described in Fig. 3.6, that is, convergence of the error-correction algorithm.

The iterative adjustment to the memory matrix described in Eq. (3.39) is continued until the error vector $\mathbf{e}_k(n)$ *is negligibly small;* that is, the actual response $\hat{\mathbf{M}}(n)\mathbf{a}_k$ approaches the desired response $\mathbf{b}_k$.

The supervised learning procedure based on the use of error correction, as described here, is repeated for each of the q associations in Eq. (3.35), with each association being picked at random. This procedure is called the *least-mean-square* (*LMS*) *rule* or *delta rule* (Widrow and Hoff, 1960). The latter terminology is in recognition of the fact that the algorithm described in Eq. (3.39) learns from the difference between the desired and actual responses. We shall have more to say on the LMS algorithm in Chapter 5.

Autoassociation

In an autoassociative memory, each key pattern is associated with itself in memory; that is,

$$\mathbf{b}_k = \mathbf{a}_k, \qquad k = 1, 2, \ldots, q \tag{3.40}$$

In such a case, Eq. (3.39) takes on the form

$$\hat{\mathbf{M}}(n+1) = \hat{\mathbf{M}}(n) + \eta[\mathbf{a}_k - \hat{\mathbf{M}}(n)\mathbf{a}_k]\mathbf{a}_k^T \tag{3.41}$$

Ideally, as the number of iterations, n, approaches infinity, the error vector $\mathbf{e}_k(n)$ approaches zero, and the memory characterized by the memory matrix $\hat{\mathbf{M}}$ autoassociates perfectly, as shown by

$$\hat{\mathbf{M}}(\infty)\mathbf{a}_k = \mathbf{a}_k \qquad \text{for } k = 1, 2, \ldots, q \tag{3.42}$$

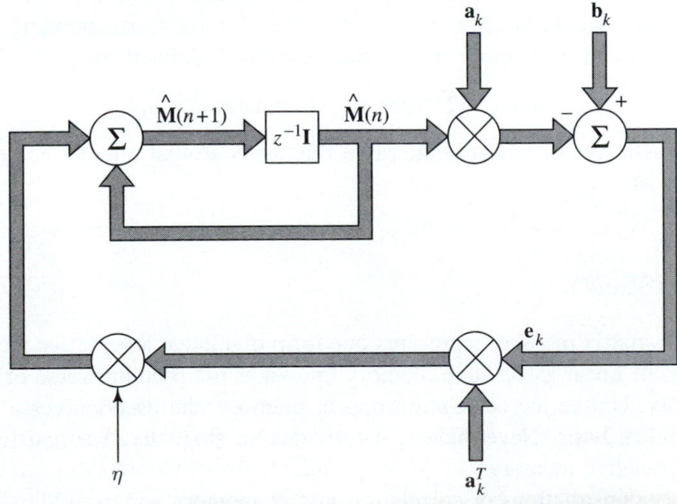

FIGURE 3.6 Signal-flow graph representation of error-correction mechanism defined by Eq. (3.39).

Digressing for a moment, the *eigenvalue problem* involving a matrix $\mathbf{A}$ is described by the relation (Strang, 1980)

$$\mathbf{A}\mathbf{x} = \lambda\mathbf{x} \tag{3.43}$$

where λ is called an *eigenvalue* of matrix $\mathbf{A}$, and $\mathbf{x}$ is called the associated *eigenvector.* Transposing the term $\lambda\mathbf{x}$ to the left-hand side, we have

$$[\mathbf{A} - \lambda\mathbf{I}]\mathbf{x} = 0 \tag{3.44}$$

where $\mathbf{I}$ is the identity matrix. This equation can be satisfied if and only if

$$\det[\mathbf{A} - \lambda\mathbf{I}] = 0 \tag{3.45}$$

where $\det(\cdot)$ denotes the determinant of the matrix enclosed within. Equation (3.45) is called the *characteristic equation,* whose roots define the eigenvalues of the matrix $\mathbf{A}$.

Returning to the autoassociation problem described in Eq. (3.42), we now see that it describes an eigenvalue problem involving the square matrix $\hat{\mathbf{M}}(\infty)$ of dimension p, with two properties:

1. Each of the key vectors is an eigenvector of the memory matrix $\hat{\mathbf{M}}(\infty)$, defined by

$$\hat{\mathbf{M}}(\infty) = \sum_{k=1}^{q} \lambda_k \mathbf{a}_k \mathbf{a}_k^T \tag{3.46}$$

2. The eigenvalues of the matrix $\hat{\mathbf{M}}(\infty)$ are all equal to unity; that is, the characteristic equation

$$\det[\hat{\mathbf{M}}(\infty) - \lambda\mathbf{I}] = 0 \tag{3.47}$$

has a root $\lambda = 1$ that is of multiplicity q.

Since the eigenvectors of a square matrix form an orthogonal set, it follows from the discussion presented in Section 3.3 that a network having the memory matrix $\hat{\mathbf{M}}(\infty)$ autoassociates perfectly, which reconfirms the statement we made previously on perfect autoassociation.

In practice, however, the condition described in Eq. (3.42) is never satisfied exactly. Rather, as the number of iterations approaches infinity, the error vector for each association becomes small but remains finite. Indeed, the error vector $\mathbf{e}_k(n)$ is a stochastic vector, whose final value fluctuates around a mean value of zero. Correspondingly, the actual activity pattern stored in memory (i.e., actual response), defined by

$$\hat{\mathbf{a}}_k(n) = \hat{\mathbf{M}}(n)\mathbf{a}_k, \qquad k = 1, 2, \ldots, q \tag{3.48}$$

is also a stochastic vector whose final value fluctuates around a mean value equal to an eigenvector of $\hat{\mathbf{M}}(\infty)$.

3.5 Discussion

The correlation matrix memory represents one form of a linear associative memory. There is another type of linear associative memory known as the pseudoinverse or generalized-inverse memory. Unlike the correlation matrix memory, the pseudoinverse memory has no neurobiological basis. Nevertheless, it provides an alternative method for the design of a linear associative memory.

The memory constructions of correlation matrix memory and pseudoinverse memory are different. Given a key matrix $\mathbf{A}$ and a memorized matrix $\mathbf{B}$, the estimate of the memory matrix constructed by the *correlation matrix memory* is given by Eq. (3.14), reproduced here for convenience of presentation,

$$\hat{\mathbf{M}}_{\text{cmm}} = \mathbf{B}\mathbf{A}^T \tag{3.49}$$

where the superscript T denotes transposition. On the other hand, the estimate of the memory matrix constructed by the *pseudoinverse memory* is given by

$$\hat{\mathbf{M}}_{\text{pim}} = \mathbf{B}\mathbf{A}^+ \tag{3.50}$$

where $\mathbf{A}^+$ is the *pseudoinverse matrix* of the key matrix $\mathbf{A}$; see Appendix A at the end of the book for a description of the pseudoinverse memory and the derivation of Eq. (3.50).

Cherkassky et al. (1991) present a detailed comparative analysis of the correlation matrix memory and the pseudoinverse memory in the presence of additive noise. The training set vectors are assumed to be error free, and these vectors are used for memory construction. In the recall phase, it is assumed that the unknown stimulus vector $\mathbf{a}$ is described by

$$\mathbf{a} = \mathbf{a}_j + \boldsymbol{\nu} \tag{3.51}$$

where $\mathbf{a}_j$ is one of the known key vectors, and $\boldsymbol{\nu}$ is an additive input noise vector. Components of the noise vector $\boldsymbol{\nu}$ are assumed to be *independent and identically distributed* (i.i.d.) random variables with mean μ_i and variance σ_i^2. The resulting response of the associative memory with memory matrix $\hat{\mathbf{M}}$ is

$$\begin{aligned}\mathbf{b} &= \hat{\mathbf{M}}\mathbf{a} \\ &= \hat{\mathbf{M}}(\mathbf{a}_j + \boldsymbol{\nu})\end{aligned} \tag{3.52}$$

In light of Eq. (3.22), we may express the matrix product $\hat{\mathbf{M}}\mathbf{a}_j$ as the vector $\mathbf{b}_j$ plus a noise term that accounts for crosstalk between the key vector $\mathbf{a}_j$ and all the other key vectors stored in memory. Let this crosstalk term be denoted by $\mathbf{v}_j$. Accordingly, we may rewrite Eq. (3.52) as follows:

$$\mathbf{b} = \mathbf{b}_j + \mathbf{v}_j + \hat{\mathbf{M}}\boldsymbol{\nu} \tag{3.53}$$

For performance measure, the output signal-to-noise ratio, $(\text{SNR})_o$, is divided by the input signal-to-noise ratio, $(\text{SNR})_i$, as shown by

$$\begin{aligned}\frac{(\text{SNR})_o}{(\text{SNR})_i} &= \frac{s_o^2/(\sigma_o^2 + \sigma_c^2)}{s_i^2/\sigma_i^2} \\ &= \frac{s_o^2\sigma_i^2}{s_i^2(\sigma_o^2 + \sigma_c^2)}\end{aligned} \tag{3.54}$$

where σ_i^2 is the input noise variance due to $\boldsymbol{\nu}$, σ_o^2 is the output noise variance due to $\hat{\mathbf{M}}\boldsymbol{\nu}$, σ_c^2 is the variance of the crosstalk term $\mathbf{v}_j$, s_o^2 is the variance of elements in the response vectors, and s_i^2 is the variance of all elements in the key vectors. Equation (3.54) is applicable to autoassociative as well as heteroassociative memory.

The results obtained by Cherkassy et al. (1991) may be summarized as follows:

1. In the case of an autoassociative memory, the pseudoinverse memory provides better noise performance than the correlation matrix memory; this result is in agreement with earlier findings (Kohonen, 1988b).
2. In the case of a many-to-one classifier, in which a number of key vectors are mapped into one class and which includes the unary classifier as a special case, the correlation matrix memory provides a better noise performance than the pseudoinverse memory.

These results are based on certain assumptions about the key vectors. First, it is assumed that the key vectors are of approximately the same Euclidean length; this can be achieved by simple preprocessing (normalization) of the input data. Second, it is assumed that the key vectors have statistically independent components.

PROBLEMS

3.1 The theory of the correlation matrix memory developed in Section 3.3 assumed that the input space dimensionality and output space dimensionality are the same. How is this theory modified by assuming different values, L and M, say, for these two dimensionalities?

3.2 Consider the following orthonormal sets of key patterns, applied to a correlation matrix memory:

$$\mathbf{a}_1 = [1, 0, 0, 0]^T$$

$$\mathbf{a}_2 = [0, 1, 0, 0]^T$$

$$\mathbf{a}_3 = [0, 0, 1, 0]^T$$

The respective stored patterns are

$$\mathbf{b}_1 = [5, 1, 0]^T$$

$$\mathbf{b}_2 = [-2, 1, 6]^T$$

$$\mathbf{b}_3 = [-2, 4, 3]^T$$

(a) Calculate the memory matrix $\mathbf{M}$.
(b) Show that the memory associates perfectly.

3.3 Consider again the correlation matrix memory of Problem 3.2. The stimulus applied to the memory is a noisy version of the key pattern $\mathbf{a}_1$, as shown by

$$\mathbf{a} = [0.8, \ -0.15, \ 0.15, \ -0.20]^T$$

(a) Calculate the memory response $\mathbf{b}$.
(b) Show that the response $\mathbf{b}$ is closest to the stored pattern $\mathbf{b}_1$ in a Euclidean sense.

3.4 An autoassociative memory is trained on the following key vectors:

$$\mathbf{a}_1 = \tfrac{1}{4}[-2, -3, \sqrt{3}]^T$$

$$\mathbf{a}_2 = \tfrac{1}{4}[2, -2, -\sqrt{8}]^T$$

$$\mathbf{a}_3 = \tfrac{1}{4}[3, -1, \sqrt{6}]^T$$

(a) Calculate the angles between these vectors. How close are they to orthogonality with respect to each other?
(b) Using the generalization of Hebb's rule (i.e., the outer product rule), calculate the memory matrix of the network. Hence, investigate how close to perfect the memory autoassociates.
(c) A masked version of the key vector $\mathbf{a}_1$, namely,

$$\mathbf{a} = [0, -3, \sqrt{3}]^T$$

is applied to the memory. Calculate the response of the memory, and compare your result with the desired response $\mathbf{a}_1$.

3.5 The autoassociative memory of Problem 3.4 is modified to include an error-correction mechanism. The learning-rate parameter η equals 0.1.

(a) Calculate the modified version of the memory matrix of the memory. Using this new result, investigate how close to perfect the memory autoassociates, and compare your finding with that of Problem 3.4, part (b).

(b) Repeat part (c) of Problem 3.4.

3.6 Consider an orthonormal set of vectors $\mathbf{a}_1, \mathbf{a}_2, \ldots, \mathbf{a}_q$, the dimension of each of which is p. Using the outer product rule, determine the memory matrix $\hat{\mathbf{M}}$ of an autoassociative memory based on this set of vectors.

(a) How are the eigenvectors of the memory matrix $\hat{\mathbf{M}}$ related to the vectors $\mathbf{a}_1, \mathbf{a}_2, \ldots, \mathbf{a}_q$? Assuming that $q < p$, what are the eigenvalues of $\hat{\mathbf{M}}$?

(b) What is the maximum value of vectors that can be stored in the autoassociative memory for reliable recall to be possible?

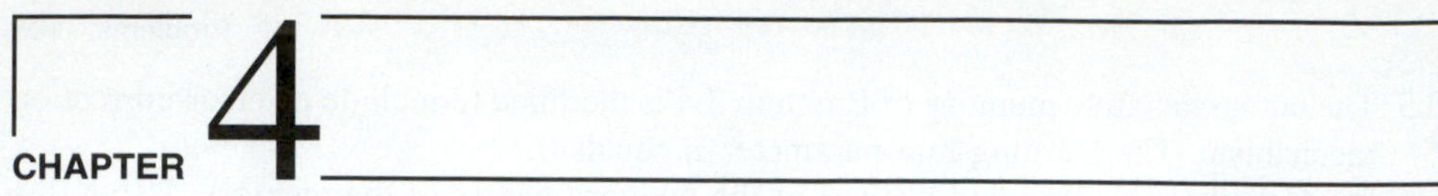

The Perceptron

4.1 Introduction

The *perceptron* is the simplest form of a neural network used for the classification of a special type of patterns said to be *linearly separable* (i.e., patterns that lie on opposite sides of a hyperplane). Basically, it consists of a single neuron with adjustable synaptic weights and threshold, as shown in Fig. 4.1. The algorithm used to adjust the free parameters of this neural network first appeared in a learning procedure developed by Rosenblatt (1958, 1962) for his *perceptron* brain model.[1] Indeed, Rosenblatt proved that if the patterns (vectors) used to train the perceptron are drawn from two linearly separable classes, then the perceptron algorithm converges and positions the decision surface in the form of a hyperplane between the two classes. The proof of convergence of the algorithm is known as the *perceptron convergence theorem.*

The single-layer perceptron depicted in Fig. 4.1 has a single neuron. Such a perceptron is limited to performing pattern classification with only two classes. By expanding the output (computation) layer of the perceptron to include more than one neuron, we may correspondingly form classification with more than two classes. However, the classes would have to be linearly separable for the perceptron to work properly. Accordingly, insofar as the basic theory of a single-layer perceptron as a pattern classifier is concerned, we need consider only the single-neuron configuration shown in Fig. 4.1. The extension of the theory so developed to the case of more than one neuron is a trivial matter.

Organization of the Chapter

This chapter on the single-layer perceptron is relatively short, but it is important for historical and theoretical reasons. In Section 4.2 we present some basic considerations involved in the operation of the perceptron. Then, in Section 4.3 we describe Rosenblatt's original algorithm for adjusting the synaptic weight vector of the perceptron for pattern classification of linearly separable classes, and demonstrate convergence of the algorithm. This is followed by the description of a performance measure for the single-layer perceptron in Section 4.4. In Section 4.5 we consider the relationship between the single-layer perceptron and the maximum-likelihood Gaussian classifier. The chapter concludes with general discussion in Section 4.6.

[1] The network organization of the original version of the perceptron, as envisioned by Rosenblatt (1962), has three types of units: sensory units, association units, and response units. The connections from the sensory units to the association units have fixed weights, and the connections from the association units to the response units have variable weights. The association units act as preprocessors designed to extract a pattern from the environmental input. Insofar as the variable weights are concerned, the operation of Rosenblatt's original perceptron is essentially the same as that depicted in Fig. 4.1 for the case of a single response unit.

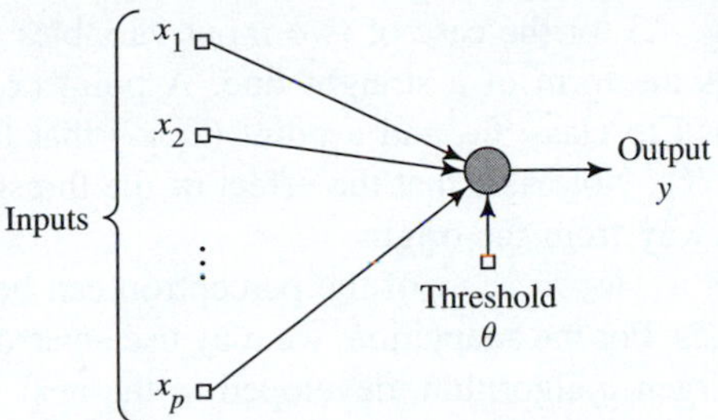

FIGURE 4.1 Single-layer perceptron.

4.2 Basic Considerations

Basic to the operation of Rosenblatt's perceptron is the *McCulloch–Pitts model* of a neuron. From Chapter 1, we recall that such a neuron model consists of a linear combiner followed by a hard limiter, as depicted in Fig. 4.2. The summing node of the neuron model computes a linear combination of the inputs applied to its synapses, and also accounts for an externally applied threshold. The resulting sum is applied to a hard limiter. Accordingly, the neuron produces an output equal to $+1$ if the hard limiter input is positive, and -1 if it is negative.

In the signal-flow graph model of Fig. 4.2, the synaptic weights of the single-layer perceptron are denoted by $w_1, w_2, \ldots, w_p$. (We have simplified the notation here by not including an additional subscript to identify the neuron, since we only have to deal with a single neuron.) Correspondingly, the inputs applied to the perceptron are denoted by $x_1, x_2, \ldots, x_p$. The externally applied threshold is denoted by θ. From the model of Fig. 4.2 we thus find that the linear combiner output (i.e., hard limiter input) is

$$v = \sum_{i=1}^{p} w_i x_i - \theta \tag{4.1}$$

The purpose of the perceptron is to classify the set of externally applied stimuli $x_1, x_2, \ldots, x_p$ into one of two classes, $\mathscr{C}_1$ or $\mathscr{C}_2$, say. The decision rule for the classification is to assign the point represented by the inputs $x_1, x_2, \ldots, x_p$ to class $\mathscr{C}_1$ if the perceptron output y is $+1$ and to class $\mathscr{C}_2$ if it is -1.

To develop insight into the behavior of a pattern classifier, it is customary to plot a map of the decision regions in the p-dimensional signal space spanned by the p input variables $x_1, x_2, \ldots, x_p$. In the case of an elementary perceptron, there are two decision regions separated by a *hyperplane* defined by

$$\sum_{i=1}^{p} w_i x_i - \theta = 0 \tag{4.2}$$

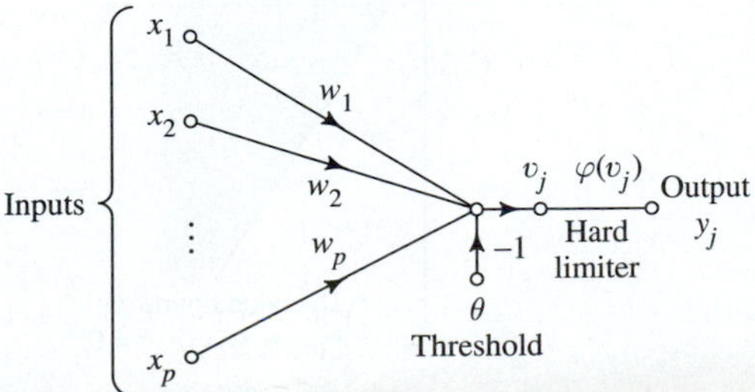

FIGURE 4.2 Signal-flow graph of the perceptron.

This is illustrated in Fig. 4.3 for the case of two input variables x_1 and x_2, for which the decision boundary takes the form of a straight line. A point (x_1,x_2) that lies above the boundary line is assigned to class $\mathscr{C}_1$, and a point (x_1,x_2) that lies below the boundary line is assigned to class $\mathscr{C}_2$. Note also that the effect of the threshold θ is merely to shift the decision boundary away from the origin.

The synaptic weights $w_1, w_2, \ldots, w_p$ of the perceptron can be fixed or adapted on an iteration-by-iteration basis. For the adaptation, we may use an error-correction rule known as the perceptron convergence algorithm, developed in the next section.

4.3 The Perceptron Convergence Theorem

For the development of the error-correction learning algorithm for a single-layer perceptron, we find it more convenient to work with the modified signal-flow graph model of Fig. 4.4. In this second model, which is equivalent to that of Fig. 4.2, the threshold $\theta(n)$ is treated as a synaptic weight connected to a fixed input equal to -1. We may thus define the $(p + 1)$-by-1 input vector

$$\mathbf{x}(n) = [-1, x_1(n), x_2(n), \ldots, x_p(n)]^T \tag{4.3}$$

Correspondingly, we define the $(p + 1)$-by-1 weight vector

$$\mathbf{w}(n) = [\theta(n), w_1(n), w_2(n), \ldots, w_p(n)]^T \tag{4.4}$$

Accordingly, the linear combiner output is written in the compact form

$$v(n) = \mathbf{w}^T(n)\mathbf{x}(n) \tag{4.5}$$

For fixed n, the equation $\mathbf{w}^T\mathbf{x} = 0$, plotted in a p-dimensional space with coordinates $x_1, x_2, \ldots, x_p$, defines a hyperplane as the decision surface between two different classes of inputs.

Suppose then the input variables of the single-layer perceptron originate from two *linearly separable classes* that fall on the opposite sides of some hyperplane. Let X_1 be the subset of training vectors $\mathbf{x}_1(1), \mathbf{x}_1(2), \ldots$ that belong to class $\mathscr{C}_1$, and let X_2 be the

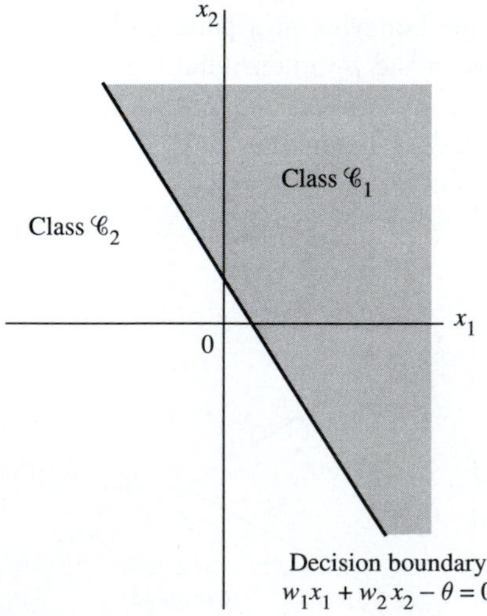

FIGURE 4.3 Illustrating linear reparability for a two-dimensional, two-class pattern-classification problem.

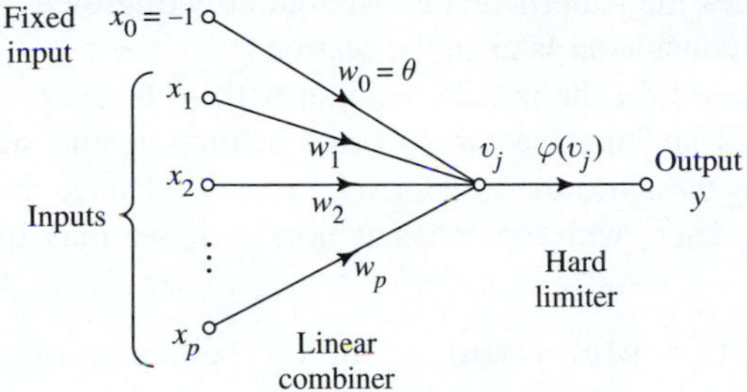

FIGURE 4.4 Equivalent signal-flow graph of the perceptron.

subset of training vectors $\mathbf{x}_2(1)$, $\mathbf{x}_2(2)$, . . . that belong to class $\mathscr{C}_2$. The union of X_1 and X_2 is the complete training set X. Given the sets of vectors X_1 and X_2 to train the classifier, the training process involves the adjustment of the weight vector $\mathbf{w}$ in such a way that the two classes $\mathscr{C}_1$ and $\mathscr{C}_2$ are separable. These two classes are said to be *linearly separable* if a realizable setting of the weight vector $\mathbf{w}$ exists. Conversely, if the two classes $\mathscr{C}_1$ and $\mathscr{C}_2$ are known to be linearly separable, then there exists a weight vector $\mathbf{w}$ such that we may state

$$\mathbf{w}^T\mathbf{x} \geq 0 \text{ for every input vector } \mathbf{x} \text{ belonging to class } \mathscr{C}_1$$

and (4.6)

$$\mathbf{w}^T\mathbf{x} < 0 \text{ for every input vector } \mathbf{x} \text{ belonging to class } \mathscr{C}_2$$

Given the subsets of training vectors X_1 and X_2, the training problem for the elementary perceptron is then to find a weight vector $\mathbf{w}$ such that the two inequalities of Eq. (4.6) are satisfied.

The algorithm for adapting the weight vector of the elementary perceptron may now be formulated as follows:

1. If the nth member of the training vector, $\mathbf{x}(n)$, is correctly classified by the weight vector $\mathbf{w}(n)$ computed at the nth iteration of the algorithm, no correction is made to the weight vector of the perceptron, as shown by

$$\mathbf{w}(n+1) = \mathbf{w}(n) \qquad \text{if } \mathbf{w}^T(n)\mathbf{x}(n) \geq 0 \text{ and } \mathbf{x}(n) \text{ belongs to class } \mathscr{C}_1$$

and (4.7)

$$\mathbf{w}(n+1) = \mathbf{w}(n) \qquad \text{if } \mathbf{w}^T(n)\mathbf{x}(n) < 0 \text{ and } \mathbf{x}(n) \text{ belongs to class } \mathscr{C}_2$$

2. Otherwise, the weight vector of the perceptron is updated in accordance with the rule

$$\mathbf{w}(n+1) = \mathbf{w}(n) - \eta(n)\mathbf{x}(n) \qquad \text{if } \mathbf{w}^T(n)\mathbf{x}(n) \geq 0 \text{ and } \mathbf{x}(n) \text{ belongs to class } \mathscr{C}_2$$

and (4.8)

$$\mathbf{w}(n+1) = \mathbf{w}(n) + \eta(n)\mathbf{x}(n) \qquad \text{if } \mathbf{w}^T(n)\mathbf{x}(n) < 0 \text{ and } \mathbf{x}(n) \text{ belongs to class } \mathscr{C}_1$$

where the *learning-rate parameter* $\eta(n)$ controls the adjustment applied to the weight vector at iteration n.

If $\eta(n) = \eta > 0$, where η is a constant independent of the iteration number n, we have a *fixed increment adaptation rule* for the perceptron.

In the sequel, we first prove the convergence of a fixed increment adaptation rule for which $\eta = 1$. Clearly, the value of η is unimportant, so long as it is positive. A value of $\eta \neq 1$ merely scales the pattern vectors without affecting their separability. The case of a variable $\eta(n)$ is considered later in the section.

The proof is presented for the initial condition $\mathbf{w}(0) = \mathbf{0}$. Suppose that $\mathbf{w}^T(n)\mathbf{x}(n) < 0$ for $n = 1, 2, \ldots$ and an input vector $\mathbf{x}(n)$ that belongs to the subset X_1. That is, the perceptron incorrectly classifies the vectors $\mathbf{x}(1), \mathbf{x}(2), \ldots,$ since the second condition of Eq. (4.6) is violated. Then, with the constant $\eta(n) = 1$, we may use the second line of Eq. (4.8) to write

$$\mathbf{w}(n+1) = \mathbf{w}(n) + \mathbf{x}(n) \qquad \text{for } \mathbf{x}(n) \text{ belonging to class } \mathscr{C}_1 \tag{4.9}$$

Given the initial condition $\mathbf{w}(0) = \mathbf{0}$, we may iteratively solve this equation for $\mathbf{w}(n+1)$, obtaining the result

$$\mathbf{w}(n+1) = \mathbf{x}(1) + \mathbf{x}(2) + \cdots + \mathbf{x}(n) \tag{4.10}$$

Since the classes $\mathscr{C}_1$ and $\mathscr{C}_2$ are assumed to be linearly separable, there exists a solution $\mathbf{w}_0$ for which $\mathbf{w}^T\mathbf{x}(n) > 0$ for the vectors $\mathbf{x}(1), \ldots, \mathbf{x}(n)$ belonging to the subset X_1. For a fixed solution $\mathbf{w}_0$, we may then define a positive number α by the relation

$$\alpha = \min_{\mathbf{x}(n) \in X_1} \mathbf{w}_0^T\mathbf{x}(n) \tag{4.11}$$

where $\mathbf{x}(n) \in X_1$ stands for "$\mathbf{x}(n)$ belongs to subset X_1." Hence, multiplying both sides of Eq. (4.10) by the row vector $\mathbf{w}_0^T$, we get

$$\mathbf{w}_0^T\mathbf{w}(n+1) = \mathbf{w}_0^T\mathbf{x}(1) + \mathbf{w}_0^T\mathbf{x}(2) + \cdots + \mathbf{w}_0^T\mathbf{x}(n) \tag{4.12}$$

Accordingly, in light of the definition given in Eq. (4.11), we have

$$\mathbf{w}_0^T\mathbf{w}(n+1) \geq n\alpha \tag{4.13}$$

Next, we make use of an inequality known as the Cauchy–Schwarz inequality. Given two vectors $\mathbf{w}_0$ and $\mathbf{w}(n+1)$, the *Cauchy–Schwarz inequality* states that

$$\|\mathbf{w}_0\|^2 \|\mathbf{w}(n+1)\|^2 \geq [\mathbf{w}_0^T\mathbf{w}(n+1)]^2 \tag{4.14}$$

where $\|\cdot\|$ denotes the Euclidean norm of the enclosed argument vector, and the inner product $\mathbf{w}_0^T\mathbf{w}(n+1)$ is a scalar quantity. We now note from Eq. (4.13) that $[\mathbf{w}_0^T\mathbf{w}(n+1)]^2$ is equal to or greater than $n^2\alpha^2$. Moreover, from Eq. (4.14) we note that $\|\mathbf{w}_0\|^2\|\mathbf{w}(n+1)\|^2$ is equal to or greater than $[\mathbf{w}_0^T\mathbf{w}(n+1)]^2$. It follows therefore that

$$\|\mathbf{w}_0\|^2 \|\mathbf{w}(n+1)\|^2 \geq n^2\alpha^2$$

or, equivalently,

$$\|\mathbf{w}(n+1)\|^2 \geq \frac{n^2\alpha^2}{\|\mathbf{w}_0\|^2} \tag{4.15}$$

Next, we follow another development route. In particular, we rewrite Eq. (4.9) in the form

$$\mathbf{w}(k+1) = \mathbf{w}(k) + \mathbf{x}(k) \qquad \text{for } k = 1, \ldots, n \quad \text{and} \quad \mathbf{x}(k) \in X_1 \tag{4.16}$$

Hence, taking the squared Euclidean norm of both sides of Eq. (4.16), we get

$$\|\mathbf{w}(k+1)\|^2 = \|\mathbf{w}(k)\|^2 + \|\mathbf{x}(k)\|^2 + 2\mathbf{w}^T(k)\mathbf{x}(k) \tag{4.17}$$

But, under the assumption that the perceptron incorrectly classifies an input vector $\mathbf{x}(k)$ belonging to the subset X_1, we have $\mathbf{w}^T(k)\mathbf{x}(k) < 0$. We therefore deduce from Eq. (4.17) that

$$\|\mathbf{w}(k+1)\|^2 \leq \|\mathbf{w}(k)\|^2 + \|\mathbf{x}(k)\|^2$$

or, equivalently,

$$\|\mathbf{w}(k+1)\|^2 - \|\mathbf{w}(k)\|^2 \le \|\mathbf{x}(k)\|^2, \qquad k = 1, \ldots, n \tag{4.18}$$

Adding these inequalities for $k = 1, \ldots, n$, and assuming that the initial condition $\mathbf{w}(0) = \mathbf{0}$, we get the following condition:

$$\begin{aligned}\|\mathbf{w}(n+1)\|^2 &\le \sum_{k=1}^{n} \|\mathbf{x}(k)\|^2 \\ &\le n\beta \end{aligned} \tag{4.19}$$

where β is a positive number defined by

$$\beta = \max_{\mathbf{x}(k) \in X_1} \|\mathbf{x}(k)\|^2 \tag{4.20}$$

Equation (4.19) states that the squared Euclidean norm of the weight vector $\mathbf{w}(n+1)$ grows at most linearly with the number of iterations n.

Clearly, the second result of Eq. (4.19) is in conflict with the earlier result of Eq. (4.15) for sufficiently large values of n. Indeed, we can state that n cannot be larger than some value n_{max} for which Eqs. (4.15) and (4.19) are both satisfied with the equality sign. That is, n_{max} is the solution of the equation

$$\frac{n_{max}^2 \alpha^2}{\|\mathbf{w}_0\|^2} = n_{max}\beta$$

Solving for n_{max} for a solution vector $\mathbf{w}_0$, we find that

$$n_{max} = \frac{\beta \|\mathbf{w}_0\|^2}{\alpha^2} \tag{4.21}$$

We have thus proved that for $\eta(n) = 1$ for all n, and $\mathbf{w}(0) = \mathbf{0}$, and given that a solution vector $\mathbf{w}_0$ exists, the rule for adapting the synaptic weights connecting the associator units to the response unit of the perceptron must terminate after at most n_{max} iterations. Note also from Eqs. (4.11), (4.20), and (4.21) that there is *no* unique solution for $\mathbf{w}_0$ or n_{max}.

We may now state the *fixed-increment convergence theorem* for a single-layer perceptron as follows (Rosenblatt, 1962):

> *Let the subsets of training vectors X_1 and X_2 be linearly separable. Let the inputs presented to the single-layer perceptron originate from these two subsets. The perceptron converges after some n_0 iterations, in the sense that*
>
> $$\mathbf{w}(n_0) = \mathbf{w}(n_0+1) = \mathbf{w}(n_0+2) = \ldots$$
>
> *is a solution vector for $n_0 \le n_{max}$.*

Consider next the *absolute error-correction procedure* for the adaptation of a single-layer perceptron, for which $\eta(n)$ is variable. In particular, let $\eta(n)$ be the smallest integer for which

$$\eta(n)\mathbf{x}^T(n)\mathbf{x}(n) > |\mathbf{w}^T(n)\mathbf{x}(n)|$$

With this procedure we find that if the inner product $\mathbf{w}^T(n)\mathbf{x}(n)$ at iteration n has an incorrect sign, then $\mathbf{w}^T(n+1)\mathbf{x}(n)$ at iteration $n+1$ would have the correct sign. This suggests that if $\mathbf{w}^T(n)\mathbf{x}(n)$ has an incorrect sign, we may modify the training sequence at iteration $n+1$ by setting $\mathbf{x}(n+1) = \mathbf{x}(n)$. In other words, each pattern is presented repeatedly to the perceptron until that pattern is classified correctly.

Note also that the use of an initial value $\mathbf{w}(0)$ different from the null condition merely results in a decrease or increase in the number of iterations required to converge, depending on how $\mathbf{w}(0)$ relates to the solution $\mathbf{w}_0$. Hence, regardless of the value assigned to $\mathbf{w}(0)$, the single-layer perceptron of Fig. 4.1 is assured of convergence.

Summary

In Table 4.1 we present a summary of the *perceptron convergence algorithm* (Lippmann, 1987). The symbol $\text{sgn}(\cdot)$, used in step 3 of the table for computing the actual response of the perceptron, stands for the *signum function:*

$$\text{sgn}(v) = \begin{cases} +1 & \text{if } v > 0 \\ -1 & \text{if } v < 0 \end{cases} \tag{4.22}$$

TABLE 4.1 Summary of the Perceptron Convergence Algorithm

Variables and Parameters

$$\mathbf{x}(n) = (p+1)\text{-by-1 input vector}$$
$$= [-1, x_1(n), x_2(n), \ldots, x_p(n)]^T$$
$$\mathbf{w}(n) = (p+1)\text{-by-1 weight vector}$$
$$= [\theta(n), w_1(n), w_2(n), \ldots, w_p(n)]^T$$
$$\theta(n) = \text{threshold}$$
$$y(n) = \text{actual response (quantized)}$$
$$d(n) = \text{desired response}$$
$$\eta = \text{learning-rate parameter, a positive constant less than unity}$$

Step 1: Initialization

Set $\mathbf{w}(0) = \mathbf{0}$. Then perform the following computations for time $n = 1, 2, \ldots$.

Step 2: Activation

At time n, activate the perceptron by applying continuous-valued input vector $\mathbf{x}(n)$ and desired response $d(n)$.

Step 3: Computation of Actual Response

Compute the actual response of the perceptron:

$$y(n) = \text{sgn}[\mathbf{w}^T(n)\mathbf{x}(n)]$$

where $\text{sgn}(\cdot)$ is the signum function.

Step 4: Adaptation of Weight Vector

Update the weight vector of the perceptron:

$$\mathbf{w}(n+1) = \mathbf{w}(n) + \eta[d(n) - y(n)]\mathbf{x}(n)$$

where

$$d(n) = \begin{cases} +1 & \text{if } \mathbf{x}(n) \text{ belongs to class } \mathscr{C}_1 \\ -1 & \text{if } \mathbf{x}(n) \text{ belongs to class } \mathscr{C}_2 \end{cases}$$

Step 5

Increment time n by one unit, and go back to step 2.

In effect, the signum function is a shorthand notation for the asymmetric form of hard limiting. Accordingly, the *quantized response* $y(n)$ of the perceptron is written in the compact form

$$y(n) = \operatorname{sgn}(\mathbf{w}^T(n)\mathbf{x}(n)) \tag{4.23}$$

Note that the input vector $\mathbf{x}(n)$ is a $(p + 1)$-by-1 vector whose first element is fixed at -1 throughout the computation in accordance with the definition of Eq. (4.3). Correspondingly, the weight vector $\mathbf{w}(n)$ is a $(p + 1)$-by-1 vector whose first element equals the threshold $\theta(n)$, as defined in Eq. (4.4). In Table 4.1 we have also introduced a *quantized desired response* $d(n)$, defined by

$$d(n) = \begin{cases} +1 & \text{if } \mathbf{x}(n) \text{ belongs to class } \mathscr{C}_1 \\ -1 & \text{if } \mathbf{x}(n) \text{ belongs to class } \mathscr{C}_2 \end{cases} \tag{4.24}$$

Thus, the adaptation of the weight vector $\mathbf{w}(n)$ is summed up nicely in the form of an *error-correction learning rule,* as shown by

$$\mathbf{w}(n + 1) = \mathbf{w}(n) + \eta[d(n) - y(n)]\mathbf{x}(n) \tag{4.25}$$

where η is the *learning-rate parameter,* and the difference $d(n) - y(n)$ plays the role of an *error signal.* The learning-rate parameter is a positive constant limited to the range $0 < \eta \leq 1$. In assigning a value to it inside this range, we have to keep in mind two conflicting requirements (Lippmann, 1987):

- *Averaging* of past inputs to provide stable weight estimates, which requires a small η
- *Fast adaptation* with respect to real changes in the underlying distributions of the process responsible for the generation of the input vector $\mathbf{x}$, which requires a large η

4.4 Performance Measure

In the previous section we derived the perceptron convergence algorithm without any reference to a performance measure, yet in Chapter 2 we emphasized that improvement in the performance of a learning machine takes place over time in accordance with a performance measure. What then is a suitable performance measure for the single-layer perceptron? An obvious choice would be the *average probability of classification error,* defined as the average probability of the perceptron making a decision in favor of a particular class when the input vector is drawn from the other class. Unfortunately, such a performance measure does not lend itself readily to the analytic derivation of a learning algorithm. Shynk (1990) has proposed the use of a performance function that befits the operation of a perceptron, as shown by the statistical expectation

$$J = -E[e(n)v(n)] \tag{4.26}$$

where $e(n)$ is the error signal defined as the difference between the desired response $d(n)$ and the actual response $y(n)$ of the perceptron, and $v(n)$ is the linear combiner output (i.e., hard-limiter input). Note that the error signal $e(n)$ is not a quantized signal, but rather the difference between two quantized signals. The *instantaneous estimate* of the performance function is the time-varying function

$$\begin{aligned} \hat{J}(n) &= -e(n)v(n) \\ &= -[d(n) - y(n)]v(n) \end{aligned} \tag{4.27}$$

The *instantaneous gradient vector* is defined as the derivative of the estimate $\hat{J}(n)$ with respect to the weight vector $\mathbf{w}(n)$, as shown by

$$\nabla_{\mathbf{w}}\hat{J}(n) = \frac{\partial J(n)}{\partial \mathbf{w}(n)} \tag{4.28}$$

Hence, recognizing that the desired response $d(n)$ is independent of $\mathbf{w}(n)$ and the fact that the actual response $y(n)$ has a constant value equal to -1 or $+1$, we find that the use of Eq. (4.27) in (4.28) yields[2]

$$\nabla_{\mathbf{w}}\hat{J}(n) = -[d(n) - y(n)]\frac{\partial v(n)}{\partial \mathbf{w}(n)} \tag{4.29}$$

For the defining equation (4.5), we readily find that[3]

$$\frac{\partial v(n)}{\partial \mathbf{w}(n)} = \mathbf{x}(n) \tag{4.30}$$

Thus the use of Eq. (4.30) in (4.29) yields the result

$$\nabla_{\mathbf{w}}\hat{J}(n) = -[d(n) - y(n)]\mathbf{x}(n) \tag{4.31}$$

Hence, according to the error-correction rule described in Chapter 2 we may now express the change applied to the weight vector as

$$\begin{aligned} \Delta\mathbf{w}(n) &= -\eta\nabla_{\mathbf{w}}\hat{J}(n) \\ &= \eta[d(n) - y(n)]\mathbf{x}(n) \end{aligned} \tag{4.32}$$

---

[2] To be precise, we should also include a Dirac delta function (i.e., impulse function) whenever the perceptron output $y(n)$ goes through a transition at $v(n) = 0$. Averaged over a long sequence of iterations, however, such a transition has a negligible effect.

[3] Consider a scalar quantity v defined as the inner product of two real-valued p-by-1 vectors $\mathbf{w}$ and $\mathbf{x}$, as shown by

$$v = \mathbf{w}^T\mathbf{x} = \sum_{i=1}^{p} w_i x_i$$

where w_i and x_i are the ith elements of the vectors $\mathbf{w}$ and $\mathbf{x}$, respectively. The partial derivative of the quantity v with respect to the vector $\mathbf{w}$ is defined by (Haykin, 1991)

$$\frac{\partial v}{\partial \mathbf{w}} = \begin{bmatrix} \partial v/\partial w_1 \\ \partial v/\partial w_2 \\ \vdots \\ \partial v/\partial w_p \end{bmatrix}$$

From the given definition of v, we note that

$$\frac{\partial v}{\partial w_i} = x_i, \qquad i = 1, 2, \ldots, p$$

We therefore have

$$\frac{\partial v}{\partial \mathbf{w}} = \begin{bmatrix} x_1 \\ x_2 \\ \vdots \\ x_p \end{bmatrix} = \mathbf{x}$$

where η is the learning-rate parameter. This is precisely the correction made to the weight vector as we progress from iteration n to $n + 1$, as described in Eq. (4.25). We have thus demonstrated that the instantaneous performance function $\hat{J}(n)$ defined in Eq. (4.27) is indeed the correct performance measure for a single-layer perceptron (Shynk, 1990).

4.5 Maximum-Likelihood Gaussian Classifier

A single-layer perceptron bears a close relationship to a classical pattern classifier known as the *maximum-likelihood Gaussian classifier,* in that they are both examples of *linear classifiers* (Duda and Hart, 1973).

The *maximum-likelihood method* is a classical parameter-estimation procedure that views the parameters as quantities whose values are *fixed* but *unknown.* The best estimate is defined to be the one that maximizes the probability of obtaining the samples actually observed. To be specific, suppose that we separate a set of samples according to class, so that we have M subsets of samples denoted by $X_1, X_2, \ldots, X_M$. Let the samples in subset X_j be drawn independently according to a probability law of known parametric form. Let this probability law be described by the *conditional probability density function* $f(\mathbf{x}|\mathbf{w}_j)$, where $\mathbf{x}$ is an observation vector and $\mathbf{w}_j$ represents an unknown parameter vector associated with class $\mathscr{C}_j$, $j = 1, 2, \ldots, M$. We further assume that the samples in X_i give no information about $\mathbf{w}_j$ if $i \neq j$, that is, the parameters for the different classes are functionally independent. Now, viewed as a function of $\mathbf{w}$, $f(\mathbf{x}|\mathbf{w})$ is called the *likelihood* of $\mathbf{w}$ with respect to the observation vector $\mathbf{x}$. The *maximum-likelihood estimate* of $\mathbf{w}$ is, by definition, that value $\hat{\mathbf{w}}$ which maximizes the likelihood $f(\mathbf{x}|\mathbf{w})$.

To proceed with the issue at hand, consider a p-by-1 observation vector $\mathbf{x}$ defined by

$$\mathbf{x} = [x_1, x_2, \ldots, x_p]^T \tag{4.33}$$

Note that the vector $\mathbf{x}$ as defined here is confined exclusively to the externally applied inputs. The observation vector $\mathbf{x}$ is described in terms of a *mean vector* $\boldsymbol{\mu}$ and *covariance matrix* $\mathbf{C}$, which are defined by, respectively,

$$\boldsymbol{\mu} = E[\mathbf{x}] \tag{4.34}$$

and

$$\mathbf{C} = E[(\mathbf{x} - \boldsymbol{\mu})(\mathbf{x} - \boldsymbol{\mu})^T] \tag{4.35}$$

where E is the expectation operator. Assuming that the vector $\mathbf{x}$ is *Gaussian-distributed,* we may express the *joint-probability density function* of the elements of $\mathbf{x}$ as follows (Van Trees, 1968):

$$f(\mathbf{x}) = \frac{1}{(2\pi)^{p/2}(\det \mathbf{C})^{1/2}} \exp\left[-\frac{1}{2}(\mathbf{x} - \boldsymbol{\mu})^T\mathbf{C}^{-1}(\mathbf{x} - \boldsymbol{\mu})\right] \tag{4.36}$$

where $\det \mathbf{C}$ is the determinant of the covariance matrix $\mathbf{C}$, the matrix $\mathbf{C}^{-1}$ is the inverse of $\mathbf{C}$, and p is the dimension of the vector $\mathbf{x}$.

To be more specific, suppose that we have a two-class problem, with the vector $\mathbf{x}$ characterized as follows, depending on whether it belongs to class $\mathscr{C}_1$ or class $\mathscr{C}_2$:

$$\begin{aligned}
\mathbf{x} \in X_1: \quad & \text{mean vector} = \boldsymbol{\mu}_1 \\
& \text{covariance matrix} = \mathbf{C} \\
\mathbf{x} \in X_2: \quad & \text{mean vector} = \boldsymbol{\mu}_2 \\
& \text{covariance matrix} = \mathbf{C}
\end{aligned}$$

In other words, the vector **x** has a mean vector the value of which depends on whether it belongs to class $\mathscr{C}_1$ or class $\mathscr{C}_2$, and a covariance matrix that is the same for both classes. It is further assumed that:

- The classes $\mathscr{C}_1$ and $\mathscr{C}_2$ are equiprobable.
- The samples of class $\mathscr{C}_1$ or $\mathscr{C}_2$ are correlated, so that the covariance matrix **C** is nondiagonal.
- The covariance matrix **C** is nonsingular, so that the inverse matrix $\mathbf{C}^{-1}$ exists.

We may then use Eq. (4.36) to express the joint-probability density function of the input vector **x** as follows:

$$f(\mathbf{x}|\mathscr{C}_i) = \frac{1}{(2\pi)^{p/2}(\det \mathbf{C})^{1/2}} \exp\left[-\frac{1}{2}(\mathbf{x}-\boldsymbol{\mu}_i)^T\mathbf{C}^{-1}(\mathbf{x}-\boldsymbol{\mu}_i)\right] \tag{4.37}$$

where the index $i = 1, 2$. Taking the natural logarithm of both sides of Eq. (4.37) and then expanding terms, we get

$$\ln f(\mathbf{x}|\mathscr{C}_i) = -\frac{p}{2}\ln(2\pi) - \frac{1}{2}\ln(\det \mathbf{C}) - \frac{1}{2}\mathbf{x}^T\mathbf{C}^{-1}\mathbf{x} + \boldsymbol{\mu}_i^T\mathbf{C}^{-1}\mathbf{x} - \frac{1}{2}\boldsymbol{\mu}_i^T\mathbf{C}^{-1}\boldsymbol{\mu}_i \tag{4.38}$$

The first three terms on the right-hand side of Eq. (4.38) are independent of the index i. Hence, for the purpose of pattern classification considered here, we may define a *log-likelihood* as follows:

$$l_i(\mathbf{x}) = \boldsymbol{\mu}_i^T\mathbf{C}^{-1}\mathbf{x} - \frac{1}{2}\boldsymbol{\mu}_i^T\mathbf{C}^{-1}\boldsymbol{\mu}_i \tag{4.39}$$

where $i = 1, 2$. For class $\mathscr{C}_1$, the log-likelihood is

$$l_1(\mathbf{x}) = \boldsymbol{\mu}_1^T\mathbf{C}^{-1}\mathbf{x} - \frac{1}{2}\boldsymbol{\mu}_1^T\mathbf{C}^{-1}\boldsymbol{\mu}_1 \tag{4.40}$$

For class $\mathscr{C}_2$, the log-likelihood is

$$l_2(\mathbf{x}) = \boldsymbol{\mu}_2^T\mathbf{C}^{-1}\mathbf{x} - \frac{1}{2}\boldsymbol{\mu}_2^T\mathbf{C}^{-1}\boldsymbol{\mu}_2 \tag{4.41}$$

Hence, subtracting Eq. (4.41) from (4.40), we get

$$\begin{aligned} l &= l_1(\mathbf{x}) - l_2(\mathbf{x}) \\ &= (\boldsymbol{\mu}_1 - \boldsymbol{\mu}_2)^T\mathbf{C}^{-1}\mathbf{x} - \frac{1}{2}(\boldsymbol{\mu}_1^T\mathbf{C}^{-1}\boldsymbol{\mu}_1 - \boldsymbol{\mu}_2^T\mathbf{C}^{-1}\boldsymbol{\mu}_2) \end{aligned} \tag{4.42}$$

which is linearly related to the input vector **x**. To emphasize this property of the composite log-likelihood l, we rewrite Eq. (4.42) in the equivalent form

$$\begin{aligned} l &= \hat{\mathbf{w}}^T\mathbf{x} - \hat{\theta} \\ &= \sum_{i=1}^{p} \hat{w}_i x_i - \hat{\theta} \end{aligned} \tag{4.43}$$

where $\hat{\mathbf{w}}$ is the *maximum-likelihood estimate* of the unknown parameter vector **w**, defined by

$$\hat{\mathbf{w}} = \mathbf{C}^{-1}(\boldsymbol{\mu}_1 - \boldsymbol{\mu}_2) \tag{4.44}$$

and $\hat{\theta}$ is a constant threshold, defined by

$$\hat{\theta} = \frac{1}{2}(\boldsymbol{\mu}_1^T\mathbf{C}^{-1}\boldsymbol{\mu}_1 - \boldsymbol{\mu}_2^T\mathbf{C}^{-1}\boldsymbol{\mu}_2) \tag{4.45}$$

The *maximum-likelihood Gaussian classifier* or *Gaussian classifier* (for short) may thus be implemented by a linear combiner as shown in the signal-flow graph of Fig. 4.5.

Equations (4.44) and (4.45) simplify considerably for the following special case. All the samples of the vector **x** are uncorrelated with each other, and also have a common variance σ^2, regardless of the associated class; that is, the covariance matrix **C** is a diagonal matrix defined by

$$\mathbf{C} = \sigma^2 \mathbf{I} \tag{4.46}$$

where **I** is the p-by-p identity matrix. We now have

$$\mathbf{C}^{-1} = \frac{1}{\sigma^2}\mathbf{I} \tag{4.47}$$

Accordingly, Eqs. (4.44) and (4.45) simplify as, respectively,

$$\hat{\mathbf{w}} = \frac{1}{\sigma^2}(\boldsymbol{\mu}_1 - \boldsymbol{\mu}_2) \tag{4.48}$$

and

$$\hat{\theta} = \frac{1}{2\sigma^2}(\|\boldsymbol{\mu}_1\|^2 - \|\boldsymbol{\mu}_2\|^2) \tag{4.49}$$

where $\|\cdot\|$ denotes the Euclidean norm of the enclosed vector.

In any case, treating l as the overall classifier output, the Gaussian classifier, characterized by the parameter vector $\hat{\mathbf{w}}$ and threshold $\hat{\theta}$, solves the pattern-classification problem in accordance with the following rule:

$$\begin{aligned} &\text{If } l \geq 0, \text{ then } l_1 \geq l_2 \text{ and therefore assign } \mathbf{x} \text{ to class } \mathscr{C}_1 \\ &\text{If } l < 0, \text{ then } l_2 > l_1 \text{ and therefore assign } \mathbf{x} \text{ to class } \mathscr{C}_2 \end{aligned} \tag{4.50}$$

The operation of the Gaussian classifier is analogous to that of the single-layer perceptron in that they are both linear classifiers; see Eqs. (4.2) and (4.43). There are, however, some subtle and important differences between them, which should be carefully noted as discussed here:

- The single-layer perceptron operates on the premise that the patterns to be classified are *linearly separable.* The Gaussian distribution of the two patterns assumed in the derivation of the maximum-likelihood Gaussian classifier do certainly *overlap* each other and are therefore *not* exactly separable; the extent of the overlap is determined by the mean vectors $\boldsymbol{\mu}_1$ and $\boldsymbol{\mu}_2$, and the covariance matrices $\mathbf{C}_1$ and $\mathbf{C}_2$. The nature of this overlap is illustrated in Fig. 4.6 for the special case of a scalar input x (i.e., input dimension $p = 1$). When the inputs are nonseparable and their distributions overlap as described here, the perceptron convergence algorithm develops a problem

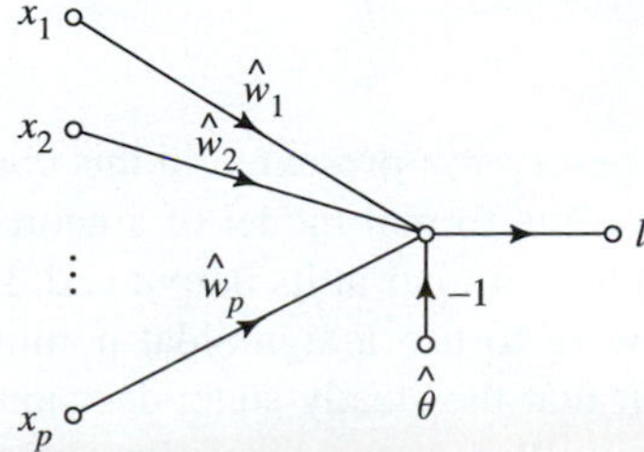

FIGURE 4.5 Signal-flow graph of Gaussian classifier.

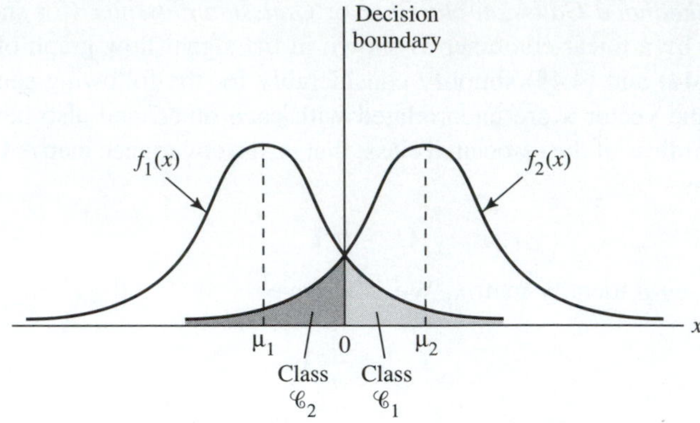

FIGURE 4.6 Two overlapping, one-dimensional Gaussian distributions.

in that the decision boundaries between the different classes may oscillate continuously (Lippmann, 1987).

- The maximum-likelihood Gaussian classifier minimizes the average probability of classification error. This minimization is independent of the overlap between the underlying Gaussian distributions of the two classes. For example, in the special case illustrated in Fig. 4.6, the maximum-likelihood Gaussian classifier always positions the decision boundary at the point where the two Gaussian distributions cross each other. This positioning of the decision boundary is perfectly in accord with the optimum *Bayes's hypothesis-testing procedure* on the assumption that the two classes are equiprobable (i.e., there is no prior information to be incorporated into the decision making).
- The perceptron convergence algorithm is *nonparametric* in the sense that it makes no assumptions concerning the form of the underlying distributions; it operates by concentrating on errors that occur where the distributions overlap. It may thus be more robust than classical techniques, and work well when the inputs are generated by nonlinear physical mechanisms, and whose distributions are heavily skewed and non-Gaussian (Lippmann, 1987). In contrast, the maximum-likelihood Gaussian classifier is *parametric;* its derivation is contingent on the assumption that the underlying distributions are Gaussian, which may limit its area of application.
- The perceptron convergence algorithm is both adaptive and simple to implement; its storage requirement is confined to the set of synaptic weights and threshold. On the other hand, the design of the maximum-likelihood Gaussian classifier is fixed; it can be made adaptive, but at the expense of increased storage requirement and more complex computations (Lippmann, 1987).

4.6 Discussion

The study of the single-layer perceptron presented in this chapter has been formulated in the context of the McCulloch–Pitts formal model of a neuron. The nonlinear element of this model is represented by a hard limiter at its output end. It would be tempting to think that we can do better if we were to use a sigmoidal nonlinear element in place of the hard limiter. Well, it turns out that the steady-state, decision-making characteristics of a single-layer perceptron are basically the same, regardless of whether we use hard-limiting or soft-limiting as the source of nonlinearity in the neural model (Shynk and Bershad,

1991, 1992; Shynk, 1990). We may therefore state formally that so long as we limit ourselves to the model of a neuron that consists of a linear combiner followed by a nonlinear element, then regardless of the form of nonlinearity used, a single-layer perceptron can perform pattern classification only on linearly separable patterns.

Linear separability requires that the patterns to be classified must be sufficiently separated from each other to ensure that the decision surfaces consist of hyperplanes. This requirement is illustrated in Fig. 4.7a for the case of a two-dimensional, single-layer perceptron. If now the two patterns $\mathscr{C}_1$ and $\mathscr{C}_2$ are allowed to move too close to each other, as in Fig. 4.7b, they become nonlinearly separable and the elementary perceptron fails to classify them.

The first real critique of Rosenblatt's perceptron was presented by Minsky and Selfridge (1961). Minsky and Selfridge pointed out that the perceptron as defined by Rosenblatt could not even generalize toward the notion of binary parity, let alone make general abstractions. They also suggested the roles that connectionist networks might play in the implementation of larger systems.

The computational limitations of Rosenblatt's perceptron were subsequently put on a solid mathematical foundation in the famous book by Minsky and Papert (1969, 1988). This is a thorough and well-written book. After the presentation of some brilliant and highly detailed mathematical analysis of the perceptron, Minsky and Papert proved that the perceptron as defined by Rosenblatt is inherently incapable of making some global generalizations on the basis of locally learned examples. In the last chapter of their book, Minsky and Papert go on to make the conjecture that the limitations of the kind they had discovered for Rosenblatt's perceptron would also hold true for its variants, more specifically, multilayer neural networks. Quoting from Section 13.2 of the book by Minsky and Papert (1969):

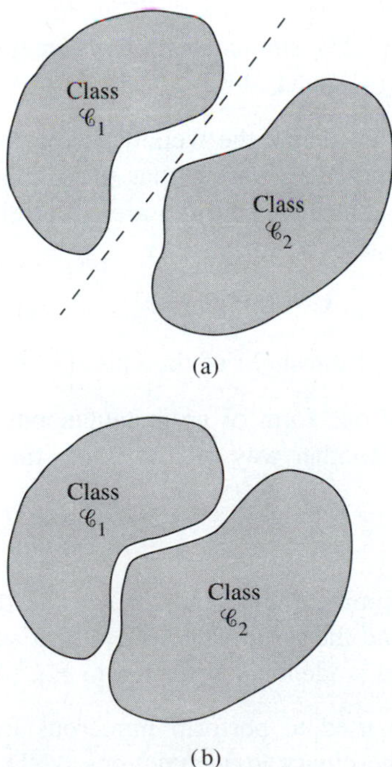

FIGURE 4.7 (a) A pair of linearly separable patterns. (b) A pair of nonlinearly separable patterns.

> The perceptron has shown itself worthy of study despite (and even because of !) its severe limitations. It has many features to attract attention: its linearity; its intriguing learning theorem; its clear paradigmatic simplicity as a kind of parallel computation. There is no reason to suppose that any of these virtues carry over to the many-layered version. Nevertheless, we consider it to be an important research problem to elucidate (or reject) our intuitive judgement that the extension to multilayer systems is sterile.

This conjecture cast serious doubt on the computational capabilities of not only the perceptron but neural networks in general up to the mid-1980s.

History has shown, however, that the conjecture made by Minsky and Papert seems to be unjustified in that we now have several advanced forms of neural networks that are computationally more powerful than Rosenblatt's perceptron. For example, multilayer perceptrons trained with the back-propagation algorithm discussed in Chapter 6 and the radial basis-function networks discussed in Chapter 7 overcome the computational limitations of the single-layer perceptron.

PROBLEMS

4.1 The single-layer perceptron is a linear pattern classifier. Justify this statement.

4.2 Consider two one-dimensional, Gaussian-distributed classes $\mathscr{C}_1$ and $\mathscr{C}_2$ that have a common variance equal to 1. Their mean values are as follows:

$$\mu_1 = -10$$

$$\mu_2 = +10$$

These two classes are essentially linearly separable. Design a classifier that separates these two classes.

4.3 Verify that Eqs. (4.22)–(4.25), summarizing the perceptron convergence algorithm, are consistent with Eqs. (4.7) and (4.8).

4.4 Equations (4.44) and (4.45) define the weight vector and threshold of a maximum-likelihood Gaussian classifier, assuming that the samples of classes $\mathscr{C}_1$ or $\mathscr{C}_2$ are correlated. Suppose now that these samples are uncorrelated but have different variances, so that for both classes we may write

$$\mathbf{C} = \text{diag}[\sigma_1^2, \sigma_2^2, \ldots, \sigma_p^2]$$

Find the weight vector and threshold of the classifier so defined.

4.5 In Eq. (4.27) we defined one form of an instantaneous performance function for a single-layer perceptron. Another way of expressing this performance measure is as follows (Shynk, 1990):

$$\hat{J}(n) = |v(n)| - d(n)\, v(n)$$

where $v(n)$ is the hard-limiter input, and $d(n)$ is the desired response. Using this performance measure, find the instantaneous gradient vector $\nabla_{\mathbf{w}}\hat{J}(n)$, and show that the expression so derived is identical with that in Eq. (4.31).

4.6 The perceptron may be used to perform numerous logic functions. Demonstrate the implementation of the binary logic functions AND, OR, and COMPLEMENT. However, a basic limitation of the perceptron is that it cannot implement the EXCLUSIVE OR function. Explain the reason for this limitation.

CHAPTER 5

Least-Mean-Square Algorithm

5.1 Introduction

In this chapter we study a primitive class of neural networks consisting of a single neuron and operating under the assumption of linearity. This class of networks is important for three reasons. First, the theory of *linear adaptive filters* employing a single linear neuron model is well developed, and it has been applied successfully in such diverse fields as communications, control, radar, sonar, and biomedical engineering (Haykin, 1991; Widrow and Stearns, 1985). Second, it is a by-product of the pioneering work done on neural networks during the 1960s. Last, but no means least, a study of linear adaptive filters (alongside that of single-layer perceptrons, covered in Chapter 4) paves the way for the theoretical development of the more general case of multilayer perceptrons that includes the use of nonlinear elements, which is undertaken in Chapter 6.

We begin our study by reviewing briefly the linear optimum filtering problem. We then formulate the highly popular *least-mean-square* (*LMS*) *algorithm,* also known as the *delta rule* or the *Widrow–Hoff rule* (Widrow and Hoff, 1960). The LMS algorithm operates with a single linear neuron model. The design of the LMS algorithm is very simple, yet a detailed analysis of its convergence behavior is a challenging mathematical task.

The LMS algorithm was originally formulated by Widrow and Hoff for use in *adaptive switching circuits.* The machine used to perform the LMS algorithm was called an *Adaline,* the development of which was inspired by Rosenblatt's perceptron. Subsequently, the application of the LMS algorithm was extended to *adaptive equalization* of telephone channels for high-speed data transmission (Lucky, 1965, 1966), *adaptive antennas* for the suppression of interfering signals originating from unknown directions (Widrow et al., 1967), *adaptive echo cancellation* for the suppression of echoes experienced on long-distance communication circuits (Sondhi and Berkley, 1980; Sondhi, 1967), *adaptive differential pulse code modulation* for efficient encoding of speech signals in digital communications (Jayant and Noll, 1984), *adaptive signal detection* in a nonstationary environment (Zeidler, 1990), and *adaptive cross-polar cancellation* applied to radar polarimetry for precise navigation along a confined waterway (Ukrainec and Haykin, 1989). Indeed, the LMS algorithm has established itself as an important functional block in the ever-expanding field of *adaptive signal processing.*

Organization of the Chapter

The main body of the chapter is organized as follows. The development of the Wiener–Hopf equations for linear optimum filtering is presented in Section 5.2. This is followed by a description of the method of steepest descent in Section 5.3, which is a deterministic algorithm for the recursive computation of the optimum filter solution. The method of steepest descent provides the heuristics for deriving the LMS algorithm; this is done in Section 5.4. The essential factors affecting the convergence behavior of the LMS algorithm are considered briefly in Section 5.5. In Section 5.6 we consider the learning curve of the LMS algorithm, which is then followed by a discussion on the use of learning-rate annealing schedules in Section 5.7. In Section 5.8 we describe the Adaline based on the LMS algorithm. The chapter concludes with some final remarks in Section 5.9.

5.2 Wiener–Hopf Equations

Consider a set of p *sensors* located at different points in space, as depicted in Fig. 5.1. Let $x_1, x_2, \ldots, x_p$ be the individual signals produced by these sensors. These signals are applied to a corresponding set of weights $w_1, w_2, \ldots, w_p$. The weighted signals are then summed to produce the output signal y. The requirement is to determine the optimum setting of the weights $w_1, w_2, \ldots, w_p$ so as to minimize the difference between the system output y and some desired response d in a mean-square sense. The solution to this fundamental problem lies in the Wiener–Hopf equations.

The system described in Fig. 5.1 may be viewed as a *spatial filter.* The input–output relation of the filter is described by the summation

$$y = \sum_{k=1}^{p} w_k x_k \tag{5.1}$$

Let d denote the *desired response* or *target output* for the filter. We may then define the *error signal,*

$$e = d - y \tag{5.2}$$

As performance measure or cost function, we introduce the *mean-squared error* defined as follows:

$$J = \frac{1}{2} E[e^2] \tag{5.3}$$

where E is the statistical expectation operator. The factor $\frac{1}{2}$ is included for convenience of presentation, which will become apparent later. We may now state the *linear optimum filtering problem* as follows:

Determine the optimum set of weights $w_{o1}, w_{o2}, \ldots, w_{op}$ for which the mean-squared error J is minimum.

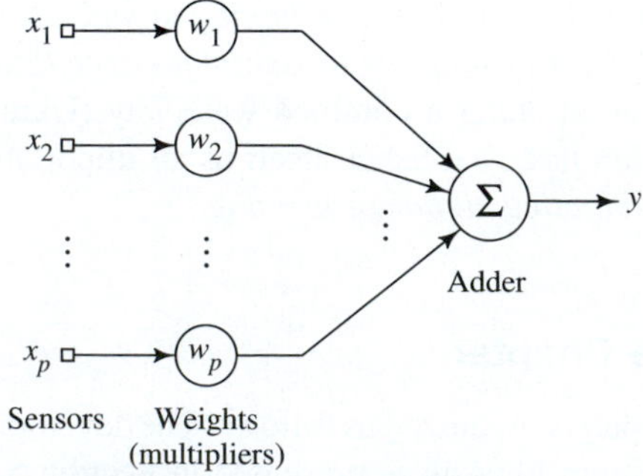

FIGURE 5.1 Spatial filter.

The solution of this filtering problem is referred to in the signal processing literature as the *Wiener filter,* in recognition of the pioneering work done by Wiener (Haykin, 1991; Widrow and Stearns, 1985).

Substituting Eqs. (5.1) and (5.2) in (5.3), then expanding terms, we get

$$J = \frac{1}{2}E[d^2] - E\left[\sum_{k=1}^{p} w_k x_k d\right] + \frac{1}{2}E\left[\sum_{j=1}^{p}\sum_{k=1}^{p} w_j w_k x_j x_k\right] \tag{5.4}$$

where the double summation is used to represent the square of a summation. Since mathematical expectation is a linear operation, we may interchange the order of expectation and summation in Eq. (5.4). Accordingly, we may rewrite Eq. (5.4) in the equivalent form

$$J = \frac{1}{2}E[d^2] - \sum_{k=1}^{p} w_k E[x_k d] + \frac{1}{2}\sum_{j=1}^{p}\sum_{k=1}^{p} w_j w_k E[x_j x_k] \tag{5.5}$$

where the weights are treated as constants and therefore taken outside the expectations.

At this point, we find it convenient to introduce some definitions that account for the three different expectations appearing in Eq. (5.5), as described here:

- The expectation $E[d^2]$ is the *mean-square value* of the desired response d; let

$$r_d = E[d^2] \tag{5.6}$$

- The expectation $E[dx_k]$ is the *cross-correlation function* between the desired response d and the sensory signal x_k; let

$$r_{dx}(k) = E[dx_k], \qquad k = 1, 2, \ldots, p \tag{5.7}$$

- The expectation $E[x_j x_k]$ is the *autocorrelation function* of the set of sensory signals themselves; let

$$r_x(j,k) = E[x_j x_k], \qquad j, k = 1, 2, \ldots, p \tag{5.8}$$

In light of these definitions, we may now simplify the format of Eq. (5.5) as follows:

$$J = \frac{1}{2}r_d - \sum_{k=1}^{p} w_k r_{dx}(k) + \frac{1}{2}\sum_{j=1}^{p}\sum_{k=1}^{p} w_j w_k r_x(j,k) \tag{5.9}$$

A multidimensional plot of the cost function J versus the weights (free parameters) w_1, $w_2, \ldots, w_p$ constitutes the *error-performance surface,* or simply the *error surface* of the filter. The error surface is bowl-shaped, with a well-defined bottom or global minimum point. It is precisely at this point where the spatial filter of Fig. 5.1 is optimum in the sense that the mean-squared error attains its minimum value $J_{\min}$.

To determine this optimum condition, we differentiate the cost function J with respect to the weight w_k and then set the result equal to zero for all k. The derivative of J with respect to w_k is called the *gradient* of the error surface with respect to that particular weight. Let $\nabla_{w_k} J$ denote this gradient, as shown by

$$\nabla_{w_k} J = \frac{\partial J}{\partial w_k}, \qquad k = 1, 2, \ldots, p \tag{5.10}$$

Differentiating Eq. (5.9) with respect to w_k, we readily find that

$$\nabla_{w_k} J = -r_{dx}(k) + \sum_{j=1}^{p} w_j r_x(j,k) \tag{5.11}$$

The optimum condition of the filter is thus defined by

$$\nabla_{w_k} J = 0, \qquad k = 1, 2, \ldots, p \tag{5.12}$$

Let w_{ok} denote the optimum setting of weight w_k. Then, from Eq. (5.11), we find that the optimum weights of the spatial filter in Fig. 5.1 are determined by the following set of simultaneous equations:

$$\sum_{j=1}^{p} w_{oj} r_x(j,k) = r_{xd}(k), \qquad k = 1, 2, \ldots, p \tag{5.13}$$

This system of equations is known as the *Wiener–Hopf equations,* and the filter whose weights satisfy the Wiener–Hopf equations is called a *Wiener filter.*

5.3 Method of Steepest Descent

To solve the Wiener–Hopf equations (5.13) for tap weights of the optimum spatial filter, we basically need to compute the inverse of a p-by-p matrix made up of the different values of the autocorrelation function $r_x(j,k)$ for j, k = 1, 2, . . . , p. We may avoid the need for this matrix inversion by using the *method of steepest descent.* According to this method, the weights of the filter assume a time-varying form, and their values are adjusted in an *iterative* fashion along the error surface with the aim of moving them progressively toward the optimum solution. The method of steepest descent has the task of continually seeking the bottom point of the error surface of the filter. Now it is intuitively reasonable that successive adjustments applied to the tap weights of the filter be in the direction of steepest descent of the error surface, that is, in a *direction opposite to the gradient vector* whose elements are defined by $\nabla_{w_k} J$ for k = 1, 2, . . . , p. Such an adjustment is illustrated in Fig. 5.2 for the case of a single weight.

Let $w_k(n)$ denote the value of weight w_k of the spatial filter calculated at iteration or discrete time n by the method of steepest descent. In a corresponding way, the gradient of the error surface of the filter with respect to this weight takes on a time-varying form of its own, as shown by [in light of Eq. (5.11)]

$$\nabla_{w_k} J(n) = -r_{dx}(k) + \sum_{j=1}^{p} w_j(n) r_x(j,k) \tag{5.14}$$

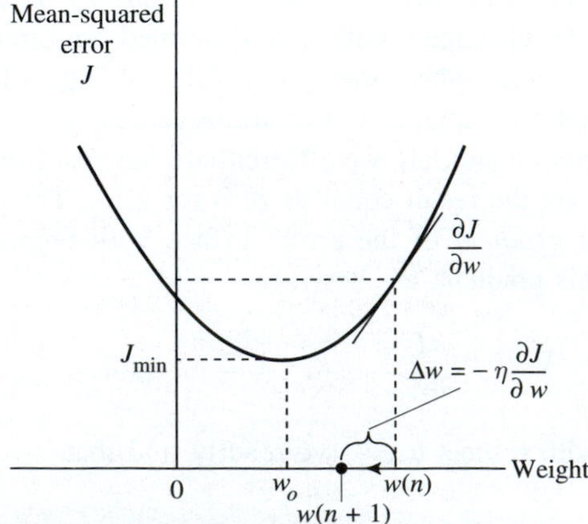

FIGURE 5.2 Illustrating the mean-squared error criterion for a single weight.

Note that the indices j and k refer to locations of different sensors in space, whereas the index n refer to iteration number. According to the method of steepest descent, the adjustment applied to the weight $w_k(n)$ at iteration n is defined by

$$\Delta w_k(n) = -\eta \nabla_{w_k} J(n), \qquad k = 1, 2, \ldots, p \tag{5.15}$$

where η is a positive constant called the *learning-rate parameter.* Given the *old* value of the kth weight $w_k(n)$ at iteration n, the *updated* value of this weight at the next iteration $n + 1$ is computed as

$$\begin{aligned} w_k(n+1) &= w_k(n) + \Delta w_k(n) \\ &= w_k(n) - \eta \nabla_{w_k} J(n), \qquad k = 1, 2, \ldots, p \end{aligned} \tag{5.16}$$

We may thus state the method of steepest descent as follows:

> *The updated value of the kth weight of a Wiener filter (designed to operate in a minimum mean-square error sense) equals the old value of the tap weight plus a correction that is proportional to the negative of the gradient of the error surface with respect to that particular weight.*

Substituting Eq. (5.14) in (5.16), we may finally formulate the method of steepest descent in terms of the correlation functions $r_x(j,k)$ and $r_{dx}(k)$ as follows:

$$w_k(n+1) = w_k(n) + \eta \left[r_{dx}(k) - \sum_{j=1}^{M} w_j(n) r_x(j,k) \right], \qquad k = 1, 2, \ldots, p \tag{5.17}$$

The method of steepest descent is *exact* in the sense that there are no approximations made in its derivation. The derivation presented here is based on minimizing the mean-squared error, defined as

$$J(n) = \frac{1}{2} E[e^2(n)] \tag{5.18}$$

This cost function is an *ensemble average,* taken at a particular instant of time n and over an *ensemble* of spatial filters of an identical design but with different inputs drawn from the same population. The method of steepest descent may also be derived by minimizing the *sum of error squares:*

$$\begin{aligned} \mathscr{E}_{\text{total}}(n) &= \sum_{i=1}^{n} \mathscr{E}(i) \\ &= \frac{1}{2} \sum_{i=1}^{n} e^2(i) \end{aligned} \tag{5.19}$$

where the integration is now taken over all iterations of the algorithm, but for a particular realization of the spatial filter. This second approach yields a result identical to that described in Eq. (5.17), but with a new interpretation of the correlation functions. Specifically, the autocorrelation function r_x and cross-correlation function r_{dx} are now defined as *time averages* rather than as ensemble averages. If the physical processes responsible for the generation of the input signals and desired response are *jointly ergodic,* then we are justified in substituting time averages for ensemble averages (Gray and Davisson, 1986; Papoulis, 1984).

In any event, care has to be exercised in the selection of the learning-rate parameter η for the method of steepest descent to work. Also, a practical limitation of the method of steepest descent is that it requires knowledge of the spatial correlation functions $r_{dx}(k)$ and $r_x(j,k)$. Now, when the filter operates in an *unknown* environment, these correlation functions are not available, in which case we are forced to use *estimates* in their place. The least-mean-square algorithm, described in the next section, results from a simple and yet effective method of providing for these estimates.

5.4 Least-Mean-Square Algorithm

The *least-mean-square* (*LMS*) *algorithm* is based on the use of *instantaneous estimates* of the autocorrelation function $r_x(j,k)$ and the cross-correlation function $r_{xd}(k)$. These estimates are deduced directly from the defining equations (5.8) and (5.7) as follows:

$$\hat{r}_x(j,k;n) = x_j(n)x_k(n) \tag{5.20}$$

and

$$\hat{r}_{dx}(k;n) = x_k(n)d(n) \tag{5.21}$$

The use of a hat in $\hat{r}_x$ and $\hat{r}_{dx}$ is intended to signify that these quantities are "estimates." The definitions introduced in Eqs. (5.20) and (5.21) have been generalized to include a *nonstationary environment,* in which case all the sensory signals and the desired response assume time-varying forms too. Thus, substituting $\hat{r}_x(j,k;n)$ and $\hat{r}_{dx}(k;n)$ in place of $r_x(j,k)$ and $r_{dx}(k)$ in Eq. (5.17), we get

$$\begin{aligned}\hat{w}_k(n+1) &= \hat{w}_k(n) + \eta\left[x_k(n)\,d(n) - \sum_{j=1}^{p}\hat{w}_j(n)x_j(n)x_k(n)\right] \\ &= \hat{w}_k(n) + \eta\left[d(n) - \sum_{j=1}^{p}\hat{w}_j(n)x_j(n)\right]x_k(n) \\ &= \hat{w}_k(n) + \eta[d(n) - y(n)]x_k(n), \qquad k = 1, 2, \ldots, p\end{aligned} \tag{5.22}$$

where $y(n)$ is the output of the spatial filter computed at iteration n in accordance with the LMS algorithm; that is,

$$y(n) = \sum_{j=1}^{p}\hat{w}_j(n)x_j(n) \tag{5.23}$$

Note that in Eq. (5.22) we have used $\hat{w}_k(n)$ in place of $w_k(n)$ to emphasize the fact that Eq. (5.22) involves "estimates" of the weights of the spatial filter.

Figure 5.3 illustrates the operational environment of the LMS algorithm, which is completely described by Eqs. (5.22) and (5.23). A summary of the LMS algorithm is presented in Table 5.1, which clearly illustrates the simplicity of the algorithm. As indicated in this table, for the *initialization* of the algorithm, it is customary to set all the initial values of the weights of the filter equal to zero.

In the method of steepest descent applied to a "known" environment, the weight vector $\mathbf{w}(n)$, made up of the weights $w_1(n), w_2(n), \ldots, w_p(n)$, starts at some initial value $\mathbf{w}(0)$, and then follows a precisely defined trajectory (along the error surface) that eventually terminates on the optimum solution $\mathbf{w}_o$, provided that the learning-rate parameter η is chosen properly. In contrast, in the LMS algorithm applied to an "unknown" environment, the weight vector $\hat{\mathbf{w}}(n)$, representing an "estimate" of $\mathbf{w}(n)$, follows a random trajectory. For this reason, the LMS algorithm is sometimes referred to as a "stochastic gradient algorithm." As the number of iterations in the LMS algorithm approaches infinity, $\hat{\mathbf{w}}(n)$ performs a random walk (Brownian motion) about the optimum solution $\mathbf{w}_o$; see Appendix D.

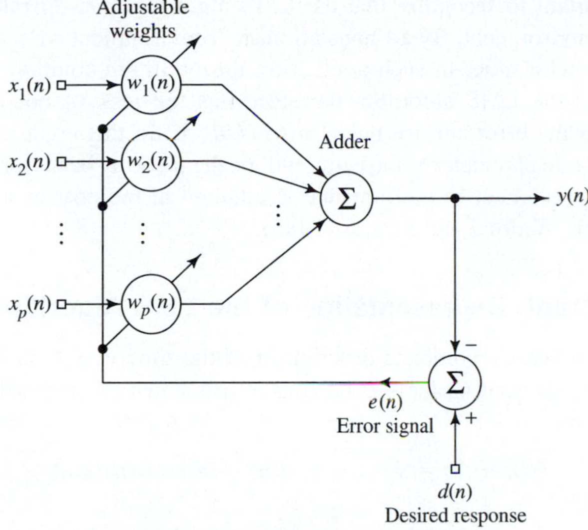

FIGURE 5.3 Adaptive spatial filter.

Another way of stating the basic difference between the method of steepest descent and the LMS algorithm is in terms of the error calculations involved. At any iteration n, the method of steepest descent minimizes the mean-squared error $J(n)$. This cost function involves ensemble averaging, the effect of which is to give the method of steepest descent an "exact" gradient vector that improves in pointing accuracy with increasing n. The LMS algorithm, on the other hand, minimizes an instantaneous estimate of the cost function $J(n)$. Consequently, the gradient vector in the LMS algorithm is "random," and its pointing accuracy improves "on the average" with increasing n.

The basic difference between the method of steepest descent and the LMS algorithm may also be stated in terms of time-domain ideas, emphasizing other aspects of the adaptive filtering problem. The method of steepest descent minimizes the sum of error squares $\mathscr{E}_{\text{total}}(n)$, integrated over all previous iterations of the algorithm up to and including iteration n. Consequently, it requires the storage of information needed to provide running estimates of the autocorrelation function r_x and cross-correlation function r_{dx}. In contrast, the LMS algorithm simply minimizes the instantaneous error squared $\mathscr{E}(n)$, defined as $(\frac{1}{2})e^2(n)$, thereby reducing the storage requirement to the minimum possible. In particular, it does not require storing any more information than is present in the weights of the filter.

TABLE 5.1 Summary of the LMS Algorithm

1. Initialization. Set

$$\hat{w}_k(1) = 0 \qquad \text{for } k = 1, 2, \ldots, p$$

2. Filtering. For time $n = 1, 2, \ldots$, compute

$$y(n) = \sum_{j=1}^{p} \hat{w}_j(n)x_j(n)$$

$$e(n) = d(n) - y(n)$$

$$\hat{w}_k(n+1) = w_k(n) + \eta e(n)x_k(n) \qquad \text{for } k = 1, 2, \ldots, p$$

It is also important to recognize that the LMS algorithm can operate in a stationary or nonstationary environment. By a ''nonstationary'' environment we mean one in which the statistics vary with time. In such a situation the optimum solution assumes a time-varying form, and the LMS algorithm therefore has the task of not only *seeking* the minimum point of the error surface but also *tracking* it. In this context, the smaller we make the learning-rate parameter η, the better will be the tracking behavior of the algorithm. However, this improvement in performance is attained at the cost of a slow adaptation rate (Haykin, 1991; Widrow and Stearns, 1985).

Signal-Flow Graph Representation of the LMS Algorithm

Equation (5.22) provides a complete description of the time evolution of the weights in the LMS algorithm. Rewriting the second line of this equation in matrix form, we may express it as follows:

$$\hat{\mathbf{w}}(n+1) = \hat{\mathbf{w}}(n) + \eta[d(n) - \mathbf{x}^T(n)\hat{\mathbf{w}}(n)]\mathbf{x}(n) \tag{5.24}$$

where

$$\hat{\mathbf{w}}(n) = [\hat{w}_1(n), \hat{w}_2(n), \ldots, \hat{w}_p]^T \tag{5.25}$$

and

$$\mathbf{x}(n) = [x_1(n), x_2(n), \ldots, x_p(n)]^T \tag{5.26}$$

Rearranging terms in Eq. (5.24), we have

$$\hat{\mathbf{w}}(n+1) = [\mathbf{I} - \eta\mathbf{x}(n)\mathbf{x}^T(n)]\hat{\mathbf{w}}(n) + \eta\mathbf{x}(n)\, d(n) \tag{5.27}$$

where $\mathbf{I}$ is the identity matrix. In using the LMS algorithm, we note that

$$\hat{\mathbf{w}}(n) = z^{-1}[\hat{\mathbf{w}}(n+1)] \tag{5.28}$$

where z^{-1} is the *unit-delay operator* implying storage. Using Eqs. (5.27) and (5.28), we may thus represent the LMS algorithm by the signal-flow graph depicted in Fig. 5.4.

The signal-flow graph of Fig. 5.4 reveals that the LMS algorithm is an example of a *stochastic feedback system.* The presence of feedback has a profound impact on the convergence behavior of the LMS algorithm, as discussed next.

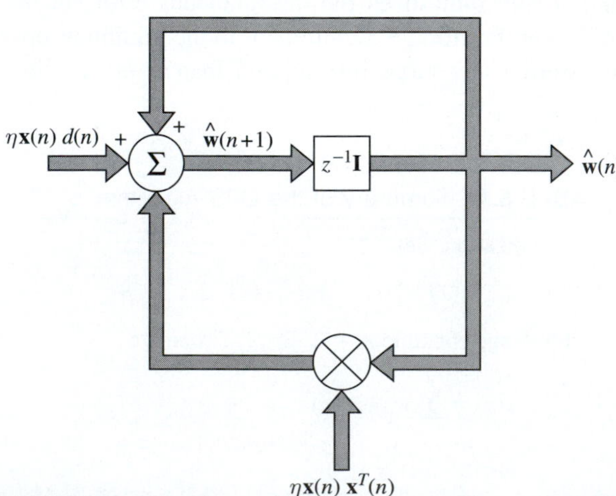

FIGURE 5.4 Signal-flow graph representation of the LMS algorithm.

5.5 Convergence Considerations of the LMS Algorithm

From control theory, we know that the stability of a feedback system is determined by the parameters that constitute its feedback loop. From Fig. 5.4 we see that it is the lower feedback loop that adds variability to the behavior of the LMS algorithm. In particular, there are two distinct quantities, namely, the learning-rate parameter η and the input vector $\mathbf{x}(n)$, that determine the transmittance of this feedback loop. We therefore deduce that the convergence behavior (i.e., stability) of the LMS algorithm is influenced by the statistical characteristics of the input vector $\mathbf{x}(n)$ and the value assigned to the learning-rate parameter η. Casting this observation in a different way, we may state that for a specified environment that supplies the input vector $\mathbf{x}(n)$, we have to exercise care in the selection of the learning-rate parameter η for the LMS algorithm to be convergent.

There are two distinct aspects of the convergence problem in the LMS algorithm that require special attention (Haykin, 1991):

1. The LMS algorithm is said to be *convergent in the mean* if the mean value of the weight vector $\hat{\mathbf{w}}(n)$ approaches the optimum solution $\mathbf{w}_o$ as the number of iterations n approaches infinity; that is,

$$E[\hat{\mathbf{w}}(n)] \rightarrow \mathbf{w}_o \qquad \text{as } n \rightarrow \infty \tag{5.29}$$

2. The LMS algorithm is said to be *convergent in the mean square* if the mean-square value of the error signal $e(n)$ approaches a constant value as the number of iterations n approaches infinity; that is,

$$E[e^2(n)] \rightarrow \text{constant} \qquad \text{as } n \rightarrow \infty \tag{5.30}$$

It turns out that the condition for convergence in the mean square is tighter than the condition for convergence in the mean. In other words, if the LMS algorithm is convergent in the mean square, then it is convergent in the mean; however, the converse of this statement is not necessarily true. Both of these issues are considered in the remainder of this section.

Convergence in the Mean

We begin this convergence analysis of the LMS algorithm by making the following assumption: The weight vector $\mathbf{w}$ computed by the LMS algorithm is uncorrelated with the input vector $\mathbf{x}(n)$, as shown by

$$E[\hat{\mathbf{w}}(n)\mathbf{x}(n)] = \mathbf{0} \tag{5.31}$$

Then, taking the expectation of both sides of Eq. (5.27) and then applying this assumption, we get

$$E[\hat{\mathbf{w}}(n+1)] = (\mathbf{I} - \eta\mathbf{R}_x)E[\hat{\mathbf{w}}(n)] + \eta\mathbf{r}_{dx} \tag{5.32}$$

where $\mathbf{R}_x$ and $\mathbf{r}_{dx}$ are defined, respectively, by

$$\mathbf{R}_x = E[\mathbf{x}(n)\mathbf{x}^T(n)] \tag{5.33}$$

and

$$\mathbf{r}_{dx} = E[\mathbf{x}(n)d(n)] \tag{5.34}$$

We refer to $\mathbf{R}_x$ as the *correlation matrix* of the input vector $\mathbf{x}(n)$, and to $\mathbf{r}_{dx}$ as the *cross-correlation vector* between the input vector $\mathbf{x}(n)$ and the desired response $d(n)$.

To find the condition for the convergence of the LMS algorithm in the mean, we perform an *orthogonal similarity transformation* on the correlation matrix $\mathbf{R}_x$, as shown by (Strang, 1980)

$$\mathbf{Q}^T\mathbf{R}_x\mathbf{Q} = \mathbf{\Lambda} \tag{5.35}$$

or, equivalently,

$$\mathbf{R}_x = \mathbf{Q}\mathbf{\Lambda}\mathbf{Q}^T \tag{5.36}$$

where $\mathbf{\Lambda}$ is a *diagonal matrix* made up of the *eigenvalues* of the correlation matrix $\mathbf{R}_x$, and $\mathbf{Q}$ is an *orthogonal matrix* whose columns are the associated *eigenvectors* of $\mathbf{R}_x$. An important property of an orthogonal matrix is that its inverse and transpose have the same value; that is,

$$\mathbf{Q}^{-1} = \mathbf{Q}^T \tag{5.37}$$

or, equivalently,

$$\mathbf{Q}\mathbf{Q}^T = \mathbf{I} \tag{5.38}$$

Rewriting the Wiener–Hopf equations (5.13) in matrix form, we have

$$\mathbf{R}_x\mathbf{w}_o = \mathbf{r}_{dx} \tag{5.39}$$

where $\mathbf{R}_x$ and $\mathbf{r}_{dx}$ are as defined previously, and $\mathbf{w}_o$ is the weight vector of the optimum (Wiener) filter. Using Eq. (5.39) for the cross-correlation vector $\mathbf{r}_{dx}$ in Eq. (5.32), then substituting the orthogonal similarity transformation of Eq. (5.36) for the correlation matrix $\mathbf{R}_x$, and then using the relation of Eq. (5.37), we get

$$\mathbf{Q}^T E[\hat{\mathbf{w}}(n+1)] = (\mathbf{I} - \eta\mathbf{\Lambda})\mathbf{Q}^T E[\hat{\mathbf{w}}(n)] + \eta\mathbf{\Lambda}\mathbf{Q}^T\mathbf{w}_o \tag{5.40}$$

Let a new vector $\mathbf{v}(n)$ be defined as a *transformed version of the deviation between the expectation* $E[\hat{\mathbf{w}}(n)]$ *and the Wiener solution* $\mathbf{w}_o$, as shown by

$$\mathbf{v}(n) = \mathbf{Q}^T(E[\hat{\mathbf{w}}(n)] - \mathbf{w}_o) \tag{5.41}$$

Equivalently, we have the affine transformation

$$E[\mathbf{w}(n)] = \mathbf{Q}\mathbf{v}(n) + \mathbf{w}_o \tag{5.42}$$

We may then rewrite Eq. (5.40) in the simplified form

$$\mathbf{v}(n+1) = (\mathbf{I} - \eta\mathbf{\Lambda})\mathbf{v}(n) \tag{5.43}$$

The recursive vector equation (5.43) represents a system of *uncoupled homogeneous first-order difference equations,* as shown by

$$v_k(n+1) = (1 - \eta\lambda_k)v_k(n), \qquad k = 1, 2, \ldots, p \tag{5.44}$$

where the λ_k are the eigenvalues of the correlation matrix $\mathbf{R}_x$ and $v_k(n)$ is the kth element of the vector $\mathbf{v}(n)$. Let $v_k(0)$ denote the initial value of $v_k(n)$. We may then solve Eq. (5.44) for $v_k(n)$, obtaining

$$v_k(n) = (1 - \eta\lambda_k)^n v_k(0), \qquad k = 1, 2, \ldots, p \tag{5.45}$$

For the LMS algorithm to be convergent in the mean, we require that for an arbitrary choice of $v_k(0)$ the following condition be satisfied:

$$|1 - \eta\lambda_k| < 1 \qquad \text{for } k = 1, 2, \ldots, p \tag{5.46}$$

Under this condition, we find that

$$v_k(n) \to 0 \qquad \text{as } n \to \infty \tag{5.47}$$

which, in the light of Eq. (5.41), is equivalent to the condition described in Eq. (5.29).

The condition of Eq. (5.44), in turn, requires that we choose the learning-rate parameter η as follows (Haykin, 1991; Widrow and Stearns, 1985):

$$0 < \eta < \frac{2}{\lambda_{max}} \tag{5.48}$$

where λ_{max} is the *largest eigenvalue* of the autocorrelation matrix $\mathbf{R}_x$.

In summary, *the LMS algorithm is convergent in the mean* provided that the learning-rate parameter η is a positive constant with an upper bound defined by $2/\lambda_{max}$. Note that η is measured in units equivalent to the inverse of variance (power).

Convergence in the Mean Square

A detailed analysis of convergence of the LMS algorithm in the mean square is much more complicated than convergence analysis of the algorithm in the mean. This analysis is also much more demanding in the assumptions made concerning the behavior of the weight vector $\mathbf{w}(n)$ computed by the LMS algorithm (Haykin, 1991). In this subsection we present a simplified result of the analysis.

The LMS algorithm is *convergent in the mean square* if the learning-rate parameter η satisfies the following condition (Haykin, 1991; Widrow and Stearns, 1985):

$$0 < \eta < \frac{2}{\text{tr}[\mathbf{R}_x]} \tag{5.49}$$

where $\text{tr}[\mathbf{R}_x]$ is the *trace* of the correlation matrix $\mathbf{R}_x$. From matrix algebra, we know that (Strang, 1980)

$$\text{tr}[\mathbf{R}_x] = \sum_{k=1}^{p} \lambda_k \geq \lambda_{max} \tag{5.50}$$

It follows therefore that if the learning-rate parameter η satisfies the condition of Eq. (5.49), then it also satisfies the condition of Eq. (5.48). In other words, if the LMS algorithm is convergent in the mean square, then it is also convergent in the mean.

From matrix algebra we also know that the trace of a square matrix equals the sum of its diagonal elements. The kth diagonal element of the correlation matrix $\mathbf{R}_x$ equals the mean-square value of the input signal $x(n)$. Hence, the trace of the correlation matrix $\mathbf{R}_x$ equals the *total input power* measured over all the p sensory inputs of the spatial filter in Fig. 5.3. Accordingly, we may reformulate the condition for convergence of the LMS algorithm in the mean square given in Eq. (5.49) as follows:

$$0 < \eta < \frac{2}{\text{total input power}} \tag{5.51}$$

For the instrumentation of this condition, we simply have to ensure that the learning-rate parameter η is a positive constant whose value is less than twice the reciprocal of the total input power.

5.6 Learning Curve

A curve obtained by plotting the mean squared error $J(n)$ versus the number of iterations n is called the *ensemble-averaged learning curve*. Such a curve can be highly informative, as it vividly displays important characteristics of the learning process under study.

The learning curve of the LMS algorithm consists of the sum of exponentials only. The precise form of this sum depends on the correlation structure of the input vector $\mathbf{x}(n)$.

In any event, to obtain the learning curve, we average the squared error over an ensemble of identical LMS filters with their inputs represented by different realizations of the vector $\mathbf{x}(n)$, which are drawn individually from the same population. For a single realization of the LMS algorithm, the learning curve consists of noisy exponentials; the ensemble averaging has the effect of smoothing out the noise.

For an LMS algorithm convergent in the mean square, the final value $J(\infty)$ of the mean-squared error $J(n)$ is a positive constant, which represents the *steady-state condition* of the learning curve. In fact, $J(\infty)$ is always in excess of the minimum mean-squared error $J_{\min}$ realized by the corresponding Wiener filter for a stationary environment. The difference between $J(\infty)$ and $J_{\min}$ is called the *excess mean-squared error:*

$$J_{\text{ex}} = J(\infty) - J_{\min} \tag{5.52}$$

The ratio of J_{ex} to $J_{\min}$ is called the *misadjustment:*

$$M = \frac{J_{\text{ex}}}{J_{\min}} \tag{5.53}$$

It is customary to express the misadjustment M as a percentage. Thus, for example, a misadjustment of 10 percent means that the LMS algorithm produces a mean-squared error (after completion of the learning process) that is 10 percent greater than the minimum mean squared error $J_{\min}$. Such a performance is ordinarily considered to be satisfactory.

Another important characteristic of the LMS algorithm is the *settling time.* However, there is no unique definition for the settling time. We may, for example, *approximate* the learning curve by a single exponential with *average time constant* τ_{av}, and so use τ_{av} as a rough measure of the settling time. The smaller the value of τ_{av} is, the faster will be the settling time.

To a good degree of approximation, the misadjustment M of the LMS algorithm is directly proportional to the learning-rate parameter η, whereas the average time constant τ_{av} is inversely proportional to the learning-rate parameter η (Widrow and Stearns, 1985; Haykin, 1991). We therefore have conflicting results in the sense that if the learning-rate parameter is reduced so as to reduce the misadjustment, then the settling time of the LMS algorithm is increased. Conversely, if the learning-rate parameter is increased so as to accelerate the learning process, then the misadjustment is increased. Careful attention has therefore to be given to the choice of the learning parameter η in the design of the LMS algorithm in order to produce a satisfactory overall performance.

5.7 Learning-Rate Annealing Schedules

The difficulties encountered with the LMS algorithm may be attributed to the fact that the learning-rate parameter is maintained constant throughout the computation, as shown by

$$\eta(n) = \eta_0 \qquad \text{for all } n \tag{5.54}$$

This is the simplest possible form the learning-rate parameter can assume. In contrast, in *stochastic* approximation, which goes back to the classic paper by Robbins and Monro (1951), the learning-rate parameter is time-varying. The particular time-varying form most commonly used in the stochastic approximation literature is described by

$$\eta(n) = \frac{c}{n} \tag{5.55}$$

where c is a constant. Such a choice is indeed sufficient to guarantee convergence of the stochastic approximation algorithm (Kushner and Clark, 1978; Ljung, 1977). However, when the constant c is large, there is a danger of parameter blowup for small n.

Darken and Moody (1992) have proposed the use of a so-called *search-then-converge schedule,* defined by

$$\eta(n) = \frac{\eta_0}{1 + (n/\tau)} \tag{5.56}$$

where η_0 and τ are constants. In the early stages of adaptation involving a number of iterations n small compared to the *search time constant* τ, the learning-rate parameter $\eta(n)$ is approximately equal to η_0 and the algorithm operates essentially as the "standard" LMS algorithm, as indicated in Fig. 5.5. Hence, by choosing a high value for η_0 within the permissible range, it is hoped that the adjustable weights of the filter will find and hover about a "good" set of values. Then, for a number of iterations n large compared to the search time constant τ, the learning-rate parameter $\eta(n)$ approximates as c/n, where $c = \tau\eta_0$, as shown in Fig. 5.5. The algorithm now operates as a traditional stochastic approximation algorithm, and the weights converge to their optimum values. It thus appears that the search-then-converge scheme combines the desirable features of the standard LMS and traditional stochastic approximation algorithms. The specific learning-rate parameter $\eta(n)$ given in Eq. (5.56) is the simplest member of a class of search-and-converge schedules described in Darken and Moody (1992).

Sutton (1992b) has proposed even more elaborate schemes for adjusting the learning-rate parameter $\eta(n)$, which are based in part on connectionist learning methods, and which result in a significant improvement in performance. The new algorithms described by Sutton are of the same order of complexity as the standard LMS algorithm, $O(p)$, where p is the number of adjustable parameters.

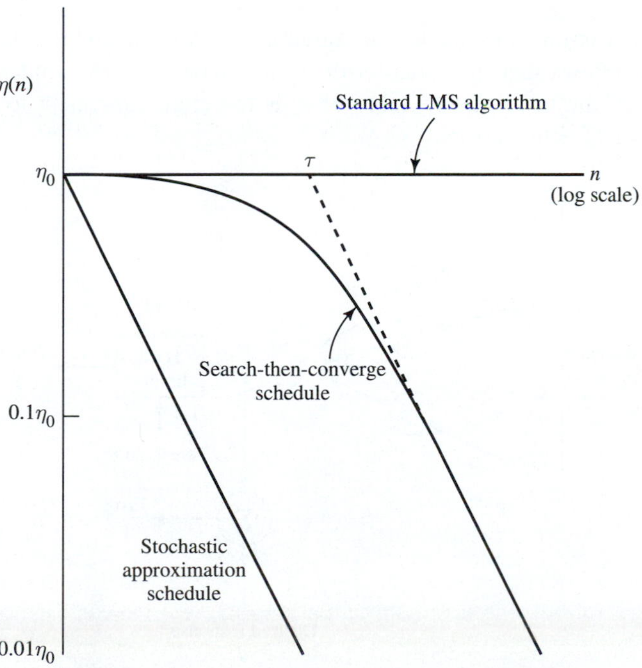

FIGURE 5.5 Learning-rate annealing schedules.

5.8 Adaline

The *Adaline* (*ada*ptive *line*ar element), originally conceived by Widrow and Hoff, is an adaptive pattern-classification machine that uses the LMS algorithm for its operation (Widrow and Lehr, 1990; Widrow and Hoff, 1960).

A block diagram of the Adaline is shown in Fig. 5.6. It consists of a linear combiner, a hard limiter, and a mechanism for adjusting the weights. The inputs $x_1, x_2, \dots, x_p$ applied to the linear combiner are assigned the value -1 or $+1$. A variable threshold θ (whose value lies somewhere between 0 and $+1$) is applied to the hard limiter. The Adaline is also supplied with a desired output d whose value is $+1$ or -1. The weights $w_1, w_2, \dots, w_p$ and threshold θ are all adjusted in accordance with the LMS algorithm. In particular, the linear combiner output u, produced in response to the inputs $x_1, x_2, \dots,$ x_p, is subtracted from the desired output d to produce the error signal e. The error signal e is, in turn, used to actuate the LMS algorithm in the manner described in Section 5.4.

The Adaline output y is obtained by passing the linear combiner output u through the hard limiter. We thus have

$$y = \begin{cases} +1 & \text{if } u \geq \theta \\ -1 & \text{if } u < \theta \end{cases} \tag{5.57}$$

Note, however, that the control action of the LMS algorithm depends on the error signal e measured as the difference between the desired output d and the linear combiner output u *before* quantization rather than the actual error e_a between the desired output d and the actual Adaline output y.

The objective of the adaptive process in the Adaline may be stated as follows:

> *Given a set of input patterns and the associated desired outputs, find the optimum set of synaptic weights* $w_1, w_2, \dots, w_p$, *and threshold* θ, *to minimize the mean-square value of the actual error* e_a.

Since the values assumed by the actual output of the Adaline and the desired output are $+1$ or -1, it follows that the actual error e_a may have only the values $+2$, 0, or -2. Minimization of the mean-square value of e_a is therefore equivalent to minimizing the average number of actual errors.

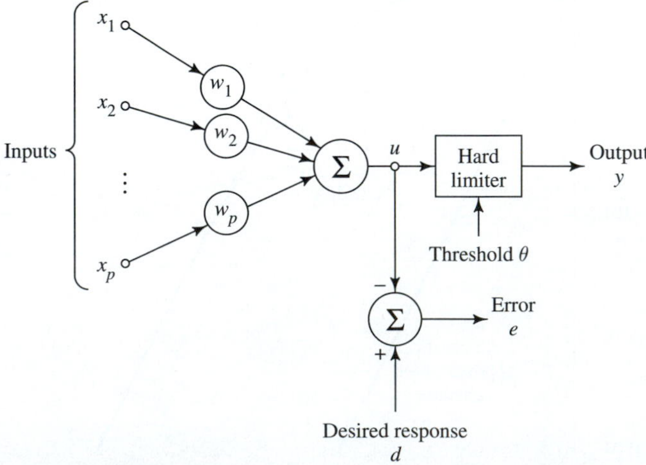

FIGURE 5.6 Block diagram of Adaline.

During the training phase of the Adaline, crude geometric patterns are fed to the machine. The machine then learns something from each pattern, and thereby experiences a change in its design. The total experience gained by the machine is stored in the values assumed by the weights $w_1, w_2, \ldots, w_p$ and the threshold θ. The Adaline may be trained on undistorted, noise-free patterns by repeating them over and over until the iterative search process for the optimum setting of the weights converges, or it can be trained on a sequence of noisy patterns on a one-pass basis such that the process converges in a statistical manner (Widrow and Hoff, 1960). Combinations of these methods may also be accommodated simultaneously. After training of the Adaline is completed, it may be used to classify the original patterns and noisy or distorted versions of them.

5.9 Discussion

The LMS algorithm has established itself as an important functional block of *adaptive signal processing.* It offers some highly desirable features:

- Simplicity of implementation, be that in software or hardware form.
- Ability to operate satisfactorily in an unknown environment.
- Ability to track time variations of input statistics.

Indeed, the simplicity of the LMS algorithm has made it the *standard* against which other linear adaptive filtering algorithms are benchmarked.

The formulation of the LMS algorithm presented in this chapter has been from the viewpoint of *spatial filtering.* It may equally well be applied to solve *temporal* filtering problems. In the latter case, the filter takes on the form of a *tapped-delay-line filter,* as depicted in the signal-flow graph of Fig. 5.7. The input vector $\mathbf{x}(n)$ is now defined by the tap inputs of the filter, as shown by

$$\mathbf{x}(n) = [x(n), x(n-1), \ldots, x(n-p+1)]^T \tag{5.58}$$

where p is the number of taps. Thus, the tap-input $x(n-k)$ in the tapped-delay-line filter of Fig. 5.7 plays a role similar to that of the sensor input $x_k(n)$ in the spatial filter of Fig. 5.1. The function of the LMS algorithm is to adjust the tap weights of the filter in Fig. 5.7 so as to make the filter output $y(n)$ approximate a desired response $d(n)$ in a least-mean-square sense.

Regardless of the form of the LMS algorithm, its operation consists of two basic processes forming a feedback loop:

- *Adaptive process,* which involves the adjustments of the free parameters of a filter.
- *Filtering process,* which culminates in the computation of an error signal; the error signal is in turn used to actuate the adaptive process, thereby closing the feedback loop.

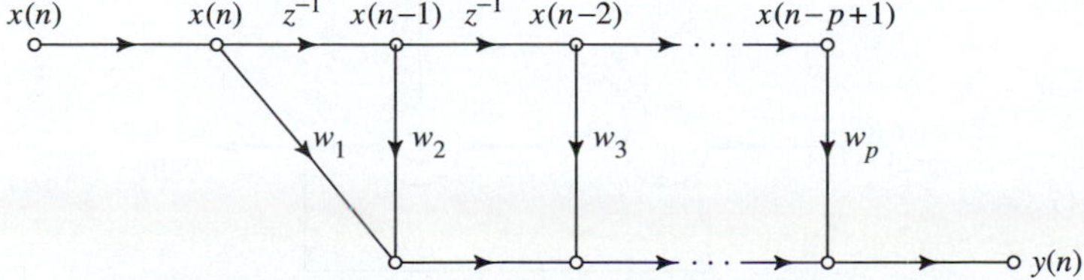

FIGURE 5.7 Signal-flow graph of tapped-delay-line filter.

For a detailed study of the LMS algorithm and other linear adaptive filtering algorithms, and their various applications, the reader is referred to Haykin (1991), and Widrow and Stearns (1985).

PROBLEMS

5.1 Consider the method of steepest descent involving a single weight $w(n)$. Do the following:

(a) Determine the mean-squared error $J(n)$ as a function of $w(n)$.

(b) Find the optimum solution $w_o(n)$ and the minimum mean-squared error $J_{\min}$.

5.2 The correlation matrix $\mathbf{R}_x$ of the input vector $\mathbf{x}(n)$ in the LMS algorithm is defined by

$$\mathbf{R}_x = \begin{bmatrix} 1 & 0.5 \\ 0.5 & 1 \end{bmatrix}$$

Define the range of values for the learning-rate parameter η of the LMS algorithm for (a) the algorithm to be convergent in the mean, and (b) for it to be convergent in the mean square.

5.3 The *normalized LMS algorithm* is described by the following recursion for the weight vector:

$$\hat{\mathbf{w}}(n+1) = \hat{\mathbf{w}}(n) + \frac{\eta}{\|\mathbf{x}(n)\|^2} e(n)\mathbf{x}(n)$$

where η is a positive constant and $\|\mathbf{x}(n)\|$ is the Euclidean norm of the input vector $\mathbf{x}(n)$. The error signal $e(n)$ is defined by

$$e(n) = d(n) - \mathbf{w}^T(n)\mathbf{x}(n)$$

where $d(n)$ is the desired response. For the normalized LMS algorithm to be convergent in the mean square, show that

$$0 < \eta < 2$$

5.4 The LMS algorithm is used to implement the dual-input, single-weight adaptive noise canceller shown in Fig. P5.4. Set up the equations that define the operation of this algorithm.

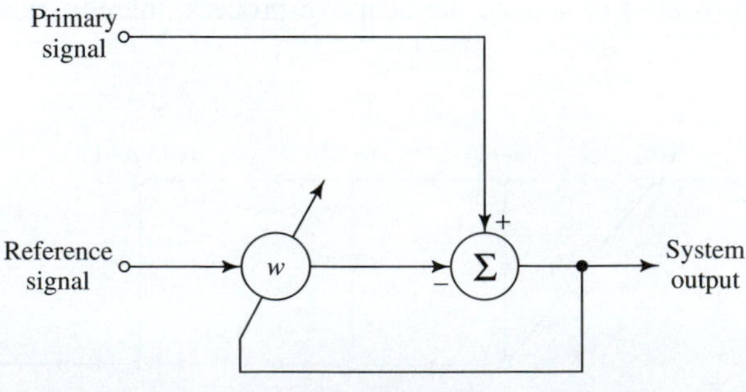

FIGURE P5.4

5.5 The signal-flow graph of Fig. P5.5 shows a linear predictor with its input vector made up of the samples $x(n-1), x(n-2), \ldots, x(n-p)$, where p is the prediction order. The requirement is to use the LMS algorithm to make a prediction $\hat{x}(n)$ of the input sample $x(n)$. Set up the recursions that may be used to compute the tap weight $w_1, w_2, \ldots, w_p$ of the predictor.

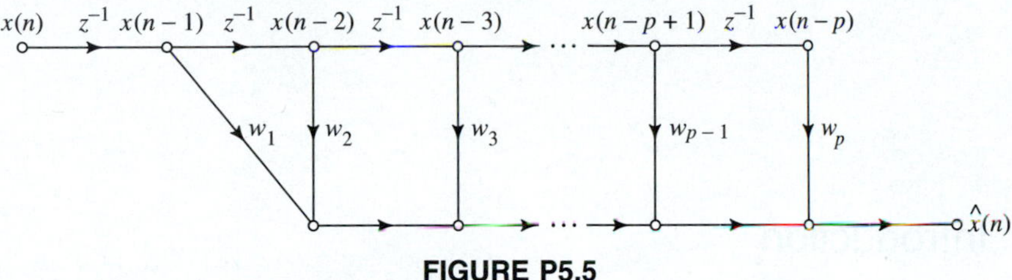

FIGURE P5.5

5.6 Compare the distinguishing features of the LMS algorithm and those of a single-layer perceptron involving the use of a single neuron.

CHAPTER 6

Multilayer Perceptrons

6.1 Introduction

In this chapter we study an important class of neural networks, namely, multilayer feedforward networks. Typically, the network consists of a set of sensory units (source nodes) that constitute the *input layer,* one or more *hidden layers* of computation nodes, and an *output layer* of computation nodes. The input signal propagates through the network in a forward direction, on a layer-by-layer basis. These neural networks are commonly referred to as *multilayer perceptrons* (MLPs), which represent a generalization of the single-layer perceptron considered in Chapter 4.

Multilayer perceptrons have been applied successfully to solve some difficult and diverse problems by training them in a supervised manner with a highly popular algorithm known as the *error back-propagation algorithm.* This algorithm is based on the *error-correction learning rule.* As such, it may be viewed as a generalization of an equally popular adaptive filtering algorithm: the ubiquitous least-mean-square (LMS) algorithm described in Chapter 5 for the special case of a single linear neuron model.

Basically, the error back-propagation process consists of two passes through the different layers of the network: a forward pass and a backward pass. In the *forward pass,* an activity pattern (input vector) is applied to the sensory nodes of the network, and its effect propagates through the network, layer by layer. Finally, a set of outputs is produced as the actual response of the network. During the forward pass the synaptic weights of the network are all fixed. During the *backward pass,* on the other hand, the synaptic weights are all adjusted in accordance with the error-correction rule. Specifically, the actual response of the network is subtracted from a desired (target) response to produce an *error signal.* This error signal is then propagated backward through the network, against the direction of synaptic connections—hence the name "error back-propagation." The synaptic weights are adjusted so as to make the actual response of the network move closer to the desired response. The error back-propagation algorithm is also referred to in the literature as the *back-propagation algorithm,* or simply *back-prop.* Henceforth, we will refer to it as the back-propagation algorithm. The learning process performed with the algorithm is called *back-propagation learning.*

A multilayer perceptron has three distinctive characteristics:

1. The model of each neuron in the network includes a *nonlinearity* at the output end. The important point to emphasize here is that the nonlinearity is *smooth* (i.e., differentiable everywhere), as opposed to the hard-limiting used in Rosenblatt's perceptron. A commonly used form of nonlinearity that satisfies this requirement is a *sigmoidal nonlinearity* defined by the *logistic function:*

$$y_j = \frac{1}{1 + \exp(-v_j)}$$

where v_j is the net internal activity level of neuron j, and y_j is the output of the neuron. The presence of nonlinearities is important because, otherwise, the input–output relation of the network could be reduced to that of a single-layer perceptron. Moreover, the use of the logistic function is biologically motivated, since it attempts to account for the refractory phase of real neurons (Pineda, 1988b).

2. The network contains one or more layers of *hidden neurons* that are not part of the input or output of the network. These hidden neurons enable the network to learn complex tasks by extracting progressively more meaningful features from the input patterns (vectors).

3. The network exhibits a high degree of *connectivity,* determined by the synapses of the network. A change in the connectivity of the network requires a change in the population of synaptic connections or their weights.

Indeed, it is through the combination of these characteristics together with the ability to learn from experience through training that the multilayer perceptron derives its computing power. These same characteristics, however, are also responsible for the deficiencies in our present state of knowledge on the behavior of the network. First, the presence of a distributed form of nonlinearity and the high connectivity of the network make the theoretical analysis of a multilayer perceptron difficult to undertake. Second, the use of hidden neurons makes the learning process harder to visualize. In an implicit sense, the learning process must decide which features of the input pattern should be represented by the hidden neurons. The learning process is therefore made more difficult because the search has to be conducted in a much larger space of possible functions, and a choice has to be made between alternative representations of the input pattern (Hinton, 1987).

Research interest in multilayer feedforward networks dates back to the pioneering work of Rosenblatt (1962) on *perceptrons* and that of Widrow and his students on Madalines (Widrow, 1962). *Madalines* were constructed with many inputs, many Adaline elements in the first layer, and with various logic devices such as AND, OR, and majority-vote-taker elements in the second layer; the Adaline was described in Section 5.8. The Madalines of the 1960s had adaptive first layers and fixed threshold functions in the second (output) layers (Widrow and Lehr, 1990). However, the tool that was missing in those early days of multilayer feedforward networks was what we now call back-propagation learning.

The usage of the term ''back-propagation'' appears to have evolved after 1985. However, the basic idea of back-propagation was first described by Werbos in his Ph.D. thesis (Werbos, 1974), in the context of general networks with neural networks representing a special case. Subsequently, it was rediscovered by Rumelhart, Hinton, and Williams (1986b), and popularized through the publication of the seminal book entitled *Parallel Distributed Processing* (Rumelhart and McClelland, 1986). A similar generalization of the algorithm was derived independently by Parker in 1985, and interestingly enough, a roughly similar learning algorithm was also studied by LeCun (1985).

The development of the back-propagation algorithm represents a ''landmark'' in neural networks in that it provides a *computationally efficient* method for the training of multilayer perceptrons. Although it cannot be claimed that the back-propagation algorithm can provide a solution for all solvable problems, it is fair to say that it has put to rest the pessimism about learning in multilayer machines that may have been inferred from the book by Minsky and Papert (1969).

Organization of the Chapter

In this rather long chapter we consider both the theory and applications of multilayer perceptrons. We begin with some preliminaries in Section 6.2 to pave the way for the derivation of the back-propagation algorithm. In Section 6.3 we present a detailed derivation of the algorithm, using the chain rule of calculus. We take a traditional approach in the derivation presented here. A summary of the back-propagation algorithm is presented in Section 6.4. Then, in Section 6.5, we address the issue of initialization, which plays a key role in successful applications of the back-propagation algorithm. In Section 6.6 we illustrate the use of the back-propagation algorithm by solving the XOR problem, an interesting problem that cannot be solved by the single-layer perceptron.

In Section 6.7 we present some practical hints for making the back-propagation algorithm work better.

In Section 6.8 we address the development of a decision rule for the use of a back-propagation network to solve the statistical pattern-recognition problem. Then, in Section 6.9, we use a computer experiment to illustrate the application of back-propagation learning to distinguish between two classes of overlapping two-dimensional Gaussian distributions.

In Sections 6.10 through 6.14 we consider some basic issues relating to back-propagation learning. In Section 6.10 we discuss the issue of generalization, which is the very essence of back-propagation learning. This is naturally followed by Section 6.11 with a brief discussion of cross-validation, a standard tool in statistics, and how it can be applied to the design of neural networks. In Section 6.12 we consider the approximate realization of any continuous input–output mapping by a multilayer perceptron. In Section 6.13 we discuss the fundamental role of back-propagation in computing partial derivatives. In Section 6.14 we pause to summarize the important advantages and limitations of back-propagation learning.

In Section 6.15 we discuss some heuristics that provide guidelines for how to accelerate the rate of convergence of back-propagation learning. These heuristics are used to formulate a form of learning called fuzzy back-propagation, which is presented in Section 6.16. In Section 6.17 we describe procedures to orderly "prune" a multilayer perceptron and maintain (and frequently, improve) overall performance; network pruning is desirable when the use of VLSI technology is being considered for the hardware implementation of multilayer perceptrons.

In Sections 6.18 and 6.19 we reexamine the supervised learning of a multilayer perceptron as a problem in system identification or function optimization, respectively. In Section 6.20 we consider the use of a multilayer perceptron for learning a probability distribution. We conclude the chapter with some general discussion in Section 6.21 and important applications of back-propagation learning in Section 6.22.

6.2 Some Preliminaries

Figure 6.1 shows the architectural graph of a multilayer perceptron with two hidden layers. To set the stage in its general form, the network shown here is *fully connected,* which means that a neuron in any layer of the network is connected to all the nodes/neurons in the previous layer. Signal flow through the network progresses in a forward direction, from left to right and on a layer-by-layer basis.

Figure 6.2 depicts a portion of the multilayer perceptron. In this network, two kinds of signals are identified (Parker, 1987):

1. *Function Signals.* A function signal is an input signal (stimulus) that comes in at the input end of the network, propagates forward (neuron-by-neuron) through the network, and emerges at the output end of the network as an output signal. We refer to such a signal as a "function signal" for two reasons. First, it is presumed

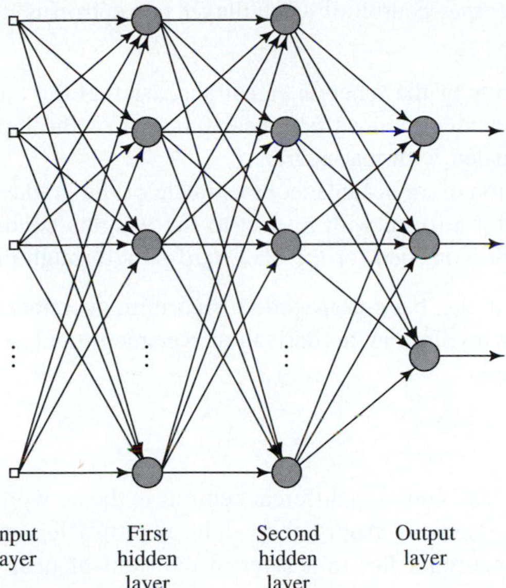

FIGURE 6.1 Architectural graph of a multilayer perceptron with two hidden layers.

to perform a useful function at the output of the network. Second, at each neuron of the network through which a function signal passes, the signal is calculated as a function of the inputs and associated weights applied to that neuron.

2. *Error Signals.* An error signal originates at an output neuron of the network, and propagates backward (layer by layer) through the network. We refer to it as an "error signal" because its computation by every neuron of the network involves an error-dependent function in one form or another.

The output neurons (computational nodes) constitute the output layer of the network. The remaining neurons (computational nodes) constitute hidden layers of the network. Thus the hidden units are not part of the output or input of the network—hence their designation as "hidden." The first hidden layer is fed from the input layer made up of sensory units (source nodes); the resulting outputs of the first hidden layer are in turn applied to the next hidden layer; and so on for the rest of the network.

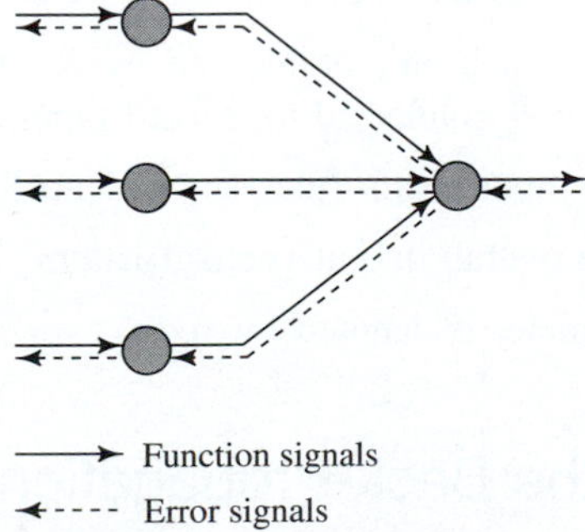

FIGURE 6.2 Illustration of the directions of two basic signal flows in a multilayer perceptron, namely, forward propagation of function signals and back-propagation of error signals.

Each hidden or output neuron of a multilayer perceptron is designed to perform two computations:

1. The computation of the function signal appearing at the output of a neuron, which is expressed as a continuous nonlinear function of the input signals and synaptic weights associated with that neuron
2. The computation of an instantaneous estimate of the gradient vector (i.e., the gradients of the error surface with respect to the weights connected to the inputs of a neuron), which is needed for the backward pass through the network

The derivation of the back-propagation algorithm is rather involved. To ease the mathematical burden involved in this derivation, we first present a summary of the notations used in the derivation.

Notation

- The indices i, j, and k refer to different neurons in the network; with signals propagating through the network from left to right, neuron j lies in a layer to the right of neuron i, and neuron k lies in a layer to the right of neuron j when neuron j is a hidden unit.
- The iteration n refers to the nth training pattern (example) presented to the network.
- The symbol $\mathscr{E}(n)$ refers to the instantaneous sum of error squares at iteration n. The average of $\mathscr{E}(n)$ over all values of n (i.e., the entire training set) yields the average squared error $\mathscr{E}_{av}$.
- The symbol $e_j(n)$ refers to the error signal at the output of neuron j for iteration n.
- The symbol $d_j(n)$ refers to the desired response for neuron j and is used to compute $e_j(n)$.
- The symbol $y_j(n)$ refers to the function signal appearing at the output of neuron j at iteration n.
- The symbol $w_{ji}(n)$ denotes the synaptic weight connecting the output of neuron i to the input of neuron j at iteration n. The correction applied to this weight at iteration n is denoted by $\Delta w_{ji}(n)$.
- The net internal activity level of neuron j at iteration n is denoted by $v_j(n)$; it constitutes the signal applied to the nonlinearity associated with neuron j.
- The activation function describing the input–output functional relationship of the nonlinearity associated with neuron j is denoted by $\varphi_j(\cdot)$.
- The threshold applied to neuron j is denoted by θ_j; its effect is represented by a synapse of weight $w_{j0} = \theta_j$ connected to a fixed input equal to -1.
- The ith element of the input vector (pattern) is denoted by $x_i(n)$.
- The kth element of the overall output vector (pattern) is denoted by $o_k(n)$.
- The learning-rate parameter is denoted by η.

6.3 Derivation of the Back-Propagation Algorithm

The error signal at the output of neuron j at iteration n (i.e., presentation of the nth training pattern) is defined by

$$e_j(n) = d_j(n) - y_j(n), \qquad \text{neuron } j \text{ is an output node} \tag{6.1}$$

We define the instantaneous value of the squared error for neuron j as $\frac{1}{2}e_j^2(n)$. Correspondingly, the instantaneous value $\mathscr{E}(n)$ of the sum of squared errors is obtained by summing $\frac{1}{2}e_j^2(n)$ over *all neurons in the output layer;* these are the only "visible" neurons for which error signals can be calculated. The *instantaneous sum of squared errors* of the network is thus written as

$$\mathscr{E}(n) = \frac{1}{2} \sum_{j \in C} e_j^2(n) \tag{6.2}$$

where the set C includes all the neurons in the output layer of the network. Let N denote the total number of patterns (examples) contained in the training set. The *average squared error* is obtained by summing $\mathscr{E}(n)$ over all n and then normalizing with respect to the set size N, as shown by

$$\mathscr{E}_{\text{av}} = \frac{1}{N} \sum_{n=1}^{N} \mathscr{E}(n) \tag{6.3}$$

The instantaneous sum of error squares $\mathscr{E}(n)$, and therefore the average squared error $\mathscr{E}_{\text{av}}$, is a function of all the free parameters (i.e., synaptic weights and thresholds) of the network. For a given training set, $\mathscr{E}_{\text{av}}$ represents the *cost function* as the measure of training set learning performance. The objective of the learning process is to adjust the free parameters of the network so as to minimize $\mathscr{E}_{\text{av}}$. To do this minimization we use an approximation similar in rationale to that we used for the derivation of the LMS algorithm in Chapter 5. Specifically, we consider a simple method of training in which the weights are updated on a *pattern-by-pattern* basis. The adjustments to the weights are made in accordance with the respective errors computed for *each* pattern presented to the network. The arithmetic average of these individual weight changes over the training set is therefore an *estimate* of the true change that would result from modifying the weights based on minimizing the cost function $\mathscr{E}_{\text{av}}$ over the entire training set.

Consider then Fig. 6.3, which depicts neuron j being fed by a set of function signals produced by a layer of neurons to its left. The net internal activity level $v_j(n)$ produced

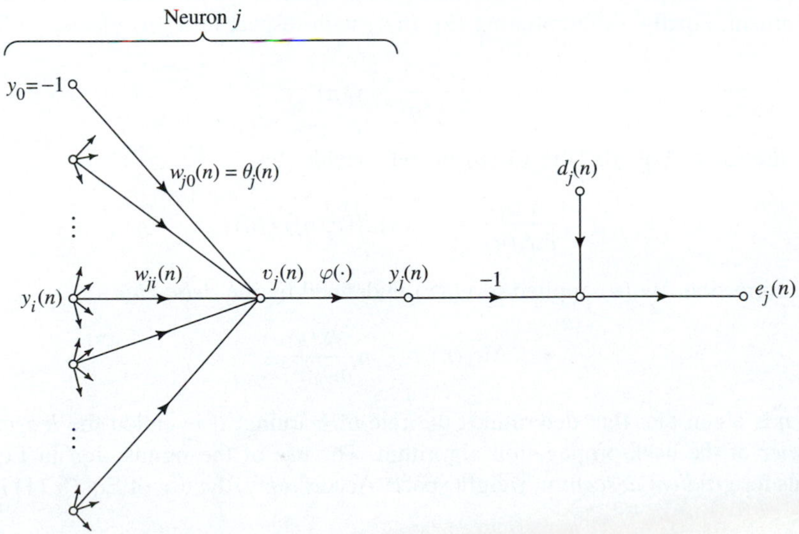

FIGURE 6.3 Signal-flow graph highlighting the details of output neuron *j*.

at the input of the nonlinearity associated with neuron j is therefore

$$v_j(n) = \sum_{i=0}^{p} w_{ji}(n) y_i(n) \tag{6.4}$$

where p is the total number of inputs (excluding the threshold) applied to neuron j. The synaptic weight w_{j0} (corresponding to the fixed input $y_0 = -1$) equals the threshold θ_j applied to neuron j. Hence the function signal $y_j(n)$ appearing at the output of neuron j at iteration n is

$$y_j(n) = \varphi_j(v_j(n)) \tag{6.5}$$

In a manner similar to the LMS algorithm, the back-propagation algorithm applies a correction $\Delta w_{ji}(n)$ to the synaptic weight $w_{ji}(n)$, which is proportional to the instantaneous gradient $\partial \mathscr{E}(n)/\partial w_{ji}(n)$. According to the chain rule, we may express this gradient as follows:

$$\frac{\partial \mathscr{E}(n)}{\partial w_{ji}(n)} = \frac{\partial \mathscr{E}(n)}{\partial e_j(n)} \frac{\partial e_j(n)}{\partial y_j(n)} \frac{\partial y_j(n)}{\partial v_j(n)} \frac{\partial v_j(n)}{\partial w_{ji}(n)} \tag{6.6}$$

The gradient $\partial \mathscr{E}(n)/\partial w_{ji}(n)$ represents a *sensitivity factor*, determining the direction of search in weight space for the synaptic weight w_{ji}.

Differentiating both sides of Eq. (6.2) with respect to $e_j(n)$, we get

$$\frac{\partial \mathscr{E}(n)}{\partial e_j(n)} = e_j(n) \tag{6.7}$$

Differentiating both sides of Eq. (6.1) with respect to $y_j(n)$, we get

$$\frac{\partial e_j(n)}{\partial y_j(n)} = -1 \tag{6.8}$$

Next, differentiating Eq. (6.5) with respect to $v_j(n)$, we get

$$\frac{\partial y_j(n)}{\partial v_j(n)} = \varphi_j'(v_j(n)) \tag{6.9}$$

where the use of prime (on the right-hand side) signifies differentiation with respect to the argument. Finally, differentiating Eq. (6.4) with respect to $w_{ji}(n)$ yields

$$\frac{\partial v_j(n)}{\partial w_{ji}(n)} = y_i(n) \tag{6.10}$$

Hence, the use of Eqs. (6.7) to (6.10) in (6.6) yields

$$\frac{\partial \mathscr{E}(n)}{\partial w_{ji}(n)} = -e_j(n)\varphi_j'(v_j(n))y_i(n) \tag{6.11}$$

The correction $\Delta w_{ji}(n)$ applied to $w_{ji}(n)$ is defined by the *delta rule*

$$\Delta w_{ji}(n) = -\eta \frac{\partial \mathscr{E}(n)}{\partial w_{ji}(n)} \tag{6.12}$$

where η is a constant that determines the rate of learning; it is called the *learning-rate parameter* of the back-propagation algorithm. The use of the minus sign in Eq. (6.12) accounts for *gradient descent* in weight space. Accordingly, the use of Eq. (6.11) in (6.12) yields

$$\Delta w_{ji}(n) = \eta \delta_j(n) y_i(n) \tag{6.13}$$

where the *local gradient* $\delta_j(n)$ is itself defined by

$$\delta_j(n) = -\frac{\partial \mathscr{E}(n)}{\partial e_j(n)} \frac{\partial e_j(n)}{\partial y_j(n)} \frac{\partial y_j(n)}{\partial v_j(n)}$$

$$= e_j(n)\varphi_j'(v_j(n)) \tag{6.14}$$

The local gradient points to required changes in synaptic weights. According to Eq. (6.14), the local gradient $\delta_j(n)$ for output neuron j is equal to the product of the corresponding error signal $e_j(n)$ and the derivative $\varphi_j'(v_j(n))$ of the associated activation function.

From Eqs. (6.13) and (6.14) we note that a key factor involved in the calculation of the weight adjustment $\Delta w_{ji}(n)$ is the error signal $e_j(n)$ at the output of neuron j. In this context, we may identify two distinct cases, depending on where in the network neuron j is located. In case I, neuron j is an output node. This case is simple to handle, because each output node of the network is supplied with a desired response of its own, making it a straightforward matter to calculate the associated error signal. In case II, neuron j is a hidden node. Even though hidden neurons are not directly accessible, they share responsibility for any error made at the output of the network. The question, however, is to know how to penalize or reward hidden neurons for their share of the responsibility. This problem is indeed the *credit-assignment problem* considered in Section 2.6. It is solved in an elegant fashion by back-propagating the error signals through the network.

In the sequel, cases I and II are considered in turn.

Case I: Neuron *j* Is an Output Node

When neuron j is located in the output layer of the network, it would be supplied with a desired response of its own. Hence we may use Eq. (6.1) to compute the error signal $e_j(n)$ associated with this neuron; see Fig. 6.3. Having determined $e_j(n)$, it is a straightforward matter to compute the local gradient $\delta_j(n)$ using Eq. (6.14).

Case II: Neuron *j* Is a Hidden Node

When neuron j is located in a hidden layer of the network, there is no specified desired response for that neuron. Accordingly, the error signal for a hidden neuron would have to be determined recursively in terms of the error signals of all the neurons to which that hidden neuron is directly connected; this is where the development of the back-propagation algorithm gets complicated. Consider the situation depicted in Fig. 6.4, which depicts neuron j as a hidden node of the network. According to Eq. (6.14), we may redefine the local gradient $\delta_j(n)$ for hidden neuron j as

$$\delta_j(n) = -\frac{\partial \mathscr{E}(n)}{\partial y_j(n)} \frac{\partial y_j(n)}{\partial v_j(n)}$$

$$= -\frac{\partial \mathscr{E}(n)}{\partial y_j(n)} \varphi_j'(v_j(n)), \qquad \text{neuron } j \text{ is hidden} \tag{6.15}$$

where, in the second line, we have made use of Eq. (6.9). To calculate the partial derivative $\partial \mathscr{E}(n)/\partial y_j(n)$, we may proceed as follows. From Fig. 6.4 we see that

$$\mathscr{E}(n) = \frac{1}{2}\sum_{k \in C} e_k^2(n), \qquad \text{neuron } k \text{ is an output node} \tag{6.16}$$

which is a rewrite of Eq. (6.2) except for the use of index k in place of index j. We have done so in order to avoid confusion with the use of index j that refers to a hidden neuron

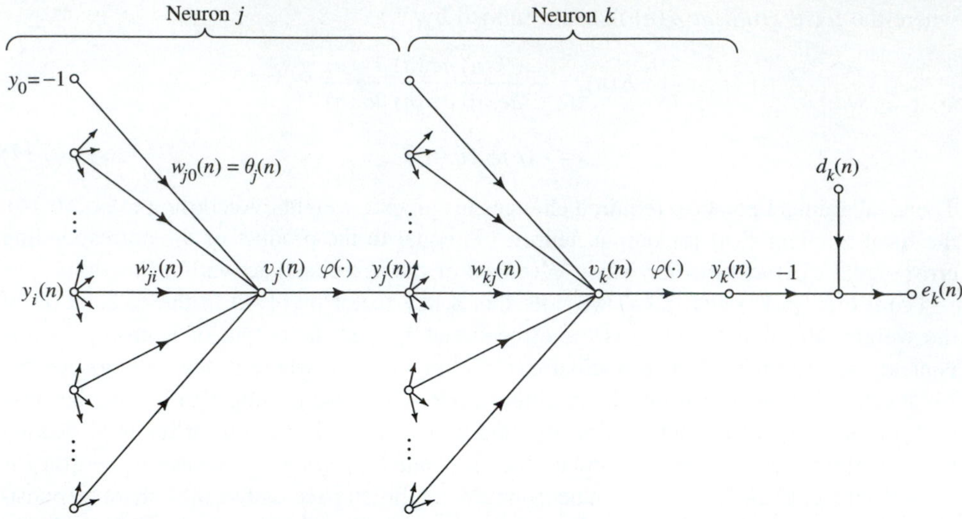

FIGURE 6.4 Signal-flow graph highlighting the details of output neuron *k* connected to hidden neuron *j*.

under case II. In any event, differentiating Eq. (6.16) with respect to the function signal $y_j(n)$, we get

$$\frac{\partial \mathscr{E}(n)}{\partial y_j(n)} = \sum_k e_k \frac{\partial e_k(n)}{\partial y_j(n)} \tag{6.17}$$

Next, we use the chain rule for the partial derivative $\partial e_k(n)/\partial y_j(n)$, and thus rewrite Eq. (6.17) in the equivalent form

$$\frac{\partial \mathscr{E}(n)}{\partial y_j(n)} = \sum_k e_k(n) \frac{\partial e_k(n)}{\partial v_k(n)} \frac{\partial v_k(n)}{\partial y_j(n)} \tag{6.18}$$

However, from Fig. 6.4, we note that

$$\begin{aligned} e_k(n) &= d_k(n) - y_k(n) \\ &= d_k(n) - \varphi_k(v_k(n)), \qquad \text{neuron } k \text{ is an output node} \end{aligned} \tag{6.19}$$

Hence

$$\frac{\partial e_k(n)}{\partial v_k(n)} = -\varphi_k'(v_k(n)) \tag{6.20}$$

We also note from Fig. 6.4 that for neuron k, the net internal activity level is

$$v_k(n) = \sum_{j=0}^{q} w_{kj}(n) y_j(n) \tag{6.21}$$

where q is the total number of inputs (excluding the threshold) applied to neuron k. Here again, the synaptic weight $w_{k0}(n)$ is equal to the threshold $\theta_k(n)$ applied to neuron k, and the corresponding input y_0 is fixed at the value -1. In any event, differentiating Eq. (6.21) with respect to $y_j(n)$ yields

$$\frac{\partial v_k(n)}{\partial y_j(n)} = w_{kj}(n) \tag{6.22}$$

Thus, using Eqs. (6.20) and (6.22) in (6.18), we get the desired partial derivative:

$$\begin{aligned}\frac{\partial \mathscr{E}(n)}{\partial y_j(n)} &= -\sum_k e_k(n)\varphi_k'(v_k(n))w_{kj}(n) \\ &= -\sum_k \delta_k(n)w_{kj}(n) \end{aligned} \tag{6.23}$$

where, in the second line, we have used the definition of the local gradient $\delta_k(n)$ given in Eq. (6.14) with the index k substituted for j.

Finally, using Eq. (6.23) in (6.15), we get the local gradient $\delta_j(n)$ for hidden neuron j, after rearranging terms, as follows:

$$\delta_j(n) = \varphi_j'(v_j(n))\sum_k \delta_k(n)w_{kj}(n), \qquad \text{neuron } j \text{ is hidden} \tag{6.24}$$

The factor $\varphi_j'(v_j(n))$ involved in the computation of the local gradient $\delta_j(n)$ in Eq. (6.24) depends solely on the activation function associated with hidden neuron j. The remaining factor involved in this computation, namely, the summation over k, depends on two sets of terms. The first set of terms, the $\delta_k(n)$, requires knowledge of the error signals $e_k(n)$, for all those neurons that lie in the layer to the immediate right of hidden neuron j, and that are directly connected to neuron j; see Fig. 6.4. The second set of terms, the $w_{kj}(n)$, consists of the synaptic weights associated with these connections.

We may now summarize the relations that we have derived for the back-propagation algorithm. First, the correction $\Delta w_{ji}(n)$ applied to the synaptic weight connecting neuron i to neuron j is defined by the delta rule:

$$\begin{pmatrix} \textit{Weight} \\ \textit{correction} \\ \Delta w_{ji}(n) \end{pmatrix} = \begin{pmatrix} \textit{learning-} \\ \textit{rate parameter} \\ \eta \end{pmatrix} \cdot \begin{pmatrix} \textit{local} \\ \textit{gradient} \\ \delta_j(n) \end{pmatrix} \cdot \begin{pmatrix} \textit{input signal} \\ \textit{of neuron } j \\ y_i(n) \end{pmatrix} \tag{6.25}$$

Second, the local gradient $\delta_j(n)$ depends on whether neuron j is an output node or a hidden node:

1. If neuron j is an output node, $\delta_j(n)$ equals the product of the derivative $\varphi_j'(v_j(n))$ and the error signal $e_j(n)$, both of which are associated with neuron j; see Eq. (6.14).
2. If neuron j is a hidden node, $\delta_j(n)$ equals the product of the associated derivative $\varphi_j'(v_j(n))$ and the weighted sum of the δ's computed for the neurons in the next hidden or output layer that are connected to neuron j; see Eq. (6.24).

The Two Passes of Computation

In the application of the back-propagation algorithm, two distinct passes of computation may be distinguished. The first pass is referred to as the forward pass, and the second one as the backward pass.

In the *forward pass* the synaptic weights remain unaltered throughout the network, and the function signals of the network are computed on a neuron-by-neuron basis. Specifically, the function signal appearing at the output of neuron j is computed as

$$y_j(n) = \varphi(v_j(n)) \tag{6.26}$$

where $v_j(n)$ is the net internal activity level of neuron j, defined by

$$v_j(n) = \sum_{i=0}^{p} w_{ji}(n)y_i(n) \tag{6.27}$$

where p is the total number of inputs (excluding the threshold) applied to neuron j, and $w_{ji}(n)$ is the synaptic weight connecting neuron i to neuron j, and $y_i(n)$ is the input signal of neuron j or, equivalently, the function signal appearing at the output of neuron i. If neuron j is in the first hidden layer of the network, then the index i refers to the ith input terminal of the network, for which we write

$$y_i(n) = x_i(n) \tag{6.28}$$

where $x_i(n)$ is the ith element of the input vector (pattern). If, on the other hand, neuron j is in the output layer of the network, the index j refers to the jth output terminal of the network, for which we write

$$y_j(n) = o_j(n) \tag{6.29}$$

where $o_j(n)$ is the jth element of the output vector (pattern). This output is compared with the desired response $d_j(n)$, obtaining the error signal $e_j(n)$ for the jth output neuron. Thus the forward phase of computation begins at the first hidden layer by presenting it with the input vector, and terminates at the output layer by computing the error signal for each neuron of this layer.

The backward pass, on the other hand, starts at the output layer by passing the error signals leftward through the network, layer by layer, and recursively computing the δ (i.e., the local gradient) for each neuron. This recursive process permits the synaptic weights of the network to undergo changes in accordance with the delta rule of Eq. (6.25). For a neuron located in the output layer, the δ is simply equal to the error signal of that neuron multiplied by the first derivative of its nonlinearity. Hence we use Eq. (6.25) to compute the changes to the weights of all the connections feeding into the output layer. Given the δ's for the neurons of the output layer, we next use Eq. (6.24) to compute the δ's for all the neurons in the penultimate layer and therefore the changes to the weights of all connections feeding into it. The recursive computation is continued, layer by layer, by propagating the changes to all synaptic weights made.

Note that for the presentation of each training example, the input pattern is fixed (''clamped'') throughout the round-trip process, encompassing the forward pass followed by the backward pass.

Sigmoidal Nonlinearity

The computation of the δ for each neuron of the multilayer perceptron requires knowledge of the derivative of the activation function $\varphi(\cdot)$ associated with that neuron. For this derivative to exist, we require the function $\varphi(\cdot)$ to be continuous. In basic terms, *differentiability* is the only requirement that an activation function would have to satisfy. An example of a continuously differentiable nonlinear activation function commonly used in multilayer perceptrons is the *sigmoidal nonlinearity,* a particular form of which is defined for neuron j by the *logistic function*

$$\begin{aligned} y_j(n) &= \varphi_j(v_j(n)) \\ &= \frac{1}{1 + \exp(-v_j(n))}, \qquad -\infty < v_j(n) < \infty \end{aligned} \tag{6.30}$$

where $v_j(n)$ is the net internal activity level of neuron j. According to this nonlinearity, the amplitude of the output lies inside the range $0 \leq y_j \leq 1$. Another type of sigmoidal nonlinearity is the *hyperbolic tangent,* which is antisymmetric with respect to the origin and for which the amplitude of the output lies inside the range $-1 \leq y_j \leq +1$. We will have more to say on this latter form of nonlinearity in Section 6.7. For the time being, we are going to concentrate on the logistic function of Eq. (6.30) as the source of nonlinearity.

Differentiating both sides of Eq. (6.30) with respect to $v_j(n)$, we get

$$\begin{aligned}\frac{\partial y_j(n)}{\partial v_j(n)} &= \varphi_j'(v_j(n)) \\ &= \frac{\exp(-v_j(n))}{[1 + \exp(-v_j(n))]^2}\end{aligned} \tag{6.31}$$

Using Eq. (6.30) to eliminate the exponential term $\exp(-v_j(n))$ from Eq. (6.31), we may express the derivative $\varphi_j'(v_j(n))$ as

$$\varphi_j'(v_j(n)) = y_j(n)[1 - y_j(n)] \tag{6.32}$$

For a neuron j located in the output layer, we note that $y_j(n) = o_j(n)$. Hence, we may express the local gradient for neuron j as

$$\begin{aligned}\delta_j(n) &= e_j(n)\varphi_j'(v_j(n)) \\ &= [d_j(n) - o_j(n)]o_j(n)[1 - o_j(n)], \qquad \text{neuron } j \text{ is an output node}\end{aligned} \tag{6.33}$$

where $o_j(n)$ is the function signal at the output of neuron j, and $d_j(n)$ is the desired response for it. On the other hand, for an arbitrary hidden neuron j, we may express the local gradient as

$$\begin{aligned}\delta_j(n) &= \varphi_j'(v_j(n)) \sum_k \delta_k(n) w_{kj}(n) \\ &= y_j(n)[1 - y_j(n)] \sum_k \delta_k(n) w_{kj}(n), \qquad \text{neuron } j \text{ is hidden}\end{aligned} \tag{6.34}$$

Note from Eq. (6.32) that the derivative $\varphi_j'(v_j(n))$ attains its maximum value at $y_j(n) = 0.5$, and its minimum value (zero) at $y_j(n) = 0$, or $y_j(n) = 1.0$. Since the amount of change in a synaptic weight of the network is proportional to the derivative $\varphi_j'(v_j(n))$, it follows that for a sigmoidal activation function the synaptic weights are changed the most for those neurons in the network for which the function signals are in their midrange. According to Rumelhart et al. (1986a), it is this feature of back-propagation learning that contributes to its stability as a learning algorithm.

Rate of Learning

The back-propagation algorithm provides an "approximation" to the trajectory in weight space computed by the method of steepest descent. The smaller we make the learning-rate parameter η, the smaller will the changes to the synaptic weights in the network be from one iteration to the next and the smoother will be the trajectory in weight space. This improvement, however, is attained at the cost of a slower rate of learning. If, on the other hand, we make the learning-rate parameter η too large so as to speed up the rate of learning, the resulting large changes in the synaptic weights assume such a form that the network may become unstable (i.e., oscillatory). A simple method of increasing the rate of learning and yet avoiding the danger of instability is to modify the delta rule of Eq. (6.13) by including a *momentum* term, as shown by[1] (Rumelhart et al., 1986a)

$$\Delta w_{ji}(n) = \alpha \Delta w_{ji}(n-1) + \eta \delta_j(n) y_i(n) \tag{6.35}$$

[1] For the special case of the LMS algorithm, which is a linear adaptive filtering algorithm, it has been shown that use of the momentum constant α reduces the stable range of the learning-rate parameter η, and could thus lead to instability if η is not adjusted appropriately. Moreover, the misadjustment increases with increasing α (for details, see Roy and Shynk, 1990).

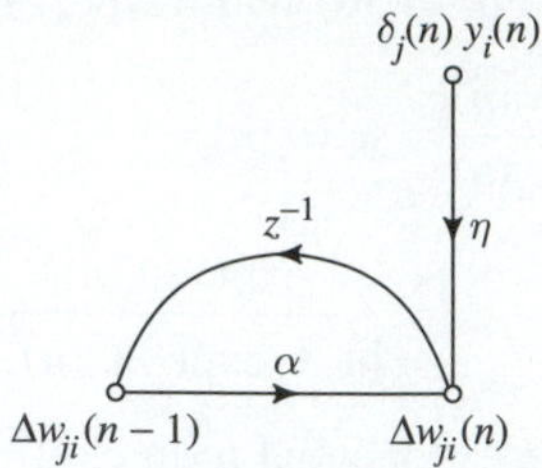

FIGURE 6.5 Signal-flow graph illustrating the effect of momentum constant α.

where α is usually a positive number called the *momentum constant.* It controls the feedback loop acting around $\Delta w_{ji}(n)$, as illustrated in Fig. 6.5, where z^{-1} is the unit-delay operator. Equation (6.35) is called the *generalized delta rule*[2]; it includes the delta rule of Eq. (6.13) as a special case (i.e., $\alpha = 0$).

In order to see the effect of the sequence of pattern presentations on the synaptic weights due to the momentum constant α, we rewrite Eq. (6.35) as a time series with index t. The index t goes from the initial time 0 to the current time n. Equation (6.35) may be viewed as a first-order difference equation in the weight correction $\Delta w_{ji}(n)$. Hence, solving this equation for $\Delta w_{ji}(n)$, we have

$$\Delta w_{ji}(n) = \eta \sum_{t=0}^{n} \alpha^{n-t} \delta_j(t) y_i(t) \tag{6.36}$$

which represents a time series of length $n + 1$. From Eqs. (6.11) and (6.14) we note that the product $\delta_j(n) y_i(n)$ is equal to $-\partial\mathscr{E}(n)/\partial w_{ji}(n)$. Accordingly, we may rewrite Eq. (6.36) in the equivalent form

$$\Delta w_{ji}(n) = -\eta \sum_{t=0}^{n} \alpha^{n-t} \frac{\partial\mathscr{E}(t)}{\partial w_{ji}(t)} \tag{6.37}$$

Based on this relation, we may make the following insightful observations (Watrous, 1987; Jacobs, 1988; Goggin et al., 1989):

1. The current adjustment $\Delta w_{ji}(n)$ represents the sum of an exponentially weighted time series. For the time series to be *convergent,* the momentum constant must be restricted to the range $0 \le |\alpha| < 1$. When α is zero, the back-propagation algorithm operates without momentum. Note also that the momentum constant α can be positive or negative, although it is unlikely that a negative α would be used in practice.

2. When the partial derivative $\partial\mathscr{E}(t)/\partial w_{ji}(t)$ has the same algebraic sign on consecutive iterations, the exponentially weighted sum $\Delta w_{ji}(n)$ grows in magnitude, and so the weight $w_{ji}(n)$ is adjusted by a large amount. Hence the inclusion of momentum in the back-propagation algorithm tends to *accelerate descent* in steady downhill directions.

3. When the partial derivative $\partial\mathscr{E}(t)/\partial w_{ji}(t)$ has opposite signs on consecutive iterations, the exponentially weighted sum $\Delta w_{ji}(n)$ shrinks in magnitude, and so the weight $w_{ji}(n)$ is adjusted by a small amount. Hence the inclusion of momentum in the back-propagation algorithm has a *stabilizing effect* in directions that oscillate in sign.

Thus, the incorporation of momentum in the back-propagation algorithm represents a minor modification to the weight update, and yet it can have highly beneficial effects on learning behavior of the algorithm. The momentum term may also have the benefit of

[2] For a derivation of the back-propagation algorithm including the momentum constant from first principles, see Hagiwara (1992).

preventing the learning process from terminating in a shallow local minimum on the error surface.

Additional Notes. In deriving the back-propagation algorithm, it was assumed that the learning-rate parameter is a constant denoted by η. In reality, however, it should be defined as η_{ji}; that is, the learning-rate parameter should be *connection-dependent.* Indeed, many interesting things can be done by making the learning-rate parameter different for different parts of the network. We shall have more to say on this issue in Sections 6.7 and 6.15.

It is also noteworthy that in the application of the back-propagation algorithm we may choose all the synaptic weights in the network to be adjustable, or we may constrain any number of weights in the network to remain fixed during the adaptation process. In the latter case, the error signals are back-propagated through the network in the usual manner; however, the fixed synaptic weights are left unaltered. This can be done simply by making the learning-rate parameter η_{ji} for synaptic weight w_{ji} equal to zero.

Another point of interest concerns the manner in which the various layers of the back-propagation network are interconnected. In the development of the back-propagation algorithm presented here, we proceeded on the premise that the neurons in each layer of the network receive their inputs from other units in the previous layer, as illustrated in Fig. 6.1. In fact, there is no reason why a neuron in a certain layer may not receive inputs from other units in earlier layers of the network. In handling such a neuron, there are two kinds of error signals to be considered: (1) an error signal that results from the direct comparison of the output signal of that neuron with a desired response; and (2) an error signal that is passed through the other units whose activation it affects. In this situation, the correct procedure to deal with the network is simply to add the changes in synaptic weights dictated by the direct comparison to those propagated back from the other units (Rumelhart et al., 1986b).

Pattern and Batch Modes of Training

In a practical application of the back-propagation algorithm, learning results from the many presentations of a prescribed set of training examples to the multilayer perceptron. One complete presentation of the entire training set during the learning process is called an *epoch.* The learning process is maintained on an epoch-by-epoch basis until the synaptic weights and threshold levels of the network stabilize and the average squared error over the entire training set converges to some minimum value. It is good practice to *randomize the order of presentation of training examples* from one epoch to the next. This randomization tends to make the search in weight space stochastic over the learning cycles, thus avoiding the possibility of limit cycles in the evolution of the synaptic weight vectors.

For a given training set, back-propagation learning may thus proceed in one of two basic ways:

1. *Pattern Mode.* In the *pattern mode* of back-propagation learning, weight updating is performed after the presentation of each training example; this is indeed the very mode of operation for which the derivation of the back-propagation algorithm presented here applies. To be specific, consider an epoch consisting of N training examples (patterns) arranged in the order $[\mathbf{x}(1),\mathbf{d}(1)], \dots, [\mathbf{x}(N),\mathbf{d}(N)]$. The first example $[\mathbf{x}(1),\mathbf{d}(1)]$ in the epoch is presented to the network, and the sequence of forward and backward computations described previously is performed, resulting in certain adjustments to the synaptic weights and threshold levels of the network. Then, the second example $[\mathbf{x}(2),\mathbf{d}(2)]$ in the epoch is presented, and the sequence of forward and backward computations is repeated, resulting in further adjustments to the synaptic weights and threshold levels. This process is continued until the last example $[\mathbf{x}(N),\mathbf{d}(N)]$ in the epoch is accounted for. Let $\Delta w_{ji}(n)$ denote the change applied to synaptic weight w_{ji} after the presentation of pattern n. Then the net weight change $\Delta \hat{w}_{ji}$, *averaged* over the entire training set of N patterns, is given by

$$\begin{aligned}\Delta \hat{w}_{ji} &= \frac{1}{N}\sum_{n=1}^{N} \Delta w_{ji}(n) \\ &= -\frac{\eta}{N}\sum_{n=1}^{N} \frac{\partial \mathscr{E}(n)}{\partial w_{ji}(n)} \\ &= -\frac{\eta}{N}\sum_{n=1}^{N} e_j(n)\frac{\partial e_j(n)}{\partial w_{ji}(n)} \end{aligned} \tag{6.38}$$

where in the second and third lines we have made use of Eqs. (6.12) and (6.2), respectively.

2. *Batch Mode.* In the *batch mode* of back-propagation learning, weight updating is performed *after* the presentation of *all* the training examples that constitute an epoch. For a particular epoch, we define the cost function as the average squared error of Eqs. (6.2) and (6.3), reproduced here in the composite form:

$$\mathscr{E}_{\text{av}} = \frac{1}{2N}\sum_{n=1}^{N}\sum_{j\in C} e_j^2(n) \tag{6.39}$$

where the error signal $e_j(n)$ pertains to output neuron j for training example n and which is defined by Eq. (6.1). The error $e_j(n)$ equals the difference between $d_j(n)$ and $y_j(n)$, which represent the jth element of the desired response vector $\mathbf{d}(n)$ and the corresponding value of the network output, respectively. In Eq. (6.39) the inner summation with respect to j is performed over all the neurons in the output layer of the network, whereas the outer summation with respect to n is performed over the entire training set in the epoch at hand. For a learning-rate parameter η, the adjustment applied to synaptic weight w_{ji}, connecting neuron i to neuron j, is defined by the delta rule

$$\begin{aligned}\Delta w_{ji} &= -\eta\frac{\partial \mathscr{E}_{\text{av}}}{\partial w_{ji}} \\ &= -\frac{\eta}{N}\sum_{n=1}^{N} e_j(n)\frac{\partial e_j(n)}{\partial w_{ji}} \end{aligned} \tag{6.40}$$

To calculate the partial derivative $\partial e_j(n)/\partial w_{ji}$ we proceed in the same way as before. According to Eq. (6.40), in the batch mode the weight adjustment Δw_{ji} is made only after the entire training set has been presented to the network.

Comparing Eqs. (6.38) and (6.40), we clearly see that the average weight change $\Delta \hat{w}_{ji}$ made in the pattern mode of training is different from the corresponding value Δw_{ji} made in the batch mode, presumably for the same reduction in the average squared error $\mathscr{E}_{\text{av}}$ that results from the presentation of the entire training set. Indeed, $\Delta \hat{w}_{ji}$ for the pattern-to-pattern mode represents an *estimate* of Δw_{ji} for the batch mode.

From an "on-line" operational point of view, the pattern mode of training is preferred over the batch mode, because it requires *less* local storage for each synaptic connection. Moreover, given that the patterns are presented to the network in a random manner, the use of pattern-by-pattern updating of weights makes the search in weight space *stochastic* in nature, which, in turn, makes it less likely for the back-propagation algorithm to be trapped in a local minimum. On the other hand, the use of batch mode of training provides a more accurate estimate of the gradient vector. In the final analysis, however, the relative effectiveness of the two training modes depends on the problem at hand (Hertz et al., 1991).

Stopping Criteria

The back-propagation algorithm cannot, in general, be shown to converge, nor are there well-defined criteria for stopping its operation. Rather, there are some reasonable criteria, each with its own practical merit, which may be used to terminate the weight adjustments. To formulate such a criterion, the logical thing to do is to think in terms of the unique properties of a local or global minimum of the error surface. Let the weight vector $\mathbf{w}^*$ denote a minimum, be it local or global. A necessary condition for $\mathbf{w}^*$ to be a minimum is that the gradient vector $\mathbf{g}(\mathbf{w})$ (i.e., first-order partial derivative) of the error surface with respect to the weight vector $\mathbf{w}$ be zero at $\mathbf{w} = \mathbf{w}^*$. Accordingly, we may formulate a sensible convergence criterion for back-propagation learning as follows (Kramer and Sangiovanni-Vincentelli, 1989):

- The back-propagation algorithm is considered to have converged when the Euclidean norm of the gradient vector reaches a sufficiently small gradient threshold.

The drawback of this convergence criterion is that, for successful trials, learning times may be long. Also, it requires the computation of the gradient vector $\mathbf{g}(\mathbf{w})$.

Another unique property of a minimum that we can use is the fact that the cost function or error measure $\mathscr{E}_{av}(\mathbf{w})$ is stationary at the point $\mathbf{w} = \mathbf{w}^*$. We may therefore suggest a different criterion of convergence:

- The back-propagation algorithm is considered to have converged when the absolute rate of change in the average squared error per epoch is sufficiently small.

Typically, the rate of change in the average squared error is considered to be small enough if it lies in the range of 0.1 to 1 percent per epoch; sometimes, a value as small as 0.01 percent per epoch is used.

A variation of this second criterion for convergence of the algorithm is to require that the maximum value of the average squared error $\mathscr{E}_{av}(\mathbf{w})$ be equal to or less than a sufficiently small threshold. Kramer and Sangiovanni-Vincentelli (1989) suggest a hybrid criterion of convergence consisting of this latter threshold and a gradient threshold, as stated here:

- The back-propagation algorithm is terminated at the weight vector $\mathbf{w}_{\text{final}}$ when $\|\mathbf{g}(\mathbf{w}_{\text{final}})\| \leq \varepsilon$, where ε is a sufficiently small gradient threshold, or $\mathscr{E}_{av}(\mathbf{w}_{\text{final}}) \leq \tau$, where τ is a sufficiently small error energy threshold.

Another useful criterion for convergence is as follows. After each learning iteration, the network is tested for its generalization performance. The learning process is stopped when the generalization performance is adequate, or when it is apparent that the generalization performance has peaked; see Section 6.11 for more details.

6.4 Summary of the Back-Propagation Algorithm

Figure 6.1 presents the architectural layout of a multilayer perceptron. The corresponding architecture for back-propagation learning, incorporating both the forward and backward phases of the computations involved in the learning process, is presented in Fig. 6.6. The multilayer network shown in the top part of the figure accounts for the forward phase.

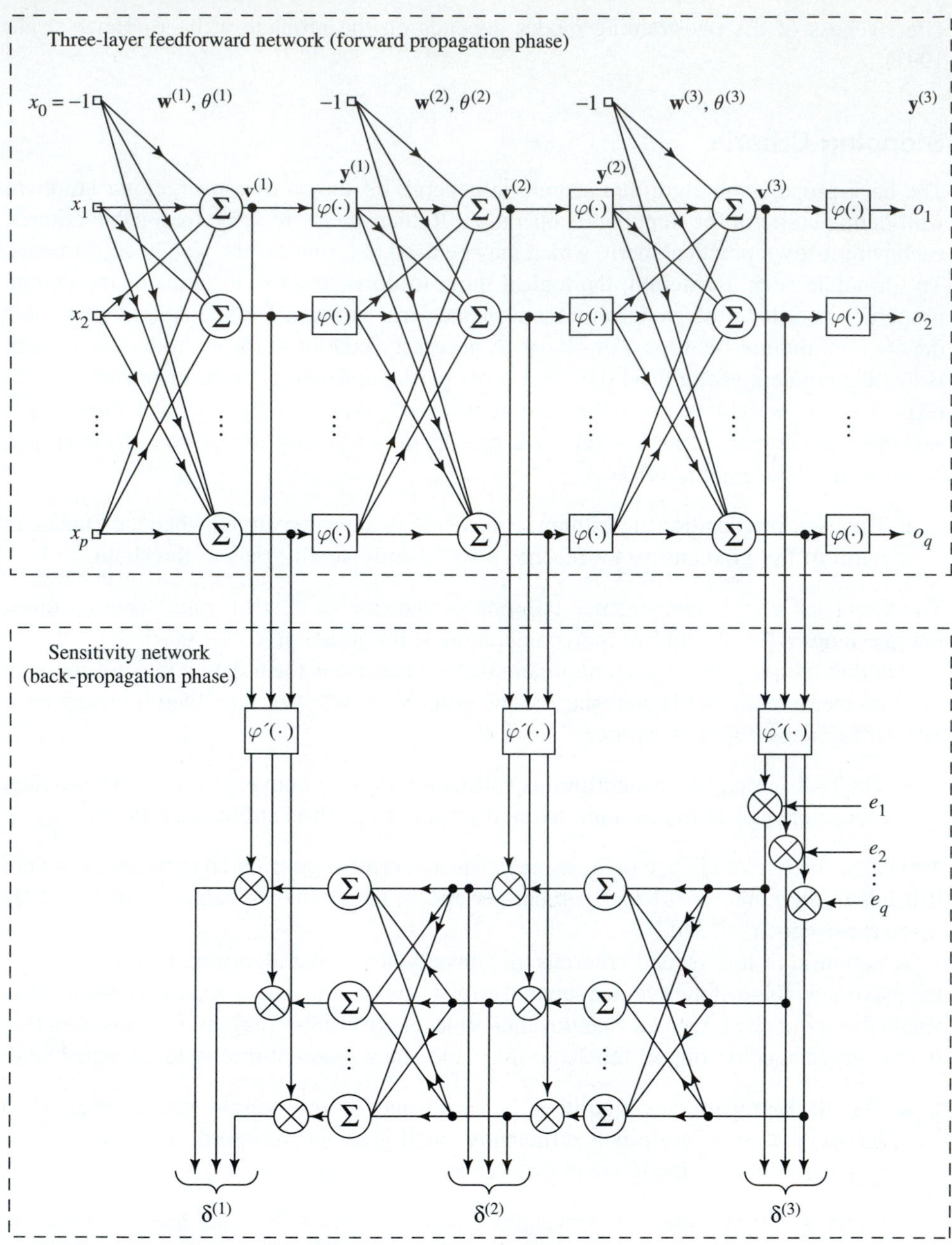

FIGURE 6.6 Architectural graph of three-layer feedforward network and associated sensitivity network (back-propagating error signals).

The notations used in this part of the figure are as follows:

$\mathbf{w}^{(l)}$ = synaptic weight vector of a neuron in layer l
$\theta^{(l)}$ = threshold of a neuron in layer l
$\mathbf{v}^{(l)}$ = vector of net internal activity levels of neurons in layer l
$\mathbf{y}^{(l)}$ = vector of function signals of neurons in layer l

The layer index l extends from the input layer ($l = 0$) to the output layer ($l = L$); in Fig. 6.6 we have $L = 3$; we refer to L as the *depth* of the network. The lower part of the figure accounts for the backward phase, which is referred to as a *sensitivity network* for computing the local gradients in the back-propagation algorithm. The notations used in this second part of the figure are as follows:

$\boldsymbol{\delta}^{(l)}$ = vector of local gradients of neurons in layer l
$\mathbf{e}$ = error vector represented by $e_1, e_2, \ldots, e_q$ as elements

While the network of Fig. 6.6 is merely an architectural layout of the back-propagation algorithm, it is found to have substantial advantages in dynamic situations where the algorithmic representation becomes cumbersome (Narendra and Parthasarathy, 1990).

Earlier we mentioned that the pattern-by-pattern updating of weights is the preferred method for on-line implementation of the back-propagation algorithm. For this mode of operation, the algorithm cycles through the training data $\{[\mathbf{x}(n),\mathbf{d}(n)];\ n = 1, 2, \ldots, N\}$ as follows.

1. *Initialization.* Start with a reasonable network configuration, and set all the synaptic weights and threshold levels of the network to small random numbers that are uniformly distributed.[3]

2. *Presentations of Training Examples.* Present the network with an epoch of training examples. For each example in the set ordered in some fashion, perform the following sequence of forward and backward computations under points 3 and 4, respectively.

3. *Forward Computation.* Let a training example in the epoch be denoted by $[\mathbf{x}(n),\mathbf{d}(n)]$, with the input vector $\mathbf{x}(n)$ applied to the input layer of sensory nodes and the desired response vector $\mathbf{d}(n)$ presented to the output layer of computation nodes. Compute the activation potentials and function signals of the network by proceeding forward through the network, layer by layer. The net internal activity level $v_j^{(l)}(n)$ for neuron j in layer l is

$$v_j^{(l)}(n) = \sum_{i=0}^{p} w_{ji}^{(l)}(n)\, y_i^{(l-1)}(n)$$

where $y_i^{(l-1)}(n)$ is the function signal of neuron i in the previous layer $l - 1$ at iteration n and $w_{ji}^{(l)}(n)$ is the synaptic weight of neuron j in layer l that is fed from neuron i in layer $l - 1$. For $i = 0$, we have $y_0^{(l-1)}(n) = -1$ and $w_{j0}^{(l)}(n) = \theta_j^{(l)}(n)$, where $\theta_j^{(l)}(n)$ is the threshold applied to neuron j in layer l. Assuming the use of a logistic function for the sigmoidal nonlinearity, the function (output) signal of neuron j in layer l is

$$y_j^{(l)}(n) = \frac{1}{1 + \exp(-v_j^{(l)}(n))}$$

If neuron j is in the first hidden layer (i.e., $l = 1$), set

$$y_j^{(0)}(n) = x_j(n)$$

where $x_j(n)$ is the jth element of the input vector $\mathbf{x}(n)$. If neuron j is in the output layer (i.e., $l = L$), set

$$y_j^{(L)}(n) = o_j(n)$$

[3] Note that this form of initialization is different from that used for the LMS algorithm.

Hence, compute the error signal

$$e_j(n) = d_j(n) - o_j(n)$$

where $d_j(n)$ is the jth element of the desired response vector $\mathbf{d}(n)$.

4. *Backward Computation.* Compute the δ's (i.e., the local gradients) of the network by proceeding backward, layer by layer:

$$\delta_j^{(L)}(n) = e_j^{(L)}(n)o_j(n)[1 - o_j(n)] \qquad \text{for neuron } j \text{ in output layer } L$$

$$\delta_j^{(l)}(n) = y_j^{(l)}(n)[1 - y_j^{(l)}(n)] \sum_k \delta_k^{(l+1)}(n)w_{kj}^{(l+1)}(n) \qquad \text{for neuron } j \text{ in hidden layer } l$$

Hence, adjust the synaptic weights of the network in layer l according to the generalized delta rule:

$$w_{ji}^{(l)}(n + 1) = w_{ji}^{(l)}(n) + \alpha[w_{ji}^{(l)}(n) - w_{ji}^{(l)}(n - 1)] + \eta\delta_j^{(l)}(n)y_i^{(l-1)}(n)$$

where η is the learning-rate parameter and α is the momentum constant.

5. *Iteration.* Iterate the computation by presenting new epochs of training examples to the network until the free parameters of the network stabilize their values and the average squared error $\mathscr{E}_{\text{av}}$ computed over the entire training set is at a minimum or acceptably small value. The order of presentation of training examples should be randomized from epoch to epoch. The momentum and the learning-rate parameter are typically adjusted (and usually decreased) as the number of training iterations increases.

6.5 Initialization

The first step in back-propagation learning is, of course, to *initialize* the network. A good choice for the initial values of the free parameters (i.e., adjustable synaptic weights and threshold levels) of the network can be of tremendous help in a successful network design. In cases where prior information is available, it may be better to use the prior information to guess the initial values of the free parameters. But how do we initialize the network if no prior information is available? The customary practice is to set all the free parameters of the network to random numbers that are *uniformly distributed* inside a small range of values, as stated in the summary presented in Section 6.4.

The wrong choice of initial weights can lead to a phenomenon known as *premature saturation* (Lee et al., 1991). This phenomenon refers to a situation where the instantaneous sum of squared errors $\mathscr{E}(n)$ remains almost constant for some period of time during the learning process. Such a phenomenon cannot be considered as a local minimum, because the squared error continues to decrease after this period is finished. (In more direct terms, the premature saturation phenomenon corresponds to a ''saddle point'' in the error surface.)

When a training pattern is applied to the input layer of a multilayer perceptron, the output values of the network are calculated through a sequence of forward computations that involves inner products and sigmoidal transformations. This is followed by a sequence of backward computations that involves the calculation of error signals and pertinent slope of the sigmoidal activation function, and culminates in synaptic weight adjustments. Suppose that, for a particular training pattern, the net internal activity level of an output neuron (computation node) is computed to have a large magnitude. Then, assuming that the sigmoidal activation function of the neuron has the limiting values -1 and $+1$, we find that the corresponding slope of the activation function for that neuron will be very small, and the output value for the neuron will be close to -1 or $+1$. In such a situation, we say that the neuron is in ''saturation.'' If the output value is close to $+1$ when the target value (desired response) is -1, or vice versa, we say that the neuron is "incorrectly saturated." When this happens, the adjustment applied to the synaptic weights of the neuron will be small (even though the magnitude of the associated error signal is large), and the network may take a long time to escape from it (Lee et al., 1991).

At the initial stage of back-propagation learning, depending on the prevalent conditions, both unsaturated neurons and incorrectly saturated ones may exist in the output layer of the network. As the learning process continues, the synaptic weights associated with the unsaturated output neurons change rapidly, because the corresponding error signals and gradients have relatively large magnitudes, thereby resulting in a reduction in the instantaneous sum of squared errors $\mathscr{E}(n)$. If, however, at this point in time the incorrectly saturated output neurons remain saturated for some particular training patterns, then the phenomenon of premature saturation may arise with $\mathscr{E}(n)$ remaining essentially constant.

In Lee et al. (1991), a formula for the *probability of premature saturation* in back-propagation learning has been derived for the batch mode of updating, and it has been verified using computer simulation. The essence of this formula may be summarized as follows:

1. Incorrect saturation is avoided by choosing the initial values of the synaptic weights and threshold levels of the network to be uniformly distributed inside a *small* range of values.
2. Incorrect saturation is less likely to occur *when the number of hidden neurons is maintained low,* consistent with a satisfactory operation of the network.
3. Incorrect saturation rarely occurs when the neurons of the network operate in their *linear regions.*

For pattern-by-pattern updating, computer simulation results show similar trends to the batch mode of operation referred to herein.

Russo (1991) recommends an empirical formula for the initial size of the weights that helps avoid the saturation of the neurons. This formula is described under point 3 of Section 6.7.

6.6 The XOR Problem

In the elementary (single-layer) perceptron there are no hidden neurons. Consequently, it cannot classify input patterns that are not linearly separable. However, nonlinearly separable patterns are of common occurrence. For example, it arises in the *Exclusive OR (XOR) problem,* which may be viewed as a special case of a more general problem, namely, that of classifying points in the *unit hypercube.* Each point in the hypercube is either in class 0 or class 1. However, in the special case of the XOR problem, we need consider only the four corners of the *unit square* that correspond to the input patterns (0,0), (0,1), (1,1), and (1,0). The first and third input patterns are in class 0, as shown by

$$0 \text{ XOR } 0 = 0$$

and

$$1 \text{ XOR } 1 = 0$$

The input patterns (0,0) and (1,1) are at opposite corners of the unit square, and yet they produce the identical output 0. On the other hand, the input patterns (0,1) and (1,0) are also at opposite corners of the square, but they are in class 1, as shown by

$$0 \text{ XOR } 1 = 1$$

and

$$1 \text{ XOR } 0 = 1$$

We first recognize that the use of a single neuron with two inputs results in a straight line for decision boundary in the input space. For all points on one side of this line, the neuron outputs 1; for all points on the other side of the line, it outputs 0. The position and orientation of the line in the input space are determined by the synaptic weights of the neuron connected to the input nodes, and the threshold applied to the neuron. With the input patterns (0,0) and (1,1) located on opposite corners of the unit square, and likewise for the other two input patterns (0,1) and (1,0), it is clear that we cannot construct a straight line for a decision boundary so that (0,0) and (0,1) lie in one decision region, and (0,1) and (1,0) lie in the other decision region. In other words, an elementary perceptron cannot solve the XOR problem.

We may solve the XOR problem by using a single hidden layer with two neurons, as in Fig. 6.7a (Touretzky and Pomerleau, 1989). The signal-flow graph of the network is shown in Fig. 6.7b. The following assumptions are made here:

- Each neuron is represented by a McCulloch–Pitts model.
- Bits 0 and 1 are represented by the levels 0 and +1, respectively.

The top neuron, labeled 1, in the hidden layer is characterized as follows:

$$w_{11} = w_{12} = +1$$

$$\theta_1 = +\tfrac{3}{2}$$

The slope of the decision boundary constructed by this hidden neuron is equal to -1, and positioned as in Fig. 6.8a. The bottom neuron, labeled 2 in the hidden layer, is

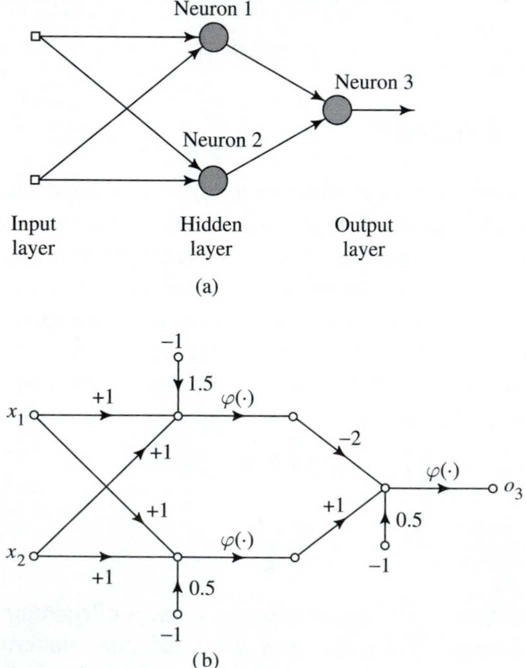

FIGURE 6.7 (a) Architectural graph of network for solving the XOR problem. (b) Signal-flow graph of the network.

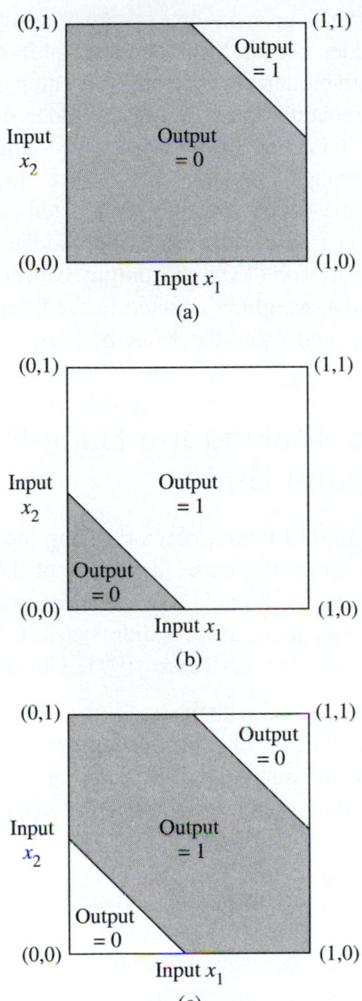

FIGURE 6.8 (a) Decision boundary constructed by hidden neuron 1 of the network in Fig. 6.7. (b) Decision boundary constructed by hidden neuron 2 of the network. (c) Decision boundaries constructed by the complete network.

characterized as follows:

$$w_{21} = w_{22} = +1$$

$$\theta_2 = +\tfrac{1}{2}$$

The orientation and position of the decision boundary constructed by this second hidden neuron is as shown in Fig. 6.8b.

The output neuron, labeled 3 in Fig. 6.7a, is characterized as follows:

$$w_{31} = -2$$

$$w_{32} = +1$$

$$\theta_3 = +\tfrac{1}{2}$$

The function of the output neuron is to construct a linear combination of the decision boundaries formed by the two hidden neurons. The result of this computation is shown in Fig. 6.8c. The bottom hidden neuron has an excitatory (positive) connection to the output neuron, whereas the top hidden neuron has a stronger inhibitory (negative) connection to the output neuron. When both hidden neurons are off, which occurs when the input pattern is (0,0), the output neuron remains off. When both hidden neurons are on, which occurs when the input pattern is (1,1), the output neuron is switched off again, because the inhibitory effect of the larger negative weight connected to the top hidden neuron overpowers the excitatory effect of the positive weight connected to the bottom hidden neuron. When the top hidden neuron is off and the bottom hidden neuron is on, which occurs when the input pattern is (0,1) or (1,0), the output neuron is switched on due to the excitatory effect of the positive weight connected to the bottom hidden neuron. Thus, the network of Fig. 6.7a does indeed solve the XOR problem.

6.7 Some Hints for Making the Back-Propagation Algorithm Perform Better

It is often said that the design of a neural network using the back-propagation algorithm is more of an art than a science in the sense that many of the numerous factors involved in the design are indeed the results of one's own personal experience. There is some truth in this statement. Nevertheless, there are possible ways in which the back-propagation algorithm may be made to work better (Russo, 1991; Guyon, 1991).

1. A multilayer perceptron trained with the back-propagation algorithm may, in general, learn faster (in terms of the number of training iterations required) when the sigmoidal activation function built into the neuron model of the network is asymmetric than when it is nonsymmetric. We say that an activation function $\varphi(v)$ is asymmetric if

$$\varphi(-v) = -\varphi(v)$$

as depicted in Fig. 6.9a. This condition is not satisfied by the logistic function, depicted in Fig. 6.9b.

A popular example of an asymmetric activation function is a sigmoidal nonlinearity in the form of a *hyperbolic tangent,* defined by

$$\varphi(v) = a \tanh(bv)$$

where a and b are constants. Note that the hyperbolic tangent is just the logistic function biased and rescaled, as shown by

$$\begin{aligned} a \tanh(bv) &= a\left[\frac{1-\exp(-bv)}{1+\exp(-bv)}\right] \\ &= \frac{2a}{1+\exp(-bv)} - a \end{aligned} \tag{6.41}$$

Accordingly, the modifications made in the formulation of the back-propagation algorithm using this form of sigmoidal nonlinearity are of a minor nature; see Problem 6.9.

Suitable values for the constants a and b are (Guyon, 1991)

$$a = 1.716$$

and

$$b = \tfrac{2}{3}$$

2. It is important that the target values (desired response) are chosen within the range of the sigmoidal activation function. More specifically, the desired response d_j for neuron

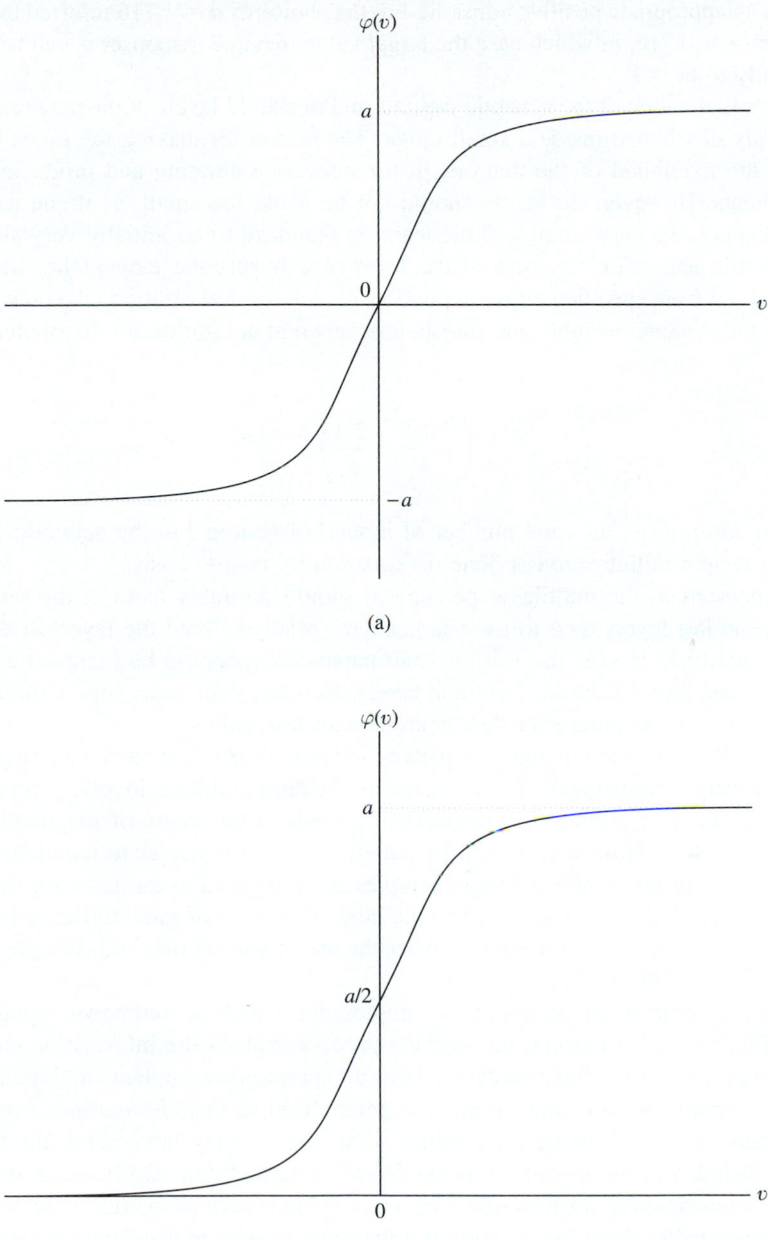

FIGURE 6.9 (a) Asymmetric activation (hyperbolic) function. (b) Nonsymmetric activation (logistic) function.

j in the output layer of the multilayer perceptron should be *offset* by some amount ε away from the limiting value of the sigmoidal activation function, depending on whether the limiting value is positive or negative. Otherwise, the back-propagation algorithm tends to drive the free parameters of the network to infinity, and thereby slow down the learning process by orders of magnitude. To be specific, consider the asymmetric activating function of Fig. 6.9a. For the limiting value $+a$, we set

$$d_j = a - \varepsilon$$

where ε is an appropriate positive constant. For the choice of $a = 1.716$ referred to earlier, we may set $\varepsilon = 0.716$, in which case the target value (desired response) d_j can be chosen conveniently to be ± 1.

3. The initialization of the synaptic weights and threshold levels of the network should be uniformly distributed inside a small range. The reason for making the range small is to reduce the likelihood of the neurons in the network saturating and producing small error gradients. However, the range should not be made too small, as it can cause the error gradients to be very small and the learning therefore to be initially very slow. For an asymmetric activation function in the form of a hyperbolic tangent for which the constants a and b are specified above, a possible choice for initialization is to pick random values for the synaptic weights and threshold levels that are uniformly distributed inside the range

$$\left(-\frac{2.4}{F_i}, +\frac{2.4}{F_i}\right)$$

where F_i is *fan-in* (i.e., the total number of inputs) of neuron i in the network; in other words, the weight initialization is done on a neuron-by-neuron basis.

4. All neurons in the multilayer perceptron should desirably learn at the same rate. Typically, the last layers tend to have larger local gradients than the layers at the front end of the network. Hence, the learning-rate parameter η should be assigned a smaller value in the last layers than the front-end layers. Neurons with many inputs should have a smaller learning-rate parameter than neurons with few inputs.

5. For on-line operation, pattern-by-pattern updating rather than batch updating should be used for weight adjustments. For pattern-classification problems involving a large and redundant database, pattern-by-pattern updating tends to be orders of magnitude faster than batch updating. However, pattern-by-pattern updating is harder to parallelize.

6. The order in which the training examples are presented to the network should be randomized (shuffled) from one epoch to the next. This form of randomization is critical for improving the speed of convergence. Also, the use of *queries* may improve the training efficiency (Baum, 1991).

7. Learning from a set of training examples deals with an unknown input–output mapping function $f(\cdot)$. In effect, the learning process exploits the information contained in the examples about the function $f(\cdot)$ to *infer* an approximate implementation of it. The process of learning from examples may be generalized to *include learning from hints,* which is achieved by allowing prior information that we may have about the function $f(\cdot)$ to be included in the learning process (Abu-Mostafa, 1990; Al-Mashouq and Reed, 1991). Such information, for example, may include invariance properties, symmetries, or any other knowledge about the function $f(\cdot)$ that may be used to accelerate the search for its approximate realization; the idea of invariances was discussed in Section 1.7.

6.8 Output Representation and Decision Rule

In theory, for an m-class *classification problem* in which the union of the m distinct classes forms the entire input space, we need a total of m outputs to represent all possible classification decisions, as depicted in Fig. 6.10. In this figure, the vector $\mathbf{x}_j$ denotes the jth *prototype* (i.e., unique sample) of a p-dimensional random vector $\mathbf{x}$ to be classified by a multilayer perceptron. The kth of m possible classes to which $\mathbf{x}$ can belong is denoted by $\mathscr{C}_k$. Let $y_{k,j}$ be the kth output of the network produced in response to the prototype $\mathbf{x}_j$, as shown by

$$y_{k,j} = F_k(\mathbf{x}_j), \qquad k = 1, 2, \dots, m \tag{6.42}$$

where the function $F_k(\cdot)$ defines the mapping learned by the network from the input to the kth output. For convenience of presentation, let

$$\begin{aligned}\mathbf{y}_j &= [y_{1,j}, y_{2,j}, \dots, y_{m,j}]^T \\ &= [F_1(\mathbf{x}_j), F_2(\mathbf{x}_j), \dots, F_m(\mathbf{x}_j)]^T \\ &= \mathbf{F}(\mathbf{x}_j)\end{aligned} \tag{6.43}$$

where $\mathbf{F}(\cdot)$ is a vector-valued function. A basic question that we wish to address in this section is the following:

> *After the training of a multilayer perceptron, what should the optimum decision rule be for classifying the m outputs of the network?*

Clearly, any reasonable output decision rule ought to be based on knowledge of the vector-valued function:

$$\mathbf{F}: \mathbb{R}^p \ni \mathbf{x} \rightarrow \mathbf{y} \in \mathbb{R}^m \tag{6.44}$$

In general, all that is certain about the vector-valued function $\mathbf{F}(\cdot)$ is that it is a continuous function that minimizes the mean-squared error defined as the value of the *cost* (*loss*) *functional:*

$$L(\mathbf{F}) = \frac{1}{2N} \sum_{j=1}^{N} \|\mathbf{d}_j - \mathbf{F}(\mathbf{x}_j)\|^2 \tag{6.45}$$

where $\mathbf{d}_j$ is the desired (target) output pattern for the prototype $\mathbf{x}_j$, $\|\cdot\|$ is the Euclidean norm of the enclosed vector, and N is the total number of input–output patterns presented to the network in training. The essence of the mean-squared error criterion of Eq. (6.45) is the same as the cost function of Eq. (6.3). The vector-valued function $\mathbf{F}(\cdot)$ is strongly dependent on the choice of input–output pairs $(\mathbf{x}_j,\mathbf{d}_j)$ used to train the network, so that different values of $(\mathbf{x}_j,\mathbf{d}_j)$ will indeed lead to different vector-valued functions $\mathbf{F}(\cdot)$. Note that the terminology $(\mathbf{x}_j,\mathbf{d}_j)$ used here is the same as that of $[\mathbf{x}(j),\mathbf{d}(j)]$ used previously.

Suppose now that the network is trained with *binary* target values (which incidently correspond to the upper and lower bounds on the network outputs when using the logistic function), written as follows:

$$d_{k,j} = \begin{cases} 1 & \text{when the prototype } \mathbf{x}_j \text{ belongs to class } \mathscr{C}_k \\ 0 & \text{when the prototype } \mathbf{x}_j \text{ does not belong to class } \mathscr{C}_k \end{cases} \tag{6.46}$$

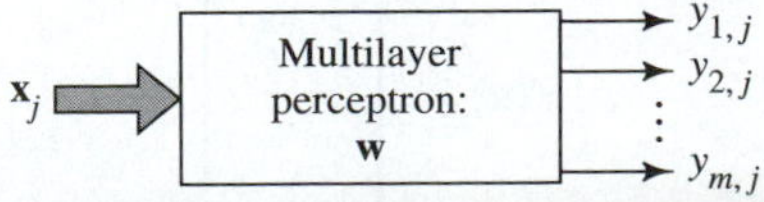

FIGURE 6.10 Block diagram of a pattern classifier.

Based on this notation, class $\mathscr{C}_k$ is represented by the m-dimensional target vector

$$\begin{bmatrix} 0 \\ \vdots \\ 1 \\ \vdots \\ 0 \end{bmatrix} \leftarrow k\text{th element}$$

It is tempting to suppose that a multilayer perceptron classifier trained with the back-propagation algorithm on a finite set of independently and identically distributed (i.i.d.) examples may lead to an asymptotic approximation of the underlying *a posteriori* class probabilities. This property may be justified on the following grounds (White, 1989; Richard and Lippmann, 1991):

- The *law of large numbers* is invoked to show that, as the size of the training set, N, approaches infinity, the weight vector $\mathbf{w}$ that minimizes cost functional $L(\mathbf{F})$ of Eq. (6.45) approaches the optimum weight vector $\mathbf{w}^*$ that minimizes the expectation of the random quantity $\frac{1}{2}\|\mathbf{d} - \mathbf{F}(\mathbf{w},\mathbf{x})\|^2$, where $\mathbf{d}$ is the desired response vector and $\mathbf{F}(\mathbf{w},\mathbf{x})$ is the approximation realized by a multilayer perceptron with weight vector $\mathbf{w}$ and vector $\mathbf{x}$ as input (White, 1989). The function $\mathbf{F}(\mathbf{w},\mathbf{x})$, showing explicit dependence on the weight vector $\mathbf{w}$, is the same as $\mathbf{F}(\mathbf{x})$ used previously.
- The optimum weight vector $\mathbf{w}^*$ has the property that the corresponding vector of actual network outputs, $\mathbf{F}(\mathbf{w}^*,\mathbf{x})$, is a mean-squared, error-minimizing approximation to the conditional expectation $E[\mathbf{d}|\mathbf{x}]$ (White, 1989); this issue was discussed in Chapter 2.
- For a 1 *of m pattern classification problem,* the kth element of desired response vector $\mathbf{d}$ equals one if the input vector belongs to class $\mathscr{C}_k$ and zero otherwise. Under this condition, the conditional expectation $E[\mathbf{d}_k|\mathbf{x}]$ equals the *a posteriori* class probability $P(\mathscr{C}_k|\mathbf{x})$, $k = 1, 2, \ldots, m$ (Richard and Lippmann, 1991).

It follows therefore that a multilayer perceptron classifier (using the logistic function for nonlinearity) does indeed approximate the *a posteriori* class probabilities, provided that the size of the training set is large enough and the back-propagation learning process does not get stuck at a local minimum. Accordingly, we may proceed to answer the question we posed earlier. Specifically, we may say that the most appropriate output decision rule is

Classify the random vector $\mathbf{x}$ *as belonging to class* $\mathscr{C}_k$ *if*

$$F_k(\mathbf{x}) > F_j(\mathbf{x}) \qquad \textit{for all } j \neq k \tag{6.47}$$

where $F_k(\mathbf{x})$ *and* $F_j(\mathbf{x})$ *are elements of the vector-valued mapping function*

$$\mathbf{F}(\mathbf{x}) = \begin{bmatrix} F_1(\mathbf{x}) \\ F_2(\mathbf{x}) \\ \vdots \\ F_m(\mathbf{x}) \end{bmatrix}$$

A unique largest output value exists with probability one[4] when the underlying posterior class distributions are distinct. Hence this decision rule has the advantage of rendering *unambiguous* decisions over the common *ad hoc* rule of selecting class membership based on the concept of output "firing," that is, the vector $\mathbf{x}$ is assigned membership in a particular class if the corresponding output value is greater than some fixed threshold (usually, 0.5 for the logistic form of activation function), which can lead to multiple class assignments.

In Section 6.6 we pointed out that the binary target values [0,1], corresponding to the logistic function of Eq. (6.30), are perturbed by a small amount ε as a practical measure, to avoid the saturation of synaptic weights (due to finite numerical precision) during training of the network. As a result of this perturbation, the target values are now nonbinary, and the asymptotic approximations $F_k(\mathbf{x})$ are no longer exactly the *a posteriori* probabilities $P(\mathscr{C}_k|\mathbf{x})$ of the m classes of interest (Hampshire and Pearlmutter, 1990). Instead, $P(\mathscr{C}_k|\mathbf{x})$ is linearly mapped to the closed interval $[\varepsilon, 1 - \varepsilon]$, such that $P(\mathscr{C}_k|\mathbf{x}) = 0$ is mapped to an output of ε and $P(\mathscr{C}_k|\mathbf{x}) = 1$ is mapped to an output of $1 - \varepsilon$. Because this linear mapping preserves relative ordering, it does *not* affect the result of applying the output decision rule of Eq. (6.47).

It is also of interest to note that when a decision boundary is formed by thresholding the outputs of a multilayer perceptron against some fixed values, the overall shape and orientation of the decision boundary may be explained heuristically (for the case of a single hidden layer) in terms of the number of hidden neurons and the ratios of synaptic weights connected to them (Lui, 1989). Such an analysis, however, is not applicable to a decision boundary formed in accordance with the output decision rule of Eq. (6.47). A more appropriate approach is to consider the hidden neurons as *nonlinear feature detectors* that attempt to map classes from the original input space $\mathbb{R}^p$, where the classes may not be linearly separable, into the space of hidden-layer activations, where it is more likely for them to be linearly separable (Yee, 1992).

6.9 Computer Experiment

In this section we use a computer experiment to illustrate the learning behavior of a multilayer perceptron used as a pattern classifier. The objective of the experiment is to distinguish between two classes of "overlapping," two-dimensional, Gaussian-distributed patterns labeled 1 and 2. Let $\mathscr{C}_1$ and $\mathscr{C}_2$ denote the set of events for which a random vector $\mathbf{x}$ belongs to patterns 1 and 2, respectively. We may then express the conditional probability density functions for the two classes as follows:

Class $\mathscr{C}_1$:
$$f(\mathbf{x}|\mathscr{C}_1) = \frac{1}{2\pi\sigma_1^2} \exp\left(-\frac{1}{2\sigma_1^2}\|\mathbf{x} - \boldsymbol{\mu}_1\|^2\right) \tag{6.48}$$

where

$$\boldsymbol{\mu}_1 = \text{mean vector} = [0,0]^T$$

$$\sigma_1^2 = \text{variance} = 1$$

Class $\mathscr{C}_2$:
$$f(\mathbf{x}|\mathscr{C}_2) = \frac{1}{2\pi\sigma_2^2} \exp\left(-\frac{1}{2\sigma_2^2}\|\mathbf{x} - \boldsymbol{\mu}_2\|^2\right) \tag{6.49}$$

[4] Here it is assumed that infinite-precision arithmetic is used; ties are possible with finite precision.

where

$$\boldsymbol{\mu}_2 = [2,0]^T$$

$$\sigma_2^2 = 4$$

The two classes are assumed to be equally likely; that is,

$$P(\mathscr{C}_1) = P(\mathscr{C}_2) = 0.5$$

Figure 6.11a shows three-dimensional plots of the two Gaussian distributions defined by Eqs. (6.48) and (6.49). Figure 6.11b shows individual scatter diagrams for classes $\mathscr{C}_1$ and $\mathscr{C}_2$ and the joint scatter diagram representing the superposition of scatter plots of 540 points taken from each of the two processes. This latter diagram shows clearly that the two distributions overlap each other significantly, indicating that there is a significant probability of misclassification.

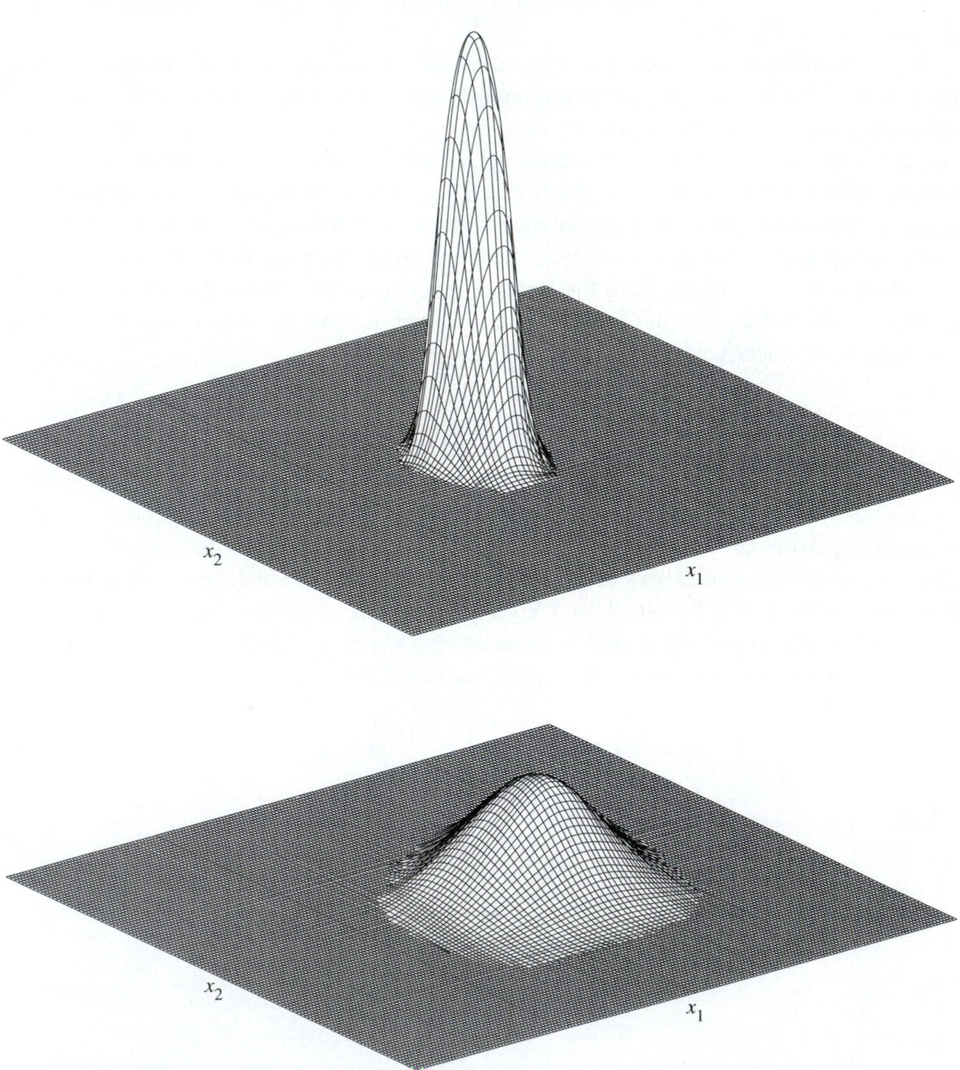

FIGURE 6.11a Top: the probability density function $f(\mathbf{x}|\mathscr{C}_1)$; bottom: the probability density function $f(\mathbf{x}|\mathscr{C}_2)$.

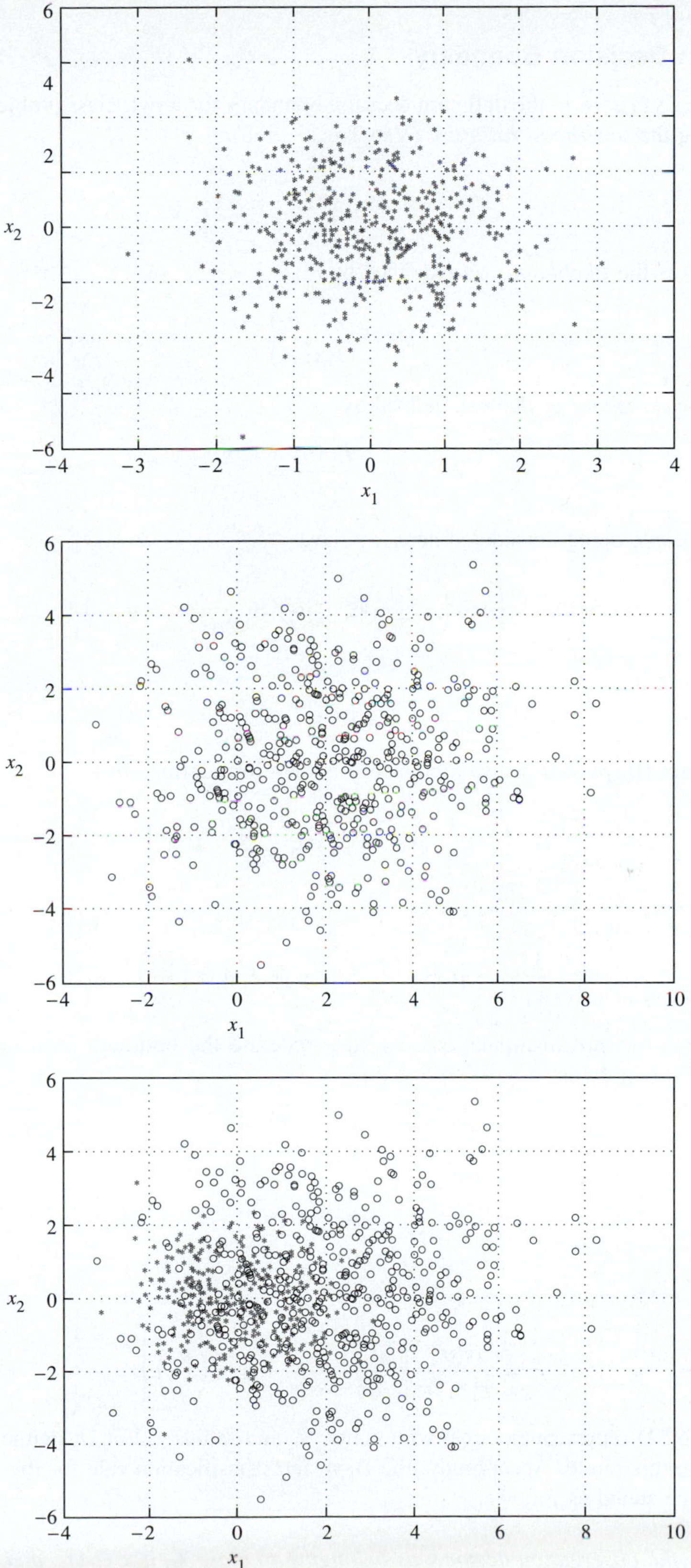

FIGURE 6.11b Top: scatter plot of class $\mathscr{C}_1$; middle: scatter plot of class $\mathscr{C}_2$; bottom: joint scatter plot of classes $\mathscr{C}_1$ and $\mathscr{C}_2$ (* = $\mathscr{C}_1$, ○ = $\mathscr{C}_2$).

Bayesian Decision Boundary

Using *Bayes's criterion,* the optimum decision boundary for a two-class problem is found by applying the *likelihood ratio test* (Van Trees, 1968):

$$\Lambda(\mathbf{x}) \underset{\mathscr{C}_2}{\overset{\mathscr{C}_1}{\lesseqgtr}} \lambda \tag{6.50}$$

where $\Lambda(\mathbf{x})$ is the *likelihood ratio,* defined by

$$\Lambda(\mathbf{x}) = \frac{f(\mathbf{x}|\mathscr{C}_2)}{f(\mathbf{x}|\mathscr{C}_1)} \tag{6.51}$$

and λ is the *threshold of the test,* defined by

$$\lambda = \frac{P(\mathscr{C}_1)}{P(\mathscr{C}_2)} \tag{6.52}$$

For the example being considered here, we have

$$\Lambda(\mathbf{x}) = \frac{\sigma_1^2}{\sigma_2^2} \exp\left(-\frac{1}{2\sigma_2^2}\|\mathbf{x} - \boldsymbol{\mu}_2\|^2 + \frac{1}{2\sigma_1^2}\|\mathbf{x} - \boldsymbol{\mu}_1\|^2\right)$$

and

$$\lambda = 1$$

The optimum (Bayesian) decision boundary is therefore defined by

$$\frac{\sigma_1^2}{\sigma_2^2} \exp\left(-\frac{1}{2\sigma_2^2}\|\mathbf{x} - \boldsymbol{\mu}_2\|^2 + \frac{1}{2\sigma_1^2}\|\mathbf{x} - \boldsymbol{\mu}_1\|^2\right) = 1$$

or, equivalently,

$$\frac{1}{\sigma_1^2}\|\mathbf{x} - \boldsymbol{\mu}_1\|^2 - \frac{1}{\sigma_2^2}\|\mathbf{x} - \boldsymbol{\mu}_2\|^2 = 4 \ln\left(\frac{\sigma_2}{\sigma_1}\right) \tag{6.53}$$

Using straightforward manipulations, we may redefine the optimum decision boundary of Eq. (6.53) simply as

$$\|\mathbf{x} - \mathbf{x}_c\|^2 = r^2 \tag{6.54}$$

where

$$\mathbf{x}_c = \frac{\sigma_2^2\boldsymbol{\mu}_1 - \sigma_1^2\boldsymbol{\mu}_2}{\sigma_2 - \sigma_1} \tag{6.55}$$

and

$$r^2 = \frac{\sigma_1^2\sigma_2^2}{\sigma_2^2 - \sigma_1^2}\left[\frac{\|\boldsymbol{\mu}_1 + \boldsymbol{\mu}_2\|^2}{\sigma_2^2 - \sigma_1^2} + 4 \ln\left(\frac{\sigma_2}{\sigma_1}\right)\right] \tag{6.56}$$

Equation (6.54) represents a circle with center $\mathbf{x}_c$ and radius r. Let Ω_1 define the region lying inside this circle. Accordingly, the Bayesian classification rule for the problem at hand may be stated as follows:

> *Classify the observation vector* $\mathbf{x}$ *as belonging to class* $\mathscr{C}_1$ *if* $\mathbf{x} \in \Omega_1$, *and to class* $\mathscr{C}_2$ *otherwise.*

For the particular parameters of this experiment, we have a circular decision boundary whose center is located at

$$\mathbf{x}_c = [-\tfrac{2}{3}, 0]^T$$

and whose radius is

$$r \simeq 2.34$$

Let c denote the set of correct classification outcomes, and e the set of erroneous classification outcomes. The *average probability of error* (misclassification), P_e, of a classifier operating according to the Bayesian decision rule is

$$P_e = P(e|\mathscr{C}_1)P(\mathscr{C}_1) + P(e|\mathscr{C}_2)P(\mathscr{C}_2) \tag{6.57}$$

where $P(e|\mathscr{C}_1)$ is the conditional probability of error given that the classifier input data was drawn from the distribution of class $\mathscr{C}_1$, and similarly for $P(e|\mathscr{C}_2)$. For the problem at hand, we find that

$$P(e|\mathscr{C}_1) \simeq 0.1056$$

and

$$P(e|\mathscr{C}_2) \simeq 0.2642$$

The average probability of misclassification is therefore

$$P_e \simeq 0.1849$$

Equivalently, the *average probability of correct classification* is

$$\begin{aligned} P_c &= 1 - P_e \\ &\simeq 0.8151 \end{aligned}$$

Experimental Determination of Optimal Multilayer Perceptron[5]

Table 6.1 lists the variable parameters of a multilayer perceptron (MLP) involving a single layer of hidden neurons, and trained with the back-propagation algorithm. Since the ultimate objective of a pattern classifier is to achieve an acceptable rate of correct classification, this criterion is used to judge when the variable parameters of the MLP (used as a pattern classifier) are optimal.

Optimal Number of Hidden Neurons. Reflecting practical approaches to the problem of determining the optimal number of hidden neurons, M, the criterion used is the smallest number of hidden neurons that yields a performance "close" to the optimal Bayesian classifier—say, within 1 percent. Thus, the experimental study begins with two hidden neurons as the starting point for the simulation results summarized in Table 6.2. Since the purpose of the first set of simulations is merely to ascertain the sufficiency of two hidden neurons or otherwise, the learning-rate parameter η and momentum constant α are arbitrarily set to some nominal values. For each simulation run, a training set of input–output pairs, randomly generated from the Gaussian distributions for classes $\mathscr{C}_1$ and $\mathscr{C}_2$ with equal probability, is repeatedly cycled through the network, with each training cycle representing an *epoch.* The number of epochs is chosen so that the total number of training patterns used for each run is constant. By so doing, any potential effects arising from variations of the training set sizes are averaged out.

[5] The experimental results reported in this computer experiment are based on Yee (1992).

TABLE 6.1 Variable Parameters of Multilayer Perceptron

Parameter	Symbol	Typical Range
Number of hidden neurons	M	$(2,\infty)$
Learning-rate parameter	η	$(0,1)$
Momentum constant	α	$(0,1)$

In Table 6.2 and subsequent tables, the *mean-squared error* is computed precisely as the error functional defined in Eq. (6.45). It should be emphasized that the mean-squared error is included in these tables only as a matter of record, since a *small mean-squared error does not necessarily imply good generalization* (i.e., good performance with data not seen before).

After convergence of a network trained with a total number of N patterns, the probability of correct classification can, in theory, be calculated as follows:

$$P(c;N) = P(c;N|\mathscr{C}_1)P(\mathscr{C}_1) + P(c;N|\mathscr{C}_2)P(\mathscr{C}_2) \tag{6.58}$$

where

$$P(c;N|\mathscr{C}_1) = \int_{\Omega_1(N)} f(\mathbf{x}|\mathscr{C}_1)\, d\mathbf{x} \tag{6.59}$$

$$P(c;N|\mathscr{C}_2) = 1 - \int_{\Omega_1(N)} f(\mathbf{x}|\mathscr{C}_2)\, d\mathbf{x} \tag{6.60}$$

and $\Omega_1(N)$ is the region in decision space over which the multilayer perceptron (trained with N patterns) classifies the vector $\mathbf{x}$ as belonging to class $\mathscr{C}_1$. Usually, this region is found experimentally by evaluating the mapping function learned by the network and applying the output decision rule of Eq. (6.47). Unfortunately, the numerical evaluation of $P(c;N|\mathscr{C}_1)$ and $P(c;N|\mathscr{C}_2)$ is problematic, because closed-form expressions describing the decision boundary $\Omega_1(N)$ cannot be easily found.

Accordingly, we resort to the use of an experimental approach that involves testing the trained multilayer perceptron against another independent set of input–output pairs that are again drawn randomly from the distributions for classes $\mathscr{C}_1$ and $\mathscr{C}_2$ with equal probability. Let A be a random variable that counts the number of patterns out of the N test patterns that are classified correctly. Then the ratio

$$p_N = \frac{A}{N}$$

is a random variable that provides the maximum-likelihood unbiased estimate of the actual classification performance p of the network. Assuming that p is constant over the N input–output pairs, we may apply the *Chernoff bound* (Devroye, 1991) to the estimator

TABLE 6.2 Simulation Results for Two Hidden Neurons[a]

Run Number	Training Set Size	Number of Epochs	Mean-Squared Error	Probability of Correct Classification, P_c
1	500	320	0.2331	79.84%
2	2000	80	0.2328	80.34%
3	8000	20	0.2272	80.23%

[a] Learning rate parameter $\eta = 0.1$ and momentum $\alpha = 0$.

p_N of p, obtaining

$$\text{Prob}(|p_N - p| > \varepsilon) < 2\exp(-2\varepsilon^2 N) = \delta$$

The application of the Chernoff bound yields $N \simeq 26{,}500$ for $\varepsilon = 0.01$, and $\delta = 0.01$ (i.e., 99 percent certainty that the estimate p has the given tolerance). We thus picked a test set of size $N = 32{,}000$. The last column of Table 6.2 presents the average probability of correct classification estimated for this test set size.

The average classification performance presented in Table 6.2 for a multilayer perceptron using two hidden neurons is already reasonably close to the Bayesian performance $P_c = 81.51$ percent. On this basis, we may conclude that for the pattern-classification problem described here, the use of two hidden neurons is adequate. To emphasize this conclusion, in Table 6.3 we present the results of simulations repeated for the case of four hidden neurons, with all other parameters held constant. Although the average mean-squared error in Table 6.3 for four hidden neurons is slightly lower than that in Table 6.2 for two hidden neurons, the average rate of correct classification does not show a significant improvement. Accordingly, for the remainder of the computer experiment described here, the number of hidden neurons is held at two.

Optimal Learning and Momentum Constants. For the "optimal" values of the learning-rate parameter η and momentum constant α, we may use any one of three definitions:

1. The η and α that, on average, yield convergence to a local minimum in the error surface of the network with the least number of epochs.
2. The η and α that, for either the worst-case or on average, yield convergence to the global minimum in the error surface with the least number of epochs.
3. The η and α that, on average, yield convergence to the network configuration that has the best generalization, over the entire input space, with the least number of epochs

The terms "average" and "worst-case" used here refer to the distribution of the training input–output pairs. Definition 3 is the ideal; in practice, however, it is difficult to apply, since minimizing the mean-squared error is usually the mathematical criterion for optimality during network training and, as stated previously, a lower mean-squared error over a training set does not necessarily imply good generalization. From a research point of view, definition 2 has generated more interest than definition 1. For example, in Luo (1991), rigorous results are presented for the optimal adaptation of the learning-rate parameter η such that the smallest number of epochs is needed for the multilayer perceptron to approximate the globally optimum synaptic weight matrix to a desired accuracy, albeit for the special case of linear neurons. In general, however, heuristic and experimental procedures presently dominate the optimal selection of η and α, using definition 1. For the experiment described here, we therefore consider optimality in the sense of definition 1.

TABLE 6.3 Simulation Results for Multilayer Perceptron Using Four Hidden Neurons[a]

Run Number	Training Set Size	Number of Epochs	Mean-Squared Error	Probability of Correct Classification
1	500	320	0.2175	80.43%
2	2000	80	0.2175	80.45%
3	8000	20	0.2195	80.99%

[a] Learning-rate parameter $\eta = 0.1$ and momentum constant $\alpha = 0$.

Using a multilayer perceptron with two hidden neurons, combinations of learning-rate parameter $\eta \in \{0.01, 0.1, 0.5, 0.9\}$ and momentum constant $\alpha \in \{0.0, 0.1, 0.5, 0.9\}$ are simulated to observe their effect on network convergence. Each combination is trained with the same set of initial random weights and the same set of 500 input–output patterns, so that the results of the experiment may be compared directly. As stated previously, a network is considered to have "converged" when the absolute rate of change of mean-squared error per epoch is sufficiently "small"; in this experiment, this is defined as less than 0.01 percent. The ensemble-averaged learning curves so computed are plotted in Figs. 6.12a–6.12d, which are individually grouped by η.

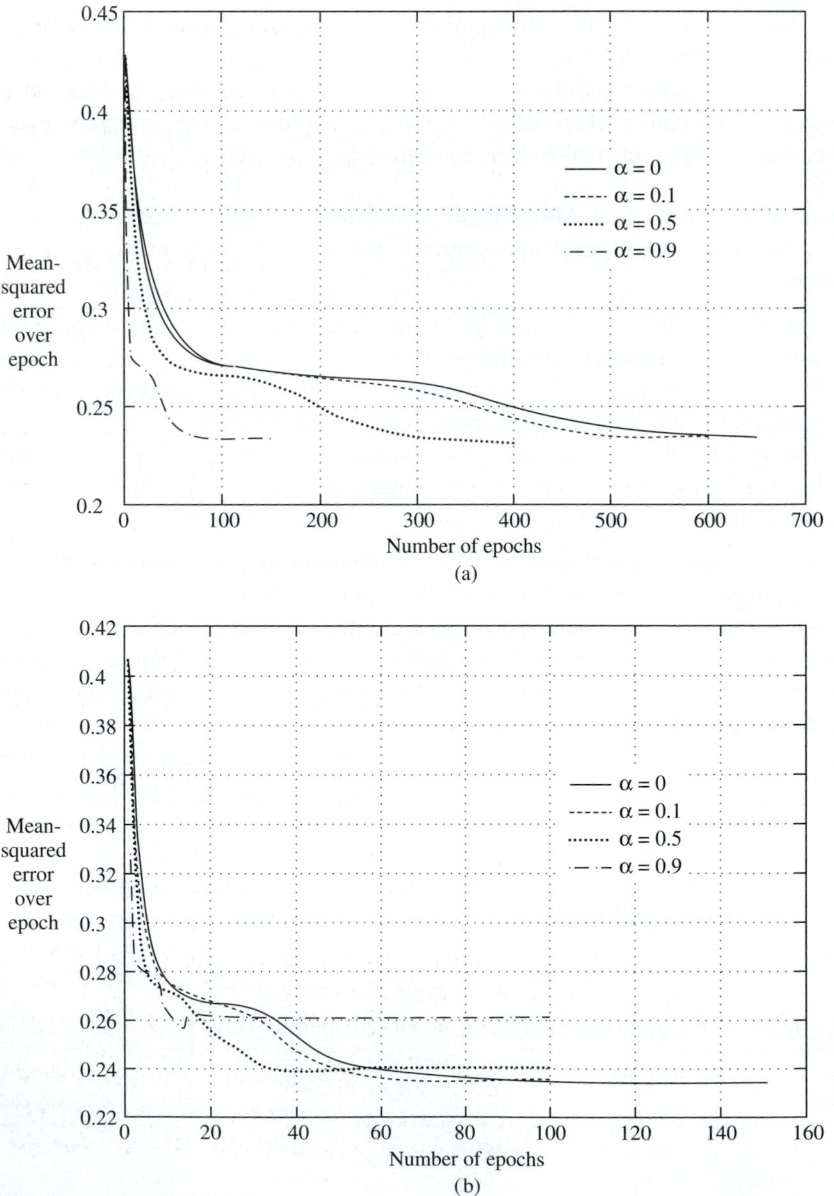

FIGURE 6.12 Ensemble-averaged learning curves for varying momentum constant α, and the following values of learning-rate parameters: (a) $\eta = 0.01$; (b) $\eta = 0.1$.

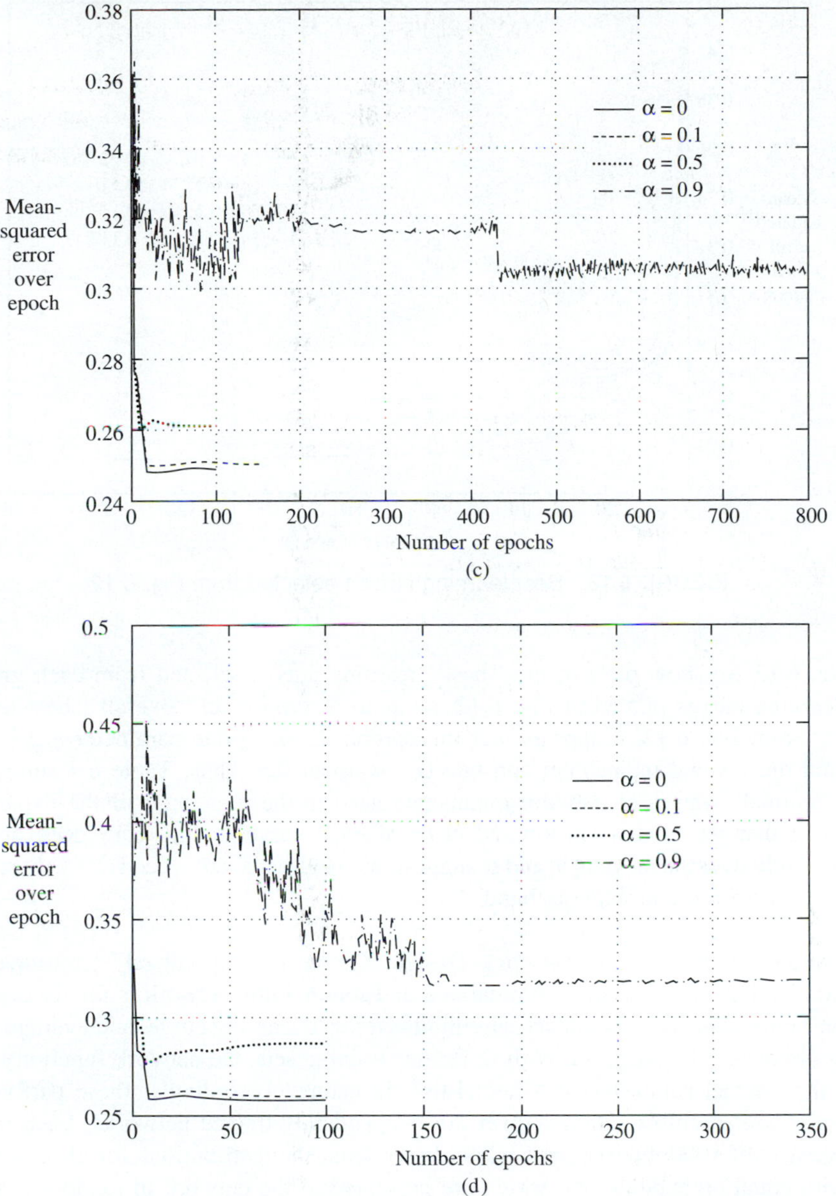

FIGURE 6.12 (continued) (c) $\eta = 0.5$; (d) $\eta = 0.9$.

The experimental learning curves shown here suggest the following trends:

- While, in general, a smaller learning-rate parameter η results in slower convergence, it can locate ''deeper'' local minima in the error surface than a larger η. This finding is intuitively satisfying, since a smaller η implies that the search for a minimum should cover more of the error surface than would be the case for a larger η.
- For $\eta \rightarrow 0$, the use of $\alpha \rightarrow 1$ produces increasing speed of convergence. On the other hand, for $\eta \rightarrow 1$, the use of $\alpha \rightarrow 0$ is required to ensure learning stability.
- The use of the constants $\eta = \{0.5, 0.9\}$ and $\alpha = 0.9$ causes oscillations in the mean-squared error during learning and a higher value for the final mean-squared error at convergence, both of which are undesirable effects.

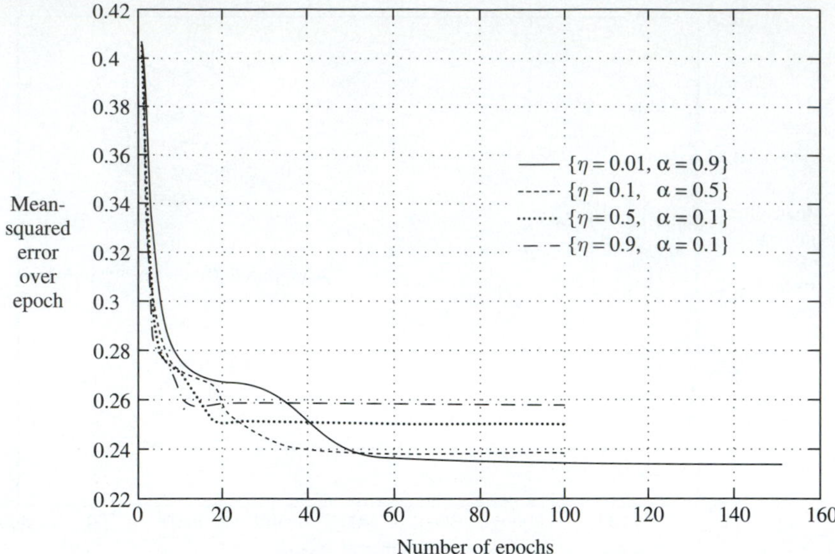

FIGURE 6.13 Best learning curves selected from Fig. 6.12.

In Fig. 6.13 we show plots of the "best" learning curves selected from each group of the learning curves plotted in Fig. 6.12, so as to determine an "overall" best learning curve. From Fig. 6.13, it appears that the optimal learning-rate parameter η_{opt} is about 0.1 and the optimal momentum constant α_{opt} is about 0.5. Thus, Table 6.4 summarizes the "optimal" values of network parameters used in the remainder of the experiment. The fact that the final mean-squared error of each curve in Fig. 6.13 does not vary significantly over the range of η and α suggests a "well-behaved" (i.e., relatively smooth) error surface for the problem at hand.

Evaluation of Optimal Network Design. Given the "optimized" multilayer perceptron having the parameters summarized in Table 6.4, the network is finally evaluated to determine its decision boundary, ensemble-averaged learning curve, and average probability of correct classification. With finite-size training sets, the network function learned with the optimal parameters is "stochastic" in nature. Accordingly, these performance measures are ensemble-averaged over 20 independently trained networks. Each training set consists of 1000 input–output pairs, drawn from the distributions for classes $\mathscr{C}_1$ and $\mathscr{C}_2$ with equal probability, and which are presented to the network in random order. As before, the criterion used for network convergence is an absolute rate of change in mean-squared error of less than 0.01 percent per epoch. For the experimental determination of the average probabilities of correct classification, the same test set of 32,000 input–output pairs used previously is used once more.

TABLE 6.4 Configuration of Optimized Multilayer Perceptron

Parameter	Symbol	Value
Optimum number of hidden neurons	M_{opt}	2
Optimum learning-rate parameter	η_{opt}	0.1
Optimum momentum constant	α_{opt}	0.5

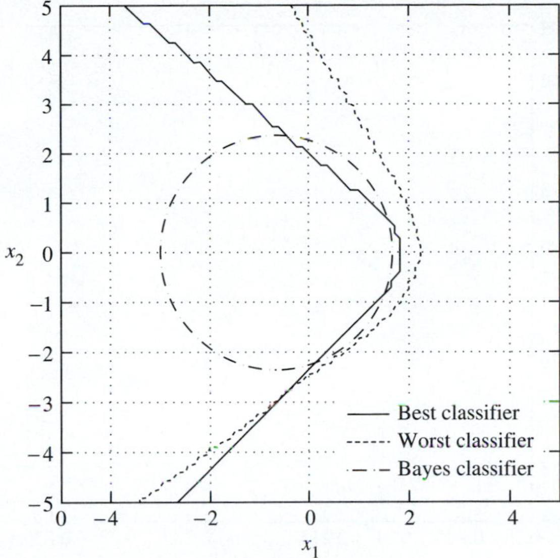

FIGURE 6.14 Decision boundaries constructed by multilayer perceptron.

Figure 6.14 shows the decision boundaries for the two networks in the ensemble of 20 with the worst and best classification performance; this figure also includes, for reference, the (circular) Bayesian decision boundary. Both decision boundaries (for the worst and best classification performance) are convex with respect to the region where they classify the vector **x** as belonging to class $\mathscr{C}_1$ or class $\mathscr{C}_2$. Each boundary appears to comprise two linear segments with a nonlinear segment joining them near their projected intersection.

Figure 6.15 shows the ensemble-averaged, slowest and fastest learning curves observed during training of the "optimized" network. Despite the superior final mean-squared error

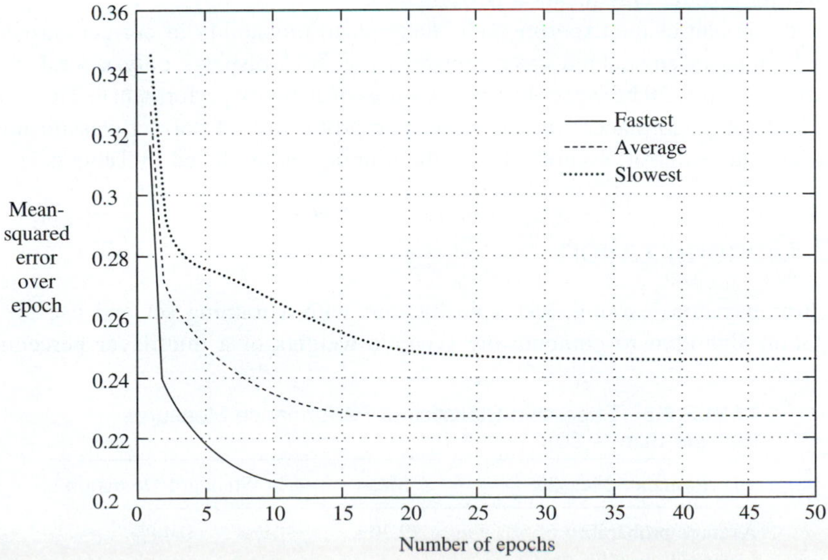

FIGURE 6.15 Ensemble-averaged learning curves; slowest and fastest performances for the optimized network.

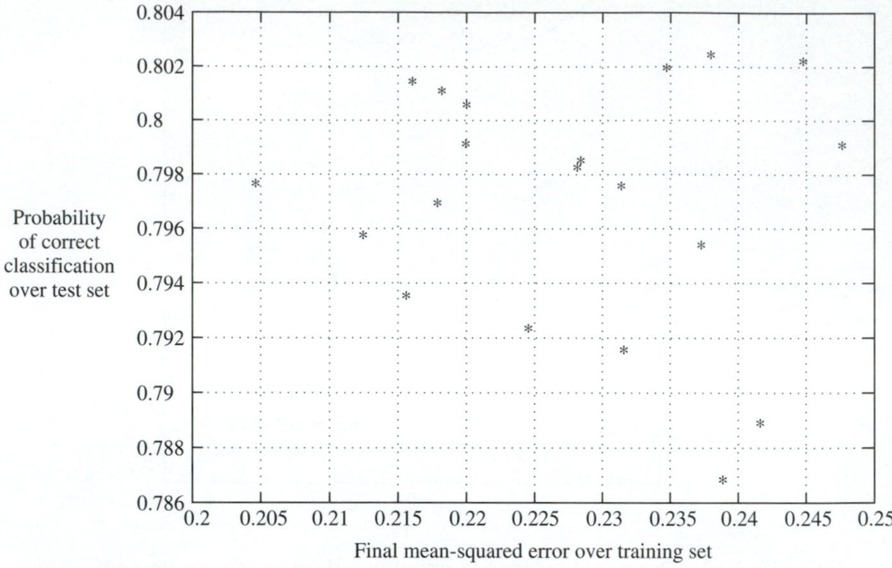

FIGURE 6.16 Average correct classification probability versus mean-squared error.

of the network with the fastest learning curve (0.2047 versus 0.2477 for the network with the slowest learning curve), this apparent advantage produces no gain in classification performance; in fact, the fastest learning network has a marginally *worse* classification performance than the slowest learning network (79.78 versus 79.90 percent). A similar situation occurs when the mean-squared error of the network in the ensemble with the best classification performance is compared with that of the network with the worst classification performance: the former has a P_c of 80.23 percent with a final mean-squared error of 0.2380, whereas the latter has a P_c of 78.68 percent with a final mean-squared error of 0.2391, not significantly different from the former. These results reinforce the notion that a lower mean-squared error over the training set is not in itself a sufficient condition for a better classification performance.

Indeed, the plot of the experimentally determined probability of correct classification versus the final mean-squared error shown in Fig. 6.16 displays only a weak negative correlation of -0.1220 between the two measures of network performance. The ensemble statistics of the performance measures, average probability of correct classification and final mean-squared error, computed over the training set are listed in Table 6.5.

6.10 Generalization

In back-propagation learning, we typically start with a training set and use the back-propagation algorithm to compute the synaptic weights of a multilayer perceptron by

TABLE 6.5 Ensemble Statistics of Performance Measures (Sample Size = 20)

Performance Measure	Mean	Standard Deviation
Average probability of correct classification	79.70%	0.44%
Final mean-squared error	0.2277	0.0118

loading (encoding) as many of the training examples as possible into the network. The hope is that the neural network so designed will generalize. A network is said to *generalize* well when the input–output relationship computed by the network is correct (or nearly so) for input/output patterns (test data) never used in creating or training the network; the term ''generalization'' is borrowed from psychology. Here, of course, it is assumed that the test data are drawn from the same population used to generate the training data.

The learning process (i.e., training of a neural network) may be viewed as a ''curve-fitting'' problem. The network itself may be considered simply as a nonlinear input–output mapping. Such a viewpoint then permits us to look on generalization not as a mystical property of neural networks but rather simply as the effect of a good nonlinear interpolation of the input data (Wieland and Leighton, 1987). The network performs useful interpolation

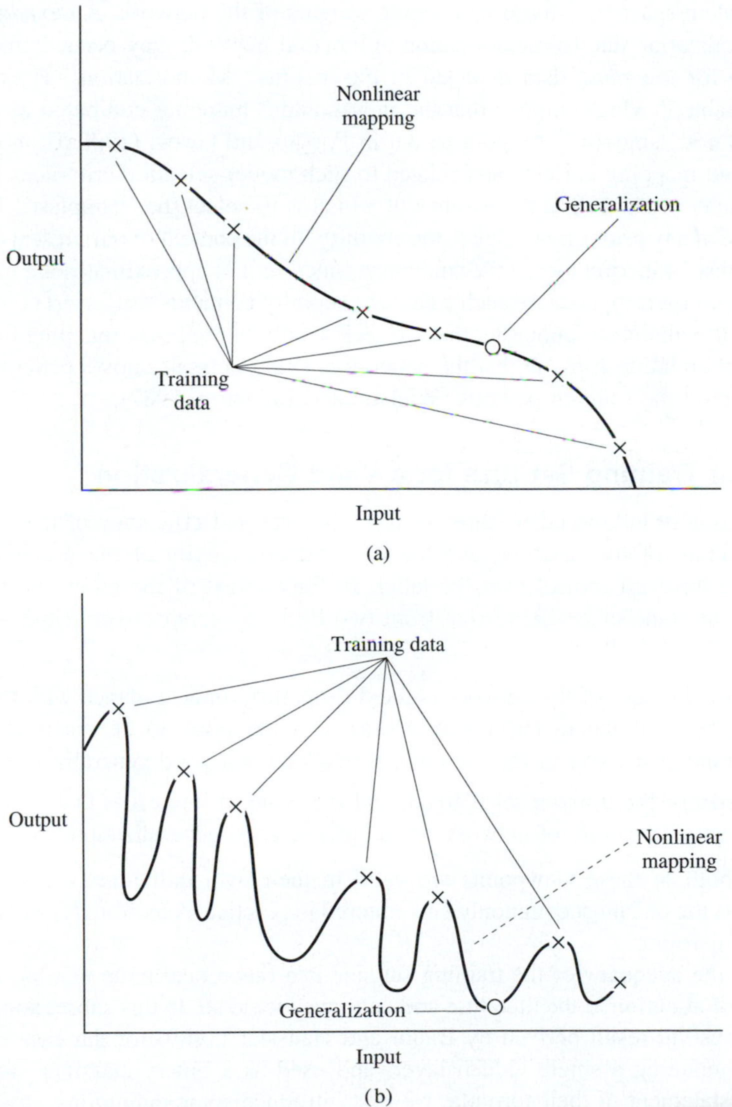

FIGURE 6.17 (a) Properly fitted data (good generalization). (b) Overfitted data (poor generalization).

primarily because multilayer perceptrons with continuous activation functions lead to output functions that are also continuous.

Figure 6.17a illustrates how generalization may occur in a hypothetical network. The nonlinear input–output mapping represented by the curve depicted in this figure is computed by the network as a result of learning the points labeled as "training data." The point marked on the curve as "generalization" is thus seen to be simply as the result of interpolation performed by the network.

A neural network that is designed to generalize well will produce a correct input–output mapping even when the input is slightly different from the examples used to train the network, as illustrated in Fig. 6.17a. When, however, a neural network learns too many specific input–output relations (i.e., it is overtrained), the network may memorize the training data and therefore be less able to generalize between similar input–output patterns. Ordinarily, loading data into a multilayer perceptron in such a fashion requires the use of more hidden neurons than is actually necessary, with the result that unintended curves in the problem space are stored in synaptic weights of the network. An example of how poor generalization due to memorization in a neural network may occur is illustrated in Fig. 6.17b for the same data depicted in Fig. 6.17a. "Memorization" is essentially a "look-up table," which implies that the input–output mapping computed by the neural network is not "smooth." As pointed out in Poggio and Girosi (1990a), smoothness of input–output mapping is intimately related to such model-selection criteria as the *Occam razor* (Blumer et al., 1987), the essence of which is to select the "simplest" function in the absence of any prior knowledge to the contrary. In the context of our present discussion, the "simplest" function means the smoothest function that approximates the mapping for a given error criterion, because such a choice generally demands the fewest computational resources. It is therefore important that we seek a smooth nonlinear mapping for ill-posed input–output relationships, so that the network is able to classify novel patterns correctly with respect to the training patterns (Wieland and Leighton, 1987).

Sufficient Training Set Size for a Valid Generalization

Generalization is influenced by three factors: the size and efficiency of the training set, the architecture of the network, and the physical complexity of the problem at hand. Clearly, we have no control over the latter. In the context of the other two factors, we may view the issue of generalization from two different perspectives (Hush and Horne, 1993):

- The architecture of the network is fixed (hopefully in accordance with the physical complexity of the underlying problem), and the issue to be resolved is that of determining the size of the training set needed for a good generalization to occur.
- The size of the training set is fixed, and the issue of interest is that of determining the best architecture of network for achieving good generalization.

Although both of these viewpoints are valid in their own individual ways, the former viewpoint is the one most commonly encountered in practice. Accordingly, we concentrate on it from here on.

Indeed, the adequacy of the training set size is a theoretical issue that has attracted a great deal of attention in the literature and continues to do so. In this subsection we briefly describe a useful result derived by Baum and Haussler (1989) for the case of a neural network containing a single hidden layer, and used as a binary classifier. To pave the way for a statement of their formula, we first introduce some definitions.

An example is defined as a pair $\{\mathbf{x}, d\}$ where the input vector $\mathbf{x} \in \mathbb{R}^p$, and the desired output $d \in [-1,1]$. In other words, the network acts as a binary classifier. An epoch is defined as a sequence of examples drawn independently at random from some distribution D. Let f be a function from the space $\mathbb{R}^p$ into $[-1,1]$, with $d = f(\mathbf{x})$. An *error* of the function f, with respect to the distribution D, is defined as the probability that the output $y \neq d$ for a pair $(\mathbf{x}, d)$ picked at random. Let M denote the total number of hidden computation nodes. Let W be the total number of synaptic weights in the network. Let N denote the number of random examples used to train the network. Let ε denote the fraction of errors permitted on test. Then, according to Baum and Haussler, the network will almost certainly provide generalization, provided that two conditions are met:

1. The fraction of errors made on the training set is less than $\varepsilon/2$.
2. The number of examples, N, used in training is

$$N \geq \frac{32W}{\varepsilon} \ln\left(\frac{32M}{\varepsilon}\right) \tag{6.61}$$

where ln denotes the natural logarithm.

Equation (6.61) provides a *distribution-free, worst-case* formula for estimating the training set size for a single-layer neural network that is sufficient for a good generalization. We say "worst case" because in practice there can be a huge numerical gap between the actual size of the training set needed and that predicted by the criterion of Eq. (6.61). It should be emphasized, however, that this gap is merely a reflection of the worst-case nature of the criterion; *on average,* we can do much better in terms of bounding the size of the training set.

Ignoring the logarithmic factor in Eq. (6.61), we see that the appropriate number of training examples is, to a first order of approximation, directly proportional to the number of weights in the network and inversely proportional to the accuracy parameter ε. Indeed, it seems that in practice all we need for a good generalization is to satisfy the condition

$$N > \frac{W}{\varepsilon} \tag{6.62}$$

Thus, with an error of 10 percent, say, the number of training examples should be approximately 10 times the number of synaptic weights in the network. Equation (6.62) is in accordance with *Widrow's rule of thumb* for the LMS algorithm, which states that the settling time for adaptation in adaptive temporal filtering is approximately equal to the memory time span of an adaptive tapped-delay-line filter divided by the misadjustment (Widrow and Stearns, 1985). The misadjustment in the LMS algorithm plays a role somewhat analogous to the accuracy parameter ε in Eq. (6.62).

6.11 Cross-Validation

The essence of back-propagation learning is to encode an input–output relation, represented by a set of examples $\{\mathbf{x}, \mathbf{d}\}$, with a multilayer perceptron (MLP) well trained in the sense that it learns enough about the past to generalize to the future. From such a perspective, the learning process amounts to a choice of network parameterization for this data set. More specifically, we may view the MLP selection problem as choosing, within a set of candidate model structures (parameterizations), the "best" one according to a certain criterion.

In this context, a standard tool in statistics, known as *cross-validation,* provides an appealing guiding principle (Stone, 1974; Janssen et al., 1988). First, as usual, the available data set is randomly partitioned into a training set and a test set. The training set is further partitioned into two subsets:

1. A subset used for *estimation of the model* (i.e., training the network).
2. A subset used for *evaluation of the performance of the model* (i.e., validation); the validation subset is typically 10 to 20 percent of the training set.

The motivation here is to *validate* the model on a data set different from the one used for parameter estimation. In this way, we may use the training set to assess the performance of various candidate model structures, and thereby choose the ''best'' one. The particular model with the best-performing parameter values is then trained on the full training set, and the generalization performance of the resulting network is measured on the test set. It is of interest to note that cross-validation follows a two-step procedure, the first step of which is basically the same as that of the structural risk-minimization procedure described in Section 2.13.

Cross-validation may be used for large neural networks with good generalization as the goal in different ways, as described next.

Network Complexity

Consider first the problem of choosing network complexity measured in terms of the number of hidden neurons used in a multilayer perceptron. Statistically, this problem may be interpreted as that of choosing the size of the parameter set used to model the data set (Hanson and Solamon, 1990; Smith, 1993). Measured in terms of the ability of the network to generalize, there is obviously a limit on the size of the network. This follows from the basic observation that it may not be an optimal strategy to train the network to perfection on a given data set, because of the ill-posedness of any finite set of data representing a target function, a condition that is true for both ''noisy'' and ''clean'' data. Rather, it would be better to train the network in order to produce the ''best'' generalization. To do so, we may use cross-validation. Specifically, the training data set is partitioned into training and test subsets, in which case ''overtraining'' will show up as poorer performance on the cross-validation set.

Size of Training Set

Another way in which cross-validation may be used is to decide when the training of a network on the training set should be actually stopped. In this case, the error performance of the network on generalization is exploited to determine the size of the data set used in training (Hinton, 1990b; Smith, 1993). The idea of cross-validation as used in this case is illustrated in Fig. 6.18, where two curves are shown for the mean-squared error in generalization, plotted versus the number of epochs used in training. One curve relates to the use of few adjustable parameters (i.e., underfitting), and the other relates to the use of many parameters (i.e., overfitting). In both cases, we usually find that (1) the error performance on generalization exhibits a minimum point, and (2) the minimum mean-squared error for overfitting is smaller and better defined than that for underfitting. Accordingly, we may achieve good generalization even if the neural network is designed to have too many parameters, provided that training of the network on the training set is stopped at a number of epochs corresponding to the minimum point of the error-performance curve on cross-validation.

Size of Learning-Rate Parameter

Cross-validation may also be used to adjust the size of the learning-rate parameter of a multilayer perceptron with back-propagation learning used as a pattern classifier (Renals et al., 1992b). In particular, the network is first trained on the subtraining set, and the

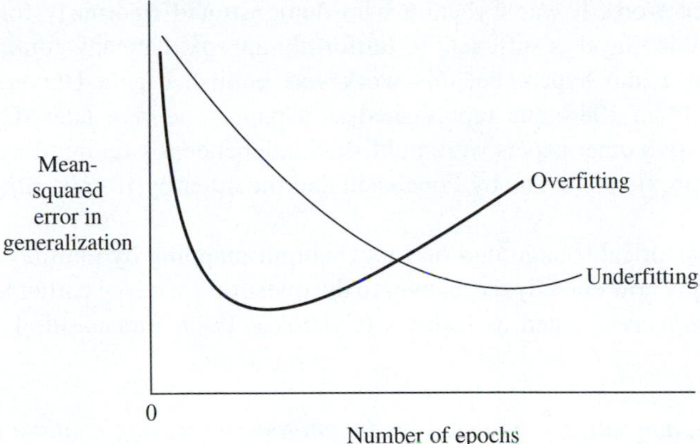

FIGURE 6.18 Illustration of the idea of cross validation.

cross-validation set is then used to validate the training after each epoch. When the classification performance of the network on the cross-validation set fails to improve by a certain amount (typically, 0.5 percent), the size of the learning-rate parameter is reduced; typically, a factor of 2 is used for the parameter reduction. After each succeeding epoch, the learning-rate parameter is further reduced, until once again there is no further improvement in classification performance on the cross-validation set. When that point is reached, training of the network is halted.

6.12 Approximations of Functions

A multilayer perceptron trained with the back-propagation algorithm may be viewed as a practical vehicle for performing a *nonlinear input–output mapping* of a general nature. To be specific, let p denote the number of input (source) nodes of a multilayer perceptron, and let q denote the number of neurons in the output layer of the network. The input–output relationship of the network defines a mapping from a p-dimensional Euclidean input space to a q-dimensional Euclidean output space, which is infinitely continuously differentiable. In assessing the capability of the multilayer perceptron from the viewpoint of input–output mapping, the following fundamental question arises:

> *What is the minimum number of hidden layers in a multilayer perceptron with an input–output mapping that provides an approximate realization of any continuous mapping?*

In this section we address the answer to this question and related issues.

Universal Approximation Theorem

Research interest in the virtues of multilayer perceptrons as devices for the representation of arbitrary continuous functions was perhaps first put into focus by Hecht-Nielsen (1987), who invoked an improved version of Kolomogorov's superposition theorem due to Sprecher (1965). Then, Gallant and White (1988) showed that a single-hidden-layer feedforward network with monotone ''cosine'' squashing at the hidden layer and no squashing at the output embeds as a special case a ''Fourier network'' that yields a Fourier series approximation to a given function as its output. However, in the context of traditional multilayer perceptrons, it was Cybenko who demonstrated rigorously for the first time that a single hidden layer is sufficient to uniformly approximate any continuous function with support in a unit hypercube; this work was published as a University of Illinois Technical Report in 1988, and republished as a paper one year later (Cybenko, 1988, 1989). In 1989, two other papers were published independently on multilayer perceptrons as universal approximators, one by Funahashi and the other by Hornik, Stinchcombe, and White.

Given this historical background on input–output mapping by multilayer feedforward networks, we may now embody the answer to the question we raised earlier in the *universal approximation theorem* stated as follows (Cybenko, 1989; Funahashi, 1989; Hornik et al., 1989):

Let $\varphi(\cdot)$ be a nonconstant, bounded, and monotone-increasing continuous function. Let I_p denote the p-dimensional unit hypercube $[0,1]^p$. The space of continuous functions on I_p is denoted by $C(I_p)$. Then, given any function $f \in C(I_p)$ and $\varepsilon > 0$, there exist an integer M and sets of real constants α_i, θ_i, and w_{ij}, where $i = 1, \ldots, M$ and $j = 1, \ldots, p$ such that we may define

$$F(x_1, \ldots, x_p) = \sum_{i=1}^{M} \alpha_i \varphi\left(\sum_{j=1}^{p} w_{ij}x_j - \theta_i\right) \tag{6.63}$$

as an approximate realization of the function $f(\cdot)$; that is,

$$|F(x_1, \ldots, x_p) - f(x_1, \ldots, x_p)| < \varepsilon$$

for all $\{x_1, \ldots, x_p\} \in I_p$.

This theorem is directly applicable to multilayer perceptrons. We first note that the logistic function $1/[1 + \exp(-v)]$ used as the nonlinearity in a neuron model for the construction of a multilayer perceptron is indeed a nonconstant, bounded, and monotone-increasing function; it therefore satisfies the conditions imposed on the function $\varphi(\cdot)$. Next, we note that Eq. (6.63) represents the output of a multilayer perceptron described as follows:

1. The network has p input nodes and a single hidden layer consisting of M neurons; the inputs are denoted by $x_1, \ldots, x_p$.
2. Hidden neuron i has synaptic weights $w_{i1}, \ldots, w_{ip}$ and threshold θ_i.
3. The network output is a linear combination of the outputs of the hidden neurons, with $\alpha_1, \ldots, \alpha_M$ defining the coefficients of this combination.

The universal approximation theorem is an *existence theorem* in the sense that it provides the mathematical justification for the approximation of an arbitrary continuous function as opposed to exact representation. Equation (6.63), which is the backbone of the theorem, merely generalizes approximations by finite Fourier series. In effect, the theorem states that a *single hidden layer is sufficient for a multilayer perceptron to compute a uniform ε approximation to a given training set represented by the set of inputs* $x_1, \ldots, x_p$ and a desired (target) output $f(x_1, \ldots, x_p)$. However, the theorem does not say that a single hidden layer is optimum in the sense of learning time or ease of implementation.

Bounds on Approximation Errors

Barron (1991, 1992) has established the approximation properties of a multilayer perceptron, assuming that the network has a single layer of hidden neurons using sigmoidal nonlinearities and a linear output neuron. The network is trained using the back-propagation algorithm and then tested with new data. During training, the network learns specific points of a target function f in accordance with the training data, and thereby produces the approximating function F defined in Eq. (6.63). When the network is exposed to test data that has not been seen before, the network function F acts as an "estimator" of new points of the target function; that is, $F = \hat{f}$. According to Barron (1991, 1992), the *total risk R*, defined as the mean integrated squared error between the target function f and the estimated network function $\hat{f}$, is bounded by

$$O\left(\frac{C_f^2}{M}\right) + O\left(\frac{Mp}{N}\log N\right) \tag{6.64}$$

where $O(\cdot)$ denotes "order of," and C_f is the first absolute moment of the Fourier magnitude distribution of the target function f; that is, C_f quantifies the "regularity" of f. The network parameters used to define the bound are as follows: M is the total number of hidden neurons, p is the number of input (source) nodes, and N is the number of training examples. The total risk R quantifies the ability of the network to generalize to new data. In particular, the two terms in the bound on the risk R express the trade-off between two conflicting requirements concerning the size of the hidden layer (Barron, 1991, 1992):

- *The accuracy of best approximation,* which requires a large M (number of hidden neurons) in accordance with the universal approximation theorem
- *The accuracy of the empirical fit to this approximation,* which requires a small M/N (ratio of hidden layer size to training set size)

The approach taken by Barron in deriving these important results involves a form of complexity regularization that is closely related to Vapnik's method of structural risk minimization, which was discussed in Section 2.13.

The implication of the bound on the mean-squared approximation error is that exponentially large sample sizes are *not* required to get accurate estimates for multilayer perceptrons as universal approximators, which makes them all the more important.

The error between the empirical fit and the best approximation may be viewed as an *estimation error.* Let ε_0 denote the mean-squared value of this error. It follows therefore that the bound on ε_0 is on the order of Mp/N, ignoring the logarithmic factor $\log N$, which is justifiable for a large training set. Reformulating this result, we may thus state that the size N of the training set for good generalization should be larger than Mp/ε_0, which interestingly has a mathematical structure similar to that of Eq. (6.62). In other words, as a rule of thumb, we may state that for good generalization the number of training examples should desirably be larger than the ratio of the total number of free parameters in the network to the mean-squared estimation error.

Another interesting result that emerges from the bounds described in (6.64) is that when the size of the hidden layer is optimized (i.e., the total risk is minimized with respect to N) by setting

$$M \simeq C_f\left(\frac{N}{p\log N}\right)^{1/2}$$

then the total risk R is bounded by $O(C_f\sqrt{p\log N/N})$. A surprising aspect of this result is that, in terms of the first-order behavior of the total risk R, the rate of convergence expressed as a function of the training set size N is of order $(1/N)^{1/2}$ (times a logarithmic factor). In contrast, for traditional smooth functions (i.e., those with bounded norms of the derivatives of order s for some $s > 0$), the minimax rate of convergence of the total risk is of order $(1/N)^{2s/(2s+p)}$. The dependence of the rate on p (i.e., dimension of the input space) in the exponent is a *curse of dimensionality* (Duda and Hart, 1973), which severely restricts the practical application of traditional smooth functions. The curse of dimensionality does not appear to apply to the class of functions described in Eq. (6.63) (Barron, 1991), confirming another important property of multilayer perceptrons.

Practical Considerations

The universal approximation theorem is important from a theoretical viewpoint, because it provides the *necessary mathematical tool* for the viability of feedforward networks with a single hidden layer as a class of approximate solutions. Without such a theorem, we could conceivably be searching for a solution that cannot exist. However, the theorem is only an existence proof; it does not tell us how to construct the multilayer perceptron to do the approximation.[6]

Nevertheless, the universal approximation theorem has limited practical value. The theorem assumes that the continuous function to be approximated is given and that a hidden layer of unlimited size is available for the approximation. Both of these assumptions are violated in most practical applications of multilayer perceptrons.

The problem with multilayer perceptrons using a single hidden layer is that the neurons therein tend to interact with each other globally. In complex situations this interaction makes it difficult to improve the approximation at one point without worsening it at some other point. On the other hand, with two hidden layers the approximation (curve-fitting) process becomes more manageable. In particular, we may proceed as follows (Chester, 1990; Funahashi, 1989):

1. *Local features* are extracted in the first hidden layer. Specifically, some neurons in the first hidden layer are used to partition the input space into regions, and other neurons in that layer learn the local features characterizing those regions.
2. *Global features* are extracted in the second hidden layer. Specifically, a neuron in the second hidden layer combines the outputs of neurons in the first hidden layer operating on a particular region of the input space, and thereby learns the global features for that region and outputs zero elsewhere.

This two-stage approximation process is similar in philosophy to the spline technique for curve fitting (Schumaker, 1981), in the sense that the effects of neurons are isolated and the approximations in different regions of the input space may be individually adjusted.

Sontag (1992) provides further justification for the use of two hidden layers in the context of *inverse problems.* Specifically, the following inverse problem is considered:

Given a continuous vector-valued function $\mathbf{f}: \mathbb{R}^p \rightarrow \mathbb{R}^m$, *a compact subset* $C \subseteq \mathbb{R}^m$ *that is included in the image of* $\mathbf{f}$, *and an* $\varepsilon > 0$, *find a vector-valued function* $\boldsymbol{\varphi}: \mathbb{R}^m \rightarrow \mathbb{R}^p$ *such that the following condition is satisfied:*

$$\|\boldsymbol{\varphi}(\mathbf{f}(\mathbf{u})) - \mathbf{u}\| < \varepsilon \qquad \text{for } \mathbf{u} \in C$$

This problem arises in *inverse kinematics* (dynamics), where the observed state $\mathbf{x}(n)$ of a system is a function of current actions $\mathbf{u}(n)$ and the previous state $\mathbf{x}(n-1)$ of the system, as shown by

$$\mathbf{x}(n) = \mathbf{f}(\mathbf{x}(n-1), \mathbf{u}(n))$$

It is assumed that $\mathbf{f}$ is *invertible,* so that we may solve for $\mathbf{u}(n)$ as a function of $\mathbf{x}(n)$ for any $\mathbf{x}(n-1)$. The function $\mathbf{f}$ represents the direct kinematics, whereas the function $\boldsymbol{\varphi}$

[6] Takahaski (1993) has developed a theory for constructing a multilayer perceptron with two input (source) nodes, a single hidden layer, and two output neurons. The theory permits the specification of the training data set and the free parameters of the network so as to generalize and approximate any given continuous mapping between sets of contours on a plane with any given permissible error.

represents the inverse kinematics. In practical terms, the motivation is to find a function φ that is computable by a multilayer feedforward network. In general, discontinuous functions φ are needed to solve the inverse kinematics problem. Interestingly, however, even if the use of neuron models with discontinuous activation functions is permitted, one hidden layer is *not* enough to guarantee the solution of all such inverse problems, whereas multilayer feedforward networks with two hidden layers are indeed sufficient, for every possible $\mathbf{f}$, C, and ε (Sontag, 1992).

6.13 Back-Propagation and Differentiation

Back-propagation is a specific technique for implementing *gradient descent* in weight space for a multilayer feedforward network. The basic idea of the technique is to efficiently compute *partial derivatives* of an approximating function $F(\mathbf{w};\mathbf{x})$ realized by the network with respect to all the elements of the adjustable weight vector $\mathbf{w}$ for a given value of input vector $\mathbf{x}$. Herein lies the computational power of the back-propagation algorithm. The first documented description of the use of such an approach for efficient gradient evaluation is due to Werbos (1974). The material presented in this section follows the treatment given in Saarinen et al. (1992); a more general discussion of the topic is presented by Werbos (1990).

To be specific, consider a multilayer perceptron with an input layer of p nodes, two hidden layers, and a single output neuron, as depicted in Fig. 6.19. The elements of the weight vector $\mathbf{w}$ are ordered by layer (starting from the first hidden layer), then by neurons in a layer, and then by the number of a synapse within a neuron. Let $w_{ji}^{(l)}$ denote the synaptic weight from neuron i to neuron j in layer l. For $l = 1$, corresponding to the first hidden layer, the index i refers to a source node rather than a neuron. For $l = 3$, corresponding to the output layer in Fig. 6.19, we have $j = 1$. We wish to evaluate the derivatives of the function $F(\mathbf{w};\mathbf{x})$ with respect to all the elements of the weight vector $\mathbf{w}$, for a specified input vector $\mathbf{x} = [x_1, x_2, \ldots, x_p]^T$. Note that for $l = 2$ (i.e., a single hidden layer), the function $F(\mathbf{w};\mathbf{x})$ has exactly the form defined in Eq. (6.63). We have included the weight vector $\mathbf{w}$ as an argument of the function F to focus attention on it.

The multilayer perceptron of Fig. 6.19 is parameterized by an *architecture* A (representing a discrete parameter) and a *weight vector* $\mathbf{w}$ (made up of continuous elements). Let $A_j^{(l)}$ denote that part of the architecture extending from the input layer ($l = 0$) to node j

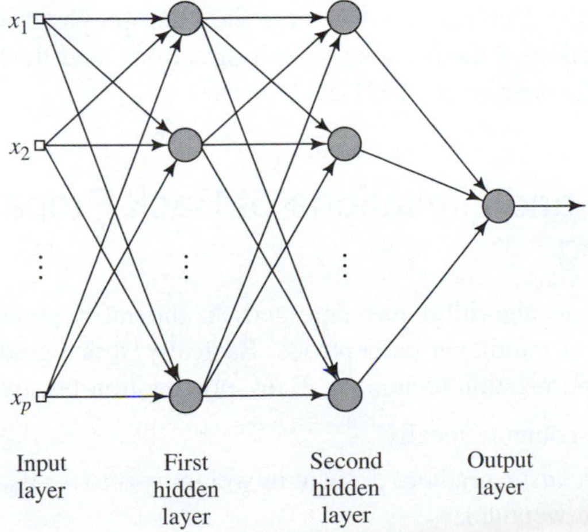

FIGURE 6.19 Multilayer perceptron with two hidden layers and one output neuron.

in layer $l = 1, 2, 3$. Accordingly, we may write

$$F(\mathbf{w};\mathbf{x}) = \varphi(A_1^{(3)}) \tag{6.65}$$

where φ is the activation function, assumed to have the sigmoidal form defined in Eq. (6.30). Note, however, $A_1^{(3)}$ is to be interpreted merely as an architectural symbol rather than a variable. Thus, adapting Eqs. (6.1), (6.2), (6.11), and (6.23) for use in the situation at hand, we obtain the following results (Saarinen et al., 1992):

$$\frac{\partial F(\mathbf{w};\mathbf{x})}{\partial w_{1k}^{(3)}} = \varphi'(A_1^{(3)})\varphi(A_k^{(2)}) \tag{6.66}$$

$$\frac{\partial F(\mathbf{w};\mathbf{x})}{\partial w_{kj}^{(2)}} = \varphi'(A_1^{(3)})\varphi'(A_k^{(2)})\varphi(A_j^{(1)})w_{1k}^{(3)} \tag{6.67}$$

$$\frac{\partial F(\mathbf{w};\mathbf{x})}{\partial w_{ji}^{(1)}} = \varphi'(A_1^{(3)})\varphi'(A_j^{(1)})x_i\left[\sum_k w_{1k}^{(3)}\varphi'(A_k^{(2)})w_{kj}^{(2)}\right] \tag{6.68}$$

where φ' is the partial derivative of the nonlinearity φ with respect to its input, and x_i is the ith element of the input vector $\mathbf{x}$. In a similar way, we may derive the equations for the partial derivatives of a general network with more hidden layers and more neurons in the output layer.

Jacobian of Multilayer Perceptron

Let W denote the total number of free parameters (i.e., synaptic weights and thresholds) of a multilayer perceptron, which are ordered in the manner described to form the weight vector $\mathbf{w}$. Let N denote the total number of examples used to train the network. Using back-propagation, we may compute a set of W partial derivatives of the approximating function $F[\mathbf{w};\mathbf{x}(n)]$ with respect to the elements of the weight vector $\mathbf{w}$ for a specific example $\mathbf{x}(n)$ in the training set. Repeating these computations for $n = 1, 2, \ldots, N$, we end up with an N-by-W matrix of partial derivatives. This matrix is called the *Jacobian* $\mathbf{J}$ of the multilayer perceptron. Each row of the Jacobian corresponds to a particular example in the training set.

There is experimental evidence to suggest that many neural network training problems are intrinsically *ill-conditioned,* leading to a Jacobian $\mathbf{J}$ that is almost *rank-deficient* (Saarinen et al., 1991). The rank of $\mathbf{J}$ is equal to the number of nonzero singular values of $\mathbf{J}$. The Jacobian $\mathbf{J}$ is said to be rank-deficient if its rank is less than $\min(N,W)$. Any rank deficiency in the Jacobian would cause the back-propagation algorithm to obtain only partial information of the possible search directions, and thus would cause training times to be long (Saarinen et al., 1991).

6.14 Virtues and Limitations of Back-Propagation Learning

The back-propagation algorithm has emerged as the most popular algorithm for the supervised training of multilayer perceptrons. Basically, it is a gradient (derivative) technique and *not* an optimization technique. Back-propagation has two distinct properties:

- It is simple to compute locally.
- It performs *stochastic* gradient descent in weight space (for pattern-by-pattern updating of synaptic weights).

These two properties of back-propagation learning in the context of a multilayer perceptron are indeed responsible for its very advantages and disadvantages, as described next.

Connectionism

The back-propagation algorithm is an example of a *connectionist paradigm* that relies on local computations to discover the information-processing capabilities of neural networks. This form of computational restriction is referred to as the *locality constraint,* in the sense that the computation performed by a neuron is influenced solely by those neurons that are in physical contact with it. The use of local computations in the design of artificial neural networks is usually advocated for three principal reasons:

1. Artificial neural networks that perform local computations are often held up as metaphors for biological neural networks.
2. The use of local computations permits a graceful degradation in performance due to hardware errors, and therefore a fault-tolerant network design.
3. Local computations favor the use of parallel architectures as an efficient method for the implementation of artificial neural networks.

Taking these three points in reverse order, point 3 is perfectly justified in the case of back-propagation learning. In particular, the back-propagation algorithm has been implemented successfully on parallel computers by many investigators, and VLSI architectures have been developed for the hardware realization of multilayer perceptrons (Tomlinson et al., 1990; Hammerstrom, 1992). Point 2 is justified so long as certain precautions are taken in the application of the back-propagation algorithm, such as injecting small numbers of ''transient faults'' at each step (Bolt, 1992). As for point 1, relating to the biological plausibility of back-propagation learning, it has indeed been seriously questioned on the following grounds (Shepherd, 1990b; Crick, 1989; Stork, 1989):

1. The reciprocal synaptic connections between the neurons of a multilayer perceptron may assume weights that are excitatory or inhibitory. In the real nervous system, however, neurons appear usually to be the one or the other. This is one of the most serious of the unrealistic assumptions made in neural network models.
2. In a multilayer perceptron, hormonal and other types of global communications are ignored. In real nervous systems, these types of global communication are critical for state-setting functions, such as arousal, attention, and learning.
3. In back-propagation learning, a synaptic weight is modified by a presynaptic activity and an error (learning) signal independent of postsynaptic activity. There is evidence from neurobiology to suggest otherwise.
4. In a neurobiological sense, the implementation of back-propagation learning requires the rapid transmission of information backward along an axon. It appears highly unlikely that such an operation actually takes place in the brain.
5. Back-propagation learning implies the existence of a ''teacher,'' which in the context of the brain would presumably be another set of neurons with novel properties. The existence of such neurons is biologically implausible.

However, these neurobiological misgivings do not belittle the engineering importance of back-propagation learning as a tool for information processing, as evidenced by its successful application in numerous and highly diverse fields, including the simulation of neurobiological phenomena.

Hidden Units

Hidden units play a critical role in the operation of multilayer perceptrons with back-propagation learning in that they act as *feature detectors.* A novel way in which this important attribute of back-propagation learning can be exploited is in the ''discovery'' of significant features that characterize input patterns of interest. Moreover, because the learning process can sometimes be performed without an external teacher, the feature

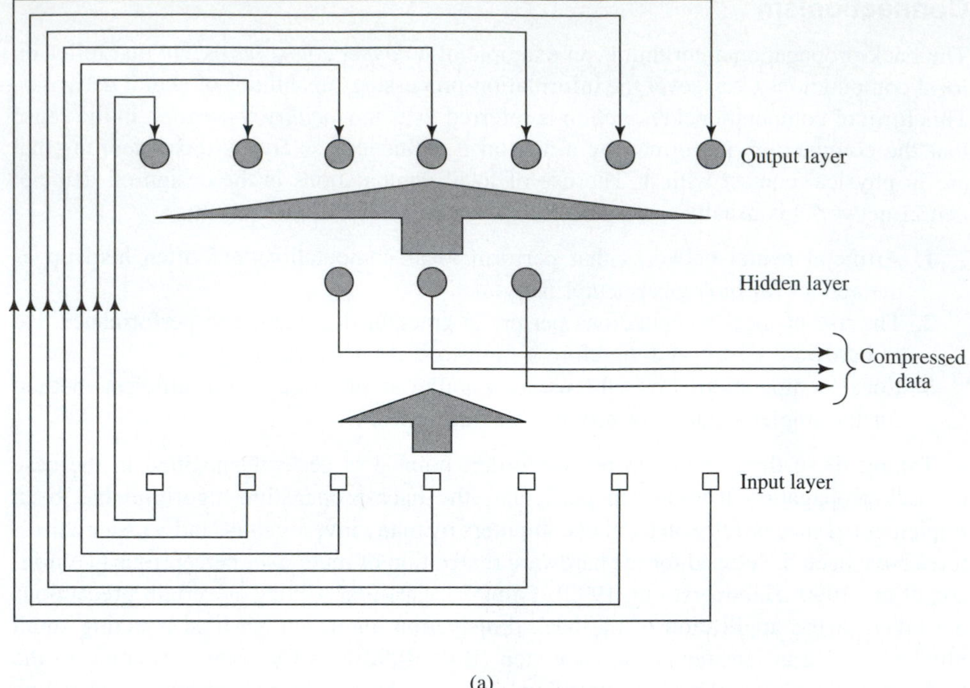

(a)

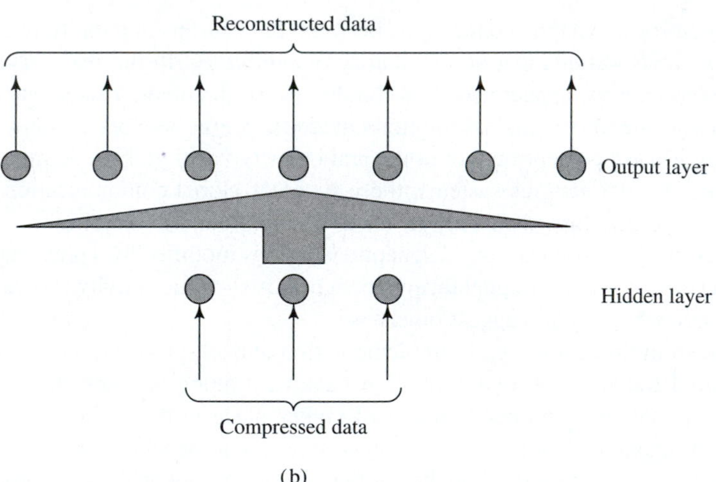

(b)

FIGURE 6.20 Autoencoder with a single hidden layer. (a) Input–output connections of the autoencoder. (b) Layout of network for reconstructing the original data.

extraction is accomplished without detailed knowledge of the output pattern or the underlying physics.

One of the simplest ways to avoid the need for an external teacher in back-propagation learning is to learn the *identity map* over some set of inputs (Rumelhart et al., 1986b). To do this, we let the input pattern and the target (desired) pattern be exactly the same, as illustrated in Fig. 6.20. Specifically, the network is constrained to perform the identity mapping through a narrow channel (hidden layer) of the network, forcing it to develop an efficient encoding in that channel. There are two interesting aspects to this operation:

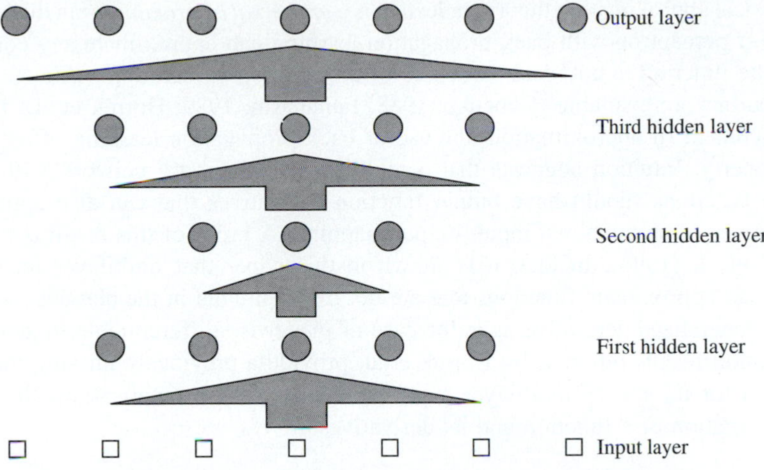

FIGURE 6.21 Autoencoder with three hidden layers.

1. The network develops a compact representation (encoding) of its environment.
2. The representation is learned in a self-organized manner.

Reconstruction of the original data by feeding the encoded data into the hidden layer is illustrated in Fig. 6.20b. Based on the idea of identity mapping, as described here, back-propagation learning can be used to perform image compression (Cottrell et al., 1987), and program neural-like networks as models of real brain networks (Zipser and Rumelhart, 1990).

A multilayer perceptron operating in the self-organized manner described in Fig. 6.20 is referred to as an *autoencoder* or *autoassociator*. Basically, such a structure computes the *principal components*[7] of the input data, which provides the optimum basis for *linear* dimensionality reduction (data compression). The addition of a pair of hidden layers, one between the input and *representation* (i.e., second hidden) layer and the other between the representation layer and the output, as shown in Fig. 6.21, permits the autoencoder to perform nonlinear representations of the data (DeMers and Cottrell, 1993). By so doing, fewer nodes in the representation layer may be needed, and therefore a more effective data compression may be performed than in the case of the single-hidden-layer autoencoder of Fig. 6.20.

Universal Approximation

A multilayer perceptron trained with the back-propagation algorithm manifests itself as a *nested sigmoidal scheme,* written in the following compact form for the case of a single output:

$$F(\mathbf{x},\mathbf{w}) = \varphi\left(\sum_j w_{oj}\varphi\left(\sum_k w_{jk}\varphi\left(\cdots\varphi\left(\sum_i w_{li}x_i\right)\cdots\right)\right)\right) \tag{6.69}$$

where $\varphi(\cdot)$ is a sigmoidal activation function, w_{oj} is the synaptic weight from neuron j in the last hidden layer to the single output neuron o, and so on for the other synaptic weights, and x_i is the ith element of the input vector $\mathbf{x}$. The weight vector $\mathbf{w}$ denotes the entire set of synaptic weights ordered by layer, then neurons in a layer, and then number in a neuron. The scheme of nested nonlinear functions described in Eq. (6.69) is unusual

[7] A detailed exposition of *principal components analysis* is presented in Chapter 9.

in the classical approximation theory. Indeed, it is a *universal approximator* in the sense that a multilayer perceptron with back-propagation learning can approximate any continuous multivariate function to any desired degree of accuracy, provided that sufficiently many hidden neurons are available (Cybenko, 1988; Funahashi, 1989; Hornik et al., 1989).

In the context of approximation, the use of back-propagation learning offers another useful property. Intuition suggests that a multilayer feedforward network with smooth activation functions should have output function derivatives that can also approximate the derivatives of an unknown input–output mapping. A proof of this result is presented in Hornik et al. (1990). In fact, it is shown in this paper that multilayer feedforward networks can approximate functions that are not differentiable in the classical sense, but possess a generalized derivative as in the case of piecewise differentiable functions. The approximation results reported by Hornik et al. provide a previously missing theoretical justification for the use of multilayer feedforward networks in applications that require the approximation of a function and its derivatives.

Convergence

The back-propagation algorithm is a first-order approximation of the steepest-descent technique in the sense that it depends on the gradient of the instantaneous error surface in weight space. The algorithm is therefore *stochastic* in nature; that is, it has a tendency to zigzag its way about the true direction to a minimum on the error surface. Indeed, back-propagation learning is an application of a statistical method known as *stochastic approximation* that was originally proposed by Robbins and Monro (1951). Consequently, it suffers from a *slow convergence* property. We may identify two fundamental causes for this property (Jacobs, 1988):

1. The error surface is fairly flat along a weight dimension, which means that the derivative of the error surface with respect to that weight is small in magnitude. In such a situation, the adjustment applied to the weight is small and, consequently, many iterations of the algorithm may be required to produce a significant reduction in the error performance of the network. Alternatively, the error surface is highly curved along a weight dimension, in which case the derivative of the error surface with respect to that weight is large in magnitude. In this second situation, the adjustment applied to the weight is large, which may cause the algorithm to overshoot the minimum of the error surface.
2. The direction of the negative gradient vector (i.e., the negative derivative of the cost function with respect to the vector of weights) may point away from the minimum of the error surface; hence the adjustments applied to the weights may induce the algorithm to move in the wrong direction.

Consequently, the rate of convergence in back-propagation learning tends to be relatively slow, which in turn makes it computationally expensive. According to the empirical study of Saarinen et al. (1992), the local convergence rates of the back-propagation algorithm are *linear,* which is justified on the grounds that the Jacobian (matrix of first-order partial derivatives) is almost rank-deficient, and so is the Hessian matrix (second-order partial derivatives of the error surface with respect to the weights); these are consequences of the intrinsically ill-conditioned nature of neural-network training problems. Saarinen et al. interpret the linear local convergence rates of back-propagation learning in two ways:

- It is a vindication of back-propagation (gradient descent) in the sense that higher-order methods may not converge much faster while requiring more computational effort; or

- Large-scale neural-network training problems are so inherently difficult to perform that no supervised learning strategy is feasible, and other approaches such as the use of preprocessing may be necessary.

Local Minima

Another peculiarity of the error surface that impacts the performance of the back-propagation algorithm is the presence of *local minima* (i.e., isolated valleys) in addition to global minima. Since back-propagation is basically a hill-climbing technique, it runs the risk of being trapped in a local minimum, where every small change in synaptic weights increases the cost function. But somewhere else in the weight space there exists another set of synaptic weights for which the cost function is smaller than the local minimum in which the network is stuck. Clearly, it is undesirable to have the learning process terminate at a local minimum, especially if it is located far above a global minimum.

The issue of local minima in back-propagation learning has been raised in the epilogue of the enlarged edition of the classic book by Minsky and Papert (1988), where most of the attention is focused on a discussion of the two-volume book, *Parallel Distributed Processing,* by Rumelhart and McClelland (1986). In Chapter 8 of the latter book it is observed that getting trapped in a local minimum is rarely a practical problem for back-propagation learning. Minsky and Papert counter by pointing out that the entire history of pattern recognition shows otherwise. Gori and Tesi (1992) describe a simple example where, although a nonlinearly separable set of patterns could be learned by the chosen network with a single hidden layer, back-propagation learning can get stuck in a local minimum.

What we basically need is a theoretical framework of back-propagation learning that explains the local-minima problem. This is a difficult task to accomplish. Nevertheless, some progress has been reported in the literature on this issue. Baldi and Hornik (1989) have considered the problem of learning in layered linear feedforward neural networks using back-propagation learning. The main result of their paper is that the error surface has only one minimum, corresponding to an orthogonal projection onto the subspace spanned by the first principal eigenvectors of a covariance matrix associated with the training patterns; all other critical points of the error surface are saddle points. Gori and Tesi (1992) have considered the more general case of back-propagation learning that involves the use of nonlinear neurons. The main result of this latter paper is that for linearly separable patterns, convergence to an optimal solution (i.e., global minimum) is ensured by using the batch mode of back-propagation learning, and the network exceeds Rosenblatt's perceptron in generalization to new examples.

Scaling

In principle, neural networks such as multilayer perceptrons trained with the back-propagation algorithm offer the potential of universal computing machines. However, for that potential to be fully realized, we have to overcome the *scaling problem,* which addresses the issue of how well the network behaves (e.g., as measured by the time required for training or the best generalization performance attainable) as the computational task increases in size and complexity. Among the many possible ways of measuring the size or complexity of a computational task, the predicate order defined by Minsky and Papert (1969, 1988) provides the most useful and important measure.

To explain what we mean by a predicate, let $\psi(X)$ denote a function that can have only two values. Ordinarily, we think of the two values of $\psi(X)$ as 0 and 1. But by taking the values to be FALSE or TRUE, we may think of $\psi(X)$ as a *predicate,* that is, a variable statement whose falsity or truth depends on the choice of argument X. For example, we may write

$$\psi_{\text{CIRCLE}}(X) = \begin{cases} 1 & \text{if the figure } X \text{ is a circle} \\ 0 & \text{if the figure } X \text{ is not a circle} \end{cases} \tag{6.70}$$

Using the idea of a predicate, Tesauro and Janssens (1988) performed an empirical study involving the use of a multilayer perceptron trained with the back-propagation algorithm to learn to compute the parity function. The *parity function* is a Boolean predicate defined by

$$\psi_{\text{PARITY}}(X) = \begin{cases} 1 & \text{if } |X| \text{ is an odd number} \\ 0 & \text{otherwise} \end{cases} \tag{6.71}$$

and whose order is equal to the number of inputs. The experiments performed by Tesauro and Janssens appear to show that the time required for the network to learn to compute the parity function scales exponentially with the number of inputs (i.e., the predicate order of the computation), and that projections of the use of the back-propagation algorithm to learn arbitrarily complicated functions may be overly optimistic.

It is generally agreed that it is inadvisable for a multilayer perceptron to be fully connected. In this context, we may therefore raise the following question: Given that a multilayer perceptron should not be fully connected, how should the synaptic connections of the network be allocated? This question is of no major concern in the case of small-scale applications, but it is certainly crucial to the successful application of back-propagation learning for solving large-scale, real-world problems.

One way of alleviating the scaling problem is to develop insight into the problem at hand and use it to put ingenuity into the architectural design of the multilayer perceptron. Specifically, the network architecture and the constraints imposed on synaptic weights of the network should be designed so as to incorporate prior information about the task into the makeup of the network. Such a design strategy is well illustrated by the way in which back-propagation learning has been successfully applied to the optical character recognition problem (LeCun et al., 1990a); this strategy is discussed in Section 6.22.

Another way of dealing with the scaling problem is to reformulate the back-propagation learning process with modularity built into the network architecture (Ballard, 1990; Jacobs et al., 1991a); *modularity* appears to be an important principle in the architecture of vertebrate nervous systems (Houk, 1992; Van Essen et al., 1992). A computational system is said to have a *modular* architecture if it can be broken down into two or more subsystems that perform computation on distinct inputs in the absence of communication with each other. Moreover, the connection process inside each module can be made "dynamic," that is, synaptic connections can be made or broken as part of the learning process. Modular networks are treated in Chapter 12.

6.15 Accelerated Convergence of Back-Propagation Through Learning-Rate Adaptation

In the previous section we identified the main causes for the possible slow rate of convergence of the back-propagation algorithm. In this section we describe procedures for increasing the rate of convergence while maintaining the locality constraint that is an inherent characteristic of back-propagation learning. We begin the discussion by describing four *heuristics* due to Jacobs (1988), which should be viewed as useful "guidelines" for thinking about how to accelerate the convergence of back-propagation learning through learning rate adaptation:

HEURISTIC 1. Every adjustable network parameter of the cost function should have its own individual learning-rate parameter.

Here we note that the back-propagation algorithm may be slow to converge, because the use of a fixed learning-rate parameter may not suit all portions of the error surface. In other words, a learning-rate parameter appropriate for the adjustment of one synaptic weight is not necessarily appropriate for the adjustment of other synaptic weights in the network. Heuristic 1 recognizes this fact by assigning a different learning-rate parameter to each adjustable synaptic weight (parameter) in the network.

HEURISTIC 2. Every learning-rate parameter should be allowed to vary from one iteration to the next.

Typically, the error surface behaves differently along different regions of a single weight dimension. In order to match this variation, heuristic 2 states that the learning-rate parameter needs to vary from iteration to iteration. It is of interest to note that this heuristic is well founded in the case of linear units; see Luo (1991).

HEURISTIC 3. When the derivative of the cost function with respect to a synaptic weight has the same algebraic sign for several consecutive iterations of the algorithm, the learning-rate parameter for that particular weight should be increased.

The current operating point in weight space may lie on a relatively flat portion of the error surface along a particular weight dimension. This may, in turn, account for the derivative of the cost function (i.e., the gradient of the error surface) with respect to that weight maintaining the same algebraic sign, and therefore pointing in the same direction, for several consecutive iterations of the algorithm. Heuristic 3 states that in such a situation the number of iterations required to move across the flat portion of the error surface may be reduced by increasing the learning-rate parameter appropriately.

HEURISTIC 4. When the algebraic sign of the derivative of the cost function with respect to a particular synaptic weight alternates for several consecutive iterations of the algorithm, the learning-rate parameter for that weight should be decreased.

When the current operating point in weight space lies on a portion of the error surface along a weight dimension of interest that exhibits peaks and valleys (i.e., the surface is highly curved), then it is possible for the derivative of the cost function with respect to that weight to change its algebraic sign from one iteration to the next. In order to prevent the weight adjustment from oscillating, heuristic 4 states that the learning-rate parameter for that particular weight should be decreased appropriately.

It is noteworthy that the use of a different and time-varying learning-rate parameter for each synaptic weight in accordance with these heuristics modifies the back-propagation algorithm in a fundamental way. Specifically, the modified algorithm no longer performs a steepest-descent search. Rather, the adjustments applied to the synaptic weights are based on (1) the partial derivatives of the error surface with respect to the weights, and (2) estimates of the curvatures of the error surface at the current operating point in weight space along the various weight dimensions.

Furthermore, all four heuristics satisfy the locality constraint. Adherence to the locality constraint limits the domain of usefulness of these heuristics in that error surfaces exist for which they do not work. Nevertheless, modifications of the back-propagation algorithm in light of these heuristics, as shown next, do have practical value.

Delta-Bar-Delta Learning Rule

To derive the modification to the back-propagation algorithm, we follow a procedure similar to that described in Section 6.3 for the conventional form of the algorithm. We begin by defining the cost function as the instantaneous sum of squared errors,

$$E(n) = \frac{1}{2}\sum_j e_j^2(n) = \frac{1}{2}\sum_j [d_j(n) - y_j(n)]^2 \tag{6.72}$$

where $y_j(n)$ is the output of neuron j, and d_j is the desired (target) response for that neuron. Although the definition of $E(n)$ in Eq. (6.72) is mathematically similar to that of the cost function $\mathscr{E}(n)$ in Eq. (6.2), the parameter space pertaining to the new cost function $E(n)$ is assumed to consist of different learning rates. Let $\eta_{ji}(n)$ denote the learning-rate parameter assigned to synaptic weight $w_{ji}(n)$ at iteration number n. Applying the chain rule to $E(n)$, we may write

$$\frac{\partial E(n)}{\partial \eta_{ji}(n)} = \frac{\partial E(n)}{\partial y_j(n)} \frac{\partial y_j(n)}{\partial v_j(n)} \frac{\partial v_j(n)}{\partial \eta_{ji}(n)} \tag{6.73}$$

For convenience of presentation, we reproduce Eqs. (6.4) and (6.12) here as follows:

$$v_j(n) = \sum_i w_{ji}(n) y_i(n) \tag{6.74}$$

$$w_{ji}(n) = w_{ji}(n-1) - \eta_{ji}(n) \frac{\partial \mathscr{E}(n-1)}{\partial w_{ji}(n-1)} \tag{6.75}$$

Substituting Eq. (6.75) in (6.74), we get

$$v_j(n) = \sum_i y_i(n) \left[w_{ji}(n-1) - \eta_{ji}(n) \frac{\partial \mathscr{E}(n-1)}{\partial w_{ji}(n-1)} \right] \tag{6.76}$$

Hence, differentiating Eq. (6.76) with respect to $\eta_{ji}(n)$, and rewriting Eq. (6.5), we have

$$\frac{\partial v_j(n)}{\partial \eta_{ji}(n)} = -y_i(n) \frac{\partial \mathscr{E}(n-1)}{\partial w_{ji}(n-1)} \tag{6.77}$$

$$\frac{\partial y_j(n)}{\partial v_j(n)} = \varphi_j'(v_j(n)) \tag{6.78}$$

Next, we evaluate the partial derivative $\partial E(n)/\partial y_j(n)$. For the case when neuron j lies in the output layer of the network, the desired response $d_j(n)$ is supplied externally. Accordingly, we may differentiate Eq. (6.72) with respect to $y_j(n)$, obtaining the result

$$\begin{aligned} \frac{\partial E(n)}{\partial y_j(n)} &= -[d_j - y_j(n)] \\ &= -e_j(n) \end{aligned} \tag{6.79}$$

where $e_j(n)$ is the error signal. Thus, using the partial derivatives of Eqs. (6.77), (6.78), and (6.79) in (6.73), and then rearranging terms, we obtain

$$\frac{\partial E(n)}{\partial \eta_{ji}(n)} = -\varphi_j'(v_j(n))e_j(n)y_i(n)\left[-\frac{\partial \mathscr{E}(n-1)}{\partial w_{ji}(n-1)}\right] \tag{6.80}$$

Note that the partial derivative $\partial \mathscr{E}(n-1)/\partial w_{ij}(n-1)$ on the right-hand side of Eq. (6.80) refers to the cost functions $\mathscr{E}(n-1)$ describing the error surface at time $n-1$; the differentiation is with respect to synaptic weight $w_{ji}(n-1)$.

From Eq. (6.11) we note that the factor

$$-\varphi_j'(v_j(n))e_j(n)y_i(n)$$

equals the partial derivative $\partial \mathscr{E}(n)/\partial w_{ji}(n)$. Using this relation in Eq. (6.80), we may redefine $\partial E(n)/\partial \eta_{ji}(n)$ simply as

$$\frac{\partial E(n)}{\partial \eta_{ji}(n)} = -\frac{\partial \mathscr{E}(n)}{\partial w_{ji}(n)}\frac{\partial \mathscr{E}(n-1)}{\partial w_{ji}(n-1)} \tag{6.81}$$

Equation (6.81) defines the derivative of the error surface with respect to the learning-rate parameter $\eta_{ji}(n)$, assuming that neuron j lies in the output layer of the network. In fact, we can show that this same formula also applies to a neuron j that lies in a hidden layer of the network; see Problem 6.14. In other words, Eq. (6.81) applies to all neurons in the network.

We are now ready to formulate a learning-rate update rule that performs steepest descent on an error surface over the parameter space, where the parameter of interest is the learning-rate parameter $\eta_{ji}(n)$. Specifically, we define the adjustment applied to $\eta_{ji}(n)$ as

$$\begin{aligned}\Delta\eta_{ji}(n+1) &= -\gamma\frac{\partial E(n)}{\partial \eta_{ji}(n)}\\ &= \gamma\frac{\partial \mathscr{E}(n)}{\partial w_{ji}(n)}\frac{\partial \mathscr{E}(n-1)}{\partial w_{ji}(n-1)}\end{aligned} \tag{6.82}$$

where γ is a positive constant, called the *control step-size parameter for the learning-rate adaptation procedure.*

The partial derivatives $\partial \mathscr{E}(n-1)/\partial w_{ji}(n-1)$ and $\partial \mathscr{E}(n)/\partial w_{ji}(n)$ refer to the derivative (negative gradient) of the error surface with respect to the synaptic weight w_{ji} (connecting neuron i to neuron j), evaluated at iterations $n-1$ and n, respectively. Accordingly, we may make two important observations:

1. When the derivative of the error surface with respect to the weight w_{ji} has the same algebraic sign on two consecutive iterations, the adjustment $\Delta\eta_{ji}(n+1)$ has a positive value. The adaptation procedure therefore increases the learning-rate parameter for the weight w_{ji}. Correspondingly, the back-propagation learning along that direction will be fast.
2. When the derivative of the error surface with respect to the weight w_{ji} alternates on two consecutive iterations, the adjustment $\Delta\eta_{ji}(n+1)$ assumes a negative value. In this case, the adaptation procedure decreases the learning-rate parameter for the weight w_{ji}. Correspondingly, the back-propagation learning along that direction will be slow.

These two observations are in perfect accord with heuristics 3 and 4, respectively.

The learning-rate adaptation procedure described by Eq. (6.82) is called the *delta-delta learning rule* (Jacobs, 1988). Although this learning rule satisfies the heuristics mentioned above, it has some potential problems. If the derivative of the error surface with respect to a particular weight has the same sign but small magnitudes at two consecutive iterations, the positive adjustment applied to the learning rate for that weight is very small. On the other hand, if the derivative of the error surface with respect to a weight has opposite signs and large magnitudes at two consecutive iterations, the negative adjustment applied to that weight will be very large. Under these circumstances, it is very difficult to choose an appropriate value for the step-size parameter γ. This limitation of the delta-delta learning rule is overcome by introducing a further modification, as described next.

Let $w_{ji}(n)$ denote the value of the synaptic weight connecting neuron i to neuron j, measured at iteration n. Let $\eta_{ji}(n)$ denote the learning-rate parameter assigned to this weight at this iteration. The learning-rate update rule is now defined as follows:

$$\Delta\eta_{ji}(n+1) = \begin{cases} \kappa & \text{if } S_{ji}(n-1)D_{ji}(n) > 0 \\ -\beta\eta_{ji}(n) & \text{if } S_{ji}(n-1)D_{ji}(n) < 0 \\ 0 & \text{otherwise} \end{cases} \tag{6.83}$$

where $D_{ji}(n)$ and $S_{ji}(n)$ are themselves defined as, respectively

$$D_{ji}(n) = \frac{\partial \mathscr{E}(n)}{\partial w_{ji}(n)} \tag{6.84}$$

and

$$S_{ji}(n) = (1-\xi)D_{ji}(n-1) + \xi S_{ji}(n-1) \tag{6.85}$$

where ξ is a positive constant. The quantity $D_{ji}(n)$ is the current value of the partial derivative of the error surface with respect to the weight $w_{ji}(n)$. The second quantity $S_{ji}(n)$ is an exponentially weighted sum of the current and past derivatives of the error surface with respect to w_{ji}, and with ξ as the base and iteration number n as the exponent. The learning-rate adaptation procedure described in Eqs. (6.83) to (6.85) is called the *delta-bar-delta learning rule*[8] (Jacobs, 1988). Note that if we set the control parameters κ and β both equal to zero, the learning-rate parameters assume a constant value as in the standard back-propagation algorithm.

From these defining equations we may make the following observations:

1. The delta-bar-delta learning rule uses a mechanism similar to the delta-delta learning role to satisfy the heuristics 3 and 4. Specifically, if for a synaptic weight w_{ji} the derivative $D_{ji}(n)$ at iteration n and the exponentially weighted sum $S_{ji}(n-1)$ at the previous iteration $n-1$ have the same sign, then the learning-rate parameter for that weight is incremented by the constant κ. If, on the other hand, the quantities $D_{ji}(n)$ and $S_{ji}(n-1)$ have opposite signs, then the learning-rate parameter for the weight w_{ji} is decremented by a proportion, β, of its current value $\eta_{ji}(n)$. Otherwise, the learning-rate parameter remains unchanged.
2. The learning-rate parameter $\eta_{ji}(n)$ is incremented linearly but decremented exponentially. A linear increase prevents the learning-rate parameter from growing too fast, whereas an exponential decrease means that the learning-rate parameter remains positive and that it is reduced rapidly.

A strict application of back-propagation learning calls for the computation of weight and parameter updates for each input pattern. For a large network and sizable training database, this form of updating results in a significant increase in memory storage size

[8] Minai and Williams (1990) describe a further improvement of the delta-bar-delta learning rule. In particular, it is shown that the advantages of momentum can be retained without significant drawbacks.

and computational complexity when the delta-bar-delta rule for learning-rate adaptation is incorporated into the back-propagation algorithm. To be specific, we have to allocate additional memory storage for (1) the parameters $\eta_{ji}(n)$ and $\Delta\eta_{ji}(n)$ assigned to every synaptic weight in the network, and (2) the associated partial derivatives $\partial\mathscr{E}(n-1)/\partial w_{ji}(n-1)$. All of this may make it difficult to justify the use of the delta-bar-delta learning rule in practice.

However, we note that the weight changes due to the application of each training-pattern point are usually small compared to the magnitudes of the weights themselves. This is merely a manifestation of the *principle of minimal disturbance* (Widrow and Lehr, 1990). We may therefore simplify implementation of the back-propagation algorithm incorporating the delta-bar-delta learning rule by exploiting an idea similar to the gradient reuse method (Hush and Salas, 1988). In particular, we note that when batch updating is used, the gradient estimate may be formed by averaging the gradient contributions computed from several patterns. Weights and learning-rate parameters are then updated once every B patterns, where B is the epoch (batch) size. The basic idea of the *gradient reuse method* is that gradients are reused several times until the resulting weight updates and learning-rate updates no longer lead to a reduction in error performance. By so doing, the number of gradients computed per iteration is significantly reduced, on average. Moreover, with batch updating a more accurate estimate of the true gradient is computed, and the update of interest is therefore more likely to be in the correct downhill direction.

Thus, let $\delta_j^{(b)}(n)$ and $y_i^{(b)}(n)$ denote the local gradient and the output signal computed for neuron j and neuron i, respectively; the superscript b refers to the presentation of the bth pattern point, and the index n refers to the current iteration. From Eqs. (6.11) and (6.14) we note that the partial derivative of the error surface with respect to the jith synaptic weight and corresponding to the presentation of the bth pattern point is equal to $-\delta_j^{(b)}(n)y_i^{(b)}(n)$. According to the gradient reuse method, we may then set the average gradient with respect to the jith weight as follows:

$$\frac{\partial\mathscr{E}(n)}{\partial w_{ji}(n)} = -\sum_{b=1}^{B} \delta_j^{(b)}(n)y_i^{(b)}(n) \tag{6.86}$$

where B is the epoch (batch) size over which the gradient averaging is performed. We may therefore redefine the update formula for the jith synaptic weight as

$$w_{ji}(n+1) = w_{ji}(n) + \alpha\Delta w_{ji}(n-1) + \eta_{ji}(n+1)\sum_{b=1}^{B} \delta_j^{(b)}(n)y_i^{(b)}(n) \tag{6.87}$$

Correspondingly, we may reformulate Eq. (6.84) in light of the gradient reuse method as

$$D_{ji}(n) = -\sum_{b=1}^{B} \delta_j^{(b)}(n)y_i^{(b)}(n) \tag{6.88}$$

The computational complexity of the modified back-propagation algorithm incorporating the delta-bar-delta training rule is therefore greatly reduced through the use of epoch updating (i.e., the gradient reuse method) as described herein, without sacrificing network learning performance (Haykin and Deng, 1991).

Computer Experiment

In this computer experiment, we study a two-dimensional classification problem that involves nonconvex decision regions. The distribution of the pattern classes $\mathscr{C}_1$ and $\mathscr{C}_2$ is shown in Fig. 6.22a. Class $\mathscr{C}_1$ consists of pattern points inside the area marked $\mathscr{C}_1$, and class $\mathscr{C}_2$ consists of the pattern points inside the area marked $\mathscr{C}_2$. The requirement is to

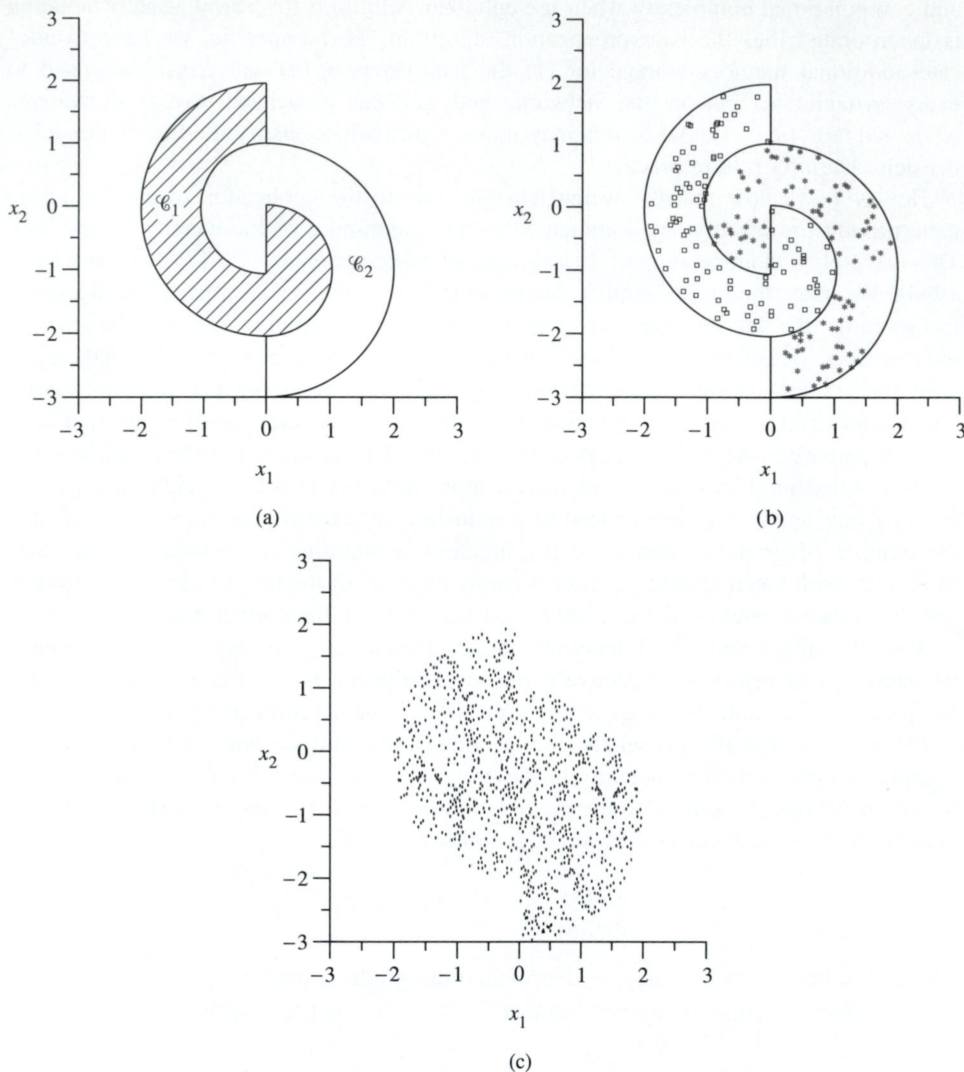

FIGURE 6.22 Pattern classification using multilayer perceptron: (a) distribution of classes $\mathscr{C}_1$ and $\mathscr{C}_2$; (b) the training data of classes $\mathscr{C}_1$ and $\mathscr{C}_2$ ($\mathscr{C}_1$ = 100 points; $\mathscr{C}_2$ = 100 points); and (c) the testing data of classes $\mathscr{C}_1$ and $\mathscr{C}_2$ ($\mathscr{C}_1$ = 482 points, $\mathscr{C}_2$ = 518 points).

design a neural network classifier that decides whether an input pattern belongs to class $\mathscr{C}_1$ or class $\mathscr{C}_2$.

The composition of the neural network used in the study is as follows:

Number of input (source) nodes	= 2
Number of neurons in the first hidden layer	= 12
Number of neurons in the second hidden layer	= 4
Number of neurons in the output layer	= 2

Figure 6.22b depicts the pattern set used to train the network. Figure 6.22c depicts the test pattern set used to evaluate the performance of the network after training. Both sets consist of uniformly distributed random points. There are 100 class $\mathscr{C}_1$ points and 100

class $\mathscr{C}_2$ points in the training set, and there are 482 class $\mathscr{C}_1$ points and 518 class $\mathscr{C}_2$ points in the test set.

In Fig. 6.23 we present learning curves that compare the use of pattern updates with batch updates. In particular, Fig. 6.23a compares the error performance of the standard back-propagation algorithm using pattern updates and batch updates. Figure 6.23b presents corresponding curves for the modified back-propagation algorithm incorporating the delta-bar-delta training rule. From Fig. 6.23a we see that for the standard back-propagation algorithm, the use of pattern updates yields slightly better results than batch updates. On

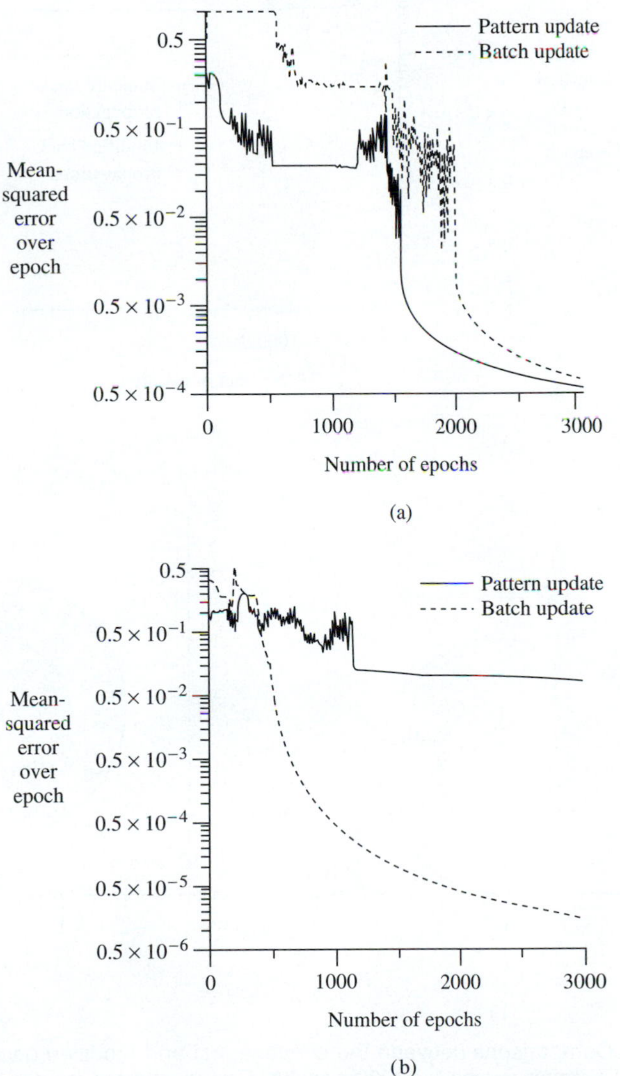

FIGURE 6.23 Learning curves for pattern update and batch update methods. (a) Learning curves for the standard back-propagation algorithm for 3000 epochs. Continuous curve: $\eta_0 = 0.75$, $\alpha = 0.25$, $\kappa = 0.0$, $p = 0.0$, $\xi = 0.0$; dashed curve: $\eta_0 = 0.75$, $\alpha = 0.25$, $\kappa = 0.0$, $p = 0.0$, $\xi = 0.0$. (b) Learning curves for the modified back-propagation algorithm for 3000 epochs. Continuous curve: $\eta_0 = 0.75$, $\alpha = 0.05$, $\kappa = 0.002$, $\beta = 0.05$, $\xi = 0.7$; dashed curve: $\eta_0 = 0.75$, $\alpha = 0.3$, $\kappa = 0.01$, $\beta = 0.1$, $\xi = 0.7$.

the other hand, in Fig. 6.23b we have opposite results in that, for the modified back-propagation algorithm, the use of batch updates yields a better performance than pattern updates.

In Fig. 6.24 we compare the conventional and modified forms of the back-propagation algorithm, using batch updates. In particular, this figure compares their learning curves for the following values of control parameters.

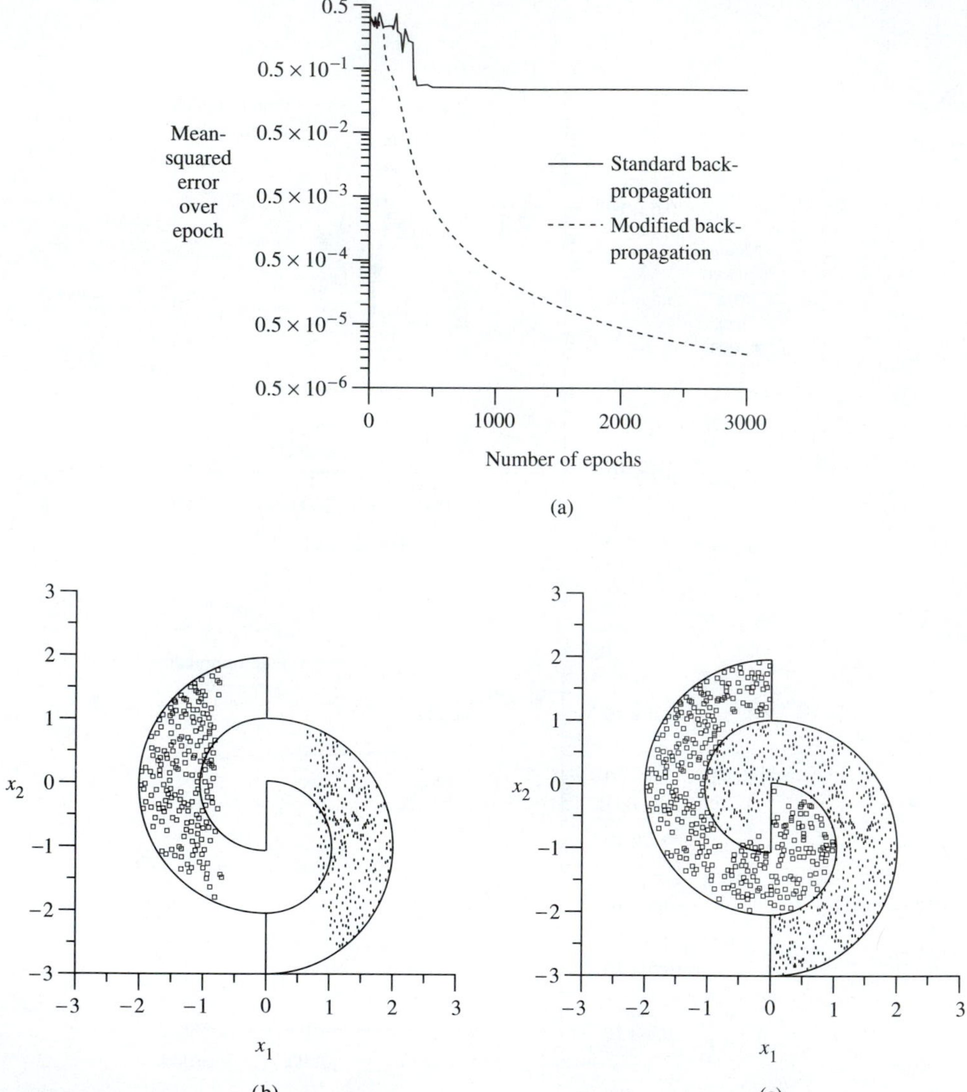

FIGURE 6.24 Comparisons between the conventional and modified back-propagation algorithms. (a) Learning curves for 3000 epochs. Continuous curve: standard back-propagation algorithm, $\eta_0 = 0.75$, $\alpha = 0.75$, $\kappa = 0.0$, $\beta = 0.0$, $\xi = 0.0$; dashed curve: modified back-propagation algorithm, $\eta_0 = 0.75$, $\alpha = 0.75$, $\kappa = 0.01$, $\beta = 0.2$, $\xi = 0.7$. (b) Classified results for standard back-propagation at $n = 150$ for $\eta_0 = 0.75$, $\alpha = 0.75$, $\kappa = 0$, $\beta = 0$, $\xi = 0$; $\mathscr{C}_1 = 258$ points, $\mathscr{C}_2 = 268$ points, error $= 474$ points. (c) Classified results for modified back-propagation at $n = 150$ for $\eta_0 = 0.75$, $\alpha = 0.75$, $\kappa = 0.01$, $\beta = 0.2$, $\xi = 0.7$; $\mathscr{C}_1 = 449$ points, $\mathscr{C}_2 = 455$ points, error $= 96$ points.

1. Standard back-propagation:

$$\eta_0 = 0.75$$

$$\alpha = 0.75$$

2. Modified back-propagation (incorporating the delta-bar-delta training rule):

$$\eta_0 = 0.75$$

$$\alpha = 0.75$$

$$\kappa = 0.01$$

$$\beta = 0.2$$

$$\xi = 0.7$$

In Fig. 6.24a we see that the improvement in the error performance of the modified back-propagation algorithm over that of the standard form of the algorithm is indeed quite significant.

In Figs. 6.24b and 6.24c we show the classified results obtained using the standard and modified forms of the back-propagation algorithm for the same sets of parameter values listed above. The classified results presented here are quite dramatic; they were obtained after the presentation of 150 training epochs. In the case of standard back-propagation, we see from Fig. 6.24b that the shapes of class $\mathscr{C}_1$ and class $\mathscr{C}_2$ have not fully developed. In sharp contrast, the shapes of class $\mathscr{C}_1$ and class $\mathscr{C}_2$ can be clearly seen from the classified results of Fig. 6.24c obtained using the modified back-propagation algorithm. Note that in Figs. 6.24b and 6.24c, only correctly classified test data points are shown.

6.16 Fuzzy Control of Back-Propagation Learning

The heuristics for accelerating the rate of convergence of back-propagation learning, described in the previous section, lend themselves to implementation by means of a fuzzy logic controller.

Fuzzy set theory[9] was originated by Zadeh (1965, 1973) to provide a mathematical tool for dealing with *linguistic variables* (i.e., concepts described in natural language). A *fuzzy set* is defined as a set whose boundary is not sharp. Let X be a universal set, where generic elements are denoted by x. Let A be a fuzzy set characterized by a *membership function* $\mu_A(x)$ that maps the universal set X to the real interval [0,1]. The closer $\mu_A(x)$ is to 1, the more x belongs to A. We may therefore also view $\mu_A(x)$ as the degree of compatibility of x with the concept represented by A. The set-theoretic operations of union ($\cup$), intersection ($\cap$), and complement for fuzzy sets are defined via their membership functions. Let A and B denote a pair of fuzzy sets in X with membership functions $\mu_A(x)$ and $\mu_B(x)$, respectively. The membership function $\mu_{A\cup B}(x)$ of the union $A \cup B$ and the membership function $\mu_{A\cap B}(x)$ of the intersection $A \cap B$ are defined as follows:

$$\mu_{A\cup B}(x) = \max(\mu_A(x), \mu_B(x)) \tag{6.89}$$

[9] For a book on fuzzy set theory, see Dubois and Prade (1980). The interplay between neural networks and fuzzy systems, in general, has received a great deal of attention in recent years (Kosko, 1992). Building on the theoretical result that fuzzy systems are universal approximators, Wang and Mendel (1992) have shown that fuzzy systems may be viewed as a layered feedforward network. Moreover, they have developed a back-propagation algorithm for training this form of fuzzy system, so as to match desired input–output pairs of patterns.

$$\mu_{A\cap B}(x) = \min(\mu_A(x), \mu_B(x)) \tag{6.90}$$

The complement of the fuzzy set A is defined by the membership function

$$\mu_{\bar{A}}(x) = 1 - \mu_A(x) \tag{6.91}$$

One other term that we need to introduce is a universe of discourse generated by a kernel space referring to any prescribed set of objects or constructs. Let K be a kernel space, and let E be a set that contains K and that is generated from K by a finite application of set-theoretic operations. Then a *universe of discourse* is a designated subset of E (Dubois and Prade, 1980).

Returning to the issue at hand, consider Fig. 6.25, which presents the block diagram of a *hybrid learning system,* in which an on-line fuzzy logic controller is used to adapt the learning parameters of a multilayer perceptron with back-propagation learning. The objective here is to provide a significant improvement in the rate of convergence of the learning process (Choi et al., 1992). The fuzzy logic controller in Fig. 6.25 incorporates human linguistic descriptions about the unknown learning parameters of the back-propagation algorithm. In particular, it consists of four principal components, as depicted in Fig. 6.26 (Lee, 1990):

1. *Fuzzification interface,* which performs the following functions:
   - A scale mapping that changes the range of values of input variables into corresponding universe of discourse
   - Fuzzification that converts nonfuzzy (crisp) input data into suitable linguistic values, which may be viewed as labels of fuzzy sets
2. *Fuzzy rule base,* which consists of a set of linguistic control rules written in the form:

   "IF a set of conditions are satisfied, THEN a set of consequences are inferred."

3. *Fuzzy inference machine,* which is a decision-making logic that employs rules from the fuzzy rule base to infer fuzzy control actions in response to fuzzified inputs.
4. *Defuzzification interface,* which performs the following functions:
   - A scale mapping that converts the range of values of output variables into corresponding universe of discourse
   - Defuzzification that yields a nonfuzzy (crisp) control action from an inferred fuzzy control action

A commonly used defuzzification rule is the *centroid method,* according to which the defuzzification interface produces a crisp output defined as the center of gravity of the distribution of possible actions.

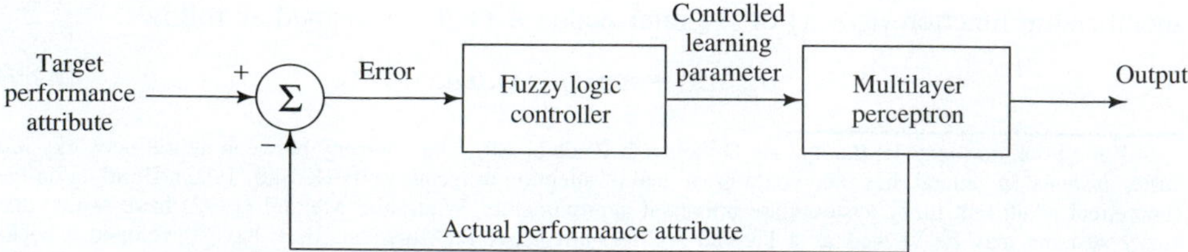

FIGURE 6.25 Fuzzy control of back-propagation learning.

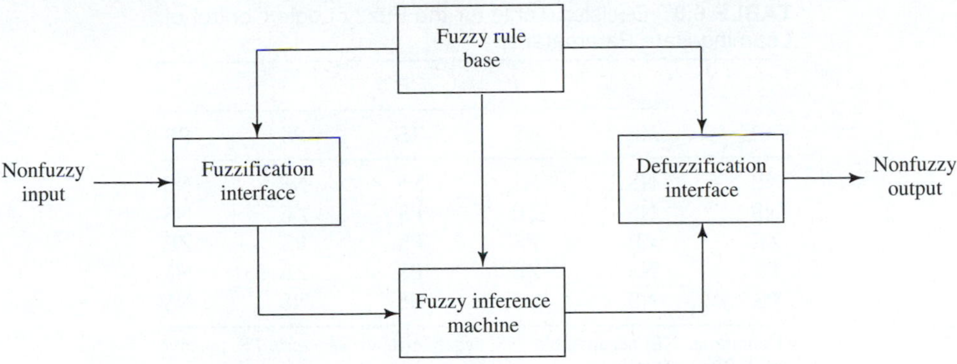

FIGURE 6.26 Block diagram of a fuzzy system.

The main idea behind the fuzzy control of back-propagation learning is the implementation of heuristics in the form of fuzzy "IF . . . , THEN . . ." rules that are used for the purpose of achieving a faster rate of convergence. The heuristics are driven by the behavior of the instantaneous sum of squared errors E given in Eq. (6.72). In the following heuristics, the *change of error* (denoted by CE) is an approximation to the gradient of the error surface, and the *change of CE* (denoted by CCE) is an approximation to the second-order gradient information related to the acceleration of convergence (Choi et al., 1992):

- IF CE is small with no sign changes in several consecutive iterations of the algorithm, THEN the value of the learning-rate parameter should be increased.
- IF sign changes occur in CE in several consecutive iterations of the algorithm, THEN the value of the learning-rate parameter should be decreased, regardless of the value of CCE.
- IF CE is small AND CCE is small, with no sign changes for several consecutive iterations of the algorithm, THEN the values of both the learning-rate parameter and the momentum constant should be increased.

The first two heuristics are recognized as heuristics 3 and 4 as presented in the previous section, respectively. The last heuristic, involving the momentum constant, is new.

The sign change of the gradient to the error surface is identical to the sign change of CE. Consider, for example, a situation where we have

$$E(n-2) \leq E(n-1)$$

and

$$E(n-1) > E(n)$$

We may then write

$$\text{CE}(n-1) = E(n-1) - E(n-2) \geq 0$$

and

$$\text{CE}(n) = E(n) - E(n-1) < 0$$

The implication here is that there has been a sign change from iteration $n-2$ to iteration n of the algorithm.

A fuzzy rule base for fuzzy back-propagation learning is given in Tables 6.6 and 6.7. The associated *membership functions,* labeled by linguistic terms, are shown in parts (a)

TABLE 6.6 Decision Table for the Fuzzy Logic Control of Learning-Rate Parameter η[a]

	CE				
CCE	NB	NS	ZE	PS	PB
NB	NS	NS	NS	NS	NS
NS	NS	ZE	PS	ZE	NS
ZE	ZE	PS	PS	PS	ZE
PS	NS	ZE	PS	ZE	NS
PB	NS	NS	NS	NS	NS

[a] Definitions: NB, negative big; NS, negative small; ZE, zero; PS, positive small; PB, positive big.

and (b) of Fig. 6.27. Table 6.6 and Fig. 6.27a pertain to changes applied to the learning-rate parameter η of the back-propagation algorithm, whereas Table 6.7 pertains to changes applied to the momentum constant α of the algorithm. The details of these two tables are as follows:

- The contents of Table 6.6 represent the value of the fuzzy variable $\Delta\eta$, denoting the change applied to the learning-rate parameter η, for fuzzified values of CE and CCE. For instance, we may read the following fuzzy rule from Table 6.6:
  - If CE is zero, AND IF CCE is negative small, THEN $\Delta\eta$ is positive small.
- The contents of Table 6.7 represent the value of the fuzzy variable $\Delta\alpha$, denoting the change applied to the momentum constant α, for fuzzified values of CE and CCE. For instance, we may read the following fuzzy rule from Table 6.7:
  - IF CE is negative small, AND CCE is negative small, THEN $\Delta\alpha$ is zero.

From the membership function shown in Fig. 6.27 we note that the universe of discourse for both CE and CCE is $[-0.3, 0.3]$; values of CE and CCE outside of this range are clamped to -0.3 and 0.3, respectively.

Having determined whether $\Delta\eta$, the change in the learning-rate parameter, is positive small, zero, or negative small, we may then assign an appropriate value to the change $\Delta\eta$ using the membership functions presented in Fig. 6.27b.

Choi et al. (1992) present computer simulation results, comparing the performance of fuzzy back-propagation learning to that of standard back-propagation learning. The experiments involved the detection of a constant signal in the presence of additive Laplacian

TABLE 6.7 Decision Table for the Fuzzy Control of Momentum Constant α[a]

	CE				
CCE	NB	NS	ZE	PS	PB
NB	NS	NS	ZE	ZE	ZE
NS	NS	ZE	ZE	ZE	ZE
ZE	ZE	PS	PS	PS	ZE
PS	ZE	ZE	ZE	ZE	NS
PB	ZE	ZE	ZE	NS	NS

[a] Definitions: NB, negative big; NS, negative small; ZE, zero; PS, positive small; PB, positive big.

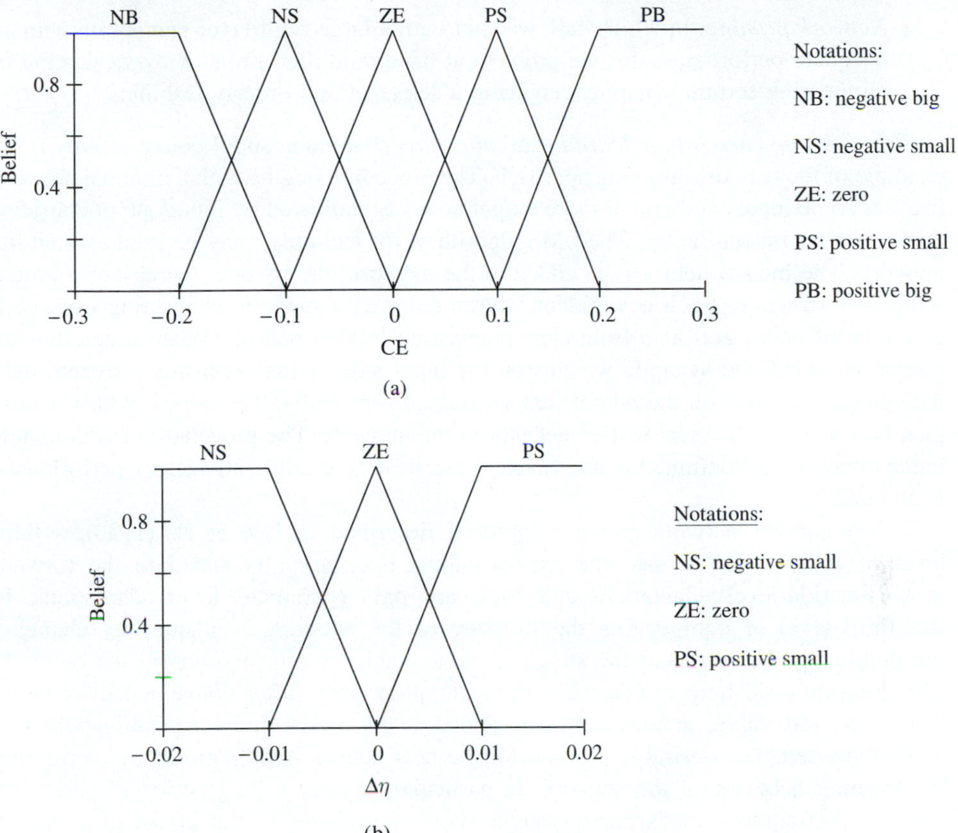

FIGURE 6.27 (a) Membership functions for CE; the same membership functions are used for CCE. (b) Membership functions for $\Delta\eta$.

noise.[10] The results of the computer simulations appear to show that the convergence of fuzzy back-propagation learning is dramatically faster, and the steady-state value of the mean-squared error is significantly smaller than standard back-propagation learning.

6.17 Network-Pruning Techniques

To solve real-world problems with neural networks, we usually require the use of highly structured networks of a rather large size. A practical issue that arises in this context is that of minimizing the size of the network and yet maintaining good performance. A neural network with minimum size is less likely to learn the idiosyncrasies or noise in the training data, and may thus generalize better to new data. We may achieve this design objective in one of two ways:

- *Network growing,* in which case we start with a small multilayer perceptron, small for accomplishing the task at hand, and then add a new neuron or a new layer of hidden neurons only when we are unable to meet the design specification.

[10] A sample ν drawn from a *Laplacian noise* process is governed by the probability density function

$$f(\nu) = \frac{\alpha}{2}\exp(-\alpha|\nu|), \qquad -\infty < \nu < \infty$$

where α is a constant of the distribution.

- *Network pruning,* in which case we start with a large multilayer perceptron with an adequate performance for the problem at hand, and then prune it by weakening or eliminating certain synaptic weights in a selective and orderly fashion.

The *cascade-correlation learning architecture* (Fahlman and Lebiere, 1990) is an example of the network-growing approach. The procedure begins with a minimal network that has some inputs and one or more output nodes as indicated by input/output considerations, but no hidden nodes. The LMS algorithm, for example, may be used to train the network. The hidden neurons are added to the network one by one, thereby obtaining a multilayer structure. Each new hidden neuron receives a synaptic connection from each of the input nodes and also from each preexisting hidden neuron. When a new hidden neuron is added, the synaptic weights on the input side of that neuron are frozen; only the synaptic weights on the output side are trained repeatedly. The added hidden neuron then becomes a permanent feature detector in the network. The procedure of adding new hidden neurons is continued in the manner described here until satisfactory performance is attained.

In yet another network-growing approach described in Lee et al. (1990), a third level of computation termed the *structure-level adaptation* is added to the forward pass (function-level adaptation) and backward pass (parameter-level adaptation). In this third level of computation the structure of the network is adapted by changing the number of neurons and the structural relationship among neurons in the network. The criterion used here is that when the estimation error (after convergence) is larger than a desired value, a new neuron is added to the network in a position where it is most needed. The desirable position for the new neuron is determined by monitoring the learning behavior of the network. In particular, if after a long period of parameter adaptation (training), the synaptic weight vector pertaining to the inputs of a neuron continues to fluctuate significantly, it may be inferred that the neuron in question does not have enough representation power to learn its proper share of the task. The structure-level adaptation also includes a provision for the possible annihilation of neurons. Specifically, a neuron is annihilated when it is not a functioning element of the network or it is a redundant element of the network. This method of network growing appears to be computationally intensive.

In this section we focus on two network-pruning approaches. In the first approach, generalization is improved through the use of *complexity regularization.* This approach is exemplified by the weight-decay (Hinton, 1987) and the weight-elimination (Weigend et al., 1991) procedures. In the second approach, synaptic weights are removed from the network on the basis of their saliencies, the calculations of which involve the use of the *Hessian* matrix of the error surface. This latter approach is exemplified by the so-called optimal brain damage (LeCun et al., 1990) and the optimal brain surgeon (Hassibi et al., 1993) procedures.

Complexity Regularization

In designing a multilayer perceptron by whatever method, we are in effect building a nonlinear *model* of the physical phenomenon responsible for the generation of the input–output examples used to train the network. Insofar as the network design is statistical in nature, we need an appropriate measure of the fit between the model (network) and the observed data. This implies that unless we have some prior information, the design procedure should include a criterion for selecting the *model complexity* (i.e., the number of independently adjusted parameters of the network). Various criteria for model-complexity selection are described in the statistics literature, important examples of which include the *minimum description length* (MDL) *criterion* (Rissanen, 1978, 1989), and *an information-theoretic criterion* (AIC) (Akaike, 1974). Although these criteria do indeed differ from each other in their exact details, they share a common form of composition, as described here (Haykin, 1991; Priestley, 1981):

$$\begin{pmatrix}\text{Model-complexity}\\ \text{criterion}\end{pmatrix} = \begin{pmatrix}\text{log-likelihood}\\ \text{function}\end{pmatrix} + \begin{pmatrix}\text{model-complexity}\\ \text{penalty}\end{pmatrix} \tag{6.92}$$

The basic difference between the various criteria lies in the definition of the model-complexity penalty term.

In the context of back-propagation learning, or any other supervised learning procedure for that matter, we may follow a similar approach. Specifically, the learning objective is to find a weight vector that minimizes the total *risk*

$$R(\mathbf{w}) = \mathscr{E}_s(\mathbf{w}) + \lambda\mathscr{E}_c(\mathbf{w}) \tag{6.93}$$

The first term, $\mathscr{E}_s(\mathbf{w})$, is the standard *performance measure,* which depends on both the network (model) and the input data. In back-propagation learning it is typically defined as a mean-squared error whose evaluation extends over the output neurons of the network and that is carried out for all the training examples on an epoch-by-epoch basis. The second term, $\mathscr{E}_c(\mathbf{w})$, is the *complexity penalty,* which depends on the network (model) alone; its evaluation extends over all the synaptic connections in the network. In fact, the form of the total risk defined in Eq. (6.93) is simply a statement of Tikhonov's *regularization theory;* this subject is treated in detail in Chapter 7. For the present discussion, it suffices to think of λ as a *regularization parameter,* which represents the relative importance of the complexity-penalty term with respect to the performance-measure term. When λ is zero, the back-propagation learning process is unconstrained, with the network being completely determined from the training examples. When λ is made infinitely large, on the other hand, the implication is that the constraint imposed by the complexity penalty is by itself sufficient to specify the network, which is another way of saying that the training examples are unreliable. In practical applications of the weight-decay procedure, the regularization parameter λ is assigned a value somewhere between these two limiting cases. The viewpoint described here for the use of complexity regularization for improved generalization is perfectly consistent with the structural minimization procedure discussed in Section 2.13.

In the sequel, we describe three different complexity-regularization procedures of increasing level of sophistication.

Weight Decay. In the *weight-decay procedure* (Hinton, 1987), the complexity regularization is defined as the squared norm of the weight vector **w** in the network, as shown by

$$\begin{aligned}\mathscr{E}_c(\mathbf{w}) &= \|\mathbf{w}\|^2 \\ &= \sum_{i\in C_{\text{total}}} w_i^2 \end{aligned} \tag{6.94}$$

where the set C_{total} refers to all the synaptic weights in the network. This procedure operates by forcing some of the synaptic weights in the network to take on values close to zero, while permitting other weights to retain their relatively large values. Accordingly, the weights of the network are grouped roughly into two categories: those that have a large influence on the network (model), and those that have little or no influence on it. The weights in the latter category are referred to as *excess weights.* In the absence of complexity regularization, these weights result in poor generalization by virtue of a high likelihood of taking on completely arbitrary values or causing the network to overfit the data in order to produce a slight reduction in the training error (Hush and Horne, 1993). The use of complexity regularization encourages the excess weights to assume values close to zero, and thereby improve generalization.

Weight Elimination. In this second complexity-regularization procedure, the complexity penalty is defined by (Weigend et al., 1991)

$$\mathscr{E}_c(\mathbf{w}) = \sum_{i \in C_{\text{total}}} \frac{(w_i/w_0)^2}{1 + (w_i/w_0)^2} \tag{6.95}$$

where w_0 is a free parameter of the weight-decay procedure that is preassigned, and w_i refers to the weight of some synapse i in the network. The set C_{total} refers to all the synaptic connections in the network. An individual penalty term varies with w_i/w_0 in a symmetric fashion, as shown in Fig. 6.28. When $|w_i| \ll w_0$, the complexity penalty (cost) for that weight approaches zero. The implication of this condition is that insofar as learning from examples is concerned, the ith synaptic weight is unreliable and should therefore be eliminated from the network. On the other hand, when $|w_i| \gg w_0$, the complexity penalty (cost) for that weight approaches the maximum value of unity, which means that w_i is important to the back-propagation learning process. We thus see that the complexity penalty term of Eq. (6.95) does indeed serve the desired purpose of identifying the synaptic weights of the network that are of significant influence. Note also that the weight-elimination procedure includes the weight-decay procedure as a special case; specifically, for large w_0, Eq. (6.95) reduces to the form shown in Eq. (6.94), except for a scaling factor.

The weight-elimination procedure is particularly sensitive to the choice of the regularization parameter λ. Weigend et al. (1991) describe a set of three heuristics for the incremental adjustment of λ. The procedure starts with $\lambda = 0$, enabling the network to use all of its resources initially, and then λ is adjusted by a small amount after the presentation of each epoch. Let n denote the iteration for a particular epoch that has just finished. Let $R(n)$

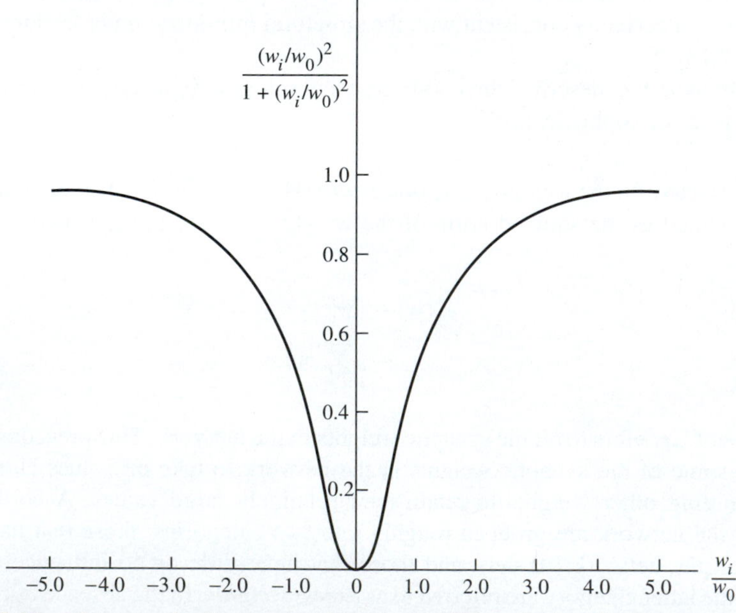

FIGURE 6.28 The complexity penalty term $(w_i/w_0)^2/[1 + (w_i/w_0)^2]$ plotted versus w_i/w_0.

denote the corresponding value of the total risk. Since $R(n)$ can increase or decrease from one iteration to the next, it is compared to three quantities:

- *Previous risk,* $R(n - 1)$
- *Average risk,* defined by

$$R_{av}(n) = \gamma R_{av}(n - 1) + (1 - \gamma)R(n)$$

  where $0 < \gamma < 1$
- *Desired risk, D.*

The first two quantities, $R(n - 1)$ and $R_{av}(n)$, are derived from previous values of the risk itself, whereas D is supplied externally. The choice of D depends on the problem at hand. Thus, given $R(n - 1)$, $R_{av}(n)$, and D, the risk $R(n)$ is compared to these three quantities and, depending on the results of the comparison, one of three possible actions is taken as follows (Weigend et al., 1991):

1. *Increment* the regularization parameter λ by a fairly small amount $\Delta\lambda$, and thereby attach slightly more importance to the complexity penalty term. This action corresponds to situations where things are going well; that is,

$$R(n) < D \quad \text{and/or} \quad R(n) < R(n - 1)$$

   The adjustment $\Delta\lambda$ is typically of order 10^{-6}.
2. *Decrement* the regularization parameter λ by a fairly small amount $\Delta\lambda$, and thereby attach slightly more importance to the performance measure term. This action is taken when the risk increases slightly but is still improving with respect to the long-term average; that is,

$$R(n) \geq R(n - 1), \quad R(n) < R_{av}(n), \quad \text{and} \quad R(n) \geq D$$

3. Make a *drastic reduction* in the value of the regularization parameter λ by 10 percent, say, and thereby attach much more importance to the performance measure term. This action is taken when the risk has increased and also exceeds its long-term average; that is,

$$R(n) \geq R(n - 1), \quad R(n) \geq R_{av}(n), \quad \text{and} \quad R(n) \geq D$$

   Such a situation may arise if there was a large increase in the risk in the previous iteration, or if there has not been much improvement in the risk in the whole period covered by the long-term average. The drastic cut in λ is made so as (hopefully) to prevent the weight elimination from compromising the performance of the whole network.

Weigend et al. (1991) have used the weight-elimination procedure for predicting two different kinds of time series:

- *Sunspot time series,* describing the famous yearly sunspot averages. For this prediction, the weight-decay procedure reduces the number of hidden neurons in the multilayer perceptron to three.
- *Currency exchange rates,* which are known to constitute notoriously noisy time series. In this case, it is shown that the weight-decay procedure results in out-of-sample prediction that is significantly better than chance.

Curvature-Driven Smoothing. In the curvature-driven smoothing approach, the complexity-regularization term depends on the geometric properties of the approximating function that defines the network output in terms of the input (Bishop, 1990). Intuitively, we expect that the smoother this function is, the smaller will be the influence of the complexity regularization. Thus, using a second-order derivative to approximate the curvature of the approximating function realized by the network (model), the complexity regularization is defined by

$$\mathscr{E}_c(\mathbf{w}) = \frac{1}{2}\sum_{i=1}^{p}\sum_{j=1}^{q}\int \left(\frac{\partial^2 y_j(\mathbf{w})}{\partial x_i^2}\right)^2 dx_1 \cdots dx_p \tag{6.96}$$

where $y_j(\mathbf{w})$ is the output of neuron j in the output layer of the network, p is the number of source nodes, and q is the number of output neurons. The curvature-driven smoothing procedure improves generalization by reducing the tendency of the network to overfit the training data. Moreover, it makes it possible to produce a solution whose properties are controlled by a single scalar parameter, namely, the regularization parameter λ. Bishop (1990) describes a generalized form of back-propagation learning that can be used to minimize the total risk $R(\mathbf{w})$ of Eq. (6.93) with the complexity regularization defined as in Eq. (6.96). No network pruning is used here; improvement in generalization performance is attained by assigning a suitable value to the regularization parameter λ.

Hessian Matrix of Error Surface

The basic idea of this second approach to network pruning is to use information on second-order derivatives of the error surface in order to make a trade-off between network complexity and training-error performance. In particular, a local model of the error surface is constructed for analytically predicting the effect of perturbations in synaptic weights. The starting point in the construction of such a model is the local approximation of the cost surface using a *Taylor series* about the operating point. Let δw_i denote the perturbation in the synaptic weight w_i. The corresponding change in the cost function $\mathscr{E}$ describing the error surface is given by the Taylor series

$$\delta\mathscr{E} = \sum_i g_i\,\delta w_i(n) + \frac{1}{2}\sum_i\sum_j h_{ji}\,\delta w_i\,\delta w_j + \text{higher-order terms} \tag{6.97}$$

where g_i is the ith component of the *gradient vector* of $\mathscr{E}$, and h_{ji} is the jith component of the *Hessian matrix* of $\mathscr{E}$, both measured with respect to the parameters of the network. That is, we have

$$g_i = \frac{\partial\mathscr{E}}{\partial w_i} \tag{6.98}$$

and

$$h_{ji} = \frac{\partial^2\mathscr{E}}{\partial w_j\,\partial w_i} \tag{6.99}$$

The requirement is to identify a set of parameters whose deletion from the multilayer perceptron will cause the least increase in the value of the cost function $\mathscr{E}$. To solve this problem in practical terms, we make the following approximations:

1. *Extremal Approximation.* We assume that parameters are deleted from the network only after the training process has converged. The implication of this assumption is that the parameters have a set of values corresponding to a local minimum or global minimum of the error surface. In such a case, the $g_i(n)$ may be set equal to zero, and the first summation on the right-hand side of Eq. (6.97) may therefore be ignored. Otherwise, the saliency measures (defined later) will be invalid for the problem at hand.

2. *Quadratic Approximation.* We assume that the error surface around a local minimum or global minimum is nearly "quadratic." Hence the higher-order terms in Eq. (6.97) may also be neglected.

Under these two assumptions, Eq. (6.97) is approximated simply as

$$\delta\mathscr{E} \simeq \frac{1}{2}\sum_i \sum_j h_{ji}\,\delta w_i\,\delta w_j$$

$$= \frac{1}{2}\,\delta\mathbf{w}^T\,\mathbf{H}\,\delta\mathbf{w} \tag{6.100}$$

where $\delta\mathbf{w}$ is the perturbation applied to the weight vector $\mathbf{w}$, and $\mathbf{H}$ is the *Hessian matrix* containing all second-order derivatives of $\mathscr{E}$ with respect to the elements of the weight vector $\mathbf{w}$. The *optimal brain damage* (*OBD*) *procedure* (LeCun et al., 1990) simplifies the computations by making a further assumption: The Hessian matrix $\mathbf{H}$ is a diagonal matrix. On the other hand, no such assumption is made in the *optimal brain surgeon* (*OBS*) *procedure* (Hassibi et al., 1993); accordingly, it contains the OBD procedure as a special case. From here on, we follow the OBS strategy.

The goal of OBS is to set one of the synaptic weights to zero so as to minimize the incremental increase in $\mathscr{E}$ given in Eq. (6.100). Let $w_i(n)$ denote this particular synaptic weight. The elimination of this weight is equivalent to the condition

$$\delta w_i + w_i = 0$$

or

$$\mathbf{1}_i^T\,\delta\mathbf{w} + w_i = 0 \tag{6.101}$$

where $\mathbf{1}_i$ is the *unit vector* whose elements are all zero, except for the ith element, which is equal to unity. We may now restate the goal of OBS as follows (Hassibi et al., 1993):

> *Minimize the quadratic form* $\frac{1}{2}\,\delta\mathbf{w}^T\mathbf{H}\,\delta\mathbf{w}$ *with respect to the incremental change in the weight vector,* $\delta\mathbf{w}$, *subject to the constraint that* $\mathbf{1}_i^T\,\delta\mathbf{w} + w_i$ *is zero, and then minimize the resultant with respect to the index* i.

To solve this constrained optimization problem, we first construct the *Lagrangian*

$$S = \frac{1}{2}\,\delta\mathbf{w}^T\,\mathbf{H}\,\delta\mathbf{w} + \lambda(\mathbf{1}_i^T\,\delta\mathbf{w} + w_i) \tag{6.102}$$

where λ is the *Lagrangian multiplier.* Then, taking the derivative of the Lagrangian S with respect to $\delta\mathbf{w}$, applying the constraint of Eq. (6.101), and using matrix inversion, we find that the optimum change in the weight vector $\mathbf{w}$ is

$$\delta\mathbf{w} = -\frac{w_i}{[\mathbf{H}^{-1}]_{ii}}\,\mathbf{H}^{-1}\mathbf{1}_i \tag{6.103}$$

and the corresponding optimum value of the Lagrangian S is

$$S_i = \frac{1}{2}\,\frac{w_i^2}{[\mathbf{H}^{-1}]_{ii}} \tag{6.104}$$

where $\mathbf{H}^{-1}$ is the inverse of the Hessian matrix $\mathbf{H}$, and $[\mathbf{H}^{-1}]_{ii}$ is the iith element of this inverse matrix. The Lagrangian S_i optimized with respect to $\delta\mathbf{w}$, subject to the constraint that the ith synaptic weight w_i is eliminated, is called the *saliency* of w_i. In effect, the saliency S_i represents the increase in the squared error (performance measure) that results from the deletion of w_i.

The difficult computational aspect of the OBS procedure lies in the inversion of the Hessian matrix **H**. The Hessian matrix would have to be nonsingular for its inverse to be computable. In general, for back-propagation learning the Hessian matrix is always nonsingular. Moreover, there is experimental evidence suggesting that neural network training problems are intrinsically ill-conditioned, leading to a Hessian matrix that is almost rank-deficient (Saarinen et al., 1991, 1992) which may raise computational difficulties of its own.

Hassibi et al. (1993) compute the Hessian matrix **H** for the batch mode of learning by proceeding as follows. First, they derive an approximate formula for the Hessian matrix evaluated at a local minimum of the error surface. The approximation is made up of a sum of outer product terms, with each such term requiring structural information of the network in the form of first-order partial derivatives only; see Problem 6.17. Second, they use a result in matrix algebra known as the matrix inversion lemma to calculate the inverse matrix $\mathbf{H}^{-1}$. The OBS procedure is thus more precise than the OBD procedure, but computationally more intensive.

In their paper, Hassibi et al. report that on some benchmark problems, the OBS procedure resulted in smaller networks than those obtained using the weight-decay procedure. It is also reported that as a result of applying the OBS procedure to the NETtalk multilayer perceptron involving a single hidden layer and 18,000 weights (Sejnowski and Rosenberg, 1987), the network was pruned to a mere 1560 weights, which represents a dramatic reduction in the size of the network.

6.18 Supervised Learning Viewed as a Nonlinear Identification Problem

The supervised training of a multilayer perceptron may be viewed as a *global nonlinear identification problem,* the solution of which requires the *minimization of a certain cost function.* The cost function $\mathscr{E}$ is defined in terms of deviations of the network outputs from desired (target) outputs, and expressed as a function of the weight vector **w** representing the free parameters (i.e., synaptic weights and thresholds) of the network. The goal of the training is to adjust these free parameters so as to make the actual outputs of the network match the desired outputs as closely as possible. The standard back-propagation algorithm, operating in the on-line (pattern) mode, adjusts a particular parameter by using an instantaneous estimate of the gradient of the cost function with respect to that parameter, and thereby provides an efficient method for implementing the training process. In so doing, however, it uses *the minimum amount of available information.* The convergence speed of the training process should be proportional to the amount of information used about the cost function. Consequently, when the size of the network is large, the time taken to train the network becomes so excessively long that the algorithm is simply impractical to use. As a remedy, we may expand the pool of information by building heuristics into the constitution of the algorithm, as described in Sections 6.15 and 6.16.

The slow nature of network training with the standard back-propagation algorithm is rather reminiscent of the slow speed of convergence exhibited by its close relative, the least-mean-square (LMS) algorithm. Owing to this basic limitation of the LMS algorithm, a great deal of research effort has been expended in the *linear adaptive filtering* literature on an alternative approach known collectively as *recursive least-squares (RLS) algorithms,* which are a special case of the *Kalman filter* (Haykin, 1991). A linear adaptive filtering algorithm of the RLS type differs from the LMS algorithm in that it utilizes information contained in the input data more effectively, going back to the first iteration of the algorithm. The use of an RLS filtering algorithm offers the following advantages:

- Fast speed of convergence
- Built-in learning-rate parameter
- Insensitivity to variations in the condition number of the input data; the condition number refers to the ratio of the largest eigenvalue to the smallest eigenvalue of the covariance matrix of the input data

In a similar sort of way, we may train a multilayer perceptron using an *extended* RLS (Kalman) filtering algorithm applied to back-propagation learning (Palmieri et al., 1991; Shah and Palmieri, 1990). The term "extended" is used here to account for the fact that the neurons of a multilayer perceptron are nonlinear, and would therefore have to be *linearized* in order to accommodate the application of the standard RLS filtering algorithm.

Extended Kalman Type of Back-Propagation Learning

Consider a multilayer perceptron characterized by a weight vector **w** representing the free parameters of all the neurons in the network. The cost function, to be minimized during training, is defined in terms of a total of N input–output examples as follows:

$$\mathscr{E}_{\text{av}}(\mathbf{w}) = \frac{1}{2N} \sum_{n=1}^{N} \sum_{j \in C} [d_j(n) - y_j(n)]^2 \tag{6.105}$$

where $d_j(n)$ and $y_j(n)$ are the desired response and actual response of output neuron j for pattern n, respectively, and the set C includes all the output neurons of the network; the dependence of the cost function $\mathscr{E}_{\text{av}}(\mathbf{w})$ on the weight vector $\mathbf{w}$ arises because the output $y_j(n)$ is itself dependent on $\mathbf{w}$. Now we could apply the extended form of RLS (Kalman) filtering algorithm to the problem at hand by linearizing the cost function $\mathscr{E}_{\text{av}}(\mathbf{w})$ at each working point, as described by Singhal and Wu (1989). Unfortunately, the resulting computational complexity becomes prohibitive, because such an approach requires the storage and updating of the error covariance matrix whose size is the square of the number of synaptic connection in the network. To overcome this problem, we may simplify the application of extended Kalman filtering by partitioning the global problem into a number of subproblems, each one at the neuron level (Palmieri et al., 1991; Shah and Palmieri, 1990).

Consider then neuron i, which may be located anywhere in the network. During training, the behavior of neuron i may be viewed as a *nonlinear dynamical system,* which in the context of Kalman filter theory may be described by the state and measurement equations as follows (Haykin, 1991; Anderson and Moore, 1979):

$$\mathbf{w}_i(n + 1) = \mathbf{w}_i(n) \tag{6.106}$$

$$d_i(n) = \varphi(\mathbf{x}_i^T(n)\mathbf{w}_i(n)) + e_i(n) \tag{6.107}$$

where the iteration n corresponds to the presentation of the nth pattern, $\mathbf{x}_i(n)$ is the input vector of neuron i, the activation function $\varphi(\cdot)$ is responsible for the nonlinearity in the neuron, and $e_i(n)$ is the measurement error at the output of neuron i. The weight vector $\mathbf{w}_i$ of the optimum model for neuron i is to be "estimated" through training with examples. It is assumed that the activation function $\varphi(\cdot)$ is differentiable. Accordingly, we may use the Taylor series to expand the measurement equation (6.107) about the current estimate

$\hat{\mathbf{w}}_i(n)$, and thereby *linearize* the activation function as follows:

$$\varphi(\mathbf{x}_i^T(n)\mathbf{w}_i(n)) \simeq \mathbf{q}_i^T(n)\mathbf{w}_i(n) + [\varphi(\mathbf{x}_i^T(n)\hat{\mathbf{w}}_i(n)) - \mathbf{q}_i^T(n)\hat{\mathbf{w}}_i(n)] \tag{6.108}$$

where

$$\begin{aligned}\mathbf{q}_i(n) &= \left[\frac{\partial\varphi(\mathbf{x}_i^T(n)\mathbf{w}_i(n))}{\partial\mathbf{w}_i(n)}\right]_{\mathbf{w}_i(n)=\hat{\mathbf{w}}_i(n)} \\ &= \hat{y}_i(n)[1-\hat{y}_i(n)]\mathbf{x}_i(n)\end{aligned} \tag{6.109}$$

and where $\hat{y}_i(n)$ is the output of neuron i that results from the use of estimate $\hat{\mathbf{w}}_i(n)$, and $\mathbf{x}_i(n)$ is the input vector. In the last line of Eq. (6.109) we have assumed the use of a logistic function for the activation function φ. The first term on the right-hand side of Eq. (6.108) is the desired linear term; the remaining term represents a modeling error. Thus, substituting Eq. (6.108) in (6.107) and ignoring the modeling error, we may rewrite the measurement equation (6.107) as

$$d_i(n) = \mathbf{q}_i^T(n)\mathbf{w}_i(n) + e_i(n) \tag{6.110}$$

where the vector $\mathbf{q}_i$ is defined in Eq. (6.109).

The pair of equations (6.106) and (6.110) describes the linearized dynamic behavior of neuron i. The measurement error $e_i(n)$ in Eq. (6.110) is a *localized error,* the instantaneous estimate of which is given by

$$e_i(n) = -\frac{\partial\mathscr{E}(n)}{\partial y_i(n)} \tag{6.111}$$

where

$$\mathscr{E}(n) = \frac{1}{2}\sum_{j\in C}[d_j(n) - y_j(n)]^2 \tag{6.112}$$

The differentiation in Eq. (6.111) corresponds to the *back-propagation of the global error to the output of neuron i,* just as is done in standard back-propagation. Given the pair of equations (6.106) and (6.110), we may use the standard RLS algorithm (Haykin, 1991) to make an estimate of the synaptic weight vector $\mathbf{w}_i(n)$ of neuron i. The resulting solution is defined by the following system of recursive equations (Palmieri et al., 1991; Shah and Palmieri, 1990):

$$\mathbf{r}_i(n) = \lambda^{-1}\mathbf{P}_i(n)\mathbf{q}_i(n) \tag{6.113}$$

$$\mathbf{k}_i(n) = \mathbf{r}_i(n)[1 + \mathbf{r}_i^T(n)\mathbf{q}_i(n)]^{-1} \tag{6.114}$$

$$\mathbf{w}_i(n+1) = \mathbf{w}_i(n) + e_i(n)\mathbf{k}_i(n) \tag{6.115}$$

$$\mathbf{P}_i(n+1) = \lambda^{-1}\mathbf{P}_i(n) - \mathbf{k}_i(n)\mathbf{r}_i^T(n) \tag{6.116}$$

where iteration $n = 1, 2, \ldots, N$, and N is the total number of examples. The vector $\mathbf{q}_i(n)$ represents the linearized neuron function given in Eq. (6.109), $\mathbf{P}_i(n)$ is the current estimate of the inverse of the covariance matrix of $\mathbf{q}_i(n)$, and $\mathbf{k}_i(n)$ is the *Kalman gain.* The parameter λ is a *forgetting factor,* whose value lies inside the range $0 < \lambda \leq 1$. Equation (6.116) is called the *Riccatti difference equation.* Each neuron in the network perceives its own *effective input* $\mathbf{q}_i(n)$; hence it has to maintain its own copy of $\mathbf{P}_i(n)$ even if it shares some of its inputs with other neurons in the network.

The algorithm described by Eqs. (6.113) through (6.116) is called the *multiple extended Kalman algorithm* (MEKA) (Palmieri et al., 1991; Shah and Palmieri, 1990). Computer simulation results for fairly difficult pattern-classification problems are presented in Shah and Palmieri (1990), which demonstrate the superior performance of MEKA compared to the global version of the extended Kalman filter algorithm (Shinghal and Wu, 1989).

6.19 Supervised Learning as a Function Optimization Problem

The viewpoint that supervised learning is a nonlinear identification problem directs our attention toward *nonlinear optimum filtering* for relevant literature. Equivalently, we may view the supervised training of a multilayer perceptron as an *unconstrained nonlinear function optimization problem.* This latter viewpoint directs our attention to the literature on *numerical optimization theory,* with particular reference to optimization techniques that use higher-order information such as the conjugate-gradient method and Newton's method (Luenberger, 1969; Dorny, 1975). Both of these methods use the gradient vector (first-order partial derivatives) and the Hessian matrix (second-order partial derivatives) of the cost function $\mathscr{E}_{\text{av}}(\mathbf{w})$ to perform the optimization, albeit in different ways. A survey of first- and second-order optimization techniques applied to supervised learning is presented by Battiti (1992).

Conjugate-Gradient Method

In the first-order method of gradient descent, the direction vector (along which an adjustment to the weight vector is made) is simply the negative of the gradient vector. Consequently, the approach to a minimum taken by the solution may follow a zigzag path. The *conjugate-gradient method* avoids this problem by incorporating an intricate relationship between the direction and gradient vectors. The method was first applied to the general unconstrained minimization problem by Fletcher and Reeves (1964). The conjugate-gradient method is guaranteed to locate the minimum of any quadratic function of N variables in at most N steps. For nonquadratic functions, as exemplified by the cost function used in the training of a multilayer perceptron, the process is iterative rather than N-step, and a criterion for convergence is required.

Let $\mathbf{p}(n)$ denote the direction vector at iteration n of the algorithm. Then the weight vector of the network is updated in accordance with the rule

$$\mathbf{w}(n+1) = \mathbf{w}(n) + \eta(n)\mathbf{p}(n) \tag{6.117}$$

where $\eta(n)$ is the learning-rate parameter, on which we shall have more to say later. The initial direction vector $\mathbf{p}(0)$ is set equal to the negative gradient vector $\mathbf{g}(n)$ at the initial point $n = 0$; that is,

$$\mathbf{p}(0) = -\mathbf{g}(0) \tag{6.118}$$

Each successive direction vector is then computed as a linear combination of the current gradient vector and the previous direction vector. We thus write

$$\mathbf{p}(n+1) = -\mathbf{g}(n+1) + \beta(n)\mathbf{p}(n) \tag{6.119}$$

where $\beta(n)$ is a time-varying parameter. There are various rules for determining $\beta(n)$ in terms of the gradient vectors $\mathbf{g}(n)$ and $\mathbf{g}(n+1)$; two alternate rules are the following.

- The *Fletcher–Reeves formula* (Fletcher and Reeves, 1964):

$$\beta(n) = \frac{\mathbf{g}^T(n+1)\mathbf{g}(n+1)}{\mathbf{g}^T(n)\mathbf{g}(n)} \tag{6.120}$$

- The *Polak–Ribière formula* (Polak and Ribière, 1969):

$$\beta(n) = \frac{\mathbf{g}^T(n+1)[\mathbf{g}(n+1) - \mathbf{g}(n)]}{\mathbf{g}^T(n)\mathbf{g}(n)} \tag{6.121}$$

Both of these rules for determining the parameter $\beta(n)$ reduce to the same form in the case of a quadratic function (Shanno, 1978).

The computation of the learning-rate parameter $\eta(n)$ in the update formula of Eq. (6.117) involves a *line search,* the purpose of which is to find the particular value of η for which the cost function $\mathscr{E}_{\text{av}}(\mathbf{w}(n) + \eta\mathbf{p}(n))$ is minimized, given fixed values of $\mathbf{w}(n)$ and $\mathbf{p}(n)$. That is, $\eta(n)$ is defined by

$$\eta(n) = \arg\min_{\eta}\{\mathscr{E}_{\text{av}}(\mathbf{w}(n) + \eta\mathbf{p}(n))\} \tag{6.122}$$

The accuracy of the line search has a profound influence on the performance of the conjugate-gradient method (Johansson et al., 1990).

The use of the conjugate-gradient method for the supervised training of multilayer perceptrons has been studied by Kramer and Sangiovanni-Vincentelli (1989), Johansson et al. (1990), and other researchers. The findings reported in these two papers on small Boolean learning problems seem to show that back-propagation learning based on the conjugate-gradient method requires fewer epochs than the standard back-propagation algorithm, but it is computationally more complex.

Newton's Method

The conjugate-gradient method uses the Hessian matrix in its derivation, and yet the algorithm is formulated in such a way that the estimation and storage of the Hessian matrix are completely avoided. In direct contrast, the Hessian matrix plays a prominent role in *Newton's method* and its variants.

Using the Taylor series expansion, we may approximate an incremental change $\Delta\mathscr{E}_{\text{av}}(\mathbf{w})$ in the cost function $\mathscr{E}_{\text{av}}(\mathbf{w})$ as a quadratic function of $\Delta\mathbf{w}$, an incremental change in the weight vector $\mathbf{w}$, as follows:

$$\begin{aligned}\Delta\mathscr{E}_{\text{av}}(\mathbf{w}) &= \mathscr{E}_{\text{av}}(\mathbf{w} + \Delta\mathbf{w}) - \mathscr{E}_{\text{av}}(\mathbf{w}) \\ &\simeq \mathbf{g}^T\,\Delta\mathbf{w} + \frac{1}{2}\Delta\mathbf{w}^T\,\mathbf{H}\,\Delta\mathbf{w}\end{aligned} \tag{6.123}$$

where $\mathbf{g}$ is the gradient vector

$$\mathbf{g} = \frac{\partial\mathscr{E}_{\text{av}}(\mathbf{w})}{\partial\mathbf{w}} \tag{6.124}$$

and $\mathbf{H}$ is the Hessian matrix

$$\mathbf{H} = \frac{\partial^2\mathscr{E}_{\text{av}}(\mathbf{w})}{\partial\mathbf{w}^2} \tag{6.125}$$

Differentiating Eq. (6.123) with respect to $\Delta\mathbf{w}$, the change $\Delta\mathscr{E}_{\text{av}}(\mathbf{w})$ is minimized when

$$\mathbf{g} + \mathbf{H}\,\Delta\mathbf{w} = \mathbf{0}$$

which yields the optimum value of $\Delta\mathbf{w}$ to be

$$\Delta\mathbf{w} = -\mathbf{H}^{-1}\mathbf{g} \tag{6.126}$$

where $\mathbf{H}^{-1}$ is the inverse of the Hessian matrix. Thus, given a "previous estimate" $\mathbf{w}_o$ of the optimum solution to the minimization of the cost function $\mathscr{E}_{\text{av}}(\mathbf{w})$, an "improved estimate'' of the solution is obtained by using the result

$$\begin{aligned} \mathbf{w} &= \mathbf{w}_o + \Delta\mathbf{w} \\ &= \mathbf{w}_o - \mathbf{H}^{-1}\mathbf{g} \end{aligned} \tag{6.127}$$

Equation (6.127) provides the basis of *Newton's method.* This equation is applied iteratively, with the computed value of $\mathbf{w}$ being used repeatedly as the ''new'' $\mathbf{w}_o$.

The application of Newton's method to the training of multilayer perceptrons is hindered by the requirement of having to calculate the Hessian matrix and its inverse, which can be computationally expensive. The problem is further complicated by the fact that the Hessian matrix $\mathbf{H}$ would have to be nonsingular for its inverse to be computable. Unfortunately, there is no guarantee that the Hessian matrix of a multilayer perceptron with supervised training is always nonsingular. Moreover, there is the potential problem of the Hessian matrix being almost rank-deficient, which results from the intrinsically ill-conditioned nature of neural network training problems (Saarinen et al., 1991, 1992); this can only make the computational task more difficult. Battiti (1992) discusses various modifications to Newton's method to accommodate its use for multilayer perceptrons.

6.20 Supervised Learning of Probability Distributions by Multilayer Perceptrons

The training of a multilayer perceptron is usually performed with the error back-propagation algorithm, which involves the use of a mean-square error criterion as described in Section 6.3. In general, however, such an approach lacks any precise notion of probability. Yet there are many important applications where we would like to train a multilayer perceptron and be able to generalize from a limited and possibly noisy set of examples, to interpret the outputs of the network in probabilistic terms. For example, the need for learning the underlying probability distribution arises in medical diagnosis, where the pattern (vector) applied to the network input corresponds to the *symptoms* of a patient, and an output of the network corresponds to a particular *illness.*

How, then, can a multilayer perceptron learn a probability distribution? The answer to this fundamental question lies in the use of *relative entropy* as the performance measure for the supervised learning process (Baum and Wilczek, 1988; Hopfield, 1987b). To be specific, consider a multilayer perceptron consisting of an input layer, a single hidden layer, and an output layer, as shown in Fig. 6.29. According to the notation described in

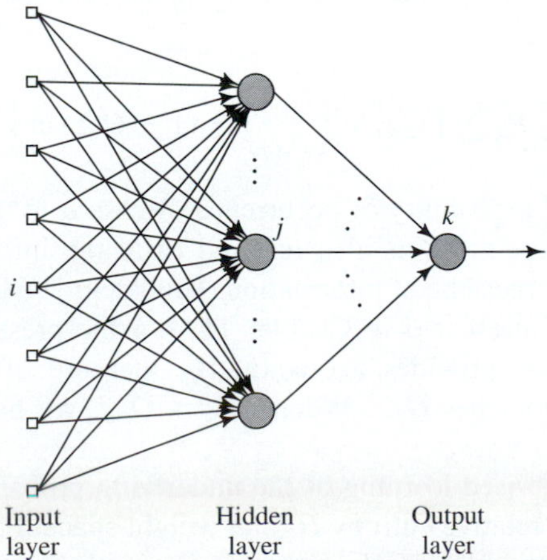

FIGURE 6.29 Multilayer perceptron with a single hidden layer and an output layer.

this figure, node i refers to the input layer, neuron j refers to the hidden layer, and neuron k refers to the output layer. It is assumed that all the hidden and output neurons of the network use the same sigmoidal nonlinearity in the form of a logistic function. Let w_{ji} denote the synaptic weight of hidden neuron j connected to node i in the input layer. Let $x_{i|\alpha}$ denote the ith component of the input pattern (vector), given case α. Then, the net internal activity of neuron j is given by

$$v_{j|\alpha} = \sum_i w_{ji} x_{i|\alpha} \tag{6.128}$$

Correspondingly, the output of hidden neuron j for case α is given by

$$y_{j|\alpha} = \varphi(v_{j|\alpha}) \tag{6.129}$$

where $\varphi(\cdot)$ is the logistic function

$$\varphi(v) = \frac{1}{1 + \exp(-v)} \tag{6.130}$$

Consider next the output layer of the network. Let w_{kj} denote the synaptic weight of output neuron k connected to hidden neuron j. The net internal activity of output neuron k is thus given by

$$v_{k|\alpha} = \sum_j w_{kj} y_{j|\alpha} \tag{6.131}$$

The kth output of the network, given case α at the input, is therefore

$$y_{k|\alpha} = \varphi(v_{k|\alpha}) \tag{6.132}$$

The output $y_{k|\alpha}$ is assigned a probabilistic interpretation as follows. Define

$$P_{k|\alpha} = y_{k|\alpha} \tag{6.133}$$

as the *estimate* of the conditional probability that the proposition k is *true,* given the case α at the input. On this basis, we may interpret

$$1 - P_{k|\alpha} = 1 - y_{k|\alpha}$$

as the estimate of the conditional probability that the proposition k is *false,* given the input case α. Correspondingly, let $Q_{k|\alpha}$ denote the *actual* (true) value of the conditional probability that the proposition k is true, given the input case α. This means that $1 - Q_{k|\alpha}$ is the actual value of the conditional probability that the proposition k is false, given the input case α. Thus, we may define the *relative entropy* for the multilayer perceptron of Fig. 6.29 as follows:

$$H_{P\|Q} = \sum_\alpha P_\alpha \sum_k \left[Q_{k|\alpha} \ln\left(\frac{Q_{k|\alpha}}{P_{k|\alpha}}\right) + (1 - Q_{k|\alpha}) \ln\left(\frac{1 - Q_{k|\alpha}}{1 - P_{k|\alpha}}\right)\right] \tag{6.134}$$

where P_α is the *a priori* probability of occurrence of case α at the input of the multilayer perceptron. The relative entropy is also referred to in the information theory literature as the *Kullback–Leibler* measure of information (Kullback, 1968). A more detailed discussion of this criterion is presented in Chapter 11. For the present it suffices to say that the relative entropy $H_{P\|Q}$ provides a quantitative measure of how closely the conditional probability $P_{k|\alpha}$ matches $Q_{k|\alpha}$. When $P_{k|\alpha} = Q_{k|\alpha}$, we have $H_{P\|Q} = 0$; otherwise, $H_{P\|Q} > 0$.

To perform the supervised learning of the underlying probability distribution, we use gradient descent on the relative entropy $H_{P\|Q}$ in weight space. First, we use the chain rule to express the partial derivative of $H_{P\|Q}$ with respect to the synaptic weight w_{kj} of output neuron k as follows:

$$\frac{\partial H_{P\|Q}}{\partial w_{kj}} = \frac{\partial H_{P\|Q}}{\partial P_{k|\alpha}} \frac{\partial P_{k|\alpha}}{\partial y_{k|\alpha}} \frac{\partial y_{k|\alpha}}{\partial v_{k|\alpha}} \frac{\partial v_{k|\alpha}}{\partial w_{kj}} \tag{6.135}$$

Hence, using Eqs. (6.131) to (6.135) and simplifying, we get

$$\frac{\partial H_{P\|Q}}{\partial w_{kj}} = -\sum_{\alpha} P_{\alpha}(Q_{k|\alpha} - P_{k|\alpha}) y_{j|\alpha} \tag{6.136}$$

Next, we use Eq. (6.134) to express the partial derivative of $H_{P\|Q}$ with respect to the synaptic weight w_{ji} of hidden neuron j as follows:

$$\frac{\partial H_{P\|Q}}{\partial w_{ji}} = -\sum_{\alpha} P_{\alpha} \sum_{k} \left(\frac{Q_{k|\alpha}}{P_{k|\alpha}} - \frac{1 - Q_{k|\alpha}}{1 - P_{k|\alpha}} \right) \frac{\partial P_{k|\alpha}}{\partial w_{ji}} \tag{6.137}$$

Via the chain rule, the partial derivative $\partial P_{k|\alpha}/\partial w_{ji}$ is itself written as

$$\frac{\partial P_{k|\alpha}}{\partial w_{ji}} = \frac{\partial P_{k|\alpha}}{\partial y_{k|\alpha}} \frac{\partial y_{k|\alpha}}{\partial v_{k|\alpha}} \frac{\partial v_{k|\alpha}}{\partial y_{j|\alpha}} \frac{\partial y_{j|\alpha}}{\partial v_{j|\alpha}} \frac{\partial v_{j|\alpha}}{\partial w_{ji}} \tag{6.138}$$

Hence, using Eqs. (6.128) through (6.133) in (6.138) and then substituting the result in Eq. (6.137), we get the desired partial derivative:

$$\frac{\partial H_{P\|Q}}{\partial w_{ji}} = -\sum_{\alpha} P_{\alpha} x_{i|\alpha} \varphi' \left(\sum_{i} w_{ji} x_{i|\alpha} \right) \sum_{k} (P_{k|\alpha} - Q_{k|\alpha}) w_{kj} \tag{6.139}$$

where $\varphi'(\cdot)$ is the derivative of the logistic function $\varphi(\cdot)$ with respect to its argument.

Assuming the use of the same learning-rate parameter η for all weight changes made in the network, the weight change applied to the synaptic weights w_{kj} and w_{ji} are computed, respectively, in accordance with the gradient-descent rules:

$$\begin{aligned} \Delta w_{kj} &= -\eta \frac{\partial H_{P\|Q}}{\partial w_{kj}} \\ &= \eta \sum_{\alpha} P_{\alpha}(Q_{k|\alpha} - P_{k|\alpha}) y_{j|\alpha} \end{aligned} \tag{6.140}$$

and

$$\begin{aligned} \Delta w_{ji} &= -\eta \frac{\partial H_{P\|Q}}{\partial w_{ji}} \\ &= \eta \sum_{\alpha} P_{\alpha} x_{i|\alpha} \varphi' \left(\sum_{i} w_{ji} x_{i|\alpha} \right) \sum_{k} (P_{k|\alpha} - Q_{k|\alpha}) w_{kj} \end{aligned} \tag{6.141}$$

Note that according to the assignment described in Eq. (6.134), the *a posteriori* conditional probability $Q(k|\alpha)$ plays the role of a desired (target) response for the output of the multilayer perceptron, given that the input data are taken from class α. Thus, using the relative entropy as the criterion for training, and assuming that the multilayer perceptron has enough free parameters, enough training data, and that the training does not get stuck at a local minimum, then the outputs of the multilayer perceptron will approximate the *a posteriori* conditional probabilities of the underlying distribution. It is important for the multilayer perceptron to converge to a global minimum, because it is only then that we are assured of the relative entropy $H_{P\|Q}$ being close to zero, which in turn means that the estimated conditional probability $P_{k|\alpha}$ is a close match for the true conditional probability $Q_{k|\alpha}$; it is difficult, if not virtually impossible, to guarantee this condition in practice.

6.21 Discussion

Back-propagation learning has indeed emerged as the *standard* algorithm for the training of multilayer perceptrons, against which other learning algorithms are often benchmarked. The back-propagation algorithm derives its name from the fact that the partial derivatives of the cost function (performance measure) with respect to the free parameters (synaptic weights and thresholds) of the network are determined by back-propagating the error signals (computed by the output neurons) through the network, layer by layer. In so doing, it solves the credit-assignment problem in a most elegant fashion. The computing power of the algorithm lies in its two main attributes:

- *Local* method for updating the synaptic weights and thresholds of the multilayer perceptron
- *Efficient* method for computing *all* the partial derivatives of the cost function with respect to these free parameters

For the cost function we may use a criterion based on (1) mean-square error, or (2) relative entropy. The mean-square error criterion is well suited for solving pattern-classification and nonlinear regression problems. On the other hand, the relative entropy criterion is particularly useful for estimating the conditional *a posteriori* probabilities of an underlying distribution.

The specific details involved in the design of a multilayer perceptron naturally depend on the application of interest. We may, however, make two distinctions:

1. In pattern classification, *all* the neurons of the network are *nonlinear.* When the nonlinearity is in the form of the logistic function, the output of neuron k in the output layer of the network is an asymptotic approximation of the *a posteriori probability* of class k, provided that the network has enough free parameters, enough training data, and does not get stuck in a local minimum.
2. In nonlinear regression, all the neurons in the *output layer* are *linear.* This particular choice is justified as follows. Assuming that all the information content of the training vectors is transferred to the synaptic weights and thresholds of the neurons, the residue (approximation error) would ideally be modeled as a realization of *white Gaussian noise.* The white property means that the power spectrum of the residue is constant and therefore independent of frequency. The Gaussian property means that the amplitude of the residue is Gaussian distributed. Now, the Gaussian distribution occupies the complete amplitude range $(-\infty, \infty)$. It follows therefore that the dynamic range of the network output must likewise be $(-\infty, \infty)$, which in turn requires that the neurons in the output layer of the network be all linear.

In the context of nonlinear regression, various methods have been proposed for improving performance by combining two or more neural networks into a single composite structure. One such method is the *basic ensemble method* (BEM) that uses the simple idea of ensemble averaging (Perrone and Cooper, 1993). Suppose that we have an ensemble of K regression estimators (e.g., multilayer perceptrons) *trained on different data sets drawn from the same population.* Let $F_k(\mathbf{x})$ denote the kth regression estimator, where $\mathbf{x}$ is the input vector and $k = 1, 2, \ldots, K$. The ensemble-averaged regression estimator is defined simply as

$$F_{\text{av}}(\mathbf{x}) = \frac{1}{K}\sum_{k=1}^{K} F_k(\mathbf{x}) \tag{6.142}$$

Perrone and Cooper (1993) demonstrate the generality of this method by showing that it is applicable to a very wide class of cost functions.

6.22 Applications

Multilayer perceptrons, trained with the back-propagation algorithm, have been applied successfully in a variety of diverse areas. These applications include the following:

- NETtalk: Neural networks that learn to pronounce English text (Sejnowski and Rosenberg, 1987)
- Speech recognition (Cohen et al., 1993; Renals et al., 1992a, b)
- Optical character recognition (Säckinger et al., 1992; LeCun et al., 1990a)
- On-line handwritten character recognition (Guyon, 1990)
- Combining visual and acoustic speech signals for improved intelligibility (Sejnowski et al., 1990)
- System identification (Narendra and Parthasarathy, 1990)
- Control (Werbos, 1989, 1992; Nguyen and Widrow, 1989; Jordan and Jacobs, 1990)
- Steering of an autonomous vehicle (Pomerleau, 1992)
- Radar target detection and classification (Haykin and Bhattacharya, 1992; Haykin and Deng, 1991; Orlando et al., 1990)
- Passive sonar detection and classification with a low false alarm rate (Casselman et al., 1991)
- Medical diagnosis of heart attacks (Baxt, 1993; Harrison et al., 1991)
- Modeling of the control of eye movements (Robinson, 1992)

To document all of these applications in full and others not mentioned here, we would need a whole book to do justice to them all. Instead, we have chosen to present detailed discussions of two specific applications: optical character recognition and speech recognition, the needs for both of which are rather pervasive.

Optical Character Recognition

The *optical character recognition* (OCR) problem is a relatively simple vision task, and yet it is difficult to accomplish with machines. The input consists of black or white pixels representing handwritten digits, and the output has only 10 output categories (digits). The problem is of significant practical value, dealing with objects in a real two-dimensional space. The requirement is to map the image space onto the category space with a high enough classification accuracy, given the considerable regularity and complexity of the problem.

LeCun et al. (1990a) have shown that a large multilayer perceptron can be used to solve this problem. The images are applied directly to the network, bypassing the need for preprocessing such as feature extraction, and thereby demonstrating the ability of a multilayer perceptron to deal with large amounts of low-level information.

The OCR network is a multilayer perceptron whose general structure is shown in Fig. 6.30 (Säckinger et al., 1992). It consists of an input layer, four hidden layers, and an output layer. The input layer has 400 source nodes that correspond directly to the 20×20 pixel image (i.e., no preprocessing is done). The 10 outputs of the network code the 10 digits in a "1 out of 10" code. The output neurons compute real-valued outputs, such that the network provides information not only about which particular digit to *select,* but also about the *confidence* in the decision made. In fact, the difference between the output levels of the most active and the second most active output neurons is an accurate measure

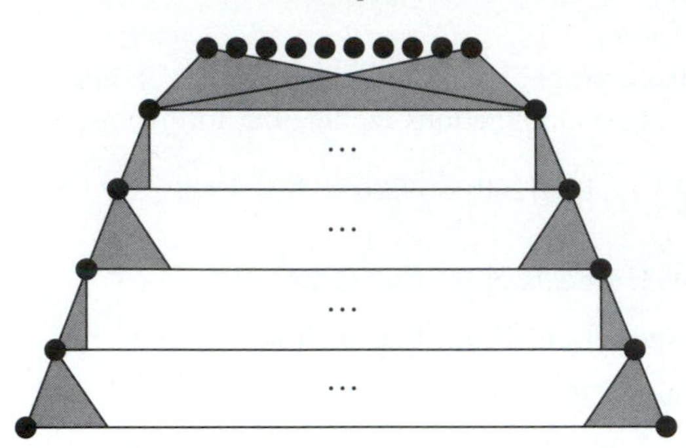

Layer	Neurons	Synapses
5	10	3,000
4	300	1,200
3	1,200	50,000
2	784	3,136
1	3,136	78,400

20 × 20 (= 400) inputs

● Neuron   Receptive field of neuron

FIGURE 6.30 General structure of the optical character recognition (OCR) network. (From E. Säckinger et al., 1992a, with permission of IEEE.)

of the confidence that can be used to reject ambiguous digits. Moreover, since the network has no feedback, the classification is accomplished in a single pass.

Figure 6.31 represents an example depicting all the states of the OCR network for the case of a handwritten digit 4. The states of the input and four hidden layers are shown as gray levels, whereas the states of the output layer are proportional to the size of the black (negative) and the white (positive) squares.

Of all the five computation layers of the network, only the output layer is fully connected with independent synaptic weights. The four hidden layers are carefully constrained to

0 1 2 3 4 5 6 7 8 9

Output layer
3,000 connection eval. by DSP

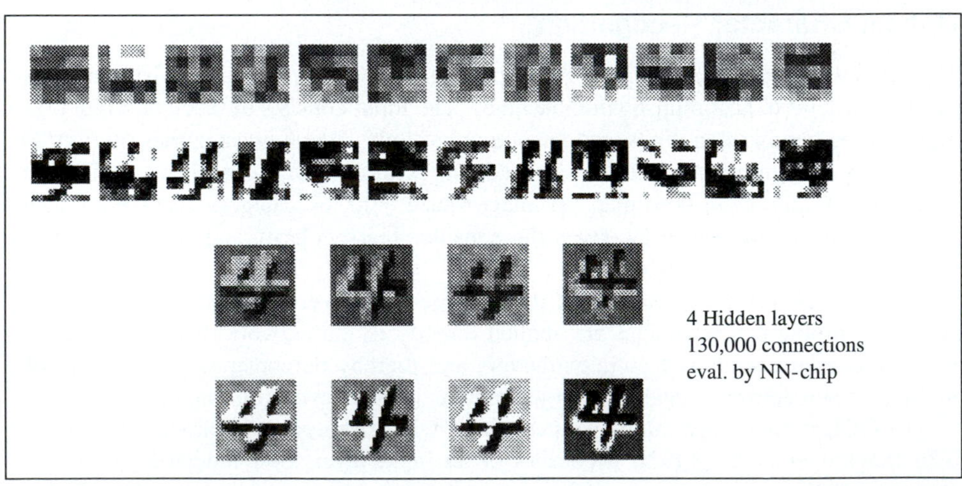

Input (20 × 20 pixels)

FIGURE 6.31 Example for the states of the OCR network with a number four as input. (From E. Säckinger et al., 1992a, with permission of IEEE.)

improve the generalization capability of the network for input patterns that are not used during training. This is accomplished by the use of *local receptive fields,* shown shaded in Fig. 6.30. *Weight sharing* is also used in these four layers, which consists of having several synapses of the network controlled by a single weight. This has the beneficial effect of reducing the number of "free" parameters, with the result that the network has many synapses but relatively few free parameters. Owing to the redundant nature of the input data and the constraints imposed on the network, the learning time is reduced significantly.

Each neuron in the first hidden layer has 25 inputs connected to a local receptive field made up of 5×5 pixel neighborhood in the input (image) layer. The neurons in this layer are grouped into four *feature maps.* Two adjacent neurons, belonging to the same feature map, have their local receptive fields displaced by *one* pixel, as illustrated in Fig. 6.32. *Weight sharing* in this layer is achieved by assigning an identical set of synaptic weights to all the neurons within each feature map. Hence the characterization of the first hidden layer is completely determined by just $4 \times 25 = 100$ free parameters, plus four bias values. The operation performed by the first hidden layer may thus be viewed essentially as four separate, two-dimensional, nonlinear convolutions of the four feature maps with the pixel image.

The second hidden layer is designed to reduce the spatial resolution of the four feature maps generated by the first layer, resulting in four new feature maps that are a quarter of the original size. The purpose of this layer is to provide some degree of *translational and rotational invariance,* which is accomplished as follows. The neurons in this layer are, as before, grouped into four feature maps, but now each neuron averages four inputs. Again, the architecture of local receptive fields and weight sharing is used, with one important change: The local receptive fields of adjacent neurons in a feature map do *not* overlap; rather, they are now displaced by *two* input units, as illustrated in Fig. 6.33. This has the effect of reducing the spatial resolution.

The third hidden layer performs feature extraction using a 5×5 receptive field in a manner similar to the first hidden layer. However, there are some basic differences to be

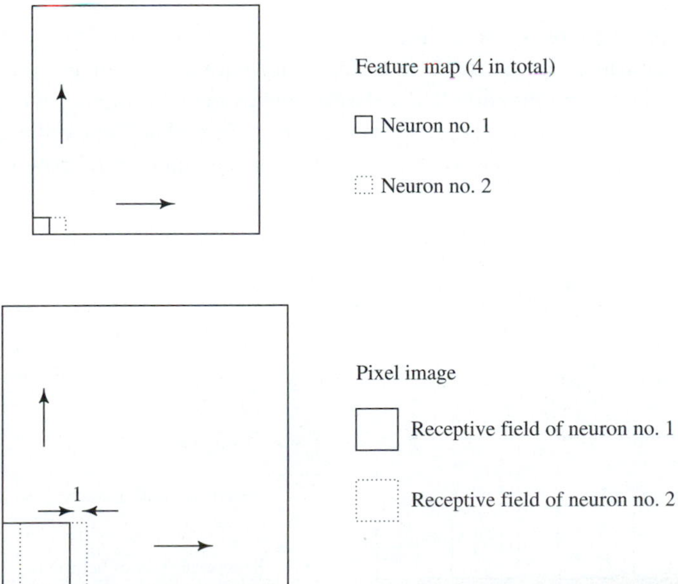

FIGURE 6.32 Illustration of the layout of the first hidden layer of the OCR network. (From E. Säckinger et al., 1992a, with permission of IEEE.)

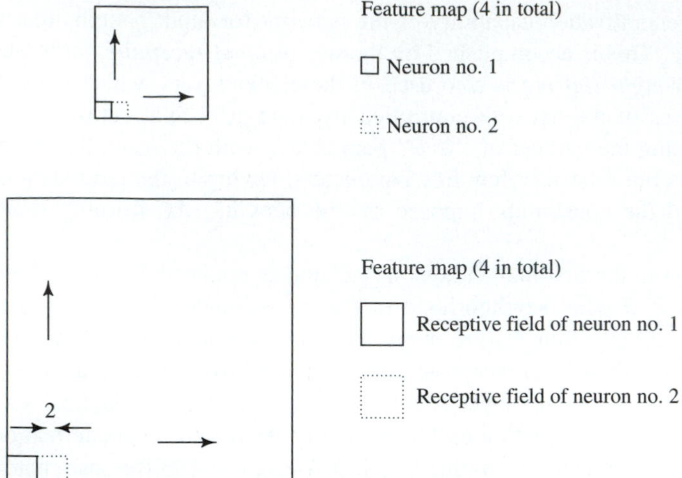

FIGURE 6.33 Illustration of the layout of the second hidden layer of the OCR network. (From E. Säckinger et al., 1992a, with permission of IEEE.)

noted. First, the neurons in the third hidden layer are grouped into 12 feature maps. Second, the inputs from one or two feature maps generated in the second hidden layer are *combined.* Most of the neurons in the third hidden layer have 50 inputs, with 25 of them connected to one feature map and the other 25 connected to a similar spatial area in another feature map, as illustrated in Fig. 6.34.

The fourth hidden layer, made up of 12 feature maps, performs the same averaging and subsampling function as explained for the second hidden layer.

Finally, the output layer has 300 inputs and 10 output neurons. This layer is the only one in the OCR network that is fully connected; that is, it contains 3000 independent synaptic weights. The output layer classifies the input patterns by computing 10 hyperplanes in the 300-dimensional feature space generated by the four hidden layers of the network.

Now that we understand the architecture of the OCR network, we next consider its performance, for which the error rate is a customary parameter. The *error rate* measures how many misclassifications the OCR network makes per 100 input patterns when it is tested on a test set of data never seen by the network before. Another even more important performance measure is the *reject rate,* defined as the number of patterns, with low

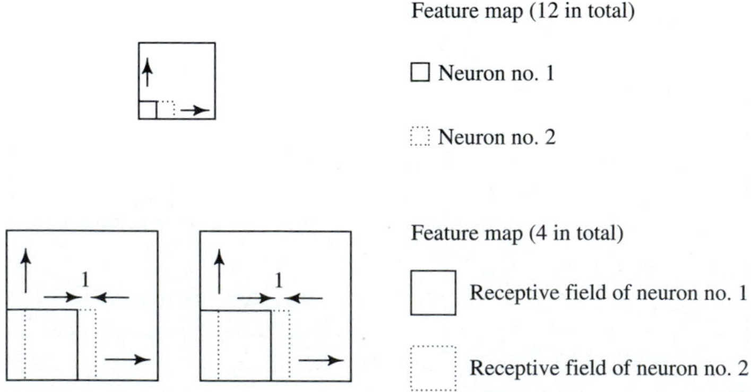

FIGURE 6.34 Illustration of the layout of the third hidden layer of the OCR network. (From E. Säckinger et al., 1992a, with permission of IEEE.)

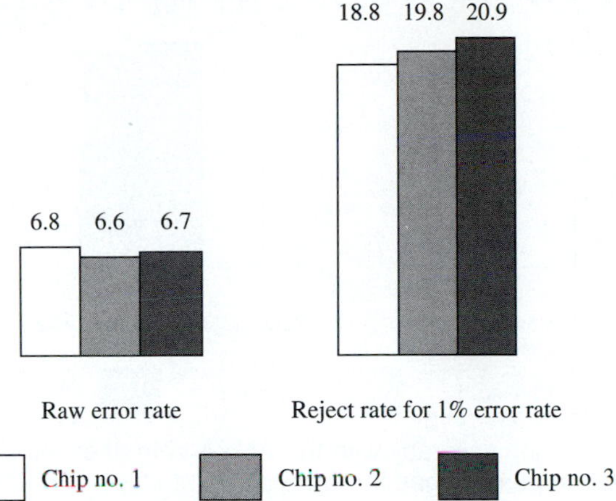

FIGURE 6.35 Recognition accuracy of the ANNA chip; the error and reject rates are given in percentages for three different chips. (From E. Säckinger et al., 1992a, with permission of IEEE.)

classification confidence, that have to be rejected in order to achieve a specified error rate—say, 1 percent. This parameter is important, since classification errors are usually related to a cost that must be kept under a certain limit. For example, the rejected patterns may be classified manually.

Figure 6.35 presents the performance figures measured for three ANNA[11] (for *a*nalog *n*eural *n*etwork *a*rithmetic and logic) chips. The first four computation layers (i.e., all the hidden layers) are on the ANNA chip, and the output layer (i.e., the last computation layer) is on a 32-bit floating-point digital signal processing (DSP) chip. The error rate and reject rate shown in Fig. 6.35 were achieved on a test set taken from segmented, handwritten ZIP codes that appeared on real-life U.S. mail (LeCun et al., 1990a). The test set is rather difficult to classify in that human performance on it is 2.5 percent raw error rate and 3.5 percent reject rate (for 1 percent error rate) (Säckinger et al., 1992). The OCR network working on a SUN SPARC workstation using 32-bit floating-point arithmetic achieved an error rate of 4.9 percent and a reject rate of 9.1 percent (for an error rate of 1 percent) on the same test set. The degradation in the performance of the ANNA chip compared to the SUN implementation is small in the case of the error rate; this degradation is due to the ANNA having less than 32-bit arithmetic. The reject rate, on the other hand, is affected more seriously by the low-resolution arithmetic of the ANNA chip. This may be explained by the fact that the error rate depends only on the most active output of the OCR network, whereas the reject rate depends on the precise values of the most active and the second most active outputs of the network and therefore requires more precision for its calculation.

Säckinger et al. (1992) describe a simple and effective method to improve the performance of the OCR network as implemented by ANNA. The method involves *retraining the output layer* of the network. During retraining with back-propagation, the chip is used for the forward pass, and the backward pass affects only the output layer that is off-chip; the weights on the chip are frozen. This method is simple to apply, since back-propagation is used for a single layer (i.e., the output layer), in which case it reduces to the simple delta rule. Figure 6.36 presents a summary of the recognition results obtained with the ANNA chip after retraining. These results, compared to those of Fig. 6.35, are encouraging.

[11] ANNA is a hybrid analog-digital chip (Säckinger et al., 1992); a description of this chip used to implement the OCR network is presented in Chapter 15.

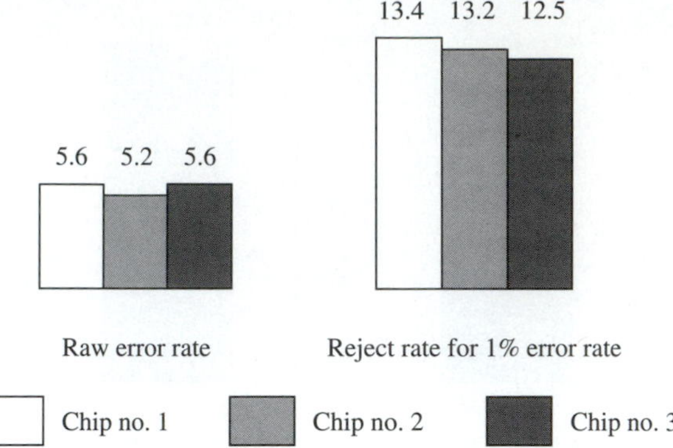

FIGURE 6.36 Recognition accuracy with the ANNA chip after retraining. The error and reject rates are given in percentages for three different chips. (From E. Säckinger et al., 1992a, with permission of IEEE.)

After retraining just the output layer, both the error rate and the reject rate are close to the original performance of the OCR network without quantization, as measured on the SUN workstation. The results shown in Fig. 6.36 also show that ''chip-to-chip'' matching is sufficiently good for one chip to be replaced by another without adversely affecting performance of the network.

The special form of multilayer perceptron, involving the use of nonlinear convolution in one layer alternating with subsampling in the next layer as described here, is called a *convolutional network* that extracts its own features. The architectural layout of the network is similar to that of a neocognitron (Fukushima, 1975, 1988b), the development of which was motivated by neurobiological considerations (Hubel and Wiesel, 1962, 1977). However, there is one important difference between the convolutional network and the neocognitron: Learning in the neocognitron is self-organized, proceeding on a layer-by-layer basis, whereas in a convolutional network learning is supervised, proceeding on an epoch-by-epoch basis.

Speech Recognition

Speech is the principal means of human communication. It is more than just a string of words; it reflects the moods, the ideas, and the personality of the speaker. For humans, speech recognition is a natural and simple process. However, to make a computer respond to even simple spoken commands has proved to be an extremely complex and difficult task. The use of a computer for solving the *speech-recognition problem* is hampered by variations in pronunciations; even single words are rarely pronounced in the same way twice. The speech-recognition problem is complicated further by concatenation, where consonants adopt aspects of neighboring consonants and vowels in fluent speech (Wheddon, 1990).

Another source of difficulty is the size of the vocabulary. The vocabulary size varies in an inverse manner with the system accuracy and efficiency, in the sense that more words introduce more confusion and require more time to process (Waibel and Lee, 1990).

In addition to linguistic and vocabulary factors, there is the issue of *speaker dependence* versus *speaker independence* to be considered. A speaker-dependent system uses speech from a target speaker for training. Accordingly, it results in good accuracy, but requires an inconvenient period for new speakers. On the other hand, a speaker-independent system is trained to handle a variety of speakers. Typically, a speaker-independent system is less accurate than a speaker-dependent system (Waibel and Lee, 1990).

All of these factors make speech recognition a continuing challenge to the speech research community (Lippmann, 1989a).

Hidden Markov models are widely used for continuous speech recognition by virtue of their inherent ability to incorporate the sequential and statistical character of the speech signal (Bahl et al., 1983; Jelinek, 1976). Such a model is formally defined as follows (Rabiner and Juang, 1986):

> A hidden Markov model (HMM) is a doubly stochastic process with an underlying stochastic process that is *not* observable (i.e., it is *hidden*), but can only be observed through another set of stochastic processes that generates the sequence of observed symbols.

An HMM provides a probabilistic framework for the modeling of a time-varying process (e.g., speech). It is characterized by the following (Rabiner, 1989):

- *A finite number of states:* Although the states are hidden, some physical significance is usually attached to the states of the model.
- *A finite number of distinct observation symbols per state* (i.e., a discrete alphabet of finite size): The observation symbols correspond to the physical output of the system being modeled.
- *A transition probability distribution:* The transition probability defines the probability of transition of the model from one state to another.
- *Observation symbol probability distributions:* After each transition, the model produces an observation (output) symbol in accordance with a probability distribution that depends on the current state. The observation symbol probability distribution is held fixed for each state, regardless of how and when a particular state is entered. Thus, with K states there are K observation symbol probability distributions to be considered.
- *An initial state probability distribution.*

Figure 6.37 presents a particular type of HMM called a *left–right* or a *Bakis model*, because the underlying state sequence associated with the model has the property that as time increases, the states proceed from left to right. Such a model has the desirable property that it can readily model a time-varying process (e.g., speech).

In the HMM formalism of speech recognition, it is assumed that the speech signal is produced by a stochastic *automaton* (finite state machine) that is built up from a set of states,

$$\mathbf{Q} = \{\mathbf{q}_1, \mathbf{q}_2, \ldots, \mathbf{q}_K\}$$

and that it is governed by statistical laws. Specifically, for each unit of speech (e.g., vocabulary word or phoneme) we have a particular HMM made up of L states $\mathbf{q}_l \in \mathbf{Q}$, with $l = 1, 2, \ldots, L$, according to a prescribed topology (Bourlard, 1990; Bourlard and Wellekens, 1990). A preprocessor is used to transform the speech signal into a sequence

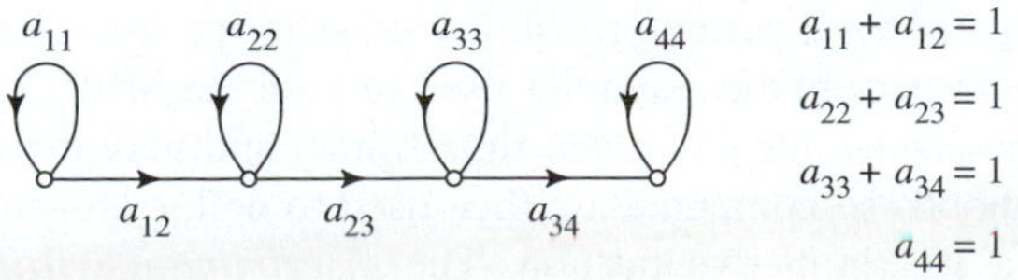

a_{11} a_{22} a_{33} a_{44}

a_{12} a_{23} a_{34}

$a_{11} + a_{12} = 1$

$a_{22} + a_{23} = 1$

$a_{33} + a_{34} = 1$

$a_{44} = 1$

FIGURE 6.37 A four-state, left–right Markov model.

of *acoustic vectors,*

$$\mathbf{X} = \{\mathbf{x}_1, \mathbf{x}_2, \ldots, \mathbf{x}_N\}$$

with the individual vectors of acoustic parameters being extracted by the preprocessor at regular intervals, typically every 10 ms. The acoustic vectors include local speech features such as spectra and related parameters. The transition probabilities, on the other hand, are used to model the displacement of these features through time. The main limitation of the HMM approach is the requirement of stringent statistical assumptions that are unlikely to be valid for speech (Cohen et al., 1993).

Another way in which we may approach speech recognition is to use neural networks, particularly multilayer perceptrons based on back-propagation learning. The main advantages of this latter approach are a powerful discrimination-based learning procedure, a flexible architecture that permits easy use of contextual information, and relatively weak hypotheses about statistical distributions. However, the temporal structure of speech signals remains difficult to handle with neural networks, and in the framework of continuous speech recognition it is still impossible to recognize a sentence in terms of speech units with multilayer perceptrons (Bourlard, 1990). This temporal problem is solved very efficiently in the HMM approach by a technique known as the dynamic time-warping algorithm, which captures the dynamics of speech (Ney, 1984).

As an alternative, the idea of a *hybrid* approach has been proposed for continuous speech recognition, involving the combined use of multilayer perceptrons (MLP) and hidden Markov models (Morgan and Bourlard, 1990; Bourlard and Wellekens, 1990). This hybrid approach exploits the advantages of back-propagation learning applied to MLP, while preserving the HMM formalism to integrate over time and to segment continuous speech signals. Such a combination is referred to as an *MLP-HMM speech-recognition system.*

The MLP is used to provide estimates of the conditional probability distribution $P(\mathbf{q}_j|\mathbf{x}_i)$, which refers to the *a posteriori* probability of state $\mathbf{q}_j$ given the input vector $\mathbf{x}_i$. Let $y(j,i)$ denote the actual value of the jth output produced by $\mathbf{x}_i$. Let $d(j,k)$ denote the desired (target) value of the jth output associated with the class $\mathbf{q}_k$; it is defined by

$$d(j,k) = \begin{cases} 1, & k = j \\ 0, & k \neq j \end{cases} \tag{6.143}$$

Using the relative entropy between the *a posteriori* target (desired) distribution and *a posteriori* output distribution as the training criterion, and assuming that the network has enough free parameters, enough training data, and that the training does not get stuck in a local minimum, then the optimized MLP output $y_{\text{opt}}(j,i)$ approximates the *a posteriori* class probability $P(\mathbf{q}_j|\mathbf{x}_i)$, as shown by

$$y_{\text{opt}}(j,i) = P(\mathbf{q}_j|\mathbf{x}_i) \tag{6.144}$$

Using Bayes' rule, we may then compute the required HMM probabilities as follows:

$$P(\mathbf{x}_i|\mathbf{q}_j) = \frac{P(\mathbf{q}_j|\mathbf{x}_i)P(\mathbf{x}_i)}{P(\mathbf{q}_j)} \tag{6.145}$$

The probability $P(\mathbf{q}_j)$ is the *a priori* probability of state $\mathbf{q}_j$; it is estimated by counting the state (class) occurrences in the examples used to train the MLP. The probability $P(\mathbf{x}_i)$ is common to all the classes for any given time frame, and may therefore be ignored.

The scaled likelihoods so computed are then used to define an acoustic model for the HMM, derived in a discriminative fashion. The *discriminative training* of the HMM involves maximizing the likelihood of the correct state sequence generating the acoustic data, and minimizing the probability of the data being generated by all incorrect state sequences.

Cohen et al. (1993) have applied a hybrid MLP-HMM approach to *context-dependent modeling* of continuous speech, in which the realization of individual phonemes is highly dependent on phonetic context. For example, the sound of the vowel /ae/ in the words "map" and "tap" is quite different. Context-dependent effects are referred to as *co-articulation.* The use of context-dependent phonetic models has been shown to improve the recognition accuracy of an HMM significantly (Schwartz et al., 1985). In a context-dependent HMM, different probability distributions are used for each phoneme in every different relevant context. The hybrid MLP-HMM system described in Cohen et al. (1993) uses an MLP with an input layer of 234 nodes, spanning 9 frames (with 26 coefficients per frame) of various spectrum- and energy-related parameters that are normalized to have zero mean and unit variance. The hidden layer has 1000 neurons, and the output layer has 69 neurons, one for each context-independent phonetic class in the SRI-DECIPHER™ system, a state-of-the-art continuous speech-recognition system. Both the hidden and output neurons use sigmoidal nonlinearities. The MLP is purposely trained to estimate the conditional probability $P(\mathbf{q}_j|\mathbf{x}_i)$, where $\mathbf{q}_j$ is the state (class) associated with the middle frame of the input $\mathbf{x}_i$. The desired (target) probability distribution is defined as 1 for the index corresponding to the phoneme class label and 0 for other classes (states). The experimental results reported in Cohen et al. (1993) and earlier experimental results reported in Renals et al. (1992b) indicate that the use of neural networks can significantly improve the performance of a context-independent HMM speech recognition system. The development of the hybrid MLP-HMM system is based on a general method of decomposing a multilayer classification network with a large output layer into a number of smaller networks, with no statistical independence assumptions. It has been demonstrated that this method may be used to estimate likelihoods for context-dependent phoneme models. Moreover, it appears that scaling is no longer considered to be a problem. It should be noted, however, that the use of MLP involves more intensive computations during training and recognition than the corresponding Gaussian mixture models used in standard HMMs.

PROBLEMS

6.1 Figure P6.1 shows a neural network, involving a single hidden neuron, for the implementation of the XOR pattern; this network may be viewed as an alternative to that considered in Section 6.6. Show that the network of Fig. P6.1 solves the XOR problem by constructing (a) decision regions, and (b) a truth table for the network.

6.2 Use the back-propagation algorithm for computing a set of synaptic weights and thresholds for a neural network structured as in Fig. 6.6 to solve the XOR problem. Assume the use of a logistic function for the nonlinearity.

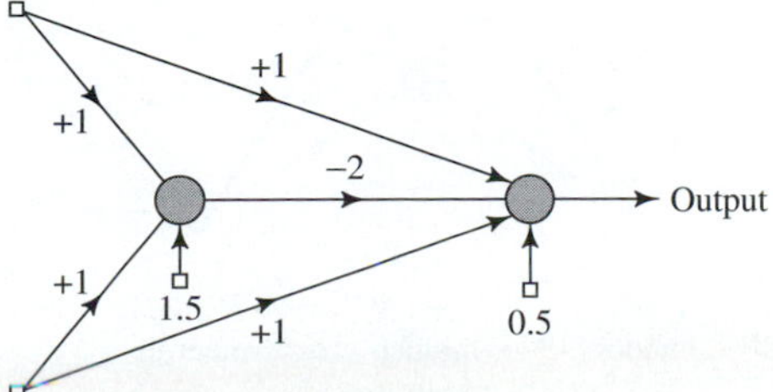

FIGURE P6.1

6.3 Consider the functions

$$\varphi(x) = \frac{1}{\sqrt{2\pi}} \int_{-\infty}^{x} e^{-t^2/2}\, dt \qquad \text{(i)}$$

and

$$\varphi(x) = \frac{2}{\pi} \tan^{-1}(x) \qquad \text{(ii)}$$

Explain why both of these functions fit the requirements of a sigmoid function. How do these two functions differ from each other?

6.4 The inclusion of a momentum term in the weight update may be viewed as a mechanism for satisfying heuristics 3 and 4 that provide guidelines for accelerating the convergence of the back-propagation algorithm, which was discussed in Section 6.15. Demonstrate the validity of this statement.

6.5 The momentum constant α is normally assigned a positive value in the range $0 \leq \alpha < 1$. Investigate the difference that would be made in the behavior of Eq. (6.37) with respect to time t if α was assigned a negative value in the range $-1 < \alpha \leq 0$.

6.6 Consider the *encoding problem* in which a set of orthogonal input patterns are mapped with a set of orthogonal output patterns through a small set of hidden neurons (Rumelhart and McClelland, 1986). Figure P6.6 shows the basic architecture for solving this problem. Essentially, the problem is to learn an encoding of a p-bit pattern into a $\log_2 p$-bit pattern, and then learn to decode this representation into the output pattern. Construct the mapping generated by the back-propagation algorithm applied to the network of Fig. P6.6 for the case of identity mapping illustrated below:

Input pattern	Output pattern
1 0 0 0 0 0 0 0	1 0 0 0 0 0 0 0
0 1 0 0 0 0 0 0	0 1 0 0 0 0 0 0
0 0 1 0 0 0 0 0	0 0 1 0 0 0 0 0
0 0 0 1 0 0 0 0	0 0 0 1 0 0 0 0
0 0 0 0 1 0 0 0	0 0 0 0 1 0 0 0
0 0 0 0 0 1 0 0	0 0 0 0 0 1 0 0
0 0 0 0 0 0 1 0	0 0 0 0 0 0 1 0
0 0 0 0 0 0 0 1	0 0 0 0 0 0 0 1

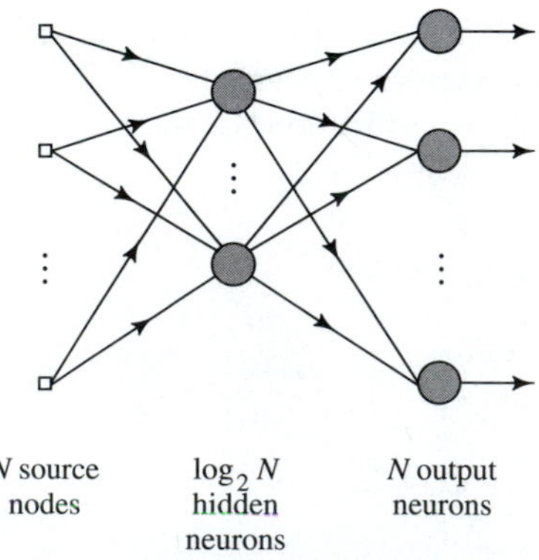

FIGURE P6.6

6.7 Consider the simple example of a network involving a single weight, for which the cost function is

$$\mathscr{E}(w) = k_1(w - w_0)^2 + k_2$$

where w_0, k_1, and k_2 are constants. A back-propagation algorithm with momentum is used to minimize $\mathscr{E}(w)$.

Explore the way in which the inclusion of the momentum constant α influences the learning process, with particular reference to the number of epochs required for convergence versus α.

6.8 Consider a two-layer network containing no hidden neurons. Assume that the network has p inputs and a single output neuron. Let x_k denote the kth input signal; the output signal is defined by

$$y = \varphi\left(\sum_{k=0}^{p} w_k x_k\right)$$

where w_0 is a threshold, and

$$\varphi(v) = \frac{1}{1 + \exp(-v)}$$

Show that this network implements a linear decision boundary that consists of a hyperplane in the input space $\mathbb{R}^p$. Illustrate your conclusions for the case of $p = 2$.

6.9 In Section 6.3 we derived the back-propagation algorithm assuming the use of the sigmoid function of Eq. (6.30), the amplitude of which lies inside the range [0,1]. Repeat the derivation of the algorithm for the asymmetric sigmoid function of Eq. (6.41), whose amplitude lies in the range [−1,1].

6.10 Equations (6.66) through (6.68) define the partial derivatives of the approximating function $F(\mathbf{w};\mathbf{x})$ realized by the multilayer perceptron of Fig. 6.19. Derive these equations from the following first principles.

(a) *Cost function:*

$$\mathscr{E}(n) = \frac{1}{2}[d - F(\mathbf{w};\mathbf{x})]^2$$

(b) *Output of neuron j:*

$$y_j = \varphi\left(\sum_i w_{ji} y_i\right)$$

where w_{ji} is synaptic weight from neuron i to neuron j, and y_i is output of neuron i;

(c) *Nonlinearity:*

$$\varphi(v) = \frac{1}{1 + \exp(-v)}$$

6.11 Investigate the use of back-propagation learning using a sigmoidal nonlinearity to achieve one-to-one mappings, as described here:

1. $f(x) = \dfrac{1}{x}, \qquad 1 \le x \le 100$

2. $f(x) = \log_{10} x, \qquad 1 \le x \le 10$

3. $f(x) = \exp(-x), \qquad 1 \le x \le 10$

4. $f(x) = \sin x, \qquad 0 \le x \le \frac{\pi}{2}$

For each mapping, do the following:

(a) Set up two sets of data, one for network training, and the other for testing.

(b) Use the training data set to compute the synaptic weights of the network, assumed to have a single hidden layer.

(c) Evaluate the computation accuracy of the network by using the test data.

Use a single hidden layer but with a variable number of hidden neurons. Investigate how the network performance is affected by varying the size of the hidden layer.

6.12 In this problem we use the back-propagation algorithm to solve a difficult nonlinear prediction problem and compare its performance with that of the LMS algorithm. The time series to be considered is created using a discrete *Volterra model* that has the form

$$x(n) = \sum_i g_i \nu(n-i) + \sum_i \sum_j g_{ij} \nu(n-i)\nu(n-j) + \cdots$$

where g_i, g_{ij}, . . . are the Volterra coefficients, the $\nu(n)$ are samples of a white, independently distributed Gaussian noise sequence, and $x(n)$ is the resultant Volterra model output. The first summation term is the familiar moving-average (MA) time-series model, and the remaining summation terms are nonlinear components of ever-increasing order. In general, the estimation of the Volterra coefficients is considered to be difficult, primarily because of their nonlinear relationship to the data.

In this problem we consider the simple example

$$x(n) = \nu(n) + \beta\nu(n-1)\nu(n-2)$$

The time series has zero mean, and is uncorrelated and therefore has a white spectrum. However, the time-series samples are not independent of each other, and therefore a higher-order predictor can be constructed. The variance of the model output is

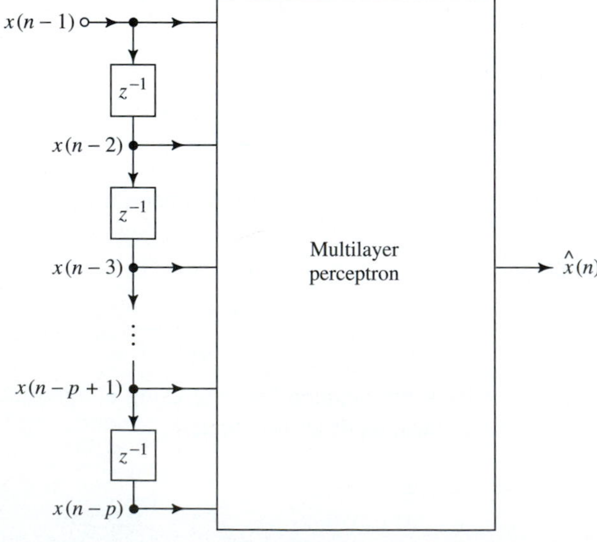

FIGURE P6.12

given by

$$\sigma_x^2 = \sigma_v^2 + \beta^2 \sigma_v^4$$

where σ_v^2 is the white-noise input variance.

(a) Construct a multilayer perceptron (MLP) with an input layer of 6 nodes, a hidden layer of 16 neurons, and a single output neuron. Figure P6.12 shows the network architecture of the MLP used as a predictor, where a tapped delay line is used to feed the input layer of the network. The hidden neurons use sigmoidal nonlinearities limited to the interval [0,1], whereas the output neuron operates as a linear combiner. The network is trained with the back-propagation algorithm having the following description:

Learning rate-parameter	$\eta = 0.001$
Momentum constant	$\alpha = 0.9$
Total number of samples processed	100,000
Number of samples per epoch	1,000
Total number of epochs	100

The white-noise input variance σ_v^2 is set equal to unity. Hence, with $\beta = 0.5$, we find that the output variance of the predictor is $\sigma_x^2 = 0.5$.

Compute the learning curve of the nonlinear predictor, with the variance of the predictor output $\hat{x}(n)$ plotted as a function of the number of epochs of training samples up to 100 epochs.

(b) Repeat the experiment using the LMS algorithm designed to perform a linear prediction on an input of 6 samples. The learning-rate parameter of the algorithm is set equal to $\eta = 0.9$.

The results of the experiment should reveal that initially the back-propagation algorithm and the LMS algorithm follow a similar path, and then the back-propagation algorithm continues to improve, finally producing a prediction variance close to the ideal value $\sigma_x^2 = 0.25$.

6.13 Consider a fully connected multilayer perceptron consisting of an input layer of two nodes, a hidden layer of two neurons, and an output layer of one neuron as shown in Fig. P6.13. Assume the use of a hyperbolic tangent for the nonlinearity. We wish to use this particular network structure to study some aspects of *double back-propagation learning* for improving generalization performance (Drucker and LeCun, 1992).

(a) Determine the partial derivatives of the instantaneous sum of squared errors $\mathscr{E}$ with respect to all 6 synaptic weights of the network, and comment on their compositions. In normal back-propagation, these are the only gradient terms that we need.

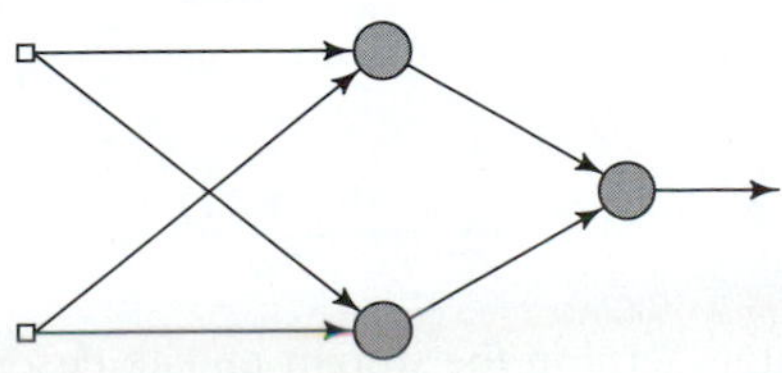

FIGURE P6.13

(b) Suppose that we proceed one more step and calculate the partial derivatives of $\mathscr{E}$ with respect to the input signals. Show that these new partial derivatives involve all the synaptic weights in the network.

(c) Now formulate a total risk R defined as the sum of $\mathscr{E}$ and another function $\mathscr{E}_b$ defined as follows:

$$\mathscr{E}_b = \frac{1}{2}\left(t_1 - \frac{\partial \mathscr{E}}{\partial x_1}\right)^2 + \frac{1}{2}\left(t_2 - \frac{\partial \mathscr{E}}{\partial x_2}\right)^2$$

where x_1 and x_2 are the input signals, and t_1 and t_2 are the corresponding target derivatives. Hence, recalculate the partial derivatives of the risk R with respect to the synaptic weights of the network.

(d) We wish to force the gradients of $\mathscr{E}$ with respect to the input signals to become zero even if the gradients of $\mathscr{E}$ with respect to the synaptic weights are nonzero. What would be the result of such a constraint imposed on the network?

6.14 Equation (6.81), defining the derivative of the error surface with respect to the learning-rate parameter $\eta_{ji}(n)$, was derived assuming that neuron j lies in the output layer of the multilayer perceptron. Show that this same formula also applies to a neuron j that lies in a hidden layer of the network.

6.15 Write the fuzzy set rule for the fuzzy back-propagation network represented by Table 6.6.

6.16 **(a)** Derive the formula for the saliency S_i given in Eq. (6.104).

(b) Assume that the Hessian matrix of the average squared error of a multilayer perceptron with respect to its weights may be approximated by a diagonal matrix as follows:

$$\mathbf{H} = \text{diag}[h_{11}, h_{22}, \ldots, h_{WW}]$$

where W is the total number of weights in the network. Determine the saliency S_i of weight w_i in the network.

6.17 Consider a multilayer perceptron with a single output neuron, defined by the function

$$y = F(\mathbf{w}, \mathbf{x})$$

where $\mathbf{x}$ is the input vector and $\mathbf{w}$ is the vector of synaptic weights in the network. The average squared error on the training set of size N is defined by

$$\mathscr{E}_{\text{av}} = \frac{1}{2N}\sum_{k=1}^{N}(d_k - y_k)^2$$

where d_k is the desired response for the input vector $\mathbf{x}_k$ pertaining to the kth example and y_k is the actual response of the network produced by the input vector $\mathbf{x}_k$. Show that the Hessian $\mathbf{H}$, evaluated at a local minimum of the error surface, may be approximated as follows (Hassibi et al., 1993):

$$\mathbf{H} \simeq \frac{1}{N}\sum_{k=1}^{N}\mathbf{g}_k\mathbf{g}_k^T$$

where

$$\mathbf{g}_k = \frac{\partial F(\mathbf{w}, \mathbf{x}_k)}{\partial \mathbf{w}}$$

6.18 The use of a momentum term in the weight update described in Eq. (6.35) may be considered as an approximation to the conjugate-gradient method (Battiti, 1992). Discuss the validity of this statement.

6.19 In describing the optical character recognition problem in Section 6.20, we mentioned that the function of the first hidden layer in the multilayer feedforward network of Fig. 6.28 may be interpreted as that of performing two-dimensional nonlinear convolutions of the four feature maps (characterizing that layer) with the pixel image. Justify the validity of this interpretation.

How would you describe the role of the second hidden layer? Justify your answer.

6.20 Consider a multilayer perceptron designed to operate as a pattern classifier, on the basis of minimizing the mean-square error $\mathscr{E}$ defined by

$$\mathscr{E} = \frac{1}{2N}\sum_{i=1}^{N}\sum_{j=1}^{K}\sum_{k=1}^{K} n_{ik}[d(j,k) - y(j,k)]^2$$

where n_{ik} is the number of times the input vector $\mathbf{x}_i$ is classified $\mathbf{q}_k$, K refers to both the total numbers of output neurons and classes, and N is the size of the training set. The desired response $d(j,k)$, pertaining to the jth output associated with the class $\mathbf{q}_k$, is defined by

$$d(j,k) = \begin{cases} 1, & k = j \\ 0, & k \neq j \end{cases}$$

Show that, regardless of the MLP topology, the minimization of $\mathscr{E}$ with respect to the actual outputs of the network yields the optimum values for the outputs given by

$$y_{\text{opt}}(j,i) = \frac{n_{ij}}{\sum_{k=1}^{K} n_{ik}}$$

What is the probabilistic interpretation of this result?

6.21 In Section 6.9 we presented qualitative arguments for the property of a multilayer perceptron classifier (using a logistic function for nonlinearity) that its outputs provide estimates of the *a posteriori* class probabilities. This property assumes that the size of the training set is large enough, and that the back-propagation algorithm used to train the network does not get stuck at a local minimum. Fill in the mathematical details of this property.

CHAPTER 7

Radial-Basis Function Networks

7.1 Introduction

The design of a supervised neural network may be pursued in a variety of different ways. The back-propagation algorithm for the design of a multilayer perceptron (under supervision) as described in the previous chapter may be viewed as an application of an optimization method known in statistics as *stochastic approximation.* In this chapter we take a different approach by viewing the design of a neural network as a *curve-fitting (approximation) problem* in a high-dimensional space. According to this viewpoint, learning is equivalent to finding a surface in a multidimensional space that provides a best fit to the training data, with the criterion for "best fit" being measured in some statistical sense. Correspondingly, generalization is equivalent to the use of this multidimensional surface to interpolate the test data. Such a viewpoint is indeed the motivation behind the method of radial-basis functions in the sense that it draws upon research work on traditional strict interpolation in a multidimensional space. In the context of a neural network, the hidden units provide a set of "functions" that constitute an arbitrary "basis" for the input patterns (vectors) when they are expanded into the hidden-unit space; these functions are called *radial-basis functions.* Radial-basis functions were first introduced in the solution of the real multivariate interpolation problem. The early work on this subject is surveyed by Powell (1985). It is now one of the main fields of research in numerical analysis.

Broomhead and Lowe (1988) were the first to exploit the use of radial-basis functions in the design of neural networks. Other major contributions to the theory, design, and application of radial-basis function networks include papers by Moody and Darken (1989), Renals (1989), and Poggio and Girosi (1990a). The paper by Poggio and Girosi emphasizes the use of regularization theory applied to this class of neural networks as a method for improved generalization to new data.

The construction of a *radial-basis function (RBF) network* in its most basic form involves three entirely different layers. The input layer is made up of source nodes (sensory units). The second layer is a hidden layer of high enough dimension, which serves a different purpose from that in a multilayer perceptron. The output layer supplies the response of the network to the activation patterns applied to the input layer. The transformation from the input space to the hidden-unit space is *nonlinear,* whereas the transformation from the hidden-unit space to the output space is *linear.* A mathematical justification for this rationale may be traced back to an early paper by Cover (1965). In particular, we note from this paper that a pattern-classification problem cast in a high-dimensional space nonlinearly is more likely to be linearly separable than in a low-dimensional space—hence the reason for making the dimension of the hidden-unit space in an RBF network high. Through careful design, however, it is possible to reduce the dimension of the hidden-unit space, especially if the centers of the hidden units are made adaptive.

Organization of the Chapter

The main body of the chapter is organized as follows. In Section 7.2 we describe Cover's theorem on the separability of patterns, and revisit the XOR problem in light of Cover's theorem; we thus pave the way for the introduction of RBF networks, which we take up in Section 7.3 by considering the interpolation problem and its relationship to RBF networks. Then, in Section 7.4, we discuss the viewpoint that supervised learning is an ill-posed hypersurface-reconstruction problem. In Section 7.5 we present a detailed treatment of Tikhonov's regularization theory and its application to RBF networks, which leads naturally to the formulation of regularization RBF networks that are described in Section 7.6. This is followed by a detailed discussion of generalized RBF networks in Section 7.7. In Section 7.8 we revisit the XOR problem once more and show how it can be solved using an RBF network. In Section 7.9 we present a comparison between RBF networks and multilayer perceptrons representing two different examples of layered feedforward networks. In Section 7.10 we discuss the relationship between RBF networks and Gaussian mixture models. In Section 7.11 we present different learning strategies for the design of RBF networks. In Section 7.12 we describe a computer experiment on a simple pattern-recognition problem involving the use of RBF networks. In Section 7.13 we discuss the idea of factorizable radial-basis functions, for which the Gaussian description is so well suited. Section 7.14 on discussion and Section 7.15 on applications conclude the chapter.

7.2 Cover's Theorem on the Separability of Patterns

When a standard radial-basis function (RBF) network is used to perform a complex pattern-classification task, the problem is basically solved by transforming it into a high-dimensional space in a nonlinear manner. The underlying justification for so doing is provided by *Cover's theorem* on the *separability of patterns,* which states that a complex pattern-classification problem cast in high-dimensional space nonlinearly is more likely to be linearly separable than in a low-dimensional space (Cover, 1965). From the work we did on the perceptron in Chapter 4, we know that once we have linearly separable patterns, then the classification problem is relatively easy to solve. Accordingly, we may develop a great deal of insight into the operation of an RBF network as a pattern classifier by studying the separability of patterns, which we do in this section.

Consider a family of surfaces, each of which naturally divides an input space into two regions. Let X denote a set of N patterns (points) $\mathbf{x}_1, \mathbf{x}_2, \ldots, \mathbf{x}_N$, each of which is assigned to one of two classes X^+ and X^-. This *dichotomy* (binary partition) of the points is said to be separable with respect to the family of surfaces if there exists a surface in the family that separates the points in the class X^+ from those in the class X^-. For each pattern $\mathbf{x} \in X$, define a vector made up of a set of real-valued functions $\{\varphi_i(\mathbf{x}) | i = 1, 2, \ldots, M\}$, as shown by

$$\boldsymbol{\varphi}(\mathbf{x}) = [\varphi_1(\mathbf{x}), \varphi_2(\mathbf{x}), \ldots, \varphi_M(\mathbf{x})]^T \tag{7.1}$$

Suppose that the pattern $\mathbf{x}$ is a vector in a p-dimensional input space. The vector $\boldsymbol{\varphi}(\mathbf{x})$ then maps points in p-dimensional input space into corresponding points in a new space of dimension M. We refer to $\varphi_i(\mathbf{x})$ as a *hidden function,* because it plays a role similar to that of a hidden unit in a feedforward neural network.

A dichotomy $\{X^+, X^-\}$ of X is said to be $\boldsymbol{\varphi}$-*separable* if there exists an m-dimensional vector $\mathbf{w}$ such that we may write (Cover, 1965)

$$\mathbf{w}^T\boldsymbol{\varphi}(\mathbf{x}) \geq 0, \qquad \mathbf{x} \in X^+$$

and (7.2)

$$\mathbf{w}^T\boldsymbol{\varphi}(\mathbf{x}) < 0, \qquad \mathbf{x} \in X^-$$

The hyperplane defined by the equation

$$\mathbf{w}^T\boldsymbol{\varphi}(\mathbf{x}) = 0 \tag{7.3}$$

describes the separating surface in the $\boldsymbol{\varphi}$ space. The inverse image of this hyperplane, that is,

$$\{\mathbf{x}: \mathbf{w}^T\boldsymbol{\varphi}(\mathbf{x}) = \mathbf{0}\} \tag{7.4}$$

defines the separating surface in the input space.

Consider a natural class of mappings obtained by using a linear combination of r-wise products of the pattern vector coordinates. The separating surfaces corresponding to such mappings are referred to as *rth-order rational varieties.* A rational variety of order r in a space of dimension p is described by an rth-degree homogeneous equation in the coordinates of the input vector $\mathbf{x}$, as shown by

$$\sum_{0 \le i_1 \le i_2 \le \cdots \le i_r \le p} a_{i_1 i_2 \cdots i_r} x_{i_1} x_{i_2} \cdots x_{i_r} = 0 \tag{7.5}$$

where x_i is the ith component of the input vector $\mathbf{x}$, and x_0 is set equal to unity in order to express the equation in a homogeneous form. Examples of separating surfaces of this type are *hyperplanes* (first-order rational varieties), *quadrics* (second-order rational varieties), and *hyperspheres* (quadrics with certain linear constraints on the coefficients). These examples are illustrated in Fig. 7.1 for a configuration of five points in a two-dimensional input space. Note that, in general, linear separability implies spherical separability, which in turn implies quadric separability; however, the converses are not necessarily true.

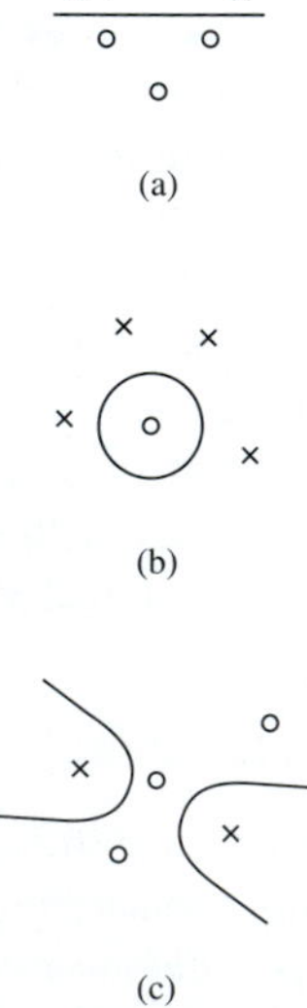

FIGURE 7.1 Three examples of φ-separable dichotomies of different sets of five points in two dimensions: (a) linearly separable dichotomy; (b) spherically separable dichotomy; (c) quadrically separable dichotomy.

Polynomial separability, as described here, may be viewed as a natural generalization of linear separability. The important point to note here is that, given a set of patterns $\mathbf{x}$ in an input space of arbitrary dimension p, we can usually find a nonlinear mapping $\boldsymbol{\varphi}(\mathbf{x})$ of high enough dimension M such that we have linear separability in the $\boldsymbol{\varphi}$ space.

Separability of Random Patterns

Consider next the separability of patterns that are randomly distributed in the input space. The desired dichotomization may be fixed or random. Under these conditions the separability of the set of pattern vectors becomes a random event that depends on the dichotomy chosen and the distribution of the patterns.

Suppose that the input vectors (patterns) $\mathbf{x}_1, \mathbf{x}_2, \ldots, \mathbf{x}_N$ are chosen independently according to a probability measure μ on the input (pattern) space. The set $X = \{\mathbf{x}_1, \mathbf{x}_2, \ldots, \mathbf{x}_N\}$ is said to be in *$\boldsymbol{\varphi}$-general position* if every m-element subset of the set of M-dimensional vectors $\{\varphi(\mathbf{x}_1), \varphi(\mathbf{x}_2), \ldots, \varphi(\mathbf{x}_N)\}$ is linearly independent for all $m \leq M$. The necessary and sufficient condition on the probability measure μ such that, with probability 1, the vectors $\mathbf{x}_1, \mathbf{x}_2, \ldots, \mathbf{x}_N$ are in $\boldsymbol{\varphi}$-general position in M-space is that the probability be zero that any point will fall in any given $(M - 1)$-dimensional subspace. Equivalently, in terms of the $\boldsymbol{\varphi}$ surfaces, we may state that a set of vectors $\mathbf{x}_1, \mathbf{x}_2, \ldots, \mathbf{x}_N$ chosen independently according to a probability measure μ is in $\boldsymbol{\varphi}$-general position with probability 1 if, and only if, every $\boldsymbol{\varphi}$ surface has μ measure zero.

Suppose, next, that a dichotomy of $X = \{\mathbf{x}_1, \mathbf{x}_2, \ldots, \mathbf{x}_N\}$ is chosen at random with equal probability from the 2^N equiprobable possible dichotomies of X. Let X be in $\boldsymbol{\varphi}$-general position with probability 1. Let $P(N, M)$ be the probability that the particular dichotomy picked at random is $\boldsymbol{\varphi}$-separable, where the class of $\boldsymbol{\varphi}$ surfaces has M degrees of freedom. Then, we may make the following two statements (Cover, 1965):

1. *With probability* 1 *there are* $C(N, M)$ *homogeneously* $\boldsymbol{\varphi}$*-separable dichotomies, defined by*

$$C(N, M) = 2 \sum_{m=0}^{M-1} \binom{N-1}{m} \tag{7.6}$$

where the binomial coefficients comprising N and M are themselves defined for all real l and integer m by

$$\binom{l}{m} = \frac{l(l-1)\cdots(l-m+1)}{m!}$$

2. *The probability that the random dichotomy is* $\boldsymbol{\varphi}$*-separable is given by*

$$P(N, M) = \left(\frac{1}{2}\right)^{N-1} \sum_{m=0}^{M-1} \binom{N-1}{m} \tag{7.7}$$

which is just the cumulative binomial distribution corresponding to the probability that $N - 1$ *flips of a fair coin will result in* $M - 1$ *or fewer heads.*

Equation (7.6) is *Schläfli's formula* for function-counting, and Eq. (7.7) is *Cover's separability theorem* for random patterns.

The proof of Cover's formula follows immediately from (1) Schläfli's formula for linearly separable dichotomies, and (2) the reflection invariance of the joint probability distribution of X. This invariance implies that the probability (conditional on X) that a random dichotomy of X be separable is equal to the unconditional probability that a particular dichotomy of X (all N points in one category) be separable (Cover, 1965).

The important point to note from Eq. (7.7) is that the higher M is, the closer will be the probability $P(N, M)$ to unity.

To sum up, Cover's separability theorem encompasses two basic ingredients:

1. Nonlinear formulation of the hidden function defined by $\varphi_i(\mathbf{x})$, where $\mathbf{x}$ is the input vector and $i = 1, 2, \ldots, M$.
2. High dimensionality of the hidden-unit space compared to the input space, which is determined by the value assigned to M (i.e., the number of hidden units).

Thus, in general, a complex pattern-classification problem cast in high-dimensional space nonlinearly is more likely to be linearly separable than in a low-dimensional space. It should be stressed, however, that in some cases the use of nonlinear mapping (i.e., point 1) may be sufficient to produce linear separability without having to increase the dimensionality of the hidden-unit space; see Example 1.

Separating Capacity of a Surface

Let $\{\mathbf{x}_1, \mathbf{x}_2, \ldots\}$ be a sequence of random patterns, and define the random variable N to be the largest integer such that the set $\{\mathbf{x}_1, \mathbf{x}_2, \ldots, \mathbf{x}_N\}$ is $\boldsymbol{\varphi}$-separable, where the function $\boldsymbol{\varphi}$ has M degrees of freedom. Then, using Eq. (7.7), we find that the probability that $N = k$ is given by the negative binomial distribution:

$$\begin{aligned} \Pr\{N = k\} &= P(k, M) - P(k+1, M) \\ &= \left(\frac{1}{2}\right)^k \binom{k-1}{M-1}, \qquad k = 0, 1, 2, \ldots \end{aligned} \tag{7.8}$$

Thus N corresponds to the waiting time for the Mth failure in a series of tosses of a fair coin, and

$$\begin{aligned} E[N] &= 2M \\ \text{median}[N] &= 2M \end{aligned} \tag{7.9}$$

The asymptotic probability that N patterns are separable in a space of dimension

$$M \approx \frac{N}{2} + \frac{\alpha}{2}\sqrt{N}$$

is given by

$$P\left(N, \frac{N}{2} + \frac{\alpha}{2}\sqrt{N}\right) \approx \Phi(\alpha) \tag{7.10}$$

where $\Phi(\alpha)$ is the cumulative Gaussian distribution; that is,

$$\Phi(\alpha) = \frac{1}{\sqrt{2\pi}} \int_{-\infty}^{\alpha} e^{-x^2/2}\, dx \tag{7.11}$$

In addition, for $\varepsilon > 0$ we have

$$\begin{aligned} \lim_{M\to\infty} P(2M(1+\varepsilon), M) &= 0 \\ P(2M, M) &= \frac{1}{2} \\ \lim_{M\to\infty} P(2M(1-\varepsilon), M) &= 1 \end{aligned} \tag{7.12}$$

Thus the probability of separability shows a pronounced threshold effect when the number of patterns is equal to twice the number of dimensions. This result suggests that $2M$ is a natural definition for the *separating capacity* of a family of decision surfaces having M degrees of freedom (Cover, 1965).

EXAMPLE 1. The XOR Problem

To illustrate the significance of the idea of φ-separability of patterns, consider the simple and yet important XOR problem. In the XOR problem there are four points (patterns), namely, (1,1), (0,1), (0,0), and (1,0), in a two-dimensional input space, as depicted in Fig. 7.2a. The requirement is to construct a pattern classifier that produces the binary output 0 in response to the input pattern (1,1), or (0,0), and the binary output 1 in response to the input pattern (0,1) or (1,0). Thus points that are closest in the input space, in terms of the Hamming distance, map to regions that are maximally apart in the output space.

Define a pair of Gaussian hidden functions as follows:

$$\varphi_1(\mathbf{x}) = e^{-\|\mathbf{x}-\mathbf{t}_1\|^2}, \qquad \mathbf{t}_1 = [1,1]^T$$

$$\varphi_2(\mathbf{x}) = e^{-\|\mathbf{x}-\mathbf{t}_2\|^2}, \qquad \mathbf{t}_2 = [0,0]^T$$

We may then construct the results summarized in Table 7.1 for the four different input patterns of interest. Accordingly, the input patterns are mapped onto the φ_1-φ_2 plane as shown in Fig. 7.2b. Here we now see that the input patterns (0,1) and (1,0) are indeed linearly separable from the remaining input patterns (1,1) and (0,0). Thereafter, the XOR problem may be readily solved by using the functions $\varphi_1(\mathbf{x})$ and $\varphi_2(\mathbf{x})$ as the inputs to a linear classifier such as the perceptron.

In this example there is no increase in the dimensionality of the hidden-unit space compared to the input space. In other words, nonlinearity exemplified by the use of Gaussian hidden functions is sufficient to transform the XOR problem into a linearly separable one.

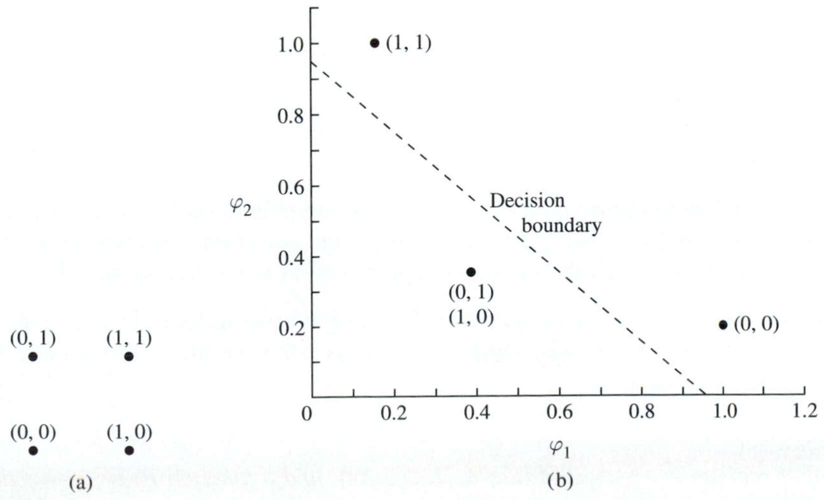

FIGURE 7.2 (a) The four patterns of the XOR problem. (b) Decision-making diagram.

TABLE 7.1 Specification of the Hidden Functions for the XOR Problem of Example 1

Input Pattern, $\mathbf{x}$	First Hidden Function, $\varphi_1(\mathbf{x})$	Second Hidden Function, $\varphi_2(\mathbf{x})$
(1,1)	1	0.1353
(0,1)	0.3678	0.3678
(0,0)	0.1353	1
(1,0)	0.3678	0.3678

7.3 Interpolation Problem

The important point that emerges from Cover's theorem on the separability of patterns is that in solving a nonlinearly separable pattern-classification problem, there is, in general, practical benefit to be gained in mapping the input space into a new space of high enough dimension. Basically, a nonlinear mapping is used to transform a nonlinearly separable classification problem into a linearly separable one. In a similar fashion, we may use a nonlinear mapping to transform a difficult nonlinear filtering problem into an easier one that involves linear filtering.

Consider then a feedforward network with an input layer, a single hidden layer, and an output layer consisting of a single unit. We have purposely chosen a single output unit to simplify the exposition without loss of generality. The network is designed to perform a *nonlinear mapping* from the input space to the hidden space, followed by a *linear mapping* from the hidden space to the output space. Let p denote the dimension of the input space. Then, in an overall fashion, the network represents a map from the p-dimensional input space to the single-dimensional output space, written as

$$s\colon \mathbb{R}^p \to \mathbb{R}^1 \tag{7.13}$$

We may think of the map s as a *hypersurface* (graph) $\Gamma \subset \mathbb{R}^{p+1}$, just as we think of the elementary map $s\colon \mathbb{R}^1 \to \mathbb{R}^1$, where $s(x) = x^2$, as a parabola drawn in $\mathbb{R}^2$ space. The surface Γ is a multidimensional plot of the output as a function of the input. In a practical situation, the surface Γ is unknown and the training data are usually contaminated with noise. Accordingly, the training phase and generalization phase of the learning process may be respectively viewed as follows (Broomhead and Lowe, 1988):

- The training phase constitutes the optimization of a fitting procedure for the surface Γ, based on known data points presented to the network in the form of input–output examples (patterns).
- The generalization phase is synonymous with interpolation between the data points, with the interpolation being performed along the constrained surface generated by the fitting procedure as the optimum approximation to the true surface Γ.

Thus we are led to the theory of *multivariable interpolation* in high-dimensional space, which has a long history (Davis, 1963). The interpolation problem, in its *strict* sense, may be stated as follows:

Given a set of N different points $\{\mathbf{x}_i \in \mathbb{R}^p | i = 1, 2, \ldots, N\}$ *and a corresponding set of N real numbers* $\{d_i \in \mathbb{R}^1 | i = 1, 2, \ldots, N\}$, *find a function* $F\colon \mathbb{R}^N \to \mathbb{R}^1$ *that satisfies the interpolation condition:*

$$F(\mathbf{x}_i) = d_i, \qquad i = 1, 2, \ldots, N \tag{7.14}$$

Note that for strict interpolation as specified here, the interpolating surface (i.e., function F) is constrained to pass through *all* the training data points.

The *radial-basis functions* (RBF) technique consists of choosing a function F that has the following form (Powell, 1988):

$$F(\mathbf{x}) = \sum_{i=1}^{N} w_i \varphi(\|\mathbf{x} - \mathbf{x}_i\|) \tag{7.15}$$

where $\{\varphi(\|\mathbf{x} - \mathbf{x}_i\|) | i = 1, 2, \ldots, N\}$ is a set of N arbitrary (generally nonlinear) functions, known as *radial-basis functions,* and $\|\cdot\|$ denotes a *norm* that is usually taken to be Euclidean. The known data points $\mathbf{x}_i \in \mathbb{R}^p$, $i = 1, 2, \ldots, N$ are taken to be the *centers* of the radial-basis functions.

Inserting the interpolation conditions of Eq. (7.14) in (7.15), we obtain the following set of simultaneous linear equations for the unknown coefficients (weights) of the expansion $\{w_i\}$:

$$\begin{bmatrix} \varphi_{11} & \varphi_{12} & \cdots & \varphi_{1N} \\ \varphi_{21} & \varphi_{22} & \cdots & \varphi_{2N} \\ \vdots & \vdots & \vdots & \vdots \\ \varphi_{N1} & \varphi_{N2} & \cdots & \varphi_{NN} \end{bmatrix} \begin{bmatrix} w_1 \\ w_2 \\ \vdots \\ w_N \end{bmatrix} = \begin{bmatrix} d_1 \\ d_2 \\ \vdots \\ d_N \end{bmatrix} \tag{7.16}$$

where

$$\varphi_{ji} = \varphi(\|\mathbf{x}_j - \mathbf{x}_i\|), \qquad j, i = 1, 2, \ldots, N \tag{7.17}$$

Let

$$\mathbf{d} = [d_1, d_2, \ldots, d_N]^T \tag{7.18}$$

$$\mathbf{w} = [w_1, w_2, \ldots, w_N]^T \tag{7.19}$$

The N-by-1 vectors $\mathbf{d}$ and $\mathbf{w}$ represent the *desired response vector* and *linear weight vector,* respectively. Let $\boldsymbol{\Phi}$ denote an N-by-N matrix with elements φ_{ji}:

$$\boldsymbol{\Phi} = \{\varphi_{ji} | j, i = 1, 2, \ldots, N\} \tag{7.20}$$

We call this matrix the *interpolation matrix.* We may then rewrite Eq. (7.16) in the compact form

$$\boldsymbol{\Phi}\mathbf{w} = \mathbf{x} \tag{7.21}$$

There is a class of radial-basis functions that enjoys the following remarkable property (Light, 1992):

> *Let* $\mathbf{x}_1, \mathbf{x}_2, \ldots, \mathbf{x}_N$ *be distinct points in* $\mathbb{R}^p$. *Then the N-by-N interpolation matrix* $\boldsymbol{\Phi}$ *whose jith element is* $\varphi_{ji} = \varphi(\|\mathbf{x}_j - \mathbf{x}_i\|)$ *is positive definite.*

This theorem is more powerful than a previous result due to Micchelli (1986) stating that the interpolation matrix $\boldsymbol{\Phi}$ is nonsingular. Light's theorem applies to the following cases (among others):

1. *Inverse multiquadrics* (Hardy, 1971)

$$\varphi(r) = \frac{1}{(r^2 + c^2)^{1/2}} \qquad \text{for some } c > 0, \text{ and } r \geq 0 \tag{7.22}$$

2. *Gaussian functions*

$$\varphi(r) = \exp\left(-\frac{r^2}{2\sigma^2}\right) \qquad \text{for } \sigma > 0, \text{ and } r \geq 0 \tag{7.23}$$

Theoretical investigations and practical results, however, seem to show that the type of nonlinearity $\varphi(\cdot)$ is not crucial to the performance of RBF networks (Powell, 1988).

Returning to the implication of Light's theorem, we note that, provided that the data points are all distinct, the interpolation matrix $\boldsymbol{\Phi}$ is positive definite, and so we may solve Eq. (7.21) for the weight vector $\mathbf{w}$, obtaining

$$\mathbf{w} = \boldsymbol{\Phi}^{-1}\mathbf{d} \tag{7.24}$$

where $\boldsymbol{\Phi}^{-1}$ is the inverse of the interpolation matrix $\boldsymbol{\Phi}$. Although in theory we are always assured a solution to the strict interpolation problem, in practice we cannot solve Eq. (7.21) when the matrix $\boldsymbol{\Phi}$ is arbitrarily close to singular. At this point, regularization theory can help by perturbing the matrix $\boldsymbol{\Phi}$ to $\boldsymbol{\Phi} + \lambda\mathbf{I}$, as we shall see in Section 7.5.

7.4 Supervised Learning as an Ill-Posed Hypersurface Reconstruction Problem

The strict interpolation procedure as described here may not be a good strategy for the training of RBF networks for certain classes of tasks because of poor generalization to new data for the following reason. When the number of data points in the training set is much larger than the number of degrees of freedom of the underlying physical process, and we are constrained to have as many radial-basis functions as data points, the problem is overdetermined. Consequently, the network may end up fitting misleading variations due to idiosyncrasies or noise in the input data, thereby resulting in a degraded generalization performance (Broomhead and Lowe, 1988).

To develop a deep understanding of the overfitting problem described here and how to cure it, we first go back to the viewpoint that the design of a neural network (more precisely, an associative memory) trained to retrieve an output pattern when presented with an input pattern is equivalent to learning a hypersurface (i.e., multidimensional mapping) that defines the output in terms of the input. In other words, *learning is viewed as a problem of hypersurface reconstruction, given a set of data points that may be sparse.* According to this viewpoint, the hypersurface reconstruction or approximation problem belongs to a generic class of problems called *inverse problems.*

An inverse problem may be well-posed or ill-posed. The term "well-posed" has been used in applied mathematics since the time of Hadamand in the early 1900s. To explain what we mean by this terminology, assume that we have a domain X and a range Y taken to be metric spaces, and that are related by a fixed but unknown mapping F. The problem of reconstructing the mapping F is said to be *well posed* if three conditions are satisfied (Morozov, 1993; Tikhonov and Arsenin, 1977):

1. *Existence.* For every input vector $\mathbf{x} \in X$, there does exist an output $y = F(\mathbf{x})$, where $y \in Y$.
2. *Uniqueness.* For any pair of input vectors $\mathbf{x}, \mathbf{t} \in X$, we have $F(\mathbf{x}) = F(\mathbf{t})$ if, and only if, $\mathbf{x} = \mathbf{t}$.
3. *Continuity.* The mapping is continuous, that is, for any $\varepsilon > 0$ there exists $\delta = \delta(\varepsilon)$ such that the condition $\rho_X(\mathbf{x},\mathbf{t}) < \delta$ implies that $\rho_Y(F(\mathbf{x}),F(\mathbf{t})) < \varepsilon$, where $\rho(\cdot,\cdot)$ is the symbol for distance between the two arguments in their respective spaces. This criterion is illustrated in Fig. 7.3.

If these conditions are not satisfied, the inverse problem is said to be ill-posed.

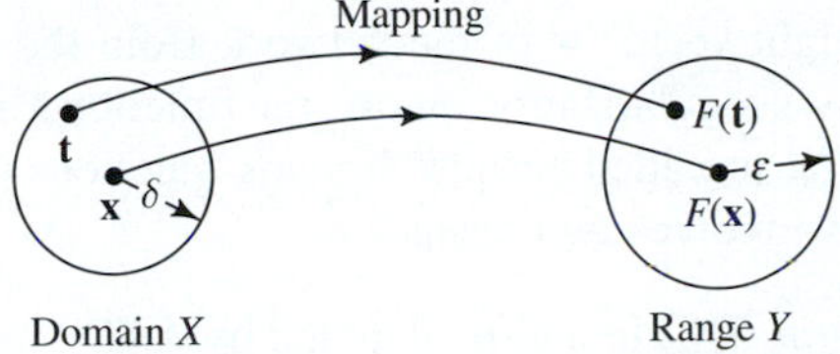

FIGURE 7.3 Illustration of the mapping of (input) domain X onto (output) range Y.

Learning, viewed as a hypersurface reconstruction problem, is an ill-posed inverse problem for the following reasons. First, there is not as much information in the training data as we really need to reconstruct the input–output mapping uniquely, hence the uniqueness criterion is violated. Second, the presence of noise or imprecision in the input data adds uncertainty to the reconstructed input–output mapping. In particular, if the noise level in the input is too high, it is possible for the neural network to produce an output outside of the range Y for a specified input $\mathbf{x}$ in the domain X; in other words, the continuity criterion is violated. To make the learning problem well posed so that generalization to new data is feasible, some form of prior information about the input–output mapping is needed (Poggio and Girosi, 1990a). This, in turn, means that the process responsible for the generation of input–output examples used to train a neural network must exhibit *redundancy* in an information-theoretic sense. This requirement is indeed satisfied by the physical processes with which we have to deal in practice (e.g., speech, pictures, radar signals, sonar signals, seismic data), which are all redundant by their very nature. Furthermore, for a physical process, the *generator* of the data is usually *smooth.* Indeed, so long as the data generation is smooth, then small changes in the input can give rise to large changes in the output and still be approximated adequately (Lowe, 1992); this point is well illustrated by a chaotic map. The important point to note here is that the smoothness of data generation is a basic form of functional redundancy.

7.5 Regularization Theory

In 1963, Tikhonov proposed a new method called *regularization for solving ill-posed problems.*[1] In the context of approximation problems, the basic idea of regularization is to *stabilize* the solution by means of some auxiliary nonnegative functional that embeds prior information, e.g., smoothness constraints on the input–output mapping (i.e., solution to the approximation problem), and thereby make an ill-posed problem into a well-posed one (Poggio and Girosi, 1990a).

To be specific, let the set of input–output data available for approximation be described by

$$\text{Input signal:} \qquad \mathbf{x}_i \in \mathbb{R}^p, \qquad i = 1, 2, \ldots, N \tag{7.25}$$

$$\text{Desired response:} \qquad d_i \in \mathbb{R}^1, \qquad i = 1, 2, \ldots, N \tag{7.26}$$

Note that the output is assumed to be one-dimensional; this assumption does not in any way limit the general applicability of the regularization theory being developed here. Let the approximating function be denoted by $F(\mathbf{x})$, where (for convenience of presentation)

[1] Regularization theory is discussed in book form by Tikhonov and Arsenin (1977), and Morozov (1993).

we have omitted the weight vector $\mathbf{w}$ of the network from the argument of the function F. According to Tikhonov's regularization theory, the function F is determined by minimizing a *cost functional* $\mathscr{E}(F)$, so-called because it maps functions (in some suitable function space) to the real line. It involves two terms.

1. *Standard Error Term.* This first term, denoted by $\mathscr{E}_s(F)$, measures the standard error (distance) between the desired (target) response d_i and the actual response y_i for training example $i = 1, 2, \ldots, N$. Specifically, we define

$$\mathscr{E}_s(F) = \frac{1}{2}\sum_{i=1}^{N} (d_i - y_i)^2$$
$$= \frac{1}{2}\sum_{i=1}^{N} [d_i - F(\mathbf{x}_i)]^2 \qquad (7.27)$$

where we have introduced the scaling factor $\frac{1}{2}$ for the sake of consistency with material presented in previous chapters.

2. *Regularizing Term.* This second term, denoted by $\mathscr{E}_c(F)$, depends on the geometric properties of the approximating function $F(\mathbf{x})$. Specifically, we write

$$\mathscr{E}_c(F) = \frac{1}{2}\|\mathbf{P}F\|^2 \qquad (7.28)$$

where $\mathbf{P}$ is a linear (pseudo) differential operator. Prior information about the form of the solution [i.e., the function $F(\mathbf{x})$] is embedded in the operator $\mathbf{P}$, which naturally makes the selection of $\mathbf{P}$ problem-dependent. We refer to $\mathbf{P}$ as a *stabilizer* in the sense that it stabilizes the solution F, making it smooth and therefore continuous. Note, however, that smoothness implies continuity, but the reverse is not necessarily true.

The analytic approach used for the situation described here draws a strong analogy between linear differential operators and matrices, thereby placing both types of models in the same conceptual framework. Thus, the symbol $\|\cdot\|$ in Eq. (7.28) denotes a norm imposed on the function space to which $\mathbf{P}F$ belongs. By a *function space* we mean a normed vector space of functions. Ordinarily, the function space used here is the L^2 *space* that consists of all real-valued functions $f(\mathbf{x})$, $\mathbf{x} \in \mathbb{R}^p$, for which $|f(\mathbf{x})|^2$ is Lebesgue integrable. The function $f(\mathbf{x})$ denotes the actual function that defines the underlying physical process responsible for the generation of the input–output pairs $(\mathbf{x}_1, d_1)$, $(\mathbf{x}_2, d_2)$, $\ldots$, $(\mathbf{x}_N, d_N)$. Strictly speaking, however, we require the function $f(\mathbf{x})$ to be a member of a *reproducing kernel Hilbert space* (RKHS)[2] with a reproducing kernel in the form of the Dirac delta distribution δ (Tapia and Thompson, 1978). We need to do this because, further on in the derivations, we require that the Dirac delta distribution δ to be in the dual of the function space. The simplest RKHS satisfying our needs is the *space of rapidly decreasing, infinitely continuously differentiable functions,* that is, the classical space S of rapidly decreasing test functions for the *Schwarz theory of distributions,* with finite $\mathbf{P}$-induced norm, as shown by

$$H_{\mathbf{P}} = \{f \in S: \|\mathbf{P}f\| < \infty\} \qquad (7.29)$$

[2] Generally speaking, engineers tend to think of only the L^2 space whenever Hilbert space is mentioned, perhaps on the grounds that L^2 space is isomorphic to any Hilbert space. But the *norm* is the most important feature of a Hilbert space, and *isometrics* (i.e., norm-preserving isomorphism) are more important than simply additive isomorphism (Kailath, 1974). The theory of RKHS shows that there are many other different and quite useful Hilbert spaces besides the L^2 space. For a tutorial review of RKHS, see Kailath (1971).

where the norm of $\mathbf{P}f$ is taken with respect to the range of $\mathbf{P}$, assumed to be another Hilbert space. By a "rapidly decreasing" function φ we mean one that satisfies the condition

$$\lim_{\|\mathbf{x}\|\to\infty} |\mathbf{x}^{\alpha}\partial^{\beta}\varphi(\mathbf{x})| = 0$$

for all pairs of multi-indices[3] α and β. In what follows we shall refer to the $H_{\mathbf{P}}$ of Eq. (7.29) simply as H when the operator $\mathbf{P}$ is clear from context.

The total cost functional to be minimized is

$$\begin{aligned}\mathscr{E}(F) &= \mathscr{E}_s(F) + \lambda\mathscr{E}_c(F) \\ &= \frac{1}{2}\sum_{i=1}^{N} [d_i - F(\mathbf{x}_i)]^2 + \frac{1}{2}\lambda\|\mathbf{P}F\|^2\end{aligned} \tag{7.30}$$

where λ is a positive real number called the *regularization parameter.*

In a sense, we may view the regularization parameter λ as an indicator of the sufficiency of the given data set as examples that specify the solution $F(\mathbf{x})$. In particular, the limiting case $\lambda \to 0$ implies that the problem is unconstrained, with the solution $F(\mathbf{x})$ being completely determined from the examples. The other limiting case, $\lambda \to \infty$, on the other hand, implies that the *a priori* smoothness constraint is by itself sufficient to specify the solution $F(\mathbf{x})$, which is another way of saying that the examples are unreliable. In practical applications, the regularization parameter λ is assigned a value somewhere between these two limiting conditions, so that both the sample data and the *a priori* information contribute to the solution $F(\mathbf{x})$. Thus, the regularizing term $\mathscr{E}_c(F)$ represents a *model complexity-penalty function,* the influence of which on the final solution is controlled by the regularization parameter λ.

As we remarked previously in Section 6.17, regularization theory is closely linked with the *model order-selection problem* in statistics, which is exemplified by the *minimum description length* (MDL) criterion (Rissanen, 1978) and *an information-theoretic criterion* (AIC) (Akaike, 1973).

Solution to the Regularization Problem

The *principle of regularization* may now be stated as follows:

Find the function $F(\mathbf{x})$ that minimizes the cost functional $\mathscr{E}(F)$, defined by

$$\mathscr{E}(F) = \mathscr{E}_s(F) + \lambda\mathscr{E}_c(F)$$

where $\mathscr{E}_s(F)$ is the standard error term, $\mathscr{E}_c(F)$ is the regularizing term, and λ is the regularization parameter.

To proceed with the minimization of the cost functional $\mathscr{E}(F)$, we need a rule for evaluating the differential of $\mathscr{E}(F)$. We can take care of this matter by using the *Fréchet differential,* which for this functional is defined by (Dorny, 1975; de Figueiredo and Chen, 1993):

$$d\mathscr{E}(F,h) = \left[\frac{d}{d\beta}\mathscr{E}(F + \beta h)\right]_{\beta=0} \tag{7.31}$$

[3] A *multi-index* $\alpha = (\alpha_1, \alpha_2, \ldots, \alpha_n)$ of *order* $|\alpha| = \sum_{i=1}^{n} \alpha_i$ is a set of whole numbers used to abbreviate the following notations (Al-Gwaiz, 1992):

1. $\mathbf{x}^{\alpha} = \mathbf{x}_1^{\alpha_1}\mathbf{x}_2^{\alpha_2}\cdots\mathbf{x}_n^{\alpha_n}$ for $\mathbf{x} \in \mathbb{R}^n$
2. $\partial^{\alpha} f = \dfrac{\partial^{|\alpha|} f}{\partial\mathbf{x}_1^{\alpha_1}\partial\mathbf{x}_2^{\alpha_2}\cdots\partial\mathbf{x}_n^{\alpha_n}}$ for $f: \mathbb{R}^n \to \mathbb{R}^1$

where $h(\mathbf{x})$ is a fixed function of the vector $\mathbf{x}$. In Eq. (7.31), the ordinary rules of differentiation are used. A necessary condition for the function $F(\mathbf{x})$ to be a relative extremum of the functional $\mathscr{E}(F)$ is that the Fréchet differential $d\mathscr{E}(F,h)$ be zero at $F(\mathbf{x})$ for all $h \in H$, as shown by

$$d\mathscr{E}(F,h) = d\mathscr{E}_s(F,h) + \lambda\, d\mathscr{E}_c(F,h) = 0 \tag{7.32}$$

where $d\mathscr{E}_s(F,h)$ and $d\mathscr{E}_c(F,h)$ are the Fréchet differentials of the functionals $\mathscr{E}_s(F)$ and $\mathscr{E}_c(F)$, respectively.

Evaluating the Fréchet differential of the standard error term $\mathscr{E}_s(F,h)$ of Eq. (7.27), we have

$$\begin{aligned} d\mathscr{E}_s(F,h) &= \left[\frac{d}{d\beta}\mathscr{E}_s(F+\beta h)\right]_{\beta=0} \\ &= \left[\frac{1}{2}\frac{d}{d\beta}\sum_{i=1}^{N}[d_i - F(\mathbf{x}_i) - \beta h(\mathbf{x}_i)]^2\right]_{\beta=0} \\ &= -\sum_{i=1}^{N}[d_i - F(\mathbf{x}_i) - \beta h(\mathbf{x}_i)]h(\mathbf{x}_i)\big|_{\beta=0} \\ &= -\sum_{i=1}^{N}[d_i - F(\mathbf{x}_i)]h(\mathbf{x}_i) \end{aligned} \tag{7.33}$$

At this point in the discussion, we find it instructive to invoke the *Riesz representation theorem,* which may be stated as follows (Debnath and Mikusiński, 1990):

> *Let f be a bounded linear functional in a general Hilbert space denoted by H. There exists one $h_0 \in H$ such that*
>
> $$f = (h, h_0)_H \qquad \textit{for all } h \in H$$
>
> *Moreover, we have*
>
> $$\|f\|_{H^*} = \|h_0\|_H$$
>
> *where H^* is the dual or conjugate of the Hilbert space H.*

The symbol $(\cdot,\cdot)_H$ used here refers to the *inner product* in H space. Hence, in light of the Riesz representation theorem, we may rewrite the Fréchet differential $d\mathscr{E}_s(F,h)$ of Eq. (7.33) in the equivalent form

$$d\mathscr{E}_s(F,h) = -\left(h, \sum_{i=1}^{N}(d_i - F)\delta_{\mathbf{x}_i}\right)_H \tag{7.34}$$

where $\delta_{\mathbf{x}_i}$ denotes the *Dirac delta distribution* centered at $\mathbf{x}_i$; that is,

$$\delta_{\mathbf{x}_i}(\mathbf{x}) = \delta(\mathbf{x} - \mathbf{x}_i) \tag{7.35}$$

Consider next the evaluation of the Fréchet differential of the regularizing term $\mathscr{E}_c(F)$ of Eq. (7.28), where the norm is defined in accordance with Eq. (7.29). Thus, proceeding in a manner similar to that described above, we have

$$\begin{aligned} d\mathscr{E}_c(F,h) &= \frac{d}{d\beta}\mathscr{E}_c(F+\beta h)|_{\beta=0} \\ &= \frac{1}{2}\frac{d}{d\beta}\int_{\mathbb{R}^p} (\mathbf{P}[F+\beta h])^2\, d\mathbf{x}|_{\beta=0} \\ &= \int_{\mathbb{R}^p} \mathbf{P}[F+\beta h]\mathbf{P}h\, d\mathbf{x}|_{\beta=0} \\ &= \int_{\mathbb{R}^p} \mathbf{P}F\mathbf{P}h\, d\mathbf{x} \\ &= (\mathbf{P}h,\mathbf{P}F)_H \end{aligned} \tag{7.36}$$

Using the definition of an *adjoint* differential operator, we may equivalently write

$$d\mathscr{E}_c(F,h) = (h,\mathbf{P}^*\mathbf{P}F)_H \tag{7.37}$$

where $\mathbf{P}^*$ is the *adjoint* of the differential operator $\mathbf{P}$. In a loose sense, taking adjoints is similar to conjugation of complex numbers.

Returning to the extremum condition described in Eq. (7.32) and substituting the Fréchet differentials of Eqs. (7.34) and (7.37) in that equation, we may now make the following statements:

- The Fréchet differential $d\mathscr{E}(F,h)$ is

$$d\mathscr{E}(F,h) = 2\left[h,\mathbf{P}^*\mathbf{P}F - \frac{1}{\lambda}\sum_{i=1}^{N}(d_i - F)\delta_{\mathbf{x}_i}\right]_H \tag{7.38}$$

- Since the regularization parameter λ is ordinarily assigned a value somewhere in the open interval $(0,\infty)$, the Fréchet differential $d\mathscr{E}(F,h)$ is zero for every $h(\mathbf{x})$ in H space if and only if the following condition is satisfied in the distributional sense:

$$\mathbf{P}^*\mathbf{P}F - \frac{1}{\lambda}\sum_{i=1}^{N}(d_i - F)\delta_{\mathbf{x}_i} = 0 \tag{7.39}$$

  or, equivalently,

$$\mathbf{P}^*\mathbf{P}F(\mathbf{x}) = \frac{1}{\lambda}\sum_{i=1}^{N}[d_i - F(\mathbf{x}_i)]\delta(\mathbf{x}-\mathbf{x}_i) \tag{7.40}$$

Equation (7.40) is referred to as the *Euler–Lagrange equation* for the cost functional $\mathscr{E}(F)$ defined in Eq. (7.30) (Poggio and Girosi, 1990a).

EXAMPLE 2. Spline Functions

Consider the simple example of one-dimensional data, for which the differential operator $\mathbf{P}$ is defined by

$$\|\mathbf{P}F\|^2 = \int_{\mathbb{R}^1}\left[\frac{d^2F(x)}{dx^2}\right]^2 dx$$

In this case, the function $F(x)$ that minimizes the cost functional of Eq. (7.30) is a cubic spline.

Spline functions are examples of piecewise polynomial approximators (Schumaker, 1981). The basic idea behind the method of splines is as follows. An approximation region of interest is broken up into a finite number of subregions via the use of *knots;*

the knots can be fixed, in which case the approximators are *linearly* parameterized, or they can be variable, in which case the approximators are *nonlinearly* parameterized. In both cases, in each region of the approximation a polynomial of degree at most n is used, with the additional requirement that the overall function be $n - 1$ times differentiable. Among the spline functions used in practice, *cubic splines* (for which $n = 3$) are the most popular; here, the overall function must be continuous with second-order derivatives at the knots.

Green's Functions

Equation (7.40) represents a partial pseudodifferential equation in F. The solution of this equation is known to consist of the integral transformation of the right-hand side of the equation with a kernel given by the *influence function* or *Green's function* for the self-adjoint differential operator $\mathbf{P}^*\mathbf{P}$ (Poggio and Girosi, 1990a; Courant and Hilbert, 1970; Dorny, 1975). The Green's function plays the same role for a linear differential equation as does the inverse matrix for a matrix equation.

Let $G(\mathbf{x};\mathbf{x}_i)$ denote the Green's function centered at $\mathbf{x}_i$. By definition, the Green's function $G(\mathbf{x};\mathbf{x}_i)$ satisfies the partial differential equation

$$\mathbf{P}^*\mathbf{P}G(\mathbf{x};\mathbf{x}_i) = 0$$

everywhere except at the point $\mathbf{x} = \mathbf{x}_i$, where the Green's function has a singularity. That is, the Green's function $G(\mathbf{x};\mathbf{x}_i)$ must satisfy the following partial differential equation (taken in the sense of distributions):

$$\mathbf{P}^*\mathbf{P}G(\mathbf{x};\mathbf{x}_i) = \delta(\mathbf{x} - \mathbf{x}_i) \tag{7.41}$$

where, as defined previously, $\delta(\mathbf{x} - \mathbf{x}_i)$ is a delta function located at $\mathbf{x} = \mathbf{x}_i$.

The solution $F(\mathbf{x})$ for the partial differential equation (7.40) may now be expressed in the form of a multiple integral transformation as follows (Courant and Hilbert, 1970):

$$F(\mathbf{x}) = \int_{\mathbb{R}^p} G(\mathbf{x};\boldsymbol{\xi})\varphi(\boldsymbol{\xi})\, d\boldsymbol{\xi} \tag{7.42}$$

where the function $\varphi(\boldsymbol{\xi})$ denotes the right-hand side of Eq. (7.40) with $\mathbf{x}$ replaced by $\boldsymbol{\xi}$, that is,

$$\varphi(\boldsymbol{\xi}) = \frac{1}{\lambda}\sum_{i=1}^{N} [d_i - F(\boldsymbol{\xi}_i)]\, \delta(\boldsymbol{\xi} - \mathbf{x}_i) \tag{7.43}$$

Substituting Eq. (7.43) in (7.42), interchanging the order of summation and integration, and then using the *sifting property* of a delta function, we get the desired result (Girosi and Poggio, 1990a):

$$F(\mathbf{x}) = \frac{1}{\lambda}\sum_{i=1}^{N} [d_i - F(\mathbf{x}_i)]G(\mathbf{x};\mathbf{x}_i) \tag{7.44}$$

Equation (7.44) states that the minimizing solution $F(\mathbf{x})$ to the regularization problem is a linear superposition of N Green's functions. The $\mathbf{x}_i$ represent the *centers of the expansion,* and the weights $[d_i - F(\mathbf{x}_i)]/\lambda$ represent the *coefficients of the expansion.* In other words, the solution to the regularization problem lies in an N-dimensional subspace of the space of smooth functions, and the set of Green's functions $\{G(\mathbf{x};\mathbf{x}_i)\}$ centered at $\mathbf{x}_i$, $i = 1, 2, \ldots, N$, constitutes a basis for this subspace.

The next issue to be resolved is the determination of the unknown coefficients in the expansion of Eq. (7.44). Let

$$w_i = \frac{1}{\lambda}[d_i - F(\mathbf{x}_i)], \qquad i = 1, 2, \ldots, N \tag{7.45}$$

Accordingly, we may recast the minimizing solution of Eq. (7.44) simply as follows:

$$F(\mathbf{x}) = \sum_{i=1}^{N} w_i G(\mathbf{x};\mathbf{x}_i) \tag{7.46}$$

Evaluating Eq. (7.46) at $\mathbf{x}_j$, $j = 1, 2, \ldots, N$, we get

$$F(\mathbf{x}_j) = \sum_{i=1}^{N} w_i G(\mathbf{x}_j;\mathbf{x}_i), \qquad j = 1, 2, \ldots, N \tag{7.47}$$

We now introduce the following definitions:

$$\mathbf{F} = [F(\mathbf{x}_1), F(\mathbf{x}_2), \ldots, F(\mathbf{x}_N)]^T \tag{7.48}$$

$$\mathbf{d} = [d_1, d_2, \ldots, d_N]^T \tag{7.49}$$

$$\mathbf{G} = \begin{bmatrix} G(\mathbf{x}_1;\mathbf{x}_1) & G(\mathbf{x}_1;\mathbf{x}_2) & \ldots & G(\mathbf{x}_1;\mathbf{x}_N) \\ G(\mathbf{x}_2;\mathbf{x}_1) & G(\mathbf{x}_2;\mathbf{x}_2) & \ldots & G(\mathbf{x}_2;\mathbf{x}_N) \\ \vdots & \vdots & & \vdots \\ G(\mathbf{x}_N;\mathbf{x}_1) & G(\mathbf{x}_N;\mathbf{x}_2) & \ldots & G(\mathbf{x}_N;\mathbf{x}_N) \end{bmatrix} \tag{7.50}$$

$$\mathbf{w} = [w_1, w_2, \ldots, w_N]^T \tag{7.51}$$

Then we may rewrite Eqs. (7.45) and (7.47) in matrix form as follows, respectively:

$$\mathbf{w} = \frac{1}{\lambda}(\mathbf{d} - \mathbf{F}) \tag{7.52}$$

and

$$\mathbf{F} = \mathbf{G}\mathbf{w} \tag{7.53}$$

Eliminating **F** between Eqs. (7.52) and (7.53) and rearranging terms, we get

$$(\mathbf{G} + \lambda\mathbf{I})\mathbf{w} = \mathbf{d} \tag{7.54}$$

where **I** is the N-by-N identity matrix. We call the matrix **G** the *Green's matrix.*

Since the combined operator $\mathbf{P}^*\mathbf{P}$ in Eq. (7.40) is self-adjoint, it follows that the associated Green's function $\mathbf{G}(\mathbf{x};\mathbf{x}_i)$ is a *symmetric function,* as shown by (Courant and Hilbert, 1970)

$$G(\mathbf{x}_i;\mathbf{x}_j) = G(\mathbf{x}_j;\mathbf{x}_i) \qquad \text{for all } i \text{ and } j \tag{7.55}$$

Equivalently, the Green's matrix **G** defined in Eq. (7.50) is a *symmetric matrix;* that is,

$$\mathbf{G}^T = \mathbf{G} \tag{7.56}$$

where the superscript T denotes matrix transposition. We now invoke Light's theorem, which was described in Section 7.3 in the context of the interpolation matrix $\boldsymbol{\Phi}$. We first note that Green's matrix **G** plays a role in regularization theory similar to that of $\boldsymbol{\Phi}$ in RBF interpolation theory. Both **G** and $\boldsymbol{\Phi}$ are N-by-N symmetric matrices. Accordingly, we may state that the matrix **G**, for certain classes of Green's functions, is positive definite provided that the data points $\mathbf{x}_1, \mathbf{x}_2, \ldots, \mathbf{x}_N$ are distinct. The classes of Green's functions covered by Light's theorem include multiquadrics and Gaussian functions. In practice, we may always choose λ sufficiently large to ensure that $\mathbf{G} + \lambda\mathbf{I}$ is positive definite and, therefore, invertible. This, in turn, means that the linear system of equations (7.54) will have a unique solution given by (Poggio and Girosi, 1990a)

$$\mathbf{w} = (\mathbf{G} + \lambda\mathbf{I})^{-1}\mathbf{d} \tag{7.57}$$

Thus, having selected the pseudodifferential operator $\mathbf{P}$ and therefore identified the associated Green's function $G(\mathbf{x}_j;\mathbf{x}_i)$, where $i = 1, 2, \ldots, N$, we may use Eq. (7.57) to obtain the weight vector $\mathbf{w}$ for a specified desired response vector $\mathbf{d}$ and an appropriate value of regularization parameter λ.

In conclusion, we may state that the solution to the regularization problem is given by the expansion

$$F(\mathbf{x}) = \sum_{i=1}^{N} w_i G(\mathbf{x};\mathbf{x}_i) \tag{7.58}$$

where $G(\mathbf{x};\mathbf{x}_i)$ is the Green's function for the self-adjoint differential operator $\mathbf{P}^*\mathbf{P}$, and w_i is the ith element of the weight vector $\mathbf{w}$; these two quantities are themselves defined by Eq. (7.41) and (7.57), respectively. Equation (7.58) states the following (Poggio and Girosi, 1990a):

- The regularization approach is equivalent to the expansion of the solution in terms of a set of Green's functions, whose characterization depends only on the form adopted for the stabilizer $\mathbf{P}$ and the associated boundary conditions.
- The number of Green's functions used in the expansion is equal to the number of examples used in the training process.

It should be noted, however, that the solution of the regularization problem given in Eq. (7.58) is incomplete, as it represents a solution *modulo* a term $g(\mathbf{x})$ that lies in the null space of the operator $\mathbf{P}$ (Poggio and Girosi, 1990a). We say this because all the functions that lie in the null space of $\mathbf{P}$ are indeed "invisible" to the smoothing term $\|\mathbf{P}F\|^2$ in the cost functional $\mathscr{E}(F)$ of Eq. (7.30); by the *null space* of $\mathbf{P}$, we mean the set of all functions $g(\mathbf{x})$ for which $\mathbf{P}g$ is zero. The exact form of the additional term $g(\mathbf{x})$ is problem-dependent in the sense that it depends on the stabilizer chosen and the boundary conditions of the problem at hand. For example, it is not needed in the case of a stabilizer $\mathbf{P}$ corresponding to a bell-shaped Green's function such as a Gaussian or inverse multiquadric. For this reason, and since its inclusion does not modify the main conclusions, we will disregard it in the sequel.

The characterization of the Green's function $G(\mathbf{x};\mathbf{x}_i)$, for a specified center $\mathbf{x}_i$, depends only on the form of the stabilizer $\mathbf{P}$, that is, on the *a priori* assumption made concerning the input–output mapping. If the stabilizer $\mathbf{P}$ is *translationally invariant,* then the Green's function $G(\mathbf{x};\mathbf{x}_i)$ centered at $\mathbf{x}_i$ will depend only on the difference between the arguments $\mathbf{x}$ and $\mathbf{x}_i$; that is,

$$G(\mathbf{x};\mathbf{x}_i) = G(\mathbf{x} - \mathbf{x}_i) \tag{7.59}$$

If the stabilizer $\mathbf{P}$ is both *translationally and rotationally invariant,* then the Green's function $G(\mathbf{x};\mathbf{x}_i)$ will depend only on the *Euclidean norm* of the difference vector $\mathbf{x} - \mathbf{x}_i$, as shown by

$$G(\mathbf{x};\mathbf{x}_i) = G(\|\mathbf{x} - \mathbf{x}_i\|) \tag{7.60}$$

Under these conditions, the Green's function must be a *radial-basis function.* In such a case, the regularized solution of Eq. (7.58) takes on the following special form (Poggio and Girosi, 1990a):

$$F(\mathbf{x}) = \sum_{i=1}^{N} w_i G(\|\mathbf{x} - \mathbf{x}_i\|) \tag{7.61}$$

The solution described in Eq. (7.61) constructs a linear function space that depends on the known data points according to the Euclidean distance measure.

The solution described by Eq. (7.61) is termed *strict interpolation,* since all the N data points available for training are used to generate the interpolating function $F(\mathbf{x})$. It is important, however, to realize that this solution differs from that of Eq. (7.15) in a fundamental respect: The solution of Eq. (7.61) is *regularized* by virtue of the definition given in Eq. (7.57) for the weight vector $\mathbf{w}$. It is only when we set the regularization parameter λ equal to zero that the two solutions may become one and the same.

Multivariate Gaussian Functions

A special class of differential operators $\mathbf{P}$ that are invariant under both rotations and translations is defined by (Poggio and Girosi, 1990a):

$$\|\mathbf{P}F\|^2 = \sum_{k=0}^{K} a_k \|D^k F(\mathbf{x})\|^2 \tag{7.62}$$

where, using standard multi-index notation (see footnote 3), the norm of the differential operator D^k is defined as

$$\|D^k F\|^2 = \sum_{|\alpha|=k} \int_{\mathbb{R}^p} |\partial^\alpha F(\mathbf{x})|^2 \, d\mathbf{x} \tag{7.63}$$

The integral in Eq. (7.63) is a multiple integral defined over the p coordinates of the input vector $\mathbf{x}$. The Green's function $G(\mathbf{x};\mathbf{x}_i)$ associated with this differential operator satisfies the following differential equation (in the sense of distributions)

$$\sum_{k=0}^{K} (-1)^k a_k \nabla^{2k} G(\mathbf{x};\mathbf{x}_i) = \delta(\mathbf{x} - \mathbf{x}_i) \tag{7.64}$$

where ∇^{2k} is the k-iterated Laplacian operator in p dimensions, and

$$\nabla^2 = \frac{\partial^2}{\partial x_1^2} + \frac{\partial^2}{\partial x_2^2} + \cdots + \frac{\partial^2}{\partial x_p^2} \tag{7.65}$$

Specializing to the case of *Gaussian radial basis functions,* we permit the upper limit K in the summation of Eq. (7.64) to approach infinity, and define the coefficient a_k as

$$a_k = \frac{\sigma_i^{2k}}{k!2^k} \tag{7.66}$$

where σ_i is some constant associated with the data point $\mathbf{x}_i$. In such a case the Green's function $G(\mathbf{x};\mathbf{x}_i)$ satisfies the pseudodifferential equation

$$\sum_{k=0}^{\infty} (-1)^k \frac{\sigma_i^{2k}}{k!2^k} \nabla^{2k} G(\mathbf{x};\mathbf{x}_i) = \delta(\mathbf{x} - \mathbf{x}_i) \tag{7.67}$$

To solve Eq. (7.67) for the Green's function $G(\mathbf{x};\mathbf{x}_i)$, we use the multidimensional Fourier transform. To simplify matters, we put $\mathbf{x}_i = 0$ and $\sigma_i^2 = 1$; their effects will be accounted for later. We may then reduce Eq. (7.67) to its basic form:

$$(\mathbf{P}^*\mathbf{P})G(\mathbf{x}) = \delta(\mathbf{x}) \tag{7.68}$$

where

$$\mathbf{P}^*\mathbf{P} = \sum_{k=0}^{\infty} (-1)^k \frac{\nabla^{2k}}{k!2^k} \tag{7.69}$$

The *multidimensional Fourier transform* of $G(\mathbf{x})$ is defined by (Debnath and Mikusiński, 1990)

$$\hat{G}(\mathbf{s}) = \int_{\mathbb{R}^p} G(\mathbf{x}) \exp(-i\mathbf{s}^T\mathbf{x})\, d\mathbf{x} \tag{7.70}$$

where $i = \sqrt{-1}$ and $\mathbf{s}$ is the p-dimensional *transform variable;* the notation $i = \sqrt{-1}$ only applies to Eqs. (7.70) through (7.74). Then, recognizing that the multidimensional Fourier transform of the Dirac delta distribution $\delta(\mathbf{x})$ is unity, and using the differentiation property of the multidimensional Fourier transform, we find that Eq. (7.68) is transformed as follows:

$$\sum_{k=0}^{\infty} \frac{1}{k!2^k} \left(\sum_{n=1}^{p} s_n^2 \right)^k \hat{G}(\mathbf{s}) = 1 \tag{7.71}$$

where s_n is the nth element of the vector $\mathbf{s}$, and differentiation of $G(\mathbf{x})$ with respect to the nth element of the vector $\mathbf{x}$ has the effect of multiplying the Fourier transform by is_n. We next note that the infinite series in the transform variable $\mathbf{s}$ in Eq. (7.71) converges for all $\mathbf{s} \in \mathbb{R}^p$ to the following:

$$\sum_{k=0}^{\infty} \frac{1}{k!} \left(\frac{1}{2} \mathbf{s}^T\mathbf{s} \right)^k = \exp\left(\frac{1}{2} \mathbf{s}^T\mathbf{s} \right) \tag{7.72}$$

Hence, substituting Eq. (7.72) in (7.71), and solving for the multidimensional Fourier transform $\hat{G}(\mathbf{s})$, we get

$$\hat{G}(\mathbf{s}) = \exp\left(-\frac{1}{2} \mathbf{s}^T\mathbf{s} \right) \tag{7.73}$$

Next, we use the *inverse multidimensional Fourier transform* to obtain

$$\begin{aligned}
G(\mathbf{x}) &= \left(\frac{1}{2\pi} \right)^p \int_{\mathbb{R}^p} \hat{G}(\mathbf{s}) \exp(i\mathbf{s}^T\mathbf{x})\, d\mathbf{s} \\
&= \left(\frac{1}{2\pi} \right)^p \int_{\mathbb{R}^p} \exp\left(-\frac{1}{2} \mathbf{s}^T\mathbf{s} \right) \exp(i\mathbf{s}^T\mathbf{x})\, d\mathbf{s} \\
&= \prod_{n=1}^{p} \mathcal{F}^{-1} \left[\exp\left(-\frac{1}{2} s_n^2 \right) \right] \\
&= \prod_{n=1}^{p} \exp\left(-\frac{1}{2} x_n^2 \right) \\
&= \exp\left(-\frac{1}{2} \|\mathbf{x}\|^2 \right)
\end{aligned} \tag{7.74}$$

where the symbol $\mathcal{F}^{-1}$, in the third line, denotes inverse Fourier transformation. Finally, we replace $G(\mathbf{x})$ with $G(\mathbf{x};\mathbf{x}_i) = G(\|\mathbf{x} - \mathbf{x}_i\|)$, and reintroduce the scaling factor σ_i^{2m}, the combined effort of which is to yield the following solution for Eq. (7.67):

$$G(\mathbf{x};\mathbf{x}_i) = \exp\left(-\frac{1}{2\sigma_i^2}\|\mathbf{x}-\mathbf{x}_i\|^2\right)$$

$$= \exp\left[-\frac{1}{2\sigma_i^2}\sum_{k=1}^{p}(x_k - x_{i,k})^2\right] \tag{7.75}$$

Since the coefficient $a_0 = 1 > 0$ in Eq. (7.67), it follows that $G(\mathbf{x};\mathbf{x}_i)$ is positive definite[4] for all i. Hence the terms in the null space of the stabilizer $\mathbf{P}$ are not necessary for the function $F(\mathbf{x})$ to minimize the functional $\mathscr{E}(F)$.

The Green's function $G(\mathbf{x};\mathbf{x}_i)$ defined in Eq. (7.75) is recognized to be a *multivariate Gaussian function* characterized by a *mean vector* $\mathbf{x}_i$ and common *variance* σ_i^2, except for a scaling factor that may be absorbed in the weight w_i. Correspondingly, the regularized solution defined by Eq. (7.58) takes on the following special form:

$$F(\mathbf{x}) = \sum_{i=1}^{N} w_i \exp\left(-\frac{1}{2\sigma_i^2}\|\mathbf{x}-\mathbf{x}_i\|^2\right) \tag{7.76}$$

which consists of a linear superposition of multivariate Gaussian basis functions with centers $\mathbf{x}_i$ (located at the data points) and widths σ_i.

7.6 Regularization Networks

The expansion of the approximating function $F(\mathbf{x})$ given in Eq. (7.58) in terms of the Green's function $G(\mathbf{x};\mathbf{x}_i)$ centered at $\mathbf{x}_i$ suggests the network structure shown in Fig. 7.4 as a method for its implementation. For obvious reasons, this network is called a *regularization network* (Poggio and Girosi, 1990a). It consists of three layers. The first layer is composed of input (source) nodes whose number is equal to the dimension p of the input vector $\mathbf{x}$ (i.e., the number of independent variables of the problem). The second layer is a hidden layer, composed of nonlinear units that are connected *directly* to all of the nodes in the input layer. There is one hidden unit for each data point $\mathbf{x}_i$, $i = 1, 2, \ldots, N$, where N is the number of training examples. The activation functions of the individual hidden units are defined by the Green's functions. Accordingly, the output of the ith hidden unit is $G(\mathbf{x};\mathbf{x}_i)$. The output layer consists of a single linear unit, being fully connected to the hidden layer. By "linearity" we mean that the output of the network is a linearly weighted sum of the outputs of the hidden units. The weights of the output layer are the unknown coefficients of the expansion, defined in terms of the Green's functions $G(\mathbf{x};\mathbf{x}_i)$ and the regularization parameter λ by Eq. (7.57). Figure 7.4 depicts the architecture of the regularization network for a single output. Clearly, such an architecture can be readily extended to accommodate any number of network outputs desired.

The regularization network shown in Fig. 7.4 assumes that the Green's function $G(\mathbf{x};\mathbf{x}_i)$ is *positive definite* for all i. Provided that this condition is satisfied, which it is in the case of the $G(\mathbf{x};\mathbf{x}_i)$ having the Gaussian form given in Eq. (7.76), for example, then the solution produced by this network will be an "optimal" interpolant in the sense that it minimizes the functional $\mathscr{E}(F)$. Moreover, from the viewpoint of approximation theory, the regularization network has three desirable properties (Poggio and Girosi, 1990a):

1. The regularization network is a *universal approximator* in that it can approximate arbitrarily well any multivariate continuous function on a compact subset of $\mathbb{R}^p$, given a sufficiently large number of hidden units.

[4] A continuous function $f(t)$, defined on the interval $(0,\infty)$, is said to be *positive definite* if, for any distinct points $\mathbf{x}_1, \mathbf{x}_2, \ldots, \mathbf{x}_N \in \mathbb{R}^p$ and certain scalars $c_1, c_2, \ldots, c_N$, the quadratic form $\sum_{i=1}^{N}\sum_{j=1}^{N} c_i c_j f(\|\mathbf{x}_i - \mathbf{x}_j\|)$ is positive definite; the selection of the scalars is constrained by the *order* of positive definiteness of the function $f(t)$ (Poggio and Girosi, 1990a).

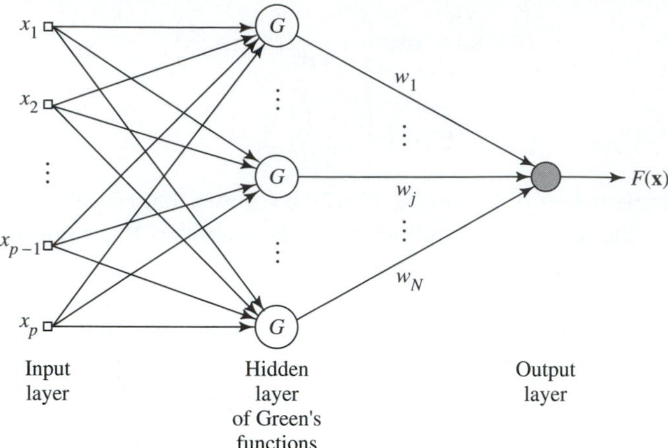

FIGURE 7.4 Regularization network.

2. Since the approximation scheme derived from regularization theory is linear in the unknown coefficients, it follows that the regularization network has the *best-approximation property.* This means that given an unknown nonlinear function f, there always exists a choice of coefficients that approximates f better than all other possible choices.
3. The solution computed by the regularization network is *optimal.* Optimality here means that the regularization network minimizes a functional that measures how much the solution deviates from its true value as represented by the training data.

7.7 Generalized Radial-Basis Function Networks

The one-to-one correspondence between the training input date $\mathbf{x}_i$ and the Green's function $G(\mathbf{x};\mathbf{x}_i)$ for $i = 1, 2, \ldots, N$ produces a regularization network that is prohibitively expensive to implement in computational terms for large N. Specifically, the computation of the linear weights of the network [i.e., the coefficients of the expansion in Eq. (7.58)] requires the inversion of an N-by-N matrix, which therefore grows polynomially with N (roughly as N^3). Furthermore, the likelihood of *ill conditioning* is higher for larger matrices; the *condition number* of a matrix is defined as the ratio of the largest eigenvalue to the smallest eigenvalue of the matrix. To overcome these computational difficulties, the complexity of the network would have to be reduced, which requires an approximation to the regularized solution, as discussed next.

The approach taken involves searching for a suboptimal solution in a lower-dimensional space that approximates the regularized solution of Eq. (7.58). This is done by using a standard technique known in variational problems as *Galerkin's method.* According to this technique, the approximated solution $F^*(\mathbf{x})$ is expanded on a finite basis, as shown by (Poggio and Girosi, 1990a),

$$F^*(\mathbf{x}) = \sum_{i=1}^{M} w_i \varphi_i(\mathbf{x}) \tag{7.77}$$

where $\{\varphi_i(\mathbf{x}) | i = 1, 2, \ldots, M\}$ is a new set of basis functions that we assume to be linearly independent without loss of generality. Typically, the number of basis functions is less than the number of data points (i.e., $M \leq N$), and the w_i constitute a new set of weights. With radial-basis functions in mind, we set

$$\varphi_i(\mathbf{x}) = G(\|\mathbf{x} - \mathbf{t}_i\|), \qquad i = 1, 2, \ldots, M \tag{7.78}$$

where the set of centers $\{\mathbf{t}_i | i = 1, 2, \ldots, M\}$ is to be determined. This particular choice of basis functions is the only one that guarantees that in the case of $M = N$, and

$$\mathbf{t}_i = \mathbf{x}_i, \qquad i = 1, 2, \ldots, N$$

the correct solution of Eq. (7.58) is consistently recovered. Thus, using Eq. (7.78) in (7.77), we may redefine $F^*(\mathbf{x})$ as

$$\begin{aligned} F^*(\mathbf{x}) &= \sum_{i=1}^{M} w_i G(\mathbf{x}; \mathbf{t}_i) \\ &= \sum_{i=1}^{M} w_i G(\|\mathbf{x} - \mathbf{t}_i\|) \end{aligned} \tag{7.79}$$

Given the expansion of Eq. (7.79) for the approximating function $F^*(\mathbf{x})$, the problem we have to address is the determination of the new set of weights $\{w_i | i = 1, 2, \ldots, M\}$ so as to minimize the new cost functional $\mathscr{E}(F^*)$ defined by

$$\mathscr{E}(F^*) = \sum_{i=1}^{N} \left(d_i - \sum_{j=1}^{M} w_j G(\|\mathbf{x}_i - \mathbf{t}_j\|) \right)^2 + \lambda \|\mathbf{P}F^*\|^2 \tag{7.80}$$

The first term on the right-hand side of Eq. (7.80) may be expressed as the squared Euclidean norm $\|\mathbf{d} - \mathbf{G}\mathbf{w}\|^2$, where

$$\mathbf{d} = [d_1, d_2, \ldots, d_N]^T \tag{7.81}$$

$$\mathbf{G} = \begin{bmatrix} G(\mathbf{x}_1; \mathbf{t}_1) & G(\mathbf{x}_1; \mathbf{t}_2) & \ldots & G(\mathbf{x}_1; \mathbf{t}_M) \\ G(\mathbf{x}_2; \mathbf{t}_1) & G(\mathbf{x}_2; \mathbf{t}_2) & \ldots & G(\mathbf{x}_2; \mathbf{t}_M) \\ \vdots & \vdots & & \vdots \\ G(\mathbf{x}_N; \mathbf{t}_1) & G(\mathbf{x}_N; \mathbf{t}_2) & \ldots & G(\mathbf{x}_N; \mathbf{t}_M) \end{bmatrix} \tag{7.82}$$

$$\mathbf{w} = [w_1, w_2, \ldots, w_M]^T \tag{7.83}$$

The desired response vector $\mathbf{d}$ is N-dimensional as before. However, the matrix $\mathbf{G}$ of Green's functions and the weight vector $\mathbf{w}$ have different dimensions; the matrix $\mathbf{G}$ is now N-by-M and therefore no longer symmetric, and the vector $\mathbf{w}$ is M-by-1. From Eq. (7.79) we note that the approximating function F^* is a linear combination of the Green's functions for the stabilizer $\mathbf{P}$. Accordingly, we may express the second term on the right-hand side of Eq. (7.80) as

$$\begin{aligned} \|\mathbf{P}F^*\|^2 &= (\mathbf{P}F^*, \mathbf{P}F^*)_H \\ &= \left[\sum_{i=1}^{M} w_i G(\mathbf{x}; \mathbf{t}_i), \mathbf{P}^*\mathbf{P} \sum_{i=1}^{M} w_i G(\mathbf{x}; \mathbf{t}_i) \right]_H \\ &= \left[\sum_{i=1}^{M} w_i G(\mathbf{x}; \mathbf{t}_i), \sum_{i=1}^{M} w_i \delta_{\mathbf{t}_i} \right]_H \\ &= \sum_{j=1}^{M} \sum_{i=1}^{M} w_j w_i G(\mathbf{t}_j; \mathbf{t}_i) \\ &= \mathbf{w}^T \mathbf{G}_0 \mathbf{w} \end{aligned} \tag{7.84}$$

where, in the second and third lines, we made use of the definition of an adjoint operator and Eq. (7.41), respectively. The matrix $\mathbf{G}_0$ is a symmetric M-by-M matrix, defined by

$$\mathbf{G}_0 = \begin{bmatrix} G(\mathbf{t}_1;\mathbf{t}_1) & G(\mathbf{t}_1;\mathbf{t}_2) & \dots & G(\mathbf{t}_1;\mathbf{t}_M) \\ G(\mathbf{t}_2;\mathbf{t}_1) & G(\mathbf{t}_2;\mathbf{t}_2) & \dots & G(\mathbf{t}_2;\mathbf{t}_M) \\ \vdots & \vdots & & \vdots \\ G(\mathbf{t}_M;\mathbf{t}_1) & G(\mathbf{t}_M;\mathbf{t}_2) & \dots & G(\mathbf{t}_M;\mathbf{t}_M) \end{bmatrix} \tag{7.85}$$

Thus the minimization of Eq. (7.80) with respect to the weight vector $\mathbf{w}$ yields the result (see Problem 7.10)

$$(\mathbf{G}^T\mathbf{G} + \lambda\mathbf{G}_0)\mathbf{w} = \mathbf{G}^T\mathbf{d} \tag{7.86}$$

Note that as the regularization parameter λ approaches zero, the weight vector $\mathbf{w}$ converges to the pseudoinverse (minimum-norm) solution to the overdetermined least-squares data-fitting problem, as shown by (Broomhead and Lowe, 1988)

$$\mathbf{w} = \mathbf{G}^+\mathbf{d}, \qquad \lambda = 0 \tag{7.87}$$

where $\mathbf{G}^+$ is the pseudoinverse of matrix $\mathbf{G}$; that is,

$$\mathbf{G}^+ = (\mathbf{G}^T\mathbf{G})^{-1}\mathbf{G}^T \tag{7.88}$$

Weighted Norm

The norm in the approximate solution of Eq. (7.80) is ordinarily intended to be a Euclidean norm. When, however, the individual elements of the input vector $\mathbf{x}$ belong to different classes, it is more appropriate to consider a general *weighted norm,* the squared form of which is defined as (Poggio and Girosi, 1990a)

$$\begin{aligned}\|\mathbf{x}\|_C^2 &= (\mathbf{C}\mathbf{x})^T(\mathbf{C}\mathbf{x}) \\ &= \mathbf{x}^T\mathbf{C}^T\mathbf{C}\mathbf{x}\end{aligned} \tag{7.89}$$

where $\mathbf{C}$ is a p-by-p *norm weighting matrix,* and p is the dimension of the input vector $\mathbf{x}$. Depending on how the weighting matrix $\mathbf{C}$ is defined, we may identify three specific cases of interest.

1. The matrix $\mathbf{C}$ is equal to the identity matrix $\mathbf{I}$, for which the standard Euclidean norm is obtained; that is,

$$\|\mathbf{x}\|_C^2 = \|\mathbf{x}\|^2, \qquad \mathbf{C} = \mathbf{I} \tag{7.90}$$

2. The matrix $\mathbf{C}$ is a diagonal matrix, in which case the diagonal elements assign a specific weight to each input coordinate, as shown by

$$\|\mathbf{x}\|_C^2 = \sum_{k=1}^{p} c_k^2 x_k^2 \tag{7.91}$$

   where x_k is the kth element of the input vector $\mathbf{x}$ and c_k is the kth diagonal element of the matrix $\mathbf{C}$.
3. The matrix $\mathbf{C}$ is a nondiagonal matrix, in which case the weighted norm takes on a quadratic form as shown by

$$\|\mathbf{x}\|_C^2 = \sum_{k=1}^{p} \sum_{l=1}^{p} a_{kl} x_k x_l \tag{7.92}$$

where a_{kl} is the klth element of the matrix product $\mathbf{C}^T\mathbf{C}$.

Using the definition of weighted norm, we may now rewrite the approximation to the regularized solution given in Eq. (7.80) in the more generalized form (Poggio and Girosi, 1990a; Lowe, 1989)

$$F^*(\mathbf{x}) = \sum_{i=1}^{M} w_i G(\|\mathbf{x} - \mathbf{t}_i\|_{C_i}) \tag{7.93}$$

The use of a weighted norm may be interpreted in two ways. We may simply view it as applying an *affine transformation* to the original input space. In principle, allowing for such a transformation cannot degrade results from the default case, since it actually corresponds to an identity norm-weighting matrix. On the other hand, the weighted norm follows directly from a slight generalization of the p-dimensional Laplacian in the definition of the pseudodifferential operator $\mathbf{P}$ in Eq. (7.69); see Problem 7.11. In any event, the use of a weighted norm may also be justified in the context of Gaussian radial-basis functions on the following grounds. A Gaussian radial-basis function $G(\|\mathbf{x} - \mathbf{t}_i\|_{C_i})$ centered at $\mathbf{t}_i$ and with norm weighting matrix $\mathbf{C}_i$ may be expressed as

$$\begin{aligned} G(\|\mathbf{x} - \mathbf{t}_i\|_{C_i}) &= \exp[-(\mathbf{x} - \mathbf{t}_i)^T \mathbf{C}_i^T \mathbf{C}_i (\mathbf{x} - \mathbf{t}_i)] \\ &= \exp\left[-\frac{1}{2}(\mathbf{x} - \mathbf{t}_i)^T \boldsymbol{\Sigma}_i^{-1} (\mathbf{x} - \mathbf{t}_i)\right] \end{aligned} \tag{7.94}$$

where the inverse matrix $\boldsymbol{\Sigma}_i^{-1}$ is defined by

$$\frac{1}{2}\boldsymbol{\Sigma}_i^{-1} = \mathbf{C}_i^T \mathbf{C}_i \tag{7.95}$$

Equation (7.94) represents a multivariate Gaussian distribution with mean vector $\mathbf{t}_i$ and covariance matrix $\boldsymbol{\Sigma}_i$. As such, it represents a generalization of the distribution described in Eq. (7.76).

The solution to the approximation problem given in Eq. (7.80) provides the framework for the *generalized radial-basis function* (*RBF*) *network* having the structure shown in Fig. 7.5. In this network, provision is made for a bias (i.e., data-independent variable) applied to the output unit. This is done simply by setting one of the linear weights in the output layer of the network equal to the bias and treating the associated radial-basis function as a constant equal to +1. (The bias is the negative of a threshold.)

In structural terms, the generalized RBF network of Fig. 7.5 is similar to the regularization RBF network of Fig. 7.4. However, these two networks differ from each other in two important respects:

1. The number of nodes in the hidden layer of the generalized RBF network of Fig. 7.5 is M, where M is ordinarily smaller than the number N of examples available for training. On the other hand, the number of hidden nodes in the regularization RBF network of Fig. 7.4 is exactly N.
2. In the generalized RBF network of Fig. 7.5, the linear weights associated with the output layer, and the positions of the centers of the radial-basis functions and the norm weighting matrix associated with the hidden layer, are all unknown parameters that have to be learned. On the other hand, the activation functions of the hidden layer in the regularization RBF network of Fig. 7.4 are known, being defined by a

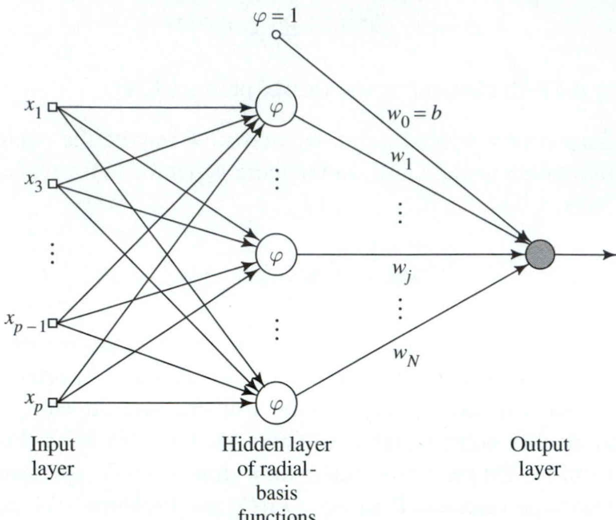

FIGURE 7.5 Radial-basis function network.

set of Green's functions centered at the training data points; the linear weights of the output layer are the only unknown parameters of the network.

7.8 The XOR Problem (Revisited)

Consider again the XOR (Exclusive OR) problem, which we solved in Chapter 6 using a multilayer perceptron with a single hidden layer. Here we are going to present a solution of this same problem using an RBF network.

The RBF network to be investigated consists of a pair of Gaussian functions, defined as follows:

$$G(\|\mathbf{x} - \mathbf{t}_i\|) = \exp(-\|\mathbf{x} - \mathbf{t}_i\|^2), \qquad i = 1, 2 \tag{7.96}$$

where the centers $\mathbf{t}_1$ and $\mathbf{t}_2$ are

$$\mathbf{t}_1 = [1,1]^T$$

$$\mathbf{t}_2 = [0,0]^T$$

For the characterization of the output unit, we assume the following:

1. The output unit uses *weight sharing,* which is justified by virtue of the symmetry of the problem; this is a form of prior information being built into the design of the network. With only two hidden units, we therefore only have a single weight w to be determined.
2. The output unit includes a bias b (i.e., data-independent variable). The significance of this bias is that the desired output values of the XOR function have nonzero mean.

Thus the structure of the RBF network proposed for solving the XOR problem is as shown in Fig. 7.6. The input–output relation of the network is defined by

$$y(\mathbf{x}) = \sum_{i=1}^{2} wG(\|\mathbf{x} - \mathbf{t}_i\|) + b \tag{7.97}$$

To fit the training data of Table 7.2, we require that

$$y(\mathbf{x}_j) = d_j, \qquad j = 1, 2, 3, 4 \tag{7.98}$$

where $\mathbf{x}_j$ is an input vector and d_j is the corresponding value of the desired output. Let

$$g_{ji} = G(\|\mathbf{x}_j - \mathbf{t}_i\|), \qquad j = 1, 2, 3, 4;\ i = 1, 2 \tag{7.99}$$

Then, using the values of Table 7.2 in Eq. (7.99), we get the following set of equations written in matrix form:

$$\mathbf{Gw} = \mathbf{d} \tag{7.100}$$

where

$$\mathbf{G} = \begin{bmatrix} g_{11} & g_{12} & 1 \\ g_{21} & g_{22} & 1 \\ g_{31} & g_{32} & 1 \\ g_{41} & g_{42} & 1 \end{bmatrix}$$

$$= \begin{bmatrix} 1 & 0.1353 & 1 \\ 0.3678 & 0.3678 & 1 \\ 0.1353 & 1 & 1 \\ 0.3678 & 0.3678 & 1 \end{bmatrix} \tag{7.101}$$

$$\mathbf{d} = [1 \quad 0 \quad 1 \quad 0]^T \tag{7.102}$$

$$\mathbf{w} = [w \quad w \quad b]^T \tag{7.103}$$

The problem described here is *overdetermined in the sense that we have more data points than free parameters.* This explains why the matrix **G** is not square. Consequently, no

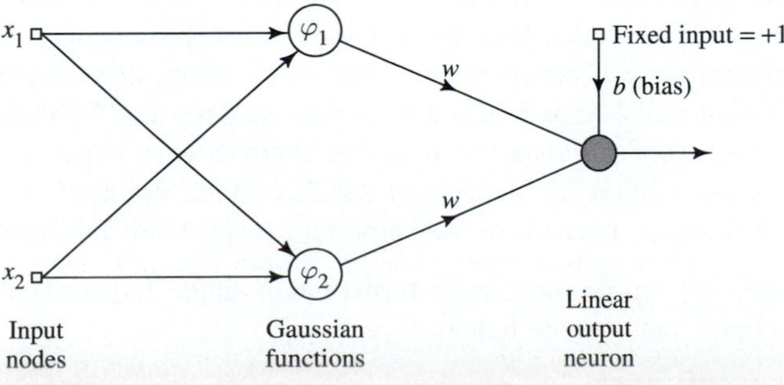

FIGURE 7.6 RBF network for solving the XOR problem.

TABLE 7.2 Input–Output Transformation Computed for Example 1

Data Point, j	Input Pattern, $\mathbf{x}_j$	Desired Output, d_j	Actual Output, y_i
1	(1,1)	1	+0.901
2	(0,1)	0	−0.01
3	(0,0)	1	+0.901
4	(1,0)	0	−0.01

unique inverse exists for the matrix **G**. To overcome this difficulty, we use the *minimum-norm* solution of Eq. (7.88), and so write

$$\begin{aligned}\mathbf{w} &= \mathbf{G}^{+}\mathbf{d} \\ &= (\mathbf{G}^{T}\mathbf{G})^{-1}\mathbf{G}^{T}\mathbf{d}\end{aligned} \tag{7.104}$$

Note that $\mathbf{G}^T\mathbf{G}$ is a square matrix with a unique inverse of its own. Substituting Eq. (7.101) in (7.104), we get

$$\mathbf{G}^{+} = \begin{bmatrix} 1.656 & -1.158 & 0.628 & -1.158 \\ 0.628 & -1.158 & 1.656 & -1.158 \\ -0.846 & 1.301 & -0.846 & 1.301 \end{bmatrix} \tag{7.105}$$

Finally, substituting Eqs. (7.102) and (7.105) in (7.104), we get

$$\mathbf{w} = \begin{bmatrix} 2.284 \\ 2.284 \\ -1.692 \end{bmatrix}$$

which completes the specification of the RBF network.

The last column of Table 7.2 includes the actual values of the RBF network output produced in response to the four input patterns. These results show that the RBF network of Fig. 7.6 successfully discriminates states of opposite polarity, and the XOR problem is therefore solved.

7.9 Comparison of RBF Networks and Multilayer Perceptrons

Radial-basis function (RBF) networks and multilayer perceptrons are examples of nonlinear layered feedforward networks. They are both universal approximators. The universality of multilayer perceptrons was considered in Chapter 6. There also exists a formal proof for the universality of radial-basis function networks, as described by Park and Sandberg (1991). It is therefore not surprising to find that there always exists an RBF network capable of accurately mimicking a specified MLP, or vice versa. However, these two networks differ from each other in several important respects, as outlined here.

1. An RBF network (in its most basic form) has a single hidden layer,[5] whereas an MLP may have one or more hidden layers.

[5] An RBF network has been proposed by He and Lapedes (1991) that involves two hidden layers. The second hidden layer and output layer are both linear, performing successive approximations on the activation functions of the first hidden layer. See Problem 7.4 for more details.

2. Typically, the computation nodes of an MLP, be they located in a hidden or output layer, share a common neuron model. On the other hand, the computation nodes in the hidden layer of an RBF network are quite different and serve a different purpose from those in the output layer of the network.
3. The hidden layer of an RBF network is nonlinear, whereas the output layer is linear. On the other hand, the hidden and output layers of an MLP used as a classifier are usually all nonlinear; however, when the MLP is used to solve nonlinear regression problems, a linear layer for the output is usually the preferred choice.
4. The argument of the activation function of each hidden unit in an RBF network computes the *Euclidean norm* (*distance*) between the input vector and the center of that unit. On the other hand, the activation function of each hidden unit in an MLP computes the *inner product* of the input vector and the synaptic weight vector of that unit.[6]
5. MLPs construct *global* approximations to nonlinear input–output mapping. Consequently, they are capable of generalization in regions of the input space where little or no training data are available. On the other hand, RBF networks using exponentially decaying localized nonlinearities (e.g., Gaussian functions) construct *local* approximations to nonlinear input–output mapping, with the result that these networks are capable of fast learning and reduced sensitivity to the order of presentation of training data. In many cases, however, we find that in order to represent a mapping to some desired degree of smoothness, the number of radial-basis functions required to span the input space adequately may have to be very large.[7]

The linear characteristic of the output layer of the RBF network means that such a network is more closely related to Rosenblatt's perceptron than the multilayer perceptron. However, the RBF network differs from the perceptron in that it is capable of implementing arbitrary nonlinear transformations of the input space. This is well illustrated by the XOR problem, which cannot be solved by any linear perceptron but can be solved by an RBF network.

7.10 Mixture Models

The expansion described in Eq. (7.93) is closely related to *mixture models,* that is, mixtures of Gaussian distributions. Mixtures of probability distributions, in particular Gaussian distributions, have been used extensively as models in a wide variety of applications where the data of interest arise from two or more populations mixed together in some varying properties (McLachlan and Basford, 1988). According to the *mixture model,* we have a superpopulation S that is a mixture of finite number—say, n—of populations S_1, $S_2, \ldots, S_n$ in some proportions $\pi_1, \pi_2, \ldots, \pi_n$, respectively, where

$$\sum_{i=1}^{n} \pi_i = 1 \quad \text{and} \quad \pi_i \geq 0 \qquad \text{for all } i \tag{7.106}$$

The probability density function (pdf) of a random vector $\mathbf{x}$ in S is represented by

$$f(\mathbf{x}; \varphi) = \sum_{i=1}^{n} \pi_i f_i(\mathbf{x}; \boldsymbol{\theta}) \tag{7.107}$$

[6] Simard et al. (1992, 1993) have proposed a new distance measure for radial-basis functions, which can be made locally invariant to any set of transformations of the input and which can be computed efficiently. The new distance measure is called *target distance;* see Problem 1.16.

[7] Lane et al. (1991) discuss a general neural network formulation that combines the generalization capability of *global* multilayer feedforward networks with the computational efficiency and learning speed of *local* networks.

where $f_i(\mathbf{x};\boldsymbol{\theta})$ is the pdf corresponding to S_i and $\boldsymbol{\theta}$ represents the vector of all unknown associated parameters. The vector $\boldsymbol{\varphi}$ is made up of $\boldsymbol{\theta}$ and the mixing proportions $\pi_1, \pi_2, \ldots, \pi_n$. We are given a set of observation vectors $\alpha_1, \alpha_2, \ldots, \alpha_N$, say, and the problem is to estimate the unknown parameter vector $\boldsymbol{\varphi}$. We thus see that the mixture model problem is indeed similar to the problem of finding the w_i, the $\mathbf{t}_i$, and the $\boldsymbol{\Sigma}_i$ in the expansion of Eq. (7.93).

This analogy suggests that we may develop insight into the characterization of RBF networks from the literature on probability density function estimation. A particular paper that we have in mind here is that of Parzen (1962), who considered the estimation of a probability density function $f(x)$, given a sequence of independent and identically distributed random variables with common probability density function $f(x)$. Lowe (1991a) uses Parzen's basic exposition of the problem to derive the radial-basis function network. Lowe also points out that the traditional method of expectation-maximation (EM) (Dempster et al., 1977), based on maximizing the likelihood of the data given the model, may be used to optimize the positions and spreads of the centers in the hidden layer of an RBF network in an unsupervised manner; the EM algorithm is explained in Chapter 12.

7.11 Learning Strategies

The learning process undertaken by a radial-basis function (RBF) network may be visualized as follows. The linear weights associated with the output unit(s) of the network tend to evolve on a different "time scale" compared to the nonlinear activation functions of the hidden units. Thus, as the hidden layer's activation functions evolve slowly in accordance with some *nonlinear* optimization strategy, the output layer's weights adjust themselves rapidly through a *linear* optimization strategy. The important point to note here is that the different layers of an RBF network perform different tasks, and so it is reasonable to separate the optimization of the hidden and output layers of the network by using different techniques, and perhaps operating on different time scales (Lowe, 1991a).

There are different learning strategies that we can follow in the design of an RBF network, depending on how the centers of the radial basis functions of the network are specified. Essentially, we may identify three approaches, as discussed below.

1. Fixed Centers Selected at Random

The simplest approach is to assume *fixed* radial-basis functions defining the activation functions of the hidden units. Specifically, the locations of the centers may be chosen *randomly* from the training data set. This is considered to be a "sensible" approach, provided that the training data are distributed in a representative manner for the problem at hand (Lowe, 1989). For the radial-basis functions themselves, we may employ an *isotropic* Gaussian function whose standard deviation is fixed according to the spread of the centers. Specifically, a (normalized) radial-basis function centered at $\mathbf{t}_i$ is defined as

$$G(\|\mathbf{x} - \mathbf{t}_i\|^2) = \exp\left(-\frac{M}{d^2}\|\mathbf{x} - \mathbf{t}_i\|^2\right), \qquad i = 1, 2, \ldots, M \tag{7.108}$$

where M is the number of centers and d is the maximum distance between the chosen centers. In effect, the standard deviation (i.e., width) of all the Gaussian radial-basis functions is fixed at

$$\sigma = \frac{d}{\sqrt{2M}} \tag{7.109}$$

Such a choice for the standard deviation σ merely ensures that the Gaussian functions are not too peaked or too flat; both of these extremes are to be avoided.

The only parameters that would need to be learned in this approach are the linear weights in the output layer of the network. A straightforward procedure for doing this is to use the *pseudoinverse method* (Broomhead and Lowe, 1988). Specifically, we have [see also Eqs. (7.87) and (7.88)]

$$\mathbf{w} = \mathbf{G}^{+}\mathbf{d} \tag{7.110}$$

where $\mathbf{d}$ is the desired response vector in the training set. The matrix $\mathbf{G}^{+}$ is the pseudoinverse of the matrix $\mathbf{G}$, which is itself defined as

$$\mathbf{G} = \{g_{ji}\} \tag{7.111}$$

where

$$g_{ji} = \exp\left(-\frac{M}{d^2}\|\mathbf{x}_j - \mathbf{t}_i\|^2\right), \qquad j = 1, 2, \ldots, N; i = 1, 2, \ldots, M \tag{7.112}$$

where $\mathbf{x}_j$ is the jth input vector of the training set.

Basic to all algorithms for the computation of a pseudoinverse of a matrix is the *singular-value decomposition* (Golub and Van Loan, 1989; Haykin, 1991):

If $\mathbf{G}$ *is a real N-by-M matrix, then there exist orthogonal matrices*

$$\mathbf{U} = \{\mathbf{u}_1, \mathbf{u}_2, \ldots, \mathbf{u}_N\}$$

and

$$\mathbf{V} = \{\mathbf{v}_1, \mathbf{v}_2, \ldots, \mathbf{v}_M\}$$

such that

$$\mathbf{U}^T\mathbf{G}\mathbf{V} = \text{diag}(\sigma_1, \sigma_2, \ldots, \sigma_K), \qquad K = \min(M, N) \tag{7.113}$$

where

$$\sigma_1 \geq \sigma_2 \geq \cdots \geq \sigma_K > 0$$

The column vectors of the matrix $\mathbf{U}$ are called the *left singular vectors* of $\mathbf{G}$, and the column vectors of the matrix $\mathbf{V}$ are called its *right singular vectors*. The $\sigma_1, \sigma_2, \ldots, \sigma_K$ are called the *singular values* of the matrix $\mathbf{G}$. According to the singular value decomposition theorem, the M-by-N pseudoinverse of matrix $\mathbf{G}$ is defined by

$$\mathbf{G}^{+} = \mathbf{V}\boldsymbol{\Sigma}^{+}\mathbf{U}^T \tag{7.114}$$

where $\boldsymbol{\Sigma}^{+}$ is itself an N-by-N matrix defined in terms of the singular values of $\mathbf{G}$ by

$$\boldsymbol{\Sigma}^{+} = \text{diag}\left(\frac{1}{\sigma_1}, \frac{1}{\sigma_2}, \ldots, \frac{1}{\sigma_K}, 0, \ldots, 0\right) \tag{7.115}$$

Efficient algorithms for the computation of a pseudoinverse matrix are discussed in the books by Golub and Van Loan (1989) and Haykin (1991).

2. Self-Organized Selection of Centers

In the second approach, the radial-basis functions are permitted to move the locations of their centers in a *self-organized* fashion, whereas the linear weights of the output layer are computed using a *supervised learning* rule. In other words, the network undergoes a *hybrid learning process* (Moody and Darken, 1989; Lippmann, 1989b). The self-organized component of the learning process serves to allocate network resources in a meaningful way by placing the centers of the radial-basis functions in only those regions of the input space where significant data are present.

For the self-organized selection of the hidden units' centers, we may use the standard *k-nearest-neighbor rule* (Moody and Darken, 1989). This rule classifies an input vector $\mathbf{x}$ by assigning it the label most frequently represented among the k nearest samples; in other words, a decision is made by examining the labels on the k nearest neighbors and taking a vote (Duda and Hart, 1973).

For the supervised learning operation to compute the linear weights of the output layer, we may use an error-correction learning rule such as the simple and yet highly effective *least-mean-square* (*LMS*) algorithm; this algorithm was discussed in Chapter 5. The outputs of the hidden units in the RBF network serve as the inputs of the LMS algorithm.

3. Supervised Selection of Centers

In the third approach, the centers of the radial-basis functions and all other free parameters of the network undergo a supervised learning process; in other words, the RBF network takes on its most generalized form. A natural candidate for such a process is error-correction learning, which is most conveniently implemented using a gradient-descent procedure that represents a generalization of the LMS algorithm.

The first step in the development of such a learning procedure is to define the instantaneous value of the cost function

$$\mathscr{E} = \frac{1}{2}\sum_{j=1}^{N} e_j^2 \tag{7.116}$$

where N is the number of training examples used to undertake the learning process, and e_j is the error signal, defined by

$$\begin{aligned} e_j &= d_j - F^*(\mathbf{x}_j) \\ &= d_j - \sum_{i=1}^{M} w_i G(\|\mathbf{x}_j - \mathbf{t}_i\|_{\mathbf{C}_i}) \end{aligned} \tag{7.117}$$

The requirement is to find the free parameters w_i, $\mathbf{t}_i$, and $\mathbf{\Sigma}_i^{-1}$ (the latter being related to the norm-weighting matrix $\mathbf{C}_i$) so as to minimize $\mathscr{E}$. The results of this minimization are summarized in Table 7.3; the derivations of these results are presented as an exercise to the reader as Problem 7.12. The following points are noteworthy in Table 7.3.

- The cost function $\mathscr{E}$ is convex with respect to the linear parameters w_i, but nonconvex with respect to the centers $\mathbf{t}_i$ and matrix $\mathbf{\Sigma}_i^{-1}$; in the latter case, the search for the optimum values of $\mathbf{t}_i$ and $\mathbf{\Sigma}_i^{-1}$ may get stuck at a local minimum in parameter space.
- The update equations for w_i, $\mathbf{t}_i$, and $\mathbf{\Sigma}_i^{-1}$ are (in general) assigned different learning-rate parameters η_1, η_2, and η_3, respectively.
- Unlike the back-propagation algorithm, the gradient-descent procedure described in Table 7.3 for an RBF network does *not* involve error back-propagation.
- The gradient vector $\partial\mathscr{E}/\partial\mathbf{t}_i$ has an effect similar to a *clustering effect* that is task-dependent (Poggio and Girosi, 1990a).

For the *initialization* of the gradient-descent procedure, it is often desirable to begin the search in parameter space from a *structured* initial condition that limits the region of

TABLE 7.3 Adaptation Formulas for the Linear Weights and the Positions and Spreads of Centers for RBF Network[a]

1. *Linear weights* (output layer)

$$\frac{\partial \mathscr{E}(n)}{\partial w_i(n)} = \sum_{j=1}^{N} e_j(n) G(\|\mathbf{x}_j - \mathbf{t}_i(n)\|_{C_i})$$

$$w_i(n+1) = w_i(n) - \eta_1 \frac{\partial \mathscr{E}(n)}{\partial w_i(n)}, \qquad i = 1, 2, \ldots, M$$

2. *Positions of centers* (hidden layer)

$$\frac{\partial \mathscr{E}(n)}{\partial \mathbf{t}_i(n)} = 2w_i(n) \sum_{j=1}^{N} e_j(n) G'(\|\mathbf{x}_j - \mathbf{t}_i(n)\|_{C_i}) \, \mathbf{\Sigma}_i^{-1}[\mathbf{x}_j - \mathbf{t}_i(n)]$$

$$\mathbf{t}_i(n+1) = \mathbf{t}_i(n) - \eta_2 \frac{\partial \mathscr{E}(n)}{\partial \mathbf{t}_i(n)}, \qquad i = 1, 2, \ldots, M$$

3. *Spreads of centers* (hidden layer)

$$\frac{\partial \mathscr{E}(n)}{\partial \mathbf{\Sigma}_i^{-1}(n)} = -w_i(n) \sum_{j=1}^{N} e_j(n) G'(\|\mathbf{x}_j - \mathbf{t}_i(n)\|_{C_i}) \mathbf{Q}_{ji}(n)$$

$$\mathbf{Q}_{ji}(n) = [\mathbf{x}_j - \mathbf{t}_i(n)][\mathbf{x}_j - \mathbf{t}_i(n)]^T$$

$$\mathbf{\Sigma}_i^{-1}(n+1) = \mathbf{\Sigma}_i^{-1}(n) - \eta_3 \frac{\partial \mathscr{E}(n)}{\partial \mathbf{\Sigma}_i^{-1}(n)}$$

[a] The term $e_j(n)$ is the error signal of output unit j at time n. The term $G'(\cdot)$ is the first derivative of the Green's function $G(\cdot)$ with respect to its argument.

parameter space to be searched to an already known useful area, which may be achieved by implementing a standard pattern-classification method as an RBF network (Lowe, 1991a). In so doing, the likelihood of converging to an undesirable local minimum in weight space is reduced. For example, we may begin with a *standard Gaussian classifier,* which assumes that each pattern in each class is drawn from a full Gaussian distribution.

An obvious question that arises at this stage of the discussion is: What can be gained by adapting the positions of the centers of the radial-basis functions? The answer to this question naturally depends on the application of interest. Nevertheless, on the basis of some results reported in the literature, there is practical merit to the idea of allowing the centers to move. Work done by Lowe (1989) on speech recognition using RBF networks indicates that nonlinear optimization of the parameters that define the activation functions of the hidden layer is beneficial when a minimal network configuration is required. However, according to Lowe, the same performance on generalization may be achieved by using a larger RBF network, that is, a network with a larger number of fixed centers in the hidden layer, and only adapting the output layer of the network by linear optimization.

Wettschereck and Dietterich (1992) have compared the performance of (Gaussian) radial-basis function networks with fixed centers to that of generalized radial-basis function networks with adjustable centers; in the latter case, the positions of the centers are determined by supervised learning. The performance comparison was made for the NETtalk task. The original NETtalk experiment was carried out by Sejnowski and Rosenberg (1987) using a multilayer perceptron trained with the back-propagation algorithm; the purpose of the experiment was to understand how a neural network could learn to map English spelling into its phonetic pronunciation. The experimental study by Wettschereck and Dietterich in the NETtalk domain may be summarized as follows:

- RBF networks (with unsupervised learning of the centers' locations and supervised learning of the output-layer weights) did *not* generalize nearly as well as multilayer perceptrons trained with the back-propagation algorithm.
- Generalized RBF networks (with supervised learning of the centers' locations as well as the output-layer weights) were able to exceed substantially the generalization performance of multilayer perceptrons.

7.12 Computer Experiment

In this section we use a computer experiment to illustrate the design of a regularization RBF network based on the use of fixed centers selected randomly from the training data. The computer experiment[8] involves a binary classification problem based on data drawn from two equiprobable overlapping two-dimensional Gaussian distributions corresponding to classes $\mathscr{C}_1$ and $\mathscr{C}_2$. Details of the Gaussian distributions are the same as those described in Section 6.9. Class $\mathscr{C}_1$ is characterized by mean vector $[0,0]^T$ and common variance 1, whereas class $\mathscr{C}_2$ is characterized by mean vector $[0,2]^T$ and common variance 4. The experiment described in this section may thus be viewed as the regularization RBF counterpart to the back-propagation learning experiment of Section 6.9.

With two classes $\mathscr{C}_1$ and $\mathscr{C}_2$, the regularization RBF network is constructed to have two output functions, one for each class. Also, binary-valued class indicator outputs are used as the desired output values, as shown by

$$d_k^{(p)} = \begin{cases} 1 & \text{if pattern } p \text{ belongs to class } \mathscr{C}_k \\ 0 & \text{otherwise} \end{cases}$$

where $k = 1, 2$.

Before we proceed with the experiment, however, we have to resolve the issue of an output decision rule for performing the pattern classification. In Yee and Haykin (1993) it is shown that the outputs of a regularization RBF network classifier provide estimates of the posterior class probabilities. This is true only under the condition that the network is trained with the binary-valued class indictor vector type of desired outputs. Accordingly, we may proceed to apply the decision rule of Eq. (6.47) for this class of networks:

Select the class corresponding to the maximum output function.

The method of random selection of fixed centers is tested with different values of regularization parameter λ. For a prescribed λ, Eq. (7.86) is used to compute the weight vector of the output layer in the RBF network, as shown by

$$\mathbf{w} = (\mathbf{G}^T\mathbf{G} + \lambda\mathbf{G}_0)^{-1}\mathbf{G}^T\mathbf{d}$$

where $\mathbf{G}$ is an N-by-M matrix whose jith element is equal to the radially symmetric function $G(\mathbf{x}_j;\mathbf{t}_i)$, and $\mathbf{G}_0$ is a symmetric M-by-M matrix whose jith element is equal to $G(\mathbf{t}_j;\mathbf{t}_i)$.

For each λ, the ensemble comprises 50 independent networks, each of which is tested against the same reference set of 1000 patterns. The norm weighting matrix $\mathbf{C}$ for a trial is assumed to be a diagonal matrix, defined by the diagonal elements of the sample covariance matrix that is computed from the particular trial's training input data.

[8] The results of the computer experiment described here are based on Yee (1992).

TABLE 7.4 Size of Hidden Layer M = 20 Centers: Average Probability of Correct Classification, P_c (%)

Ensemble Statistic	Regularization Parameter, λ					
	0	0.1	1	10	100	1000
Mean	80.01	80.26	80.48	80.14	78.79	76.83
Std. dev.[a]	1.20	1.14	1.00	0.98	1.43	2.64
Minimum	76.70	77.20	78.40	77.50	74.10	70.70
Maximum	81.80	81.90	82.20	81.60	80.50	80.10

[a] Std. dev.: Standard deviation.

Table 7.4 presents the ensemble statistics for the average probability of correct classification P_c, computed for the case of $M = 20$ centers that are randomly selected from $N = 200$ sized training input sets for each network trial. The ensemble statistics are computed for different values of the regularization parameter λ.

Table 7.5 presents the corresponding results computed for the case of a smaller regularization RBF network with $M = 10$ centers that are selected randomly for $N = 200$ training input sets.

Figure 7.7 displays the decision boundaries formed by the network outputs for a regularization parameter $\lambda = 1$, for which we have the best statistics. The two parts of Fig. 7.7 correspond to the best- and worst-performing network within the ensemble under test; both parts of the figure are for the case of $M = 20$ units.

Comparing the results of Table 7.4 with those of Table 7.5, we see that the classification performance of the regularization RBF network is only marginally improved as a result of doubling the number of centers. Moreover, we note from both Tables 7.4 and 7.5 that an RBF network trained in accordance with the method of fixed centers selected at random is relatively insensitive to the regularization parameter λ. This observation suggests that the use of randomly selected centers from a fixed training set is actually a regularization method in its own right!

7.13 Factorizable Radial-Basis Functions

From an implementation point of view, it would be highly attractive if the radial-basis functions used in the construction of a neural network are *factorizable.* Given such a property, we may then synthesize a multidimensional radial-basis function as the product of lower-dimensional (e.g., one-dimensional and two-dimensional) radial-basis functions. Indeed, *the only radial-basis function that is factorizable is the Gaussian function* (Poggio

TABLE 7.5 Size of Hidden Layer M = 10 Centers: Average Probability of Correct Classification, P_c (%)

Ensemble Statistic	Regularization Parameter, λ					
	0	0.1	1	10	100	1000
Mean	78.53	78.65	79.06	78.65	76.03	74.48
Std. dev.[a]	1.53	1.49	1.51	1.49	3.78	4.77
Minimum	75.00	75.50	75.70	74.30	64.30	61.30
Maximum	80.90	81.70	81.70	81.50	80.40	79.70

[a] Std. dev.: Standard deviation.

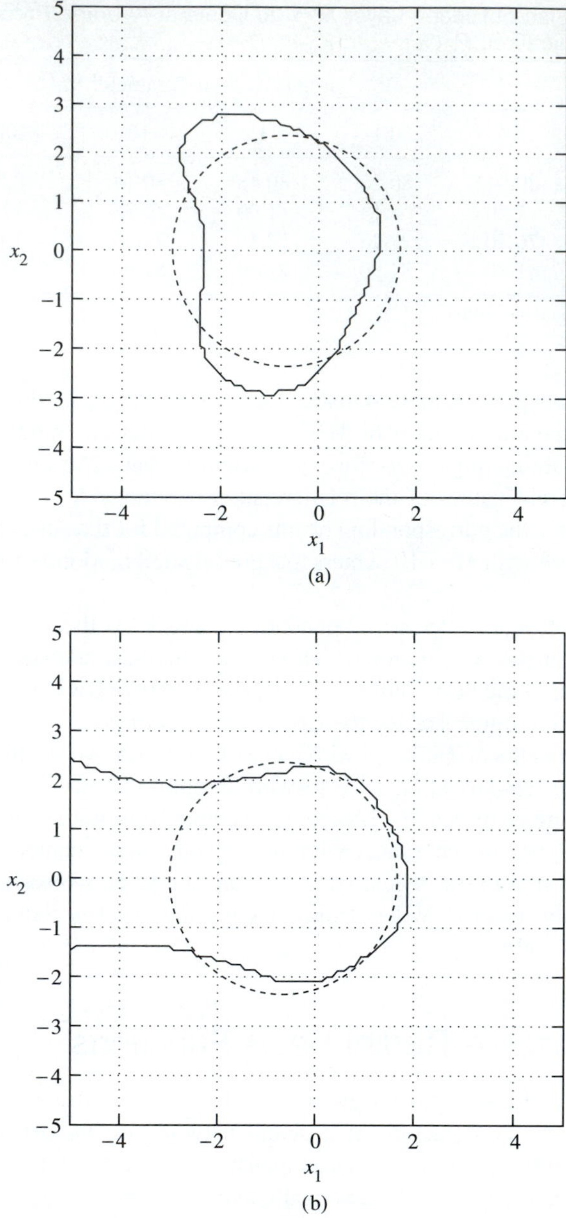

FIGURE 7.7 Decision boundaries constructed by RBF network for the computer experiment. (a) Best case. (b) Worst case.

and Girosi, 1990a, b). To demonstrate this important property of Gaussian radial-basis functions, consider the simple case of a Gaussian function in two dimensions:

$$\begin{aligned} G(\mathbf{x};\mathbf{t}) &= G(\|\mathbf{x}-\mathbf{t}\|^2) \\ &= e^{-\|\mathbf{x}-\mathbf{t}\|^2} \\ &= e^{-(x_1-t_1)^2-(x_2-t_2)^2} \\ &= e^{-(x_1-t_1)^2}e^{-(x_2-t_2)^2} \\ &= G(x_1;t_1)G(x_2;t_2) \end{aligned} \tag{7.118}$$

Equation (7.118) shows that a two-dimensional Gaussian activation function $G(\mathbf{x};\mathbf{t})$ with a center $\mathbf{t} = [t_1,t_2]^T$ is equivalent to the product of a pair of one-dimensional Gaussian activation functions $G(x_1;t_1)$ and $G(x_2;t_2)$, where x_1 and x_2 are the elements of the input vector $\mathbf{x}$, and t_1 and t_2 are the elements of the center $\mathbf{t}$.

We may readily generalize the result of Eq. (7.118) for the case of a multivariate Gaussian activation function $G(\mathbf{x};\mathbf{t})$ that computes the weighted norm, assuming that the weighting matrix $\mathbf{C}$ is a diagonal matrix. To be specific, suppose that we have

$$\mathbf{C} = \text{diag}[c_1, c_2, \ldots, c_p] \tag{7.119}$$

We may then factorize $G(\mathbf{x};\mathbf{t})$ as follows:

$$\begin{aligned} G(\mathbf{x};\mathbf{t}) &= G(\|\mathbf{x} - \mathbf{t}\|_C^2) \\ &= \prod_{k=1}^{p} \exp\left(-\frac{(x_k - t_k)^2}{2\sigma_k^2}\right) \end{aligned} \tag{7.120}$$

where the kth element t_k of the center $\mathbf{t}$ plays the role of a "mean." The variance σ_k^2 is defined in terms of the kth diagonal element of the matrix $\mathbf{C}$ by

$$\sigma_k^2 = \frac{1}{2c_k^2} \tag{7.121}$$

For the more general case of a norm weighting matrix $\mathbf{C}$ that is nondiagonal, we may proceed as follows. Referring to Eq. (7.89), we first express the weighted norm $\|\mathbf{x} - \mathbf{t}\|_C^2$ as

$$\begin{aligned} \|\mathbf{x} - \mathbf{t}\|_C^2 &= (\mathbf{x} - \mathbf{t})^T\mathbf{C}^T\mathbf{C}(\mathbf{x} - \mathbf{t}) \\ &= (\mathbf{x} - \mathbf{t})^T\boldsymbol{\Sigma}^{-1}(\mathbf{x} - \mathbf{t}) \end{aligned} \tag{7.122}$$

where

$$\boldsymbol{\Sigma}^{-1} = \mathbf{C}^T\mathbf{C}$$

In the context of a multivariate Gaussian function, the matrix $\boldsymbol{\Sigma}$ plays the role of a covariance matrix. In any event, we use the *similarity transformation* to factorize the inverse matrix $\boldsymbol{\Sigma}^{-1}$ in terms of its eigenvalues $\lambda_1, \lambda_2, \ldots, \lambda_p$ and associated eigenvectors $\mathbf{q}_1, \mathbf{q}_2, \ldots, \mathbf{q}_p$ as follows (Strang, 1980):

$$\boldsymbol{\Sigma}^{-1} = \mathbf{Q}\boldsymbol{\Lambda}\mathbf{Q}^T \tag{7.123}$$

where

$$\mathbf{Q} = [\mathbf{q}_1, \mathbf{q}_2, \ldots, \mathbf{q}_p] \tag{7.124}$$

$$\boldsymbol{\Lambda} = \text{diag}[\lambda_1, \lambda_2, \ldots, \lambda_p] \tag{7.125}$$

Accordingly, we may rewrite the weighted norm of Eq. (7.122) in the new form

$$\|\mathbf{x} - \mathbf{t}\|_C^2 = (\mathbf{x}' - \mathbf{t}')^T\boldsymbol{\Lambda}(\mathbf{x}' - \mathbf{t}') \tag{7.126}$$

where

$$\mathbf{x}' = \mathbf{Q}^T\mathbf{x} \tag{7.127}$$

and

$$\mathbf{t}' = \mathbf{Q}^T\mathbf{t} \tag{7.128}$$

We now recognize that the matrix $\boldsymbol{\Lambda}$ is a diagonal matrix. We may therefore use our previous result to factorize the multivariate Gaussian activation function $G(\mathbf{x},\mathbf{t})$

as follows:

$$G(\mathbf{x};\mathbf{t}) = \prod_{k=1}^{p} \exp\left(-\frac{(x_k' - t_k')^2}{2\sigma_k^2}\right) \tag{7.129}$$

where

$$x_k' = \mathbf{q}_k^T \mathbf{x} \tag{7.130}$$

$$t_k' = \mathbf{q}_k^T \mathbf{t} \tag{7.131}$$

$$\sigma_k^2 = \frac{1}{2\lambda_k} \tag{7.132}$$

Knowing the norm weighting matrix **C**, we may precompute the transformed centers and the spreads. Then, the multivariate Gaussian function $G(\mathbf{x};\mathbf{t})$ may be computed using a set of one-dimensional Gaussian functions as shown in the block diagram of Fig. 7.8.

7.14 Discussion

The structure of an RBF network is unusual in that the constitution of its hidden units is entirely different from that of its output units. With radial-basis functions providing the foundation for the design of the hidden units, the theory of RBF networks is linked intimately with that of radial-basis functions, which is nowadays one of the main fields of study in numerical analysis (Singh, 1992). Another interesting point to note is that with linear weights of the output layer providing a set of adjustable parameters, much can be gained by ploughing through the extensive literature on linear adaptive filtering (Haykin, 1991).

Curse of Dimensionality

Kernel-type approximations, such as standard RBF networks, suffer from the so-called *curse of dimensionality,* referring to the exponential increase in the number of hidden units with the dimension of the input space. The curse of dimensionality becomes particu-

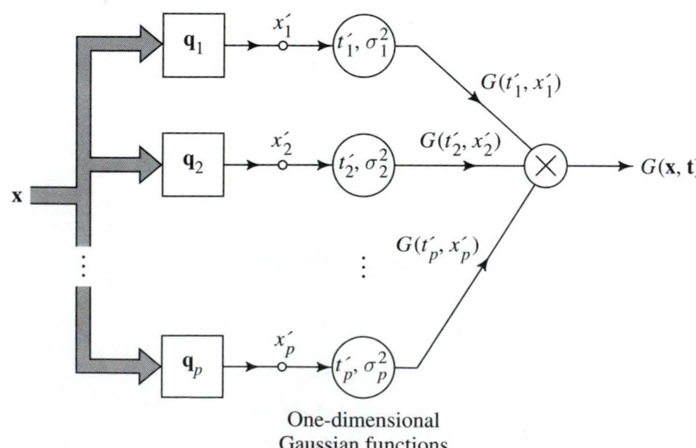

FIGURE 7.8 Factorization of radial-basis function for the general case of a nondiagonal norm-weighting matrix.

larly acute in trying to solve large-scale problems such as image recognition and speech recognition. Standard RBF networks, using fixed Gaussian radial-basis functions with their exponents based on the Euclidean distance matrix, operate by constructing *hyperspheres* around the centers of the basis functions, and therefore suffer from the curse of dimensionality. We may alleviate this problem by replacing the hyperspheres with *hyperellipses* that have adjustable orientations. This is achieved, for example, by using generalized Gaussian radial-basis functions based on the notion of a weighted norm (Poggio and Girosi, 1990a; Lowe, 1989). Thus, in the case of hypersurface estimation (reconstruction), such a scheme permits the use of a smaller number of hidden units, but more parameters to adapt. Saha et al. (1991) describe another scheme referred to as *oriented nonradial-basis function* (ONRBF) *networks,* in which case the exponent of the Gaussian radial-basis function is replaced by a polynomial. Specifically, the activation function of the ith hidden unit is defined by

$$\varphi_i(\mathbf{x}) = \exp(-\|\mathbf{T}_i[x_1, x_2, \ldots, x_p, 1]^T\|^2) \tag{7.133}$$

where $x_1, x_2, \ldots, x_p$ are the elements of the input vector $\mathbf{x}$, and $\mathbf{T}_i$ is a p-by-$(p + 1)$ matrix. The matrices $\mathbf{T}_i$, $i = 1, 2, \ldots, M$, transform the input vectors, and these transformations correspond to translation, scaling, and rotation of the input vectors.

Orthogonal Least-Squares Method

Another important issue that occupied much of our attention in this chapter was the use of regularization to discourage the RBF network from overfitting the training data. An alternative way in which this objective may be achieved is to use the *orthogonal least squares* (OLS) *learning procedure* (Chen et al., 1991). This method is rooted in *linear regression models,* according to which a desired response $d(n)$ is defined by (Haykin, 1991):

$$d(n) = \sum_{i=1}^{M} x_i(n)a_i + e(n), \qquad n = 1, 2, \ldots, N \tag{7.134}$$

where the a_i are the *model parameters,* the $x_i(n)$ are the *regressors,* and $e(n)$ is the *residue* (error). Using matrix notation, we may rewrite Eq. (7.134) as

$$\mathbf{d} = \mathbf{X}\mathbf{a} + \mathbf{e} \tag{7.135}$$

where

$$\mathbf{d} = [d(1), d(2), \ldots, d(N)]^T$$

$$\mathbf{a} = [a_1, a_2, \ldots, a_M]^T$$

$$\mathbf{X} = [\mathbf{x}_1, \mathbf{x}_2, \ldots, \mathbf{x}_M]$$

$$\mathbf{x}_i = [x_i(1), x_i(2), \ldots, x_i(N)]^T, \qquad 1 \le i \le M$$

$$\mathbf{e} = [e(1), e(2), \ldots, e(N)]^T$$

The regressor vectors $\mathbf{x}_i$ form a set of basis vectors, and the least-squares solution of Eq. (7.135) satisfies the condition that the matrix product $\mathbf{Xa}$ be the *projection* of the desired response vector $\mathbf{d}$ onto the space spanned by the basis vectors—hence the name of the method. The OLS method involves the transformation of the regressor vectors $\mathbf{x}_1, \mathbf{x}_2, \ldots, \mathbf{x}_M$ into a corresponding set of orthogonal basis vectors denoted by $\mathbf{u}_1, \mathbf{u}_2, \ldots, \mathbf{u}_M$. For example, the standard *Gram–Schmidt orthogonalization procedure* may be used to perform this transformation, as shown by

$$\mathbf{u}_1 = \mathbf{x}_1$$

$$\alpha_{ik} = \frac{\mathbf{u}_i^T \mathbf{x}_k}{\mathbf{u}_i^T \mathbf{u}_k}, \qquad 1 \le i < k$$

$$\mathbf{u}_k = \mathbf{x}_k - \sum_{i=1}^{k-1} \alpha_{ik} \mathbf{x}_i$$

where $k = 2, \ldots, M$.

In the context of a neural network, the OLS learning procedure chooses the radial-basis function centers $\mathbf{t}_1, \mathbf{t}_2, \ldots, \mathbf{t}_M$ as a subset of the training data vectors $\mathbf{x}_1, \mathbf{x}_2, \ldots, \mathbf{x}_N$, where $M < N$. The centers are determined one-by-one in a well-defined manner (e.g., following the Gram–Schmidt orthogonalization procedure), until a network of adequate performance is constructed. At each step of the procedure, the increment to the explained variance of the desired response is maximized. In so doing, the OLS learning procedure will generally produce an RBF network whose hidden layer is smaller than that of an RBF network with randomly selected centers, for a specified level of unexplained variance of the desired response. Furthermore, the problem of numerical ill-conditioning encountered in the random selection of centers method is avoided. Thus, the OLS learning procedure provides another useful approach for the construction of a parsimonious RBF network with good numerical properties.

7.15 Applications

Radial-basis function (RBF) networks have been applied to a wide variety of problems, though perhaps not as many as those involving multilayer perceptrons. Nevertheless, the range of applications of RBF networks covered in the literature is quite broad, as illustrated by the following representative list:

- Image processing (Saha et al., 1991; Poggio and Edelman, 1990)
- Speech recognition (Ng and Lippmann, 1991; Niranjan and Fallside, 1990)
- Time-series analysis (He and Lapedes, 1991; Kadirkamanathan et al., 1991; Moody and Darken, 1989; Broomhead and Lowe, 1988)
- Adaptive equalization (Chen et al., 1992a, b; Cid-Sueiro and Figueiras-Vidal, 1993; Kassam and Cha, 1993)
- Radar point-source location (Webb, 1993)
- Medical diagnosis (Lowe and Webb, 1990)

In this section we focus on two specific applications of RBF networks, one relating to the prediction of a chaotic time series, and the other relating to adaptive equalization of communication channels.

Prediction of Chaotic Time Series

Broomhead and Lowe (1988) and Kadirkamanathan et al. (1991), have used RBF networks successfully for the prediction of a *chaotic* time series.[9] The chaotic time series considered therein is the *logistic map* whose dynamics is governed by the difference equation:

[9] For a discussion of chaos, see Chapter 14.

$$x_n = 4x_{n-1}(1 - x_{n-1}) \tag{7.136}$$

This is a first-order nonlinear process where only the previous sample x_{n-1} determines the value of the present sample. The logistic map is known to be chaotic on the interval [0,1]. The RBF network used by Broomhead and Lowe was constructed as follows. The centers of the radial-basis function were chosen to be uniformly spaced on (0,1); the number of centers was an adjustable parameter. The linear weights of the output layer were computed using the pseudoinverse of the matrix **G** in accordance with Eq. (7.88); the pseudoinverse matrix $\mathbf{G}^+$ was itself computed using the singular value decomposition of matrix **G**. Figure 7.9 shows the actual and predicted outputs of the network over the interval [0,1] for one iterate.

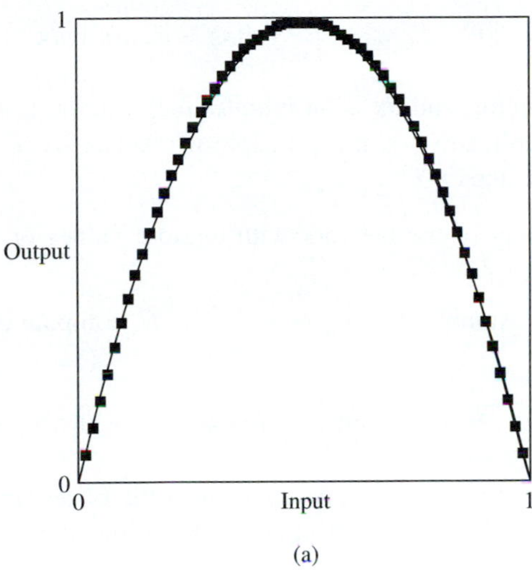

(a)

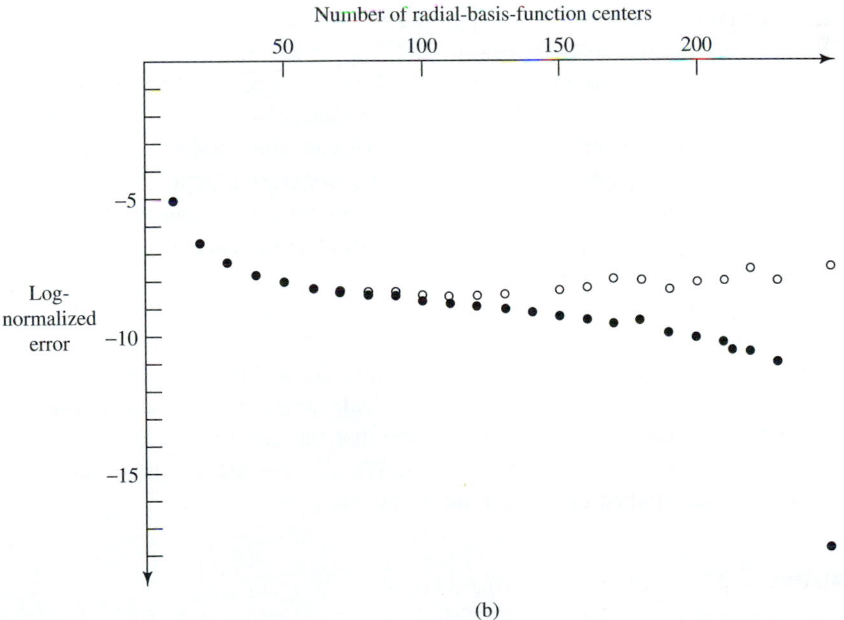

(b)

FIGURE 7.9 The quadratic map. (a) A figure showing the actual (solid lines) and predicted (filled squares) outputs of the network over the interval [0,1] for one iterate. (b) The log-normalized error showing the training (filled circles) and recognition (open circles) data as a function of the number of radial-basis function centers. (From D. S. Broomhead and D. Lowe, 1988; British Crown Copyright.)

Kadirkamanathan et al. (1991) use a sequential adaptation algorithm for Gaussian RBF networks, which is based on the *principle of successive F projections.* This is a general method of choosing a posterior function estimate of an unknown function f when there exists a prior estimate and new information about f in the form of constraints. The principle of successive F projections states that, of all the functions that satisfy the constraints, we should choose the posterior F_n that has the least L^2 norm, $\|F_n - F_{n-1}\|$, where F_{n-1} is the prior estimate of f. That is,

$$F_n = \arg \min_F \|F - F_{n-1}\| \text{ such that } F_n \in H_I \tag{7.137}$$

where H_I is the set of functions that satisfy the new constraints, and

$$\|F - F_{n-1}\|^2 = \int_{\mathbf{x}\in X} |F(\mathbf{x}) - F_{n-1}(\mathbf{x})|^2 \, d\mathbf{x} \tag{7.138}$$

where $\mathbf{x}$ is the input vector, and $d\mathbf{x}$ is an infinitesimal volume in the input space X. For RBF networks, the application of the principle of successive F projections yields an algorithm that has two steps:

- Initialize parameters of the network with random values or values based on prior knowledge.
- For each training example $(\mathbf{x}_j,d_j)$, $j = 1, 2, \ldots, N$, compute the posterior parameter estimate

$$\hat{\boldsymbol{\theta}}_j = \arg \min_{\boldsymbol{\theta}} \int_{\mathbf{x}\in X} |F(\mathbf{x},\boldsymbol{\theta}) - F(\mathbf{x};\boldsymbol{\theta}_{j-1})|^2 \, d\mathbf{x} \tag{7.139}$$

  where $(\mathbf{x}_j,d_j)$, for $j = 1, 2, \ldots, N$, constitutes the observation (training) set, $\boldsymbol{\theta}$ is the parameter set of the network, and $F(\mathbf{x},\boldsymbol{\theta})$ is the function constructed by the network.

There are two good reasons for applying the sequential adaptation algorithm to an RBF network with Gaussian hidden units (Kadirkamanathan et al., 1991). First, the method of successive F projections minimizes the volume change in the hypersurface as new patterns are learned. Since an RBF network with Gaussian hidden units provides a local approximation to the functional relationship between the desired response and input patterns, it follows that only a few hidden units undergo adaptation. The algorithm is therefore quite stable. Second, for an RBF network with Gaussian hidden units, the L^2-norm measure of volume change in the hypersurface lends itself to an analytic solution.

Kadirkamanathan et al. (1991) used an RBF network with the successive F-projections algorithm to predict the chaotic time series defined by the logistic map of Eq. (7.136). The network had a single input node and 8 Gaussian hidden units. Figure 7.10 shows the result on the map constructed by the network for 0, 20, and 60 samples; the samples used to do the training are also shown in Fig. 7.10. Each sample was presented to the network only once for training. From Fig. 7.10 we see that the algorithm provides a close fit to the logistic map after training on 20 samples. We also see that the algorithm is stable in that the map is maintained up to training on 60 samples.

Adaptive Equalization

Adaptive equalization is a well-established technique used in digital communication systems to combat the effects of imperfections in communication channels (Qureshi, 1985). The equalizer is positioned at the front end of the receiver, as depicted in the baseband discrete-time model of Fig. 7.11. A data sequence $\{a(n)\}$ is transmitted through a dispersive channel whose *transfer function* is modeled by

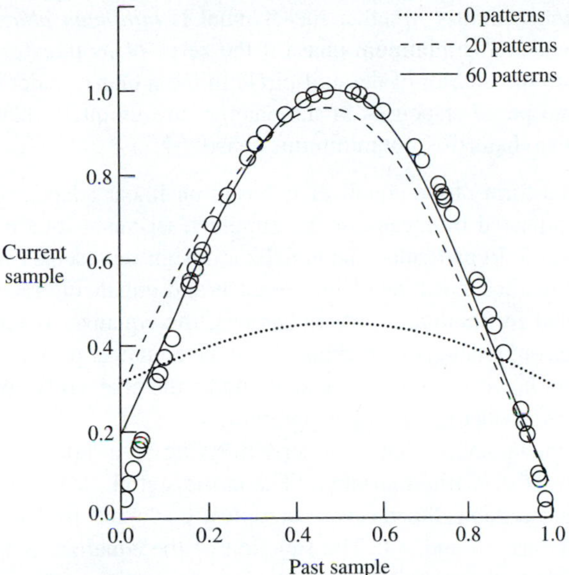

FIGURE 7.10 Map constructed by RBF network using the successive *F*-projections algorithm; small open circles are the samples used to train the network. (From Kadirkamanathan et al., 1991, with permission of Morgan Kaufmann.)

$$H(z) = \sum_{j=0}^{l} h_j z^{-j} \tag{7.140}$$

where the $\{h_j | j = 0, 1, \ldots, l\}$ represent a set of coefficients characterizing the channel, and z^{-1} is the unit-delay operator. The data sequence $\{a(n)\}$ is assumed to consist of a string of equiprobable and statistically independent binary symbols 0 and 1, represented by the levels -1 and $+1$, respectively. The channel output $s(n)$ is corrupted by front-end *receiver noise* $\nu(n)$ that is commonly modeled as *additive white Gaussian noise*. The received signal is

$$x(n) = s(n) + \nu(n) \tag{7.141}$$

whose two components are uncorrelated with each other. The signal $x(n)$ is applied to an equalizer, positioned at the front end of the receiver. The equalizer is designed to produce an *estimate* $\hat{a}(n)$ of the original symbol $a(n)$.

There are three factors to be considered in the design of the equalizer:

1. *Intersymbol interference* (ISI), which is a signal-dependent form of interference that is caused by the dispersive effects of the channel; it is because of ISI that the channel output $s(n)$ is markedly different from the transmitted symbol $a(n)$.
2. *Receiver noise,* which is always present.

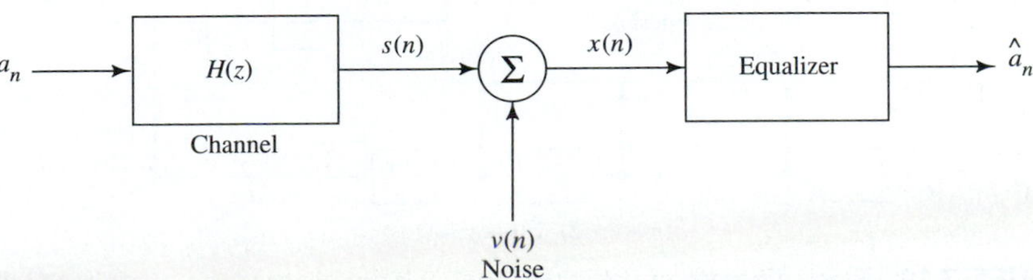

FIGURE 7.11 Baseband discrete-time model of data transmission system.

3. *Type of channel,* that is, whether the channel is *minimum phase* or *nonminimum phase.* The channel is minimum phase if the zeros of its transfer function $H(z)$ are all confined to the interior of the unit circle in the z plane; under this condition, the amplitude and phase responses of the channel are uniquely related to each other. Otherwise, the channel is nonminimum phase.

The conventional form of the equalizer is based on linear adaptive filter theory, with its weights being adjusted by means of the simple least-mean-square (LMS) algorithm discussed in Chapter 5. In particular, the equalizer design represents the "best" compromise between eliminating intersymbol interference and enhancing receiver noise. In the absence of noise and for minimum-phase channels, the equalizer operates as an *inverse model* such that the combination of the channel and the equalizer provides "distortionless" transmission. When, however, noise is present and/or the channel is nonminimum phase, the use of an inverse model is no longer optimum.

An alternative viewpoint to that of inverse filtering is to approach the equalization process as a *pattern-classification* problem (Theodoridis et al., 1992). For the simple case of bipolar data transmission, the received samples, corrupted by ISI and noise, would have to be classified as -1 and $+1$. The function of the equalizer is therefore to assign each received sample to the correct decision region. According to this viewpoint, a linear equalizer is equivalent to a linear classifier. However, in realistic situations where noise is present in the received signal and/or the communication channel is nonminimum phase, it has been shown by Gibson and Cowan (1990) that the optimum classifier is in fact nonlinear.

In order to see how the design of a nonlinear adaptive equalizer can be based on neural networks, consider first the block diagram of Fig. 7.12, which describes a *decision-feedback* equalizer. The equalizer consists of a nonlinear filter with *feedforward* inputs denoted by $x(n), x(n-1), \ldots, x(n-m)$ and *feedback* inputs denoted by $a(n-\tau-1)$, $a(n-\tau-2), \ldots, a(n-\tau-k)$, where $x(n)$ is the channel output at time n, and $a(n-\tau)$ is the equalizer output representing an estimate of the transmitted symbol $a(n)$ delayed by τ symbols. The equalizer output is produced by passing the nonlinear filter output through a *hard limiter,* whereby decisions are made on a symbol-by-symbol basis. Chen et al. (1992a) have derived an optimum form of the decision feedback equalizer shown in Fig. 7.12 for the channel described in Eq. (7.140), as described next.

For a channel modeled as a finite-duration impulse response (FIR) filter of length l as in Eq. (7.140) and an equalizer of feedforward order m as shown in Fig. 7.12, there are

$$N_s = 2^{l+m} \tag{7.142}$$

combinations of the channel input sequence

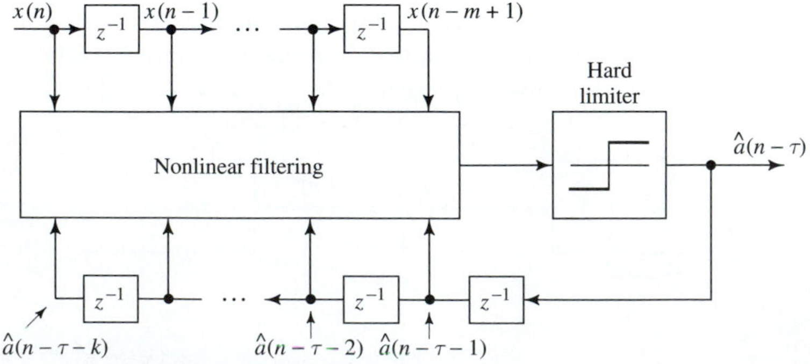

FIGURE 7.12 Block diagram of decision-feedback equalizer using a nonlinear filter.

$$\mathbf{a}(n) = [a(n), a(n-1), \ldots, a(n-m+1-l)]^T \tag{7.143}$$

Thus, the channel output vector

$$\mathbf{s}(n) = [s(n), s(n-1), \ldots, s(n-m+1)]^T \tag{7.144}$$

has N_s desired states; the vector $\mathbf{s}(n)$ is the noise-free version of the vector of feedforward inputs applied to the nonlinear filter in Fig. 7.12. It is sufficient to consider a feedback order

$$k = l + m - 1 - \tau \tag{7.145}$$

where τ is an integer representing the number of symbols by which the equalizer output is delayed with respect to the channel input. Let it be initially assumed that the decision-feedback equalizer in Fig. 7.12 uses the correct feedback vector

$$\mathbf{a}_f(n-\tau) = [a(n-\tau-1), a(n-\tau-2), \ldots, a(n-\tau-k)]^T \tag{7.146}$$

Let

$$N_f = 2^k \tag{7.147}$$

denote the number of combinations of the feedback vector $\mathbf{a}_f(n-\tau)$, which are written as

$$\{\mathbf{a}_{f,j} \mid j = 1, 2, \ldots, N_f\} \tag{7.148}$$

The set of desired channel states $S_{m,\tau}$ may now be divided into N_f subsets conditioned on $\mathbf{a}_f(n-\tau)$, as shown by

$$S_{m,\tau} = \bigcup_{1 \le j \le N_f} S_{m,\tau,j} \tag{7.149}$$

where

$$S_{m,\tau,j} = S^+_{m,\tau,j} \bigcup S^-_{m,\tau,j} \tag{7.150}$$

with $S^+_{m,\tau,j}$ and $S^-_{m,\tau,j}$ themselves defined by, respectively,

$$S^+_{m,\tau,j} = \left\{ \mathbf{s}(n) \middle| a(n-\tau) = +1 \bigcap \mathbf{a}_f(n-\tau) = \mathbf{a}_{f,j} \right\} \tag{7.151}$$

and

$$S^-_{m,\tau,j} = \left\{ \mathbf{s}(n) \middle| a(n-\tau) = -1 \bigcap \mathbf{a}_f(n-\tau) = \mathbf{a}_{f,j} \right\} \tag{7.152}$$

We are now ready to define an optimum solution for the equalizer output $a(n-\tau)$ that is conditioned on $\mathbf{a}_f(n-\tau) = \mathbf{a}_{f,j}$. Specifically, following Chen et al. (1992a, b), we may write

$$a(n-\tau) = \begin{cases} 1, & F_B[\mathbf{x}(n) | \mathbf{a}_f(n-\tau) = \mathbf{a}_{f,j}] \ge 0 \\ -1, & F_B[\mathbf{x}(n) | \mathbf{a}_f(n-\tau) = \mathbf{a}_{f,j}] < 0 \end{cases} \tag{7.153}$$

where $F_B(\cdot|\cdot)$ is an optimum conditional decision function defined by

$$F_B(\mathbf{x}(n) | \mathbf{a}_f(n-\tau) = \mathbf{a}_{f,j}) = \sum_{\mathbf{x}_i^+ \in S^+_{m,\tau,j}} \alpha \exp\left(-\frac{1}{2\sigma_\nu^2} \|\mathbf{x}(n) - \mathbf{x}_i^+\|^2 \right)$$
$$- \sum_{\mathbf{x}_i^- \in S^-_{m,\tau,j}} \alpha \exp\left(-\frac{1}{2\sigma_\nu^2} \|\mathbf{x}(n) - \mathbf{x}_i^-\|^2 \right) \tag{7.154}$$

where α is an arbitrary constant, σ_ν^2 is the variance of the noise $\nu(n)$, and $\mathbf{x}(n)$ is the feedforward input vector of the equalizer,

$$\mathbf{x}(n) = [x(n), x(-1), \ldots, x(n - m + 1)]^T \tag{7.155}$$

The important point to note is that the feedback vector does not enter Eq. (7.154); it is merely used to narrow down the number of desired states that would have to be considered at each time n (Chen et al., 1992a, b). In particular, at each n only $2^{\tau+1}$ states are required to compute the decision function of Eq. (7.154). On the other hand, all the N_s states would be required without decision feedback. Furthermore, it is shown in Chen et al. (1992a, b) that $m = \tau + 1$ is sufficient for decision feedback equalization. In general, we have $m > \tau + 1$ in the case of an adaptive equalizer without decision feedback. Hence, the use of decision feedback can result in a reduction in computational complexity of the adaptive equalizer by a factor larger than 2^l, where l is the memory span of the channel. According to Chen et al. (1992a, b), decision feedback improves the equalizer's performance by increasing the minimum distance between the Gaussian centers $\mathbf{x}_i^+$ and $\mathbf{x}_i^-$ at each time n.

The decision function defined in Eq. (7.154) is readily implemented using an RBF network. Specifically, comparing Eq. (7.154) with (7.153), we may make the following observations on the constitution of the RBF network (Chen et al., 1992a, b):

- The number M of hidden units is set equal to N_s, where N_s is defined by Eq. (7.142).
- The hidden units are grouped in accordance with the conditional subsets $S_{m,\tau,j}$, and their centers $\mathbf{t}_i$ define the corresponding channel states $\mathbf{s}_i \in S_{m,\tau,j}$. In effect, the feedback vector determines which subset of hidden units should be active at any particular time n.
- The radial-basis functions are Gaussian functions centered on $\mathbf{t}_i$, and with all their widths chosen equal to σ_ν (i.e., the standard deviation of the receiver noise).
- The weights of the output layer are set equal to -1 or $+1$.

Thus, the RBF decision-feedback equalizer described here represents a novel solution to the adaptive equalization problem. It is of interest to note that this equalizer structure is similar to the general block decision-feedback equalizer proposed by Williamson et al. (1992).

Two adaptive approaches are described by Chen et al. (1992,a b) to realize decision feedback equalization using the RBF network. The first method estimates the channel model based on the LMS algorithm, and then uses the channel estimate to compute a subset of centers for use in the RBF network. The second method uses a clustering technique to estimate the channel states directly. The first method requires a shorter training sequence, while the second method offers a lower computational load and greater immunity to nonlinear channel distortion.

Chen et al. (1992b) have used computer simulation to investigate the performance of an RBF decision feedback equalizer and compare its performance with that of a standard decision-feedback equalizer and a maximum-likelihood sequential estimator known as the Viterbi algorithm. The investigations were carried out for both stationary and nonstationary communication channels; the highly nonstationary channel considered was chosen to be representative of a mobile radio environment. The results of the investigations reported by Chen et al. (1992b) may be summarized as follows:

- The maximum-likelihood sequential estimator provides the best attainable performance for the case of a stationary channel; the corresponding performance of the RBF decision-feedback equalizer is worse off by about 2 dB, but better than that of the standard decision-feedback equalizer by roughly an equal amount.

- In the case of a highly nonstationary channel, the RBF decision-feedback equalizer outperforms the maximum-likelihood sequential estimator; it is suggested that performance degradation in the latter case may be due to the accumulation of tracking errors.

The results of this study appear to show that the RBF decision-feedback equalizer is robust and provides a viable solution for the equalization of highly nonstationary channels.

PROBLEMS

7.1 In Example 2 we pointed out that for the differential operator

$$\mathbf{P}F(x) = \frac{d^2}{dx^2}F(x)$$

the function $F(x)$ that minimizes the cost functional $\mathscr{E}(F)$ consists of a cubic spline. Develop the details of this statement.

7.2 The multiquadric

$$\varphi(r) = (r^2 + c^2)^{1/2}, \qquad c > 0;\ r \geq 0$$

and the inverse multiquadric

$$\varphi(r) = \frac{1}{(r^2 + c^2)^{1/2}}, \qquad c > 0;\ r \geq 0$$

provide two possible choices for radial-basis functions. An RBF network using the inverse multiquadric constructs local approximation to nonlinear input–output mapping. On the other hand, the use of a multiquadric represents a counterexample to this property of RBF networks. Justify the validity of these two statements.

7.3 The set of values given in Section 7.8 for the weight vector $\mathbf{w}$ of the RBF network of Fig. 7.6 presents one possible solution for the XOR problem. Investigate another set of values for the weight vector $\mathbf{w}$ for solving this problem.

7.4 In Section 7.8 we presented a solution of the XOR problem using an RBF network with two hidden units. In this problem we consider an exact solution of the XOR problem using an RBF network with four hidden units, with each radial-basis function center being determined by each piece of input data. The four possible input patterns are defined by (0,0), (0,1), (1,1), (1,0), which represent the cyclically ordered corners of a square.

(a) Construct the interpolation matrix $\boldsymbol{\Phi}$ for the resulting RBF network. Hence, compute the inverse matrix $\boldsymbol{\Phi}^{-1}$.

(b) Calculate the linear weights of the output layer of the network.

7.5 The *method of successive approximations* (He and Lapedes, 1991) is based on partitioning the N centers given for strict interpolation into N' groups of L centers each. The L centers of each group are selected randomly from the training input data, which are used to compute the first set of linear weights $\{b_{ji} | i = 1, \ldots, L;\ j = 1, \ldots, N'\}$. Next, each group of basis functions and its associated set of linear weights is viewed to be a *composite* basis function. The method of fixed centers is again applied to the set of N' composite basis functions to yield a second set of linear weights $\{a_j | j = 1, \ldots, N'\}$. The overall result, for the case of a single output node, is thus described as follows:

$$F(\mathbf{x}) = \sum_{j=1}^{N'} \left[a_j \sum_{i=1}^{L} b_{ji} G_{ji}(\mathbf{x}) \right]$$

where

$$G_{ji}(\mathbf{x}) = G(\mathbf{x}; \mathbf{x}_{ji})$$

(a) Show that the learning-time complexity for the successive approximation method is roughly $N'NL' + NN'^2$ compared to N^3 for strict interpolation.

(b) After training is completed, the two layers of linear weights can be collapsed into a single layer. Compute the linear weights of such an equivalent layer.

7.6 Compare the Boolean limiting version of an RBF network with that of a multilayer perceptron.

7.7 In this problem we continue with the computer experiment in Section 7.12 to study the method of strict interpolation for the design of an RBF network used as a binary pattern classifier. The purpose of the experiment is twofold:

- To demonstrate that the generalization performance of the network so trained is relatively poor
- To demonstrate that the generalization performance of the network can be improved using regularization

The network is intended to solve the binary pattern-recognition problem described in Section 7.12, where the requirement is to classify data drawn from a mixture model consisting of two equiprobable overlapping two-dimensional Gaussian distributions. One distribution has a mean vector $[0,0]^T$ and common variance 1, whereas the other distribution has a mean vector $[0,2]^T$ and common variance 4. The "select class with maximum function output" decision rule is used for the classification.

(a) Consider a strict interpolation network using $N = 20$ centers (selected at random). Compute the mean, standard deviation, minimum and maximum values of the average probability of correct classification P_c for different values of regularization parameter $\lambda = 0, 0.1, 1, 10, 100, 1000$. For the computation of ensemble statistics, use 50 independent network trials per ensemble, with each one tested against a fixed reference set of 1000 patterns.

(b) Construct the decision boundary computed for the configuration described in part (a) for regularization parameter $\lambda = 0$.

(c) Repeat the computations described in part (a) for $N = 100$ centers (selected at random).

(d) Construct the decision boundary computed for part (c) for regularization parameter $\lambda = 10$.

(e) In light of your results, discuss the merit of strict interpolation as a method for the design of RBF networks, and the role of regularization in the performance of the network as a pattern classifier.

(f) Compare your results with those presented in Section 7.12 that were computed using the method of fixed centers selected at random. Hence, confirm the notion that the latter method is superior to strict interpolation for the design of RBF networks.

7.8 It may be argued that in the case of the experiment described in Section 7.12 involving the classification of a pair of Gaussian-distributed classes, the RBF network considered there was able to perform well since it is using Gaussian radial-basis functions to approximate the underlying Gaussian class conditional distributions. In this problem we use a computer experiment to explore the design of a strict-interpolation Gaussian RBF network for distinctly discontinuous class conditional distributions. Specifically, consider two equiprobable classes $\mathscr{C}_1$ and $\mathscr{C}_2$ whose distributions are described by, respectively:

- $U(\mathscr{C}_1)$, where $\mathscr{C}_1 \triangleq \Omega_1$ is a circle of radius $r = 2.34$ centered at $\mathbf{x}_c = [-2,30]^T$
- $U(\mathscr{C}_2)$, where $\mathscr{C}_2 \subset \mathbb{R}^2$ is a square region centered at $\mathbf{x}_c$ with side length $r = \sqrt{2\pi}$

Here $U(\Omega)$ denotes a uniform distribution over $\Omega \subset \mathbb{R}^2$. These parameters are chosen so that the decision region for class $\mathscr{C}_1$ is the same as in the Gaussian-distributed case considered in Section 7.12. Investigate the use of regularization as a means of improving the classification performance of a Gaussian RBF network using strict interpolation.

7.9 It may be argued, by virtue of the central limit theorem, that for an RBF network the output produced by the network in response to a random input vector may be approximated by a Gaussian distribution, and that the approximation gets better as the number of centers in the network is increased. Investigate the validity of this notion.

7.10 Consider the cost functional

$$\mathscr{E}(F^*) = \sum_{i=1}^{N} \left[d_i - \sum_{j=1}^{M} w_j G(\|\mathbf{x}_j - \mathbf{t}_i\|) \right]^2 + \lambda \|\mathbf{P}F^*\|^2$$

which refers to the approximating function

$$F^*(\mathbf{x}) = \sum_{i=1}^{M} w_i G(\|\mathbf{x} - \mathbf{t}_i\|)$$

Using the Fréchet differential, show that the cost functional $\mathscr{E}(F^*)$ is minimized when

$$(\mathbf{G}^T\mathbf{G} + \lambda \mathbf{G}_0)\mathbf{w} = \mathbf{G}^T\mathbf{d}$$

where the N-by-M matrix $\mathbf{G}$, the M-by-M matrix $\mathbf{G}_0$, the M-by-1 vector $\mathbf{w}$, and the N-by-1 vector $\mathbf{d}$ are defined by Eqs. (7.82), (7.85), (7.83), and (7.49), respectively.

7.11 Suppose that we define

$$(\mathbf{P}^*\mathbf{P})_{\mathrm{U}} = \sum_{k=0}^{\infty} (-1)^k \frac{\nabla_{\mathrm{U}}^{2k}}{k!2^k}$$

where

$$\nabla_{\mathrm{U}}^2 = \sum_{j=1}^{p} \sum_{i=1}^{p} u_{ji} \frac{\partial^2}{\partial x_j \partial x_i}$$

The p-by-p matrix $\mathbf{U}$, with its jith element denoted by u_{ji}, is symmetric and positive definite. Hence the inverse matrix $\mathbf{U}^{-1}$ exists, and so it permits the following decomposition via the similarity transformation:

$$\begin{aligned} \mathbf{U}^{-1} &= \mathbf{V}^T\mathbf{D}\mathbf{V} \\ &= \mathbf{V}^T\mathbf{D}^{1/2}\mathbf{D}^{1/2}\mathbf{V} \\ &= \mathbf{C}^T\mathbf{C} \end{aligned}$$

where $\mathbf{V}$ is an orthogonal matrix, $\mathbf{D}$ is a diagonal matrix, $\mathbf{D}^{1/2}$ is the square root of $\mathbf{D}$, and the matrix $\mathbf{C}$ is defined by

$$\mathbf{C} = \mathbf{D}^{1/2}\mathbf{V}$$

The problem is to solve for the Green's function $G(\mathbf{x};\mathbf{t})$ that satisfies the following condition (in the distributional sense):

$$(\mathbf{P}^*\mathbf{P})_U G(\mathbf{x};\mathbf{t}) = \delta(\mathbf{x} - \mathbf{t})$$

Using the multidimensional Fourier transform to solve this equation for $G(\mathbf{x};\mathbf{t})$, show that

$$G(\mathbf{x};\mathbf{t}) = \exp\left(-\frac{1}{2}\|\mathbf{x} - \mathbf{t}\|_C^2\right)$$

where

$$\|\mathbf{x}\|_C^2 = \mathbf{x}^T\mathbf{C}^T\mathbf{C}\mathbf{x}$$

7.12 Consider the cost functional

$$\mathscr{E} = \frac{1}{2}\sum_{j=1}^{N} e_j^2$$

where

$$\begin{aligned} e_j &= d_j - F^*(x_j) \\ &= d_j - \sum_{i=1}^{M} w_i G(\|\mathbf{x}_j - \mathbf{t}_i\|_{C_i}) \end{aligned}$$

The free parameters are the linear weights w_i, the centers $\mathbf{t}_i$ of the Green's functions, and the inverse covariance matrix $\mathbf{\Sigma}_i^{-1} = \mathbf{C}_i^T\mathbf{C}_i$, where $\mathbf{C}_i$ is the norm weighting matrix. The problem is to find the values of these free parameters that minimize the cost functional $\mathscr{E}$. Derive the following partial derivatives:

(a) $\dfrac{\partial \mathscr{E}}{\partial w_i} = \sum_{j=1}^{N} e_j G(\|\mathbf{x}_j - \mathbf{t}_i\|_{C_i})$

(b) $\dfrac{\partial \mathscr{E}}{\partial \mathbf{t}_i} = 2w_i \sum_{j=1}^{N} e_j G'(\|\mathbf{x}_j - \mathbf{t}_i\|_{C_i})\, \mathbf{\Sigma}_i^{-1}(\mathbf{x}_j - \mathbf{t}_i)$

(c) $\dfrac{\partial \mathscr{E}}{\partial \mathbf{\Sigma}_i^{-1}} = -w_i \sum_{j=1}^{N} e_j G'(\|\mathbf{x}_j - \mathbf{t}_i\|_{C_i})\mathbf{Q}_{ji}$

where $\mathbf{G}'(\cdot)$ is the derivative of $G(\cdot)$ with respect to its argument, and

$$\mathbf{Q}_{ji} = (\mathbf{x}_j - \mathbf{t}_i)(\mathbf{x}_j - \mathbf{t}_i)^T$$

For differentiation with respect to a vector as in part (b), you may use the rule: If $v = \mathbf{x}^T\mathbf{x}$, then

$$\frac{\partial v}{\partial \mathbf{x}} = 2\mathbf{x}$$

For differentiation with respect to a matrix as in part (c), you may use the rule: If $v = \mathbf{x}^T\mathbf{A}\mathbf{x}$, then

$$\frac{\partial v}{\partial \mathbf{A}} = \mathbf{x}\mathbf{x}^T$$

CHAPTER 8

Recurrent Networks Rooted in Statistical Physics

8.1 Introduction

The multilayer perceptron and the radial-basis function network considered in the previous two chapters represent important examples of a class of neural networks known as nonlinear layered feedforward networks. In this chapter we consider another important class of neural networks that have a *recurrent* structure, and the development of which is inspired by different ideas from *statistical physics*. In particular, they share the following distinctive features:

- Nonlinear computing units
- Symmetric synaptic connections
- Abundant use of feedback

All the characteristics described herein are exemplified by the Hopfield network, the Boltzmann machine, and the mean-field-theory machine.

The *Hopfield network* is a recurrent network that embodies a profound physical principle, namely, that of *storing information in a dynamically stable configuration.* Prior to the publication of Hopfield's influential paper in 1982, this approach to the design of a neural network had occupied the attention of several investigators—Grossberg (1967, 1968), Amari (1972), Little (1974), and Cowan (1968), among others; the work of some of these pioneers predated that of Hopfield by more than a decade. Nevertheless, it was in Hopfield's 1982 paper that the physical principle of storing information in a dynamically stable network was formulated in precise terms for the first time. Hopfield's idea of locating each pattern to be stored at the bottom of a "valley" of an energy landscape, and then permitting a dynamical procedure to minimize the energy of the network in such a way that the valley becomes a basin of attraction is novel indeed!

The standard discrete-time version of the Hopfield network uses the McCulloch–Pitts model for its neurons. Retrieval of information stored in the network is accomplished via a dynamical procedure of updating the state of a neuron selected from among those that want to change, with that particular neuron being picked *randomly* and one at a time. This asynchronous dynamical procedure is repeated until there are no further state changes to report. In a more elaborate version of the Hopfield network, the firing mechanism of the neurons (i.e., switching them on or off) follows a *probabilistic law.* In such a situation, we refer to the neurons as *stochastic neurons.* The use of stochastic neurons permits us to develop further insight into the statistical characterization of the Hopfield network by linking its behavior with the well-established subject of statistical physics.

The *Boltzmann machine* represents a generalization of the Hopfield network (Hinton and Sejnowski, 1983, 1986; Ackley et al., 1985). It combines the use of symmetric synaptic connections (a distinctive feature of the Hopfield network) with the use of hidden neurons (a distinctive feature of multilayer feedforward networks). For its operation, the Boltzmann machine relies on a stochastic concept rooted in statistical thermodynamics that is known as *simulated annealing* (Kirkpatrick et al., 1983). The Boltzmann machine was named by Hinton and Sejnowski in honor of Boltzmann. The general discipline of statistical thermodynamics grew out of the work of Boltzmann who, in 1872, made the discovery that the random motion of the molecules of a gas has an energy related to temperature.

The *mean-field-theory* (MFT) machine is derived from the Boltzmann machine by invoking a ''naive'' approximation known as the *mean-field approximation* (Peterson and Hartman, 1989; Peterson and Anderson, 1987). According to this approximation, the stochastic binary units of the Boltzmann machine are replaced by deterministic analog units. The motivation for the mean-field approximation is to circumvent the excessive computer time required for the implementation of the Boltzmann machine.

The Hopfield network operates in an unsupervised manner. As such, it may be used as a content-addressable memory or as a computer for solving optimization problems of a combinatorial kind. In a *combinatorial optimization problem* we have a discrete system with a large but finite number of possible solutions; the requirement is to find the solution that minimizes a cost function providing a measure of system performance. The Boltzmann machine and its derivative, the mean-field-theory machine, on the other hand, may require supervision by virtue of using input and output units.

The Hopfield network, the Boltzmann machine, and the mean-field-theory machine require time to settle to an equilibrium condition; they may therefore be excessively slow, unless special-purpose chips or hardware are used for their implementation. Moreover, they are *relaxation networks with a local learning rule.* Above all, however, they are all rooted in statistical physics.

Organization of the Chapter

The main body of this chapter is organized as follows. In Section 8.2 we present an overview of the dynamics of the class of recurrent networks considered here. In Section 8.3 we describe the Hopfield network, which uses the formal neuron of McCulloch and Pitts (1943) as its processing unit. The convergence properties of the Hopfield network are given particular attention here. This is followed by a computer experiment illustrating the behavior of the Hopfield network in Section 8.4. Then, in Section 8.5, we discuss the energy function of the Hopfield network and the related issue of spurious states. In Section 8.6 we present a probabilistic treatment of associative recall in a Hopfield network. The material covered in this latter section establishes a fundamental limit on the storage capacity of the Hopfield network as an associative memory for correlated patterns. In Section 8.7 we discuss the ''isomorphism'' between the Hopfield network and the *spin-glass model* that is rooted in statistical mechanics. This is followed by a description of *stochastic neurons* in Section 8.8, and then a qualitative discussion of the *phase diagram* of a stochastic Hopfield network in Section 8.9. The phase diagram delineates the lines across which the network changes its computational behavior.

In Section 8.10 we describe the stochastic simulated annealing algorithm. This material paves the way for a detailed description of the Boltzmann machine in Section 8.11 from a statistical physics perspective. In Section 8.12 we view the Boltzmann machine as a Markov chain model. Next, we describe the mean-field-approximation theory in Section 8.13. In Section 8.14 we describe a computer experiment comparing the Boltzmann and mean-field-theory machines. The chapter concludes with some general discussion in Section 8.15.

8.2 Dynamical Considerations

Consider a recurrent network (i.e., a neural network with feedback) made up of N neurons with *symmetric coupling* described by $w_{ji} = w_{ij}$, where w_{ji} is the synaptic weight connecting neuron i to neuron j. The symmetry of the synaptic connections results in a powerful theorem about the behavior of the network, as discussed here. Let $v_j(t)$ denote the activation potential acting on neuron j, and let $x_j(t)$ denote the corresponding value of the neuron's output. These two variables are related by

$$x_j = \varphi_j(v_j) \tag{8.1}$$

where $\varphi_j(\cdot)$ is the sigmoidal nonlinearity of neuron j. Both v_j and x_j are functions of the continuous-time variable t. The *state* of neuron j may be described in terms of the activation potential $v_j(t)$ or, equivalently, the output signal $x_j(t)$. In the former case, the *dynamics* of the recurrent network is described by a set of coupled nonlinear differential equations as follows (Hopfield, 1984a; Cohen and Grossberg, 1983):

$$C_j \frac{dv_j}{dt} = \sum_{\substack{i=1 \\ i \neq j}}^{N} w_{ji} \varphi_j(v_j) - \frac{v_j}{R_j} - \theta_j, \qquad j = 1, 2, \ldots, N \tag{8.2}$$

where θ_j is a threshold applied to neuron j from an external source. The finite rate of change of the activation potential $v_j(t)$ with respect to time t is due to the *capacitive* effects C_j associated with neuron j, which are an intrinsic property of biological neurons or the physical implementation of artificial neurons. According to Eq. (8.2), three factors contribute to the rate of change dv_j/dt:

1. Postsynaptic effects induced in neuron j due to the presynaptic activities of neurons $i = 1, 2, \ldots, N$, excluding $i = j$
2. Leakage due to finite input resistance R_j of the nonlinear element of neuron j
3. Threshold θ_j

For the recurrent network with symmetric coupling as described here, we may define an *energy function* or *Liapunov function* as follows (Hopfield, 1984a):

$$E = -\frac{1}{2} \sum_{i} \sum_{\substack{j \\ i \neq j}} w_{ji} x_i x_j + \sum_{j=1}^{N} \frac{1}{R_j} \int_0^{x_j} \varphi_j^{-1}(x_j)\, dx_j + \sum_{j=1}^{N} \theta_j x_j \tag{8.3}$$

where x_j is the output of neuron j, related to the activation potential v_j by Eq. (8.1). The energy function of Eq. (8.3) is a special case of a theorem due to Cohen and Grossberg (1983), which is considered in Chapter 14 devoted to neurodynamics. The importance of the energy function E is that it provides the basis for a deep understanding of how specific problems may be solved by recurrent networks. For now, it suffices to note that the energy function E is fully descriptive of the recurrent network under study in that it includes all the synaptic weights and all the state variables of the network, and that we may state the following theorem for the case when the threshold θ_j changes slowly over the time of computation (Hopfield, 1984a; Cohen and Grossberg, 1983):

> *The energy function E is a monotonically decreasing function of the network state $\{x_j | j = 1, 2, \ldots, N\}$.*

When the network is started in any initial state, it will move in a *downhill* direction of the energy function E until it reaches a *local minimum*; at that point, it stops changing with time. Simply put, a recurrent network with symmetric coupling *cannot* oscillate despite the abundant presence of feedback.

We refer to the space of *all* possible states of the network as the *phase space,* a terminology borrowed from physics; it is also referred to as the *state space.* The local minima of the energy function E represent the *stable points* of the phase space. These stable points are also referred to as *attractors* in the sense that each attractor exercises a substantial domain of influence (i.e., basin of attraction) around it. Accordingly, symmetric recurrent networks are sometimes referred to as *attractor neural networks* (Amit, 1989).

Figure 8.1 presents a graphical portrayal of the above theorem for a two-dimensional phase space (Hopfield and Tank, 1986). Each *trajectory* of the *flow map* shown in Fig. 8.1b corresponds to a possible time history of the network, with arrows indicating the directions of motion. Each trajectory terminates at a stable point, which is due to the network moving in a downhill direction of the energy function E toward the bottom of a local valley and then stopping there. Figure 8.1a shows the *energy landscape* for the flow map of Fig. 8.1b. Each *contour line* of the energy landscape corresponds to a constant

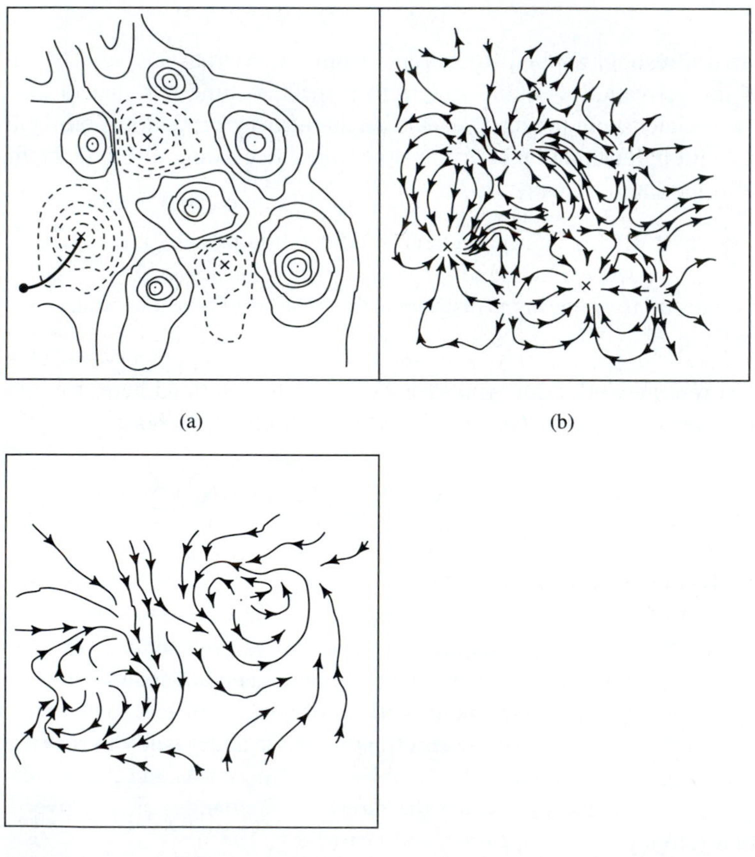

FIGURE 8.1 (a) Energy landscape of a symmetric recurrent network; solid lines indicate a hill, whereas dashed lines indicate a valley. (b) Flow lines of the network dynamics, corresponding to the energy landscape (a). (c) More complicated dynamics that can occur for an asymmetric recurrent network. (From J.J. Hopfield and T.W. Tank, 1986; copyright 1986 by the AAAS.)

value of the energy function E. The solid contour lines of Fig. 8.1a indicate *hills,* whereas the dashed contour lines indicate *valleys.* The bottom points of the valleys represent stable points of the phase space; that is, the valleys are located where the trajectories in Fig. 8.1b terminate. When the network is presented a pattern that is inside the domain of influence of an attractor of the phase space, the network relaxes to that attractor, as illustrated in the bottom left-hand corner of Fig. 8.1a.

The picture portrayed by the flow map of Fig. 8.1b corresponds to a recurrent network with symmetric coupling. What if the coupling is asymmetric? In such a situation it is possible for complications to arise, as illustrated in the flow map of Fig. 8.1c, which exhibits trajectories representative of complicated oscillatory behaviors (Hopfield and Tank, 1986). It is important to recognize, however, that it is possible to design stable recurrent networks that are asymmetric (Carpenter et al., 1987). Nevertheless, the use of symmetric coupling does indeed help by simplifying the class of behaviors that are exhibited by neural networks having feedback. It is for this reason that in this chapter we focus our attention exclusively on recurrent networks that are symmetric. A simple and yet important example of this special class of recurrent networks is represented by the Hopfield network, which is considered next.

8.3 The Hopfield Network

The *Hopfield network* may be viewed as a nonlinear *associative memory* or *content-addressable memory,* the primary function of which is to retrieve a pattern (item) stored in memory in response to the presentation of an incomplete or noisy version of that pattern. To illustrate the meaning of this statement in a succinct way, we can do no better than quote from the 1982 paper of Hopfield:

> Suppose that an item stored in memory is "H.A. Kramers & G.H. Wannier *Physi Rev. 60,* 252 (1941)." A general content-addressable memory would be capable of retrieving this entire memory item on the basis of sufficient partial information. The input "& Wannier (1941)" might suffice. An ideal memory could deal with errors and retrieve this reference even from the input "Wannier, (1941)."

An important property of a content-addressable memory is therefore the ability to retrieve a stored pattern, given a reasonable subset of the information content of that pattern. Moreover, a content-addressable memory is *error-correcting* in the sense that it can override inconsistent information in the cues presented to it.

The essence of a content-addressable memory (CAM) is to map a fundamental memory $\boldsymbol{\xi}_\mu$ onto a fixed (stable) point $\mathbf{s}_\mu$ of a dynamic system, as illustrated in Fig. 8.2. Mathematically, we may express this mapping in the form

$$\boldsymbol{\xi}_\mu \rightleftharpoons \mathbf{s}_\mu$$

The arrow from left to right describes an *encoding* operation, whereas the arrow from right to left describes a *decoding* operation. The stable points of the phase space of the network are the *fundamental memories* or *prototype states* of the network. Suppose now that the network is presented a pattern containing partial but sufficient information about one of the fundamental memories. We may then represent that particular pattern as a starting point in the phase space. In principle, provided that the starting point is close to the stable point representing the memory being retrieved, the system should evolve with

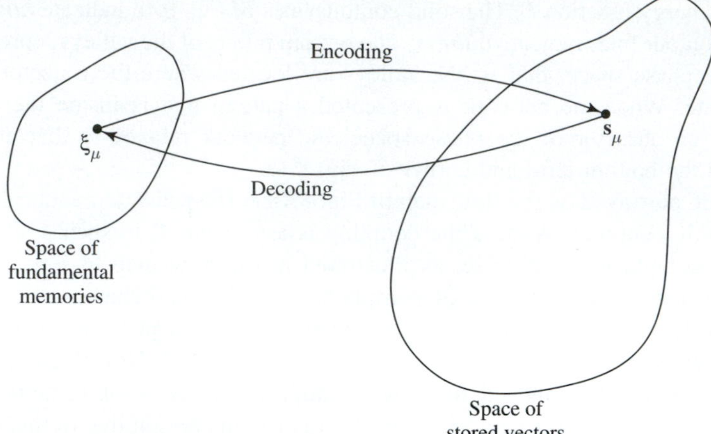

FIGURE 8.2 Illustration of the coding–decoding performed by a recurrent network.

time and finally converge onto the memory state itself, at which point the entire memory is generated by the network. We may therefore describe a Hopfield network as a *dynamic system whose phase space contains a set of fixed (stable) points representing the fundamental memories of the system.* Consequently, the Hopfield network has an *emergent* property, which helps it retrieve information and cope with errors.

Operational Features of the Hopfield Network

The Hopfield model uses the formal neuron of McCulloch and Pitts (1943) as its basic processing unit. Each such neuron has two states determined by the level of the activation potential acting on it. The "on" or "firing" state of a neuron i is denoted by the output $s_i = +1$, and the "off" or "quiescent" state is represented by $s_i = -1$. For a network made up of N neurons, the *state* of the network is thus defined by the vector

$$\mathbf{s} = [s_1, s_2, \ldots, s_N]^T$$

where the superscript T denotes matrix transposition. With $s_i = \pm 1$, the state of neuron i represents one *bit* of information, and the N-by-1 state vector $\mathbf{s}$ represents a binary word of N bits of information. Note that s_i is the limiting form of the state variable x_i used in Section 8.2, under the following two conditions:

- Time t approaches infinity so as to permit the recursive network to relax to a stable (equilibrium) condition.

- The slope of the nonlinearity $\varphi_i(\cdot)$ at the origin is made infinitely large, so that the sigmoidal nonlinearity assumes the form of a hard limiter in accordance with the McCulloch–Pitts model.

A pair of neurons i and j in the network are connected by a synaptic weight w_{ji}, which specifies the contribution of the output signal s_i of neuron i to the potential acting on neuron j. The contribution so made may be positive (excitatory synapse) or negative (inhibitory synapse). The net potential v_j acting on neuron j is the sum of all postsynaptic potentials delivered to it, as illustrated in the signal-flow graph of Fig. 8.3. Specifically, we may write

$$v_j = \sum_{i=1}^{N} w_{ji} s_i - \theta_j \tag{8.4}$$

where θ_j is a fixed *threshold* applied externally to neuron j. Hence, neuron j modifies its state s_j according to the *deterministic rule*

$$s_j = \begin{cases} +1 & \text{if } v_j > 0 \\ -1 & \text{if } v_j < 0 \end{cases} \tag{8.5}$$

This relation may be rewritten in the compact form

$$s_j = \operatorname{sgn}[v_j] \tag{8.6}$$

where sgn is the *signum function,* defined graphically in Fig. 8.4. What if v_j is exactly zero? The action taken here can be quite arbitrary. For example, we may set $s_j = \pm 1$ if $v_j = 0$. However, we will use the following convention: If v_j is zero, neuron j remains in its previous state, regardless of whether it is on or off. The significance of this assumption is that the resulting flow diagram is symmetrical, as will be demonstrated later.

There are two phases to the operation of the Hopfield network, namely, the storage phase and the retrieval phase, as described here.

1. *Storage Phase.* Suppose that we wish to store a set of N-dimensional vectors (binary words), denoted by $\{\boldsymbol{\xi}_\mu | \mu = 1, 2, \ldots, p\}$. We call these p vectors *fundamental memories,* representing the patterns to be memorized by the network. Let $\xi_{\mu,i}$ denote the ith element of the fundamental memory $\boldsymbol{\xi}_\mu$, where the class $\mu = 1, 2, \ldots, p$. According to the *outer product rule* of storage, that is, the generalization of *Hebb's postulate of learning,* the synaptic weight from neuron i to neuron j is defined by

$$w_{ji} = \frac{1}{N} \sum_{\mu=1}^{p} \xi_{\mu,j} \xi_{\mu,i} \tag{8.7}$$

The reason for using $1/N$ as the constant of proportionality is to simplify the mathematical description of information retrieval. Note also that the learning rule of Eq. (8.7) is a "one-shot" computation. In the normal operation of the Hopfield network, we set

$$w_{ii} = 0 \qquad \text{for all } i \tag{8.8}$$

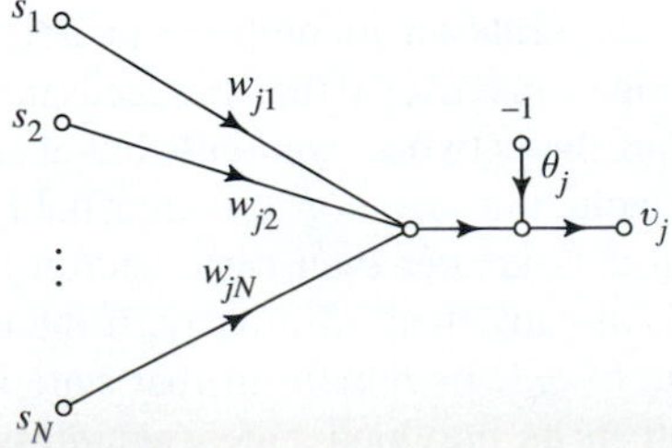

FIGURE 8.3 Signal-flow graph of the net activation potential v_j of neuron j.

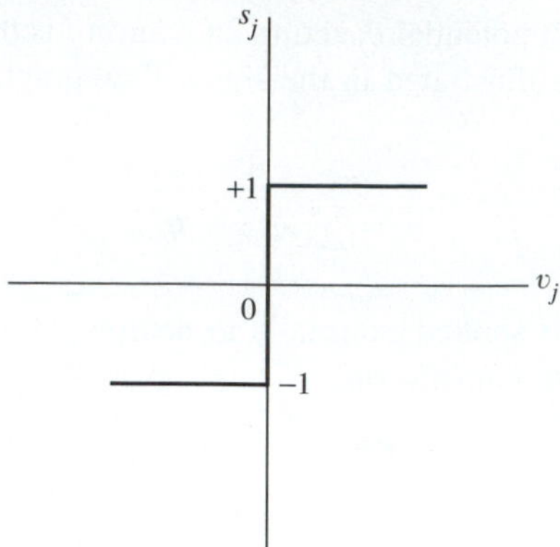

FIGURE 8.4 The signum function.

which means that the neurons have *no* self-feedback. Let **W** denote the *N*-by-*N* *synaptic weight matrix* of the network, with w_{ji} as its jith element. We may then combine Eqs. (8.7) and (8.8) into a single equation written in matrix form as follows:

$$\mathbf{W} = \frac{1}{N} \sum_{\mu=1}^{p} \boldsymbol{\xi}_\mu \boldsymbol{\xi}_\mu^T - \frac{p}{N}\mathbf{I} \tag{8.9}$$

where $\boldsymbol{\xi}_\mu \boldsymbol{\xi}_\mu^T$ represents the outer product of the vector $\boldsymbol{\xi}_\mu$ with itself, and **I** denotes the identity matrix. From these defining equations of the synaptic weights/weight matrix, we note the following:

- The output of each neuron in the network is fed back to all other neurons.
- There is no self-feedback in the network (i.e., $w_{ii} = 0$).
- The weight matrix of the network is symmetric in that we have

$$w_{ij} = w_{ji} \tag{8.10}$$

  that is, the influence of neuron i on neuron j is equal to the influence of neuron j on neuron i. Equivalently, in matrix form we may write

$$\mathbf{W}^T = \mathbf{W}$$

The first two conditions are illustrated in the Hopfield network of Fig. 8.5 for the case of $N = 4$; the boxes labeled z^{-1} represent unit delays.

2. *Retrieval Phase.* During the retrieval phase, an N-dimensional vector **x**, called a *probe,* is imposed on the Hopfield network as its state. The probe vector has elements equal to ± 1. Typically, it represents an incomplete or noisy version of a fundamental memory of the network. Information retrieval then proceeds in accordance with a *dynamical rule* in which each neuron j of the network *randomly* but at some fixed rate examines the net activation potential v_j (including any nonzero threshold θ_j) applied to it. If, at that instant of time, the potential v_j is greater than zero, neuron j will switch its state to $+1$, or remain in that state if it is already there. Similarly, if the potential v_j is less than zero, neuron j will switch its state to -1, or remain in that state if it is already there. If v_j is exactly zero, neuron j is left in its previous state, regardless of whether it is on or off. The state updating from one iteration to the next is therefore deterministic, but the selection

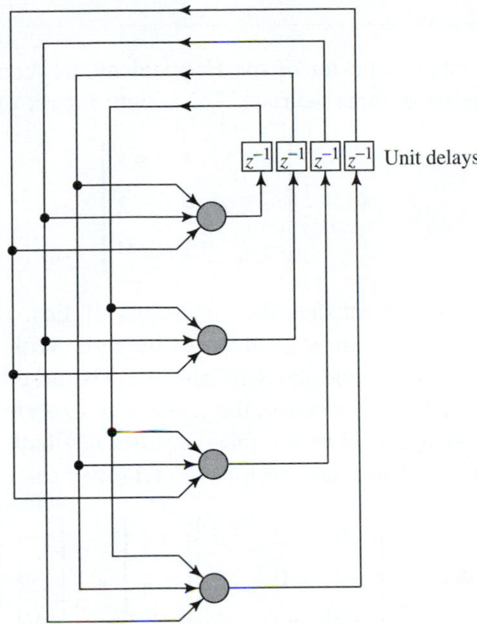

FIGURE 8.5 Architectural graph of Hopfield network for $N = 4$ neurons.

of a neuron to perform the updating is done randomly. The *asynchronous* (serial) updating procedure described here is continued until there are no further changes to report. That is, starting with the probe vector **x**, the network finally produces a time-invariant state vector **y** whose individual elements satisfy the *condition for stability:*

$$y_j = \operatorname{sgn}\left(\sum_{i=1}^{N} w_{ji} y_i - \theta_j\right), \qquad j = 1, 2, \ldots, N \tag{8.11}$$

or, in matrix form,

$$\mathbf{y} = \operatorname{sgn}(\mathbf{W}\mathbf{y} - \boldsymbol{\theta}) \tag{8.12}$$

where **W** is the synaptic weight matrix of the network, and $\boldsymbol{\theta}$ is the externally applied *threshold vector.* The stability condition described here is also referred to as the *alignment condition.* The state vector **y** that satisfies it is called a *stable state* or *fixed point* of the phase space of the system. We may therefore make the statement that the Hopfield network will always converge to a stable state when the retrieval operation is performed *asynchronously.*

The *Little model* (Little and Shaw, 1975; Little, 1974) uses the same synaptic weights as the Hopfield model. However, they differ from each other in that the Hopfield model uses *asynchronous (serial) dynamics,* whereas the Little model uses *synchronous (parallel) dynamics.* Accordingly, they exhibit different convergence properties (Bruck, 1990; Goles and Martinez, 1990): The Hopfield network will always converge to a stable state, whereas the Little model will always converge to a stable state or a limit cycle of length at most 2. By such a ''limit cycle'' we mean that the cycles in the state space of the network are of a length less than or equal to 2.

EXAMPLE 1

To illustrate the emergent behavior of the Hopfield model, consider the network of Fig. 8.6a, which consists of three neurons. The weight matrix of the network is

$$\mathbf{W} = \frac{1}{3}\begin{bmatrix} 0 & -2 & +2 \\ -2 & 0 & -2 \\ +2 & -2 & 0 \end{bmatrix}$$

which is legitimate, since it satisfies the conditions of Eqs. (8.8) and (8.10). The threshold applied to each neuron is assumed to be zero. With three neurons in the network, there are $2^3 = 8$ possible states to consider. Of these 8 states, only the two states $(1,-1,1)$ and $(-1,1,-1)$ are stable; the remaining six states are all unstable. We say that these two particular states are stable, because they both satisfy the alignment condition of Eq. (8.12). For the state vector $(1,-1,1)$ we have

$$\mathbf{Wy} = \frac{1}{3}\begin{bmatrix} 0 & -2 & +2 \\ -2 & 0 & -2 \\ +2 & -2 & 0 \end{bmatrix}\begin{bmatrix} +1 \\ -1 \\ +1 \end{bmatrix} = \frac{1}{3}\begin{bmatrix} +4 \\ -4 \\ +4 \end{bmatrix}$$

Hard-limiting this result yields

$$\text{sgn}[\mathbf{Wy}] = \begin{bmatrix} +1 \\ -1 \\ +1 \end{bmatrix} = \mathbf{y}$$

Similarly, for the state vector $(-1,1,-1)$ we have

$$\mathbf{Wy} = \frac{1}{3}\begin{bmatrix} 0 & -2 & +2 \\ -2 & 0 & -2 \\ +2 & -2 & 0 \end{bmatrix}\begin{bmatrix} -1 \\ +1 \\ -1 \end{bmatrix} = \frac{1}{3}\begin{bmatrix} -4 \\ +4 \\ -4 \end{bmatrix}$$

which, after hard limiting, yields

$$\text{sgn}[\mathbf{Wy}] = \begin{bmatrix} -1 \\ +1 \\ -1 \end{bmatrix} = \mathbf{y}$$

Hence, both of these state vectors satisfy the alignment condition.

Moreover, following the asynchronous updating procedure described earlier, we get the flow described in Fig. 8.6b. This flow map exhibits symmetry with respect to the two stable states of the network, which is intuitively satisfying. This symmetry is the result of leaving a neuron in its previous state if the net potential acting on it is exactly zero.

Figure 8.6b also shows that if the network of Fig. 8.6a is in the initial state $(1,1,1)$, $(-1,-1,1)$, or $(1,-1,-1)$, it will converge onto the stable state $(1,-1,1)$ after one iteration. If the initial state is $(-1,-1,-1)$, $(-1,1,1)$, or $(1,1,-1)$, it will converge onto the second stable state $(-1,1,-1)$, also after one iteration.

The network therefore has two fundamental memories $(1,-1,1)$ and $(-1,1,-1)$,

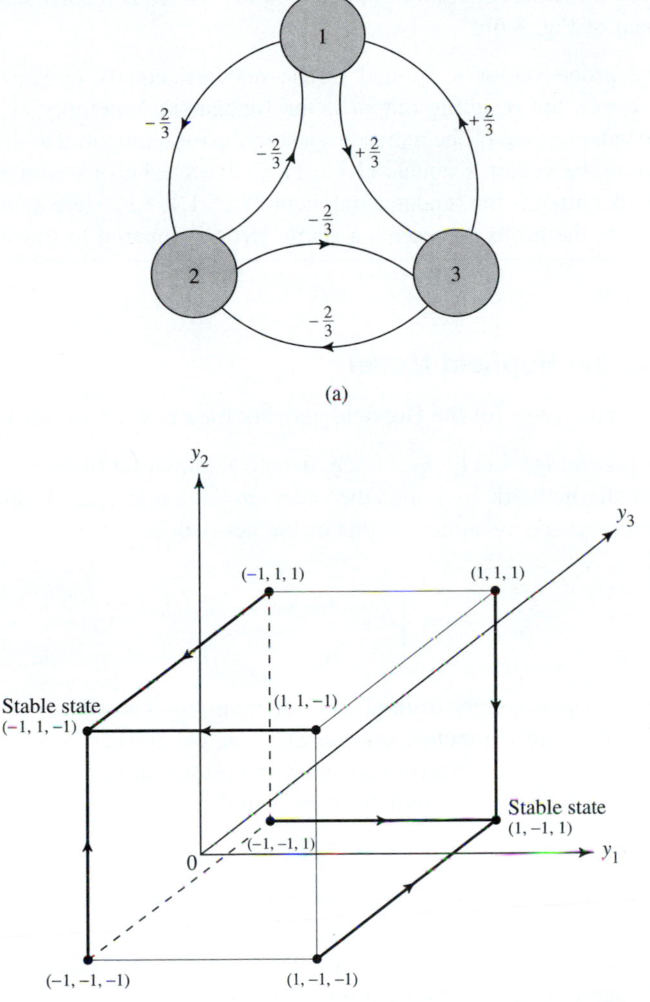

FIGURE 8.6 (a) Architectural graph of Hopfield network for $N = 3$ neurons. (b) Diagram depicting the two stable states and "flow" of the network.

representing the two stable states. Hence, the application of Eq. (8.9) yields the synaptic weight matrix

$$\mathbf{W} = \frac{1}{3}\begin{bmatrix} +1 \\ -1 \\ +1 \end{bmatrix}[+1, -1, +1] + \frac{1}{3}\begin{bmatrix} -1 \\ +1 \\ -1 \end{bmatrix}[-1, +1, -1] - \frac{2}{3}\begin{bmatrix} 1 & 0 & 0 \\ 0 & 1 & 0 \\ 0 & 0 & 1 \end{bmatrix}$$

$$= \frac{1}{3}\begin{bmatrix} 0 & -2 & +2 \\ -2 & 0 & -2 \\ +2 & -2 & 0 \end{bmatrix}$$

which checks with the synaptic weights shown in Fig. 8.6a.

The error-correcting capability of the Hopfield network is readily seen by examining the flow map of Fig. 8.6b:

1. If the probe vector $\mathbf{x}$ applied to the network equals $(-1,-1,1)$, $(1,1,1)$, or $(1,-1,-1)$, the resulting output is the fundamental memory $(1,-1,1)$. Each of these values of the probe represents a single error, compared to the stored pattern.
2. If the probe vector $\mathbf{x}$ equals $(1,1,-1)$, $(-1,-1,-1)$, or $(-1,1,1)$, the resulting network output is the fundamental memory $(-1,1,-1)$. Here again, each of these values of the probe represents a single error, compared to the stored pattern.

Summary of the Hopfield Model

The operational procedure for the Hopfield network may now be summarized as follows:

1. *Storage (Learning).* Let $\boldsymbol{\xi}_1, \boldsymbol{\xi}_2, \ldots, \boldsymbol{\xi}_p$ denote a known set of N-dimensional memories. Construct the network by using the outer product rule (i.e., Hebb's postulate of learning) to compute the synaptic weights of the network as

$$w_{ji} = \begin{cases} \dfrac{1}{N} \displaystyle\sum_{\mu=1}^{p} \xi_{\mu,j}\, \xi_{\mu,i}, & j \neq i \\ 0, & j = i \end{cases}$$

where w_{ji} is the synaptic weight from neuron i to neuron j. The elements of the vector $\boldsymbol{\xi}_\mu$ equal ± 1. Once they are computed, the synaptic weights are kept fixed.

2. *Initialization.* Let $\mathbf{x}$ denote an unknown N-dimensional input vector (probe) presented to the network. The algorithm is initialized by setting

$$s_j(0) = x_j, \qquad j = 1, \ldots, N$$

where $s_j(0)$ is the state of neuron j at time $n = 0$, and x_j is the jth element of the probe vector $\mathbf{x}$.

3. *Iteration until Convergence.* Update the elements of state vector $\mathbf{s}(n)$ asynchronously (i.e., randomly and one at a time) according to the rule

$$s_j(n+1) = \operatorname{sgn}\left[\sum_{i=1}^{N} w_{ji}\, s_i(n)\right]$$

Repeat the iteration until the state vector $\mathbf{s}$ remains unchanged.

4. *Outputting.* Let $\mathbf{s}_{\text{fixed}}$ denote the fixed point (stable state) computed at the end of step 3. The resulting output vector $\mathbf{y}$ of the network is

$$\mathbf{y} = \mathbf{s}_{\text{fixed}}$$

8.4 Computer Experiment I

In this section we use a computer experiment to illustrate the behavior of the Hopfield network as a content-addressable memory. The network used in the experiment consists of $N = 120$ neurons, and therefore $N^2 - N = 12{,}280$ synaptic weights. It was trained to retrieve the eight digitlike black-and-white patterns shown in Fig. 8.7, with each pattern containing 120 pixels (picture elements) and designed specially to produce good performance (Lippmann, 1987). The inputs applied to the network assume the value $+1$ for black pixels and -1 for white pixels. The eight patterns of Fig. 8.7 were used as fundamental memories in the storage (learning) phase of the Hopfield network to create the synaptic weight matrix **W**, which was done using Eq. (8.9). The retrieval phase of the network's operation was performed asynchronously, as described in Section 8.3.

During the first stage of the retrieval part of the experiment, the fundamental memories were presented to the network to test its ability to recover them correctly from the information stored in the synaptic weight matrix. In each case, the desired pattern was produced by the network after one iteration.

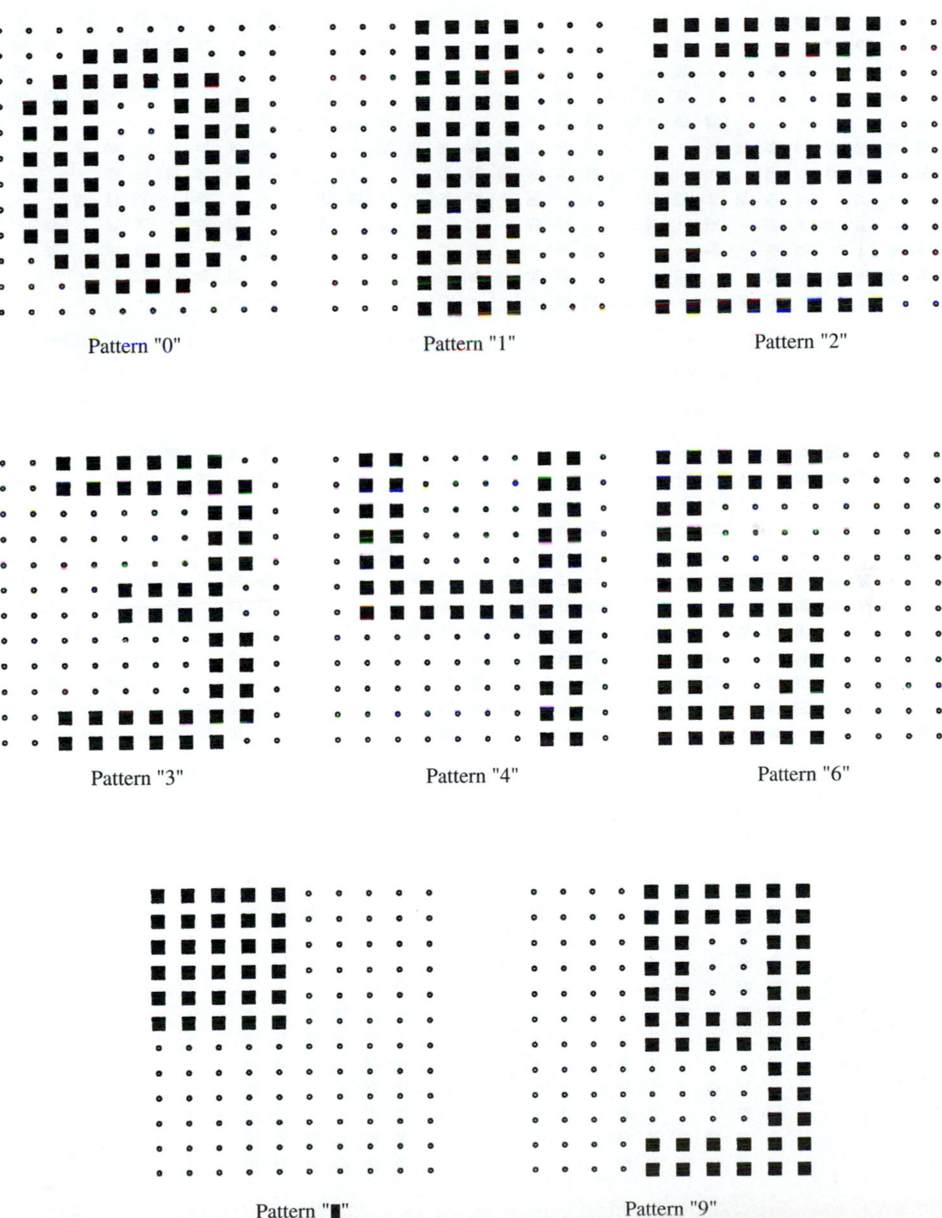

FIGURE 8.7 Set of handcrafted patterns for computer experiment on the Hopfield network.

Next, to demonstrate the error-correcting capability of the Hopfield network, a pattern of interest was distorted by randomly and independently reversing each pixel of the pattern from $+1$ to -1 and vice versa with a probability of 0.25, and then using the corrupted pattern as a probe for the network. The result of this experiment for digit 6 is presented in Fig. 8.8. The pattern in the top left hand-corner of this figure represents a corrupted version of digit 6, which is applied to the network at zero time. The patterns produced by the network after 5, 10, 15, 20, 25, 30, and 37 iterations are presented in the rest of the figure. As the number of iterations is increased, we see that the resemblance of the

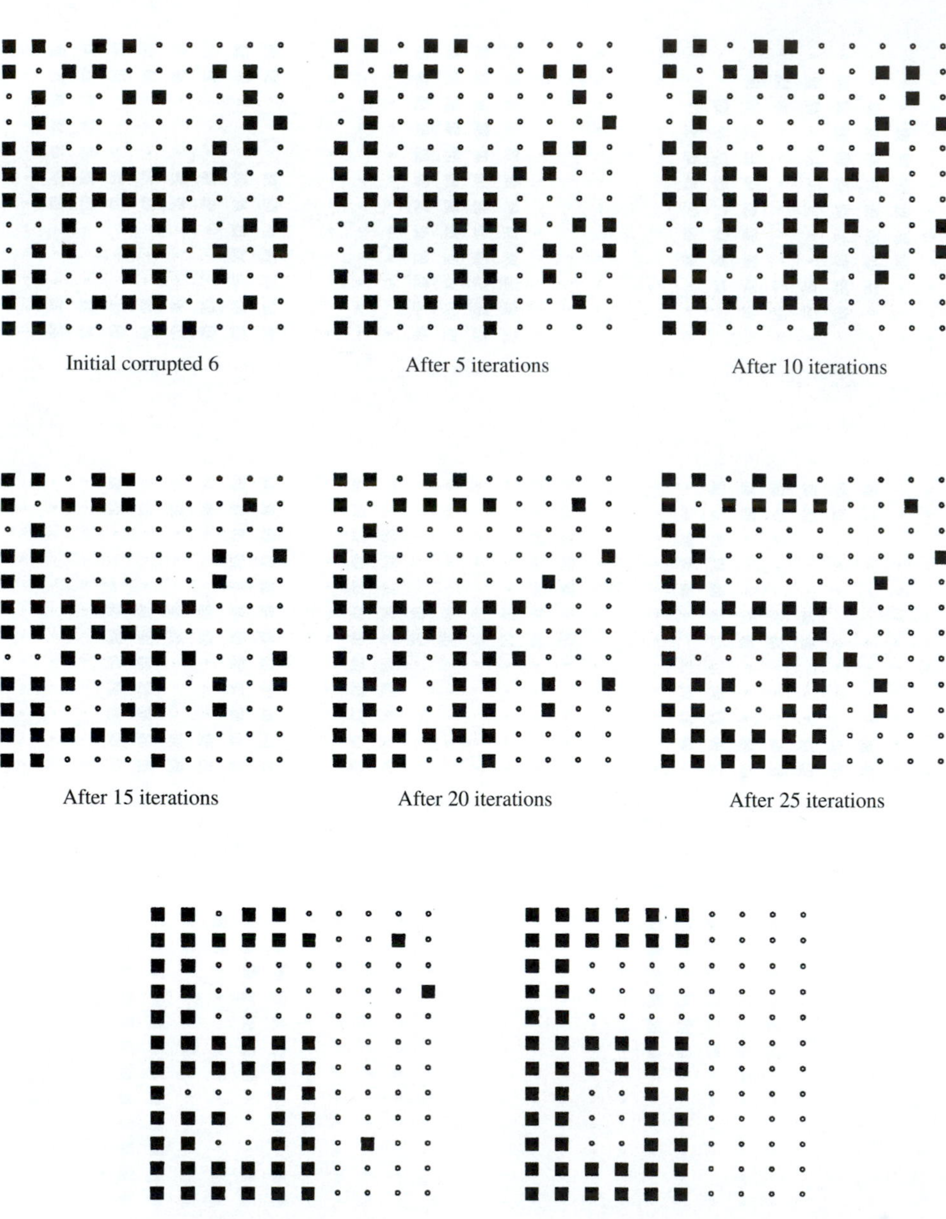

FIGURE 8.8 Correct recollection of corrupted pattern 6.

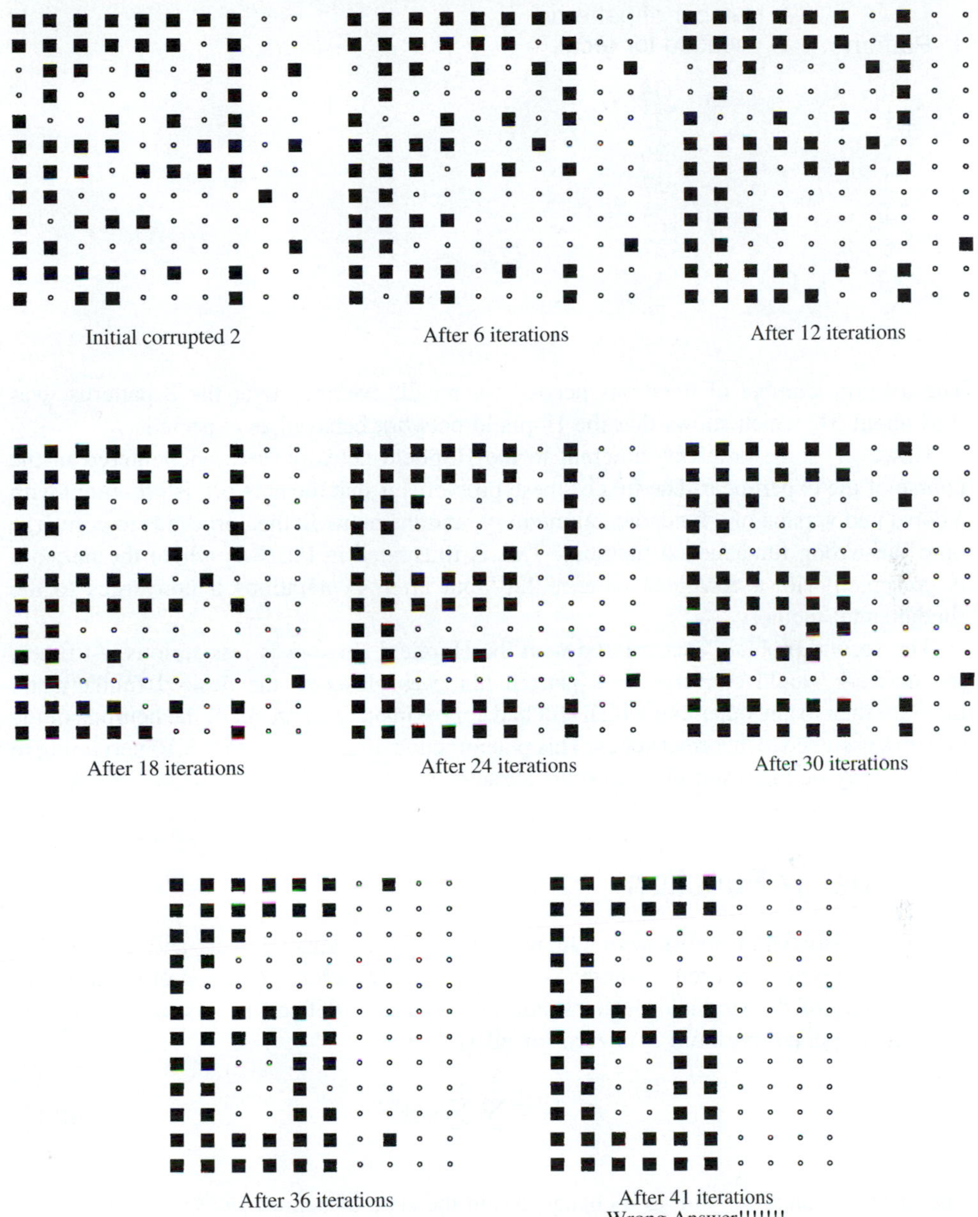

FIGURE 8.9 Incorrect recollection of corrupted pattern 2.

network output to digit 6 is progressively improved. Indeed, after 37 iterations, the network converges onto the correct form of digit 6.

Since, in theory, one-quarter of the 120 neurons of the Hopfield network end up changing state for each corrupted pattern, the number of iterations needed for recall, on average, is 30. In our experiment, the number of iterations needed for the recall of the different patterns from their corrupted versions were as follows:

Pattern	Number of patterns needed for recall
0	34
1	32
2	26
3	37
4	25
6	37
"□"	32
9	26

The average number of iterations needed for recall, averaged over the 8 patterns, was thus about 31, which shows that the Hopfield network behaved as expected.

However, some problems inherent to the Hopfield network were encountered in the course of the experiment. The first of these problems is that the network is presented with a corrupted version of a fundamental memory, and the network then proceeds to converge onto the wrong fundamental memory. This is illustrated in Fig. 8.9, where the network is presented with a corrupted pattern "2," but after 41 iterations it converges to the fundamental memory "6."

The second problem encountered with the Hopfield network is less serious. At times, the network would converge to a pattern that was closer to the desired fundamental memory than to any other, but which still had approximately 5 percent of the neurons of the network assigned to incorrect states. This phenomenon, illustrated in Fig. 8.10 pertaining to digit 9, may be the result of a spurious attractor.

8.5 Energy Function

Consider a Hopfield network with symmetric synaptic weights $w_{ji} = w_{ij}$ and $w_{ii} = 0$. Let s_i denote the state of neuron i, where $i = 1, 2, \ldots, N$. The *energy function* of the discrete-time version of the Hopfield network considered here is defined by (assuming that the externally applied threshold θ_j is zero for all j)

$$E = -\frac{1}{2}\sum_{i=1}^{N}\sum_{\substack{j=1 \\ i\neq j}}^{N} w_{ji} s_i s_j \tag{8.13}$$

The energy change ΔE due to a change Δs_j in the state of neuron j is given by

$$\Delta E = -\Delta s_j \sum_{\substack{i=1 \\ i\neq j}}^{N} w_{ji} s_i \tag{8.14}$$

Thus the action of the algorithm, responsible for changes in the network state during the information retrieval, causes the energy function E to be a *monotonically decreasing function* of the network state $\{s_j | j = 1, 2, \ldots, N\}$. State changes will continue until a local minimum of the energy landscape is reached, at which point the network stops. The *energy landscape* describes the dependence of the energy function E on the network state for a specified set of synaptic weights.

The local minima of the energy landscape correspond to the *attractors* of the phase space, which are the nominally assigned memories of the network. To guarantee the emergence of associative memory, two conditions must be satisfied:

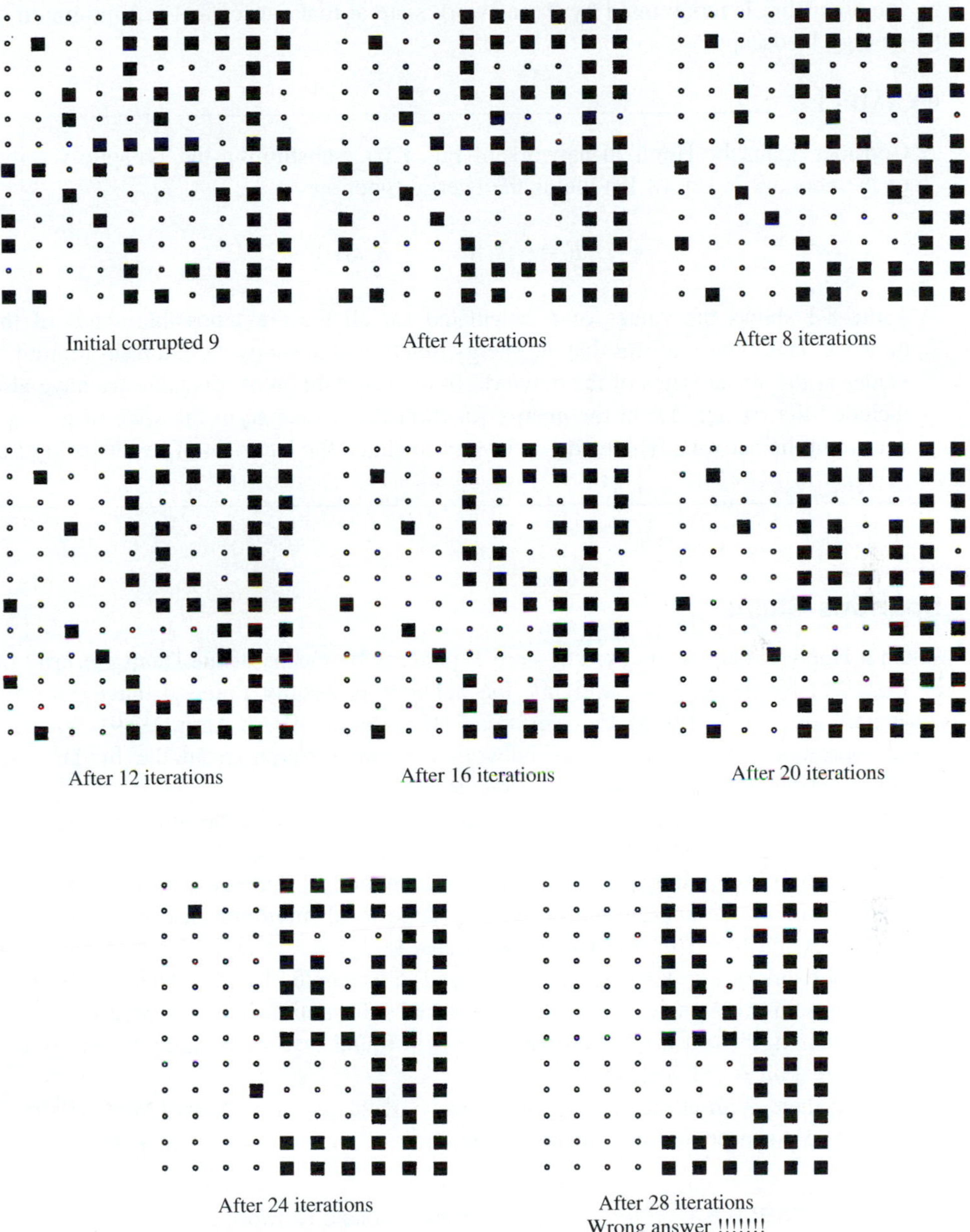

FIGURE 8.10 Illustration of another aspect of the recollection phenomenon exhibited by the Hopfield network.

- The fundamental patterns memorized by the network are all stable.
- The stable patterns have a sizeable basin of attraction (region of influence).

Suppose that the retrieval algorithm is initiated with a probe (i.e., unknown input pattern), representing a starting point in the energy landscape. Then, as the algorithm iterates its way to a solution, the starting point moves through the energy landscape toward a local minimum. When the local minimum is actually reached, the algorithm stays there, because everywhere else in the close vicinity is an uphill climb. The solution produced by the algorithm is represented by the network state at that particular local minimum of the energy landscape.

EXAMPLE 2

Consider again the Hopfield network of Fig. 8.6a. Substituting the synaptic weights of the network in Eq. (8.13) yields the energy function

$$E = \frac{2}{3}(s_1 s_2 - s_2 s_3 + s_1 s_3)$$

Table 8.1 shows the values of E calculated for all the eight possible states of the network. This table confirms that the energy function of the network attains its minimum values at the stable states of the network. In the last column of this table we have also included the change ΔE in the energy function due a change in the state of a single neuron in the network. The reader is invited to check the latter set of results using Eq. (8.14).

Spurious States

When a Hopfield network is used to store K patterns by means of the Hebb prescription of Eq. (8.7) for the synaptic weights, the network is usually found to have *spurious attractors,* also referred to as *spurious states* (Hertz et al., 1991; Amit, 1989). Spurious states represent stable states of the network that are different from the fundamental memories of the network. How do spurious states arise?

First of all, we note that the energy function E is symmetric in the sense that its value remains unchanged if the states of the neurons are reversed (i.e., the state s_i is replaced by $-s_i$ for all i). Accordingly, if the fundamental memory ξ_μ corresponds to a particular local minimum of the energy landscape, that same local minimum also corresponds to $-\xi_\mu$. This is illustrated by the two stable states $(-1,+1,-1)$ and $(+1,-1,+1)$ of the Hopfield network of Fig. 8.6 that was considered in Examples 1 and 2. This sign reversal need not pose a problem in the retrieval of stored information if it is agreed to reverse all the remaining bits of a retrieval pattern if it is found that a particular bit designated as the "sign" bit is -1 instead of $+1$.

Second, there is an attractor for every *mixture* of the stored patterns (Amit, 1989). A mixture state corresponds to a linear combination of an *odd* number of patterns. As a

TABLE 8.1 Energy Function of the Hopfield Network of Fig. 8.6a

Network State			Energy Function,	
s_1	s_2	s_3	E	ΔE
−1	−1	−1	2/3	
+1	−1	−1	2/3	0
−1	+1	−1	−2	−8/3
+1	+1	−1	2/3	8/3
−1	−1	+1	2/3	0
+1	−1	+1	−2	−8/3
−1	+1	+1	2/3	8/3
+1	+1	+1	2/3	0

simple example, consider the network state

$$s_i = \text{sgn}(\xi_{1,i} + \xi_{2,i} + \xi_{3,i}) \tag{8.15}$$

This is a *3-mixture spurious state.* It is a state formed out of three random patterns $\boldsymbol{\xi}_1$, $\boldsymbol{\xi}_2$, and $\boldsymbol{\xi}_3$ by a majority rule. The stability condition of Eq. (8.11) is indeed satisfied by the 3-mixture state of Eq. (8.15) for a large network (Amit, 1989).

Third, for a large number p of fundamental memories, the energy landscape has local minima that are not correlated with any of these memories embedded in the network. Such spurious states are sometimes referred to as *spin-glass states,* by analogy with spin-glass models of statistical mechanics; the idea of spin-glass models is discussed in Sections 8.7 and 8.8.

It is of interest to note that the absence of self-feedback, as described in Eq. (8.8), has a beneficial effect insofar as spurious states are concerned. Specifically, if we were to set $w_{ii} \neq 0$ for all i, additional stable spurious states might be produced in the neighborhood of a desired attractor (Kanter and Sompolinsky, 1987).

8.6 Error Performance of the Hopfield Network

Unfortunately, the fundamental memories of a Hopfield network are not always stable. Moreover, spurious states representing other stable states that are different from the fundamental memories can arise. These two phenomena, the probable instability of fundamental memories and the possible existence of spurious states, tend to decrease the efficiency of a Hopfield network as a content-addressable memory. In this section we use probabilistic considerations to explore the first of these two phenomena.

The summation in Eq. (8.7), defining the synaptic weights w_{ji} from neuron i to neuron j, is taken over all the fundamental memories. This equation is reproduced here for convenience of presentation:

$$w_{ji} = \frac{1}{N} \sum_{\mu=1}^{p} \xi_{\mu,j} \xi_{\mu,i}$$

Let a probe denoted by the vector $\mathbf{x}$ be presented to the network. Then, assuming that the threshold θ_j applied to neuron j is zero, we find that the potential v_j acting on this neuron is

$$\begin{aligned} v_j &= \sum_{i=1}^{N} w_{ji} x_i \\ &= \frac{1}{N} \sum_{i=1}^{N} \sum_{\mu=1}^{p} \xi_{\mu,j} \xi_{\mu,i} x_i \\ &= \frac{1}{N} \sum_{\mu=1}^{p} \xi_{\mu,j} \sum_{i=1}^{N} \xi_{\mu,i} x_i \end{aligned} \tag{8.16}$$

where, for the purpose of generality, the use of self-feedback (i.e., $w_{ii} \neq 0$) is permitted. Consider the special case when the probe $\mathbf{x}$ equals one of the fundamental memories stored in the network; that is, $\mathbf{x} = \boldsymbol{\xi}_\nu$. We may then rewrite Eq. (8.16) as

$$\begin{aligned} v_j &= \frac{1}{N} \sum_{\mu=1}^{p} \xi_{\mu,j} \sum_{i=1}^{N} \xi_{\mu,i} \xi_{\nu,i} \\ &= \xi_{\nu,j} + \frac{1}{N} \sum_{\substack{\mu=1 \\ \mu \neq \nu}}^{p} \xi_{\mu,j} \sum_{i=1}^{N} \xi_{\mu,i} \xi_{\nu,i} \end{aligned} \tag{8.17}$$

The first term on the right-hand side of Eq. (8.17) is simply the jth element of the fundamental memory $\boldsymbol{\xi}_\nu$; now we can see why the scaling factor $1/N$ was introduced in the definition of the synaptic weight w_{ji} in Eq. (8.7). This term may therefore be viewed as the desired "signal" component. The second term on the right-hand side of Eq. (8.17) is the result of "crosstalk" between the elements of the fundamental memory $\boldsymbol{\xi}_\nu$ under test and those of some other fundamental memory $\boldsymbol{\xi}_\mu$. This second term may therefore be viewed as the "noise" component of v_j. We therefore have a situation similar to the classical "signal-in-noise detection problem" in communication theory (Haykin, 1983).

We assume that the fundamental memories are random, being generated as a sequence of pN Bernoulli trials. The noise term of Eq. (8.17) then consists of a sum of $N(p - 1)$ independent random variables, taking on values ± 1 divided by N. This is a situation where the central limit theorem of probability theory applies. The *central limit theorem* states (Feller, 1968):

> *Let $\{X_k\}$ be a sequence of mutually independent random variables with a common distribution. Suppose that X_k has mean μ and variance σ^2, and let $Y = X_1 + X_2 + \cdots + X_n$. Then, as n approaches infinity, the probability distribution of the sum random variable Y approaches a Gaussian distribution.*

Hence, applying the central limit theorem to the noise term in Eq. (8.17), we find that the noise is asymptotically Gaussian distributed. Each of the $N(p - 1)$ random variables constituting the noise term in Eq. (8.17) has a mean of zero and a variance of $1/N^2$. It follows, therefore, that the statistics of the Gaussian distribution are

- Zero mean
- Variance equal to $(p - 1)/N$, which is $N(p - 1)$ times $1/N^2$

The signal component $\xi_{\nu,j}$ has a value of $+1$ or -1 with equal probability, and therefore a mean of zero and variance of unity. The *signal-to-noise ratio* is thus defined by

$$\begin{aligned}\rho &= \frac{\text{variance of signal}}{\text{variance of noise}} \\ &= \frac{1}{(p-1)/N} \\ &= \frac{N}{p-1} \\ &\simeq \frac{N}{p} \qquad \text{for large } p \end{aligned} \tag{8.18}$$

The components of the fundamental memory $\boldsymbol{\xi}_\nu$ will be *stable* if, and only if, the signal-to-noise ratio ρ is high. Now, the number p of fundamental memories provides a direct measure of the *storage capacity* of the network. Therefore, it follows from Eq. (8.18) that so long as the storage capacity of the network is not overloaded—that is, the number p of fundamental memories is small compared to the number N of neurons in the network—the fundamental memories are stable in a probabilistic sense.

Storage Capacity of the Hopfield Network

Let the jth bit of the probe $\mathbf{x} = \boldsymbol{\xi}_\nu$ be a "1," that is, $\xi_{\nu,j} = +1$. Then the *conditional probability of bit error* is defined by the shaded area shown in Fig. 8.11. The rest of the

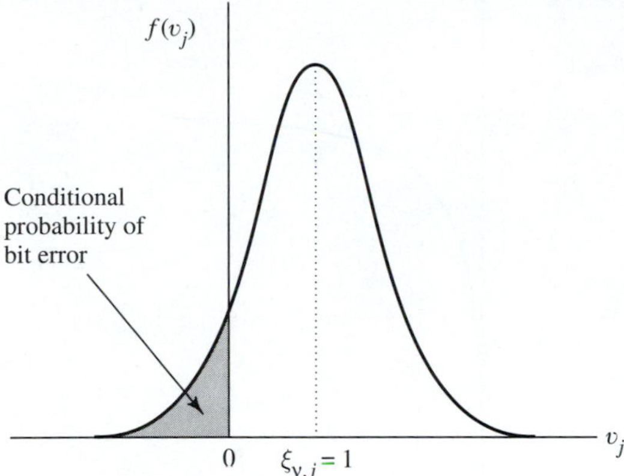

FIGURE 8.11 Conditional probability of bit error, assuming a Gaussian distribution for the net activation potential v_j of neuron j.

area under this curve is the *conditional probability that bit j of the probe is retrieved correctly*. Using the well-known formula for a Gaussian distribution, this latter conditional probability is given by

$$\text{Prob}(v_j > 0 | \xi_{\nu,j} = +1) = \frac{1}{\sqrt{2\pi}\sigma} \int_0^\infty \exp\left(-\frac{(v_j - \mu)^2}{2\sigma^2}\right) dv_j \tag{8.19}$$

With $\xi_{\nu,j}$ set to $+1$, and the mean of the noise term in Eq. (8.17) equal to zero, it follows that the mean of the random variable v_j is

$$\mu = 1$$

and its variance is

$$\sigma^2 = \frac{p-1}{N}$$

From the definition of the *error function* commonly used in calculations involving the Gaussian distribution, we have

$$\text{erf}(y) = \frac{2}{\sqrt{\pi}} \int_0^y e^{-z^2} \, dz \tag{8.20}$$

where y is a variable defining the upper limit of integration. A plot of erf(y) versus y is presented in Fig. 8.12. Note that as y approaches infinity, the error function erf(y) approaches unity.

We may now simplify the expression for the conditional probability of correctly retrieving the jth bit of the fundamental memory $\boldsymbol{\xi}_\nu$ by rewriting Eq. (8.19) in terms of the error function as follows:

$$\text{Prob}(v_j > 0 | \xi_{\nu,j} = +1) = \frac{1}{2}\left[1 + \text{erf}\left(\sqrt{\frac{\rho}{2}}\right)\right] \tag{8.21}$$

where ρ is the signal-to-noise ratio defined in Eq. (8.18).

Each fundamental memory consists of n bits. Also, the fundamental memories are usually equiprobable. It follows therefore that the *average probability of stable patterns*

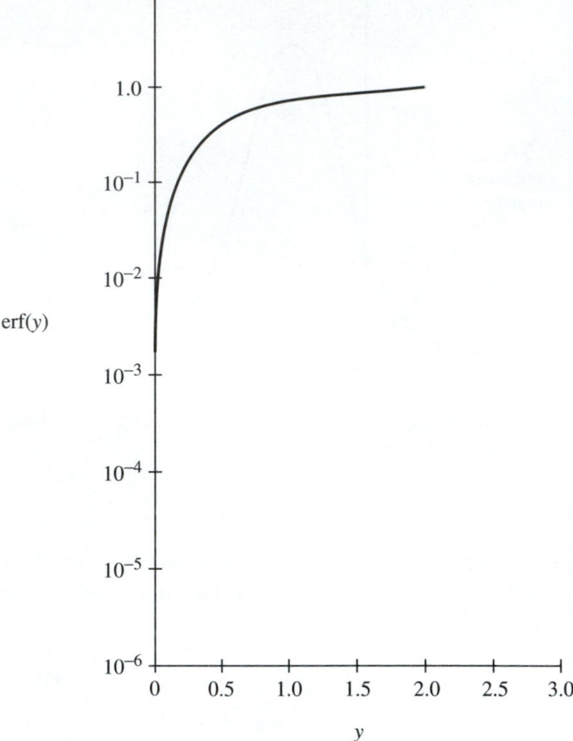

FIGURE 8.12 Error function.

is defined by

$$P_{\text{stab}} = [\text{Prob}(v_j > 0 | \xi_{\nu,j} = +1)]^N \tag{8.22}$$

We may use this probability to formulate an expression for capacity of a Hopfield network. Specifically, we define the *storage capacity* as the largest number of fundamental memories $p_{\max}$ that can be stored in the network, and yet insist that most of them be recalled correctly. For example, we may require that

$$P_{\text{stab}} \simeq 0.99$$

which, in effect, states that all N bits of each fundamental memory are retrieved correctly with 99 percent probability. This suggests that for the calculation of the storage capacity, we may consider the asymptotic behavior of the error function for large values of its argument. This asymptotic behavior is closely described by the approximation (Haykin, 1983)

$$\text{erf}(y) \simeq 1 - \frac{1}{\sqrt{\pi} y} e^{-y^2} \qquad \text{as } y \to \infty \tag{8.23}$$

Correspondingly, we may approximate the conditional probability of Eq. (8.21) as

$$\text{Prob}(v_j > 0 | \xi_{\nu,j} = +1) \simeq 1 - \frac{1}{\sqrt{2\pi\rho}} e^{-\rho/2} \tag{8.24}$$

Hence, substituting Eq. (8.24) in (8.22), we get

$$
\begin{aligned}
P_{\text{stab}} &\simeq \left(1 - \frac{1}{\sqrt{2\pi\rho}} e^{-\rho/2}\right)^N \\
&\simeq 1 - \frac{N}{\sqrt{2\pi\rho}} e^{-\rho/2}
\end{aligned}
\tag{8.25}
$$

where, in the second line, we have used the approximation to the binomial expansion.

The second term in Eq. (8.25) must be negligible compared to the unity term as the network N is made infinitely large in order to ensure that the average probability of stable patterns P_{stab} is close to unity. We note that the second term in Eq. (8.24) is the average probability that a bit in a fundamental memory will be unstable. Now, it is not enough to require the probability for one unstable bit be small, but rather it must be small compared with $1/N$. This requirement is satisfied provided that we choose

$$
\frac{1}{\sqrt{2\pi\rho}} e^{-\rho/2} < \frac{1}{N}
$$

or, equivalently,

$$
\rho > 2 \ln N + \frac{1}{2} \ln(2\pi\rho)
$$

To ensure the stability of *most* of the fundamental memories, we must therefore choose the signal-to-noise ratio such that its minimum value satisfies the condition (Amit, 1989)

$$
\rho_{\min} = 2 \ln N \tag{8.26}
$$

We may then rewrite Eq. (8.25) simply as

$$
P_{\text{stab}} \simeq 1 - \frac{1}{2\sqrt{\pi \ln N}} \tag{8.27}
$$

Equation (8.27) shows that, in the limit as the number of neurons N approaches infinity, the probability that there will be an unstable bit in a state of the Hopfield network corresponding to any of the fundamental memories approaches zero. This result, however, is subject to the requirement that the signal-to-noise ratio ρ is not permitted to drop below the minimum value $\rho_{\min}$ of Eq. (8.26) or, equivalently, that the number of fundamental memories p does not exceed a critical value $p_{\max}$. In light of this requirement, we may use the definition of ρ given in the last line of Eq. (8.18) to write

$$
\begin{aligned}
p_{\max} &\simeq \frac{N}{\rho_{\min}} \\
&= \frac{N}{2 \ln N}
\end{aligned}
\tag{8.28}
$$

Equation (8.28) defines the storage capacity of a Hopfield network on the basis that *most of the fundamental memories are recalled perfectly.*

In our definition of the storage capacity, we could be even more stringent by requiring that *all* the fundamental memories be recalled perfectly. Such a definition requires that all pN bits of the fundamental memories are retrieved correctly with a probability of 99 percent, say. Using this definition, it can be shown that the maximum number of fundamental memories is given by (Amit, 1989)

$$
p_{\max} \simeq \frac{N}{4 \ln N} \tag{8.29}
$$

The important point to note is that whether we use the definition of Eq. (8.28) or the more stringent one of Eq. (8.29) for the storage capacity of a Hopfield network, the asymptotic storage capacity of the network has to be maintained small for the fundamental memories to be recoverable. This is indeed a major limitation of the Hopfield network.

How to Increase the Storage Capacity

One way of suppressing the adverse effects of correlated patterns in the Hopfield network is to modify the outer product rule of learning by making it *nonlocal* in character. In particular, the synaptic weight w_{ji} is redefined by (Personnaz et al., 1985)

$$w_{ji} = \frac{1}{N} \sum_{\mu=1}^{p} \sum_{\nu=1}^{p} \xi_{\mu,j} (\mathbf{C}^{-1})_{\mu\nu} \xi_{\nu,i} \tag{8.30}$$

where $(\mathbf{C}^{-1})_{\mu\nu}$ is the $\mu\nu$th element of the inverse matrix $\mathbf{C}^{-1}$. The $\mu\nu$th element of the *overlap matrix* $\mathbf{C}$ is defined by

$$(\mathbf{C})_{\mu\nu} = \sum_{i} \xi_{\mu,i} \xi_{\nu,i} \tag{8.31}$$

Dynamics of the network so defined is not governed by the energy function of Eq. (8.13) because of the presence of self-coupling terms. The self-coupling severely restricts the size of the basins of attraction of the fundamental memories, especially for large p. Kanter and Sompolinsky (1987) have introduced a modification of the model of Personnaz et al. by eliminating the self-coupling terms from the dynamics. The resulting network has the ability to retrieve perfectly any p linearly independent patterns for all $p < N$, where N is the number of neurons. The fact that the patterns memorized by the network can be retrieved without errors and that correlated patterns can also be stored is a good advantage. The price paid for this improvement is that the learning rule is nonlocal, which makes the model unattractive from a biological viewpoint.

8.7 Isomorphism Between a Hopfield Network and a Spin-Glass Model

A Hopfield model consists of a large assembly of identical neurons, each characterized by an internal state (i.e., firing rate), and interconnected by synapses of varying weights in accordance with a dynamic rule. Such a model is reminiscent of some simple models of magnetic materials encountered in statistical mechanics.

Consider a solid consisting of N identical atoms arranged in a regular lattice. Each atom has a net electronic *spin* and associated magnetic moment. In a well-known example in statistical mechanics referred to as the *Ising-spin model,* the spin σ_j of each atom j can only take on the value ± 1. In addition, each atom is assumed to interact with neighboring atoms. The predominant iteration is usually the so-called *exchange iteration,* which is a quantum mechanical effect. If the spin–spin interactions extend over large distances and take on random values, we speak of a *spin-glass model.*

Much research in condensed matter physics has been directed at "frustrated" systems, in which atoms are not all alike. The term "frustration" refers to the feature that interactions favoring different and incompatible kinds of ordering may be simultaneously present. The magnetic alloys known as "spin glasses," which exhibit competition between ferromagnetic and antiferromagnetic spin ordering, are the best example of frustrated systems. These systems stand in the same relation to conventional magnets as glasses do to crystals—hence the name ''spin glass'' (Kirkpatrick et al., 1983). The ferromagnetic use corresponds to the case for which all the w_{ij} are positive. The antiferromagnetic use, on the other hand, corresponds to the case where there is a regular change of sign between neighboring atoms. If the signs and absolute values of w_{ij} are randomly distributed, the material is called a spin glass.

The dynamics of the spin-glass model is viewed in a phase space that is spanned by the degrees of freedom and the associated moments. The system is governed by a Hamiltonian through the usual equations of motion. The internal states of the system are represented by the spin variables $\sigma_j, j = 1, 2, \ldots, N$. For the system to evolve toward an equilibrium state, we assume the existence of an unspecified mechanism that permits the spins to flip up or down, according to the following rules:

1. Every atom j in the model is associated with a quantity called the *molecular field* h_j.
2. The molecular field h_j is a linear combination of the internal states σ_j of the surrounding spins:

$$h_j = \sum_i J_{ji}\sigma_i \tag{8.32}$$

   where the coefficients J_{ji} are called the *exchange couplings.*
3. The internal state σ_j eventually flips so as to satisfy the *alignment condition:*

$$h_j\sigma_j > 0 \tag{8.33}$$

The *Hamiltonian H* representing the interaction energy between the spins of the system is defined by

$$\begin{aligned} H &= -\frac{1}{2}\sum_j h_j\sigma_j \\ &= -\frac{1}{2}\sum_i\sum_j J_{ji}\sigma_j\sigma_i \end{aligned} \tag{8.34}$$

where the factor $\frac{1}{2}$ is introduced because the interaction between the same two spins is counted twice in performing the double summation. When the exchange couplings are symmetric, that is,

$$J_{ji} = J_{ij} \tag{8.35}$$

but they have a random character, the system is known to have many locally stable states.

Comparing the equations that characterize the spin-glass model with those of the Hopfield model, we see immediately that there is indeed an *isomorphism* between these two models. The details of this isomorphism are presented in Table 8.2.

Physicists have devoted a great deal of work to the statistical mechanics of spin-glass models, which means that the formal methods and concepts of statistical mechanics are natural tools for the study of not only the Hopfield network but also other related neural networks (Peretto, 1984). The most significant results have been obtained with fully connected spin networks (Kirkpatrick and Sherrington, 1978).

8.8 Stochastic Neurons

Up to now, we have focused our attention on the ''noiseless'' dynamics of the Hopfield model—noiseless in the sense that there is no noise present in the synaptic transmission of signals. In reality, however, synaptic transmission in a nervous system is a noisy

TABLE 8.2 Dictionary Describing Isomorphism Between the Hopfield and Spin-Glass Models

Hopfield Model	Spin-Glass Model
Neuron i	Atom i
Neuron state $s_i = \pm 1$	Spin $\sigma_i = \pm 1$
Synaptic weights, w_{ji}	Exchange couplings, J_{ji}
Net activation potential, v_j	Molecular field, h_j
Excitatory synapse, $w_{ji} > 0$	$J_{ji} > 0$
Inhibitory synapse, $w_{ji} < 0$	$J_{ji} < 0$
Energy function, E	Hamiltonian, H

process brought on by random fluctuations from the release of neurotransmitters, and other probabilistic causes. The important question, of course, is how to account for the effects of synaptic noise in a neural network in a mathematically tractable manner. The traditional method for doing so in the neural network literature is to introduce a *probabilistic mechanism in the firing of neurons* and, in a loose sense, to represent the effects of synaptic noise by *thermal fluctuations.* Specifically, a neuron j decides to fire according to the value of the net potential v_j acting on it with the *probability of firing* being defined by $P(v_j)$. We thus replace the deterministic rule of Eq. (8.5) for the state s_j of neuron j by the *probabilistic rule*

$$s_j = \begin{cases} +1 & \text{with probability } P(v_j) \\ -1 & \text{with probability } 1 - P(v_j) \end{cases} \tag{8.36}$$

If the net potential v_j acting on neuron j is exactly zero, we set $s_j = \pm 1$ each with probability $\frac{1}{2}$.

For the function $P(v)$ to qualify as a probability, it must satisfy the limiting values

$$P(v) = 0 \qquad \text{as } v \to -\infty$$

and

$$P(v) = 1 \qquad \text{as } v \to +\infty$$

Moreover, between these two limits, the function $P(v)$ must increase monotonically with v. A standard choice for $P(v)$ is the sigmoid-shaped function (Little, 1974):

$$P(v) = \frac{1}{1 + \exp(-2v/T)} \tag{8.37}$$

where T is a *pseudotemperature* that is used to control the noise level and therefore the uncertainty in the firing of a neuron. It is important to realize, however, that T is not the physical temperature of a neural network, be that a biological or an artificial network. Rather, as already stated, we should think of T as a parameter that controls the thermal fluctuations representing the effects of synaptic noise. For brevity, however, we will refer to T in the context of neural networks simply as "temperature" hereafter.

When $T \to 0$, which corresponds to the *noiseless* limit, the width of the threshold region shrinks to zero. Under this condition, the probabilistic firing rule of Eq. (8.36) reduces to the deterministic rule of Eq. (8.5). Figure 8.13 displays the probability $P(v)$ that a neuron fires, which is plotted as a function of the net potential v acting on the neuron for two different values of the temperature T. The continuous curve represents a plot of Eq. (8.36) for some temperature T greater than zero, whereas the curve shown in

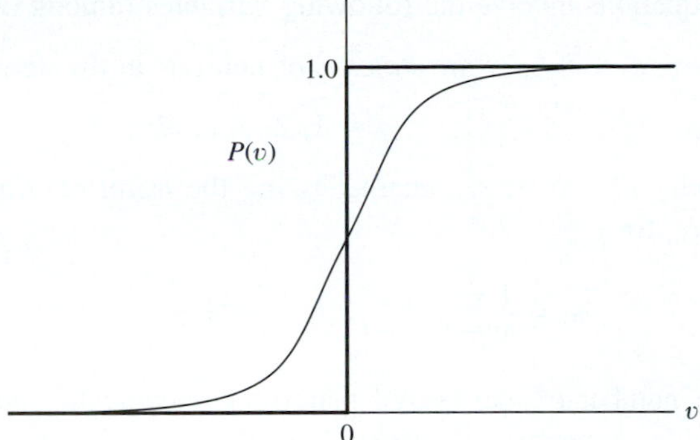

FIGURE 8.13 Sigmoid-shaped function for probability of a stochastic neuron firing; heavy solid curve corresponds to the operation of the McCulloch–Pitts neuron.

heavy solid lines represents the limiting case of $T = 0$. Note that although the continuous curve in Fig. 8.13 has the same sigmoidal shape as the activation function of a nonlinear neuron in multilayer perceptrons, it has an entirely different meaning. The sigmoid function plotted in Fig. 8.13 represents a probabilistic threshold response, whereas the sigmoidal activation function in a multilayer perceptron represents a deterministic input–output relation.

It is also of interest to note that the probabilistic rule of Eq. (8.36) is consistent with the way in which the effect of thermal fluctuations in a spin-glass model is described mathematically. Indeed, the use of the probabilistic rule for the firing of a neuron as described here makes the analogy between the Hopfield model in neural networks and the spin-glass model in statistical mechanics all the more complete and fruitful.

8.9 Phase Diagram of the Hopfield Network, and Related Properties

The striking similarity between the behavior of the Hopfield network and that of the spin-glass model has led to the discovery of an important property of the Hopfield network: It is solvable exactly. Specifically, starting with the energy function (i.e., Hamiltonian) of the Hopfield network and the generalized Hebb rule for the synaptic weights of the network, and assuming that the number N of neurons in the network is large (i.e., invoking the *thermodynamical limit* $N \rightarrow \infty$), Amit and co-workers[1] used the formal methods and concepts of statistical mechanics to derive the *mean-field equations* for associative recall in a stochastic Hopfield network (i.e., one that uses stochastic neurons). The mathematics involved in the derivation is rigorous and difficult to plough through, and unfortunately beyond the scope of this book. We will therefore content ourselves by describing highlights of the theory.

[1] The derivation of the mean-field equations for the Hopfield network was first reported in a remarkable series of papers (Amit et al., 1985a, 1985b; 1987a, 1987b), which were followed by a book (Amit, 1989). For a condensed treatment of the subject, see chaps. 16 and 17 of the book by Müller and Reinhardt, (1990), and chap. 1 by van Hemmen and Kühn in the book edited by Domany et al. (1991).

The term "mean field" in mean-field equations comes from statistical physics. It refers to the mean value of the molecular field associated with each atom in a spin-glass model.

The mean-field equations involve the following variables (among others):

- The *mean (average) values of the states* s_j of neurons in the network:

$$\langle s_j \rangle, \qquad j = 1, 2, \ldots, N$$

- A set of *auxiliary variables,* m_ν, characterizing the *mean overlap* of $\langle s_j \rangle$ with the stored pattern $\xi_{\nu,j}$ for $j = 1, 2, \ldots, N$:

$$m_\nu = \frac{1}{N} \sum_{j=1}^{N} \langle s_j \rangle \xi_{\nu,j}, \qquad \nu = 1, 2, \ldots, p \tag{8.38}$$

  where p is the number of memorized patterns (fundamental memories). In other words, m_ν provides a measure of *retrieval quality.*

- The *load parameter* or *storage efficiency,*

$$\alpha = \frac{p}{N} \tag{8.39}$$

  which expresses the number of memorized patterns, p, as a fraction of the total number of neurons in the network, N. Note that for $\alpha \neq 0$, the number p of memorized patterns scales proportionately with the number N of neurons, as $N \to \infty$. Note also that α is the reciprocal of the signal-to-noise ratio ρ for large N; see Eq. (8.18).

- The *temperature* T, which provides a measure of how noisy the network dynamics is.

For a complete description of a stochastic Hopfield network required to recall memorized patterns, we have to consider m as a function of both α and T. This evaluation leads to the formulation of the *T–α phase diagram,* depicted in Fig. 8.14. The phase diagram delineates three main critical lines labeled T_g, T_M, and T_C, across which the Hopfield network changes its qualitative behavior.

The phase boundary between the network functioning as an *associative memory* and one suffering from *total confusion* or *amnesia* is described by the curve labeled T_M in

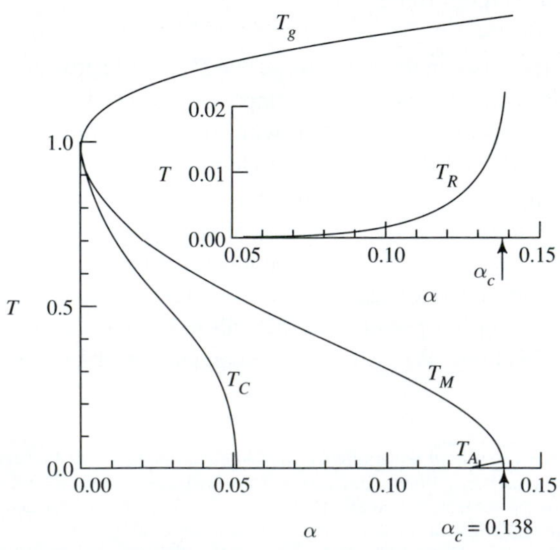

FIGURE 8.14 Phase diagram of the Hopfield network. (From E. Domany et al., 1991, with permission of Springer-Verlag.)

Fig. 8.14. This curve is bounded by the *critical load parameter* $\alpha_c = 0.138$ on the α axis and the *critical temperature* $T = 1$ on the T axis. Directly below T_M the retrieval states of the Hopfield network are *metastable,* with few spin errors. If $\alpha < 0.051$, we pass the line T_C, below which the retrieval states of the network are *globally stable,* with no spin errors. In the *no-recall area* above the curve T_M in Fig. 8.14, the only stable states are the spin-glass (spurious) states. In the no-recall area, above the line T_g, these spin-glass states "melt"; the resulting solution produced by the network has an average value of zero. Near $\alpha_c = 0.138$ there is another critical line T_R, below which the *replica symmetry* of the retrieval states breaks down. What this implies is that within the retrieval states, a fraction of the spins (neurons) freeze in a spin-glass fashion. As the inset of the phase diagram in Fig. 8.14 shows, this instability is restricted to a fairly small region and therefore has a very small impact on the quantities that are relevant to retrieval.

As mentioned previously, the variable m provides a measure of retrieval quality. More specifically, the probability that a neuron in the network is in its correct state is equal to $(1 + m)/2$. The relative error in a time-averaged recall state is therefore $(1 - m)/2$. For a fixed value of the load parameter α, the retrieval quality m decreases monotonically as the temperature T increases from $T = 0$ to $T_M(\alpha)$. Figure 8.15 shows the way in which the retrieval quality m varies as a function of T for several fixed values of α. Each curve in Fig. 8.15 stops at a value of m equal to the discontinuity at $T_M(\alpha)$; this particular value of m defines the retrieval quality just before the network runs into total confusion.

Figure 8.16 shows the relative error $(1 - m)/2$ in a time-averaged recall state plotted as a function of the load parameter α for temperature $T = 0$. As α is increased starting from zero, the recall quality of the network degrades slightly. Just before the critical point $\alpha = \alpha_c$ is reached, the relative error remains small, less than 2 percent. However, when α reaches the critical value $\alpha_c = 0.138$, there is a dramatic increase in the level of errors and the system ceases to provide associative memory. Here again, we see that at the critical point α_c the network suddenly changes its behavior from a good associative memory into a condition of total confusion.

Finally, we should point out that the problem of modeling an associative memory such as the Hopfield network is a dynamic one, whereas the phase diagram applies to a static equilibrium problem. In the latter case, properties are averaged over *all* states of the spin system, stable and unstable. Nevertheless, we expect and indeed find that many results of the dynamics of the Hopfield network agree with and can (to a large extent) be predicted

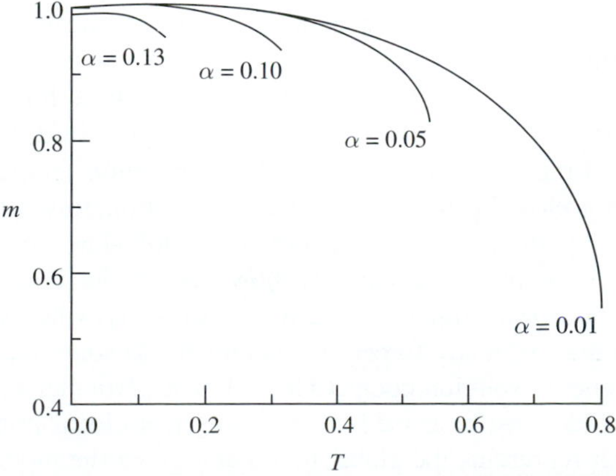

FIGURE 8.15 Recall quality m as a function of the temperature T for several load parameters α. (From D. J. Amit et al., 1987b, with permission of the American Institute of Physics.)

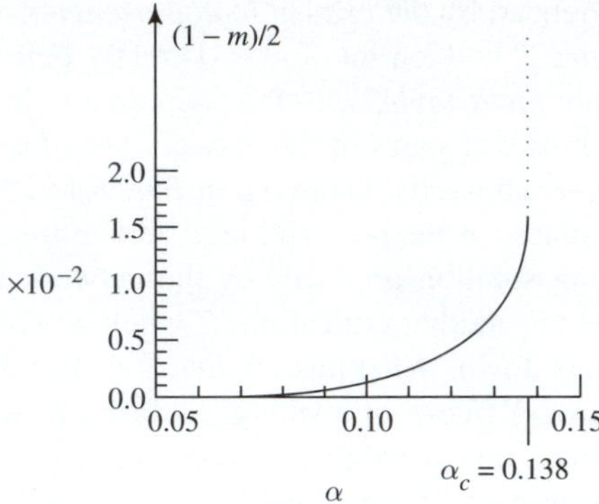

FIGURE 8.16 The quality of memory recall of the Hopfield network deteriorates with increasing load parameter $\alpha = p/N$ and breaks down at $\alpha \approx 0.138$. (From B. Müller and J. Reinhardt, 1990, with permission of Springer-Verlag.)

from the static equilibrium calculation (Domany, 1988). For instance, the critical load parameter $\alpha_c = 0.138$ is in agreement with the estimate of Hopfield (1982), where it is reported that (as a result of computer simulations) about $0.15N$ states can be recalled simultaneously before error becomes severe.

8.10 Simulated Annealing

Sections 8.3 through 8.9 were concerned strictly with different aspects of the Hopfield network. We now turn our attention to simulated annealing, which is important not only in its own right as a technique for solving combinatorial optimization problems, but also because it provides the basis for the Boltzmann machine to be considered in Section 8.11. A discussion of simulated annealing is also considered rather appropriate at this juncture, as it flows quite nicely from the stochastic notions presented in the previous two sections.

In a neural network, the objective is often that of minimizing a cost function defined as the global energy of the network. Ordinarily, the number of neurons contained in the network is very large. Thus, finding the minimum-energy solution of a neural network is not unlike that of finding the low-temperature state of a physical system. However, as mentioned previously, the concept of the temperature of a physical system has no obvious equivalent in a neural network.

Another issue of concern is that deterministic algorithms used for energy minimization suffer from a fundamental weakness of gradient descent procedures: The algorithm may get ''stuck'' in ''local minima'' that are not globally optimum. In the case of a Hopfield network used for ''noiseless'' pattern storage and recognition, this issue is not a problem, because the local energy minima of the network are exploited as a means of storing input patterns. This issue is of particular concern, however, in the case of neural networks required to perform *constraint-satisfaction tasks.* Specifically, when some of the neurons in a neural network are externally forced or ''clamped'' to some input pattern, we have to find a minimum-energy solution compatible with that particular input pattern. In such a situation, the network must be capable of escaping from local minima so as to reach the configuration that represents the global minimum, given the input pattern of interest.

Both of these issues are addressed in the *simulated annealing algorithm,* which was originally developed by Kirkpatrick et al. (1983). The basic idea of the algorithm is quite simple:

When optimizing a very large and complex system (i.e., a system with many degrees of freedom), instead of ''always'' going downhill, try to go downhill ''most of the time.''

Simulated annealing differs from conventional iterative optimization algorithms in two important respects:

- The algorithm need not get stuck, since transition out of a local minimum is always possible when the system operates at a nonzero temperature.
- Simulated annealing exhibits a *divide-and-conquer* feature that is *adaptive* in nature. Specifically, gross features of the final state of the system are seen at higher temperatures, while fine details of the state appear at lower temperatures.

The simulated annealing algorithm is based on the analogy between the behavior of a physical system with many degrees of freedom in thermal equilibrium at a series of finite temperatures as encountered in statistical physics and the problem of finding the minimum of a given function depending on many parameters as in combinatorial optimization (Kirkpatrick et al., 1983). In condensed-matter physics, *annealing* refers to a physical process that proceeds as follows (van Laarhoven and Aarts, 1988):

1. A solid in a *heat bath* is heated by raising the temperature to a maximum value at which all particles of the solid arrange themselves randomly in the liquid phase.
2. Then the temperature of the heat bath is lowered, permitting all particles to arrange themselves in the low-energy ground state of a corresponding lattice.

It is presumed that the maximum temperature in phase 1 is sufficiently high, and the cooling in phase 2 is carried out sufficiently slowly. However, if the cooling is too rapid—that is, the solid is not allowed enough time to reach thermal equilibrium at each temperature value—the resulting crystal will have many defects, or the substance may form a glass with no crystalline order and only metastable locally optimal structures (Kirkpatrick et al., 1983).

In 1953, Metropolis et al. proposed an algorithm for efficient simulation of the evolution to thermal equilibrium of a solid for a given temperature. The simulated annealing algorithm developed by Kirkpatrick et al. (1983) is a variant (with time-dependent temperature) of the Metropolis algorithm.[2]

Metropolis Algorithm

The *Metropolis algorithm,* based on Monte Carlo techniques, provides a simple method for simulating the evolution of a physical system in a heat bath (reservoir) to *thermal equilibrium.* It was introduced in the early days of scientific computation for the efficient simulation of a collection of atoms in equilibrium at a given temperature. In each step of the algorithm, an atom (unit) of a system is subjected to a small random displacement, and the resulting change ΔE in the energy of the system is computed. If we find that the change $\Delta E \leq 0$, the displacement is accepted, and the new system configuration with the displaced atom is used as the starting point for the next step of the algorithm. If, on the other hand, we find that the change $\Delta E > 0$, the algorithm proceeds in a probabilistic manner, as described next. The probability that the configuration with the displaced atom

[2] The Langevin equation (with time-dependent temperature) provides the basis for another global optimization algorithm that was proposed by Grenander (1983), and subsequently analyzed by Gidas (1985). The Langevin equation is described in Appendix D at the end of the book.

accepted is given by, except for a scaling factor,

$$P(\Delta E) = \exp\left(-\frac{\Delta E}{T}\right) \tag{8.40}$$

where T is the temperature. To implement the probabilistic part of the algorithm, we may use a generator of random numbers distributed uniformly in the interval (0,1). Specifically, one such number is selected and compared with the probability $P(\Delta E)$ of Eq. (8.40). If the random number is less than the probability $P(\Delta E)$, the new configuration with the displaced atom is accepted. Otherwise, the original system configuration is reused for the next step of the algorithm.

Provided that the temperature is lowered in a sufficiently slow manner, the system can reach thermal equilibrium at each temperature. In the Metropolis algorithm, this condition is achieved by having a large number of transitions at each temperature; a *transition* refers to some combined action that results in the transformation of a system from one state to another. Thus, by repeating the basic steps of the Metropolis algorithm, we effectively simulate the motion of the atoms in a physical system in thermal equilibrium with a heat bath of absolute temperature T. Moreover, the choice of $P(\Delta E)$ defined in Eq. (8.40) ensures that thermal equilibrium is characterized by the Boltzmann distribution, just as in statistical mechanics. According to the Boltzmann distribution, described in Appendix C at the end of the book, the probability of a physical system being in a state α with energy E_α at temperature T is given by

$$P_\alpha = \frac{1}{Z}\exp\left(-\frac{E_\alpha}{T}\right) \tag{8.41}$$

where Z is the *partition function,* defined by

$$Z = \sum_\beta \exp\left(-\frac{E_\beta}{T}\right) \tag{8.42}$$

where the summation is taken over all states β with energy E_β at temperature T. At high values of temperature T, the Boltzmann distribution exhibits a uniform preference for all states, regardless of energy. When the temperature T approaches zero, however, only the states with minimum energy have a nonzero probability of occurrence.

Markov Property of Simulated Annealing

Given a neighborhood structure, we may view the simulated annealing algorithm as an algorithm that continuously tries to transform the current configuration into one of its neighbors. In mathematical terms, such a mechanism is best described by means of a Markov chain (van Laarhoven and Aarts, 1988).

To define what we mean by a Markov chain, consider a probabilistic experiment involving a sequence of trials with possible outcomes $\{A_n, n = 0, 1, 2, \ldots\}$, which is characterized in such a way that the conditional probability of the outcome A_n depends only on A_{n-1} and is independent of all previous outcomes. More precisely, let the conditional probability of the event (outcome) A_n, given that $A_{n-1}, \ldots, A_0$ have occurred, satisfy the condition

$$\text{Prob}(A_n|A_{n-1}, \ldots, A_0) = \text{Prob}(A_n|A_{n-1}) \tag{8.43}$$

A sequence of trials whose outcomes $\{A_n, n = 0, 1, 2, \ldots\}$ satisfy this condition is said to be a *Markov chain* (Feller, 1968; Bharucha-Reid, 1960).

In the case of simulated annealing, trials correspond to transitions and outcomes correspond to system configurations (states). Since, in simulated annealing, the current state of a system that has experienced a transition depends only on the previous state, it follows that *simulated annealing has the Markov property.*

A Markov chain is described in terms of a set of one-step *transition probabilities* $p_{ji}(n, n-1)$. Specifically, $p_{ji}(n, n-1)$ is the conditional probability that the system is in state j after the nth transition, given that it was in state i after the $(n-1)$th transition. Let $P_j(n)$ denote the *absolute* or *unconditional probability* that the system is in state j after the nth transition. We may then solve for $P_j(n)$ using the recursion

$$P_j(n) = \sum_k p_{jk}(n, n-1)P_k(n-1), \qquad n = 1, 2, \ldots \tag{8.44}$$

where the summation is over all possible states of the system. If the transition probabilities $p_{jk}(n, n-1)$ do not depend on n, the Markov chain is said to be *homogeneous.*

Finite-Time Approximation

An important property of simulated annealing is that of asymptotic convergence, for which a mathematical proof was first given by Geman and Geman (1984). According to Geman and Geman, we may state the following:

> *If the temperature T_k employed in executing the kth step of the simulated annealing algorithm satisfies the bound*
>
> $$T_k \geq \frac{T_0}{\log(1+k)} \tag{8.45}$$
>
> *for every k, where T_0 is a sufficiently large constant (initial temperature) independent of k, then with probability one the system will converge to the minimum energy configuration.*

Stated in another way, the algorithm generates a Markov chain that converges in distribution to a uniform one over the minimal energy configurations. The conditions for asymptotic convergence given here are *sufficient* but not *necessary.* Similar conditions for asymptotic convergence of the simulated annealing algorithm have been derived by many other authors (Aarts and Korst, 1989).

Unfortunately, the annealing schedule specified by Eq. (8.45) is extremely slow—too slow to be of practical use. In practice, we have to resort to a *finite-time approximation* of the asymptotic convergence of the algorithm. The price paid for the approximation is that the algorithm is no longer guaranteed to find a global minimum with probability 1. Nevertheless, the resulting approximate form of the algorithm is capable of producing near-optimum solutions for many practical applications.

To implement a finite-time approximation of the simulated annealing algorithm, we need to specify a set of parameters governing the convergence of the algorithm. These parameters are combined in a so-called *annealing schedule* or *cooling schedule.* Indeed, the search for adequate annealing schedules has been the subject of an active research field for several years (van Laarhoven and Aarts, 1988). The annealing schedule that we will briefly describe here is the one originally proposed by Kirkpatrick et al. (1983), which is based on a number of conceptually simple empirical rules.[3]

---

[3] For more elaborate and theoretically oriented annealing schedules, see the books by Aarts and Korst (1989, pp. 60–75) and by van Laarhoven and Aarts (1988, pp. 62–71).

An annealing schedule specifies a finite sequence of values of the temperature and a finite number of transitions attempted at each value of the temperature. The annealing schedule due to Kirkpatrick et al. specifies the parameters of interest as follows:

- *Initial Value of the Temperature.* The initial value T_0 of the temperature is chosen high enough to ensure that virtually all proposed transitions are accepted by the simulated annealing algorithm.
- *Decrement of the Temperature.* Ordinarily, the cooling is performed *exponentially,* with the changes made in the value of the temperature being small. In particular, the *decrement function* is defined by

$$T_k = \alpha T_{k-1}, \qquad k = 1, 2, \ldots \tag{8.46}$$

  where α is a constant smaller but close to unity. Typical values of α lie between 0.8 and 0.99. At each temperature, enough transitions are attempted so that there are ten *accepted* transitions per experiment on the average.
- *Final Value of the Temperature.* The system is frozen and annealing stops if the desired number of acceptances is not achieved at three successive temperatures.

Simulated Annealing for Combinatorial Optimization

Simulated annealing is particularly well suited for solving combinatorial optimization problems. As mentioned previously, the objective of a combinatorial optimization problem is to minimize the cost function of a finite, discrete system characterized by a large number of possible solutions. Essentially, simulated annealing uses the Metropolis algorithm to generate a sequence of solutions by invoking an analogy between a physical many-particle system and a combinatorial optimization problem. Specifically, the following equivalences are invoked (Aarts and Korst, 1989):

- Solutions in a combinatorial optimization problem are equivalent to the states of a physical system.
- The cost of a solution is equivalent to the energy of a state.

The temperature T in the Metropolis algorithm plays the role of a *control parameter* in simulated annealing. The other parameter is the number of transitions generated at each iteration of the Metropolis algorithm

8.11 The Boltzmann Machine

We next turn our attention to the *Boltzmann machine,* which represents another important example of a neural network that relies on a stochastic (probabilistic) form of learning (Hinton and Sejnowski, 1983, 1986; Ackley et al., 1985). Basic to the operation of the Boltzmann machine is the idea of simulated annealing described in the previous section. The machine is so called in recognition of the formal equivalence between Boltzmann's original work on statistical thermodynamics and the network's dynamic behavior.

The Boltzmann machine and the Hopfield network share the following common features: (1) Their processing units have binary values (± 1, say) for their states; (2) all the synaptic connections between their units are symmetric; (3) the units are picked at random and one at a time for updating; and (4) they have no self-feedback. However, they differ from each other in three important respects:

- The Boltzmann machine permits the use of *hidden neurons,* whereas no such neurons exist in the Hopfield network.
- The Boltzmann machine uses *stochastic neurons* with a probabilistic firing mechanism, whereas the standard Hopfield network uses neurons based on the *McCulloch–-Pitts model* with a *deterministic* firing mechanism.
- The Hopfield network operates in an unsupervised manner, whereas the Boltzmann machine may also be trained by supervision of a probabilistic form.

The stochastic neurons of a *Boltzmann machine* partition into two functional groups: *visible,* and *hidden,* as depicted in Fig. 8.17a. The visible neurons provide an interface between the network and the environment in which it operates. During the training phase of the network, the visible neurons are all *clamped* onto specific states determined by the environment. The hidden neurons, on the other hand, always operate freely; they are used

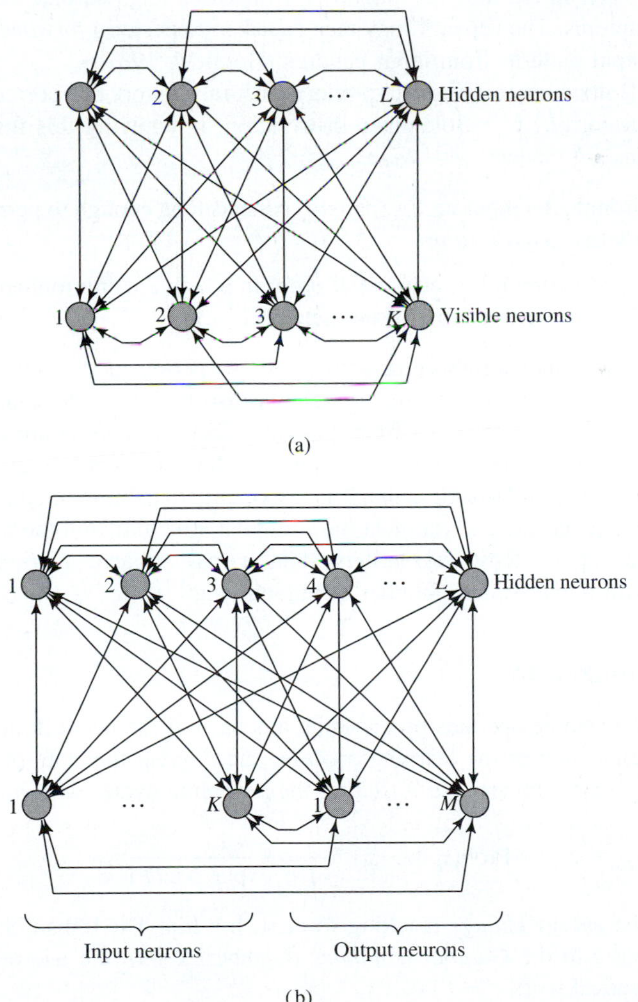

FIGURE 8.17 (a) Boltzmann machine with visible and hidden neurons. (b) Boltzmann machine with input, output, and hidden neurons; the input neurons are always clamped into states of +1 or −1 by the environment. In both configurations (a) and (b), all the synaptic connections between the neurons are symmetric.

to explain underlying constraints contained in the environmental input vectors. The hidden neurons accomplish this task by capturing higher-order statistical correlations in the clamping vectors. The network described here represents a special case of the Boltzmann machine. It may be viewed as an "unsupervised" learning procedure for modeling a probability distribution that is specified by clamping patterns onto the visible neurons with appropriate probabilities. By so doing, the network can perform *pattern completion.* Specifically, when a partial information-bearing vector is clamped onto a subset of the visible neurons, the network performs completion on the remaining visible neurons, provided that it has learned the training distribution properly (Hinton, 1987).

The visible neurons may be further subdivided into *input* and *output* neurons, as illustrated in Fig. 8.17b. In this second configuration, the Boltzmann machine performs *association* under the *supervision* of a teacher, with the input neurons receiving information from the environment and the output neurons reporting the outcome of the computation to an end user. In particular, the information that we may have as to what the "correct" output pattern is for each input pattern may be probabilistic in nature. Such a situation arises, for example, in the medical diagnosis of diseases (e.g., cardiac conditions) from patterns of symptoms. The network may then be asked to perform *forward inference,* that is, inferring output patterns from input patterns (Hopfield, 1987b).

The goal of Boltzmann learning is to produce a neural network that correctly categorizes input patterns according to a Boltzmann distribution. In applying this form of learning, two assumptions are made:

- Each environmental input vector (pattern) persists long enough to permit the network to reach *thermal equilibrium.*
- There is *no* structure in the sequential order in which the environmental vectors are clamped into the visible units of the network.

A particular set of synaptic weights is said to constitute a perfect model of the environmental structure if it leads to exactly the same probability distribution of the states of the visible units (when the network is running freely) as that when these units are clamped by the environmental input vectors. Unless the number of hidden units is exponentially large compared to the number of visible units, it is impossible to achieve such a perfect model, in general. If, however, the environment has a regular structure, and the network uses its hidden units to capture these regularities, then it may achieve a good match to the environment with a manageable number of hidden units.

Energy Minimization

The Boltzmann machine operates by choosing a neuron of the network at random—say, neuron j—at some step of the learning process, and *flipping* the state of neuron j from state s_j to state $-s_j$ at temperature T (during the annealing cycle) with probability

$$\text{Prob}(s_j \rightarrow -s_j) = \frac{1}{1 + \exp(-\Delta E_j/T)} \tag{8.47}$$

where ΔE_j is the *energy change* resulting from such a flip. The transition probability of Eq. (8.47) is basic to the *Glauber dynamics* (Glauber, 1963), the use of which is well suited for theoretical work.

Although the probability of Eq. (8.47) is different in appearance from that of Eq. (8.37), they are in fact equivalent in meaning. To show this equivalence, we first note that since the Boltzmann machine uses symmetric connections, we may define an energy function for it similar to that for the Hopfield network. Specifically, we define the energy function of the Boltzmann machine as follows:

$$E = -\frac{1}{2}\sum_{i}\sum_{\substack{j \\ i\neq j}} w_{ji}s_j s_i \tag{8.48}$$

Hence, the energy change produced by neuron j flipping from state s_j to $-s_j$ equals

$$\begin{aligned}\Delta E_j &= (\text{energy with neuron } j \text{ in state } s_j) - (\text{energy with neuron } j \text{ in state } -s_j)\\ &= -(s_j)\sum_i w_{ji}s_i + (-s_j)\sum_i w_{ji}s_i\\ &= -2s_j\sum_i w_{ji}s_i\\ &= -2s_j v_j\end{aligned}$$

where v_j is the net activation potential applied to neuron j. We may therefore rewrite Eq. (8.47) as

$$\text{Prob}(s_j \rightarrow -s_j) = \frac{1}{1 + \exp(2s_j v_j/T)}$$

This means that for an initial state $s_j = -1$, the probability that neuron j is flipped into state $+1$ is

$$\frac{1}{1 + \exp(-2v_j/T)}$$

Similarly, for an initial state of $s_j = +1$, the probability that neuron j is flipped into state -1 is

$$\frac{1}{1 + \exp(+2v_j/T)} = 1 - \frac{1}{1 + \exp(-2v_j/T)}$$

The latter probability and the one previous to it are in perfect agreement with the two lines of Eq. (8.36), respectively.

Returning to the task at hand, we recognize that in Eq. (8.48) the double summation runs over both visible (input–output) and hidden neurons. The condition $i \neq j$ implies that the network has no self-feedback; w_{ji} is the synaptic weight from neuron i to neuron j, and N is the total number of neurons in the network. An external threshold θ_j applied to neuron j is readily taken into account by setting one of the synaptic weights equal to θ_j and feeding that particular weight from a fixed input equal to -1. The value of the energy function E depends on the global state of the network. A *global state* is defined as a set of states of all the neurons in the network. With the network assumed to consist of N neurons and each neuron taking on the value ± 1, there are 2^N global states.

If the probabilistic rule described in Eq. (8.47) is applied repeatedly to the neurons, the network will reach *thermal equilibrium*. At thermal equilibrium the neurons will change state, but the probability of finding the network in any particular global state remains constant and obeys the *Boltzmann distribution*. The simplicity of this distribution and the fact that it is independent of the path followed in reaching thermal equilibrium are the properties that make the Boltzmann machine interesting.

The minima of the energy function E correspond to stable configurations of the Boltzmann machine. To find a stable configuration that is well suited to the problem at hand, Boltzmann learning proceeds by first operating the network at a high temperature, and then gradually lowering it until the network eventually reaches thermal equilibrium at a series of temperatures, as prescribed by the simulated annealing procedure. At high temperatures, the network ignores small energy differences and therefore tends to approach thermal equilibrium rapidly. In so doing, it performs a "coarse search" of the space of global states, and thereby finds a good minimum. As the temperature is lowered, the network begins to perform a "fine search" by responding to small energy differences, and thus finds a better minimum in the neighborhood of the coarse-search minimum discovered at high temperature. It is this property of the Boltzmann machine learning procedure that makes it well suited to *constraint-satisfaction tasks* involving a large number of weak constraints (Hinton and Sejnowski, 1986). The term "weak constraints" refers to a situation where the distinction between the cost function to be minimized and the set of constraints to be satisfied is not clear-cut. Consider, for example, computer vision, where it is usually helpful to constrain neighboring areas of a continuous surface to be at similar depths. This is not an absolute constraint, as it does not apply to the edge of an object. Accordingly, a computer vision system may generate interpretations that violate this constraint if, by so doing, it can satisfy many other requirements. Constraints that may be broken at a cost are referred to as *weak* (*soft*) *constraints* (Blake, 1983). Thus, in a situation of this kind, an optimum solution is the most "plausible" solution that fits the set of weak constraints not exactly but as well as possible.

The Boltzmann Learning Rule

The use of hidden neurons enhances the computing power of the Boltzmann machine by acting as useful *feature detectors.* However, their inclusion requires that we treat the Boltzmann machine differently from the Hopfield network. In particular, Hebb's postulate of learning is no longer suitable, since it does not tell us how to adjust the synaptic weights between the visible and hidden neurons, and those between the hidden neurons themselves. Moreover, the idea of error-correction learning, which works well for multilayer feedforward networks (with one-way flow of information) is not applicable to the Boltzmann machine based on symmetrical connections (i.e., two-way flow of information). To deal with Boltzmann learning, we therefore require a completely *new* concept.

The operation of the Boltzmann machine depends on whether the network simply has visible and hidden neurons as in Fig. 8.17a, or whether it has input, hidden, and output neurons as in Fig. 8.17b. These two network configurations are considered in turn.

Stochastic Network with Visible and Hidden Neurons. To proceed with the formal development of Boltzmann learning, we will first introduce some new notations. Let the states of the visible neurons be denoted by α, and those of the hidden neurons by β. Assuming that the network has K visible neurons and L hidden neurons, α runs from 1 to 2^K and β runs from 1 to 2^L. Let P_α^+ denote the probability that the visible neurons of the Boltzmann machine are collectively in state α, given that the network is operating in its clamped condition (i.e., under the influence of the environment). Let P_α^- denote the probability that these same neurons are in state α, given that the network is allowed to run freely, but with no environmental input. Thus, P_α^+ and P_α^- are both *conditional probabilities,* measured at thermal equilibrium. The use of a $+$ sign as superscript indicates that the network is in a *clamped condition,* whereas the use of a $-$ sign as superscript indicates that the network is *running freely.* Accordingly, we may view the set of probabilities

$$\{P_\alpha^+ | \alpha = 1, 2, \ldots, 2^K\}$$

as the *desired probabilities* that represent the environment (i.e., the training set), and the set of probabilities

$$\{P_\alpha^- | \alpha = 1, 2, \ldots, 2^K\}$$

as the *actual probabilities* computed by the network. In Boltzmann learning, we adjust the synaptic weights w_{ji} of the network so as to give the visible neurons a desired probability distribution. That is, the learning task is to make the actual probabilities P_α^- take on the desired probabilities P_α^+. To do so, we need a suitable measure of the discrepancy between the environment and the network's internal model. For such a measure, we may use the *relative entropy* defined by (Gray, 1990):

$$H_{P^+\|P^-} = \sum_{\alpha=1}^{2^K} P_\alpha^+ \ln\left(\frac{P_\alpha^+}{P_\alpha^-}\right) \tag{8.49}$$

where K is the number of visible neurons. The relative entropy $H_{P^+\|P^-}$ is referred to in the information-theory literature as the *Kullback–Leibler measure of information* (Kullback, 1968); it may also be given a statistical thermodynamics interpretation. In any event, it always has a positive value or zero. For the special case when $P_\alpha^+ = P_\alpha^-$ for all α, it equals zero exactly. Under this special condition, there is a perfect match between the environment and the network's internal model.

The distribution P_α^+ is naturally independent of the synaptic weights w_{ji}, whereas P_α^- depends on the w_{ji}. Hence, the relative entropy $H_{P^+\|P^-}$ may be minimized by adjusting the synaptic weights w_{ji}. To perform a gradient descent in the H space, we need to know the derivative of $H_{P^+\|P^-}$ with respect to w_{ji}. In the general case of a cross-coupled network, it is difficult to find the partial derivative $\partial H_{P^+\|P^-}/\partial w_{ji}$. However, it is a straightforward matter to evaluate this derivative for a Boltzmann machine because of the simple probability distributions that exist when the network is in thermal equilibrium.

Differentiating both sides of Eq. (8.49) with respect to the synaptic weight w_{ji} and recognizing that the clamped probability distribution P_α^+ over the visible neurons is independent of w_{ji}, we get

$$\frac{\partial H_{P^+\|P^-}}{\partial w_{ji}} = -\sum_\alpha \frac{P_\alpha^+}{P_\alpha^-}\frac{\partial P_\alpha^-}{\partial w_{ji}} \tag{8.50}$$

where, from here on, it is understood that α runs over the range 1 to 2^K. To minimize the relative entropy $H_{P^+\|P^-}$, we use gradient descent:

$$\begin{aligned} \Delta w_{ji} &= -\varepsilon \frac{\partial H_{P^+\|P^-}}{\partial w_{ji}} \\ &= \varepsilon \sum_\alpha \frac{P_\alpha^+}{P_\alpha^-}\frac{\partial P_\alpha^-}{\partial w_{ji}}, \qquad \begin{matrix} i, j = 1, 2, \ldots, N \\ i \neq j \end{matrix} \end{aligned} \tag{8.51}$$

where ε is some positive constant. To evaluate the change Δw_{ji} in the synaptic weight w_{ji}, we require the partial derivative $\partial P_\alpha^-/\partial w_{ji}$, which is considered next.

Let $P_{\alpha\beta}^-$ denote the *joint* probability that the visible neurons are in state α and the hidden neurons are in state β, given that the network is operating in its clamped condition. In this condition, we may then express the probability P_α^- of finding the visible neurons in state α regardless of β as follows:

$$P_\alpha^- = \sum_\beta P_{\alpha\beta}^- \tag{8.52}$$

where, from here on, it is understood that β runs over the range 1 to 2^L and L is the number of hidden neurons. Assuming that the network is in thermal equilibrium, we may invoke the Boltzmann distribution to calculate the probability P_α^-. In particular, extending the use of Eqs. (8.41) and (8.42) to deal with this calculation, we have

$$P_\alpha^- = \frac{1}{Z}\sum_\beta \exp\left(-\frac{E_{\alpha\beta}}{T}\right) \tag{8.53}$$

where $E_{\alpha\beta}$ is the energy of the network when the visible neurons are in state α and the hidden neurons are jointly in state β. Recognizing the fact that

$$\sum_{\alpha} P_{\alpha}^{-} = 1$$

we find that the partition function Z is defined by

$$Z = \sum_{\alpha} \sum_{\beta} \exp\left(-\frac{E_{\alpha\beta}}{T}\right) \tag{8.54}$$

As before, T is the temperature. From Eq. (8.48), the energy $E_{\alpha\beta}$ is itself defined in terms of the synaptic weights w_{ji} by

$$E_{\alpha\beta} = -\frac{1}{2} \sum_{i=1}^{N} \sum_{\substack{j=1 \\ i \neq j}}^{N} w_{ji} s_{j|\alpha\beta} s_{i|\alpha\beta} \tag{8.55}$$

where $s_{i|\alpha\beta}$ is the state of neuron i, given that the visible neurons are in state α and the hidden neurons are jointly in state β. The upper limit of the double summation in Eq. (8.55) is N, the total number of neurons in the network. Note that $N = K + L$, where K is the number of visible neurons and L is the number of hidden neurons.

The task at hand is to calculate the partial derivative $\partial P_{\alpha}^{-}/\partial w_{ji}$. Using the definition of Eq. (8.53), we get

$$\frac{\partial P_{\alpha}^{-}}{\partial w_{ji}} = -\frac{1}{ZT} \sum_{\beta} \exp\left(-\frac{E_{\alpha\beta}}{T}\right) \frac{\partial E_{\alpha\beta}}{\partial w_{ji}} - \frac{1}{Z^2} \frac{\partial Z}{\partial w_{ji}} \sum_{\beta} \exp\left(-\frac{E_{\alpha\beta}}{T}\right) \tag{8.56}$$

From Eq. (8.54), we note that

$$\frac{\partial Z}{\partial w_{ji}} = -\frac{1}{T} \sum_{\alpha} \sum_{\beta} \exp\left(-\frac{E_{\alpha\beta}}{T}\right) \frac{\partial E_{\alpha\beta}}{\partial w_{ji}} \tag{8.57}$$

From Eq. (8.55), we simply have (remembering that $w_{ij} = w_{ji}$)

$$\frac{\partial E_{\alpha\beta}}{\partial w_{ji}} = -s_{j|\alpha\beta} s_{i|\alpha\beta} \tag{8.58}$$

Consider now the first term on the right-hand side of Eq. (8.56). This term, except for the multiplying factor $-1/T$, may be written in light of Eq. (8.58) as follows:

$$\begin{aligned} \frac{1}{Z} \sum_{\beta} \exp\left(-\frac{E_{\alpha\beta}}{T}\right) \frac{\partial E_{\alpha\beta}}{\partial w_{ji}} &= -\frac{1}{Z} \sum_{\beta} \exp\left(-\frac{E_{\alpha\beta}}{T}\right) s_{j|\alpha\beta} s_{i|\alpha\beta} \\ &= -\sum_{\beta} P_{\alpha\beta}^{-} s_{j|\alpha\beta} s_{i|\alpha\beta} \end{aligned} \tag{8.59}$$

where, in the second line, we have made use of the Boltzmann distribution

$$P_{\alpha\beta}^{-} = \frac{1}{Z} \exp\left(-\frac{E_{\alpha\beta}}{T}\right) \tag{8.60}$$

where Z is the partition function defined in Eq. (8.54). The definition of $P_{\alpha\beta}^{-}$ given in Eq. (8.60) is perfectly consistent with that of P_{α}^{-} in Eq. (8.53).

Consider next the second term on the right-hand side of Eq. (8.56). This term, except for the minus sign, may be expressed as the product of two factors:

$$\frac{1}{Z^2}\frac{\partial Z}{\partial w_{ji}}\sum_\beta \exp\left(-\frac{E_{\alpha\beta}}{T}\right) = \left[\frac{1}{Z}\sum_\beta \exp\left(-\frac{E_{\alpha\beta}}{T}\right)\right]\left(\frac{1}{Z}\frac{\partial Z}{\partial w_{ji}}\right) \tag{8.61}$$

From Eq. (8.53), the first factor is recognized as the Boltzmann distribution P_α^-. To evaluate the second factor, we use Eqs. (8.57) and (8.58), obtaining

$$\begin{aligned}\frac{1}{Z}\frac{\partial Z}{\partial w_{ji}} &= \frac{1}{TZ}\sum_\alpha\sum_\beta \exp\left(-\frac{E_{\alpha\beta}}{T}\right) s_{j|\alpha\beta}s_{i|\alpha\beta} \\ &= \frac{1}{T}\sum_\alpha\sum_\beta P_{\alpha\beta}^- s_{j|\alpha\beta}s_{i|\alpha\beta}\end{aligned} \tag{8.62}$$

where, in the second line, we have made use of the Boltzmann distribution of Eq. (8.60). Hence, the use of Eqs. (8.53) and (8.62) in (8.61) yields

$$\frac{1}{Z^2}\frac{\partial Z}{\partial w_{ji}}\sum_\beta \exp\left(-\frac{E_{\alpha\beta}}{T}\right) = \frac{P_\alpha^-}{T}\sum_\alpha\sum_\beta P_{\alpha\beta}^- s_{j|\alpha\beta}s_{i|\alpha\beta} \tag{8.63}$$

We are now ready to formulate the expression for the partial derivative $\partial P_\alpha^-/\partial w_{ji}$. Substituting Eqs. (8.59) and (8.63) in (8.56) yields the desired result:

$$\begin{aligned}\frac{\partial P_\alpha^-}{\partial w_{ji}} &= \frac{1}{T}\sum_\beta P_{\alpha\beta}^- s_{j|\alpha\beta}s_{i|\alpha\beta} \\ &\quad - \frac{P_\alpha^-}{T}\sum_\alpha\sum_\beta P_{\alpha\beta}^- s_{j|\alpha\beta}s_{i|\alpha\beta}\end{aligned} \tag{8.64}$$

Returning to Eq. (8.51), the use of Eq. (8.64) in this equation yields (after the cancellation of common terms)

$$\begin{aligned}\Delta w_{ji} &= \frac{\varepsilon}{T}\sum_\alpha \frac{P_\alpha^+}{P_\alpha^-}\sum_\beta P_{\alpha\beta}^- s_{j|\alpha\beta}s_{i|\alpha\beta} \\ &\quad - \frac{\varepsilon}{T}\sum_\alpha P_\alpha^+ \sum_\alpha\sum_\beta P_{\alpha\beta}^- s_{j|\alpha\beta}s_{i|\alpha\beta}\end{aligned} \tag{8.65}$$

Next, we make the following observations that enable us to simplify this expression:

- The sum of the probabilities P_α^+ over the states α is unity:

$$\sum_\alpha P_\alpha^+ = 1 \tag{8.66}$$

- Application of Bayes' rule to the joint probability $P_{\alpha\beta}^-$ yields

$$P_{\alpha\beta}^- = P_{\beta|\alpha}^- P_\alpha^- \tag{8.67}$$

  where $P_{\beta|\alpha}^-$ is the conditional probability that the hidden neurons are in state β, given that the visible neurons are in state α and the network is running freely. Similarly, given that the network is clamped to its environment, we have

$$P_{\alpha\beta}^+ = P_{\beta|\alpha}^+ P_\alpha^+ \tag{8.68}$$

  where $P_{\beta|\alpha}^+$ is the conditional probability that the hidden neurons are in state β, given that the visible neurons are in state α and the network is in its clamped condition.

- The probability of a hidden state, given some visible state, is naturally the same whether the visible neurons of the network in thermal equilibrium are clamped in that state by the environment or arrive at that state by free running of the network;

that is,[4]

$$P^-_{\beta|\alpha} = P^+_{\beta|\alpha} \tag{8.69}$$

In light of this relation, we may therefore rewrite Eq. (8.67) in the equivalent form,

$$P^-_{\alpha\beta} = P^+_{\beta|\alpha} P^-_{\alpha} \tag{8.70}$$

- Invoking the use of Eqs. (8.70) and (8.68), in that order, we have

$$\begin{aligned} \frac{P^+_\alpha}{P^-_\alpha} P^-_{\alpha\beta} &= P^+_\alpha P^+_{\beta|\alpha} \\ &= P^+_{\alpha\beta} \end{aligned} \tag{8.71}$$

Accordingly, using Eq. (8.66) in the second term on the right-hand side of (8.65), and using Eq. (8.71) in the first term on the right-hand side of (8.65), we get the simplified result

$$\Delta w_{ji} = \frac{\varepsilon}{T}\left(\sum_\alpha \sum_\beta P^+_{\alpha\beta} s_{j|\alpha\beta} s_{i|\beta} - \sum_\alpha \sum_\beta P^-_{\alpha\beta} s_{j|\alpha\beta} s_{i|\alpha\beta}\right) \tag{8.72}$$

To simplify matters further, we introduce the following two definitions:

$$\begin{aligned} \rho^+_{ji} &= \langle s_j s_i \rangle^+ \\ &= \sum_\alpha \sum_\beta P^+_{\alpha\beta} s_{j|\alpha\beta} s_{i|\alpha\beta}, \qquad \begin{matrix} i, j = 1, 2, \ldots, N \\ i \neq j \end{matrix} \end{aligned} \tag{8.73}$$

$$\begin{aligned} \rho^-_{ji} &= \langle s_j s_i \rangle^- \\ &= \sum_\alpha \sum_\beta P^-_{\alpha\beta} s_{j|\alpha\beta} s_{i|\alpha\beta}, \qquad \begin{matrix} i, j = 1, 2, \ldots, N \\ i \neq j \end{matrix} \end{aligned} \tag{8.74}$$

where α runs over the range from 1 to 2^K, and β runs over the range from 1 to 2^L; K is the number of visible neurons, L is the number of hidden neurons, and $N = K + L$ is the total number of neurons in the network. The first average, ρ^+_{ji}, is the *correlation* between the states of neuron i and j, *conditional* on the visible neurons being clamped onto the environment; this average is taken over all possible states. The second average, ρ^-_{ji}, is the *unconditional correlation* between the states of neurons i and j. Note that both correlations ρ^+_{ji} and ρ^-_{ji} range in value from -1 to $+1$. Using these definitions in Eq. (8.72), we finally obtain the simple result

$$\Delta w_{ji} = \eta(\rho^+_{ji} - \rho^-_{ji}), \qquad \begin{matrix} i, j = 1, 2, \ldots, N \\ i \neq j \end{matrix} \tag{8.75}$$

where η is a *learning-rate parameter,* related to ε as follows:

$$\eta = \frac{\varepsilon}{T} \tag{8.76}$$

The gradient descent rule of Eq. (8.75) is called the *Boltzmann learning rule.* This

[4] The *clamping assumption* described in Eq. (8.69) is not an intrinsic property of a stochastic machine being clamped to a fixed state. Livesey (1991) argues that the clamping assumption is essentially an assertion of the *time reversibility* of a certain Markov chain underlying the behavior of the machine. This assumption can fail in general, and holds only for the case of a Boltzmann machine by virtue of the particular choice of transition probabilities.

definition is based on counting *correlations,* which is consistent with that described by Peterson and Anderson (1987). It is different from the original description of the Boltzmann machine (Hinton, 1987; Ackley et al., 1985), which is based on counting *occurrences.* In the latter case, positive increments are assigned to ρ_{ji} only when both of the neurons i and j are on simultaneously. By expanding these occurrence measurements to correlations, negative increments (arising when the neurons i and j have different states) are also captured. It appears that this generalization improves the learning properties of the algorithm (Peterson and Anderson, 1987).

According to the learning rule of Eq. (8.75), the synaptic weights of a Boltzmann machine are adjusted using only locally available observations under two different conditions: (1) clamped, and (2) free running. This important feature of Boltzmann learning greatly simplifies the network architecture, particularly when dealing with large networks. Another useful feature of Boltzmann learning, which may come as a surprise, is that the rule for adjusting the synaptic weight from neuron i to neuron j is independent of whether these two neurons are both visible, both hidden, or one of each. All of these nice features of Boltzmann learning result from a key insight by Hinton and Sejnowski (1983, 1986), which was to tie the abstract mathematical model of the Boltzmann machine to neural networks by doing a combination of two things:

- The use of Eq. (8.47) to define the flipping probability for each neuron
- The use of Hopfield's energy function [namely, Eq. (8.48)] to calculate the $E_{\alpha\beta}$ in Eqs. (8.53) and (8.54) that define the Boltzmann distribution

From a learning point of view, the two terms that constitute the Boltzmann learning rule of Eq. (8.75) have opposite meaning. We may view the first term, corresponding to the clamped condition of the network, as essentially a Hebbian *learning* rule; and view the second term, corresponding to the free-running condition of the network, as an *unlearning* or *forgetting* term. Indeed, the Boltzmann learning rule represents a *generalization* of the *repeated forgetting and relearning rule* described by Pöppel and Krey (1987) for the case of symmetric networks with no hidden neurons.

It is also of interest that since the Boltzmann machine learning algorithm requires that hidden neurons know the difference between stimulated and free-running activity, and given that there is a (hidden) external network that signals to hidden neurons that the machine is being stimulated, we have a primitive form of *attention* mechanism (Cowan and Sharp, 1988).

Stochastic Network with Input, Hidden, and Output Neurons. The treatment of Boltzmann learning just presented applies to a network that has only visible and hidden neurons. When the visible neurons of the network are subdivided into input and output neurons, as illustrated in Fig. 8.17b, we have to make certain modifications to the formulation of Boltzmann learning, as described next.

Let the states of the input, hidden, and output neurons of such a network be denoted by α, β, and γ, respectively. With the numbers of the input, hidden, and output neurons assumed to be K, L, and M, respectively, α, β, and γ run from 1 to 2^K, 1 to 2^L, and 1 to 2^M, respectively. Let $P^+_{\alpha\gamma}$ denote the probability that the input neurons are in state α and the output neurons are jointly in state γ, given that both the *input and output neurons are clamped* onto the environment. Let $P^-_{\alpha\gamma}$ denote the probability that the input neurons are in state α and the output neurons are jointly in state γ, given that *only the input neurons are clamped* onto the environment. Both of these conditional probabilities are measured at thermal equilibrium. For the situation described here, we may extend the definition of relative entropy given in Eq. (8.49) as follows:

$$H_{P^+\|P^-} = \sum_{\alpha=1}^{2^K} \sum_{\gamma=1}^{2^M} P_{\alpha\gamma}^+ \ln\left(\frac{P_{\alpha\gamma}^+}{P_{\alpha\gamma}^-}\right) \tag{8.77}$$

This relative entropy provides a measure of the mismatch between the desired probabilities $P_{\alpha\gamma}^+$ supplied by the environment and the actual probabilities $P_{\alpha\gamma}^-$ computed by the network. Using Bayes' rule, and recognizing that in Fig. 8.17b the input neurons are always clamped, that is,

$$P_\alpha^+ = P_\alpha^- \tag{8.78}$$

we may rewrite Eq. (8.77) in the equivalent form (see Problem 8.9)

$$H_{P^+\|P^-} = \sum_{\alpha} P_\alpha^+ \sum_{\gamma} P_{\gamma|\alpha}^+ \ln\left(\frac{P_{\gamma|\alpha}^+}{P_{\gamma|\alpha}^-}\right) \tag{8.79}$$

where P_α^+ is the probability of the state α over the input neurons; $P_{\gamma|\alpha}^+$ is the conditional probability that the output neurons are clamped in state γ, given an input state α; and $P_{\gamma|\alpha}^-$ is the conditional probability that the output neurons of the network in thermal equilibrium are in state γ, given that only the input neurons are in clamped state α. Both P_α^+ and $P_{\gamma|\alpha}^+$ are determined by the environment.

Following through an analysis similar to, but somewhat more involved than, that presented in the previous subsection, we may show that the Boltzmann learning rule for adjusting the synaptic weight w_{ji} from neuron i to neuron j takes a form similar to that in Eq. (8.75) except that the correlations ρ_{ji}^+ and ρ_{ji}^- are now defined as follows:

- The correlation ρ_{ji}^+ between neurons i and j, averaged over all possible states, is measured under the condition that the input and output neurons are clamped onto the environment.
- The correlation ρ_{ji}^- between neurons i and j is defined similarly, except that only the input neurons are now clamped onto the environment.

As before, correlations are measured when the network is in thermal equilibrium. Note, however, that according to Eq. (8.79), the adjustment Δw_{ji} applied to the synaptic weight w_{ji} of a Boltzmann machine with separate input and output neurons requires that we do two additional things: First, we multiply $\eta(\rho_{ji}^+ - \rho_{ji}^-)$ by the probability P_α^+ of state α over the input neurons (i.e., P_α^+ acts as a weighting factor assigned to state α); and second, we sum the product over all states α.

The Boltzmann Machine Learning Procedure and Related Issues

A summary of the major steps in the Boltzmann machine learning procedure (in the context of a network made up of input, hidden, and output neurons) is presented in Table 8.3 (Hinton, 1987).

From this table we see clearly that the Boltzmann machine is very computation intensive. Basically, there are two interwoven computations performed by the machine (Hinton and Sejnowski, 1986):

1. Each point in the H space, defining the dependence of the relative entropy $H_{P^+\|P^-}$ on the synaptic weight w_{ji}, represents an energy landscape. At each such point, the network performs simulated annealing in accordance with a specified annealing schedule. In reaching thermal equilibrium, the network searches for plausible interpretations of some perceptual input. If the bidirectional interactions between the

TABLE 8.3 Summary of the Boltzmann Machine Learning Procedure

1. *Initialization.* Initialize the network by setting the weights w_{ji} to random values uniformly distributed in the range $[-a, a]$; a typical value for a is 0.5 or 1.
2. *Clamping Phase.* Present the network the mapping, which it is required to learn, by clamping the input and output neurons to corresponding patterns. (If there are several possible output patterns for the input, then each such possibility must be clamped to the output neurons with the appropriate frequency.) For each input–output pattern, perform simulated annealing for a finite sequence of decreasing temperatures $T_0, T_1, \ldots, T_{\text{final}}$. At each value of the temperature T, let the network relax according to the Boltzmann distribution

$$P_\alpha = \frac{1}{Z}\exp\left(-\frac{E_\alpha}{T}\right)$$

where P_α is the probability that the network is in state α with energy E_α, and Z is the partition function. Perform the relaxation by updating the states of the unclamped (hidden) neurons according to the rule

$$s_j = \begin{cases} +1 \text{ with probability } P(v_j) \\ -1 \text{ with probability } 1 - P(v_j) \end{cases}$$

where

$$P(v_j) = \frac{1}{1 + \exp(-2v_j/T)}$$

and

$$v_j = \sum_{\substack{i=1 \\ i \neq j}}^{N} w_{ji} s_i$$

where w_{ji} is the synaptic weight from neuron i to neuron j, and N is the total number of neurons in the network. At each temperature, relax the network for a length of time determined by the annealing schedule. At the final temperature T_{final}, collect statistics to estimate the correlations

$$\rho_{ji}^{+} = \langle s_j s_i \rangle^{+}, \qquad \begin{array}{l} j, 1 = 1, 2, \ldots, N \\ j \neq i \end{array}$$

where $+$ refers to the clamped condition.
3. *Free-Running Phase.* Repeat the computations performed in step 2, but this time clamp only the input neurons of the network. Hence, at the final temperature T_{final}, estimate the correlations

$$\rho_{ji}^{-} = \langle s_j s_i \rangle^{-}$$

where $-$ refers to the condition when the output neurons are free-running.
4. *Updating of Synaptic Weights.* Update the synaptic weights of the network according to the Boltzmann learning rule

$$\Delta w_{ji} = \eta(\rho_{ji}^{+} - \rho_{ji}^{-}), \qquad \begin{array}{l} j, i = 1, 2, \ldots, N \\ j \neq i \end{array}$$

where η is the learning-rate parameter.
5. *Iteration Until Convergence.* Iterate steps 2 through 4 until the learning procedure converges with no more changes taking place in the synaptic weights w_{ji} for all j,i.

neurons of the network evade the plausible constraints of the environment, then the more probable states of the network are the ones that satisfy the constraints best. The computation of these states is naturally influenced by the choice of the parameters that specify the annealing schedule (i.e., the finite sequence of values of the temperature T and the finite number of transitions at each value of the temperature).

2. The synaptic weights of the network are adjusted so as to evade the environmental constraints. The adjustments are accomplished by using gradient descent in H space. This second computation is influenced by two major factors:

   - The *learning-rate parameter* η, which controls the size of each step taken for gradient descent in the H space
   - The *estimates* of the clamped and free-running correlations, namely, ρ_{ji}^{+} and ρ_{ji}^{-}, which always contain some "noise."

The presence of noise in these estimates results in "occasional" uphill steps in the minimization of the relative entropy $H_{P^+\|P^-}$. The effect of this noise is reduced by using a small value for the learning-rate parameter η or increasing the sample size. The latter approach, however, may pose a practical problem, because if the variance of the estimates of the correlations is to be reduced by a factor N, say, we have to increase the sample size by a factor N^2.

8.12 A Markov Chain Model of the Boltzmann Machine

The Boltzmann distribution is at the heart of the Boltzmann machine, as is shown clearly by the derivation of the Boltzmann learning rule presented in the previous section. Indeed, this derivation was made possible largely because of some beautiful mathematical properties of the Boltzmann distribution. As mentioned previously, the Boltzmann distribution is rooted in statistical physics. This same exponential distribution may also be derived using a self-contained mathematical approach that does not rely on concepts from statistical physics. In particular, a *two-step probabilistic Markov chain model* of a stochastic neural network may be used to formalize the assumptions that yield the unique properties of the Boltzmann machine (Mazaika, 1987). This should not come as a surprise, since the simulated annealing procedure that is basic to the operation of the Boltzmann machine is known to have a Markov property, as pointed out in Section 8.10.

The mathematical approach taken here rests on a fundamental assumption that is intuitively satisfying in the context of the Boltzmann machine (Mazaika, 1987):

The transition model between states of a neuron in a stochastic network is composed of two random processes:

- *The first process decides which state transition should be attempted.*
- *The second process decides if the transition succeeds.*

An attractive feature of this model is that it is easy to solve for the stationary distribution of the network, subject to two requirements: pairwise solutions to the steady-state equation, and a simple condition imposed on the second process. It turns out that the resulting stationary state probabilities follow an exponential distribution.

We begin by recalling the Markov chain model for the state transition process, which was introduced in Section 8.10. A *Markov chain* is defined by assigning a *transition probability* $p_{\beta\alpha}$ from state α to state β. The transition probability $p_{\beta\alpha}$ is the conditional probability that the network is in state β, given that it was in state α. We may thus define a matrix of transition probabilities for all states β and α, as shown by Feller (1968) and Bharucha-Reid (1960):

$$\mathbf{P} = \begin{bmatrix} p_{\alpha\alpha} & p_{\alpha\beta} & p_{\alpha\gamma} & \cdots \\ p_{\beta\alpha} & p_{\beta\beta} & p_{\beta\gamma} & \cdots \\ p_{\gamma\alpha} & p_{\gamma\beta} & p_{\gamma\gamma} & \cdots \\ \vdots & \vdots & \vdots & \ddots \end{bmatrix} \tag{8.80}$$

The first subscript of the individual elements of the matrix **P** stands for a row, and the second for a column. It has the following properties:

- The matrix **P** is a square matrix with nonnegative elements, since

$$p_{\beta\alpha} \geq 0 \qquad \text{for all } \alpha \text{ and } \beta \tag{8.81}$$

- The column sums of the matrix **P** equal unity, since

$$\sum_{\beta} p_{\beta\alpha} = 1 \qquad \text{for all } \alpha \tag{8.82}$$

A matrix satisfying these conditions is called a *stochastic matrix* or *Markov matrix.* Together with the initial distribution (i.e., the probability distribution for the possible states of the network at the initial or zeroth transition), *the stochastic matrix* **P** *completely defines a Markov chain with states* α, β, ... Note that with a network made up of N stochastic neurons, there are 2^N possible states, and so **P** is a 2^N-by-2^N matrix, which is a large matrix. Thus, the summation in Eq. (8.82) is over β from 1 to 2^N.

A Markov chain always has a stationary probability distribution of states (Feller, 1968). By definition, a probability distribution $\{P_\alpha\}$ is called a *stationary* or *equilibrium distribution* if it satisfies the condition

$$P_\alpha = \sum_{\beta} p_{\alpha\beta} P_\beta \tag{8.83}$$

A necessary requirement here is that the matrix of transition probabilities define an *ergodic* chain. To explain what we mean by this class of Markov chains, let $p_{\beta\gamma}^{(n)}$ denote *the probability of a transition from state* γ *to state* β *in exactly n steps.* In other words, $p_{\beta\gamma}^{(n)}$ is the conditional probability of the network entering state β at the nth step, given the initial state γ. *If the Markov chain is ergodic, then for every pair of states* γ *and* β, *the limit*

$$P_\beta = \lim_{n \to \infty} p_{\beta\gamma}^{(n)} \tag{8.84}$$

exists, the probability P_β *is positive for all* β, *and*

$$\sum_{\beta} P_\beta = 1 \tag{8.85}$$

The physical implication of the ergodic condition is that there always exists a transition from any state to another state, and all the states will be part of a single system.

In order to solve explicitly for the probability distribution $\{P_\alpha\}$ from the matrix of transition probabilities $\{p_{\beta\alpha}\}$, we assume *pairwise solutions* of the following form (Mazaika, 1987):

$$p_{\alpha\beta} P_\beta = p_{\beta\alpha} P_\alpha \tag{8.86}$$

It is straightforward to show that pairwise solutions do indeed satisfy Eq. (8.83). Specifically, we may multiply both sides of Eq. (8.82) by the probability P_α, and so write

$$\begin{aligned} P_\alpha &= P_\alpha \sum_\beta p_{\beta\alpha} \\ &= \sum_\beta p_{\beta\alpha} P_\alpha \\ &= \sum_\beta p_{\alpha\beta} P_\beta \end{aligned} \tag{8.87}$$

where, in the last line, we have made use of Eq. (8.86). The result obtained in Eq. (8.87) is recognized to be exactly the condition of Eq. (8.83) for the stationarity of the probability distribution $\{P_\alpha\}$. The idea of pairwise solutions in Eq. (8.86) was introduced as an artifact to solve explicitly for the stationary distribution of the network, yet it should be recognized that this assumption has a fundamental meaning in statistical physics. There it is known as the *detailed balance principle,* according to which the rate of occurrence of any transition equals the corresponding rate of occurrence of the *inverse* transition (Reif, 1965). The detailed balance principle is a sufficient condition for equilibrium.

We next factor the transition process from state α to state β into a two-step process by expressing the transition probability $p_{\beta\alpha}$ as the product of two factors:

$$p_{\beta\alpha} = r_{\beta\alpha} q_{\beta\alpha}, \qquad \beta \neq \alpha \tag{8.88}$$

where $r_{\beta\alpha}$ is the probability that a transition from state α to state β is *attempted,* and $q_{\beta\alpha}$ is the conditional probability that the attempt is *successful* given that it was attempted. When $\beta = \alpha$, the "unity column sum" property of the stochastic matrix **P** given in Eq. (8.80) implies that

$$\begin{aligned} p_{\alpha\alpha} &= 1 - \sum_{\beta \neq \alpha} p_{\beta\alpha} \\ &= 1 - \sum_{\beta \neq \alpha} r_{\beta\alpha} q_{\beta\alpha} \end{aligned} \tag{8.89}$$

Moreover, we require that the attempt rate matrix be *symmetric:*

$$r_{\beta\alpha} = r_{\alpha\beta} \qquad \text{for all } \alpha \neq \beta \tag{8.90}$$

and that it satisfies the *normalization condition*

$$\sum_\beta r_{\beta\alpha} = 1 \qquad \text{for all } \alpha \neq \beta \tag{8.91}$$

Our last requirement is that the probability of a successful attempt satisfies the property of *complementary conditional transition probability:*

$$q_{\beta\alpha} = 1 - q_{\alpha\beta} \tag{8.92}$$

We may now summarize the list of conditions that we have imposed on the matrix of transition probabilities:

- Condition of stationary distribution, Eq. (8.83)
- Condition of detailed balance, Eq. (8.86)
- Factorization into a two-step process with symmetric attempt rate matrix, Eqs. (8.88) and (8.90)
- Property of complementary conditional transition probability, Eq. (8.92)

Then, starting with Eq. (8.83), and using Eqs. (8.88), (8.90), and (8.92) in that order, we may write

$$\begin{aligned} P_\alpha &= \sum_\beta p_{\alpha\beta} P_\beta \\ &= \sum_\beta r_{\alpha\beta} q_{\alpha\beta} P_\beta \\ &= \sum_\beta r_{\beta\alpha}(1 - q_{\beta\alpha}) P_\beta \end{aligned} \tag{8.93}$$

Next, using Eq. (8.88) in the second line of (8.87) yields

$$\begin{aligned} P_\alpha &= \sum_\beta p_{\beta\alpha} P_\alpha \\ &= \sum_\beta r_{\beta\alpha} q_{\beta\alpha} P_\alpha \end{aligned} \tag{8.94}$$

Hence, combining Eqs. (8.93) and (8.94) and then rearranging terms, we get

$$\sum_\beta r_{\beta\alpha}(q_{\beta\alpha} P_\beta + q_{\beta\alpha} P_\alpha - P_\beta) = 0 \tag{8.95}$$

For $r_{\beta\alpha} \neq 0$, the condition of Eq. (8.95) can be satisfied only if

$$q_{\beta\alpha} P_\beta + q_{\beta\alpha} P_\alpha - P_\beta = 0$$

Hence, solving for $q_{\beta\alpha}$ yields the unique result

$$q_{\beta\alpha} = \frac{1}{1 + (P_\alpha / P_\beta)} \tag{8.96}$$

Finally, we make a change of variables as shown by

$$E_\alpha = -T \ln P_\alpha + T^* \tag{8.97}$$

where E_α is a new variable corresponding to the probability P_α that the network is in state α, and T and T^* are arbitrary constants. We may now express P_α in terms of E_α as follows:

$$P_\alpha = \frac{1}{Z} \exp\left(-\frac{E_\alpha}{T}\right) \tag{8.98}$$

where Z is a constant defined by

$$Z = \exp\left(-\frac{T^*}{T}\right) \tag{8.99}$$

Hence, we may reformulate Eq. (8.96) as follows:

$$\begin{aligned} q_{\beta\alpha} &= \frac{1}{1 + \exp(-(E_\alpha - E_\beta)/T)} \\ &= \frac{1}{1 + \exp(-\Delta E / T)} \end{aligned} \tag{8.100}$$

where $\Delta E = E_\alpha - E_\beta$. To evaluate the constant Z we use the condition of Eq. (8.85), obtaining

$$Z = \sum_\beta \exp\left(-\frac{E_\beta}{T}\right) \tag{8.101}$$

We may therefore finally express P_α as

$$P_\alpha = \frac{\exp(-E_\alpha/T)}{\sum_\beta \exp(-E_\beta/T)} \tag{8.102}$$

which is recognized as the Boltzmann distribution. According to the mathematical approach taken here, the variable E_α is the long-time average probability of state α.

The most significant point that emerges from the mathematically inspired Markov chain model of the Boltzmann machine derived here is perhaps the following (Mazaika, 1987):

> *Subject to the conditions imposed on the matrix of transition probabilities, the update rule of Eq. (8.100) is the only possible distribution for state transitions in the Boltzmann machine.*

In other words, the formula for the transition function $q_{\beta\alpha}$ is unique. Another significant point is the fact that, except for the assumed symmetry of the attempt rate matrix, the stationary-state probabilities of the Boltzmann machine do not depend on the r's at all. This fact is exploited next.

Unequal Update Rates

The conventional Boltzmann machine learning procedure applies when it is equally likely to try any neuron in the network for an update of its state. We may make a simple modification of the learning procedure by permitting a different update attempt rate on each neuron (Mazaika, 1987). To be specific, let v_i denote the update attempt rate on neuron i. Suppose also that the time step τ used in the learning procedure is small enough to justify the inequality

$$\sum_{i=1}^{N} v_i \tau \ll 1 \tag{8.103}$$

where N is the number of neurons in the network. Then, to a first-order of approximation in τ, we may express the probability to attempt a transition from state α to state β as follows:

$$r_{\beta\alpha} \simeq \begin{cases} v_i \tau & \text{for } \beta \text{ differing from } \alpha \text{ only on neuron } i \\ 0 & \text{for all other } \beta \neq \alpha \end{cases} \tag{8.104}$$

Clearly, the condition for symmetry (i.e., $r_{\beta\alpha} = r_{\alpha\beta}$) is maintained, and so the special formula of Eq. (8.100) for the $q_{\beta\alpha}$ transition function still applies, and the stationary probability distribution of Eq. (8.102) remains valid. We also note from Eq. (8.91) that

$$r_{\alpha\alpha} = 1 - \sum_{\substack{\beta=1 \\ \beta\neq\alpha}}^{2^N} r_{\beta\alpha}$$

Hence, in light of Eq. (8.104), we may write (Mazaika, 1987)

$$r_{\alpha\alpha} \simeq 1 - \sum_{i=1}^{N} v_i \tau \tag{8.105}$$

which defines the probability of no change being attempted on neuron i during a time step τ if the system is in state α.

The elements on the main diagonal of the stochastic matrix **P** are given by Eq. (8.80). If the energy E_α of state α is low, we find from Eq. (8.100) that the factors $q_{\beta\alpha}$ are small compared to unity. Hence $p_{\alpha\alpha}$ is relatively large (i.e., close to unity). We therefore make the observation that a state α with low energy tends to persist more, despite the fact it has the identical probability $r_{\alpha\alpha}$ of no attempted update in time step τ (Mazaika, 1987).

8.13 The Mean-Field-Theory Machine

A highly attractive feature of the Boltzmann machine is that it can avoid local minima by incorporating a relaxation technique based on simulated annealing into its learning procedure. However, the use of simulated annealing is also responsible for an excessive computation time requirement that has hindered experimentation with the Boltzmann machine. Not only does simulated annealing require measurements at a sequence of temperatures that defines the annealing cycle, but also each measurement requires many sweeps of its own. To overcome this major limitation of the Boltzmann machine, we may use a *mean-field approximation,* according to which the stochastic, binary-state neurons of the Boltzmann machine are replaced by deterministic, analog ones (Peterson and Anderson, 1987).

The idea of mean-field approximation is well known in statistical physics (Glauber, 1963). While it cannot be denied that in the context of a stochastic machine it would be desirable to know the states of all the neurons in the network at all times, we must nevertheless recognize that, in the case of a network with a large number of neurons, the neural states contain vastly more information than we usually require in practice. In fact, to answer the most familiar physical questions about the stochastic behavior of the network, we need only know the average values of neural states or the average products of pairs of neural states.

In this section we develop the *mean-field-theory learning rule* by proceeding as follows:

- First, we develop the idea of mean-field approximation in a rather simple-minded way.
- Then, we use a technique known in physics as the saddle-point method to shed more light on the mean-field approximation.
- Finally, we consider the issues involved in the implementation of mean-field-theory learning.

Mean-Field Approximation

In Section 8.8 we introduced the idea of a stochastic neuron. With the firing mechanism of such a neuron model described by the probabilistic rule of Eq. (8.36), it is rational for us to enquire about the *average* of the state s_j of neuron j. To be precise, we should speak of the average as a "thermal" average, since the synaptic noise is modeled in terms of thermal fluctuations. In any event, let $\langle s_j \rangle$ denote the average (mean) of s_j. Then, invoking the probabilistic rule of Eq. (8.36) and using the definition of Eq. (8.37), we may express the average $\langle s_j \rangle$ for some *specified* value of activation potential v_j as follows:

$$\begin{aligned} \langle s_j \rangle &= (+1)P(v_j) + (-1)[1 - P(v_j)] \\ &= 2P(v_j) - 1 \\ &= \frac{1 - \exp(-2v_j/T)}{1 + \exp(-2v_j/T)} \\ &= \tanh(v_j/T) \end{aligned} \tag{8.106}$$

where $\tanh(v_j/T)$ is the hyperbolic tangent of v_j/T. Figure 8.18 shows two plots of the average $\langle s_j \rangle$ versus the potential v_j. The continuous curve is for some temperature T greater than zero, and the plot shown in heavy solid lines is for the limiting case of $T = 0$. In the latter case, Eq. (8.106) takes on the limiting form

$$\langle s_j \rangle \rightarrow \text{sgn}(v_j) \qquad \text{as } T \rightarrow 0 \tag{8.107}$$

which corresponds to the deterministic rule of Eq. (8.6).

The discussion so far has focused on the simple case of a single stochastic neuron. In the more general case of a stochastic machine composed of a large assembly of neurons, we have a much more difficult task on our hands. The difficulty arises because of the combination of two factors:

- The probability function $P(v_j)$ that neuron j is on is a nonlinear function of the activation potential v_j.
- The activation potential v_j is now a random variable, being influenced by the stochastic action of other neurons connected to the inputs of neuron j.

In general, it is safe to say that there is no mathematical method that we can use to evaluate the behavior of a stochastic neural network in exact terms. But there is an approximation, known as the *mean-field approximation,* that we can use, which often yields adequately good results. The basic idea of mean-field approximation is to replace the actual fluctuating activation potential v_j for each neuron j in the network by its average $\langle v_j \rangle$, as shown by

$$v_j \rightarrow \langle v_j \rangle = \left\langle \sum_i w_{ji} s_i \right\rangle = \sum_i w_{ji} \langle s_i \rangle \tag{8.108}$$

where the arrow signifies ''replacement'' of one quantity by another. Accordingly, we may compute the average state $\langle s_j \rangle$ for neuron j embedded in a stochastic machine made up of a total of N neurons, just as we did in Eq. (8.106) for a single stochastic neuron, by writing

$$\langle s_j \rangle = \tanh\left(\frac{1}{T} v_j\right) \rightarrow \tanh\left(\frac{1}{T} \langle v_j \rangle\right) = \tanh\left(\frac{1}{T} \sum_i w_{ji} \langle s_i \rangle\right) \tag{8.109}$$

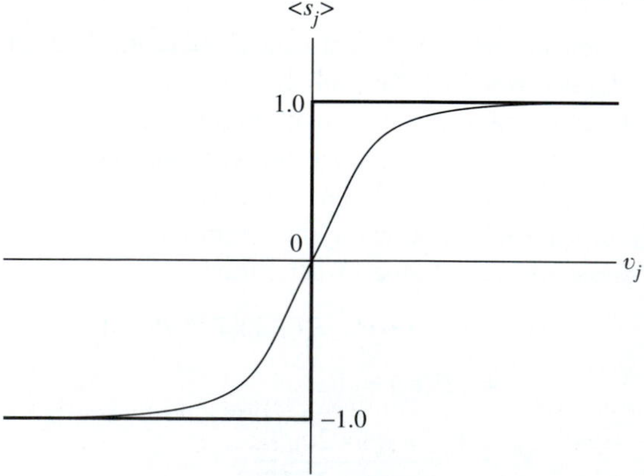

FIGURE 8.18 Graph of the thermal average $\langle s_j \rangle$ versus the activation potential v_j; heavy solid curve corresponds to normal operation of the McCulloch–Pitts neuron.

In light of Eq. (8.109), we may formally state the mean-field approximation as follows:

The average of some function of a random variable is approximated as the function of the average of that random variable.

For $j = 1, 2, \ldots, N$, Eq. (8.109) represents a set of nonlinear equations with N unknowns $\langle s_j \rangle$ that captures the notion of noise. The solution of this set of nonlinear equations is now a manageable proposition, because the unknowns are all *deterministic* rather than stochastic variables, which they are in the original network.

Equation (8.109) is called the *mean-field-theory equation* for the average state of neuron j in a stochastic machine made up of N neurons. We may also derive this equation in a more rigorous manner using the saddle-point method, as described next.

Saddle-Point Method

Let $\mathbf{s}_\alpha$ denote the N-by-1 state vector of a stochastic machine residing in state α. The discrete probability P_α that the system is in state $\mathbf{s}_\alpha$ at a temperature T is given by the Boltzmann distribution of Eq. (8.41). The probability P_α acts as a statistical weight in the sense that the *average* of a state-dependent function $g(\mathbf{s}_\alpha)$ is defined by

$$\begin{aligned}\langle g(\mathbf{s}_\alpha)\rangle &= \sum_\alpha P_\alpha g(\mathbf{s}_\alpha) \\ &= \frac{1}{Z}\sum_\alpha \exp\left(-\frac{E_\alpha}{T}\right) g(\mathbf{s}_\alpha)\end{aligned} \tag{8.110}$$

where the summation extends over all possible states (configurations) of the system; E_α is the energy of the system in state α, and Z is the partition function defined in Eq. (8.42). For convenience of presentation, the latter definition is reproduced here as

$$Z = \sum_\alpha \exp\left(-\frac{E_\alpha}{T}\right) \tag{8.111}$$

Basically, mean-field approximation provides an efficient method of computing the average $\langle g(\mathbf{s}_\alpha)\rangle$. Its derivation relies on a manipulation of the summations in Eqs. (8.110) and (8.111).

Consider first the simple case of a stochastic neuron j with state s_j. We wish to replace the discrete function $g(s_j)$ summed over s_j by an integral over a pair of new continuous variables U_j and V_j. To do so, we begin by invoking the *sifting property of the Dirac delta function* $\delta(U_j)$, written as follows:

$$g(s_j) = \int_{-\infty}^{\infty} g(U_j)\,\delta(s_j - U_j)\,dU_j \tag{8.112}$$

Next, we use the following definition of the Dirac delta function:

$$\delta(U_j) = \frac{1}{2\pi i}\int_{-i\infty}^{i\infty} \exp(U_j V_j)\,dV_j \tag{8.113}$$

where i is the square root of -1, and the integration with respect to V_j runs over the imaginary axis. Accordingly, the use of this definition in Eq. (8.112) yields

$$g(s_j) = \frac{1}{2\pi i}\int_{-\infty}^{\infty}\int_{-i\infty}^{i\infty} g(U_j)\exp(-U_j V_j + s_j V_j)\,dU_j\,dV_j \tag{8.114}$$

We next use this formulation to evaluate the discrete sum of the function $g(s_j)$ over the possible values of s_j, and thus write

$$\sum_{s_j=\pm 1} g(s_j) = \frac{1}{2\pi i} \sum_{s_j=\pm 1} \int_{-\infty}^{\infty} \int_{-i\infty}^{i\infty} g(U_j) \exp(-U_j V_j + s_j V_j)\, dU_j\, dV_j$$

$$= \frac{1}{2\pi i} \int_{-\infty}^{\infty} \int_{-i\infty}^{i\infty} g(U_j) \exp(-U_j v_j) \left[\sum_{s_j=\pm 1} \exp(s_j V_j) \right] dU_j\, dV_j \tag{8.115}$$

where, in the last line, we have interchanged the order of summation and integrations, and also rearranged terms. We now recognize the following identity:

$$\sum_{s_j=\pm 1} \exp(s_j V_j) = \exp(V_j) + \exp(-V_j)$$

$$= 2 \cosh V_j$$

$$= 2 \exp(\ln(\cosh V_j)) \tag{8.116}$$

where $\cosh V_j$ is the hyperbolic cosine of V_j, and ln denotes the natural logarithm. Hence, in light of the identity in Eq. (8.116), we may rewrite Eq. (8.115) as

$$\sum_{s_j=\pm 1} g(s_j) = \frac{1}{\pi i} \int_{-\infty}^{\infty} \int_{-i\infty}^{i\infty} g(U_j) \exp(-U_j V_j + \ln(\cosh V_j))\, dU_j\, dV_j \tag{8.117}$$

where we have added the exponents in the integrand. Equation (8.117) is the desired result for a single stochastic neuron. It reformulates a discrete sum over two possible values of neuronal state $s_j = \pm 1$ as a double integral over two continuous variables U_j and V_j.

Equation (8.117) applies to a single neuron. It is a straightforward matter to extend it to a stochastic machine made up of N neurons. For this evaluation, we use the definition of the partition function Z to write

$$Z = \sum_{\alpha} \exp\left(-\frac{E_\alpha}{T}\right)$$

$$= \sum_{s_1=\pm 1} \cdots \sum_{s_j=\pm 1} \cdots \sum_{s_N=\pm 1} \exp\left(-\frac{E_\alpha}{T}\right)$$

$$= c \prod_{j=1}^{N} \int_{-\infty}^{\infty} \int_{-i\infty}^{i\infty} \exp\left(-\frac{1}{T} E_{\text{eff}}(\mathbf{U}, \mathbf{V}, T)\right) dU_j\, dV_j \tag{8.118}$$

where c is a normalization constant, and $E_{\text{eff}}(\mathbf{U}, \mathbf{V}, T)$ is the *effective energy*, defined by

$$E_{\text{eff}}(\mathbf{U}, \mathbf{V}, T) = E(\mathbf{U}) + T \sum_{j=1}^{N} [U_j V_j - \ln(\cosh V_j)] \tag{8.119}$$

where $\mathbf{U}$ and $\mathbf{V}$ are both N-by-1 vectors with elements U_j and V_j, respectively, and the state energy E_α corresponds to $E(\mathbf{U})$. The elements U_j and V_j are called the *mean-field variables,* for reasons that will become apparent momentarily.

The effective energy $E_{\text{eff}}(\mathbf{U}, \mathbf{V}, T)$ in the exponent of the integrand in Eq. (8.118) can be large for machines with a large number of neurons. Consequently, we may solve the integral using the *saddle-point method,* which is a well-known technique in theoretical physics. According to this method, we recognize two things: (1) The double integral of

Eq. (8.118) is *dominated by saddle points* in the integration intervals specified here, and (2) the saddle points of the partition function Z will be found among the roots of the equations (Courant and Hilbert, 1970):

$$\frac{\partial}{\partial U_j} E_{\text{eff}}(\mathbf{U}, \mathbf{V}, T) = 0 \tag{8.120}$$

and

$$\frac{\partial}{\partial V_j} E_{\text{eff}}(\mathbf{U}, \mathbf{V}, T) = 0 \tag{8.121}$$

In other words, the saddle points of the partition function Z are determined by the simultaneous stationarity of the effective energy $E_{\text{eff}}(\mathbf{U}, \mathbf{V}, T)$ in both of the mean field variables U_j and V_j. Using the definition of Eq. (8.119) in (8.120) and (8.121) yields, respectively,

$$V_j = \frac{1}{T} \frac{\partial E(\mathbf{U})}{\partial U_j} \tag{8.122}$$

and

$$U_j = \tanh V_j \tag{8.123}$$

where $\tanh V_j$ is the hyperbolic tangent that results from the differentiation of $\ln(\cosh V_j)$ with respect to V_j. In general, the solutions of Eqs. (8.122) and (8.123) are real, because the effective energy $E_{\text{eff}}(\mathbf{U}, \mathbf{V}, T)$ is real for real U_j and V_j.

For a Boltzmann machine whose energy function is defined by Eq. (8.48), application of (8.122) and (8.123) yields the *mean-field-theory equations*:

$$U_j = \tanh\left(\frac{1}{T}\sum_i w_{ji} U_i\right), \qquad j = 1, 2, \ldots, N \tag{8.124}$$

where the state variables s_j of individual neurons have been replaced by the mean-field variables U_j through the use of Eq. (8.122); the index i is not to be confused with the square root of -1 used in Eqs. (8.113) to (8.115). It is of interest to note that the mean-field-theory equations (8.124) are the steady-state solutions of the resistance–capacitance (RC) equations:

$$\frac{dU_j}{dt} = -U_j + \tanh\left(\frac{1}{T}\sum_{i=1}^{N} w_{ji} U_i\right), \qquad j = 1, 2, \ldots, N \tag{8.125}$$

which are seen to have a mathematical form similar to Eq. (8.2). Also, comparison of Eq. (8.124) with (8.108) immediately reveals that the mean-field variable U_j is identically the same as the average state $\langle s_j \rangle$. As for the other mean-field variable V_j, it is identically the same as the average value of the activation potential v_j. We may thus formally write

$$U_j = \langle s_j \rangle \tag{8.126}$$

and

$$V_j = \langle v_j \rangle \tag{8.127}$$

Equations (8.126) and (8.127) justify the terminology of "mean-field variables" to describe U_j and V_j.

An important property of the effective energy function $E_{\text{eff}}(\mathbf{U}, \mathbf{V}, T)$ is that it has a *smoother landscape* than the energy function E of the original Boltzmann machine due to the presence of extra terms. Consequently, there is less likelihood of getting stuck in local minima.

Mean-Field-Theory Learning Rule

Thus far, we have shown how to compute the mean-field variable $U_j = \langle s_j \rangle$. But, the parameters that we really need for the implementation of the Boltzmann machine are the correlations $\langle s_j s_i \rangle$. We may, of course, determine these correlations by formal manipulations of the partition function Z along similar lines to those we used for the derivation of Eq. (8.124). Specifically, it may be shown that (Peterson and Anderson, 1987)

$$\langle s_j s_i \rangle \rightarrow U_{ji} = \frac{1}{2}\left[\tanh\left(\frac{1}{T}\sum_k w_{jk} U_k\right) + \tanh\left(\frac{1}{T}\sum_k w_{ik} U_k\right)\right] \tag{8.128}$$

which represents a system of N-by-N nonlinear equations for $j, i = 1, 2, \ldots, N$. For large N, we therefore have a large system of equations with deterministic variables. Experience with the computation of large systems shows that such systems, in general, tend to converge rather slowly. It is therefore tempting to go one step further in the approximation and factorize the correlation U_{ji} as the product of two mean-field variables U_j and U_i as follows (Peterson and Anderson, 1987):

$$\langle s_j s_i \rangle \rightarrow U_{ji} \rightarrow U_j U_i, \qquad j, i = 1, 2, \ldots, N \tag{8.129}$$

where U_j is itself defined by Eq. (8.124).

The deterministic form of Boltzmann learning in which the computation of the correlations is approximate in accordance with Eqs. (8.129) and (8.124) is called mean-field-theory learning. Specifically, we may reformulate Eq. (8.75) to define the *mean-field-theory* (MFT) *learning rule* as follows:

$$\Delta w_{ji} = \eta(U_j^+ U_i^+ - U_j^- U_i^-) \tag{8.130}$$

where U_j^+ and U_j^- are the average outputs of visible neuron j (on a single pattern) in the clamped and free-running conditions, respectively, and η is the learning-rate parameter. The MFT learning algorithm is summarized in Table 8.4.

Mean-field-theory learning, as described here, is expected to improve in accuracy with increasing N, the number of neurons in the network. What is amazing, however, is that it appears to work well even for relatively small networks on the order of $N = 10$ neurons (Peterson and Anderson, 1987). At first glance, this observation may seem to contradict what is known about the dynamics of spin-glass models—namely, that the mean-field approximation yields relatively inaccurate results for small systems (Mézard et al., 1987). The reason why mean-field-theory learning appears to work well for small neural networks is that it is likely that small discrepancies in the settling process are averaged out.

We may now summarize the main attributes of mean-field-theory learning compared to Boltzmann learning as follows:

- Mean-field-theory learning is a deterministic form of Boltzmann learning, from which it is derived through the use of mean-field approximation. It therefore provides a substantial speedup over the Boltzmann machine learning procedure (Peterson and Anderson, 1987)
- The Boltzmann machine learning procedure performs steepest descent in the relative entropy (H) space if the learning-rate parameter η is sufficiently small, as shown in Section 8.11. By making η sufficiently small, the mean-field-theory learning procedure may also be made to approximate steepest descent in the H space arbitrarily closely, except at rare discontinuities (Hinton, 1989).

TABLE 8.4 Summary of the Mean-Field-Theory Learning Algorithm

1. *Initialization.* Initialize the network by setting the synaptic weights w_{ji} to uniformly distributed random values in the range $(-a, a)$, where a is typically 0.5 or 1.
2. *Clamping Phase.* For a sequence of decreasing temperatures $T_0, T_1, \ldots, T_{\text{final}}$, solve Eq. (8.124) iteratively for the mean-field variable $U_j = \langle s_j \rangle$ of each free-running neuron j in the network. For this solution, use the recursion

$$U_j^{\text{new}} = \tanh\left(\frac{1}{T}\sum_i w_{ji}U_i^{\text{old}}\right), \qquad j = 1, 2, \ldots, N$$

For a clamped neuron j, simply set $U_j = \pm 1$ depending on whether neuron j is on or off. Hence, at the final temperature T_{final} compute the clamped correlations,

$$\rho_{ji}^{+} = U_j^{+}U_i^{+}, \qquad \begin{array}{l} j, i = 1, 2, \ldots, N \\ j \neq i \end{array}$$

where N is the total number of neurons in the network, and U_j^{+} is the average output of visible neuron j in the clamped phase of operation.
3. *Free-Running Phase.* Similarly, in the free-running phase, compute the correlations

$$\rho_{ji}^{-} = U_j^{-}U_i^{-}, \qquad \begin{array}{l} j, i = 1, 2, \ldots, N \\ j \neq i \end{array}$$

where U_j^{-} is the average output of visible neuron j in the free-running phase of operation.
4. *Weight Updating.* After each input pattern has passed through steps 2 and 3, update the synaptic weights of the network according to the Boltzmann learning rule,

$$\Delta w_{ji} = \eta(\rho_{ji}^{+} - \rho_{ji}^{-}), \qquad \begin{array}{l} j, i = 1, 2, \ldots, N \\ j \neq i \end{array}$$

where η is the learning-rate parameter.
5. *Iteration Until Convergence.* Repeat steps 2 through 4 until there are no further changes in the synaptic weights reported.

8.14 Computer Experiments II

Here we present the results of computer experiments on the two-dimensional *mirror symmetry problem* to provide two performance comparisons: (1) between Boltzmann and mean-field-theory machines, and (2) between a mean-field-theory machine and a multilayer perceptron using the relative entropy criterion; the latter network was considered in Section 6.20. As depicted in Fig. 8.19, the mirror symmetry problem requires that the network detect which one of three possible axes of symmetry is present in an N-by-N binary-pixel input pattern (Sejnowski et al., 1986).

Input patterns made up of N-by-N arrays of binary pixels are generated with one of three possible axes of symmetry: vertical, horizontal, or one of the diagonals. Only input patterns with exactly one axis of symmetry are used in the experiment. For an N-by-N array of binary pixels there are $2^{N^2/2}$ such input patterns. The task is to train a neural network so as to classify these input patterns correctly according to their axes of symmetry. The potential difficulty in this pattern-classification problem lies in the fact that single pixels by themselves carry no information about the solution to the problem, but pairs of pixels related by a mirror symmetry can be used to extract the information needed for classification. In other words, the mirror symmetry problem is a second-order problem in the sense of Minsky and Papert (1969).

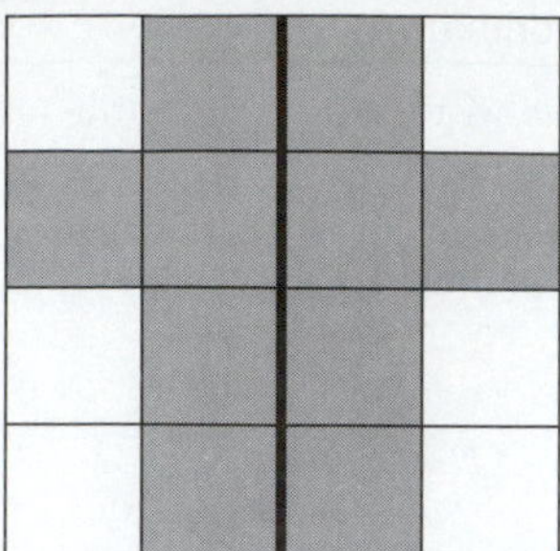
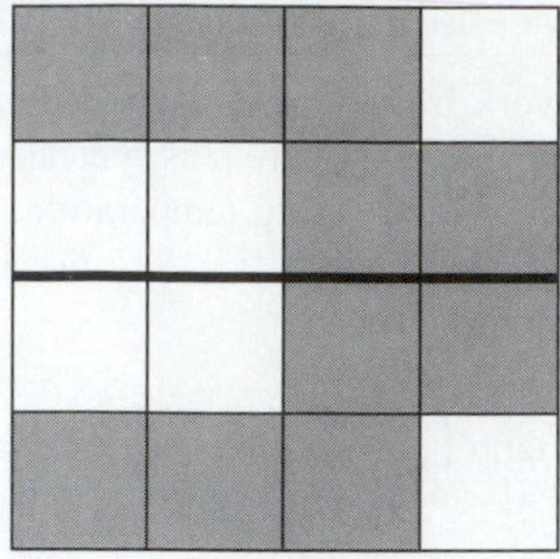
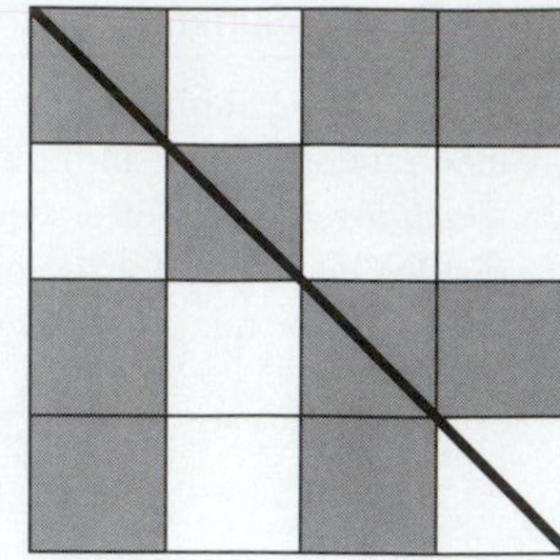

FIGURE 8.19 The two-dimensional mirror symmetry problem. The figure (from left to right) displays symmetry with respect to the following axes: vertical, horizontal, and a diagonal.

The results of computer experiments described here follow Peterson (1991b), using a network architecture of N-by-N input nodes, a single hidden layer of 12 neurons, and an output layer of 3 neurons (one for each axis of symmetry). The experiments were performed with two problem sizes:

- 4-by-4, with about 1.5×10^3 patterns
- 10-by-10, with about 3.7×10^{16} patterns

In this comparative study involving the mean-field-theory machine and multilayer perceptron, there are two subtle but important issues that need to be considered:

1. *The* $[-1, +1]$ *Versus* $[0,1]$ *Representation.* For the training of the Boltzmann and mean-field-theory machines described in this chapter, we used the $[-1, +1]$ representation for the output of a neuron. In this form of representation, both "on–on" and "off–off" correlations are counted as positive correlations in the learning rule of Eq. (8.75). This makes the learning faster than would be the case if we were to use the $[0,1]$ representation, for which only the "on–on" correlations are counted. For the multilayer perceptron we also expect the $[-1, +1]$ representation to allow faster learning. However, with respect to generalization, the use of $[0,1]$ may be preferred over $[-1, +1]$ in cases where two neurons are undecided—that is, their outputs have values near 0.5 and 0.0, respectively. In such a situation, the uncertainty is emphasized in the $[0,1]$ case, whereas no learning takes place in $[-1, +1]$ case. For these reasons, the $[-1, +1]$ representation was chosen for both the Boltzmann and mean-field theory learning machines and the $[0,1]$ representation for the multilayer perceptron in the computer experiments reported in Peterson (1991b).

2. *Endpoint Versus Midpoint Success Criterion.* By an "endpoint" criterion we mean a success criterion in the learning process in which we require that the network provide an output y_k for the kth class whose value is fairly close to the desired (target) response. For example, in the $[-1, +1]$ representation, we may require $|y_k| > 0.8$ for the endpoint criterion. On the other hand, in the "midpoint" criterion, we simply require that the output y_k be on the correct side of zero in the $[-1, +1]$ representation. It turns out that the performance of the mean-field-theory machine is insensitive to such a choice because its units tend to settle to extreme states, whereas the multilayer perceptron is sensitive to it. Accordingly, in the experiments performed by Peterson (1991b), the midpoint criterion was used for the comparison of the mean-field-theory machine and multilayer perceptron.

Figures 8.20a and 8.20b compare the learning curves of the Boltzmann and mean-field-theory machines using the $[-1, +1]$ representation and the endpoint criterion for the 4-by-4 and 10-by-10 mirror symmetry problems, respectively. These results show that the mean-field-theory machine offers superior performance compared to the Boltzmann machine for the mirror symmetry problem. The learning curves of Fig. 8.20c for the 4-by-4 mirror symmetry problem show that the mean-field-theory machine using [−1, +1] representation is slightly superior to the multilayer perceptron using [0,1] representation. The learning curves of Fig. 8.20c were computed using the midpoint criterion. The results of this latter experiment point to the interesting property that a mean-field-theory machine and a multilayer perceptron using the relative entropy criterion have approximately an

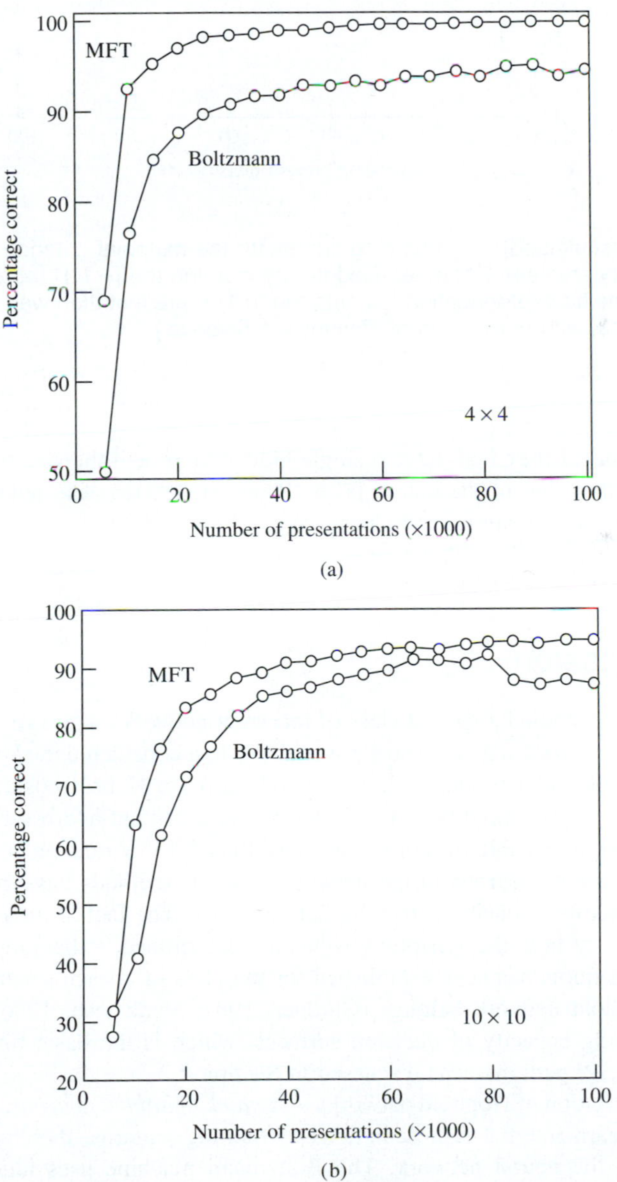

FIGURE 8.20 Learning curves using the endpoint criterion for (a) the 4 × 4 and (b) 10 × 10 mirror symmetry problems. The [−1,1] representation was used for both the mean-field-theory learning machine and the Boltzmann machine.

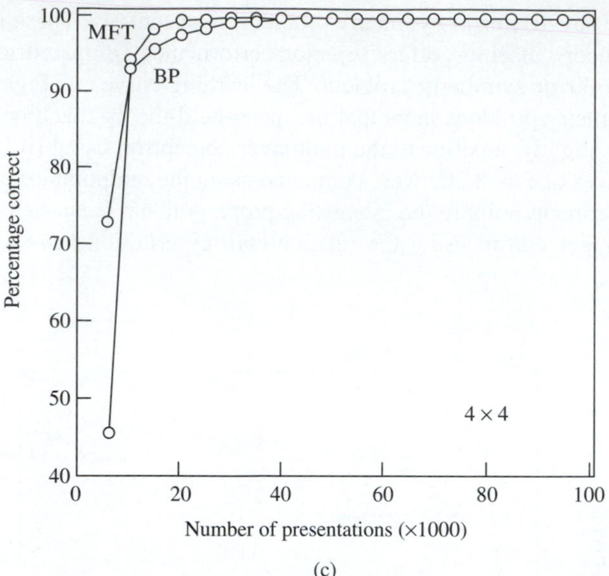

(c)

FIGURE 8.20 (continued) (c) Learning curves for the midpoint criterion for the 4 × 4 mirror symmetry problem. For mean-field-theory learning the [−1,1] representation was used and for the back-propagation learning the [0,1] representation was used. (From C. Peterson, 1991b, with permission of *Connection Science*.)

equal performance if they both have a single hidden layer and the size of the input layer is much larger than that of the output layer (Peterson, 1991b). The reader is referred to Problem 8.15 for a derivation of this property.

8.15 Discussion

In this chapter we studied a special class of recurrent networks with symmetric coupling, and whose theory is rooted in statistical physics. We first considered the Hopfield network, which employs the outer product rule (a generalization of Hebb's postulate of learning) for setting the synaptic weights of the network. As a content-addressable memory, the Hopfield network is capable of storing no more than $0.138N$ random patterns, where N is the total number of neurons in the network. Various methods have been devised for increasing the storage capacity of the Hopfield network. The fact of the matter, however, is that regardless of how the synaptic weights are determined, a theoretical storage limit of $2N$ random patterns has been established for the class of attractor neural networks, to which the Hopfield network belongs (Gardner, 1987; Venkatesh, 1986; Cover, 1965). Cover's separating capacity of decision surfaces, which is the basis for the theoretical storage limit of $2N$ patterns, was discussed in Section 7.2.

The main limitation of Hopfield networks is the *lack of hidden neurons*. Hidden neurons are known to learn internal representations of training patterns, thereby enhancing the performance of the neural network. The Boltzmann machine uses hidden and visible neurons that are in the form of stochastic, binary-state units. It cleverly links the simulated annealing algorithm with a neural network, and thereby exploits the beautiful properties of the Boltzmann distribution. The Boltzmann machine has some appealing features:

- Through training, the probability distribution of the network is matched to that of the environment. This is achieved by using the relative entropy, rooted in information theory, as the measure of performance.
- The network offers a generalized approach that is applicable to the basic issues of *search, representation,* and *learning* (Hinton, 1987).
- The network is guaranteed to find the global minimum of the energy function, provided that the annealing schedule in the learning process is performed slowly enough (Geman and Geman, 1984).

The annealing schedule referred to here is described in Eq. (8.45). Unfortunately, this schedule is much too slow to be of practical value. In practice, a faster annealing schedule is used so as to produce reasonably good solutions, though not necessarily optimal.

The mean-field-theory machine is derived from the Boltzmann machine by analogy. Specifically, the stochastic binary-state neurons of the Boltzmann machine are replaced by deterministic analog ones. The end result is a new neural network that offers the following practical advantages (Hartman, 1991; Peterson and Anderson, 1987):

- Being deterministic, the mean-field-theory machine is one to two orders of magnitude faster than the corresponding Boltzmann machine.
- The mean-field-theory equations (8.124) are isomorphic to the steady-state solutions of the *RC* circuit described by Eqs. (8.125). This property, coupled with the local nature of the Boltzmann learning algorithm, makes the mean-field-theory machine a strong candidate for implementation in analog VLSI form. Indeed, Alspector et al. (1991a, b) describe a general-purpose neural network chip that can be used for implementing the mean-field-theory (and the Boltzmann) machine, on which we have more to say in Chapter 15.
- Mean-field-theory machines can be used for content-addressable memory (Alspector et al., 1992b; Hartman, 1991), pattern recognition, and combinatorial optimization problems (Peterson and Söderberg, 1989; Peterson and Anderson, 1987).

In a content-addressable memory, which we wish to discuss here, the aim is to correct errors in the state of visible neurons. Each visible neuron functions both as an input unit and an output unit of the network. The initial state of the visible neurons is determined by the input to the network, and their final state supplies the output of the network. In a Hopfield network which has no hidden neurons, retrieval proceeds simply by initializing the network and then allowing the network to evolve under its own dynamics. In the case of a mean-field-theory machine, we require a more elaborate retrieval procedure on account of the hidden neurons. Specifically, we would like to exploit the internal representation of the stored pattern learned by the hidden neurons, as an adjunct in the correction of errors in the state of visible neurons. The learning process itself needs consideration because, unlike a Boltzmann machine, a mean-field-theory machine is deterministic. In particular, a completely free-running phase is ruled out, because it is identical for all training patterns in the sense that the annealing process ends in the same single, final state. To resolve these peculiarities of learning and retrieval, we may follow a robust procedure that was originally described by Hartman (1991) and applied to a general-purpose neural network chip by Alspector et al. (1992b):

- *Learning* (storage). In the clamping phase, the visible neurons are all clamped to a training pattern, and the hidden neurons are updated at low temperature. In the free-running phase, half the visible neurons (picked at random) are clamped to the training pattern, and the remaining half are free.

- *Retrieval* (recall). The visible neurons are clamped to a new pattern (which may include errors), thereby initializing the hidden neurons in accordance with the clamped state of the visible neurons. Then the whole network is annealed to an intermediate temperature, at which point the state of the hidden neurons approximates the learned internal representation of the stored pattern, and the visible neurons are released. Finally, the annealing process is finished, and the whole network is allowed to settle. The visible neurons are thus able to correct errors by virtue of the evoked internal representation of stored pattern learned by the hidden neurons.

It has been demonstrated by Hartman (1991) using a detailed computer simulation study and verified by Alspector et al. (1992b) using a general-purpose neural network chip that the mean-field-theory machine has a larger capacity for storage and error-correcting retrieval of random patterns than any other network. The key to this significant increase in storage capacity lies in the use of hidden neurons that assist in the storage and error-correction process. The storage capacity has also been found empirically to improve considerably with the use of more hidden neurons.

We conclude this discussion of mean-field-theory learning by summarizing its fundamental limitations in light of a study by Gallard (1993):

1. When a supervised Boltzmann machine (i.e., one with input and output neurons) reaches thermal equilibrium, we have a probability of an output vector, given a clamped input vector that is defined previously in terms of the Boltzmann distribution. However, the analogous definition for this conditional probability in mean-field-theory learning is *not* similarly valid. The problem arises due to the fact that in the latter case the unclamped, interconnected hidden and output neurons of the machine in its free-running condition (i.e., negative phase) are no longer independent, and the true stochastic system is not well represented. That is, the probability of an output vector, given a clamped input vector, has different values for these two machines. The situation is made worse by adding more hidden layers or more intra-hidden-layer connections to a single-hidden-layer network. Although superficially it would seem that these additions increase the complexity potential of the functions that may be learned by a mean-field-theory machine, in reality all that the new neural connections accomplish is to erode the representational fidelity of the mean-field-theory machine. This is indeed borne out by computer simulation results.

2. Learning in a mean-field-theory machine is restricted to the simple gradient search; advanced optimization techniques such as the conjugate gradient method (discussed in Chapter 6) are of no value.

It thus appears that the use of mean-field-theory learning is restricted to neural networks with a single hidden layer, which limits the scope of their applications.

PROBLEMS

8.1 Consider a Hopfield network made up of five neurons, which is required to store the following three fundamental memories:

$$\boldsymbol{\xi}_1 = [+1, +1, +1, +1, +1]^T$$

$$\boldsymbol{\xi}_2 = [+1, -1, -1, +1, -1]^T$$

$$\boldsymbol{\xi}_3 = [-1, +1, -1, +1, +1]^T$$

(a) Evaluate the 5-by-5 synaptic weight matrix of the network.

(b) Demonstrate that all three fundamental memories, $\boldsymbol{\xi}_1$, $\boldsymbol{\xi}_2$, and $\boldsymbol{\xi}_3$, satisfy the alignment condition, using asynchronous updating.

(c) Investigate the retrieval performance of the network when it is presented with a noisy version of $\boldsymbol{\xi}_1$ in which the second element is reversed in polarity.

8.2 Investigate the use of synchronous updating for the retrieval performance of the Hopfield network described in Problem 8.1.

8.3 **(a)** Show that

$$\boldsymbol{\xi}_1 = [-1, -1, -1, -1, -1]^T$$
$$\boldsymbol{\xi}_2 = [-1, +1, +1, -1, +1]^T$$
$$\boldsymbol{\xi}_3 = [+1, -1, +1, -1, -1]^T$$

are also fundamental memories of the Hopfield network described in Problem 8.1. How are these fundamental memories related to those of Problem 8.1?

(b) Suppose that the first element of the fundamental memory $\boldsymbol{\xi}_3$ in Problem 1 is masked (i.e., reduced to zero). Determine the resulting pattern produced by the Hopfield network. Compare this result with the original form of $\boldsymbol{\xi}_3$.

8.4 Equation (8.30) defines the synaptic weight w_{ji} produced by a modification of the outer product rule of storage. Demonstrate that a network based on this formula satisfies the alignment condition described in Eq. (8.11).

8.5 Consider a simple Hopfield network made up of two neurons. The synaptic weight matrix of the network is

$$\mathbf{W} = \begin{bmatrix} 0 & -1 \\ -1 & 0 \end{bmatrix}$$

The threshold applied to each neuron is zero. The four possible states of the network are

$$\mathbf{s}_1 = [+1, +1]^T$$
$$\mathbf{s}_2 = [-1, +1]^T$$
$$\mathbf{s}_3 = [-1, -1]^T$$
$$\mathbf{s}_4 = [+1, -1]^T$$

(a) Demonstrate that states $\mathbf{s}_2$ and $\mathbf{s}_4$ are stable, whereas states $\mathbf{s}_1$ and $\mathbf{s}_3$ exhibit a limit cycle. Do this demonstration using the following tools:

1. The alignment (stability) condition

2. The energy function

(b) What is the length of the limit cycle characterizing states $\mathbf{s}_1$ and $\mathbf{s}_3$?

8.6 Derive Eq. (8.29) defining the maximum number of fundamental memories that are all retrieved correctly by a Hopfield network with a probability of 99 percent.

8.7 Show that the energy function of a Hopfield network may be expressed as

$$E = -\frac{N}{2}\sum_{\nu=1}^{p} m_\nu^2$$

where m_ν are the overlaps, defined by

$$m_\nu = \frac{1}{N}\sum_{j=1}^{N} s_j \xi_{\nu,j}, \qquad \nu = 1, 2, \ldots, p$$

where s_j is the jth element of the state vector $\mathbf{s}$ and $\xi_{\nu,j}$ is the jth element of the fundamental memory $\boldsymbol{\xi}_\nu$.

8.8 In this problem we continue with the computer experiment described in Section 8.4, pertaining to the use of the Hopfield network as a content-addressable memory. The network is trained to retrieve the eight digitlike black-and-white patterns shown in Fig. 8.7, with each pattern containing 120 pixels. Continue with this computer

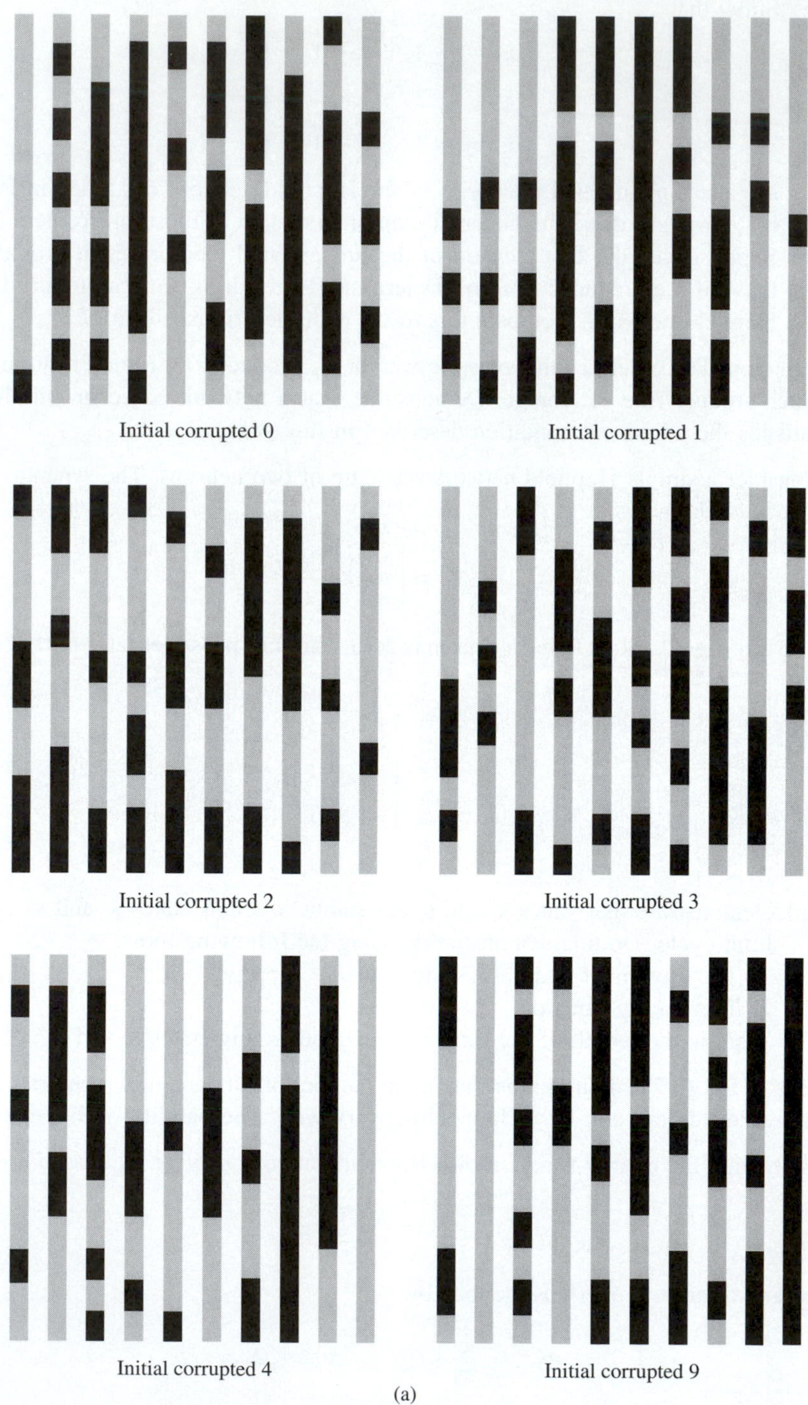

FIGURE P8.8 Different shades are used for the states $+1$ and -1, compared to those in Fig. 8.7.

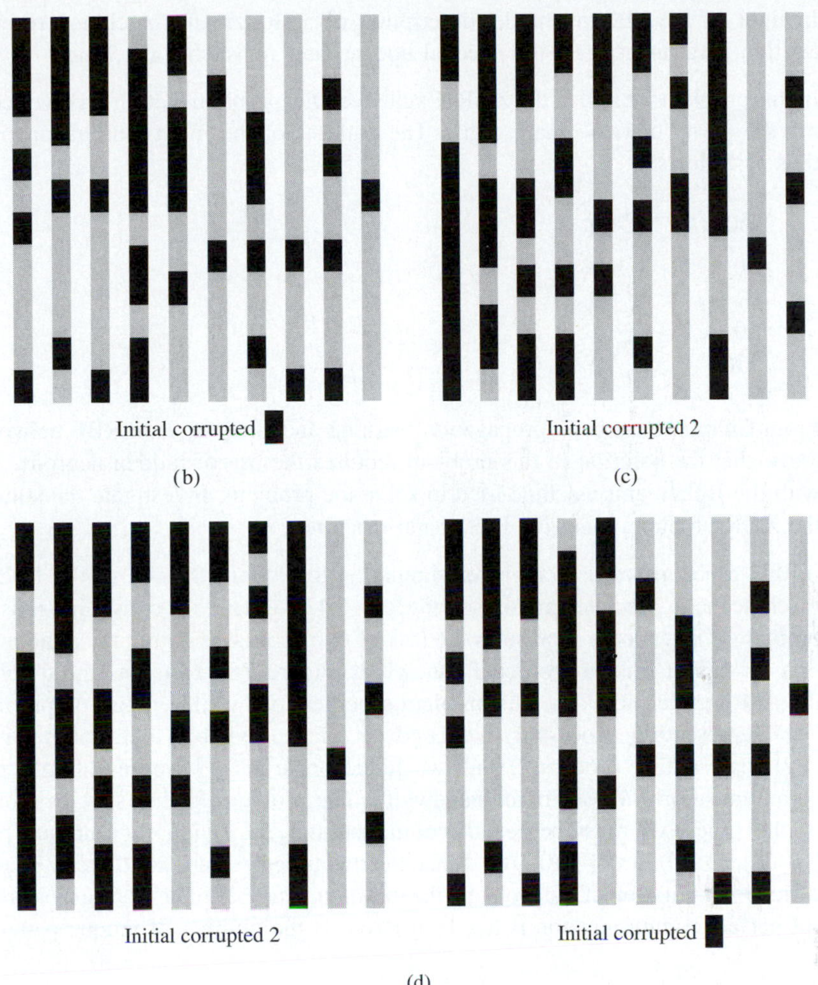

FIGURE P8.8 (continued)

experiment for the following situations:

(a) The network is presented with initial corrupted versions of 0, 1, 2, 3, 4, 9 that are shown in Fig. P8.8a.

(b) The network is presented with the initial corrupted version of ▮ shown in Fig. P8.8b.

(c) The network is presented with the initial corrupted version of 2 shown in Fig. P8.8c.

(d) The network is presented with the initial corrupted versions of ▮ and 2 shown in Fig. P8.8d.

8.9 **(a)** Derive Eq. (8.79) defining the relative entropy of a Boltzmann machine that includes input, hidden, and output neurons.

(b) Show that the Boltzmann learning rule for adjusting the synaptic weight w_{ji} in this network configuration may still be expressed in the same form as that described in Eq. (8.75), with new interpretations for the correlations ρ_{ji}^{+} and ρ_{ji}^{-}.

8.10 In light of the Markov model description of a Boltzmann machine presented in Section 8.12, investigate the unequal update rates for such a machine.

8.11 In this problem we revisit the XOR (Exclusive-OR) problem, which involves computing the parity of two binary digits. The patterns of the input–output mapping are thus as follows:

Input	Output
00	0
01	1
10	1
11	0

From Chapter 6 on back-propagation learning and Chapter 7 on RBF networks we know that the solution to this problem requires the use of hidden neurons. So it is with the Boltzmann machine used to solve the problem. Investigate the solution of the XOR problem using the Boltzmann machine.

8.12 In this problem we use computer simulation to explore the use of the Boltzmann machine as a mechanism for solving the "424 encoder" constraint-satisfaction problem. The encoder represents the task of two processes communicating information through a link of restricted bandwidth. Figure P8.12 depicts the topology of the 424 encoder network. The problem specifies four visible input–output neurons ($V1$) representing process 1, a second set of four visible input–output neurons ($V2$) representing process 2, and two hidden neurons (H) representing a parallel communication link of limited bandwidth. The problem further specifies that each of the processes must be capable of transmitting/receiving four unique patterns {(1000), (0100), (0010), (0001)}. Since the two processes are not directly connected, which is a limitation of the problem, the minimum number of hidden neurons required for perfect communication is $\log_2 v$, where v is the number of unique patterns.

Input layer

Hidden layer

Output layer

FIGURE P8.12

The purpose of the experiment is to reproduce the results for the 424 encoder problem presented by Ackley et al. (1985) under the following specifications:

(a) Twenty random binary input vectors from the set {(1000), (0100), (0010), (0001)}; noise is added to the vectors with a probability of 0.15 that "on" bits are turned "off," and a probability of 0.05 that "off" bits are turned "on." The addition of noise is intended to prevent the synaptic weights from growing too large.

(b) Number of updates = 10, such that, on the average, all neurons are updated on each annealing cycle.

(c) Annealing schedule:

$$\{2 \,@\, 20,\ 2 \,@\, 15,\ 2 \,@\, 12,\ 4 \,@\, 10,\ 2 \,@\, 20,\ 2 \,@\, 15,\ 2 \,@\, 12,\ 4 \,@\, 10\}$$

8.13 Using the saddle-point method, derive the formula for the correlation $\langle s_i s_j \rangle$ given in Eq. (8.128) for mean-field-theory learning.

8.14 The Boltzmann machine performs gradient descent (in weight space) on the relative entropy between the underlying probability distribution of the environment and the probability distribution learned by the network. On what function does the mean-field-theory machine perform its gradient descent? You may refer to Hinton (1989) for a discussion of this issue.

8.15 Consider a network architecture consisting of an input layer, a single hidden layer, and an output layer. The size of the input layer is much larger than that of the output layer. Consequently, in the case of a mean-field-theory machine we may say that insofar as a hidden neuron is concerned, the feedback signal from an output neuron has a minor influence compared to the feedforward signal from an input neuron. For such a network architecture, show that the mean-field-theory machine has a behavior approximately the same as that of a multilayer perceptron using the relative entropy criterion; the latter network was considered in Section 6.20. In particular, show that for these two different neural networks:

(a) The update formulas for the synaptic weights of an output neuron have the same approximate form.

(b) Likewise, the update formulas for the synaptic weights of a hidden neuron have the same approximate form.

8.16 Consider a recurrent network that is asymmetric in that $w_{ij} \neq w_{ji}$. Show that the mean-field-theory learning algorithm will automatically symmetrize the network provided that, after each weight update, each weight is decayed toward zero by a small amount proportional to its magnitude (Hinton, 1989).

CHAPTER 9

Self-Organizing Systems I: Hebbian Learning

9.1 Introduction

An important feature of neural networks is the ability to *learn* from their environment, and through learning to *improve* performance in some sense. In Chapter 6 on multilayer perceptrons and Chapter 7 on radial-basis function networks, the focus was on algorithms for supervised learning, for which a set of targets of interest is provided by an external teacher. The targets may take the form of a desired input–output mapping that the algorithm is required to approximate. In this chapter and the next two chapters, we study algorithms for *self-organized learning* or *unsupervised learning.* The purpose of an algorithm for self-organized learning is to *discover* significant patterns or features in the input data, and to do the discovery *without* a teacher. To do so, the algorithm is provided with a set of rules of a *local* nature, which enables it to learn to compute an input–output mapping with specific desirable properties; the term ''local'' means that the change applied to the synaptic weight of a neuron is confined to the immediate neighborhood of that neuron. It frequently happens that the desirable properties represent goals of a neurobiological origin. Indeed, the modeling of network structures used for self-organized learning tends to follow neurobiological structures to a much greater extent than is the case for supervised learning. This may not be surprising, because the process of network organization is fundamental to the organization of the brain.

The structure of a self-organizing system may take on a variety of different forms. It may, for example, consist of an *input* (*source*) *layer* and an *output* (*representation*) *layer,* with feedforward connections from input to output and lateral connections between neurons in the output layer. Another example is a feedforward network with multiple layers, in which the self-organization proceeds on a layer-by-layer basis. In both examples, the learning process consists of repeatedly modifying the synaptic weights of all the connections in the system in response to input (activation) patterns and in accordance with prescribed rules, until a final configuration develops.

This chapter on self-organizing systems is restricted to Hebbian learning. In the next chapter we consider another class of self-organizing systems, which are based on competitive learning.

Organization of the Chapter

The material in this chapter is organized as follows. In Section 9.2 we describe some basic principles of self-organization, using qualitative arguments. Then, in Section 9.3 we consider a multilayer feedforward network, the self-organization of which is motivated by the mammalian visual system (Linsker, 1986). Linsker's model is a nice example of how self-organized neural networks can be so closely related to a neurobiological structure. It also provides motivation for understanding linear self-organizing algorithms. In Section 9.4 we discuss the attributes and limitations of Linsker's model, and set the stage for principal components analysis.

In Section 9.5 we present introductory material on *principal components analysis,* which is a standard method in statistical pattern recognition; this technique is basic to many of the self-organizing networks discussed in the rest of the chapter. One such network is a rather simple model consisting of a single linear neuron (Oja, 1982), which is described in Section 9.6. In Section 9.7 we consider a self-organizing network consisting of a feedforward structure with a single layer of neurons, which extract all the principal components in a sequential fashion (Sanger, 1989a, b). Next, in Section 9.8, we describe another neural network with lateral inhibitions that performs a similar set of operations (Kung and Diamantaras, 1990). In Section 9.9 we present a classification of algorithms for principal components analysis using neural networks. In Section 9.10 we complete the discussion of principal components analysis by presenting some final thoughts on the subject.

9.2 Some Intuitive Principles of Self-Organization

As mentioned previously, self-organized (unsupervised) learning consists of repeatedly modifying the synaptic weights of a neural network in response to activation patterns and in accordance with prescribed rules, until a final configuration develops. The key question, of course, is how a useful configuration can finally develop from self-organization. The answer lies essentially in the following observation (Turing, 1952):

Global order can arise from local interactions.

This observation is of fundamental importance; it applies to the brain and just as well to artificial neural networks. In particular, many originally random local interactions between neighboring neurons of a network can coalesce into states of global order and ultimately lead to coherent behavior, which is the essence of self-organization.

Network organization takes place at two different levels that interact with each other in the form of a *feedback* loop. The two levels are

- *Activity.* Certain activity patterns are produced by a given network in response to input signals.
- *Connectivity.* Connection strengths (synaptic weights) of the network are modified in response to neuronal signals in the activity patterns, due to synaptic plasticity.

The feedback between changes in synaptic weights and changes in activity patterns must be *positive,* in order to achieve self-organization (instead of stabilization) of the network. Accordingly, we may abstract the first principle of self-organization (von der Malsburg, 1990a):

PRINCIPLE 1. Modifications in synaptic weights tend to self-amplify.

The process of self-amplification is constrained by the requirement that modifications in synaptic weights have to be based on locally available signals, namely, the presynaptic signal and postsynaptic signal. The requirements of self-reinforcement and locality suffice to specify the mechanism whereby a strong synapse leads to coincidence of presynaptic and postsynaptic signals and, in turn, the synapse is increased in strength by such a coincidence. The mechanism described here is in fact a restatement of Hebb's postulate of learning!

In order to stabilize the system, there has to be competition for some "limited" resources (e.g., number of inputs, energy resources). Specifically, an increase in the strength of some synapses in the network must be compensated for by a decrease in others. Accordingly, only the "successful" synapses can grow, while the less successful ones tend to weaken and may eventually disappear. This observation leads us to abstract the second principle of self-organization (von der Malsburg, 1990a):

PRINCIPLE 2. Limitation of resources leads to competition among synapses and therefore the selection of the most vigorously growing synapses (i.e., the fittest) at the expense of the others.

This principle is also made possible by synaptic plasticity.

For our final observation, we note that a single synapse on its own cannot efficiently produce favorable events. To do so, we need cooperation among a set of synapses converging onto a particular neuron and carrying coincident signals strong enough to activate that neuron. We may therefore abstract the third principle of self-organization (von der Malsburg, 1990a):

PRINCIPLE 3. Modifications in synaptic weights tend to cooperate.

The presence of a vigorous synapse can enhance the fitness of other synapses, in spite of the overall competition in the network. This form of cooperation may arise due to synaptic plasticity, or due to simultaneous stimulation of presynaptic neurons brought on by the existence of the right conditions in the external environment.

All three principles of self-organization mentioned above relate to the network itself. However, for self-organized learning to perform a useful information-processing function, there has to be *redundancy* in the activation patterns fed into the network by the environment. From the perspective of self-organization, the following arguments may be made (Barlow, 1989):

- The redundancy of input patterns (vectors) provides the knowledge incorporated in the neural network.
- Some of this knowledge may be obtained by observations of such statistical parameters as the mean, variance, and correlation matrix of the input data vector.
- Knowledge of this sort incorporated in the neural network results in a model of "what usually happens," against which incoming messages are compared, and unexpected discrepancies are thereby identified.
- Such knowledge is a necessary prerequisite of self-organized learning.

9.3 Self-Organized Feature Analysis

Now that we have some understanding of what self-organized learning is, it seems appropriate that we consider a self-organized model motivated by the mammalian visual system, and that incorporates the three principles of self-organization that we have just described. The visual system has been elucidated experimentally by many investigators since the pioneering work of Hubel and Wiesel (1977). We therefore have known results in light of which we may assess the behavior of the model.

The processing of information in the visual system is performed in stages. In particular, simple features, such as contrast and edge orientation, are analyzed in the early stages of the system, whereas more elaborate complex features are analyzed in later stages. It is tempting to ask if there are self-organizing rules that can lead to the development of artificial neuronal responses with properties that are qualitatively similar to those observed in the first few processing stages of the visual system. The answer to this question is indeed yes, in light of some interesting work by Linsker (1986).

Figure 9.1 shows the gross structure of a modular network that resembles the visual system. Specifically, the neurons of the network are organized into two-dimensional layers indexed as A (input layer), B, C, and so on, with local feedforward connections from one layer to the next. Each neuron of layer M, $M = B, C, \ldots$, receives inputs from a limited number of neurons located in an overlying region of the previous layer L, $L = A, B, \ldots$, which is called the *receptive field* of that neuron. The receptive fields of the network play a crucial role in the synaptic development process in that they make it possible for neurons in one layer to respond to *spatial correlations* of neuronal activities in the previous layer.

For our present discussion, two assumptions of a structural nature are made:

1. The positions of the connections, once they are chosen, are fixed for the duration of the neuronal development process.
2. Each neuron acts as a linear combiner.

The purpose of our present discussion is to apply a rule to the model of Fig. 9.1, which combines aspects of Hebb-like modification with cooperative and competitive learning in such a way that the network's outputs optimally discriminate among an ensemble of

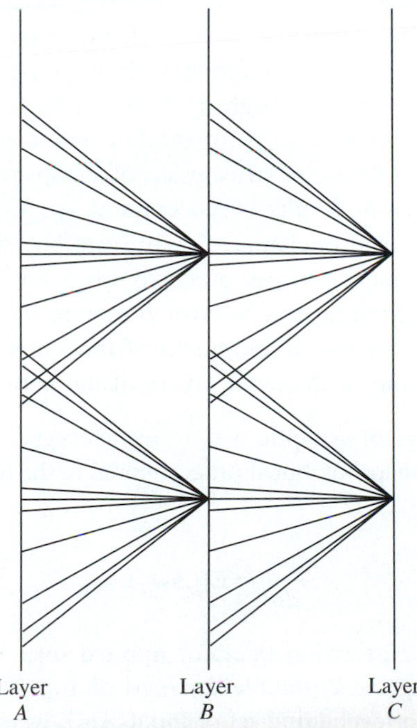

FIGURE 9.1 Layout of modular self-adaptive network.

inputs in a self-organized manner. Thus, all three principles of self-organization, described in the previous section, are involved in the operation of the model.

Consider a neuron j in layer M, and let neurons $1, 2, \ldots, N$ in the previous layer L provide inputs to neuron j. In effect, the latter neurons provide the receptive field for neuron j. To simplify the analysis, we ignore effects due to the time sequence in which the signaling activities of the neurons occur. Rather, we think of the activity history of a layer as a set of *snapshots,* with each snapshot representing the set of signaling activities of the various neurons in that layer and the order of occurrence of the snapshots having no importance. For snapshot π, say, let the inputs applied to neuron j be denoted by $x_1^\pi, x_2^\pi, \ldots, x_N^\pi$. The corresponding value of the neuron's output may be written as

$$y_j^\pi = a_1 + \sum_{i=1}^{N} w_{ji} x_i^\pi \tag{9.1}$$

where a_1 is a fixed bias and w_{ji} is the synaptic weight of neuron j connected to the ith input. According to a modified form of Hebb's postulate of learning, the change in the synaptic weight w_{ji} as a result of the presentation of snapshot π may be written in the form

$$(\Delta w_{jk})^\pi = a_2(y_j^\pi - y_j^0)(x_k^\pi - x_k^0) + a_3 \tag{9.2}$$

where a_2, a_3, y_j^0, and x_k^0 are new constants. These constants are tuned to produce different types of behavior. Most important, the constant a_2 is positive, playing the role of a learning-rate parameter and therefore responsible for self-amplification in accordance with Principle 1.

To proceed with the analysis, it is assumed that the synaptic development process satisfies the following conditions (Linsker, 1986):

1. The synaptic weights operate under a *saturation constraint,* intended to prevent them from becoming infinitely large during the development process. Specifically, each synaptic weight has the same pair of limiting values, one negative denoted by w_- and the other positive denoted by w_+. All the features of interest emerge with this simple assumption, even though it is biologically less reasonable than the assumption that each synaptic weight is bounded by the two values 0 and w_+ for excitatory synapses, and w_- and 0 for inhibitory synapses. Insofar as the overall behavior is concerned, the use of two classes of synapses (excitatory and inhibitory) yields the same simulation results as one class of synapses with bounds w_- and w_+.
2. The synaptic weights tend to change slowly from one snapshot to the next.
3. The synaptic development process proceeds on a layer-by-layer basis. First, the synaptic connections from layer A to layer B mature (develop) to their final values. This is then followed by the development of the synaptic connections from layer B to layer C, and so on for the other layers of the network.

Define the *rate of change* of synaptic weight w_{jk} averaged over a time long compared to the presentation of each snapshot, but short compared to the time required for maturation of the layer, as follows:

$$\frac{dw_{jk}}{dt} = E[(\Delta w_{jk})^\pi] \tag{9.3}$$

where E is the statistical expectation operator applied over the ensemble of snapshots denoted by π. Thus, taking the ensemble average of Eq. (9.3) and using Eq. (9.1) to express y_j^π in terms of the corresponding set of inputs $\{x_i^\pi\}$, we obtain (after some algebraic manipulations)

$$\frac{dw_{jk}}{dt} = \sum_{i=1}^{N} w_{ji}c_{ik} + k_1 + \frac{k_2}{N}\sum_{i=1}^{N} w_{ji} \tag{9.4}$$

where k_1 and k_2 are new constants defined in terms of the previous set of constants a_1, a_2, a_3, and x_k^0, y_j^0, and N is the total number of synaptic weights of neuron j. The parameter c_{ik} is the ensemble-averaged *covariance* of the activities of neurons i and k, which is defined as

$$c_{ik} = E[(x_i^\pi - \bar{x})(x_k^\pi - \bar{x})] \tag{9.5}$$

where $\bar{x}$ is the ensemble average for the input activity x_i^π, taken to be the same for all i; that is,

$$\bar{x} = E[x_i^\pi] \qquad \text{for all } i \tag{9.6}$$

The covariance c_{ik} is the ikth element of an N-by-N *covariance matrix* denoted by $\mathbf{C}$. This matrix plays an important role in what follows. Note, however, that the appearance of c_{ik} does not mean that there is a direct connection between node i in layer L and node k in layer M. Rather, the covariance c_{ik} arises because Hebb's rule causes the rate of change dw_{jk}/dt to depend on the ensemble-averaged product $E[y_j^\pi x_k^\pi]$ and y_j^π, in turn, depends on the set of inputs $\{x_i^\pi\}$ by virtue of Eq. (9.1).

To compute the synaptic development of each layer in turn, we proceed as follows (Linsker, 1986, 1988b):

1. For an ensemble of random presentations applied to input layer A, we use Eq. (9.5) to calculate the covariance c_{ik} for all i and k.
2. For a postsynaptic neuron j in layer B with synapses placed at random according to a specified density distribution, we choose a random set of values for the synaptic weights of that neuron. Hence, we use Eq. (9.4) for the development of neuron j, using the c_{ik} that applies to layer A activity. For this calculation, we need to specify values for the constants k_1 and k_2, and the size of the receptive field that provides inputs to neuron j in layer B under development:

   - The values assigned to the constants k_1 and k_2 determine the mature value of the weight sum $\sum_i w_{ji}$ for the synapses of neuron j. In other words, the constants k_1 and k_2 define the limit on the available resources for which the individual synapses would have to compete in the formation of the model in accordance with Principle 2.

   - The receptive field usually decreases as we proceed away from the overlying point in any direction. For example, we may assume that the synaptic distribution is Gaussian, that is, it has an average density proportional to $\exp(-r^2/r_B^2)$, where r is the distance from the overlying point and r_B is the effective radius of the distribution in layer B.

3. We explore the sensitivity of the mature neuron morphologies of layer B to the random initial choices. A mature layer B is considered to be populated by neurons of uniform morphology if it is substantially independent of the random choices made in step 2.
4. Given this insensitivity to random synaptic positions and initial synaptic weight values, we go back to step 1 and compute the synaptic development from layer B to layer C. This process is repeated until all the layers of the network are taken care of.

Tendency of Synaptic Weights to Reach Boundary Values

An important aspect of the learning rule described in Eq. (9.4) is that at *equilibrium,* that is, when

$$\frac{dw_{jk}}{dt} = 0 \qquad \text{for neuron } j \text{ and all synapses } k \tag{9.7}$$

then neuron j in layer M, $M = B, C, \ldots$, must have all, or all but one, of its synaptic weights "pinned" at one of the boundary values, w_- or w_+ (Linsker, 1986).

We prove this result by contradiction. Suppose that the synaptic weights w_{j1} and w_{j2} of neuron j in layer M are at intermediate values and that they satisfy the stability condition

$$\frac{dw_{j1}}{dt} = \frac{dw_{j2}}{dt} = 0$$

To check stability against small perturbations, let w_{j1} be increased by a small amount ε and let w_{j2} be decreased by the same amount, so that $\sum_i w_{ji}$ remains unchanged. Then, from Eq. (9.4) we readily find that (see Problem 9.2)

$$\frac{dw_{j1}}{dt} = \varepsilon(c_{11} - c_{21}) \tag{9.8}$$

where c_{11} refers to the variance of the output signal of neuron 1 in layer L, $L = A, B, \ldots$, and c_{21} refers to the covariance between the output signals of neurons 2 and 1 in that same layer. For the perceptual system being considered here, c_{11} is greater than c_{21}. It follows therefore that dw_{j1}/dt is positive. Similarly, we find that

$$\frac{dw_{j2}}{dt} = \varepsilon(c_{12} - c_{22}) \tag{9.9}$$

which is negative. The new values of dw_{j1}/dt and dw_{j2}/dt tend to cause the perturbations $+\varepsilon$ and $-\varepsilon$ applied to w_{j1} and w_{j2}, respectively, to amplify; the system is therefore unstable against this perturbation. In other words, any synaptic weight vector $\mathbf{w}_j$ with two or more elements not at a boundary (w_- or w_+) is unstable under the learning rule described in Eq. (9.4).

Simulation Results

When the parameter space of the layered network is explored, we find that there are a limited number of ways in which each layer of the network can develop. Basically, a sequence of feature-analyzing neuron types emerges as one layer matures after another. This phenomenon was first illustrated by Linsker (1986) by focusing on a situation in which there is only random activity in layer A, with no correlation of activity from one input node to the next. That is,

$$c_{ik} = \begin{cases} 1, & k = i \\ 0, & k \neq i \end{cases} \tag{9.10}$$

for nodes i and k in the input layer A. The motivation for considering this case was to understand how known feature-analyzing neurons may arise even before birth, which have been observed in certain primates.

The synaptic weights from layer A to layer B depend on the parameters k_1 and k_2 and the size of the receptive fields assigned to the neurons of layer B. To proceed further,

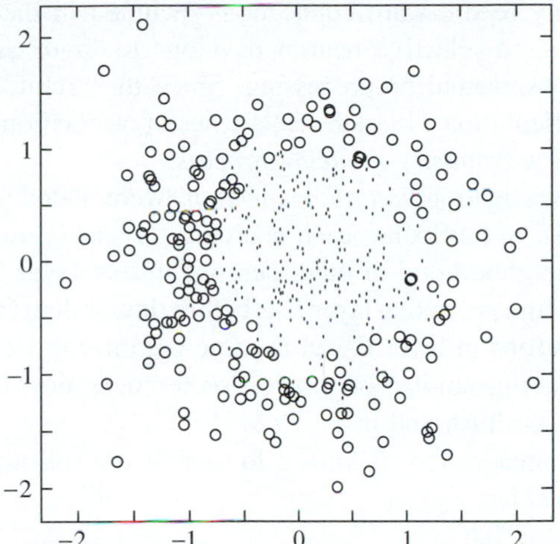

FIGURE 9.2 Synaptic positions and mature synaptic weights for a single neuron of layer *C* having 600 synapses. Parameter values are $k_1 = 0.45$, $k_2 = -3$, $r_C/r_B = 3^{1/2}$, and each *w* value is allowed to range between -0.5 and $+0.5$. Random initial *w* values are chosen from uniform distribution on the interval -0.5 to $+0.5$. At maturity, every *w* reaches an extreme value: 0.5 (indicated by a circle) or -0.5 (dot). Axes are labeled by distance from neuron center (in units of r_C). (From R. Linsker, 1986, with permission of the National Academy of Sciences of the U.S.A.)

these parameters were chosen in a regime such that the neurons of layer *B* are all-excitatory (i.e., all the synaptic weights saturated to w_+). This made nearby neurons in layer *B* have highly correlated activity, with the result that each activity pattern in layer *B* is a ''blurred'' image of the random ''snow'' appearing in layer *A*. If a neuron's activity in layer *B* is high at a given time, then its neighbor's activities are likely to be high too. Consequently, a new type of feature-analyzing neuron, namely, a *center-surround neuron,* was found to emerge in layer *C*. Center-surround neurons act as a contrast-sensitive filter, responding maximally either to a bright circular spot in the center of their receptive field surrounded by a dark area or the reverse, a dark circular spot on a bright background. Figure 9.2 illustrates the pattern of synaptic connections computed for a resulting mature neuron in layer *C*. At maturity, every synaptic weight reaches an extreme value: $w_+ = 0.5$ (indicated by a circle) or $w_- = -0.5$ (indicated by a dot). The axes are labeled by distance from the neuron center, in units of r_C (the effective radius of the synaptic distribution in layer *C*). Figure 9.2 illustrates the *antagonistic* nature of a center-surround structure; that is, an inhibitory center is accompanied by an excitatory surround (or vice versa). The synapses in the inhibitory area *cooperate* with each other in accordance with Principle 3; likewise, for the synapses in the excitatory area. But these two sets of synapses are in *competition* with others for their respective areas of influence.

Moreover, the different neurons of layer *C* were found to have a Mexican hat form of covariance function (Linsker, 1986, pp. 8390–8394). Specifically, nearby neurons were positively correlated; farther away, there was a ring of neurons that were negatively correlated. The ''Mexican hat'' character of the covariance function became progressively more pronounced as we proceed through succeeding layers *D*, *E*, and *F*. Finally, in layer *G*, another type of feature-analyzing neuron, an *orientation-selective neuron,*[1] was found to emerge. This latter neuron responds maximally to a bright edge or bar against a dark

[1] Yuille et al. (1989) have demonstrated another method for obtaining orientation selective neurons by using a form of Hebbian learning different from that used in Linsker's model.

background. With only feedforward connections included in the layered network as in Fig. 9.1, each orientation-selective neuron develops to favor an arbitrary orientation, because of the center-surround preprocessing. Since the architecture and development rules do not possess orientational bias, the emergence of orientation selectivity as described here is an example of a *symmetry-breaking process.*

In a subsequent investigation, *lateral connections* were added within layer G (Linsker, 1986, pp. 8779–8783). In particular, each neuron in layer G now receives lateral inputs from a surrounding neighborhood of other neurons in that layer, as well as feedforward inputs from neurons of the preceding layer F as before. It was then found that the orientation preferences of the neurons in layer G can become organized in certain arrangements. In particular, neurons having similar orientation preferences develop to occupy irregular band-shaped regions, as illustrated in Fig. 9.3.

The mammalian visual system is known to exhibit the following distinctive features (Hubel and Wiesel, 1977):

- Center-surround neurons in the retina
- Orientation-selective neurons in the visual cortex
- Irregular band-shaped regions of neurons of similar orientation called *orientation columns,* in subsequent layers.

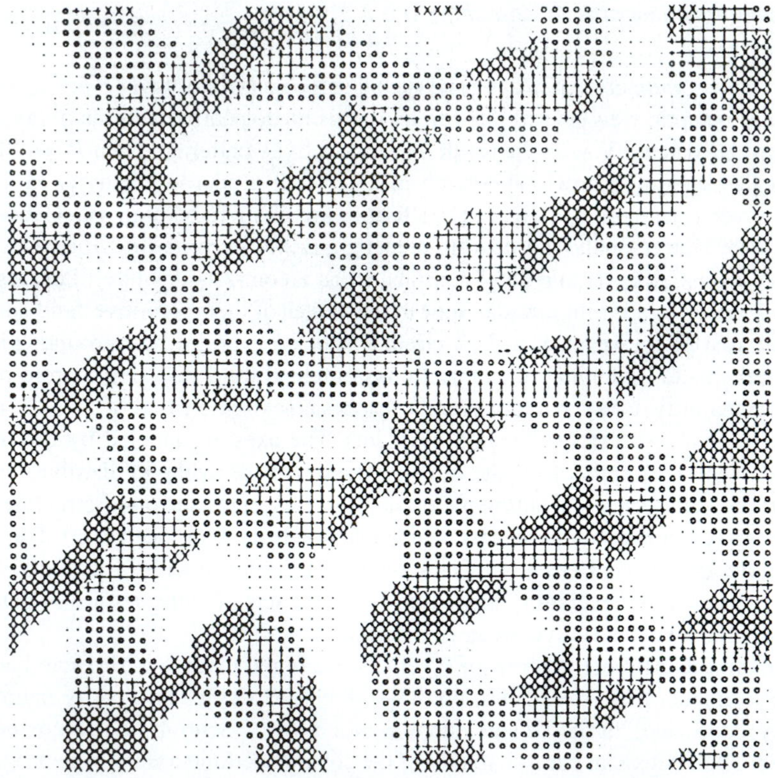

FIGURE 9.3 A nearly Hebb-optimal solution for an array of orientation neurons. Each neuron is "stained" according to its orientation preference θ (measured counterclockwise from the vertical): 9–45° (dot); 45–81° (small circle); 81–117° (+); 117–153° (×); 153–189° (blank). Adjacent grid positions are separated by distance $0.1493r_G$, where r_G is the effective radius of the synaptic distribution in layer G. Array is 72 by 72 with periodic boundary conditions. (From R. Linsker, 1986, with permission of the National Academy of Sciences of the U.S.A.)

Recognizing the highly complex nature of the visual system, it is indeed remarkable that the simple model considered by Linsker is capable of developing similar feature-analyzing neurons. The point is not to imply that feature-analyzing neurons in the mammalian visual system develop in exactly the manner described here. Rather, such structures may be produced by a relatively simple layered network whose synaptic connections develop in accordance with a Hebbian form of learning.

Optimization Properties of Hebbian Learning

The learning rule of Eq. (9.4), based on Hebb's postulate, has some remarkable optimization properties, as shown here. Consider a neuron j in layer M that receives inputs from neurons $1, 2, \ldots, N$ in the previous layer L, where $M = B, C, \ldots$, and $L = A, B, \ldots$. The neuron's development is described by Eqs. (9.4)–(9.6), with a saturation constraint on the range of values assumed by each synaptic weight. We assume that the ensemble statistical properties of the neural activities that supply the inputs to neuron j are not affected by the values assigned to its synaptic weights; this assumption is valid provided that there is no feedback from neuron j in layer M to the neurons in the previous layer L.

Define a *cost function* E to have the following property (Linsker, 1988):

$$-\frac{dE}{dw_{jk}} = \frac{dw_{jk}}{dt} \tag{9.11}$$

where w_{jk} is the synaptic weight from neuron k in layer L to neuron j in layer M. The meaning of this property is that as Hebb's rule causes the value of synaptic weight w_{jk} to change with time, the value of E as a function of w_{jk} decreases along the path of locally steepest descent. In particular, if the rate of change of a synaptic weight, dw_{jk}/dt, is positive, then the partial derivative dE/dw_{jk} is negative; in this case w_{jk} increases and E decreases with time. If, on the other hand, dw_{jk}/dt is negative, then dE/dw_{jk} is positive, in which case w_{jk} decreases and E again decreases with time. Thus, using Eqs. (9.4) and (9.11) yields the relation

$$\frac{dE}{dw_{jk}} = -\sum_{i=1}^{N} w_{ji}c_{ik} - k_1 - \frac{k_2}{N}\sum_{i=1}^{N} w_{ji} \tag{9.12}$$

Solving this equation for the cost function E, we therefore have (to within a constant):

$$E = E_c + E_k \tag{9.13}$$

where E_c and E_k are defined, respectively, by

$$E_c = -\frac{1}{2}\sum_{i=1}^{N}\sum_{k=1}^{N} w_{ji}c_{ik}w_{jk} \tag{9.14}$$

and

$$E_k = -k_1\sum_{i=1}^{N} w_{ji} - \frac{k_2}{2N}\left(\sum_{i=1}^{N} w_{ji}\right)^2 \tag{9.15}$$

When neuron j reaches maturity (full development), the rate of change of its synaptic weights, dw_{jk}/dt, is zero for all k. Under this condition, the cost function E reaches a *local minimum*. The cost function E is made up of two terms, E_c and E_k. The quadratic form (i.e., double summation) involved in the definition of E_c in Eq. (9.14) is just the variance of the output y_j of neuron j, as shown by

$$\sigma_j^2 = E[(y_j - \bar{y})^2]$$
$$= \sum_{i=1}^{N} \sum_{k=1}^{N} w_{ji} c_{ik} w_{jk} \tag{9.16}$$

where the covariance c_{ik} is itself defined in Eq. (9.5). The term E_k defined in Eq. (9.15) may be viewed as a *model-penalty* function, which is parabolic in the weight sum $\sum_i w_{ji}$. There is no explicit constraint imposed on the mature value of $\sum_i w_{ji}$; rather, the constraint emerges from the tuning of the constants k_1 and k_2. Now, for any fixed value of $\sum_i w_{ji}$, the cost function E is minimized when the variance σ_j^2 is maximized. Accordingly, the minimization of the cost function E may be interpreted as a *constrained optimization problem,* stated formally as follows (Linsker, 1988a):

Find the synaptic weights of neuron j so as to maximize the variance σ_j^2 of its output, defined by the quadratic form

$$\sigma_j^2 = \sum_{i=1}^{N} \sum_{k=1}^{N} w_{ji} c_{ik} w_{jk}$$

subject to two constraints:

$$\sum_i w_{ji} = \text{constant}$$

and

$$w_- \leq w_{ji} \leq w_+ \qquad \text{for all } i$$

The parameter c_{ik} is the covariance of the activities of neurons i and k that feed neuron j.

The implication of this statement is that, in the context of a layered feedforward model that is trained on a layer-by-layer basis, a Hebbian form of learning causes a neuron to develop in such a way that the variance of its output is maximized, subject to certain constraints. In general, however, the variance is not guaranteed to have a unique local maximum, because of the constraints.

9.4 Discussion

Linsker's model is based on a linear multilayer feedforward network with Hebb-modifiable synapses. Self-organization of the model is performed on a layer-by-layer basis, with the result that each layer has a distinct role. Thus, in response to a random uncorrelated signaling activity in the input layer of the network, center-surround neurons and orientation-selective target neurons emerge in different layers of the network, which are qualitatively similar to properties found in the early stages of visual processing in cat and monkey. The two parameters that determine which neuron type develops are (1) the radius of the source region that supplies input to each target neuron, and (2) the degree of correlation needed to cause increase in synaptic weights via the Hebb-like rule.

It would be tempting to say that since the model is linear, the transformations computed by successive layers of the model may be combined into a single layer of weights. If we were to do so, however, the self-organized feature analyzing properties of the different layers would disappear, and the model would then lose its impact.

Linsker's model for an adaptive perceptual system is important for three reasons (Becker, 1991):

1. It is remarkable that the model based on the application of Hebbian learning in multiple stages is capable of providing interesting classes of feature detectors.
2. Given certain architectural constraints, the model demonstrates a learning mechanism for explaining how a perceptual system may evolve in response to a purely random input.
3. The model may account for some of the neurobiological findings on early development of the perceptual system.

Indeed, the model offers a great deal of potential for future research in neurobiological modeling. In its present form, however, the model may be criticized on two accounts. First, the model is entirely linear; it therefore suffers from limited computational power. Second, the model involves a large number of parameters that have to be tuned on a layer-by-layer basis in order to produce the desired receptive fields in the output layer. In his later work, Linsker (1988a) adopted a more principled approach for the study of self-organized learning that is rooted in information theory. Details of this latter approach are presented in Chapter 11.

Earlier we mentioned that, in mathematical terms, the Hebbian learning algorithm used to produce the layered model causes the synaptic weights w_{ji} of a neuron j to develop with time so as to maximize the variance σ_j^2 of its output subject to the two constraints $\sum_i w_{ji} = \text{constant}$ and $w_- \leq w_{ji} \leq w_+$ for all i. We may visualize this constrained optimization geometrically as follows (Linsker, 1989a, 1990a):

- The synaptic weights w_{ji} constitute a vector $\mathbf{w}_j$ that lies within a hypercube bounded by w_- and w_+.
- The variance σ_j^2 is to be maximized on the hyperplane $\sum_i w_{ji} = \text{constant}$.
- The variance σ_j^2 is guaranteed to have a maximum occurring at a point in the boundary of the hypercube, at which all, or all but one, of the synaptic weights w_{ji} are extremal.

It should be emphasized, however, that a neuron in Linsker's model, as described here, does *not* perform principal components analysis on its inputs. To do so, we would need to maximize the variance σ_j^2 of the neuron's output on a hypersphere rather than a hypercube. In other words, the maximization of σ_j^2 is constrained by the requirement that $\sum_i w_{ji}^2 = \text{constant}$, with no additional constraint imposed on the w_{ji}. Principal components analysis is a form of data compression, designed to identify a specific set of features that is characteristic of the input data. In order to perform it, there has to be redundancy in the input data. The remainder of the chapter is devoted to the important subject of principal components analysis, and how it can be performed using self-organizing systems based on Hebbian learning.

9.5 Principal Components Analysis

A key problem in statistical pattern recognition is that of feature selection or feature extraction. *Feature selection* refers to a process whereby a *data space* is transformed into a *feature space* that, in theory, has exactly the same dimension as the original data space. However, the transformation is designed in such a way that the data set may be represented by a reduced number of "effective" features and yet retain most of the intrinsic information content of the data; in other words, the data set undergoes a *dimensionality reduction.* To be specific, suppose we have a p-dimensional vector $\mathbf{x}$ and wish to transmit it using m numbers, where $m < p$. If we simply truncate the vector $\mathbf{x}$, we will cause a mean-squared error equal to the sum of the variances of the elements eliminated from $\mathbf{x}$. So we ask the following question: Does there exist an invertible *linear* transformation $\mathbf{T}$ such that the truncation of $\mathbf{Tx}$ is optimum in the mean-squared error sense? Clearly, the transformation $\mathbf{T}$ should have the property that some of its components have low variance. Principal components analysis (also known as the *Karhunen–Loève transformation* in communication theory) maximizes the rate of decrease of variance and is therefore the right choice. In this chapter we will show some algorithms using neural networks that can perform principal components analysis on a data vector of interest.

Principal components analysis (PCA) is perhaps the oldest and best-known technique in multivariate analysis (Preisendorfer, 1988; Jolliffe, 1986). It was first introduced by Pearson (1901), who used it in a biological context to recast linear regression analysis into a new form. It was then developed by Hotelling (1933) in work done on psychometry. It appeared once again and quite independently in the setting of probability theory, as considered by Karhunen (1947); and was subsequently generalized by Loève (1963).

Let $\mathbf{x}$ denote a p-dimensional *random vector* representing the data set of interest. We assume that the random vector $\mathbf{x}$ has zero mean:

$$E[\mathbf{x}] = 0$$

where E is the statistical expectation operator. If $\mathbf{x}$ has a nonzero mean, then we subtract the mean from it before proceeding with the analysis. Let $\mathbf{u}$ denote a *unit vector,* also of dimension p, onto which the vector $\mathbf{x}$ is to be *projected.* This projection is defined by the inner product of the vectors $\mathbf{x}$ and $\mathbf{u}$, as shown by

$$a = \mathbf{x}^T\mathbf{u} = \mathbf{u}^T\mathbf{x} \tag{9.17}$$

subject to the constraint

$$\|\mathbf{u}\| = (\mathbf{u}^T\mathbf{u})^{1/2} = 1 \tag{9.18}$$

The projection a is a *random variable* with a mean and variance related to the statistics of the data vector $\mathbf{x}$. Under the assumption that the random data vector $\mathbf{x}$ has zero mean, it follows that the mean value of the projection a is zero too:

$$E[a] = \mathbf{u}^T E[\mathbf{x}] = 0$$

The variance of a is therefore the same as its mean-square value, and so we may write

$$\begin{aligned}\sigma^2 &= E[a^2] \\ &= E[(\mathbf{u}^T\mathbf{x})(\mathbf{x}^T\mathbf{u})] \\ &= \mathbf{u}^T E[\mathbf{x}\mathbf{x}^T]\mathbf{u} \\ &= \mathbf{u}^T\mathbf{R}\mathbf{u}\end{aligned} \tag{9.19}$$

The p-by-p matrix $\mathbf{R}$ is the *correlation matrix* of the data vector, formally defined as the expectation of the outer product of the vector $\mathbf{x}$ with itself, as shown by

$$\mathbf{R} = E[\mathbf{x}\mathbf{x}^T] \tag{9.20}$$

We observe that the correlation matrix $\mathbf{R}$ is *symmetric,* which means that

$$\mathbf{R}^T = \mathbf{R} \tag{9.21}$$

From this property it follows that if $\mathbf{a}$ and $\mathbf{b}$ are any p-by-1 vectors, then

$$\mathbf{a}^T\mathbf{R}\mathbf{b} = \mathbf{b}^T\mathbf{R}\mathbf{a} \tag{9.22}$$

From Eq. (9.19) we see that the variance σ^2 of the projection a is a function of the unit vector $\mathbf{u}$; we may thus write

$$\begin{aligned}\psi(\mathbf{u}) &= \sigma^2 \\ &= \mathbf{u}^T\mathbf{R}\mathbf{u}\end{aligned} \tag{9.23}$$

on the basis of which we may think of $\psi(\mathbf{u})$ as a *variance probe.*

Eigenstructure of Principal Components Analysis

The next issue to be considered is that of finding the unit vectors $\mathbf{u}$ along which $\psi(\mathbf{u})$ has *extremal* or *stationary* values (local maxima or minima), subject to a constraint on the Euclidean norm of $\mathbf{u}$. The solution to this problem lies in the eigenstructure of the correlation matrix $\mathbf{R}$ (Preisendorfer, 1988). If $\mathbf{u}$ is a unit vector such that the variance probe $\psi(\mathbf{u})$ has an extremal value, then for any small perturbation $\delta\mathbf{u}$ of the unit vector $\mathbf{u}$, we find that, to a first-order in $\delta\mathbf{u}$,

$$\psi(\mathbf{u} + \delta\mathbf{u}) = \psi(\mathbf{u}) \tag{9.24}$$

Now, from the definition of the variance probe given in Eq. (9.23), we have

$$\begin{aligned}\psi(\mathbf{u} + \delta\mathbf{u}) &= (\mathbf{u} + \delta\mathbf{u})^T\mathbf{R}(\mathbf{u} + \delta\mathbf{u}) \\ &= \mathbf{u}^T\mathbf{R}\mathbf{u} + 2(\delta\mathbf{u})^T\mathbf{R}\mathbf{u} + (\delta\mathbf{u})^T\mathbf{R}\,\delta\mathbf{u}\end{aligned}$$

where, in the second line, we have made use of Eq. (9.22). Ignoring the second-order term $(\delta\mathbf{u})^T\mathbf{R}\,\delta\mathbf{u}$ and invoking the definition of Eq. (9.23), we may therefore write

$$\begin{aligned}\psi(\mathbf{u} + \delta\mathbf{u}) &= \mathbf{u}^T\mathbf{R}\mathbf{u} + 2(\delta\mathbf{u})^T\mathbf{R}\mathbf{u} \\ &= \psi(\mathbf{u}) + 2(\delta\mathbf{u})^T\mathbf{R}\mathbf{u}\end{aligned} \tag{9.25}$$

Hence, the use of Eq. (9.24) in (9.25) implies that

$$(\delta\mathbf{u})^T\mathbf{R}\mathbf{u} = 0 \tag{9.26}$$

Just any perturbations $\delta\mathbf{u}$ of $\mathbf{u}$ are not admissible; rather, we are restricted to use only those perturbations for which the Euclidean norm of the perturbed vector $\mathbf{u} + \delta\mathbf{u}$ remains equal to unity; that is,

$$\|\mathbf{u} + \delta\mathbf{u}\| = 1$$

or, equivalently,

$$(\mathbf{u} + \delta\mathbf{u})^T(\mathbf{u} + \delta\mathbf{u}) = 1$$

Hence, in light of Eq. (9.18), we require that to a first order in $\delta\mathbf{u}$,

$$(\delta\mathbf{u})^T\mathbf{u} = 0 \tag{9.27}$$

This means that the perturbations $\delta\mathbf{u}$ must be orthogonal to $\mathbf{u}$, and therefore only a change in the direction of $\mathbf{u}$ is permitted.

By convention, the elements of the unit vector $\mathbf{u}$ are dimensionless in a physical sense. If, therefore, we are to combine Eqs. (9.26) and (9.27), we have to introduce a scaling factor λ into the latter equation with the same dimensions as the entries in the correlation matrix $\mathbf{R}$. Doing all of this, we may then write

$$(\delta\mathbf{u})^T\mathbf{R}\mathbf{u} - \lambda(\delta\mathbf{u})^T\mathbf{u} = 0$$

or, equivalently,

$$(\delta \mathbf{u})^T(\mathbf{R}\mathbf{u} - \lambda \mathbf{u}) = 0 \tag{9.28}$$

For the condition of Eq. (9.28) to hold, it is necessary and sufficient that we have

$$\mathbf{R}\mathbf{u} = \lambda \mathbf{u} \tag{9.29}$$

This is the equation that governs the unit vectors $\mathbf{u}$ for which the variance probe $\psi(\mathbf{u})$ has extremal values.

Equation (9.29) is recognized as the *eigenvalue problem*, commonly encountered in linear algebra (Strang, 1980). The problem has nontrivial solutions (i.e., $\mathbf{u} \neq \mathbf{0}$) only for special values of λ that are called the *eigenvalues* of the correlation matrix $\mathbf{R}$. The associated values of $\mathbf{u}$ are called *eigenvectors*. A correlation matrix is characterized by real, nonnegative eigenvalues. The associated eigenvectors are unique, assuming that the eigenvalues are distinct. Let the eigenvalues of the p-by-p matrix $\mathbf{R}$ be denoted by λ_0, $\lambda_1, \ldots, \lambda_{p-1}$, and the associated eigenvectors be denoted by $\mathbf{u}_0, \mathbf{u}_1, \ldots, \mathbf{u}_{p-1}$, respectively. We may then write

$$\mathbf{R}\mathbf{u}_j = \lambda_j \mathbf{u}_j, \qquad j = 0, 1, \ldots, p - 1 \tag{9.30}$$

Let the corresponding eigenvalues be arranged in decreasing order:

$$\lambda_0 > \lambda_1 > \cdots > \lambda_j > \cdots > \lambda_{p-1} \tag{9.31}$$

so that $\lambda_0 = \lambda_{\max}$. Let the associated eigenvectors be used to construct a p-by-p matrix:

$$\mathbf{U} = [\mathbf{u}_0, \mathbf{u}_1, \ldots, \mathbf{u}_j, \ldots, \mathbf{u}_{p-1}] \tag{9.32}$$

We may then combine the set of p equations represented in (9.30) into a single equation:

$$\mathbf{R}\mathbf{U} = \mathbf{U}\boldsymbol{\Lambda} \tag{9.33}$$

where $\boldsymbol{\Lambda}$ is a diagonal matrix defined by the eigenvalues of matrix $\mathbf{R}$:

$$\boldsymbol{\Lambda} = \text{diag}[\lambda_0, \lambda_1, \ldots, \lambda_j, \ldots, \lambda_{p-1}] \tag{9.34}$$

The matrix $\mathbf{U}$ is an *orthogonal matrix* in the sense that its column vectors (i.e., the eigenvectors of $\mathbf{R}$) satisfy the *conditions of orthonormality:*

$$\mathbf{u}_i^T \mathbf{u}_j = \begin{cases} 1, & j = i \\ 0, & j \neq i \end{cases} \tag{9.35}$$

Equation (9.35) requires distinct eigenvalues. Equivalently, we may write

$$\mathbf{U}^T\mathbf{U} = \mathbf{I}$$

from which we deduce that the inverse of matrix $\mathbf{U}$ is the same as its transpose, as shown by

$$\mathbf{U}^T = \mathbf{U}^{-1} \tag{9.36}$$

This, in turn, means that we may rewrite Eq. (9.33) in a form known as the *orthogonal similarity transformation:*

$$\mathbf{U}^T\mathbf{R}\mathbf{U} = \boldsymbol{\Lambda} \tag{9.37}$$

or, in expanded form,

$$\mathbf{u}_j^T \mathbf{R} \mathbf{u}_k = \begin{cases} \lambda_j, & k = j \\ 0, & k \neq j \end{cases} \tag{9.38}$$

From Eqs. (9.23) and (9.38) it therefore follows that the variance probes and eigenvalues are equal, as shown by

$$\psi(\mathbf{u}_j) = \lambda_j, \qquad j = 0, 1, \ldots, p-1 \tag{9.39}$$

We may summarize the two important findings we have made from the eigenstructure of principal components analysis:

- The eigenvectors of the correlation matrix **R** pertaining to the zero-mean data vector **x** define the unit vectors $\mathbf{u}_j$, representing the principal directions along which the variance probes $\psi(\mathbf{u}_j)$ have their extremal values.
- The associated eigenvalues define the extremal values of the variance probes $\psi(\mathbf{u}_j)$.

Basic Data Representations

With p possible solutions for the unit vector **u**, we find that there are p possible projections of the data vector **x** to be considered. Specifically, from Eq. (9.17) we note that

$$a_j = \mathbf{u}_j^T\mathbf{x} = \mathbf{x}^T\mathbf{u}_j, \qquad j = 0, 1, \ldots, p-1 \tag{9.40}$$

where the a_j are the projections of **x** onto the principal directions represented by the unit vectors $\mathbf{u}_j$. The a_j are called the *principal components;* they have the same physical dimensions as the data vector **x**. The formula of Eq. (9.40) may be viewed as one of *analysis.*

To reconstruct the original data vector **x** exactly from the projections a_j, we proceed as follows. First, we combine the set of projections $\{a_j | j = 0, 1, \ldots, p-1\}$ into a single vector, as shown by

$$\begin{aligned}\mathbf{a} &= [a_0, a_1, \ldots, a_{p-1}]^T \\ &= [\mathbf{x}^T\mathbf{u}_0, \mathbf{x}^T\mathbf{u}_1, \ldots, \mathbf{x}^T\mathbf{u}_{p-1}]^T \\ &= \mathbf{U}^T\mathbf{x}\end{aligned} \tag{9.41}$$

Next, we premultiply both sides of Eq. (9.41) by the matrix **U**, and then use the relation of Eq. (9.36). Accordingly, the original data vector **x** may be reconstructed as follows:

$$\begin{aligned}\mathbf{x} &= \mathbf{U}\mathbf{a} \\ &= \sum_{j=0}^{p-1} a_j\mathbf{u}_j\end{aligned} \tag{9.42}$$

which may be viewed as the formula for *synthesis.* In this sense, the unit vectors $\mathbf{u}_j$ represent a *basis* of the data space. Indeed, Eq. (9.42) is nothing but a coordinate transformation, according to which a point **x** in the data space is transformed into a corresponding point **a** in the feature space.

Dimensionality Reduction

From the perspective of statistical pattern recognition, the practical value of principal components analysis is that it provides an effective technique for *dimensionality reduction.* In particular, we may reduce the number of features needed for effective data representation by discarding those linear combinations in Eq. (9.42) that have small variances and retain only those terms that have large variances (Oja, 1983). Let $\lambda_0, \lambda_1, \ldots, \lambda_{m-1}$ denote the largest m eigenvalues of the correlation matrix $\mathbf{R}$. We may then approximate the data vector $\mathbf{x}$ by *truncating* the expansion of Eq. (9.42) after m terms as follows:

$$\mathbf{x}' = \sum_{j=0}^{m-1} a_j \mathbf{u}_j, \qquad m < p \tag{9.43}$$

Note that the largest eigenvalues $\lambda_0, \lambda_1, \ldots, \lambda_{m-1}$ do not enter the computation of the approximating vector $\mathbf{x}'$; they merely determine the number of the terms retained in the actual expansion used to compute $\mathbf{x}'$.

The *approximation error vector* $\mathbf{e}$ equals the difference between the original data vector $\mathbf{x}$ and the approximating date vector $\mathbf{x}'$, as shown by

$$\mathbf{e} = \mathbf{x} - \mathbf{x}' \tag{9.44}$$

Substituting Eqs. (9.42) and (9.43) in (9.44) yields

$$\mathbf{e} = \sum_{j=m}^{p-1} a_j \mathbf{u}_j \tag{9.45}$$

The error vector $\mathbf{e}$ *is orthogonal to the approximating data vector* $\mathbf{x}'$, as illustrated graphically in Fig. 9.4. In other words, the inner product of the vectors $\mathbf{x}'$ and $\mathbf{e}$ is zero. This property is readily shown by using Eqs. (9.43) and (9.45) as follows:

$$\begin{aligned} \mathbf{e}^T\mathbf{x}' &= \sum_{i=m}^{p-1} a_i \mathbf{u}_i^T \sum_{j=0}^{m-1} a_j \mathbf{u}_j \\ &= \sum_{i=m}^{p-1} \sum_{j=0}^{m-1} a_i a_j \mathbf{u}_i^T \mathbf{u}_j \\ &= 0 \end{aligned} \tag{9.46}$$

where we have made use of the second condition in Eq. (9.35). Equation (9.46) is known as the *principle of orthogonality.*

The total variance of the p components of the random vector $\mathbf{x}$ is, via Eq. (9.23) and the first line of Eq. (9.38),

$$\sum_{j=0}^{p-1} \sigma_j^2 = \sum_{j=0}^{p-1} \lambda_j \tag{9.47}$$

where σ_j^2 is the variance of the jth principal component a_j. The total variance of the m elements of the approximating vector $\mathbf{x}'$ is

$$\sum_{j=0}^{m-1} \sigma_j^2 = \sum_{j=0}^{m-1} \lambda_j \tag{9.48}$$

The total variance of the $(m - p)$ elements in the approximation error vector $\mathbf{x} - \mathbf{x}'$ is therefore

$$\sum_{j=m}^{p-1} \sigma_j^2 = \sum_{j=m}^{p-1} \lambda_j \tag{9.49}$$

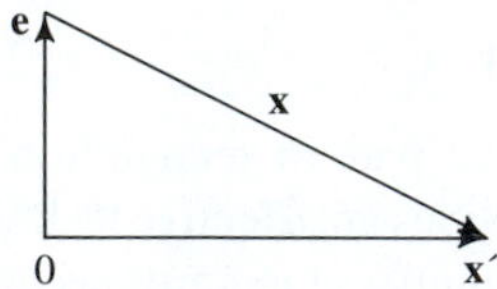

FIGURE 9.4 Illustration of the relationship between vector $\mathbf{x}$, its reconstructed version $\mathbf{x}'$, and error vector $\mathbf{e}$.

The eigenvalues $\lambda_m, \ldots, \lambda_{p-1}$ are the *smallest* $(p - m)$ eigenvalues of the correlation matrix $\mathbf{R}$; they correspond to the terms discarded from the expansion of Eq. (9.43) used to construct the approximating vector $\mathbf{x}'$. The closer all these eigenvalues are to zero, the more effective will be the dimensionality reduction (resulting from the application of the principal components analysis to the data vector $\mathbf{x}$) in preserving the information content of the input data. Thus, to perform dimensionality reduction on some input data, we *compute the eigenvalues and eigenvectors of the correlation matrix of the input data vector, and then project the data orthogonally onto the subspace spanned by the eigenvectors belonging to the largest eigenvalues.* This method of data representation is commonly referred to as *subspace decomposition* (Oja, 1983).

EXAMPLE 1. Bivariate Data Set

To illustrate the application of the principal components analysis, consider the example of a bivariate (two-dimensional) data set depicted in Fig. 9.5. The horizontal and vertical axes of the diagram represent the natural coordinates of the data set. The rotated axes labeled 1 and 2 result from the application of principal components analysis to this data set. From Fig. 9.5 we see that projecting the data set onto axis 1 captures the salient feature of the data, namely, the fact that the data set is bimodal (i.e., there are two clusters in its structure). Indeed, the variance of the projections of the data points onto axis 1 is greater than that for any other projection axis in the figure. By contrast, the inherent bimodal nature of the data set is completely obscured when it is projected onto the orthogonal axis 2.

The important point to note from this simple example is that although the cluster structure of the data set is evident from the two-dimensional plot of the raw data displayed in the framework of the horizontal and vertical axes, this is not always the case in practice. In the more general case of high-dimensional data sets, it is quite conceivable to have the intrinsic cluster structure of the data concealed, and to see it

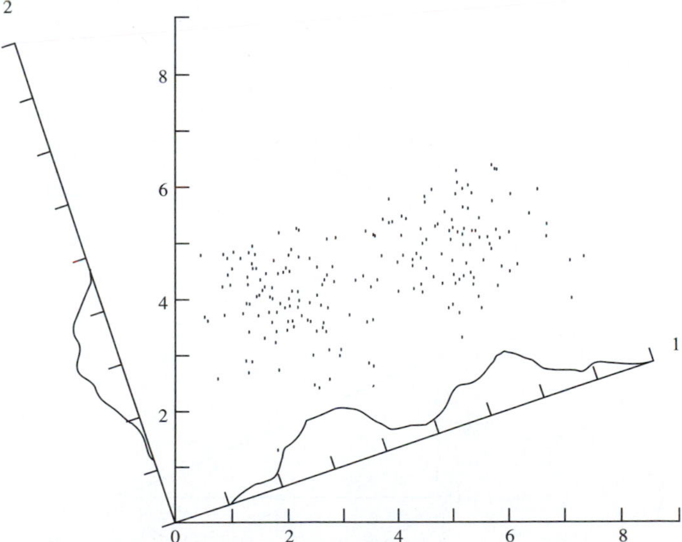

FIGURE 9.5 Illustration of principal components analysis. A cloud of data points is shown in two dimensions, and the density plots formed by projecting this cloud onto each of two axes 1 and 2 are indicated. The projection onto axis 1 has maximum variance, and clearly shows the bimodal, or clustered, character of the data. (From R. Linsker, 1988, with permission of IEEE.)

we have to perform a statistical analysis similar to principal components analysis. It should be noted, however, that there are cases in which principal components analysis does not separate clustered data correctly; its use in these cases is clearly only a heuristic (Linsker, 1988).

9.6 A Linear Neuron Model as a Maximum Eigenfilter

There is a close correspondence between the behavior of self-organized neural networks and the statistical method of principal components analysis. In this section we demonstrate this correspondence by establishing a remarkable result: A single linear neuron with a Hebbian-type adaptation rule for its synaptic weights can evolve into a filter for the first principal component of the input distribution (Oja, 1982).

To proceed with the demonstration, consider the simple neuron model depicted in Fig. 9.6a. The model is *linear* in the sense that the model output is a linear combination of its inputs. The neuron receives a set of p input signals $x_0, x_1, \ldots, x_{p-1}$ through a corresponding set of p synapses with weights $w_0, w_1, \ldots, w_{p-1}$, respectively. The resulting model output y is thus defined by

$$y = \sum_{i=0}^{p-1} w_i x_i \tag{9.50}$$

Note that in the situation described here we have a single neuron to deal with, and so there is no need to use double subscripts to identify the synaptic weights of the network.

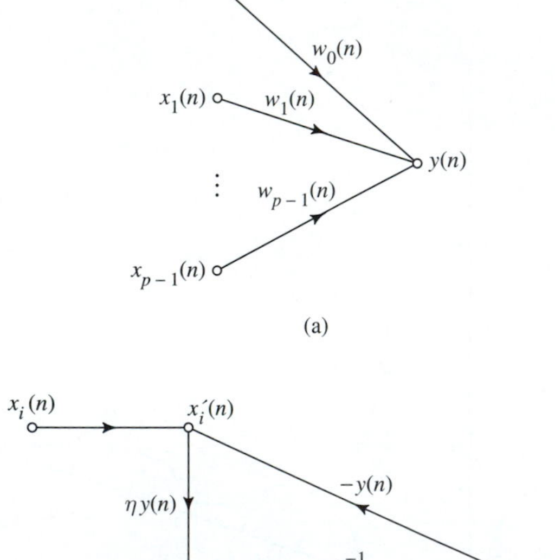

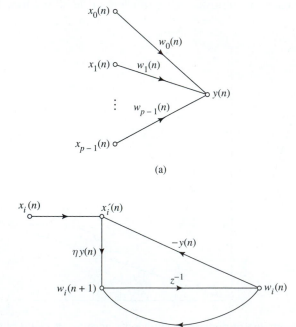

FIGURE 9.6 Signal-flow graph representation of maximum eigenfilter. (a) Graph of Eq. (9.50). (b) Graph of Eqs. (9.55) and (9.56).

In accordance with Hebb's postulate of learning, a synaptic weight w_i varies with time, growing strong when the presynaptic signal x_i and postsynaptic signal y coincide with each other. Specifically, we write

$$w_i(n + 1) = w_i(n) + \eta y(n)x_i(n), \qquad i = 0, 1, \ldots, p - 1 \tag{9.51}$$

where n denotes discrete time and η is the *learning-rate parameter*. However, this learning rule in its basic form leads to unlimited growth of the synaptic weight w_i, which is unacceptable on physical grounds. We may overcome this problem by incorporating some form of *saturation* or *normalization* in the learning rule for the adaptation of synaptic weights. The use of normalization has the effect of introducing competition among the synapses of the neuron over limited resources, which is essential for stabilization. From a mathematical point of view, a convenient form of normalization is described by (Oja, 1982):

$$w_i(n + 1) = \frac{w_i(n) + \eta y(n)x_i(n)}{\left(\sum_{i=0}^{p-1} [w_i(n) + \eta y(n)x_i(n)]^2\right)^{1/2}} \tag{9.52}$$

where the summation in the denominator extends over the complete set of synapses associated with the neuron. Assuming that the learning-rate parameter η is small, we may expand Eq. (9.52) as a power series in η, and so write

$$w_i(n + 1) = w_i(n) + \eta y(n)[x_i(n) - y(n)w_i(n)] + O(\eta^2) \tag{9.53}$$

where the term $O(\eta^2)$ represents second- and higher-order effects in η. For small η, we may justifiably ignore this term, and therefore approximate Eq. (9.52) to first order in η as follows:

$$w_i(n + 1) = w_i(n) + \eta y(n)[x_i(n) - y(n)w_i(n)] \tag{9.54}$$

The term $\eta y(n)x_i(n)$ on the right-hand side of Eq. (9.54) represents the usual Hebbian modifications to synaptic weight w_i, and therefore accounts for the self-amplification effect dictated by Principle 1 of self-organization. The inclusion of the negative term $-y(n)w_i(n)$ is responsible for stabilization in accordance with Principle 2; it modifies the input $x_i(n)$ into a form that is dependent on the associated synaptic weight $w_i(n)$ and the output $y(n)$, as shown by

$$x_i'(n) = x_i(n) - y(n)w_i(n) \tag{9.55}$$

which may be viewed as the *effective input* of the ith synapse. We may now use the definition given in Eq. (9.55) to rewrite the learning rule of Eq. (9.54) as follows:

$$w_i(n + 1) = w_i(n) + \eta y(n)x_i'(n) \tag{9.56}$$

The overall operation of the neuron is represented by a combination of two signal-flow graphs, as shown in Fig. 9.6. The signal-flow graph of Fig. 9.6a shows the dependence of the output $y(n)$ on the weights $w_0(n), w_1(n), \ldots, w_{p-1}(n)$, in accordance with Eq. (9.50). The signal-flow graph of Fig. 9.6b provides a portrayal of Eqs. (9.55) and (9.56); the transmittance z^{-1} in the middle portion of the graph represents a unit-delay operator. The output signal $y(n)$ produced in Fig. 9.6a acts as a transmittance in Fig. 9.6b. The graph of Fig. 9.6b clearly exhibits the following two forms of internal feedback acting on the neuron:

- Positive feedback for self-amplification and therefore growth of the synaptic weight $w_i(n)$, according to its external input $x_i(n)$
- Negative feedback due to $-y(n)$ for controlling the growth, thereby resulting in stabilization of the synaptic weight $w_i(n)$

The product term $-y(n)w_i(n)$ is related to a *forgetting* or *leakage factor* that is frequently used in learning rules, but with a difference: The forgetting factor becomes more pronounced with a stronger response $y(n)$. This kind of control appears to have neurobiological support (Stent, 1973).

Properties of the Model

For convenience of presentation, let

$$\mathbf{x}(n) = [x_0(n), x_1(n), \dots, x_{p-1}(n)]^T \tag{9.57}$$

and

$$\mathbf{w}(n) = [w_0(n), w_1(n), \dots, w_{p-1}(n)]^T \tag{9.58}$$

Typically, the input vector $\mathbf{x}(n)$ and the synaptic weight vector $\mathbf{w}(n)$ are both random vectors. Using this vector notation, we may rewrite Eq. (9.50) in the form of an inner product as follows:

$$y(n) = \mathbf{x}^T(n)\mathbf{w}(n) = \mathbf{w}^T(n)\mathbf{x}(n) \tag{9.59}$$

Similarly, we may rewrite Eq. (9.54) as

$$\mathbf{w}(n+1) = \mathbf{w}(n) + \eta y(n)[\mathbf{x}(n) - y(n)\mathbf{w}(n)] \tag{9.60}$$

Hence, substituting Eq. (9.59) in (9.60) yields

$$\mathbf{w}(n+1) = \mathbf{w}(n) + \eta[\mathbf{x}(n)\mathbf{x}^T(n)\mathbf{w}(n) - \mathbf{w}^T(n)\mathbf{x}(n)\mathbf{x}^T(n)\mathbf{w}(n)\mathbf{w}(n)] \tag{9.61}$$

The learning algorithm of Eq. (9.61) is a recursive, stochastic, time-varying difference equation. A convergence analysis of this algorithm is in general difficult; details of the convergence analysis are presented in Appendix B. For now it suffices to say that the self-organized learning algorithm described here is indeed *asymptotically stable* in the sense that the solution to Eq. (9.61) converges to a stable fixed point as the number of iterations n approaches infinity, as shown by

$$\mathbf{w}(n) \rightarrow \mathbf{q}_0 \qquad \text{as } n \rightarrow \infty \tag{9.62}$$

The proof of convergence relies on three *fundamental assumptions*:

1. The rate of learning is slow enough for the synaptic weights to be treated as stationary insofar as short-term statistics are concerned, as shown by

$$E[\mathbf{w}(n+1)|\mathbf{w}(n)] = \mathbf{w}(n) + \Delta\mathbf{w}(n) \tag{9.63}$$

2. The input vector $\mathbf{x}(n)$ is drawn from a stationary stochastic process, whose correlation matrix $\mathbf{R}$ has distinct eigenvalues.
3. The input vector $\mathbf{x}(n)$ and the synaptic weight vector $\mathbf{w}(n)$ are statistically independent. This assumption is not strictly true; nevertheless, it is commonly made in the convergence analysis of linear adaptive filters (Haykin, 1991).

Hence, taking the statistical expectation of both sides of Eq. (9.61), we find that in the limit as n approaches infinity,

$$\mathbf{0} = \mathbf{R}\mathbf{q}_0 - (\mathbf{q}_0^T\mathbf{R}\mathbf{q}_0)\mathbf{q}_0 \tag{9.64}$$

where $\mathbf{R}$ is the *correlation matrix* of the input vector $\mathbf{x}(n)$, as defined by

$$\mathbf{R} = E[\mathbf{x}(n)\mathbf{x}^T(n)] \tag{9.65}$$

We may therefore state that at equilibrium the average asymptotic value $\mathbf{q}_0$ of the synaptic weight vector satisfies the condition

$$\mathbf{R}\mathbf{q}_0 = \lambda_0 \mathbf{q}_0 \tag{9.66}$$

where

$$\lambda_0 = \mathbf{q}_0^T \mathbf{R}\mathbf{q}_0 \tag{9.67}$$

In light of Eqs. (9.30) and (9.38) describing properties of the principal components analysis, we immediately deduce that $\mathbf{q}_0$ is an eigenvector of the correlation matrix $\mathbf{R}$. Moreover, substituting Eq. (9.66) in (9.67) yields

$$\lambda_0 = \lambda_0 \mathbf{q}_0^T \mathbf{q}_0 = \lambda_0 \|\mathbf{q}_0\|^2$$

where $\|\mathbf{q}_0\|$ is the Euclidean norm (length) of vector $\mathbf{q}_0$. Cancelling the common factor λ_0, we therefore have

$$\|\mathbf{q}_0\|^2 = 1 \tag{9.68}$$

which states that the average asymptotic value $\mathbf{q}_0$ of the synaptic weight vector $\mathbf{w}$ has unit length.

Let $\mathbf{q}_0, \mathbf{q}_1, \ldots, \mathbf{q}_{p-1}$ denote the p *normalized* eigenvectors of the correlation matrix $\mathbf{R}$. Now, Eq. (9.64) is satisfied by any of these eigenvectors. However, only the eigenvector $\mathbf{q}_0$ corresponding to the largest eigenvalue $\lambda_0 = \lambda_{\max}$ represents a stable solution. To demonstrate this property, suppose that after a large number of iterations n the weight vector $\mathbf{w}(n)$ is in the neighborhood of eigenvector $\mathbf{q}_j$, as shown by

$$\mathbf{w}(n) = \mathbf{q}_j + \boldsymbol{\varepsilon}, \qquad n \to \infty \tag{9.69}$$

where $\boldsymbol{\varepsilon}$ is a small vector. Then, taking the statistical expectation of both sides of Eq. (9.61) and proceeding as before, we get

$$\begin{aligned} E[\Delta\mathbf{w}(n)] &= E[\mathbf{w}(n+1) - \mathbf{w}(n)] \\ &= \eta[\mathbf{R}(\mathbf{q}_j + \boldsymbol{\varepsilon}) - (\mathbf{q}_j + \boldsymbol{\varepsilon})^T \mathbf{R}(\mathbf{q}_j + \boldsymbol{\varepsilon})(\mathbf{q}_j + \boldsymbol{\varepsilon})], \qquad n \to \infty \end{aligned} \tag{9.70}$$

where η is the learning-rate parameter. Invoking the symmetric property of the correlation matrix [i.e., using Eq. (9.21)] and ignoring second- and higher-order terms in $\boldsymbol{\varepsilon}$, we may approximate Eq. (9.70) to first order in $\boldsymbol{\varepsilon}$ as follows:

$$E[\Delta\mathbf{w}(n)] \simeq \eta(\mathbf{R}\mathbf{q}_j + \mathbf{R}\boldsymbol{\varepsilon} - \mathbf{q}_j^T \mathbf{R}\mathbf{q}_j \mathbf{q}_j - 2\boldsymbol{\varepsilon}^T \mathbf{R}\mathbf{q}_j \mathbf{q}_j - \mathbf{q}_j^T \mathbf{R}\mathbf{q}_j \boldsymbol{\varepsilon}), \qquad n \to \infty \tag{9.71}$$

Since $\mathbf{q}_j$ is a normalized eigenvector of the correlation matrix $\mathbf{R}$, we have

$$\mathbf{R}\mathbf{q}_j = \lambda_j \mathbf{q}_j, \qquad j = 1, 2, \ldots, p-1 \tag{9.72}$$

and

$$\mathbf{q}_i^T \mathbf{q}_j = \begin{cases} 1, & i = j \\ 0, & \text{otherwise} \end{cases} \tag{9.73}$$

Accordingly, we may simplify Eq. (9.71) as follows:

$$\begin{aligned} E[\Delta\mathbf{w}(n)] &\simeq \eta(\mathbf{R}\boldsymbol{\varepsilon} - 2\lambda_j \boldsymbol{\varepsilon}^T \mathbf{q}_j \mathbf{q}_j - \lambda_j \boldsymbol{\varepsilon}) \\ &= \eta(\mathbf{R}\boldsymbol{\varepsilon} - 2\lambda_j \mathbf{q}_j \mathbf{q}_j^T \boldsymbol{\varepsilon} - \lambda_j \boldsymbol{\varepsilon}), \qquad n \to \infty \end{aligned} \tag{9.74}$$

where, in the second line, we have used the scalar property of $\boldsymbol{\varepsilon}^T \mathbf{q}_j$ and the fact that this inner product may also be expressed as $\mathbf{q}_j^T \boldsymbol{\varepsilon}$. The average change $E[\Delta\mathbf{w}(n)]$ in the synaptic vector projected onto the coordinate represented by another eigenvector $\mathbf{q}_i$ of the correlation matrix $\mathbf{R}$ is obtained by premultiplying it by $\mathbf{q}_i^T$, as shown by

$$\mathbf{q}_i^T E[\Delta \mathbf{w}(n)] \simeq \eta(\mathbf{q}_i^T \mathbf{R} \boldsymbol{\varepsilon} - 2\lambda_j \mathbf{q}_i^T \mathbf{q}_j \mathbf{q}_j^T \boldsymbol{\varepsilon} - \lambda_j \mathbf{q}_i^T \boldsymbol{\varepsilon})$$

$$= \begin{cases} -2\eta\lambda_j \mathbf{q}_j^T \boldsymbol{\varepsilon}, & i = j \\ \eta(\lambda_i - \lambda_j)\mathbf{q}_i^T \boldsymbol{\varepsilon}, & i \neq j \end{cases} \tag{9.75}$$

where in the second line we have made use of Eqs. (9.72) and (9.73), and also the symmetric property of the correlation matrix $\mathbf{R}$. Equation (9.75) tells us the following. For $i \neq j$, the component of $\boldsymbol{\varepsilon}$ along the direction of the eigenvector $\mathbf{q}_i$ tends to grow, and the solution is therefore unstable, if $\lambda_i > \lambda_j$. If, on the other hand, $i = j$ and λ_j corresponds to the largest eigenvalue $\lambda_0 = \lambda_{\max}$, then the solution represented by the associated eigenvector $\mathbf{q}_0$ is *stable in all possible directions.*

In conclusion, we may state that a linear neuron model governed by the self-organizing learning rule of Eq. (9.54) or, equivalently, that of Eq. (9.60), tends to extract the first principal component from a stationary input vector, that is, the one corresponding to the largest eigenvalue of the correlation matrix of the input vector (Oja, 1982).

EXAMPLE 2. Matched Filter

Consider a random input vector $\mathbf{x}(n)$ composed as follows:

$$\mathbf{x}(n) = \mathbf{s} + \mathbf{v}(n) \tag{9.76}$$

where $\mathbf{s}$ is a fixed unit vector representing the *signal component,* and $\mathbf{v}(n)$ is a zero-mean *white-noise component.* The correlation matrix of the input vector is

$$\mathbf{R} = E[\mathbf{x}(n)\mathbf{x}^T(n)]$$

$$= \mathbf{s}\mathbf{s}^T + \sigma^2\mathbf{I} \tag{9.77}$$

where σ^2 is the variance of the elements of the noise vector $\mathbf{v}(n)$, and $\mathbf{I}$ is the identity matrix. The largest eigenvalue of the correlation matrix $\mathbf{R}$ is therefore

$$\lambda_0 = 1 + \sigma^2 \tag{9.78}$$

The associated eigenvector $\mathbf{q}_0$ is

$$\mathbf{q}_0 = \mathbf{s} \tag{9.79}$$

It is readily shown that this solution satisfies the eigenvalue problem

$$\mathbf{R}\mathbf{q}_0 = \lambda_0 \mathbf{q}_0$$

Hence, for the situation described in this example, the self-organized linear neuron (upon convergence to its stable condition) acts as a *matched filter* in the sense that its impulse response (represented by the synaptic weights) is matched to the signal component $\mathbf{s}$ of the input vector $\mathbf{x}(n)$.

9.7 Self-Organized Principal Components Analysis

In the previous section we showed that the synaptic weight vector $\mathbf{w}(n)$ of a self-organized linear neuron, operating under the modified Hebbian learning rule of Eq. (9.54), converges with probability 1 to a vector of unit Euclidean length, which lies in the maximal eigenvector direction of the correlation matrix of the input vector (Oja, 1982). In the present section we describe a generalization of this learning rule that may be used to train a feedforward network composed of a single layer of linear neurons. The goal here is to produce a network that performs principal components analysis of arbitrary size on the input vector (Sanger, 1989b).

To be specific, consider the feedforward network shown in Fig. 9.7. The following two assumptions of a structural nature are made:

1. Each neuron in the output layer of the network is *linear*.
2. The network has p inputs and m outputs, both of which are specified. Moreover, the network has fewer outputs than inputs (i.e., $m < p$).

The only aspect of the network that is subject to training is the set of synaptic weights $\{w_{ji}\}$ connecting source nodes i in the input layer to computation nodes j in the output layer, where $i = 0, 1, \ldots, p - 1$, and $j = 0, 1, \ldots, m - 1$.

The output $y_j(n)$ of neuron j at time n, produced in response to the set of inputs $\{x_i(n) | i = 0, 1, \ldots, p - 1\}$, is given by (see Fig. 9.8a)

$$y_j(n) = \sum_{i=0}^{p-1} w_{ji}(n) x_i(n), \qquad j = 0, 1, \ldots, m - 1 \tag{9.80}$$

The synaptic weight $w_{ji}(n)$ is adapted in accordance with a generalized form of Hebbian learning, as shown by (Sanger, 1989b):

$$\Delta w_{ji}(n) = \eta \left[y_j(n) x_i(n) - y_j(n) \sum_{k=0}^{j} w_{ki}(n) y_k(n) \right], \qquad \begin{array}{l} i = 0, 1, \ldots, p - 1 \\ j = 0, 1, \ldots, m - 1 \end{array} \tag{9.81}$$

where $\Delta w_{ji}(n)$ is the change applied to the synaptic weight $w_{ji}(n)$ at time n, and η is the learning-rate parameter. The *generalized Hebbian algorithm* (GHA) of Eq. (9.81) for a layer of m neurons includes the algorithm of Eq. (9.54) for a single neuron as a special case, that is, $j = 0$.

To develop insight into the behavior of the generalized Hebbian algorithm, we follow the discussion in Sanger (1989b). Specifically, we rewrite Eq. (9.81) in the form

$$\Delta w_{ji}(n) = \eta y_j(n) [x_i'(n) - w_{ji}(n) y_j(n)], \qquad \begin{array}{l} i = 0, 1, \ldots, p - 1 \\ j = 0, 1, \ldots, m - 1 \end{array} \tag{9.82}$$

where $x_i'(n)$ is a modified version of the ith element of the input vector $\mathbf{x}(n)$; it is a function of the index j, as shown by

$$x_i'(n) = x_i(n) - \sum_{k=0}^{j-1} w_{ki}(n) y_k(n) \tag{9.83}$$

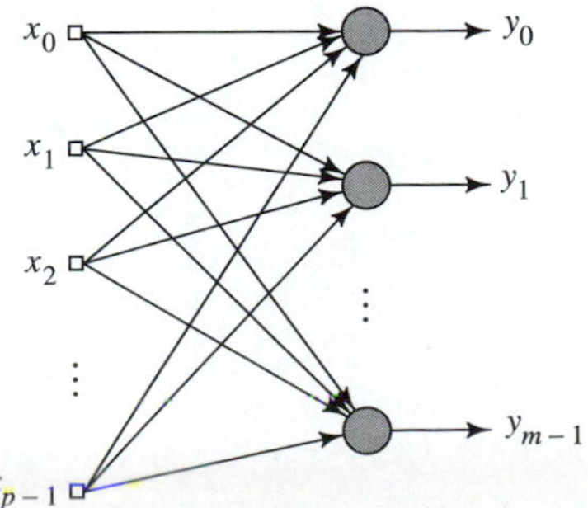

FIGURE 9.7 Feedforward network with a single layer of computation nodes.

For a specified neuron j, the algorithm described in Eq. (9.82) has exactly the same mathematical form as that of Eq. (9.54), except for the fact that the input signal $x_i(n)$ is replaced by its modified value $x_i'(n)$ in Eq. (9.82). We may go on one step further and rewrite Eq. (9.82) in a form that corresponds to Hebb's postulate of learning, as shown by

$$\Delta w_{ji}(n) = \eta y_j(n) x_i''(n) \tag{9.84}$$

where

$$x_i''(n) = x_i' - w_{ji}(n) y_j(n) \tag{9.85}$$

Thus, noting that

$$w_{ji}(n + 1) = w_{ji}(n) + \Delta w_{ji}(n) \tag{9.86}$$

and

$$w_{ji}(n) = z^{-1}[w_{ji}(n + 1)] \tag{9.87}$$

where z^{-1} is the unit-delay operator, we may construct the signal-flow graph of Fig. 9.8b for the generalized Hebbian algorithm described here. From this graph, we see that the algorithm lends itself to a *local* form of implementation, provided that it is formulated as in Eq. (9.84). Note also that $y_j(n)$, responsible for feedback in the signal-flow graph of Fig. 9.8b, is itself determined by Eq. (9.80); signal-flow graph representation of this latter equation is shown in Fig. 9.8a.

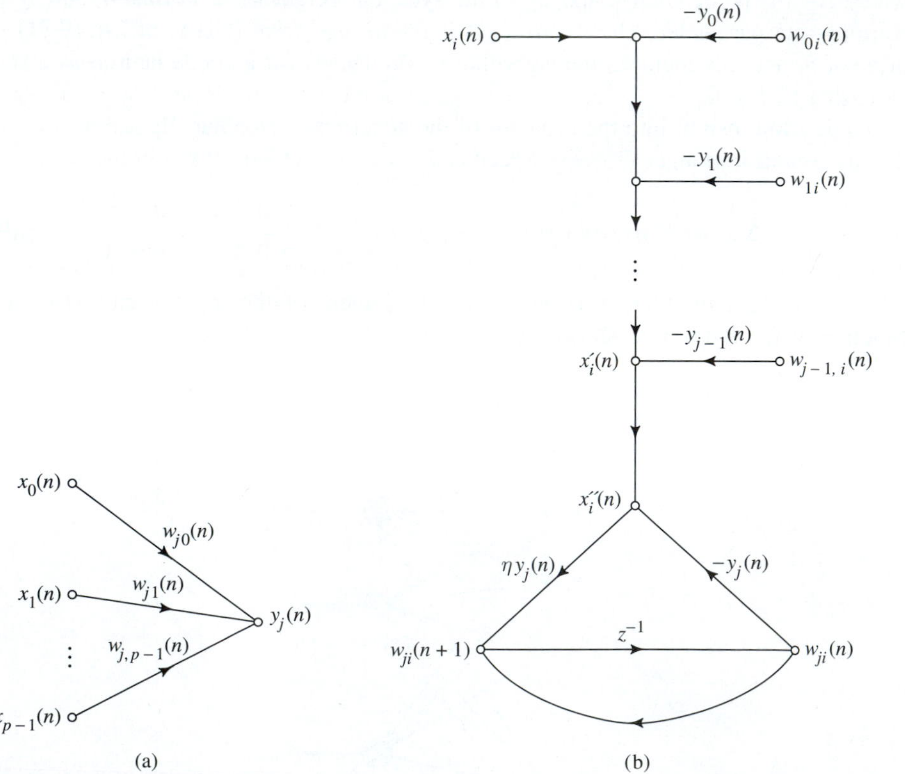

FIGURE 9.8 The signal-flow graph representation of generalized Hebbian algorithm. (a) Graph of Eq. (9.80). (b) Graph of Eqs. (9.81) through (9.87).

For a heuristic understanding of how the generalized Hebbian algorithm actually operates, we first use matrix notation to rewrite the version of the algorithm defined in Eq. (9.82) as follows:

$$\Delta \mathbf{w}_j(n) = \eta y_j(n)\mathbf{x}'(n) - \eta y_j^2(n)\mathbf{w}_j(n), \qquad j = 0, 1, \ldots, m-1 \tag{9.88}$$

where

$$\mathbf{x}'(n) = \mathbf{x}(n) - \sum_{k=0}^{j-1} \mathbf{w}_k(n) y_k(n) \tag{9.89}$$

The vector $\mathbf{x}'(n)$ represents a modified form of the input vector. Based on the representation given in Eq. (9.88), we may make the following observations (Sanger, 1989b):

1. For the first neuron of the feedforward network shown in Fig. 9.7, we have

$$j = 0: \qquad \mathbf{x}'(n) = \mathbf{x}(n) \tag{9.90}$$

In this case, the generalized Hebbian algorithm reduces to that of Eq. (9.60) for a single neuron. From the material presented in Section 9.6 we already know that this neuron will discover the first principal component (i.e., the largest eigenvalue and associated eigenvector) of the input vector $\mathbf{x}(n)$.

2. For the second neuron of the network in Fig. 9.7, we write

$$j = 1: \qquad \mathbf{x}'(n) = \mathbf{x}(n) - \mathbf{w}_0(n) y_0(n) \tag{9.91}$$

Provided that the first neuron has already converged to the first principal component, the second neuron sees an input vector $\mathbf{x}'(n)$ from which the first eigenvector of the correlation matrix $\mathbf{R}$ has been removed. The second neuron therefore extracts the first principal component of $\mathbf{x}'(n)$, which is equivalent to the second principal component (i.e., the second largest eigenvalue and associated eigenvector) of the original input vector $\mathbf{x}(n)$.

3. For the third neuron, we write

$$j = 2: \qquad \mathbf{x}'(n) = \mathbf{x}(n) - \mathbf{w}_0(n) y_0(n) - \mathbf{w}_1(n) y_1(n) \tag{9.92}$$

Suppose that the first two neurons have already converged to the first and second principal components, as explained in steps 1 and 2. The third neuron now sees an input vector $\mathbf{x}'(n)$ from which the first two eigenvectors have been removed. Therefore, it extracts the first principal component of the vector $\mathbf{x}'(n)$ defined in Eq. (9.92), which is equivalent to the third principal component (i..e, the third largest eigenvalue and associated eigenvector) of the original input vector $\mathbf{x}(n)$.

4. Proceeding in this fashion for the remaining neurons of the feedforward network in Fig. 9.7, it is now apparent that each output of the network trained in accordance with the generalized Hebbian algorithm of Eq. (9.82) represents the response to a particular eigenvector of the correlation matrix of the input vector, and that the individual outputs are ordered by decreasing eigenvalue.

This method of computing eigenvectors is similar to a technique known as *Hotelling's deflation technique* (Kreyszig, 1988); it follows a procedure similar to Gram–Schmidt orthogonalization (Strang, 1980).

The neuron-by-neuron description presented here is intended merely to simplify the explanation. In practice, all the neurons in the generalized Hebbian algorithm tend to converge together, and the total training time is less than if the neurons are trained one at a time. However, the second neuron (eigenvector) is unlikely to converge correctly until the first neuron is at least part way toward the first eigenvector.

Convergence Theorem

Let $\mathbf{W}(n) = \{w_{ji}(n)\}$ denote the m-by-p synaptic weight matrix of the feedforward network shown in Fig. 9.7; that is,

$$\mathbf{W}(n) = [\mathbf{w}_0(n), \mathbf{w}_1(n), \dots, \mathbf{w}_{m-1}(n)]^T \tag{9.93}$$

Let the learning-rate parameter of the generalized Hebbian algorithm of Eq. (9.82) take on a time-varying form $\eta(n)$, such that in the limit we have

$$\lim_{n\to\infty} \eta(n) = 0 \quad \text{and} \quad \sum_{n=0}^{\infty} \eta(n) = \infty \tag{9.94}$$

We may then rewrite this algorithm in the matrix form

$$\Delta\mathbf{W}(n) = \eta(n)\{\mathbf{y}(n)\mathbf{x}^T(n) - \text{LT}[\mathbf{y}(n)\mathbf{y}^T(n)]\mathbf{W}(n)\} \tag{9.95}$$

where the operator LT[·] sets all the elements above the diagonal of its matrix argument to zero, thereby making that matrix *lower triangular*. Under these conditions, and invoking the fundamental assumptions made in Section 9.6, we may state the following theorem (Sanger, 1989b):

> *If the synaptic weight matrix* $\mathbf{W}(n)$ *is assigned random values at time* $n = 0$, *then with probability* 1, *the generalized Hebbian algorithm of Eq. (9.95) will converge in the mean, and in the limit* $\mathbf{W}^T(n)$ *will approach a matrix whose columns are the first m eigenvectors of the p-by-p correlation matrix* $\mathbf{R}$ *of the p-by-*1 *input vector* $\mathbf{x}(n)$, *ordered by decreasing eigenvalue.*

A proof of this convergence theorem is considered in Appendix B.

The practical significance of this theorem is that it guarantees the generalized Hebbian algorithm to find the first m eigenvectors of the correlation matrix $\mathbf{R}$, assuming that the associated eigenvalues are distinct. Equally important is the fact that we do not need to compute the correlation matrix $\mathbf{R}$. Rather, the first m eigenvectors of $\mathbf{R}$ are computed by the algorithm directly from the input data. The resulting computational savings can be enormous especially if the number of elements p in the input vector $\mathbf{x}(n)$ is very large, and the required number of the eigenvectors associated with the m largest eigenvalues of the correlation matrix $\mathbf{R}$ is a small fraction of p.

The convergence theorem is formulated in terms of a time-varying learning-rate parameter $\eta(n)$. In practice, the learning-rate parameter is chosen to be a small constant η, in which case convergence is guaranteed with mean-squared error in synaptic weights of order η.

Optimality of the Generalized Hebbian Algorithm

Suppose that in the limit we write

$$\Delta\mathbf{w}_j(n) \to \mathbf{0} \quad \text{and} \quad \mathbf{w}_j(n) \to \mathbf{q}_j \qquad \text{as } n \to \infty \qquad \text{for } j = 0, 1, \dots, m-1 \tag{9.96}$$

and that we have

$$\|\mathbf{w}_j(n)\| = 1 \qquad \text{for all } j \tag{9.97}$$

Then the limiting values $\mathbf{q}_0, \mathbf{q}_1, \dots, \mathbf{q}_{m-1}$ of the synaptic weight vectors of the neurons in the feedforward network of Fig. 9.7 represent the *normalized eigenvectors* associated with the largest m eigenvalues of the correlation matrix $\mathbf{R}$ of the input vector $\mathbf{x}(n)$, and which are ordered in descending eigenvalue. At equilibrium, we may therefore write

$$\mathbf{q}_j^T\mathbf{R}\mathbf{q}_k = \begin{cases} \lambda_j, & k = j \\ 0, & k \neq j \end{cases} \tag{9.98}$$

where $\lambda_0 > \lambda_1 > \cdots > \lambda_{m-1}$.

For the output of neuron j, we have the limiting value

$$\lim_{n\to\infty} y_j(n) = \mathbf{x}^T(n)\mathbf{q}_j = \mathbf{q}_j^T\mathbf{x}(n) \tag{9.99}$$

In light of the property described in Eq. (9.38) we may thus express the cross-correlation between the outputs $y_j(n)$ and $y_k(n)$ at equilibrium as follows:

$$\begin{aligned}\lim_{n\to\infty} E[y_j(n)y_k(n)] &= E[\mathbf{q}_j^T\mathbf{x}(n)\mathbf{x}^T(n)\mathbf{q}_k] \\ &= \mathbf{q}_j^T E[\mathbf{x}(n)\mathbf{x}^T(n)]\mathbf{q}_k \\ &= \mathbf{q}_j^T\mathbf{R}\mathbf{q}_k \\ &= \begin{cases} \lambda_j, & k = j \\ 0, & k \neq j \end{cases}\end{aligned} \tag{9.100}$$

Hence, we may state that, at equilibrium, the generalized Hebbian algorithm of Eq. (9.81) acts as an *eigen-analyzer* of the input data.

Let $\hat{\mathbf{x}}(n)$ denote the particular value of the input vector $\mathbf{x}(n)$ for which the limiting conditions of Eq. (9.96) are satisfied for $j = m - 1$. Hence, from the matrix form of Eq. (9.81), we find that in the limit

$$\hat{\mathbf{x}}(n) = \sum_{k=0}^{m-1} y_k(n)\mathbf{q}_k \tag{9.101}$$

This means that given two sets of quantities, the limiting values $\mathbf{q}_0, \mathbf{q}_1, \ldots, \mathbf{q}_{m-1}$ of the synaptic weight vectors of the neurons in the feedforward network of Fig. 9.7 and the corresponding outputs $y_0(n), y_1(n), \ldots, y_{m-1}(n)$, we may then construct a *linear least-squares estimate* $\hat{\mathbf{x}}(n)$ of the input vector $\mathbf{x}(n)$. In effect, the formula of Eq. (9.101) may be viewed as one of *data reconstruction,* as depicted in Fig. 9.9. Note that, in light of the discussion presented in Section 9.5, this method of data reconstruction is subject to an approximation error vector that is orthogonal to the estimate $\hat{\mathbf{x}}(n)$.

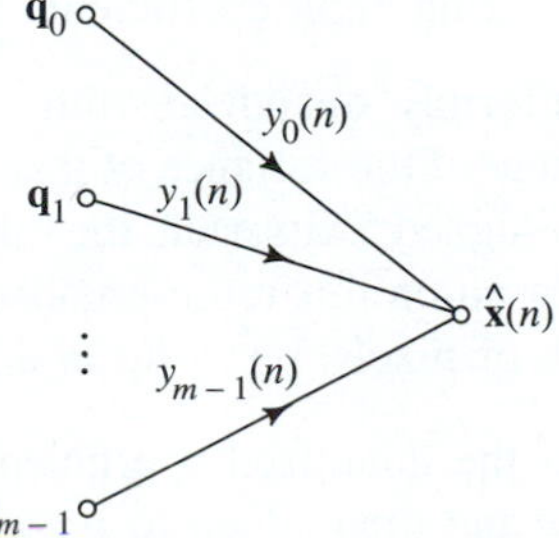

FIGURE 9.9 Signal-flow graph representation of how the reconstructed vector $\hat{\mathbf{x}}$ is computed.

Summary of the GHA

The computations involved in the generalized Hebbian algorithm (GHA) are simple; they may be summarized as follows:

1. Initialize the synaptic weights of the network, w_{ji}, to small random values at time $n = 1$. Assign a small positive value to the learning-rate parameter η.
2. For $n = 1, j = 0, 1, \ldots, m - 1$, and $i = 0, 1, \ldots, p - 1$, compute

$$y_j(n) = \sum_{i=0}^{p-1} w_{ji}(n)x_i(n)$$

$$\Delta w_{ji}(n) = \eta \left[y_j(n)x_i(n) - y_j(n) \sum_{k=0}^{j} w_{kj}(n)y_k(n) \right]$$

   where $x_i(n)$ is the ith component of the p-by-1 input vector $\mathbf{x}(n)$ and m is the desired number of principal components.
3. Increment n by 1, go to step 2, and continue until the synaptic weights w_{ji} reach their steady-state values. For large n, the synaptic weight w_{ji} of neuron j converges to the ith component of the eigenvector associated with the jth eigenvalue of the correlation matrix of the input vector $\mathbf{x}(n)$.

Application: Image Coding

We complete discussion of the generalized Hebbian learning algorithm by examining its use for solving an *image coding* problem (Sanger, 1989b). Figure 9.10a shows an image of children used for "training." It was digitized to form a 256 × 256 image with 256 gray levels. The image was coded using a linear feedforward network with a single layer of 8 neurons, each with 64 inputs. To train the network, 8 × 8 nonoverlapping blocks of the image were used, with the image scanned from left to right and top to bottom. To allow the network time to converge, the image was scanned twice.

Figure 9.11 shows the 8 × 8 masks representing the synaptic weights learned by the network. Each of the eight masks displays the set of synaptic weights associated with a particular neuron of the network. Specifically, excitatory synapses (positive weights) are shown white, whereas inhibitory synapses (negative weights) are shown black; gray indicates zero weights. In our notation, the masks represent the columns of the 64 × 8 synaptic weight matrix $\mathbf{W}^T$ after the generalized Hebbian algorithm has converged.

To code the image, the following procedure was used (Sanger, 1989b):

- Each 8 × 8 block of the image was multiplied by each of the eight masks shown in Fig. 9.11, thereby generating eight coefficients for image coding.
- Each coefficient was uniformly quantized with a number of bits approximately proportional to the logarithm of the variance of that coefficient over the image. Thus, the first two masks were assigned 5 bits each, the third mask 3 bits, and the remaining five masks 2 bits each. Based on this representation, a total of 23 bits were needed to code each 8 × 8 block of pixels, resulting in a data rate of 0.36 bits per pixel.

To reconstruct the image from the quantized coefficients, all the masks were weighted by their quantized coefficients, and then added to reconstitute each block of the image. The reconstructed children's image is shown in Fig. 9.10b.

To test the "generalization" performance of the network, the same set of masks shown in Fig. 9.11 were used to code an image that had not been previously seen by the network.

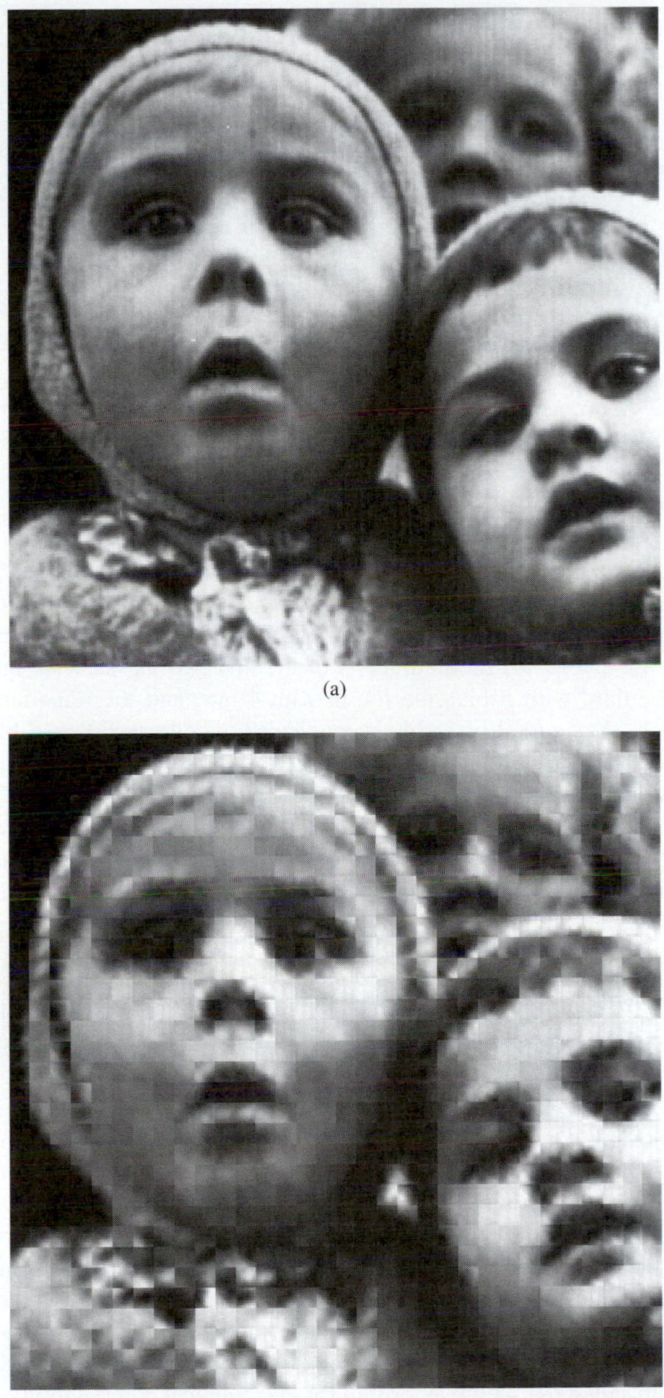

(a)

(b)

FIGURE 9.10 (a) 256 × 256-pixel (8-bit) test image for coding. (b) Image of part (a) coded at 0.36 bits per pixel. (From *Neural Networks* **2,** Optimal unsupervised learning in a single-layer linear feedforward neural network, pp. 459–473, copyright 1989, with kind permission from Pergamon Press, Ltd, Headington Hill Hall, Oxford 0X3 0BW, UK.)

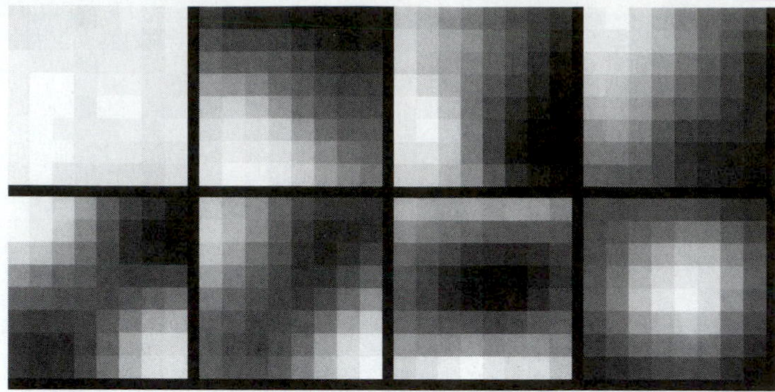

FIGURE 9.11 8 × 8 masks learned by a network trained on the image of Fig. 9.10a. (From *Neural Networks* **2,** Optimal unsupervised learning in a single-layer linear feedforward neural network, pp. 459–473, copyright 1989, with kind permission from Pergamon Press, Ltd, Headington Hill Hall, Oxford 0X3 0BW, UK.)

Figure 9.12a shows the image of a dog with statistics probably similar to those of the children's image in Fig. 9.10a. But these statistics are untested and in some sense untestable, which motivated the choice of images shown in Figs. 9.10a and 9.12a. In the test case involving the use of Fig. 9.12a, the outputs of the first two masks were quantized using 7 bits each, the third with 5 bits, the fourth with 4 bits, and the remaining four masks with 3 bits each. Thus a total of 35 bits were needed to code each 8 × 8 block of pixels, resulting in a bit rate of 0.55 bits per pixel. Figure 9.12b shows the reconstructed image of the dog, using the quantized coefficients derived from the masks of Fig. 9.11. The generalization property of the linear feedforward network considered here, exemplified by the results shown in Fig. 9.12, is a direct consequence of the statistical similarity of the images shown in Figs. 9.10a and 9.12a.

9.8 Adaptive Principal Components Analysis Using Lateral Inhibition

The generalized Hebbian learning described in the previous section relies on the exclusive use of feedforward connections for finding successive eigenvectors. Földiák (1989) expanded the neural network configuration for such an application by including anti-Hebbian feedback connections. The motivation for this modification was derived from some earlier work by Barlow and Földiák (1989) on adaptation and decorrelation in the visual cortex; there it was argued that if the neurons interact according to an anti-Hebbian rule, then the outputs of the neurons define a coordinate system in which there are no correlations even when the incoming signals have strong correlations. Kung and Diamantaras (1990), building on the earlier works of Oja (1982) and Földiák (1989), developed a new algorithm called the APEX algorithm for the recursive computation of the principal components; the acronym APEX stands for *A*daptive *P*rincipal components *Ex*traction. An attractive feature of the APEX algorithm is that if we are given the first j principal components, the algorithm computes the $(j + 1)$th principal component in an iterative manner. In this section we develop the APEX algorithm as an algorithm for the adaptive computation of principal components.

Figure 9.13 shows the network model used for the derivation of the algorithm. As before, the input vector $\mathbf{x}$ has dimension p, with its components denoted by $x_0, x_1, \ldots,$

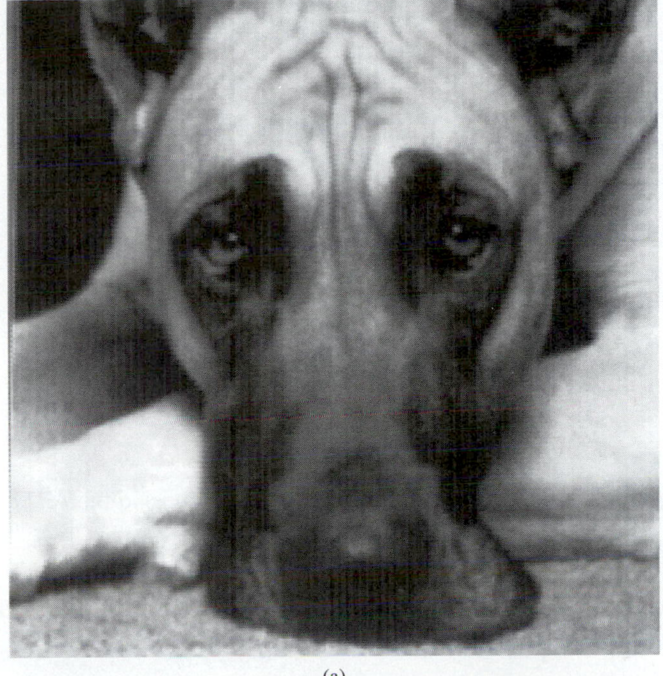

(a)

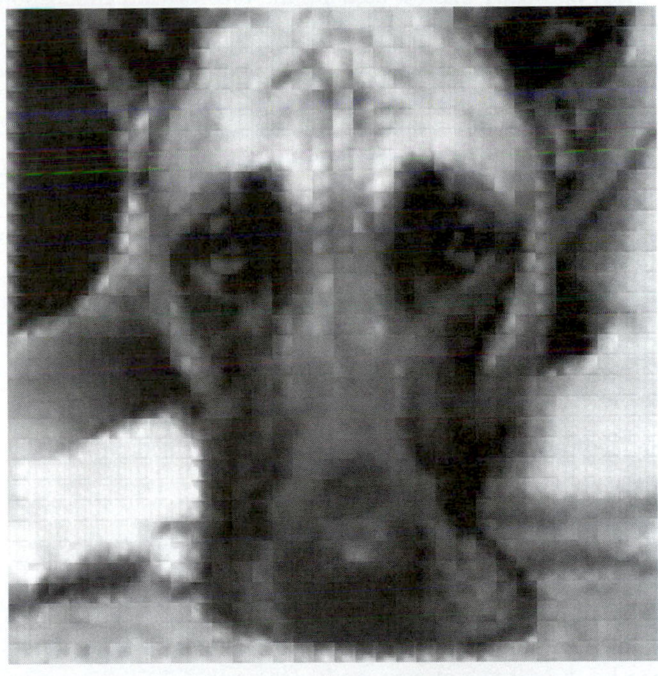

(b)

FIGURE 9.12 (a) 256 × 256-pixel (8-bit) test image. (b) Image of part (a) coded at 0.55 bits per pixel using the same masks as in Fig. 9.11. (From *Neural Networks* **2,** Optimal unsupervised learning in a single-layer linear feedforward neural network, pp. 459–473, copyright 1989, with kind permission from Pergamon Press, Ltd, Headington Hill Hall, Oxford 0X3 0BW, UK.)

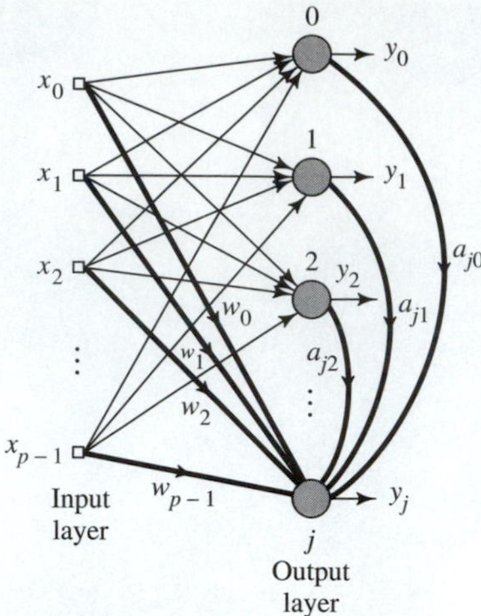

FIGURE 9.13 Network with lateral connections for deriving the APEX algorithm.

x_{p-1}. Each neuron in the network is assumed to be linear. As depicted in Fig. 9.13, there are two kinds of synaptic connections in the network:

- *Feedforward connections* from the input nodes to each of the neurons 0, 1, . . . , j, with $j < p$. Of particular interest here are the feedforward connections to neuron j; these connections are represented by the feedforward weight vector

$$\mathbf{w}_j = [w_0(n), w_1(n), \ldots, w_{p-1}(n)]^T$$

The feedforward connections operate in accordance with a *Hebbian learning rule*; they are *excitatory* and therefore provide for self-amplification.

- *Lateral connections* from the individual outputs of neurons 0, 1, . . . , $j - 1$ to neuron j, thereby applying *feedback* to the network. These connections are represented by the feedback weight vector

$$\mathbf{a}_j(n) = [a_{j0}(n), a_{j1}(n), \ldots, a_{j,j-1}(n)]^T$$

The lateral connections operate in accordance with an *anti-Hebbian learning rule,* which has the effect of making them *inhibitory.*

In Fig. 9.13 the feedforward and feedback connections of neuron j are shown boldfaced merely to emphasize that neuron j is the subject of study.

The output $y_j(n)$ of neuron j is given by

$$y_j(n) = \mathbf{w}_j^T(n)\mathbf{x}(n) + \mathbf{a}_j^T(n)\mathbf{y}_{j-1}(n) \tag{9.102}$$

where the contribution $\mathbf{w}_j^T(n)\mathbf{x}(n)$ is due to the feedforward connections, and the remaining contribution $\mathbf{a}_j^T(n)\mathbf{y}_{j-1}(n)$ is due to the lateral connections. The feedback signal vector $\mathbf{y}_{j-1}(n)$ is defined by the outputs of neurons 0, 1, . . . , $j - 1$:

$$\mathbf{y}_{j-1}(n) = [y_0(n), y_1(n), \ldots, y_{j-1}(n)]^T \tag{9.103}$$

It is assumed that the input vector $\mathbf{x}(n)$ is drawn from a wide-sense stationary process, whose correlation matrix $\mathbf{R}$ has *distinct eigenvalues arranged in decreasing order* as follows:

$$\lambda_0 > \lambda_1 > \cdots > \lambda_{j-1} > \lambda_j > \cdots > \lambda_{p-1} \tag{9.104}$$

It is further assumed that neurons $0, 1, \ldots, j-1$ of the network in Fig. 9.13 have *already converged to their respective stable conditions,* as shown by

$$\mathbf{w}_k(0) = \mathbf{q}_k, \qquad k = 0, 1, \ldots, j-1 \tag{9.105}$$

$$\mathbf{a}_k(0) = \mathbf{0}, \qquad k = 0, 1, \ldots, j-1 \tag{9.106}$$

where $\mathbf{q}_k$ is the eigenvector associated with the kth eigenvalue of the correlation matrix $\mathbf{R}$, and time $n = 0$ refers to the start of computations by neuron j of the network. We may then use Eqs. (9.102), (9.103), (9.105), and (9.106) to write

$$\begin{aligned}\mathbf{y}_{j-1}(n) &= [\mathbf{q}_0^T\mathbf{x}(n), \mathbf{q}_1^T\mathbf{x}(n), \ldots, \mathbf{q}_{j-1}^T\mathbf{x}(n)] \\ &= \mathbf{Q}\mathbf{x}(n)\end{aligned} \tag{9.107}$$

where $\mathbf{Q}$ is a j-by-p matrix defined in terms of the eigenvectors $\mathbf{q}_0, \mathbf{q}_1, \ldots, \mathbf{q}_{j-1}$ associated with the j largest eigenvalues $\lambda_0, \lambda_1, \ldots, \lambda_{j-1}$ of the correlation matrix $\mathbf{R}$; that is,

$$\mathbf{Q} = [\mathbf{q}_0, \mathbf{q}_1, \ldots, \mathbf{q}_{j-1}]^T \tag{9.108}$$

The requirement is to use neuron j in the network of Fig. 9.13 to compute the next largest eigenvalue λ_j of the correlation matrix $\mathbf{R}$ of the input vector $\mathbf{x}(n)$ and the associated eigenvector $\mathbf{q}_j$.

The update equations for the feedforward weight vector $\mathbf{w}_j(n)$ and the feedback weight vector $\mathbf{a}_j(n)$ for neuron j are defined as, respectively,

$$\mathbf{w}_j(n+1) = \mathbf{w}_j(n) + \eta[y_j(n)\mathbf{x}(n) - y_j^2(n)\mathbf{w}_j(n)] \tag{9.109}$$

and

$$\mathbf{a}_j(n+1) = \mathbf{a}_j(n) - \eta[y_j(n)\mathbf{y}_{j-1}(n) + y_j^2(n)\mathbf{a}_j(n)] \tag{9.110}$$

where η is the *learning-rate parameter,* assumed to be the same for both update equations. The term $y_j(n)\mathbf{x}(n)$ on the right-hand side of Eq. (9.109) represents Hebbian learning, whereas the term $-y_j(n)\mathbf{y}_{j-1}(n)$ on the right-hand side of Eq. (9.110) represents anti-Hebbian learning. The remaining terms, $-y_j^2(n)\mathbf{w}_j(n)$ and $y_j^2(n)\mathbf{a}_j(n)$, are included in these two equations so as to assure the stability of the algorithm. Basically, Eq. (9.109) is the vector form of Oja's learning rule described in Eq. (9.54), whereas Eq. (9.110) is *new,* accounting for the use of lateral inhibition (Kung and Diamantaras, 1990).

We prove absolute stability of the neural network of Fig. 9.13 by *induction,* as follows:

- First, we prove that if neurons $0, 1, \ldots, j-1$ have converged to their stable conditions, then neuron j converges to its own stable condition by extracting the next largest eigenvalue λ_j of the correlation matrix $\mathbf{R}$ of the input vector $\mathbf{x}(n)$ and the associated eigenvector $\mathbf{q}_j$.

- Next, we complete the proof by induction by recognizing that neuron 0 has no feedback and therefore the feedback weight vector $\mathbf{a}_0$ is zero. Hence this particular neuron operates in exactly the same way as Oja's neuron, and from Section 9.6 we know that this neuron is absolutely stable under certain conditions.

The only matter that requires attention is therefore the first point.

To proceed then, we invoke the fundamental assumptions made in Section 9.6, and so state the following theorem in the context of neuron j in the neural network of Fig.

9.13 operating under the conditions described by Eqs. (9.105) and (9.106) (Kung and Diamantaras, 1990):

Given that the learning-rate parameter η is assigned a sufficiently small value to ensure that the adjustments to the weight vectors proceed slowly, then, in the limit, the feedforward weight vector and the average output power of neuron j approach the normalized eigenvector $\mathbf{q}_j$ and corresponding eigenvalue λ_j of the correlation matrix $\mathbf{R}$, as shown by, respectively,

$$\lim_{n\to\infty} \mathbf{w}_j(n) \to \mathbf{q}_j$$

and

$$\lim_{n\to\infty} \sigma_j^2(n) \to \lambda_j$$

where $\sigma_j^2(n) = E[y_j^2(n)]$, and $\lambda_0 > \lambda_1 > \cdots > \lambda_j > \cdots > \lambda_{p-1} > 0$. In other words, given the eigenvectors $\mathbf{q}_0, \ldots, \mathbf{q}_{j-1}$, neuron j of the network of Fig. 9.13 computes the next largest eigenvalue λ_j and associated eigenvector $\mathbf{q}_j$.

To prove this theorem we follow the discussion in (Kung and Diamantaras, 1990). Consider first Eq. (9.109). Using Eqs. (9.102) and (9.103), and recognizing that

$$\mathbf{a}_j^T(n)\mathbf{y}_{j-1}(n) = \mathbf{y}_{j-1}^T(n)\mathbf{a}_j(n)$$

we may recast Eq. (9.109) as follows:

$$\mathbf{w}_j(n+1) = \mathbf{w}_j(n) + \eta[\mathbf{x}(n)\mathbf{x}^T(n)\mathbf{w}_j(n) + \mathbf{x}(n)\mathbf{x}^T(n)\mathbf{Q}^T\mathbf{a}_j(n) - y_j^2(n)\mathbf{w}_j(n)] \tag{9.111}$$

where the matrix $\mathbf{Q}$ is defined by Eq. (9.108). The term $y_j^2(n)$ in Eq. (9.111) has not been touched for a reason that will become apparent presently. Invoking the fundamental assumptions described in Section 9.6, we find that applying the statistical expectation operator to both sides of Eq. (9.111) yields

$$\mathbf{w}_j(n+1) = \mathbf{w}_j(n) + \eta[\mathbf{R}\mathbf{w}_j(n) + \mathbf{R}\mathbf{Q}^T\mathbf{a}_j(n) - \sigma_j^2(n)\mathbf{w}_j(n)] \tag{9.112}$$

where $\mathbf{R}$ is the correlation matrix of the input vector $\mathbf{x}(n)$, and $\sigma_j^2(n)$ is the average output power of neuron j. Let the synaptic weight vector $\mathbf{w}_j(n)$ be expanded in terms of the entire orthonormal set of eigenvectors of the correlation matrix $\mathbf{R}$ as follows:

$$\mathbf{w}_j(n) = \sum_{k=0}^{p-1} \theta_{jk}(n)\mathbf{q}_k \tag{9.113}$$

where $\mathbf{q}_k$ is the eigenvector associated with the eigenvalue λ_k of matrix $\mathbf{R}$, and $\theta_{jk}(n)$ is a time-varying coefficient of the expansion. We may then use the basic relation [see Eq. (9.30)]

$$\mathbf{R}\mathbf{q}_k = \lambda_k\mathbf{q}_k$$

to express the matrix product $\mathbf{R}\mathbf{w}_j(n)$ as follows:

$$\begin{aligned}\mathbf{R}\mathbf{w}_j(n) &= \sum_{k=0}^{p-1} \theta_{jk}(n)\mathbf{R}\mathbf{q}_k \\ &= \sum_{k=0}^{p-1} \lambda_k\theta_{jk}(n)\mathbf{q}_k \end{aligned} \tag{9.114}$$

Similarly, using Eq. (9.108), we may express the matrix product $\mathbf{RQ}^T\mathbf{a}_j(n)$ as

$$\mathbf{RQ}^T\mathbf{a}_j(n) = \mathbf{R}[\mathbf{q}_0, \mathbf{q}_1, \ldots, \mathbf{q}_{j-1}]\mathbf{a}_j(n)$$

$$= [\lambda_0\mathbf{q}_0, \lambda_1\mathbf{q}_1, \ldots, \lambda_{j-1}\mathbf{q}_{j-1}]\begin{bmatrix} a_{j0}(n) \\ a_{j2}(n) \\ \vdots \\ a_{j,j-1}(n) \end{bmatrix}$$

$$= \sum_{k=0}^{j-1} \lambda_k a_{jk}(n)\mathbf{q}_k \tag{9.115}$$

Hence, substituting Eqs. (9.113), (9.114), and (9.115) in (9.112), and simplifying, we get (Kung and Diamantaras, 1990)

$$\sum_{k=0}^{p-1} \theta_{jk}(n+1)\mathbf{q}_k = \sum_{k=0}^{p-1} \{1 + \eta[\lambda_k - \sigma_j^2(n)]\}\theta_{jk}(n)\mathbf{q}_k + \eta \sum_{k=0}^{j-1} \lambda_k a_{jk}(n)\mathbf{q}_k \tag{9.116}$$

Following a procedure similar to that described above, it is a straightforward matter to show that the update equation (9.110) for the feedback weight vector $\mathbf{a}_j(n)$ may be transformed as follows (see Problem 9.8):

$$\mathbf{a}_j(n+1) = -\eta\lambda_k\theta_{jk}(n)\mathbf{1}_k + \{1 - \eta[\lambda_k + \sigma_j^2(n)]\}\mathbf{a}_j(n) \tag{9.117}$$

where $\mathbf{1}_k$ is a vector all of whose j elements are zero, except for the kth element, which is equal to 1. The index k is restricted to lie in the range $0 \le k \le j-1$.

There are two cases to be considered, depending on the value assigned to index k in relation to $j-1$. Case I refers to $0 \le k \le j-1$, which pertains to the analysis of the "old" principal modes of the network. Case II refers to $j \le k \le p-1$, which pertains to the analysis of the remaining "new" principal modes. The total number of principal modes is p, the dimension of the input vector $\mathbf{x}(n)$.

Case I: $0 \le k \le j-1$

In this case, we readily deduce the following update equations for the coefficient $\theta_{jk}(n)$ associated with eigenvector $\mathbf{q}_k$ and the feedback weight $a_{jk}(n)$ from Eqs. (9.116) and (9.117), respectively:

$$\theta_{jk}(n+1) = \eta\lambda_k a_{jk}(n) + \{1 + \eta[\lambda_k - \sigma_j^2(n)]\}\theta_{jk}(n) \tag{9.118}$$

and

$$a_{jk}(n+1) = -\eta\lambda_k\theta_{jk}(n) + \{1 - \eta[\lambda_k + \sigma_j^2(n)]\}a_{jk}(n) \tag{9.119}$$

Figure 9.14 presents a signal-flow graph representation of Eqs. (9.118) and (9.119).

In matrix form, we may rewrite Eqs. (9.118) and (9.119) as

$$\begin{bmatrix} \theta_{jk}(n+1) \\ a_{jk}(n+1) \end{bmatrix} = \begin{bmatrix} 1 + \eta[\lambda_k - \sigma_j^2(n)] & \eta\lambda_k \\ -\eta\lambda_k & 1 - \eta[\lambda_k + \sigma_j^2(n)] \end{bmatrix} \begin{bmatrix} \theta_{jk}(n) \\ a_{jk}(n) \end{bmatrix} \tag{9.120}$$

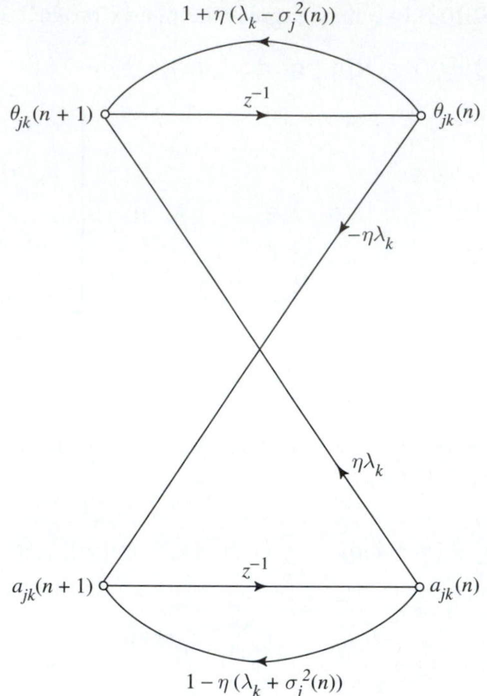

FIGURE 9.14 Signal-flow graph representation of Eqs. (9.118) and (9.119).

The system matrix described in Eq. (9.120) has a double eigenvalue at

$$\rho_{jk} = [1 - \eta\sigma_j^2(n)]^2 \tag{9.121}$$

From Eq. (9.121) we can make two important observations:

1. The double eigenvalue ρ_{jk} of the system matrix in Eq. (9.120) is independent of all the eigenvalues λ_k of the correlation matrix **R**, corresponding to $k = 0, 1, \ldots, j - 1$.
2. For all k, the double eigenvalue ρ_{jk} depends solely on the learning-rate parameter η and the average output power σ_j^2 of neuron j. It is therefore less than unity, provided that η is a sufficiently small, positive number.

Hence, *given that* $\rho_{jk} < 1$, *the coefficients* $\theta_{jk}(n)$ *of the expansion in Eq. (9.113) and the feedback weights* $a_{jk}(n)$ *will for all k approach zero asymptotically with the same speed, since all the principal modes of the network have the same eigenvalue* (Kung and Diamantaras, 1990). This is indeed a remarkable result. It is a consequence of the property that the orthogonality of eigenvectors of a correlation matrix does *not* depend on the eigenvalues. In other words, the expansion of $\mathbf{w}_j(n)$ in terms of the orthonormal set of eigenvectors of the correlation matrix **R** given in Eq. (9.113), which is basic to the result described in Eq. (9.121), is *invariant* to the choice of eigenvalues $\lambda_0, \lambda_1, \ldots, \lambda_{j-1}$.

Case II: $j \leq k \leq p - 1$

In this second case, the feedback weights $a_{jk}(n)$ have *no* influence on the modes of the network, as shown by

$$a_{jk}(n) = 0 \qquad \text{for } j \leq k \leq p - 1 \tag{9.122}$$

Hence, for every principal mode $k \geq j$ we have a very simple equation:

$$\theta_{jk}(n+1) = \{1 + \eta[\lambda_k - \sigma_j^2(n)]\}\theta_{jk}(n) \tag{9.123}$$

which follows directly from Eqs. (9.116) and (9.122). According to case I, both $\theta_{jk}(n)$ and $a_{jk}(n)$ will eventually converge to zero for $k = 0, 1, \ldots, j - 1$. We may therefore use Eqs. (9.102) and (9.113) to express the average output power of neuron j as follows:

$$\begin{aligned}
\sigma_j^2(n) &= E[y_j^2(n)] \\
&= E[\mathbf{w}_j^T(n)\mathbf{x}(n)\mathbf{x}^T(n)\mathbf{w}_j(n)] \\
&= \mathbf{w}_j^T(n)E[\mathbf{x}(n)\mathbf{x}^T(n)]\mathbf{w}_j(n) \\
&= \mathbf{w}_j^T(n)\mathbf{R}\mathbf{w}_j(n) \\
&= \sum_{k=j}^{p-1}\sum_{l=j}^{p-1} \theta_{jk}(n)\theta_{jl}(n)\mathbf{q}_k^T\mathbf{R}\mathbf{q}_l \\
&= \sum_{k=j}^{p-1} \lambda_k\theta_{jk}^2(n)
\end{aligned} \tag{9.124}$$

where, in the last line, we have made use of the following relation [see Eqs. (9.72) and (9.73)]:

$$\mathbf{q}_k^T\mathbf{R}\mathbf{q}_l = \begin{cases} \lambda_k, & l = k \\ 0, & \text{otherwise} \end{cases}$$

It follows therefore that Eq. (9.123) cannot diverge, because whenever $\theta_{jk}(n)$ becomes large such that $\sigma_j^2(n) > \lambda_k$, then $1 + \eta[\lambda_k - \sigma_j^2(n)]$ becomes smaller than unity, in which case $\theta_{jk}(n)$ will decrease in magnitude. Let the algorithm be initialized, with $\theta_{jj}(0) \neq 0$. Also, define

$$r_{jk}(n) = \frac{\theta_{jk}(n)}{\theta_{jj}(n)}, \qquad k = j+1, \ldots, p-1 \tag{9.125}$$

We may then use Eq. (9.123) to write

$$r_{jk}(n+1) = \frac{1 + \eta[\lambda_k - \sigma_j^2(n)]}{1 + \eta[\lambda_j - \sigma_j^2(n)]} r_{jk}(n) \tag{9.126}$$

With the eigenvalues of the correlation matrix arranged in the descending order

$$\lambda_0 > \lambda_1 > \cdots > \lambda_k > \cdots > \lambda_j \cdots > \lambda_{p-1}$$

it follows that

$$\frac{\theta_{jk}(n)}{\theta_{jj}(n)} < 1 \qquad \text{for all } n \text{, and for } k = j+1, \ldots, p-1 \tag{9.127}$$

Moreover, we note from Eqs. (9.123) and (9.124) that $\theta_{jj}(n + 1)$ remains bounded; therefore,

$$r_{jk}(n) \to 0 \qquad \text{as } n \to \infty \text{ for } k = j+1, \ldots, p-1 \tag{9.128}$$

Equivalently, in light of the definition given in Eq. (9.125), we may state that

$$\theta_{jk}(n) \to 0 \qquad \text{as } n \to \infty \text{ for } k = j+1, \ldots, p-1 \tag{9.129}$$

Under this condition, Eq. (9.124) simplifies as

$$\sigma_j^2(n) = \lambda_j \theta_{jj}^2(n) \tag{9.130}$$

and so Eq. (9.123) for $k = j$ becomes

$$\theta_{jj}(n + 1) = \{1 + \eta\lambda_j[1 - \theta_{jj}(n)]\}\theta_{jj}(n) \tag{9.131}$$

From this equation we immediately deduce that

$$\theta_{jj}(n) \rightarrow 1 \qquad \text{as } n \rightarrow \infty \tag{9.132}$$

The implications of this limiting condition and that of Eq. (9.129) are twofold:

1. From Eq. (9.130) we have

$$\sigma_j^2(n) \rightarrow \lambda_j \qquad \text{as } n \rightarrow \infty \tag{9.133}$$

2. From Eq. (9.113) we have

$$\mathbf{w}_j(n) \rightarrow \mathbf{q}_j \qquad \text{as } n \rightarrow \infty \tag{9.134}$$

In other words, the neural network model of Fig. 9.13 extracts the jth eigenvalue and associated eigenvector of the correlation matrix $\mathbf{R}$ of the input vector $\mathbf{x}(n)$ as the number of iterations n approaches infinity. This, of course, assumes that neurons $0, 1, \ldots, j - 1$ of the network have already converged to the respective eigenvalues and associated eigenvectors of the correlation matrix $\mathbf{R}$.

In the APEX algorithm described in Eqs. (9.109) and (9.110), the same learning-rate parameter η is used for updating both the feedforward weight vector $\mathbf{w}_j(n)$ and feedback weight vector $\mathbf{a}_j(n)$. The relationship of Eq. (9.121) may be exploited to define an optimum value for the learning-rate parameter for each neuron j by setting the double eigenvalue ρ_{jk} equal to zero. In such a case, we have

$$\eta_{j,\text{opt}}(n) = \frac{1}{\sigma_j^2(n)} \tag{9.135}$$

where $\sigma_j^2(n)$ is the average output power of neuron j. A more practical proposition, however, is to set (Kung and Diamantaras, 1990)

$$\eta_j = \frac{1}{\lambda_{j-1}} \tag{9.136}$$

which yields an underestimated value for the learning-rate parameter, since $\lambda_{j-1} > \lambda_j$ and $\sigma_j^2(n) \rightarrow \lambda_j$ as $n \rightarrow \infty$. Note that the eigenvalue λ_{j-1} is computed by neuron $j - 1$ and therefore available for use in updating the feedforward and feedback weights of neuron j. A more refined estimate of the learning-rate parameter, based on recursive least-squares estimation, is described in Diamantaras (1992).

Summary of the APEX Algorithm

1. Initialize the feedforward weight vector $\mathbf{w}_j$ and the feedback weight vector $\mathbf{a}_j$ to small random values at time $n = 1$. Assign a small positive value to the learning-rate parameter η.
2. Set $j = 0$, and for $n = 1, 2, \ldots,$ compute

$$y_0(n) = \mathbf{w}_0^T(n)\mathbf{x}(n)$$

$$\mathbf{w}_0(n + 1) = \mathbf{w}_0(n) + \eta[y_0(n)\mathbf{x}(n) - y_0^2(n)\mathbf{w}_0(n)]$$

where $\mathbf{x}(n)$ is the input vector. For large n, we have

$$\mathbf{w}_0(n) \rightarrow \mathbf{q}_0$$

where $\mathbf{q}_0$ is the eigenvector associated with the largest eigenvalue of the correlation matrix of $\mathbf{x}(n)$.

3. Set $j = 1$, and for $n = 1, 2, \ldots,$ compute

$$\mathbf{y}_{j-1}(n) = [y_0(n), y_1(n), \ldots, y_{j-1}(n)]^T$$

$$y_j(n) = \mathbf{w}_j^T(n)\mathbf{x}(n) + \mathbf{a}_j^T(n)\mathbf{y}_{j-1}(n)$$

$$\mathbf{w}_j(n+1) = \mathbf{w}_j(n) + \eta[y_j(n)\mathbf{x}(n) - y_j^2(n)\mathbf{w}_j(n)]$$

$$\mathbf{a}_j(n+1) = \mathbf{a}_j(n) - \eta[y_j(n)\mathbf{y}_{j-1}(n) + y_j^2(n)\mathbf{a}_j(n)]$$

4. Increment j by 1, go to step 3, and continue until $j = m - 1$, where m is the desired number of principal components. (Note that $j = 0$ corresponds to the eigenvector associated with the largest eigenvalue, which is taken care of in step 2.) For large n we have

$$\mathbf{w}_j(n) \rightarrow \mathbf{q}_j$$

$$\mathbf{a}_j(n) \rightarrow \mathbf{0}$$

where $\mathbf{q}_j$ is the eigenvector associated with the jth eigenvalue of the correlation matrix of $\mathbf{x}(n)$.

9.9 Two Classes of PCA Algorithms

In addition to the generalized Hebbian algorithm (GHA), discussed in Section 9.7, and the APEX algorithm, discussed in Section 9.8, several other algorithms for principal components analysis (PCA) have been reported in the literature (Oja, 1992; Xu and Yuille, 1992; Chen and Liu, 1992; Brockett, 1991; Rubner and Tavan, 1989; Földiák, 1989). The various PCA algorithms using neural networks may be categorized into two classes: *reestimation algorithms* and *decorrelating algorithms* (Becker and Plumbley, 1993).

According to this classification, the GHA is a reestimation algorithm in that Eqs. (9.88) and (9.89) may be recast in the equivalent form

$$\mathbf{w}_j(n+1) = \mathbf{w}_j(n) + \eta y_j(n)[\mathbf{x}(n) - \hat{\mathbf{x}}_j(n)] \tag{9.137}$$

where $\hat{\mathbf{x}}_j(n)$ is the *reestimator* defined by

$$\hat{\mathbf{x}}_j(n) = \sum_{k=0}^{j} \mathbf{w}_k(n)\, y_k(n) \tag{9.138}$$

In a reestimation algorithm the neural network has only forward connections, whose strengths (weights) are modified in a Hebbian manner. The successive outputs of the network are forced to learn different principal components by subtracting estimates of the earlier components from the input before the data is involved in the learning process.

In contrast, the APEX algorithm is a decorrelating algorithm. In such an algorithm the neural network has both forward and feedback connections. The strengths of the forward connections follow a Hebbian law, whereas the strengths of the feedback connections follow an anti-Hebbian law. The successive outputs of the network are decorrelated, forcing the network to respond to the different principal components.

As pointed out in Section 9.7, all the neurons in the GHA tend to converge simultaneously. On the other hand, in the APEX algorithm as described in Section 9.8, the neurons tend to converge in a sequential manner. Chen and Liu (1992) describe an extension of the APEX algorithm in which the principal components are obtained simultaneously.

Principal Subspace

In situations where only the *principal subspace* (i.e., the space of the principal components) is required, we may use a *symmetric model* in which the reestimator $\hat{\mathbf{x}}_j(n)$ in the GHA algorithm is replaced by

$$\hat{\mathbf{x}}(n) = \sum_{k=0}^{m} \mathbf{w}_k(n) y_k(n) \qquad \text{for all } j \tag{9.139}$$

In the symmetric model defined by Eqs. (9.137) and (9.139), the network converges to a set of outputs that span the principal subspace, rather than the principal components themselves. At convergence, the weight vectors of the network are orthogonal to each other, as in the GHA. The principal subspace, as described here, may be viewed as a generalization of the classical Oja rule defined in Eq. (9.60).

9.10 How Useful Is Principal Components Analysis?

At this point in our discussion, it is rather appropriate that we reflect over the material presented in the previous four sections on principal components analysis and ask the question: How useful is principal components analysis? The answer to this question, of course, depends on the application of interest.[2]

If the main objective is to achieve good data compression while preserving as much information about the inputs as possible, then the use of principal components analysis offers a useful unsupervised learning procedure. Here we note from the material presented in Section 9.4 that the use of a subspace decomposition method based on the "first m principal components" of the input data provides a linear transformation, which is optimum in the sense that it permits reconstruction of the original input data within a mean-squared error. Moreover, a representation based on the first m principal components is preferable to an arbitrary subspace representation, because the principal components of the input data are naturally ordered in decreasing eigenvalue or, equivalently, decreasing variance [see Eqs. (9.23) and (9.39)]. Accordingly, we may optimize the use of principal components analysis for *data compression* by employing the greatest numerical precision to encode the first principal component of the input, and progressively less precision to encode the remaining $m - 1$ components.

A related issue is the representation of a data set made up of an aggregate of several *clusters*. For the clusters to be individually visible, the separation between them has to be larger than the internal scatter of the clusters. If it so happens that there are only a few clusters in the data set, then the leading principal axes found by using the principal components analysis will tend to pick projections of clusters with good separations, thereby providing an effective basis for *feature extraction*. There are, however, certain situations where the use of principal components can go astray (Huber, 1985):

[2] The critique of principal components analysis presented here is largely based on Becker (1991).

- If there are too many isotropically distributed clusters, or
- If there are meaningless variables (outliers) with a high noise level

The latter problem is particularly serious in real-life situations, since practical data usually contain outliers. To overcome this limitation, Xu and Yuille (1992) have adapted the application of a statistical physics approach to the problem of *robust* principal components analysis; they also present experimental results that demonstrate a significant improvement in performance over existing techniques.

In the context of biological perceptual systems, Linsker (1990a) questions the "sufficiency" of principal components analysis as a principle for determining the response property developed by a neuron to analyze an ensemble of input "scenes." In particular, the optimality of principal components analysis with respect to the accurate reconstruction of an input signal from a neuron's response is considered to be of questionable relevance. It appears that in general a brain does much more than simply try to reproduce the input scenes received by its sensory units. Rather, some underlying "meaningful variables" or features are extracted so as to permit high-level interpretations of the inputs. We may therefore sharpen the question we raised earlier and ask: How useful is principal components analysis for perceptual processing?

Several investigators have explored some general properties of solutions obtained by applying the method of principal components analysis to input ensembles of biological interest. Here, particular mention should be made of the work done by Linsker (1987, 1990a), Miller et al. (1989), Sanger (1990), and Yuille et al. (1989) on the relationships between principal components analysis and the emergence of feature-analyzing properties of neurons found in the early stages of a sensory processing pathway.

Ambros-Ingerson et al. (1990) point out that the algorithms set forth by Oja (1982) and Sanger (1989b) for principal components analysis (i.e., the Hebbian-inspired algorithms discussed in Sections 9.6 and 9.7) may be cast as distinct special cases of a *hierarchical clustering algorithm* based on competitive learning. They put forward the hypothesis that hierarchical clustering may emerge as a fundamental property (at least in part) of memories based on long-term potentiation (LTP)-like synaptic modifications of the kind found in cortico-bulbar networks and circuitry of similar design in other regions of the brain, and which property may be used for recognizing environmental cues. The point to note here is that self-organized principal components analysis, however it is performed, may be a useful tool for understanding some aspects of perceptual processing not because of its optimal reconstruction property, but rather by virtue of its intrinsic property of picking projections of clusters with good separations.

Moreover, since the set of projections so formed are *uncorrelated* with each other, a self-organizing network for principal components analysis may also provide a useful *preprocessor* for a supervised or unsupervised neural network (Becker, 1991). This kind of preprocessing, for example, may be helpful for a supervised learning procedure such as back-propagation, which relies on steepest descent. The convergence process in back-propagation learning is typically slow due to interacting effects of a multilayer perceptron's synaptic weights on the error signal, even with the use of simple local accelerating procedures such as momentum and adaptive learning rates for individual weights (see Section 6.15). If, however, the inputs to the multilayer perceptron consist of uncorrelated components, then the Hessian matrix of the cost function $\mathscr{E}(n)$ with respect to the free parameters of the network is more nearly diagonal than would be the case otherwise. With this form of diagonalization in place, the use of simple local accelerating procedures permits a considerable speedup in the convergence process, which is made possible by appropriate scaling of the learning rates along each weight axis independently.

Specific applications of principal components analysis as a preprocessor for supervised classification include the following.

- Leen et al. (1990) employ Sanger's generalized Hebbian algorithm for principal components analysis to reduce the dimension of speech signals; the compressed signals are then used to train a multilayer perceptron for vowel recognition. The results show that a significant reduction in training time can be achieved without a sacrifice in classification accuracy.
- Yang and Dumont (1991) also employ Sanger's generalized Hebbian algorithm for feature extraction and data compression of acoustic emission signals; the compressed signals are then applied to a multilayer perceptron (trained with the back-propagation algorithm) for automatic classification. Here again, significant reductions in network size and training time are reported without affecting classification accuracy.
- Cottrell and Metcalfe (1991) and Golomb et al. (1991) use the PCA projection generated by an autoassociator to reduce the dimension of input vectors for image recognition systems. The *autoassociator* consists of a multilayer perceptron with a single hidden layer acting as the feature extraction layer, and with the original data used as the input to the network and at the same time as the desired response for back-propagation learning; see Section 6.14 for a more detailed description of the autoassociator.

Baldi and Hornik (1989) discuss the relationship between the autoassociator (using linear neurons) and principal components analysis. In particular, they show that the synaptic weight vector corresponding to the "first" hidden neuron of the autoassociator is exactly equal to the dominant eigenvector of the correlation matrix of the input data, which is exactly the same result obtained using Oja's self-organized neuron. In other words, the solution sought by back-propagation learning in the autoassociative case and by Hebbian learning are identical on one single linear "neuron."

The material presented in this chapter on principal components analysis (PCA) has been based on *linear models* using Hebbian learning. Oja et al. (1991) have proposed a new class of *nonlinear PCA networks* in which a sigmoidal activation function is added to the model of a neuron. Such a modification makes it possible to extract higher-order statistics and adds robustness to the expansion. The eigenvectors computed by a nonlinear PCA network form a subspace of their own; however, they are no longer orthogonal to each other. Nonlinear PCA has been successfully applied to the separation of sinusoidal signals (Karhunen and Joutsensalo, 1992).

PROBLEMS

9.1 Equations (9.2) and (9.51) represent two different ways of describing Hebbian learning.

(a) Expand Eq. (9.2) and, hence, relate the constants a_2, a_3, x_k^0, and y_j^0 in this equation to those in Eq. (9.51).

(b) Given the representation defined in Eq. (9.2), evaluate the constants k_1 and k_2 used in Eq. (9.4), defining the rate of change of a synaptic weight, dw_{jk}/dt.

9.2 Prove the results described in Eqs. (9.8) and (9.9).

9.3 **(a)** Explain the reason for the emergence of orientation-selective neurons in Linsker's model for the perceptual system described in Section 9.3.

(b) Even if we were to use a Hebb-like rule different from the particular one used in this model, orientation-selective neurons can still emerge. What is the mathematical reason for this phenomenon?

9.4 A neuron operating under a Hebb-like rule has an *optimal inference property,* stated as follows: The average error incurred when the output of the neuron is used to estimate its inputs is less for such a neuron than any other linear neuron. Prove the validity of this property.

9.5 For the matched filter considered in Example 2, the eigenvalue λ_0 and associated eigenvector $\mathbf{q}_0$ are defined by

$$\lambda_0 = 1 + \sigma^2$$

$$\mathbf{q}_0 = \mathbf{s}$$

Show that these parameters satisfy the basic relation

$$\mathbf{R}\mathbf{q}_0 = \lambda_0\mathbf{q}_0$$

where $\mathbf{R}$ is the correlation matrix of the input vector $\mathbf{x}$.

9.6 Construct a signal-flow graph to represent the vector-valued Eqs. (9.88) through (9.92).

9.7 In this problem we explore the use of the generalized Hebbian algorithm to study two-dimensional receptive fields produced by a random input (Sanger, 1990). The random input consists of a two-dimensional field of independent Gaussian noise with zero mean and unit variance, which is convolved with a Gaussian mask (filter) and then multiplied by a Gaussian window. The Gaussian mask has a standard deviation of 2 pixels, and the Gaussian window has a standard deviation of 8 pixels. The resulting random input $x(r, s)$ at position (r, s) may thus be written as follows:

$$x(r, s) = m(r, s)[g(r, s) * w(r, s)]$$

where $w(r, s)$ is the field of independent and identically distributed Gaussian noise, $g(r, s)$ is the Gaussian mask, and $m(r, s)$ is the Gaussian window function. The circular convolution of $g(r, s)$ and $w(r, s)$ is defined by

$$g(r, s) * w(r, s) = \sum_{p=0}^{N-1}\sum_{q=0}^{N-1} g(p, q)w(r - p, s - q)$$

where $g(r, s)$ and $w(r, s)$ are both assumed to be periodic.

Use 2000 samples of the random input $x(r, s)$ to train a single-layer feedforward network by means of the generalized Hebbian algorithm. The network has 4096 inputs arranged as a 64-by-64 grid of pixels, and 16 outputs. The resulting synaptic weights of the trained network are represented as 64-by-64 arrays of numbers. Perform the computations described herein and display the 16 arrays of synaptic weights as two-dimensional masks. Comment on your results.

9.8 Equation (9.117) defines the transformed version of the update equation (9.110) for computing the feedback weight vector $\mathbf{a}_j(n)$. The transformation is based on the definition of the synaptic weight vector $\mathbf{w}_j(n)$ in terms of the p principal modes of the network given in Eq. (9.113). Derive Eq. (9.117).

9.9 Consider the system matrix of Eq. (9.120), represented by the signal-flow graph of Fig. 9.13 which corresponds to $0 \leq k \leq j - 1$.

(a) Formulate the characteristic equation of this 2-by-2 matrix.

(b) Show that the matrix has a double eigenvalue.

(c) Justify the statement that all the principal modes of the network have the same eigenvalue.

9.10 The GHA uses forward connections only, whereas the APEX algorithm uses both forward and lateral connections. Yet, despite these differences, the long-term convergence behavior of the APEX algorithm is in theory exactly the same as that of the GHA. Justify the validity of this statement.

CHAPTER 10

Self-Organizing Systems II: Competitive Learning

10.1 Introduction

In this chapter we continue our study of self-organizing systems by considering a special class of artificial neural networks known as self-organizing feature maps. These networks are based on *competitive learning;* the output neurons of the network compete among themselves to be activated or fired, with the result that only *one* output neuron, or one neuron per group, is on at any one time. The output neurons that win the competition are called *winner-takes-all neurons.* One way of inducing a winner-takes-all competition among the output neurons is to use lateral inhibitory connections (i.e., negative feedback paths) between them; such an idea was originally proposed by Rosenblatt (1958).

In a *self-organizing feature map,* the neurons are placed at the nodes of a *lattice* that is usually one- or two-dimensional; higher-dimensional maps are also possible but not as common. The neurons become *selectively tuned* to various input patterns (vectors) or classes of input patterns in the course of a competitive learning process. The locations of the neurons so tuned (i.e., the winning neurons) tend to become ordered with respect to each other in such a way that a meaningful coordinate system for different input *features* is created over the lattice (Kohonen, 1990a). A self-organizing feature map is therefore characterized by the formation of a *topographic map* of the input patterns, in which *the spatial locations (i.e., coordinates) of the neurons in the lattice correspond to intrinsic features of the input patterns,* hence the name "self-organizing feature map."

The development of this special class of artificial neural networks is motivated by a distinct feature of the human brain; simply put, the brain is organized in many places in such a way that different sensory inputs are represented by *topologically ordered computational maps.* In particular, sensory inputs such as tactile (Kaas et al., 1983), visual (Hubel and Wiesel, 1962, 1977), and acoustic (Suga, 1985) are mapped onto different areas of the cerebral cortex in a topologically ordered manner. Thus the computational map constitutes a basic building block in the information-processing infrastructure of the nervous system. A computational map is defined by an array of neurons representing slightly differently tuned processors or filters, which operate on the sensory information-bearing signals in parallel. Consequently, the neurons transform input signals into a *place-coded probability distribution* that represents the computed values of parameters by sites of maximum relative activity within the map (Knudsen et al., 1987). The information so derived is of such a form that it can be readily accessed by higher-order processors using relatively simple connection schemes.

Organization of the Chapter

The material presented in this chapter on computational maps is organized as follows: In Section 10.2 we expand on the idea of computational maps in the brain. Then, in Section

10.3, we describe two feature-mapping models, one originally developed by Willshaw and von der Malsburg (1976) and the other by Kohonen (1982a), which are able to explain or capture the essential features of computational maps in the brain. The two models differ from each other in the form of the inputs used.

The rest of the chapter is devoted to detailed considerations of Kohonen's model that has attracted a great deal of attention in the literature. In Section 10.4 we describe the formation of ''activity bubbles,'' which refers to the modification of the primary excitations by the use of lateral feedback. This then paves the way for the mathematical formulation of Kohonen's model in Section 10.5. In Section 10.6 we describe some important properties of the model, followed by additional notes of a practical nature in Section 10.7 on the operation of the model. In Section 10.8 we describe a hybrid combination of the Kohonen model and supervised linear filter for adaptive pattern classification. Learning vector quantization, an alternative method of improving the pattern-classification performance of the Kohonen model, is described in Section 10.9. The chapter concludes with Section 10.10 on applications of the Kohonen model, and some final thoughts on the subject in Section 10.11.

10.2 Computational Maps in the Cerebral Cortex

Anyone who examines a human brain cannot help but be impressed by the extent to which the brain is dominated by the cerebral cortex. The brain is almost completely enveloped by the cortex, tending to obscure the other parts. Although it is only about 2 mm thick, its surface area, when spread out, is about 2400 cm^2 (i.e., about six times the size of this page). What is even more impressive is the fact that there are billions of neurons and hundreds of billions of synapses in the cortex. For sheer complexity, the cerebral cortex probably exceeds any other known structure (Hubel and Wiesel, 1977).

Figure 10.1 presents a cytoarchitectural map of the cerebral cortex as worked out by Brodmann (Shepherd, 1988; Brodal, 1981). The different areas of the cortex are identified by the thickness of their layers and the types of neurons within them. Some of the most important specific areas are as follows:

Motor cortex:	motor strip, area 4; premotor area, area 6; frontal eye fields, area 8.
Somatosensory cortex:	areas 3, 1, and 2.
Visual cortex:	areas 17, 18, and 19.
Auditory cortex:	areas 41 and 42.

Figure 10.1 shows clearly that different sensory inputs (motor, somatosensory, visual, auditory, etc.) are mapped onto corresponding areas of the cerebral cortex in an orderly fashion. These cortical maps are not entirely genetically predetermined; rather, they are sketched in during the early development of the nervous system. However, it is uncertain how cortical maps are sketched in this manner. Four major hypotheses have been advanced by neurobiologists (Udin and Fawcett, 1988):

1. The target (postsynaptic) structure possesses addresses (i.e., chemical signals) that are actively searched for by the ingrowing connections (axons).
2. The structure, starting from zero (i.e., an informationless target structure), self-organizes using learning rules and system interactions.

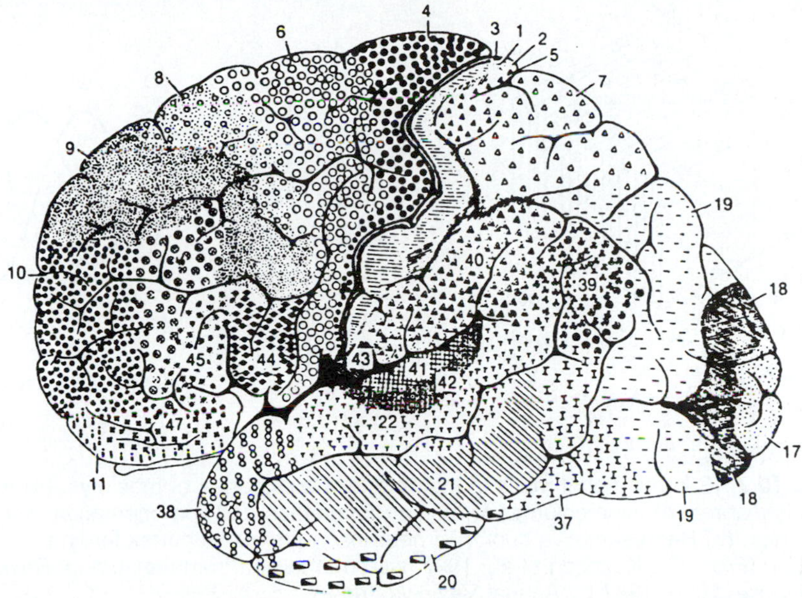

FIGURE 10.1 Cytoarchitectural map of the cerebral cortex. The different areas are identified by the thickness of their layers and types of cells within them. Some of the most important specific areas are as follows. Motor cortex: motor strip, area 4; premotor area, area 6; frontal eye fields, area 8. Somatosensory cortex: areas 3, 1, 2. Visual cortex: areas 17, 18, 19. Auditory cortex: areas 41 and 42. (From G.M. Shepherd, 1988; A. Brodal, 1981; with permission of Oxford University Press.)

3. Axons, as they grow, physically maintain neighborhood relationships, and therefore arrive at the target structure already topographically arranged.
4. Axons grow out in a topographically arranged time sequence, and connect to a target structure that is generated in a matching temporal fashion.

All these hypotheses have experimental support of their own, and appear to be correct to some extent. In fact, different structures may use one mechanism or another, or it could be that multiple mechanisms are involved.

Once the cortical maps have been formed, they remain "plastic" to a varying extent, and therefore adapt to subsequent changes in the environment or the sensors themselves. The degree of plasticity, however, depends on the type of system in question. For example, a *retinotopic map* (i.e., the map from the retina to the visual cortex) remains plastic for only a relatively short period of time after its formation, whereas the somatosensory map remains plastic longer (Kaas et al., 1983).

An example of a cortical mapping is shown in Figure 10.2. This figure is a schematic representation of computational maps in the primary visual cortex of cats and monkeys. The basis of this representation was discovered originally by Hubel and Wiesel (1962). In Fig. 10.2 we recognize two kinds of repeating computational maps:

1. *Maps of preferred line orientation,* representing the angle of tilt of a line stimulus
2. *Maps of ocular dominance,* representing the relative strengths of excitatory influence of each eye

The major point of interest here is the fact that line orientation and ocular dominance are mapped across the cortical surface along independent axes. Although in Fig. 10.2 (for

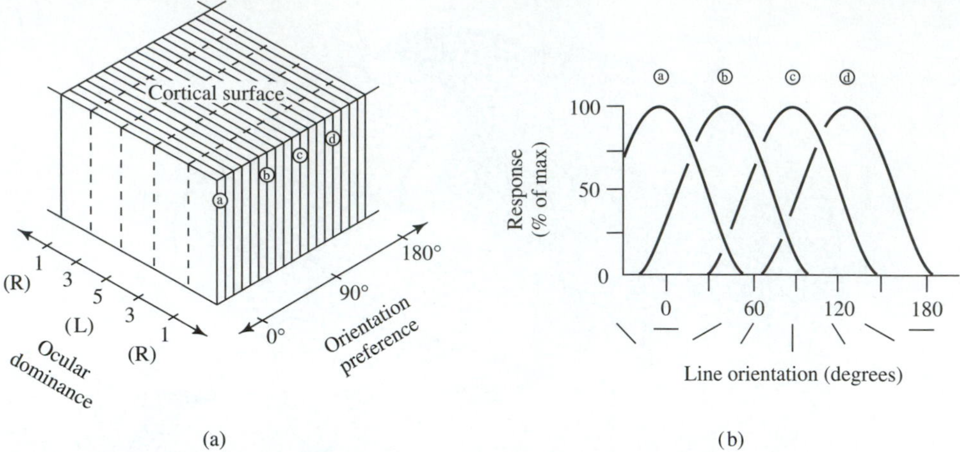

FIGURE 10.2 Computational maps in the primary visual cortex of monkeys. (a) A schematic diagram of hypercolumns for ocular dominance and line orientation in the visual cortex. (b) Representative curves of neurons in the visual cortex for line orientation. (From E.I. Knudsen et al., 1987, with permission from the *Annual Review of Neuroscience,* **10,** © 1987 by Annual Reviews, Inc.)

convenience of presentation), we have shown these two maps to be orthogonal to each other, there is no direct evidence to suggest that they are related in this fashion.

The use of computational maps offers the following advantages (Knudsen et al., 1987):

- *Efficient Information Processing*. The nervous system is required to analyze complex events arising in a dynamic environment on a continuous basis. This, in turn, requires the use of processing strategies that permit the rapid handling of large amounts of information. Computational maps, performed by parallel processing arrays, are ideally suited for this task. In particular, computational maps provide a method for the rapid sorting and processing of complex stimuli, and representing the results obtained in a simple and systematic form.
- *Simplicity of Access to Processed Information*. The use of computational maps simplifies the schemes of connectivity required to utilize the information by higher-order processors.
- *Common Form of Representation*. A common, mapped representation of the results of different kinds of computations permits the nervous system to employ a single strategy for making sense of information.
- *Facilitation of Additional Interactions*. By representing a feature of interest in topographic form, maps enable us to sharpen tuning of the processor in ways that would not be possible otherwise. For example, regional interactions such as excitatory facilitation and lateral inhibitions can work only on sensory information that is mapped.

10.3 Two Basic Feature-Mapping Models

What can we deduce from the above discussion of computational maps in the brain that would guide the self-building of topographic maps? The answer essentially lies in the *principle of topographic map formation,* which may be stated as follows (Kohonen,

1990a):

The spatial location of an output neuron in the topographic map corresponds to a particular domain or feature of the input data.

The output neurons are usually arranged in a one- or two-dimensional *lattice,* a topology that ensures that each neuron has a set of neighbors.

The manner in which the input patterns are specified determines the nature of the feature-mapping model. In particular, we may distinguish two basic models, as illustrated in Fig. 10.3 for a two-dimensional lattice of output neurons that are fully connected to the inputs. Both models were inspired by the pioneering self-organizing studies of von der Malsburg (1973), who noted that a model of the visual cortex could not be entirely genetically predetermined; rather, a self-organizing process involving synaptic learning may be responsible for the *local* ordering of feature-sensitive cortical cells. However, global topographic ordering was *not* achieved, because the model used a fixed (small) neighborhood. The computer simulation by von der Malsburg was perhaps the first to demonstrate self-organization.

The model of Fig. 10.3a was originally proposed by Willshaw and von der Malsburg (1976) on biological grounds to explain the problem of retinotopic mapping from the retina to the visual cortex (in higher vertebrates). Specifically, there are two separate two-dimensional lattices of neurons connected together, with one projecting onto the other. One

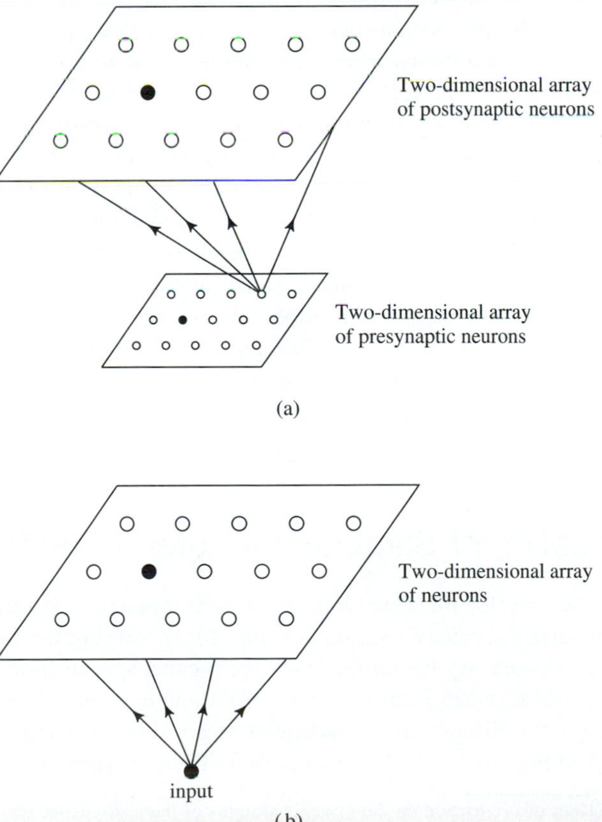

FIGURE 10.3 (a) Willshaw–von der Malsburg's model. (b) Kohonen's model.

lattice represents presynaptic (input) neurons, and the other lattice represents postsynaptic (output) neurons. The postsynaptic lattice uses a *short-range excitatory mechanism* as well as a *long-range inhibitory mechanism.* These two mechanisms are local in nature and critically important for self-organization. The two lattices are interconnected by modifiable synapses of a Hebbian type. Strictly speaking, therefore, the postsynaptic neurons are not winner-takes-all; rather, a threshold is used to ensure that only a few postsynaptic neurons will fire at any one time. Moreover, to prevent a steady buildup in the synaptic weights that may lead to network instability, the total weight associated with each postsynaptic neuron is limited by an upper boundary condition.[1] Thus, for each neuron, some synaptic weights increase while others are made to decrease. The basic idea of the Willshaw–von der Malsburg model is for the geometric proximity of presynaptic neurons to be coded in the form of correlations in their electrical activity, and to use these correlations in the postsynaptic lattice so as to connect neighboring presynaptic neurons to neighboring postsynaptic neurons. A topologically ordered mapping is thereby produced by self-organization. Note, however, that the Willshaw–von der Malsburg model is specialized to mappings where the input dimension is the same as the output dimension.

The second model, of Fig. 10.3b, introduced by Kohonen (1982a), is not meant to explain neurobiological details. Rather, the model tries to capture the essential features of computational maps in the brain and yet remain computationally tractable. The model's neurobiological feasibility is discussed in Kohonen (1993). It appears that the Kohonen model is more general than the Willshaw–von der Malsburg model in the sense that it is capable of performing data compression (i.e., dimensionality reduction on the input).

In reality, the Kohonen model belongs to the class of *vector coding* algorithms. We say so because the model provides a topological mapping that optimally places a fixed number of vectors (i.e., codewords) into a higher-dimensional input space, and thereby facilitates data compression. The Kohonen model may therefore be derived in two ways. We may use basic ideas of self-organization, motivated by neurobiological considerations, to derive the model, which is the traditional approach (Kohonen, 1982a, 1988b, 1990a). Alternatively, we may use a vector quantization approach that uses a model involving an encoder and a decoder, which is motivated by communication-theoretic considerations (Luttrell, 1989b, 1991). In this chapter, we consider both approaches.

The Kohonen model has received much more attention in the literature than the Willshaw–von der Malsburg model. The model possesses certain properties discussed later in the chapter, which make it particularly interesting for understanding and modeling cortical maps in the brain. The remainder of the chapter is devoted to the Kohonen model, the derivation of the *self-organizing feature map* (SOFM) usually associated with the Kohonen model, its basic properties, and applications.

10.4 Modification of Stimulus by Lateral Feedback

In order to pave the way for the development of self-organizing feature maps, we first discuss the use of *lateral feedback* as a mechanism for modifying the form of excitation applied to a neural network. By lateral feedback we mean a special form of feedback that is dependent on lateral distance from the point of its application.

For the purpose of this discussion, it is adequate to consider the one-dimensional lattice of neurons shown in Fig. 10.4, which contains two different types of connections. There

[1] Amari (1980) relaxes this restriction on the synaptic weights of the postsynaptic neurons somewhat. The mathematical analysis presented by Amari elucidates the dynamical stability of a cortical map formed by self-organization.

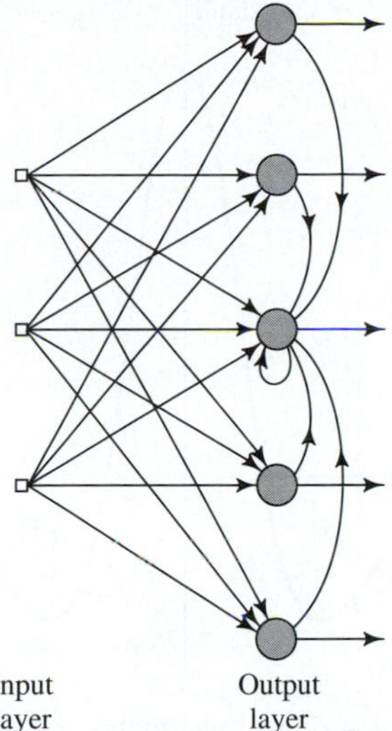

FIGURE 10.4 One-dimension lattice of neurons with feedforward connections and lateral feedback connections; the latter connections are shown only for the neuron at the center of the array.

are forward connections from the primary source of excitation, and those that are internal to the network by virtue of self-feedback and lateral feedback. In Fig. 10.4, the input signals are applied in parallel to the neurons. These two types of local connections serve two different purposes. The weighted sum of the input signals at each neuron is designed to perform feature detection. Hence each neuron produces a selective response to a particular set of input signals. The feedback connections, on the other hand, produce excitatory or inhibitory effects, depending on the distance from the neuron.

Following biological motivation, the lateral feedback is usually described by a *Mexican hat function,* the form of which is depicted in Fig. 10.5. According to this figure, we may distinguish three distinct areas of lateral interaction between neurons:[2]

1. A short-range lateral excitation area.
2. A penumbra of inhibitory action.
3. An area of weaker excitation that surrounds the inhibitory penumbra; this third area is usually ignored.

These areas are designated as 1, 2, and 3, respectively, in Fig. 10.5.

The neural network described here exhibits two important characteristics. First, the network tends to concentrate its electrical activity into local clusters, referred to as *activity bubbles* (Kohonen, 1988b). Second, the locations of the activity bubbles are determined by the nature of the input signals.

Let $x_1, x_2, \dots, x_p$ denote the input signals (excitations) applied to the network, where p is the number of input terminals. Let $w_{j1}, w_{j2}, \dots, w_{jp}$ denote the corresponding synaptic weights of neuron j. Let $c_{j,-K}, \dots, c_{j,-1}, c_{j,0}, c_{j1}, \dots, c_{jK}$ denote the lateral feedback weights connected to neuron j, where K is the "radius" of the lateral interaction. Let $y_1, y_2, \dots, y_N$ denote the output signals of the network, where N is the number of

[2] In the visual cortex, the short-range lateral excitation extends up to a radius of 50 to 100 μm, the penumbra of inhibitory action reaches up to a radius of 200 to 500 μm, and the area of weaker excitation surrounding the penumbra reaches up to a radius of several centimeters (Kohonen, 1982a).

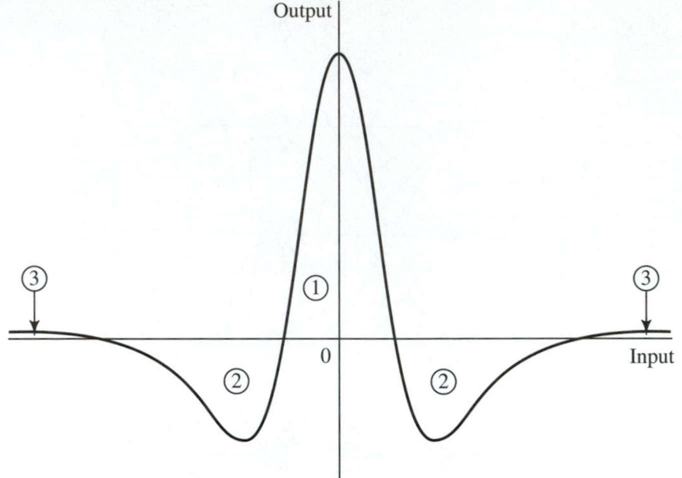

FIGURE 10.5 The Mexican hat function of lateral interconnections.

neurons in the network. We may thus express the output signal (response) of neuron j as follows:

$$y_j = \varphi\left(I_j + \sum_{k=-K}^{K} c_{jk} y_{j+k}\right), \qquad j = 1, 2, \ldots, N \tag{10.1}$$

where $\varphi(\cdot)$ is some nonlinear function that limits the value of y_j and ensures that $y_j \geq 0$. The term I_j serves the function of a *stimulus*, representing the total external control exerted on neuron j by the weighted effect of the input signals; that is,

$$I_j = \sum_{l=1}^{p} w_{jl} x_l \tag{10.2}$$

Typically, the stimulus I_j is a *smooth function* of the spatial index j.

The solution to the nonlinear equation (10.1) is found iteratively, using a *relaxation* technique. Specifically, we reformulate it as a difference equation as follows:

$$y_j(n+1) = \varphi\left(I_j + \beta \sum_{k=-K}^{K} c_{jk} y_{j+k}(n)\right), \qquad j = 1, 2, \ldots, N \tag{10.3}$$

where n denotes discrete time. Thus, $y_j(n + 1)$ is the output of neuron j at time $n + 1$, and $y_{j+k}(n)$ is the output of neuron $j + k$ at the previous time n. The parameter β in the argument on the right-hand side of Eq. (10.3) controls the rate of convergence of the relaxation process.

The relaxation equation (10.3) represents a *feedback system* as illustrated in the signal-flow graph shown in Fig. 10.6, where z^{-1} is the unit-delay operator. The parameter β plays the role of a *feedback factor* of the system. The system includes both positive and negative feedback, corresponding to the excitatory and inhibitory parts of the Mexican hat function, respectively. The limiting action of the nonlinear activation function $\varphi(\cdot)$ causes the spatial response $y_j(n)$ to stabilize in a certain fashion, dependent on the value assigned to β. If β is large enough, then in the final state corresponding to $n \rightarrow \infty$, the values of y_j tend to concentrate inside a spatially bounded cluster, that is, an "activity bubble." The bubble is centered at a point where the initial response $y_j(0)$ due to the stimulus I_j is maximum. The width of the activity bubble depends on the ratio of the excitatory to inhibitory lateral interconnections. In particular, we may state the following:

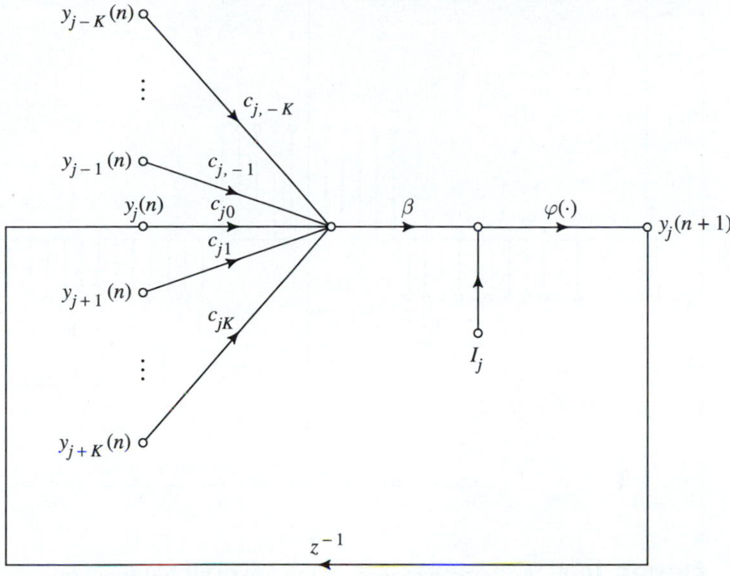

FIGURE 10.6 Signal-flow graph depicting the relaxation equation (10.3) as a feedback system.

- If the positive feedback is made stronger, the activity bubble becomes wider.
- If, on the other hand, the negative feedback is enhanced, the activity bubble becomes sharper.

Of course, if the net feedback acting around the system is too negative, formation of the activity bubble is prevented. The various aspects of the bubble formation are illustrated in the computer experiment presented next.

Computer Experiment on Bubble Formation

To simplify the computation involved in the formation of activity bubble by lateral feedback, the Mexican hat function is approximated by the function shown in Fig. 10.7. Two specific points should be noted here:

- The area of weak excitation surrounding the inhibitory region is *ignored.*
- The areas of excitatory feedback and inhibitory feedback are *normalized* to unity.

To further simplify the simulations, the function $\varphi(\cdot)$ is taken to be a piecewise-linear function shown in Fig. 10.8. Specifically, we have

$$\varphi(x) = \begin{bmatrix} a, & x \geq a \\ x, & 0 \leq x < a \\ 0, & x < 0 \end{bmatrix} \tag{10.4}$$

with $a = 10$.

The one-dimensional lattice of Fig. 10.4 is assumed to consist of $N = 51$ neurons. The stimulus I_j acting on neuron j is assumed to be half a sinusoid, as shown by

$$I_j = 2 \sin\left(\frac{\pi j}{50}\right), \qquad 0 \leq j \leq 50 \tag{10.5}$$

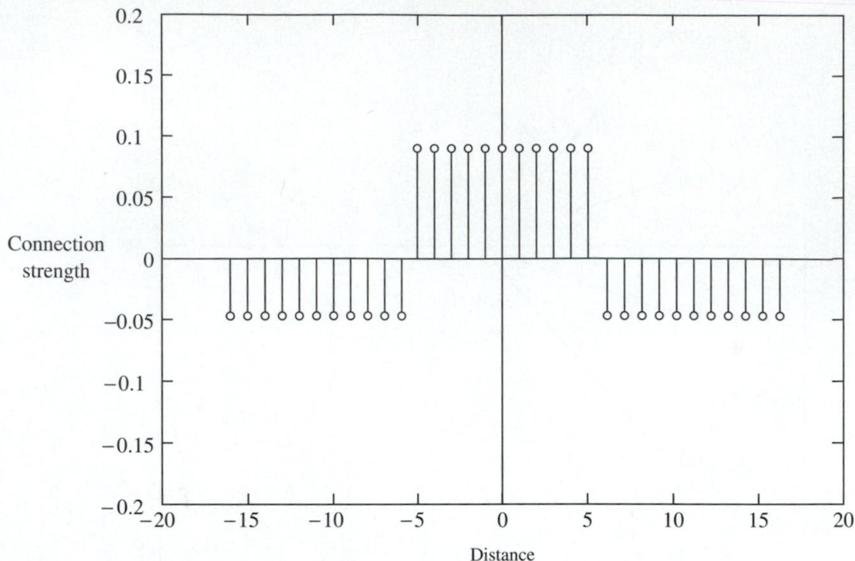

FIGURE 10.7 An approximation of the Mexican hat function.

The stimulus I_j so defined is zero at both ends of the lattice, and has a peak value of 2 at its mid-point. For convenience of presentation we have redefined the range occupied by j in Eq. (10.5) as the closed interval $[0, N - 1]$.

Figure 10.9 shows 10 steps of the relaxation equation (10.3) for the conditions described herein, and for two different values of the feedback factor:

Feedback Factor $\beta = 2$. The simulation results for this feedback factor are presented in Fig. 10.9a. The spatial response $y_j(n)$ begins with a width of 50, corresponding to $n = 0$. Then, with increasing n, it becomes narrower and higher. The limiting action of the function $\varphi(\cdot)$ causes the response $y_j(n)$ to stabilize, such that in the final state (corresponding to $n \to \infty$), a bubble is formed with all the neurons located inside it effectively having an activation of $a = 10$ and all the neurons located outside it having essentially zero activation. From the simulation results presented in Fig. 10.9a, it is apparent that the activity bubble so formed is centered around the highest value of the stimulus I_j, occurring at the mid-point of the lattice.

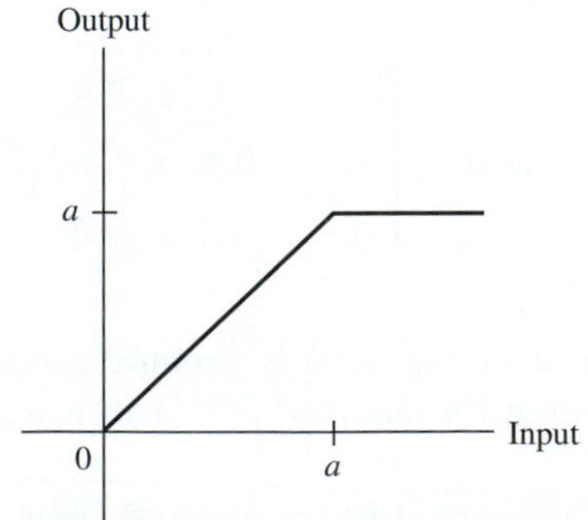

FIGURE 10.8 Piecewise-linear function.

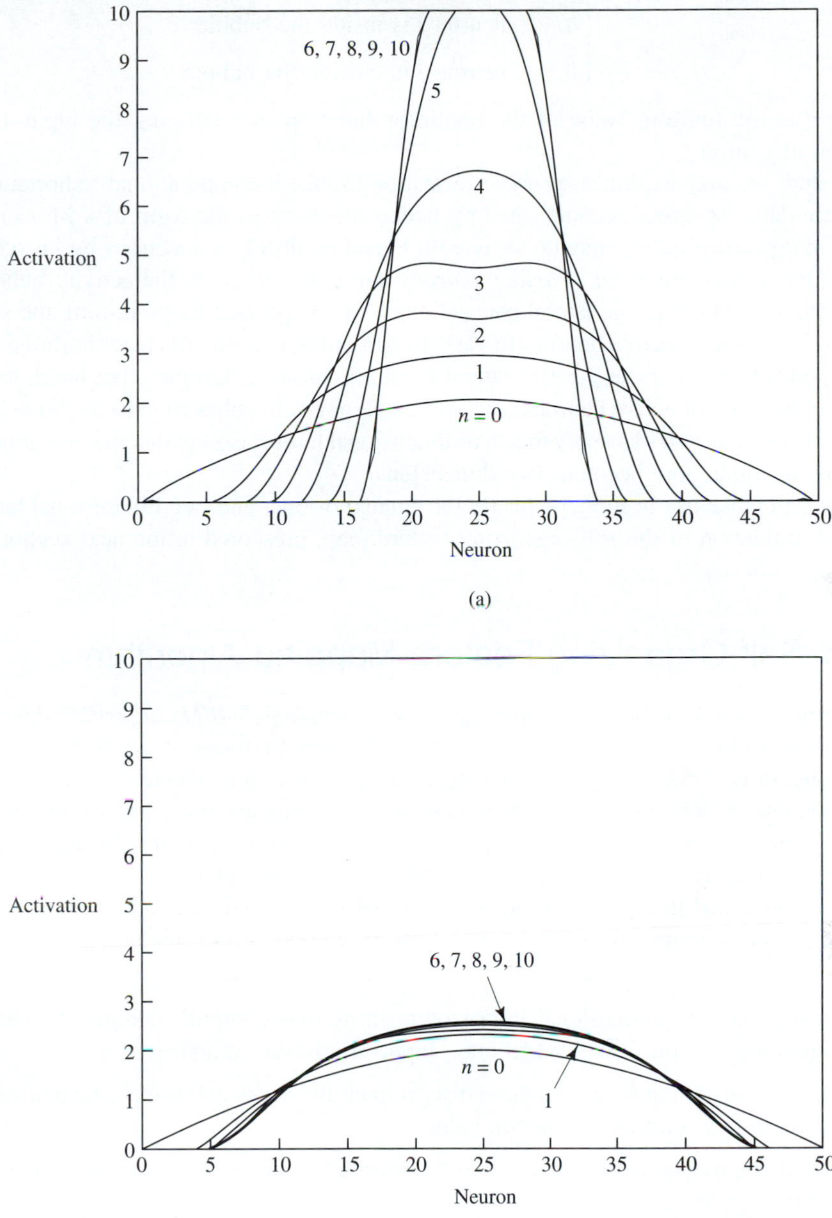

FIGURE 10.9 Bubble formation for (a) feedback factor $\beta = 2$ and (b) feedback factor $\beta = 0.75$. The iteration numbers are shown on the graphs.

Feedback Factor $\beta = 0.75$. If the feedback factor β is smaller than a critical value, the net gain of the system will not be enough to permit the formation of an activity bubble. This behavior is illustrated in Fig. 10.9b for $\beta = 0.75$.

Consequences of Bubble Formation

Given that an activity bubble is formed as illustrated in Fig. 10.9a, what can we learn from it? First, we may idealize the output of neuron j as follows:

$$y_j = \begin{cases} a, & \text{neuron } j \text{ is inside the bubble} \\ 0, & \text{neuron } j \text{ is outside the bubble} \end{cases} \tag{10.6}$$

where a is the limiting value of the nonlinear function $\varphi(\cdot)$ defining the input–output relation of neuron j.

Second, we may exploit the bubble formation to take a computational "shortcut," so as to emulate the effect accomplished by lateral feedback in the form of a Mexican hat function. Specifically, we may do away with lateral feedback connections by introducing a *topological neighborhood of active neurons* that corresponds to the activity bubble.

Third, adjustment of the lateral connections is accomplished by permitting the size of the neighborhood of active neurons to vary. In particular, making this neighborhood wider corresponds to making the positive lateral feedback stronger. On the other hand, making the neighborhood of active neurons narrower corresponds to enhancing the negative lateral feedback. Similar remarks apply to a two-dimensional lattice, except that the neighborhood of active neurons now becomes two-dimensional.

We shall make use of these points (in the context of one- and two-dimensional lattices) in the formulation of the self-organizing feature map, presented in the next section.

10.5 Self-Organizing Feature-Mapping Algorithm

The principal goal of the *self-organizing feature-mapping (SOFM) algorithm* developed by Kohonen (1982a) is to transform an incoming signal pattern of arbitrary dimension into a one- or two-dimensional discrete map, and to perform this transformation adaptively in a topological ordered fashion. Many activation patterns are presented to the network, *one at a time*. Typically, each input presentation consists simply of a localized region, or "spot," of activity against a quiet background. Each such presentation causes a corresponding localized group of neurons in the output layer of the network to be active.

The essential ingredients of the neural network embodied in such an algorithm are as follows:

- A one- or two-dimensional lattice of neurons that computes simple discriminant functions of inputs received from an input of arbitrary dimension
- A mechanism that compares these discriminant functions and selects the neuron with the largest discriminant function value
- An interactive network that activates the selected neuron and its neighbors simultaneously
- An adaptive process that enables the activated neurons to increase their discriminant function values in relation to the input signals

In this section we develop the SOFM algorithm; the properties of the algorithm are discussed in the next section.

To proceed with the development of the algorithm, consider Fig. 10.10, which depicts a two-dimensional lattice of neurons. In this figure we have connected the same set of input (sensory) signals to all the neurons in the lattice. The input vector, representing the set of input signals, is denoted by

$$\mathbf{x} = [x_1, x_2, \ldots, x_p]^T \tag{10.7}$$

The synaptic weight vector of neuron j is denoted by

$$\mathbf{w}_j = [w_{j1}, w_{j2}, \ldots, w_{jp}]^T, \qquad j = 1, 2, \ldots, N \tag{10.8}$$

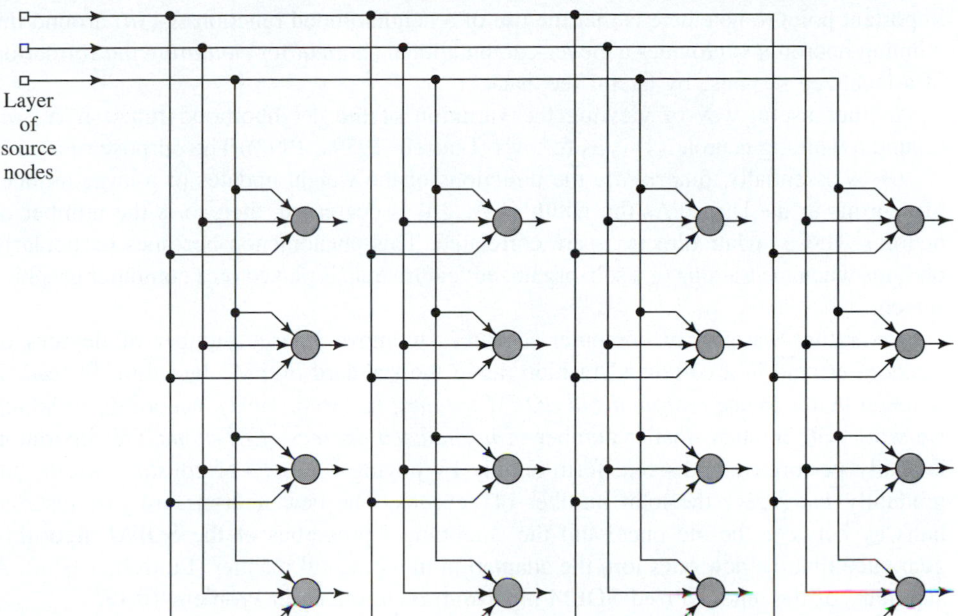

FIGURE 10.10 Two-dimensional lattice of neurons.

To find the best match of the input vector $\mathbf{x}$ with the synaptic weight vectors $\mathbf{w}_j$, we simply compare the inner products $\mathbf{w}_j^T\mathbf{x}$ for $j = 1, 2, \ldots, N$ and select the largest. This assumes that the same threshold is applied to all the neurons. Note also that $\mathbf{w}_j^T\mathbf{x}$ is identical with the stimulus I_j in Eq. (10.2). Thus, by selecting the neuron with the largest inner product $\mathbf{w}_j^T\mathbf{x}$, we will have in effect determined the location where the activity bubble is to be formed.

In the formulation of an adaptive algorithm, we often find it convenient to *normalize* the weight vectors $\mathbf{w}_j$ to constant Euclidean norm (length). In such a situation, *the best-matching criterion* described here is equivalent to the *minimum Euclidean distance between vectors.* Specifically, if we use the index $i(\mathbf{x})$ to identify the neuron that best matches the input vector $\mathbf{x}$, we may then determine $i(\mathbf{x})$ by applying the condition

$$i(\mathbf{x}) = \arg\min_j \|\mathbf{x} - \mathbf{w}_j\|, \qquad j = 1, 2, \ldots, N \tag{10.9}$$

where $\|\cdot\|$ denotes the Euclidean norm of the argument vector. According to Eq. (10.9), $i(\mathbf{x})$ is the subject of attention, for after all it is the value of i that we want. The particular neuron i that satisfies this condition is called the *best-matching* or *winning neuron* for the input vector $\mathbf{x}$. By using Eq. (10.9), a continuous input space is mapped onto a discrete set of neurons. Depending on the application of interest, the response of the network could be either the index of the winning neuron (i.e., its position in the lattice), or the synaptic weight vector that is closest to the input vector in a Euclidean sense.

The topology of iterations in the SOFM algorithm defines which neurons in the two-dimensional lattice are in fact neighbors. Let $\Lambda_{i(\mathbf{x})}(n)$ denote the *topological neighborhood* of winning neuron $i(\mathbf{x})$. The neighborhood $\Lambda_{i(\mathbf{x})}(n)$ is chosen to be a function of the discrete time n; hence we may also refer to $\Lambda_{i(\mathbf{x})}(n)$ as a *neighborhood function.* Numerous simulations have shown that the best results in self-organization are obtained if the neighborhood function $\Lambda_{i(\mathbf{x})}(n)$ is selected fairly wide in the beginning and then permitted to shrink with time n (Kohonen, 1990a). This behavior is equivalent to initially using a strong positive lateral feedback, and then enhancing the negative lateral feedback. The important point to note here is that the use of a neighborhood function $\Lambda_{i(\mathbf{x})}(n)$ around the winning neuron $i(\mathbf{x})$ provides a clever computational shortcut for *emulating* the formation of a localized response by lateral feedback.

Another useful way of viewing the variation of the neighborhood function $\Lambda_{i(\mathbf{x})}(n)$ around a winning neuron $i(\mathbf{x})$ is as follows (Luttrell, 1989a, 1992). The purpose of a wide $\Lambda_{i(\mathbf{x})}(n)$ is essentially to *correlate* the directions of the weight updates of a large number of neurons in the lattice. As the width of $\Lambda_{i(\mathbf{x})}(n)$ is decreased, then so is the number of neurons whose update directions are correlated. This phenomenon becomes particularly obvious when the training of a self-organized feature map is played on a computer graphics screen.

It is rather wasteful of computer resources to move a large number of degrees of freedom around in a correlated fashion, as in the standard SOFM algorithm. Instead, it is much better to use *renormalized SOFM training* (Luttrell, 1992), according to which we work with a much smaller number of *normalized degrees of freedom.* This operation is easily performed in discrete form simply by having a $\Lambda_{i(\mathbf{x})}(n)$ of *constant* width, but gradually *increasing* the total number of neurons. The new neurons are just inserted halfway between the old ones, and the smoothness properties of the SOFM algorithm guarantee that the new ones join the adaptation in a graceful manner (Luttrell, 1989a). A summary of the renormalized SOFM algorithm is presented in Problem 10.18.

Adaptive Process

For the network to be self-organizing, the synaptic weight vector $\mathbf{w}_j$ of neuron j is required to change in relation to the input vector $\mathbf{x}$. The question is how to make the change. In Hebb's postulate of learning, a synaptic weight is increased with a simultaneous occurrence of presynaptic and postsynaptic activities. The use of such a rule is well suited for associative learning. For the type of unsupervised learning being considered here, however, the Hebbian hypothesis in its basic form is unsatisfactory for the following reason; changes in connectivities occur in one direction only, which finally drive all the synaptic weights into saturation. To overcome this problem, we may modify the Hebbian hypothesis simply by including a nonlinear *forgetting term* $-g(y_j)\mathbf{w}_j$, where $\mathbf{w}_j$ is the synaptic weight vector of neuron j and $g(y_j)$ is some positive scalar function of its response y_j. The only requirement imposed on the function $g(y_j)$ is that the constant term in the Taylor series expansion of $g(y_j)$ be zero, so that we may write

$$g(y_j) = 0 \qquad \text{for } y_j = 0 \text{ and for all } j \tag{10.10}$$

The significance of this requirement will become apparent momentarily. Given such a function, we may then express the differential equation that defines the *computational map* produced by the SOFM algorithm as

$$\frac{d\mathbf{w}_j}{dt} = \eta y_j \mathbf{x} - g(y_j)\mathbf{w}_j, \qquad j = 1, 2, \ldots, N \tag{10.11}$$

where t denotes the continuous time and η is the *learning-rate parameter* of the algorithm.

We may further simplify Eq. (10.11) in light of the "activity bubble formation" phenomenon described previously. To be specific, if the input vector $\mathbf{x}$ is changing at a rate that is slow compared to the synaptic weight vector $\mathbf{w}_j$ for all j, we may justifiably assume that due to the clustering effect (i.e., the formation of an activity bubble), the response y_j of neuron j is at either a low or high saturation value, depending on whether neuron j is outside or inside the bubble, respectively. Correspondingly, the function $g(y_j)$ takes on a binary character. Thus, identifying the neighborhood function $\Lambda_{i(\mathbf{x})}$ (around the winning neuron $i(\mathbf{x})$] with the activity bubble, we may write

$$y_j = \begin{cases} 1, & \text{neuron } j \text{ is active (i.e., inside the neighborhood } \Lambda_{i(\mathbf{x})}) \\ 0, & \text{neuron } j \text{ is inactive (i.e., outside the neighborhood } \Lambda_{i(\mathbf{x})}) \end{cases} \tag{10.12}$$

In a corresponding way, we may express the function $g(y_j)$ as

$$g(y_j) = \begin{cases} \alpha, & \text{neuron } j \text{ is active (on)} \\ 0, & \text{neuron } j \text{ is inactive (off)} \end{cases} \tag{10.13}$$

where α is some positive constant, and the second line is a consequence of the conditions described in Eqs. (10.10) and (10.12). Accordingly we may simplify Eq. (10.11) as follows:

$$\frac{d\mathbf{w}_j}{dt} = \begin{cases} \eta\mathbf{x} - \alpha\mathbf{w}_j, & \text{neuron } j \text{ is inside the neighborhood } \Lambda_{i(\mathbf{x})} \\ 0, & \text{neuron } j \text{ is outside the neighborhood } \Lambda_{i(\mathbf{x})} \end{cases} \tag{10.14}$$

Without loss of generality, we may use the same scaling factor for the input vector $\mathbf{x}$ and the weight vector $\mathbf{w}_j$. In other words, we may put $\alpha = \eta$, in which case Eq. (10.14) further simplifies as

$$\frac{d\mathbf{w}_j}{dt} = \begin{cases} \eta(\mathbf{x} - \mathbf{w}_j), & \text{neuron } j \text{ is inside the neighborhood } \Lambda_{i(\mathbf{x})} \\ 0, & \text{neuron } j \text{ is outside the neighborhood } \Lambda_{i(\mathbf{x})} \end{cases} \tag{10.15}$$

According to Eq. (10.15), the weight vector $\mathbf{w}_j$ tends to follow the input vector $\mathbf{x}$ with increasing time t.

Finally, using discrete-time formalism, Eq.(10.15) is cast in a form whereby, given the synaptic weight vector $\mathbf{w}_j(n)$ of neuron j at discrete time n, we may compute the updated value $\mathbf{w}_j(n + 1)$ at time $n + 1$ as follows (Kohonen, 1982a, 1990a):

$$\mathbf{w}_j(n+1) = \begin{cases} \mathbf{w}_j(n) + \eta(n)[\mathbf{x} - \mathbf{w}_j(n)], & j \in \Lambda_{i(\mathbf{x})}(n) \\ \mathbf{w}_j(n), & \text{otherwise} \end{cases} \tag{10.16}$$

Here, $\Lambda_{i(\mathbf{x})}(n)$ is the neighborhood function around the winning neuron i at time n, and $\eta(n)$ is the corresponding value of the learning-rate parameter; the reason for making the learning-rate parameter time-dependent is explained later. The update equation (10.16) is the desired formula for computing the feature map.

The effect of the update equation (10.16) is to move the synaptic weight vector $\mathbf{w}_i$ of the winning neuron i toward the input vector $\mathbf{x}$. Upon repeated presentations of the training data, the synaptic weight vectors tend to follow the distribution of the input vectors due to the neighborhood updating. The algorithm therefore leads to a *topological ordering* of the feature map in the input space in the sense that neurons that are adjacent in the lattice will tend to have similar synaptic weight vectors. We will have much more to say on this issue in Section 10.6.

Summary of the SOFM Algorithm

The essence of Kohonen's SOFM algorithm is that it substitutes a simple geometric computation for the more detailed properties of the Hebb-like rule and lateral interactions. There are three basic steps involved in the application of the algorithm after initialization, namely, sampling, similarity matching, and updating. These three steps are repeated until the map formation is completed. The algorithm is summarized as follows (Kohonen 1988b, 1990a):

1. *Initialization.* Choose random values for the initial weight vectors $\mathbf{w}_j(0)$. The only restriction here is that the $\mathbf{w}_j(0)$ be different for $j = 1, 2, \ldots, N$, where N is the

number of neurons in the lattice. It may be desirable to keep the magnitude of the weights small.

2. *Sampling*. Draw a sample $\mathbf{x}$ from the input distribution with a certain probability; the vector $\mathbf{x}$ represents the sensory signal.
3. *Similarity Matching*. Find the best-matching (winning) neuron $i(\mathbf{x})$ at time n, using the minimum-distance Euclidean criterion:

$$i(\mathbf{x}) = \arg\min_j \|\mathbf{x}(n) - \mathbf{w}_j\|, \qquad j = 1, 2, \ldots, N$$

4. *Updating*. Adjust the synaptic weight vectors of all neurons, using the update formula

$$\mathbf{w}_j(n+1) = \begin{cases} \mathbf{w}_j(n) + \eta(n)[\mathbf{x}(n) - \mathbf{w}_j(n)], & j \in \Lambda_{i(\mathbf{x})}(n) \\ \mathbf{w}_j(n), & \text{otherwise} \end{cases}$$

where $\eta(n)$ is the learning-rate parameter, and $\Lambda_{i(\mathbf{x})}(n)$ is the neighborhood function centered around the winning neuron $i(\mathbf{x})$; both $\eta(n)$ and $\Lambda_{i(\mathbf{x})}(n)$ are varied dynamically during learning for best results.

5. *Continuation*. Continue with step 2 until no noticeable changes in the feature map are observed.

Selection of Parameters

The learning process involved in the computation of a feature map is stochastic in nature, which means that the accuracy of the map depends on the number of iterations of the SOFM algorithm. Moreover, the success of map formation is critically dependent on how the main parameters of the algorithm, namely, the learning-rate parameter η and the neighborhood function Λ_i, are selected. Unfortunately, there is no theoretical basis for the selection of these parameters. They are usually determined by a process of trial and error. Nevertheless, the following observations provide a useful guide (Kohonen, 1988b, 1990a).

1. The learning-rate parameter $\eta(n)$ used to update the synaptic weight vector $\mathbf{w}_j(n)$ should be time-varying. In particular, during the first 1000 iterations or so, $\eta(n)$ should begin with a value close to unity; thereafter, $\eta(n)$ should decrease gradually, but staying above 0.1. The exact form of variation of $\eta(n)$ with n is not critical; it can be linear, exponential, or inversely proportional to n. It is during this initial phase of the algorithm that the topological ordering of the weight vectors $\mathbf{w}_j(n)$ takes place. This phase of the learning process is called the *ordering phase.* The remaining (relatively long) iterations of the algorithm are needed principally for the fine tuning of the computational map; this second phase of the learning process is called the *convergence phase.* For good statistical accuracy, $\eta(n)$ should be maintained during the convergence phase at a small value (on the order of 0.01 or less) for a fairly long period of time, which is typically thousands of iterations.

2. For topological ordering of the weight vectors $\mathbf{w}_j$ to take place, careful consideration has to be given to the neighborhood function $\Lambda_i(n)$. Generally, the function $\Lambda_i(n)$ is taken to include neighbors in a square region around the winning neuron, as illustrated in Fig. 10.11. For example, a ''radius'' of one includes the winning neuron plus the eight neighbors. However, the function $\Lambda_i(n)$ may take other forms, such as hexagonal or even a *continuous* Gaussian shape. In any case, the neighborhood function $\Lambda_i(n)$ usually begins such that it includes all neurons in the network and then gradually shrinks with time. To be specific, during the initial phase of 1000 iterations or so, when topological ordering of the synaptic weight vectors takes place, the radius of $\Lambda_i(n)$ is permitted to shrink

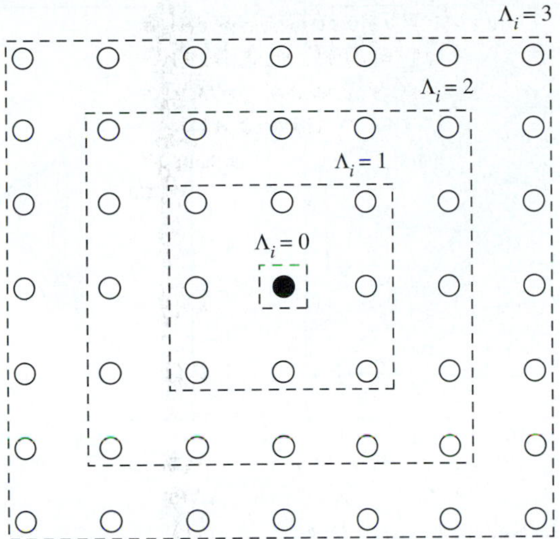

FIGURE 10.11 Square topological neighborhood Λ_i, of varying size, around "winning" neuron *i*, identified as a black circle.

linearly with time n to a small value of only a couple of neighboring neurons. During the convergence phase of the algorithm, $\Lambda_i(n)$ should contain only the nearest neighbors of winning neuron i, which may eventually be 1 or 0 neighboring neurons.

It is of interest to note that, by the appropriate use of topological neighborhoods, the SOFM algorithm ensures that the neurons in the network are *not* underutilized, a problem that plagues other competitive learning networks (Ahalt et al., 1990). Also, as mentioned previously, we may improve the utilization of computer resources by using the *renormalized* SOFM training scheme in place of varying the neighborhood function $\Lambda_i(n)$ with n (Luttrell, 1989a).

Computer Simulations

We illustrate the behavior of the SOFM algorithm by using computer simulations to study a network with 100 neurons, arranged in the form of a two-dimensional lattice with 10 rows and 10 columns. The network is trained with a two-dimensional input vector $\mathbf{x}$, whose elements x_1 and x_2 are uniformly distributed in the region $\{-1 < x_1 < +1; -1 < x_2 < +1\}$. To initialize the network, the synaptic weights are chosen from a random set.

Figure 10.12 shows four stages of training as the network learns to represent the input distribution. Figure 10.12a shows the initial values of the synaptic weights, randomly chosen. Figures 10.12b, 10.12c, and 10.12d present the values of the synaptic weight vectors, plotted as dots in the input space, after 50, 1000, and 10,000 iterations, respectively. The lines drawn in Fig. 10.12 connect neighboring neurons (across rows and columns) in the network.

The results shown in Fig. 10.12 demonstrate the ordering phase and the convergence phase that characterize the learning process of the SOFM algorithm. During the ordering phase, the map *unfolds* to form a mesh, as shown in Figs. 10.12b and 10.12c. At the end of this phase, the neurons are mapped in the correct order. During the convergence phase, the map spreads out to fill the input space. At the end of this second phase, shown in Fig. 10.12d, the statistical distribution of the neurons in the map approaches that of the input vectors, except for some edge effects. This property holds for a uniform distribution

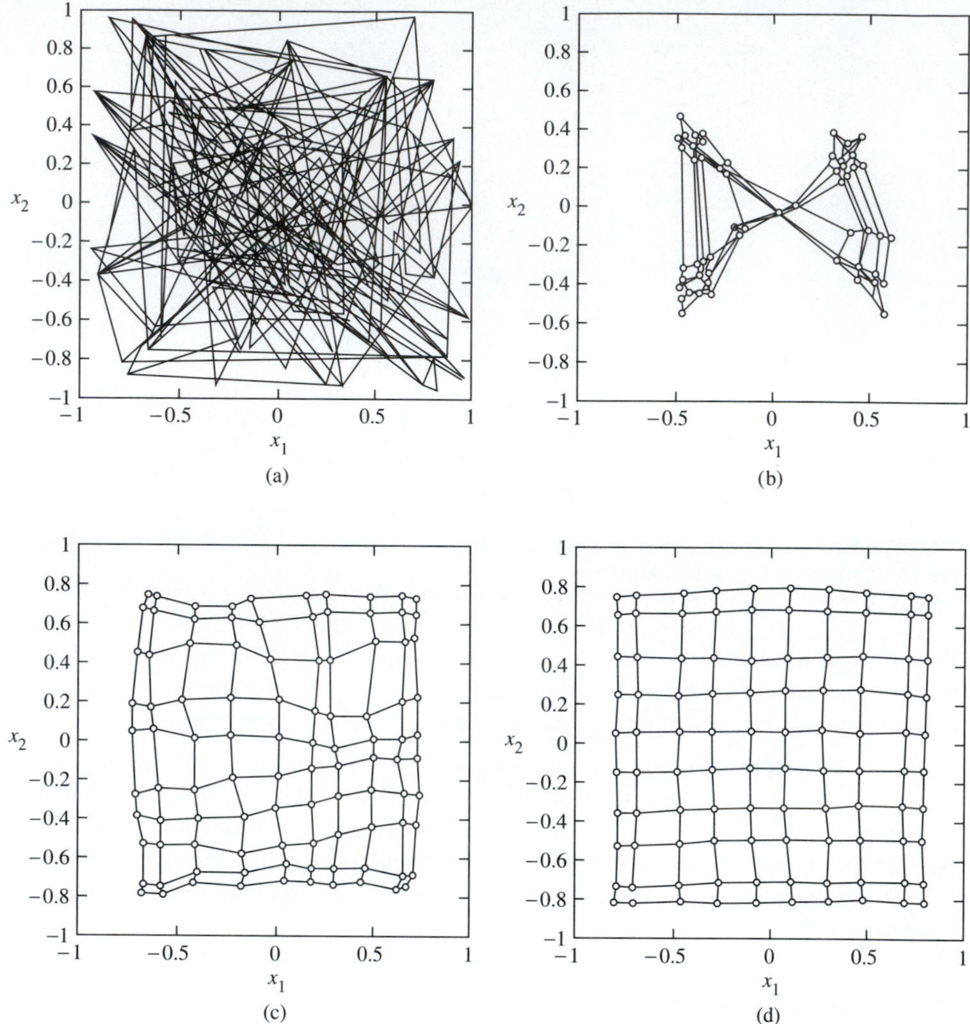

FIGURE 10.12 Demonstration of the SOFM algorithm for a uniformly distributed two-dimensional input, using a two-dimensional lattice. (a) Initial random weights. (b) Network after 50 iterations. (c) After 1000 iterations. (d) After 10,000 iterations.

of input vectors, but would *not* be the case for any other input distribution, as discussed later.

10.6 Properties of the SOFM Algorithm

Once the SOFM algorithm has converged, the *feature map* computed by the algorithm displays important statistical characteristics of the input, as discussed in this section.

To begin with, let X denote a spatially *continuous input (sensory) space,* the topology of which is defined by the metric relationship of the vectors $\mathbf{x} \in X$. Let A denote a *spatially discrete output space,* the topology of which is endowed by arranging a set of neurons as the computation nodes of a lattice. Let Φ denote a nonlinear transformation called a *feature map,* which maps the input space X onto the output space A, as shown by

$$\Phi: X \rightarrow A \tag{10.17}$$

Equation (10.17) may be viewed as an abstraction of Eq. (10.9) that defines the location of a winning neuron $i(\mathbf{x})$ developed in response to an input vector $\mathbf{x}$. For example, in a neurobiological context, the input space X may represent the coordinate set of somatosensory receptors distributed densely over the entire body surface. Correspondingly, the output space A represents the set of neurons located in that layer of the cerebral cortex to which the somatosensory receptors are confined.

Given an input vector $\mathbf{x}$, the SOFM algorithm proceeds by first identifying a best-matching or winning neuron $i(\mathbf{x})$ in the output space A, in accordance with the feature map Φ. The synaptic weight vector $\mathbf{w}_i$ of neuron $i(\mathbf{x})$ may then be viewed as a *pointer* for that neuron into the input space X. These two operations are depicted in Fig. 10.13.

The self-organizing feature mapping Φ has some important properties, as described here:

PROPERTY 1. Approximation of the Input Space
The self-organizing feature map Φ, represented by the set of synaptic weight vectors $\{\mathbf{w}_j | j = 1, 2, \ldots, N\}$, in the output space A, provides a good approximation to the input space X.

The basic aim of the SOFM algorithm is to store a large set of input vectors $\mathbf{x} \in X$ by finding a smaller set of prototypes $\mathbf{w}_j \in A$, so as to provide a "good" approximation to the original input space X. The theoretical basis of the idea just described is rooted in *vector quantization theory,* the motivation for which is dimensionality reduction or data compression (Gray, 1984). It is therefore appropriate that we present a brief discussion of this theory.

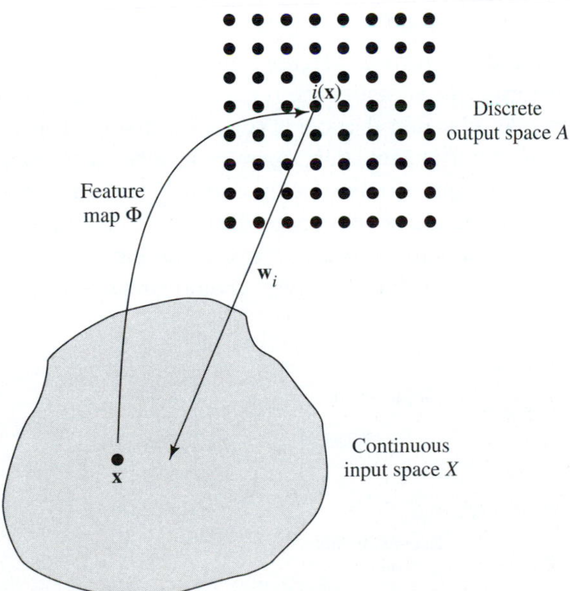

FIGURE 10.13 Illustration of a relationship between the feature map Φ and weight vector $\mathbf{w}_i$ of winning neuron i.

Consider Fig. 10.14, where $\mathbf{c}(\mathbf{x})$ acts as an *encoder* for the input vector $\mathbf{x}$ and $\mathbf{x}'(\mathbf{c})$ acts as a *decoder* for $\mathbf{c}(\mathbf{x})$. The vector $\mathbf{x}$ is selected at random from a training set (i.e., input space X), subject to an underlying probability density function $f(\mathbf{x})$. The optimum encoding–decoding scheme is determined by varying the functions $\mathbf{c}(\mathbf{x})$ and $\mathbf{x}'(\mathbf{c})$, so as to minimize an *average distortion*, defined by

$$D = \frac{1}{2}\int_{-\infty}^{\infty} d\mathbf{x}\, f(\mathbf{x})\, d(\mathbf{x},\mathbf{x}') \tag{10.18}$$

where the factor $\frac{1}{2}$ has been introduced for convenience of presentation, and $d(\mathbf{x},\mathbf{x}')$ is a *distortion* measure; and the integration is performed over the entire input space X. A popular choice for the distortion measure $d(\mathbf{x},\mathbf{x}')$ is the square of the Euclidean distance between the input vector $\mathbf{x}$ and the reproduction (reconstruction) vector $\mathbf{x}'$; that is,

$$\begin{aligned} d(\mathbf{x},\mathbf{x}') &= \|\mathbf{x} - \mathbf{x}'\|^2 \\ &= (\mathbf{x} - \mathbf{x}')^T(\mathbf{x} - \mathbf{x}') \end{aligned} \tag{10.19}$$

Thus we may rewrite Eq. (10.18) as

$$D = \frac{1}{2}\int_{-\infty}^{\infty} d\mathbf{x}\, f(\mathbf{x})\|\mathbf{x} - \mathbf{x}'\|^2 \tag{10.20}$$

The necessary conditions for the minimization of the average distortion D are embodied in the *LBG algorithm,* so named in recognition of its originators, Linde, Buzo, and Gray (1980). The conditions are two-fold:

CONDITION 1. Given the input vector $\mathbf{x}$, choose the code $\mathbf{c} = \mathbf{c}(\mathbf{x})$ to minimize the squared error distortion $\|\mathbf{x} - \mathbf{x}'(\mathbf{c})\|^2$.

CONDITION 2. Given the code $\mathbf{c}$, compute the reproduction vector $\mathbf{x}' = \mathbf{x}'(\mathbf{c})$ as the centroid of those input vectors $\mathbf{x}$ that satisfy condition 1.

Condition 1 is recognized as a *nearest-neighbor* encoding rule. Conditions 1 and 2 imply that the average distortion D is stationary (i.e., at a local minimum) with respect to variations in the encoder $\mathbf{c}(\mathbf{x})$ and decoder $\mathbf{x}'(\mathbf{c})$, respectively. The LBG algorithm, for the implementation of vector quantization, operates in a *batch* training mode. Basically, the algorithm consists of alternately adjusting the encoder $\mathbf{c}(\mathbf{x})$ in accordance with condition 1, and then adjusting the decoder $\mathbf{x}'(\mathbf{c})$ in accordance with condition 2, until the average distortion D reaches a minimum. In order to overcome the local-minimum problem, it may be necessary to run the LBG algorithm several times with different initial code vectors.

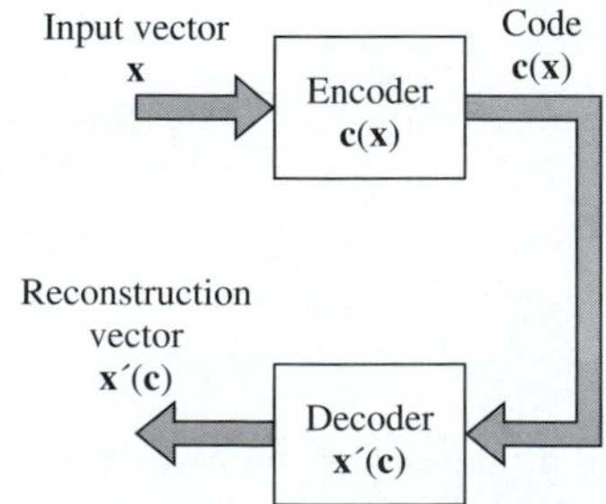

FIGURE 10.14 Encoder–decoder model.

The LBG algorithm described briefly here is closely related to the SOFM algorithm. Following Luttrell (1989b), we may delineate the form of this relationship by considering the scheme shown in Fig. 10.15, where we have introduced a signal-independent *noise* process $\boldsymbol{\nu}$ following the encoder $\mathbf{c}(\mathbf{x})$. The noise $\boldsymbol{\nu}$ is associated with the "communication channel" between the encoder and the decoder, the purpose of which is to account for the possibility that the output code $\mathbf{c}(\mathbf{x})$ may be distorted. On the basis of the model shown in Fig. 10.15, we may consider a *modified* form of average distortion as follows:

$$D_1 = \frac{1}{2}\int_{-\infty}^{\infty} d\mathbf{x}\, f(\mathbf{x}) \int_{-\infty}^{\infty} d\boldsymbol{\nu}\,\pi(\boldsymbol{\nu}) \|\mathbf{x} - \mathbf{x}'(\mathbf{c}(\mathbf{x}) + \boldsymbol{\nu})\|^2 \tag{10.21}$$

where $\pi(\boldsymbol{\nu})$ is the probability density function of the noise $\boldsymbol{\nu}$, and the second integration is over all possible realizations of the noise.

We wish to minimize the average distortion D_1 with respect to the function $\mathbf{x}'(\mathbf{c})$ in the model of Fig. 10.15. Differentiating Eq. (10.21) with respect to $\mathbf{x}'(\mathbf{c})$, we get the following partial derivative:

$$\frac{\partial D_1}{\partial \mathbf{x}'(\mathbf{c})} = -\int_{-\infty}^{\infty} d\mathbf{x}\, f(\mathbf{x})\pi(\mathbf{c}' - \mathbf{c}(\mathbf{x}))[\mathbf{x} - \mathbf{x}'(\mathbf{c})] \tag{10.22}$$

Thus, in order to minimize the average distortion D_1, conditions 1 and 2 stated earlier for the LBG algorithm must be modified as follows (Luttrell, 1989b):

CONDITION I. Given the input vector $\mathbf{x}$, choose the code $\mathbf{c} = \mathbf{c}(\mathbf{x})$ to minimize the distortion measure

$$\int_{-\infty}^{\infty} d\boldsymbol{\nu}\,\pi(\boldsymbol{\nu}) \|\mathbf{x} - \mathbf{x}'(\mathbf{c}(\mathbf{x}) + \boldsymbol{\nu})\|^2 \tag{10.23}$$

CONDITION II. Given the code $\mathbf{c}'$, compute the reconstruction vector $\mathbf{x}'(\mathbf{c})$ to satisfy the condition

$$\mathbf{x}'(\mathbf{c}) = \frac{\int_{-\infty}^{\infty} d\mathbf{x}\, f(\mathbf{x})\pi(\mathbf{c}' - \mathbf{c}(\mathbf{x}))\mathbf{x}}{\int_{-\infty}^{\infty} d\mathbf{x}\, f(\mathbf{x})\pi(\mathbf{c}' - \mathbf{c}(\mathbf{x}))} \tag{10.24}$$

Equation (10.24) is obtained simply by setting the partial derivative $\partial D_1/\partial \mathbf{x}'(\mathbf{c})$ in Eq. (10.22) equal to zero and then solving for $\mathbf{x}'(\mathbf{c})$ in closed form.

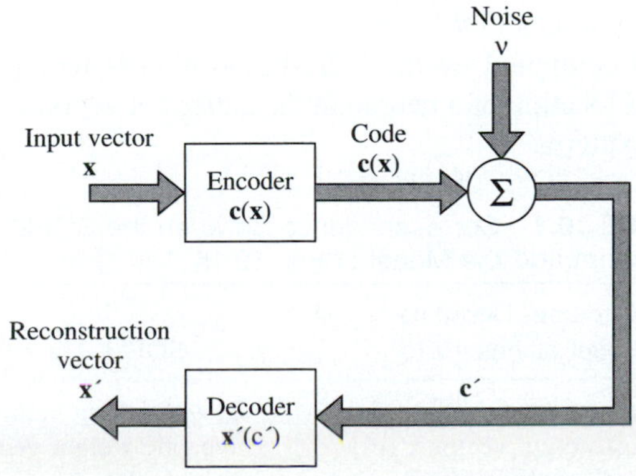

FIGURE 10.15 Noisy encoder–decoder model.

The model described in Fig. 10.14 may be viewed as a special case of that shown in Fig. 10.15. In particular, if we set the probability density function $\pi(\boldsymbol{\nu})$ equal to a Dirac delta function $\delta(\boldsymbol{\nu})$, conditions I and II reduce to conditions 1 and 2 for the LBG algorithm, respectively.

To simplify condition I, we assume that $\pi(\boldsymbol{\nu})$ is a smooth function of $\boldsymbol{\nu}$. It may then be shown that, to a second-order of approximation, the distortion measure defined in Eq. (10.23) consists of two components (Luttrell, 1989b):

- The *conventional* distortion term, defined by the squared error distortion $\|\mathbf{x} - \mathbf{x}'(\mathbf{c})\|^2$
- A *curvature* term that arises from the noise model $\pi(\boldsymbol{\nu})$

Consider next condition II. A straightforward approach to realize this condition is to use stochastic gradient descent learning. In particular, we pick input vectors $\mathbf{x}$ at random from the input space X using the factor $\int d\mathbf{x} f(\mathbf{x})$, and update the reconstruction vector $\mathbf{x}'(\mathbf{c}')$ as follows (Luttrell, 1989b):

$$\mathbf{x}'(\mathbf{c}') \leftarrow \mathbf{x}'(\mathbf{c}') + \eta\pi(\mathbf{c}' - \mathbf{c}(\mathbf{x}))[\mathbf{x} - \mathbf{x}'(\mathbf{c}')] \tag{10.25}$$

where η is the learning-rate parameter and $\mathbf{c}(\mathbf{x})$ is the nearest-neighbor encoding approximation to condition (1). The update equation (10.25) is obtained by inspection of the partial derivative in Eq. (10.22). This update is applied to all $\mathbf{c}'$, for which we have

$$\pi(\mathbf{c}' - \mathbf{c}(\mathbf{x})) > 0 \tag{10.26}$$

We may think of the gradient descent procedure described in Eq. (10.25) as a way of minimizing the distortion measure D_1 in Eq. (10.21). That is, Eqs. (10.24) and (10.25) are essentially of the same type, except for the fact that (10.24) is batch and (10.25) is continuous.

The update equation (10.25) is identical to Kohonen's SOFM algorithm, bearing in mind the correspondences listed in Table 10.1. Accordingly, we may state that the LBG algorithm for vector quantization is the batch training version of the SOFM algorithm with zero neighborhood size; for zero neighborhood, $\pi(0) = 1$. Note that in order to obtain the LBG algorithm from the batch version of the SOFM algorithm we do *not* need to make any approximations, because the curvature terms (and all higher-order terms) make no contribution when the neighborhood has *zero* width.

The important point to note from the discussion presented here is that the SOFM algorithm is a vector quantization algorithm, which provides a good approximation to the input space X. Indeed, this viewpoint provides another approach for deriving the SOFM algorithm, as exemplified by Eq. (10.25). We will have more to say on the factor $\pi(\cdot)$ of this update equation in Section 10.7.

PROPERTY 2. Topological Ordering
The feature map Φ computed by the SOFM algorithm is topologically ordered in the sense that the spatial location of a neuron in the lattice corresponds to a particular domain or feature of input patterns.

TABLE 10.1 Correspondence Between the SOFM Algorithm and the Model of Fig. 10.15

Encoding–Decoding Model of Fig. 10.15	SOFM Algorithm
Encoder $\mathbf{c}(\mathbf{x})$	Best-matching neuron $i(\mathbf{x})$
Reconstruction vector $\mathbf{x}'(\mathbf{c}')$	Synaptic weight vector $\mathbf{w}_j$
Function $\pi(\mathbf{c}' - \mathbf{c}(\mathbf{x}))$	Neighborhood function $\Lambda_{i(\mathbf{x})}$

The topological ordering property[3] is a direct consequence of the update equation (10.16) that forces the synaptic weight vector $\mathbf{w}_i$ of the winning neuron $i(\mathbf{x})$ to move toward the input vector $\mathbf{x}$. It also has the effect of moving the synaptic weight vectors $\mathbf{w}_j$ of the closest neurons j along with the winning neuron $i(\mathbf{x})$. We may therefore visualize the feature map Φ as an *elastic net* with the topology of a one- or two-dimensional lattice as prescribed in the output space A, and whose nodes have weights as coordinates in the input space X (Hertz et al., 1991). The overall aim of the algorithm may thus be stated as follows:

> *Approximate the input space X by* pointers *or* prototypes *in the form of synaptic weight vectors $\mathbf{w}_j$, in such a way that the feature map Φ provides a faithful representation of the important features that characterize the input vectors $\mathbf{x} \in X$.*

The feature map Φ is usually displayed in the input space X. Specifically, all the pointers (i.e., synaptic weight vectors) are shown as dots, and the pointers of neighboring neurons are connected with lines in accordance with the topology of the lattice. Thus, by using a line to connect two pointers $\mathbf{w}_i$ and $\mathbf{w}_j$, we are indicating that the corresponding neurons i and j are neighboring neurons in the lattice.

The topological ordering property of the SOFM algorithm is well illustrated in Fig. 10.12d. In particular, we observe that the algorithm (after convergence) captures the underlying topology of the uniform distribution at the input. In the computer simulations presented in Fig. 10.12, the input space X and output space A are both two-dimensional.

We now examine the case when the dimension of the input space X is greater than the dimension of the output space A. In spite of this mismatch, the feature map Φ is often able to form a topological representation of the input distribution. Figure 10.16 shows three different stages in the evolution of a feature map trained with input data drawn from a uniform distribution inside a square as in Fig. 10.12, but this time the computation is performed with a one-dimensional lattice of 100 neurons. The final stage of the computation is shown in Fig. 10.16c, at which point the algorithm appears to have converged. Here we see that the feature map computed by the algorithm is very distorted, in order to fill the square as densely as possible and thereby provide a good approximation to the underlying topology of the two-dimensional input space X. The approximating curve shown in Fig. 10.16c resembles a *Peano curve* (Kohonen, 1990a). An operation of the kind exemplified by the feature map of Fig. 10.16, where an input space X is represented by projecting it onto a lower-dimensional output space A, is referred to as *dimensionality reduction*. Note that in Fig. 10.16a we have initialized the algorithm on a scale different from that in Fig. 10.12a; such a charge does not affect the operation of the algorithm.

The topological ordering property of the SOFM algorithm, coupled with its computational tractability, makes it a valuable tool for the simulation of computational maps in the brain. Indeed, the self-organizing feature maps are perhaps the simplest model that can account for the adaptive formation of such topographic representations (Ritter et al., 1992).

PROPERTY 3. Density Matching

The feature map Φ reflects variations in the statistics of the input distribution: regions in the input space X from which sample vectors $\mathbf{x}$ are drawn with a high probability of occurrence are mapped onto larger domains of the output space A, and therefore with

[3] The topological property of a self-organizing feature map may be assessed quantitatively in different ways. One such quantitative measure, called the *topographic product*, is described by Bauer and Pawelzik (1992).

better resolution than regions in X from which sample vectors $\mathbf{x}$ are drawn with a low probability of occurrence.

Let $f(\mathbf{x})$ denote the multidimensional probability density function (pdf) of the input vector $\mathbf{x}$. The pdf, integrated over the entire input space X, must equal unity, as shown by

$$\int_{-\infty}^{\infty} f(\mathbf{x})\, d\mathbf{x} = 1 \tag{10.27}$$

Let $m(\mathbf{x})$ denote the map *magnification factor,* defined as the number of neurons in a small volume $d\mathbf{x}$ of the input space X. The magnification factor, integrated over the input space X, must contain the total number N of neurons in the network, as shown by

$$\int_{-\infty}^{\infty} m(\mathbf{x})\, d\mathbf{x} = N \tag{10.28}$$

For the SOFM algorithm to *match the input density* exactly, we require that (Amari, 1980)

$$m(\mathbf{x}) \propto f(\mathbf{x}) \tag{10.29}$$

This property implies that if a particular region of the input (source) layer is stimulated by an activity "spot" more often than another, then that region is mapped onto a larger region of neurons in the output layer.

In general, in the case of a two-dimensional feature map the magnification factor $m(\mathbf{x})$ is not expressible as a simple function of the pdf $f(\mathbf{x})$ of the input vector $\mathbf{x}$. Indeed, it is only in the case of a one-dimensional feature map that it is possible to derive such a relationship. For this special case, we find that, contrary to earlier supposition (Kohonen, 1982a), the magnification factor $m(\mathbf{x})$ is *not* proportional to the pdf $f(\mathbf{x})$. Two different

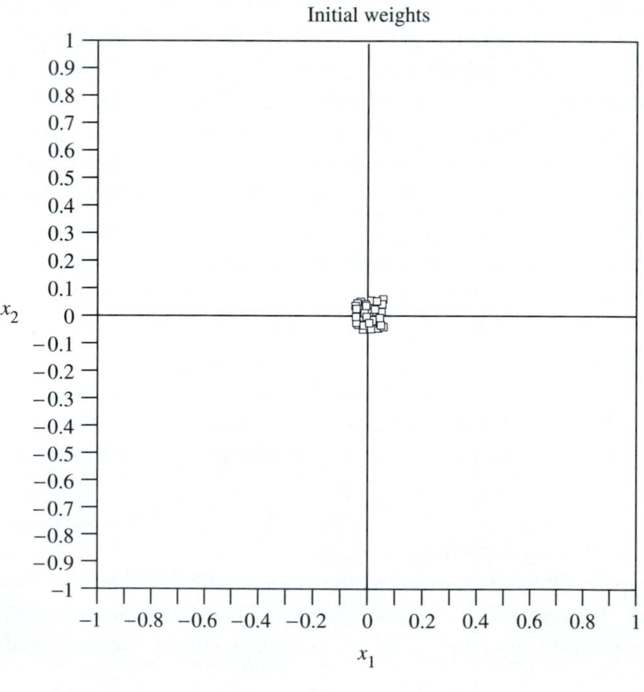

FIGURE 10.16 Another demonstration of the SOFM algorithm for a uniformly distributed two-dimensional input using a one-dimensional lattice. (a) Initial pattern.

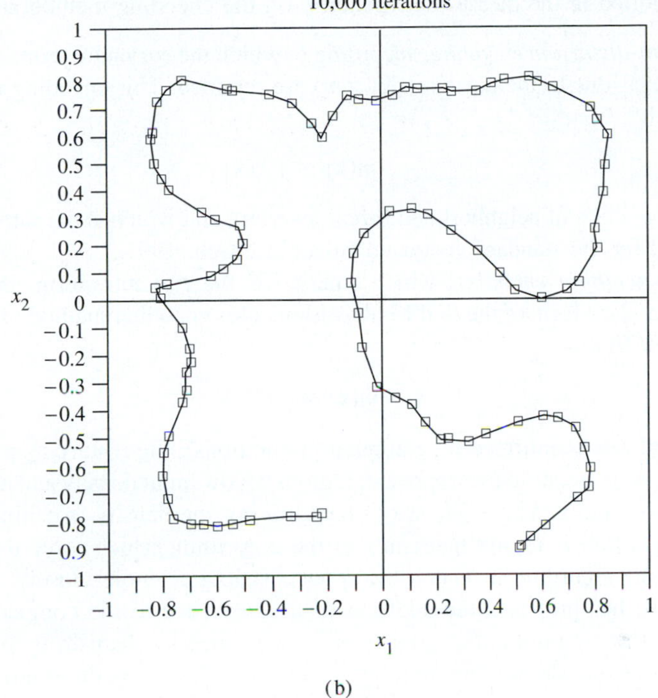

(b)

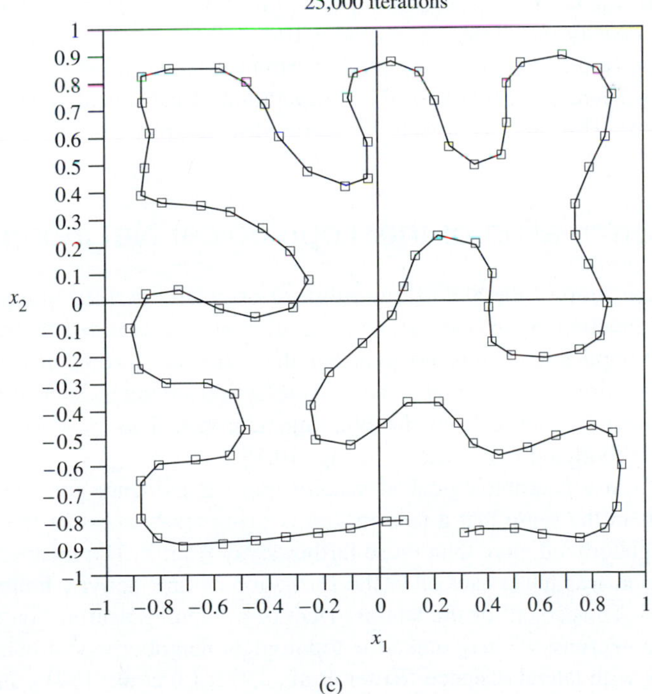

(c)

FIGURE 10.16 (continued) (b) Network after 10,000 iterations. (c) After 25,000 iterations.

results are reported in the literature, depending on the encoding method advocated:

1. *Minimum-distortion encoding,* according to which the curvature terms and all higher-order terms due to the noise model $\pi(\boldsymbol{\nu})$ are retained. This encoding method yields the result

$$m(\mathbf{x}) \propto f^{1/3}(\mathbf{x}) \tag{10.30}$$

for a large class of neighborhood functions $\pi(\boldsymbol{\nu})$, and which is the same as the result obtained for the standard vector quantizer (Luttrell, 1991a).

2. *Nearest-neighbor encoding,* which emerges if the curvature terms are ignored, as in the standard form of the SOFM algorithm. This encoding method yields the result (Ritter, 1991)

$$m(\mathbf{x}) \propto f^{2/3}(\mathbf{x}) \tag{10.31}$$

As a general rule (confirmed by computer simulations), the feature map computed by the SOFM algorithm tends to overrepresent regions of low input density and underrepresent regions of high input density. One way of improving the density-matching property of the SOFM algorithm is to add heuristics to the algorithm, which force the distribution computed by the algorithm to match the input distribution more closely. For example, DeSieno (1988) has proposed the addition of a *conscience* to the competitive learning mechanism of the algorithm. The goal of the conscience mechanism is to bring all the available neurons into the solution quickly, and to bias the competition process such that each neuron, regardless of its location in the lattice, has the chance to win the competition with a probability close to the ideal of $1/N$, where N is the total number of neurons. For a description of the conscience algorithm, and comparison with the SOFM algorithm in the context of density matching, see Problem 10.9.

Another way of matching the computed distribution to the input distribution is to use an information-theoretic approach for the computation of the self-organizing feature map (Linsker, 1989b). This latter approach is described in Chapter 11.

10.7 Reformulation of the Topological Neighborhood

In the traditional form of the SOFM algorithm as originally derived in Section 10.5, the neighborhood function Λ_i around the winning neuron i is assumed to have a constant amplitude. The implication of this model is that all the neurons located inside this topological neighborhood fire at the same rate, and the interaction among those neurons is independent of their lateral distance from the winning neuron i. This most simple form of a topological neighborhood is illustrated in Fig. 10.17.

However, from a neurobiological viewpoint there is evidence for lateral interaction among neurons in the sense that a neuron that is firing tends to excite the neurons in its immediate neighborhood more than those farther away from it. The feedback form of this lateral interaction was taken care of in the formation of an ‘‘activity bubble’’ discussed in Section 10.4. To account for the lateral effect of a winning neuron i on the activity of its neighboring neurons, we may make the topological neighborhood around the winning neuron i decay with lateral distance (Ritter et al., 1992; Lo et al., 1991). Justification for this form of topological neighborhood is also found in the update equation (10.25) derived from the vector quantization approach.

Let $d_{j,i}$ denote the lateral distance of neuron j from the winning neuron i, which is a Euclidean measure in the output space $\mathcal{A}$. Let $\pi_{j,i}$ denote the amplitude of the topological

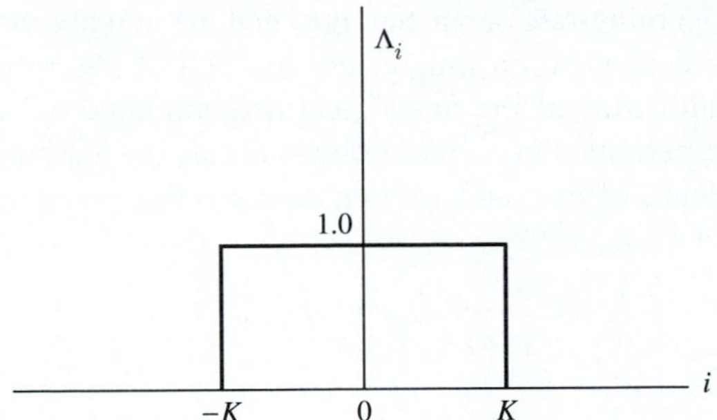

FIGURE 10.17 Simple form of a topological neighborhood.

neighborhood centered on the winning neuron i. The amplitude $\pi_{j,i}$ is (usually) a unimodal function of the lateral distance $d_{j,i}$, such that it satisfies two distinct requirements:

- The topological neighborhood $\pi_{j,i}$ is maximum at $d_{i,i} = 0$; in other words, it attains its maximum value at the winning neuron i for which the distance $d_{i,i}$ is of course zero.
- The amplitude of the topological neighborhood $\pi_{j,i}$ decreases with increasing lateral distance $d_{j,i}$, decaying to zero for $d_{j,i} \rightarrow \infty$.

A typical choice of $\pi_{j,i}$ that satisfies these two requirements is the Gaussian-type function

$$\pi_{j,i} = \exp\left(-\frac{d_{j,i}^2}{2\sigma^2}\right) \tag{10.32}$$

where the parameter σ is the "effective width" of the topological neighborhood, as illustrated in Fig. 10.18. Except for a scaling factor, the nonnegative function $\pi_{j,i}$ of Eq. (10.32) is in the form of a density function, as implied by the update equation (10.25).

Given the new form of the topological neighborhood, we may now rewrite the recursive equation (10.16) of the SOFM algorithm for updating the synaptic weight vector $\mathbf{w}_j$ of neuron j at lateral distance $d_{j,i}$ from the winning neuron $i(\mathbf{x})$ as follows:

$$\mathbf{w}_j(n + 1) = \mathbf{w}_j(n) + \eta(n)\pi_{j,i(\mathbf{x})}(n)[\mathbf{x}(n) - \mathbf{w}_j(n)] \tag{10.33}$$

where n denotes discrete time. The rest of the SOFM algorithm is the same as in the summary presented in Section 10.5.

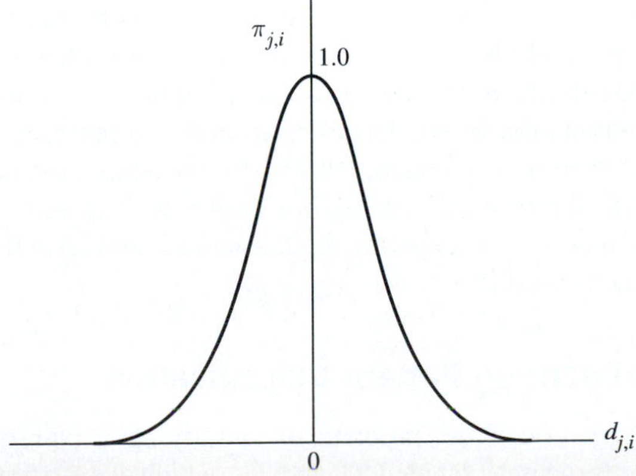

FIGURE 10.18 Gaussian neighborhood function.

In Eq. (10.33) the learning-rate parameter $\eta(n)$ and the neighborhood function $\pi_{j,i(\mathbf{x})}(n)$ are both shown to be dependent on time n. For the SOFM algorithm to converge, it is important that the width $\sigma(n)$ of the topological neighborhood as well as the learning-rate parameter $\eta(n)$ be permitted to decrease slowly during the learning process. A popular choice for the dependence of $\sigma(n)$ and $\eta(n)$ on time n is the exponential decay described as, respectively (Ritter et al., 1992),

$$\sigma(n) = \sigma_0 \exp\left(-\frac{n}{\tau_1}\right) \tag{10.34}$$

and

$$\eta(n) = \eta_0 \exp\left(-\frac{n}{\tau_2}\right) \tag{10.35}$$

The constants σ_0 and η_0 are the respective values of $\sigma(n)$ and $\eta(n)$ at the initiation of the SOFM algorithm (i.e., at $n = 0$), and τ_1 and τ_2 are their respective *time constants.* Even though it is not optimal, the exponential decay formulas described in Eqs. (10.34) and (10.35) for the width of the topological neighborhood and the learning-rate parameter often turn out to be adequate for the problem at hand. Note that Eqs. (10.34) and (10.35) are applied to the neighborhood function and the learning-rate parameter, respectively, only during the ordering phase (i.e., the first thousand iterations or so), after which small values are used for a very long time.

10.8 Adaptive Pattern Classification

In *pattern classification,* the requirement is to classify the signal sets presented to an observer into a finite number of classes (patterns) such that the average probability of misclassification is minimized. In such a task, the issue of particular importance is to delineate the class boundaries where decisions are made. The solution to the pattern classification problem may be obtained by using a Bayesian approach, which (typically) assumes a Gaussian distribution. Alternatively, we may use a nonparametric approach based on the self-organizing feature map, by exploiting the density-matching property of the map. However, from the outset, it should be emphasized that the feature map is intended only to visualize metric-topological relationships of input vectors $\mathbf{x}$. As such, it is *not* recommended that the feature map be used by itself for pattern classification or other decision-making processes. Rather, to achieve the best results for pattern classification, the use of the feature map should be accompanied by a supervised learning scheme (Kangas et al., 1990). One possibility is the use of a *hybrid* approach as shown in Fig. 10.19, which involves a combination of the feature map and a supervised linear classifier for adaptive pattern classification (Lippmann, 1989b). For the adaptation of the linear classifier we may use the LMS algorithm described in Chapter 5. The scheme of Fig. 10.19 is illustrated by way of a computer experiment, considered next. Another hybrid approach is considered in the next section.

Computer Experiment on Pattern Classification

For this experiment we revisit the problem of classifying a pair of overlapping two-dimensional Gaussian processes labeled $\mathscr{C}_1$ and $\mathscr{C}_2$, which we first studied in Chapter 6 using a multilayer perceptron and then again in Chapter 7 using an RBF network. Class $\mathscr{C}_1$ has a mean of (0,0) and a variance of 1. Class $\mathscr{C}_2$ has a mean of (2,0) and a variance

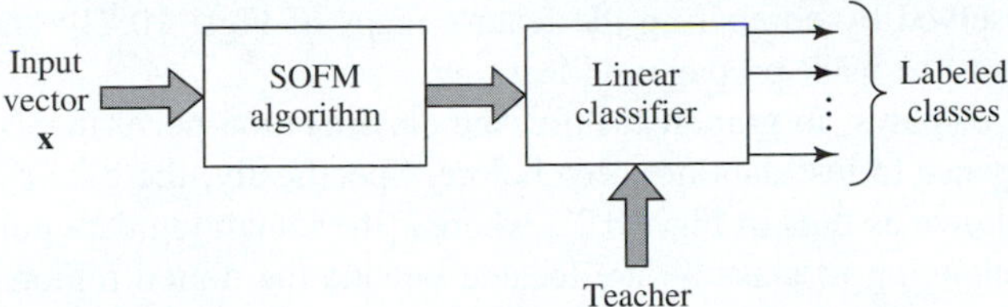

FIGURE 10.19 Two-stage adaptive pattern classifier.

of 4. In Fig. 10.20 we show a scatter plot of both processes, consisting of 1000 points. To classify these two processes, assumed to be equiprobable, we propose to use a hybrid network consisting of two components:

- A self-organizing feature map, acting as a preprocessor: The map consists of a two-dimensional lattice made up of 3-by-3 neurons, with each neuron having two inputs. Thus, both the input space X and the output space A are two-dimensional in this experiment. The feature map Φ, representing the projection of the neurons onto the input space X, provides a nonlinear transformation of the input space.
- A linear adaptive classifier consisting of two neurons fed by the outputs of the neurons constituting the 3-by-3 lattice; the linear classifier is trained with the LMS algorithm. The outputs of the two neurons represent the decisions made by the classifier in favor of class $\mathscr{C}_1$ or class $\mathscr{C}_2$.

Figure 10.21 illustrates the formation of the two-dimensional feature map captured by the SOFM algorithm at various stages of the self-organization process. Figure 10.21a displays the initial state of the feature map chosen in a random fashion. Figures 10.21b–10.21d display the states of the feature map computed after 400 iterations, 1,000 iterations, and 20,000 iterations, respectively. From the experimental results shown in Fig. 10.21, we observe that a self-organizing feature map does not suffer from overtraining,

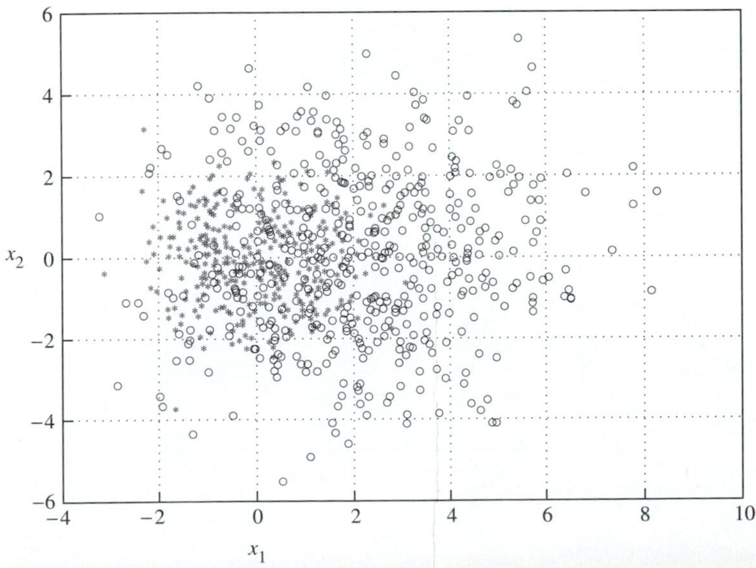

FIGURE 10.20 Joint scalar plot of classes $\mathscr{C}_1$ and $\mathscr{C}_2$ used for computer experiment on the SOFM algorithm: * = $\mathscr{C}_1$, ○ = $\mathscr{C}_2$.

as is readily observed by comparing the feature maps of Figs. 10.21c and 10.21d. This is in direct contrast to back-propagation learning.

Figure 10.22 displays, in graphical form, the classification performance of the hybrid classifier in response to test data not seen before. Specifically, the data points belonging to class $\mathscr{C}_1$ are shown as dots in Fig. 10.22, whereas the remaining data points (not shown in the figure) belonging to class $\mathscr{C}_2$ are located outside the dotted region. Thus, for this computer experiment, the decision boundary constructed by the hybrid classifier is defined by the boundary of the dotted region shown in Fig. 10.22. This decision boundary is seen to be fairly close to that of the optimum Bayesian classifier, which is defined by the circle

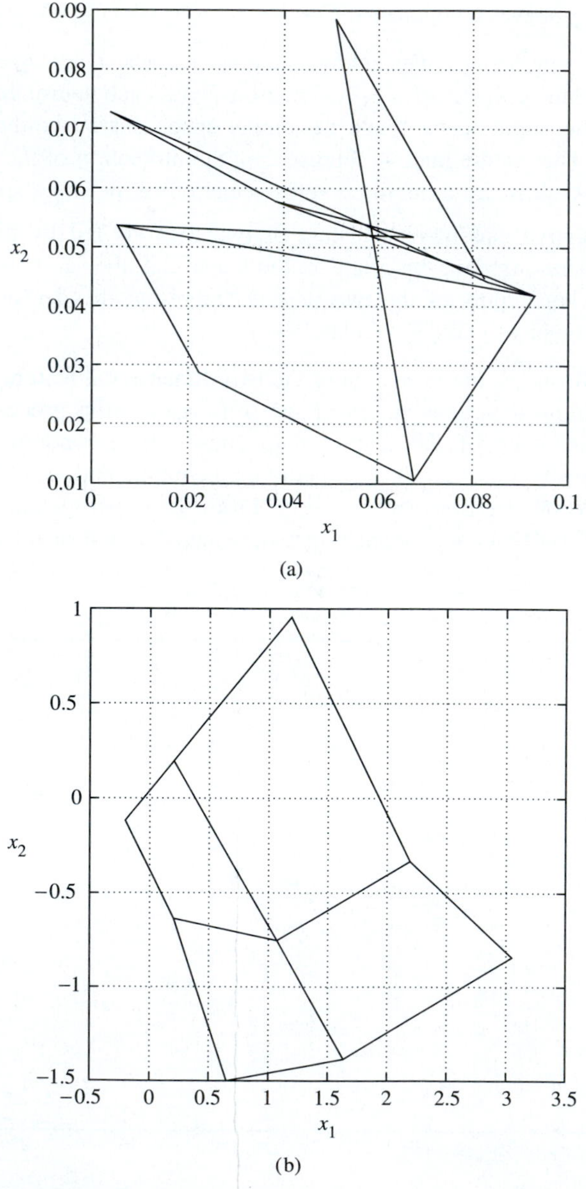

FIGURE 10.21 Results of computer experiment on pattern classification using the combination of a two-dimensional feature map and supervised linear classifier. (a) Initial random weights of 3-by-3 lattice. (b) Feature map after 400 iterations.

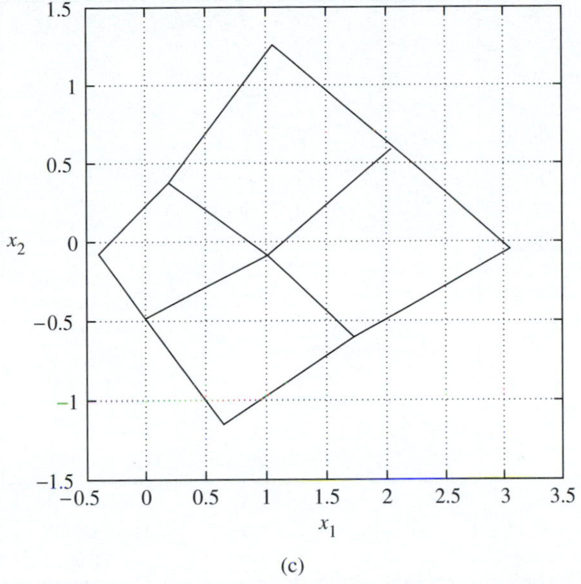

(c)

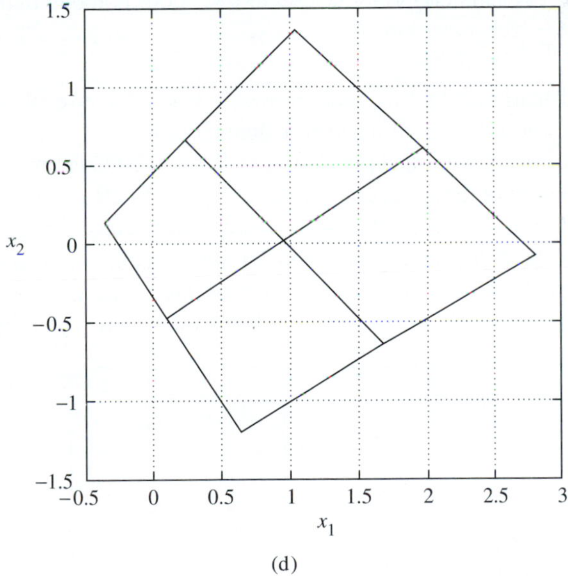

(d)

FIGURE 10.21 (continued) (c) Feature map after 1,000 iterations. (d) After 20,000 iterations.

shown in Fig. 10.22. The average classification accuracy of the hybrid classifier is estimated to be 80.3 percent, a result that is close to a classification accuracy of 81.51 percent for the optimum Bayesian classifier.

10.9 Learning Vector Quantization

As mentioned in the previous section, improved classification performance with a self-organizing feature map can be obtained by using it in conjunction with a supervised learning technique. In that section we considered the use of a linear adaptive classifier

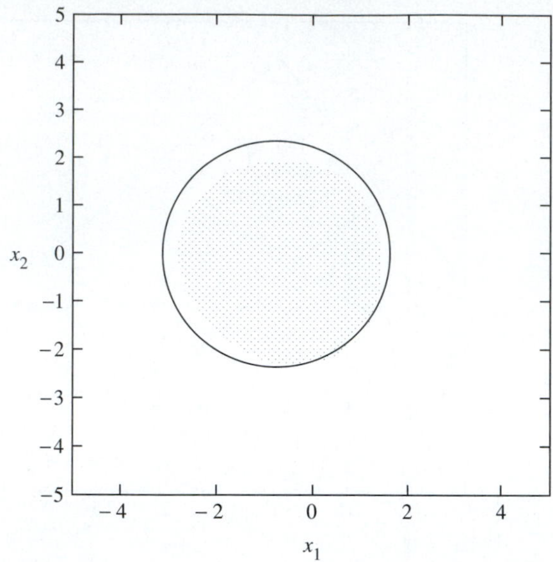

FIGURE 10.22 Graphical portrayal of the decision boundary constructed by the hybrid classifier for the computer experiment, which is defined by the boundary of the dotted region. The circular decision boundary shown in the figure pertains to the optimum Bayesian classifier.

for the supervised learning; in this section we consider the use of another supervised learning technique known as learning vector quantization.

Vector quantization, as discussed previously in Section 10.6, is a technique that exploits the underlying structure of input vectors for the purpose of data compression or equivalent bandwidth compression (Linde et al., 1980; Gray, 1984). Specifically, an input space is divided into a number of distinct regions, and for each region a *reproduction (reconstruction) vector* is defined. When the quantizer is presented a new input vector, the region in which the vector lies is first determined, and it is then represented by the reproduction

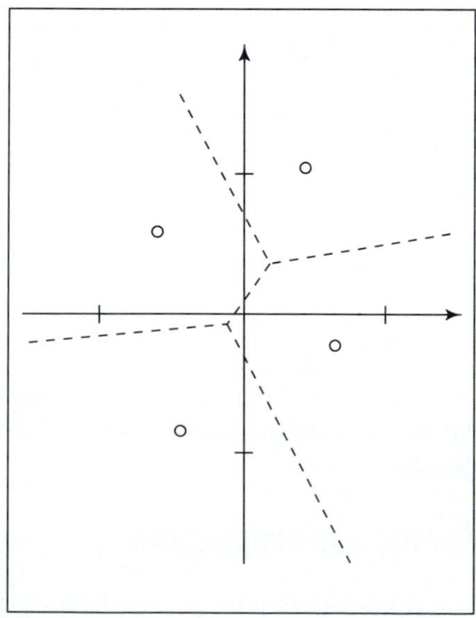

FIGURE 10.23 Voronoi diagram involving four cells. (Adapted from R.M. Gray, 1984, with permission of IEEE.)

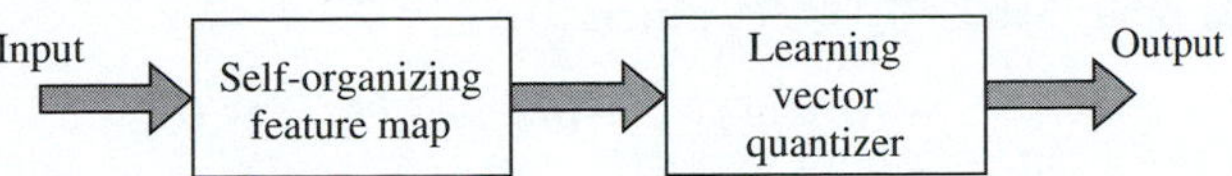

FIGURE 10.24 Another method of adaptive pattern classification, using a self-organizing feature map and learning vector quantizer.

vector for that region. Thus, by using an encoded version of this reproduction vector for storage or transmission in place of the original input vector, considerable savings in storage or transmission bandwidth can be realized, albeit at the expense of some distortion. The collection of possible reproduction vectors is called the *reproduction codebook* or, simply, *codebook* of the quantizer, and its members are called *codewords*, or *templates*.

A vector quantizer with minimum encoding distortion is called a *Voronoi quantizer*, since the *Voronoi cells* about a set of points in an input space correspond to a partition of that space according to the *nearest-neighbor rule* based on the Euclidean metric (Gersho, 1982). Figure 10.23 shows an example of an input space divided into four Voronoi cells with their associated Voronoi vectors (i.e., reproduction vectors). Each Voronoi cell contains those points of the input space that are the closest to the Voronoi vector among the totality of such points.

The SOFM algorithm provides an "approximate" method for computing the Voronoi vectors in an unsupervised manner, with the approximation being specified by the synaptic weight vectors of the neurons in the feature map; this is merely restating Property 1 of the SOFM algorithm discussed in Section 10.6. The computation of the feature map may therefore be viewed as the first of two stages for solving the pattern-classification problem, as depicted in Fig. 10.24. The second stage is provided by learning vector quantization, which is described next.

Learning vector quantization[4] (LVQ) is a supervised learning technique that uses class information to move the Voronoi vectors slightly, so as to improve the quality of the classifier decision regions. An input vector $\mathbf{x}$ is picked at random from the input space. If the class labels of the input vector $\mathbf{x}$ and a Voronoi vector $\mathbf{w}$ agree, then the Voronoi vector $\mathbf{w}$ is moved in the direction of the input vector $\mathbf{x}$. If, on the other hand, the class labels of the input vector $\mathbf{x}$ and the Voronoi vector $\mathbf{w}$ disagree, the Voronoi vector $\mathbf{w}$ is moved away from the input vector $\mathbf{x}$.

Let $\{\mathbf{w}_j | j = 1, 2, \ldots, N\}$ denote the set of Voronoi vectors, and $\{\mathbf{x}_i \| 1, 2, \ldots, L\}$ denote the set of input (observation) vectors. We assume that there are many more input vectors than Voronoi vectors. The learning vector quantization (LVQ) algorithm proceeds as follows:

- Suppose that the Voronoi vector $\mathbf{w}_c$ is the closest to the input vector $\mathbf{x}_i$. Let $\mathscr{C}_{\mathbf{w}_c}$ denote the class associated with the Voronoi vector $\mathbf{w}_c$, and $\mathscr{C}_{\mathbf{x}_i}$ denote the class label of the input vector $\mathbf{x}_i$. The Voronoi vector $\mathbf{w}_c$ is adjusted as follows:
  - If $\mathscr{C}_{\mathbf{w}_c} = \mathscr{C}_{\mathbf{x}_i}$, then

$$\mathbf{w}_c(n + 1) = \mathbf{w}_c(n) + \alpha_n[\mathbf{x}_i - \mathbf{w}_c(n)] \qquad (10.36)$$

where $0 < \alpha_n < 1$.

[4] The idea of learning vector quantization was originated by Kohonen in 1986; three versions of this algorithm are described by Kohonen (1990b). The version of the algorithm discussed in this section is the first version of learning vector quantization, referred to as LVQ1 by Kohonen.

Kohonen et al. (1992) describe a package that contains all the computer programs for the correct application of LVQ1 and certain other versions of the learning vector quantization algorithm. The package also includes a program for the monitoring of the codebook vectors at any time during the learning process.

- If, on the other hand, $\mathscr{C}_{\mathbf{w}_c} \neq \mathscr{C}_{\mathbf{x}_i}$, then

$$\mathbf{w}_c(n + 1) = \mathbf{w}_c(n) - \alpha_n[\mathbf{x}_i - \mathbf{w}_c(n)] \tag{10.37}$$

- The other Voronoi vectors are not modified.

It is desirable for the learning constant α_n to decrease monotonically with the number of iterations n. For example, α_n may initially be about 0.1 or smaller, and then decrease linearly with n. After several passes through the input data, the Voronoi vectors would typically converge, and the training is complete.

The learning vector quantization algorithm is a stochastic approximation algorithm. Baras and LaVigna (1990) discuss the convergence properties of the algorithm using a tool rooted in the theory of stochastic approximation; this special tool is described in Appendix B.

10.10 Applications

The properties of self-organizing feature maps discussed in Section 10.6 make them an interesting tool for two distinct classes of applications:

- Simulators used for the purpose of understanding and modeling of computational maps in the brain
- Subsystems for practical applications such as robot movement, speech recognition, vector coding, and adaptive equalization

A large variety of applications of self-organizing feature maps have been reported in the literature (Kohonen, 1990a), which include the following:

- Control of robot arms (Martinetz et al., 1990)
- Phonetic typewriter (Kohonen, 1988c)
- Vector quantization (Luttrell, 1989a; Chiueh et al., 1993)
- Adaptive equalization (Kohonen et al., 1992) and blind equalization (Haykin, 1992)
- Texture segmentation (Oja, 1992)
- Radar classification of sea ice (Orlando et al., 1991)
- Brain modeling (Ritter et al., 1992; Obermayer et al., 1991; Cottrell and Fort, 1986).
- Biosequencing (Ferrán and Ferrara, 1991).
- Clone detection in large telecommunication software systems (Carter et al., 1993)

In this section we focus on one important application of the SOFM algorithm, namely, hierarchical vector quantization that involves the hybrid use of the SOFM and LBG algorithms, as described next.

Hierarchical Vector Quantization

We begin a discussion of this application by stating a fundamental result of Shannon's *rate distortion theory,* a branch of information theory devoted to data compression (Gray, 1984):

> Better data compression performance can always be achieved by coding vectors instead of scalars, even if the source of data is memoryless (e.g., it provides a sequence of independent

random variables), or if the data compression system has memory (i.e., the action of an encoder depends on past encoder inputs or outputs).

Because of this fundamental result, there has been an extensive research effort devoted to vector quantization (Makhoul et al., 1985; Gray, 1984; Linde et al., 1980).

However, conventional vector quantization algorithms require a prohibitive amount of computation, which has hindered their practical use. The most time-consuming part of vector quantization is the encoding operation. For encoding, the input vector must be compared with each code vector in the codebook in order to determine which particular code yields the minimum distortion. For a codebook containing N code vectors, the time taken for encoding is on the order of N, which can therefore be large for large N. Luttrell (1989a) describes a *multistage hierarchical vector quantizer* that trades off accuracy for speed of encoding. This scheme is not simply the standard tree search of a codebook; it is genuinely new. The multistage hierarchical vector quantizer attempts to factorize the overall vector quantization into a number of suboperations, each of which requires very little computation. Desirably, the factorization is reduced to a single table look up per suboperation. By clever use of the SOFM algorithm to train each stage of the quantizer, the loss in accuracy can be small (as low as a fraction of a decibel), while the gain in speed of computation is large.

Consider two vector quantizers VQ_1 and VQ_2, with VQ_1 feeding its output into VQ_2. The output from VQ_2 is the final encoded version of the original input signal applied to VQ_1. In performing its quantization, it is inevitable for VQ_2 to discard some information. Insofar as VQ_1 is concerned, the sole effect of VQ_2 is therefore to distort the information output by VQ_1. It thus appears that the appropriate training method for VQ_1 is the SOFM algorithm, which accounts for the signal distortion induced by VQ_2 (Luttrell, 1989a). In order to use the LBG algorithm to train VQ_2 we need only assume that the output of VQ_2 is not corrupted before we do the reconstruction. Then we do not need to introduce any noise model (at the output of VQ_2) with its associated finite-width neighborhood function.

It is a straightforward matter to generalize this heuristic argument to a multistage vector quantizer (Luttrell, 1989a). Specifically, each stage must be designed to account for the distortion induced by all *subsequent* stages, and model it as noise. To do so, the SOFM algorithm is used to train all the stages of the quantizer, except for the last stage for which the LBG algorithm is adequate.

Hierarchical vector quantization is a special case of multistage vector quantization (Luttrell, 1989a). As an illustration, consider the quantization of 4-by-1 input vector

$$\mathbf{x} = [x_1, x_2, x_3, x_4]^T$$

In Fig. 10.25a we show a single-stage vector quantizer for $\mathbf{x}$. Alternatively, we may use a two-stage hierarchical vector quantizer as depicted in Fig. 10.25b. The significant difference between these two schemes is that the input dimension of the quantizer in Fig. 10.25a is four, whereas for the quantizer in Fig. 10.25b it is two. Accordingly, the quantizer of Fig. 10.25b requires a look-up table of smaller sizes, and is therefore simpler to implement than that of Fig. 10.25a. This is the advantage of a hierarchical quantizer over a conventional quantizer.

Luttrell (1989a) has demonstrated the performance of a multistage hierarchical vector quantizer applied to various stochastic time series, with little loss in encoding accuracy. In Fig. 10.26 we have reproduced Luttrell's results for the case of a correlated Gaussian noise process generated by using a *first-order autoregressive (AR) model*:

$$x(n + 1) = \rho x(n) + e(n) \tag{10.38}$$

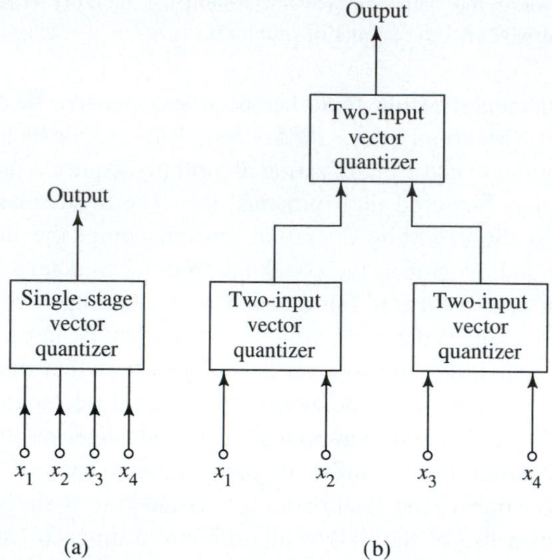

FIGURE 10.25 (a) Single-stage vector quantizer with four-dimensional input. (b) Two-stage hierarchical vector quantizer using two-input vector quantizers. (From S.P. Luttrell, 1989a, British Crown copyright.)

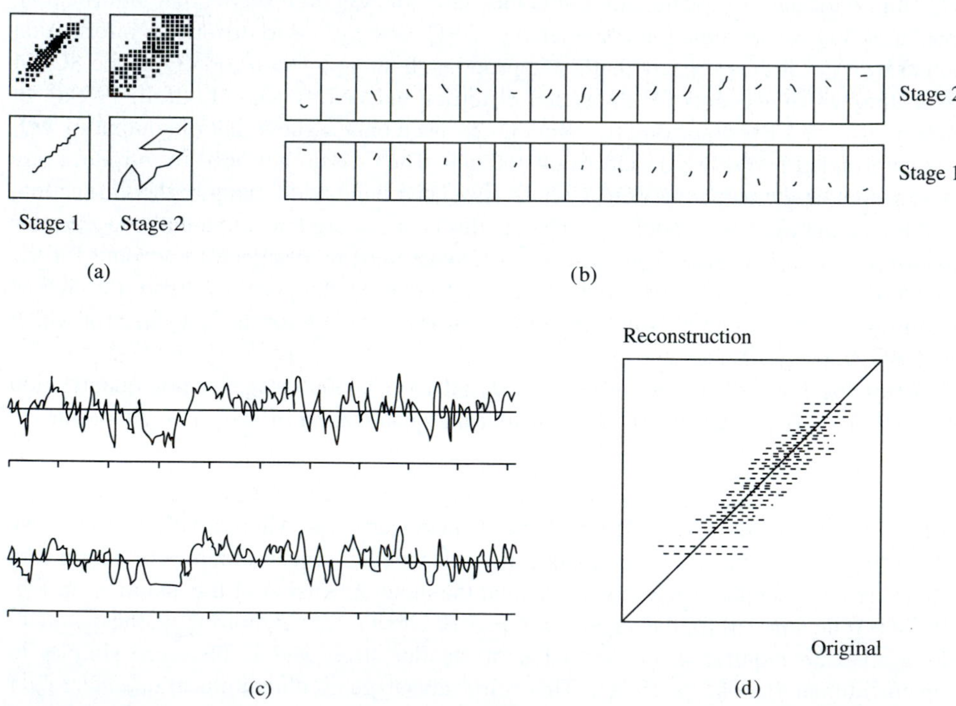

FIGURE 10.26 Two-stage encoding/decoding results for correlated Gaussian noise input. Correlation coefficient $\rho = 0.85$. (From S.P. Luttrell, 1989a, British Crown Copyright.)

where ρ is the AR coefficient and the $e(n)$ are independent and identically distributed (i.i.d.) Gaussian random variables of zero mean and unit variance. Hence, we may readily show that $x(n)$ is characterized as follows:

$$E[x(n)] = 0 \tag{10.39}$$

$$E[x^2(n)] = \frac{1}{1 - \rho^2} \tag{10.40}$$

$$\frac{E[x(n+1)x(n)]}{E[x^2(n)]} = \rho \tag{10.41}$$

Thus ρ may also be viewed as the *correlation coefficient* of the time series $\{x(n)\}$. To initiate the generation of the time series according to Eq. (10.38), a Gaussian random variable of zero mean and variance $1/(1 - \rho^2)$ was used for $x(0)$, and the value $\rho = 0.85$ was used for the correlation coefficient.

For the vector quantization, a hierarchical encoder with a four-dimensional input space, like the binary tree of Fig. 10.25b, was used. For the AR time series $\{x(n)\}$, translational symmetry implies that only *two* distinct look-up tables are needed. The size of each look-up table depends exponentially on the number of input bits, and linearly on the number of output bits. During training, a large number of bits is needed to represent numbers for a correct computation of the updates described in Eq. (10.25); so the look-up tables are not used during training. Once training is complete, however, the number of bits may be reduced to their normal level, and the look-up table entries filled in as required. For the encoder shown in Fig. 10.25b, the input samples were approximated by using four bits per sample. For all stages of the encoder, N (= 17) code vectors were used, and so the number of output bits from each look-up table was approximately four too. Thus, the address space size of both the first stage and second stage look-up tables is 256 ($= 2^{4+4}$), which means that the overall memory requirements for representing the look-up tables are modest.

Figure 10.26 shows the encoding–decoding results obtained with $x(n)$ as the input. The lower half of Fig. 10.26a shows the code vectors for each of the two stages as a curve embedded in a two-dimensional input space; the upper half of Fig. 10.26a presents estimates of the corresponding co-occurrence matrices using 16-by-16 bins. Figure 10.26b presents, as fragments of the time series, the following:

- The code vector computed by the first encoder stage
- The reconstruction vector computed by the second stage that minimizes the mean-squares distortion, while keeping all other variables fixed

Figure 10.26c presents 512 samples of both the original time series (top curve) and its reconstruction (bottom curve) from the output of the last encoder stage; the horizontal scale in Fig. 10.26c is half that in Fig. 10.26b. Finally, Fig. 10.26d presents a co-occurrence matrix created from a pair of samples: an original time series sample and its corresponding reconstruction. The width of the band in Fig. 10.26d indicates the extent of the distortion produced by the hierarchical vector quantization.

Examining the waveforms in Fig. 10.26c, we see that the reconstruction is a very good representation of the original time series, except for some positive and negative peaks that were clipped. According to Luttrell (1989a), the normalized mean-squared distortion was computed to be 0.15, which is almost as good (0.05 dB loss) as the 8.8 dB obtained with a single-stage four-sample block encoder using 1 bit per sample (Jayant and Noll, 1984).

10.11 Discussion

The weight update equation (10.16) is basic to the formation of a self-organizing feature map. This update formula represents a combination of three distinct ideas:

- The selection of a winning neuron $i(\mathbf{x})$, which is achieved (in the first place) by applying the similarity-matching formula of Eq. (10.9).
- The formulation of a neighborhood function $\Lambda_{i(\mathbf{x})}(n)$ around the winning neuron $i(\mathbf{x})$, an idea that was first introduced by Kohonen (1982a).
- A competitive learning rule, according to which the adjustment $\Delta w_{jk}(n)$ applied to the synaptic weight $w_{jk}(n)$ of neuron j inside the neighborhood function $\Lambda_{i(\mathbf{x})}(n)$ is equal to $\eta(n)[x_k(n) - w_{jk}(n)]$, where $x_k(n)$ is the input signal and $\eta(n)$ is the learning-rate parameter. In fact, this learning rule was first introduced into the neural network literature by Grossberg (1969).

It is the combination of these three ideas that endows the SOFM algorithm with its selective tuning capability.

The SOFM algorithm is simple to implement, yet a mathematical analysis of its convergence behavior is a difficult undertaking.[5] Unfortunately, in general, there is no well-defined criterion that we can use to assure the stability of the map formed by the algorithm. Rather, we have some heuristics along the lines described in Section 10.5, which have been developed on the basis of experience gained from extensive computer simulations, and the use of which is intended to minimize the risk of the map becoming unstable. In order to pursue a mathematical analysis of the convergence problem in a general context, we may begin by viewing the learning process involved in the formation of the map as a stochastic process. Specifically, the state of the model at time n is given by the set of synaptic weight vectors

$$\mathbf{w}(n) = \{\mathbf{w}_1(n), \mathbf{w}_2(n), \ldots, \mathbf{w}_N(n)\}$$

where N is the total number of neurons in the model. Indeed, the SOFM algorithm used to update the state $\mathbf{w}(n)$ is a *Markov process,* defined by a set of possible states and a set of transition probabilities between states; see the discussion in Section 8.10. To proceed further, we invoke the use of a mathematical tool known as the *Fokker–Planck equation,* a description of which is presented in Appendix D. The use of the Fokker–Planck equation provides a means to describe the time evolution of the underlying weight-space probability distribution of the model. We thus have a firm foundation for the study of the SOFM algorithm. Such an approach is described by Ritter and Schulten (1988), who have derived a Fokker–Planck equation for the SOFM algorithm in the vicinity of equilibrium condition and for small values of the learning-rate parameter. They have used this approach to investigate the conditions for convergence and the stability properties of the algorithm. Good agreement between theory and statistical measurements based on computer simulations is reported. A description of this work is also presented in the book by Ritter et al. (1992).

PROBLEMS

10.1 What would happen in a competitive learning network if a limit is imposed on the number of patterns to which each output neuron can respond?

[5] Lo et al. (1993) present a step-by-step constructive proof that demonstrates the asymptotic convergence of the SOFM algorithm to a unique solution for the special case of a one-dimensional lattice fed from a uniform, one-dimensional input distribution. The proof of convergence is extended to a two-dimensional lattice fed from a uniform, two-dimensional input distribution.

10.2 It is said that the SOFM algorithm based on competitive learning lacks any tolerance against hardware failure, yet the algorithm is error-tolerant in that a small perturbation applied to the input vector causes the output to jump from the winning neuron to a neighboring one. Discuss the implications of these two statements.

10.3 Show that the Mexican hat function may be generated as the difference between two Gaussian functions of the same mean but different variances, plus a small positive constant.

10.4 The function $g(y_j)$ denotes a nonlinear function of the response y_j, which is used in the SOFM algorithm as described in Eq. (10.11). Discuss the implication of what could happen if the constant term in the Taylor series expansion of $g(y_j)$ is nonzero.

10.5 Figure P10.5 shows six different patterns for lateral interconnections used for the formulation of an activity bubble. Using these patterns, investigate the effect of the shape of the lateral interaction on the bubble-formation phenomenon.

10.6 In this experiment we extend the idea of activity bubble formation to a two-dimensional lattice. Figure P10.6 shows the two-dimensional Mexican hat function. Use a two-dimensional lattice made up of 20-by-20 neurons. The input signal applied to the network is a two-dimensional sinusoid of amplitude 2, given by

$$x_{ij} = 2 \sin \left(\frac{\pi}{14.4} (i^2 + j^2)^{1/2} \right)$$

Using computer simulations, plot the activity bubble after 0, 3, and 20 iterations.

10.7 Assume that $\pi(\boldsymbol{\nu})$ is a smooth function of $\boldsymbol{\nu}$ in the model of Fig. 10.15. Using a Taylor expansion of the distortion measure of Eq. (10.23), determine the curvature term that arises from the noise model $\pi(\boldsymbol{\nu})$.

10.8 The *k-means algorithm* (MacQueen, 1967) provides a simple mechanism for minimizing the sum of squared errors with k clusters, with each cluster consisting of a set of N samples $\mathbf{x}_1, \mathbf{x}_2, \ldots, \mathbf{x}_N$ that are similar to each other. The algorithm proceeds as follows:

1. Choose a set of clusters $\{\mathbf{y}_1, \mathbf{y}_2, \ldots, \mathbf{y}_k\}$ arbitrarily.
2. Assign the N samples to the k clusters using the minimum Euclidean distance rule:

$$\mathbf{x} \text{ belongs to cluster } \mathscr{C}_i \text{ if } \|\mathbf{x} - \mathbf{y}_i\| < \|\mathbf{x} - \mathbf{y}_j\|, \qquad j \neq i$$

3. Compute new cluster prototypes so as to minimize the cost function

$$J_i = \sum_{\mathbf{x} \in \mathscr{C}_i} \|\mathbf{x} - \mathbf{y}_i\|^2$$

4. If any cluster prototype changes, return to step 2; otherwise, stop.

Show that the SOFM algorithm is equivalent to k-means clustering for a neighborhood function Λ_i of size 1.

10.9 The *conscience algorithm* is a modification of the SOFM algorithm, which forces the density matching to be "exact" (DeSieno, 1988). In the conscience algorithm, summarized in Table P10.9 (p. 439), each neuron keeps track of how many times it has won the competition (i.e., how many times its synaptic weight vector has been the neuron closest to the input vector in Euclidean distance). The notion used here is that if a neuron wins too often, it "feels guilty" and therefore pulls itself out of the competition.

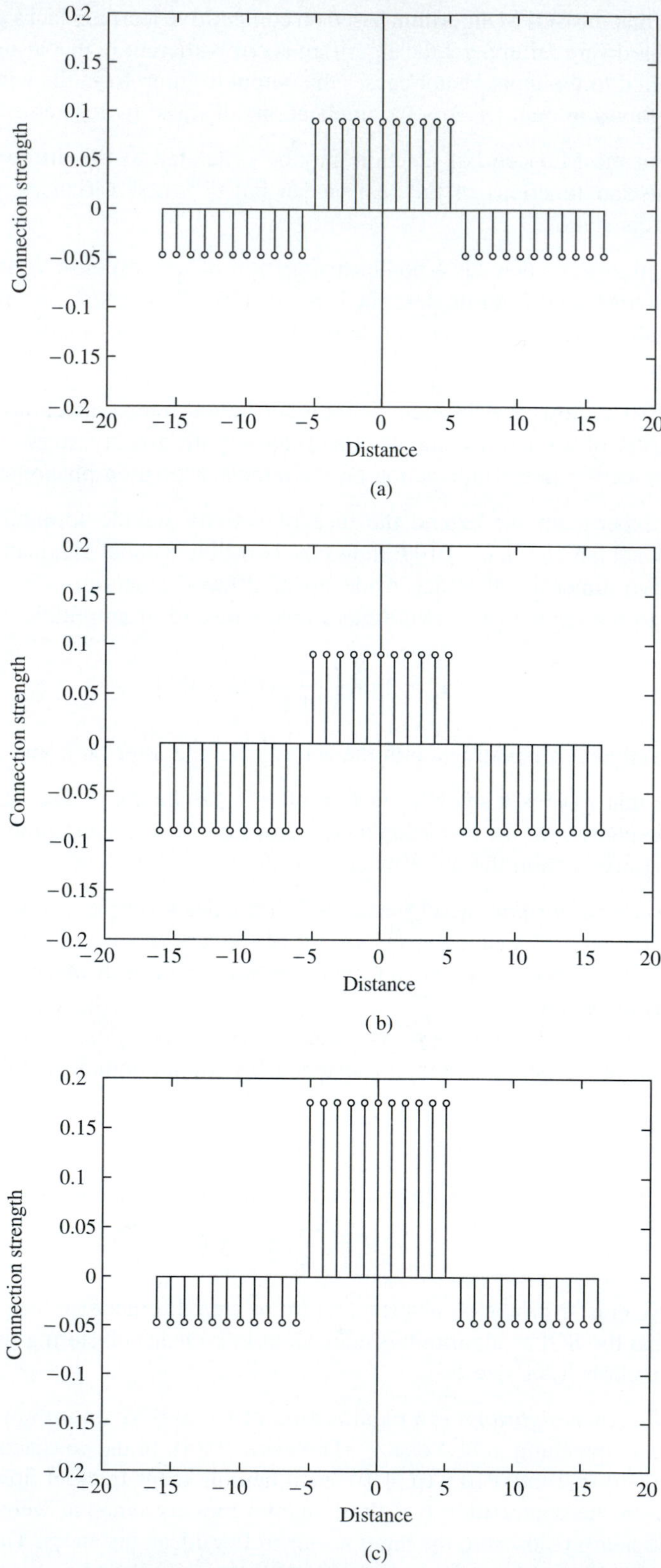

(a)

(b)

(c)

FIGURE P10.5

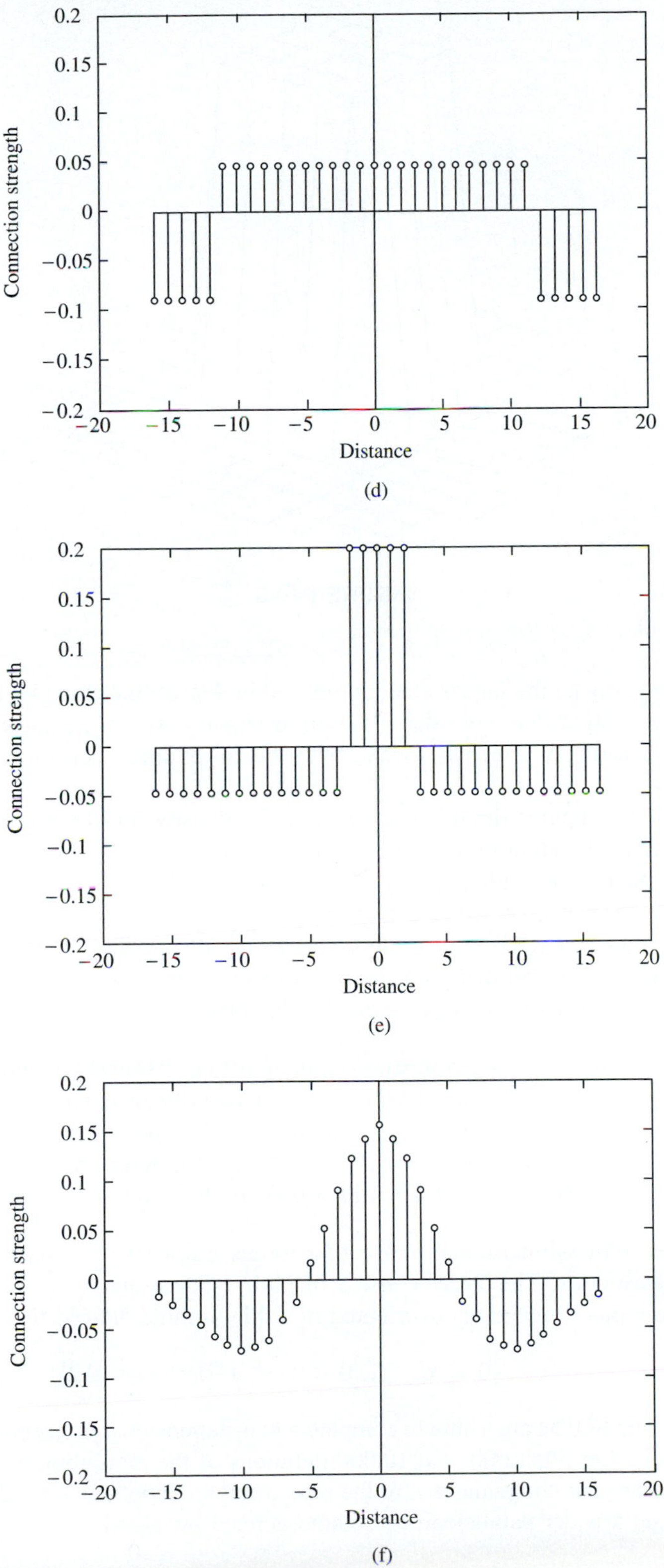

(d)

(e)

(f)

FIGURE P10.5 (continued)

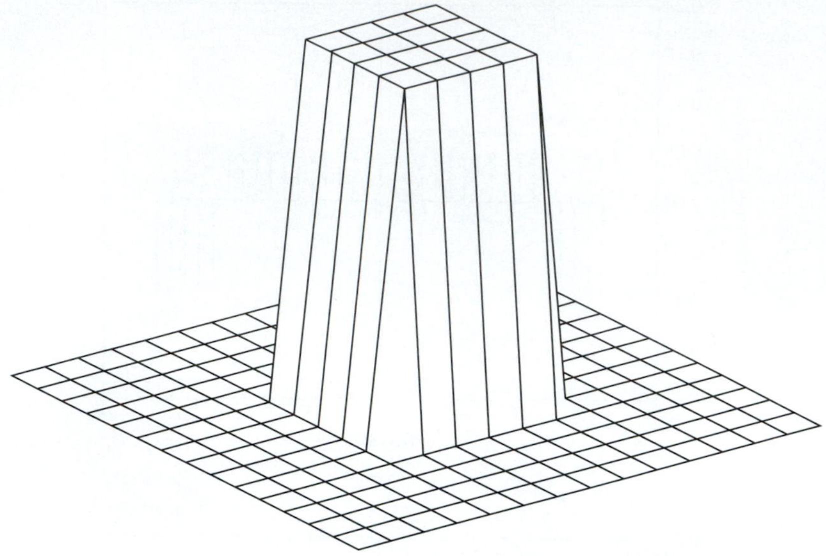

FIGURE P10.6

To investigate the improvement produced in density matching by the use of the conscience algorithm, consider a one-dimensional lattice (i.e., linear array) made up of 20 neurons, which is trained with the linear input density plotted in Fig. P10.9.

(a) Using computer simulations, compare the density matching produced by the conscience algorithm with that produced by the SOFM algorithm. For the SOFM algorithm use $\eta = 0.05$, and for the conscience algorithm use $B = 0.0001$, $C = 1.0$, and $\eta = 0.05$.

(b) As frames of reference for this comparison, include the "exact" match to the input density and that predicted from theory using Eq. (10.29).

Discuss the results of your computer simulations.

10.10 In this experiment we use computer simulations to investigate the SOFM algorithm applied to a one-dimensional lattice with a two-dimensional input. The lattice consists of 65 neurons. The inputs consist of random points uniformly distributed inside the triangular area shown in Fig. P10.10. Compute the map produced by the SOFM algorithm after 0, 20, 100, 1,000, 10,000, and 25,000 iterations.

10.11 Consider a two-dimensional lattice of neurons trained with a three-dimensional input distribution. The lattice consists of 10-by-10 neurons.

(a) The input is uniformly distributed in a thin volume defined by

$$\{0 < x_1 < 1,\ 0 < x_2 < 1,\ 0 < x_3 < 0.2\}$$

Use the SOFM algorithm to compute a two-dimensional projection of the input space after 50, 1,000, and 10,000 iterations of the algorithm.

(b) Repeat your computations for the case when the input is uniformly distributed inside a wider parallelepiped volume defined by

$$\{0 < x_1 < 1,\ 0 < x_2 < 1,\ 0 < x_3 < 0.4\}$$

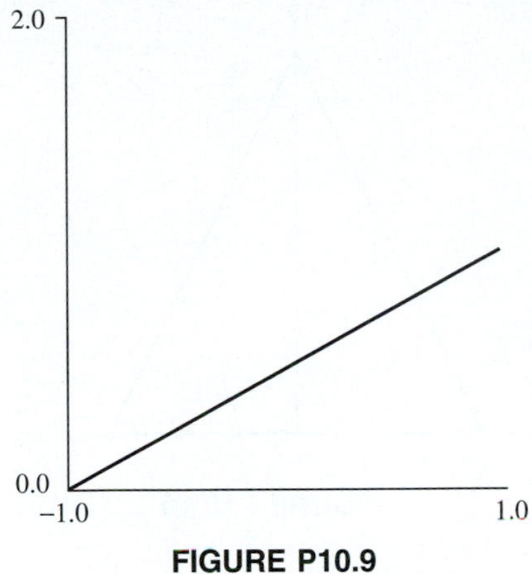

FIGURE P10.9

TABLE P10.9 Summary of the Conscience Algorithm

1. Find the synaptic weight vector $\mathbf{w}_i$ closest to the input vector $\mathbf{x}$:

$$\|\mathbf{x} - \mathbf{w}_i\| = \min_j \|\mathbf{x} - \mathbf{w}_j\|, \qquad j = 1, 2, \ldots, N$$

2. Keep a running total of the fraction of time, p_j, that neuron j wins the competition:

$$p_j^{\text{new}} = p_j^{\text{old}} + B(y_j - p_j^{\text{old}})$$

where $0 < B \ll 1$ and

$$y_j = \begin{cases} 1 & \text{if neuron } j \text{ is the winning neuron} \\ 0 & \text{otherwise} \end{cases}$$

The p_j are initialized to zero at the beginning of the algorithm.

3. Find the new winning neuron using the conscience mechanism

$$\|\mathbf{x} - \mathbf{w}_i\| = \min_j(\|\mathbf{x} - \mathbf{w}_j\| - b_j)$$

where b_j is a *bias* term introduced to modify the competition; it is defined by

$$b_j = C\left(\frac{1}{N} - p_j\right)$$

where C is a bias factor and N is the total number of neurons in the network.

4. Update the synaptic weight vector of the winning neuron:

$$\mathbf{w}_i^{\text{new}} = \mathbf{w}_i^{\text{old}} + \eta(\mathbf{x} - \mathbf{w}_i^{\text{old}})$$

where η is the usual learning-rate parameter used in the SOFM algorithm.

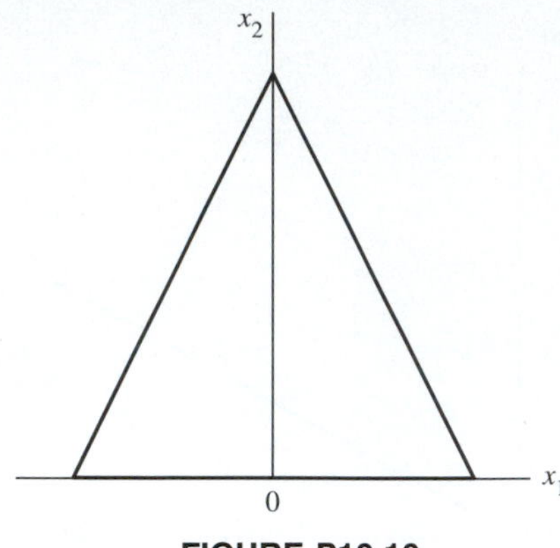

FIGURE P10.10

(c) Repeat your computations one more time for the case when the input is uniformly distributed inside a cube defined by

$$\{0 < x_1 < 1, 0 < x_2 < 1, 0 < x_3 < 1\}$$

Discuss the implications of the results of your computer simulations.

10.12 A problem that occasionally arises in the application of the SOFM algorithm is the failure of topological ordering by creating a "folded" map. This problem arises when the neighborhood size is permitted to decay too rapidly. The creation of a folded map may be viewed as some form of a "local minimum" of the topological ordering process.

To investigate this phenomenon, consider a two-dimensional lattice of 10-by-10 neurons trained on a two-dimensional input uniformly distributed inside the square $\{-1 < x_1 < +1, -1 < x_2 < +1\}$. Compute the map produced by the SOFM algorithm, permitting the neighborhood function around the winning neuron to decay much faster than that normally used. You may have to repeat the experiment several times in order to see a failure of the ordering process.

10.13 In this experiment we investigate the use of the SOFM algorithm combined with learning vector quantization for pattern classification.

The input consists of a mixture of two-dimensional Gaussian processes. One process is centered at the origin with a variance of 1. The other process is centered at the point (2.32, 0) with a variance of 2. The two processes are equiprobable. Data drawn from this mixture model are used to train a one-dimensional lattice of 20 neurons. The network is trained with $\Lambda_i = 0$ to match the input distribution as closely as possible; the parameter Λ_i is defined in Fig. 10.11.

(a) Compute the steady-state map produced by the SOFM algorithm.

(b) Construct the decision region formed by labeling each of the neurons in the lattice and drawing borders equidistant between neurons with different class labels.

(c) Repeat the construction of the decision region, using the LVQ algorithm.

(d) Compare the classification error rates computed in parts (b) and (c) with those produced by a Bayesian classifier.

10.14 The topological ordering property of the SOFM algorithm may be used to form an abstract two-dimensional representation of a high-dimensional input space. To investigate this form of a representation, consider a two-dimensional lattice consisting of 10-by-10 neurons that is trained with an input consisting of four Gaussian clouds, $\mathscr{C}_1$, $\mathscr{C}_2$, $\mathscr{C}_3$, and $\mathscr{C}_4$, in an eight-dimensional input space. All the clouds have unit variance but different centers. The centers are located at the points $(0, 0, 0, \dots, 0)$, $(4, 0, 0, \dots, 0)$, $(4, 4, 0, \dots, 0)$, and $(0, 4, 0, \dots, 0)$. Compute the map produced by the SOFM algorithm, with each neuron in the map being labeled with the particular class most represented by the input points around it.

10.15 Repeat the computer experiment for adaptive pattern classification described in Section 10.8 for a two-dimensional lattice made up of 6-by-6 neurons. In particular, compute the feature map after 0, 100, 700, 1,000, 50,000, and 200,000 iterations.

10.16 In this problem we consider the optimized form of the learning vector quantization algorithm of Section 10.9 (Kohonen et al., 1992). In particular, we wish to arrange for the effects of the corrections to the Voronoi vectors, made at different times, to have equal influence when referring to the end of the learning period.

(a) First, show that Eqs. (10.36) and (10.37) may be integrated into a single equation, as follows:

$$\mathbf{w}_c(n+1) = (1 - s_n\alpha_n)\mathbf{w}_c(n) + s_n\alpha_n\mathbf{x}_n$$

where

$$s_n = \begin{cases} +1 & \text{if the classification is correct} \\ -1 & \text{if the classification is wrong} \end{cases}$$

(b) Hence, show that the optimization criterion described at the beginning of the problem is satisfied if

$$\alpha_n = (1 - s_n\alpha_n)\alpha_{n-1}$$

which yields the optimized value of the learning constant α_n as

$$\alpha_n^{\text{opt}} = \frac{\alpha_{n-1}^{\text{opt}}}{1 + s_n\alpha_{n-1}^{\text{opt}}}$$

10.17 Consider the signal-space diagram shown in Fig. P10.17 corresponding to *M-ary pulse-amplitude modulation* (PAM) with $M = 8$. The signal points correspond to Gray-encoded data blocks. Each signal point is represented by a rectangular pulse signal with appropriate amplitude scaling:

$$p(t) = \pm\tfrac{7}{2}, \pm\tfrac{5}{2}, \pm\tfrac{3}{2}, \pm\tfrac{1}{2}, \qquad 0 \le t \le T$$

where T is the signaling interval. At the receiver input, white Gaussian noise of zero mean is added to the transmitted signal, with varying signal-to-noise ratio (SNR). The SNR is defined as the ratio of the "average" transmitted signal power to the average noise power.

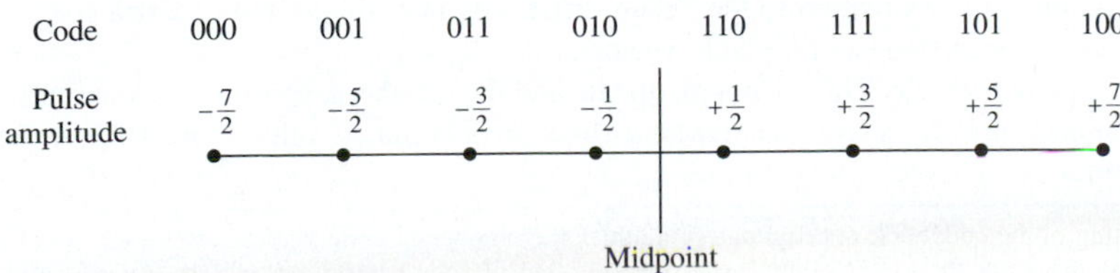

FIGURE P10.17

(a) Using a random binary sequence as the transmitter input, generate data representing the received signal for SNR = 10, 20, and 30 dB.

(b) For each of these SNRs, set up a self-organizing feature map. For typical values, you may use:

- Input vector made up of eight elements obtained by sampling the received signal at a rate equal to eight times the signaling rate (i.e., 8 samples per signaling interval). Do not assume knowledge of timing information.
- One-dimensional lattice of 64 neurons (i.e., eight times the size of the input vector).

(c) Display the feature maps for each of the three SNRs, and thereby demonstrate the topological ordering property of the Kohonen algorithm.

10.18 Table P10.18 presents a summary of the *renormalized SOFM algorithm* (Luttrell, 1992); a very brief description of the algorithm was given in Section 10.5. Compare the conventional and renormalized SOFM algorithms, keeping in mind the following two issues:

1. The coding complexity involved in algorithmic implementation.

2. The computer time taken to do the training.

Illustrate the comparison between these two algorithms using data drawn from a uniform distribution inside a square and the following two network configurations:

(a) One-dimensional lattice of 257 neurons.

(b) One-dimensional lattice of 2049 neurons.

In both cases, start with an initial number of code vectors equal to 2.

TABLE P10.18 Summary of Renormalized Training Algorithm (one-dimensional version)

1. *Initialization.* Set the number of code vectors to be some small number (e.g., use 2 for simplicity or some other value more representative of the problem at hand). Initialize their positions to be those of a corresponding number of training vectors chosen randomly from the training set.
2. *Selection of an input vector.* Choose an input vector randomly from the training set.
3. *Encoding of the input vector.* Determine the ''winning'' code vector (i.e., the synaptic weight vector of the winning neuron). To do this, use either the ''nearest neighbor'' or the ''minimum distortion'' encoding prescription as required.
4. *Updating of the codebook.* Do the usual ''winner and its topological neighbors'' update. You may find it sufficient to keep the learning-rate parameter η fixed (0.125, say) and to update the winning neuron using η, and its nearest neighbors using $\eta/2$, say.
   (Note: A neighborhood radius of 1 is sufficient for proper map formation.)
5. *Splitting of the codebook.*[a] Continue with the codebook update (step 4), each time using a new input vector chosen randomly from the training set, until the number of codebook updates is about 10–30 times the number of code vectors. When this number is reached, the codebook has probably settled down, and then it is time to split the codebook. You may do so by taking the ''Peano string'' of code vectors that you have got and interpolating their positions to generate a finer grained approximation to the Peano string; you may simply put an extra code vector half way between each two existing code vectors.
6. *Completion of training.* The codebook update and the codebook splitting are continued until the total number of code vectors has reached some predetermined value (e.g., 100), at which time the training is all over.

[a] The splitting of the codebook approximately doubles the number of code vectors after each epoch, so it does not take too many epochs to get to any prescribed number of code vectors.

10.19 It is sometimes said that the SOFM algorithm *preserves* the topological relationships that exist in the input space. Strictly speaking, this property can be guaranteed only for an input space of equal or lower dimensionality than that of the neural lattice. Discuss the validity of this statement in light of the Peano curve of Fig. 10.16 and those computed in Problem 10.18.

CHAPTER 11

Self-Organizing Systems III: Information-Theoretic Models

11.1 Introduction

In 1988, Linsker (1988a) proposed a principle of self-organization that is rooted in information theory. The principle is that the synaptic connections of a multilayered neural network develop in such a way as to *maximize the amount of information that is preserved when signals are transformed at each processing stage of the network, subject to certain constraints.* The idea that information theory may offer an explanation for perceptual processing is not new.[1] For instance, we may mention an early paper by Attneave (1954), in which the following information-theoretic function is proposed for the perceptual system:

> A major function of the perceptual machinery is to strip away some of the redundancy of stimulation, to describe or encode information in a form more economical than that in which it impinges on the receptors.

The main idea behind Attneave's paper is the recognition that encoding of data from a scene for the purpose of redundancy reduction is related to the identification of specific features in the scene. This important insight is related to a view of the brain described in Craik (1943), where a model of the external world is constructed so as to incorporate the regularities and constraints of the world.

Indeed, the application of information-theoretic ideas to the perceptual system has been a subject of research almost as far back as Shannon's 1948 classic paper, which laid down the foundations of information theory. Shannon's original work on *information theory,*[2] and its refinement by other researchers, was in direct response to the need of electrical engineers to design communication systems that are both *efficient* and *reliable.* In spite of its practical origins, information theory as we know it today is a deep mathematical theory concerned with the very essence of the *communication process.* Indeed, the theory provides a framework for the study of fundamental issues such as the efficiency of information representation and the limitations involved in the reliable transmission of information over a communication channel. Moreover, the theory encompasses a multitude of powerful theorems for computing ideal *bounds* on the optimum representation and transmission of information-bearing signals; these bounds are important because they

[1] For a review of the literature on the relation between information theory and perception, see Linsker (1990b) and Atick (1992).

[2] For detailed treatment of information theory, see the book by Cover and Thomas (1991); see also Gray (1990). For a collection of papers on the development of information theory (including the 1948 classic paper by Shannon), see Slepian (1973). Shannon's paper is also reproduced, with minor revisions, in the book by Shannon and Weaver (1949).

For a brief review of the important principles of information theory with neural processing in mind, see Atick (1992). For a treatment of information theory from a biology perspective, see Yockey (1992).

provide benchmarks for the improved design of information-processing systems. The main purpose of this chapter is to use Shannon's information theory to derive Linsker's principle of maximum information preservation, which represents a fundamental principle of self-organization.

Organization of the Chapter

The main body of the chapter is organized as follows. In Section 11.2 we present an introductory treatment of Shannon's information theory to pave the way for the mathematical derivation of the principle of maximum information preservation. This latter development is presented in Section 11.3. Next, in Section 11.4, we use the principle of maximum information preservation to generate a topologically ordered map; the important point to note here is that the map so generated is superior (in certain respects) to Kohonen's SOFM algorithm, which was the center of attention in Chapter 10. In Section 11.5 we present a discussion of the principle of maximum information preservation in light of some related work.

In Section 11.6 we extend the principle of maximum information preservation to image processing, the aim of which is to discover properties of a sensory input that exhibit coherence across both space and time (Becker and Hinton, 1992). Then, in Section 11.7 we discuss another information-theoretic model proposed by Atick and Redlich (1990a, b) for the study of perceptual systems. The chapter concludes with some final thoughts on the subject presented in Section 11.8.

11.2 Shannon's Information Theory

Consider a random variable x, each presentation of which may be regarded as a *message*. Strictly speaking, if the random variable x was continuous in its amplitude range, then it would carry an infinite amount of information. However, on physical and biological grounds we recognize that it is meaningless to think in terms of amplitude measurements with infinite precision, which suggests that x may be uniformly *quantized* into a finite number of discrete levels. Accordingly, we may view x as a *discrete* random variable, modeled as follows:

$$x = \{x_k | k = 0, \pm 1, \ldots, \pm K\} \tag{11.1}$$

where x_k is a discrete number and $(2K + 1)$ is the total number of discrete levels. The separation δx between the discrete levels is assumed to be small enough for the model of Eq. (11.1) to provide an adequate representation for the variable of interest. We may, of course, pass to the continuum limit by letting δx approach zero and K approach infinity, in which case we have a continuous random variable and (as we will see later in the section) sums become integrals.

To complete the model, let the event $x = x_k$ occur with *probability*

$$p_k = \text{Prob}(x = x_k) \tag{11.2}$$

with the requirement that

$$0 \le p_k \le 1 \qquad \text{and} \qquad \sum_{k=-K}^{K} p_k = 1 \tag{11.3}$$

Can we find a measure of how much "information" is produced by the random variable x taking on the discrete value x_k? The idea of information is closely related to that of "uncertainty" or "surprise," as described next.

Suppose that the event $x = x_k$ occurs with probability $p_k = 1$, which therefore requires that $p_i = 0$ for all $i \neq k$. In such a situation there is no "surprise" and therefore no "information" conveyed by the occurrence of the event $x = x_k$, since we know what the message must be. If, on the other hand, the various discrete levels were to occur with different probabilities and, in particular, the probability p_k is low, then there is more "surprise" and therefore "information" when x takes on the value x_k rather than another value x_i with higher probability p_i, $i \neq k$. Thus, the words "uncertainty," "surprise," and "information" are all related. Before the occurrence of the event $x = x_k$, there is an amount of uncertainty. When the event $x = x_k$ occurs, there is an amount of surprise. After the occurrence of the event $x = x_k$, there is a gain in the amount of information. All these three amounts are obviously the same. Moreover, the amount of information is related to the *inverse* of the probability of occurrence.

Entropy

We define the amount of information gained after observing the event $x = x_k$ with probability p_k as the logarithmic function

$$I(x_k) = \log\left(\frac{1}{p_k}\right) = -\log p_k \tag{11.4}$$

where the base of the logarithm is arbitrary. When the natural logarithm is used, the units for information are *nats,* and when the base 2 logarithm is used the units are *bits.* In any case, the definition of information given in Eq. (11.4) exhibits the following properties:

1.

$$I(x_k) = 0 \qquad \text{for } p_k = 1 \tag{11.5}$$

Obviously, if we are absolutely certain of the outcome of an event, there is *no* information gained by its occurrence.

2.

$$I(x_k) \geq 0 \qquad \text{for } 0 \leq p_k \leq 1 \tag{11.6}$$

That is, the occurrence of an event $x = x_k$ either provides some or no information, but it never results in a loss of information.

3.

$$I(x_k) > I(x_i) \qquad \text{for } p_k < p_i \tag{11.7}$$

That is, the less probable an event is, the more information we gain through its occurrence.

The amount of information $I(x_k)$ is a discrete random variable with probability p_k. The mean value of $I(x_k)$ over the complete range of $2K + 1$ discrete values is given by

$$\begin{aligned} H(x) &= E[I(x_k)] \\ &= \sum_{k=-K}^{K} p_k I(x_k) \\ &= -\sum_{k=-K}^{K} p_k \log p_k \end{aligned} \tag{11.8}$$

The quantity $H(x)$ is called the *entropy* of a random variable x permitted to take on a finite set of discrete values; it is so called in recognition of the analogy between the definition given in Eq. (11.8) and that of entropy in statistical thermodynamics. The entropy $H(x)$ is a measure of the *average amount of information conveyed per message.* Note, however, that the x in $H(x)$ is not an argument of a function but rather a label for a random variable. Note also that in the definition of Eq. (11.8) we take 0 log 0 to be 0.

The entropy $H(x)$ is bounded as follows:

$$0 \le H(x) \le \log(2K + 1) \tag{11.9}$$

where $(2K + 1)$ is the total number of discrete levels. Furthermore, we may make the following statements:

1. $H(x) = 0$ if and only if the probability $p_k = 1$ for some k, and the remaining probabilities in the set are all zero; this lower bound on entropy corresponds to no *uncertainty.*
2. $H(x) = \log_2(2K + 1)$, if and only if $p_k = 1/(2K + 1)$ for all k (i.e., all the discrete levels are equiprobable); this upper bound on entropy corresponds to *maximum uncertainty.*

The proof of property 2 follows from the following lemma (Gray, 1990):

Given any two probability distributions $\{p_k\}$ and $\{q_k\}$ for a discrete random variable x, then

$$\sum_k p_k \log\left(\frac{p_k}{q_k}\right) \ge 0 \tag{11.10}$$

which is satisfied with equality if and only if $q_k = p_k$ for all k.

The quantity used in this lemma is of such fundamental importance that we pause to recast it in a form suitable for use in the study of stochastic networks. Let P_α and Q_α denote the probabilities that a network is in state α under two different operating conditions. The *relative entropy* of the probability distribution P_α with respect to the second probability distribution Q_α is defined by (Gray, 1990)

$$H_{P\|Q} = \sum_\alpha P_\alpha \log\left(\frac{P_\alpha}{Q_\alpha}\right) \tag{11.11}$$

where the sum is over all possible states α of the network. The probability distribution Q_α plays the role of a *reference measure.* The idea of relative entropy was introduced by Kullback (1968); it is also referred to in the literature by other names such as the *Kullback–Leibler information criterion, cross entropy,* and *directed divergence.* The relative entropy of Eq. (11.11) was used in Chapter 6 to derive a special form of the back-propagation algorithm, and also in Chapter 8 for the derivation of Boltzmann learning.

Conditional Entropy and Mutual Information

We next turn our attention to other notions of information theory. We begin by adding a second random variable y to our previous model. Consider, then, a dynamical system with the output y representing a noisy version of the input x. Both x and y are permitted to take on only discrete values. The entropy $H(x)$ is a measure of the prior uncertainty about x. How can we measure the uncertainty about x after observing y? In order to answer this question, we define the *conditional entropy* of x given y as follows (Gray, 1990):

$$H(x|y) = H(x,y) - H(y) \tag{11.12}$$

with the property that

$$0 \leq H(x|y) \leq H(x) \tag{11.13}$$

The conditional entropy $H(x|y)$ represents the *amount of uncertainty remaining about the system input x after the system output y has been observed.*

Since the entropy $H(x)$ represents our uncertainty about the system input *before* observing the system output, and the conditional entropy $H(x|y)$ represents our uncertainty about the system input *after* observing the system output, it follows that the difference $H(x) - H(x|y)$ must represent our uncertainty about the system input that is resolved by observing the system output. This quantity is called the *average mutual information* between x and y. Denoting it by $I(x; y)$, we may thus write[3]

$$I(x; y) = H(x) - H(x|y) \tag{11.14}$$

Entropy is a special case of mutual information, since we have

$$H(x) = I(x; x) \tag{11.15}$$

The mutual information $I(x; y)$ between two discrete random variables x and y has the following properties (Cover and Thomas, 1991; Gray, 1990).

1. *The mutual information between x and y is symmetric;* that is,

$$I(y; x) = I(x; y) \tag{11.16}$$

where the mutual information $I(y; x)$ is a measure of the uncertainty about the system output y that is resolved by observing the system input x, and the mutual information $I(x; y)$ is a measure of the uncertainty about the system input that is resolved by observing the system output.

2. *The mutual information between x and y is always nonnegative;* that is,

$$I(x; y) \geq 0 \tag{11.17}$$

This property, in effect, states that we cannot lose information, on the average, by observing the system output y. Moreover, the mutual information is zero if and only if the input and output of the system are statistically independent.

3. *The mutual information between x and y may be expressed in terms of the entropy of y as*

$$I(x:y) = H(y) - H(y|x) \tag{11.18}$$

where $H(y|x)$ is a *conditional entropy.* The right-hand side of Eq. (11.18) is the ensemble average of the information conveyed by the system output y, minus the ensemble average of the information conveyed by y given that we already know the system input x. This latter system output y conveys information about the processing noise, rather than about the system input x.

Figure 11.1 provides a diagrammatic interpretation of Eqs. (11.14) and (11.18). The entropy of the system input x is represented by the circle on the left. The entropy of the

[3] The term $I(x; y)$ was originally referred to as the *rate of information transmission* by Shannon (1948). Today, however, this term is commonly referred to as the mutual information between the random variables x and y.

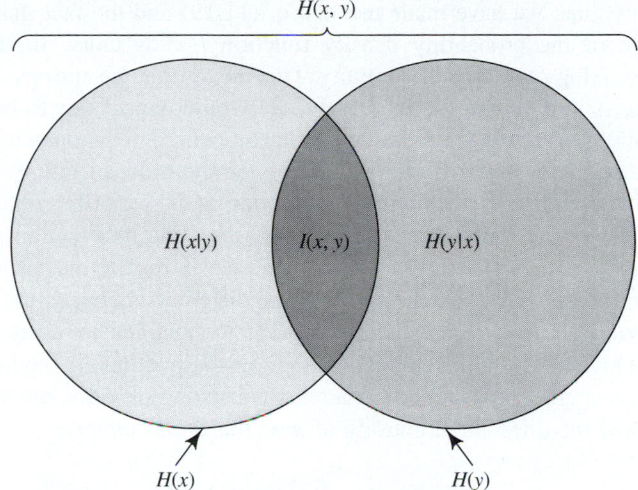

FIGURE 11.1 Illustration of the relations among the mutual information $I(x; y)$ and the entropies $H(x)$ and $H(y)$.

system output y is represented by the circle on the right. The mutual information between x and y is represented by the overlap between these two circles.

Differential Entropy of Continuous Random Variables

The discussion of information-theoretic concepts has thus far involved ensembles of random variables that are discrete in their amplitude values. We now extend some of these concepts to continuous random variables.

Consider a continuous random variable x with the *probability density function* $f(x)$. By analogy with the entropy of a discrete random variable, we introduce the following definition:

$$h(x) = -\int_{-\infty}^{\infty} f(x) \log f(x)\, dx \tag{11.19}$$

We refer to $h(x)$ as the *differential entropy* of x to distinguish it from the ordinary or *absolute entropy*. We do so in recognition of the fact that although $h(x)$ is a useful mathematical quantity to know, it is *not* in any sense a measure of the randomness of x.

We justify the use of Eq. (11.19) as follows. We begin by viewing the continuous random variable x as the limiting form of a discrete random variable that assumes the value $x_k = k\,\delta x$, where $k = 0, \pm 1, \pm 2, \ldots$, and δx approaches zero. By definition, the continuous random variable x assumes a value in the interval $[x_k, x_k + \delta x]$ with probability $f(x_k)\,\delta x$. Hence, permitting δx to approach zero, the ordinary entropy of the continuous random variable x may be written in the limit as

$$\begin{aligned}
H(x) &= -\lim_{\delta x \to 0} \sum_{k=-\infty}^{\infty} f(x_k)\,\delta x \log(f(x_k)\,\delta x) \\
&= -\lim_{\delta x \to 0} \left[\sum_{k=-\infty}^{\infty} f(x_k)(\log f(x_k))\,\delta x + \log \delta x \sum_{k=-\infty}^{\infty} f(x_k)\,\delta x \right] \\
&= -\int_{-\infty}^{\infty} f(x) \log f(x)\, dx - \lim_{\delta x \to 0} \log \delta x \int_{-\infty}^{\infty} f(x)\, dx \\
&= h(x) - \lim_{\delta x \to 0} \log \delta x
\end{aligned} \tag{11.20}$$

where, in the last line, we have made use of Eq. (11.19) and the fact that the total area under the curve of the probability density function $f(x)$ is unity. In the limit as δx approaches zero, $-\log \delta x$ approaches infinity. This means that the entropy of a continuous random variable is infinitely large. Intuitively, we would expect this to be true, because a continuous random variable may assume a value anywhere in the open interval $(-\infty,\infty)$ and the uncertainty associated with the variable is on the order of infinity. We avoid the problem associated with the term $\log \delta x$ by adopting $h(x)$ as a differential entropy, with the term $-\log \delta x$ serving as reference. Moreover, since the information processed by a dynamical system is actually the difference between two entropy terms that have a common reference, the information will be the same as the difference between the corresponding differential entropy terms. We are therefore perfectly justified in using the term $h(x)$, defined in Eq. (11.19), as the differential entropy of the continuous random variable x.

When we have a continuous random vector $\mathbf{x}$ consisting of n random variables $x_1, x_2, \ldots, x_n$, we define the differential entropy of $\mathbf{x}$ as the *n-fold integral*

$$h(\mathbf{x}) = -\int_{-\infty}^{\infty} f(\mathbf{x}) \log f(\mathbf{x})\, d\mathbf{x} \tag{11.21}$$

where $f(\mathbf{x})$ is the joint probability density function of $\mathbf{x}$.

EXAMPLE 1. Maximum Differential Entropy for Specified Variance

In this example we solve an important *constrained optimization problem.* We determine the form that the probability density function of a random variable x must have for the differential entropy of x to assume its largest value for some prescribed variance. In mathematical terms, we may restate the problem as follows:

With the differential entropy of a random variable x defined by

$$h(x) = -\int_{-\infty}^{\infty} f(x) \log f(x)\, dx \tag{11.22}$$

find the probability density function $f(x)$ for which $h(x)$ is maximum, subject to the two constraints

$$\int_{-\infty}^{\infty} f(x)\, dx = 1 \tag{11.23}$$

and

$$\int_{-\infty}^{\infty} (x-\mu)^2 f(x)\, dx = \sigma^2 = \text{constant} \tag{11.24}$$

where μ is the mean of x and σ^2 is its variance.

The first constraint, Eq. (11.23) simply states that the area under $f(x)$, a probability density function, must equal unity. The second constraint, Eq. (11.24), recognizes that the variance of x has a prescribed value.

We use the *method of Lagrange multipliers* to solve this constrained optimization problem. Specifically, the differential entropy $h(x)$ will attain its maximum value only when the integral

$$\int_{-\infty}^{\infty} [-f(x) \log f(x) + \lambda_1 f(x) + \lambda_2 (x-\mu)^2 f(x)]\, dx$$

is *stationary.* The parameters λ_1 and λ_2 are known as *Lagrange multipliers.* That is, $h(x)$ is maximum only when the derivative of the integrand

$$-f(x) \log f(x) + \lambda_1 f(x) + \lambda_2 (x-\mu)^2 f(x)$$

with respect to $f(x)$ is zero. This yields the result

$$-1 + \lambda_1 + \lambda_2(x - \mu)^2 = \log f(x)$$

where the logarithm is taken to be the natural logarithm. Solving for $f(x)$, we get

$$f(x) = \exp[-1 + \lambda_1 + \lambda_2(x - \mu)^2] \tag{11.25}$$

Note that λ_2 has to be negative if the integrals of $f(x)$ and $(x - \mu)^2 f(x)$ with respect to x are to converge. Substituting Eq. (11.25) in (11.23) and (11.24), and then solving for λ_1 and λ_2, we get

$$\lambda_1 = 1 - \log(2\pi\sigma^2)$$

and

$$\lambda_2 = -\frac{1}{2\sigma^2}$$

The desired form for $f(x)$ is therefore described by

$$f(x) = \frac{1}{\sqrt{2\pi}\sigma} \exp\left(-\frac{(x-\mu)^2}{2\sigma^2}\right) \tag{11.26}$$

which is recognized as the probability density of a *Gaussian random variable x of mean μ and variance σ^2*. The maximum value of the differential entropy of such a random variable is obtained by substituting Eq. (11.26) in (11.22). The result of this substitution is given by

$$h(x) = \frac{1}{2}[1 + \log(2\pi\sigma^2)] \tag{11.27}$$

We may thus summarize the results of this example, as follows:

1. *For a given variance σ^2, the Gaussian random variable has the largest differential entropy attainable by any random variable.* That is, if x is a Gaussian random variable and y is any other random variable with the same mean and variance, then for all y,

$$h(x) \geq h(y) \tag{11.28}$$

with the equality holding only if $y = x$.

2. *The entropy of a Gaussian random variable x is uniquely determined by the variance of x* (i.e., it is independent of the mean of x).

Mutual Information for Continuous Random Variables

Consider next a pair of continuous random variables x and y. By analogy with Eq. (11.19), we define the *average mutual information* between the random variables x and y as

$$I(x; y) = \int_{-\infty}^{\infty}\int_{-\infty}^{\infty} f(x,y) \log\left(\frac{f(x|y)}{f(x)}\right) dx\, dy \tag{11.29}$$

where $f(x, y)$ is the *joint probability density function* of x and y, and $f(x|y)$ is the *conditional* probability density function of x given y. Also, by analogy with our previous discussion for discrete random variables, the mutual information $I(x; y)$ between the continuous random variables x and y has the following properties:

$$\begin{aligned} I(x; y) &= h(x) - h(x|y) \\ &= h(y) - h(y|x) \\ &= h(x) + h(y) - h(x,y) \end{aligned} \tag{11.30}$$

$$I(y; x) = I(x; y) \tag{11.31}$$

$$I(x; y) \geq 0 \tag{11.32}$$

The parameter $h(x)$ is the differential entropy of x; likewise for $h(y)$. The parameter $h(x|y)$ is the *conditional differential entropy* of x given y; it is defined by the double integral

$$h(x|y) = -\int_{-\infty}^{\infty}\int_{-\infty}^{\infty} f(x,y) \log f(x|y)\, dx\, dy \tag{11.33}$$

The parameter $h(y|x)$ is the conditional differential entropy of y given x; it is defined in a manner similar to $h(x|y)$. The parameter $h(x,y)$ is the joint differential entropy of x and y.

11.3 The Principle of Maximum Information Preservation

Now that we have developed an adequate understanding of Shannon's information theory, we are ready to formulate the principle of maximum information preservation, which is a fundamental principle of self-organization. To make a statement of this important principle in specific terms, consider a two-layer network required to process incoming sensory signals in a self-organized fashion. The input (source) layer has forward connections to the output (target) layer; lateral connections are permitted within the output layer. Let $\mathbf{x}$ denote an L-by-1 random vector representing the activities observed in the input layer; the elements of the vector $\mathbf{x}$ are $x_1, x_2, \ldots, x_L$. Let $\mathbf{y}$ denote an M-by-1 random vector representing the resulting activities produced in the output layer; the elements of the vector $\mathbf{y}$ are $y_1, y_2, \ldots, y_M$. The *principle of maximum information preservation* may be stated as follows (Linsker, 1987, 1988a):

> *The transformation of a vector* $\mathbf{x}$ *observed in the input layer of a neural network to a vector* $\mathbf{y}$ *produced in the output layer of the network should be so chosen that the activities of the neurons in the output layer jointly maximize information about the activities in the input layer. The parameter to be maximized is the average mutual information between the input vector* $\mathbf{x}$ *and the output vector* $\mathbf{y}$*, in the presence of processing noise.*

The principle of maximum information preservation is clearly independent of the learning rule used for its implementation. Also, this principle may be viewed as the neural-network counterpart of the concept of *channel capacity,* which defines the Shannon limit on the rate of information transmission through a communication channel.

A Single Neuron Corrupted by Processing Noise

To illustrate the application of the principle of maximum information preservation, consider the simple case of a single neuron that receives its inputs from a set of L source nodes in the input layer of the network. Let the output of this neuron in the presence of *processing noise* be expressed as (Linsker, 1988a)

$$y = \left(\sum_{i=1}^{L} w_i x_i\right) + \nu \tag{11.34}$$

where w_i is the synaptic weight from source node i in the input layer to the neuron in the output layer, and ν is the processing noise, as modeled in Fig. 11.2. It is assumed that:

- The output y of the neuron is a Gaussian random variable with variance σ_y^2.
- The processing noise ν is also a Gaussian random variable with zero mean and variance σ_ν^2.
- The processing noise is uncorrelated with any of the input components, that is,

$$E[\nu x_i] = 0 \qquad \text{for all } i \tag{11.35}$$

To proceed with the analysis, we first note from the second line of Eq. (11.30) that the average mutual information $I(y; \mathbf{x})$ between the output y of the neuron in the output layer and the input vector $\mathbf{x}$ is given by

$$I(y; \mathbf{x}) = h(y) - h(y|\mathbf{x}) \tag{11.36}$$

In view of Eq. (11.34), we note that the probability density function of y, given the input vector $\mathbf{x}$, is the same as the probability density function of a constant plus a Gaussian-distributed random variable ν. Accordingly, the conditional entropy $h(y|\mathbf{x})$ is the "information" that the output neuron conveys about the processing noise ν rather than about the signal vector $\mathbf{x}$. We may thus write

$$h(y|\mathbf{x}) = h(\nu) \tag{11.37}$$

and therefore rewrite Eq. (11.36) simply as

$$I(y; \mathbf{x}) = h(y) - h(\nu) \tag{11.38}$$

Applying Eq. (11.27) for the differential entropy of a Gaussian random variable to the problem at hand, we have

$$h(y) = \frac{1}{2}[1 + \log(2\pi\sigma_y^2)] \tag{11.39}$$

and

$$h(\nu) = \frac{1}{2}[1 + \log(2\pi\sigma_\nu^2)] \tag{11.40}$$

Hence the use of Eqs. (11.39) and (11.40) in (11.38) yields, after simplification (Linsker, 1988a),

$$I(y; \mathbf{x}) = \frac{1}{2}\log\left(\frac{\sigma_y^2}{\sigma_\nu^2}\right) \tag{11.41}$$

where σ_y^2 depends on σ_ν^2.

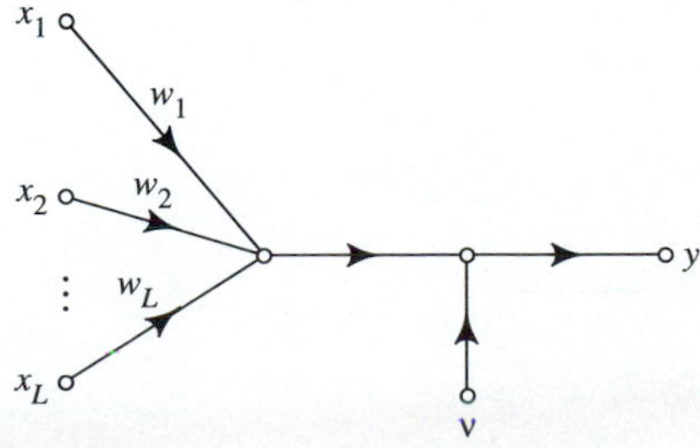

FIGURE 11.2 Signal-flow graph of a noisy neuron.

The ratio σ_y^2/σ_ν^2 may be viewed as a *signal-to-noise ratio.* Imposing the constraint that the noise variance σ_ν^2 is fixed, we see from Eq. (11.41) that the average mutual information $I(y; \mathbf{x})$ is maximized by maximizing the output variance σ_y^2 of the output neuron. We may therefore state that, under certain conditions, maximizing the output variance of a neuron maximizes the average mutual information between the output signal of that neuron and its inputs (Linsker, 1988a). However, this result does not always hold, as illustrated by the model considered next.

A Single Neuron Corrupted by Additive Input Noise

Suppose that the noise corrupting the output of a neuron in the output layer originates at the input ends of the synapses connected to the neuron as shown in the model of Fig. 11.3. According to this second noise model, we have (Linsker, 1988a)

$$y = \sum_{i=1}^{L} w_i(x_i + \nu_i) \tag{11.42}$$

where each noise ν_i is assumed to be an independent Gaussian random variable with zero mean and variance σ_ν^2. We may rewrite Eq. (11.42) in a form similar to that of Eq. (11.34), as shown by

$$y = \left(\sum_{i=1}^{L} w_i x_i\right) + \nu' \tag{11.43}$$

where ν' is a composite noise component, defined by

$$\nu' = \sum_{i=1}^{L} w_i \nu_i \tag{11.44}$$

The noise ν' has a Gaussian distribution with zero mean and a variance equal to the sum of the variances of its independent noise components; that is,

$$\sigma_{\nu'}^2 = \left(\sum_{i=1}^{L} w_i\right)^2 \sigma_\nu^2 \tag{11.45}$$

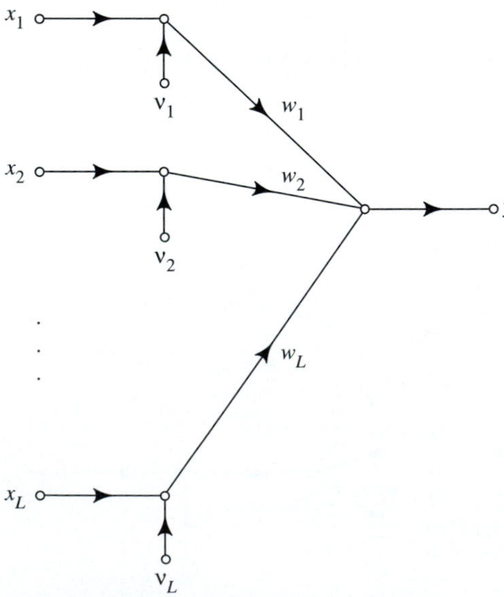

FIGURE 11.3 Another noise model.

As before, we assume that the output y of the neuron in the output layer has a Gaussian distribution with variance σ_y^2. The average mutual information $I(y; \mathbf{x})$ between y and $\mathbf{x}$ is still given by Eq. (11.36). This time, however, the conditional entropy $h(y|\mathbf{x})$ is defined by

$$\begin{aligned} h(y|\mathbf{x}) &= h(\nu') \\ &= \frac{1}{2}(1 + 2\pi\sigma_{\nu'}^2) \\ &= \frac{1}{2}\left[1 + 2\pi\sigma_\nu^2\left(\sum_{i=1}^{L} w_i\right)^2\right] \end{aligned} \tag{11.46}$$

Thus, using Eqs. (11.39) and (11.45) in (11.36), and simplifying terms, we get (Linsker, 1988a)

$$I(y; \mathbf{x}) = \frac{1}{2}\log\left(\frac{\sigma_y^2}{\sigma_\nu^2(\sum_{i=1}^{L} w_i)^2}\right) \tag{11.47}$$

Under the constraint that the noise variance σ_ν^2 is maintained constant, the mutual information $I(y; \mathbf{x})$ is now maximized by maximizing the ratio $\sigma_y^2/(\sum_{i=1}^{L} w_i)^2$.

These two simple models illustrate that the consequences of the principle of maximum information preservation are indeed problem-dependent. We next turn our attention to other issues related to the principle.

Redundancy and Diversity

Consider the noise model of Fig. 11.4, which shows L source nodes in the input layer of the network coupled to two neurons in the output layer. The outputs y_1 and y_2 of the latter two neurons are defined by, respectively (Linsker, 1988a),

$$y_1 = \left(\sum_{i=1}^{L} w_{1i}x_i\right) + \nu_1 \tag{11.48}$$

and

$$y_2 = \left(\sum_{i=1}^{L} w_{2i}x_i\right) + \nu_2 \tag{11.49}$$

where the w_{1i} are the synaptic weights from the input layer to neuron 1 in the output layer, and the w_{2i} are similarly defined. Note that the model of Fig. 11.4 may be expanded to include lateral connections between the output nodes, the effect of which is merely to modify the weights in the linear combinations of Eqs. (11.48) and (11.49). To proceed with the analysis, we make the following assumptions (Linsker, 1988a):

- The additive noise terms ν_1 and ν_2 are each Gaussian distributed, with zero mean and common variance σ_ν^2. Moreover, these two noise terms are uncorrelated with each other, as shown by

$$E[\nu_1\nu_2] = 0 \tag{11.50}$$

- Each noise term is uncorrelated with any of the input signals, as shown by

$$E[\nu_i x_j] = 0 \qquad \text{for all } i \text{ and } j \tag{11.51}$$

- The output signals y_1 and y_2 are both Gaussian random variables with zero mean.

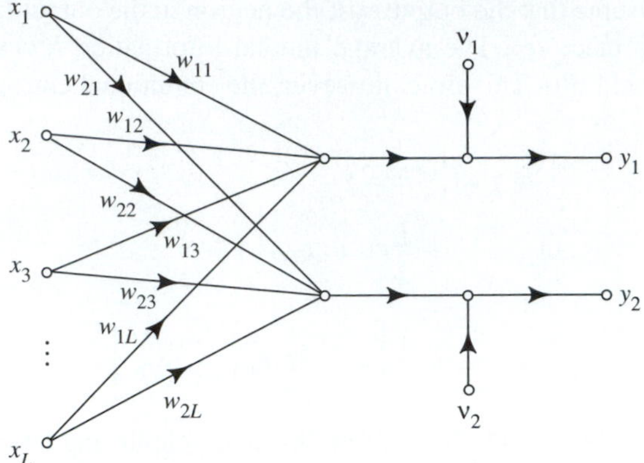

FIGURE 11.4 A more elaborate noise model.

The issue we wish to address is to see how the principle of maximum information preservation may be used to understand the behavior of the model so described.

The average mutual information between the output vector $\mathbf{y} = [y_1, y_2]^T$ and the input vector $\mathbf{x} = [x_1, x_2, \ldots, X_L]^T$ is defined by [see second line of Eq. (11.30)]

$$I(\mathbf{x}; \mathbf{y}) = h(\mathbf{y}) - h(\mathbf{y}|\mathbf{x}) \tag{11.52}$$

The noise model shown in Fig. 11.4 is an extension of the noise model of Fig. 11.2. Hence, using a rationale similar to that presented for the model of Fig. 11.2, we may rewrite Eq. (11.52) in the form

$$I(\mathbf{x}; \mathbf{y}) = h(\mathbf{y}) - h(\boldsymbol{\nu}) \tag{11.53}$$

The differential entropies $h(\boldsymbol{\nu})$ and $h(\mathbf{y})$ are each considered in turn; the noise vector $\boldsymbol{\nu}$ is made up of the elements ν_1 and ν_2.

Since the noise terms ν_1 and ν_2 are assumed to be Gaussian and uncorrelated, it follows that they are also statistically independent from each other. For the differential entropy $h(\boldsymbol{\nu})$, we therefore have

$$\begin{aligned} h(\boldsymbol{\nu}) &= h(\nu_1, \nu_2) \\ &= h(\nu_1) + h(\nu_2) \\ &= 1 + \log(2\pi\sigma_\nu^2) \end{aligned} \tag{11.54}$$

where, in the last line, we have made use of Eq. (11.40).

The differential entropy of the output vector $\mathbf{y}$ is given by

$$\begin{aligned} h(\mathbf{y}) &= h(y_1, y_2) \\ &= -\int_{-\infty}^{\infty}\int_{-\infty}^{\infty} f(y_1, y_2) \log[f(y_1, y_2)]\, dy_1\, dy_2 \end{aligned} \tag{11.55}$$

where $f(y_1, y_2)$ is the joint probability density function of y_1 and y_2. According to the model of Fig. 11.4, the output signals y_1 and y_2 are both dependent on the same set of input signals; it follows, therefore, that y_1 and y_2 can be correlated with each other. Let $\mathbf{R}$ denote the correlation matrix of the output vector:

$$\begin{aligned} \mathbf{R} &= E[\mathbf{y}\mathbf{y}^T] \\ &= \begin{bmatrix} r_{11} & r_{12} \\ r_{21} & r_{22} \end{bmatrix} \end{aligned} \tag{11.56}$$

where

$$r_{ij} = E[y_i y_j], \qquad i, j = 1, 2 \tag{11.57}$$

Using the definitions given in Eqs. (11.48) and (11.49), and invoking the assumptions made in Eqs. (11.50) and (11.51), we find that the individual elements of the correlation matrix **R** have the following values:

$$r_{11} = \sigma_1^2 + \sigma_\nu^2 \tag{11.58}$$

$$r_{12} = r_{21} = \sigma_1 \sigma_2 \rho_{12} \tag{11.59}$$

$$r_{22} = \sigma_2^2 + \sigma_\nu^2 \tag{11.60}$$

where σ_1^2 and σ_2^2 are the respective variances of the output signals y_1 and y_2 in the *absence of noise;* and ρ_{12} is the *correlation coefficient* of the output signals y_1 and y_2, also in the absence of noise.

Consider the general case of an *N-dimensional Gaussian distribution,* defined by

$$f(\mathbf{y}) = \frac{1}{2\pi \det(\mathbf{R})} \exp\left(-\frac{1}{2}\mathbf{y}^T\mathbf{R}^{-1}\mathbf{y}\right) \tag{11.61}$$

where $\det(\mathbf{R})$ is the determinant of the correlation matrix **R**, and $\mathbf{R}^{-1}$ is its inverse. The differential entropy of the N-dimensional vector **y** so described is given by (Shannon, 1948)

$$h(\mathbf{y}) = \log((2\pi e)^{N/2} \det(\mathbf{R})) \tag{11.62}$$

where e is the base of the natural logarithm. For the problem at hand, we have $N = 2$. Hence, for the output vector **y** made up of the elements y_1 and y_2, Eq. (11.62) reduces to

$$h(\mathbf{y}) = 1 + \log(2\pi \det(\mathbf{R})) \tag{11.63}$$

Accordingly, the use of Eqs. (11.54) and (11.63) in (11.53) yields (Linsker, 1988a)

$$I(\mathbf{x}; \mathbf{y}) = \log\left(\frac{\det(\mathbf{R})}{\sigma_\nu^2}\right) \tag{11.64}$$

To maximize the mutual information $I(\mathbf{x}; \mathbf{y})$ between the output vector **y** and the input vector **x** for a fixed noise variance σ_ν^2, we must maximize the determinant of the 2-by-2 correlation matrix **R**. From Eqs. (11.58) to (11.59) we note that

$$\begin{aligned} \det(\mathbf{R}) &= r_{11}r_{22} - r_{12}r_{21} \\ &= \sigma_\nu^4 + \sigma_\nu^2(\sigma_1^2 + \sigma_2^2) + \sigma_1^2\sigma_2^2(1 - \rho_{12}^2) \end{aligned} \tag{11.65}$$

Depending on the prevalent value of the noise variance σ_ν^2, we may identify two distinct situations (Linsker, 1988a), as described here.

1. *Large Noise Variance.* When the noise variance σ_ν^2 is large, the third term on the right-hand side of Eq. (11.65), which is independent of σ_ν^2, may be neglected. In such a case, maximizing $\det(\mathbf{R})$ requires that we maximize $(\sigma_1^2 + \sigma_2^2)$. In the absence of any specific constraints, this requirement may be achieved simply by maximizing the variance σ_1^2 of the output y_1 or the variance σ_2^2 of the second output y_2, separately. Since the variance of the output y_i, $i = 1, 2$, is equal to σ_i^2 in the absence of noise and $\sigma_i^2 + \sigma_\nu^2$ in the presence of noise, it follows that, in accordance with the principle of maximum information preservation, the optimum solution for a fixed noise variance is to maximize the variance of either output, y_1 or y_2.

2. *Low Noise Variance.* When, on the other hand, the noise variance σ_ν^2 is small, the third term $\sigma_1^2\sigma_2^2(1 - \rho_{12}^2)$ on the right-hand side of Eq. (11.65) becomes particularly important relative to the other two terms. The mutual information $I(\mathbf{x}; \mathbf{y})$ is then maximized by making an optimal trade-off between two options: keeping the output variance σ_1^2 and σ_2^2 large, and making the outputs y_1 and y_2 of the two output neurons uncorrelated.

Based on these observations, we may therefore make the following two statements (Linsker, 1988a).

- *A high noise level favors redundancy of response,* in which case the two output neurons in the model of Fig. 11.4 compute the same linear combination of inputs, given that there is only one such combination that yields a response with maximum variance.
- *A low noise level favors diversity of response,* in which case the two output neurons in the model of Fig. 11.4 compute different linear combinations of inputs, even though such a choice may result in a reduced output variance.

Justification of the Multivariate Gaussian Model

In general, the computation of the average mutual information $I(\mathbf{x}; \mathbf{y})$ between the output vector $\mathbf{y}$ of a neural network and the input vector $\mathbf{x}$ is mathematically intractable. To overcome this difficulty in the applications of the principle of maximum information preservation described above, we adopted a *multivariate Gaussian model,* assuming the presence of Gaussian-distributed processing noise. In essence, we used a "surrogate" mutual information, which was computed on the premise that the output vector $\mathbf{y}$ has a multivariate Gaussian distribution with the same mean vector and covariance matrix as the actual distribution. Linsker (1993) uses the idea of relative entropy to provide a principled justification for the use of such a surrogate mutual information, under the condition that the network has stored information about the mean vector and covariance matrix of the output vector $\mathbf{y}$, but not about higher-order statistics.

11.4 Generation of Topologically Ordered Maps

In Chapter 10 we discussed the topological ordering property of a self-organizing feature map that is an inherent property of Kohonen's model based on competitive learning. This desirable property may also be realized in a fundamentally different way. Specifically, we may use the principle of maximum information preservation. In this section we revisit the idea of a topologically ordered map and use this principle for its generation (Linsker, 1989b).

Let $\mathbf{x}$ denote an input vector drawn from a stationary ensemble, which is characterized by the probability density function $f(\mathbf{x})$. The input vector $\mathbf{x}$ is applied simultaneously to a set of neurons $j = 1, 2, \ldots, N$, which are arranged in the form of a lattice. The response of neuron j to the input vector $\mathbf{x}$ occurs in three steps (Linsker, 1989b).

1. *Feedforward Activation.* The input vector $\mathbf{x}$ acting on node j produces an output signal y_j defined by a Gaussian radial-basis function:

$$y_j \propto \exp(-\alpha\|\mathbf{x} - \mathbf{t}_j\|^2), \qquad j = 1, 2, \ldots, N \tag{11.66}$$

where α is a fixed parameter, and the *center* $\mathbf{t}_j$ is subject to adaptation.

2. *Lateral Interaction.* The activity of neuron j is modified by lateral interaction with neighboring neurons as follows:

$$a_j = \sum_k c_{jk} y_k, \qquad j = 1, 2, \ldots, N \tag{11.67}$$

where c_{jk} is the excitatory strength of the lateral connection from neuron k to neuron j; it is specified, subject to two requirements:

$$c_{jk} \geq 0 \qquad \text{for all } j \text{ and } k \tag{11.68}$$

and

$$\sum_j c_{jk} = 1 \qquad \text{for all } k \tag{11.69}$$

For definiteness, we may choose c_{jk} to be proportional to $\exp(-\beta|j - k|^2)$, where β is another fixed parameter, and choose the constant of proportionality to satisfy Eq. (11.69).

3. *Selection of Firing Neuron.* An output neuron i is selected to be fired with conditional probability

$$P(i|\mathbf{x}) = \frac{a_i}{\sum_j a_j} \tag{11.70}$$

Lateral inhibitory connections are implicit in the selection of a single firing neuron at step 3.

The use of Eq. (11.67) in (11.70) yields

$$\begin{aligned} P(i|\mathbf{x}) &= \frac{\sum_k c_{ik} y_k}{\sum_j \sum_k c_{jk} y_k} \\ &= \frac{\sum_k c_{ik} y_k}{\sum_k y_k} \end{aligned} \tag{11.71}$$

where, in the second line, we have made use of Eq. (11.69). According to Eq. (11.71), the conditional probability that neuron i is selected for firing, given the input vector $\mathbf{x}$, equals the normalized average strength of the *active* lateral connections to neuron i, with each excitatory lateral strength c_{ik} weighted by the feedforward response y_k of neuron k.

The average mutual information $I(\mathbf{x}; \{j\})$ between the input vector $\mathbf{x}$ and the set of output neurons $\{j\}$ is defined by

$$\begin{aligned} I(\mathbf{x}; \{j\}) &= \int_{-\infty}^{\infty} d\mathbf{x} \sum_j P(j,\mathbf{x}) \log \frac{P(j|\mathbf{x})}{P(j)} \\ &= \int_{-\infty}^{\infty} d\mathbf{x}\, f(\mathbf{x}) \sum_j P(j|\mathbf{x}) \log \frac{P(j|\mathbf{x})}{P(j)} \end{aligned} \tag{11.72}$$

The probability $P(j)$ that node j has fired is defined in terms of the conditional probability $P(j|\mathbf{x})$ by

$$P(j) = \int_{-\infty}^{\infty} d\mathbf{x}\, f(\mathbf{x})\, P(j|\mathbf{x}) \tag{11.73}$$

Let S denote a set of allowed input–output mappings:

$$S \ni \Phi : X \rightarrow A \tag{11.74}$$

where X denotes the input space, and A denotes the output space defined by the lattice of computational nodes. The requirement is to choose a mapping $\Phi \in S$ that maximizes the average mutual information $I(\mathbf{x}; \{j\})$. By so doing, the values of the output signals of the network discriminate optimally, in an information-theoretic sense, among the possible sets of input signals applied to the network.

To be specific, we wish to derive a learning rule that, when averaged over the input ensemble, performs gradient ascent on $I(\mathbf{x}; \{j\})$. The derivative of $I(\mathbf{x}; \{j\})$ with respect to the center $\mathbf{t}_i$ of neuron i is given by (Linsker, 1989b)

$$\frac{\partial I(\mathbf{x}; \{j\})}{\partial \mathbf{t}_i} = \int_{-\infty}^{\infty} d\mathbf{x}\, f(\mathbf{x})\, \mathbf{z}_i(\mathbf{x}) \tag{11.75}$$

where the vector $\mathbf{z}_i(\mathbf{x})$ is itself defined by

$$\mathbf{z}_i(\mathbf{x}) = \frac{\partial y_i / \partial \mathbf{t}_i}{\sum_k y_k} \sum_j [\log P(j|\mathbf{x}) - \log P(j)][c_{ji} - P(j|\mathbf{x})] \tag{11.76}$$

In order to reduce boundary effects, *periodic boundary conditions* are imposed on the formation of the map. Specifically, the input space and output space are each regarded as the *surface of a torus* (Linsker, 1989b); this kind of assumption is commonly made in image processing. Accordingly, in calculating the Euclidean distance $\|\mathbf{x} - \mathbf{t}_i\|$ we go the "short way around" the input space or output space. A similar remark applies to the calculation of the derivative $\partial y_i / \partial \mathbf{t}_i$.

The learning rule for the map generation may now be formulated as follows (Linsker, 1989b).

- To initialize the algorithm, select the center $\mathbf{t}_i$ of neuron i from a uniform distribution on a square of small side $s = 0.7$ centered at (0.1,0.1), say.
- Select input presentations $\mathbf{x}$ from the ensemble X according to the probability density functions $f(\mathbf{x})$.
- For each input vector in turn, modify the center $\mathbf{t}_i$ of neuron i by a small amount $\eta \mathbf{z}_i(\mathbf{x})$, where η is a small positive constant.

Note that if the centers $\mathbf{t}_j$ are permitted to change slowly over many presentations, the firing incidence of neuron j averaged over an appropriate number of recent input presentations may provide a suitable approximation to $P(j)$.

For an interpretation of Eq. (11.76), consider neuron $j = 1, 2, \ldots, N$, where N is the total number of neurons in the network. Let it be supposed that for neuron j we have (Linsker, 1989b)

1. $P(j|\mathbf{x}) > P(j)$; that is, the occurrence of input pattern $\mathbf{x}$ is conducive to the firing of neuron j
2. $c_{ji} > P(j|\mathbf{x})$; that is, the excitatory lateral connection from neuron i to neuron j is stronger than the conditional probability that neuron j would fire given the input $\mathbf{x}$.

Under these two conditions, term j in Eq. (11.76) has the effect of tending to move the center $\mathbf{t}_i$ of neuron i in the direction of increase of the output signal y_i of that neuron. If, on the other hand, the reverse of condition 2 holds, the effect of term j tends to decrease the output signal y_i.

We may thus sum up the essence of the information-theoretic learning rule described here as follows (Linsker, 1989b):

> *Each neuron i develops to become more responsive to input patterns* **x** *if it is relatively strongly coupled to neurons j that are themselves relatively strongly responsive to* **x**. *Similarly, it develops to become less responsive to input patterns* **x** *if it is weakly coupled to neurons j.*

There are three distinct elements apparent in this statement: *self-amplification* (i.e., *Hebb-like modification*), *cooperation,* and *competition* among the output nodes of the network for ''territory'' in the input space (Linsker, 1989b). It is rather striking that a learning rule rooted in information theory would embody the three basic principles of self-organization that were identified in Section 9.2.

Qualitative Aspects of the Learning Rule

From the review of Shannon's information theory presented in Section 11.2, we know that the average mutual information $I(\mathbf{x}; \{j\})$ may be expressed as the entropy of the probability distribution $\{P(j)\}$ minus the entropy of the conditional probability distribution $\{P(j|\mathbf{x})\}$. It follows, therefore, that $I(\mathbf{x}; \{j\})$ is maximum if two conditions hold (Linsker, 1989b).

1. *The entropy of* $\{P(j)\}$ *is maximum.* An example of an embedding that achieves this condition is one in which the density of nodes j mapped onto each region of the input space X is proportional to the probability density function $f(\mathbf{x})$.
2. *The entropy of* $\{P(j|\mathbf{x})\}$ *is minimum.* This second condition is achieved by choosing an embedding for which the conditional probability distribution $P(j|\mathbf{x})$ for each input vector $\mathbf{x}$ is sharply localized to a small region of the output space A. The intuitive idea here is that if each input vector $\mathbf{x}$ activates fewer neurons, then the ability of the network to discriminate among the possible input vectors, given knowledge of which particular neuron fired, is improved. The sharpened localization of $P(j|\mathbf{x})$ is achieved in two ways:

   - The spread of output signals y_j due to feedforward activation has a fixed extent in the input space X; hence, lowering the density of neuron j in the vicinity of $\mathbf{x}$ tends to localize y_j, and thereby $P(j|\mathbf{x})$, to a small region of the output space A.
   - The contour lines of the lateral connection strengths c_{jk}, viewed in the input space X, tend to become circular, which is the optimum condition; hence the conditional probability $P(j|\mathbf{x})$, which is proportional to the convolution of c_{jk} and y_j, becomes more sharply localized.

The maximization of the average mutual information $I(\mathbf{x}; \{j\})$ between the input and the output, resulting from the combination of these effects, is the basis of a self-organized learning process that produces a topologically ordered input–output mapping similar to the SOFM algorithm described in Chapter 10. However, unlike the SOFM algorithm, the maximization of $I(\mathbf{x}; \{j\})$ yields a distribution of neurons for which it is possible to satisfy the ideal condition of Eq. (10.29) for the magnification factor (Linsker, 1989b). On the other hand, the SOFM algorithm has the advantage of simplicity of implementation.

11.5 Discussion

Shannon's information theory is endowed with some important concepts and powerful theorems that befit them for the study of different aspects of neural networks. In Chapter 6 we used the idea of relative entropy to derive a special form of the back-propagation algorithm. In Chapter 8 we used it to derive the *Boltzmann learning rule;* this latter rule is basic to the operation of the Boltzmann and mean-field-theory machines.

Information theory is well equipped to explain many aspects of sensory processing (Atick, 1992). Consider, for example, the *information bottleneck* phenomenon that may arise at some point along a sensory pathway, which means that somewhere along the pathway there exists a restriction on the rate of data flow onto higher levels. This phenomenon may arise because of a limitation on the bandwidth or dynamic range of a neural link, which is not unlikely given the limited resources available to neurons in the human brain. Another way in which an information bottleneck can arise is the existence of a computational bottleneck at higher levels of the sensory pathway, imposing a limitation on the number of bits of data per second needed to perform the requisite analysis.

In previous sections of this chapter we focused much of our attention on mutual information, which provides the theoretical basis of Linsker's *principle of maximum information preservation.* According to this principle, any layer of a perceptual system should adapt itself so as to maximize the information conveyed to that layer about the input patterns. It is striking that, as demonstrated in Section 11.4, this principle exhibits properties of Hebb-like modification, and cooperative and competitive learning, combined in a particular way, even though no assumptions are made concerning the form of the learning rule or its component properties (Linsker, 1989b).

Plumbley and Fallside (1988) change the emphasis in the principle of maximum information preservation slightly by redefining it as a *minimization of information loss.* Expressed in this form, they apply a minimax approach to the information loss, relating it to the more familiar criterion of minimizing mean-squared error. In particular, they use this approach to analyze a linear network with a single layer of neurons that performs dimensionality reduction. The analysis assumes the presence of additive Gaussian noise. The conclusion drawn from this analysis is that the information loss due to the input–output mapping is upper-bounded by the entropy of the reconstruction error. Hence the entropy is minimized by minimizing the mean-square value of the reconstruction error. The net result is that the information loss limitation problem is changed into one related to principal components analysis; the subject of principal components analysis was discussed in Chapter 9.

In a subsequent paper, Plumbley and Fallside (1989) examine the goals of the early stages of a perceptual system before the signal reaches the cortex, and describe their operation in information-theoretic terms. It is argued that in such a system, optimal transmission of information involves the temporal and spatial decorrelation of the signal before transmission. That is, the temporal and spatial power spectra should be uniform up to the available bandwidth. Recognizing that most real-world signals contain a large proportion of low spatial and temporal frequencies, it is noted that the processes of temporal adaptation and spatial lateral inhibition are required to filter the input signal so as to produce the desired flat output power spectrum.

In Chapter 9 we also discussed how Linsker's layered feedforward model, based on Hebbian learning, may be used to explain the emergence of different receptive fields in early visual systems. The results presented in that chapter were all based on computer simulations. Tang (1991) has extended Linsker's layered model by using information-theoretic ideas to derive analytic solutions for the problems posed by Linsker's model. Tang's theory builds on the principle of maximum information preservation. Moreover, it is proposed that the layered network may be an *active* multimode communication channel that participates in the decision-making process, with the result that some modes of the input are selected for their relevant functional characteristics. Applications of the theory to edge detection and motion detection are demonstrated in Tang (1991).

Linsker (1993) extends the principle of maximum information preservation by applying it to a class of weakly nonlinear input–output mappings. The *weakly nonlinear input–output relation* considered by Linsker is defined by

$$y_j = v_j + \varepsilon v_j^3 + \sum_i w_{ji}\nu_i + \nu_j' \tag{11.77}$$

where y_j is the output of neuron j and v_j is the internal activity level of neuron j defined in terms of the inputs x_i by

$$v_j = \sum_i w_{ji} x_i \tag{11.78}$$

The ε is assumed to be a small constant. The noise at the ith input of neuron j is denoted by ν_i and that at its output by ν_j'. On the basis of this nonlinear, noisy model of a neuron, it is shown that the application of the principle of maximum information preservation results in the generation of optimum filters with some interrelated properties, as summarized here (Linsker, 1993):

- A type of *sparse coding* exemplified by the concentration of activity among a relatively small number of neurons
- Sensitivity to higher-order statistics of the input
- Emergence of *multiresolution* capability with subsampling at spatial frequencies, as favored solutions for certain types of input ensembles.

Such a model may be useful for a better understanding of the formation of place-coded representations in biological systems (Linsker, 1993).

Contextual Supervision

Kay (1992) has considered a neural network for which the input data may be divided into two sets: a *primary input* denoted by vector $\mathbf{x}_1$ of dimension p_1, and a *contextual input* denoted by vector $\mathbf{x}_2$ of dimension p_2. In practice, there would be several realizations of the overall input vector $\mathbf{x} = (\mathbf{x}_1, \mathbf{x}_2)$ available for use. The goal of the exercise is to discover the structure of the information contained in the primary vector $\mathbf{x}_1$ in light of the contextual input vector $\mathbf{x}_2$ used as a "teacher." The key question is: Given the vectors $\mathbf{x}_1$ and $\mathbf{x}_2$, how do we proceed? As a first step, we may wish to find those linear functions of the primary input vector $\mathbf{x}_1$ that are maximally correlated with the contextual input vector $\mathbf{x}_2$. The strength of this relationship is measured using the average mutual information between $\mathbf{x}_1$ and $\mathbf{x}_2$. Let

$$y_i = \mathbf{a}_i^T \mathbf{x}_1 \tag{11.79}$$

and

$$z_i = \mathbf{b}_i^T \mathbf{x}_2 \tag{11.80}$$

A case of interest arises when the input vector $\mathbf{x}$ is random, and it follows a multivariate, elliptically symmetric probability model of the form

$$cf((\mathbf{x} - \boldsymbol{\mu})^T \boldsymbol{\Sigma}^{-1} (\mathbf{x} - \boldsymbol{\mu})), \qquad \mathbf{x} \in \mathbb{R}^{p_1 + p_2} \tag{11.81}$$

where c is a constant, $\boldsymbol{\mu}$ and $\boldsymbol{\Sigma}$ are the mean vector and covariance matrix of $\mathbf{x}$, respectively, and $f(\cdot)$ is a real-valued function. The covariance matrix $\boldsymbol{\Sigma}$ may be written as

$$\boldsymbol{\Sigma} = \begin{bmatrix} \boldsymbol{\Sigma}_{11} & \boldsymbol{\Sigma}_{12} \\ \boldsymbol{\Sigma}_{21} & \boldsymbol{\Sigma}_{22} \end{bmatrix} \tag{11.82}$$

where

$$\boldsymbol{\Sigma}_{11} = \mathrm{cov}[\mathbf{x}_1]$$

$$\boldsymbol{\Sigma}_{22} = \mathrm{cov}[\mathbf{x}_2]$$

$$\boldsymbol{\Sigma}_{12} = \mathrm{cov}[\mathbf{x}_1, \mathbf{x}_2] = \boldsymbol{\Sigma}_{21}^T$$

It is assumed that the covariance matrix $\mathbf{\Sigma}$ is positive definite, which implies that the inverse matrices $\mathbf{\Sigma}_{11}^{-1}$ and $\mathbf{\Sigma}_{22}^{-1}$ exist. For the particular situation described here, it may be shown that the mutual information $I(\mathbf{x}_1; \mathbf{x}_2)$ between $\mathbf{x}_1$ and $\mathbf{x}_2$ is linked to the mutual information $I(y_i; z_i)$ between y_i and z_i as follows (Kay, 1992):

$$\begin{aligned} I(\mathbf{x}_1; \mathbf{x}_2) &= \sum_{i=1}^{r} I(y_i; z_i) + \text{constant} \\ &= -\sum_{i=1}^{r} \log(1 - \rho_i^2) + \text{constant} \end{aligned} \tag{11.83}$$

where r is the *rank* of the cross-covariance matrix $\mathbf{\Sigma}_{12}$, and ρ_i is the *normalized correlation coefficient* between y_i and z_i for $i = 1, 2, \ldots, r$. The set of correlations $\{\rho_i | i = 1, 2, \ldots, r\}$ are called the *canonical correlations* between $\mathbf{x}_1$ and $\mathbf{x}_2$ (Rao, 1973). The definition of canonical correlations hinges on the mutual uncorrelatedness of the pairs $\{y_i, z_i | i = 1, 2, \ldots, r\}$. The property described in Eq. (11.83) may be exploited to form a simple index for finding the number of pairs required to summarize the structure of linear dependence between the input vectors $\mathbf{x}_1$ and $\mathbf{x}_2$. Following the earlier work of Sanger (1989b) on principal components analysis that was described in Section 9.7, Kay (1992) proposes a neural network for computing the canonical correlations, based on the following pair of recursive equations:

$$\mathbf{a}_i(n+1) = \mathbf{a}_i(n) + \eta(n) z_i(n)[g_{i-1}(y) - y_i^2(n)]\mathbf{x}_1(n) \tag{11.84}$$

$$\mathbf{b}_i(n+1) = \mathbf{b}_i(n) + \eta(n) y_i(n)[h_{i-1}(z) - z_i^2(n)]\mathbf{x}_2(n) \tag{11.85}$$

where n denotes discrete time, $\eta(n)$ is a learning-rate parameter that tends to zero at a suitable rate as $n \to \infty$, and

$$g_i(y) = g_{i-1}(y) - y_i^2(n) \tag{11.86}$$

$$h_i(z) = h_{i-1}(z) - z_i^2(n) \tag{11.87}$$

For the initialization of the algorithm, we set

$$g_0(y) = h_0(z) = 1 \tag{11.88}$$

To realize a local implementation of the recursions described in Eqs. (11.84) and (11.85), we may arrange the $\{y_i(n), z_i(n)\}$ in pairs, and then update $\mathbf{a}_i(n)$ and $\mathbf{b}_i(n)$ using outputs $y_i(n)$ and $z_i(n)$ plus a local lateral connection between neighboring output pairs. The ith canonical correlation $\rho_i(n)$ is obtained from the product $y_i(n)z_i(n)$. The feature discovery procedure under contextual supervision described here has potential applications involving the fusion of data from two different two-dimensional projections of a three-dimensional object, or the integration of visual and aural data recorded from the same stimulus (Kay, 1992).

11.6 Spatially Coherent Features

Becker and Hinton (1992) have extended the idea of maximizing mutual information to unsupervised processing of the image of a natural scene. An unprocessed pixel of such an image contains a wealth of information about the scene of interest, albeit in complex form. In particular, the intensity of each pixel is affected by such intrinsic parameters as depth, reflectance, and surface orientation, as well as background noise and illumination. The goal is to design a self-organizing system that is capable of learning to encode this complex information in a simpler form. To be more specific, the objective is to extract higher-order features that exhibit *simple coherence across space* in such a way that the representation of information in one spatially localized patch of the image makes it easy to produce the presentation of information in neighboring patches. Becker and Hinton use this approach to design a network made up of a number of modules receiving inputs from nearby patches of the image, with each module learning to discover higher-order features for displaying spatial coherence.

Consider Fig. 11.5, which shows two modules receiving inputs from adjacent, nonoverlapping patches of an image. Let y_a and y_b denote the outputs of the two modules. The unsupervised learning procedure developed by Becker and Hinton (1992) for image processing is to maximize the mutual information between the network outputs y_a and y_b. This mutual information, in light of the last line of Eq. (11.30), is defined by

$$I(y_a; y_b) = h(y_a) + h(y_b) - h(y_a, y_b) \tag{11.89}$$

where $h(y_a)$ and $h(y_b)$ are the entropies of y_a and y_b, respectively, and $h(y_a, y_b)$ is their joint entropy. The requirement is to maximize the mutual information $I(y_a; y_b)$ with respect to the synaptic weights of both modules in Fig. 11.5. Under Gaussian assumptions, a simple objective function based on $I(y_a; y_b)$ can be derived for the self-organized learning process. Specifically, it is assumed that both modules receive input that is produced by some common signal s corrupted by independent Gaussian noise in each input patch, and that the modules transform the input into outputs y_a and y_b that are noisy versions of the common signal s, as shown by

$$y_a = s + \nu_a \tag{11.90}$$

and

$$y_b = s + \nu_b \tag{11.91}$$

where ν_a and ν_b are the additive noise components. According to this model, the two modules make consistent assumptions about each other. It may be readily shown that the

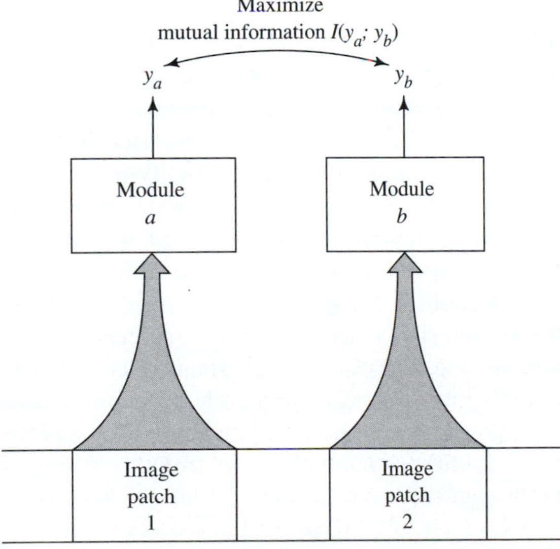

FIGURE 11.5 Illustration of the idea of an image processor using two neural modules *a* and *b* that receive their inputs from two adjacent, nonoverlapping patches of an image; the learning process is designed to maximize the average mutual information between the outputs of the two modules.

mutual information between y_a and y_b is (Becker, 1992)

$$I(y_a; y_b) = \frac{1}{2}\log\left(\frac{\text{var}[y_a] + \text{var}[y_b]}{\text{var}[y_a] + \text{var}[y_b] - \text{var}[s]}\right) \tag{11.92}$$

where var[·] denotes the variance of the enclosed random variable. Under the same model, a simpler measure of performance that appears to work in practice as well as $I(y_a; y_b)$ is the following (Becker, 1992):

$$I^* = \frac{1}{2}\log\left(\frac{\text{var}[y_a + y_b]}{\text{var}[y_a - y_b]}\right) \tag{11.93}$$

The mutual information I^* defines the amount of information the average of the outputs y_a and y_b conveys about the common underlying signal s (i.e., the particular feature that is *coherent* in the two input patches). By maximizing the mutual information I^*, the two modules are forced to extract as pure a version of the underlying common signal as possible. An algorithm based on this maximization has been used by Becker and Hinton (1992) to discover higher-order features such as stereo disparity and surface curvature in random-dot stereograms. Moreover, under the assumption of a Gaussian mixture model of the underlying coherent feature, the algorithm has been extended to develop population codes of spatially coherent features such as stereo disparity (Becker and Hinton, 1992), and to model the locations of discontinuities in depth (Becker and Hinton, 1993); Gaussian mixture models were discussed in Section 7.10.

It is of interest to note that in the case of linear networks assuming a multidimensional Gaussian distribution, the self-organizing model due to Becker and Hinton is equivalent to canonical correlations between the inputs (Becker, 1992). A similar result is obtained in the model described in Section 11.5 due to Kay (1992). However, while Kay's model is an attractive model for self-organization because of its simple learning rule, the Becker–Hinton model is more general in that it can be applied to multilayer networks.

Signal Separation

Inspired by the earlier work of Becker and Hinton (1989, 1992) on the extraction of spatially coherent features just described, Ukrainec and Haykin (1992) have successfully developed an information-theoretic model for the enhancement of a polarization target in dual-polarized radar images. The sample radar scene used in the study is described as follows. An incoherent radar transmits in a horizontally polarized fashion, and receives radar returns on both horizontal and vertical polarization channels. The target of interest is a *cooperative, polarization-twisting reflector* designed to rotate the incident polarization through 90°. In the normal operation of a radar system, the detection of such a target is made difficult by imperfections in the system as well as reflections from unwanted polarimetric targets on the ground (i.e., radar clutter). It is perceived that a nonlinear mapping is needed to account for the non-Gaussian distribution common to radar returns. The target enhancement problem is cast as a variational problem involving the minimization of a quadratic cost functional with constraints. The net result is a processed cross-polarized image that exhibits a significant improvement in target visibility, far more pronounced than that attainable through the use of a linear technique such as principal components analysis.

The model used by Ukrainec and Haykin assumes Gaussian statistics for the transformed data, since a model-free estimate of the probability density function is a computationally challenging task. The mutual information between two Gaussian variables y_a and y_b is defined by (see Problem 11.4):

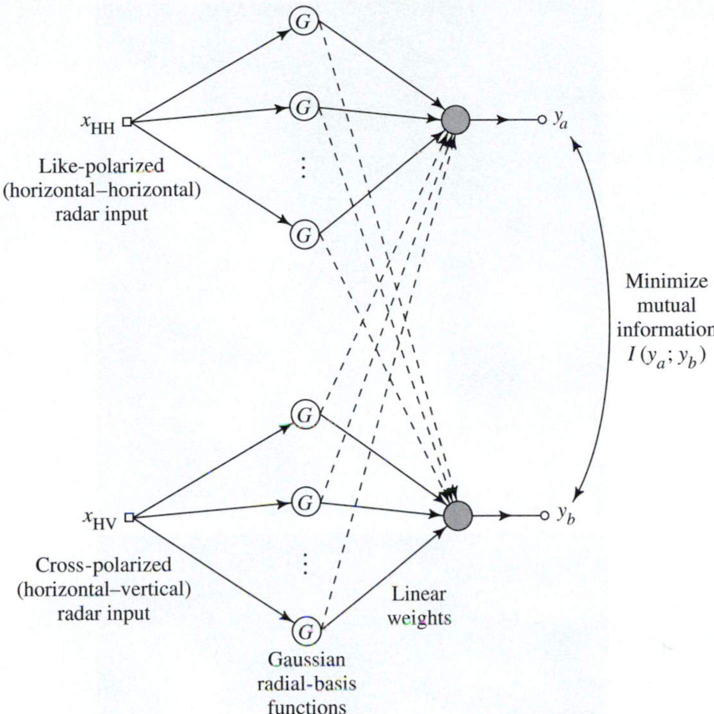

FIGURE 11.6 Block diagram of a neural processor, the goal of which is to suppress background clutter using a pair of polarimetric, noncoherent radar inputs; clutter suppression is attained by minimizing the average mutual information between the outputs of the two modules.

$$I(y_a; y_b) = -\frac{1}{2}\log(1 - \rho_{ab}^2) \tag{11.94}$$

where ρ_{ab} is the correlation coefficient between the two random variables y_a and y_b. To learn the synaptic weights of the two modules, a variational approach is taken. The requirement is to *suppress* the radar clutter that is common to the horizontally polarized and vertically polarized radar images. To satisfy this requirement, we *minimize* the mutual information $I(y_a; y_b)$, subject to a *constraint* imposed on the synaptic weights as shown by

$$P = (\text{tr}[\mathbf{W}^T\mathbf{W}] - 1)^2 \tag{11.95}$$

where $\mathbf{W}$ is the overall weight matrix of the network, and tr[·] is the trace of the enclosed matrix. A stationary point is reached when we have

$$\nabla_\mathbf{W} I(y_a; y_b) + \lambda\, \nabla_\mathbf{W} P = 0 \tag{11.96}$$

where λ is the Lagrange multiplier. A quasi-Newton optimization routine was used to find the minimum; Newton's method was discussed in Chapter 6.

Figure 11.6 shows the architecture of the neural network used by Ukrainec and Haykin (1992). A Gaussian radial basis function (RBF) network was chosen for each of the two modules because it has the advantage of providing a set of fixed basis functions (i.e., a nonadaptive hidden layer). The input data is expanded onto the basis functions and then combined using layers of *linear* weights; the dashed lines shown in Fig. 11.6 represent the cross-coupling connections between the two modules. The centers of the Gaussian

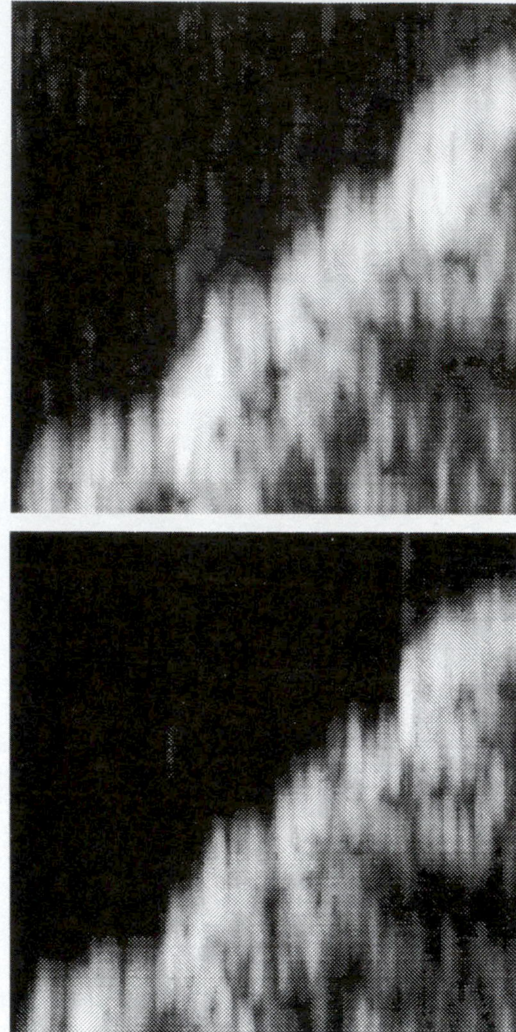

FIGURE 11.7a Raw B-scan radar images (azimuth plotted versus range) for horizontal–horizontal (top) and horizontal–vertical (bottom) polarizations.

functions were chosen at evenly spaced intervals to cover the entire input domain, and their widths were chosen using a heuristic.

Figure 11.7a shows the raw horizontally polarized and vertically polarized (both on receive) radar images of a parklike setting on the shore of Lake Ontario. The range coordinate is along the horizontal axis of each image, increasing from left to right; the azimuth coordinate is along the vertical axis, increasing down the image. Figure 11.7b shows the combined image obtained by minimizing the mutual information between the horizontally and vertically polarized radar images, as just described. The bright spot clearly visible in this image corresponds to the radar return from a cooperative, polarization-twisting reflector placed along the lake shore. The clutter-suppression performance of the information-theoretic model described here exceeds that of commonly used projections using principal components analysis (Ukrainec and Haykin, 1992).

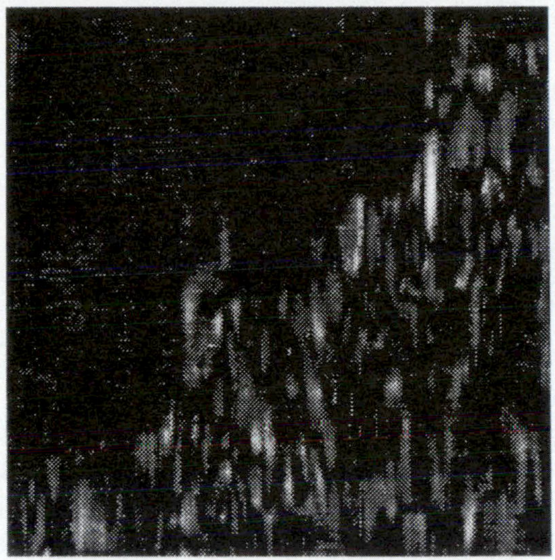

FIGURE 11.7b Composite image computed by minimizing the average mutual information between the two polarized radar images of Fig. 11.7a.

11.7 Another Information-Theoretic Model of the Perceptual System

In Section 11.5 we discussed a model of the perceptual system proposed by Plumbley and Fallside (1988), based on a modification of the principle of maximum information preservation. In yet another approach to the study of perceptual systems, Atick and Redlich (1990a) have investigated the *principle of minimum redundancy* that applies to noisy channels. Figure 11.8 depicts a model of the perceptual system used in the study. The model consists of three components: *input channel, recoding system,* and *output channel.* The output of the input channel is described by

$$\mathbf{x} = \mathbf{s} + \mathbf{n}_1 \tag{11.97}$$

where $\mathbf{s}$ is an ideal signal received by the input channel and $\mathbf{n}_1$ is assumed to be the source of all noise in the input. The signal $\mathbf{x}$ is subsequently transformed (recoded) by a linear matrix operator $\mathbf{A}$. It is then transmitted through the optic nerve, or output channel, producing the output $\mathbf{y}$, as shown by

$$\mathbf{y} = \mathbf{A}\mathbf{x} + \mathbf{n}_2 \tag{11.98}$$

where $\mathbf{n}_2$ denotes the postencoding intrinsic noise. The approach taken by Atick and Redlich was inspired by Barlow's hypothesis for the goal of sensory transformations

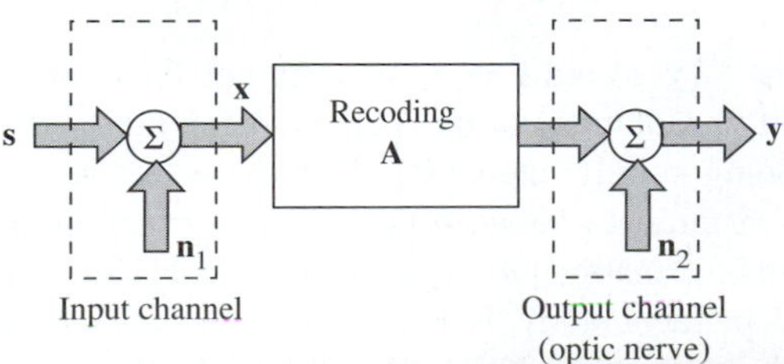

FIGURE 11.8 A model of a perceptual system.

(Barlow, 1989). The idea behind the approach is based on the fact that light signals arriving at the retina contain useful sensory information in a highly redundant form. Moreover, it is hypothesized that the purpose of retinal signal processing is to reduce or eliminate the "redundant" bits of data due to both correlations and noise, before sending the signal along the optic nerve. To quantify this notion, Atick and Redlich introduced the redundancy measure

$$R = 1 - \frac{I(\mathbf{y}; \mathbf{s})}{C(\mathbf{y})} \tag{11.99}$$

where $I(\mathbf{y}; \mathbf{s})$ is the mutual information between $\mathbf{y}$ and $\mathbf{s}$, and $C(\mathbf{y})$ is the channel capacity of the optic nerve (output channel). Equation (11.99) is justified on the grounds that the information the brain is interested in is the ideal signal $\mathbf{s}$, while the physical channel through which this information must pass is in reality the optic nerve. It is assumed that there is no dimensionality reduction in the input–output mapping performed by the perceptual system, which means that $C(\mathbf{y}) > I(\mathbf{y}; \mathbf{s})$. The requirement is to find an input–output mapping (i.e., matrix $\mathbf{A}$) that minimizes the redundancy measure R, subject to the constraint of no information loss, as shown by

$$I(\mathbf{y}; \mathbf{x}) = I(\mathbf{x}; \mathbf{x}) - \varepsilon \tag{11.100}$$

where ε is some small positive parameter. The *channel capacity* $C(\mathbf{y})$ is defined as the maximum rate of information flow possible through the optic nerve, ranging over all probability distributions of inputs applied to it, and keeping the average input power fixed.

When the signal vector $\mathbf{s}$ and the output vector $\mathbf{y}$ have the same dimensionality, and there is noise in the system, Atick and Redlich's principle of minimum redundancy and Linsker's principle of maximum information preservation are essentially equivalent, provided that a similar constraint is imposed on the computational capability of the output neurons in both cases (Linsker, 1992). To be specific, suppose that [as in Atick and Redlich (1990b)] the channel capacity is measured in terms of the dynamic range of the output of each neuron in the model of Fig. 11.8. Then, according to the principle of minimum redundancy, the quantity to be minimized is

$$1 - \frac{I(\mathbf{y}; \mathbf{s})}{C(\mathbf{y})}$$

for a given permissible information loss, and therefore for a given $I(\mathbf{y}; \mathbf{s})$. Thus the quantity to be minimized is essentially

$$F_1(\mathbf{y}; \mathbf{s}) = C(\mathbf{y}) - \lambda I(\mathbf{y}; \mathbf{s}) \tag{11.101}$$

On the other hand, according to the principle of maximum information preservation, the quantity to be maximized in the model of Fig. 11.8 is

$$F_2(\mathbf{y}; \mathbf{s}) = I(\mathbf{y}; \mathbf{s}) + \lambda C(\mathbf{y}) \tag{11.102}$$

Although the functions $F_1(\mathbf{y}; \mathbf{s})$ and $F_2(\mathbf{y}; \mathbf{s})$ are different, their optimizations yield identical results: They are both formulations of the method of Lagrange multipliers, with the roles of $I(\mathbf{y}; \mathbf{s})$ and $C(\mathbf{y})$ being simply interchanged.

Thus, despite the differences between the principle of minimum redundancy and the principle of maximum information preservation, they lead to similar results. It is of interest to note that in an independent study, Nadal and Parga (1993) reach a similar conclusion; they consider a single-layer perceptron (using the McCulloch–Pitts model of a neuron) in the context of an unsupervised learning task.

11.8 Concluding Remarks

In this chapter we introduced several information-theoretic models for self-organized learning. The most common theme of these models is Shannon's notion of *mutual information* (Shannon, 1948). In Linsker's principle of maximum information preservation (Linsker, 1988a), self-organized learning is achieved by maximizing the mutual information between the input and output vectors of the model of interest; this optimization principle is referred to in the literature as *infomax*. In the self-organized learning model proposed by Becker and Hinton (1992), the mutual information between the outputs of two modules is maximized, with adjacent, nonoverlapping patches of an image providing the inputs applied to the two modules; this latter optimization principle is referred to in the literature as the I_{max} *learning procedure*. Both self-organized learning procedures, *infomax* and I_{max}, rely on the use of *noisy models*. Most frequently, the noise is assumed to be produced by Gaussian sources that operate in an additive manner, an assumption that is made for mathematical tractability.

Infomax is well suited for the development of self-organized models and feature maps. On the other hand, I_{max} is well suited for image processing, with emphasis on the discovery of properties of a noisy sensory input that exhibit coherence across space and time. The challenge for future research, inspired by information-theoretic ideas, is to develop more powerful learning procedures involving the use of *nonlinear models* that can extract higher-order features and that are applicable to a variety of signal classification and signal separation problems (Becker and Plumbley, 1993).

PROBLEMS

11.1 Derive the properties of the average mutual information $I(x; y)$ between two continuous-valued random values x and y as shown in Eqs. (11.30) through (11.32).

11.2 Consider two channels whose outputs are represented by the random variables x and y. The requirement is to maximize the mutual information between x and y. Show that this requirement is achieved by satisfying two conditions:

(a) The probability of occurrence of x or that of y is 0.5.

(b) The joint probability distribution of x and y is concentrated in a small region of the probability space.

11.3 Prove the result described in Eq. (11.62) for the relative entropy of an N-dimensional Gaussian distribution.

11.4 Consider two random variables, x_1 and x_2, that are noisy versions of some underlying signal s, as described by

$$y_a = s + \nu_a, \qquad y_b = s + \nu_b$$

where ν_a and ν_b denote additive, independent, and zero-mean Gaussian noise components.

(a) Show that the average mutual information between y_a and y_b is given by

$$I(y_a; y_b) = -\frac{1}{2}\log(1 - \rho_{ab}^2)$$

where ρ_{ab} is the *correlation coefficient* between y_a and y_b; that is,

$$\rho_{ab} = \frac{E[y_a y_b]}{(E[y_a^2]E[y_b^2])^{1/2}}$$

(b) What is the condition for which the average mutual information $I(y_a; y_b)$ is (i) maximum and (ii) minimum?

11.5 Consider the average mutual information $I(\mathbf{x}; \{j\})$ defined in Eq. (11.72). Show that the derivative of $I(\mathbf{x}; \{j\})$ with respect to center $\mathbf{t}_i$ of node i is as shown in Eq. (11.75) with vector $\mathbf{z}_i(\mathbf{x})$ defined in Eq. (11.76).

11.6 Show that the topologically ordered map produced by applying the principle of maximum information preservation satisfies the ideal condition of Eq. (10.29) for the map magnification factor. You may refer to Linsker (1989b), where this issue is discussed in detail.

11.7 In this problem we use the information-theoretic rule described in Section 11.5 to generate a topologically ordered map for a two-dimensional uniform distribution. At each iteration of the algorithm, the center $\mathbf{t}_{i,j}$ of node (i,j) is changed by a small amount

$$\Delta\mathbf{t}_{i,j} = \frac{1}{K}\sum_{k=1}^{K} \mathbf{z}_{i,j}(\mathbf{x}_k), \qquad i,j = 1, 2, \ldots, 10$$

where $\{\mathbf{x}_k\}$ is an ensemble of input vectors; see Eq. (11.76). The parameter values are as follows (Linsker, 1989b):

$$\alpha = 20$$

$$\beta = \tfrac{4}{9}$$

$$K = 900$$

Starting with a random selection of centers $\mathbf{t}_{i,j}$, plot the map produced by the learning rule after 0, 10, 15, and 40 iterations.

11.8 Consider an input vector $\mathbf{x}$ made up of a primary component $\mathbf{x}_1$ and a contextual component $\mathbf{x}_2$. Define

$$y_i = \mathbf{a}_i^T\mathbf{x}_1$$

$$z_i = \mathbf{b}_i^T\mathbf{x}_2$$

Show that the mutual information between $\mathbf{x}_1$ and $\mathbf{x}_2$ is related to the mutual information between y_i and z_i as described in Eq. (11.83). Assume the probability model of Eq. (11.81) for the input vector $\mathbf{x}$.

11.9 Equation (11.92) defines the mutual information between two continuous random variables y_a and y_b, assuming the Gaussian model described by Eqs. (11.90) and (11.91). Derive the formula of Eq. (11.92).

Equation (11.93) provides a simpler measure of performance than that of Eq. (11.92). Derive the alternative formula of Eq. (11.93).

CHAPTER 12

Modular Networks

12.1 Introduction

The hierarchical levels of organization in artificial neural networks may be classified as follows. At the most fundamental level are synapses, followed by neurons, then layers of neurons in the case of a layered network, and finally the network itself. The design of neural networks that we have pursued up to this point has been of a modular nature at the level of neurons or layers only. It may be argued that the architecture of a neural network should go one step higher in the hierarchical level of organization. Specifically, it should consist of a multiplicity of networks, and that learning algorithms should be designed to take full advantage of the resulting modular structure. The present chapter is devoted to a particular class of *modular networks* that relies on the combined use of supervised and unsupervised learning paradigms.

We may justify the rationale for the use of modular networks by considering the approximation problem. The approximation of a prescribed input–output mapping may be realized using a *local* method that captures the underlying local structure of the mapping. Such a model is exemplified by radial-basis function (RBF) networks, which were studied in Chapter 7. The use of a local method offers the advantage of fast learning and therefore the ability to operate in real time, since it usually requires relatively few training examples to learn a single task. However, a limitation of local methods is that they tend to be memory intensive. Alternatively, the approximation may be realized using a *global* method that captures the underlying global structure of the mapping. This second model is exemplified by back-propagation learning applied to multilayer perceptrons, which were studied in Chapter 6. The use of global methods offers the advantages of a smaller storage requirement and better generalization performance. However, they suffer from a slow learning process that limits their range of applications. In light of this dichotomy between local and global methods of approximation, it is natural to ask: How can we combine the advantages of these two methods? The answer appears to lie in the use of a *modular* architecture that captures the underlying structure of an input–output mapping at an intermediate level of granularity. The idea of using a modular network for realizing a complex mapping function was discussed by Hinton and Jacobs as far back as the mid-1980s (Jacobs et al., 1991a). Mention should also be made of a *committee machine* consisting of a layer of elementary perceptrons followed by a vote-taking perceptron in the second layer, which was described in Nilsson (1965). However, it appears that the class of modular networks discussed in this chapter was first described in Jacobs and Jordan (1991), and the architecture for it was presented by Jacobs et al. (1991a).

A useful feature of a modular approach is that it also provides a better fit to a discontinuous input–output mapping. Consider, for example, Fig. 12.1, which depicts a

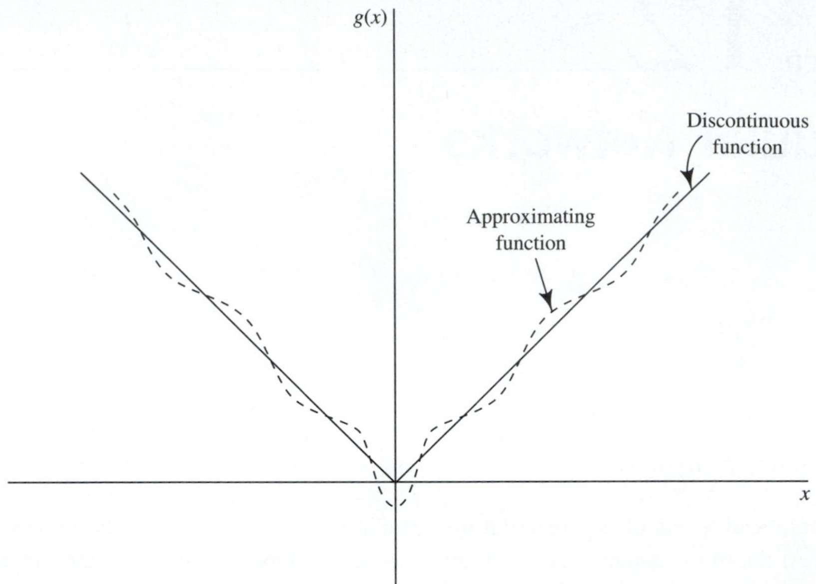

FIGURE 12.1 A discontinuous (piecewise-linear) function and its approximation.

one-dimensional function $g(x)$ with a discontinuity, as described by

$$g(x) = \begin{cases} x, & x > 0 \\ -x, & x \leq 0 \end{cases} \tag{12.1}$$

If we were to use a single fully connected network to approximate this function, the approximation may exhibit erratic behavior near the discontinuity, as illustrated by the dashed curve in Fig. 12.1. In a situation of this kind, it would be preferable to split the function into two separate pieces, and use a modular network to learn each piece separately (Jacobs et al., 1991b).

The use of a modular approach may also be justified on neurobiological grounds. Modularity appears to be an important principle in the architecture of vertebrate nervous systems, and there is much that can be gained from the study of learning in modular networks in different parts of the nervous system (Houk, 1992). For example, the existence of hierarchical representations of information is particularly evident in the cortical visual areas (Van Essen et al., 1992; Van Essen, 1985; Fodor, 1983). The highly complex computation performed by the visual system is broken down into pieces, just like any good engineer would do when designing a complex system, as evidenced by the following (Van Essen et al., 1992):

1. Separate modules are created in the visual system for different subtasks, allowing the neural architecture to be optimized for particular types of computation.
2. The same module is replicated many times, as exemplified by the internal structure of area VI of the visual cortex.
3. Coordinated and efficient routing of information between modules is maintained.

Modularity may therefore be viewed as an *additional variable,* which would permit the formation of *higher-order computational units* that can perform complex tasks. Referring back to the hierarchical levels of organization in the brain as described in Chapter 1, and recognizing the highly complex nature of the computational vision and motor control tasks that a human being can perform so efficiently and effortlessly, it is apparent that modularity as a computational technique *is* the key to understanding complex tasks performed by artificial neural networks. Unfortunately, the scope of our knowledge of this important subject is rather limited at the present. This chapter on a very special kind of modular networks should therefore be viewed as a good beginning.

Organization of the Chapter

The main body of this chapter on modular networks is organized as follows. In Section 12.2 we formally define what we mean by a modular network, and discuss the implications of modularity. In Section 12.3 we describe an associative Gaussian mixture model for a specific configuration of modular networks. This is followed by the derivation of a stochastic-gradient learning algorithm (based on maximization of a log-likelihood function) for the network, which we do in Section 12.4. In Section 12.5 we extend the concept of modularity by developing a hierarchical structure of modular representations. In Section 12.6 we describe an application of modular networks in control. The chapter concludes in Section 12.7 with a summary of the properties of modular networks and some final thoughts on the subject

12.2 Basic Notions of Modularity

A modular network is formally defined as follows.[1]

> *A neural network is said to be modular if the computation performed by the network can be decomposed into two or more modules (subsystems) that operate on distinct inputs without communicating with each other. The outputs of the modules are mediated by an integrating unit that is not permitted to feed information back to the modules. In particular, the integrating unit both (1) decides how the outputs of the modules should be combined to form the final output of the system, and (2) decides which modules should learn which training patterns.*

Modularity may therefore be viewed as a manifestation of the *principle of divide and conquer,* which permits us to solve a complex computational task by dividing it into simpler subtasks and then combining their individual solutions.

A modular network fuses supervised and unsupervised learning paradigms in a seamless fashion. Specifically, we have the following.

- *Supervised learning,* exemplified by an external ''teacher'' that supplies the desired responses (target patterns) needed to train the different modules of the network. However, the teacher does not specify which module of the network should produce each desired response; rather, it is the function of the unsupervised learning paradigm to do this assignment.
- *Unsupervised learning,* exemplified by the modules ''competing'' with each other for the right to produce each desired response. The integrating unit has the role of ''mediating'' among the different modules for this right.

Consequently, the modules of the network tend to *specialize* by learning different regions of the input space. However, the form of competitive learning described here does not necessarily enforce the specialization; rather, it is done naturally. In the competition, roughly speaking, the winner is the module whose output most closely matches the desired

[1] This definition is adapted from Osherson et al. (1990); Jacobs and Jordan (1991); and Jacobs et al. (1991a).

response, and the other modules are the losers. Furthermore, each module receives an amount of training information that is proportional to its relative ability to learn. This means that the winning module receives more training information than the losing modules.

From Chapter 10 we recall that unsupervised learning involves the use of positive feedback. So it is with a modular network in that the competition among the modules for the right to learn the training patterns involves a *positive feedback* effect. More precisely, if a particular module learns a great deal about some training patterns, then it will likely perform well when presented with related training patterns and thus learn a great deal about them too. By the same token, the module will perform poorly when presented with unrelated training patterns, in which case it will learn little or nothing about them. In both cases, the positive feedback effect manifests itself by some form of self-amplification.

The Credit-Assignment Problem

In a neurobiological system, a large network needs constraints to limit the number of synapses to the space available on the surfaces of the dendrites and cell body (soma) of neurons in the system. An additional, and perhaps more restrictive, constraint stems from the difficulty of implementing learning algorithms in large networks (Houk, 1992). This is because of the credit-assignment problem, which was discussed in Chapter 1. This problem refers to the issue of getting the right training information to the right synapses in a network so as to improve the overall system performance. It appears that modularity may serve to organize a network in a manner that is beneficial to credit assignment (Houk and Barto, 1992).

In the case of artificial neural networks, we also expect to find that modularity provides a viable solution to the credit-assignment problem by having the integrating unit learn to properly allocate the training data to the different modules of the network. This allocation is carried out in accordance with the inherent complexity of the input data and the learning capacity of the expert networks acting as estimators.

From statistical estimation theory, we know that (unless we have some prior information) the estimation procedure should include a criterion for selecting the model order (i.e., the number of free parameters in the model). The *minimum description length (MDL) criterion,* which describes the process of searching for a model with the shortest code length, has several attributes that befit its use for model-order selection (Rissanen, 1978, 1989). Most important, since the MDL criterion permits the shortest encoding of the data, a model based on it captures best all the properties in the data that we wish to learn—indeed, can learn. In its most essential form, the MDL criterion may be written as (Rissanen, 1989):

$$\text{MDL}(k) = -\ln f(\mathbf{x}|\hat{\boldsymbol{\theta}})\,\pi(\hat{\boldsymbol{\theta}}) + \frac{k}{2}\ln N \tag{12.2}$$

where k is the number of free parameters in the model, $\hat{\boldsymbol{\theta}}$ is the estimate of the parameter vector $\boldsymbol{\theta}$ characterizing the model, $f(\mathbf{x}|\hat{\boldsymbol{\theta}})$ is the conditional probability density function of the input vector $\mathbf{x}$ given the estimate $\hat{\boldsymbol{\theta}}$, the probability distribution $\pi(\hat{\boldsymbol{\theta}})$ expresses our prior knowledge about the estimate $\hat{\boldsymbol{\theta}}$, and N is the length of data available for processing. The first term in Eq. (12.2) decreases with k, whereas the second term increases with k. Accordingly, the optimum model order k is the value of k for which MDL(k) is minimum. Returning to the issue at hand, it would be highly desirable to have the overall learning capacity of the modular network match the complexity of the input data. For this to happen, the total number of free parameters in the modular network should ideally satisfy the MDL criterion. With the modular network containing a multitude of expert networks and an integrating unit, it is obvious that each expert network is too simple to deal with the complexity of the input data by itself. Accordingly, when an expert network is faced with complex data, it will unavoidably yield large *residuals* (i.e., estimation errors). This will, in turn, fuel the competitive process in the modular network and thereby permit the other expert networks to try to describe the residuals. This is accomplished under the direction of the integrating unit, thereby providing a viable solution to the credit-assignment problem.

Advantages of Modular Networks

The use of modular architecture has an important implication: *The structure of each module in the network biases the set of training data for which it is likely to win the competition.* In other words, the network is sensitive to structure–function relationships characterizing the training patterns, and such relationships can be exploited to bias the nature of the decomposition discovered by the network and thereby develop specialization among the different modules. Thus, by its very design and implications, a modular network offers several advantages over a single neural network in terms of learning speed, representation capability, and the ability to deal with hardware constraints, as explained here (Jacobs et al., 1991b).

1. *Speed of Learning.* If a complex function is naturally decomposable into a set of simpler functions, then a modular network has the built-in ability to discover the decomposition. Accordingly, a modular network is able to learn the set of simpler functions faster than a multilayer perceptron can learn the undecomposed complex function. Consider, for example, the piecewise-linear function defined in Eq. (12.1) and depicted in Fig. 12.1. This function can be learned by a multilayer perceptron with at least a single hidden layer. Alternatively, it can be learned by a modular network consisting simply of two linear neurons and an integrating unit. One neuron learns the function $g(x) = x$ for $x > 0$, and the other neuron learns the remaining function $g(x) = -x$ for $x \leq 0$. The role of the integrating unit is to select the appropriate neuron in the appropriate context. Assuming that the integrating unit is able to learn its role relatively easily, a modular network should be able to learn the function $g(x)$ faster than a multilayer perceptron for two reasons: (1) It has no hidden neurons, and (2) each of its two modules (made up of single neurons) is required to learn only a linear function (Jacobs et al., 1991b).

2. *Data Representation.* The representation of input data developed by a modular network tends to be easier to understand than in the case of an ordinary multilayer perceptron, by virtue of the ability of a modular network to decompose a complex task into a number of simpler tasks. This property was demonstrated by Rueckl et al. (1989), who used simulated retinal images to perform two relatively independent tasks: object recognition (''what'' task), and spatial location (''where'' task). Comparative computations involving two different models were investigated:

- An *unsplit model,* consisting of a fully connected multilayer perceptron with a single hidden layer
- A *split model,* in which the synaptic weights between the hidden and output layers were partitioned into two equal subsets, one subset connected only to the output neurons representing the ''what'' task and the other subset connected only to the remaining output neurons representing the ''where'' task.

The two models were tested on the same simulated retinal data. At each time step of the simulation, one of nine objects is placed at one of nine corners of a simulated retina. The ''what'' task is to identify the object, and the ''where'' task is to identify its location in the retina. When the unsplit model is used to resolve these two relatively independent tasks, the same set of hidden neurons is forced to represent information about both tasks. On the other hand, in the case of the split model, different sets of hidden neurons are used to represent information about the two tasks. Provided that enough computational resources were available in both cases, the split model was found to develop more efficient internal representations.

3. *Hardware Constraints.* In a brain, there is a physical limit on the number of neurons that can be accommodated in the available space. In a related discussion on representations employed by the brain, it is suggested by Ballard (1986) that such a limitation compels the brain to adopt a modular structure, and that the brain uses a coarse code to represent multidimensional spaces. To represent a space of dimension k, it is hypothesized that the number of neurons required to do the representation is N^k/D^{k-1}, where N is the number of just-noticeable differences in each dimension of the space and D is the diameter of the receptive field of each neuron. With a limit imposed on the number of neurons in a cortical area of the brain, the representation of high-dimensional spaces is distributed in different areas that compute different functions. In an analogous manner, it may be argued that, in order to reduce the number of neurons in an artificial neural network, the representation of multidimensional spaces may be distributed among multiple networks (Jacobs et al., 1991b).

With the background on modularity described in this section and the previous one, we are ready to undertake a detailed analysis of a special class of modular networks, which we do in the remaining sections of the chapter.[2]

12.3 Associative Gaussian Mixture Model

Consider the specific configuration of a modular network shown in Fig. 12.2. The structure consists of K supervised modules called *expert networks,* and an integrating unit called a *gating network* that performs the function of a mediator among the expert networks.

Let the training examples be denoted by input vector $\mathbf{x}$ of dimension p and desired response (target output) vector $\mathbf{d}$ of dimension q. The input vector $\mathbf{x}$ is applied to the expert networks and the gating network simultaneously. Let $\mathbf{y}_i$ denote the q-by-1 output vector of the ith expert network, let g_i denote the activation of the ith output neuron of the gating network, and let $\mathbf{y}$ denote the q-by-1 output vector of the whole modular network. We may then write

$$\mathbf{y} = \sum_{i=1}^{K} g_i \mathbf{y}_i \tag{12.3}$$

The goal of the learning algorithm used to train the modular network of Fig. 12.2 is to model the probability distribution of the set of training patterns $\{\mathbf{x},\mathbf{d}\}$. We assume that the patterns $\{\mathbf{x},\mathbf{d}\}$ used to do the training are generated by a number of different regressive processes.

To do the learning, the expert networks and the gating network in Fig. 12.2 are all trained simultaneously. For this purpose, we may use a learning algorithm that proceeds as follows (Jacobs and Jordan, 1991).

1. An input vector $\mathbf{x}$ is selected at random from some prior distribution.
2. A rule or expert network is chosen from the distribution $P(i|\mathbf{x})$; this is the probability of the ith rule given the input vector $\mathbf{x}$.

[2] Much of the material presented in the remainder of this chapter is based on Jacobs and Jordan (1991), and Jordan and Jacobs (1992). The approach taken in these two papers is statistical in nature, being based on maximum-likelihood estimation. Some similar results are reported by Szymanski and Lemmon (1993), using an information-theoretic approach.

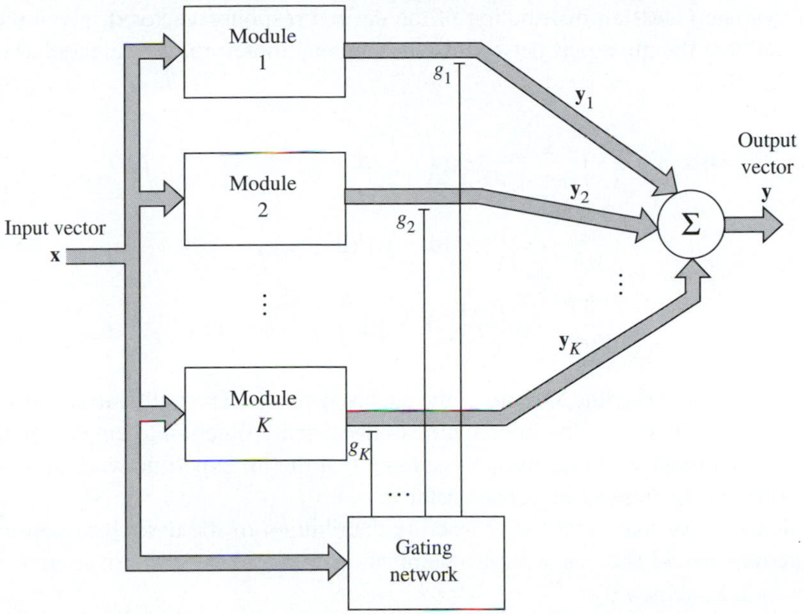

FIGURE 12.2 Block diagram of a modular network; the outputs of the expert networks (modules) are mediated by a gating network.

3. A desired response vector $\mathbf{d}$ is generated by the selected rule i according to the regressive process

$$\mathbf{d} = \mathbf{F}_i(\mathbf{x}) + \boldsymbol{\varepsilon}_i, \qquad i = 1, 2, \ldots, K \tag{12.4}$$

   where $\mathbf{F}_i(\mathbf{x})$ is a deterministic, vector-valued function of the input vector $\mathbf{x}$, and $\boldsymbol{\varepsilon}_i$ is a random vector. For simplicity, it may be assumed that the random vector $\boldsymbol{\varepsilon}_i$ is Gaussian-distributed with zero mean and covariance matrix $\sigma^2\mathbf{I}$, where $\mathbf{I}$ is the identity matrix and σ^2 is a common variance. To simplify matters further, we may set $\sigma^2 = 1$.

Note that the output vector of each expert is *not* modeled as a multivariate Gaussian distribution. Rather, it is viewed as the *conditional mean* of a multivariate Gaussian distribution. Specifically, the output vector $\mathbf{y}_i$ of the ith expert network is written as

$$\mathbf{y}_i = \boldsymbol{\mu}_i, \qquad i = 1, 2, \ldots, K \tag{12.5}$$

The vector $\boldsymbol{\mu}_i$ is the conditional mean of the desired response $\mathbf{d}$ given the input vector $\mathbf{x}$ and that the ith expert network is picked for training, as shown by [in light of Eq. (12.4)]

$$\begin{aligned} \boldsymbol{\mu}_i &= E[\mathbf{d}|\mathbf{x},i] \\ &= \mathbf{F}_i(\mathbf{x}), \qquad i = 1, 2, \ldots, K \end{aligned} \tag{12.6}$$

Note also that, in general, the elements of the output vector of each expert are *not* uncorrelated. Rather, the covariance matrix of the ith expert network's output vector $\mathbf{y}_i$ is the covariance matrix of $\boldsymbol{\varepsilon}_i$. For the sake of simplicity, however, it is assumed that for all K expert networks we have

$$\boldsymbol{\varepsilon}_1 = \boldsymbol{\varepsilon}_2 = \cdots = \boldsymbol{\varepsilon}_K$$

and that the covariance matrix of $\boldsymbol{\varepsilon}_i$ is the identity matrix, as shown by

$$\boldsymbol{\Lambda}_i = \mathbf{I}, \qquad i = 1, 2, \ldots, K \tag{12.7}$$

The multivariate Gaussian distribution of the desired response vector **d**, given the input vector **x** and that the ith expert network is chosen, may therefore be expressed as (Wilks, 1962)

$$\begin{aligned} f(\mathbf{d}|\mathbf{x},i) &= \frac{1}{(2\pi \det \mathbf{\Lambda}_i)^{q/2}} \exp\left(-\frac{1}{2} (\mathbf{d} - \mathbf{y}_i)^T \mathbf{\Lambda}_i^{-1} (\mathbf{d} - \mathbf{y}_i) \right) \\ &= \frac{1}{(2\pi)^{q/2}} \exp\left(-\frac{1}{2} (\mathbf{d} - \mathbf{y}_i)^T (\mathbf{d} - \mathbf{y}_i) \right) \\ &= \frac{1}{(2\pi)^{q/2}} \exp\left(-\frac{1}{2} \|\mathbf{d} - \mathbf{y}_i\|^2 \right), \qquad i = 1, 2, \ldots, K \end{aligned} \tag{12.8}$$

where $\|\cdot\|$ denotes the Euclidean norm of the enclosed vector. The multivariate distribution in Eq. (12.8) is written as a conditional probability density function to emphasize the fact that, for a given input vector **x**, we are assuming that the ith expert network produces the closest match to the desired response vector **d**.

On this basis, we may treat the probability distribution of the desired response vector **d** as a *mixture model* (i.e., as a linear combination of K different multivariate Gaussian distributions), as shown by

$$\begin{aligned} f(\mathbf{d}|\mathbf{x}) &= \sum_{i=1}^{K} g_i f(\mathbf{d}|\mathbf{x},i) \\ &= \frac{1}{(2\pi)^{q/2}} \sum_{i=1}^{K} g_i \exp\left(-\frac{1}{2} \|\mathbf{d} - \mathbf{y}_i\|^2 \right) \end{aligned} \tag{12.9}$$

The probability distribution of Eq. (12.9) is called an *associative Gaussian mixture model*[3]; the term "associative" refers to the fact that the model is associated with a set of training patterns represented by the input vector **x** and desired response vector **d**.

The goal of the learning algorithm is to model the distribution of a given set of training patterns. To do so, we first recognize the fact that the output vector $\mathbf{y}_i$ of the ith expert network is a function of the synaptic weight vector $\mathbf{w}_i$ of that network. Let the vector **w** of appropriate dimension denote the synaptic weights of all the expert networks arranged as follows:

$$\mathbf{w} = \begin{bmatrix} \mathbf{w}_1 \\ \mathbf{w}_2 \\ \vdots \\ \mathbf{w}_K \end{bmatrix} \tag{12.10}$$

Similarly, let the vector **g** denote the activations of all the output neurons in the gating network, as shown by

$$\mathbf{g} = \begin{bmatrix} g_1 \\ g_2 \\ \vdots \\ g_K \end{bmatrix} \tag{12.11}$$

[3] For a discussion of nonassociative Gaussian mixture models, see McLachlan and Basford (1988).

We may thus view the conditional probability density function $f(\mathbf{d}|\mathbf{x})$ as a *likelihood function,* with the whole synaptic weight vector $\mathbf{w}$ and the activation vector $\mathbf{g}$ playing the roles of unknown parameters. In situations of the kind described by Eq. (12.9), it is preferrable to work with the natural logarithm of $f(\mathbf{d}|\mathbf{x})$ rather than $f(\mathbf{d}|\mathbf{x})$; we may do so since the logarithm is a monotone increasing function of its argument. Accordingly, we may define a *log-likelihood function* as follows:

$$l(\mathbf{w}, \mathbf{g}) = \ln f(\mathbf{d}|\mathbf{x}) \tag{12.12}$$

Substituting Eq. (12.9) in (12.12) and ignoring the constant term $-\ln(2\pi)^{q/2}$, we may formally express the log-likelihood function $l(\mathbf{w},\mathbf{g})$ as follows (Jacobs and Jordan, 1991; Jacobs et al., 1991a):

$$l(\mathbf{w},\mathbf{g}) = \ln \sum_{i=1}^{K} g_i \exp\left(-\frac{1}{2}\|\mathbf{d} - \mathbf{y}_i\|^2\right) \tag{12.13}$$

where it is understood that $\mathbf{y}_i$ depends on $\mathbf{w}_i$ (i.e., the ith portion of $\mathbf{w}$). We may thus view $l(\mathbf{w},\mathbf{g})$ as an objective function, the maximization of which yields *maximum-likelihood estimates* of all the free parameters of the modular network in Fig. 12.2, represented by the synaptic weights of the different expert networks and those of the gating network.

We may now offer the following interpretations for some of the modular network's unknown quantities (Jacobs and Jordan, 1991):

1. The optimized module's output vectors $\mathbf{y}_1, \mathbf{y}_2, \ldots, \mathbf{y}_K$ of the expert networks are unknown *conditional mean vectors.*
2. The optimized gating network's outputs $g_1, g_2, \ldots, g_K$ are the conditional *a priori probabilities* that the respective modules generated the current training pattern.

The probabilistic parameters referred to under points 1 and 2 are all conditional on the input vector $\mathbf{x}$.

Whereas the different expert networks of the modular structure in Fig. 12.2 are permitted to have an arbitrary connectivity, the activations of the output neurons of the gating network are constrained to satisfy two requirements (Jacobs and Jordan, 1991):

$$0 \le g_i \le 1 \qquad \text{for all } i \tag{12.14}$$

and

$$\sum_{i=1}^{K} g_i = 1 \tag{12.15}$$

These two constraints are necessary if the activations g_i are to be interpreted as *a priori* probabilities.

Given a set of unconstrained variables, $\{u_j | j = 1, 2, \ldots, K\}$, we may satisfy the two constraints of Eqs. (12.14) and (12.15) by defining the activation g_i of the ith output neuron of the gating network as follows (Bridle, 1990a):

$$g_i = \frac{\exp(u_i)}{\sum_{j=1}^{K} \exp(u_j)} \tag{12.16}$$

where u_i is the weighted sum of the inputs applied to the ith output neuron of the gating network. This normalized exponential transformation may be viewed as a multiinput generalization of the logistic function. It preserves the rank order of its input values, and is a differentiable generalization of the "winner-takes-all" operation of picking the maximum value. For this reason, the transformation of Eq. (12.16) is referred to as *softmax* (Bridle, 1990a, b).

12.4 Stochastic-Gradient Learning Algorithm

To assist in the formulation of the learning algorithm for the modular network of Fig. 12.2, we define the *a posteriori probability* associated with the output of the ith expert network as (Jacobs and Jordan, 1991)

$$h_i = \frac{g_i \exp(-\frac{1}{2}\|\mathbf{d} - \mathbf{y}_i\|^2)}{\sum_{j=1}^{K} g_j \exp(-\frac{1}{2}\|\mathbf{d} - \mathbf{y}_j\|^2)}, \qquad i = 1, 2, \ldots, K \tag{12.17}$$

This probability is conditional on both the input vector $\mathbf{x}$ and the desired response vector $\mathbf{d}$. From this definition, we also note that as with the *a priori* probabilities represented by the activations g_i, the *a posteriori* probabilities h_i satisfy the two necessary conditions:

$$0 \leq h_i \leq 1 \qquad \text{for all } i \tag{12.18}$$

and

$$\sum_{i=1}^{K} h_i = 1 \tag{12.19}$$

There are two different parameter adjustments to be performed in the modular network of Fig. 12.2:

1. Modifications of the synaptic weights in the different expert networks
2. Modifications of the synaptic weights in the gating network

All these parameter adjustments are performed simultaneously. We may do so using a stochastic gradient algorithm based on the associative Gaussian mixture model of Eq. (12.9), as described next.

Adapting the Expert Networks

The log-likelihood function l for the modular network of Fig. 12.2 is defined by Eq. (12.13). Hence, differentiating this equation with respect to the output vector $\mathbf{y}_i$ of the ith expert network, we get the following q-by-1 partial derivative (after simplification):

$$\frac{\partial l}{\partial \mathbf{y}_i} = h_i(\mathbf{d} - \mathbf{y}_i), \qquad i = 1, 2, \ldots, K \tag{12.20}$$

Equation (12.20) states that, during the training process, the synaptic weights of the ith expert network in Fig. 12.2 are adjusted to correct the error between the output vector $\mathbf{y}_i$ and the desired response vector $\mathbf{d}$, but in proportion to the *a posteriori* probability h_i that the ith expert network generated the training pattern in current use (Jacobs and Jordan, 1991).

Suppose now that each expert network consists of a single layer of neurons, as depicted in the architectural graph of Fig. 12.3a. The specification of the neurons in Fig. 12.3a depends on whether we are solving a regression or classification problem, as explained here:

- *Regression.* In a nonlinear regression problem the residuals are generally assumed to have a *multivariate Gaussian distribution.* In a corresponding way, the output neurons of the expert networks are modeled as linear.
- *Classification.* In a pattern-classification problem, the output neurons are usually assumed to have a sigmoidal nonlinearity. In this case, a mixture of Bernoulli

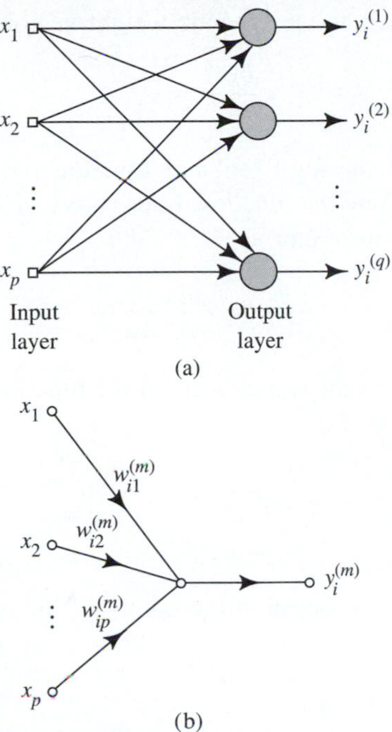

FIGURE 12.3 (a) Single layer of linear neurons constituting the expert network. (b) Signal-flow graph of a linear neuron.

distributions[4] rather than a multivariate Gaussian distribution is generally used to formulate the log-likelihood function.

In all cases, of course, the gating networks use the softmax nonlinearity.

In the discussion that follows we consider a nonlinear regression problem, assuming a multivariate Gaussian model. The nonlinear nature of the problem is taken care of by the softmax nonlinearity of the gating network in Fig. 12.2. The Gaussian assumption is taken care of by using linear output neurons for the implementation of the expert networks.

We may thus define the mth element of the output vector $\mathbf{y}_i$ of the ith expert network as the inner product of the corresponding synaptic weight vector $\mathbf{w}_i^{(m)}$ and the input vector $\mathbf{x}$, as depicted in the signal flow graph of Fig. 12.3b; that is,

$$y_i^{(m)} = \mathbf{x}^T \mathbf{w}_i^{(m)}, \qquad \begin{cases} i = 1, 2, \ldots, K \\ m = 1, 2, \ldots, q \end{cases} \tag{12.21}$$

where the superscript T denotes transposition, and the weight vector $\mathbf{w}_i^{(m)}$ is made up of the elements $w_{i1}^{(m)}, w_{i2}^{(m)}, \ldots, w_{ip}^{(m)}$ of the mth neuron in the ith expert network. Hence,

[4] In binary classification, the classifier output y is a discrete random variable with one of two possible outcomes: 1 or 0. It is generally assumed that the probabilistic component of the model has a *Bernoulli distribution.* Let p_i denote the conditional probability that the ith expert network reports outcome 1 given the input vector $\mathbf{x}$. The resulting probability distribution of the modular network may then be described by a Bernoulli mixture model (Jordan and Jacobs, 1993):

$$P(\mathbf{d}|\mathbf{x}) = \sum_{i=1}^{K} g_i p_i^y (1 - p_i)^y$$

differentiating $y_i^{(m)}$ with respect to the synaptic weight vector $\mathbf{w}_i^{(m)}$, we get

$$\frac{\partial y_i^{(m)}}{\partial \mathbf{w}_i^{(m)}} = \mathbf{x} \tag{12.22}$$

The *sensitivity vector* of the log-likelihood function l with respect to the synaptic weight vector $\mathbf{w}_i^{(m)}$ is defined by the functional derivative $\partial l/\partial \mathbf{w}_i^{(m)}$. Using the chain rule, we may express this sensitivity vector as

$$\frac{\partial l}{\partial \mathbf{w}_i^{(m)}} = \frac{\partial l}{\partial y_i^{(m)}} \frac{\partial y_i^{(m)}}{\partial \mathbf{w}_i^{(m)}} \tag{12.23}$$

The partial derivative $\partial l/\partial y_i^{(m)}$ is the mth element of the functional derivative $\partial l/\partial \mathbf{y}_i$ defined in Eq. (12.20); that is,

$$\begin{aligned} \frac{\partial l}{\partial y_i^{(m)}} &= h_i(d^{(m)} - y_i^{(m)}) \\ &= h_i e_i^{(m)} \end{aligned} \tag{12.24}$$

where $e_i^{(m)}$ is the *error signal* produced at the output of the mth neuron in the ith expert network, as shown by

$$e_i^{(m)} = d^{(m)} - y_i^{(m)} \tag{12.25}$$

We are now ready to formulate the expression for the sensitivity vector $\partial l/\partial \mathbf{w}_i^{(m)}$. Specifically, substituting Eqs. (12.22) and (12.24) in (12.23), we get

$$\frac{\partial l}{\partial \mathbf{w}_i^{(m)}} = h_i e_i^{(m)} \mathbf{x}, \qquad \begin{cases} i = 1, 2, \ldots, K \\ m = 1, 2, \ldots, q \end{cases} \tag{12.26}$$

To maximize the log-likelihood function l with respect to the synaptic weights of the different expert networks, we may use *gradient ascent* in weight space. In particular, we modify the synaptic weight vector $\mathbf{w}_i^{(m)}$ by applying a small adjustment $\Delta\mathbf{w}_i^{(m)}$, defined by

$$\Delta\mathbf{w}_i^{(m)} = \eta \frac{\partial l}{\partial \mathbf{w}_i^{(m)}}, \qquad \begin{cases} i = 1, 2, \ldots, K \\ m = 1, 2, \ldots, q \end{cases} \tag{12.27}$$

where η is a small *learning-rate parameter*. Note that the scaling factor on the right-hand side of Eq. (12.27) is $+\eta$, since we are using gradient *ascent* to maximize l. Thus, using $\mathbf{w}_i^{(m)}(n)$ to denote the value of the synaptic weight vector $\mathbf{w}_i^{(m)}$ at iteration n of the learning algorithm, the updated value of this synaptic weight vector at iteration $n + 1$ is computed in accordance with the recursion

$$\begin{aligned} \mathbf{w}_i^{(m)}(n+1) &= \mathbf{w}_i^{(m)}(n) + \Delta\mathbf{w}_i^{(m)}(n) \\ &= \mathbf{w}_i^{(m)}(n) + \eta h_i e_i^{(m)}(n)\mathbf{x}, \qquad \begin{cases} m = 1, 2, \ldots, q \\ i = 1, 2, \ldots, K \end{cases} \end{aligned} \tag{12.28}$$

This is the desired recursive formula for adapting the expert networks of the modular architecture shown in Fig. 12.2.

Adapting the Gating Network

Consider next the way in which the gating network is adapted. As with the expert networks, we assume that the gating network consists of a single layer of output neurons, as shown in the architectural graph of Fig. 12.4a. This structure differs from that of Fig. 12.3a for

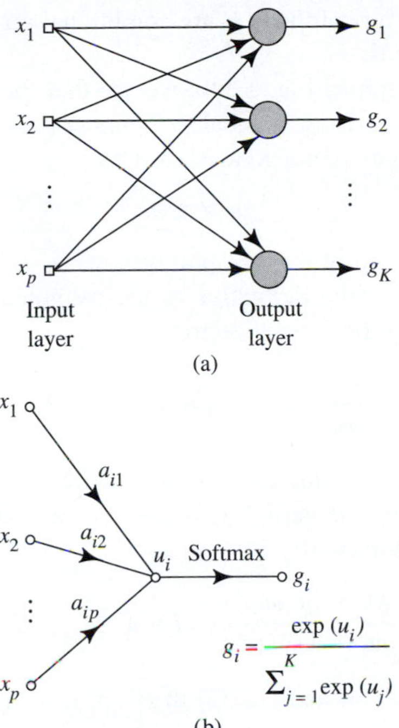

FIGURE 12.4 (a) Single layer of softmax neurons for the gating network. (b) Signal-flow graph of a softmax neuron.

the expert networks in two respects. First, the gating network has K output neurons, whereas each expert network has q output neurons. Second, the gating network uses a softmax for the activation function of its output neurons as depicted in the signal-flow graph of Fig. 12.4b, whereas the expert networks use linear output neurons as shown in the signal-flow graph of Fig. 12.3b. In any event, we note that at the ith output neuron of the gating network, say, the unconstrained variables are represented by the weighted sum u_i of the inputs applied to that neuron. The activation g_i of the ith output neuron is related to the weighted sum u_i by the softmax of Eq. (12.16). Hence, substituting Eq. (12.16) in the definition of the log-likelihood function l given in Eq. (12.13), and recognizing that the summation term $\Sigma_{j=1}^{K} \exp(u_j)$ is the same for all i, we may rewrite the expression for the log-likelihood function l as

$$l = \ln \sum_{i=1}^{K} \exp(u_i) \cdot \exp\left(-\frac{1}{2} \|\mathbf{d} - \mathbf{y}_i\|^2 \right) - \ln \sum_{j=1}^{K} \exp(u_j) \tag{12.29}$$

The partial derivative of the log-likelihood function l with respect to the ith weighted sum u_i of the inputs applied to the ith output neuron of the gating network is therefore found to be (after simplification)

$$\frac{\partial l}{\partial u_i} = h_i - g_i \tag{12.30}$$

where we have made use of the definitions of g_i and h_i given in Eqs. (12.16) and (12.17), respectively. Equation (12.30) states that the synaptic weights of the ith output neuron of the gating network are adjusted such that the activations of the network (i.e., the *a priori* probabilities g_i) move toward the corresponding *a posteriori* probabilities h_i (Jacobs and Jordan, 1991). Note that the *a priori* probabilities g_i are conditional on the input vector

x, whereas the *a posteriori* probabilities h_i are conditional on both the input vector **x** and the desired response vector **d**.

From the signal-flow graph of Fig. 12.4b, we see that the weighted sum u_i of the ith output neuron of the gating network is equal to the inner product of the pertinent synaptic weight vector $\mathbf{a}_i$ and the input vector **x**, as shown by

$$u_i = \mathbf{x}^T\mathbf{a}_i \tag{12.31}$$

where the vector $\mathbf{a}_i$ is made up of the synaptic weights $a_{i1}, a_{i2}, \ldots, a_{ip}$ of neuron i in the gating network. Hence the partial derivative of the weighted sum u_i with respect to the weight vector $\mathbf{a}_i$ is given by the p-by-1 vector

$$\frac{\partial u_i}{\partial \mathbf{a}_i} = \mathbf{x}, \qquad i = 1, 2, \ldots, K \tag{12.32}$$

The *sensitivity vector* of the log-likelihood function l with respect to the synaptic weight vector $\mathbf{a}_i$ is defined by the partial derivative $\partial l/\partial \mathbf{a}_i$. Using the chain rule, we may express this sensitivity vector as

$$\frac{\partial l}{\partial \mathbf{a}_i} = \frac{\partial l}{\partial u_i}\frac{\partial u_i}{\partial \mathbf{a}_i}, \qquad i = 1, 2, \ldots, K \tag{12.33}$$

Hence, substituting Eqs. (12.30) and (12.32) in (12.33), we get

$$\frac{\partial l}{\partial \mathbf{a}_i} = (h_i - g_i)\mathbf{x} \tag{12.34}$$

Correspondingly, the adjustment applied to the synaptic weight vector $\mathbf{a}_i$ is defined by

$$\begin{aligned} \Delta\mathbf{a}_i &= \eta\frac{\partial l}{\partial \mathbf{a}_i} \\ &= \eta(h_i - g_i)\mathbf{x} \end{aligned} \tag{12.35}$$

where we have used the same learning-rate parameter for adapting the expert networks. We may, if we so wish, use a different learning-rate parameter here.

Let $\mathbf{a}_i(n)$ be the value of the synaptic weight vector $\mathbf{a}_i$ of the ith output neuron in the gating network at iteration n of the learning algorithm. The value of this weight vector at iteration $n + 1$ is updated by using the recursion

$$\mathbf{a}_i(n + 1) = \mathbf{a}_i(n) + \eta\big(h_i(n) - g_i(n)\big)\mathbf{x} \tag{12.36}$$

This is the desired formula for adapting the gating network.

Note that there is no back-propagation of error terms in the formulas of Eqs. (12.28) and (12.36), which simplifies the recursive computations of the various synaptic weights in the modular network of Fig. 12.2. The reason there is no back-propagation here is because we chose to make the expert and gating networks single-layered. This is not part of the model; rather, it is a simplification in network design that we have made in order to make an important point.

Summary of the Learning Algorithm for Fig. 12.2

We may now summarize the procedure for adapting the different expert networks and the gating network of the modular structure of Fig. 12.2.

1. *Initialization.* Assign initial values to the synaptic weights of the different expert networks and those of the gating network by using small values that are uniformly distributed.

2. *Adapting the Expert and Gating Networks.* Present the network a task example represented by the input vector $\mathbf{x}$ and desired response vector $\mathbf{d}$. Hence, compute for iteration $n = 0, 1, 2, \ldots,$ output $i = 1, 2, \ldots, K$, and neuron $m = 1, 2, \ldots, q$:

$$u_i(n) = \mathbf{x}^T\mathbf{a}_i(n)$$

$$g_i(n) = \frac{\exp(u_i(n))}{\sum_{j=1}^{K}\exp(u_j(n))}$$

$$y_i^{(m)}(n) = \mathbf{x}^T\mathbf{w}_i^{(m)}(n)$$

$$\mathbf{y}_i(n) = [y_i^{(1)}(n), y_i^{(2)}(n), \ldots, y_i^{(q)}(n)]^T$$

$$h_i(n) = \frac{g_i(n)\exp(-\frac{1}{2}\|\mathbf{d} - \mathbf{y}_i(n)\|^2)}{\sum_{j=1}^{K} g_j(n)\exp(-\frac{1}{2}\|\mathbf{d} - \mathbf{y}_j(n)\|^2)}$$

$$e_i^{(m)}(n) = d^{(m)} - y_i^{(m)}(n)$$

$$\mathbf{w}_i^{(m)}(n+1) = \mathbf{w}_i^{(m)}(n) + \eta h_i(n)e_i^{(m)}(n)\mathbf{x}$$

$$\mathbf{a}_i(n+1) = \mathbf{a}_i(n) + \eta[h_i(n) - g_i(n)]\mathbf{x}$$

3. Repeat step 2 for all the available training examples.
4. Iterate the computations in steps 2 and 3 until the networks reach a steady state.

12.5 Hierarchical Structure of Adaptive Expert Networks

In perceptual studies, it appears that human subjects robustly recognize objects first at categorical levels and then at successively subordinate levels; this notion suggests the presence of structured memories that are organized and searched in a hierarchical manner during recognition (Van Essen et al., 1992; Ambros-Ingerson et al., 1990). In other words, *hierarchy* is another important principle in the architecture of vertebrate nervous systems.

The motivation for building hierarchy into the architecture of a modular network is to have the expert networks take on a general structure of their own. The most logical procedure for doing so is to continue with the principle of divide and conquer by structuring the expert networks themselves in modular form in a manner similar to that described in Section 12.3 (Jordan and Jacobs, 1992). This approach is illustrated in Fig. 12.5, involving *two hierarchical levels* of network architecture. The network consists of K *clusters* of adaptive expert networks, with each cluster containing L adaptive expert networks. The outputs of the isolated clusters are mediated by a *top-level* gating network as before. Likewise, the outputs of the isolated expert networks in each cluster are mediated by a gating network incorporated into the cluster, as illustrated in Fig. 12.5. We may readily generalize the divide-and-conquer policy used in Fig. 12.5 to construct a *treelike architecture* with an arbitrary number of hierarchical levels.

To simplify the discussion, however, we confine ourselves in this section to adaptive modular networks involving two hierarchical levels, as illustrated in Fig. 12.5. Nevertheless, the learning algorithm developed here may be readily extended to cover a tree of arbitrary depth.

As in Section 12.4, we assume that all the gating networks inside and outside the clusters in Fig. 12.5 consist of a single layer of neurons, and whose activation functions are modeled to be softmax. In particular, the activation g_i of the ith output neuron of the *top-level* gating network is defined by

$$g_i = \frac{\exp(u_i)}{\sum_{j=1}^{K}\exp(u_j)}, \qquad i = 1, 2, \ldots, K \tag{12.37}$$

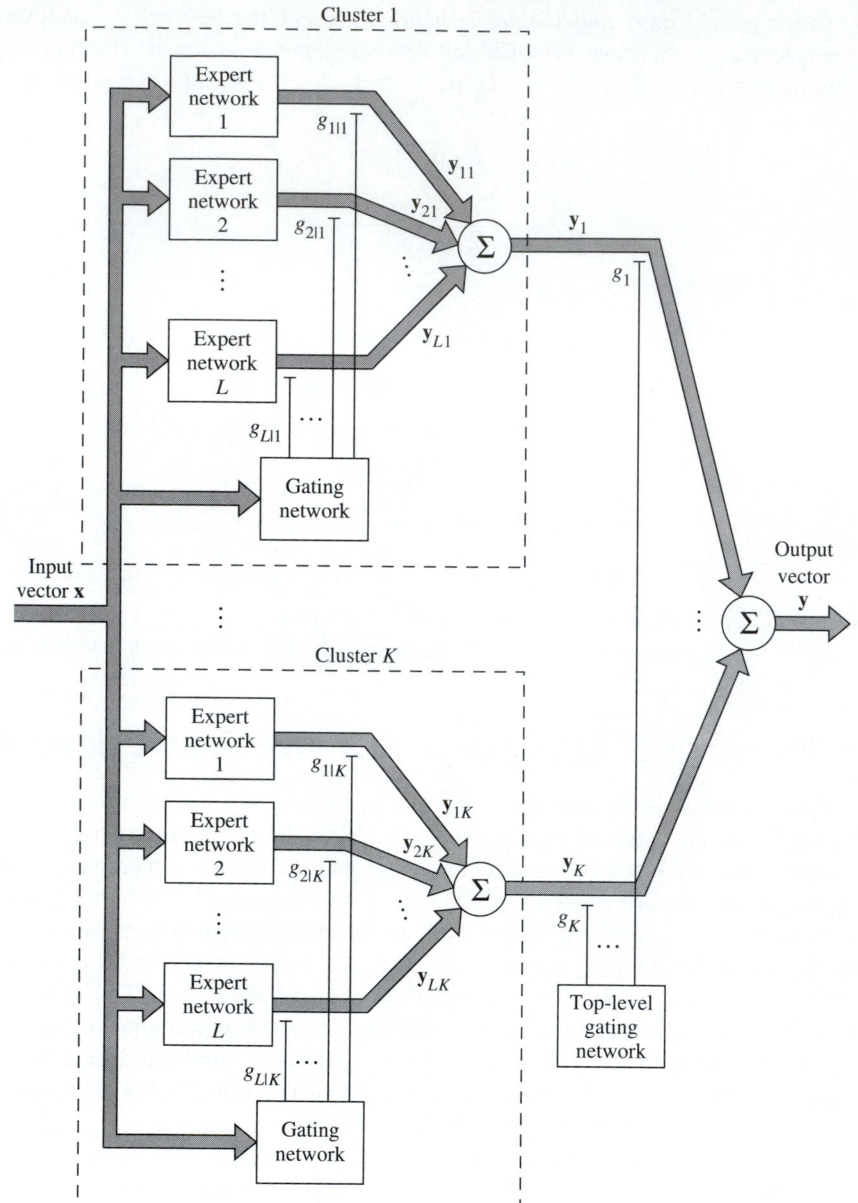

FIGURE 12.5 Two-level hierarchical network, combining modularity and hierarchy.

where u_i is the weighted sum of the inputs applied to that neuron; basically, this equation is a reproduction of Eq. (12.16) for the case of the single level of hierarchy shown in Fig. 12.2. Similarly, the activation of the jth output neuron in the ith cluster of the hierarchical network shown in Fig. 12.5 is defined by

$$g_{j|i} = \frac{\exp(u_{j|i})}{\sum_{k=1}^{L} \exp(u_{k|i})}, \qquad \begin{cases} j = 1, 2, \ldots, L \\ i = 1, 2, \ldots, K \end{cases} \tag{12.38}$$

where $u_{j|i}$ is the weighted sum of the inputs applied to this particular neuron in the ith cluster.

The expert networks in each cluster of Fig. 12.5 are also assumed to consist of a single layer of linear neurons. Let $\mathbf{y}_{ji}$ denote the output vector of the jth expert network in the ith cluster. We may then express the output vector $\mathbf{y}_i$ of the ith cluster of output networks as

$$\mathbf{y}_i = \sum_{j=1}^{L} g_{j|i}\mathbf{y}_{ji}, \qquad i = 1, 2, \ldots, K \tag{12.39}$$

where $g_{j|i}$ is as defined in Eq. (12.38). Correspondingly, the output vector $\mathbf{y}$ of the whole network in Fig. 12.5 is defined by

$$\mathbf{y} = \sum_{i=1}^{K} g_i\mathbf{y}_i \tag{12.40}$$

where g_i is as defined in Eq. (12.37).

For a probabilistic interpretation of the problem being considered in this section, presumed to be more complex than that considered in Section 12.3, we assume that the training patterns $\{\mathbf{x},\mathbf{d}\}$ are generated by a set of *nested regressive processes* (Jordan and Jacobs, 1992). To be precise, the rules (i.e., expert networks) within the same cluster are assumed to have commonalities in their input–output parameterizations. At each time, we assume that the following holds:

1. An input vector $\mathbf{x}$ is selected at random from some prior distribution.
2. A cluster is chosen from the distribution $P(i|\mathbf{x})$; this is the probability of the ith cluster given the input vector $\mathbf{x}$.
3. A rule (i.e., expert network) is chosen from the distribution $P(j|\mathbf{x},i)$; this is the probability of the jth rule given the input vector $\mathbf{x}$ and the ith cluster.
4. A desired response vector $\mathbf{d}$ is generated according to the regressive relation:

$$\mathbf{d} = \mathbf{F}_{ji}(\mathbf{x}) + \boldsymbol{\varepsilon}, \qquad \begin{cases} i = 1, 2, \ldots, K \\ j = 1, 2, \ldots, L \end{cases} \tag{12.41}$$

   where $\mathbf{F}_{ji}(\cdot)$ is a vector-valued nonlinear function of its argument vector, and $\boldsymbol{\varepsilon}$ is a zero-mean, Gaussian-distributed random vector.

The goal is to model the probability distribution of the set of training examples $\{\mathbf{x},\mathbf{d}\}$.

For the objective function appropriate to the learning problem at hand, we use a log-likelihood function defined as the expanded form of an associative Gaussian mixture model. Specifically, we write (except for a constant)

$$l = \ln \sum_{i=1}^{K} g_i \sum_{j=1}^{L} g_{j|i} \exp\left(-\frac{1}{2}\|\mathbf{d} - \mathbf{y}_{ji}\|^2\right) \tag{12.42}$$

where $\mathbf{d}$ is the desired response vector associated with the input vector $\mathbf{x}$ applied simultaneously to all the expert networks and gating networks in Fig. 12.5; the outputs $\mathbf{y}_{ji}$ and the activations g_i and $g_{j|i}$ are as defined before. Given the training data $\{\mathbf{x},\mathbf{d}\}$, we wish to maximize the log-likelihood function l with respect to the unknown quantities $\mathbf{y}_{ji}$, g_i, and $g_{i|j}$. These quantities, pertaining to the structure of Fig. 12.5, may be given the following probabilistic interpretations (Jordan and Jacobs, 1992):

- The output vectors $\mathbf{y}_{ji}$ of the individual expert networks are the unknown conditional mean vectors of multivariate Gaussian distributions.
- The activation g_i of the top-level gating network and the activations $g_{j|i}$ of the gating networks inside the isolated clusters are the unknown conditional *a priori* probabilities

that the ith cluster and the i,jth expert networks generated the current training pattern $\{\mathbf{x},\mathbf{d}\}$.

All of these unknown probabilistic quantities are conditional on the input vector $\mathbf{x}$.

To assist in the formulation of the learning algorithm, we introduce two probabilistic definitions. First, we define the conditional *a posteriori* probability that the ith cluster of expert networks generates a particular desired response vector $\mathbf{d}$ as

$$h_i = \frac{g_i \sum_{j=1}^{L} g_{j|i} \exp(-\frac{1}{2}\|\mathbf{d} - \mathbf{y}_{ji}\|^2)}{\sum_{i=1}^{K} g_i \sum_{j=1}^{L} g_{j|i} \exp(-\frac{1}{2}\|\mathbf{d} - \mathbf{y}_{ji}\|^2)}, \qquad i = 1, 2, \ldots, K \tag{12.43}$$

Second, we define the conditional *a posteriori* probability that the jth expert network in the ith cluster generates a particular desired response vector $\mathbf{d}$ as

$$h_{j|i} = \frac{g_{j|i} \exp(-\frac{1}{2}\|\mathbf{d} - \mathbf{y}_{ji}\|^2)}{\sum_{j=1}^{L} g_{j|i} \exp(-\frac{1}{2}\|\mathbf{d} - \mathbf{y}_{ji}\|^2)}, \qquad \begin{cases} i = 1, 2, \ldots, K \\ j = 1, 2, \ldots, L \end{cases} \tag{12.44}$$

The *a posteriori* probabilities h_i and $h_{j|i}$ are both conditional on the input vector $\mathbf{x}$ and the desired response vector $\mathbf{d}$.

The output vectors $\mathbf{y}_{ji}$ and the activations g_i and $g_{j|i}$ depend on the synaptic weights of the neural networks that constitute the respective expert networks and gating networks. The log-likelihood function l defined in Eq. (12.42) may therefore be viewed as a log-likelihood function with these synaptic weights as the unknown parameters. Hence, maximizing the log-likelihood function l yields the *maximum likelihood estimates* of these parameters. The maximization of l may be performed in an iterative fashion, using gradient ascent for the computation of small adjustments applied simultaneously to all the synaptic weights in the network.

We may compute these synaptic modifications in Fig. 12.5 by proceeding in three stages, as follows (Jordan and Jacobs, 1992):

1. *Adapting the Top-Level Gating Network.* Here we differentiate the log-likelihood function l of Eq. (12.42) with respect to the weighted sum u_i of the inputs applied to the ith output neuron of the top-level gating network, obtaining the scalar partial derivative

$$\frac{\partial l}{\partial u_i} = h_i - g_i, \qquad i = 1, 2, \ldots, K \tag{12.45}$$

   Hence, during the training process the *a priori* probability g_i tries to move toward the corresponding a posteriori probability h_i.

2. *Adapting the Gating Networks in the Clusters.* In this case, we differentiate the log-likelihood function l of Eq. (12.42) with respect to the weighted sum $u_{j|i}$ of the inputs applied to the jth output neuron of the gating network in the ith cluster, obtaining the scalar partial derivative

$$\frac{\partial l}{\partial u_{j|i}} = h_i(h_{j|i} - g_{j|i}), \qquad \begin{cases} i = 1, 2, \ldots, K \\ j = 1, 2, \ldots, L \end{cases} \tag{12.46}$$

   Consequently, during training the *a priori* probability $g_{j|i}$ tries to move toward the corresponding *a posteriori* probability $h_{j|i}$.

3. *Adapting the Expert Networks.* Next, we differentiate the log-likelihood function l of Eq. (12.42) with respect to the output vector $\mathbf{y}_{ji}$ of the jth expert network in the

ith cluster, obtaining the q-by-1 partial derivative

$$\frac{\partial l}{\partial \mathbf{y}_{ji}} = h_i h_{j|i}(\mathbf{d} - \mathbf{y}_{ji}), \qquad \begin{cases} i = 1, 2, \ldots, K \\ j = 1, 2, \ldots, L \end{cases} \tag{12.47}$$

Thus, during training the synaptic weights of the jth expert network in the ith cluster are updated by an amount proportional to the *a posteriori* probability that this particular expert network generated the training pattern in current use.

The partial derivative $\partial l/\partial u_{j|i}$ of Eq. (12.46) and the partial derivative $\partial l/\partial \mathbf{y}_{ji}$ of Eq. (12.47) share a common factor, namely, the *a posteriori* probability h_i. This means that the expert networks within a cluster are tied to each other. Consequently, the expert networks within a cluster tend to learn similar mappings early in the training process. However, when the probabilities associated with a cluster to which the expert networks belong assume larger values later in the training process, they start to specialize in what they learn. Thus the hierarchical network of Fig. 12.5 tends to evolve in a *coarse-to-fine* structural fashion. This property is important, because it implies that a deep hierarchical network is naturally robust with respect to the overfitting problem (Jordan and Jacobs, 1992).

The final step in the development of the stochastic-gradient learning algorithm for the network of Fig. 12.5 involves the determination of the sensitivity factors $\partial l/\partial \mathbf{a}_i$, $\partial l/\partial \mathbf{c}_{j|i}$, and $\partial l/\partial \mathbf{w}_{ji}^{(m)}$. The vector $\mathbf{a}_i$ denotes the synaptic weight vector of the ith output neuron of the top-level gating network, $\mathbf{c}_{j|i}$ denotes the synaptic weight vector of the jth output neuron of the gating network in the ith cluster, and $\mathbf{w}_{ji}^{(m)}$ denotes the synaptic weight vector of the mth output neuron of the jth expert network in the ith cluster; the index $m = 1, 2, \ldots, q$, where q is the total number of output neurons in each expert network. To find the formulas for these sensitivity factors, we use chain rules to express them as the products of certain functional derivatives, as shown here:

$$\frac{\partial l}{\partial \mathbf{a}_i} = \frac{\partial l}{\partial u_i}\frac{\partial u_i}{\partial \mathbf{a}_i}, \qquad i = 1, 2, \ldots, K \tag{12.48}$$

$$\frac{\partial l}{\partial \mathbf{c}_{j|i}} = \frac{\partial l}{\partial u_{j|i}}\frac{\partial u_{j|i}}{\partial \mathbf{c}_{j|i}}, \qquad \begin{cases} i = 1, 2, \ldots, K \\ j = 1, 2, \ldots, L \end{cases} \tag{12.49}$$

$$\frac{\partial l}{\partial \mathbf{w}_{ji}^{(m)}} = \frac{\partial l}{y_{ji}^{(m)}}\frac{\partial y_{ji}^{(m)}}{\partial \mathbf{w}_{ji}^{(m)}}, \qquad \begin{cases} i = 1, 2, \ldots, K \\ j = 1, 2, \ldots, L \\ m = 1, 2, \ldots, q \end{cases} \tag{12.50}$$

The derivations of the functional derivatives in Eqs. (12.48) through (12.50) and their use in the determination of these three sensitivity factors, and therefore the development of a learning algorithm for the network of Fig. 12.5, follow a procedure similar to that described in Section 12.4; this derivation is presented as an exercise to the reader as Problem 12.7.

12.6 Piecewise Control Using Modular Networks

Jacobs and Jordan (1993) describe the use of a modular network that learns to perform nonlinear control tasks using a piecewise control strategy called *gain scheduling*. This

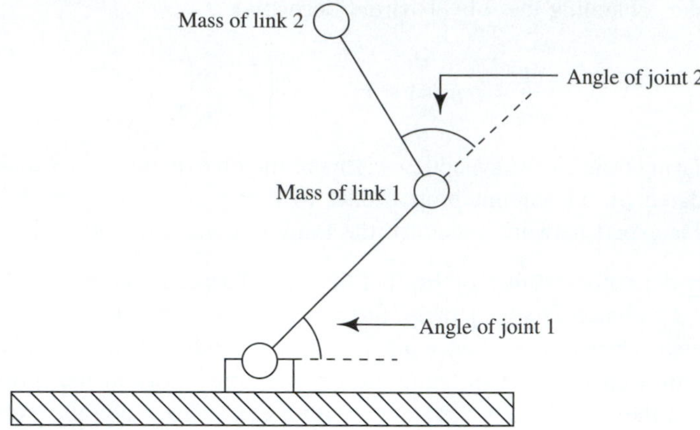

FIGURE 12.6 Two-joint planar arm. (From R.A. Jacobs and M.I. Jordan, 1993, with permission of IEEE.)

control strategy is applicable to situations where it is known how the dynamics of a plant change with its operating points.

An important advantage of a modular network over a multilayer perceptron as feedforward controller for the kind of plant described here is that it is relatively robust with respect to *temporal crosstalk* (Jacobs and Jordan, 1993; Jacobs et al., 1991b). To explain what we mean by this phenomenon, suppose that a multilayer perceptron is trained on a particular task using the back-propagation algorithm, and then it is switched to another task that is incompatible with the first one. Ideally, we would like to have the network learn the second task without its performance being unnecessarily impaired with respect to the first task. However, according to Sutton (1986), back-propagation learning has the opposite effect in the sense that it tends to preferentially modify the synaptic weights of hidden neurons that have already developed useful properties. Consequently, after learning the second task, the multilayer perceptron is no longer able to perform the first task. We may of course alternate the training process between tasks, and carry on in this way until the multilayer perceptron eventually learns both tasks. However, the price that we have to pay for it is a prolonged learning process. The generalization performance of the multilayer perceptron may also be affected by the blocked presentation of incompatible training data.

In contrast, when a modular network is trained on a number of incompatible tasks, it has the ability to partition the parameter space of the plant into a number of regions and assign different expert networks to learn a control law for each region (Jacobs and Jordan, 1993). The end result is that the network is relatively immune to temporal crosstalk between tasks.

Jacobs and Jordan (1993) have compared the performance of a single network and a modular network as feedforward controllers for a robot arm in the form of the two-joint planar manipulator shown in Fig. 12.6. These two networks were specified as follows[5]:

- A fully connected multilayer perceptron with 19 input nodes (corresponding to the joint variables and payload identity), 10 hidden neurons, and 2 output neurons (corresponding to the feedforward torques).

[5] In the study reported by Jacobs and Jordan (1993), two other modifications of the modular network were also considered, which are referred to as modular architectures with a *share network*. During training the share network learns a strategy that is useful to all tasks. One of these two networks was constrained to discover a particular type of decomposition. The performance of these two configurations was almost the same, and superior to that of the conventional modular network.

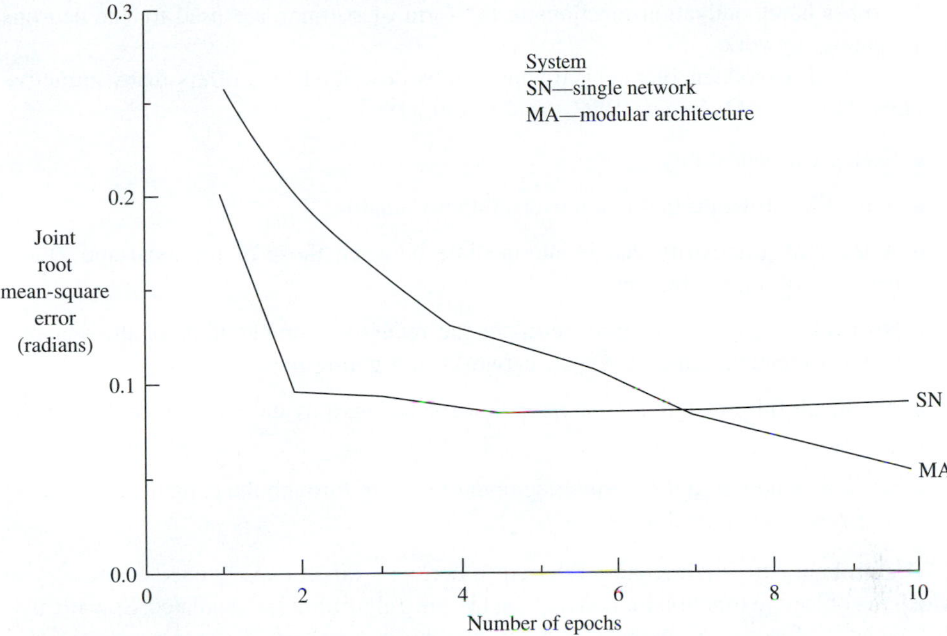

FIGURE 12.7 Learning curves for a single network and a modular network, both of which are trained on the two-joint planar arm. (From R.A. Jacobs and M.I. Jordan, 1993, with permission of IEEE.)

- A modular network, consisting of 6 expert networks and 1 gating network; each expert network receives the joint variables and has two output neurons, and the gating network receives the payload identity and has 2 output neurons.

Figure 12.7 shows the learning curves for these two systems. The horizontal axis gives the number of epochs used for training. The vertical axis gives the joint root-mean-square error (RMSE) in radians, averaged over 25 runs. The curves show that the modular network achieves significantly better performance than the multilayer perceptron after 7 epochs.

12.7 Summary and Discussion

In this chapter we have introduced modularity and hierarchy as two important principles in the design of neural networks. In particular, we have described a maximum-likelihood procedure for building a hierarchy of adaptive expert networks through the repeated use of modularity to implement the principle of divide and conquer. The end result is a hierarchical neural network made up of isolated clusters of expert networks whose individual outputs are mediated by corresponding gating networks and finally the outputs of the clusters themselves are mediated by a top-level gating network, as illustrated in Fig. 12.5 for the case of two levels of hierarchy. We may, of course, go one step further than that shown in Fig. 12.5 and build clusters of expert networks inside larger clusters, and thereby expand the level of hierarchy. The ultimate objective is to build a hierarchical structure in which all the expert networks and the gating networks consist of a single layer of neurons, thereby avoiding the need for the back-propagation of error terms. For the expert networks, the neurons are linear, assuming that the problem at hand is a regressive problem;

on the other hand, activation functions in the form of softmax are used for the neurons in the gating networks.

The use of a modular hierarchical approach as described here offers many attractive features (Houk, 1992; Jordan, 1992; Jacobs et al., 1991b):

- Biological plausibility
- A treelike structure that is a universal approximator
- A level of granularity that is intermediate between those of the local and global methods of approximation
- No back-propagation of error terms in the recursive computations of the synaptic weights characterizing the expert networks and gating networks
- An insightful probabilistic interpretation for the various unknown quantities of the network
- A viable solution to the credit-assignment problem through the computation of a set of *a posteriori* probabilities

The probabilistic interpretation referred to here is a direct consequence of the way in which the objective function for deriving the learning algorithm is formulated. Specifically, the objective function is defined as a log-likelihood function of the synaptic weights of the expert networks and those of the gating networks. Accordingly, maximization of the objective function results in *maximum-likelihood estimates* of these unknown free parameters of the network. Maximum-likelihood parameter estimation is a well-developed branch of statistics, which means that we have a wealth of knowledge at our disposal for the computation and interpretation of these estimates. In particular, if the estimates are known to be *unbiased,* then the maximum-likelihood estimates of the synaptic weights of the various network components satisfy an inequality referred to as the Cramér–Rao lower bound (Van Trees, 1968). If this bound is satisfied with an equality, the estimates are said to be *efficient.* At this point a logical question to ask is: Do parameter estimation procedures better than the maximum-likelihood procedure exist? Certainly, if an efficient procedure does *not* exist, then there may be unbiased estimates with lower variances than the maximum-likelihood estimates. The difficulty, however, is that there is no general rule for finding them. It is for this reason that the maximum-likelihood procedure enjoys a great deal of popularity as a tool for parameter estimation.

A practical limitation of the maximum-likelihood procedure is that it can be computationally intensive. We may overcome this limitation by following a gradient ascent procedure, as described in Sections 12.4 and 12.5. However, by doing so there is no guarantee that we reach the globally maximum value of the objective function (i.e., log-likelihood function), as there is the real possibility of being trapped in a local minimum. To guard against such a possibility, we may add small amounts of noise to the sensitivity factors so as to help the stochastic-gradient algorithm escape local minima (Jelinek and Reilly, 1990).

Alternatively, we may use the *expectation-maximization (EM) algorithm* (Dempster et al., 1977), which is well suited for mixture models. The EM algorithm is a general approach to iterative computation of maximum-likelihood estimates when the observed data can be viewed as incomplete data. The term ''incomplete data'' has two implications:

1. The existence of two sample spaces X and Y represented by the *observed data vector* $\mathbf{x}$ and the *complete data vector* $\mathbf{y}$, respectively
2. The *one-to-many mapping* $\mathbf{y} \rightarrow \mathbf{x}(\mathbf{y})$ from space Y to space X

The complete data vector **y** is not observed directly, but only through the vector **x**. Each iteration of the EM algorithm is composed of two steps: an expectation (E) step and a maximization (M) step—hence the name of the algorithm. Suppose that $\hat{\boldsymbol{\theta}}(n)$ denotes the current value of a parameter vector after n cycles of the algorithm. Let l_c denote the log-likelihood of the complete data vector **y**. The next cycle of the EM algorithm may then be described as follows:

E STEP. Compute the expected value of the complete-data log-likelihood l_c, given the observed data vector **x** and the current model represented by the parameter vector $\hat{\boldsymbol{\theta}}(n)$ by finding the deterministic quantity

$$Q(\boldsymbol{\theta},\hat{\boldsymbol{\theta}}(n)) = E[l_c(\boldsymbol{\theta}|\mathbf{x})] \tag{12.51}$$

where E is the expectation operator and $\boldsymbol{\theta}$ is an unknown parameter vector.

M STEP. Determine the updated value $\hat{\boldsymbol{\theta}}(n+1)$ of the parameter vector as the solution of the equations

$$\hat{\boldsymbol{\theta}}(n+1) = \arg_{\boldsymbol{\theta}}\max Q[\boldsymbol{\theta},\hat{\boldsymbol{\theta}}(n)] \tag{12.52}$$

Jordan and Jacobs (1993) describe the application of the EM algorithm to the design of hierarchical mixtures of experts for solving nonlinear regression problems.[6] They compare the performance of a modular network so trained with that of a multilayer perceptron trained with the back-propagation algorithm for a four-joint robot arm moving in three-dimensional space. Computer simulations were carried out for both batch and on-line modes of operations. In both cases, learning based on the EM algorithm outperformed back-propagation learning.

The material presented in this chapter represents one particular viewpoint of how to design modular networks for solving nonlinear regression problems. The notions of modularity described here represent an important step in the development of a powerful approach to the design of neural networks. There is much that remains to be explored on this highly important subject.

PROBLEMS

12.1 Figure P12.1 shows a modular network with a treelike structure. Reduce this network to its most basic form involving the minimum number of components.

12.2 Consider the modular network of Fig. 12.2. Derive the expressions for the partial derivatives $\partial l/\partial \mathbf{y}_i$ and $\partial l/\partial u_i$ given in Eqs. (12.20) and (12.30), respectively.

12.3 A modular network is trained with a particular data set, and the same module is found to win the competition for all the training data. What is the implication of such a phenomenon?

12.4 Consider the modular network of Fig. 12.2, in which each expert network consists of a feedforward network with two layers of computation nodes. The modular network is designed to perform nonlinear regression.

[6] Another useful application of the EM algorithm is described in Xu and Jordan (1993a). In this paper, the EM algorithm is used to combine multiple classifiers for a particular pattern recognition task. In a related paper, Xu and Jordan (1993b) propose the use of the EM algorithm and the model of a finite mixture of Gaussian distributions for unsupervised learning.

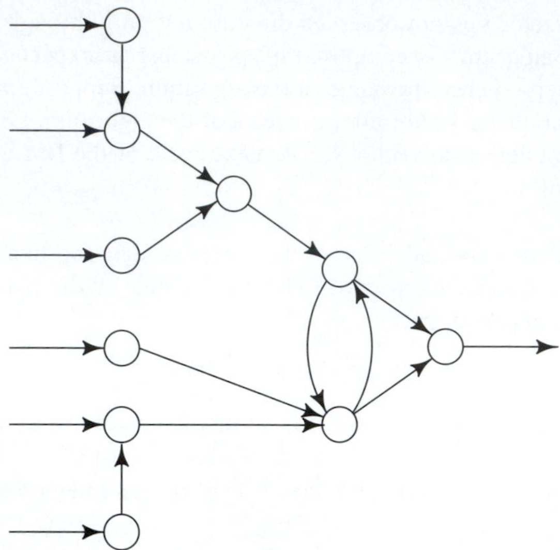

FIGURE P12.1

(a) Describe the types of neurons that are used in the two layers of each expert network.

(b) How would you design such a network in light of the theory presented in Sections 12.3 and 12.4?

12.5 Consider a piecewise-linear task described by

$$F(x_1, x_2, \ldots, x_{10}) = \begin{cases} 3x_2 + 2x_3 + x_4 + 3 + \varepsilon & \text{if } x_1 = 1 \\ 3x_5 + 2x_6 + x_7 - 3 + \varepsilon & \text{if } x_1 = -1 \end{cases}$$

For comparison, the following network configurations are used:

1. Multilayer perceptron:	"10 → 10 → 1" network
2. Single-level hierarchical network, as in Fig. 12.2:	Gating networks: 10 → 2; Expert networks: 10 → 1
3. Two-level hierarchical network, as in Fig. 12.5:	Two levels: Gating networks: 10 → 2; Expert networks: 10 → 1

Compare the computational complexities of these three networks.

12.6 Construct the block diagram of a hierarchical network with three levels of hierarchy. Level 3 has four clusters of expert networks, and level 2 has two clusters.

12.7 Consider the hierarchical structure of Fig. 12.5, involving two levels of modularity.

(a) Derive the expressions for the partial derivatives $\partial l/\partial u_i$, $\partial l/\partial u_{j|i}$, and $\partial l/\partial \mathbf{y}_{ji}$, given in Eqs. (12.45), (12.46), and (12.47), respectively.

(b) Hence, develop a stochastic gradient algorithm for the recursive computation of the synaptic weights of the expert networks and the gating networks shown in Fig. 12.5. Assume that all of these networks consist of single layers of output neurons.

12.8 The learning algorithm derived in Section 12.4 for the modular network of Fig. 12.2 was formulated for the on-line mode of operation. Describe the changes that would have to be made to this algorithm for the batch mode of operation.

12.9 For unbiased estimates and therefore improved performance of the modular network in Fig. 12.2, it may be necessary to adapt the variances of the multivariate Gaussian distribution. To do so, we redefine the covariance matrix $\mathbf{\Lambda}_i$ of the ith expert network's output vector $\mathbf{y}_i$ in the modular network of Fig. 12.2 as follows:

$$\mathbf{\Lambda}_i = \sigma_i^2 \mathbf{I}$$

where σ_i^2 is the variance to be adapted, and $\mathbf{I}$ is the identity matrix. Accordingly, we reformulate the objective function of Eq. (12.13) as

$$l = \ln \sum_{i=1}^{K} \frac{g_i}{\sigma_i} \exp\left(-\frac{1}{2\sigma_i^2} \|\mathbf{d} - \mathbf{y}_i\|^2\right)$$

(a) Derive the partial derivative $\partial l / \partial \sigma_i^2$.
(b) Formulate a procedure for the adjustment of σ_i^2.

12.10 In Section 12.6 we discussed how temporal crosstalk can arise in a multilayer perceptron trained with the back-propagation algorithm. The spatial counterpart of this phenomenon, *spatial crosstalk,* can also arise in such a neural network. Describe an example of this latter phenomenon (Jacobs et al., 1991b).

CHAPTER 13

Temporal Processing

13.1 Introduction

The back-propagation algorithm described in Chapter 6 has established itself as the most popular method for the design of neural networks. However, a major limitation of the standard back-propagation algorithm described there is that it can only learn an input–output mapping that is *static*. Consequently, the multilayer perceptron so trained has a static structure that maps an input vector **x** onto an output vector **y**, as depicted in Fig. 13.1a. This form of static input–output mapping is well suited for pattern-recognition applications (e.g., optical character recognition), where both the input vector **x** and the output vector **y** represent *spatial* patterns that are independent of time.

The standard back-propagation algorithm may also be used to perform nonlinear prediction on a stationary time series. A time series is said to be *stationary* when its statistics do *not* change with time. In such a case we may also use a static multilayer perceptron, as depicted in Fig. 13.1b, where the input elements labeled z^{-1} represent unit delays. The input vector **x** is now defined in terms of the past samples $x(n-1), x(n-2), \ldots, x(n-p)$ as follows:

$$\mathbf{x} = [x(n-1), x(n-2), \ldots, x(n-p)]^T \tag{13.1}$$

We refer to p as the *prediction order*. Thus the scalar output $y(n)$ of the multilayer perceptron produced in response to the input vector **x** equals the *one-step prediction* $\hat{x}(n)$, as shown by

$$y(n) = \hat{x}(n) \tag{13.2}$$

The actual value $x(n)$ of the input signal represents the desired response.

The important point to note from both Figs. 13.1a and 13.1b is that the multilayer perceptron represents a *static model*, all of whose free parameters have *fixed* values.

However, we know that *time* is important in many of the cognitive tasks encountered in practice, such as vision, speech, signal processing, and motor control. The question is how to represent time. In particular, how can we extend the design of a multilayer perceptron so that it assumes a time-varying form and therefore will be able to deal with time-varying signals? Indeed, how can we do a similar modification for other neural networks? The answer to these questions is to allow time to be represented by the effect it has on signal processing. This means providing the mapping network *dynamic* properties that make it responsive to time-varying signals.

In short, for a neural network to be dynamic, it must be given *memory* (Elman, 1990). One way in which this requirement can be accomplished is to introduce *time delays* into the synaptic structure of the network and to adjust their values during the learning phase. The use of time delays in neural networks is neurobiologically motivated, since it is well

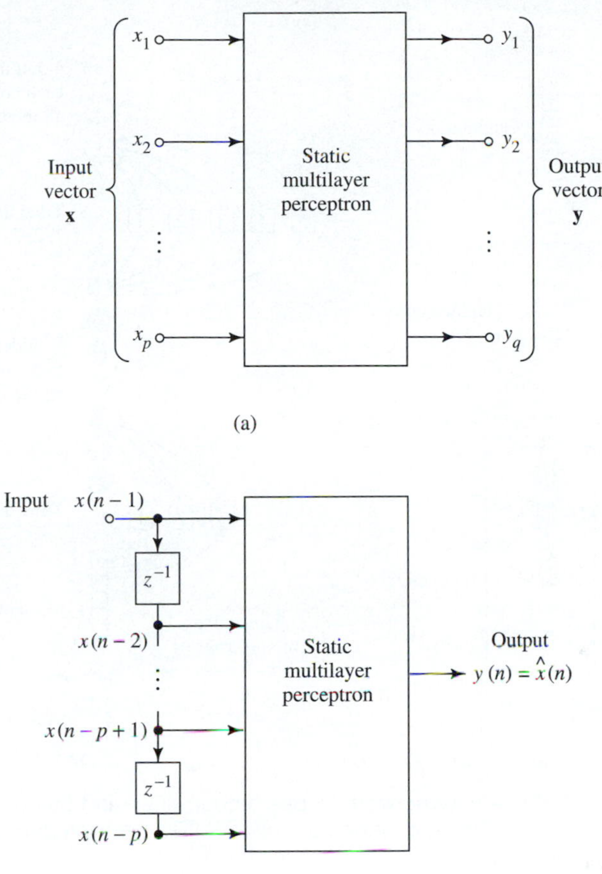

FIGURE 13.1 Static multilayer perceptron used as (a) a pattern classifier and (b) a nonlinear predictor.

known that signal delays are omnipresent in the brain and play an important role in neurobiological information processing (Braitenberg, 1967, 1977, 1986; Miller, 1987).

In this chapter we focus on error-correction learning techniques that involve the use of time delays in one form or another. One such popular technique is the so-called *time-delay neural network* (TDNN), which was first described by Lang and Hinton (1988) and Waibel et al. (1989). The TDNN is a multilayer feedforward network whose hidden neurons and output neurons are *replicated across time.* It was devised to capture explicitly the concept of time symmetry as encountered in the recognition of an isolated word (phoneme) using a spectrogram. A *spectrogram* is a two-dimensional image in which the vertical dimension corresponds to frequency and the horizontal dimension corresponds to time; the intensity (darkness) of the image corresponds to signal energy (Rabiner and Schafer, 1978). Figure 13.2a illustrates a single hidden-layer version of the TDNN (Lang and Hinton, 1988). The input layer consists of 192 (16 by 12) sensory nodes encoding the spectrogram; the hidden layer contains 10 copies of 8 hidden neurons; and the output layer contains 6 copies of 4 output neurons. The various replicas of a hidden neuron apply the same set of synaptic weights to narrow (three-time-step) windows of the spectrogram; similarly, the various replicas of an output neuron apply the same set of synaptic weights to narrow (five-time-step) windows of the pseudospectrogram computed by the hidden layer. Figure 13.2b presents a *time-delay* interpretation of the replicated neural network

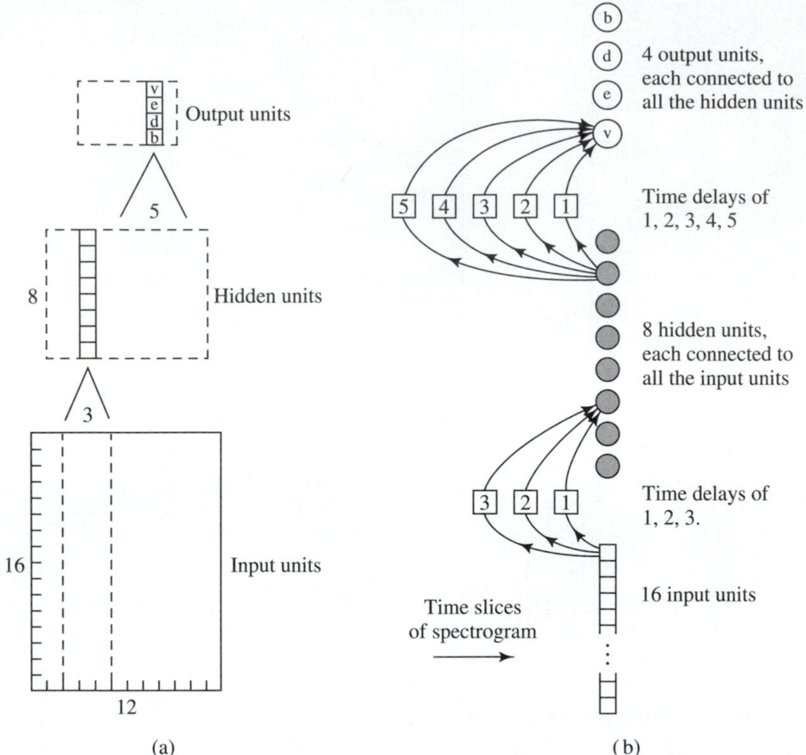

FIGURE 13.2 (a) A three-layer network whose hidden units and output units are replicated across time. (b) Time-delay neural network (TDNN) representation. (From K.J. Lang and G.E. Hinton, 1988.)

of Fig. 13.2a—hence the name "time-delay neural network." This network has a total of 544 synaptic weights. Lang and Hinton (1988) used the TDNN for the recognition of four isolated words: "bee," "dee," "ee," and "vee," which accounts for the use of four output neurons in Fig. 13.2. A recognition score of 93 percent was obtained on test data different from the training data. In a more elaborate study reported by Waibel et al. (1989), a TDNN with two hidden layers was used for the recognition of three isolated words: "bee," "dee," and "gee." In performance evaluation involving the use of test data from three speakers, the TDNN achieved an average recognition score of 98.5 percent. For comparison, various hidden Markov models (HMM) were applied to the same task, for which a recognition score of only 93.7 percent was obtained. It appears that the power of the TDNN lies in its ability to develop shift-invariant internal representations of speech and to use them for making optimal classifications (Waibel et al., 1989).

The TDNN topology is in fact embodied in a multilayer perceptron in which each synapse is represented by a *finite-duration impulse response (FIR) filter* (Wan, 1993). This latter neural network is referred to as an *FIR multilayer perceptron.* For its training, we may construct a static equivalent network by *unfolding* the FIR multilayer perceptron *in time,* and then use the standard back-propagation algorithm. A more efficient procedure, however, is to use a *temporal back-propagation algorithm* that invokes certain approximations to simplify the computation, and which was first described by Wan (1990a, b).

The FIR multilayer perceptron is a *feedforward* network; it attains dynamic behavior by virtue of the fact that each synapse of the network is designed as an FIR filter. Another way in which a neural network can assume dynamic behavior is to make it *recurrent,* that is, to build feedback into its design. Two specific approaches that may be used to train a recurrent network, and that do *not* involve the use of approximations in the computation of gradients, are as follows:

- *Back-Propagation Through Time.* The idea behind this approach is that for every recurrent network it is possible to construct a feedforward network with identical behavior over a particular time interval (Minsky and Papert, 1969). Back-propagation through time was first described in the Ph.D. thesis of Werbos (1974); see also Werbos (1990). The algorithm was rediscovered independently by Rumelhart et al. (1986b). A novel variant of the back-propagation through time algorithm is described by Williams and Peng (1990).
- *Real-Time Recurrent Learning.* A version of this algorithm is described by Williams and Zipser (1989). The origin of the algorithm may be traced, however, to an earlier paper by McBride and Nardendra (1965) on system identification for tuning the parameters of an arbitrary dynamical system.

In this chapter we study FIR multilayer perceptrons and recurrent networks; we also consider both back-propagation-through-time and real-time recurrent learning algorithms.

Organization of the Chapter

The main body of the chapter is organized as follows. In Section 13.2 we describe spatio-temporal models of a single neuron, and so motivate the discussion of FIR multilayer perceptrons in Section 13.3. Then, in Section 13.4, we describe a temporal back-propagation algorithm that does not require any constraints on the synaptic weights of the network, and that also preserves the symmetry between the forward and backward propagation phases of the network operation; in this section we also describe the use of this temporal back-propagation algorithm for modeling a chaotic time series, which can be a difficult task. In Section 13.5 we discuss a generalization of temporal back-propagation that permits the adaptation of time delays in a continuous manner.

In Section 13.6 we describe the use of back-propagation through time for a recurrent network. Then, in Section 13.7, we derive the real-time recurrent learning (RTRL) algorithm that exploits its use of feedback to provide for temporal processing. This learning algorithm is exploited in the design of a novel nonlinear adaptive predictor that operates in real time, which is described in Section 13.8. This is followed by Section 13.9 on a partially recurrent network. We conclude the chapter in Section 13.10 by presenting some final thoughts on the subject of temporal processing.

13.2 Spatio-Temporal Models of a Neuron

For much of the neural network analysis presented in previous chapters of the book, we used the nonlinear model of a neuron shown in Fig. 1.4. A limitation of this model is that it only accounts for the *spatial* behavior of a neuron by incorporating a set of fixed synaptic weights at the input end of the model. To extend the usefulness of this model for *temporal processing,* we need to modify it so as to account for the temporal nature of the input data. A general method of representing temporal behavior is to model each synapse by a *linear, time-invariant filter,* as shown in Fig. 13.3 (Shamma, 1989a). The temporal behavior of synapse i belonging to neuron j may thus be described by an impulse

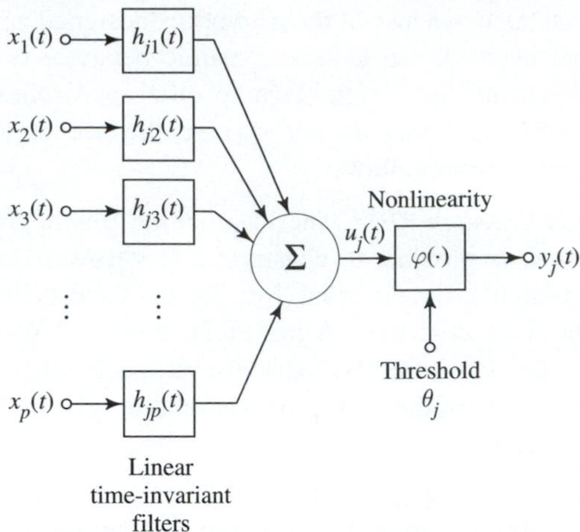

FIGURE 13.3 Dynamic model of a neuron using linear, time-invariant, low-pass filters as a synapses.

response $h_{ji}(t)$ that is a function of continuous time t. By definition, the *impulse response* of a linear time-invariant filter is the response of the filter produced by a unit impulse (Dirac delta function) applied to the filter input at time $t = 0$. Let $x_i(t)$ denote the stimulus (excitation) applied to synapse i, $i = 1, 2, \ldots, p$. The response of synapse i due to the input $x_i(t)$ is equal to the *convolution* of its impulse response $h_{ji}(t)$ with the input $x_i(t)$. Thus, using an asterisk to denote this operation, we may express the output of synapse i as

$$h_{ji}(t) * x_i(t) = \int_{-\infty}^{t} h_{ji}(\lambda)x_i(t - \lambda)\, d\lambda \tag{13.3}$$

The integral of Eq. (13.3) is referred to as the *convolution integral,* with λ playing the role of a dummy variable. Note that convolution is *commutative*, which means that we may interchange the order of the impulse response $h_{ji}(t)$ and the excitation $x_i(t)$ without affecting the final result. Given a neuron j with a total of p synapses, the net activation potential $v_j(t)$ of the neuron due to the combined effect of all the inputs and the externally applied threshold θ_j is given by

$$\begin{aligned} v_j(t) &= u_j(t) - \theta_j \\ &= \sum_{i=1}^{p} h_{ji}(t) * x_i(t) - \theta_j \\ &= \sum_{i=1}^{p} \int_{-\infty}^{t} h_{ji}(\lambda)x_i(t - \lambda)\, d\lambda - \theta_j \end{aligned} \tag{13.4}$$

Finally, $v_j(t)$ is passed through a *sigmoidal nonlinearity* $\varphi(\cdot)$ represented by the logistic function, for example, to produce the overall output

$$\begin{aligned} y_j(t) &= \varphi(v_j(t)) \\ &= \frac{1}{1 + \exp(-v_j(t))} \end{aligned} \tag{13.5}$$

Equations (13.4) and (13.5) provide a complete representation of the spatio-temporal behavior of an artificial neuron.

Finite-Duration Impulse Response (FIR) Model

The synaptic filters shown in Fig. 13.3 are continuous-time filters. Typically, each synaptic filter is characterized as follows:

- The synaptic filter is *causal,* which means that the synapse does not respond before the stimulus is applied to its input. The implication of causality is that the impulse response $h_{ji}(t)$ must vanish for negative time, as shown by

$$h_{ji}(t) = 0, \qquad t < 0 \tag{13.6}$$

- The synaptic filter has *finite memory.* Since the impulse response $h_{ji}(t)$ acts as the memory function of synapse i for neuron j, we may write

$$h_{ji}(t) = 0, \qquad t > T \tag{13.7}$$

  where T is the *memory span,* assumed to be the same for all synapses.

Accordingly, we may rewrite Eq. (13.4) as

$$v_j(t) = \sum_{i=1}^{p} \int_0^T h_{ji}(\lambda)x_i(t - \lambda)\, d\lambda - \theta_j \tag{13.8}$$

From a computational viewpoint, we find it convenient to approximate the convolution integral in Eq. (13.8) by a *convolution sum.* To do so we replace the continuous-time variable t by a discrete-time variable, as shown by

$$t = n\,\Delta t \tag{13.9}$$

where n is an integer and Δt is the *sampling period.* Then, we may approximate Eq. (13.8) as

$$\begin{aligned} v_j(n\,\Delta t) &= \sum_{i=1}^{p} \sum_{l=0}^{M} h_{ji}(l\,\Delta t)x_i(\Delta t(n - l))\,\Delta t - \theta_j \\ &= \sum_{i=1}^{p} \sum_{l=0}^{M} w_{ji}(l\,\Delta t)x_i(\Delta t(n - l)) - \theta_j \end{aligned} \tag{13.10}$$

where

$$M = \frac{T}{\Delta t} \tag{13.11}$$

and

$$w_{ji}(l\,\Delta t) = h_{ji}(l\,\Delta t)\,\Delta t \tag{13.12}$$

The sampling period Δt has a uniform value that is common to the time-varying quantities $w_{ji}(l\,\Delta t)$, $x_i[\Delta t(n - l)]$, and $v_j(n\,\Delta t)$ in Eq. (13.10). For notational convenience we may simplify matters by omitting Δt from the arguments of all three time-varying quantities, and thus rewrite Eq. (13.10) in the reduced form

$$v_j(n) = \sum_{i=1}^{p} \sum_{l=0}^{M} w_{ji}(l)x_i(n - l) - \theta_j \tag{13.13}$$

where it is customary to refer to n as the *discrete-time variable.* The inner summation in Eq. (13.13) accounts for the temporal behavior of neuron j, and the outer summation accounts for its spatial behavior.

On the basis of Eq. (13.13), together with (13.5), we may reformulate the spatio-temporal model of a neuron as shown in Fig. 13.4a, where $\mathbf{w}_{ji}$ denotes the *weight vector*

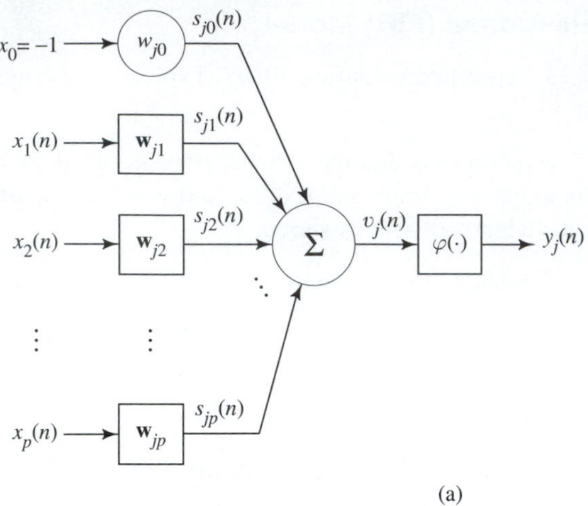

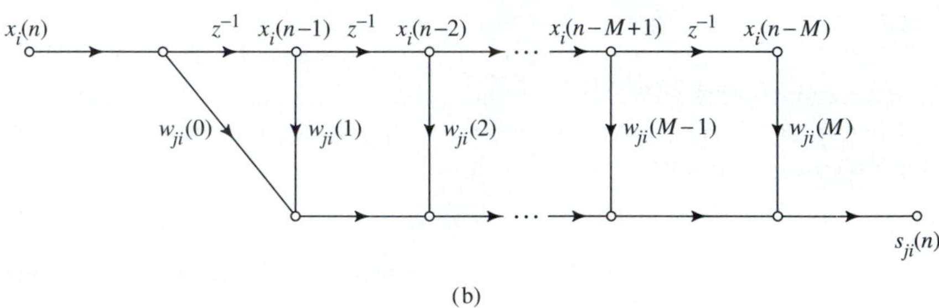

FIGURE 13.4 (a) Dynamic model of a neuron, incorporating synaptic FIR filters. (b) Signal-flow graph of a synaptic FIR filter.

of synapse i belonging to neuron j, and where $i = 1, 2, \ldots, p$. The weight w_{j0} connected to the fixed input $x_0 = -1$ represents the threshold θ_j. We refer to the model of Fig. 13.4a as the *finite-duration impulse response (FIR) model* of a single artificial neuron. This terminology is in recognition of the fact that each synapse of the neuron is itself modeled by an FIR filter having the signal-flow graph representation shown in Fig. 13.4b, where z^{-1} represents the unit-delay operator.

Resistance–Capacitance Model

The exact form of the synaptic impulse response $h_{ji}(t)$ in the general model of Fig. 13.3 depends on the modeling objectives and computational costs involved. The discrete-time approximation that led to the formulation of the model shown in Fig. 13.4a is motivated by computational considerations. Alternatively, modeling considerations may require that we simplify temporal behavior by using a scaling parameter to determine the sign and strength of a "typical" synaptic impulse response, in which case we write

$$h_{ji}(t) = w_{ji} \cdot h_o(t) \qquad \text{for all } i \text{ and } j \tag{13.14}$$

where $h_o(t)$ models the temporal characteristics of a typical postsynaptic potential, and w_{ji} is a scalar that determines its sign (excitatory or inhibitory) and the overall strength of the connection between neurons j and i (Shamma, 1989a). Once again, the form assumed by $h_o(t)$ depends on the amount of detail required. A popular choice is an *exponential* model defined by

$$h_o(t) = \frac{1}{\tau} \exp\left(-\frac{t}{\tau}\right) \tag{13.15}$$

where τ is a *time constant.* The time function $h_o(t)$ of Eq. (13.15) is recognized as the impulse response of a simple RC circuit consisting of a resistor R and capacitor C connected in parallel, and fed from a current source. The time constant of such a circuit is

$$\tau = RC \tag{13.16}$$

Thus, according to Eq. (13.14), the linear, time-invariant filter of impulse response $h_o(t)$ is common to all the synapses of neuron j. We may therefore factor out the effect of $h_o(t)$ by connecting a linear, time-invariant filter of impulse response $h_o(t)$ in cascade with a linear combiner that accounts for the w_{ji}, $i = 1, 2, \ldots, p$, as shown in the model of Fig. 13.5a. Moreover, in light of Eq. (13.15), we may represent the filter by a simple RC circuit, as shown in Fig. 13.5b. The combination of Figs. 13.5a and 13.5b represents an *RC model* of an artificial neuron; in the neural network literature, it is commonly referred to as the *additive model.* This particular model may be viewed as a lumped-circuit approximation of the distributed transmission-line model of a biological dendritic neuron (Rall, 1989). The low-pass nature of the RC circuit in Fig. 13.5b may also be justified by the fact that a biological synapse is itself a low-pass filter to an excellent approximation (Scott, 1977). In the model of Fig. 13.5a it is assumed that the inputs $x_1(t)$, $x_2(t), \ldots, x_p(t)$ are voltage signals and the corresponding weights $w_{j1}, w_{j2}, \ldots, w_{jp}$ are

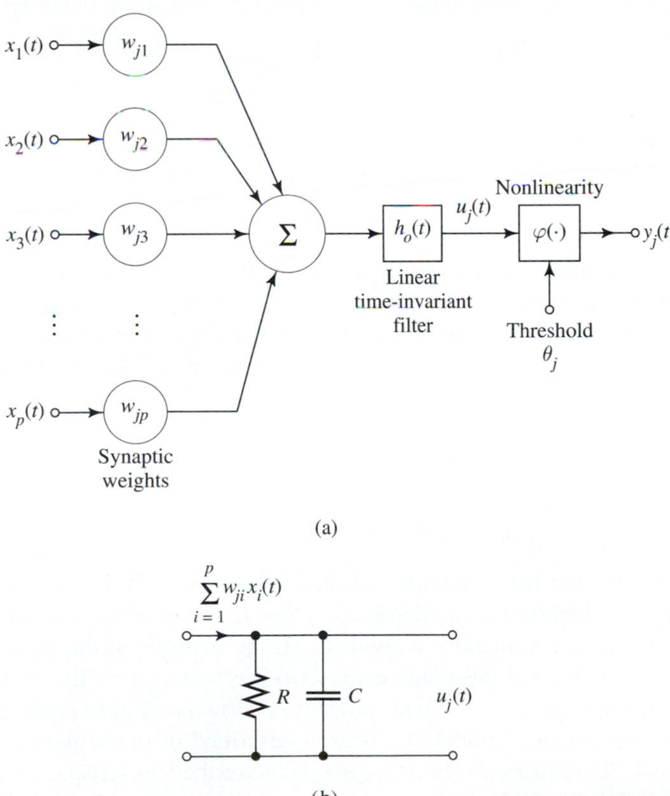

FIGURE 13.5 (a) *RC* model of a neuron. (b) *RC* model of a filter with impulse response $h_o(t)$.

conductances, in which case the linear combiner output is a current signal. It is also assumed that the nonlinear element of the model has an input resistance that is represented by the element R in the RC circuit of Fig. 13.5b.

The FIR model of Fig. 13.4 is used to develop the temporal extension of the back-propagation algorithm, which is pursued in Section 13.4. The RC model (additive model) of Fig. 13.5 provides the basis for the study of neurodynamics presented in Chapter 14.

13.3 FIR Multilayer Perceptron

Consider a multilayer perceptron whose hidden neurons and output neurons are all based on the *finite-duration impulse response (FIR) model* shown in Fig. 13.4. We refer to such a neural network structure as an *FIR multilayer perceptron.*

Let $w_{ji}(l)$ denote the weight connected to the lth *tap* of the FIR filter modeling the synapse that connects the output of neuron i to neuron j. As shown in Fig. 13.4b, the index l ranges from 0 to M, where M is the total number of delay units built into the design of the FIR filter. According to this model, the signal $s_{ji}(n)$ appearing at the output of the ith synapse of neuron j is given by a linear combination of delayed values of the input signal $x_i(n)$ as shown by the *convolution sum*

$$s_{ji}(n) = \sum_{l=0}^{M} w_{ji}(l)x_i(n - l) \tag{13.17}$$

where n denotes discrete time. We may rewrite Eq. (13.17) in matrix form by introducing the following definitions for the state vector and weight vector for synapse i, respectively:

$$\mathbf{x}_i(n) = [x_i(n), x_i(n-1), \ldots, x_i(n-M)]^T \tag{13.18}$$

$$\mathbf{w}_{ji} = [w_{ji}(0), w_{ji}(1), \ldots, w_{ji}(M)]^T \tag{13.19}$$

where the superscript T signifies matrix transposition. We may thus express the (scalar) signal $s_{ji}(n)$ as the inner product of the vectors $\mathbf{w}_{ji}(n)$ and $\mathbf{x}_i(n)$; that is,

$$s_{ji}(n) = \mathbf{w}_{ji}^T\mathbf{x}_i(n) \tag{13.20}$$

Equation (13.20) defines the output $s_{ji}(n)$ of the ith synapse in the model of Fig. 13.4a in response to the state (input) vector $\mathbf{x}_i(n)$, where $i = 1, 2, \ldots, p$. Hence, summing the contributions of the complete set of p synapses depicted in this model (i.e., summing over the index i), we may describe the output $y_j(n)$ of neuron j by the following pair of equations:

$$v_j(n) = \sum_{i=1}^{p} s_{ji}(n) - \theta_j = \sum_{i=1}^{p} \mathbf{w}_{ji}^T\mathbf{x}_i(n) - \theta_j \tag{13.21}$$

$$y_j(n) = \varphi(v_j(n)) \tag{13.22}$$

where $v_j(n)$ denotes the net activation potential of neuron j, θ_j is the externally applied threshold, and $\varphi(\cdot)$ denotes the nonlinear activation function of the neuron. It is assumed that the same form of nonlinearity is used for all the neurons in the network. Note that if the weight vector $\mathbf{w}_{ji}$ and the state vector $\mathbf{x}_i(n)$ are replaced by the scalars w_{ji} and x_i, respectively, and the operation of inner product is correspondingly replaced by ordinary multiplication, the dynamic model of a neuron described in mathematical terms of Eqs. (13.21) and (13.22) reduces to the static model described in Chapter 1. Indeed, these simple analogies between the standard and temporal versions of the back-propagation algorithm carry on throughout the derivations presented in this and the next section.

Using the dynamic model of a neuron shown in Fig. 13.4, we may construct the corresponding dynamic version of the FIR multilayer perceptron in a manner similar to that described in Chapter 6, the only difference being that the static forms of the synaptic connections between the neurons in the various layers of the network are replaced by their dynamic versions.

To train the network, we use a supervised learning algorithm in which the actual response of each neuron in the output layer is compared with a desired target response at each time instant. Assume that neuron j lies in the output layer with its actual response denoted by $y_j(n)$ and that the desired response for this neuron is denoted by $d_j(n)$, both of which are measured at time n. We may then define an *instantaneous value* for the sum of squared errors produced by the network as follows:

$$\mathscr{E}(n) = \frac{1}{2}\sum_j e_j^2(n) \tag{13.23}$$

where the index j refers to the neurons in the output layer only, and $e_j(n)$ is the error signal, defined by

$$e_j(n) = d_j(n) - y_j(n) \tag{13.24}$$

The goal is to minimize a *cost function* defined as the value of $\mathscr{E}(n)$ computed over all time:

$$\mathscr{E}_{\text{total}} = \sum_n \mathscr{E}(n) \tag{13.25}$$

The algorithm we have in mind for computing an estimate of the optimum weight vector that attains this goal is based on an approximation to the method of steepest descent. This approximation works with an instantaneous estimate of the gradient vector, an issue we discuss next.

Instantaneous Gradient Approach

An obvious way of proceeding with this development is to differentiate the cost function of Eq. (13.25) with respect to the weight vector $\mathbf{w}_{ji}$. By so doing, we get

$$\frac{\partial \mathscr{E}_{\text{total}}}{\partial \mathbf{w}_{ji}} = \sum_n \frac{\partial \mathscr{E}(n)}{\partial \mathbf{w}_{ji}} \tag{13.26}$$

To proceed further, we *unfold the network in time.* The strategy here is first to try to remove all the time delays in the network by expanding it into an equivalent but larger "static" network, and then to apply the standard back-propagation algorithm to compute the instantaneous error gradients.

To unfold the network in time, we may proceed in one of two ways, depending on which computation end of the multilayer perceptron we begin with:

- *Forward Unfolding in Time.* We start at the input (sensory) layer and move forward through the network, layer by layer.
- *Backward Unfolding in Time.* We start at the output (computation) layer, and move backward through the network, layer by layer.

In both cases, there is growth in the size of the network that results from unfolding it in time. In the forward case, the growth is of order $O(DN)$, where D is the total number of time delays and N is the total number of free parameters in the network. On the other hand, in the backward case, the size of the equivalent static network grows *geometrically*

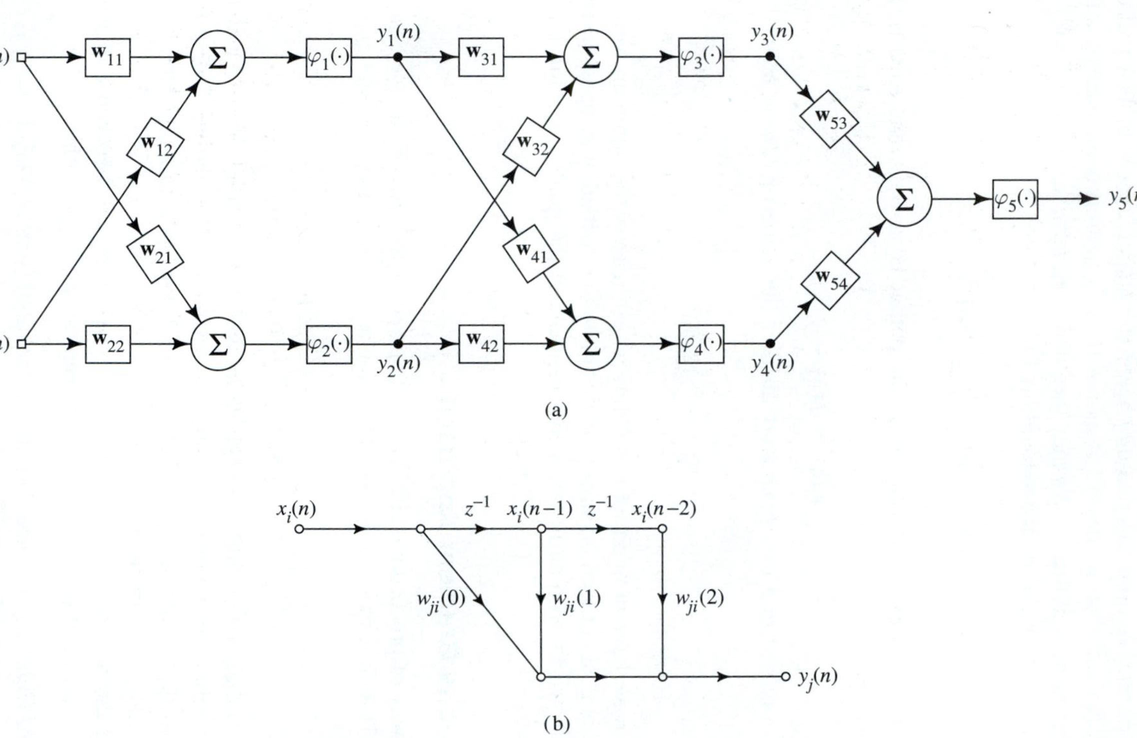

FIGURE 13.6 (a) Architectural flow graph of 2-2-2-1 FIR multilayer perceptron. (b) FIR model of a synaptic filter.

with the number of time delays and layers. Forward folding in time is therefore preferred over backward folding in time.

In unfolding the network in time, each node (tap) of a synaptic filter of a neuron in a given layer is interpreted as a *virtual neuron* with a single synaptic weight and an input delayed by an appropriate number of unit delays. In effect, a delay unit is removed by replicating previous layers in the network and delaying the inputs appropriately.

As an example, consider the 2-2-2-1 FIR multilayer perceptron shown in Fig. 13.6a, whose synaptic filter structures are all defined by the signal-flow graph of Fig. 13.6b. Specifically, each of the 10 synapses in the network is modeled as an FIR filter of length two, which results in a total of 30 adjustable weights. In Fig. 13.7 we present the signal-flow graph for a complete unfolding-in-time form of the network, with this operation initiated from the input layer and ending at the output layer. Thus, for the FIR multilayer perceptron of Fig. 13.6, the unfolding-in-time operation yields an equivalent static network where all the time dependences are made external to the network by windowing the input in time. We thus see that whereas the original FIR multilayer perceptron of Fig. 13.6 has

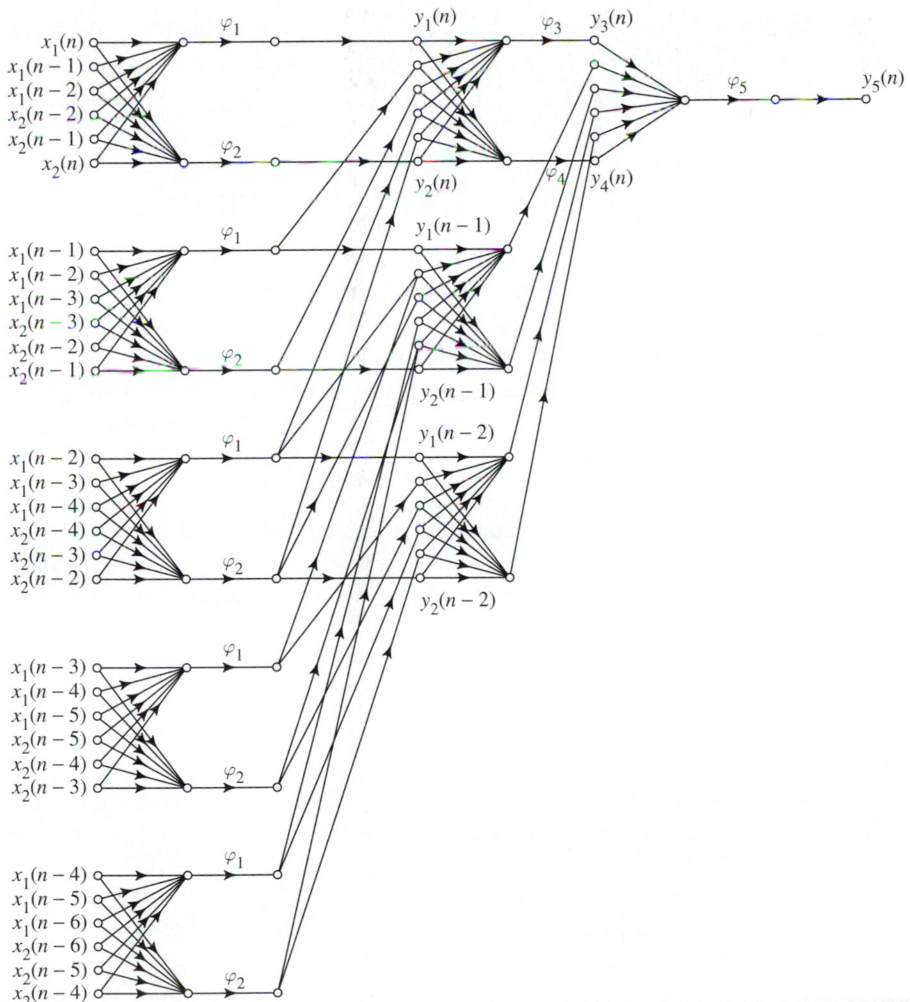

FIGURE 13.7 Signal-flow graph of 2-2-2-1 FIR multilayer perceptron that has been unfolded in time, starting from its input end.

30 adjustable weights, the equivalent network represented by Fig. 13.7 has a total of 102 "static" weights due to *redundancies* in the weights, calculated as follows:

$$(5 \times 12) + (3 \times 12) + 6 = 102$$

Having obtained the unfolded static network in the manner described, we may then proceed to calculate the instantaneous error gradients for all the weights in the network using the standard back-propagation algorithm, as described in Chapter 6. The problem with this approach, however, is that it does *not* lead to a desirable form of the temporal back-propagation algorithm. Specifically, it is handicapped by the following negative attributes (Wan, 1990a, b):

1. There is a loss of a sense of symmetry between the forward propagation of states and the backward propagation of terms needed to calculate instantaneous error gradients.
2. There is no nice recursive formula for propagating the error terms.
3. There is need for global bookkeeping, in that we have to keep track of which static weights are actually the same in the equivalent network.

We thus see that although the use of instantaneous gradient estimates is the obvious approach to develop a temporal version of back-propagation, from a practical standpoint it is *not* the way to proceed.

13.4 Temporal Back-Propagation Learning

To overcome the problems associated with the instantaneous gradient approach, we may proceed as follows (Wan, 1990a, b). First, we recognize that the expansion of the total error gradient into a sum of instantaneous error gradients, as shown in Eq. (13.26), is not unique. In particular, we may consider an alternative way of expressing the partial derivative of the cost function $\mathscr{E}_{\text{total}}$ with respect to the weight vector $\mathbf{w}_{ji}(n)$, by writing

$$\frac{\partial \mathscr{E}_{\text{total}}}{\partial \mathbf{w}_{ji}(n)} = \sum_n \frac{\partial \mathscr{E}_{\text{total}}}{\partial v_j(n)} \frac{\partial v_j(n)}{\partial \mathbf{w}_{ji}(n)} \tag{13.27}$$

where the time index n runs over $v_j(n)$ and not $\mathscr{E}(n)$. We may interpret the partial derivative $\partial \mathscr{E}_{\text{total}}/\partial v_j(n)$ as the change in the cost function $\mathscr{E}_{\text{total}}$ produced by a change in the internal activation potential v_j of neuron j at time n. Moreover, we recognize that

$$\frac{\partial \mathscr{E}_{\text{total}}}{\partial v_j(n)} \frac{\partial v_j(n)}{\partial \mathbf{w}_{ji}(n)} \neq \frac{\partial \mathscr{E}(n)}{\partial \mathbf{w}_{ji}(n)} \tag{13.28}$$

It is only when we take the sum over all n, as in Eqs. (13.26) and (13.27), that the equality holds.

Given the expansion of Eq. (13.27), we may now use the idea of gradient descent in weight space. In particular, we postulate a recursion for updating the tap-weight vector $\mathbf{w}_{ji}(n)$, as shown by

$$\mathbf{w}_{ji}(n+1) = \mathbf{w}_{ji}(n) - \eta \frac{\partial \mathscr{E}_{\text{total}}}{\partial v_j(n)} \frac{\partial v_j(n)}{\partial \mathbf{w}_{ji}(n)} \tag{13.29}$$

where η is the *learning-rate parameter*. From the defining equation (13.21), we find that for any neuron j in the network the partial derivative of the activation potential $v_j(n)$ with respect to the weight vector $\mathbf{w}_{ji}(n)$ is given by

$$\frac{\partial v_j(n)}{\partial \mathbf{w}_{ji}(n)} = \mathbf{x}_i(n) \tag{13.30}$$

where $\mathbf{x}_i(n)$ is the input vector applied to neuron j. Moreover, we may define the *local gradient* for neuron j as

$$\delta_j(n) = -\frac{\partial \mathscr{E}_{\text{total}}}{\partial v_j(n)} \tag{13.31}$$

Accordingly, we may rewrite Eq. (13.29) in the familiar form

$$\mathbf{w}_{ji}(n+1) = \mathbf{w}_{ji}(n) + \eta\delta_j(n)\mathbf{x}_i(n) \tag{13.32}$$

As in the derivation of the standard back-propagation algorithm, the explicit form of the local gradient $\delta_j(n)$ depends on whether neuron j lies in the output layer or a hidden layer of the network. These two different cases are considered next, in turn.

CASE 1. Neuron j Is an Output Unit

For the output layer, we simply have

$$\begin{aligned}\delta_j(n) &= -\frac{\partial \mathscr{E}_{\text{total}}}{\partial v_j(n)} \\ &= -\frac{\partial \mathscr{E}(n)}{\partial v_j(n)} \\ &= e_j(n)\varphi'(v_j(n))\end{aligned} \tag{13.33}$$

where $e_j(n)$ is the error signal measured at the output of neuron j, and

$$\begin{aligned}\varphi'(v_j(n)) &= \frac{\partial \varphi(v_j(n))}{\partial v_j(n)} \\ &= \frac{\partial y_j(n)}{\partial v_j(n)}\end{aligned} \tag{13.34}$$

CASE 2. Neuron j Is a Hidden Unit

For neuron j located in a hidden layer, we define $\mathscr{A}$ as the set of all neurons whose inputs are fed by neuron j in a forward manner. Let $v_m(n)$ denote the internal activation potential of neuron m that belongs to the set $\mathscr{A}$. We may then write

$$\begin{aligned}\delta_j(n) &= -\frac{\partial \mathscr{E}_{\text{total}}}{\partial v_j(n)} \\ &= -\sum_{m\in\mathscr{A}}\sum_{n}\frac{\partial \mathscr{E}_{\text{total}}}{\partial v_m(n)}\frac{\partial v_m(n)}{\partial v_j(n)}\end{aligned} \tag{13.35}$$

Using the definition of Eq. (13.31) (with index m used in place of j) in Eq. (13.35), we may thus write

$$\begin{aligned}\delta_j(n) &= \sum_{m\in\mathscr{A}}\sum_{n}\delta_m(n)\frac{\partial v_m(n)}{\partial v_j(n)} \\ &= \sum_{m\in\mathscr{A}}\sum_{n}\delta_m(n)\frac{\partial v_m(n)}{\partial y_j(n)}\frac{\partial y_j(n)}{\partial v_j(n)}\end{aligned} \tag{13.36}$$

where $y_j(n)$ is the output of neuron j. Next, using the definition given in Eq. (13.34) for $\partial y_j(n)/\partial v_j(n)$ and recognizing that this partial derivative refers to neuron j that lies outside the set $\mathcal{A}$, we may rewrite Eq. (13.36) as

$$\delta_j(n) = \varphi'(v_j(n)) \sum_{m \in \mathcal{A}} \sum_{n} \delta_m(n) \frac{\partial v_m(n)}{\partial y_j(n)} \tag{13.37}$$

As defined previously, $v_m(n)$ denotes the activation potential of neuron m fed by the output of neuron j. Hence, adapting the meaning of Eqs. (13.17) and (13.21) to the situation at hand, we may express $v_m(n)$ as

$$v_m(n) = \sum_{j=0}^{p} \sum_{l=0}^{M} w_{mj}(l) y_j(n-l) \tag{13.38}$$

In Eq.(13.38) we have included the bias θ_m applied to neuron m as the term corresponding to $j = 0$ by defining

$$w_{m0}(l) = \theta_m \quad \text{and} \quad y_0(n-l) = -1 \qquad \text{for all } l \text{ and } n \tag{13.39}$$

The index M defining the upper limit of the inner summation in Eq. (13.38) is the total number of time delays in each synaptic filter of neuron m, and every other neuron in the network. The index p defining the upper limit of the outer summation in Eq. (13.38) is the total number of synapses belonging to neuron m. Recognizing that the convolution sum with respect to l is commutative, we may rewrite Eq. (13.38) in the equivalent form

$$v_m(n) = \sum_{j=0}^{p} \sum_{l=0}^{M} y_j(l) w_{mj}(n-l) \tag{13.40}$$

Differentiating Eq. (13.40) with respect to y_j, we thus obtain

$$\frac{\partial v_m(n)}{\partial y_j(n)} = \begin{cases} w_{mj}(n-l), & 0 \le n-l \le M \\ 0, & \text{otherwise} \end{cases} \tag{13.41}$$

In light of Eq. (13.41), the partial derivatives $\partial v_m(n)/\partial y_j(n)$ in Eq. (13.37), for which n is outside the range $l \le n \le M + l$, evaluate to zero. Accordingly, for the case of a hidden neuron j, the use of Eq. (13.41) in (13.37) yields

$$\begin{aligned} \delta_j(n) &= \varphi'(v_j(n)) \sum_{m \in \mathcal{A}} \sum_{n=l}^{M+l} \delta_m(n) w_{mj}(n-l) \\ &= \varphi'(v_j(n)) \sum_{m = \mathcal{A}} \sum_{n=0}^{M} \delta_m(n+l) w_{mj}(n) \end{aligned} \tag{13.42}$$

Define a new vector

$$\boldsymbol{\Delta}_m(n) = [\delta_m(n), \delta_m(n+1), \ldots, \delta_m(n+M)]^T \tag{13.43}$$

Earlier, we defined the weight vector $\mathbf{w}_{ji}$ as in Eq. (13.19). Using matrix notation, we may therefore rewrite Eq. (13.42) as

$$\delta_j(n) = \varphi'(v_j(n)) \sum_{m \in \mathcal{A}} \boldsymbol{\Delta}_m^T(n) \mathbf{w}_{mj} \tag{13.44}$$

where $\boldsymbol{\Delta}_m^T(n)\mathbf{w}_{mj}$ is the inner product of the vectors $\boldsymbol{\Delta}_m(n)$ and $\mathbf{w}_{mj}$, both of which have dimension $(m + 1)$. Equation (13.44) completes the evaluation of $\delta_j(n)$ for a neuron j in the hidden layer.

We are now ready to summarize the weight-update equation for *temporal back-propagation* as the following pair of relations (Wan, 1990a, b):

$$\mathbf{w}_{ji}(n+1) = \mathbf{w}_{ji}(n) + \eta\delta_j(n)\mathbf{x}_i(n) \tag{13.45}$$

$$\delta_j(n) = \begin{cases} e_j(n)\varphi'(v_j(n)), & \text{neuron } j \text{ in the output layer} \\ \varphi'(v_j(n)) \sum_{m \in \mathcal{A}} \mathbf{\Delta}_m^T(n)\mathbf{w}_{mj}, & \text{neuron } j \text{ in a hidden layer} \end{cases} \tag{13.46}$$

We immediately observe that these relations represent a *vector generalization* of the standard back-propagation algorithm. Indeed, if we replace the input vector $\mathbf{x}_i(n)$, the weight vector $\mathbf{w}_{mj}$, and the local gradient vector $\mathbf{\Delta}_m$ by their scalar counterparts, the temporal back-propagation algorithm reduces to the standard form of the back-propagation algorithm derived in Chapter 6.

To compute $\delta_j(n)$ for a neuron j located in a hidden layer, we *propagate* the δ's from the next layer backwards through those synaptic filters whose excitation is derived from neuron j, in accordance with Eq. (13.44). This backward-propagation mechanism is illustrated in Fig. 13.8. We thus see that the local gradient $\delta_j(n)$ is formed not by simply taking a weighted sum but by backward filtering through each synapse. In particular, for each new set of input and desired response vectors, the forward filters are incremented one time step and the backward filters are incremented one time step.

We can now see the practical benefits gained by using the temporal back-propagation algorithm described herein (Wan, 1990a, b):

1. The symmetry between the forward propagation of states and the backward propagation of error terms is preserved, and the sense of parallel distributed processing is thereby maintained.
2. Each unique weight of synaptic filter is used only once in the calculation of the δ's; there is no redundant use of terms experienced in the instantaneous gradient method.

In deriving the temporal back-propagation algorithm described in Eqs. (13.45) and (13.46), it was assumed that the synaptic filter weights are fixed for all gradient calculations.

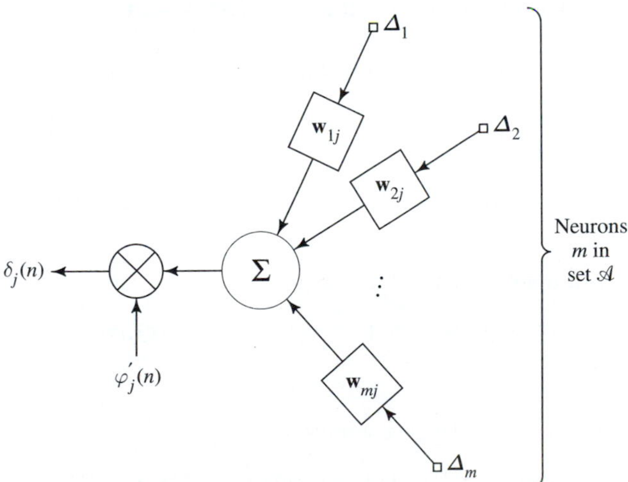

FIGURE 13.8 Back-propagation of local gradients through an FIR multilayer perceptron.

Clearly, this is not a valid assumption during actual adaptation. Accordingly, discrepancies in performance will arise between the temporal back-propagation algorithm and the temporal version obtained using the instantaneous gradient method. However, these discrepancies are usually of a minor nature (Wan, 1990a, b). For a small learning-rate parameter η, the differences in the learning characteristics of these two algorithms are negligible for all practical purposes.

Causality Constraints

Careful examination of Eq. (13.42) reveals that the computation of $\delta_j(n)$ is *noncausal*, because it requires knowledge of future values of the δ's and the w's. If we use the first line of this equation, we require future values of the w's. Alternatively, application of the second line of the equation requires knowledge of future values of the δ's.

Clearly, the exact time reference used for adaptation is unimportant. Moreover, the synaptic structures employed in the network are all FIR filters. Accordingly, the computation of $\delta_j(n)$ may be made *causal* simply by adding a finite number of unit-delay operators at various locations inside the network. As a possible solution, we thus require that the adaptation of all weight vectors be based only on the current and past values of error signals. We may therefore immediately set up $\delta_j(n)$ for neuron j in the output layer and so adapt the synaptic filter weights in that layer.

Consider now the next layer back (i.e., one hidden layer back from the output layer). Causality constraints imply that for neuron j in this layer the computation of the local gradient

$$\delta_j(n-M) = \varphi'(v_j(n-M)) \sum_{m\in\mathcal{A}} \mathbf{\Delta}_m^T(n-M)\mathbf{w}_{mj} \tag{13.47}$$

is based only on current and past values of the vector $\mathbf{\Delta}_m$; that is,

$$\mathbf{\Delta}_m(n-M) = [\delta_m(n-M), \delta_m(n+1-M), \ldots, \delta_m(n)]^T \tag{13.48}$$

Equation (13.47) is obtained simply by replacing the time index n by $n - M$, where M is the number of time delays in a synaptic filter. Note that the states $\mathbf{x}_i(n - M)$ must be stored, so that we may compute the product $\delta_j(n - M)\mathbf{x}_i(n - M)$ for the adaptation of the weight vector connecting neuron j in the last hidden layer to neuron i one layer farther back.

We may continue the operation described here for one more layer back (i.e., two layers back from the output layer) simply by making the time shift twice as long. The operation is continued in this fashion until all the computation layers in the network are accounted for.

Accordingly, we may formulate the *causal* form of the temporal back-propagation algorithm as follows:

- For neuron j in the output layer, compute

$$\mathbf{w}_{ji}(n+1) = \mathbf{w}_{ji}(n) + \eta\delta_j(n)\mathbf{x}_i(n) \tag{13.49}$$

$$\delta_j(n) = e_j(n)\varphi_j'(n) \tag{13.50}$$

- For neuron j in a hidden layer, compute

$$\mathbf{w}_{ji}(n+1) = \mathbf{w}_{ji}(n) + \eta\delta_j(n-lM)\mathbf{x}_i(n-lM) \tag{13.51}$$

$$\delta_j(n-lM) = \varphi'(v_j(n-lM)) \sum_{m\in\mathcal{A}} \mathbf{\Delta}_m^T(n-lM)\mathbf{w}_{mj} \tag{13.52}$$

where M is the total synaptic filter length, and the index l identifies the hidden layer in question. Specifically, $l = 1$ corresponds to one layer back from the output layer; $l = 2$, two layers back from the output layer; and so on.

Although the causal form of the temporal back-propagation algorithm described in Eqs. (13.49) through (13.52) is less esthetically pleasing than the noncausal form described in Eqs. (13.45) and (13.46), basically the two forms of the algorithm differ from each other only in terms of a simple change of indices.

Summarizing, then, we may state the following (Wan, 1990a, b):

- The δ's are propagated through the layers of the network backward and continuously *without* delay. This kind of propagation forces the internal values of the δ's to be shifted in time.
- To correct for this time shift, the states [i.e., the values of $\mathbf{x}_i(n)$] are stored so as to form the proper product terms needed for adaptation of the weight vectors. In other words, added storage delays are required only for the states, whereas the backward propagation of the deltas is performed without delays.
- The backward propagation of the deltas remains symmetric with respect to the forward propagation of the states.

Analogy of the Constrained Temporal Back-Propagation Algorithm with the Delayed LMS Algorithm

The discrepancies between the constrained (causal) and unconstrained (noncausal) forms of the temporal back-propagation algorithm are somewhat analogous to the least-mean-square (LMS) versus delayed LMS algorithm (Wan, 1994). In the delayed LMS algorithm applicable to a single linear neuron, the weight vector of the neuron is adapted as follows (in light of the theory described in Chapter 5):

$$\mathbf{w}(n + 1) = \mathbf{w}(n) + \eta e(n - D)\, \mathbf{x}(n - D) \tag{13.53}$$

where $\mathbf{w}(n + 1)$ is the updated value of the weight vector, $\mathbf{w}(n)$ is its old value, $\mathbf{x}(n)$ is the input vector, $e(n)$ is the error signal between the neuron's actual response and the desired response, η is the learning-rate parameter, and D is the delay. The delayed LMS algorithm exhibits a similar misadjustment as the standard LMS algorithm ($D = 0$), but a slower convergence. However, it is hard to generalize these claims to FIR multilayer perceptrons on account of the presence of nonlinearities (Wan, 1994).

Modeling of Time Series

In this subsection we illustrate an application of the FIR multilayer perceptron as a device for the nonlinear prediction of a time series, the motivation for which is to develop a nonlinear model of the underlying dynamics responsible for the physical generation of the time series.

Consider a scalar time series denoted by $\{x(n)\}$, which is described by a *nonlinear regressive model* of *order* p as follows:

$$x(n) = f(x(n - 1), x(n - 2), \ldots, x(n - p)) + \varepsilon(n) \tag{13.54}$$

where f is a *nonlinear function* of its arguments and $\varepsilon(n)$ is a *residual*. It is assumed that $\varepsilon(n)$ is drawn from a *white Gaussian noise process*. The assumption that the noise is white means that its power spectrum is *constant,* which in turn implies that any two samples of the noise are *uncorrelated.* Since it is further assumed that the noise is Gaussian, the $\varepsilon(n)$ for different n represent *statistically independent* samples of the noise process. Returning to the task at hand, the nonlinear function f is unknown, and the only thing that we have available to us is a set of *observables*: $x(1), x(2), \ldots, x(N)$, where N is the total length of the time series. The requirement is to construct a physical model of the time series, given this data set. To do so, we may use an FIR multilayer perceptron as a *one-step predictor* of some order p, as illustrated in Fig. 13.9a. Specifically, the network is designed to make a prediction of the sample $x(n)$, given the past p samples $x(n-1)$, $x(n-2), \ldots, x(n-p)$, as shown by

$$\hat{x}(n) = F(x(n-1), x(n-2), \ldots, x(n-p)) + e(n) \tag{13.55}$$

The nonlinear function F is the *approximation* of the unknown function f, which is computed by the FIR multilayer perceptron. The actual sample value $x(n)$ acts as the *desired response.* Thus the FIR multilayer perceptron is trained so as to minimize the squared value of the *prediction error*:

$$e(n) = x(n) - \hat{x}(n), \qquad p + 1 \leq n \leq N \tag{13.56}$$

Regardless of the training method used, the minimization of the squared error $e^2(n)$, in accordance with Eqs. (13.55) and (13.56), is an *open-loop adaptation scheme* in the sense that the actual output of the network is *not* fed back to the input during training. In the control and signal-processing literature, this training scheme is referred to as *equation-error formulation* (Mendel, 1973), while in the neural network literature it is referred to as *teacher forcing* (Williams and Zipser, 1989).

The open-loop adaptation method depicted in Fig. 13.9a represents *feedforward prediction.* Once the training of the FIR multilayer perceptron is completed, the *generalization* performance of the network is evaluated by performing *recursive prediction* in an autonomous fashion. Specifically, the predictive capability of the network is tested by using the *closed-loop adaptation scheme,* illustrated in Fig. 13.9b. Thus a "short-term" prediction of the time series is computed iteratively by feeding the sequence of one-step predictions

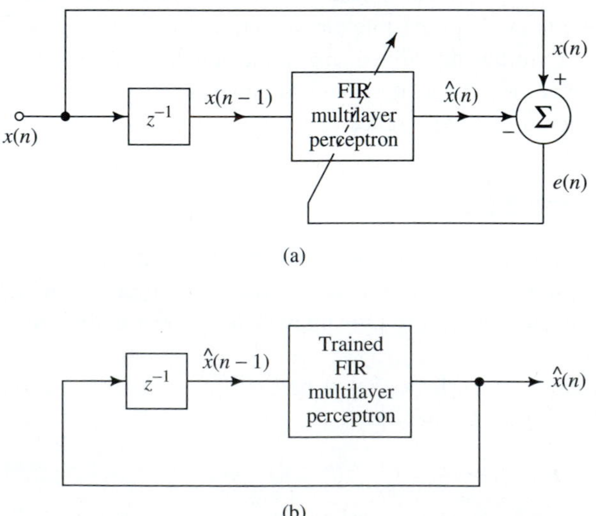

FIGURE 13.9 (a) Open-loop adaptation scheme (training). (b) Closed-loop adaptation scheme (recursive prediction).

computed by the network back into the input, as shown by

$$\hat{x}(n) = F(\hat{x}(n-1), \hat{x}(n-2), \ldots, \hat{x}(n-p)) \tag{13.57}$$

Note that (after initialization) there is *no* external input applied to the network in Fig. 13.9b. We refer to the prediction so computed as short-term, because ordinarily it is only possible to maintain a reliable prediction of the time series through a limited number of time steps into the future. In the case of chaotic phenomena, the behavior of which is *highly sensitive to initial conditions,* the quality of the prediction degrades rapidly once we go past a certain number of time steps into the future.

Wan (1994) has used an FIR multilayer perceptron to perform nonlinear prediction on the time series plotted in Fig. 13.10, which shows the chaotic intensity pulsations of an NH_3 laser. This particular time series was distributed as part of the Santa Fe Institute Time-Series Competition, which was held in the United States in 1992. For the laser data, only 1000 samples of the sequence (i.e., those to the left of the dashed line in Fig. 13.10) were provided. The requirement was to predict the next 100 samples. During the course of the competition, the physical origin of the data set, as well as the 100 point continuations, were kept secret in order to ensure that there would be no bias built into the design of the predictor.

The FIR multilayer perceptron was designed as a 1-12-12-1 fully connected feedforward network, configured as follows (Wan, 1994):

Input layer: 1 node
First hidden layer:
    Number of neurons: 12
    Number of taps per synaptic filter: 25
Second hidden layer:
    Number of neurons: 12
    Number of taps per synaptic filter: 5
Output layer:
    Number of neurons: 1
    Number of taps per synaptic filter: 5

For a model (prediction) order $p = 25$, the 100-step prediction obtained using this network is shown in Fig. 13.11a. This prediction was made on the basis of only the past 1000 samples, and no actual values were provided past 1000. Figure 13.11a shows that the prediction performed by the FIR multilayer perceptron is indeed remarkable.

For comparison, Fig. 13.11b presents the 100-point iterated prediction computed using a *linear* autoregressive (AR) model of order 25; the coefficients of the model were

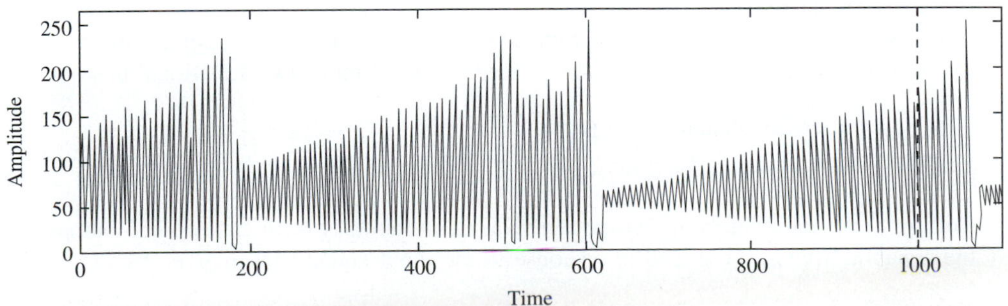

FIGURE 13.10 Chaotic time series.

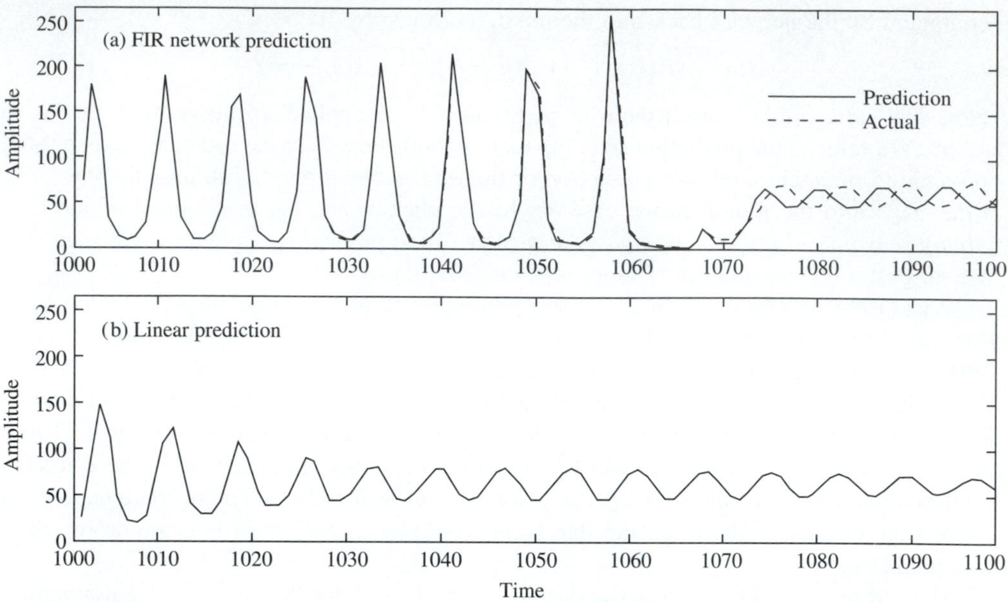

FIGURE 13.11 (a) Recursive prediction of the chaotic time series of Fig. 13.10 using an FIR multilayer perceptron trained on the first 1000 samples of the time series. (b) Prediction using a linear autoregressive model.

computed using a standard least-squares method. The linear predictions presented here are clearly no match for the nonlinear predictions made by the FIR multilayer perceptron.

It is also of interest to note that the FIR multilayer perceptron won the Santa Fe Competition from a diverse list of submissions that included standard recurrent and feedforward neural networks (Wan, 1994).

13.5 Temporal Back-Propagation with Adaptive Time Delays

The temporal back-propagation algorithm described in the previous section for training a multilayer perceptron has two distinct characteristics: (1) discrete-time operation and (2) fixed time delays. Day and Davenport (1993) and Lin et al. (1992, 1993) have independently developed generalizations of temporal back-propagation that permit the synaptic time delays to be adapted in a continuous fashion, like the way in which the synaptic weights are adapted.

Consider the *continuous-time synaptic filter* depicted in Fig. 13.12, connecting neuron i to neuron j. This filter consists of the cascade connection of two functional units:

- *Synaptic delay,* denoted by $\tau_{ji}(t)$
- *Synaptic weight,* denoted by $w_{ji}(t)$

Both of these parameters are assumed to vary continuously with time t. The output of the synaptic filter so described in response to the input signal $x_i(t)$ is given by

$$s_{ji}(t) = w_{ji}(t)x_i\big(t - \tau_{ji}(t)\big) \tag{13.58}$$

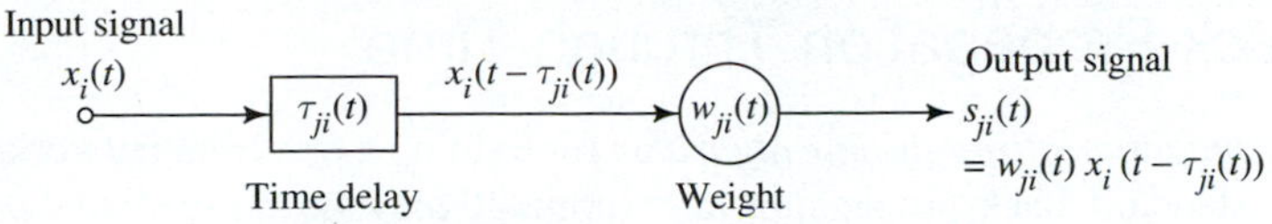

FIGURE 13.12 Another dynamic model of a neuron, with each synapse consisting of a time-varying delay followed by a time-varying weight.

Note that the impulse response of the synaptic model of Fig. 13.12 is *time-varying.* As such, the synaptic delay $\tau_{ji}(t)$ and synaptic weight $w_{ji}(t)$ are *not* interchangeable.

The total contribution to the internal activity of neuron j by the input signals $x_1(t)$, $x_2(t), \ldots, x_p(t)$ is

$$\begin{aligned} u_j(t) &= \sum_{i=1}^{p} s_{ji}(t) \\ &= \sum_{i=1}^{p} w_{ji}(t)x_i(t - \tau_{ji}(t)) \end{aligned} \tag{13.59}$$

Let $\varphi(\cdot)$ denote the activation function of neuron j, assumed to be the same for all the neurons in the multilayer perceptron. The output signal of neuron j is given by

$$y_j(t) = \varphi(u_j(t) - \theta_j) \tag{13.60}$$

where $u_j(t)$ is defined by Eq. (13.59), and θ_j is the externally applied threshold.

The adaptation of the synaptic weights and time delays is performed using the method of steepest descent and error back-propagation so as to minimize the instantaneous sum of squared errors

$$\mathscr{E}(t) = \frac{1}{2}\sum_{j\in\mathscr{A}} [d_j(t) - y_j(t)]^2 \tag{13.61}$$

where $y_j(t)$ is the actual response of output neuron j at time t, $d_j(t)$ is the corresponding desired response, and $\mathscr{A}$ is the set of output neurons. The training set consists of a sequence of spatio-temporal patterns and desired responses that vary over time t. The adjustments applied to the synaptic weights and time delays of the multilayer perceptron are defined by, respectively,

$$\Delta w_{ji}(t) = -\eta_1 \frac{\partial \mathscr{E}(t)}{\partial w_{ji}(t)} \tag{13.62}$$

$$\Delta \tau_{ji}(t) = -\eta_2 \frac{\partial \mathscr{E}(t)}{\partial \tau_{ji}(t)} \tag{13.63}$$

where η_1 and η_2 are learning-rate parameters.

As with the temporal back-propagation algorithm described in Section 13.4, special consideration has to be given to whether neuron j is an output neuron or a hidden neuron. Details of the derivation are presented in Lin et al. (1992) and Day and Davenport (1993). The important point to note here is that the use of the continuous-time temporal back-propagation with adaptive time delays provides the neural network designer another method for building dynamic multilayer perceptrons that can respond to spatio-temporal patterns in a flexible and efficient manner. Yet another method is back-propagation through time, described in the next section.

13.6 Back-Propagation Through Time

The *back-propagation-through-time algorithm* for training a recurrent network is an extension of the standard back-propagation algorithm. It may be derived by *unfolding* the temporal operation of the network into a multilayer feedforward network, the topology of which grows by one layer at every time step. To illustrate this idea, consider the simple recurrent network shown in Fig. 13.13a, consisting of two computation nodes. Unfolding the temporal operation of this network in a step-by-step manner, we get the signal-flow graph shown in Fig. 13.13b, which is representative of a multilayer feedforward network with a new layer added at every time step.

Speaking in general terms, let the data set used to train a recurrent network be partitioned into epochs. Let n_0 denote the start time of an epoch, and n_1 denote its end time. Given this epoch, we may define the cost function

$$\mathscr{E}_{\text{total}}(n_0, n_1) = \frac{1}{2} \sum_{n=n_0}^{n_1} \sum_{j \in \mathscr{A}} e_j^2(n) \tag{13.64}$$

where $\mathscr{A}$ is the set of indices j pertaining to those neurons in the network for which desired responses are specified, and $e_j(n)$ is the error signal at the output of such a neuron measured with respect to some desired response. We wish to compute the partial derivatives of the cost function $\mathscr{E}_{\text{total}}(n_0, n_1)$ with respect to synaptic weights of the network. To do so, we may use the *epochwise back-propagation-through-time algorithm,* described as follows (Williams and Peng, 1990):

- First, a single forward pass of the data through the network for the interval $[n_0, n_1]$ is performed. The complete record of input data, network state (i.e., synaptic weights of the network), and desired responses over this interval is *saved.*
- A single backward pass over this past record is performed to compute the values of the local gradients

$$\delta_j(n) = -\frac{\partial \mathscr{E}_{\text{total}}(n_0, n_1)}{\partial v_j(n)} \tag{13.65}$$

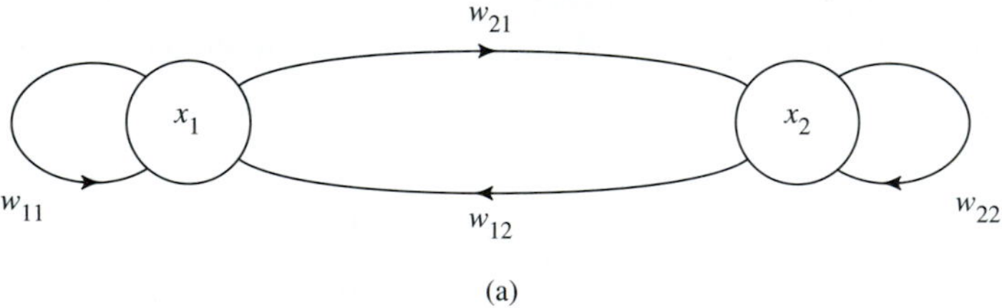

(a)

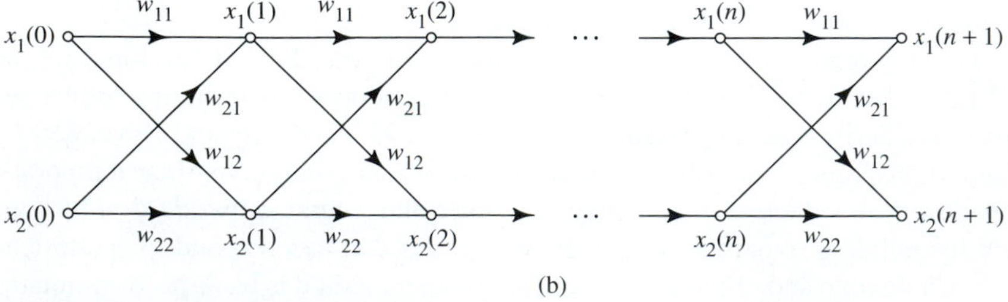

(b)

FIGURE 13.13 (a) Architectural graph of a two-neuron recurrent network. (b) Signal-flow graph of the network folded in time.

for all $j \in \mathcal{A}$ and $n_0 < n \leq n_1$ by using the equations

$$\delta_j(n) = \begin{cases} \varphi'(v_j(n))e_j(n) & \text{if } n = n_1 \\ \varphi'(v_j(n))\left[e_j(n) + \sum_{k \in \mathcal{A}} w_{kj}\delta_k(n+1)\right] & \text{if } n_0 < n < n_1 \end{cases} \tag{13.66}$$

where $\varphi'(\cdot)$ is the derivative of an activation function with respect to its argument. The use of Eq. (13.66) is repeated, starting from time n_1 and working back, step by step, to time n_0; the number of steps involved here is equal to the number of time steps contained in the epoch.

- Once the computation of back-propagation has been performed back to time $n_0 + 1$, the following adjustment is applied to the synaptic weight w_{ji} of neuron j:

$$\begin{aligned} \Delta w_{ji} &= -\eta \frac{\partial \mathscr{E}_{\text{total}}(n_0, n_1)}{\partial w_{ji}} \\ &= \eta \sum_{n=n_0+1}^{n_1} \delta_j(n) x_i(n-1) \end{aligned} \tag{13.67}$$

where η is the learning-rate parameter and $x_i(n-1)$ is the ith input of neuron j at time $n - 1$.

The computations described here may be viewed as representing the standard back-propagation algorithm applied to a multilayer feedforward network in which desired responses are specified for neurons in many layers of the network, because the actual output layer is replicated many times when the temporal behavior of the network is unfolded.

Obviously, the epochwise back-propagation-through-time algorithm is not suitable for the real-time operation of a recurrent network. Williams and Peng (1990) describe a computationally efficient variant of this algorithm, which is intended for use on an arbitrary recurrent network that runs continuously.

13.7 Real-Time Recurrent Networks

In this section we describe another algorithm for the training of a recurrent network that runs continuously. The network so trained is called a *real-time recurrent network* (Williams and Zipser, 1989). It differs from a Hopfield network considered in Chapter 8, which is also a recurrent network, in two important respects:

- The network contains hidden neurons.
- It has arbitrary dynamics.

Of particular interest is the ability of the recurrent network to deal with time-varying input or output through its own temporal operation.

Consider a network consisting of a total of N neurons with M external input connections. Let $\mathbf{x}(n)$ denote the M-by-1 external input vector applied to the network at discrete time n, and let $\mathbf{y}(n+1)$ denote the corresponding N-by-1 vector of individual neuron outputs produced one step later at time $n + 1$. The input vector $\mathbf{x}(n)$ and one-step *delayed* output vector $\mathbf{y}(n)$ are concatenated to form the $(M + N)$-by-1 vector $\mathbf{u}(n)$, whose ith element is denoted by $u_i(n)$. Let $\mathcal{A}$ denote the set of indices i for which $x_i(n)$ is an external input, and let $\mathcal{B}$ denote the set of indices i for which $u_i(n)$ is the output of a neuron. We thus

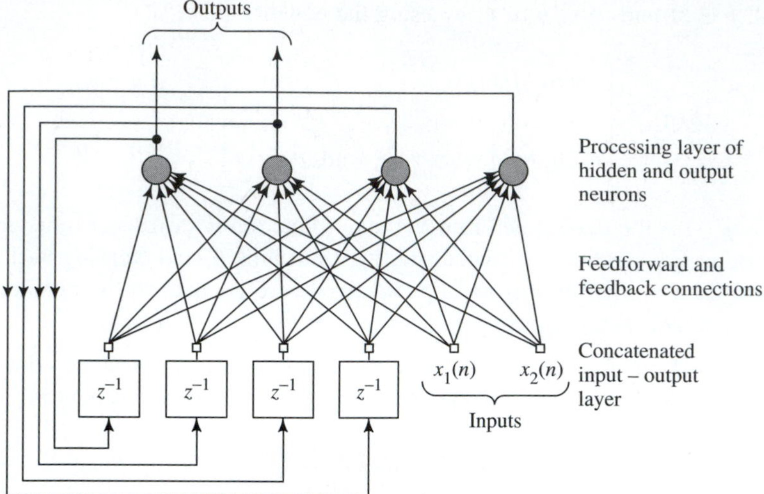

FIGURE 13.14 Architectural graph of a real-time recurrent network.

have

$$u_i(n) = \begin{cases} x_i(n) & \text{if } i \in \mathcal{A} \\ y_i(n) & \text{if } i \in \mathcal{B} \end{cases} \tag{13.68}$$

We may distinguish two distinct layers in the network, namely, a *concatenated input–output layer* and a *processing layer.* This is illustrated in Fig. 13.14 for $M = 2$ and $N = 4$. The network is fully interconnected in that there are a total of MN forward connections and N^2 feedback connections; N of the feedback connections are in actual fact *self-feedback* connections. Let $\mathbf{W}$ denote the N-by-$(M + N)$ *recurrent weight matrix* of the network. In order to make provision for a threshold for the operation of each neuron, we simply include among the M input lines one input whose value is constrained to be always -1.

The net internal activity of neuron j at time n, for $j \in \mathcal{B}$, is given by

$$v_j(n) = \sum_{i \in \mathcal{A} \cup \mathcal{B}} w_{ji}(n) u_i(n) \tag{13.69}$$

where $\mathcal{A} \cup \mathcal{B}$ is the union of sets $\mathcal{A}$ and $\mathcal{B}$. At the next time step $n + 1$, the output of neuron j is computed by passing $v_j(n)$ through the nonlinearity $\varphi(\cdot)$, obtaining

$$y_j(n + 1) = \varphi(v_j(n)) \tag{13.70}$$

The system of equations (13.69) and (13.70), where the index j ranges over the set $\mathcal{B}$ and where $u_i(n)$ is defined in terms of the external inputs and neuron outputs by Eq. (13.68), constitutes the entire *dynamics* of the network. It is important to note, however, that, as indicated in Eq. (13.70), the external input vector $\mathbf{x}(n)$ at time n does not influence the output of any neuron in the network until time $n + 1$.

With these dynamic equations on hand, we are ready to derive a temporal supervised learning algorithm, based on an approximation to the method of steepest descent, which tries to match the outputs of certain neurons in the processing layer to desired values at specific instants of time (Williams and Zipser, 1989).

Real-Time Temporal Supervised Learning Algorithm

Let $d_j(n)$ denote the desired (target) response of neuron j at time n. Let $\mathscr{C}(n)$ denote the set of neurons that are chosen to act as *visible* units in that they provide externally reachable outputs; the remaining neurons of the processing layer are *hidden*. We may then define a time-varying N-by-1 error vector $\mathbf{e}(n)$ whose jth element is

$$e_j(n) = \begin{cases} d_j(n) - y_j(n) & \text{if } j \in \mathscr{C}(n) \\ 0 & \text{otherwise} \end{cases} \tag{13.71}$$

Note that the notation $\mathscr{C}(n)$ allows for the possibility that values of desired response are specified for different neurons at different times. In other words, the set of visible neurons specified by $\mathscr{C}(n)$ can be time-varying.

Define the *instantaneous* sum of squared error at time n as

$$\mathscr{E}(n) = \frac{1}{2} \sum_{j \in \mathscr{C}} e_j^2(n) \tag{13.72}$$

The objective we have is to minimize a *cost function*, obtained by summing $\mathscr{E}(n)$ over all time n; that is,

$$\mathscr{E}_{\text{total}} = \sum_n \mathscr{E}(n) \tag{13.73}$$

To accomplish this objective we may use the method of steepest descent, which requires knowledge of the *gradient matrix*, written as

$$\begin{aligned} \nabla_{\mathbf{W}} \mathscr{E}_{\text{total}} &= \frac{\partial \mathscr{E}_{\text{total}}}{\partial \mathbf{W}} \\ &= \sum_n \frac{\partial \mathscr{E}(n)}{\partial \mathbf{W}} \\ &= \sum_n \nabla_{\mathbf{W}} \mathscr{E}(n) \end{aligned} \tag{13.74}$$

where $\nabla_{\mathbf{W}} \mathscr{E}(n)$ is the gradient of $\mathscr{E}(n)$ with respect to the weight matrix $\mathbf{W}$. We may, if desired, continue with Eq. (13.74) and derive update equations for the synaptic weights of the recurrent network without invoking approximations. However, in order to develop a learning algorithm that can be used to train the recurrent network in *real time*, we have to use an instantaneous *estimate* of the gradient, namely, $\nabla_{\mathbf{W}} \mathscr{E}(n)$, which results in an *approximation* to the method of steepest descent.

For the case of a particular weight $w_{kl}(n)$, we may thus define the incremental change $\Delta w_{kl}(n)$ made at time n as follows:

$$\Delta w_{kl}(n) = -\eta \frac{\partial \mathscr{E}(n)}{\partial w_{kl}(n)} \tag{13.75}$$

where η is the learning-rate parameter. From Eqs. (13.71) and (13.72), we note that

$$\begin{aligned} \frac{\partial \mathscr{E}(n)}{\partial w_{kl}(n)} &= \sum_{j \in \mathscr{C}} e_j(n) \frac{\partial e_j(n)}{\partial w_{kl}(n)} \\ &= -\sum_{j \in \mathscr{C}} e_j(n) \frac{\partial y_i(n)}{\partial w_{kl}(n)} \end{aligned} \tag{13.76}$$

To determine the partial derivative $\partial y_j(n)/\partial w_{kl}(n)$, we differentiate the network dynamics, that is, Eqs. (13.69) and (13.70) with respect to $w_{kl}(n)$. We do this by using the chain rule for differentiation, obtaining

$$\frac{\partial y_j(n+1)}{\partial w_{kl}(n)} = \frac{\partial y_j(n+1)}{\partial v_j(n)} \frac{\partial v_j(n)}{\partial w_{kl}(n)}$$

$$= \varphi'(v_j(n)) \frac{\partial v_j(n)}{\partial w_{kl}(n)} \tag{13.77}$$

where, as before,

$$\varphi'(v_j(n)) = \frac{\partial \varphi(v_j(n))}{\partial v_j(n)} \tag{13.78}$$

Differentiating Eq. (13.69) with respect to $w_{kl}(n)$ yields

$$\frac{\partial v_j(n)}{\partial w_{kl}(n)} = \sum_{i \in \mathcal{A} \cup \mathcal{B}} \frac{\partial}{\partial w_{kl}(n)} (w_{ji}(n) u_i(n))$$

$$= \sum_{i \in \mathcal{A} \cup \mathcal{B}} \left[w_{ji}(n) \frac{\partial u_i(n)}{\partial w_{kl}(n)} + \frac{\partial w_{ji}(n)}{\partial w_{kl}(n)} u_i(n) \right] \tag{13.79}$$

We note that the derivative $\partial w_{ji}(n)/\partial w_{kl}(n)$ equals 1 only when $j = k$ and $i = l$; otherwise, it is zero. We may therefore rewrite Eq. (13.79) as

$$\frac{\partial v_j(n)}{\partial w_{kl}(n)} = \sum_{i \in \mathcal{A} \cup \mathcal{B}} w_{ji}(n) \frac{\partial u_i(n)}{\partial w_{kl}(n)} + \delta_{kj} u_l(n) \tag{13.80}$$

where δ_{kj} is a *Kronecker delta* equal to 1 when $j = k$ and zero otherwise; this symbol is *not* to be confused with the δ used in Sections 13.4 and 13.6. From the definition of $u_i(n)$ given in Eq. (13.68), we also note that

$$\frac{\partial u_i(n)}{\partial w_{kl}(n)} = \begin{cases} 0 & \text{if } i \in \mathcal{A} \\ \dfrac{\partial y_i(n)}{\partial w_{kl}(n)} & \text{if } i \in \mathcal{B} \end{cases} \tag{13.81}$$

Accordingly, we may combine Eqs. (13.77), (13.80), and (13.81) to write

$$\frac{\partial y_j(n+1)}{\partial w_{kl}(n)} = \varphi'(v_j(n)) \left[\sum_{i \in \mathcal{B}} w_{ji}(n) \frac{\partial y_i(n)}{\partial w_{kl}(n)} + \delta_{kl} u_l(n) \right] \tag{13.82}$$

It is natural for us to assume that the initial state of the network at time $n = 0$, say, has no functional dependence on the synaptic weights; this assumption implies that

$$\frac{\partial y_i(0)}{\partial w_{kl}(0)} = 0 \tag{13.83}$$

Equations (13.82) and (13.83) hold for all $j \in \mathcal{B}$, $k \in \mathcal{B}$, and $l \in \mathcal{A} \cup \mathcal{B}$.

We may now define a dynamical system described by a triply indexed set of variables $\{\pi^j_{kl}\}$, where

$$\pi^j_{kl}(n) = \frac{\partial y_j(n)}{\partial w_{kl}(n)} \qquad \text{for all } j \in \mathcal{B}, k \in \mathcal{B}, \text{ and } l \in \mathcal{A} \cup \mathcal{B} \tag{13.84}$$

For every time step n and all appropriate j, k, and l the dynamics of the system so defined are governed by [see Eqs. (13.82) and (13.83)]:

$$\pi^j_{kl}(n+1) = \varphi'(v_j(n))\left[\sum_{i\in\mathcal{B}} w_{ji}(n)\pi^i_{kl}(n) + \delta_{kj}u_l(n)\right] \tag{13.85}$$

with *initial conditions*

$$\pi^j_{kl}(0) = 0 \tag{13.86}$$

In summary, the *real-time recurrent learning (RTRL) algorithm* for training the recurrent neural network of Fig. 13.14 proceeds as follows:

1. For every time step n, starting from $n = 0$, use the dynamic equations of the network, namely, Eqs. (13.69) and (13.70), to compute the output values of the N neurons; hence, use these output values and the specified external input values to define $u_i(n)$ for $i \in \mathcal{A} \cup \mathcal{B}$ in accordance with Eq. (13.68). For the initial values of the weights, choose them from a set of uniformly distributed random numbers.
2. Use Eqs. (13.85) and (13.86) to compute the variables $\pi^j_{kl}(n)$ for all appropriate j, k, and l.
3. Use the values of $\pi^j_{kl}(n)$ obtained in step 2, and the error signal $e_j(n)$ expressing the difference between the desired response $d_j(n)$ and neuron output $y_j(n)$, to compute the corresponding weight changes

$$\Delta w_{kl}(n) = \eta \sum_{j\in\mathcal{C}} e_j(n)\pi^j_{kl}(n) \tag{13.87}$$

4. Update the weight w_{kl} in accordance with

$$w_{kl}(n+1) = w_{kl}(n) + \Delta w_{kl}(n) \tag{13.88}$$

and repeat the computation.

Equation (13.85) applies to an arbitrary nonlinearity $\varphi(\cdot)$ that is differentiable with respect to its argument. For the special case of a sigmoidal nonlinearity in the form of a logistic function, we find that the derivative $\varphi'(\cdot)$ is given by

$$\varphi'(v_j(n)) = y_j(n+1)[1 - y_j(n+1)] \tag{13.89}$$

where $y_j(n+1)$ is the output of neuron j at time $n+1$.

The use of the instantaneous gradient $\nabla_{\mathbf{W}}\mathcal{E}(n)$ means that the real-time recurrent learning algorithm described here deviates from a non-real-time one based on the true gradient $\nabla_{\mathbf{W}}\mathcal{E}_{\text{total}}$. However, this deviation is exactly analogous to that encountered in the standard back-propagation algorithm used to train a multilayer perceptron, where weight changes are made after each pattern presentation. While the real-time recurrent learning algorithm is not guaranteed to follow the precise negative gradient of the total error function $\mathcal{E}_{\text{total}}(\mathbf{W})$ with respect to the weight matrix $\mathbf{W}$, the practical differences between the real-time and non-real-time versions are often slight; indeed, these two versions become more nearly identical as the learning-rate parameter η is reduced (Williams and Zipser, 1989). The most severe potential consequence of this deviation from the true gradient-following behavior is that the observed trajectory [obtained by plotting $\mathcal{E}(n)$ versus the elements of the weight matrix $\mathbf{W}(n)$] may itself depend on the weight changes produced by the algorithm, which may be viewed as another source of feedback and therefore a cause of instability in the system. We can avoid this effect by using a learning-rate parameter η small enough to make the time scale of the weight changes much smaller than the time scale of the network operation (Williams and Zipser, 1989).

Computational Considerations

The real-time recurrent learning algorithm described here is *nonlocal* in the sense that each weight must have access to both the complete weight matrix $\mathbf{W}(n)$ and the complete error vector $\mathbf{e}(n)$. The algorithm is, however, inherently parallel in nature, which means that implementation of the algorithm and therefore computation speed can benefit greatly from the use of parallel hardware.

With index $j \in \mathcal{B}$, $k \in \mathcal{B}$, and $l \in \mathcal{A} \cup \mathcal{B}$, we find that in the general case of a fully interconnected network with a total of N neurons and M external input connections, there are a total of $N(N^2 + NM)$ values of the dynamic variable $\pi^j_{kl}(n)$ to be considered at any time n. The triply indexed set of values $\{\pi^j_{kl}(n)\}$ may be viewed as an $(N^2 + NM)$-by-N matrix, each of whose rows corresponds to a weight and each of whose columns corresponds to a neuron in the network. Moreover, examining the update equations (13.85), we find that in general we must keep a running tally of the values π^j_{kl}, even for those j corresponding to neurons that are hidden.

13.8 Real-Time Nonlinear Adaptive Prediction of Nonstationary Signals

The prediction of a time series is synonymous with *modeling* of the underlying physical process responsible for its generation. In Section 13.4 we discussed the use of an FIR multilayer perceptron trained with the temporal back-propagation algorithm for the recursive prediction of a chaotic time series. However, in many signal processing applications (e.g., adaptive differential pulse-code modulation of speech signals) we need a different kind of prediction in that the neural network must learn to adapt to statistical variations of the incoming time series while, at the same time, the prediction is going on. In other words, the network must undergo *in-situ learning*. We may satisfy this requirement by using a real-time recurrent network. Unfortunately, the number of neurons needed is often so large that the cost of computation is too excessive. To overcome this limitation of the real-time recurrent network, we may use a *pipelined structure* (Li and Haykin, 1993; Haykin and Li, 1993a), which exploits the notion of *innovation* described in Chapter 2 (see Fig. 2.11).

Specifically, the adaptive predictor consists of a nonlinear subsystem followed by a linear one, as described here.

1. A *pipelined recurrent network* composed of M modules with *identical* synaptic weight matrices $\mathbf{W}$, which is shown in Fig. 13.15a. Each module of the network receives an input vector of p past samples of the incoming signal, as shown by

$$\mathbf{x}(n-k) = [x(n-k), x(n-k-1), \ldots, x(n-k-p+1)]^T \qquad (13.90)$$

where $k = 1, 2, \ldots, M$, and p is the *nonlinear prediction order*. Let $\mathbf{y}_k(n-k+1)$ denote the vector of output signals of all N neurons in module k that is computed at time $n-k+1$, as shown by

$$\mathbf{y}_k(n-k+1) = [y_{k,1}(n-k+1), y_{k,2}(n-k+1), \ldots, y_{k,N}(n-k+1)]^T \qquad (13.91)$$

The output vector $\mathbf{y}_M(n-M+1)$ of the neurons in the last module (i.e., module M) is fed back to its input after a delay of one time unit. Thus the last module operates as a standard real-time recurrent network. The output vector $\mathbf{y}_M(n-M+1)$ is also fed directly into module $M-1$. In effect, this output vector acts as the feedback signal vector for module $M-1$. From there on, the feedback signal vector of each module is derived directly from the previous module. Except for this modification, modules 1 to $M-1$ in

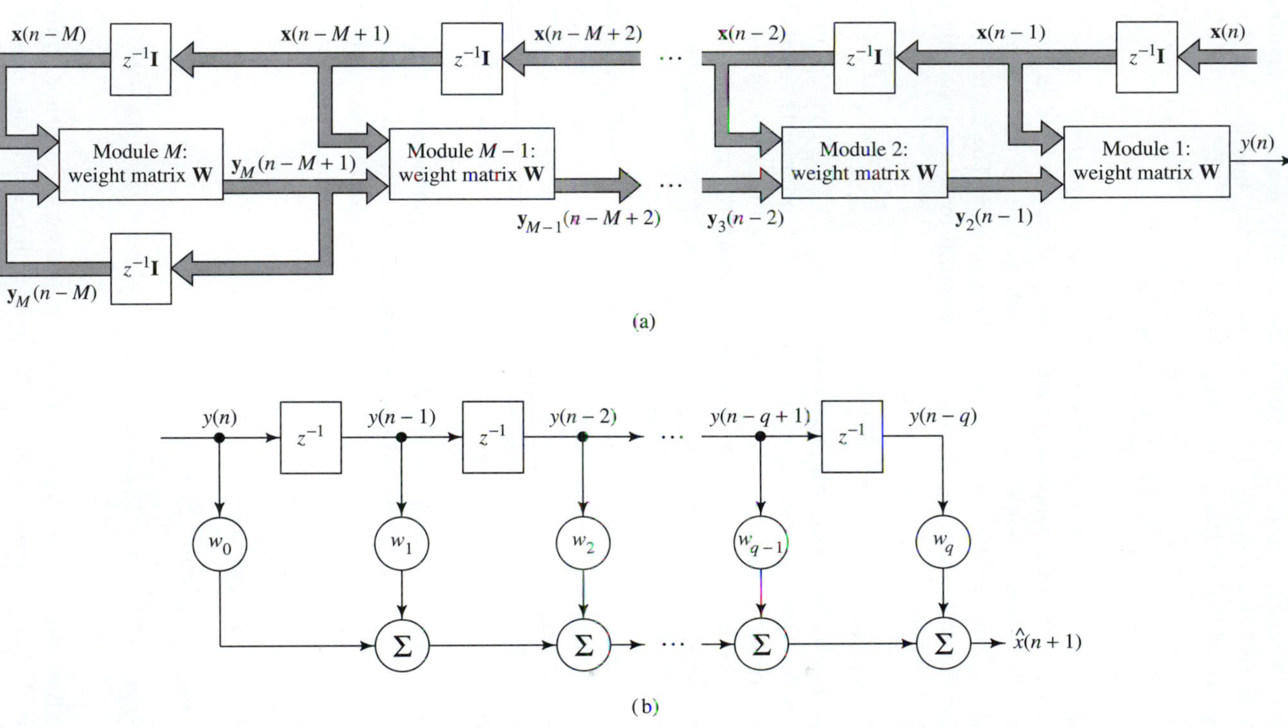

FIGURE 13.15 Real-time adaptive nonlinear predictor. (a) Pipelined recurrent network. (b) Tapped-delay-line filter.

Fig. 13.15a also learn in a real-time recurrent fashion, as described in Section 13.7. Each module computes an error signal (innovation) defined by

$$e_{k,1}(n-k+1) = x(n-k+1) - y_{k,1}(n-k+1), \qquad k = 1, 2, \ldots, M \tag{13.92}$$

where $x(n-k+1)$ is a sample of the input signal and $y_{k,1}(n-k+1)$ is the corresponding output of the only visible neuron in module k. To simplify matters, computation of the error signals is not shown in Fig. 13.15a. An overall cost function for the pipelined recurrent network of Fig. 13.15a is thus defined by

$$\mathscr{E}(n) = \sum_{k=1}^{M} \lambda^{k-1} e_{k,1}^2(n-k+1) \tag{13.93}$$

where λ is an *exponential forgetting factor* that lies in the range $0 < \lambda \leq 1$. The inverse of $1 - \lambda$ is, roughly speaking, a measure of the *memory* of the pipelined recurrent network. Adjustments to the synaptic weight matrix $\mathbf{W}$ of each module are made to minimize $\mathscr{E}(n)$ in accordance with the real-time recurrent learning algorithm. The overall output of the pipelined recurrent network in Fig. 13.15a is determined by the only visible neuron of module 1, as shown by

$$y(n) = y_{1,1}(n) \tag{13.94}$$

2. A *tapped-delay-line filter,* which is shown in Fig. 13.15b. The tap inputs of this filter consist of the output $y(n)$ computed by the pipelined recurrent network of Fig. 13.15a and q past values $y(n-1), y(n-2), \ldots, y(n-q)$. The $(q+1)$ tap weights of the filter, constituting the weight vector $\mathbf{w}_l$, are adjusted using the standard LMS algorithm (described in Chapter 5) to produce an optimum estimate of the prediction $\hat{x}(n+1)$ of the input $x(n+1)$ at time $n+1$.

The pipelined recurrent network of Fig. 13.15a performs a *global approximation* that is coarse to fine, depending on the number of modules M used and the size of each module. The tapped-delay-line filter of Fig. 13.15b fine-tunes the final result by performing a *local approximation.* The final result $\hat{x}(n+1)$ is an adaptive nonlinear prediction of the actual sample $x(n+1)$ of the input signal, which is computed in an *on-line* fashion for varying time n.

The pipelined recurrent network of Fig. 13.15a differs from the conventional real-time recurrent network of Fig. 13.14 in that it is characterized by a *nested nonlinearity.* Let it be assumed that all the neurons have a common nonlinear activation function $\varphi(\cdot)$. Accordingly, we may express the functional dependence of the output $y(n)$ of the network in Fig. 13.15a on the external inputs as follows:

$$\begin{aligned} y(n) &= \varphi(\mathbf{x}(n-1), \mathbf{y}_2(n-1)) \\ &= \varphi(\mathbf{x}(n-1), \varphi(\mathbf{x}(n-2), \mathbf{y}_3(n-2))) \\ &= \varphi(\mathbf{x}(n-1), \varphi(\mathbf{x}(n-2), \varphi(\mathbf{x}(n-3), \ldots, \varphi(\mathbf{x}(n-M), \mathbf{y}_M(n-M)), \cdots))) \end{aligned} \tag{13.95}$$

where, for convenience of presentation, we have omitted the dependence on the synaptic weight matrix $\mathbf{W}$ that is common to all the M modules. It is this nested nonlinearity that gives the pipelined recurrent network of Fig. 13.15a its enhanced computing power, compared to the conventional real-time recurrent network of Fig. 13.14.

It is also important to note that the desired response needed to perform the in-situ training of both parts of the nonlinear predictor in Fig. 13.15 is in fact derived from the incoming time series itself. Thus the nonlinear adaptive predictor described here embodies a *self-organized learning process* in the most profound sense.

To proceed with the computation, we need to *initialize* the tap-weight vector $\mathbf{w}_l$ of the tapped-delay-line filter and the synaptic weight matrix $\mathbf{W}$ of each module in the pipelined recurrent network. We also need to specify the initial value of the feedback signal vector $\mathbf{y}_M$ of module M. Initialization of the tap-weight vector $\mathbf{w}_l$ follows the customary practice of setting it equal to the null vector or a randomly distributed set of small values. However, initialization of the synaptic weight matrix $\mathbf{W}$ and the feedback signal vector $\mathbf{y}_M$ requires special attention. For this initialization, we may use the traditional epochwise training method of recurrent neural networks, which is applied to one module operating with N_0 samples of the input signal (Li and Haykin, 1993; Haykin and Li, 1993a).

Figure 13.16 illustrates the application of the novel predictor described in this section to the modeling of a male speech signal (Haykin and Li, 1993b):

When we record audio data . . .

The recorded time series corresponding to this speech signal, sampled at 8 kHz, is made up of 10,000 samples. The specifications of the predictor are as follows:

1. Pipelined-recurrent network:

   Number of modules, $M = 5$
   Number of neurons per module, $N = 2$
   Nonlinear prediction order, $p = 4$

2. Tapped-delay-line filter:

   Number of taps, $(q + 1) = 12$

Figure 13.16 displays the actual speech signal (solid curve) and its predicted version (dotted curve). This figure clearly shows that the predicted signal follows the actual signal fairly closely.

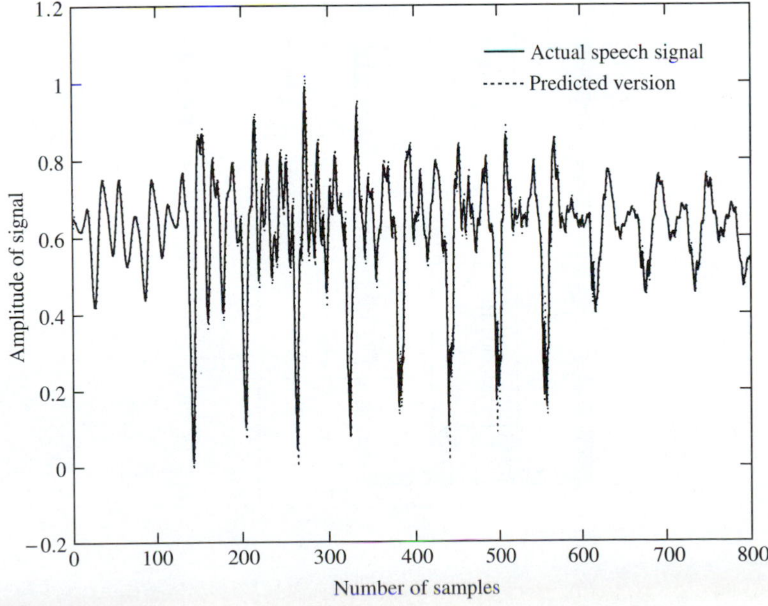

FIGURE 13.16 Actual speech signal and predicted version of it using the real-time adaptive network of Fig. 13.15.

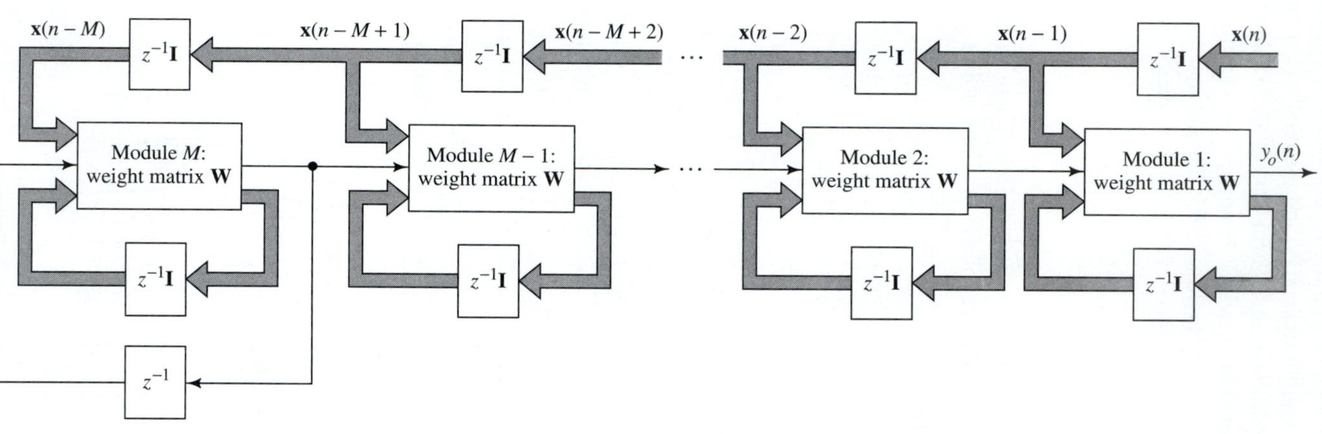

FIGURE 13.17 Another pipelined recurrent network.

A More Elaborate Pipelined Recurrent Network

In Fig. 13.17 we show another pipelined recurrent network. It differs from the structure of Fig. 13.15 in the way in which feedback is applied to each module. As before, module M operates as a conventional real-time recurrent network. Each of the other modules also operates as a real-time recurrent network, but with a *single* additional input supplied from the previous module. The network of Fig. 13.17 is slightly more demanding in storage terms than that of Fig. 13.15.

The pipelined structure of Fig. 13.15 may be viewed as an approximation to that of Fig. 13.17. Indeed, for the same number of modules and the same number of neurons per module, studies on the modeling of speech signals show that the structure of Fig. 13.17 provides a slightly more accurate prediction of the input data than that of Fig. 13.15.

13.9 Partially Recurrent Network

For our last structure, we consider a *partially recurrent network* configured as in Fig. 13.18, which was originally proposed by Robinson and Fallside (1991). This structure may be viewed as a simplified version of the recurrent network described in Elman (1990) without hidden neurons.

The network of Fig. 13.18 consists of an input layer of source and feedback nodes and an output layer of computation nodes. Moreover, the computation nodes are split into two groups: K *output neurons,* and L *context neurons.* The output neurons produce the overall output vector $\mathbf{y}(n+1)$. The context neurons produce the feedback vector $\mathbf{r}(n)$ after a delay of one time unit applied to each of its elements. The network operates by concatenating the current external input vector $\mathbf{x}(n)$ and the feedback vector $\mathbf{r}(n)$ as follows:

$$\mathbf{u}(n) = [-1, \mathbf{x}(n), \mathbf{r}(n)]^T \tag{13.96}$$

where the fixed input -1 is included for the provision of a threshold applied to each neuron in the network. The concatenated input vector $\mathbf{u}(n)$ is multiplied by a matrix of

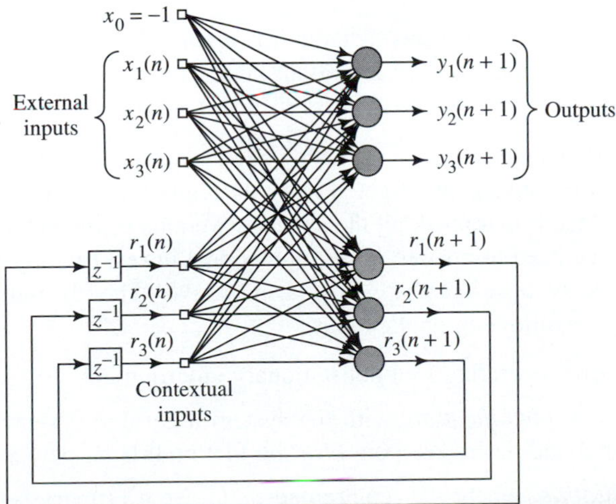

FIGURE 13.18 Partially recurrent network with $K = 3$ output neurons and $L = 3$ context neurons.

synaptic weights, $\mathbf{W}(n)$, yielding an internal activity vector defined at time n as

$$\begin{aligned}\mathbf{v}(n) &= [\mathbf{v}_o(n), \mathbf{v}_c(n)]^T \\ &= \mathbf{W}(n)\mathbf{u}(n) \end{aligned} \tag{13.97}$$

Let $\varphi(\cdot)$ denote the activation function, assumed to be the same for all the neurons in the network. Accordingly, the output vector, computed at time $n + 1$, is defined by

$$\mathbf{y}(n + 1) = \varphi(\mathbf{v}_o(n)) \tag{13.98}$$

Similarly, the feedback vector (before delay) is defined by

$$\mathbf{r}(n + 1) = \varphi(\mathbf{v}_c(n)) \tag{13.99}$$

Finally, the output vector $\mathbf{y}(n + 1)$ is compared with a desired response vector $\mathbf{d}(n + 1)$ in accordance with a cost function of interest. In the original description of the partial recurrent network presented in Robinson and Fallside (1991), the network outputs are treated as probabilities. Specifically, the relative entropy is used to define the cost function as follows (see Section 6.20):

$$\begin{aligned} H_{d\|y}(n + 1) = \sum_{k=1}^{K} \{ & d_k(n + 1) \log y_k(n + 1) \\ & - [(1 - d_k(n + 1)) \log(1 - y_k(n + 1))]\} \end{aligned} \tag{13.100}$$

where $y_k(n + 1)$ is the kth element of the output vector $\mathbf{y}(n + 1)$, and $d_k(n + 1)$ is the corresponding value of the desired response. The objective is to adapt the synaptic weight matrix $\mathbf{W}(n)$ so as to minimize the relative entropy of Eq. (13.100).

Robinson and Fallside describe the application of the partial recurrent network of Fig. 13.18 as the basis of a speaker-independent phoneme and word recognition system. Leerink and Jabri (1993) use the network as an adaptive world model to provide an evolving state for temporal difference learning applied to continuous speech recognition (temporal difference learning was described in Section 2.8).

13.10 Discussion

In this chapter we discussed various methods for temporal processing. In particular, we presented detailed treatments of two important neural networks (and their variants) that are capable of temporal processing, albeit in different ways.

1. *The FIR multilayer perceptron,* in which each synapse is modeled as an FIR filter. This neural network is conveniently trained using the temporal back-propagation algorithm (Wan, 1990a, b). Once it is trained, all the synaptic weights of the network are fixed. The network may then be used to operate on an input signal in real time by feeding the signal through the network, synapse by synapse and layer by layer. The FIR multilayer perceptron is well suited for the following applications:

- *Adaptive control* operating in a nonstationary environment
- *Dynamic system identification,* with the system input and system output providing the input signal and desired response for the FIR multilayer perceptron, respectively
- *Noise cancellation,* where the requirement is to use a primary sensor (supplying a desired signal contaminated with additive noise) and a reference sensor (supplying a correlated version of the noise) to cancel out the effect of the noise (Widrow et al., 1975)

- *Adaptive equalization* of a communication channel whose frequency response varies with time (Quereshi, 1985)
- *Modeling of nonstationary time series* by performing one-step, nonlinear prediction on the time series
- *Temporal classification of nonstationary signals*

2. *The real-time recurrent network,* the topology of which includes hidden neurons (Williams and Zipser, 1989). Its capability to provide arbitrary dynamics makes it a useful tool for real-time applications that include the following:

- *Neurobiological modeling.* Anastasio (1991) has used a three-layered recurrent neural network to explore the organization of the vestibulo-ocular reflex (VOR); the VOR stabilizes the visual image by producing eye rotations that are nearly equal and opposite to head rotations.
- *Linguistic tasks,* such as grammatical inference (Giles et al., 1991).
- *Nonlinear prediction for adaptive differential pulse-code modulation (ADPCM) of speech,* using the pipelined structure of Fig. 13.15 (Haykin and Li, 1993); in this paper it has been demonstrated that the resulting ADPCM system has a superior performance compared to the conventional version of the system using a linear predictor.

Li (1992) shows that a real-time recurrent network can be a universal approximator of a differentiable trajectory on a compact time interval. However, in the literature there is no formal proof yet for the FIR multilayer perceptron as a universal approximator of a differentiable trajectory on a compact time interval. Such a capability appears to be a natural extension of the property of an ordinary multilayer perceptron as a universal approximator of an arbitrary input–output mapping, provided that the memory span of the FIR synaptic filters is sufficiently long. Another issue that also deserves to be considered in the context of FIR multilayer perceptrons is the pruning of weights (and therefore connections). Such a pruning process is likely to be more involved than that described in Chapter 6 for the pruning of an ordinary multilayer perceptron trained with the standard back-propagation algorithm.

The FIR multilayer perceptron performs temporal processing by using the spatio-temporal model of a single neuron shown in Fig. 13.4. The real-time recurrent network, on the other hand, uses an ordinary model of a neuron, but the network develops a temporal processing capability through feedback built into its design. In a good portion of the next chapter, we continue the focus on temporal considerations, based on the spatio-temporal model of a neuron shown in Fig. 13.5.

PROBLEMS

13.1 Consider Eq. (13.14), in which the time function $h_o(t)$ is represented by the Dirac delta function

$$h_o(t) = \delta(t - \tau)$$

where τ is a fixed delay. Show that the neuron model for this particular form of $h_o(t)$ is a special case of the FIR model shown in Fig. 13.4.

13.2 Consider Eq. (13.4) defining the activation potential $v_j(t)$ of neuron j, assuming the particular form of impulse response $h_{ji}(t)$ defined in Eqs. (13.14) and (13.15).

(a) Show that $v_j(t)$ may be expressed in the equivalent form

$$v_j(t) = \frac{1}{\tau} \sum_{i=1}^{p} w_{ji} \exp\left(-\frac{t}{\tau}\right) \int_{-\infty}^{t} x_i(u) \exp\left(\frac{u}{\tau}\right) du$$

(b) By differentiating the result given in part (a) with respect to time t, derive the model described in Fig. 13.5.

13.3 The time-delay neural network (TDNN) topology is embodied in that of the FIR multilayer perceptron. Construct the FIR multilayer perceptron equivalent for the TDNN described in Fig. 13.2.

13.4 In Fig. 13.7 we unfolded the 2-2-2-1 feedforward network of Fig. 13.6 in time by starting from the input layer. Unfold this network in time starting from the output layer, and compare the resulting number of parameters with that in Fig. 13.7.

13.5 Consider a 3-2-1 feedforward network using FIR filters for its synaptic connections. Each synapse has two tap weights. Unfold this network in time by starting from (a) the input layer and (b) the output layer. Compare the numbers of free parameters in the resulting two structures.

13.6 In Section 13.3 we used the "unfolding-in-time" operation for calculating the instantaneous error gradients. The approach described there may be viewed as an indirect approach to the development of temporal back-propagation. Redo the development of Eqs. (13.45) and (13.46) using a direct mathematical procedure (Wan, 1990a).

13.7 The material presented in Section 13.3 dealt with synaptic FIR filters of equal length. How could you handle the case of synaptic FIR filters of different lengths?

13.8 Consider the *Mackey–Glass chaotic time series* (Casdagli, 1989), generated by a delay-differential equation of the form

$$\frac{dx(t)}{dt} = \frac{ax(t-\tau)}{1 + x^{10}(t-\tau)} - bx(t)$$

with the parameter values $a = 0.2$, $b = 0.1$, and delay $\tau = 30$. The requirement is to design an FIR multilayer perceptron to predict 6 samples into the future. The network has 1-15-1 neurons and 8 to 2 taps in the corresponding layers.

(a) Train the network on only the 500 points of the time series using the temporal back-propagation algorithm, with a learning-rate parameter $\eta = 0.005$ and 10,000 passes through the data.

(b) After training of the network is completed, fix all the weights and perform recursive prediction on the next 100 points of the Mackey–Glass time series. Compare your prediction with the actual values of the time series, and compute the normalized standard deviation of the prediction error using these 100 points.

13.9 Figure P13.9 illustrates the use of a *Gaussian-shaped time window* as a method for temporal processing (Bodenhausen and Waibel, 1991). The time window associated with synapse i of neuron j is denoted by $\theta(n, \tau_{ji}, \sigma_{ji})$, where τ_{ji} and σ_{ji} are measures of *time delay* and *width* of the windows, respectively, as shown by

$$\theta(n, \tau_{ji}, \sigma_{ji}) = \frac{1}{\sqrt{2\pi}\,\sigma_{ji}} \exp\left(-\frac{1}{2\sigma_{ji}^2}(n-\tau_{ji})^2\right)$$

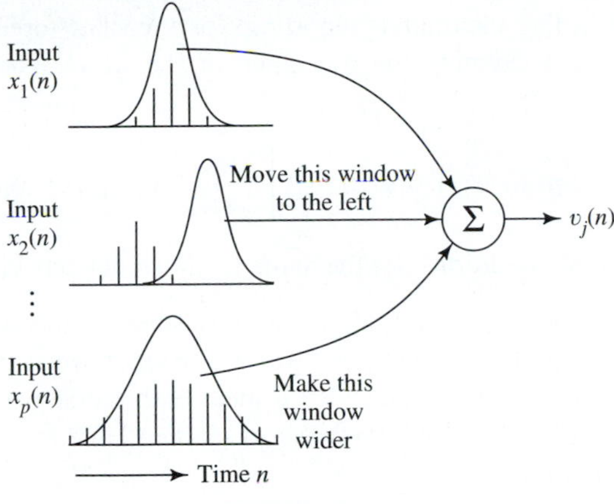

FIGURE P13.9

The output of neuron j is thus modeled as follows:

$$y_j(n) = \varphi\left(\sum_{i=1}^{p} w_{ji}u_i(n)\right)$$

where $u_i(n)$ is the convolution of the input $x_i(n)$ and the time window $\theta(n, \tau_{ji}, \sigma_{ji})$. The weight w_{ji}, time delay τ_{ji}, and width σ_{ji} of synapse i belonging to neuron j are all to be *learned* in a supervised manner.

This learning may be accomplished using the back-propagation algorithm. Demonstrate this learning process by deriving update equations for w_{ji}, τ_{ji}, and σ_{ji}.

13.10 Consider the recurrent network shown in Fig. P13.10, consisting of three computation nodes with self-feedback applied to all of them. Construct a multilayer feedforward network by unfolding the temporal behavior of this recurrent network.

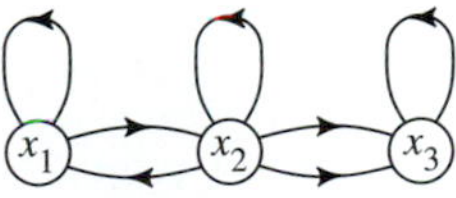

FIGURE P13.10

13.11 The dynamics of a *teacher-forced recurrent network* during training are given by Eqs. (13.69) and (13.70), except for the following change:

$$u_i(n) = \begin{cases} x_i(n) & \text{if } i \in \mathcal{A} \\ d_i(n) & \text{if } i \in \mathcal{C}(n) \\ y_i(n) & \text{if } i \in \mathcal{B} - \mathcal{C}(n) \end{cases}$$

(a) Show that for this scheme, the partial derivative $\partial y_j(n+1)/\partial w_{kl}(n)$ is given by (Williams and Zipser, 1989)

$$\frac{\partial y_j(n+1)}{\partial w_{kl}(n)} = \varphi'(v_j(n))\left[\sum_{i \in \mathcal{B} - \mathcal{C}(n)} w_{ji}(n)\frac{\partial y_i(n)}{\partial w_{kl}(n)} + \delta_{kj}u_l(n)\right]$$

(b) Hence, show that the training algorithm for a teacher-forced recurrent network is modified by defining the dynamics of the triply indexed variable π^j_{kl} as follows:

$$\pi^j_{kl}(n+1) = \varphi'(v_j(n))\left[\sum_{i\in\mathcal{B}-\mathcal{C}(n)} w_{ji}\pi^i_{kl}(n) + \delta_{kj}u_l(n)\right]$$

but the initial conditions are the same as those defined in Section 13.7.

13.12 The temporal back-propagation algorithm described in this chapter caters to the supervised learning of spatio-temporal patterns. Explore ways in which the Hebbian postulate of learning may be extended to deal with the self-organized learning of spatio-temporal patterns. You may wish to refer to Herz et al. (1988, 1989) for a discussion of this issue.

13.13 Consider the partially recurrent network of Fig. 13.18, characterized by the synaptic weight matrix $\mathbf{W}(n)$. Using gradient descent applied to the relative entropy of Eq. (13.100) as cost function, derive an algorithm for the adaptation of $\mathbf{W}(n)$. For this derivation, you may assume that all the neurons in the network have the same activation function, defined by the logistic function.

CHAPTER 14

Neurodynamics

14.1 Introduction

In the previous chapter we discussed different ways in which the use of standard neural network models such as the multilayer perceptron may be extended to incorporate the use of temporal processing. However, there are other neural network models, such as the Hopfield network, whose operation is naturally dependent on time. Whether the use of "time" is purposely added to the model or whether it is built into the model's operation, we have a nonlinear dynamical system to consider. The subject of neural networks viewed as nonlinear dynamical systems, with particular emphasis on the *stability* problem, is referred to as *neurodynamics* (Hirsch, 1989; Pineda, 1988a). An important feature of the stability (or instability) of a nonlinear dynamical system is that it is a property of the whole system. As a corollary, *the presence of stability always implies some form of coordination between the individual parts of the system* (Ashby, 1960). It appears that the study of neurodynamics began in 1938 with the work of Rashevsky, in whose visionary mind the application of dynamics to biology came into view for the first time.

The stability of a nonlinear dynamical system is a difficult issue to deal with. When we speak of the stability problem, those of us with an engineering background usually think in terms of the *bounded input–bounded output (BIBO) stability criterion.* According to this criterion, stability means that the output of a system must *not* grow without bound as a result of a bounded input, initial condition, or unwanted disturbance (Brogan, 1985). The BIBO stability criterion is well suited for a linear dynamical system. However, it is useless to apply it to neural networks, simply because all such nonlinear dynamical systems are BIBO stable because of the saturating nonlinearity built into the constitution of a neuron.

When we speak of stability in the context of a nonlinear dynamical system, we usually mean *stability in the sense of Liapunov*. In a celebrated Mémoire dated 1892, Liapunov (a Russian mathematician and engineer) presented the fundamental concepts of the stability theory known as the *direct method of Liapunov.*[1] This method is widely used for the stability analysis of linear and nonlinear systems, both time-invariant and time-varying. As such it is directly applicable to the stability analysis of neural networks (Hirsch, 1987, 1989). Indeed, much of the material presented in this chapter is concerned with the direct method of Liapunov. The reader should be forewarned, however, that its application is no easy task.

[1] The direct method of Liapunov is also referred in the literature as the second method. For an early account of this pioneering work, see the book by LaSalle and Lefschetz (1961).

The alternative spelling, Lyapunov, is frequently used in the literature; the difference in spelling arose during transliteration from Russian characters (Brogan, 1985).

The study of neurodynamics may follow one of two routes, depending on the application of interest:

- *Deterministic neurodynamics,* in which the neural network model has a deterministic behavior. In mathematical terms, it is described by a set of *nonlinear differential equations* that define the exact evolution of the model as a function of time (Grossberg, 1967; Cohen and Grossberg, 1983; Hopfield, 1984a).
- *Statistical neurodynamics,* in which the neural network model is perturbed by the presence of noise. In this case, we have to deal with *stochastic nonlinear differential equations,* expressing the solution in probabilistic terms (Amari et al., 1977; Amari, 1990; Peretto, 1984). The combination of stochasticity and nonlinearity makes the subject more difficult to handle.

In this chapter we restrict ourselves to deterministic neurodynamics. The neural network model used in the study is based on the *additive model* of a neuron that was derived in Section 13.2. As mentioned already, an important property of a dynamical system is that of stability. To understand the stability problem, we need to start with some basic concepts underlying the characterization of nonlinear dynamical systems,[2] which is how we intend to pursue the study of neurodynamics.

Organization of the Chapter

The material presented in this chapter is organized as follows. In Section 14.2 we briefly review some of the basic ideas in dynamical systems. This is followed by consideration of the stability of equilibrium states of dynamical systems in Section 14.3; here we introduce Liapunov's theorems, which are basic to the study of the stability problem. Then, in Section 14.4, we describe the notion of *attractors,* which plays an important role in the characterization of dynamic behavior of nonlinear systems. This is naturally followed by a discussion of *strange attractors* and *chaos* in Section 14.5.

Having familiarized ourselves with the behavior of dynamical systems, we move on to present general considerations of neurodynamics in Section 14.6, where we describe a neurodynamical model of recurrent networks. In Section 14.7 we discuss recurrent networks in a general neurodynamical context.

Then, in Section 14.8, we consider the continuous version of the Hopfield network, and define the Liapunov function for it. In Section 14.9 we state the *Cohen–Grossberg theorem* for nonlinear dynamical systems, which includes the Hopfield network (and other associative memory models) as special cases. In Section 14.10 we study the application of the Hopfield network as a content-addressable memory, and so revisit some of the issues discussed in Chapter 8.

In Section 14.11 we consider another recurrent network, called the brain-in-a-box-state (BSB) model (Anderson et al., 1977), and study its dynamic behavior as an associative memory.

In Section 14.12 we consider the recurrent back-propagation algorithm and the associated stability problem; the algorithm is so-called because the learning process involves the combined use of (1) a neural network with feedback connections and (2) the back-propagation of error signals to modify the synaptic weights of the network.

---

[2] For a graphical, easy-to-read treatment of nonlinear dynamics, see Abraham and Shaw (1992). For an introductory treatment of nonlinear dynamical systems with an engineering bias, see Cook (1986) and Atherton (1981). For a mathematical treatment of nonlinear dynamical systems in a more abstract setting, see Arrowsmith and Place (1990), and Hirsch and Smale (1974). The two-volume treatise by E.A. Jackson (1989, 1990) is perhaps the most complete treatment of the subject, providing a historical perspective and a readable account of nonlinear dynamics that integrates both classical and abstract ideas.

The chapter concludes with Section 14.13 with some final thoughts on the subject of neurodynamics and related issues.

14.2 Dynamical Systems

In order to proceed with the study of neurodynamics, we need a *mathematical model* for describing the dynamics of a nonlinear system. A model most naturally suited for this purpose is the so-called *state-space model.* According to this model, we think in terms of a set of *state variables* whose values (at any particular instant of time) are supposed to contain sufficient information to predict the future evolution of the system. Let $x_1(t), x_2(t), \ldots, x_N(t)$ denote the state variables of a nonlinear dynamical system, where continuous time t is the *independent variable* and N is the *order* of the system. For convenience of notation, these state variables are collected into an N-by-1 vector $\mathbf{x}(t)$ called the *state vector* of the system. The dynamics of a large class of nonlinear dynamical systems may then be cast in the form of a system of first-order differential equations written as follows:

$$\frac{d}{dt}x_j(t) = F_j(x_j(t)), \qquad j = 1, 2, \ldots, N \tag{14.1}$$

where the function F_j is, in general, a nonlinear function of its argument. We may cast this system of equations in a compact form by using vector notation, as shown by

$$\frac{d}{dt}\mathbf{x}(t) = F(\mathbf{x}(t)) \tag{14.2}$$

where the nonlinear function F operates on each element of the state vector

$$\mathbf{x}(t) = [x_1(t), x_2(t), \ldots, x_N(t)]^T \tag{14.3}$$

A nonlinear dynamical system for which the vector function $F(\mathbf{x}(t))$ does not depend *explicitly* on time t, as in Eq. (14.2), is said to be *autonomous*; otherwise, it is *nonautonomous.*[3] We will concern ourselves with autonomous systems only.

Regardless of the exact form of the nonlinear function F, the state vector $\mathbf{x}(t)$ must vary with time t; otherwise, $\mathbf{x}(t)$ is constant and the system is no longer dynamic. We may therefore formally define a dynamical system as follows:

A dynamical system is a system whose state varies with time.

Moreover, we may think of $d\mathbf{x}/dt$ as a "velocity" vector, not in a physical but rather in an abstract sense. Then, according to Eq. (14.2), we may refer to the vector function $F(\mathbf{x})$ as a velocity vector field or, simply, a *vector field.*

Phase Space

It is very informative to view the state-space equation (14.2) as describing the *motion* of a point in an N-dimensional state space, commonly referred to as the *phase space* of the

[3] A *nonautonomous* dynamical system is defined by the state equation

$$\frac{d}{dt}\mathbf{x}(t) = F(\mathbf{x}(t), t)$$

with the initial condition $\mathbf{x}(t_0) = \mathbf{x}_0$. For a nonautonomous system the vector field $F(\mathbf{x}(t), t)$ depends on time t. Therefore, unlike the case of an autonomous system, we cannot set the initial time equal to zero, in general (Parker and Chua, 1989).

system, a terminology borrowed from physics. The phase space can be a *Euclidean space* or a subset thereof. It can also be a non-Euclidean space such as a circle, a sphere, a torus, or some other *differentiable manifold.* Our interest, however, is confined to a Euclidean space.

The phase space is important, because it provides us with a visual/conceptual tool for analyzing the dynamics of a nonlinear system described by Eq. (14.2). It does so by focusing our attention on the *global characteristics* of the motion rather than the detailed aspects of analytic or numeric solutions of the equation.

At a particular instant of time t, the observed state of the system [i.e., the state vector $\mathbf{x}(t)$] is represented by a single point in the N-dimensional phase space. Changes in the state of the system with time t are represented as a curve in the phase space, with each point on the curve carrying (explicitly or implicitly) a label that records the time of observation. This curve is called a *trajectory* or *orbit* of the system. Figure 14.1 illustrates the trajectory of a two-dimensional system. The instantaneous velocity of the trajectory [i.e., the velocity vector $d\mathbf{x}(t)/dt$] is represented by the *tangent vector,* shown as a dashed line in Fig. 14.1 for time $t = t_0$. We may thus derive a velocity vector for each point of the trajectory.

The family of trajectories, for different initial conditions, is called the *phase portrait* of the system. The phase portrait includes *all* those points in the phase space where the field vector $F(\mathbf{x})$ is defined. Note that for an autonomous system there will be one and only one trajectory passing through an initial state. A useful idea that emerges from the phase portrait is the *flow* of a dynamical system, defined as the motion of the space of states within itself. In other words, we may imagine the space of states to flow, just like a fluid, around in itself, with each point (state) following a particular trajectory (Abraham and Shaw, 1992). The idea of flow, as described here, is vividly illustrated in the phase portrait of Fig. 14.2.

Given a phase portrait of a dynamical system, we may construct a field of velocity (tangent) vectors, one for each and every point of the phase space. The picture so obtained provides, in turn, a portrayal of the vector field of the system. In Fig. 14.3 we show a

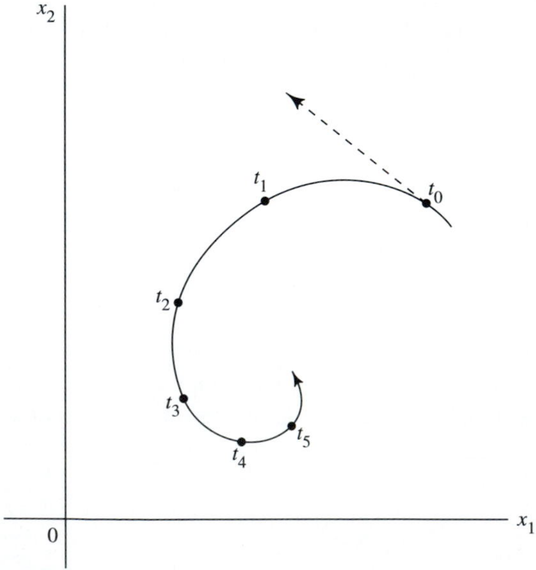

FIGURE 14.1 A two-dimensional trajectory (orbit) of a dynamical system.

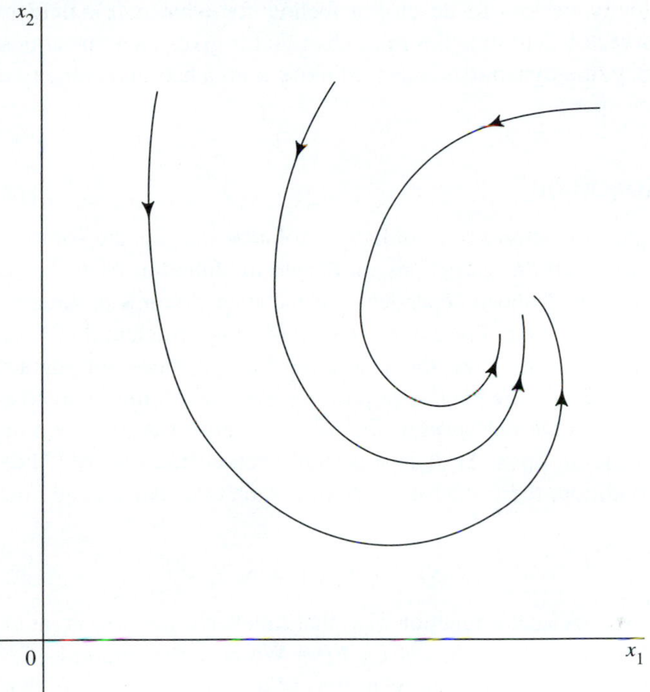

FIGURE 14.2 A two-dimensional phase portrait of a dynamical system.

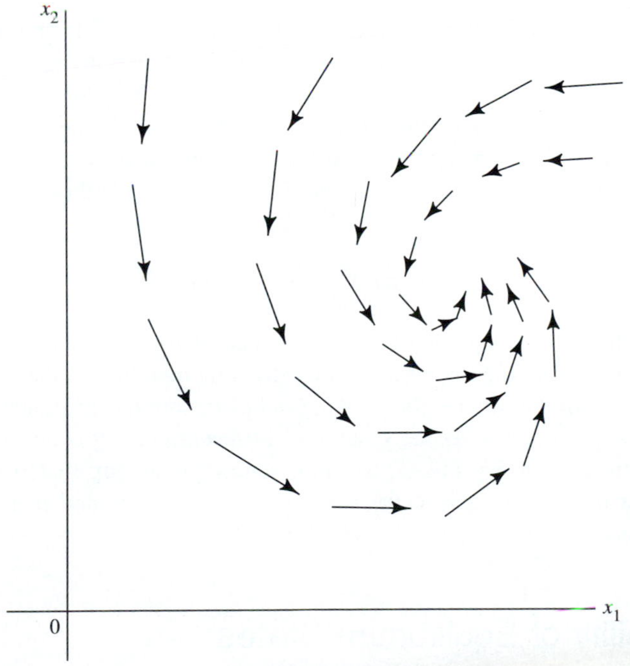

FIGURE 14.3 A two-dimensional vector field of a dynamical system.

number of velocity vectors to develop a feeling for what a full field looks like. The usefulness of a vector field thus lies in the fact that it gives us a visual description of the inherent tendency of a dynamical system to move with a habitual velocity at each specific point of a phase space.

Lipschitz Condition

For the state-space equation (14.2) to have a solution and for the solution to be unique, we have to impose certain restrictions on the vector function $F(\mathbf{x})$. For convenience of presentation, we have dropped dependence of the state vector $\mathbf{x}$ on time t, a practice that we follow from time to time. For a solution to exist, it is sufficient that $F(\mathbf{x})$ be continuous in all of its arguments. However, this restriction by itself does not guarantee uniqueness of the solution. To do so, we have to impose a further restriction, known as the *Lipschitz condition.* Let $\|\mathbf{x}\|$ denote the *norm* or *Euclidean length* of the vector $\mathbf{x}$. Let $\mathbf{x}$ and $\mathbf{u}$ be a pair of vectors in an open set $\mathcal{M}$ in a normal vector (state) space. Then, according to the Lipschitz condition, there exists a constant K such that (Hirsch and Smale, 1974; E.A. Jackson, 1989)

$$\|F(\mathbf{x}) - F(\mathbf{u})\| \leq K\|\mathbf{x} - \mathbf{u}\| \tag{14.4}$$

for all $\mathbf{x}$ and $\mathbf{u}$ in $\mathcal{M}$. A vector function $F(\mathbf{x})$ that satisfies Eq. (14.4) is said to be *Lipschitz,* and K is called the *Lipschitz constant* for $F(\mathbf{x})$. We note that Eq. (14.4) also implies the continuity of the function $F(\mathbf{x})$ with respect to $\mathbf{x}$. It follows, therefore, that in the case of autonomous systems, the Lipschitz condition guarantees both the existence and uniqueness of solutions for the state-space equation (14.2). In particular, if all partial derivatives $\partial F_i/\partial x_j$ are finite everywhere, then the function $F(\mathbf{x})$ satisfies the Lipschitz condition.

Divergence Theorem

Consider a region of volume V and surface S in the phase space of an autonomous system, and assume a "flow" of points from this region. From our earlier discussion, we recognize that the velocity vector $d\mathbf{x}/dt$ is equal to the vector field $F(\mathbf{x})$. Provided that the vector field $F(\mathbf{x})$ within the volume V is "well behaved," we may apply the *divergence theorem* from vector calculus (Jackson, 1975). Let $\mathbf{n}$ denote a unit vector normal to the surface at dS pointing outward from the enclosed volume. Then, according to the divergence theorem, the relation

$$\int_S (F(\mathbf{x}) \cdot \mathbf{n})\, dS = \int_V (\nabla \cdot F(\mathbf{x}))\, dV \tag{14.5}$$

holds between the volume integral of the divergence of $F(\mathbf{x})$ and the surface integral of the outwardly directed normal component of $F(\mathbf{x})$. The quantity on the left-hand side of Eq. (14.5) is recognized as the net *flux* flowing out of the region surrounded by the closed surface S. If this quantity is zero, the system is *conservative*; if it is negative, the system is *dissipative.* In light of Eq. (14.5), we may state equivalently that if the divergence $\nabla \cdot F(\mathbf{x})$ (which is a scalar) is zero the system is conservative, and if it is negative the system is dissipative.

14.3 Stability of Equilibrium States

Consider an autonomous dynamical system described by the state-space equation (14.2). A constant vector $\bar{\mathbf{x}} \in \mathcal{M}$ is said to be an *equilibrium (stationary) state* of the system if the following condition is satisfied:

$$F(\bar{\mathbf{x}}) = \mathbf{0} \tag{14.6}$$

where $\mathbf{0}$ is the null vector. Clearly, the velocity vector $d\mathbf{x}/dt$ vanishes at the equilibrium state $\bar{\mathbf{x}}$, and therefore the constant function $\mathbf{x}(t) = \bar{\mathbf{x}}$ is a solution of Eq. (14.2). Furthermore, because of the uniqueness property of solutions, no other solution curve can pass through the equilibrium state $\bar{\mathbf{x}}$. The equilibrium state is also referred to as a *singular point,* signifying the fact that in the case of an equilibrium point the trajectory will degenerate into the point itself.

In order to develop a deeper understanding of the equilibrium condition, suppose that the nonlinear function $F(\mathbf{x})$ is smooth enough for the state-space equation (14.2) to be linearized in the neighborhood of $\bar{\mathbf{x}}$. Specifically, let

$$\mathbf{x}(t) = \bar{\mathbf{x}} + \Delta\mathbf{x}(t) \tag{14.7}$$

where $\Delta\mathbf{x}(t)$ is a small deviation from $\bar{\mathbf{x}}$. Then, retaining the first two terms in the Taylor series expansion of $F(\mathbf{x})$, we may approximate it as follows

$$F(\mathbf{x}) \simeq \bar{\mathbf{x}} + \mathbf{A}\,\Delta\mathbf{x}(t) \tag{14.8}$$

where the matrix $\mathbf{A}$ is defined by

$$\mathbf{A} = \frac{\partial}{\partial \mathbf{x}} F(\mathbf{x})\bigg|_{\mathbf{x}=\bar{\mathbf{x}}} \tag{14.9}$$

Hence, substituting Eqs. (14.7) and (14.8) in (14.2), and then using the definition of an equilibrium state, we get

$$\frac{d}{dt}\Delta\mathbf{x}(t) \simeq \mathbf{A}\,\Delta\mathbf{x}(t) \tag{14.10}$$

Provided that the matrix $\mathbf{A}$ is nonsingular, that is, the inverse matrix $\mathbf{A}^{-1}$ exists, then the approximation described in Eq. (14.10) is sufficient to determine the *local* behavior of the trajectories of the system in the neighborhood of the equilibrium state $\bar{\mathbf{x}}$. Indeed, if $\mathbf{A}$ is nonsingular, the nature of the equilibrium state is essentially determined by its *eigenvalues,* and may therefore be classified in a corresponding fashion. In particular, when the matrix $\mathbf{A}$ has m eigenvalues with positive real parts, we say that the equilibrium state $\bar{\mathbf{x}}$ is of *type m.* For the special case of a *second-order system,* we may classify the equilibrium state as summarized in Table 14.1 and illustrated in Fig. 14.4 (Cook, 1986; Atherton, 1981). Note that in the case of a *saddle point,* shown in Fig. 14.4e, the trajectories going to the saddle point are stable, whereas the trajectories coming from the saddle point are unstable.

TABLE 14.1 Classification of the Equilibrium State of a Second-Order System

Type of Equilibrium State $\bar{\mathbf{x}}$	Eigenvalues of Matrix $\mathbf{A}$
Stable node	Real and negative
Stable focus	Complex conjugate with negative real parts
Unstable node	Real and positive
Unstable focus	Complex conjugate with positive real parts
Saddle point	Real with opposite signs
Center	Conjugate purely imaginary

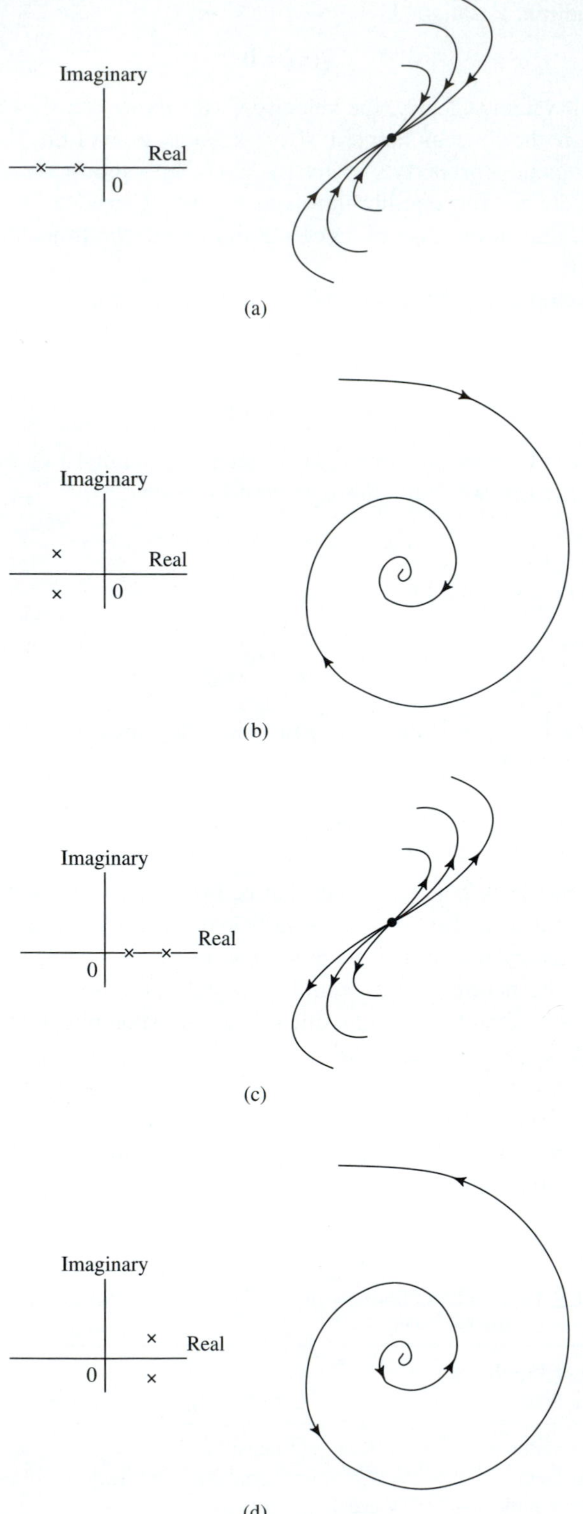

FIGURE 14.4 (a) Stable node. (b) Stable focus. (c) Unstable node. (d) Unstable focus.

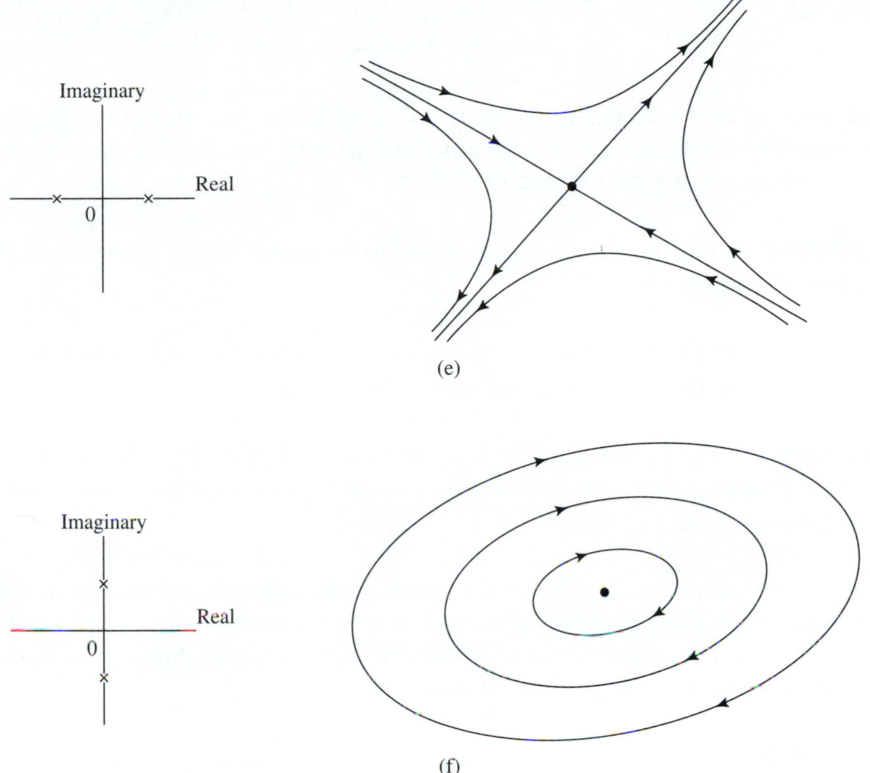

FIGURE 14.4 (continued) (e) Saddle point. (f) Center.

Definitions of Stability

Linearization of the state-space equation, as outlined above, provides useful information about the *local* stability properties of an equilibrium state. However, for us to be able to investigate the stability of a nonlinear dynamical system in a more detailed fashion, we need precise definitions of the stability and convergence of an equilibrium state.

In the context of an autonomous nonlinear dynamical system with equilibrium state $\bar{\mathbf{x}}$, the definitions of stability and convergence are as follows (Cook, 1986).

DEFINITION 1. The equilibrium state $\bar{\mathbf{x}}$ is said to be uniformly stable if for any given positive ε, there exists a positive δ such that the condition

$$\|\mathbf{x}(0) - \bar{\mathbf{x}}\| < \delta$$

implies

$$\|\mathbf{x}(t) - \bar{\mathbf{x}}\| < \varepsilon$$

for all $t > 0$.

This definition states that a trajectory of the system can be made to stay within a small neighborhood of the equilibrium state $\bar{\mathbf{x}}$ if the initial state $\mathbf{x}(0)$ is close to $\bar{\mathbf{x}}$.

DEFINITION 2. The equilibrium state $\bar{\mathbf{x}}$ is said to be convergent if there exists a positive δ such that the condition

$$\|\mathbf{x}(0) - \bar{\mathbf{x}}\| < \delta$$

implies that

$$\mathbf{x}(t) \rightarrow \bar{\mathbf{x}} \qquad \text{as } t \rightarrow \infty$$

The meaning of this second definition is that if the initial state $\mathbf{x}(0)$ of a trajectory is close enough to the equilibrium state $\bar{\mathbf{x}}$, then the trajectory described by the state vector $\mathbf{x}(t)$ will approach $\bar{\mathbf{x}}$ as time t approaches infinity.

DEFINITION 3. The equilibrium state $\bar{\mathbf{x}}$ is said to be asymptotically stable if it is both stable and convergent.

Here we note that stability and convergence are independent properties. It is only when both properties are satisfied that we have asymptotic stability.

DEFINITION 4. The equilibrium state $\bar{\mathbf{x}}$ is said to be asymptotically stable in the large, or globally asymptotically stable if it is stable and all trajectories of the system converge to $\bar{\mathbf{x}}$ as time t approaches infinity.

Clearly, this definition implies that the system cannot have other equilibrium states, and it requires that every trajectory of the system remains bounded for all time $t > 0$. In other words, global asymptotic stability implies that the system will ultimately settle down to a steady state for any choice of initial conditions.

EXAMPLE 1

Let a solution $\mathbf{u}(t)$ of the nonlinear dynamical system described by Eq. (14.2) vary with time t as indicated in Fig. 14.5. For the solution $\mathbf{u}(t)$ to be uniformly stable, we require that $\mathbf{u}(t)$ and any other solution $\mathbf{x}(t)$ remain close to each other for the same values of t (i.e., time "ticks"), as illustrated in Fig. 14.5. This kind of behavior is referred to as an *isochronous correspondence* of the two solutions $\mathbf{x}(t)$ and $\mathbf{u}(t)$ (E.A. Jackson, 1989). The solution $\mathbf{u}(t)$ is convergent provided that for every other solution $\mathbf{x}(t)$ for which $\|\mathbf{x}(0) - \mathbf{u}(0)\| \leq \delta(\boldsymbol{\varepsilon})$ at time $t = 0$, the solutions $\mathbf{x}(t)$ and $\mathbf{u}(t)$ converge to an equilibrium state as t approaches infinity.

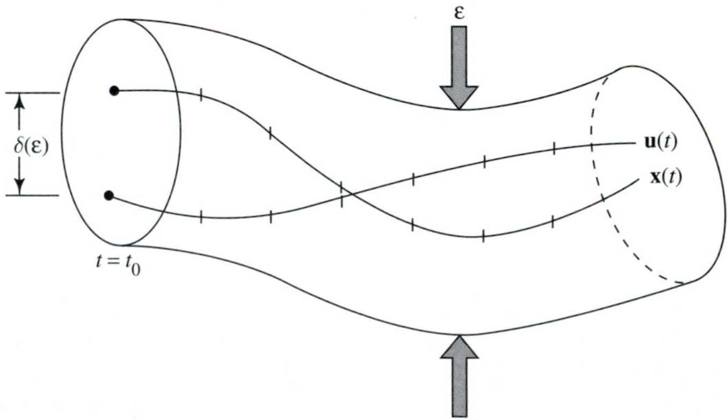

FIGURE 14.5 Illustration of the notion of uniform stability (convergence) of a state vector.

Liapunov's Theorems

Having defined stability and asymptotic stability of an equilibrium state of a dynamical system, the next issue to be considered is that of determining stability. We may obviously do so by actually finding all possible solutions to the state-space equation of the system; however, such an approach is often difficult if not impossible. A more elegant approach is to be found in *modern stability theory,* founded by Liapunov. Specifically, we may investigate the stability problem by applying the *direct method of Liapunov,* which makes use of a continuous scalar function of the state vector, called a Liapunov function.

Liapunov's theorems on the stability and asymptotic stability of the state-space equation (14.2) describing an autonomous nonlinear dynamical system with state vector $\mathbf{x}(t)$ and equilibrium state $\bar{\mathbf{x}}$ may be stated as follows:

THEOREM 1. The equilibrium state $\bar{\mathbf{x}}$ is stable if in a small neighborhood of $\bar{\mathbf{x}}$ there exists a positive definite function $V(\mathbf{x})$ such that its derivative with respect to time is negative semidefinite in that region.

THEOREM 2. The equilibrium state $\bar{\mathbf{x}}$ is asymptotically stable if in a small neighborhood of $\bar{\mathbf{x}}$ there exists a positive definite function $V(\mathbf{x})$ such that its derivative with respect to time is negative definite in that region.

A scalar function $V(\mathbf{x})$ that satisfies these requirements is called a *Liapunov function* for the equilibrium state $\bar{\mathbf{x}}$.

The above theorems require the Liapunov function $V(\mathbf{x})$ to be a positive definite function. Such a function is defined as follows: The function $V(\mathbf{x})$ is *positive definite* in the state space $\mathcal{S}$ if, for all $\mathbf{x}$ in $\mathcal{S}$, it satisfies the following requirements:

1. The function $V(\mathbf{x})$ has continuous partial derivatives with respect to the elements of the state vector $\mathbf{x}$
2. $V(\bar{\mathbf{x}}) = 0$
3. $V(\mathbf{x}) > 0$ if $\mathbf{x} \neq \bar{\mathbf{x}}$.

Given that $V(\mathbf{x})$ is a Liapunov function, then according to Theorem 1, the equilibrium state $\bar{\mathbf{x}}$ is stable if

$$\frac{d}{dt} V(\mathbf{x}) \leq 0 \qquad \text{for } \mathbf{x} \in \mathcal{U} - \bar{\mathbf{x}} \tag{14.11}$$

where $\mathcal{U}$ is a small neighborhood around $\bar{\mathbf{x}}$. Furthermore, according to Theorem 2, the equilibrium state $\bar{\mathbf{x}}$ is asymptotically stable if

$$\frac{d}{dt} V(\mathbf{x}) < 0 \qquad \text{for } \mathbf{x} \in \mathcal{U} - \bar{\mathbf{x}} \tag{14.12}$$

The important point to note from the above discussion is that Liapunov's theorems can be applied without having to solve the state-space equation of the system. Unfortunately, the theorems give no indication of how to find a Liapunov function; it is a matter of ingenuity and trial and error in each case. In many problems of interest (e.g., investigating the dynamics of Hopfield networks), the energy function can serve as a Liapunov function. The inability to find a suitable Liapunov function does not, however, prove instability of the system; that is, the existence of a Liapunov function is sufficient but not necessary for stability.

The Liapunov function $V(\mathbf{x})$ provides the mathematical basis for the *global* stability analysis of the nonlinear dynamical system described by Eq. (14.2). On the other hand, the use of Eq. (14.10) based on matrix **A** provides the basis for the *local* stability analysis of the system. Clearly, the global stability analysis is much more powerful in its conclusions than local stability analysis; that is, every globally stable system is also locally stable (but not vice versa).

14.4 Attractors

In general, a dissipative system is characterized by the convergence of its trajectories in phase space onto *manifolds* of lower dimensionality. By a ''manifold'' we simply mean a k-dimensional region embedded in the N-dimensional phase space, defined by a set of equations

$$M_j(x_1, x_2, \ldots, x_N) = 0, \qquad j = 1, 2, \ldots, N - k \tag{14.13}$$

where $x_1, x_2, \ldots, x_N$ are elements of the N-dimensional state vector of the system, and M_j is some function of these elements.

The manifold may consist of a single point in the phase space, in which case we speak of a *point attractor.* Alternatively, it may be in the form of a periodic orbit, in which case we speak of a stable *limit cycle,* stable in the sense that nearby trajectories approach it asymptotically. Figure 14.6 illustrates these two types of attractors. Attractors represent the only *equilibrium states* of a dynamical system that may be *observed experimentally.* Note, however, that in the context of attractors an equilibrium state does *not* imply a static equilibrium, nor a steady state. For example, a limit cycle represents a stable state of an attractor, but it varies continuously with time.

In Fig. 14.6 we note that each attractor is encompassed by a distinct region of its own. Such a region is called a *basin (domain) of attraction.* Note also that every initial state of the system is in the basin of some attractor. The boundary separating one basin of attraction from another is called a *separatrix.* In the case of Fig. 14.6, the basin boundary is represented by the union of the trajectory T_1, the saddle point Q, and the trajectory T_2.

A limit cycle constitutes the typical form of an oscillatory behavior that arises when an equilibrium point of a nonlinear system becomes unstable. As such, it can arise in nonlinear systems of any order. Nevertheless, limit cycles are particularly characteristic of second-order systems.

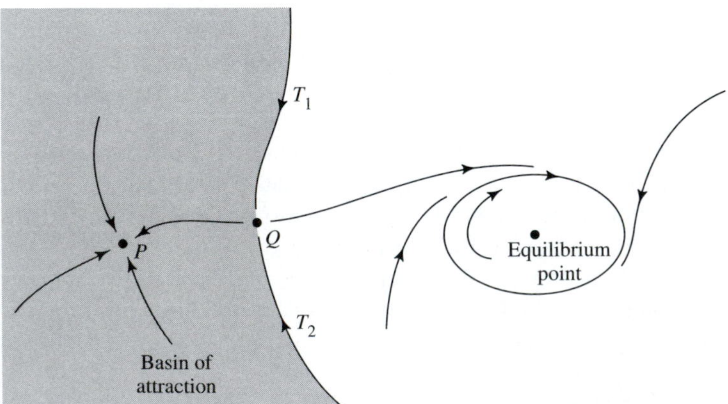

FIGURE 14.6 Illustration of the notion of a basin of attraction, and the idea of a separatrix.

EXAMPLE 2. Hopf Bifurcation

Consider a second-order nonlinear dynamical system described by the pair of state equations (Parker and Chua, 1989):

$$\frac{dx_1}{dt} = x_2 - x_1(x_1^2 + x_2^2 - c)$$

$$\frac{dx_2}{dt} = -x_1 - x_2(x_1^2 + x_2^2 - c)$$

where c is a control parameter. For the sake of simplicity, we have omitted the dependence of the state variables x_1 and x_2 on time t. The system has a fixed point at the origin; that is, $\bar{x}_1 = \bar{x}_2 = 0$. To study the local stability of this fixed point, we apply the definition of matrix $\mathbf{A}$ given in Eq. (14.9) and so obtain

$$\mathbf{A} = \begin{bmatrix} c & 1 \\ -1 & c \end{bmatrix}$$

The matrix $\mathbf{A}$ has two eigenvalues, defined by $c \pm i$, where $i = \sqrt{-1}$. When the control parameter c is less than zero, the fixed point is stable. This behavior is illustrated in Fig. 14.7a for $c = -0.2$. For $c > 0$, the fixed point is unstable. Moreover, the system

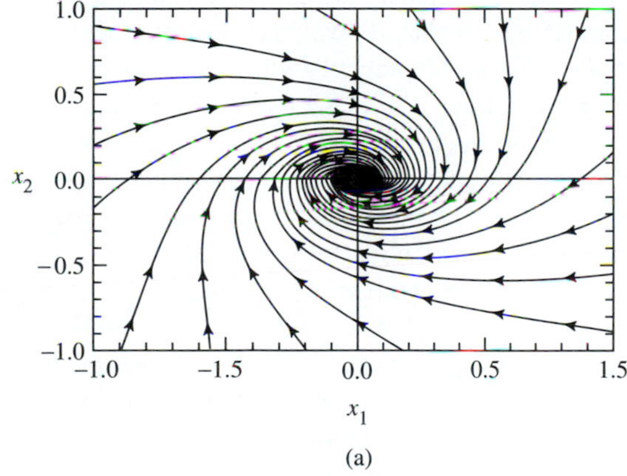

(a)

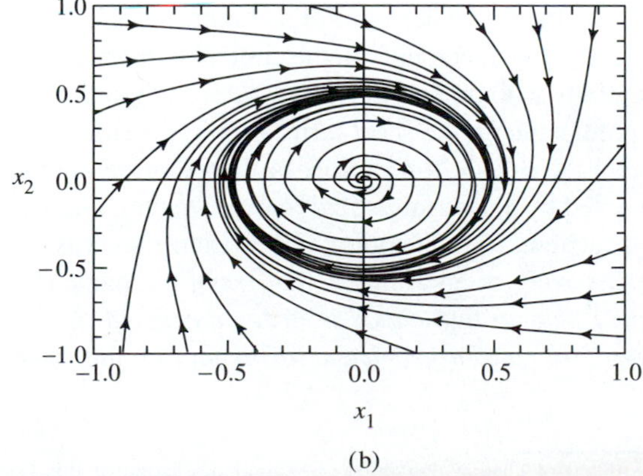

(b)

FIGURE 14.7 Phase portraits for a Hopf bifurcation: (a) $c = -0.2$; (b) $c = 0.2$. (From T.S. Parker and L.O. Chua, 1989, with permission of Springer-Verlag.)

has a stable limit cycle defined by

$$x_1^2 + x_2^2 = c, \qquad c > 0$$

At $c = 0$, the eigenvalues of the matrix $\mathbf{A}$ are purely imaginary. Thus, as the control parameter c passes through the value zero, the stability of the fixed point changes dramatically, and the system develops a stable limit cycle, as illustrated in Fig. 14.7b. This phenomenon is called the *Hopf bifurcation.*

14.5 Strange Attractors and Chaos

Nonlinear dynamical systems of order greater than 2 have the capability of exhibiting a chaotic behavior that is highly complex. This form of dynamic behavior arises by virtue of a type of attractors called strange attractors. In this section we present a qualitative treatment of what we mean by strange attractors, and fundamental characteristics of chaotic systems with which they are associated.[4]

In a nonlinear dynamical system, when the orbits in an attractor with neighboring initial conditions tend to move apart with increasing time, the system is said to possess a *strange attractor* and the system itself is said to be *chaotic.* In other words, a fundamental property that makes an attractor ''strange'' is the *sensitive dependence on initial conditions.* Sensitivity in this context means that if two identical nonlinear systems are started at slightly different initial conditions, namely, $\mathbf{x}$ and $\mathbf{x} + \boldsymbol{\varepsilon}$, where $\boldsymbol{\varepsilon}$ is a very small quantity, then their dynamic states will diverge from each other in phase space and their separation will increase exponentially on the average.

Another attribute of a chaotic system is the underlying *fractal* structure that exists in the phase space of a chaotic system. The term ''fractal'' was coined by Mandelbrot (1982), and refers to a *fractal dimension.* Unlike integer dimensions (as in a two-dimensional surface or a three-dimensional object), fractal dimensions are *not* integers.

Finally and most important, we have to recognize that a chaotic system is *deterministic* in the sense that its operation is governed by *fixed* rules, yet such a system with only a few elements can exhibit a behavior so complicated that it looks random. Indeed, the randomness is fundamental in the sense that the second-order statistics of a chaotic time series seem to indicate that it is random. However, unlike a true random phenomenon, the randomness exhibited by a chaotic system does not go away by gathering more information! In principle, the future behavior of a chaotic system is completely determined by the past but, in practice, any uncertainty in the choice of initial conditions, no matter how small, grows exponentially with time. Consequently, even though the dynamic behavior of a chaotic system is predictable in the short term, it is impossible to predict the long-term behavior of the system. A chaotic time series is therefore paradoxical in the sense that its generation is governed by a deterministic dynamic system, and yet it has a randomlike appearance. It is this attribute of a chaotic phenomenon that was originally emphasized by Lorenz with the discovery of an attractor that bears his name (Lorenz, 1963).

In summary, it may be said that *chaos is order disguised as disorder; underlying a chaotic behavior there are elegant geometric forms that create randomness* (Crutchfield et al., 1986).

[4] A mathematical treatment of chaotic dynamics is beyond the scope of this book. For an introductory treatment of chaos, see the paper by Crutchfield et al. (1986), and the books by Çambel (1993), Abraham and Shaw (1992), Schuster (1988), and Ruelle (1989). For an advanced treatment of the subject, see Guckenheimer and Holmes (1983). For a discussion of chaos in the brain, see the tutorial paper by Freeman (1992); see also the book by Başar (1990).

Chaos plays an important role in neurobiology. The brain is a nonlinear dynamical system par excellence. Indeed, there is experimental evidence that different types of chaos arise at several hierarchial levels in the brain (Freeman, 1992; Başar, 1990). Deterministic chaos is believed to play an important role in brain dynamics, as described here:

- Chaos may provide the driving activity that is essential for Hebbian learning of novel inputs (Freeman, 1992).
- The long-term unpredictability of chaos may permit the brain to create new possible responses, suggesting a role for chaos in rapid adaptation to changing environmental conditions (Mpitsos, 1990).
- Sensitive dependence of chaos on initial conditions may provide an efficient mechanism for dissipating perturbation (Mpitsos, 1990).

Chaotic dynamics also plays an important role in the study of artificial neural networks. Farmer and Sidorowich (1987), Broomhead and Lowe (1988), Casdagli (1989), Lowe and Webb (1991a), and Wan (1994) have shown that neural networks can be used to model a chaotic time series. Leung and Haykin (1990) have shown that sea clutter (radar backscatter from an ocean surface) fits a chaotic model. Using a supervised neural network to model sea clutter, Li and Haykin (1993) exploited this ''prior'' information to provide a significant improvement over conventional statistical procedures in the performance of a noncoherent marine radar for the detection of a small target embedded in an ocean environment.

One final comment is in order; stability in the sense of Liapunov, described in Section 14.3, does not apply to chaotic systems, as its use is restricted to the stability analysis of fixed-point attractors. To study the stability of chaotic systems we have to invoke other definitions (E.A. Jackson, 1989, p. 41).

14.6 Neurodynamical Models

Having familiarized ourselves with the behavior of nonlinear dynamical systems, we are ready to discuss some of the important issues involved in neurodynamics, which we do in this and the following sections. At the outset, however, we should emphasize that there is no universally agreed-upon definition of what we mean by neurodynamics. Rather than try to present such a definition, we will instead define the most general properties of the neurodynamical systems considered in this chapter. In particular, the discussion is limited to neurodynamical systems whose state variables are continuous-valued, and whose equations of motion are described by differential equations or difference equations. The systems of interest possess four general characteristics (Pineda, 1988b; Peretto and Niez, 1986):

1. *A large number of degrees of freedom.* The human cortex is a *highly parallel, distributed system* that is estimated to possess about 10 billion neurons, with each neuron modeled by one or more state variables. It is generally believed that both the computational power and the fault-tolerant capability of such a neurodynamical system are the result of the collective dynamics of the system. Indeed, the system is characterized by a very large number of coupling constants represented by the strengths (efficacies) of the individual synaptic junctions.
2. *Nonlinearity.* A neurodynamical system is nonlinear. In fact, nonlinearity is essential to create a universal computing machine.
3. *Dissipation.* A neurodynamical system is dissipative. It is therefore characterized by the convergence of the phase-space volume onto a manifold of lower dimensionality as time goes on.

4. *Noise.* Finally, noise is an intrinsic characteristic of neurodynamical systems. In real-life neurons, membrane noise is generated at synaptic junctions (Katz, 1966).

The presence of noise necessitates the use of a probabilistic treatment of neural activity, adding another level of complexity to the analysis of neurodynamical systems. A detailed treatment of stochastic neurodynamics is beyond the scope of this book. The effect of noise is therefore ignored in the material that follows.

Additive Model

Consider the noiseless, dynamical model of a neuron shown in Fig. 14.8, the mathematical basis of which was discussed in Section 13.2. In physical terms, the synaptic weights w_{j1}, w_{j2}, ..., w_{jN} represent *conductances,* and the respective inputs $x_1(t)$, $x_2(t)$, ..., $x_N(t)$ represent *potentials;* N is the number of inputs. These inputs are applied to a *current-summing junction* characterized as follows:

- Low input resistance
- Unity current gain
- High output resistance

It thus acts as a summing node for input currents. The total current flowing *toward* the input node of the nonlinearity in Fig. 14.8 is therefore

$$\sum_{i=1}^{N} w_{ji}x_i(t) + I_j$$

where the first (summation) term is due to the stimuli $x_1(t)$, $x_2(t)$, ..., $x_N(t)$, acting on the synaptic weights (conductances) w_{j1}, w_{j2}, ..., w_{jN}, respectively, and the second term is due to the current source I_j, representing an externally applied bias. Let $v_j(t)$ denote the potential developed across the input of the nonlinear element symbolized by $\varphi(\cdot)$. We may then express the total current flowing *away* from the input node of the nonlinear element as follows:

$$\frac{v_j(t)}{R_j} + C_j \frac{dv_j(t)}{dt}$$

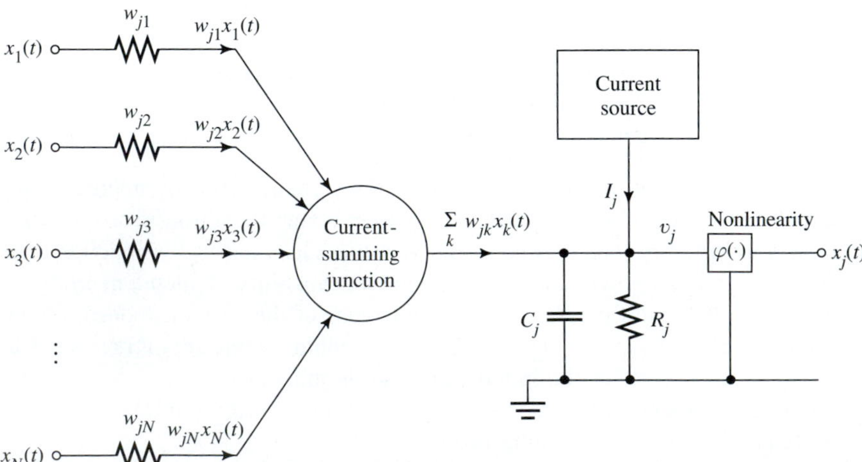

FIGURE 14.8 Additive model of a neuron.

where the first term is due to finite input resistance of the nonlinear element and the second term is due to the leakage capacitance C_j. Now, from *Kirchoff's current law,* we know that the total current flowing toward any node of an electrical circuit is zero. Accordingly, applying Kirchoff's current law to the input node of the nonlinearity in Fig. 14.8, we get

$$C_j \frac{dv_j(t)}{dt} + \frac{v_j(t)}{R_j} = \sum_{i=1}^{N} w_{ji}x_i(t) + I_j \tag{14.14}$$

The capacitive term $C_j dv_j(t)/dt$ on the left-hand side of Eq. (14.14) is the simplest way to add dynamics (memory) to the model of a neuron. Given the activation potential $v_j(t)$, we may determine the output of neuron j using the nonlinear relation

$$x_j(t) = \varphi(v_j(t)) \tag{14.15}$$

where $\varphi(\cdot)$ is a continuous nonlinear function. The *RC* model described by Eq. (14.14) is commonly referred to as the *additive model;* this terminology is used to discriminate from multiplicative (or shunting) models where w_{ji} is dependent on x_i (Grossberg, 1982).

Equations (14.14) and (14.15) may also be justified on neurobiological grounds (Hopfield, 1984a; Amari, 1972):

- $x_i(t)$ is the short-term average of the firing rate of neuron i.
- w_{ji} is the finite conductance between the output of neuron i and the cell body of neuron j.
- $v_j(t)$ is the mean soma potential of neuron j that results from the total effect of its excitatory and inhibitory inputs.
- R_j is the transmembrane resistance of neuron j.
- C_j is the capacitance of cell membranes of neuron j.
- $\varphi(\cdot)$ is the continuous nonlinear input–output characteristic of neuron j.

Returning to the issue at hand, consider now a *recurrent network* consisting of an interconnection of N neurons, each one of which is assumed to have the same mathematical model described in Eqs. (14.14) and (14.15). Then, ignoring interneuron propagation time delays, we may define the dynamics of the network by the following *system of coupled first-order differential equations:*

$$C_j \frac{dv_j(t)}{dt} = -\frac{v_j(t)}{R_j} + \sum_{i=1}^{N} w_{ji}x_i(t) + I_j, \qquad j = 1, 2, \ldots, N \tag{14.16}$$

which has the same mathematical form as the state equations (14.1), and which follows from a simple rearrangement of terms in Eq. (14.14). It is assumed that the nonlinear function $\varphi(\cdot)$ relating the output $x_j(t)$ of neuron j to its activation potential $v_j(t)$ is a continuous function and therefore differentiable. A common form of the nonlinearity φ is defined by the logistic function

$$\varphi(v_j) = \frac{1}{1 + \exp(-v_j)}, \qquad j = 1, 2, \ldots, N \tag{14.17}$$

A necessary condition for the learning algorithms described in this chapter to exist is that the recurrent network described by Eqs. (14.16) and (14.17) possesses fixed points (i.e., stable isolated attractors).

Related Model

The additive model of Eq. (14.16) is widely used in the study of neurodynamics. To simplify the exposition, we may assume that the time constant $\tau_j = R_j C_j$ of neuron j is the same for all j. Then, normalizing time t with respect to the common value of this time constant, and normalizing the w_{ji} and I_j with respect to the R_j, we may recast the model of Eq. (14.16) as follows:

$$\frac{dv_j(t)}{dt} = -v_j(t) + \sum_i w_{ji}\varphi(v_i(t)) + I_j, \qquad j = 1, 2, \ldots, N \tag{14.18}$$

where we have also incorporated Eq. (14.15). The attractor structure of the system of coupled first-order nonlinear differential equations (14.18) is basically the same as that

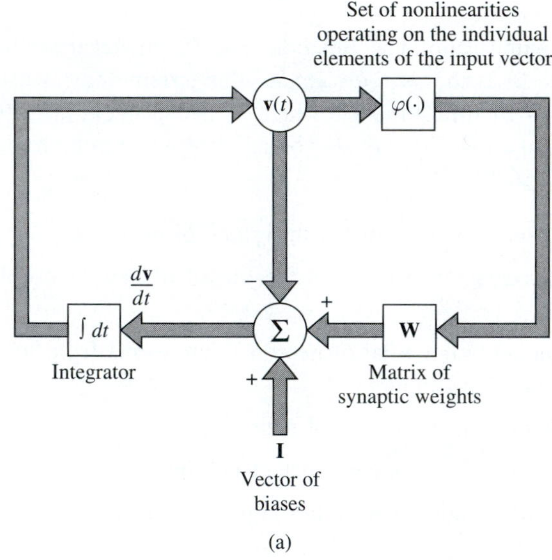

(a)

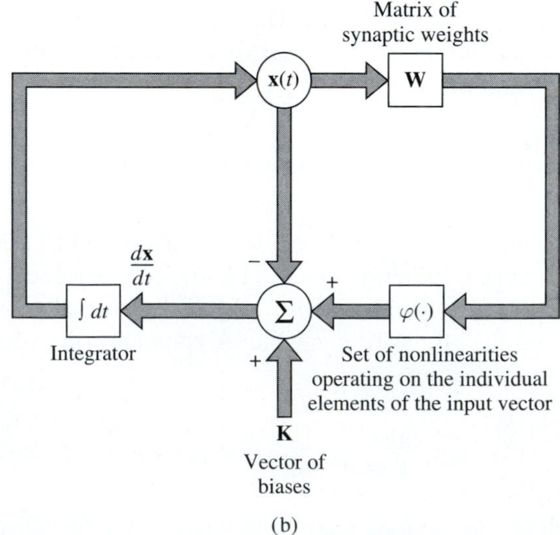

(b)

FIGURE 14.9 (a) Block diagram of a neurodynamical system represented by the coupled, first-order differential equations (14.18). (b) Block diagram of related model described by Eqs. (14.19).

of a closely related model described by (Pineda, 1987):

$$\frac{dx_j(t)}{dt} = -x_j(t) + \varphi\left(\sum_i w_{ji}x_i(t)\right) + K_j, \qquad j = 1, 2, \ldots, N \tag{14.19}$$

In the additive model described by Eq. (14.18), the activation potentials $v_1(t)$, $v_2(t)$, . . . , $v_N(t)$ of the individual neurons constitute the state vector. On the other hand, in the related model of Eq. (14.19), the outputs of the neurons $x_1(t)$, $x_2(t)$, . . . , $x_N(t)$ constitute the state vector.

These two neurodynamical models are in fact related to each other by a linear, invertible transformation. Specifically, multiplying both sides of Eq. (14.19) by w_{kj}, summing with respect to j, and then substituting the transformation

$$v_k(t) = \sum_j w_{kj}x_j(t)$$

we obtain a model of the type described by Eq. (14.18), and so find that the bias terms of the two models are related by

$$I_k = \sum_j w_{kj}K_j$$

The important point to note here is that results concerning the stability of the additive model of Eq. (14.18) are applicable to the related model of Eq. (14.19).

The close relationship between the two neurodynamical models described here is also illustrated in the block diagrams shown in Fig. 14.9. Parts (a) and (b) of this figure correspond to the matrix formulations of Eqs. (14.18) and (14.19), respectively; $\mathbf{W}$ is the matrix of synaptic weights, $\mathbf{v}(t)$ is the vector of activation potentials at time t, and $\mathbf{x}(t)$ is the vector of neuronal outputs at time t. The presence of *feedback* in both models is clearly visible in Fig. 14.9.

14.7 Manipulation of Attractors as a Recurrent Network Paradigm

With the number of neurons, N, assumed to be very large, the neurodynamical model described by Eq. (14.16) possesses, except for the effect of noise, the general properties outlined earlier in Section 14.6: very many degrees of freedom, nonlinearity, and dissipation. Accordingly, such a neurodynamical model can have complicated attractor structures and therefore exhibit useful computational capabilities.

The identification of attractors with computational objects (e.g., associative memories, input–output mappers) is one of the foundations of neural network paradigms. In order to implement this idea, we clearly need to exercise *control* over the locations of the attractors in the phase space of the network. Then, a learning algorithm takes the form of a nonlinear dynamical equation that manipulates the locations of the attractors for the purpose of encoding information in a desired form, or learning temporal structures of interest. In this way, an intimate relationship is established between the physics of the machine and the algorithms of the computation (Pineda, 1988a).

One way in which the collective properties of a neural network may be used to implement a computational task is by way of the concept of *energy minimization.* The Hopfield network (Hopfield, 1982, 1984a) and the brain-state-in-a-box model (Anderson et al., 1977) are well-known examples of such an approach. Both of these models are energy-minimizing networks; they differ from each other in their areas of application. The Hopfield network is useful as a content-addressable memory or an analog computer for solving combinatorial-type optimization problems. The brain-state-in-a-box model, on the other hand, is useful for clustering type applications. More will be said about these applications in subsequent sections of the chapter.

Another way of changing the attractor locations is to use the method of steepest descent to minimize a cost function defined in terms of the network parameters. Indeed, this general approach, reviewed in the context of statistical neurodynamics by Amari et al. (1977), forms the basis of many learning algorithms. A particular example of it has been pursued successfully in the development of a generalization of back-propagation to a recurrent neural network. In particular, an algorithm for training the network that permits the use of feedback connections was first described by Lapedes and Farber (1986a, 1986b). However, this algorithm did not use the back-propagation procedure for computing the modifications to the synaptic weights. The development of the recurrent back-propagation algorithm was carried out independently by Pineda (1987, 1988a, 1989), Rohwer and Forrest (1987), and Almeida (1987, 1988). In one way or another, these developments were all motivated by the recognition that a thorough understanding of neural networks as nonlinear dynamical systems would have to be cultivated. In terms of applications, the recurrent back-propagation algorithm is well suited for the purpose of *input–output mapping,* for which it relies on the availability of hidden neurons.

These two approaches to the design of neurodynamical systems are pursued in subsequent sections of this chapter. We begin the study in the next section by considering the dynamic behavior of continuous (analog) and discrete (digital) Hopfield networks.

14.8 Dynamics of Hopfield Models

For the discrete version of the Hopfield network studied previously in Chapter 8, we used the McCulloch–Pitts neuron model having binary outputs, 0 and 1. In this section we revisit the Hopfield network by considering the continuous version of it. In particular, we use the neurodynamical model of Eq. (14.16) to study the dynamics of the Hopfield network illustrated in Fig. 14.10 for the case of $N = 4$ neurons. As pointed out in Section

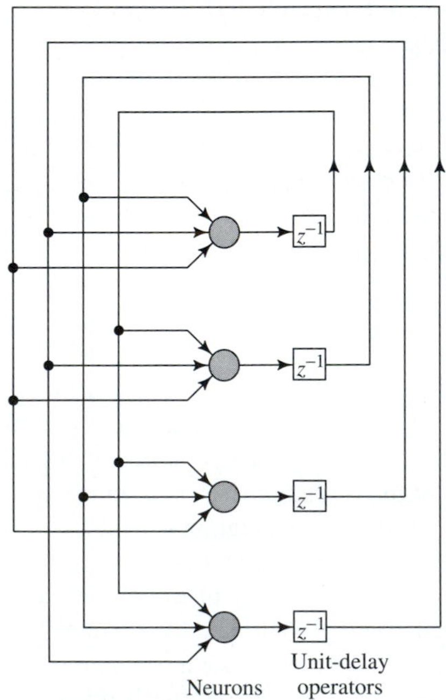

FIGURE 14.10 Architectural graph of a Hopfield network consisting of $N = 4$ neurons.

14.6, this latter model of a neuron is more realistic than the McCulloch–Pitts model in that it incorporates some important characteristics of real neurons.

Recognizing that $x_i(t) = \varphi_i(v_i(t))$, we may rewrite Eq. (14.16) in the expanded form

$$C_j \frac{d}{dt} v_j(t) = -\frac{v_j(t)}{R_j} + \sum_{i=1}^{N} w_{ji} \varphi_i(v_i(t)) + I_j, \qquad j = 1, \ldots, N \tag{14.20}$$

To proceed with the discussion, we make the following assumptions:

1. The matrix of synaptic weights is symmetric, as shown by

$$w_{ji} = w_{ij} \qquad \text{for all } i \text{ and } j \tag{14.21}$$

2. Each neuron has a nonlinear activation of its own—hence the use of $\varphi_i(\cdot)$ in Eq. (14.20).
3. The inverse of the nonlinear activation function exists, so that we may write

$$v = \varphi_i^{-1}(x) \tag{14.22}$$

Let the sigmoid function $\varphi_i(v)$ be defined by the hyperbolic tangent function

$$x = \varphi_i(v) = \frac{1 - \exp(-g_i v)}{1 + \exp(-g_i v)} \tag{14.23}$$

where g_i is the *gain* of neuron i, defined by

$$g_i = \left. \frac{d\varphi_i}{dv} \right|_{v=0} \tag{14.24}$$

The inverse output–input relation of Eq. (14.22) may thus be rewritten in the form

$$v = \varphi_i^{-1}(x) = -\frac{1}{g_i} \ln\left(\frac{1 - x}{1 + x}\right) \tag{14.25}$$

The *standard* form of the inverse output–input relation for a neuron of unity gain is defined by

$$\varphi^{-1}(x) = -\ln\left(\frac{1 - x}{1 + x}\right) \tag{14.26}$$

Hence we may rewrite Eq. (14.25) in terms of this standard relation as

$$\varphi_i^{-1}(x) = \frac{1}{g_i} \varphi^{-1}(x) \tag{14.27}$$

Figure 14.11a shows a plot of the standard sigmoidal nonlinearity $\varphi(v)$, and Fig. 14.11b shows the corresponding plot of the inverse nonlinearity $\varphi^{-1}(x)$.

According to Hopfield (1984a), the energy (Liapunov) function of the recurrent network illustrated in Fig. 14.10 is defined by

$$E = -\frac{1}{2} \sum_{i=1}^{N} \sum_{j=1}^{N} w_{ji} x_i x_j + \sum_{j=1}^{N} \frac{1}{R_j} \int_0^{x_j} \varphi_j^{-1}(x)\, dx - \sum_{j=1}^{N} I_j x_j \tag{14.28}$$

Then, differentiating E with respect to time, we get

$$\frac{dE}{dt} = -\sum_{j=1}^{N} \left(\sum_{i=1}^{N} w_{ji} x_i - \frac{v_j}{R_j} + I_j \right) \frac{dx_j}{dt} \tag{14.29}$$

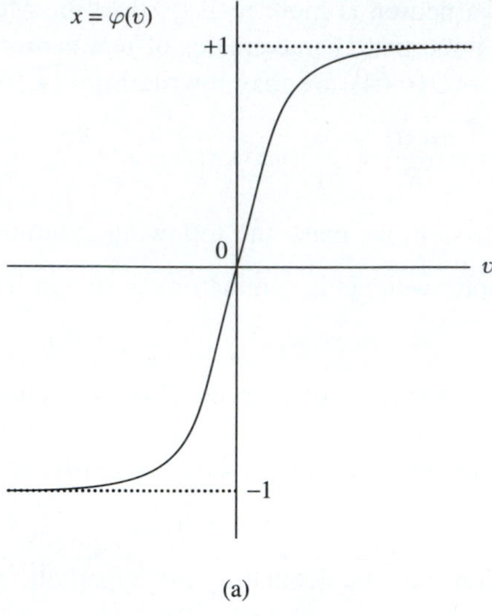

(a)

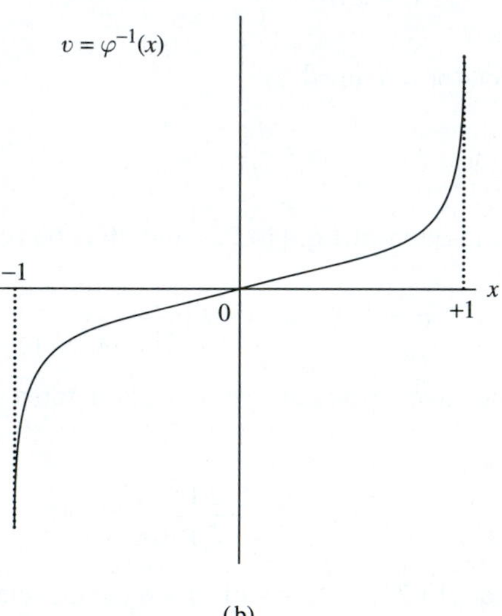

(b)

FIGURE 14.11 Plots of the standard sigmoidal nonlinearity and its inverse.

The quantity inside the parentheses on the right-hand side of Eq. (14.29) is recognized as $C_j \, dv_j/dt$ by virtue of the neurodynamical equation (14.20). Hence we may simplify Eq. (14.29) to

$$\frac{dE}{dt} = -\sum_{j=1}^{N} C_j \left(\frac{dv_j}{dt}\right) \frac{dx_j}{dt} \tag{14.30}$$

We now recognize the inverse relation that defines v_j in terms of x_j. Hence, the use of Eq. (14.22) in (14.30) yields

$$\begin{aligned} \frac{dE}{dt} &= -\sum_{j=1}^{N} C_j \left[\frac{d}{dt} \varphi_j^{-1}(x_j)\right] \frac{dx_j}{dt} \\ &= -\sum_{j=1}^{N} C_j \left(\frac{dx_j}{dt}\right)^2 \left[\frac{d}{dx_j} \varphi_j^{-1}(x_j)\right] \end{aligned} \tag{14.31}$$

From Fig. 14.11b we see that the inverse output–input relation $\varphi_j^{-1}(x_j)$ is a monotone-increasing function of the output x_j. It follows therefore that

$$\frac{d}{dx_j}\varphi_j^{-1}(x_j) \geq 0 \qquad \text{for all } x_j \tag{14.32}$$

Moreover, we note that

$$\left(\frac{dx_j}{dt}\right)^2 \geq 0 \qquad \text{for all } x_j \tag{14.33}$$

Hence, all the factors that make up the sum on the right-hand side of Eq. (14.31) are nonnegative. In other words, for the energy function E defined in Eq. (14.28), we have

$$\frac{dE}{dt} \leq 0 \qquad \text{for } x_j \neq 0 \text{ and all } j \tag{14.34}$$

From the definition of Eq. (14.28), we also note that the function E is bounded. Accordingly, we may make the following two statements:

1. The function E is a Liapunov function of the continuous Hopfield model.
2. The model is stable in accordance with Liapunov's theorem 1.

In other words, the time evolution of the continuous Hopfield model described by the system of nonlinear first-order differential equations (14.20) represents a trajectory in phase space, which seeks out the minima of the energy (Liapunov) function E and comes to a stop at such points (Hopfield, 1984a). We may therefore formally state the following theorem for a Hopfield network:

The (Liapunov) energy function E of a Hopfield network consisting of N neurons is a monotonically decreasing function of the network state $\{x_j | j = 1, 2, \ldots, N\}$.

Accordingly, the Hopfield network is globally asymptotically stable.

The use of Liapunov functions for the global stability analysis of neural networks was first introduced into the neural network literature by Grossberg (1977). Then, in 1983, Cohen and Grossberg developed a theorem that includes the Liapunov function of Eq. (14.28) as a special case. We shall discuss this latter theorem in Section 14.9.

Relation Between the Stable States of the Discrete and Continuous Versions of the Hopfield Model

We may readily establish the relationship between the stable states of the continuous Hopfield model and those of the corresponding discrete Hopfield model by redefining the input-output relation for a neuron such that we may satisfy two simplifying characteristics:

1. The output of a neuron has the asymptotic values

$$x_j = \begin{cases} +1 & \text{for } v_j = \infty \\ -1 & \text{for } v_j = -\infty \end{cases} \tag{14.35}$$

2. The midpoint of the input–output relation of a neuron lies at the origin, as shown by

$$\varphi_j(0) = 0 \tag{14.36}$$

Correspondingly, we may set the bias I_j equal to zero for all j.

In formulating the energy function E for a continuous Hopfield model, the neurons are permitted to have self-loops. A discrete Hopfield model, on the other hand, need not have self-loops. We may therefore simplify our discussion by setting $w_{jj} = 0$ for all j for both models.

In light of these observations, we may redefine the energy function of a continuous Hopfield model given in Eq. (14.28) as follows:

$$E = -\frac{1}{2}\sum_{i=1}^{N}\sum_{\substack{j=1 \\ i\neq j}}^{N} w_{ji}x_i x_j + \sum_{j=1}^{N}\frac{1}{R_j}\int_0^{x_j}\varphi_j^{-1}(x)\,dx \tag{14.37}$$

The inverse function $\varphi_j^{-1}(x)$ is defined by Eq. (14.27). Accordingly, we may rewrite the energy function of Eq. (14.37) as follows:

$$E = -\frac{1}{2}\sum_{i=1}^{N}\sum_{\substack{j=1 \\ i\neq j}}^{N} w_{ji}x_i x_j + \sum_{j=1}^{N}\frac{1}{g_j R_j}\int_0^{x_j}\varphi^{-1}(x)\,dx \tag{14.38}$$

The integral

$$\int_0^{x_j}\varphi^{-1}(x)\,dx$$

has the standard form plotted in Fig. 14.12. Its value is zero for $x_j = 0$, and positive otherwise. It assumes a very large value as x_j approaches ± 1. If however, the gain g_j of neuron j becomes infinitely large (i.e., the sigmoidal nonlinearity approaches the idealized hard-limiting form), the second term of Eq. (14.38) becomes negligibly small. Indeed, in the limiting case when $g_j = \infty$ for all j, the maxima and minima of the continuous Hopfield model become identical with those of the corresponding discrete Hopfield model. In the latter case, the energy (Liapunov) function is defined simply by

$$E = -\frac{1}{2}\sum_{i=1}^{N}\sum_{\substack{j=1 \\ i\neq j}} w_{ji}x_i x_j \tag{14.39}$$

where the jth neuron state $x_j = \pm 1$. We conclude, therefore, that the only stable points of the very high-gain, continuous, deterministic Hopfield model correspond to the stable points of the discrete stochastic Hopfield model (Hopfield, 1984a).

When, however, each neuron j has a large but finite gain g_j, we find that the second term on the right-hand side of Eq. (14.38) makes a noticeable contribution to the energy function of the continuous model. In particular, this contribution is large and positive near all surfaces, edges, and corners of the unit hypercube that defines the state space of

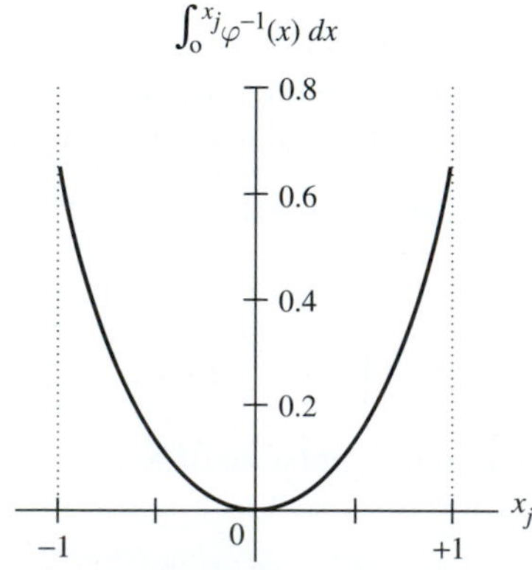

FIGURE 14.12 A plot of the integral $\int_0^{x_j}\varphi^{-1}(x)\,dx$.

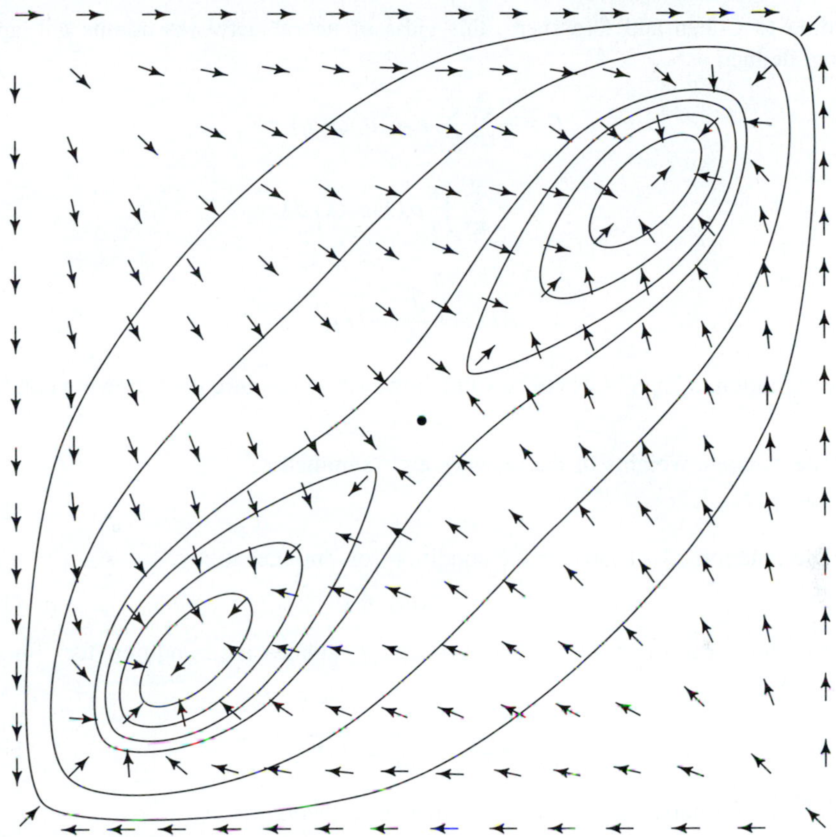

FIGURE 14.13 An energy contour map for a two-neuron, two-stable-state system. The ordinate and abscissa are the outputs of the two neurons. Stable states are located near the lower left and upper right corners, and unstable extrema at the other two corners. The arrows show the motion of the state. This motion is not in general perpendicular to the energy contours. (From J.J. Hopfield, 1984a, with permission of the National Academy of Sciences of the U.S.A.)

the model. On the other hand, the contribution is negligibly small at points that are far removed from the surface. Accordingly, the energy function of such a model has its maxima at corners, but the minima are displaced slightly toward the interior of the hypercube (Hopfield, 1984a).

Figure 14.13 depicts the energy contour map for a continuous Hopfield model using two neurons. The outputs of the two neurons define the two axes of the map. The lower left- and upper right-hand corners of Fig. 14.13 represent stable minima for the limiting case of infinite gain. The minima for the case of finite gain are displaced inward.

14.9 The Cohen–Grossberg Theorem

In 1983, Cohen and Grossberg described a general principle for assessing the stability of a certain class of neural networks, described by the following system of coupled nonlinear differential equations:

$$\frac{d}{dt}u_j = a_j(u_j)\left[b_j(u_j) - \sum_{i=1}^{N} c_{ji}\varphi_i(u_i)\right], \qquad j = 1, \ldots, N \tag{14.40}$$

According to Cohen and Grossberg, this class of neural networks admits a Liapunov function, defined as

$$E = \frac{1}{2}\sum_{i=1}^{N}\sum_{j=1}^{N} c_{ji}\varphi_i(u_i)\varphi_j(u_j) - \sum_{j=1}^{N}\int_0^{u_j} b_j(\lambda)\varphi_j'(\lambda)\, d\lambda \tag{14.41}$$

where

$$\varphi_j'(\lambda) = \frac{d}{d\lambda}(\varphi_j(\lambda))$$

For the definition of Eq. (14.41) to be valid, however, we require the following conditions to hold:

1. The synaptic weights of the network are "symmetric":
$$c_{ij} = c_{ji} \tag{14.42}$$
2. The function $a_j(u_j)$ satisfies the condition for "nonnegativity":
$$a_j(u_j) \geq 0 \tag{14.43}$$
3. The nonlinear input–output function $\varphi_j(u_j)$ satisfies the condition for "monotonicity":
$$\varphi_j'(u_j) = \frac{d}{du_j}\varphi_j(u_j) \geq 0 \tag{14.44}$$

We may now formally state the *Cohen–Grossberg theorem*:

Provided that the system of nonlinear differential equations (14.40) satisfies the conditions of symmetry, nonnegativity, and monotonicity, then the Liapunov function E of the system defined by Eq. (14.41) satisfies the condition

$$\frac{dE}{dt} \leq 0 \qquad \text{for } u_j \neq 0 \text{ and all } j$$

and the system is therefore globally asymptotically stable.

Once this basic property of the Liapunov function E is in place, global stability of the system follows from Liapunov's theorem 1.

The Hopfield Model as a Special Case of the Cohen–Grossberg Theorem

Comparing the general system of Eq. (14.40) with the system of Eq. (14.20) for a continuous Hopfield model, we may make the correspondences between the Hopfield model and the Cohen–Grossberg theorem that are summarized in Table 14.2. Hence, the use of this table in Eq. (14.41) yields the following Liapunov function for the continuous Hopfield model:

$$E = -\frac{1}{2}\sum_{i=1}^{N}\sum_{j=1}^{N} w_{ji}\varphi_i(v_i)\varphi_j(v_j) + \sum_{j=1}^{N}\int_0^{v_j}\left(\frac{v_j}{R_j} - I_j\right)\varphi_j'(v)\, dv \tag{14.45}$$

where the nonlinear activation function $\varphi_j(\cdot)$ is defined by Eq. (14.23).

TABLE 14.2 Correspondence Between the Cohen–Grossberg Theorem and the Hopfield Model

Cohen–Grossberg Theorem	Hopfield Model
u_j	$C_j v_j$
$a_j(u_j)$	1
$b_j(u_j)$	$-(v_j/R_j) + I_j$
c_{ji}	$-w_{ji}$
$\varphi_i(u_i)$	$\varphi_i(v_i)$

We next make the following observations:

1. $\varphi_i(v_i) = x_i$
2. $\int_0^{v_j} \varphi_j'(v)\, dv = \int_0^{x_j} dx = x_j$
3. $\int_0^{v_j} v\varphi_j'(v)\, dv = \int_0^{x_j} v\, dx = \int_0^{x_j} \varphi_j^{-1}(x)\, dx$

Basically, relations 2 and 3 result from the use of $x = \varphi_i(v)$. Thus the use of these observations in the Liapunov function of Eq. (14.45) yields a result identical to that we derived earlier; see Eq. (14.28). Note, however, that although $\varphi_i(v)$ must be a nondecreasing function of the input v, it does not need to have an inverse in order for the generalized Liapunov function of Eq. (14.41) to hold.

The Cohen–Grossberg theorem is a general principle of neurodynamics with a wide range of applications (Grossberg, 1990). In Section 14.11 we consider another application of this important theorem to the brain-state-in-a-box (BSB) model.

14.10 The Hopfield Model as a Content-Addressable Memory

The Hopfield network has attracted a great deal of attention as a *content-addressable memory* (Hopfield, 1982, 1984a). In this application, we know the fixed points of the network *a priori* in that they correspond to the fundamental memories to be stored. However, the synaptic weights of the network that produce the desired fixed points are unknown, and the problem is how to determine them.

In this section we closely follow the approach taken by Aiyer et al. (1990) to study the relationship between the fixed points of a Hopfield network, its Liapunov function, and the eigenvalues of its weight matrix. By so doing, we develop a deep understanding of dynamic behavior of the Hopfield network as a content-addressable memory. We begin the study by presenting an analysis of the Liapunov function of the discrete Hopfield network in terms of the eigenvalues of the weight matrix of the network and the associated eigenvectors. Then, in light of this material, we take a close look at the content-addressable memory using the discrete Hopfield network.

Eigenanalysis of the Liapunov Function of the Discrete Hopfield Network

Consider the discrete Hopfield network whose Liapunov (energy) function E is given by Eq. (14.39). Using matrix notation, we may rewrite this equation in the compact form

$$E = -\frac{1}{2}\mathbf{x}^T\mathbf{W}\mathbf{x} \tag{14.46}$$

where the N-by-1 state vector $\mathbf{x}$ represents the collective outputs of the N neurons in the network, the superscript T denotes matrix transposition, and $\mathbf{W}$ denotes the N-by-N synaptic weight matrix of the network. In the discrete Hopfield network, the weight matrix is symmetric; that is,

$$\mathbf{W}^T = \mathbf{W}$$

This condition is imposed on the network so as to have a valid Liapunov function. Using the *spectral theorem* of matrix algebra, we may represent the weight matrix $\mathbf{W}$ as follows:

$$\mathbf{W} = \sum_{i=1}^{M} \lambda_i \mathbf{q}_i \mathbf{q}_i^T \tag{14.47}$$

where λ_i is an *eigenvalue* of the matrix $\mathbf{W}$, and $\mathbf{q}_i$ is the associated N-by-1 eigenvector. The eigenvectors are all *orthogonal* to each other, and they are usually *normalized* to have a Euclidean norm of one; that is,

$$\mathbf{q}_j^T \mathbf{q}_i = \begin{cases} 1, & i = j \\ 0, & \text{otherwise} \end{cases} \tag{14.48}$$

Since the weight matrix $\mathbf{W}$ is symmetric, all the eigenvalues are *nonnegative.* However, the eigenvalues may be *degenerate,* which means that there are several eigenvectors associated with the same eigenvalue; in such a case we have a subspace (instead of an eigenvector) associated with the eigenvalue in question. Furthermore, the weight matrix $\mathbf{W}$ may have a degeneracy with a value of zero, in which case the associated eigenvectors constitute a subspace called the *null subspace.* The presence of the null subspace, and therefore $M < N$, is an intrinsic feature of the Hopfield network.

Equation (14.47) represents the eigendecomposition of the weight matrix $\mathbf{W}$. The corresponding eigenrepresentation of the state vector $\mathbf{x}$ is:

$$\mathbf{x} = \sum_{i=1}^{M} \gamma_i \mathbf{q}_i + \mathbf{x}_{\text{null}} \tag{14.49}$$

where $\gamma_i \mathbf{q}_i$ is the component of the vector $\mathbf{x}$ along the direction of the eigenvector $\mathbf{q}_i$, and $\mathbf{x}_{\text{null}}$ is the component of $\mathbf{x}$ that lies in the null subspace. Accordingly, substituting the decompositions of Eqs. (14.47) and (14.49) in (14.46) yields the following expansion for the Liapunov function:

$$E = -\frac{1}{2} \sum_{i=1}^{M} \lambda_i \gamma_i^2 \tag{14.50}$$

where we have used the orthonormal relations of Eq. (14.48) for the nonzero eigenvalues, and the fact that for the null subspace we have

$$\mathbf{x}_{\text{null}}^T \mathbf{q}_i = 0 \qquad \text{for all } i \tag{14.51}$$

Examining the expansion of Eq. (14.50), we can now describe the strategy that the network has to follow in order to minimize the energy function E. Specifically, it has to move the state vector $\mathbf{x}$ in the phase space in such a way that if the eigenvalue λ_i is negative, then γ_i is reduced to zero. If, on the other hand, the eigenvalue λ_i is positive, then γ_i is increased in magnitude. Remember that $\gamma_i \mathbf{q}_i$ defines the component of the state vector $\mathbf{x}$ that lies along the eigenvector $\mathbf{q}_i$ associated with the eigenvalue λ_i, with both $\mathbf{q}_i$ and λ_i referring to the synaptic weight matrix $\mathbf{W}$ (Aiyer et al., 1990).

Learning Rule

In a *content-addressable memory* (CAM), a stored pattern is recalled by presenting the memory with a partial or distorted form of the pattern. Let the number of stored patterns be M, with each pattern consisting of N elements that take the value ± 1. Correspondingly, a discrete Hopfield network designed to function in this fashion consists of N neurons. The weight matrix of the network is determined by a learning algorithm that operates in accordance with the memory vectors to be stored. Any such algorithm should have two desirable features:

1. The memory vectors are fixed points (stable states) of the network.
2. The initial states of the network lie inside the basins of attraction of these fixed points, so that an initial state may be connected to the appropriate memory vector in storage.

Let $\bar{\mathbf{x}}$ be a memory vector and therefore, in light of point 1, also a fixed point. Then, from the definition of a fixed point, we require that for the discrete Hopfield network,

$$\bar{\mathbf{x}} = \operatorname{sgn}(\mathbf{W}\bar{\mathbf{x}}) \tag{14.52}$$

where the signum function sgn(·) operates on each element of the column vector represented by the product $\mathbf{W}\bar{\mathbf{x}}$. According to Eq. (14.49), we may write

$$\bar{\mathbf{x}} = \sum_{i=1}^{M} \bar{\gamma}_i \mathbf{q}_i + \bar{\mathbf{x}}_{\text{null}} \tag{14.53}$$

where $\bar{\gamma}_i \mathbf{q}_i$ is the component of $\bar{\mathbf{x}}$ along the eigenvector $\mathbf{q}_i$, and $\bar{\mathbf{x}}_{\text{null}}$ is the component of $\bar{\mathbf{x}}$ that lies in the null subspace. The combined use of Eqs. (14.47) and (14.53) yields, in light of Eqs. (14.48) and (14.51), the following result:

$$\mathbf{W}\bar{\mathbf{x}} = \sum_{i=1}^{M} \lambda_i \bar{\gamma}_i \mathbf{q}_i \tag{14.54}$$

Thus, substituting Eqs. (14.53) and (14.54) in (14.52) yields

$$\sum_{i=1}^{M} \bar{\gamma}_i \mathbf{q}_i + \bar{\mathbf{x}}_{\text{null}} = \operatorname{sgn}\left(\sum_{i=1}^{M} \lambda_i \bar{\gamma}_i \mathbf{q}_i\right) \tag{14.55}$$

The only way in which Eq. (14.55) can be guaranteed for any set of memory vectors is to impose the following pair of conditions:

$$\bar{\mathbf{x}}_{\text{null}} = \mathbf{0} \tag{14.56}$$

and

$$\lambda_i = \lambda \qquad \text{for } i = 1, 2, \ldots, M \text{ with } \lambda > 0 \tag{14.57}$$

In other words, we may make the following statements (Aiyer et al., 1990):

1. For $\bar{\mathbf{x}}_{\text{null}}$ to equal the null vector **0,** the null space of the synaptic weight matrix **W** must be orthogonal to all the memory vectors.
2. If $\bar{\mathbf{x}}_{\text{null}}$ is zero, then Eq. (14.53) reveals that all the memory vectors are completely specified by the sum

$$\sum_{i=1}^{M} \bar{\gamma}_i \mathbf{q}_i$$

In other words, the eigenvectors of the weight matrix **W** must at least span the subspace spanned by the memory vectors. This is merely a restatement of point 1.

3. For $\lambda_i = \lambda$ for $i = 1, 2, \ldots, M$, the weight matrix $\mathbf{W}$ must have a single positive degenerate eigenvalue corresponding to the subspace spanned by the memory vectors.

The simplest learning rule that can satisfy the conditions of Eqs. (14.56) and (14.57) is the *outer product rule* of storage described in Chapter 8. Let $\boldsymbol{\xi}_1, \boldsymbol{\xi}_2, \ldots, \boldsymbol{\xi}_M$ denote a set of *M fundamental memory vectors* to be stored, with each vector being of length N. Then we may express the weight matrix resulting from the outer product rule as follows:

$$\mathbf{W}_M = \sum_{i=1}^{M} \boldsymbol{\xi}_i \boldsymbol{\xi}_i^T \tag{14.58}$$

where $\boldsymbol{\xi}_i \boldsymbol{\xi}_i^T$ is the outer product of $\boldsymbol{\xi}_i$ with itself; the reason for using the subscript M in the weight matrix $\mathbf{W}_M$ will become apparent later.

The N-by-1 fundamental memory vectors are assumed to have the following characteristics:

1. The elements of each fundamental memory vector take the value ± 1; hence, the inner product of $\boldsymbol{\xi}_i$ with itself is

$$\boldsymbol{\xi}_i^T \boldsymbol{\xi}_i = N \qquad \text{for all } i \tag{14.59}$$

2. The fundamental memory vectors are *linearly independent.*

Let $\mathcal{M}$ denote the subspace spanned by the fundamental memory vectors $\boldsymbol{\xi}_1, \boldsymbol{\xi}_2, \ldots, \boldsymbol{\xi}_M$, and let $\mathcal{N}$ denote the orthogonal complement of $\mathcal{M}$. Then the subspace $\mathcal{N}$ must be the null subspace of the weight matrix $\mathbf{W}_M$. Let $\bar{\boldsymbol{\xi}}$ and $\bar{\mathbf{x}}_{\text{null}}$ denote the components of a fixed point $\bar{\mathbf{x}}$ of the network that lie in the subspaces $\mathcal{M}$ and $\mathcal{N}$, respectively. We may then express $\bar{\mathbf{x}}$ as

$$\bar{\mathbf{x}} = \bar{\boldsymbol{\xi}} + \bar{\mathbf{x}}_{\text{null}} \tag{14.60}$$

Moreover, in view of the assumption that the fundamental memory vectors $\boldsymbol{\xi}_1, \boldsymbol{\xi}_2, \ldots, \boldsymbol{\xi}_M$ form a linearly independent set, we may express the component $\bar{\boldsymbol{\xi}}$ as a linear combination of them as follows:

$$\bar{\boldsymbol{\xi}} = \sum_{\alpha=1}^{M} \bar{\gamma}_\alpha \boldsymbol{\xi}_\alpha \tag{14.61}$$

Hence, using Eqs. (14.58), (14.60), and (14.61), we may express the matrix product $\mathbf{W}_M \bar{\mathbf{x}}$ as

$$\mathbf{W}_M \bar{\mathbf{x}} = \left(\sum_{\alpha=1}^{M} \boldsymbol{\xi}_\alpha \boldsymbol{\xi}_\alpha^T \right) \left(\sum_{\beta=1}^{M} \bar{\gamma}_\beta \boldsymbol{\xi}_\beta + \bar{\mathbf{x}}_{\text{null}} \right) \tag{14.62}$$

We now note the following four points (Aiyer et al., 1990):

1. The subspaces $\mathcal{M}$ and $\mathcal{N}$, where $\boldsymbol{\xi}_\alpha$ and $\bar{\mathbf{x}}_{\text{null}}$ lie, respectively, are complementary to each other by definition; hence, we have

$$\boldsymbol{\xi}_\alpha^T \bar{\mathbf{x}}_{\text{null}} = 0 \qquad \text{for all } \alpha \tag{14.63}$$

2. The inner product $\boldsymbol{\xi}_\alpha^T \boldsymbol{\xi}_\alpha$ equals N by virtue of Eq. (14.59).
3. Using the index β in place of α in the definition given in Eq. (14.61), we have

$$\sum_{\beta=1}^{M} \bar{\gamma}_\beta \boldsymbol{\xi}_\beta = \bar{\boldsymbol{\xi}}$$

4. Finally, we introduce the definition of a *noise vector*

$$\boldsymbol{\xi}_{\text{noise}} = \sum_{\substack{\alpha=1 \\ \alpha \neq \beta}}^{M} \sum_{\beta=1}^{M} \bar{\gamma}_{\beta} \boldsymbol{\xi}_{\alpha} \boldsymbol{\xi}_{\alpha}^{T} \boldsymbol{\xi}_{\beta} \tag{14.64}$$

Then, expanding the right-hand side of Eq. (14.62), and taking account of these four points, we may simplify the expression for the matrix product $\mathbf{W}_M \bar{\mathbf{x}}$ as follows:

$$\mathbf{W}_M \bar{\mathbf{x}} = N\bar{\boldsymbol{\xi}} + \boldsymbol{\xi}_{\text{noise}} \tag{14.65}$$

This equation clearly shows that for the weight matrix $\mathbf{W}_M$ to have a single positive degenerate eigenvalue equal to N, the noise term $\boldsymbol{\xi}_{\text{noise}}$ must be identically zero. The condition $\boldsymbol{\xi}_{\text{noise}} = \mathbf{0}$ can be satisfied only if the fundamental memory vectors to be stored are *orthogonal* to each other; that is,

$$\boldsymbol{\xi}_{\alpha}^{T} \boldsymbol{\xi}_{\beta} = 0 \qquad \text{for } \alpha \neq \beta \tag{14.66}$$

In other words, the simple outer product rule of Eq. (14.58) can only satisfy the condition of Eqs. (14.56) and (14.57) with orthogonal memory vectors. This reconfirms a result we established in Chapter 8.

It has been suggested by many investigators (McEliece et al., 1987; Dembo, 1989) that if the number of neurons, N, is large compared to the number of fundamental memory vectors, M, and if the memory vectors are chosen in a random fashion from a large population, then there is a high probability that the memory vectors will be orthogonal to each other or nearly so. In a situation of this kind, the conditions of Eqs. (14.56) and (14.57) are satisfied in a probabilistic sense.

Content Addressability

For the Hopfield network to operate satisfactorily as a content-addressable memory, it must possess the ability to recover a fundamental memory vector of interest upon the presentation of a *probe* vector $\boldsymbol{\xi}_{\text{probe}}$ that is close to it in Hamming distance; the *Hamming distance* refers to the number of bits in which the two vectors differ from each other. (In Chapter 8 we used the symbol $\mathbf{x}$ to denote a probe vector for the Hopfield network, whereas in this chapter we have used $\mathbf{x}$ to denote the state vector of a dynamical system; to avoid confusion in terminology, the symbol $\boldsymbol{\xi}_{\text{probe}}$ is used in this chapter to denote the probe vector for the Hopfield network.) Typically, the probe vector $\boldsymbol{\xi}_{\text{probe}}$ is a distorted version of a fundamental memory vector, in which case the Hopfield network may be viewed as an *error-correcting device.*

Earlier we used the eigenanalysis of the Liapunov function E given in Eq. (14.50) to show that all components of the state vector $\mathbf{x}$ that lie along eigenvectors associated with negative eigenvalues of the weight matrix $\mathbf{W}$ are reduced to zero by the network dynamics. It was also pointed out earlier that in the case of a weight matrix $\mathbf{W}_M$ formulated in accordance with the outer product rule, the subspace $\mathcal{N}$ (chosen to be complementary to the subspace $\mathcal{M}$ spanned by the set of fundamental memory vectors) must be the null subspace of $\mathbf{W}_M$; hence it corresponds to the zero eigenvalues of $\mathbf{W}_M$. This seems to suggest that if the weight matrix $\mathbf{W}_M$ is modified so as to introduce a negative eigenvalue into the subspace $\mathcal{N}$ then it should be possible for the network to provide a limited type of error correction by removing the component of the probe vector $\boldsymbol{\xi}_{\text{probe}}$ that lies in this subspace. In other words, the use of such a technique should correct for errors that result from the corruption of the probe vector $\boldsymbol{\xi}_{\text{probe}}$ through the addition of a component that lies in the subspace $\mathcal{N}$ (Aiyer et al., 1990).

The simplest way to introduce a negative eigenvalue into the subspace $\mathcal{N}$ is to subtract a multiple of the identify matrix $\mathbf{I}$ from the weight matrix $\mathbf{W}_M$ defined in Eq. (14.58). Specifically, we write

$$\begin{aligned}\mathbf{W} &= \mathbf{W}_M - M\mathbf{I} \\ &= \sum_{i=1}^{M} \boldsymbol{\xi}_i \boldsymbol{\xi}_i^T - M\mathbf{I}\end{aligned} \tag{14.67}$$

This modification has the effect of reducing all the diagonal terms of the new weight matrix $\mathbf{W}$ to zero. The physical implication of the modification is that the Hopfield network has *no* self-loops. Let the state vector $\mathbf{x}$ be expressed as

$$\mathbf{x} = \bar{\boldsymbol{\xi}} + \mathbf{x}_{\text{null}} \tag{14.68}$$

where $\bar{\boldsymbol{\xi}}$ is the projection of $\mathbf{x}$ onto the subspace $\mathcal{M}$, as shown by [see Eq. (14.61)]

$$\bar{\boldsymbol{\xi}} = \sum_{\alpha=1}^{M} \bar{\gamma}_\alpha \boldsymbol{\xi}_\alpha, \tag{14.69}$$

and $\mathbf{x}_{\text{null}}$ is the projection of $\mathbf{x}$ onto the subspace $\mathcal{N}$. Then, using Eqs. (14.67) through (14.69), and following a procedure similar to that described for the development of Eq. (14.65), we find that the Liapunov function for the modified weight matrix $\mathbf{W}$ is

$$\begin{aligned}E &= -\frac{1}{2}\mathbf{x}^T\mathbf{W}\mathbf{x} \\ &= -\frac{1}{2}(N - M)\|\bar{\boldsymbol{\xi}}\|^2 - \frac{1}{2}\,\bar{\boldsymbol{\xi}}^T\boldsymbol{\xi}_{\text{noise}} + \frac{1}{2}\,M\|\mathbf{x}_{\text{null}}\|^2\end{aligned} \tag{14.70}$$

where $\|\bar{\boldsymbol{\xi}}\|$ and $\|\mathbf{x}_{\text{null}}\|$ are the Euclidean norms of the vectors $\bar{\boldsymbol{\xi}}$ and $\mathbf{x}_{\text{null}}$, respectively. An error-correction capability requires that, at least, a fundamental memory vector be corrected to itself; hence the fundamental memory vectors must represent fixed points (stable states) of the network. As mentioned previously, this requirement can be satisfied by choosing an orthogonal set for the fundamental memory vectors. The effect of this choice is to reduce the noise term $\boldsymbol{\xi}_{\text{noise}}$ to zero and therefore simplify Eq. (14.70) to

$$E = -\frac{1}{2}(N - M)\|\bar{\boldsymbol{\xi}}\|^2 + \frac{1}{2}\,M\|\mathbf{x}_{\text{null}}\|^2 \tag{14.71}$$

This equation shows that the energy function E is minimized if $\|\bar{\boldsymbol{\xi}}\| \to \infty$ and $\|\mathbf{x}_{\text{null}}\| = 0$. In reality, however, the tendency to drive $\|\bar{\boldsymbol{\xi}}\|$ to infinity is counteracted by the hard-limiting actions at the individual neuron outputs, with the constraint that the energy function E is minimized at the corners of the unit hypercube. Hence the network finally stabilizes itself at one of the corners of the hypercube. The discrete Hopfield network may thus be viewed as a *vector projector* in the sense that it projects a probe vector $\boldsymbol{\xi}_{\text{probe}}$ onto the subspace $\mathcal{M}$ (spanned by the fundamental memory vectors), and then drives the resulting projected vector in a step-by-step fashion to the nearest corner of the hypercube (Aiyer et al., 1990).

Spurious Stable States

Given the interpretation of the Hopfield network as a vector projector, it is now a straightforward matter for us to explain how *spurious stable states* may arise. We first note that the fundamental memory vectors, spanning the subspace $\mathcal{M}$, constitute a set of fixed points (stable states) represented by certain corners of the unit hypercube. The other corners of the hypercube that lie in or near the subspace $\mathcal{M}$ are potential locations for spurious stable states. Specifically, the following statements are in order (Aiyer et al., 1990):

1. When a hypercube corner (representing the fixed state $\overline{\mathbf{x}}$) lies in the subspace $\mathcal{M}$, and the projection of that corner onto the null subspace $\mathcal{N}$ has a small Euclidean norm compared to its projection onto the subspace $\mathcal{M}$, that is,

$$\|\overline{\mathbf{x}}_{\text{null}}\| \ll \|\overline{\boldsymbol{\xi}}\|$$

   we then have

$$\text{sgn}\,(\mathbf{W}\overline{\mathbf{x}}) = \text{sgn}(\overline{\boldsymbol{\xi}})$$

   and the stability of that corner as a spurious state is assured.

2. When a hypercube corner, although not exactly in the subspace $\mathcal{M}$, is close enough to it for the signs of the elements of its projection $\overline{\boldsymbol{\xi}}$ onto $\mathcal{M}$ to remain unchanged, then

$$\text{sgn}(\overline{\mathbf{x}}) = \text{sgn}(\overline{\boldsymbol{\xi}})$$

   and the stability of that corner as a spurious state is assured.

Condition 1 is more strict than condition 2. Typically, we therefore find that the number of points satisfying condition 1 is small, whereas the number of points satisfying condition 2 increases rapidly (exponentially) with the number M of fundamental memory vectors (i.e., as the dimensionality of subspace $\mathcal{M}$ is increased). Moreover, the relative number of spurious stable states decreases as the dimensionality N of the memory vectors (i.e., the number of neurons) increases with respect to the number M of memory vectors to be stored (Aiyer et al., 1990).

In conclusion, there is an inherent trade-off between two conflicting requirements: (1) the need to preserve the fundamental memory vectors as fixed points in the phase space, and (2) the desire to have few spurious states. The need for stable memory vectors requires that the weight matrix $\mathbf{W}$ of the network has a single positive degenerate eigenvalue corresponding to the subspace $\mathcal{M}$ spanned by the memory vectors themselves. This requirement, in turn, causes all the other corners of the hypercube that lie in or close to the subspace $\mathcal{M}$ to act as spurious states. The Hopfield network can act as a content-addressable memory only if the number of spurious states is small enough for this operation to be indistinguishable from the operation of the network as a true vector projector (Aiyer et al., 1990).

Nonmonotonic Activation Function

There are two major flaws in the Hopfield model as a content-addressable memory:

- The network is handicapped by the unavoidable presence of *spurious states,* the number of which increases rapidly with the number of fundamental memories stored in the network; this follows from the discussion just presented.
- The *storage capacity* of the network, that is, the number of fundamental memories that can be stored in the network and then retrieved correctly with, say, 99 percent probability is only $N/(2 \ln N)$; this result was derived in Section 8.6.

Various proposals have been made in the literature for overcoming these limitations. Perhaps the most significant improvement suggested to date is that due to Morita (1993).

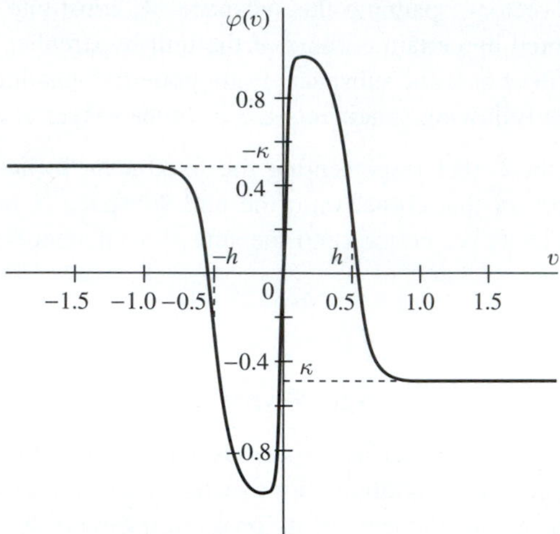

FIGURE 14.14 Nonmonotonic activation function of a neuron.

The modification introduced by Morita applies to the continuous (analog) form of the Hopfield model.[5] The modification is confined to the activation function $\varphi(\cdot)$ of a neuron, thereby retaining the simplicity of the network as an associative memory. Specifically, the usual hard-limiting or sigmoidal activation of each neuron in the network is replaced by a *nonmonotonic function,* a form of which is depicted in Fig. 14.14. In mathematical terms, the nonmonotonic activation function of Fig. 14.14 is defined as the product of two factors, as shown by (Morita, 1993)

$$\varphi(v) = \left(\frac{1 - \exp(-gv)}{1 + \exp(-gv)}\right)\left(\frac{1 + \kappa \exp(g_0(|v| - h))}{1 + \exp(g_0(|v| - h))}\right) \tag{14.72}$$

where v is the activation potential. The first factor on the right-hand side of Eq. (14.72) is the usual sigmoid function (hyperpolic tangent) used in the continuous version of the Hopfield network; the parameter g is the gain of this factor at the origin. The second factor is responsible for making the activation function $\varphi(v)$ nonmonotonic. Two of the parameters characterizing this second factor, namely, g_0 and h, are positive constants; the remaining parameter κ is usually negative. In the experiments performed by Morita (1993), the following parameter values were used:

$$g = 50; \qquad g_0 = 15$$
$$h = 0.5; \qquad \kappa = -1$$

According to Morita, the exact form of the activation function and the parameters used to describe it are not very critical; the most essential point to keep in mind is the nonmonotonic property of the activation function.

As with the continuous Hopfield model, the recalling dynamics of the *Morita model* is governed by the system of coupled first-order differential equations (14.18), reproduced here in matrix form as

$$\frac{d}{dt}\mathbf{v}(t) = -\mathbf{v}(t) + \mathbf{W}\varphi(\mathbf{v}) \tag{14.73}$$

[5] Atiya and Abu-Mostafa (1993) describe another modification of the continuous Hopfield model, which involves the addition of hidden neurons. In the case of a two-layer network, it is shown that the network is guaranteed to store any number of analog vectors that does not exceed one plus the number of neurons in the hidden layer.

where it is assumed that the bias applied to each neuron is zero. The vector $\mathbf{v}(t)$ is an N-by-1 vector representing the activation potentials of the neurons, and $\varphi(\mathbf{v})$ is a nonmonotonic function (shown in Fig. 14.14) that operates on each element of the input vector $\mathbf{v}(t)$. The matrix $\mathbf{W}$ is an N-by-N weight matrix defined in terms of the fundamental memories $\boldsymbol{\xi}_1, \boldsymbol{\xi}_2, \ldots, \boldsymbol{\xi}_M$ by Eq. (14.67). The recalling process proceeds as follows. For a probe vector $\boldsymbol{\xi}_{\text{probe}}$, Eq. (14.73) is evaluated with $\boldsymbol{\xi}_{\text{probe}}$ serving as the initial condition. Assuming that the solution converges to an equilibrium state $\bar{\mathbf{v}}$, the recalled pattern is determined, not by $\varphi(\bar{\mathbf{v}})$, but by the signum of $\bar{\mathbf{v}}$, as shown by Morita (1993) and Yoshizawa et al. (1993):

$$\bar{\mathbf{x}} = \text{sgn}(\bar{\mathbf{v}})$$

If, however, the solution does not converge, it is presumed that the retrieval process has failed and therefore a recalled pattern cannot be determined.

The Morita model of a content-addressable memory exhibits two remarkable properties (Yoshizawa et al., 1993):

1. For a network made up of N neurons, the storage capacity of the Morita model is about $0.4N$, which (for large N) is much greater than the corresponding value $N/(2 \ln N)$ of the conventional Hopfield model.
2. The Morita model exhibits *no* spurious states; instead, when it fails to recall a correct memorized pattern, the state of the network is driven into a chaotic behavior.

Yoshizawa et al. (1993) present a theoretical analysis of the Morita model, using a piecewise-linear approximation of the nonmonotonic activation function shown in Fig. 14.14; they also present computer simulations to support the theory.

14.11 Brain-State-in-a-Box Model

In this section we continue the neurodynamical analysis of an associative memory by studying the *brain-state-in-a-box (BSB) model,* which was first described by Anderson et al. (1977). Basically, the BSB model is a *positive feedback system with amplitude limitation.* It consists of a highly interconnected set of neurons that feed back upon themselves. The model operates by using the built-in positive feedback to *amplify* an input pattern, until all the neurons in the model are driven into saturation. The BSB model may thus be viewed as a *categorization* device in that an analog input pattern is given a digital representation defined by a stable state of the model.

Let $\mathbf{W}$ denote a *symmetric weight matrix* whose largest eigenvalues have positive real components. Let $\mathbf{x}(0)$ denote the *initial state vector* of the model, representing an input activation pattern. Assuming that there are N neurons in the model, the state vector of the model has dimension N, and the weight matrix $\mathbf{W}$ is an N-by-N matrix. The BSB algorithm is then completely defined by the following pair of equations:

$$\mathbf{y}(n) = \mathbf{x}(n) + \beta\mathbf{W}\mathbf{x}(n) \tag{14.74}$$

$$\mathbf{x}(n+1) = \varphi(\mathbf{y}(n)) \tag{14.75}$$

where β is a small positive constant called the *feedback factor* and $\mathbf{x}(n)$ is the state vector of the model at discrete time n. Figure 14.15a shows a block diagram of the combination of Eqs. (14.74) and (14.75); the block labeled $\mathbf{W}$ represents a single-layer linear neural network, as depicted in Fig. 14.15b. The activation function φ is a *piecewise-linear function* that operates on $y_j(n)$, the jth component of the vector $\mathbf{y}(n)$, as follows (see

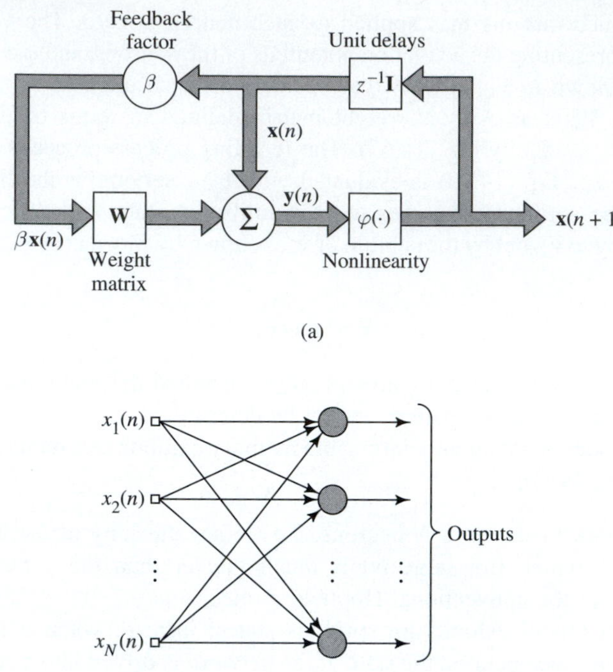

FIGURE 14.15 (a) Block diagram of the brain-state-in-a-box (BSB) model. (b) Signal-flow graph of the linear associator represented by the weight matrix **W**.

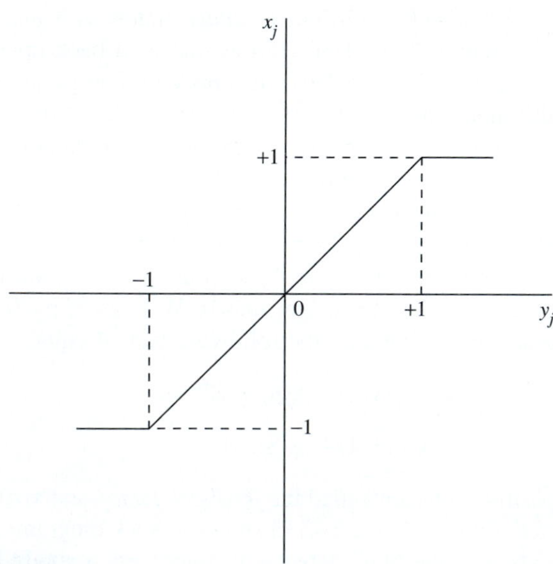

FIGURE 14.16 Piecewise-linear activation function.

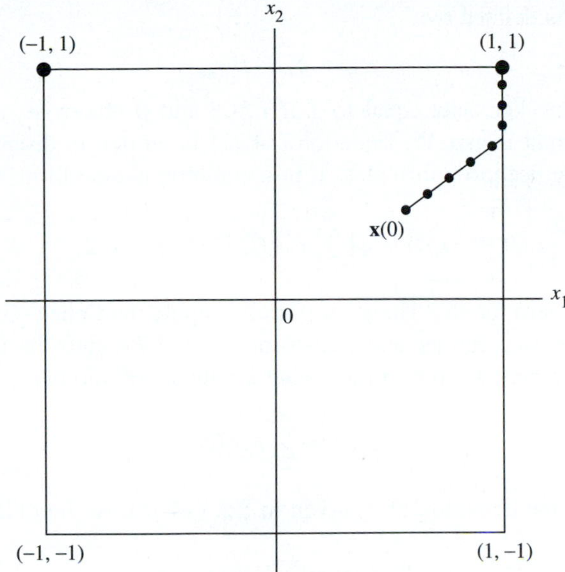

FIGURE 14.17 A possible trajectory of a BSB model using two neurons.

Fig. 14.16):

$$x_j(n+1) = \varphi(y_j(n))$$
$$= \begin{cases} +1 & \text{if } y_j(n) > +1 \\ y_j(n) & \text{if } -1 \leq y_j(n) \leq +1 \\ -1 & \text{if } y_j(n) < -1 \end{cases} \tag{14.76}$$

Equation (14.76) constrains the state vector of the BSB model to lie within an *N-dimensional unit cube centered* on the origin—hence the name of the model.

The algorithm thus proceeds as follows. An activation pattern $\mathbf{x}(0)$ is input into the BSB model as the initial state vector, and Eq. (14.74) is used to compute the vector $\mathbf{y}(0)$. Equation (14.75) is then used to truncate $\mathbf{y}(0)$, obtaining the updated state vector $\mathbf{x}(1)$. Next, $\mathbf{x}(1)$ is cycled through Eqs. (14.74) and (14.75), thereby obtaining $\mathbf{x}(2)$. This procedure is repeated until the BSB model reaches a *stable state* represented by a particular corner of the unit hypercube. Intuitively, positive feedback in the BSB model causes the initial state vector $\mathbf{x}(0)$ to increase in Euclidean length (norm) with an increasing number of iterations until it hits a wall of the box (unit hypercube), then sliding along the wall and eventually ending up in a stable corner of the box, where it keeps on "pushing" but cannot get out of the box (Kawamoto and Anderson, 1985). This dynamic behavior is illustrated in Fig. 14.17 for the simple case of $N = 2$ (Anderson, 1994).

Liapunov Function of the BSB Model

The BSB may be redefined as a special case of the neurodynamical model described in Eq. (14.16) as follows (Grossberg, 1990). To see this, we first rewrite the jth component of the BSB algorithm described by Eqs. (14.74) and (14.75) in the form

$$x_j(n+1) = \varphi\left(\sum_{i=1}^{N} c_{ji}x_i(n)\right), \qquad j = 1, 2, \ldots, N \tag{14.77}$$

The coefficient c_{ji} is defined by

$$c_{ji} = \delta_{ji} + \beta w_{ji} \tag{14.78}$$

where δ_{ji} is a Kronecker delta equal to 1 if $j = i$ and 0 otherwise, and w_{ji} is the jith element of the weight matrix $\mathbf{W}$. Equation (14.77) is written in discrete-time form. To proceed further, we need to reformulate it in a continuous-time form, as shown by

$$\frac{d}{dt}x_j(t) = -x_j(t) + \varphi\left(\sum_{i=1}^{N} c_{ji}x_i(t)\right), \qquad j = 1, 2, \ldots, N \tag{14.79}$$

where the bias I_j is zero for all j. However, for us to apply the Cohen–Grossberg theorem, we have to go one step further and transform Eq. (14.79) into the same form as the additive model. We may do so by introducing a new set of variables,

$$v_j(t) = \sum_{i=1}^{N} c_{ji}x_i(t) \tag{14.80}$$

Then, by virtue of the definition of c_{ji} given in Eq. (14.78), we find that

$$x_j(t) = \sum_{i=1}^{N} c_{ji}v_i(t) \tag{14.81}$$

Correspondingly, we may recast the model of Eq. (14.79) in the equivalent form

$$\frac{d}{dt}v_j(t) = -v_j(t) + \sum_{i=1}^{N} c_{ji}\varphi(v_i(t)), \qquad j = 1, 2, \ldots, N \tag{14.82}$$

We are now ready to apply the Cohen–Grossberg theorem to the BSB model. Comparing Eq. (14.82) with (14.40), we may deduce the correspondences listed in Table 14.3 between the BSB model and the Cohen–Grossberg theorem. Therefore, using the results of Table 14.3 in Eq. (14.41), we find that the Liapunov function of the BSB model is given by

$$E = -\frac{1}{2}\sum_{j=1}^{N}\sum_{i=1}^{N} c_{ji}\varphi(v_j)\varphi(v_i) + \sum_{j=1}^{N}\int_0^{v_j} v\varphi'(v)\,dv \tag{14.83}$$

where $\varphi'(v)$ is the first derivative of the sigmoid function $\varphi(v)$ with respect to its argument. Finally, substituting the definitions of Eqs. (14.76), (14.78), and (14.80) in (14.73), we can define the Liapunov (energy) function of the BSB model in terms of the original state variables as follows (Grossberg, 1990):

$$\begin{aligned} E &= -\frac{\beta}{2}\sum_{i=1}^{N}\sum_{j=1}^{N} w_{ji}x_jx_i \\ &= -\frac{\beta}{2}\mathbf{x}^T\mathbf{W}\mathbf{x} \end{aligned} \tag{14.84}$$

Table 14.3 Correspondence Between the Cohen–Grossberg Theorem and the BSB Model

Cohen–Grossberg Theorem	BSB Model
u_j	v_j
$a_j(u_j)$	1
$b_j(u_j)$	$-v_j$
c_{ji}	$-c_{ji}$
$\varphi_j(u_j)$	$\varphi_j(v_j)$

The evaluation of the Liapunov function for the Hopfield network presented in Section 14.8 assumed the existence of the derivative of the inverse of the model's sigmoidal nonlinearity, which is satisfied by the use of a hyperbolic tangent function. In contrast, this condition is not satisfied in the BSB model when the state variable of the jth neuron in the model is either $+1$ or -1. Despite this difficulty, the Liapunov function of the BSB model can be evaluated via the Cohen–Grossberg theorem, which clearly illustrates the general applicability of this important theorem.

Dynamics of the BSB Model

In a direct analysis carried out by Golden (1986), it is demonstrated that the BSB model is in fact a gradient descent algorithm that minimizes the energy function E defined by Eq. (14.84). This important property of the BSB model, however, presumes that the weight matrix $\mathbf{W}$ satisfies the following two conditions:

- The weight matrix $\mathbf{W}$ is *symmetric:*

$$\mathbf{W} = \mathbf{W}^T$$

- The weight matrix $\mathbf{W}$ is *positive semidefinite*; that is, in terms of the eigenvalues of $\mathbf{W}$,

$$\lambda_{\min} \geq 0$$

  where $\lambda_{\min}$ is the smallest eigenvalue of $\mathbf{W}$.

The energy function E of the BSB model thus decreases with increasing n (number of iterations) whenever the state vector $\mathbf{x}(n + 1)$ at time $n + 1$ is different from the state vector $\mathbf{x}(n)$ at time n. Moreover, the minimum points of the energy function E define the *equilibrium states* of the BSB model that are characterized by

$$\mathbf{x}(n + 1) = \mathbf{x}(n)$$

In other words, like the Hopfield model, the BSB model is an *energy-minimizing network.*

The equilibrium states of the BSB model are defined by certain corners of the unit hypercube and its origin. In the latter case, any fluctuation in the state vector, no matter how small, is amplified by positive feedback in the model, and therefore causes the state of the model to shift away from the origin in the direction of a stable configuration; in other words, the origin is a saddle point. For every corner of the hypercube to represent an equilibrium state of the BSB model, the weight matrix $\mathbf{W}$ has to satisfy a third condition (Greenberg, 1988):

- The weight matrix $\mathbf{W}$ is *diagonal dominant*, which means that

$$w_{jj} \geq \sum_{i \neq j} |w_{ij}| \qquad \text{for } j = 1, 2, \ldots, N \tag{14.85}$$

  where w_{ij} is the ijth element of $\mathbf{W}$.

For an equilibrium state $\mathbf{x}$ to be *stable*—that is, for a certain corner of the unit hypercube to be a point *attractor*—there has to be a basin of attraction $\mathcal{N}(\mathbf{x})$ in the unit hypercube such that for all initial state vectors $\mathbf{x}(0)$ in $\mathcal{N}(\mathbf{x})$ the BSB model converges onto $\mathbf{x}$. For every corner of the unit hypercube to be a point attractor, the weight matrix $\mathbf{W}$ has to satisfy a fourth condition (Greenberg, 1988):

- The weight matrix **W** is *strongly diagonal-dominant*, as shown by

$$w_{jj} \geq \sum_{i \neq j} |w_{ij}| + \alpha \qquad \text{for } j = 1, 2, \ldots, N \tag{14.86}$$

where α is a positive constant.

The important point to note from this discussion is that in the case of a BSB model for which the weight matrix **W** is symmetric and positive semidefinite, as is often the case, only some (but not all) of the corners of the unit hypercube act as point attractors. For all the corners of the unit hypercube to act as point attractors, the weight matrix **W** has to satisfy Eq. (14.86) as well, which of course subsumes the condition of Eq. (14.85).

Clustering

A natural application for the BSB model is *clustering*. This follows from the fact that the stable corners of the unit hypercube act as point attractors with well-behaved basins of attraction, which therefore divide the state space into a corresponding set of well-defined regions. Consequently, the BSB model may be used as an *unsupervised* clustering algorithm, with each stable corner of the unit hypercube representing a ''cluster'' of related data. The self-amplification provided by positive feedback (in conformity with Principle 1 of self-organization described in Chapter 9) is an important ingredient of this clustering property.

Anderson et al. (1990) describe the use of the BSB model to cluster and therefore identify radar signals from different emitters. In this application the weight matrix **W**, basic to the operation of the BSB model, is *learned* using the *linear associator (associative memory) with error-correction learning* that was described in Chapter 3. To be specific, suppose that information is represented by a set of K training vectors that are associated with themselves as follows:

$$\mathbf{x}_k \rightarrow \mathbf{x}_k, \qquad k = 1, 2, \ldots, K \tag{14.87}$$

Let a training vector $\mathbf{x}_k$ be selected at random. Then the weight matrix **W** is incremented in accordance with the error-correction algorithm [see Eq. (3.41)]

$$\Delta\mathbf{W} = \eta(\mathbf{x}_k - \mathbf{W}\mathbf{x}_k)\mathbf{x}_k \tag{14.88}$$

where η is the learning-rate parameter. According to this formula, the input vector $\mathbf{x}_k$ acts as its own ''teacher'' in that the linear associator will try to reconstruct that particular input vector. The goal of learning the set of stimuli $\mathbf{x}_1, \mathbf{x}_2, \ldots, \mathbf{x}_K$ is to have the linear associator behave as

$$\mathbf{W}\mathbf{x}_k = \mathbf{x}_k, \qquad k = 1, 2, \ldots, K \tag{14.89}$$

The error-correction algorithm described by Eq. (14.88) approximates the ideal condition of Eq. (14.89) in a least-mean-square sense. The net effect of this learning process is to force the linear associator to develop a particular set of eigenvectors (defined by the training vectors), with eigenvalues equal to unity.

To perform the radar clustering, the BSB model takes the linear associator with error-correction learning to construct the weight matrix **W**, and performs the following computation (Anderson et al., 1990):

$$\mathbf{x}(n + 1) = \varphi(\gamma\mathbf{x}(n) + \beta\mathbf{W}\mathbf{x}(n) + \delta\mathbf{x}(0)) \tag{14.90}$$

which is slightly different from the version of the BSB algorithm described in Eqs. (14.74) and (14.75). The difference is in two respects:

- The decay constant γ in the first term $\gamma\mathbf{x}(n)$ is included to cause the current state to decay slightly; provided that γ is a positive constant less than unity, the errors may eventually decay to zero.
- The third term $\delta\mathbf{x}(0)$ is included to keep the initial state vector $\mathbf{x}(0)$ constantly present; it has the effect of limiting the possible states of the BSB model.

Repeated iteration of the BSB model leads to an activity dominated by the eigenvectors of the weight matrix $\mathbf{W}$ with the largest positive eigenvalues, and therefore the vectors $\mathbf{x}_1, \mathbf{x}_2, \ldots, \mathbf{x}_K$ learned by the linear associator. The clustering ability of the BSB model develops largely as a result of signal-related eigenvectors being associated with large eigenvalues, becoming enhanced by positive feedback in the model, and thereby dominating the state of the model after a number of iterations. On the other hand, noise-related eigenvectors are usually associated with small eigenvalues, and therefore have a diminishing influence on the state of the BSB model, provided that the received signal-to-noise ratio is sufficiently high.

In a radar surveillance environment, detailed descriptions of emitters operating in the environment are not known *a priori*. Typically, hundreds of thousands of radar pulses are received for processing in fractions of seconds. Hence there is no lack of data; the challenge is how to make sense of the data. The BSB model is able to help by learning the microwave structure of the radar environment through its inherent clustering property. Clusters are formed around the point attractors of the BSB model (i.e., stable corners of the unit hypercube), with each point attractor representing a particular emitter. The BSB model may thus identify received pulses as being produced by a particular emitter.

14.12 Recurrent Back-Propagation

For our last neurodynamical model, we consider a neural network consisting of the interconnection of N continuous-valued neurons, continuous in both time and amplitude, and with the synaptic weight from neuron i to neuron j denoted by w_{ji}. All the neurons are assumed to have the same nonlinear activation function $\varphi(v)$, where v is the activation potential. (In some applications, however, different forms of nonlinearity may be used for various populations of neurons.) Unlike the standard back-propagation algorithm studied in Chapter 6, the network being considered here is permitted to have *feedback* connections among the neurons; that is, the network is recurrent.

Three subsets of neurons are identified in the recurrent network:

1. *Input neurons,* so called because they receive their stimuli directly from the externally applied pattern.
2. *Output neurons,* so called because they supply the overall response learned by the network.
3. *Hidden neurons,* which are neither input nor output neurons.

Note that a neuron can be simultaneously an input and output neuron; such neurons are said to be *autoassociative.*

Figure 14.18a illustrates the structure of the network described. In this example, neurons 1 and 2 act as input neurons, and neurons 4 and 5 act as output neurons. Neuron 3 is the only hidden neuron of the network. Note that in Fig. 14.18a output neuron 5 also receives an input; it is therefore an autoassociative unit.

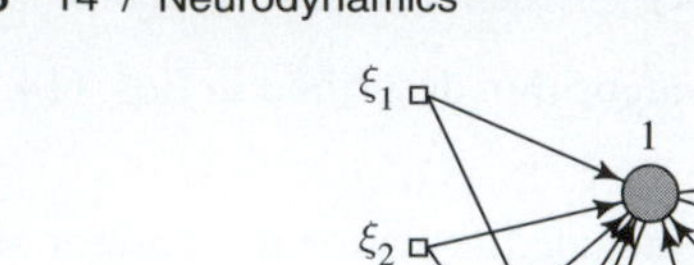
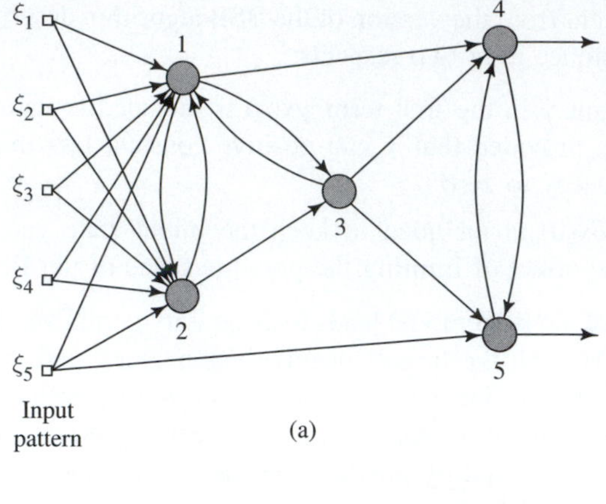

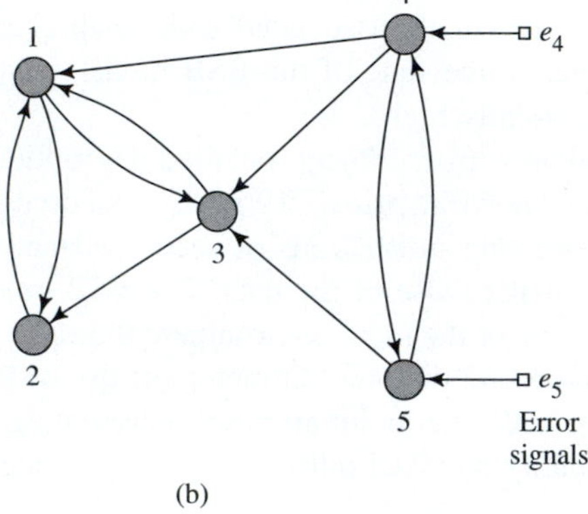

FIGURE 14.18 (a) Architectural graph of a recurrent network. (b) Architectural graph of the adjoint network.

The external environment exerts its influence on the network through the bias terms of the input neurons. If neuron j is an input neuron, the threshold term $I_j = \xi_j$, where ξ_j is an element of the input pattern applied to the network. Otherwise, we have $I_j = 0$. The input relation is thus expressed in the form

$$I_j = \begin{cases} \xi_j & \text{for input neuron } j \\ 0 & \text{otherwise} \end{cases} \tag{14.91}$$

The network provides its response through the steady-state values of the output signals produced by the output neurons. Suppose that the network has converged to a fixed point. Then, if neuron j is an output neuron, the resulting response equals the steady-state value $x_j(\infty)$ of the output signal of that neuron. The *actual* response $x_j(\infty)$ is compared to a *desired* response d_j, resulting in an *error signal* e_j. We may thus write

$$e_j = \begin{cases} d_j - x_j(\infty) & \text{for output neuron } j \\ 0 & \text{otherwise} \end{cases} \tag{14.92}$$

It is assumed that the input pattern $\{\xi_j\}$ and the desired pattern $\{d_j\}$ presented to the network are both time-invariant. Equation (14.91) is applicable if neuron j is an input neuron, and Eq. (14.92) is applicable if neuron j is an output neuron. In both cases, we speak of the neuron being *clamped.* On the other hand, if neuron j is a hidden neuron, we have

$$I_j = e_j = 0 \qquad \text{for hidden neuron } j \tag{14.93}$$

in which case we speak of neuron j being *unclamped* or *free running.*

The goal is to find a local algorithm that adjusts the synaptic weights of the network in such a way that, for a final state vector $\mathbf{x}(\infty)$ and a given input pattern $\{\xi_j\}$, it ultimately results in a point *attractor* whose components have a *desired* set of values $\{d_j\}$. This goal is accomplished by minimizing a cost function $\mathscr{E}$ that provides a measure of the Euclidean distance between the desired position of the attractor and the actual position of the attractor in the phase space of the network. The cost function $\mathscr{E}$ is defined by the sum of squared errors:

$$\mathscr{E} = \frac{1}{2}\sum_k e_k^2 \tag{14.94}$$

where the error signal e_k is itself defined by Eq. (14.92), and the factor $\frac{1}{2}$ has been introduced for convenience of presentation.

The cost function $\mathscr{E}$ depends on the synaptic weights of the network through the fixed points of the network. A dynamic way of minimizing the cost function $\mathscr{E}$ is to permit the network to evolve in the weight space along a *learning trajectory* that descends against the gradient vector of $\mathscr{E}$. Specifically, the change applied to a synaptic weight w_{rs} in accordance with the method of steepest descent, is

$$\Delta w_{rs} = -\eta \frac{\partial \mathscr{E}}{\partial w_{rs}} \tag{14.95}$$

where η is the *learning-rate parameter* that defines the time scale over which the synaptic weights of the network change. The learning-rate parameter η must be small enough to make these changes take place slowly or *adiabatically* with respect to the equations of motion (i.e., state equations). Otherwise, the cost function $\mathscr{E}$ is not a function of the point attractor.

Equation (14.95) defines the evolution of the network in the *weight space,* whose coordinates are defined by the synaptic weights of the network. Alongside this evolution, the network also evolves in the *phase space* that, for the network under consideration, is defined by the neurodynamical equation (14.18) or the related equation (14.19). The former equation is reproduced here for convenience of presentation:

$$\frac{dv_j(t)}{dt} = -v_j(t) + \sum_i w_{ji}x_i(t) + I_j, \qquad j = 1, 2, \ldots, N \tag{14.96}$$

where $x_i = \varphi(v_i)$. The elements of the state vector $\mathbf{x}$ constitute the coordinates of the phase space.

The right-hand side of Eq. (14.95) involves the partial derivative $\partial\mathscr{E}/\partial w_{rs}$. From Eqs. (14.92) and (14.94), we note that

$$\frac{\partial \mathscr{E}}{\partial w_{rs}} = -\sum_k e_k \frac{\partial x_k(\infty)}{\partial w_{rs}} \tag{14.97}$$

The use of Eq. (14.97) in (14.95) thus yields

$$\Delta w_{rs} = \eta \sum_k e_k \frac{\partial x_k(\infty)}{\partial w_{rs}} \tag{14.98}$$

To find the partial derivative $\partial x_k(\infty)/\partial w_{rs}$, we proceed as follows (Pineda, 1988a, b):

1. With the state vector $\mathbf{x}(\infty)$ representing a fixed point of the recurrent network, the jth element of $\mathbf{x}(\infty)$ is defined by

$$x_j(\infty) = \varphi(v_j(\infty)) \tag{14.99}$$

where $v_j(\infty)$ is the activation potential of neuron j at time $t = \infty$. From Eq. (14.96), we have

$$v_j(\infty) = \sum_i w_{ji}x_i(\infty) + I_j \tag{14.100}$$

2. The partial derivative $\partial x_j(\infty)/\partial w_{rs}$ is expressed, using the chain rule, as follows:

$$\frac{\partial x_j(\infty)}{\partial w_{rs}} = \frac{\partial x_j(\infty)}{\partial v_j(\infty)} \frac{\partial v_j(\infty)}{\partial w_{rs}} \tag{14.101}$$

3. From Eq. (14.99) we have

$$\frac{\partial x_j(\infty)}{\partial v_j(\infty)} = \varphi'(v_j(\infty)) \tag{14.102}$$

where $\varphi'(\cdot)$ is the derivative of the nonlinear activation function $\varphi(\cdot)$ with respect to its argument.

4. From Eq. (14.100), we have

$$\frac{\partial v_j(\infty)}{\partial w_{rs}} = \sum_i \left(\frac{\partial w_{ji}}{\partial w_{rs}} x_i(\infty) + w_{ji} \frac{\partial x_i(\infty)}{\partial w_{rs}} \right) \tag{14.103}$$

Since the synaptic weights of the network are independent of each other, it follows that the partial derivative $\partial w_{ji}/\partial w_{rs}$ equals 1 if and only if $j = r$ and $i = s$, and 0 otherwise; that is,

$$\frac{\partial w_{ji}}{\partial w_{rs}} = \delta_{jr}\delta_{is} \tag{14.104}$$

where δ_{jr} is a Kronecker delta, and likewise for δ_{is}. Substituting Eq. (14.104) in (14.103), and performing the summation over i, we get

$$\frac{\partial v_j(\infty)}{\partial w_{rs}} = \delta_{jr}x_s(\infty) + \sum_i w_{ji} \frac{\partial x_i(\infty)}{\partial w_{rs}} \tag{14.105}$$

5. The partial derivative $\partial x_j(\infty)/\partial w_{rs}$ is expressed in the equivalent form

$$\frac{\partial x_j(\infty)}{\partial w_{rs}} = \sum_i \delta_{ji} \frac{\partial x_i(\infty)}{\partial w_{rs}} \tag{14.106}$$

where δ_{ji} is a Kronecker delta.

6. Using Eq. (14.106) for the left-hand side of (14.101), and substituting Eqs. (14.102) and (14.105) in the right-hand side of (14.101), we get

$$\sum_i \delta_{ji} \frac{\partial x_i(\infty)}{\partial w_{rs}} = \varphi'(v_j(\infty)) \left[\delta_{jr}x_s(\infty) + \sum_i w_{ji} \frac{\partial x_i(\infty)}{\partial w_{rs}} \right] \tag{14.107}$$

Next, collecting all the partial derivatives in Eq. (14.107) together, we obtain

$$\sum_i L_{ji} \frac{\partial x_i(\infty)}{\partial w_{rs}} = \delta_{jr}\varphi'(v_j(\infty))x_s(\infty) \tag{14.108}$$

where L_{ji} is defined by

$$L_{ji} = \delta_{ji} - \varphi'(v_j(\infty))w_{ji} \qquad (14.109)$$

7. Equation (14.108) is defined for $j = 1, 2, \ldots, N$. Hence, rewriting this system of linear equations in matrix form, we have

$$\mathbf{L}\frac{\partial \mathbf{x}(\infty)}{\partial w_{rs}} = \begin{bmatrix} \delta_{1r}\varphi'(v_1(\infty)) \\ \delta_{2r}\varphi'(v_2(\infty)) \\ \vdots \\ \delta_{Nr}\varphi'(v_N(\infty)) \end{bmatrix} x_s(\infty) \qquad (14.110)$$

where $\mathbf{L}$ is an N-by-N matrix whose jith element is defined in Eq. (14.109). Finally, multiplying both sides of Eq. (14.110) by the inverse matrix $\mathbf{L}^{-1}$, and retaining the kth line of the resulting system of equations, we get

$$\frac{\partial x_k(\infty)}{\partial w_{rs}} = (\mathbf{L}^{-1})_{kr}\varphi'(v_r(\infty))x_s(\infty) \qquad (14.111)$$

where $(\mathbf{L}^{-1})_{kr}$ is the krth element of the inverse matrix $\mathbf{L}^{-1}$.

Equation (14.111) is the desired result.

We may now proceed with the evaluation of the change Δw_{rs} by substituting Eq. (14.111) in (14.98); the result is given in the remarkably simple form of the *delta rule* as follows:

$$\Delta w_{rs} = \eta\delta_r(\infty)x_s(\infty) \qquad (14.112)$$

where $\delta_r(\infty)$ is the *local gradient* defined by

$$\delta_r(\infty) = \varphi'(v_r(\infty))\sum_k e_k(\mathbf{L}^{-1})_{kr} \qquad (14.113)$$

The reader should be careful *not* to confuse $\delta_r(\infty)$ with the symbol for a Kronecker delta. Equations (14.112) and (14.113) formally specify a new learning rule for modifying the synaptic weights of the network. Unfortunately, however, Eq. (14.113) requires inversion of the matrix $\mathbf{L}$ in order to calculate $\delta_r(\infty)$. Recognizing that direct matrix inversion necessarily involves global computations, the learning algorithm in its present form is unsuitable for use on a neural network.

We may overcome this limitation by developing a "local" method for computing $\delta_r(\infty)$ through the introduction of an associated dynamical system. To do so, we first redefine $\delta_r(\infty)$ as

$$\delta_r(\infty) = \varphi'(v_r(\infty))y_r(\infty) \qquad (14.114)$$

where

$$y_r(\infty) = \sum_k e_k(\mathbf{L}^{-1})_{kr} \qquad (14.115)$$

We next undo the matrix inversion in Eq. (14.115) and extract a set of linear combinations for the new variable $y_r(\infty)$, as shown by

$$\sum_r L_{rj}y_r(\infty) = e_j \qquad (14.116)$$

Then, using the definition for L_{rj}, given in Eq. (14.109) albeit for a different pair of indices, we may rewrite Eq. (14.116) in the form

$$\sum_r \{\delta_{rj} - \varphi'(v_r(\infty))w_{rj}\}y_r(\infty) = e_j$$

Invoking the definition of the Kronecker delta δ_{rj}, we thus have

$$y_j(\infty) - \sum_r \varphi'(v_r(\infty))w_{rj}y_r(\infty) = e_j \tag{14.117}$$

For clarity of exposition, we do two things in Eq. (14.117): (1) replace the index r by i, and (2) rearrange terms, as shown by

$$0 = -y_j(\infty) + \sum_i \varphi'(v_i(\infty))w_{ij}y_i(\infty) + e_j, \qquad j = 1, 2, \ldots, N \tag{14.118}$$

where the range of index j has also been added for the sake of completeness.

Finally, we observe that the solutions of the system of linear equation (14.118) are indeed the fixed points of an *associated dynamical system* defined by

$$\frac{dy_j(t)}{dt} = -y_j(t) + \sum_i \varphi'(v_i(\infty))w_{ij}y_i(t) + e_j, \qquad j = 1, \ldots, N \tag{14.119}$$

The computation of $y_j(\infty)$, and therefore the local gradient $\delta_j(\infty)$, as described here is merely a relaxation method for the inversion of a matrix. Note also the step from Eq. (14.118) to (14.119) is not unique in that Eq. (14.118) may be transformed in various ways leading to related differential equations.

For the special case of an activation function $\varphi(\cdot)$ defined by the logistic function of Eq. (14.17), the evaluation of the derivative $\varphi'(\cdot)$ is readily performed using the relation

$$\varphi'(v_i(\infty)) = x_i(\infty)[1 - x_i(\infty)] \tag{14.120}$$

where $x_i(\infty)$ is the ith element of the fixed point $\mathbf{x}(\infty)$; it is represented by the steady-state output of neuron i.

With the derivation of Eq. (14.119), the construction of the new learning algorithm is completed. In order to develop a physical understanding of its operation, we make two important observations (Pineda, 1988a, b; Almeida, 1987):

1. From Eq. (14.96) we see that the given recurrent network determined by the set of synaptic weights $\{w_{ji}\}$, constitutes the network structure for computing the set of state variables $\{x_j\}$. This computation is performed in response to a specified set of input signals $\{\xi_j\}$ that defines the bias terms of the input neurons in accordance with Eq. (14.91). Hence we may view the *nonlinear* dynamical equation (14.96) or the related equation (14.19) as the *forward propagation equation* of the network.
2. From Eq. (14.119) we see that the network for computing the set of variables $\{y_j(t)\}$ is obtained by *rewiring* the given network as follows:
   (a) The synaptic weight w_{ji} from neuron i to neuron j in the original network is replaced by $\varphi'(v_i(\infty))w_{ij}$ from neuron j to neuron i. In other words, the direction of signal transmission through the network is reversed. The resulting network is referred to as the *adjoint* of the original network. Figure 14.18b illustrates the construction of this adjoint network for the structure shown in Fig. 14.18a.
   (b) The output neurons of the original network assume the role of input neurons in the adjoint network. The bias terms of these "new" input neurons are set equal to e_j, where e_j is an "error signal" defined by Eq. (14.92).

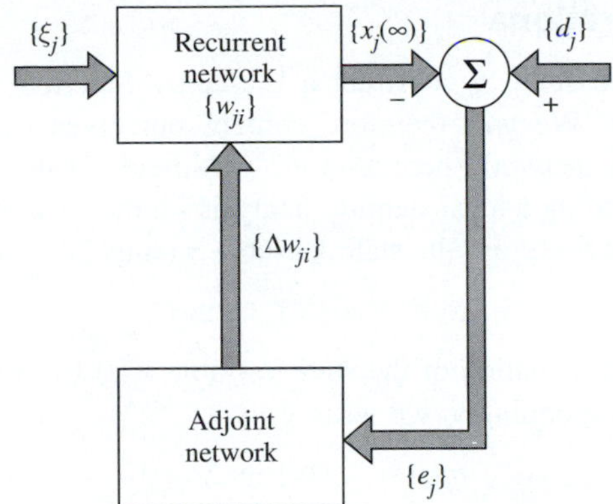

FIGURE 14.19 Block diagram illustrating the interaction between a recurrent network and its adjoint, which is trained using the recurrent back-propagation algorithm.

We may therefore view Eq. (14.119) as the *backward propagation equation* of the network. Note that, unlike the forward propagation equation, the backward propagation equation is *linear.*

It is important to stress, however, that the forward and backward propagation equations specify the dynamics of the recurrent back-propagation algorithm provided that they converge to stable fixed points, and the learning-rate parameter η is small.

The operation of the recurrent back-propagation algorithm thus involves the combined use of two network structures, the original recurrent network and the adjoint network, which work together in the manner described in Fig. 14.19. The original network viewed as a neurodynamical system is characterized by the forward propagation equation (14.96); for a given input–output example, this network computes the error vector denoted by $\{e_j\}$. The adjoint network is characterized by the backward propagation equation (14.119); the adjoint network takes the error vector from the original network and uses it to compute the adjustments to the synapatic weights of the original network, namely, $\{\Delta w_{ji}\}$.

Summary

The new algorithm is defined by Eqs. (14.91), (14.96), (14.99), (14.92), (14.119), (14.114), and (14.112), in that order. This algorithm is known as the *recurrent back-propagation algorithm* (Pineda, 1988a, b). It is so called because, first, it involves the use of a recurrent network (i.e., a neural network with feedback connections) and, second, it uses the back-propagation of error signals to modify the synaptic weights of the network.

The computational procedure for the algorithm is as follows:

1. For a specified input pattern $\{\xi_j\}$, use Eq. (14.91) to determine the set of biases $\{I_j\}$ and relax the original recurrent network in accordance with the forward propagation equation (14.96). Hence, compute the steady-state values $\{v_j(\infty)\}$ of the activation potentials and therefore the steady-state values $\{x_j(\infty)\}$ of the output signals produced by the output neurons of the network using Eq. (14.99).
2. For a specified set of desired (target) responses $\{d_j\}$, use Eq. (14.92) to compute the error signals $\{e_j\}$.
3. Relax the adjoint network in accordance with the backward propagation equation (14.119). Hence, compute the associated variables $\{y_j(\infty)\}$.
4. Finally, update the synaptic weights of the network using Eqs. (14.114) and (14.112).

Stability Considerations

In general, it is not possible to construct a Liapunov function for the recurrent back-propagation algorithm. We will therefore content ourselves by presenting a "local" stability analysis of the network; here we follow Almeida (1987).

We begin by performing a local stability analysis on the forward propagation equation (14.96). Specifically, we express the state variable $x_j(t)$ as

$$x_j(t) = x_j(\infty) + \Delta x_j(t)$$

where $\Delta x_j(t)$ is a small deviation of the state variable $x_j(t)$ from the coordinate $x_j(\infty)$ of a point attractor. Correspondingly, we write

$$v_j(t) = v_j(\infty) + \Delta v_j(t) \tag{14.121}$$

where $v_j(\infty)$ and $x_j(\infty)$ are related by Eq. (14.99). Then, linearizing the dynamical equation (14.96) around this point attractor in a manner similar to that described in Section 14.3, we obtain the following system of linear differential equations:

$$\frac{d}{dt}\Delta x_j(t) = -\sum_i L_{ji}\,\Delta x_i(t), \qquad j = 1, 2, \ldots, N \tag{14.122}$$

where L_{ji} is defined in Eq. (14.109). Using matrix notation, we may rewrite Eq. (14.122) in the compact form

$$\frac{d}{dt}\Delta\mathbf{x}(t) = -\mathbf{L}\,\Delta\mathbf{x}(t) \tag{14.123}$$

where the vector $\Delta\mathbf{x}(t)$ is the deviation of the state vector $\mathbf{x}(t)$ from the fixed point $\mathbf{x}(\infty)$, and $\mathbf{L}$ is an N-by-N matrix with element L_{ji}.

Next, we observe that the backward propagation equation (14.119) may also be expressed in the compact matrix form

$$\frac{d}{dt}\mathbf{y}(t) = -\mathbf{L}^T\mathbf{y}(t) + \mathbf{e} \tag{14.124}$$

where $\mathbf{y}(t)$ is an N-by-1 vector with element y_j, the N-by-N matrix $\mathbf{L}^T$ is the transpose of $\mathbf{L}$, and $\mathbf{e}$ is an N-by-1 vector with element e_j; here we have made use of Eq. (14.109) for the jith element of matrix $\mathbf{L}$.

From Eq. (14.123) we note that the local stability of the forward propagation equation depends on the eigenvalues of the matrix $\mathbf{L}$. From Eq. (14.124) we note that the local stability of the backward propagation equation depends on the eigenvalues of the transposed matrix $\mathbf{L}^T$. But both the matrix $\mathbf{L}$ and its transpose $\mathbf{L}^T$ have exactly the same eigenvalues. Accordingly, if a fixed point of the forward propagation equation is locally stable, then so is the corresponding fixed point of the backward propagation equation. In other words, *the local stability of the forward propagation equation* (14.96) *is a sufficient condition for the local stability of the backward propagation equation* (14.119), *and vice versa* (Almeida, 1987).

The analysis of recurrent back-propagation presented in this section is based on the premise that the recurrent network converges to a fixed point. Unfortunately, there is no general method available to guarantee this convergence. Indeed, there is a potential problem in the use of the recurrent back-propagation algorithm in that the algorithm may not converge to a stable fixed point. This means that it is possible for the algorithm to back-propagate highly incorrect error signals and therefore fail to learn properly. To guard against such a possibility, the learning-rate parameter η should be assigned a sufficiently small value. Computer experiments performed by Simard et al. (1989) tend to support this assertion. In the recurrent back-propagation algorithm, learning takes place by moving the bottom of the basins of attraction (fixed points) toward target (desired) values. As the learning process progresses, the Euclidean distance between the fixed point and the desired pattern is diminished, which in turn makes the error signals assume smaller values, and at the same time causes the learning process to slow down. If, during the learning process, the network misses the point attractor, large error signals can be injected into the back-propagation process. However, provided that the learning-rate parameter η is small, then a near miss may have a minor effect on the learning process. On the other hand, if the learning-rate parameter η is large, a near miss may have a dramatic effect on the learning process, quite possibly causing the algorithm to break down.

In the application of back-propagation learning to allocate the fixed points of a recurrent neural network as discussed in this section, stability of the network is of paramount importance. However, for certain applications, a recurrent neural network is designed to be unstable on purpose, so that it can operate as an *oscillator*. In the latter case, the objective is the learning of a temporal structure such as a limit cycle. A formulation similar to that described here may be pursued to derive the gradient descent learning algorithm for an *adaptive neural oscillator* (Doya and Yoshizawa, 1989; Urbanczik, 1991).

Comparison of the Recurrent Back-Propagation Algorithm with the Standard Back-Propagation Algorithm

The structural constraints imposed on the network topology of the standard back-propagation algorithm described in Chapter 6 make it implausible in a neurobiological sense. On the other hand, by permitting arbitrary connections, including the use of feedback, the recurrent back-propagation algorithm assumes a more neurobiologically plausible topology.

The standard back-propagation algorithm suffers from the inability to fill in patterns, because of complete reliance on feedforward connections. Thus, if (during a test) part of an input pattern applied to the network is missing or corrupted, then large errors are propagated through the network and therefore onto the output. The use of the recurrent back-propagation algorithm overcomes the pattern-completion problem by virtue of its inherent feedback connections. Almeida (1987) has confirmed experimentally that feedback structures are much better suited to this kind of problem.

The use of feedback connections in the recurrent back-propagation algorithm makes it less sensitive to noise and lack of synchronization, and also permits it to learn faster, compared to the standard back-propagation algorithm (Simard et al., 1989).

However, the standard back-propagation algorithm is more robust than the recurrent back-propagation algorithm with respect to the choice of a high learning-rate parameter (Simard et al., 1989). The reason for this behavior is that when the learning-rate parameter is large, the cost function used in the derivation of the recurrent back-propagation algorithm is not a function of the point attractor, and therefore the synaptic weights of the network no longer change in an adiabatic fashion as they should.

Finally, we note that the standard and recurrent back-propagation algorithms are both derived from the method of steepest descent. Accordingly, they both suffer from the likelihood of being trapped in local minima.

14.13 Discussion

In this chapter we studied the *nonlinear dynamics of recurrent networks* and some of their useful applications. Three models were considered: the Hopfield model, the brain-state-in-a-box (BSB) model, and recurrent back-propagation learning. Much of the richness seen in the dynamic behavior of these models is attributed directly to *feedback* built into their design.

In recurrent back-propagation learning, the inclusion of feedback means that the algorithm can be applied to a neural network with an arbitrary architecture, so long as the network has stable states. The operation of the algorithm involves two network structures: the original recurrent network and its adjoint, working together in the manner described in Fig. 14.19. For a known input–output example, the original network calculates the error vector that is fed as input into the adjoint network. Through an error back-propagation process, the adjoint network calculates the adjustments applied to the synaptic weights of the original network. We may think of the combination of the original network and its adjoint in the recurrent back-propagation algorithm as somewhat similar to the idea of a *master–slave* formalism described in Lapedes and Farber (1986b). In the latter case, a master network is used with a unit for each free parameter of the slave network, and the idea is to present known input–output pairs to the master network to determine the free parameters of the slave network; however, unlike recurrent back-propagation learning, *no* feedback is involved in the master–slave formalism of Lapedes and Farber.

Recurrent back-propagation is well suited for learning input–output mapping. In this context, an interesting application of recurrent back-propagation is described in Lockery et al. (1990). The algorithm is used to develop a nonlinear dynamical model of the sensorimotor transformations encountered in the leech; the model was trained on experimentally derived input–output patterns.

The Hopfield model and the BSB model have entirely different architectures, yet they share some common features:

- They both employ positive feedback.
- They both have an energy (Liapunov) function, and are designed to minimize it in an iterative fashion.
- They are both attractor neural networks.

Naturally, they differ in their areas of application.

We note that the BSB model is too weak for solving difficult computational problems, but its inherent clustering capability may be put to good use for data representation and concept formation. Anderson (1990) describes the use of the BSB model in experimental cognitive psychology, and Kawamoto and Anderson (1985) explore its use as a neurobiological model of multistable perception.

In contrast, the Hopfield model may be used to solve difficult computational problems, the most important two of which are summarized here:

1. *Content-addressable memory,* which involves the recall of a stored pattern by presenting a partial or distorted version of it to the memory. For this application, the usual procedure is to use the "discrete" Hopfield model that is based on the McCulloch–Pitts neuron (i.e., one using a hard-limiting activation function). However, a much better memory performance can be achieved with the "continuous" Hopfield model using a *nonmonotonic* activation function (Morita, 1993). But the network is operated in a special way in that the recalled pattern is computed by passing the steady-state values of the activation potentials through a signum function. The net result of these modifications is twofold (Yoshizawa et al., 1993):

- Increased storage capacity from $N/(2 \ln N)$ to about $0.4N$, where N is the number of neurons.
- Disappearance of spurious states and the emergence of a chaotic behavior when memory fails.

2. *Combinatorial optimization problems,* which rank among the most difficult known to mathematicians. This class of optimization problems includes the *traveling salesman problem* (TSP), considered to be a classic. Given the positions of a specified number of cities, assumed to lie in a plane, the problem is to find the shortest tour that starts and finishes at the same city. The TSP is thus simple to state but hard to solve exactly, in that there is no known method of finding the optimum tour, short of computing the length of every possible tour and then selecting the shortest one. It is said to be *NP-complete* (Hopcroft and Ullman, 1979). In a pioneering paper, Hopfield and Tank (1985) demonstrated how an analog network, based on the system of coupled first-order differential equations (14.20), can be used to represent a solution of the TSP. Specifically, the synaptic weights of the network are determined by distances between the cities visited on the tour, and the optimum solution to the problem is a fixed point of the neurodynamical equations (14.20). Herein lie the difficulties encountered with "mapping" combinatorial optimization problems onto the continuous (analog) Hopfield network. The network acts to minimize a single energy (Liapunov) function, and yet the typical combinatorial optimization problem requires the minimization of an objective function *subject to* some hard constraints (Gee et al., 1993). If any of these constraints are violated, the solution is considered to be invalid. The early mapping procedures were based on a Liapunov function constructed in an *ad hoc* manner, usually employing one term for each constraint, as shown by

$$E = E^{\text{opt}} + c_1 E_1^{\text{cns}} + c_2 E_2^{\text{cns}} + \cdots \tag{14.125}$$

The first term, E^{opt}, is the objective function to be minimized (e.g., the length of a TSP tour); it is determined by the problem at hand. The remaining terms, $E_1^{\text{cns}}, E_2^{\text{cns}}, \ldots,$ represent penalty functions whose minimization satisfies the constraints. The $c_1, c_2, \ldots,$ are constant weights assigned to the respective penalty functions $E_1^{\text{cns}}, E_2^{\text{cns}}, \ldots,$ usually by trial and error. Unfortunately, the many terms in the Liapunov function of Eq. (14.125) tend to frustrate one another, and the success of the Hopfield network is highly sensitive to the relative values of $c_1, c_2, \ldots,$ (Gee et al., 1993). It is therefore not surprising that the network often produces a large number of invalid solutions (Wilson and Pawley, 1988). In a doctoral dissertation, Gee (1993) has addressed a number of basic questions concerning the use of *optimization networks,* encompassing the continuous Hopfield network and mean field annealing (discussed in Chapter 8), as tools for solving combinatorial optimization problems. The main findings reported there may be summarized as follows (Gee, 1993):

- Given a combinatorial optimization problem expressed in terms of quadratic 0–1 programming, as in the traveling salesman problem, there is a straightforward method for programming the network for its solution, and the solution found will not violate any of the problem's constraints.
- Building on results from complexity theory and mathematical programming, hitherto ignored by the neural network community, it is shown that, except when the problem's constraints have special properties producing an integral polytope, it is not possible to force the network to converge to a valid, interpretable solution. In geometric terms, a polytope, that is, a bounded polyhedron, is said to be an *integral polytope* if all the vertices of the polytope are 0-1 points. Even when dealing with integral polytopes, if the objective function E^{opt} is quadratic, then the problem is *NP*-complete and there is no guarantee that the network will find the optimum solution; this class of problems includes the traveling salesman problem. However, a valid solution will be found and, given the nature of the descent process to this solution, there is a good chance that the solution will be quite good.

- The traveling salesman problem is the only combinatorial optimization problem considered in Gee's thesis, for which the solution produced by the network is completely reliable. There may well be other problems, not considered therein, which can also be solved reliably using optimization networks.

According to Gee (1993), optimization networks have a narrow, *potential* field of application, conditional on the development of special, parallel hardware. Suitable hardware implementation is needed to compete, in terms of speed, with other optimization techniques which, when tailor-made to specific problems, can perform extremely well (Lin, 1965).

From Local to Global Dynamics

In this chapter we have shown how the use of the additive model can be applied to entirely different topologies such as the Hopfield network and a recurrent network with hidden neurons. This *equation-based approach* provides the natural way to study important dynamical properties of neural models, such as stability.

An alternative to this traditional approach for describing neurodynamics is to decompose the global dynamics of interest into local dynamics and local rules of interaction (Lefebvre and Principe, 1993). This latter approach, called *procedural modeling,* is particularly well suited for the simulation of neurodynamics on a digital computer in an *interactive* manner. What is gained by its use is (1) simplicity in the coding, and (2) generality in the computer simulation.

The first step in decomposing the dynamics for the additive model[6] is to characterize the essential mappings embodied in the equations. This requires that we characterize the most fundamental *processing element* (PE) that we wish to construct. A neural network may then be viewed as a *coupled lattice* of PEs. The term ''coupled lattice'' is used here to represent an ensemble of ordered computations that can be mapped to sites in a graph. If we distill the global neural dynamics into rules for local interactions, network simulations can be constructed simply by arranging neural processing elements (implementing the essential mappings) on a lattice, that is, by specifying the network topology. In a computer simulation environment, each neural processing element has its own *icon*; an icon is a software entity. Thus specification of the topology can be accomplished by having the user place icons on a graphical breadboard. In so doing, the user puts in memory codes that will construct the network. Once the topology has been drawn, it is simulated immediately, since the neural processing elements (icons) know how to interact with each other locally (Lefebvre and Principe, 1993).

The coupled lattice in discrete time assumes the following geometry. The lattice exists in three dimensions with two ''spatial'' axes (x and y) lying on the plane of the paper and one ''temporal'' axis going into the plane of the paper. Present time is the first temporal plane, and each following plane is delayed by a single time step. In order to construct the lattice corresponding to a simulation topology of interest, the neural processing elements (icons) will have to fit together and live on the lattice as sites and links. The neural mappings of interest are then implemented by object classes (Lefebvre and Principe, 1993).

[6] Lefebvre and Principe (1993) use the so-called *gamma model,* which is nothing but a prewired additive model with some of the processing elements devoted to storing the past history of the inputs or activations through local recursion determined by a control parameter. A detailed description of the gamma model is presented by deVries and Principe (1992); see Problem 14.3.

New Neurodynamical Theories

We conclude this discussion of neurodynamics by briefly describing two significant contributions reported in the literature:

- Cohen (1992a) introduces two new methods for constructing systems of ordinary differential equations that can realize any fixed finite set of equilibrium states in any fixed finite dimension, and with no spurious states. One method constructs a system with the fewest number of equilibrium states, given a fixed set of attractors. The second method is more general in that it constructs a differential equation that converges to a fixed given set of equilibrium states. These two methods are applicable to the design of content-addressable memories with desired dynamic behavior. In a subsequent contribution, Cohen (1992b) describes a parameterized family of higher-order, gradientlike neural networks with a simple feedback rule that generates equilibrium points with a set of unstable manifolds of specified dimension. This latter work is used to interpolate finite sets of data on nested periodic orbits.
- Dawes (1992a, b) describes the use of *quantum neurodynamics* for (1) a neurocomputing architecture for spatio-temporal stochastic filtering, and (2) an explicit mathematical model for biological neural systems. In case (1), the nonlinear *Schrödinger equation* of quantum mechanics is used to construct a time-varying probability density function, conditioned by the history of observations; this method provides a (suboptimal) solution to stochastic filtering problems for nonlinear dynamical systems in non-Gaussian noise, which makes it directly applicable to radar and sonar target tracking systems. In case (2), quantum neurodynamics provides an essential role for the glial matrix and details of the interaction between glial cells and neurons in the cognitive processing of dynamic information streams; *glial cells* represent a variety of small cells that are considered not to generate active electrical signals as neurons do (Churchland and Sejnowski, 1992).

These two contributions are remarkable indeed in their own individual ways, which may pave the way for major advances in the theory and design of neurodynamical systems.

PROBLEMS

14.1 Restate Liapunov's theorems for the state vector $\mathbf{x}(0)$ as the equilibrium state of a dynamical system.

14.2 Verify the block diagrams of Figs. 14.9a and 14.9b for the neurodynamical equations (14.18) and (14.19), respectively.

14.3 The *discrete (time) gamma model* of a neurodynamical system is described by the following pair of equations (deVries and Principe, 1992)

$$x_j(n) = \varphi\left(\sum_{i<j}\sum_m w_{ji}^{(m)}x_i^{(m)}(n)\right) + K_j$$

and

$$x_j^{(m)}(n) = (1-\mu_j)x_j^{(m)}(n-1) + \mu_j x_j^{(m-1)}(n-1)$$

where n denotes discrete time, $j = 1, 2, \ldots, N$, and $m = 1, 2, \ldots, M$.

(a) Compare the discrete gamma model with the discrete-time form of the additive model described in Eq. (14.19).

(b) Construct a signal-flow graph for the recursive part of the gamma model.

(c) Find the value of the control parameter μ_j for which the discrete gamma model is stable.

14.4 Suppose that in the formulation of the Hopfield network as a content-addressable memory there is no bound on the magnitude of the eigenvectors of the weight matrix **W**. How would the network behave in such a case?

14.5 Fill in the details leading to the derivation of the Liapunov function E for a Hopfield network with modified weight matrix **W**, which is given in Eq. (14.70).

14.6 A Hopfield network is designed to store the two fundamental memory patterns $(+1, +1, -1, +1, +1)$ and $(+1, -1, +1, -1, +1)$. The synaptic matrix of the network is given by

$$\mathbf{W} = \begin{bmatrix} 0 & 0 & 0 & 0 & 2 \\ 0 & 0 & -2 & 2 & 0 \\ 0 & -2 & 0 & -2 & 0 \\ 0 & 2 & -2 & 0 & 0 \\ 2 & 0 & 0 & 0 & 0 \end{bmatrix}$$

(a) The sum of the eigenvalues of the matrix **W** is zero. Why?

(b) The phase space of the network is a subspace of $\mathbb{R}^5$. Specify the configuration of this space.

(c) Specify the subspace $\mathcal{M}$ spanned by the fundamental memory vectors, and the null subspace $\mathcal{N}$ of the weight matrix **W**. What are the fixed points (stable states) and spurious states of the network?

[The reader may wish to refer to the paper by deSilva and Attikiouzzel (1992) for a more detailed description of the dynamics of the network described here.]

14.7 Figure P14.7 shows a piecewise-linear approximation to the nonmonotonic activation function of Fig. 14.14. The recalling dynamics of the Hopfield network using this approximation is defined by

$$\frac{d}{dt}\mathbf{v}(t) = -\mathbf{v}(t) + \mathbf{W}\mathbf{x}(t), \qquad \mathbf{x}(t) = \text{sgn}(\mathbf{v}(t)) - k\mathbf{v}(t)$$

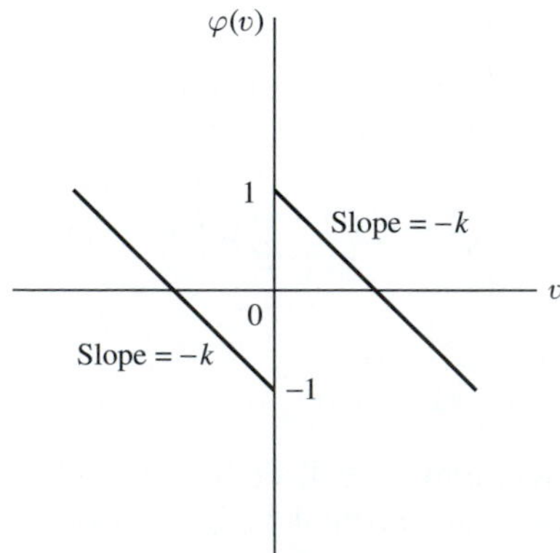

FIGURE P14.7

where $\mathbf{v}(t)$ is the vector of activation potentials, $\mathbf{W}$ is the synaptic weight matrix, $\mathbf{x}(t)$ is the state (output) vector, and $-k$ is a constant negative slope. Let $\bar{\mathbf{v}}$ be an equilibrium state of the network that lies in the quadrant of the fundamental memory $\boldsymbol{\xi}_1$, and let

$$\bar{\mathbf{x}} = \text{sgn}(\bar{\mathbf{v}}) - k\,\bar{\mathbf{v}}$$

Show that $\bar{\mathbf{x}}$ is characterized by the following three conditions (Yoshizawa et al., 1993):

(a) $\sum_{i=1}^{N} \bar{\mathbf{x}}_i \xi_{\mu,i} = 0, \qquad \mu = 2, 3, \ldots, M$

(b) $\sum_{i=1}^{N} \bar{\mathbf{x}}_i \xi_{1,i} = M$

(c) $\bar{x}_i < 1, \qquad i = 1, 2, \ldots, N$

where $\boldsymbol{\xi}_1, \boldsymbol{\xi}_2, \ldots, \boldsymbol{\xi}_M$ are the fundamental memories stored in the network, $\xi_{\mu,i}$ is the ith element of $\boldsymbol{\xi}_\mu$, $\bar{x}_i$ is the ith element of $\bar{\mathbf{x}}$, and N is the number of neurons.

14.8 Consider a BSB model for which the symmetric weight matrix $\mathbf{W}$ is defined by

$$\mathbf{W} = \begin{bmatrix} 0.035 & -0.005 \\ -0.005 & 0.035 \end{bmatrix}$$

(a) Calculate the eigenvalues and associated eigenvectors of the matrix $\mathbf{W}$.

(b) Identify the point attractors of the BSB model, and construct their individual basins of interaction.

(c) Plot the trajectory of the BSB model for each of the following initial state vectors:

$$\mathbf{x}(0) = [-0.5, 0.3]^T$$
$$\mathbf{x}(0) = [0.5, 0.3]^T$$
$$\mathbf{x}(0) = [0.7, 0.5]^T$$
$$\mathbf{x}(0) = [0.1, 0.7]^T$$

Note: This problem is taken from Anderson, 1994.

14.9 In Section 14.11 we derived the Liapunov function of the BSB model, applying the Cohen–Grossberg theorem. In carrying out the derivation, we omitted some of the details leading to Eq. (14.84). Fill in the details.

14.10 Consider a general neurodynamical system with an unspecified dependence on internal dynamical parameters, external dynamical stimuli, and state variables. The system is defined by the state equations

$$\frac{dx_j}{dt} = \varphi_j(\mathbf{W}, \mathbf{i}, \mathbf{x}), \qquad j = 1, 2, \ldots, N$$

where the matrix $\mathbf{W}$ represents the internal dynamical parameters of the system, the vector $\mathbf{i}$ represents the external dynamical stimuli, and $\mathbf{x}$ is the state vector whose jth element is denoted by x_j. Assume that trajectories of the system converge onto point attractors for values of $\mathbf{W}$, $\mathbf{i}$, and initial states $\mathbf{x}(0)$ in some operating

region of the system (Pineda, 1988a). Discuss how the system described may be used for the following applications:
(a) Continuous mapper, with **i** as input and $\mathbf{x}(\infty)$ as output
(b) Autoassociative memory, with $\mathbf{x}(0)$ as input and $\mathbf{x}(\infty)$ as output

14.11 Consider the simple neurodynamical model described by the system of equations

$$\frac{dv_j}{dt} = -v_j + \sum_i w_{ji}\varphi(v_i) + I_j, \qquad j = 1, 2, \ldots, N$$

The system described always converges to a unique point attractor, provided that the synaptic weights w_{ji} satisfy the condition

$$\sum_j \sum_i w_{ji}^2 < \frac{1}{(\max|\varphi'|)^2}$$

where $\varphi' = d\varphi/dv_j$. Explore the validity of this condition. You may refer to the paper (Atiya, 1987), where this condition is derived

14.12 What is the dimension of weight space and that of phase space for the recurrent network described in Fig. 14.18.

14.13 Develop the details involved in deriving the system of linear differential equations described in Eq. (14.119).

14.14 Using the recurrent back-propagation algorithm, develop a network for solving the XOR problem.

14.15 Consider a pattern completion problem involving 10 binary random vectors, each of which has 10 elements. The problem is to try to fill the values of two randomly selected, missing elements, given the other eight elements. Investigate this problem using the following learning procedures (Almeida, 1987):
(a) Standard back-propagation
(b) Recurrent back-propagation
In both cases, use a network with 10 hidden neurons.

14.16 In the derivation of the recurrent back-propagation algorithm presented in Section 14.12 we assumed that all the neurons of the recurrent network have the same nonlinear activation function. Rederive the recurrent back-propagation algorithm, this time assuming that each neuron has a distinct nonlinear activation function of its own.

CHAPTER 15

VLSI Implementations of Neural Networks

15.1 Introduction

In the previous chapters of this book we presented a broad exposition of neural networks, describing a variety of algorithms for implementing supervised and unsupervised learning paradigms. In the final analysis, however, neural networks can only gain acceptance as tools for solving engineering problems such as pattern classification, modeling, signal processing, and control in one of two ways:

- Compared to conventional methods, the use of a neural network makes a significant difference in the performance of a system for a real-world application, or else it provides a significant reduction in the cost of implementation without compromising performance.
- Through the use of a neural network, we are able to solve a difficult problem for which there is no other solution.

Given that we have a viable solution to an engineering problem based on a neural network approach, we need to take the next step: build the neural network in hardware, and embed the piece of hardware in its working environment. It is only when we have a working model of the system that we can justifiably say we fully understand it. The key question that arises at this point in the discussion is: What is the most cost-effective medium for the hardware implementation of a neural network? A fully digital approach that comes to mind is to use a *RISC processor*; RISC is the acronym for *reduced instruction set computer* (Cocke and Markstein, 1990). Such a processor is designed to execute a small number of simple instructions, preferably one instruction for every cycle of the computer clock. Indeed, because of the very high speed of modern-day RISC processors, their use for the emulation of neural networks is probably fast enough for some applications. However, for certain complex applications such as speech recognition and optical character recognition, a level of performance is required that is not attainable with existing RISC processors, certainly within the cost limitations of the proposed applications (Hammerstrom, 1992). Also, there are many situations such as process control, adaptive beamforming, and adaptive noise cancellation where the required speed of learning is much too fast for standard processors. To meet the computational requirements of the complex applications and highly demanding situations described here, we may have to resort to the use of *very-large-scale integrated* (VLSI) circuits, a rapidly developing technology that provides an ideal medium for the hardware implementation of neural networks.

In the use of VLSI technology, we have the capability of fabricating integrated circuits with tens of millions of transistors on a single *silicon chip,* and it is highly likely that this number will be increased by two orders of magnitude before reaching the fundamental limits of the technology imposed by the laws of physics (Hoeneisen and Mead, 1972; Keyes, 1987). We thus find that VLSI technology is well matched to neural networks for two principal reasons (Boser et al., 1992):

1. The high functional density achievable with VLSI technology permits the implementation of a large number of identical, concurrently operating neurons on a single chip, thereby making it possible to exploit the inherent parallelism of neural networks.
2. The regular topology of neural networks and the relatively small number of well-defined arithmetic operations involved in their learning algorithms greatly simplify the design and layout of VLSI circuits.

Accordingly, we find that there is a great deal of research effort devoted worldwide to VLSI implementations of neural networks on many fronts. Today, there are general-purpose chips available for the construction of multilayer perceptrons, Boltzmann machines, mean-field-theory machines, and self-organizing neural networks. Moreover, various special-purpose chips have been developed for specific information-processing functions.

VLSI technology not only provides the medium for the implementation of complex information-processing functions that are neurobiologically inspired, but also can be seen to serve a complementary and inseparable role as a synthetic element to build test beds for postulates of neural organization (Mead, 1989). The successful use of VLSI technology to create a bridge between neurobiology and information sciences will have the following beneficial effects: deeper understanding of information processing, and novel methods for solving engineering problems that are intractable by traditional computer techniques (Mead, 1989). The interaction between neurobiology and information sciences via the silicon medium may also influence the very art of electronics and VLSI technology itself by having to solve new challenges posed by the interaction.

With all these positive attributes of VLSI technology, it is befitting that we devote this final chapter of the book to its use as the medium for hardware implementations of neural networks. The discussion will, however, be at an introductory level.[1]

Organization of the Chapter

The material of the chapter is organized as follows. In Section 15.2 we discuss the basic design considerations involved in the VLSI implementation of neural networks. In Section 15.3 we categorize VLSI implementations of neural networks into analog, digital, and hybrid methods. Then, in Section 15.4 we describe commercially available general-purpose and special-purpose chips for hardware implementations of neural networks. Section 15.5 on concluding remarks completes the chapter and the book.

15.2 Major Design Considerations

The incredible functional density, ease of use, and low cost of industrial *CMOS (complementary metal oxide silicon) transistors* make CMOS technology as the technology of choice for VLSI implementations of neural networks (Mead, 1989). Regardless of whether we are considering the development of general-purpose or special-purpose chips for neural networks, there are a number of major design issues that would have to be considered in

[1] For detailed treatment of analog VLSI systems, with emphasis on neuromorphic networks, see the book by Mead (1989). For specialized aspects of the subject, see the March 1991, May 1992, and May 1993 Special Issues of the *IEEE Transactions on Neural Networks.* The report by Andreou (1992) provides an overview of analog VLSI systems with emphasis on circuit models of neurons, synapses, and neuromorphic functions.

the use of this technology. Specifically, we may identify the following items (Hammerstrom, 1992).

1. *Sum-of-Products Computation.* This is a functional requirement common to the operation of all neurons. It involves multiplying each element of an activation pattern (data vector) by an appropriate weight, and then summing the weighted inputs, as described in the standard equation

$$v_j = \sum_{i=1}^{p} w_{ji} x_i \tag{15.1}$$

where w_{ji} is the weight of synapse i belonging to neuron j, x_i is the input applied to the ith synapse, p is the number of synapses, and v_j is the resulting activation potential of neuron j.

2. *Data Representation.* Generally speaking, neural networks have low-precision requirements, the exact specification of which is algorithm/application dependent.

3. *Output Computation.* The most common form of activation function at the output of a neuron is a smooth nonlinear function such as the sigmoid function described by the logistic function,

$$\varphi(v_j) = \frac{1}{1 + \exp(-v_j)} \tag{15.2}$$

or the hyperbolic tangent,

$$\varphi(v_j) = \tanh(v_j) = \frac{1 - \exp(-v_j)}{1 + \exp(-v_j)} \tag{15.3}$$

These two forms of the sigmoidal activation function are linearly related to each other; see Chapter 6. Occasionally, the threshold function

$$\varphi(v_j) = \begin{cases} 1, & v_j > 0 \\ 0, & v_j < 0 \end{cases} \tag{15.4}$$

is considered to be sufficient.

4. *Learning Complexity.* Each learning algorithm has computational requirements of its own. Several popular learning algorithms rely on the use of *local* computations for making modifications to the synaptic weights of a neural network; this is a highly desirable feature from an implementation point of view. Some other algorithms have additional requirements, such as the back-propagation of error terms through the network, which imposes an additional burden on the implementation of the neural network, as in the case of a multilayer perceptron trained with the back-propagation algorithm.

5. *Weight Storage.* This requirement refers to the need to store the "old" values of synaptic weights of a neural network. The "new" values of the weights are computed by using the changes computed by the learning algorithm to update the old values.

6. *Communications.* Metal is expensive in terms of silicon area, which leads to significant inefficiencies if bandwidth utilization of communication (connectivity) links among neurons is low. Connectivity is perhaps one of the most serious constraints imposed on the fabrication of a silicon chip, particularly as we scale up analog or digital technology to very large neural networks. Indeed, significant innovation in communication schemes is necessary if we are to implement very large neural networks on silicon chips efficiently. The paper by Bailey and Hammerstrom (1988) discusses the fundamental issues involved in the connectivity problem with the VLSI implementation of neural networks in mind;

specifically, it shows that *multiplexing* interconnections is necessary for networks exhibiting poor locality.

7. *Implementation Costs.* The total system costs involved in the implementation of a neural network must be considered in the production of a silicon chip. The factors to be accounted for include the following:

- Input/output bandwidth requirements
- Power consumption
- Flexible use and range of applications
- Use of analog versus digital technology

The very last point, the use of analog versus digital technology, opens a new topic for discussion, which we take up in the next section.

15.3 Categories of VLSI Implementations

In an *analog* implementation of a neural network the information-bearing signals have a continuous amplitude. In a *digital* implementation, on the other hand, the signals are quantized into a finite set of discrete amplitudes. A hybrid combination of these two approaches provides the basis of other schemes for building neural networks. Accordingly, we may categorize the VLSI implementation of neural networks as follows.

Analog Techniques

In an eloquent and convincing address presented at the First IEEE International Conference on Neural Networks, Mead (1987a) argued in favor of a synthetic approach combining silicon VLSI technology and analog circuits for the implementation of neural networks. Although analog circuits do indeed suffer from lack of precision, this shortcoming is compensated by the efficiency of computations based on the principles of classical circuit theory and the laws of physics. Analog circuits can do certain computations that are difficult or time-consuming (or both) when implemented in the conventional digital paradigm, and do them with much less power (Mead, 1989).

Figure 15.1 shows the circuit symbols for the *n-channel* and *p-channel* types of MOS (metal oxide silicon) transistors, which use electrons and holes as their charge carriers, respectively. The technology so based is thus called *complementary MOS,* or CMOS. The function of a MOS transistor may be understood by examining the drain current I_d defined as a function of the gate-source voltage V_{gs}, with the drain being maintained at a fixed voltage (2V, say). Two regions may be identified in such a functional dependence (Andreou, 1992; Mead, 1989):

- The *abovethreshold region,* where the drain current I_d is a quadratic function of the gate-source voltage V_{gs}.
- The *subthreshold region,* where the transistor is operated at low gate-source voltages such that the drain current I_d is an exponential function of the gate-source voltage V_{gs}.

All things being equal, the exponential nonlinearity (i.e., operation in the subthreshold region) is preferrable, because it provides more transconductance (i.e., $\partial I_d/\partial V_{gs}$) per unit current. Moreover, in the subthreshold region, the MOS transistor can provide two useful functions, depending on the drain-source voltage, as described here:

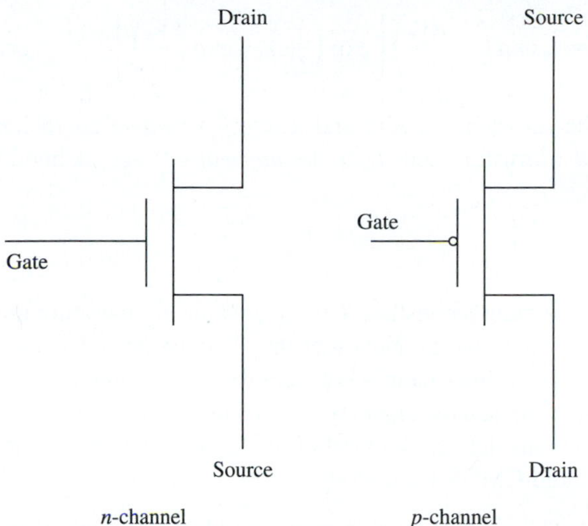

FIGURE 15.1 (a) *n*-channel transistor. (b) *p*-channel transistor.

- For small drain-source voltages (approximately, less than a few hundred millivolts), the device acts essentially as a *controlled conductance* with perfect symmetry between the source and the drain; this mode of operation is called the *ohmic* or *linear region.*
- For larger values of drain-source voltage, the device is essentially a *voltage-controlled current source* (i.e., a sink).

In analog VLSI implementations of *neuromorphic networks,* whose purpose is to mimic specific neurobiological functions, the customary practice is to operate the MOS transistors in the subthreshold region; neuromorphic networks are discussed in Section 15.4.

Subthreshold operation of CMOS transistors exhibits the following useful characteristics (Andreou, 1992; Mead, 1989):

- Exponential current gain over six orders of magnitude (10 pA $\rightarrow$ 10 μA).
- Very efficient voltage-to-current (exponential) conversion or current-to-voltage (logarithmic) conversion produced by a single transistor.
- Extremely low power dissipation (typically, 10^{-12} to 10^{-6} W).

Above all, however, it provides the basis of a design philosophy for building large-scale analog circuits that mimic a neurobiological system chosen for study.

The analog computations performed by such a neurocomputer are based on functions of *time, space, voltage, current,* and *charge,* which are related directly to the physics of the computational substrate. The functions are described at the device level, circuit level, and architectural level, as follows (Andreou, 1992; Mead, 1989):

- *Device Level.* Let I_d denote the drain current of the MOS transistor. Let V_g, V_s, and V_d denote the respective voltages of the gate, source, and drain, measured with respect to the local substrate. Then, the device behavior in the subthreshold region is defined by, depending on whether the transistor is of the *n*-channel or *p*-channel type (Mead, 1989),

$$I_d = I_0 \exp\left(\frac{\kappa V_g}{U_t}\right)\left[\exp\left(-\frac{V_s}{U_t}\right) - \exp\left(-\frac{V_d}{U_t}\right)\right] \qquad n\text{-channel} \qquad (15.5)$$

$$I_d = I_0 \exp\left(-\frac{\kappa V_g}{U_t}\right)\left[\exp\left(\frac{V_s}{U_t}\right) - \exp\left(\frac{V_d}{U_t}\right)\right] \qquad p\text{-channel} \tag{15.6}$$

where I_0 is the *zero-bias current* and κ is a *body-effect coefficient,* which depends on the type of transistor used; U_t is the *thermal voltage,* defined by

$$U_t = \frac{k_B T}{q} \tag{15.7}$$

where k_B is Boltzmann's constant, T is the absolute temperature measured in kelvins, and q is the electron charge. Note that the exponential functions in Eqs. (15.5) and (15.6) are all due to Boltzmann's law, and the *exact difference* between exponential functions inside the square brackets is a result of Ohm's law. The combination of these two equations defines the kind of analog computations that can be performed with subthreshold CMOS technology.

- *Circuit Level.* This second level is governed by the conservation of charge and the conservation of energy, which, respectively, yield the two familiar equations:

$$\sum_i I_i = 0 \tag{15.8}$$

$$\sum_i V_i = 0 \tag{15.9}$$

Equation (15.8) is recognized as *Kirchoff's current law,* and Eq. (15.9) is *Kirchoff's voltage law.*

- *Architectural Level.* At this last level, differential equations from mathematical physics are used to implement useful functions, depending on the application of interest.

In the analog approach described by Andreou (1992) and Andreou et al. (1991), a minimalistic design style is adopted. The approach is motivated by the belief that a single transistor is a powerful computational element that can provide gain and also some basic computational functions. The design methodology is based on *current-mode* subthreshold CMOS circuits, according to which the signals of interest are represented as currents, and voltages play merely an incidental role. The current-mode approach offers signal processing at the highest possible bandwidth, given the available silicon technologies and a fixed amount of energy resources (Andreou, 1992).

In contrast, in the analog approach described by Mead (1989), a *transconductance amplifier* is taken as the basic building block. This amplifier, shown in its basic form in Fig. 15.2, is a device whose output current is a function of the difference between two input voltages, V_1 and V_2. It is referred to as a transconductance amplifier because it changes a differential input voltage, $V_1 - V_2$, into an output current. This differential voltage is taken as the primary signal representation. The bottom transistor Q_b in Fig. 15.2 operates as a current source, supplying a constant current I_b. The current I_b is divided between the two top transistors Q_1 and Q_2 in a manner determined by the differential voltage, $V_1 - V_2$. Assuming that the drain-source voltages of these two transistors are large enough for them to be driven into saturation, we find that the application of Eq. (15.5) to the differential transconductance amplifier of Fig. 15.2 yields (Mead, 1989)

$$I_{\text{out}} = I_b \tanh\left(\frac{\kappa V_{\text{in}}}{2U_t}\right) \tag{15.10}$$

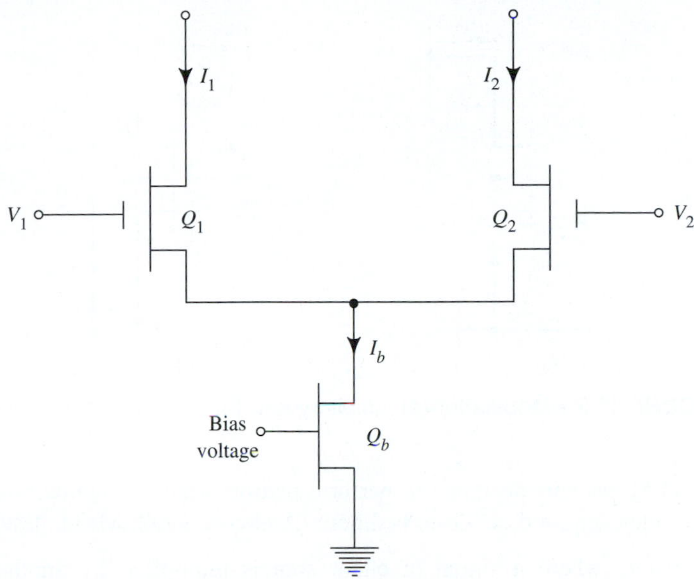

FIGURE 15.2 Circuit diagram of a differential pair used as a transconductance amplifier.

where tanh(·) is the hyperbolic tangent, and

$$V_{in} = V_1 - V_2 \tag{15.11}$$

and

$$I_{out} = I_1 - I_2 \tag{15.12}$$

Thus with the differential voltage V_{in} treated as the input signal and the differential current I_{out} treated as the output signal, we see that the circuit of Fig. 15.2 provides a simple device for the ''output computation'' in the form of a sigmoidal nonlinearity that is asymmetric about the origin.

The ''sum-of-products'' computation is equally well suited for the analog paradigm. In CMOS technology, the natural choice for a nonreciprocal synapse is a single MOS transistor driven into saturation (Boahen et al., 1989). Specifically, an input voltage applied to the insulated gate of the transistor produces a low-conductance output at the drain. This arrangement allows for a large fan-out. Figure 15.3 shows both n-channel and p-channel transistors used to model inhibitory and excitatory synapses, respectively. By convention, excitation is the supply of positive charge to a node, whereas inhibition is the drain of positive charge from a node. The input–output relation of Fig. 15.3a is defined by

$$I_{inh} = I_0 \exp(\kappa V_{inh}/U_t) \tag{15.13}$$

and that of Fig. 15.3b is defined by

$$I_{exc} = I_0 \exp(-\kappa V_{exc}/U_t) \tag{15.14}$$

In both cases each synaptic weight is modeled as a transconductance. For the final step in the sum-of-products computation, Kirchoff's current law is invoked to perform summation of output drain currents corresponding to the various synapses of a neuron.

There is one other issue that needs to be considered, namely, that of storage. This requirement, for example, may be taken care of by using the voltage difference between two floating gates to store a synaptic weight.

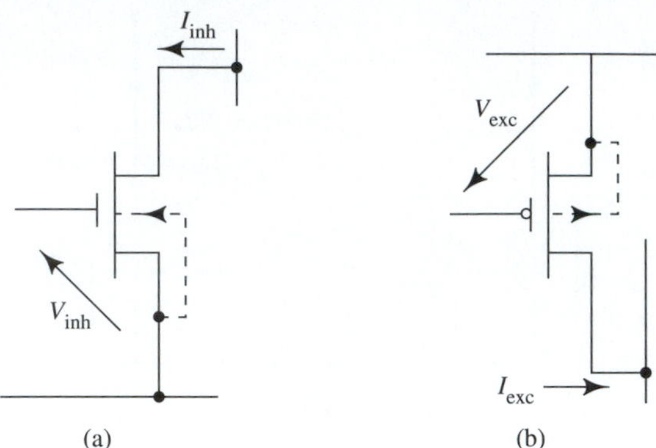

FIGURE 15.3 Models for (a) inhibitory and (b) excitatory synapses.

In analog VLSI systems designed to perform neuromorphic computations, additional operations are often required, as described here (Andreou, 1992; Mead, 1989):

- *Multiplication,* where a signal of either sign is multiplied by another signal of either sign; this operation requires the use of a *four-quadrant multiplier,* where each quadrant corresponds to a particular combination of input signals.
- *Aggregation,* where a very large number of inputs are brought together in an analog manner.
- *Scaling,* where a quantity of interest is multiplied by a scaling factor.
- *Normalization,* the purpose of which is to reduce the dynamic range of input signals to levels compatible with the needs of subsequent processing stages; normalization can be of a local or global nature.
- *Winner-takes-all,* where a particular neuron among many others wins a competitive process.

Circuits that implement these neuromorphic functions are described in Andreou (1992) and Mead (1989).

The important point to note from this brief discussion is that analog circuits, be they based on conventional CMOS technology or subthreshold CMOS technology, provide a computationally efficient technique for the implementation of neural networks and for mimicking neurobiology.

Digital Techniques

There are two key advantages to the digital approach over the analog approach (Hammerstrom, 1992):

- *Ease of Design and Manufacture.* The use of digital VLSI technology offers the advantage of high precision, ease of weight storage, and cost-performance advantage in ''programmability'' over analog VLSI technology. Moreover, digital silicon processing is more readily available than analog.
- *Flexibility.* The second and most important advantage of the digital approach is that it is much more *flexible,* permitting the use of many more complex algorithms and expanding the range of possible applications. In some cases, solving complex problems may require significant flexibility in the neural network architecture to be able to solve the problem at all. Lack of flexibility is indeed a fundamental limitation of analog systems; in particular, the level of complexity that the technology can deal

with often limits the range and scope of problems that can be solved with analog technology.

However, a disadvantage of digital VLSI technology is that the digital implementation of multiplication is both area- and power-hungry. Area requirements may be reduced by using digital, multiplexed interconnect (Hammerstrom, 1992).

The ultimate choice of digital over analog technology cannot be answered unless we know which particular algorithms are being considered for neural network applications. If, however, general-purpose use is the aim, then the use of digital VLSI technology has a distinct advantage over its analog counterpart. We have more to say on this issue in Section 15.4.

Hybrid Techniques

The use of *analog computation* is attractive for neural VLSI for reasons of compactness, potential speed, and absence of quantization effects. The use of digital techniques, on the other hand, is preferred for long-distance communications, because *digital signals* are known to be robust, easily transmitted and regenerated. These considerations encourage the use of a *hybrid* approach for the VLSI implementation of neural networks, which builds on the merits of both analog and digital technologies (Murray et al., 1991). A signaling technique that lends itself to this hybrid approach is *pulse modulation,* the theory and practice of which are well known in the field of communication systems (Haykin, 1983; Black, 1953). In pulse modulation, viewed in the context of neural networks, some characteristic of a pulse stream used as carrier is varied in accordance with a neural state. Given that the pulse amplitude, pulse duration, and pulse repetition rate are the parameters available for variation, we may distinguish three basic pulse modulation techniques as described here (Murray et al., 1991):

- *Pulse-amplitude modulation,* in which the amplitude of a pulse is modulated in time, reflecting the variation in neural state $0 < s_j < 1$. This technique is not particularly satisfactory in neural networks, because the information is transmitted as analog voltage levels, which makes it susceptible to processing variations.
- *Pulse-width modulation,* in which the width (duration) of a pulse is varied in accordance with the neural state s_j. The advantages of a hybrid scheme now become apparent, as no analog voltage is present in the modulated signal, with information being coded along the time axis. A pulse-width-modulated signal is therefore robust. Moreover, demodulation of the signal is readily accomplished via integration. The use of a constant signaling frequency, however, means that either the leading or trailing edges of the modulated signals representing neural states will occur simultaneously. The existence of this synchronism represents a drawback in massively parallel neural VLSI networks, since all the neurons (and synapses) tend to draw current on the supply lines simultaneously, with no averaging effect. It follows, therefore, that the supply lines must be oversized in order to accommodate the high instantaneous currents produced by the use of pulse-width modulation.
- *Pulse-frequency modulation,* in which the instantaneous frequency of the pulse stream is varied in accordance with the neural state s_j, with the frequency ranging from some minimum to some maximum value. In this case, both the amplitude and duration of each pulse are maintained constant. Here also the use of a hybrid scheme is advantageous for the same reasons mentioned for pulse-width modulation. Since the signaling frequency is now variable, both the leading and trailing edges of the modulated signals representing the neural states become skewed. Consequently, the

massive transient demand on supply lines is avoided, and the power requirement is averaged in time as a result of using pulse-frequency modulation.

From this discussion, it appears that pulse-frequency modulation[2] provides a practical technique for signaling in massively parallel neural VLSI networks. It is also of interest to note that it has been known for about a century that neurons in the brain signal one another using pulse-frequency modulation (Hecht-Nielsen, 1990). Thus, recognizing the benefits of pulse-frequency modulation, and being inspired by neurobiological models, Churcher et al. (1993) and Murray et al. (1991) describe integrated *pulse stream* neural networks, based on pulse-frequency modulation. In particular, the networks use *digital* signals to convey information and control *analog* circuitry, while storing *analog* information along the time axis. Thus the VLSI neural networks described therein are hybrid devices, moving between the analog and digital domains as appropriate, to optimize the robustness, compactness, and speed of the associated network chips.

There is another important hybrid technique used in the VLSI implementation of neural networks, namely, *multiplying digital-to-analog converters* (MDAC) employed as multipliers. In this technique, an *analog state* (i.e., input signal) can be multiplied with a *digital weight* as in the Bellcore chip (Alspector et al., 1991b), or a *digital state* can be multiplied with an *analog weight* as in the AT&T ANNA chip (Säckinger et al., 1992); we have more to say on these hybrid chips in Section 15.4. Thus MDACs permit the neural network designer to combine the use of analog and digital technologies in an optimal fashion to solve a particular computation problem.

15.4 Neurocomputing Hardware

Having surveyed the analog, digital, and hybrid approaches to the VLSI implementations of neural networks and identified their advantages and disadvantages, we are ready to look at some examples of neurocomputing hardware. The list of general-purpose and special-purpose neurocomputer chips/systems available presently is quite diverse, and still growing, which is indicative of the rapid acceptance of neural networks by the user community. General-purpose chips/systems include the ETANN analog chip (Holler et al., 1988), the University of Edinburgh EPSILON hybrid chip (Murray et al., 1991; Hamilton et al., 1992; Churcher et al., 1993), the Adaptive Solutions CNAPS digital system (Hammerstrom, 1992; Hammerstrom et al., 1990), the Siemens digital Neural Signal Processor (Ramacher et al., 1991; Ramacher, 1990), the Mitsubishi BNU digital chip (Arima et al., 1991), the Hitachi digital chip (Watanabe et al., 1993), the Bellcore Boltzmann/mean-field learning chip (Alspector et al., 1991b, 1992a), and the AT&T Bell Labs ANNA chip (Boser et al., 1992; Säckinger et al., 1992). Special-purpose chips include the Synaptics OCR chip, an analog implementation of Kohonen's self-organizing feature map with on-chip learning (Macq et al., 1993); VLSI processors for video machine detection (Lee et al., 1993); a programmable analog VLSI neural network for communication receivers (Choi et al., 1993); and a multilevel neural chip for analog-to-digital conversion (Yuh and Newcomb, 1993).

As examples of neurocomputing VLSI hardware, we have selected for further discussion three of these chips/systems: the CNAPS, the Boltzmann/mean-field learning chip, and the ANNA chip. The section concludes with a discussion of neuromorphic chips.

[2] Another pulse modulation technique, known as *pulse duty cycle modulation,* may be used as the basis of VLSI implementation of synaptic weighting and summing (Moon et al., 1992). In this scheme, variations in the duty cycle of a pulse stream are used to convey information.

CNAPS

For our first VLSI-based system, we have chosen a general-purpose digital machine called CNAPS (Connected Network of Adaptive ProcessorS), manufactured by Adaptive Solutions, Inc., and which is capable of high neural network performance (Hammerstrom, 1992; Hammerstrom et al., 1990).

The CNAPS system is an SIMD (Single Instruction stream, Multiple Data stream) machine, consisting of an array of processor nodes, as illustrated in Fig. 15.4. Each *processor node* (PN) is a simple digital signal processorlike computing element. The array of PNs is laid out in one dimension and operates synchronously (i.e., all the PNs execute the same instruction each clock cycle). The instructions are provided by an external *program sequencer,* which has a program memory and instruction fetch and decode capability. The program sequencer also manages all input/output to and from the PN array.

Data representation is digital *fixed-point.* Each PN has a 9-bit by 16-bit multiplier, a 32-bit adder, a logic unit, a 32-word register file, a 12-bit weight address unit, and 4K bytes of storage for weights and coefficients. The internal buses and registers are 16 bits. Each PN can compute one multiply accumulate per clock cycle. The use of fixed-point arithmetic is justified on the grounds of cost; and for practically all current learning algorithms and neural network applications, the use of arithmetic precision higher than that described here is considered unnecessary.

CNAPS uses on-chip memories, which makes it possible to perform *on-chip learning.* The total synaptic connections per chip are as follows:

- 2M 1-bit weights
- 256K 8-bit weights

At 25 MHz, a single CNAPS chip can perform 1.6 billion multiply accumulates per second. An 8-chip system can perform 12.8 billion multiply accumulates per second. Thus, in back-propagation learning, the 8-chip system can learn at 2 billion weight updates per second, assuming that all the PNs are busy. To get an idea of what these numbers imply, the NETtalk network (developed originally by Sejnowski and Rosenberg, 1987), which normally takes about 4 hours of training on a SUN SPARC workstation, would fit onto a single CNAPS chip and require only about 7 seconds to train (Hammerstrom and Rahfuss, 1992).

Boltzmann/Mean-Field-Theory Learning Chip

For our second VLSI chip, we have chosen a high-performance hybrid chip for the implementation of Boltzmann and mean-field-theory learning algorithms, fabricated by Bellcore (Alspector et al., 1991b, 1992a, 1992b). Although, indeed, this chip is restricted

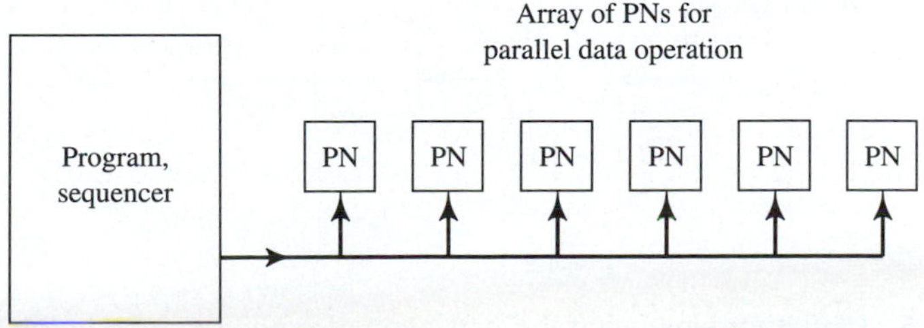

FIGURE 15.4 Single instruction stream, multiple data stream.

for use on a particular class of learning algorithms, it enjoys a wide range of applications, and in that sense it may be viewed to be of general-purpose use.

From Chapter 8 we recall that both the Boltzmann and mean-field-theory learning algorithms are as capable as the back-propagation algorithm of learning difficult problems. In computer simulation, back-propagation learning has the advantage in that it is often orders of magnitude faster than Boltzmann learning; mean-field-theory learning lies somewhere between the two, though closer to back-propagation learning. However, the *local* nature of both Boltzmann learning and mean-field-theory learning makes them easier to cast into electronics than back-propagation learning. Indeed, by implementing them in VLSI form, it becomes possible to speed up the learning process in the Boltzmann machine and mean-field-theory machine by orders of magnitude, which makes them both attractive for practical applications.

A key issue in the hardware implementation of Boltzmann learning and mean-field-theory learning is how to account for the effect of temperature T, which plays the role of a control parameter during the annealing schedule. A practical way in which this effect may be realized is to add a physical *noise* term to the activation potential of each neuron in the network. Specifically, neuron j is designed to perform the activation computation (see Fig. 15.5)

$$s_j = \varphi(v_j + n_j) \tag{15.15}$$

where v_j and s_j are the activation potential and output signal of neuron j, respectively, and n_j is an external noise term applied to neuron j. The function $\varphi(\cdot)$ is a monotonic nonlinear function such as the hyperbolic tangent $\tanh(\cdot)$ with a variable gain (midpoint slope) denoted by g. The details of the noise term n_j and the function $\varphi(\cdot)$ depend on whether Boltzmann learning or mean-field-theory learning is being simulated.

In simulations of the Boltzmann machine, the gain g is made high so as to permit the function $\varphi(\cdot)$ approach a step function. The noise term n_j is chosen from a zero-mean Gaussian distribution, whose width is proportional to the temperature T. In order to account for the role of temperature T, the noise n_j is thus slowly reduced in accordance with the prescribed annealing schedule.

In simulations of mean-field-theory learning, on the other hand, the noise term is set equal to zero. But for this application, the gain g of the function $\varphi(\cdot)$ has a finite value chosen to be proportional to the reciprocal of temperature T taken from the annealing schedule. The nonlinearity of the function $\varphi(\cdot)$ is thus "sharpened" as the annealing schedule of decreasing temperature proceeds.

Alspector et al. (1991b, 1992a) describe a microchip implementation of the Boltzmann machine. The chip contains 32 neurons with 992 connections (i.e., 496 bidirectional synapses). The chip includes a noise generator that supplies 32 uncorrelated pseudorandom noise sources simultaneously to all the neurons in the system. The traditional method for

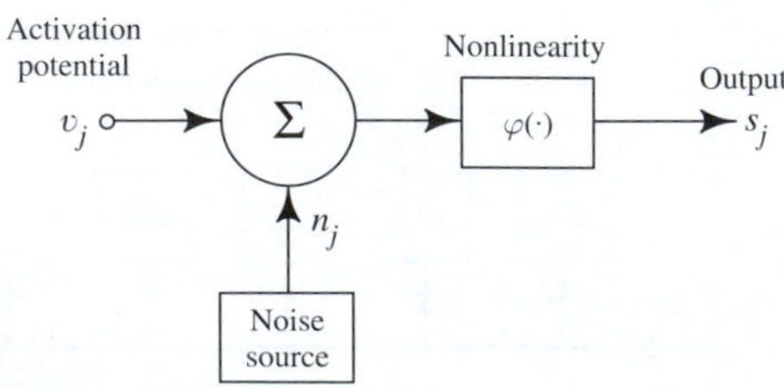

FIGURE 15.5 Circuit for simulating the activation of a neuron used in the Boltzmann machine or mean-field-theory machine.

generating a pseudorandom bit stream is to use a *linear feedback shift register* (LFSR).[3] However, the use of a separate LFSR for each neuron (in order to obtain uncorrelated noise from one neuron to another) requires an unacceptable overhead for VLSI implementation. Alspector et al. (1991a) describe a method of generating multiple, arbitrarily shifted, pseudorandom bit streams from a single LSFR, with each bit stream being obtained by tapping the outputs of selected cells (flip-flops) in the LFSR and feeding these tapped outputs through a set of exclusive-OR gates. This method enables many neurons to share a single LFSR, resulting in an acceptably small overhead for VLSI implementation.

The individual noise sources (produced in the manner described here) are summed along with the weighted postsynaptic signals from other neurons at the input to each neuron. This is done in order to implement the simulated annealing process of the stochastic Boltzmann machine. The neuron amplifiers implement a nonlinear activation function with a variable gain so as to cater to the gain-sharpening requirement of the mean-field-theory learning technique.

Most of the area covered by the ''hybrid'' microchip is occupied by the array of synapses. Each synapse *digitally* stores a weight ranging from -15 to $+15$ as binary words consisting of 4 bits plus sign. The *analog* voltage input from the presynaptic neuron is multiplied by the weight stored in the synapse, producing an output current. Although the synapses can have their weights set externally, they are designed to be adaptive. In particular, they store the ''instantaneous'' correlations produced after annealing, and therefore adjust the synaptic weight w_{ji} in an ''on-line'' fashion in accordance with the learning rule

$$\Delta w_{ji} = \kappa \cdot \text{sgn}[(s_j s_i)^+ - (s_j s_i)^-] \tag{15.16}$$

where κ is a fixed step size. The learning rule of Eq. (15.16) is called *Manhattan updating* (Peterson and Hartman, 1989). In the learning rule described in Eq. (8.75), the synaptic weights are changed according to gradient descent and therefore each gradient component (weight change) will be of different size. On the other hand, in the Manhattan learning rule of Eq. (15.16), a step is taken in a slightly different direction along a vector whose components are all of equal size. In this latter form of learning, everything about the gradient is thrown away, except for the knowledge as to which quadrant the gradient lies in, with the result that learning proceeds on a lattice. In the microchip described by Alspector et al. (1991b), the fixed step size $\kappa = 1$, and so the synaptic weight w_{ji} is changed by one unit at each iteration of the mean-field-theory learning algorithm.

An on-line procedure is used for weight updates, where only a single correlation is taken per pattern. Thus there is no basic difference between counting correlations and counting occurrences as described in Chapter 8. Also, the use of on-line weight updates avoids the problem of memory storage at synapses.

The chip is designed to be cascaded with similar chips in a board-level system that can be accessed externally by a computer. The nodes of a particular chip that sum currents

---

[3] A shift register of length m is a device consisting of m consecutive two-state memory stages (flip-flops) regulated by a single timing clock. At each clock pulse, the state (represented by binary symbol 1 or 0) of each memory stage is shifted to the next stage down the line. To prevent the shift register from emptying by the end of m clock pulses, we use a logical (i.e., Boolean) function of the states of the m memory stages to compute a *feedback term,* and apply it to the first memory stage of the shift register. The most important special form of this feedback shift register is the *linear* case in which the feedback function is obtained by using modulo-2 adders to combine the outputs of the various memory stages. A binary sequence generated by a linear feedback shift register is called a *linear maximal sequence* and is always periodic with a period defined by

$$N = 2^m - 1$$

where m is the length of the shift register. Linear maximal sequences are also referred to as *pseudorandom* or *pseudonoise* (PN) *sequences.* The term ''random'' comes from the fact that these sequences have many of the physical properties usually associated with a truly random binary sequence (Golomb, 1964).

from synapses for the net activation potential of a neuron are available externally for connection to other chips and also for external clamping of neurons. Alspector et al. (1992a) have used this system to perform learning experiments on the parity and replication (identity) problems, thereby facilitating comparisons with previous simulations (Alspector et al., 1991b). The parity problem is a generalization of the XOR problem for arbitrary input size. The goal of the replication problem is for the output to duplicate the bit pattern found on the input after being encoded by the hidden layer. For real-time operation, it is reported that the speed for on-chip learning is roughly 10^8 synaptic connections per second per chip.

In another study (Alspector et al., 1992b), a single chip was used to perform experiments on content-addressable memory using mean-field-theory learning. It is demonstrated that about 100,000 codewords per second can be stored and retrieved by the chip. Moreover, close agreement is reported between the experimental results and the computer simulations performed by Hartman (1991). These results demonstrate that mean-field-theory learning is able to provide the largest storage per neuron for error-correcting memories reported in the literature at that time.

ANNA Chip

For the description of a general-purpose hybrid chip designed with multilayer perceptrons in mind, we have chosen a reconfigurable chip called the ANNA (Analog Neural Network Arithmetic and logic unit) chip, which is a hybrid analog–digital neural network chip developed by AT&T Bell Labs (Boser et al., 1992; Säckinger et al., 1992). The hybrid architecture is designed to match the arithmetic precision of the hardware to the computational requirements of neural networks. In particular, experimental work has shown that the precision requirements of neurons within a multilayer perceptron vary, in that higher accuracy is often needed in the output layer, for example, for selective rejection of ambiguous or other unclassifiable patterns (Boser et al., 1992). A hybrid architecture may be used to deal with a situation of this kind by implementing the bulk of the neural computations with low-precision analog devices, but critical connections are implemented on a digital processor with higher accuracy.

Figure 15.6 shows a simplified architecture of the ANNA chip. The architectural layout shown in this figure leaves out many design details of the chip, but it is adequate for a description of how the multilayer perceptron designed to perform pattern classification is implemented on the chip. The ANNA chip evaluates eight inner products of state vector $\mathbf{x}$ and eight synaptic weight vectors $\mathbf{w}_j$ in parallel. The state vector is loaded into a *barrel shifter,* and the eight weight vectors are selected from a large (4096) *on-chip weight memory* by means of a multiplexer; the resulting scalar values of the inner products

$$\mathbf{w}_j^T\mathbf{x}, \qquad j = 1, 2, \ldots, 8 \tag{15.17}$$

are then passed through a *neuron function* (sigmoidal nonlinearity) denoted by $\varphi(\cdot)$, yielding a corresponding set of scalar neural outputs

$$z_j = \varphi(\mathbf{w}_j^T\mathbf{x}), \qquad j = 1, 2, \ldots, 8 \tag{15.18}$$

The whole neuron-function evaluation process takes 200 ns, or four clock cycles. The chip can be reconfigured for synaptic weight and input state vectors of varying dimension, namely, 64, 128, and 256. These figures also correspond to the number of synapses per neuron.

The input state vector $\mathbf{x}$ is supplied by a shift register that can be shifted by one, two, three, or four positions in two clock cycles (100 ns). Correspondingly, one, two, three,

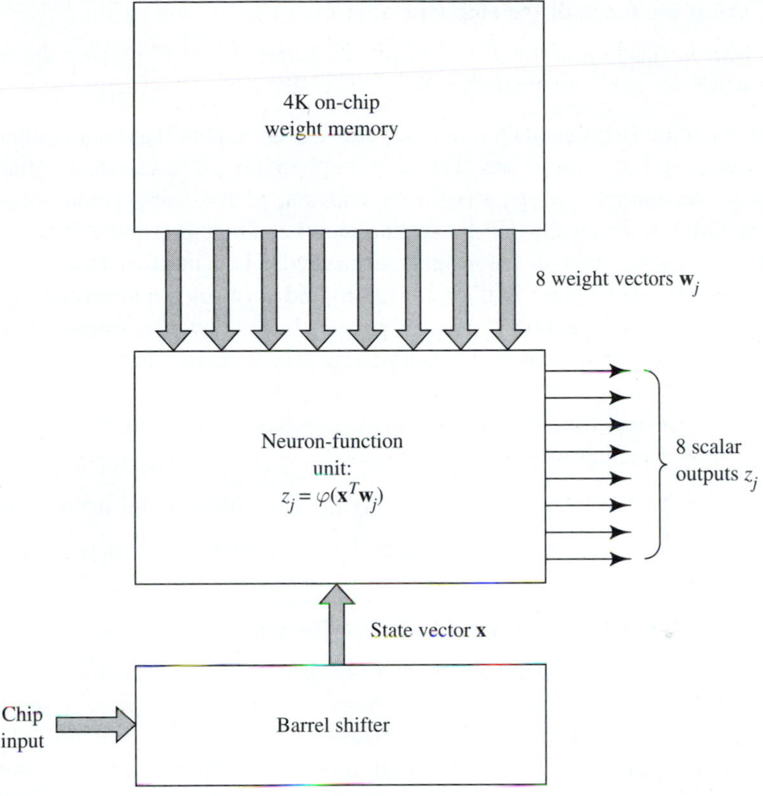

FIGURE 15.6 Simplified architecture of the ANNA chip. (From E. Säckinger et al., 1992a, with permission of IEEE.)

or four new data values are read into the input end of the shift register. Thus, this barrel shifter serves two useful purposes:

- It permits the use of sequential loading.
- It is the ideal preprocessor for convolutional networks characterized by local receptive fields and weight sharing.

The barrel shifter on the chip has length 64. It is operated in parallel with the neuron-function unit, such that a new state vector is available as soon as a new calculation cycle starts.

There are a total of 4096 analog weight values stored on the chip. These values can be grouped in a flexible way into weight vectors of varying dimension: 64, 128, and 256. Thus, on the same chip it is possible to have, for example, simultaneously thirty-two weight vectors of dimension 64, eight weight vectors of dimension 128, and four weight vectors of dimension 256.

Assuming that all neurons on the chip are configured for the maximum size of 256 synapses, the chip can evaluate a maximum of 10^{10} connections per second (C/s) as shown by the following calculation:

$$8 \text{ neurons} \times 256 \text{ synapses}/200 \text{ ns} \approx 10^{10} \text{ C/s} = 10 \text{ GC/s}$$

In practice, however, the speed of operation of the chip may be lower than this number for two reasons:

- Full use is *not* made of the chip's parallelism.
- The neuron-function unit has to wait for the barrel shifter to prepare the input state vector for the next calculation cycle.

The ANNA chip is implemented in a 0.9-μm CMOS technology, containing 180,000 transistors on a 4.5 $\times$ 7 mm^2 die. The chip implements 4096 physical synapses. The resolution of the synaptic weights is 6 bits, and that of the states (input/output of the neurons) is 3 bits. Additionally, a 4-bit scaling factor can be programmed for each neuron to extend the dynamic range of the weights, as needed. The chip uses analog computation internally, but all input/output is digital. This hybrid form of implementation combines the advantages of high synaptic density, high speed, low power consumption of analog technology, and ease of interfacing to a digital system such as a digital signal processor (DSP).

Indeed, for practical use, the chip has to be integrated into a digital system required to perform three principal functions:

- *Memory controller,* supplying and storing the state data to and from the chip.
- *Sequencer,* generating microcode words that correspond to the network topology to be evaluated.
- *Refresh controller,* refreshing the dynamic on-chip weight storage.

Boser et al. (1992) and Säckinger et al. (1992) describe an important application of the ANNA chip for the implementation of high-speed *optical character recognition* (OCR) with a total of 136,000 connections on a single chip. The general structure of the OCR network (for recognition of handwritten digits) is a multilayer perceptron consisting of an input layer, four hidden layers, and an output layer, as shown in Fig. 15.7. The input layer has 400 nodes, corresponding directly to the 20 $\times$ 20 pixel image; that is, no preprocessing, such as feature extraction, is done. The compositions of the five computation layers, expressed in terms of numbers of neurons and synapses, are given in Fig. 15.7. The 10 outputs of the network represent 10 digits in a "1 out of 10" code. The outputs of the neurons have real values (as opposed to thresholded values); hence the network output contains information not only about the classification result (the most active digit), but also about the *confidence* of the decision made. Moreover, since there is no feedback in the network, the classification can be performed in a single pass.

Of the five computation layers of the network, only the output layer is fully connected, with all synaptic weights being independent. The four hidden layers are carefully *constrained* to improve the generalization capability of the network for input patterns not seen during the training process. These constraints are symbolized by the *local receptive fields* shown shaded in Fig. 15.7, an issue that was discussed at some length in Chapter 6.

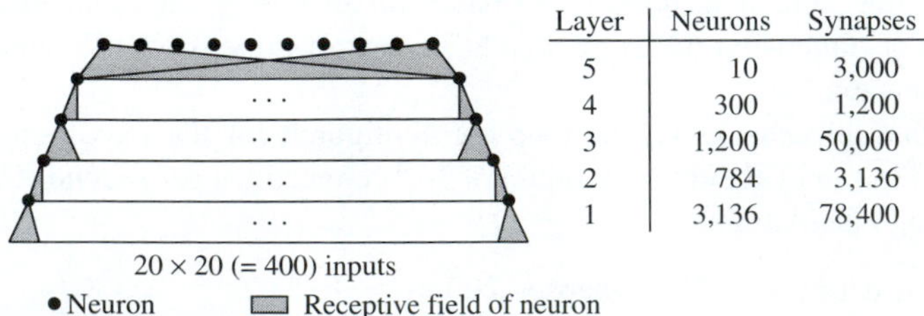

Layer	Neurons	Synapses
5	10	3,000
4	300	1,200
3	1,200	50,000
2	784	3,136
1	3,136	78,400

FIGURE 15.7 General structure of the OCR network. (From E. Säckinger et al., 1992a, with permission of IEEE.)

TABLE 15.1 Execution Time of OCR Network on ANNA Chip and SUN Workstation (adapted from Säckinger et al., 1992)

Layer	ANNA Chip	SUN SPARC 1+
Hidden layer 1	330 μs	290 ms
Hidden layer 2	210 μs	10 ms
Hidden layer 3	320 μs	190 ms
Hidden layer 4	100 μs	5 ms
Output layer	—	5 ms
Total	960 μs	0.5 s

Table 15.1 presents a summary of the execution time of the OCR network implemented using the ANNA chip, compared to a SUN SPARC 1+ workstation. This table shows that a classification rate of 1000 characters per second can be achieved using a pipelined system consisting of the ANNA chip and a DSP. This rate corresponds to a speedup factor of 500 over the SUN implementation.

Neuromorphic VLSI Chips

For our last neurocomputing hardware topic, we have opted for special-purpose *neuromorphic information-processing structures* using analog VLSI technology. The purpose of these structures is to solve a similar class of problems that nervous systems were designed to solve, in which case the approach that nature has evolved is taken seriously indeed (Faggin and Mead, 1990). The development of these structures has been pioneered by Mead and co-workers at CalTech, and which has also inspired many other researchers to follow a similar route. The silicon retina (Mahowald and Mead, 1989), the silicon cochlea (Watts et al., 1992), and the analog VLSI model of binaural hearing (Mead et al., 1991) are outstanding examples of this novel approach. A brief description of the silicon retina is presented in the sequel. The silicon retina and the other neuromorphic VLSI chips referred to herein are not only able to perform difficult signal processing computations by mimicking neurobiology, but they do so in a highly efficient manner.[4]

The *retina,* more than any other part of the brain, is where we begin to put together the relationships between the outside world represented by a visual sense, its *physical image* projected onto an array of receptors, and the first *neural images.* The retina is a thin sheet of neural tissue that lines the posterior hemisphere of the eyeball (Sterling, 1990). The retina's task is to convert an optical image into a neural image for transmission down the optic nerve to a multitude of centers for further analysis. This is a complex task, as evidenced by the synaptic organization of the retina.

[4] Faggin (1991) presents a performance assessment of neurocomputation using special-purpose VLSI chips. The following figures are presented, based on the status of VLSI technology in 1991:

Number of processors	100K
Number of weights	100K
Speed of computation	1 μs
Total computation	100×10^9 operation/s
Processing energetic efficiency	10^{-13} J/operation
Chip energetic efficiency	10^{-11} J/operation

In all vertebrate retinas the transformation from optical to neural image involves three stages (Sterling, 1990):

- Photo transduction by a layer of receptor neurons.
- Transmission of the resulting signals (produced in response to light) by chemical synapses to a layer of *bipolar cells.*
- Transmission of these signals, also by chemical synapses, to output neurons that are called *ganglion cells.*

At both synaptic stages (i.e., from receptor to bipolar cells, and from bipolar to ganglion cells), there are specialized laterally connected neurons, called *horizontal cells* and *amacrine cells,* respectively. The task of these neurons is to modify the transmission across the synaptic layers. There are also centrifugal elements, called *inter-plexiform cells*; their task is to convey signals from the inner synaptic layer back to the outer one.

Figure 15.8 shows a simplified circuit diagram of the *silicon retina* built by Mead and Mahowald (1988), which is modeled on the distal portion of the vertebrate retina. This diagram emphasizes the lateral spread of the resistive network, corresponding to the horizontal cell layer of the vertebrate retina. The primary signal pathway proceeds through the photoreceptor and the circuitry representing the bipolar cell, the latter being shown in the inset. The image signal is processed in parallel at each node of the network.

The key element in the outer plexiform layer is the *triad synapse,* which is located at the base of the photoreceptor. The triad synapse provides the point of contact among the photoreceptor, the horizontal cells, and the bipolar cells. The computation performed at the triad synapse proceeds as follows (Mahowald and Mead, 1989):

- The photoreceptor computes the logarithm of the intensity of incident light.
- The horizontal cells form a resistive network that spatio-temporally averages the output produced by the photoreceptor.
- The bipolar cell produces an output proportional to the difference between the signals generated by the photoreceptor and the horizontal cell.

The net result of these computations is that the silicon retina generates, in real time, outputs that correspond directly to signals observed in the corresponding layers of biological retinas. It demonstrates a tolerance for device imperfections that is characteristic of a collective analog system.

A commercial product resulting from the research done by Mead and co-workers on the silicon retina is the *Synaptics OCR chip,* manufactured by Synaptics Corporation for use in a device that reads the MICR code at the bottom of cheques. The chip is of an analog design, based on subthreshold CMOS technology, and customized for this specific application.

Mention should also be made of independent work done by Boahen and Andreou (1992) on a *contrast-sensitive silicon retina,* which models all major synaptic interactions in the outer plexiform of the vertebrate retina, using current-mode subthreshold CMOS technology. This silicon retina permits resolution to be traded off for enhanced signal-to-noise ratio, thereby revealing low-contrast stimuli in the presence of large transistor mismatch. It thus provides the basis of an edge-detection algorithm with a naturally built-in regularization capability.

The work of Mead and Andreou and their respective fellow researchers on silicon retinas validates an important principle enunciated by Winograd and Cowan (1963) that it is indeed possible to design reliable networks using unreliable circuit elements.

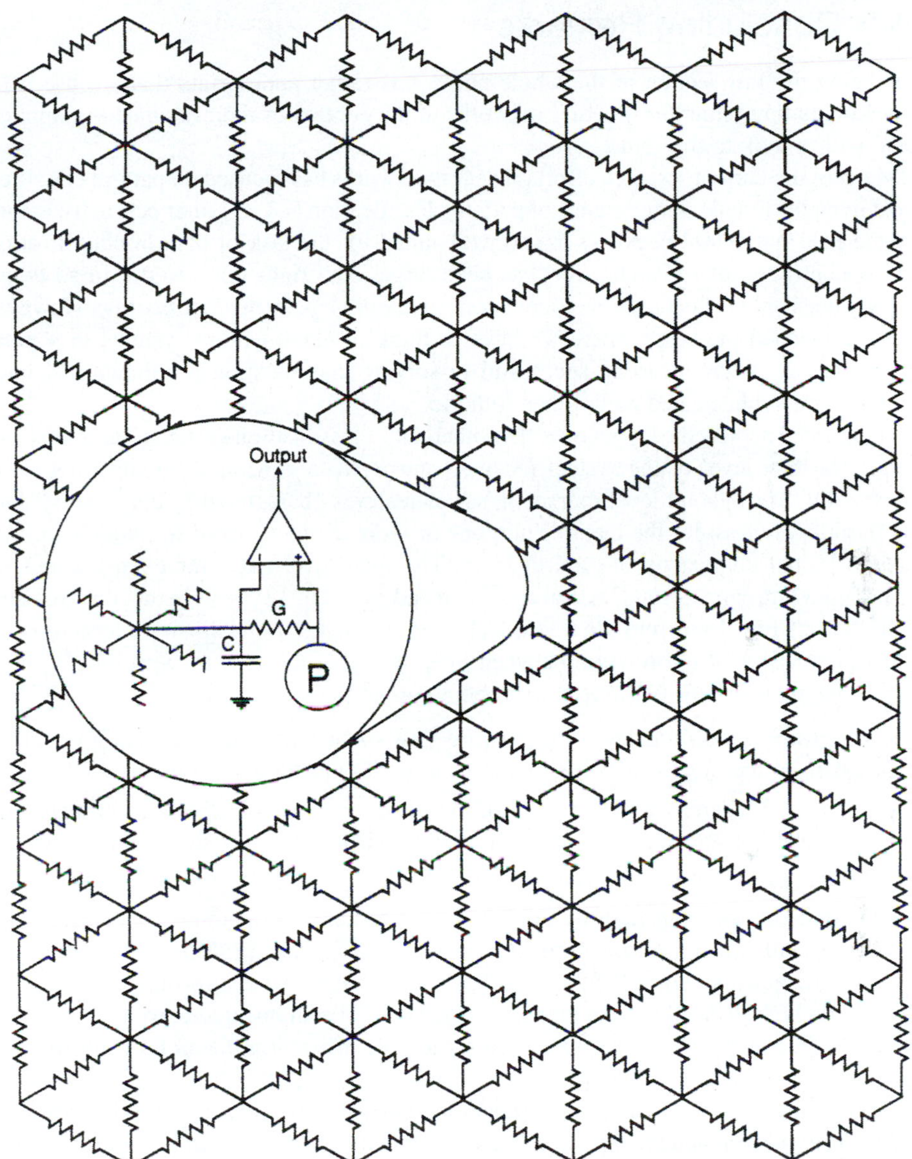

FIGURE 15.8 The silicon retina. Diagram of the resistive network and a single pixel element, shown in the circular window. The silicon model of the triad synapse consists of the conductance (G) by which the photoreceptor drives the resistive network, and the amplifier that takes the difference between the photoreceptor (P) output and the voltage on the resistive network. In addition to a triad synapse, each pixel contains six resistors and a capacitor C that represents the parasitic capacitance of the resistive network. These pixels are tiled in a hexagonal array. The resistive network results from a hexagonal tiling of pixels. (Reprinted from *Neural Networks,* **1,** C.A. Mead and M. Mahowald, "A silicon model of early visual processing," pp. 91–97, copyright 1988 with kind permission from Pergamon Press Ltd., Headington Hill Hall, Oxford 0X3 0BW, UK.)

15.5 Concluding Remarks

This being the last section of the whole book, it is rather appropriate that we use it for some concluding remarks on neural networks in the context of their engineering applications, with a look to the future.

Much of the current research effort on neural networks has focused on pattern classification. Given the practical importance of pattern classification and its rather pervasive nature, and the fact that neural networks are so well suited for the task of pattern classification, this concentration of research effort has been largely the right thing to do. In so doing, we have been able to lay down the foundations of *adaptive pattern classification.* However, we have reached the stage where we have to think of classification systems in a much broader sense, if we are to be successful in solving classification problems of a more complex and sophisticated nature than hitherto.

Figure 15.9 depicts the layout of a "hypothetical" classification system (Hammerstrom, 1992). The first level of the system receives sensory data generated by some source of information. The second level extracts a set of features characterizing the sensory data. The third level classifies the features into one or more distinct categories, which are then put into global context by the fourth level. The final level may, for example, put the parsed input into some form of a database for an end user. The key feature that distinguishes the system of Fig. 15.9 from the traditional form of a pattern classification system is the *bidirectional* flow of information between most levels of the system. Specifically, there are provisions made for two interactive operations in the system:

- *Recognition,* resulting from the forward flow of information from one level of the system to the next as in a traditional pattern classification system.
- *Focusing,*[5] whereby a higher level of the system is able selectively to influence the processing of information at a lower level by virtue of knowledge gained from past data.

The need for focusing may be argued on the grounds of a limited capacity that is ordinarily available for information processing, as Mesulam (1985) points out in the context of human attention[6]: "If the brain had infinite capacity for information processing, there would be little need for attentional mechanisms." From this quote, we may infer that the use of focusing provides a mechanism for a more efficient utilization of information-processing resources.

Thus the novelty of the pattern-classification system shown in Fig. 15.9 lies in *knowledge of the target domain* and its exploitation by lower levels of the system to improve overall system performance, given the fundamental constraint of a limited information-processing capacity. It is our belief that the evolution of pattern classification using neural networks will be in the direction of creating models that are continually influenced by knowledge of the target domain (Hammerstrom, 1992). We envision this new class of machines to have the following distinctive characteristics:

- Ability to extract *contextual knowledge,* and exploit it through the use of *focusing* mechanisms

---

[5] An example of a hierarchical focusing or selective attentional mechanism is described by Fukushima (1988a), which is a modification of the layered model *neocognitron* also pioneered by Fukushima (1975, 1988b). The mechanism described therein enables the network to focus attention on an individual character(s) in an image composed of multiple characters or a greatly deformed character that is also contaminated with noise, demonstrating a remarkable performance.

An attentional mechanism also features in the development of *adaptive resonance theory* (Carpenter and Grossberg, 1987), which involves the combination of bottom-up adaptive filtering and top-down template matching.

[6] For an essay on visual attention, what it is, and what it is for, see Allport (1989).

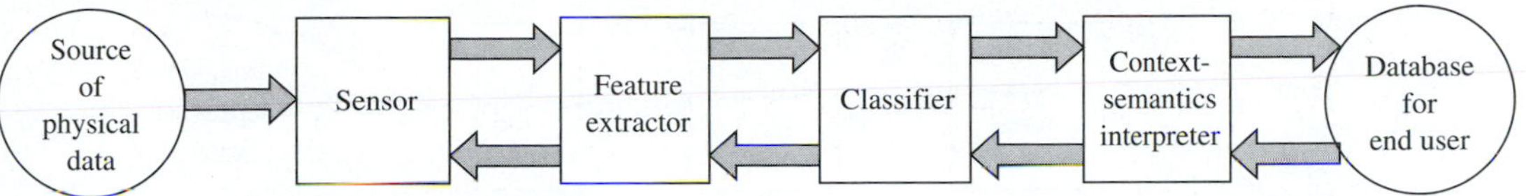

FIGURE 15.9 Block diagram of pattern classifier with contextual feedback.

- *Localized* rather than distributed representation of knowledge
- *Sparse* architecture, emphasizing network modularity and hierarchy as principles of neural network design

We refer to pattern classification performed by this new class of machines as *intelligent pattern classification,* the realization of which can only be attained by combining neural networks with other appropriate tools. A useful tool that comes to mind here is the *Viterbi algorithm* (Forney, 1973; Viterbi, 1967), which is a form of dynamic programming designed to deal with *sequential* information processing[7] that is an inherent characteristic of the system described in Fig. 15.9.

Control, another area of application naturally suited for neural networks, is also evolving in its own way in the direction of *intelligent control.* This ultimate form of control is defined as the ability of a system to *comprehend, reason, and learn* about processes, disturbances, and operating conditions (Åström and McAvoy, 1992). As with intelligent pattern classification, the key attribute that distinguishes intelligent control from classical control is the extraction and exploitation of *knowledge* for improved system performance. The fundamental goals of intelligent control may be described as follows (White and Sofge, 1992):

- Full utilization of knowledge of a system and/or feedback from a system to provide *reliable control* in accordance with some preassigned performance criterion
- Use of the knowledge to control the system in an *intelligent* manner, as a human expert may function in light of the same knowledge
- Improved ability to control the system over *time* through the accumulation of experiential knowledge (i.e., learning from experience)

This is a highly ambitious list of goals, which cannot be attained by the use of neural networks working alone. Rather, we may have to resort to the combined use of neural networks and fuzzy logic. Figure 15.10 presents one way of putting such a combination together (Werbos et al., 1992). The ''fuzzy'' tools put words from a human expert into a set of rules for use by a nonlinear controller, and the ''neural'' tools put actual operation data into physical models to further augment the capability of the nonlinear controller. Thus the fuzzy and neural tools work in a complementary fashion, accomplishing together what neither one of them can by working alone.

Turning next to signal processing, we have another fertile area for the application of neural networks by virtue of their nonlinear and adaptive characteristics. Many of the physical phenomena responsible for the generation of *information-bearing signals* encountered in practice (e.g., speech signals, radar signals, sonar signals) are governed by *nonlinear dynamics of a nonstationary and complex nature,* defying an exact mathematical

[7] The use of such an approach is described by Burges et al. (1992), where dynamic programming is combined with a neural network for segmenting and recognizing character strings.

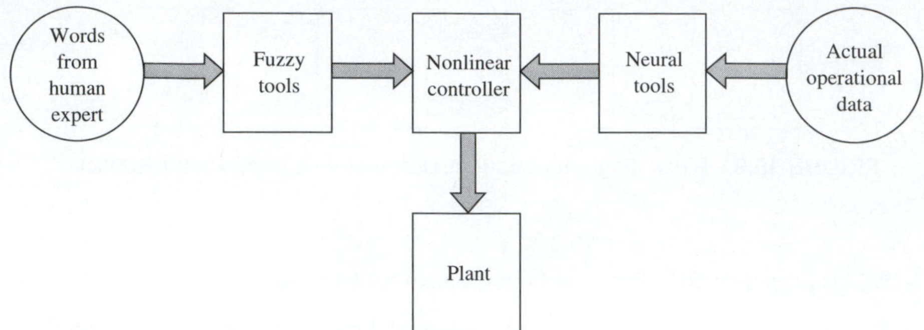

FIGURE 15.10 Block diagram of controller combining the use of neural networks and fuzzy logic.

description. To exploit the full information content of such signals at all times, we need an *intelligent signal processor,* the design of which addresses the following issues:

- *Nonlinearity,* which makes it possible to extract the higher-order statistics of the input signals.
- *Number of degrees of freedom,* which means that the system has the right number of adjustable parameters to cope with the complexity of the underlying physical process, avoiding the problems that arise due to underfitting or overfitting the input data.
- *Adaptivity,* which enables the system to respond to nonstationary behavior of the unknown environment in which it is embedded. Certain applications require that synaptic weights of the neural network be adjusted continually, while the network is being used; that is, ''training'' of the network never stops during the processing of incoming signals.
- *Prior information,* the exploitation of which specializes (biases) the system design and thereby enhances its performance.
- *Information preservation,* which requires that no useful information be discarded before the final decision-making process; such a requirement usually means that soft decision making is preferrable to hard decision making.
- *Multisensor fusion,* which makes it possible to ''fuse'' data gathered about an operational environment by a multitude of sensors, thereby realizing an overall level of performance that is far beyond the capability of any of the sensors working alone.
- *Attentional mechanism,* whereby, through interaction with a user or in a self-organized manner, the system is enabled to focus its computing power around a particular point in an image or a particular location in space for more detailed analysis

The realization of an intelligent signal processor that can provide for these needs would certainly require the hybridization of neural networks with other appropriate tools such as time-frequency analysis, chaotic dynamics, and fuzzy logic.

Needless to say, current pattern classification, control, and signal processing systems have a long way to go before they can qualify as *intelligent machines.*

The bulk of the material presented in this chapter has been devoted to VLSI implementations of neural networks. As with current applications of neural networks, we will certainly have to look to VLSI chips/systems, perhaps more sophisticated than those in use today, to build working models of intelligent machines for pattern classification, control, and signal processing applications.

PROBLEMS

15.1 Consider Eq. (15.5) describing the behavior of an *n*-channel MOS transistor. Assuming that the transistor is driven into saturation (i.e., the drain voltage is high enough), we may simplify this equation as follows:

$$I_d = I_0 \exp\left(\frac{\kappa V_g - V_s}{U_t}\right)$$

Using this relation, show that the difference between the two drain currents of the transconductance amplifier of Fig. 15.2 is related to the differential input voltage $V_1 - V_2$ as follows:

$$I_2 - I_1 = I_b \tanh\left[\frac{\kappa(V_1 - V_2)}{U_t}\right]$$

where I_b is the constant current supplied by the bottom transistor in Fig. 15.2.

15.2 The MOS transistors shown in Fig. 15.3 model inhibitory and excitatory synapses; their input–output relations are defined by Eqs. (15.13) and (15.14). Determine the transconductances realized by these transistors, and thereby confirm their respective roles.

15.3 The ETANN chip (Holler et al., 1989) and the EPSILON chip (Murray et al., 1991) use analog and hybrid approaches for the VLSI implementation of neural networks, respectively. Study the papers cited here, and make up a list comparing their individual designs and capabilities.

15.4 Moon et al. (1992) describe a pulse modulation technique known as the *pulse duty cycle modulation* for the VLSI implementation of a neural network. Referring to this paper, identify the features that distinguish this pulse modulation technique from pulse frequency modulation, emphasizing its advantages and disadvantages.

15.5 A systolic array (Kung and Leiserson, 1979) provides an architecture for the implementation of a parallel processor. A systolic emulation of learning algorithms is described by Ramacher (1990) and Ramacher et al. (1991). Study this architecture and discuss its suitability for VLSI implementation.

15.6 The contrast-sensitive silicon retina described by Boahen and Andreou (1992) appears to exhibit a regularization capability. In light of the regularization theory presented in Chapter 7, discuss this effect by referring to the paper cited here.

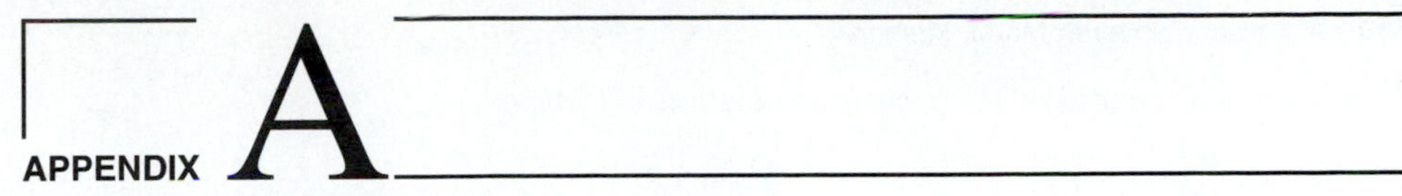

APPENDIX A

Pseudoinverse Matrix Memory

In this appendix we describe a procedure for the design of a distributed memory mapping that transforms a key pattern $\mathbf{a}_k$ into another activity pattern $\mathbf{b}_k$ that is the closest to a desired response $\mathbf{b}_k$ in the *least-squares sense.* The procedure used here is based on the classical *method of least squares,* in the context of which we may formulate the pattern-association problem as follows:

> *Given a set of key vectors denoted by* $\mathbf{a}_1, \mathbf{a}_2, \ldots, \mathbf{a}_q$ *and a corresponding set of desired response vectors* $\mathbf{b}_1, \mathbf{b}_2, \ldots, \mathbf{b}_q$, *find the linear mapping or matrix operator* $\mathbf{M}$ *that minimizes the Euclidean norm of the difference between the desired response* $\mathbf{b}_k$ *and the actual response* $\mathbf{M}\mathbf{a}_k$ *for* $k = 1, 2, \ldots, q$.

Let the matrices **A** and **B** denote the sets of input and output activity patterns, respectively, as shown by

$$\mathbf{A} = [\mathbf{a}_1, \mathbf{a}_2, \ldots, \mathbf{a}_q] \tag{A.1}$$

and

$$\mathbf{B} = [\mathbf{b}_1, \mathbf{b}_2, \ldots, \mathbf{b}_q] \tag{A.2}$$

where we note that the $\mathbf{a}_k$ and the $\mathbf{b}_k$ are p-by-1 vectors, and **A** and **B** are p-by-q matrices. We may therefore restate the least-squares formulation of the association problem as follows:

> *Given a key matrix denoted by* **A** *and a desired response matrix denoted by* **B**, *find the linear mapping or matrix operator* **M** *that minimizes the Euclidean norm of a matrix defined as the difference between the desired response* **B** *and the actual response* **MA**.

The value of the mapping **M** that satisfies this criterion is referred to as the *least-squares solution to the pattern-association problem.* It is well recognized in the literature on linear least-squares estimation that the use of a *pseudoinverse* provides a powerful method for solving the estimation problem. For the problem at hand, the matrix norm of the association error is written as $\|\mathbf{B} - \mathbf{MA}\|$. According to the pseudoinverse method, the least-squares solution $\hat{\mathbf{M}}$ that minimizes the value of this matrix norm is given by (Kohonen et al., 1976)

$$\hat{\mathbf{M}} = \mathbf{B}\mathbf{A}^+ \tag{A.3}$$

where $\mathbf{A}^+$ is the *pseudoinverse of the key matrix* **A**. Equation (A.3) is called the *pseudoinverse learning rule,* and an associative memory so designed is called a *pseudoinverse memory* (PIM).

A sufficient condition for perfect association is to have

$$\mathbf{A}^{+}\mathbf{A} = \mathbf{I} \tag{A.4}$$

where $\mathbf{I}$ is the identity matrix. When this condition is satisfied, the actual response produced by applying the key matrix $\mathbf{A}$ to the memory matrix $\hat{\mathbf{M}}$ equals the desired value $\mathbf{B}$ of the stored matrix, as shown by

$$\begin{aligned}\hat{\mathbf{M}}\mathbf{A} &= \mathbf{B}\mathbf{A}^{+}\mathbf{A} \\ &= \mathbf{B}\end{aligned} \tag{A.5}$$

where use has been made of Eq. (A.3) and then (A.4). The condition of Eq. (A.4) may be realized by using a set of key vectors (i.e., columns of the key matrix $\mathbf{A}$) that are *linearly independent.* This in turn requires that $p \geq q$, where p is the input space dimensionality and q is the number of stored associations. Under this condition, the pseudoinverse matrix $\mathbf{A}^{+}$ is defined by (Golub and Van Loan, 1989; Haykin, 1991)

$$\mathbf{A}^{+} = (\mathbf{A}^{T}\mathbf{A})^{-1}\mathbf{A}^{T} \tag{A.6}$$

where $\mathbf{A}^{T}$ is the transpose of matrix $\mathbf{A}$. We then find that the condition for perfect association given in Eq. (A.4) is immediately satisfied.

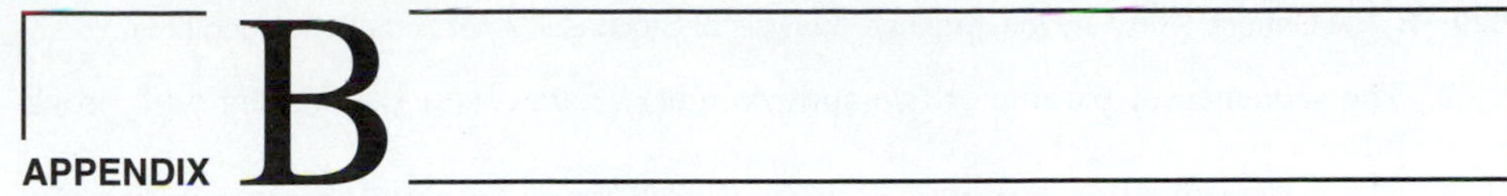

APPENDIX B

A General Tool for Convergence Analysis of Stochastic Approximation Algorithms

In this appendix we consider the issue of convergence of a class of *stochastic approximation algorithms,* examples of which are encountered in different parts of the book. The convergence analysis of these algorithms is usually quite difficult to undertake, due to the fact that the algorithms are not only stochastic but also nonlinear. We first describe a general procedure for the analysis of the asymptotic behavior of stochastic approximation algorithms. Then we apply the procedure to prove the convergence of self-organizing algorithms for principal components analysis, which are studied in Chapter 9.

We are interested specifically in the convergence analysis of stochastic approximation algorithms, the purpose of which is the *recursive* computation of *synaptic weight vectors* of neural networks, as described by

$$\mathbf{w}(n+1) = \mathbf{w}(n) + \eta(n)h\big(\mathbf{w}(n),\mathbf{x}(n)\big), \qquad n = 0, 1, 2, \ldots \tag{B.1}$$

where n is the number of iterations, $\mathbf{w}(\cdot)$ is a sequence of vectors that are the object of interest, and $\mathbf{x}(n)$ is an *observation vector* received at time n, which causes $\mathbf{w}(n)$ to be updated to take account of new information. The vectors $\mathbf{x}(n)$ and $\mathbf{w}(n)$ may or may not have the same dimension. The important point to note is that $\mathbf{x}(n)$ is a sample function (prototype) of a stochastic process. It should also be noted that although we refer to $\mathbf{w}(\cdot)$ as a synaptic weight vector, in general, it represents the "estimate" of some unknown parameter vector. The sequence $\eta(\cdot)$ is assumed to be a sequence of positive scalars.

The *update function* $h(\cdot,\cdot)$ is a deterministic function with some regularity conditions imposed on it. This function, together with the scalar sequence $\eta(\cdot)$ specify the complete structure of the algorithm.

The goal of the procedure is to associate a deterministic nonlinear differential equation with the stochastic nonlinear difference equation (B.1). The stability properties of the differential equation are then tied to the convergence properties of the algorithm. This procedure is a fairly general tool and has wide applicability. It was developed independently by Ljung (1977) and by Kushner and Clark (1978), using different approaches.

To begin with, the procedure assumes that the stochastic approximation algorithm described by Eq. (B.1) satisfies the following set of conditions, using our terminology:

1. The $\eta(n)$ is a decreasing sequence of positive real numbers, such that we have:

(a)
$$\sum_{n=1}^{\infty} \eta(n) = \infty \tag{B.2}$$

(b)
$$\sum_{n=1}^{\infty} \eta^p(n) < \infty \qquad \text{for } p > 1 \tag{B.3}$$

(c)
$$\eta(n) \to 0 \qquad \text{as } n \to \infty \tag{B.4}$$

2. The sequence of parameter (synaptic weight) vectors $\mathbf{w}(\cdot)$ is bounded with probability 1.
3. The update function $h(\mathbf{w}, \mathbf{x})$ is continuously differentiable with respect to $\mathbf{w}$ and $\mathbf{x}$, and its derivatives are bounded in time.
4. The limit

$$\bar{h}(\mathbf{w}) = \lim_{n\to\infty} E[h(\mathbf{w}, \mathbf{x})] \tag{B.5}$$

exists for each $\mathbf{w}$; the statistical expectation operator E is over $\mathbf{x}$.

5. There is a locally asymptotically stable (in the sense of Liapunov) solution to the ordinary differential equation

$$\frac{d}{dt}\mathbf{w}(t) = \bar{h}(\mathbf{w}(t)) \tag{B.6}$$

where t denotes continuous time.

6. Let $\mathbf{q}_0$ denote the solution to Eq. (B.6) with a basin of attraction $\mathcal{B}(\mathbf{q}_0)$. Then the parameter vector $\mathbf{w}(n)$ enters a compact subset $\mathcal{A}$ of the basin of attraction $\mathcal{B}(\mathbf{q}_0)$ infinitely often, with probability 1.

The six conditions described here are all reasonable. In particular, condition 1(a) is a necessary condition that makes it possible for the algorithm to move the estimate to a desired limit, regardless of the initial conditions. Condition 1(b) gives a condition on how fast $\eta(n)$ must tend to zero; it is considerably less restrictive than the usual condition

$$\sum_{n=1}^{\infty} \eta^2(n) < \infty$$

Condition 4 is the basic assumption that makes it possible to associate a differential equation with the algorithm of (B.1).

Consider, then, a stochastic approximation algorithm described by the recursive equation (B.1), subject to assumptions 1 through 6. We may then state the *asymptotic stability theorem* for this class of stochastic approximation algorithms as follows (Ljung, 1977; Kushner and Clark, 1978):

$$\lim_{n\to\infty} \mathbf{w}(n) \to \mathbf{q}_0, \qquad \text{infinitely often with probability 1} \tag{B.7}$$

It should be emphasized, however, that although the procedure described here can provide us with information about asymptotic properties of the algorithm (B.1), it usually does not tell us how large the number of iterations n has to be for the results of the analysis to be applicable. Moreover, in tracking problems, where a time-varying parameter vector is to be tracked using algorithm (B.1), it is not feasible to require

$$\eta(n) \to 0 \qquad \text{as } n \to \infty$$

as stipulated by condition 1(c). We may overcome this latter difficulty by assigning some small, positive value to η, the size of which usually depends on the application of interest. Indeed, this is what is usually done in the practical use of stochastic approximation algorithms in neural networks.

Convergence Analysis of Self-Organizing Networks for Principal Components Analysis

We now illustrate the use of the general procedure described above to perform a detailed convergence analysis[1] of a *maximum eigenfilter* that consists of a single neuron and that

[1] The convergence analysis presented here is inspired by the work of Sanger (1989b) on this subject.

operates in accordance with a Hebbian form of learning (Oja, 1982). The purpose of this network, discussed in Section 9.6, is to extract the largest eigenvalue and associated eigenvector of the correlation matrix of the stochastic process supplying the input vector to the network. We conclude this appendix by briefly discussing the convergence of a more elaborate self-organizing network consisting of a single layer of neurons, which is capable of performing a complete principal components analysis (Sanger, 1989b). This latter network is discussed in Section 9.7.

Self-Organizing Maximum Eigenfilter

Consider a neural network whose synaptic weight vector $\mathbf{w}(n)$ is adjusted in accordance with the recursive equation

$$\mathbf{w}(n + 1) = \mathbf{w}(n) + \eta(n)[\mathbf{x}(n)y(n) - y^2(n)\mathbf{w}(n)] \tag{B.8}$$

which is basically the same as Eq. (9.60), except for $\eta(n)$ written in place of η. The output $y(n)$ of the network is related to the input vector $\mathbf{x}(n)$ by

$$y(n) = \mathbf{x}^T(n)\mathbf{w}(n) = \mathbf{w}^T(n)\mathbf{x}(n) \tag{B.9}$$

To satisfy condition 1 of the asymptotic stability theorem, we let

$$\eta(n) = \frac{1}{n}$$

From Eq. (B.8), the function $h(\mathbf{w},\mathbf{x})$ is defined by

$$\begin{aligned} h(\mathbf{w},\mathbf{x}) &= \mathbf{x}(n)y(n) - y^2(n)\mathbf{w}(n) \\ &= \mathbf{x}(n)\mathbf{x}^T(n)\mathbf{w}(n) - [\mathbf{w}^T(n)\mathbf{x}(n)\mathbf{x}^T(n)\mathbf{w}(n)]\mathbf{w}(n) \end{aligned}$$

which clearly satisfies condition 3 of the theorem. For condition 4, we write

$$\begin{aligned} \bar{h}(\mathbf{w}) &= \lim_{n\to\infty} E\big[\mathbf{x}(n)\mathbf{x}^T(n)\mathbf{w}(n) - \big(\mathbf{w}^T(n)\mathbf{x}(n)\mathbf{x}^T(n)\mathbf{w}(n)\big)\mathbf{w}(n)\big] \\ &= \lim_{n\to\infty} \big(E[\mathbf{x}(n)\mathbf{x}^T(n)]\mathbf{w}(n) - \{\mathbf{w}^T(n)E[\mathbf{x}(n)\mathbf{x}^T(n)]\mathbf{w}(n)\}\mathbf{w}(n)\big) \\ &= \lim_{n\to\infty} \{\mathbf{R}\mathbf{w}(n) - [\mathbf{w}^T(n)\mathbf{R}\mathbf{w}(n)]\mathbf{w}(n)\} \\ &= \mathbf{R}\mathbf{w}(\infty) - [\mathbf{w}^T(\infty)\mathbf{R}\mathbf{w}(\infty)]\mathbf{w}(\infty) \end{aligned} \tag{B.10}$$

where $\mathbf{R}$ is the correlation matrix of the stochastic process represented by the input vector $\mathbf{x}(n)$, and $\mathbf{w}(\infty)$ is the limiting value of the synaptic weight vector. Note that, in accordance with condition 4, the expectation operator E is over $\mathbf{x}(n)$.

In accordance with condition 5 and in light of Eqs. (B.6) and (B.10), we seek stable points of the differential equation

$$\begin{aligned} \frac{d}{dt}\mathbf{w}(t) &= \bar{h}(\mathbf{w}(t)) \\ &= \mathbf{R}\mathbf{w}(t) - [\mathbf{w}^T(t)\mathbf{R}\mathbf{w}(t)]\mathbf{w}(t) \end{aligned} \tag{B.11}$$

Let $\mathbf{w}(t)$ be expanded in terms of the complete orthonormal set of eigenvectors of the correlation matrix $\mathbf{R}$ as follows:

$$\mathbf{w}(t) = \sum_{k=0}^{p-1} \theta_k(t)\mathbf{q}_k \tag{B.12}$$

where $\mathbf{q}_k$ is the kth normalized eigenvector of the matrix $\mathbf{R}$, and the coefficient $\theta_k(t)$ is the time-varying projection of the vector $\mathbf{w}(t)$ onto $\mathbf{q}_k$. Substituting Eq. (B.12) in (B.11), and using the basic definitions

$$\mathbf{R}\mathbf{q}_k = \lambda_k \mathbf{q}_k \tag{B.13}$$

and

$$\mathbf{q}_k^T \mathbf{R}\mathbf{q}_k = \lambda_k \tag{B.14}$$

where λ_k is the eigenvalue associated with $\mathbf{q}_k$, we finally get

$$\sum_{k=0}^{p-1} \frac{d\theta_k(t)}{dt} \mathbf{q}_k = \sum_{k=0}^{p-1} \lambda_k \theta_k(t) \mathbf{q}_k - \left[\sum_{l=0}^{p-1} \lambda_l \theta_l^2(t) \right] \sum_{k=0}^{p-1} \theta_k(t) \mathbf{q}_k \tag{B.15}$$

Equivalently, we may write

$$\frac{d\theta_k(t)}{dt} = \lambda_k \theta_k(t) - \theta_k(t) \sum_{l=0}^{p-1} \lambda_l \theta_l^2(t), \qquad k = 0, 1, \ldots, p-1 \tag{B.16}$$

We have thus reduced the convergence analysis of the stochastic approximation algorithm of (B.8) to the stability analysis of the system of differential equations (B.16) involving the principal modes $\theta_k(t)$.

There are two cases to be considered here, depending on the value assigned to the index k. Case I corresponds to $1 \le k \le p - 1$, and case II corresponds to $k = 0$; p is the dimension of both $\mathbf{x}(n)$ and $\mathbf{w}(n)$. These two cases are considered in turn.

Case I. $1 \le k \le p - 1$. For the treatment of this case, we define

$$\alpha_k(t) = \frac{\theta_k(t)}{\theta_0(t)}, \qquad 1 \le k \le p-1 \tag{B.17}$$

Here it is assumed that $\theta_0(t) \neq 0$, which is true with probability 1 provided that the initial values $\mathbf{w}(0)$ are chosen at random. Then, differentiating both sides of Eq. (B.17), we get

$$\begin{aligned} \frac{d\alpha_k(t)}{dt} &= \frac{1}{\theta_0(t)} \frac{d\theta_k(t)}{dt} - \frac{\theta_k(t)}{\theta_0^2(t)} \frac{d\theta_0(t)}{dt} \\ &= \frac{1}{\theta_0(t)} \frac{d\theta_k(t)}{dt} - \frac{\alpha_k(t)}{\theta_0(t)} \frac{d\theta_0(t)}{dt}, \qquad 1 \le k \le p-1 \end{aligned} \tag{B.18}$$

Next, using Eq. (B.16) in (B.18), applying the definition of Eq. (B.17), and then simplifying the result, we get

$$\frac{d\alpha_k(t)}{dt} = -(\lambda_0 - \lambda_k)\alpha_k(t), \qquad 1 \le k \le p-1 \tag{B.19}$$

With the eigenvalues of the correlation matrix $\mathbf{R}$ assumed to be distinct and arranged in decreasing order, we have

$$\lambda_0 > \lambda_1 > \cdots > \lambda_k > \cdots > \lambda_{p-1} > 0 \tag{B.20}$$

It follows therefore that the eigenvalue difference $\lambda_0 - \lambda_k$, representing the reciprocal of a time constant in Eq. (B.19) is positive, and so we find that for case I:

$$\alpha_k(t) \to 0 \qquad \text{as } t \to 0 \text{ for } 1 \le k \le p-1 \tag{B.21}$$

Case II. $k = 0$. From Eq. (B.16), this second case is described by the differential equation

$$\frac{d\theta_0(t)}{dt} = \lambda_0\theta_0(t) - \theta_0(t)\sum_{l=0}^{p-1}\lambda_l\theta_l^2(t)$$

$$= \lambda_0\theta_0(t) - \lambda_0\theta_0^3(t) - \theta_0(t)\sum_{l=1}^{p-1}\lambda_l\theta_l^2(t)$$

$$= \lambda_0\theta_0(t) - \lambda_0\theta_0^3(t) - \theta_0^3(t)\sum_{l=1}^{p-1}\lambda_l\alpha_l^2(t) \tag{B.22}$$

However, from case I we know that $\alpha_l \to 0$ for $l \neq 0$ as $t \to 0$. Hence the last term on the right-hand side of Eq. (B.22) approaches zero. We may therefore ignore this item, in which case Eq. (B.22) simplifies to

$$\frac{d\theta_0(t)}{dt} = \lambda_0\theta_0(t)[1 - \theta_0^2(t)] \tag{B.23}$$

We now assert that this differential equation has a Liapunov function defined by

$$V(t) = [\theta_0^2(t) - 1]^2 \tag{B.24}$$

To validate this assertion, we have to show that $V(t)$ satisfies two conditions:

(1) $\dfrac{dV(t)}{dt} < 0$ for all t (B.25)

(2) $V(t)$ has a minimum (B.26)

Differentiating Eq. (B.24) with respect to time, we get

$$\frac{dV(t)}{dt} = 4\theta_0(t)[\theta_0^2(t) - 1]\frac{d\theta_0}{dt}$$

$$= -4\lambda_0\theta_0^2(t)[\theta_0^2(t) - 1]^2 \tag{B.27}$$

where, in the second line, we have made use of Eq. (B.23). Since the eigenvalue λ_0 is positive, we find from Eq. (B.27) that the condition of Eq. (B.25) is indeed true for all t. Furthermore, from Eq. (B.27) we note that $V(t)$ has a minimum [i.e., $dV(t)/dt$ is zero] at $\theta_0(t) = \pm 1$, and so the condition of Eq. (B.26) is also satisfied. We may therefore conclude the analysis of case II by stating that

$$\theta_0(t) \to \pm 1 \qquad \text{as } t \to \infty \tag{B.28}$$

In light of the result described in Eq. (B.28) and the definition of Eq. (B.17), we may restate the result of case I given in Eq. (B.21) in its final form:

$$\theta_k(t) \to 0 \qquad \text{as } t \to \infty \qquad \text{for } 1 \leq k \leq p - 1 \tag{B.29}$$

The overall conclusion drawn from the analysis of cases I and II is twofold:

- The only principal mode of the stochastic approximation algorithm described in Eq. (B.8) that will converge is $\theta_0(t)$; all the other modes of the algorithm will decay to zero.
- The mode $\theta_0(t)$ will converge to ± 1.

Hence, condition 5 of the asymptotic stability theorem is satisfied. Specifically, in light of the expansion described in Eq. (B.12), we may formally state that

$$\mathbf{w}(t) \to \mathbf{q}_0 \qquad \text{as } t \to \infty \tag{B.30}$$

where $\mathbf{q}_0$ is the normalized eigenvector associated with the largest eigenvalue λ_0 of the correlation matrix $\mathbf{R}$.

We must next show that, in accordance with condition 6 of the asymptotic stability theorem, there exists a subset $\mathcal{A}$ of the set of all vectors, such that

$$\lim_{n\to\infty} \mathbf{w}(n) \to \mathbf{q}_0 \qquad \text{infinitely often with probability 1} \tag{B.31}$$

To do so, we first have to satisfy condition 2, which we do by *hard-limiting* the entries of $\mathbf{w}(n)$ so that their magnitudes remain below some threshold a. We may then define the norm of $\mathbf{w}(n)$ by writing

$$\|\mathbf{w}(n)\| = \max_j |w_j(n)| \leq a \tag{B.32}$$

Let $\mathcal{A}$ be the compact subset of $\mathbb{R}^p$ defined by the set of vectors with norm less than or equal to a. It is straightforward to show that (Sanger, 1989b)

> *If* $\|\mathbf{w}(n)\| \leq a$, *and the constant* a *is sufficiently large, then* $\|\mathbf{w}(n+1)\| < \|\mathbf{w}(n)\|$ *with probability* 1.

Thus, as the number of iterations n increases, $\mathbf{w}(n)$ will eventually be within $\mathcal{A}$, and it will remain inside $\mathcal{A}$ (infinitely often) with probability 1. Since the basin of attraction $\mathcal{B}(\mathbf{q}_0)$ includes all vectors with bounded norm, we have $\mathcal{A} \in \mathcal{B}(\mathbf{q}_0)$. In other words, condition 6 is satisfied.

We have now satisfied all six conditions of the asymptotic stability theorem, and thereby shown that (subject to the assumptions made earlier) the stochastic approximation algorithm of (B.8) will cause $\mathbf{w}(n)$ to converge with probability 1 to the eigenvector $\mathbf{q}_0$ associated with the largest eigenvalue λ_0 of the correlation matrix $\mathbf{R}$. This is not the only fixed point of the algorithm, but it is the only one that is asymptotically stable.

Self-Organizing Network for Principal Components Analysis

Consider next a network containing a single layer of neurons with forward connections only. The algorithm for adjusting the matrix of synaptic weights $\mathbf{W}(n)$ of the network is described by the recursive equation [see Eq. (9.95)]

$$\mathbf{W}(n+1) = \mathbf{W}(n) + \eta(n)\{\mathbf{y}(n)\mathbf{x}^T(n) - \text{LT}[\mathbf{y}(n)\mathbf{y}^T(n)]\mathbf{W}(n)\} \tag{B.33}$$

where $\mathbf{x}(n)$ is the input vector; $\mathbf{y}(n)$ is the output vector; and LT[$\cdot$] is a matrix operator that sets all the elements above the diagonal of the matrix argument to zero, thereby making it lower triangular. The requirement is to show that the stochastic approximation algorithm of Eq.(B.33) converges to a matrix $\mathbf{T}$ whose columns are the first m eigenvectors of the correlation matrix $\mathbf{R}$ of the input vector $\mathbf{x}(n)$ in descending eigenvalue order.

We note that the asymptotic stability theorem does not apply directly to the convergence analysis of stochastic approximation algorithms involving matrices, but rather is formulated to apply to vectors. However, we may write the elements of the parameter (synaptic weight) matrix $\mathbf{W}(n)$ in Eq. (B.33) as a vector, interpret the nonlinear function h in a corresponding way, and then proceed to apply the asymptotic stability theorem directly.

To prove the convergence of the algorithm (B.33), we may use *induction* to show that if the first j columns of the matrix $\mathbf{W}(n)$ converge to the first j eigenvectors of the correlation matrix $\mathbf{R}$, then the $(j+1)$th column will converge to the $(j+1)$ eigenvector (Sanger, 1989a). Here, we use the fact that, in light of Eq. (B.31), the first column of the matrix $\mathbf{W}(n)$ converges with probability 1 to the first principal eigenvector of $\mathbf{R}$.

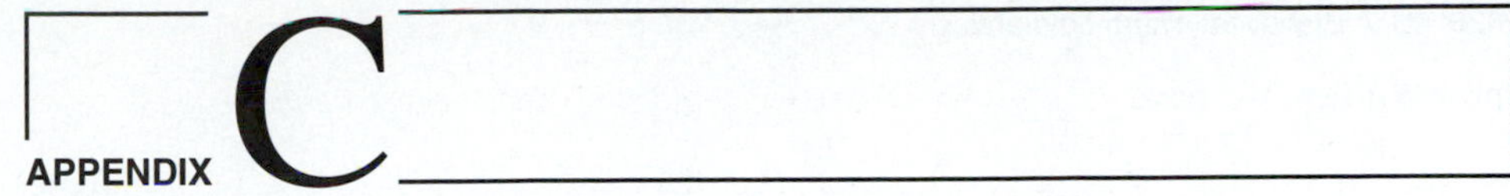

APPENDIX C

Statistical Thermodynamics

The importance of statistical thermodynamics in the study of computing machinery was well recognized by von Neumann. This is evidenced by the third of his five lectures on *Theory and Organization of Complicated Automata* at the University of Illinois in 1949. In his third lecture, on ''Statistical Theories of Information,'' von Neumann went on to say[1]:

> Thermodynamical concepts will probably enter into this new theory of information. There are strong indications that information is similar to entropy and that degenerative processes of entropy are paralleled by degenerative processes in the processing of information. It is likely that you cannot define the function of an automaton, or its efficiency, without characterizing the milieu in which it works by means of statistical traits like the ones used to characterize a milieu in thermodynamics. The statistical variables of the automaton's milieu will, of course, be somewhat more involved than the standard thermodynamic variable of temperature, but they will be similar in character.

Statistical thermodynamics is a discipline central to the study of condensed-matter physics.[2] It represents a body of methods developed for the statistical analysis of the large numbers of atoms found in samples of liquid or solid matter. The number of atoms is on the order of 10^{23} per cubic centimeter. Hence, at a given temperature, only the most probable behavior of the system in thermal equilibrium may be observed as a result of experiments performed on the system. In particular, we may characterize the system in terms of the ensemble-averaged behavior of the system and small fluctuations about this average.

Consider, for example, the case of a small system A in thermal interaction with a heat reservoir A′, with system A having many fewer degrees of freedom than A′. We ask the following question: Under conditions of thermal equilibrium, what is the probability P_α of finding the system A in any one particular state of energy E_α? The answer to this fundamental question is given by the probability distribution

$$P_\alpha = \frac{1}{Z}\exp\left(-\frac{E_\alpha}{k_B T}\right) \tag{C.1}$$

where k_B is *Boltzmann's constant*, T is the *absolute temperature* of the heat reservoir, and Z is a constant that is independent of the state α. From the normalization condition for

[1] *Papers of John von Neumann on Computing and Computer Theory,* edited by W. Aspray and A. Burks (1986), p. 465. The theory of information mentioned in the quotation refers to Shannon's information theory.

[2] For an introductory treatment of statistical thermodynamics, see the book by Reif (1967). For a concise and clearly written monograph on the subject at a more advanced level, see Schrödinger (1952).

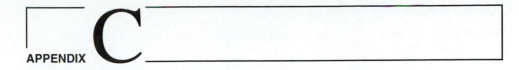

probabilities, we have

$$\sum_{\alpha} P_\alpha = 1 \tag{C.2}$$

where the sum extends over all possible states α of system A, regardless of energy. Using Eq. (C.1) in (C.2), we thus get

$$Z = \sum_{\alpha} \exp\left(-\frac{E_\alpha}{k_B T}\right) \tag{C.3}$$

Accordingly, we may rewrite the probability distribution of Eq. (C.1) explicitly in the form

$$P_\alpha = \frac{\exp(-E_\alpha/k_B T)}{\sum_\alpha \exp(-E_\alpha/k_B T)} \tag{C.4}$$

Suppose that we have a system in thermal equilibrium with its environment. Using the definition of Eq. (C.1), we find that

$$\frac{P_\alpha}{P_\beta} = \exp\left[-\frac{(E_\alpha - E_\beta)}{k_B T}\right] \tag{C.5}$$

where P_α is the probability that the system is in state α, and E_α is the energy of that state; likewise, for P_β and E_β. According to Eq. (C.5), the logarithm of the probabilities of any two states of the system is just their energy difference at a normalized temperature of 1, except for the factor $1/k_B$.

The probability of Eq. (C.4) is of fundamental importance in statistical thermodynamics. The exponential factor $\exp(-E_\alpha/k_B T)$ is called the *Boltzmann factor.* The probability distribution P_α is itself called the *Boltzmann distribution* or the *canonical distribution.* An ensemble of systems, all of which are distributed over states in accordance with Eq. (C.4), is referred to as a *canonical ensemble.*

The absolute temperature T is measured in kelvins; 0 K corresponds to $-273°$ on the Celsius scale. Boltzmann's constant has the value $k_B = 1.38 \times 10^{-23}$ J/K. Although the development of the stochastic machines considered in Chapter 8 has been motivated by ideas from statistical physics, there is a difference in terminology between neural networks and statistial physics that should be carefully noted. Specifically, in neural networks, the parameter T plays the role of a pseudotemperature that has no physical meaning. Moreover, Boltzmann's constant k_B is set equal to unity.

Partition Function, Free Energy, and Entropy

The normalizing quantity Z defined in Eq. (C.3) is called the *sum over states* or the *partition function.* (The symbol Z is used because the German name for this term is *Zustandsumme.*)

The *free energy F* of the system, defined in terms of the partition function Z, is written as

$$F = -k_B T \ln Z \tag{C.6}$$

where it is understood that the product term $k_B T$ has the dimensions of energy, and Z is dimensionless.

Consider again the two systems A and A′ that interact by exchanging heat. According to the *second law of thermodynamics,* we have

$$đS = \frac{đQ}{T} \tag{C.7}$$

The special symbol $đQ$ does *not* designate a difference; rather, it just denotes the infinitesimal amount of heat absorbed in the interaction process. The quantity S is called the *entropy*. Using the definition of Eq. (C.7), it can be shown that the entropy S may also be expressed in terms of the partition function Z as follows:

$$S = k_B \ln Z + \frac{\overline{E}}{T} \tag{C.8}$$

where $\overline{E}$ is the *mean energy* over all states of the system; that is,

$$\overline{E} = \sum_{\alpha} P_\alpha E_\alpha \tag{C.9}$$

The use of Eq. (C.6) in (C.8) shows that the mean energy $\overline{E}$, the free energy F, and the entropy S are simply related by

$$\overline{E} = F + TS \tag{C.10}$$

It is instructive to express the entropy S directly in terms of the canonical probability P_α. This can be readily done by using Eqs. (C.1), (C.8), and (C.9) to obtain the well-known formula

$$S = -k_B \sum_{\alpha} P_\alpha \ln P_\alpha \tag{C.11}$$

According to this definition, except for the multiplying factor k_B, the entropy S may be viewed as the width of the probability distribution; the more states α there are with appreciable probability, the larger will be the entropy S. It is also of interest to note that the formula of Eq. (C.11), except for the factor k_B, has exactly the same mathematical form as the definition of entropy in an information-theoretic sense; see Chapter 11.

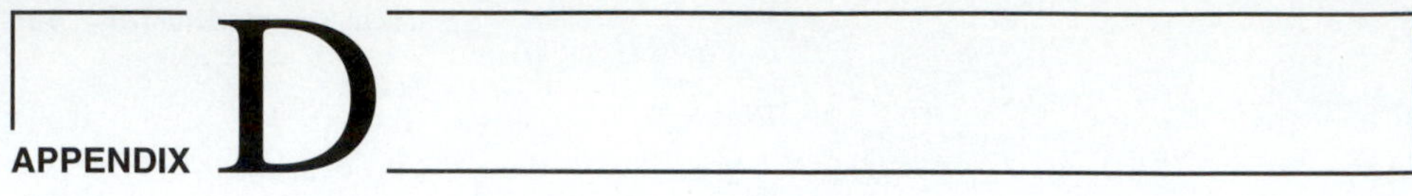

APPENDIX D

Fokker–Planck Equation

In this final appendix we discuss the Fokker–Planck equation and its implications in the context of neural networks. In its original formulation, the *Fokker–Planck equation*[1] was used to study the Brownian motion of particles. It is therefore fitting that we start our discussion by briefly describing *Brownian motion.*

Examples of Brownian motion are the fluctuating current in a resistor due to thermal agitation, or the fluctuations in the weight vector around the minimum point of the error surface as computed by the least-mean-square (LMS) algorithm.

To simplify the presentation, we treat the problem of Brownian motion in *one* dimension. We thus consider a small macroscopic particle of mass m immersed in a viscous fluid. It is assumed that the mass of the particle is small enough for its velocity due to thermal fluctuations to be significant. Let $v(t)$ denote the velocity of the particle at time t. Then, from the *equipartition law,* the mean energy of the particle (in one dimension) is given by

$$\frac{1}{2}E[v^2(t)] = \frac{1}{2}k_B T \qquad \text{for all } t \tag{D.1}$$

where E is the statistical expectation operator, k_B is Boltzmann's constant, and T is the absolute temperature.

The total force exerted by the molecules in the fluid on the particle is made up of two components:

- A continuous *damping force,* which is equal to $-\alpha v(t)$ in accordance with *Stokes' law*; α is the *coefficient of friction.*
- A *fluctuating force* $F_f(t)$, which is stochastic in nature; its properties are therefore specified only on the average.

The equation of motion of the particle, in the *absence* of an external force, is therefore given by

$$m\frac{dv(t)}{dt} = -\alpha v(t) + F_f(t) \tag{D.2}$$

[1] A Fokker–Planck equation was first derived by Fokker in 1914 and Planck in 1917 to describe the Brownian motion of particles. For a complete treatment of the many facets of the Fokker–Planck equation, a survey of methods of its solution, and its applications, see Risken (1989). The treatment of the Fokker–Planck equation presented in this appendix is summarized from Risken's book.

The theory of Brownian motion was initiated by Einstein in 1905.

Dividing both sides of this equation by m, we get

$$\frac{dv(t)}{dt} = -\gamma v(t) + \Gamma(t) \tag{D.3}$$

where

$$\gamma = \frac{\alpha}{m} \tag{D.4}$$

$$\Gamma(t) = \frac{F_f(t)}{m} \tag{D.5}$$

The term $\Gamma(t)$ is the fluctuating force per unit mass. It is a stochastic force because it depends on the positions of very many atoms in the particle that are in constant motion; $\Gamma(t)$ is called the *Langevin force.* Correspondingly, Eq. (D.3) is a stochastic differential equation, called the *Langevin equation* (Reif, 1965). The Langevin equation describes the behavior of the particle at all later times if its initial conditions are specified.

The Langevin equation was the first mathematical equation describing nonequilibrium thermodynamics.

To proceed further, we have to introduce some statistical properties of the Langevin force $\Gamma(t)$. First, we assume that its *average* over the ensemble of systems is zero; that is,

$$E[\Gamma(t)] = 0 \qquad \text{for all } t \tag{D.6}$$

This is a reasonable assumption to make, because the equation of motion of the average velocity, $E[v(t)]$, should have the following deterministic form (in the absence of an external force):

$$mE\left[\frac{dv}{dt}\right] + \alpha E[v] = 0$$

Second, we assume that the *autocorrelation function* of $\Gamma(t)$ for some lag τ is a scaled version of the Dirac delta function $\delta(\tau)$, as shown by

$$E[\Gamma(t)\Gamma(t - \tau)] = q\delta(\tau) \qquad \text{for all } t \tag{D.7}$$

where

$$q = \frac{2\gamma k_B T}{m} \tag{D.8}$$

A stochastic force $\Gamma(t)$, whose mean is zero and whose autocorrelation function is in the form of a Dirac delta function, is called *white noise*; it is so called because its power spectrum (which is defined by the Fourier transform of the autocorrelation function) is constant for all frequencies.

Since the Langevin force $\Gamma(t)$ is stochastic, it follows that the velocity $v(t)$ will be stochastic too. We therefore seek a probabilistic description for the velocity. With $v(t)$ being a continuous variable, the appropriate description is the *probability density function* $f(v,t)$, which depends on time t and the initial distribution. The equation of motion for the probability density function is given by (Risken, 1989)

$$\frac{\partial f}{\partial t} = \gamma \frac{\partial (vf)}{\partial v} + \frac{q}{2}\frac{\partial^2 f}{\partial v^2} \tag{D.9}$$

where γ and q are themselves defined by Eqs. (D.4) and (D.8), respectively. Equation (D.9) is one of the simplest Fokker–Planck equations. By solving this equation, starting with $f(v,t)$ for $t = 0$ and subject to the appropriate boundary conditions, we obtain the probability density function $f(v,t)$ for the Brownian motion of Eq. (D.3) for all later times.

General Form of the Fokker–Planck Equation

The general Fokker–Planck equation for one variable w, say, has the following form (Risken, 1989):

$$\frac{\partial f}{\partial t} = \left[-\frac{\partial}{\partial w} D^{(1)}(w) + \frac{\partial^2}{\partial w^2} D^{(2)}(w) \right] f \tag{D.10}$$

where $D^{(1)}(w)$ is called the *drift coefficient,* and $D^{(2)}(w)$ is called the *diffusion coefficient*; we always have $D^{(2)}(w) > 0$. The drift and diffusion coefficients may also depend on time t. We readily see that Eq. (D.9) is a special form of the Fokker–Planck equation (D.10), assuming that the drift coefficient is linear and the diffusion coefficient is constant. Note that the expression inside the square brackets on the right-hand side of Eq. (D.10) is an operator acting on $f(w,t)$.

Equation (D.10) is an equation of motion for a single random variable w. In mathematical terms, this equation is a linear second-order partial differential equation of parabolic type.

Consider next the general case of a random vector $\mathbf{w}$ of dimension K; that is,

$$\mathbf{w} = [w_1, w_2, \ldots, w_K]^T$$

The Fokker–Planck equation for the vector $\mathbf{w}$ has the following form (Risken, 1989):

$$\frac{\partial f}{\partial t} = \left[-\sum_{i=1}^{K} \frac{\partial}{\partial w_i} D_i^{(1)}(\mathbf{w}) + \sum_{i=1}^{K} \sum_{j=1}^{K} \frac{\partial^2}{\partial w_i \partial w_j} D_{ij}^{(2)}(\mathbf{w}) \right] f \tag{D.11}$$

where w_i is the ith element of the vector $\mathbf{w}$, and $f(\mathbf{w},t)$ is its probability density function. The drift vector $D_i^{(1)}(\mathbf{w})$ and the diffusion tensor $D_{ij}^{(2)}(\mathbf{w})$, in general, depend on the vector $\mathbf{w}$. The Fokker–Planck equation (D.11) is an equation of motion for the probability density function $f(\mathbf{w},t)$. This equation is not the only equation of motion for a probability density function; however, it is the simplest.

In the context of neural networks, the Fokker–Planck equation arises when the *learning process is viewed as a stochastic process* (Ritter et al., 1992; Leen and Orr, 1992). Specifically, the random vector $\mathbf{w}$ may represent the synaptic weights of all the neurons in the network. Ideally, we would like to know the probability density function $f(\mathbf{w},t)$ for an *ensemble* of "infinitely" many simulations (realizations) of the network at some time t during the learning process. For an intuitive picture of $f(\mathbf{w},t)$, consider the *weight space* spanned by the elements of the vector $\mathbf{w}$; for a network made up of N neurons, and with each neuron having p synaptic weights, the space is Np-dimensional. The ensemble may thus be viewed as a "cloud" of points in the weight space, and $f(\mathbf{w},t)$ is the density of the distribution of points in the cloud. Thus, at time t, an infinitesimal volume $d\mathbf{w}$ centered at $\mathbf{w}$ in the weight space contains a fraction $f(\mathbf{w},t)\, d\mathbf{w}$ of all members in the ensemble.

Given that we have solved the Fokker–Planck equation and therefore we know the probability density function $f(\mathbf{w},t)$ we can go on to compute all the statistical averages of the weight vector $\mathbf{w}$ by integration. Let $g(\mathbf{w})$ denote some function of $\mathbf{w}$. Then the average value of this function at time t is given by the multiple integral

$$E[g(\mathbf{w})]_t = \int_{-\infty}^{\infty} g(\mathbf{w}) f(\mathbf{w},t)\, d\mathbf{w} \tag{D.12}$$

Hence the probability density function $f(\mathbf{w},t)$ contains *all* the information we need to calculate the average value of any arbitrary function of the weight vector $\mathbf{w}$. Now we can see why knowledge of the Fokker–Planck equation and its solution can be so important.

Kramers–Moyal Expansion

There are several generalizations of the Fokker–Planck equation. Here we consider only one such generalization for the case of a single random variable $w(t)$; its extension to a set of random variables is straightforward. We are interested in an equation that does not stop after the second derivative with respect to the variable w; rather, it contains higher derivatives too. We may thus generalize Eq. (D.10) by writing

$$\frac{\partial f}{\partial t} = \sum_{k=1}^{\infty} \left(-\frac{\partial}{\partial w}\right)^k D_k(w) f(w,t) \tag{D.13}$$

Equation (D.13) is called the *Kramers–Moyal expansion.*

The Kramers–Moyal expansion of Eq. (D.13) reduces exactly to the Fokker–Planck equation (D.10) under the following conditions:

1. The random variable $w(t)$ satisfies the *Langevin equation*

$$\frac{dw}{dt} = g_1(w,t) + g_2(w,t)\Gamma(t) \tag{D.14}$$

where $\Gamma(t)$ is the Langevin force, and $g_1(w,t)$ and $g_2(w,t)$ are both functions of w and t.

2. The Langevin force $\Gamma(t)$ is assumed to be a Gaussian white noise; that is, its mean is zero, its autocorrelation function is a Dirac delta function, and its amplitude is Gaussian distributed.

Under these conditions, we find that (Risken, 1989)

$$D_k = 0 \qquad \text{for } k > 2$$

in which case Eq. (D.13) reduces to the same mathematical form as Eq. (D.10).

Evolution of Weight-Space Probability Density for One-Dimensional Stochastic Learning Algorithm

To illustrate the use of the Fokker–Planck equation as a tool for studying the search dynamics of the learning process, consider the one-dimensional version of the stochastic approximation algorithm written in the form of a difference equation as follows:

$$w(n+1) = w(n) + \eta h\big(w(n), x(n)\big) \tag{D.15}$$

where $w(n)$ is the old value of the synaptic weight at the discrete time n denoting the previous iteration, η is the learning-rate parameter, and $h(\cdot,\cdot)$ is an update function that is determined by $w(n)$ and the input signal $x(n)$. We make two assumptions:

- At each iteration of the algorithm, the input is drawn from an underlying distribution denoted by $\rho(x)$.
- The inputs drawn at successive iterations are statistically independent.

Equation (D.15) describes a *Markov process* for the time evolution of the synaptic weight w. This process is characterized by a single time-step *transition probability,* defined as follows (Leen and Orr, 1992; Ritter and Schulten, 1988):

$$
\begin{aligned}
P(w' \rightarrow w) &= \int_{-\infty}^{\infty} \rho(x)\delta(w - w' - h(x,w'))\, dx \\
&= E[\delta(w - w' - h(x,w'))]
\end{aligned} \tag{D.16}
$$

where the statistical expectation operator is over x, and $\delta(\cdot)$ is the Dirac delta function.

The transition probability $P(w' \rightarrow w)$ defines the probability of making a transition from the old value w' at iteration n to the new value w at iteration $n + 1$. As such, it generates the time evolution of the probability density function $f(w,n)$. Specifically, the probability density function of w after $(n + 1)$ iterations is related to the probability density function at n iterations by the *Kolmogorov equation* (Leen and Orr, 1992):

$$
f(w, n + 1) = \int_{-\infty}^{\infty} f(w', n)P(w' \rightarrow w)\, dw' \tag{D.17}
$$

Let

$$
\Delta w = w - w' \tag{D.18}
$$

We wish to recast the Kolmogorov equation as a differential-difference equation that represents the Kramers–Moyal expansion for the probability density function $f(w,n)$. To do so, we expand the transition probability of Eq. (D.17) as a power series in η, obtaining the expansion (Leen and Orr, 1992)

$$
f(w, n + 1) - f(w, n) = \sum_{k=1}^{\infty} \frac{(-\eta)^k}{k!} \frac{\partial^k}{\partial w^k}[D_k(w)f(w, n)] \tag{D.19}
$$

The coefficient D_k is itself defined by

$$
D_k(w) = E[h^k(w, x)] \tag{D.20}
$$

where the statistical expectation operator is over x. For small values of the learning-rate parameter η, the weight adjustment Δw assumes a small enough value for the expansion of Eq. (D.19) to be terminated at second order in η. In such a case, Eq. (D.19) reduces to a Fokker–Planck equation.

Applications of the Fokker–Planck Equation to Neural Networks

By viewing the stochastic learning process as a Markov process, and invoking the Fokker–-Planck equation to describe the time evolution of the weight-space probability densities $f(\mathbf{w},t)$, we have a firm foundation for the study of learning algorithms for supervised or unsupervised neural networks with the following issues in mind:

- Conditions that have to be satisfied by the learning-rate parameter for convergence of the algorithm
- Speed with which training of the network is performed
- Stability properties of the equilibrium configuration of the network

This approach is well exemplified by some papers written on the subject, as described briefly in the sequel.

Leen and Orr (1992) have used the Fokker–Planck equation to predict the statistical distribution of convergence times for (1) the back-propagation algorithm applied to the XOR problem, and (2) a simple competitive learning algorithm. The essence of the approach taken by Leen and Orr is summarized in Eqs. (D.15) through (D.20). A related study is that of Radons et al. (1990) on the use of the Fokker–Planck equation for a description of the back-propagation learning process. Finally, mention should be made of the work done by Ritter and Schulten (1988), who have derived a Fokker–Planck equation for Kohonen's self-organizing feature map (SOFM) in the vicinity of equilibrium condition and for small values of the learning-rate parameter. They have used this approach to investigate the conditions for convergence and the stability properties of the SOFM algorithm. Good agreement between theory and statistical measurements based on computer simulations is reported in all these studies.

In conclusion, we should point out that the Fokker–Planck equation and the asymptotic stability theorem (discussed in Appendix B) provide two complementary approaches to the study of stochastic learning algorithms. The asymptotic stability theorem is entirely analytic in nature, providing information about the convergence behavior of the algorithm. The Fokker–Planck equation, on the other hand, is more complete in the sense that it provides additional information on the quality of the equilibrium configuration; however, it is more intensive in application, as it involves the use of both theory and numerical integration.

Bibliography†

Aarts, E., and J. Korst, 1989. *Simulated Annealing and Boltzmann Machines: A Stochastic Approach to Combinatorial Optimization and Neural Computing.* New York: Wiley.

* Abeles, M., 1991. *Corticonics: Neural Circuits of the Cerebral Cortex.* Cambridge, UK: Cambridge University Press.

Abraham, R.H., and C.D. Shaw, 1992. *Dynamics of the Geometry of Behavior.* Reading, MA: Addison-Wesley.

Abu-Mostafa, Y.S., 1989. "The Vapnik-Chervonenkis dimension: Information versus complexity in learning." *Neural Computation* **1,** 312–317.

Abu-Mostafa, Y.S., 1990. "Learning from hints in neural networks." *Journal of Complexity* **6,** 192–198.

* Abu-Mostafa, Y.S., and J.M. St. Jacques, 1985. "Information capacity of the Hopfield model." *IEEE Transactions on Information Theory* **IT-31,** 461–464.

Ackley, D.H., G.E. Hinton, and T.J. Sejnowski, 1985. "A learning algorithm for Boltzmann machines." *Cognitive Science* **9,** 147–169.

Ahalt, S.C., A.K. Krishnamurthy, P. Chen, and D.E. Melton, 1990. "Competitive learning algorithms for vector quantization." *Neural Networks* **3,** 277–290.

* Ahmad, S., and G. Tesauro, 1989. "Scaling and generalization in neural networks: A case study." In *Advances in Neural Information Processing Systems 1* (D.S. Touretzky, ed.), pp. 160–168. San Mateo, CA: Morgan Kaufmann.

Aiyer, S.V.B., N. Niranjan, and F. Fallside, 1990. "A theoretical investigation into the performance of the Hopfield model." *IEEE Transactions on Neural Networks* **15,** 204–215.

Aizerman, M.A., E.M. Braverman, and L.I. Rozonoer, 1964a. "Theoretical foundations of the potential function method in pattern recognition learning." *Automation and Remote Control* **25,** 821–837.

Aizerman, M.A., E.M. Braverman, and L.I. Rozonoer, 1964b. "The probability problem of pattern recognition learning and the method of potential functions." *Automation and Remote Control* **25,** 1175–1193.

* Aizerman, M.A., E.M., Braverman, and L.I. Rozonoer, 1965. "The Robbins-Monro process and the method of potential functions." *Automation and Remote Control* **26,** 1882–1885.

Akaike, H., 1970. "Statistical predictor identification." *Annals of the Institute of Statistical Mathematics* **22,** 202–217.

Akaike, H., 1974. "A new look at the statistical model identification." *IEEE Transactions on Automatic Control* **AC-19,** 716–723.

Aleksander, I., and H. Morton, 1990. *An Introduction to Neural Computing.* London: Chapman & Hall.

Al-Gwaiz, M.A., 1992. *Theory of Distributions.* New York: Marcel Dekker.

Allport, A., 1989. "Visual attention." In *Foundations of Cognitive Science* (M.I. Posner, ed.), pp. 631–682. Cambridge, MA: MIT Press.

† References not cited, and included here as a source of additional information for the reader, are indicated by an asterisk.

Al-Mashouq, K.A., and I.S. Reed, 1991. ''Including hints in training neural nets.'' *Neural Computation* **3,** 418–427.

Almeida, L.B., 1987. ''A learning rule for asynchronous perceptrons with feedback in a combinatorial environment.'' *1st IEEE International Conference on Neural Networks,* Vol. 2, pp. 609–618, San Diego, CA.

Almeida, L.B., 1988. ''Backpropagation in perceptrons with feedback.'' In *Neural Computers* (R. Eckmiller and C. von der Malsburg, eds.), NATO ASI Ser., pp. 199–208. New York: Springer-Verlag.

* Alspector, J., R.B. Allen, V. Hu, and S. Satyanarayana, 1988. ''Stochastic learning networks and their electronic implementation.'' In *Neural Information Processing Systems* (D.Z. Anderson, ed.), pp. 9–21. New York: American Institute of Physics.

* Alspector, J., B. Gupta, and R.B. Allen, 1989. ''Performance of a stochastic learning microchip.'' In *Advances in Neural Information Processing Systems 1* (D.S. Touretzky, ed.), pp. 748–760. San Mateo, CA: Morgan Kaufmann.

Alspector, J., J.W. Garnett, S. Haber, M.B. Porter, and R. Chu, 1991a. ''A VLSI efficient technique for generating multiple uncorrelated noise sources and its application to stochastic neural networks.'' *IEEE Transactions on Circuits and Systems* **CAS-38,** 109–123.

Alspector, J., R.B. Allen, A. Jayakumar, T. Zeppenfeld, and R. Meir, 1991b. ''Relaxation networks for large supervised learning problems.'' In *Advances in Neural Information Processing Systems 3* (R.P. Lippmann, J.E. Moody, and D.S. Touretzky, eds.), pp. 1015–1021. San Mateo, CA: Morgan Kaufmann.

Alspector, J., A. Jayakumar, and S. Luna, 1992a. ''Experimental evaluation of learning in a neural microsystem.'' In *Advances in Neural Information Processing Systems 4* (J.E. Moody, S.J. Hanson, and R.P. Lippmann, eds.), pp. 871–878. San Mateo, CA: Morgan Kaufmann.

Alspector, J., A. Jayakumar, and B. Ngo, 1992b. ''An electronic parallel neural CAM for decoding.'' *Neural Networks for Signal Processing II, Proceedings of the 1992 IEEE Workshop,* pp. 581–587, Amsterdam, Denmark.

Alspector, J., R. Meir, B. Yuhas, A. Jayakumar, and D. Lippe, 1993. ''A parallel gradient descent method for learning in analog VLSI neural networks.'' In *Advances in Neural Information Processing Systems 5* (S.J. Hanson, J.D. Cowan, and C.L. Giles, eds.), pp. 836–844. San Mateo, CA: Morgan Kaufmann.

* Altman, J., 1987. ''A quiet revolution in thinking.'' *Nature (London)* **328,** 572.

Amarel, S., 1968. ''On representations of problems of reasoning about actions.'' In *Machine Intelligence 3* (D. Michie, ed.), pp. 131–171. New York: Elsevier.

* Amari, S., 1967. ''A theory of adaptive pattern classifiers.'' *IEEE Transactions on Electronic Computers* **EC-16,** 299–307.

Amari, S., 1972. ''Characteristics of random nets of analog neuron-like elements.'' *IEEE Transactions on Systems, Man, and Cybernetics* **SMC-2,** 643–657.

* Amari, S., 1977. ''Neural theory of association and concept-formation.'' *Biological Cybernetics* **26,** 175–185.

Amari, S., 1980. ''Topographic organization of nerve fields.'' *Bulletin of Mathematical Biology* **42,** 339–364.

* Amari, S., 1983. ''Field theory of self-organizing neural nets.'' *IEEE Transactions on Systems, Man, and Cybernetics* **SMC-13,** 741–748.

Amari, S., 1990. ''Mathematical foundations of neurocomputing.'' *Proceedings of the IEEE* **78,** 1443–1463.

Amari, S., K. Yoshida, and K.-I. Kanatani, 1977. ''A mathematical foundation for statistical neurodynamics.'' *SIAM Journal on Applied Mathematics* **33,** 95–126.

Ambros-Ingerson, J., R. Granger, and G. Lynch, 1990. ''Simulation of paleo-cortex performs hierarchical clustering.'' *Science* **247,** 1344–1348.

Amit, D.J., 1989. *Modeling Brain Function: The World of Attractor Neural Networks.* New York: Cambridge University Press.

Amit, D.J., H. Gutfreund, and H. Sompolinsky, 1985a. ''Storing infinite number of patterns in a spin-glass model of neural networks.'' *Physical Review Letters* **55,** 1530–1533.

Amit, D.J., H. Gutfreund, and H. Sompolinsky, 1985b. ''Spin-glass models of neural networks.'' *Physical Review A* **32,** 1007–1018.

Amit, D.J., H. Gutfreund, and H. Sompolinsky, 1987a. ''Statistical mechanics of neural networks near saturation.'' *Annals of Physics* **173,** 30–67.

Amit, D.J., H. Gutfreund, and H. Sompolinsky, 1987b. ''Information storage in neural networks with low levels of activity.'' *Physical Review* **A35,** 2293–2303.

Anastasio, T.J., 1991. ''A recurrent neural network model of velocity storage in the vestibulo-ocular reflex.'' In *Advances in Neural Information Processing Systems 3* (R.P. Lippmann, J.E. Moody, and D.S. Touretzky, eds.), pp. 32–38. San Mateo, CA: Morgan Kaufmann.

Anderson, B.D.O., and J.B. Moore, 1979. *Linear Optimal Control.* Englewood Cliffs, NJ: Prentice-Hall.

* Anderson, J.A., 1968. ''A memory storage model utilizing spatial correlation functions.'' *Kybernetik* **5,** 113–119.

Anderson, J.A., 1972. ''A simple neural network generating an interactive memory.'' *Mathematical Biosciences* **14,** 197–220.

Anderson, J.A., 1983. ''Cognitive and psychological computation with neural models.'' *IEEE Transactions on Systems, Man, and Cybernetics* **SMC-13,** 799–815.

Anderson, J.A., 1985. ''What Hebb synapses build.'' In *Synaptic Modification, Neuron Selectivity, and Nervous System Organization* (W.B. Levy, J.A. Anderson, and S. Lehmkuhle, eds.), pp. 153–173. Hillsdale, NJ: Erlbaum.

Anderson, J.A., 1988. ''General introduction.'' In *Neurocomputing: Foundations of Research* (J.A. Anderson and E. Rosenfeld, eds.), pp. xiii–xxi. Cambridge, MA: MIT Press.

Anderson, J.A., 1990. ''Hybrid computation in cognitive science: Neural networks and symbols.'' *Applied Cognitive Psychology* **4,** 337–347.

Anderson, J.A. 1993. ''The BSB model: A simple nonlinear autoassociative neural network.'' In *Associative Neural Memories* (M. Hassoun, ed.), pp. 77–103. Oxford: Oxford University Press.

Anderson, J.A., 1994. *Introduction to Practical Neural Modeling.* Cambridge, MA: MIT Press.

Anderson, J.A., and G.L. Murphy, 1986. ''Concepts in connectionist models.'' In *Neural Networks for Computing* (J.S. Denker, ed.), pp. 17–22. New York: American Institute of Physics.

Anderson, J.A., and E. Rosenfeld, eds., 1988. *Neurocomputing: Foundations of Research.* Cambridge, MA: MIT Press.

Anderson, J.A., J.W. Silverstein, S.A. Ritz, and R.S. Jones, 1977. ''Distinctive features, categorical perception, and probability learning: Some applications of a neural model.'' *Psychological Review* **84,** 413–451.

Anderson, J.A., A. Pellionisz, and E. Rosenfeld, eds., 1990a. *Neurocomputing 2: Directions for Research.* Cambridge, MA: MIT Press.

Anderson, J.A., M.T. Gately, P.A. Penz, and D.R. Collins, 1990b. ''Radar signal categorization using a neural network.'' *Proceedings of the IEEE* **78,** 1646–1657.

Andreou, A.G., 1992. ''Minimal circuit models of neurons, synapses and multivariable functions for analog VLSI neuromorphic computation,'' Report JHU/ECE-92-13. Johns Hopkins University, Baltimore, MD.

* Andreou, A.G., and K.A. Boahen, 1989. ''Synthetic neural circuits using current-domain signal representations.'' *Neural Computation* **1,** 489–501.

Andreou, A.G., K.A. Boahen, P.O. Pouliqueen, A. Pasavoic, R.E. Jenkins, and K. Strohbehn, 1991. ''Current-mode subthreshold MOS circuits for analog VLSI neural systems.'' *IEEE Transactions on Neural Networks* **2,** 205–213.

Arbib, M.A., 1987. *Brains, Machines, and Mathematics,* 2nd ed. New York: Springer-Verlag.

Arbib, M.A., 1989. *The Metaphorical Brain,* 2nd ed. New York: Wiley.

* Arbib, M.A., and S. Amari, eds., 1989. *Dynamic Interactions in Neural Networks: Models and Data.* New York: Springer-Verlag.

Arima, Y., K. Mashiko, K. Okada, T. Yamada, A. Maeda, H. Nontani, H. Kondoh, and S. Kayano, 1992. ''336-Neuron 28K-synapse self-learning neural network chip with branch-neuron-unit architecture.'' *IEEE Journal of Solid-State Circuits* **26,** 1637–1644.

Arrowsmith, D.K., and C.M. Place, 1990. *An Introduction to Dynamical Systems.* Cambridge, UK: Cambridge University Press.

Artola, A., and W. Singer, 1987. ''Long-term potentiation and NMDA receptors in rat visual cortex.'' *Nature (London)* **330,** 649–652.

Ashby, W.R., 1952. *Design for a Brain.* New York: Wiley.

Ashby, W.R., 1960. *Design for a Brain,* 2nd ed. New York: Wiley.

Aspray, W., and A. Burks, 1986. *Papers of John von Neumann on Computing and Computer Theory,* Charles Babbage Institute Reprint Series for the History of Computing, Vol. 12. Cambridge, MA: MIT Press.

Åström, K.J., and T.J. McAvoy, 1992. ''Intelligent control: An overview and evaluation.'' In *Handbook of Intelligent Control* (D.A. White and D.A. Sofge, eds.), New York: Van Nostrand-Reinhold.

Atherton, D.P., 1981. *Stability of Nonlinear Systems.* Chichester, UK: Research Studies Press.

Atick, J.J., 1992. ''Could information theory provide an ecological theory of sensory processing?'' *Network* **3,** 213–251.

Atick, J.J., and A.N. Redlich, 1990a. ''Towards a theory of early visual processing.'' *Neural Computation* **2,** 308–320.

Atick, J.J., and A.N. Redlich, 1990b. ''Quantitative tests of a theory of retinal processing: Contract Sensitivity Curves,'' IASSNS-HEP-90/51. School of Natural Sciences, Institute for Advanced Study, Princeton, N.J.

* Atick, J.J., and A.N. Redlich, 1992. ''What does the retina know about natural scenes.'' *Neural Computation* **4,** 196–210.

Atiya, A.F., 1988. ''Learning on a general network.'' In *Neural Information Processing Systems* (D.Z. Anderson, ed.), pp. 22–30. New York: American Institute of Physics.

Atiya, A.F., and Y.S. Abu-Mostafa, 1993. ''An analog feedback associative memory.'' *IEEE Transactions on Neural Networks* **4,** 117–126.

* Atlas, L., D. Cohn, and R. Ladner, 1990. ''Training connectionist networks with queries and selective sampling.'' In *Advances in Neural Information Processing Systems 2* (D.S. Touretzky, ed.), pp. 566–573. San Mateo, CA: Morgan Kaufmann.

Attneave, F., 1954. ''Some informational aspects of visual perception.'' *Psychological Review* **61,** 183–193.

* Babcock, K.L., and R.M. Westervelt, 1986. ''Complex dynamics in simple neural circuits.'' In *Neural Networks for Computing* (J.S. Denker, ed.), pp. 23–28. New York: American Institute of Physics.

Bahl, L.R., F. Jelinek, and R.L. Mercer, 1983. ''A maximum likelihood approach to continuous speech recognition.'' *IEEE Transactions on Pattern Analysis and Machine Intelligence* **PAMI-5,** 179–190.

Bailey, J., and D. Hammerstrom, 1988. ''Why VLSI implementations of associative VLCNs require connection multiplexing.'' *International Conference on Neural Networks,* Vol. 2, pp. 173–180, San Diego, CA.

Baldi, P., and K. Hornik, 1989. ''Neural networks and principal component analysis: Learning from examples without local minimum.'' *Neural Networks* **1,** 53–58.

Ballard, D.H., 1986. ''Cortical connections and parallel processing: Structure and function.'' *Behavioral and Brain Sciences* **9,** 67–120.

Ballard, D.H., 1990. ''Modular learning in hierarchical neural networks.'' In *Computational Neuroscience* (E.L. Schwartz, ed.), pp. 139–153. Cambridge, MA: MIT Press.

* Ballard, D.H., G.E. Hinton, and T.J. Sejnowski, 1983. ''Parallel visual computation.'' *Nature (London)* **306,** 21–26.

* Banks, S.P., and R.F. Harrison, 1989. ''Can perceptrons find Liapunov functions?—An algorithmic approach to systems stability.'' *1st IEE International Conference on Artificial Neural Networks,* pp. 364–368, London.

Baras, J.S., and A. LaVigna, 1990. ''Convergence of Kohonen's learning vector quantization.'' *International Joint Conference on Neural Networks,* Vol. 3, pp. 17–20, San Diego, CA.

* Barhen, J., S. Guleti, and M. Zak, 1989. ''Neural learning of constrained nonlinear transformations.'' *Computer* **22,** 67–76.

Barlow, H.B., 1989. ''Unsupervised learning.'' *Neural Computation* **1,** 295–311.

Barlow, H., and P. Földiák, 1989. ''Adaptation and decorrelation in the cortex.'' In *The Computing Neuron* (R. Durbin, C. Miall, and G. Mitchison, eds.) pp. 54–72. Reading, MA: Addison-Wesley.

* Barlow, R.B., Jr., 1990. ''What the brain tells the eye.'' *Scientific American* **262**(April), 90–95.

Barnard, E., and D. Casasent, 1991. ''Invariance and neural nets.'' *IEEE Transactions on Neural Networks* **2,** 498–508.

Barron, A.R., 1991. ''Complexity regularization with application to artificial neural networks.'' In *Nonparametric Functional Estimation and Related Topics* (G. Roussas, ed.), pp. 561–576.

Barron, A.R., 1992. ''Neural net approximation.'' In *Proceedings of the Seventh Yale Workshop on Adaptive and Learning Systems,* pp. 69–72. New Haven, CT: Yale University.

Barto, A.G., 1985. ''Learning by statistical cooperation of self-interested neuron-like computing elements.'' *Human Neurobiology* **4,** 229–256.

Barto, A.G., 1990. ''Some learning tasks from a control perspective.'' COINS Technical

Report 90-122, Computer and Information Science Department, University of Massachusetts, Amherst, MA. December, 1990.

Barto, A.G., 1992. ''Reinforcement learning and adaptive critic methods.'' In *Handbook of Intelligent Control* (D.A. White and D.A. Sofge, eds.), pp. 469–491. New York: Van Nostrand-Reinhold.

Barto, A.G., R.S. Sutton, and C.W. Anderson, 1983. ''Neuronlike adaptive elements that can solve difficult learning control problems.'' *IEEE Transactions on Systems, Man, and Cybernetics* **SMC-13,** 834–846.

Barto, A.R., R.S. Sutton, and C.J.C.H. Watkins, 1990. ''Learning and sequential decision making.'' In *Learning and Computational Neuroscience: Foundations of Adaptive Networks* (M. Gabriel and J. Moore, eds.), pp. 539–602. Cambridge, MA: MIT Press.

Başar, E., ed., 1990. *Chaos in Brain Function.* New York: Springer-Verlag.

Bashkirov, O.A., E.M. Braverman, and I.B. Muchnik, 1964. ''Potential function algorithms for pattern recognition learning machines.'' *Automation and Remote Control* **25,** 629–631.

Battiti, R., 1992. ''First- and second-order methods for learning: Between steepest descent and Newton's method.'' *Neural Computation* **4,** 141–166.

* Bauer, H.-U., and T. Geisel, 1990. ''Nonlinear dynamics of feedback multilayer perceptrons.'' *Physical Review A* **42,** 2401–2409.

Bauer, H.-U., and K.R. Pawelzik, 1992. ''Quantifying the neighborhood preservation of self-organizing feature maps.'' *IEEE Transactions on Neural Networks* **3,** 570–579.

Baum, E.B., 1991. ''Neural net algorithms that learn in polynomial time from examples and queries.'' *IEEE Transactions on Neural Networks,* **2,** 5–19.

Baum, E.B., and D. Haussler, 1989. ''What size net gives valid generalization?'' *Neural Computation* **1,** 151–160.

Baum, E.B., and F. Wilczek, 1988. ''Supervised learning of probability distributions by neural networks.'' (D.Z. Anderson, ed.), pp. 52–61. New York: American Institute of Physics.

Baxt, W., 1992. ''The applications of the artificial neural network to clinical decision making.'' In *Conference on Neural Information Processing Systems—Natural and Synthetic,* November 30–December 3, Denver, CO.

* Beale, R., and T. Jackson, 1990. *Neural Computing: An Introduction.* Bristol, UK: Adam Hilger.

* Bear, M.F., L.N. Cooper, and F.F. Ebner, 1987. ''A physiological basis for a theory of synapse modification.'' *Science* **237,** 42–48.

Becker, S., 1991. ''Unsupervised learning procedures for neural networks.'' *International Journal of Neural Systems* **2,** 17–33.

Becker, S., 1992. ''An Information-theoretic Unsupervised Learning Algorithm for Neural Networks.'' Ph.D. Thesis, University of Toronto, Ontario.

Becker, S., 1993. ''Learning to categorize objects using temporal coherence.'' *Advances in Neural Information Processing Systems 5* (S. J. Hanson, J.D. Cowan, and C.L. Giles, eds.), pp. 361–368. San Mateo, CA: Morgan Kaufmann.

Becker, S., and G.E. Hinton, 1989. ''Spatial coherence as an internal teacher for a neural network,'' *Technical Report GRG-TR-89-7.* Department of Computer Science, University of Toronto, Ontario.

Becker, S., and G.E. Hinton, 1992. ''A self-organizing neural network that discovers surfaces in random-dot stereograms.'' *Nature (London)* **355,** 161–163.

Becker, S., and G.E. Hinton, 1993. "Learning mixture models of spatial coherence." *Neural Computation* **5,** 267–277.

Becker, S., and M. Plumbley, 1993. "Unsupervised neural network learning procedures for feature extraction and classification." Private communication.

* Behrens, H., D. Gawronska, J. Hollatz, and B. Schürmann, 1991. "Recurrent and feedforward backpropagation for time independent pattern recognition." *International Joint Conference on Neural Networks,* Vol. 2, pp. 591–596, Seattle, WA.

* Bell, A.J., 1992. "Self-organization in real neurons: Anti-Hebb in 'Channel Space'?" In *Advances in Neural Information Processing Systems 4* (J.E. Moody, S.J. Hanson, and R.P. Lippmann, eds.), pp. 59–66. San Mateo, CA: Morgan Kaufmann.

Bellman, R., 1957. *Dynamic Programming.* Princeton, NJ: Princeton University Press.

* Bellman, R., 1961. *Adaptive Control Processes: A Guided Tour.* Princeton, NJ: Princeton University Press.

Bellman, R., and S.E. Dreyfus, 1962. *Applied Dynamic Programming.* Princeton, NJ: Princeton University Press.

* Benello, J., A.W. Mackie, and J.A. Anderson, 1989. "Synaptic category disambiguation with neural networks." *Computer Speech and Language* **3,** 203–217.

* Bertero, M., T.A. Poggio, and V. Torre, 1988. "Ill-posed problems in early vision." *Proceedings of the IEEE* **76,** 869–889.

Bertsekas, D.P., 1987. *Dynamic Programming: Deterministic and Stochastic Models."* Englewood Cliffs, NJ: Prentice-Hall.

* Bezdek, J., ed., 1992. Special Issue on Fuzzy Logic and Neural Networks. *IEEE Transactions on Neural Networks* **3,** 641–828.

Bharucha-Reid, A.T., 1960. *Elements of the Theory of Markov Processes and Their Applications.* New York: McGraw-Hill.

Bienenstock, E.L., L.N. Cooper, and P.W. Munro, 1982. "Theory for the development of neuron selectivity: Orientation specificity and binocular interaction in visual cortex." *Journal of Neuroscience* **2,** 32–48.

Bishop, C.M., 1990. "Curvature-driven smoothing in backpropagation neural networks," CLM-P-880. AEA Technology, Culham Laboratory, Abingdon, UK.

* Bishop, C.M., 1991. "Improving the generalization properties of radial basis function neural networks." *Neural Computation* **3,** 579–588.

* Bishop, C.M., 1992. "Exact calculation of the Hessian matrix for the multi-layer perceptron." *Neural Computation* **4,** 494–501.

Black, H.S., 1953. *Modulation Theory.* Princeton, NJ: Van Nostrand.

* Black, I.B., 1991. *Information in the Brain: A Molecular Perspective.* Cambridge, MA: MIT Press.

Blake, A., 1983. "The least-disturbance principle and weak constraints." *Pattern Recognition Letters* **1,** 393–399.

Blumer, A., A. Ehrenfeucht, D. Haussler, and M.K. Warmuth, 1987. "Occam's razor." *Information Processing Letters* **24,** 377–380.

Blumer, A., A. Ehrenfeucht, D. Haussler, and M.K. Warmuth, 1989. "Learnability and the Vapnik–Chervonenkis Dimension." *Journal of the Association for Computing Machinery* **36,** 929–965.

Boahen, K.A., and A.G. Andreou, 1992. "A contrast sensitive silicon retina with reciprocal synapses." In *Advances in Neural Information Processing Systems 4* (J.E. Moody, S.J. Hanson, and R.P. Lippmann, eds.), pp. 764–772. San Mateo, CA: Morgan Kaufmann.

Boahen, K.A., P.O. Pouliquen, A.G. Andreou, and R.E. Jenkins, 1989. ''A heteroassociative memory using current-mode analog VLSI circuits.'' *IEEE Transactions on Circuits and Systems* **CAS-36,** 747–755.

Bodenhausen, U., and A. Waibel, 1991. ''The tempo 2 algorithm: Adjusting time-delays by supervised learning.'' In *Advances in Neural Information Processing Systems 3* (R.P. Lippmann, J.E. Moody, and D.S. Touretzky, eds.), pp. 155–161. San Mateo, CA: Morgan Kaufmann.

Bolt, G.R., 1992. ''Fault Tolerance in Artificial Neural Networks.'' D. Phil. Thesis, York University, Ontario.

Boltzmann, L., 1872. ''Weitere studien über das Wärmegleichgewicht unter gasmolekülen,'' *Sitzungsberichte der Mathematisch-Naturwissenschaftlichen Classe der Kaiserlichen Akademie der Wissenschaften* **66,** 275–370.

* Bose, N.K., and A.K. Garga, 1992. ''Neural network design using Voronoi diagrams: Preliminaries.'' *International Joint Conference on Neural Networks,* Vol. 3, pp. 127–132, Baltimore, MD.

Boser, B.E., E. Säckinger, J. Bromley, Y. LeCun, and L.D. Jackel, 1992. ''Hardware requirements for neural network pattern classifiers.'' *IEEE Micro* **12,** 32–40.

* Boubez, T., and R.L. Peskin, 1993. ''Wavelet neural networks and receptive field partitioning.'' *IEEE International Conference on Neural Networks,* Vol. 3, pp. 1544–1549, San Francisco, CA.

Bourlard, H.A., 1990. ''How connectionist models could improve Markov models for speech recognition.'' In *Advanced Neural Computers* (R. Eckmiller, ed.), pp. 247–254. Amsterdam: North-Holland.

* Bourlard, H.A., and Y. Kamp, 1988. ''Auto-association by multilayer perceptrons and singular value decomposition.'' *Biological Cybernetics* **59,** 291–294.

Bourlard, H.A., and C.J. Wellekens, 1990. ''Links between Markov models and multilayer perceptrons.'' *IEEE Transactions on Pattern Analysis and Machine Intelligence* **PAMI-12,** 1167–1178.

Braitenberg, V., 1967. ''Is the cerebellar cortex a biological clock in the millisecond range?'' In *The Cerebellum. Progress in Brain Research* **25** (C.A. Fox and R.S. Snider, eds.), pp. 334–346. Amsterdam: Elsevier.

Braitenberg, V., 1977. *On the Texture of Brains.* New York: Springer-Verlag.

Braitenberg, V., 1984. *Vehicles: Experiments in Synthetic Psychology.* Cambridge, MA: MIT Press.

Braitenberg, V., 1986. ''Two views of the cerebral cortex.'' In *Brain Theory* (G. Palm and A. Aertsen, eds.), pp. 81–96. New York: Springer-Verlag.

Braitenberg, V., 1990. ''Reading the structure of brains.'' *Network* **1,** 1–12.

Bregman, A.S., 1990. *Auditory Scene Analysis: The Perceptual Organization of Sound.* Cambridge, MA: MIT Press.

Bridle, J.S., 1990a. ''Probabilistic interpretation of feedforward classification network outputs, with relationships to statistical pattern recognition.'' In *Neuro-computing: Algorithms, Architectures and Applications* (F. Fougelman-Soulie and J. Hérault, eds.), pp. 227–236. New York: Springer-Verlag.

Bridle, J.S., 1990b. ''Training stochastic model recognition algorithms as networks can lead to maximum mutual information estimation of parameters.'' In *Advances in Neural Information Processing Systems 2* (D.S. Touretzky, ed.), pp. 211–217. San Mateo, CA: Morgan Kaufmann.

* Bridle, J.S., A.J.R. Heading, and D.J.C. MacKay, 1992. ''Unsupervised classifiers,

mutual information, and phantom targets.'' In *Advances in Neural Information Processing Systems 4* (J.E. Moody, S.J. Hanson, and R.P. Lippmann, eds.), pp. 1096–1101. San Mateo, CA: Morgan Kaufmann.

Brockett, R.W., 1991. ''Dynamical systems that sort lists, diagonalize matrices, and solve linear programming problems.'' *Linear Algebra and Its Applications* **146,** 79–91.

Brodal, A., 1981. *Neurological Anatomy in Relation to Clinical Medicine,* 3rd ed. New York: Oxford University Press.

Brodmann, K., 1909. *Vergleichende Lokalisationslehre der Grosshirnrinde.* Leipzig: J.A. Barth.

Brogan, W.L., 1985. *Modern Control Theory,* 2nd ed. Englewood Cliffs, NJ: Prentice-Hall.

Broomhead, D.S., and D. Lowe, 1988. ''Multivariable functional interpolation and adaptive networks.'' *Complex Systems* **2,** 321–355.

* Broomhead, D.S., D. Lowe, and A.R. Webb, 1989. ''A sum rule satisfied by optimized feedforward layered networks,'' RSRE Memorandum No. 4341. Royal Signals and Radar Establishment, Malvern, UK.

* Brown, T.H., 1991. ''Neuronal plasticity and learning,'' Tutorial Notes. *International Joint Conference on Neural Networks,* Seattle, WA.

* Brown, T.H., P.F. Chapman, E.W. Kairiss, and C.L. Keenan, 1988. ''Long-term synaptic potentiation.'' *Science* **242,** 724–728.

* Brown, T.H., A.H. Ganong, E.W. Kairiss, C.L. Keenan, and S.R. Kelso, 1989. ''Long-term potentiation in two synaptic systems of the hippocampal brain slice.'' In *Neural Models of Plasticity: Experimental and Theoretical Approaches* (J.H. Byrne and W.O. Berry, eds.), pp. 266–306. San Diego, CA: Academic Press.

Brown, T.H., E.W. Kairiss, and C.L. Keenan, 1990. ''Hebbian synapses: Biophysical mechanisms and algorithms.'' *Annual Review of Neuroscience* **13,** 475–511.

Bruck, J., 1990. ''On the convergence properties of the Hopfield model.'' *Proceedings of the IEEE* **78,** 1579–1585.

* Buhman, M.D., 1988. ''Convergence of univariate quasi-interpolation using multiquadrics.'' *IMA Journal of Numerical Analysis* **8,** 365–383.

Burges, C.J.C., O. Matan, Y. LeCun, J.S. Denker, L.D. Jackal, C.E. Stenard, C.R. Nohl, and J.I. Ben, 1992. ''Shortest path segmentation: A method for training a neural network to recognize character strings.'' *International Joint Conference on Neural Networks,* Vol. 3, pp. 165–170, Seattle, WA.

* Burr, D.J., 1988. ''Experiments on neural net recognition of spoken and written text.'' *IEEE Transactions on Acoustics, Speech, and Signal Processing* **ASSP-36,** 1162–1168.

Caianiello, E.R., 1961. ''Outline of a theory of thought-processes and thinking machines.'' *Journal of Theoretical Biology* **1,** 204–235.

* Caianiello, E.R., 1990. ''Prolegomena to an analysis of form and structure.'' In *Advanced Neural Computers* (R. Eckmiller, ed.), pp. 3–10. Amsterdam: North-Holland.

Çambel, A.B., 1993. *Applied Chaos Theory: A Paradigm for Complexity.* New York: Academic Press.

Carpenter, G.A., and S. Grossberg, 1987. ''A massively parallel architecture for a self-organizing neural pattern recognition machine.'' *Computer Vision, Graphics, and Image Processing* **37,** 54–115.

* Carpenter, G.A., and S. Grossberg, 1991. *Pattern Recognition by Self-Organizing Neural Networks.* Cambridge, MA: MIT Press.

Carpenter, G.A., M.A. Cohen, and S. Grossberg, 1987. Technical comments on ''Computing with neural networks.'' *Science* **235,** 1226–1227.

Carter, S., R.J. Frank, and D.S.W. Tansley, 1993. ''Clone detection in telecommunications software systems: A neural net approach.'' In *Applications of Neural Networks to Telecommunications* (J. Alspector, R. Goodman, and T.X. Brown, eds.), pp. 273–280. Hillsdale, NJ: Lawrence Erlbaum.

Casdagli, M., 1989. ''Nonlinear prediction of chaotic time-series.'' *Physica* **35D,** 335–356.

Casselman, F.L., D.F. Freeman, D.A. Kerringan, S.E. Lane, N.H. Millstrom, and W.G. Nichols, Jr., 1991. ''A neural network-based passive sonar detection and classification design with a low false alarm rate.'' *IEEE Conference on Neural Networks for Ocean Engineering,* pp. 49–55, Washington, DC.

* Caudill, M., and C. Butler, 1992. *Understanding Neural Networks: Computer Explorations,* Vols. 1 and 2. Cambridge, MA: MIT Press.

Changeux, J.P., and A. Danchin, 1976. ''Selective stabilization of developing synapses as a mechanism for the specification of neural networks.'' *Nature* (*London*) **264,** 705–712.

Chen, H., and R.-W. Liu, 1992. ''Adaptive distributed orthogonalization processing for principal components analysis.'' *International Conference on Acoustics, Speech, and Signal Processing,* Vol. 2, pp. 293–296, San Francisco, CA.

Chen, S., B. Mulgrew, and S. McLaughlin, 1992a. ''Adaptive Bayesian feedback equalizer based on a radial basis function network.'' *IEEE International Conference on Communications* **3,** 1267–1271, Chicago, IL.

Chen, S., B. Mulgrew, S. McLaughlin, and P.M. Grant, 1992b. ''Adaptive Bayesian equalizer with feedback for mobile radio channels.'' *Workshop on Adaptive Algorithms in Communications,* Bordeaux, France.

Cherkassky, V., K. Fassett, and N. Vassilas, 1991. ''Linear algebra approach to neural associative memories and noise performance of neural classifiers.'' *IEEE Transaction on Computers* **C-40,** 1429–1435.

Chester, D.L., 1990. ''Why two hidden layers are better than one.'' *International Joint Conference on Neural Networks,* Vol. 1, pp. 265–268, Washington, DC.

Chiueh, T.-D., T.-T. Tang, and L.-G. Chen, 1993. ''Vector quantization using tree-structured self-organizing feature maps.'' In *Applications of Neural Networks to Telecommunications* (J. Alspector, R. Goodman, and T.X. Brown, eds.), pp. 259–265. Hillsdale, NJ: Lawrence Erlbaum.

Choi, J., S.H. Bang, and B.J. Sheu (1993). ''A programmable analog VLSI neural network processor for communication receivers.'' *IEEE Transactions on Neural Networks* **4,** 484–495.

Choi, J.J., P. Arabshahi, R.J. Marks, II, and T.P. Caudell, 1992. ''Fuzzy parameter adaptation in neural systems.'' *International Joint Conference on Neural Networks,* Vol. 1, pp. 232–238, Baltimore, MD.

Churcher, S., D.J. Baxter, A. Hamilton, A.F. Murray, and H.M. Reekie, 1993. ''Generic analog neural computation—The EPSILON chip.'' In *Advances in Neural Information Processing Systems* (S.J. Hanson, J.D. Cowan, and C.L. Giles, eds.), pp. 773–780. San Mateo, CA: Morgan Kaufmann.

Churchland, P.S., 1986. *Neurophilosophy: Toward a Unified Science of the Mind/Brain.* Cambridge, MA: MIT Press.

Churchland, P.S., and T.J. Sejnowski, 1992. *The Computational Brain.* Cambridge, MA: MIT Press.

* Churchland, P.S., C. Koch, and T.J. Sejnowski, 1990. ''What is computational neurosci-

ence?'' In *Computational Neuroscience* (E. Schwartz, ed.), pp. 46–55. Cambridge, MA: MIT Press.

Cid-Sueiro, J., and A.R. Figueiras-Vidal, 1993. ''Improving conventional equalizers with neural networks.'' In *Applications of Neural Networks to Telecommunications* (J. Alspector, R. Goodman, and T.X. Brown, eds.), pp. 20–26. Hillsdale, NJ: Lawrence Erlbaum.

* Cleeremans, A., and J.L. McClelland, 1991. ''Learning the structure of event sequences.'' *Journal of Experimental Psychology* **120,** 235–253.

* Cleeremans, A., D. Servan-Schreiber, and J.L. McClelland, 1989. ''Finite state automata and simple recurrent networks.'' *Neural Computation* **1,** 372–381.

Cocke, J., and V. Markstein, 1990. ''The evolution of RISC technology at IBM.'' *IBM Journal of Research and Development* **34,** 4–11. (The January 1990 issue of this journal is devoted to a description of the architecture and machine design of the IBM RISC system/6000 processor.)

Cohen, M.A., 1992a. ''The synthesis of arbitrary stable dynamics in non-linear neural networks. II. Feedback and universality.'' *International Joint Conference on Neural Networks,* Vol. 1, pp. 141–146, Baltimore, MD.

Cohen, M.A., 1992b. ''The construction of arbitrary stable dynamics in nonlinear neural networks.'' *Neural Networks* **5,** 83–103.

Cohen, M.A., and S. Grossberg, 1983. ''Absolute stability of global pattern formation and parallel memory storage by competitive neural networks.'' *IEEE Transactions on Systems, Man, and Cybernetics* **SMC-13,** 815–826.

* Cohen, M.H., P.O. Poudiqueen, and A.G. Andreou, 1992. ''Analog LSI implementation of an auto-adaptive network for real-time separation of independent signals.'' In *Advances in Neural Information Processing Systems* (J.E. Moody, S.J. Hanson, and R.P. Lippmann, eds.), pp. 805–812. San Mateo, CA: Morgan Kaufmann.

Cohen, M., H. Franco, N. Morgan, D. Rumelhart, and V. Abrash, 1993. ''Context-dependent multiple distribution phonetic modeling with MLPs.'' In *Advances in Neural Information Processing Systems* (S.J. Hanson, J.D. Cowan, and C.L. Giles, eds.), pp. 649–657. San Mateo, CA: Morgan Kaufmann.

Connor, J., 1993. ''Bootstrap methods in neural network time series prediction.'' In *Applications of Neural Networks to Telecommunications* (J. Alspector, R. Goodman, and T.X. Brown, eds.), pp. 125–131. Hillsdale, NJ: Lawrence Erlbaum.

* Connor, J., and L. Atlas, 1991. ''Recurrent neural networks and time series prediction.'' *International Joint Conference on Neural Networks,* Vol. 1, pp. 301–306, Seattle, WA.

Constantine-Paton, M., H.T. Cline, and E. Debski, 1990. ''Patterned activity, synaptic convergence, and the NMDA receptor in developing visual pathways.'' *Annual Review of Neuroscience* **13,** 129–154.

Cook, P.A., 1986. *Nonlinear Dynamical Systems.* London: Prentice-Hall International.

Cooper, L.N., 1973. ''A possible organization of animal memory and learning.'' In *Proceedings of the Nobel Symposium on Collective Properties of Physical Systems* (B. Lundquist and S. Lundquist, eds.), pp. 252–264. New York: Academic Press.

* Cooper, L.N., 1988. ''Local and global factors in learning.'' In *Brain Structure, Learning and Memory* (J.L. Davis, R.W. Newburgh, and E.S. Wegman, eds.), pp. 171–191. Washington, DC: American Association for the Advancement of Science.

Cottrell, G.W., and J. Metcalfe, 1991. ''EMPATH: Face, emotion, and gender recognition using holons.'' In *Advances in Neural Information Processing Systems 3* (R.P.

Lippmann, J.E. Moody, and D.S. Touretzky, eds.), pp. 564–571. San Mateo, CA: Morgan Kaufmann.

Cottrell, G.W., P. Munro, and D. Zipser, 1987. ''Learning internal representations from grey-scale images: An example of extensional programming.'' *Proceedings of the 9th Annual Conference of the Cognitive Science Society,* pp. 461–473.

Cottrell, M., and J.C. Fort, 1986. ''A stochastic model of retinotopy: A self organizing process.'' *Biological Cybernetics* **53,** 405–411.

Courant, R., and D. Hilbert, 1970. *Methods of Mathematical Physics,* Vols 1 and 2. New York: Wiley (Interscience).

Cover, T.M., 1965. ''Geometrical and statistical properties of systems of linear inequalities with applications in pattern recognition.'' *IEEE Transactions on Electronic Computers* **EC-14,** 326–334.

Cover, T.M., and J.A. Thomas, 1991. *Elements of Information Theory.* New York: Wiley.

* Cowan, C.F.N., P.M. Grant, S. Chen, and G.J. Gibson, 1990. ''Non-linear classification and adaptive structures.'' *Proceedings SPIE—International Society of Optical Engineering* **1348,** 62–72.

* Cowan, J.D., 1965. ''The problem of organismic reliability.'' *Progress in Brain Research* **17,** 9–63.

Cowan, J.D., 1967. ''A Mathematical Theory of Central Nervous Activity.'' Ph.D. Thesis, University of London, UK.

Cowan, J.D., 1968. ''Statistical mechanics of nervous nets.'' In *Neural Networks* (E.R. Caianiello, ed.), pp. 181–188. Berlin: Springer-Verlag.

Cowan, J.D., 1990. ''Neural networks: The early days.'' In *Advances in Neural Information Processing Systems 2* (D.S. Touretzky, ed.), pp. 828–842. San Mateo, CA: Morgan Kaufmann.

* Cowan, J.D., and M.H. Cohen, 1969. ''The role of statistical mechanics in neurobiology.'' *Journal of the Physical Society of Japan* **26,** 51–53.

Cowan, J.D., and D.H. Sharp, 1988. ''Neural nets.'' *Quarterly Reviews of Biophysics* **21,** 365–427.

Cragg, B.G., and H.N.V. Tamperley, 1954. ''The organisation of neurons: A cooperative analogy.'' *Electroencephalography and Clinical Neurophysiology* **6,** 85–92.

Cragg, B.G., and H.N.V. Tamperley, 1955. ''Memory: The analogy with ferromagnetic hysteresis.'' *Brain* **78,** Part II, 304–316.

Craik, K.J.W., 1943. *The Nature of Explanation.* Cambridge, UK: Cambridge University Press.

* Crick, F.H.C., 1984. ''Function of the thalamic reticular complex: The searchlight hypothesis.'' *Proceedings of the National Academy of Sciences of the U.S.A.* **81,** 4586–4590.

Crick, F.H.C., 1989. ''The recent excitement about neural networks.'' *Nature* (*London*), **337,** 129–132.

Crutchfield, J.P., J.D. Farmer, N.H. Packard, and R.S. Shaw, 1986. ''Chaos,'' *Scientific American* **255**(6), 38–49.

Cybenko, G., 1988. *Approximation by Superpositions of a Sigmoidal Function.* Urbana: University of Illinois.

Cybenko, G., 1989. ''Approximation by superpositions of a sigmoidal function.'' *Mathematics of Control, Signals, and Systems,* **2,** 303–314.

Darken, C., and J. Moody, 1992. ''Towards faster stochastic gradient search.'' In *Advances in Neural Information Processing Systems 4* (J.E. Moody, S.J. Hanson, and R.P. Lippmann, eds.), pp. 1009–1016. San Mateo, CA: Morgan Kaufmann.

* DARPA, 1988. *Neural Network Study.* AFCEA International Press, Fairfax, Virginia.

* Daughman, J.G., 1990. ''An information-theoretic view of analog representation in striate cortex.'' In *Computational Neuroscience* (E.L. Schwartz, ed.), pp. 403–423. Cambridge, MA: MIT Press.

Davis, P.J., 1963. *Interpolation and Approximation.* New York: Blaisdell.

Dawes, R.L., 1992a. ''Quantum neurodynamics: Neural stochastic filtering with the Schroedinger equation.'' *International Joint Conference on Neural Networks,* Vol. 1, pp. 133–140, Baltimore, MD.

Dawes, R.L., 1992b. ''Inferential reasoning through soliton properties of quantum neurodynamics.'' *IEEE International Conference on Systems, Man, and Cybernetics,* Vol. 2, pp 1314–1319, Chicago, IL.

Day, S.P., and M.R. Davenport, 1993. ''Continuous-time temporal back-propagation with adaptive time delays.'' *IEEE Transactions on Neural Networks* **4,** 348–354.

Debnath, L., and P. Mikuisiński, 1990. *Introduction to Hilbert Spaces with Applications.* San Diego, CA: Academic Press.

* deFigueiredo, R.J.P., 1992. ''The role of nonlinear operators in the structure of natural and artificial intelligence.'' *IEEE International Conference on Systems, Man, and Cybernetics,* Vol. 2, pp 1326–1331, Chicago, IL.

de Figueiredo, R.J.P., and G. Chen, 1993. *Nonlinear Feedback Control Systems.* New York: Academic Press.

Dembo, A., 1989. ''On the capacity of associative memories with linear threshold sections.'' *IEEE Transactions on Information Theory* **IT-35,** 709–720.

DeMers, D., and G. Cottrell, 1993. ''Non-linear dimensionality reduction.'' In *Advances in Neural Information Processing Systems* (S.J. Hanson, J.D. Cowan, and C.L. Giles, eds.), pp. 580–587. San Mateo, CA: Morgan Kaufmann.

Dempster, A.P., N.M. Laird, and D.B. Rubin, 1977. ''Maximum likelihood from incomplete data via the EM algorithm'' (with discussion). *Journal of the Royal Statistic Society, Series B* **39,** 1–38.

deSa, V., and D. Ballard, 1992. ''Top-down teaching enables task-relevant classification with competitive learning.'' *International Joint Conference on Neural Networks,* Vol. 3, pp. 364–371, Baltimore, MD.

DeSieno, D., 1988. ''Adding a conscience to competitive learning.'' *IEEE International Conference on Neural Networks,* Vol. 1, pp. 117–124, San Diego, CA.

deSilva, C.J.S., and Y. Attikiouzel, 1992. ''Hopfield networks as discrete dynamical systems.'' *International Joint Conference on Neural Networks,* Vol. 3, pp. 115–120, Baltimore, MD.

deVries, B., and J.C. Principe, 1992. ''The gamma model—A new neural model for temporal processing.'' *Neural Networks* **5,** 565–576.

Devroye, L., 1991. ''Exponential inequalities in nonparametric estimation.'' In *Nonparametric Functional Estimation and Related Topics* (G. Roussas, ed.), pp. 31–44. Boston, MA: Kluwer.

Diamantaras, K.I., 1992. ''Principal Component Learning Networks and Applications.'' Ph.D. dissertation, Princeton University, Princeton, NJ.

Dickerson, J.A., and B. Kosko, 1993. ''Fuzzy function approximation with supervised ellipsoidal learning.'' *World Congress on Neural Networks,* Vol. 2, pp. 9–17, Portland, OR.

Domany, E., 1988. ''Neural networks: A biased overview.'' *Journal of Statistical Physics* **51,** 743–775.

Domany, E., J.L. van Hemmen, and K. Schulten, eds., 1991. *Models of Neural Networks.* New York: Springer-Verlag.

* Dong, D.D., and J.J. Hopfield, 1992. ''Dynamic properties of neural networks with adapting synapses.'' *Network* **3,** 267–283.

Dorny, C.N., 1975. *A Vector Space Approach to Models and Optimization.* New York: Wiley (Interscience).

Doya, K., and S. Yoshizawa, 1989. ''Memorizing oscillatory patterns in the analog neural network.'' *International Joint Conference on Neural Networks,* Vol. 1, pp. 27–32, Washington, DC.

Drucker, H., and Y. LeCun, 1992. ''Improving generalization performance using double backpropagation.'' *IEEE Transactions on Neural Networks* **3,** 991–997.

Dubois, D., and H. Prade, 1980. *Fuzzy Sets and Systems: Theory and Applications.* New York: Academic Press.

Duda, R.O., and P.E. Hart, 1973. *Pattern Classification and Scene Analysis.* New York: Wiley.

* Durbin, R., and D.E. Rumelhart, 1989. ''Product units: A computationally powerful and biologically plausible extension to backpropagation networks.'' *Neural Computation* **1,** 133–142.

* Durbin, R., and D. Willshaw, 1987. ''An analogue approach to the travelling salesman problem using an elastic net method.'' *Nature* (*London*) **326,** 689–691.

Durbin, R., C. Miall, and G. Mitchison, eds., 1989. *The Computing Neuron.* Reading, MA: Addison-Wesley.

* Dyn, N., 1987. ''Interpolation of scattered data by radial functions.'' In *Topics in Multivariate Approximation* (C.K. Chui, L.L. Schumaker, and F.I. Uteras, eds.), pp. 47–61. Orlando, FL: Academic Press.

* Eckmiller, R., ed., 1990. *Advanced Neural Computers.* Amsterdam: North-Holland.

* Eckmiller, R., and C. von der Malsburg, eds., 1988. *Neural Computers,* NATO ASI Series. New York: Springer-Verlag.

Edelman, G.M., 1973. ''Antibody structure and molecular immunology.'' *Science* **180,** 830–840.

Edelman, G.M., 1987. *Neural Darwinism.* New York: Basic Books.

* Eeckman, F.H., 1988. ''The sigmoid nonlinearity in prepyriform cortex.'' In *Neural Information Processing Systems* (D.Z. Anderson, ed.), pp. 242–248. New York: American Institute of Physics.

Eeckman, F.H., and W.J. Freeman, 1986. ''The sigmoid nonlinearity in neural computation: An experimental approach.'' In *Neural Networks for Computing* (J.S. Denker, ed.), pp. 135–145. New York: American Institute of Physics.

Eggermont, J.J., 1990. *The Correlative Brain: Theory and Experiment in Neural Interaction.* New York: Springer-Verlag.

Elman, J.L. 1990. ''Finding structure in time.'' *Cognitive Science* **14,** 179–211.

* Elshafiey, I., L. Upda, and S.S. Upda, 1991. ''Development of a Hopfield network for solving integral equations.'' *International Joint Conference on Neural Networks,* Vol. 1, pp. 313–317, Seattle, WA.

* Elsner, J.B., 1991. ''Predicting time series using a neural network as a method of

distinguishing chaos from noise.'' In *Artificial Neural Networks* (T. Kohonen, K. Mäkisara, O. Simula, and J. Kangas, eds.), Vol. 1, pp. 145–150. Amsterdam: North-Holland.

* Erwin, E., K. Obermayer, and K. Schulten, 1991. ''Convergence properties of self-organizing maps.'' In *Artificial Neural Networks* (T. Kohonen, K. Mäkisara, O. Simula, and J. Kangas, eds.), Vol. 1, pp. 409–414. Amsterdam: North-Holland.

* Eveleigh, V.W., 1967. *Adaptive Control and Optimization Techniques.* New York: McGraw-Hill.

Faggin, F., 1991. ''VLSI implementation of neural networks,'' Tutorial Notes. *International Joint Conference on Neural Networks,* Seattle, WA.

Faggin, F., and C. Mead, 1990. ''VLSI implementation of neural networks.'' In *An Introduction to Neural and Electronic Networks* (S.F. Zornetzer, J.L. Davis, and C. Lau, eds.), pp. 275–292. San Diego, CA: Academic Press.

Fahlman, S.E., and C. Lebiere, 1990. ''The cascade-correlation learning architecture.'' In *Advances in Neural Information Processing Systems 2* (D.S. Touretzky, ed.), pp. 524–532. San Mateo, CA: Morgan Kaufmann.

* Fang, Y., and T.J. Sejnowski, 1990. ''Faster learning for dynamic recurrent backpropagation.'' *Neural Computation* **2,** 270–273.

* Farley, B.G., and W.A. Clark, 1954. ''Simulation of self-organizing systems by digital computer.'' *IRE Transactions on Information Theory* **IT-14,** 76–84.

Farmer, J.D., and J. Sidorowich, 1987. ''Predicting chaotic time series.'' *Physical Review Letters* **59,** 845–848.

Feldman, J.A., 1992. ''Natural computation and artificial intelligence.'' Plenary Lecture presented at the *International Joint Conference on Neural Networks,* Baltimore, MD.

Feller, W., 1968. *An Introduction to Probability Theory and its Applications,* 3rd ed., Vol. 1. New York: Wiley.

* Fels, S.S., and G.E. Hinton, 1993. ''Glove-talk: A neural network interface between a data-glove and a speech synthesizer.'' *IEEE Transactions on Neural Networks* **4,** 2–8.

Feng, J., and H. Pan, 1993. ''Analysis of Linsker-type Hebbian learning: Rigorous results.'' *IEEE International Conference on Neural Networks,* Vol. 3, pp. 1516–1521, San Francisco, CA.

Ferrán, E.A., and P. Ferrara, 1991. ''Topological maps of protein sequences.'' *Biological Cybernetics* **65,** 451–458.

Fischler, M.A., and O. Firschein, 1987. *Intelligence: The Eye, the Brain, and the Computer.* Reading, MA: Addison-Wesley.

Fletcher, R., and C.M. Reeves, 1964. ''Function minimization by conjugate gradients.'' *Computer Journal* **7,** 149–154.

Floreen, P., and P. Orponen, 1989. ''Computing stable states and sizes of attraction domains in Hopfield nets is hard.'' *International Joint Conference on Neural Networks,* Vol. 1, pp. 395–399, Washington, DC.

Fodor, J.A., 1983. *Modularity of Mind.* Cambridge, MA: MIT Press.

Fodor, J.A., and Z.W. Pylyshyn, 1988. ''Connectionism and cognitive architecture: A critical analysis.'' *Cognition* **28,** 3–72.

* Fogelman-Soulié, F., 1991. ''Neural network architectures and algorithms: A perspective.'' In *Artificial Neural Networks* (T. Kohonen, K. Mäkisara, O. Simula, and J. Kangas, eds.), Vol. 2. Amsterdam: North-Holland.

Földiak, P., 1989. ''Adaptive network for optimal linear feature extractions.'' *International Joint Conference on Neural Networks,* Vol. 1, pp. 401–405, Washington, DC.

Forney, G.D., Jr., 1973. "The Viterbi algorithm." *Proceedings of the IEEE* **61,** 268–278.

Freeman, J.A., and D.M. Sakpura, 1991. *Neural Networks: Algorithms, Applications, and Programming Techniques.* Reading, MA: Addison-Wesley.

Freeman, W.J., 1975. *Mass Action in the Nervous System.* New York: Academic Press.

* Freeman, W.J., 1987. "Simulation of chaotic EEG patterns with a dynamic model of the olfactory system." *Biological Cybernetics* **56,** 139–150.

* Freeman, W.J., 1988. "Why neural networks don't yet fly: Inquiry into the neurodynamics of biological intelligence." *International Joint Conference on Neural Networks,* Vol. 2, pp. 1–7, San Diego, CA.

Freeman, W.J., 1989. "Perpetual processing using oscillatory chaotic dynamics." *International Conference of the IEEE Engineering in Medicine and Biology Society,* Vol. 2, p. 2-AP-2-3, Seattle, WA.

* Freeman, W.J., 1991. "The physiology of perception." *Scientific American* **264**(2), 78–85.

Freeman, W.J., 1992. "Tutorial on neurobiology: From single neurons to brain chaos." *International Journal of Bifurcation and Chaos in Applied Sciences and Engineering* **2,** 451–482.

Freeman, W.J., 1993. "Chaos in the brain: Possible notes in biological intelligence." *World Congress on Neural Networks,* Vol. 4, p. 268, Portland, OR.

Freeman, W.J., and Y. Yao, 1990. "Chaos in the biodynamics of pattern recognition by neural networks." *International Joint Conference on Neural Networks,* Vol. 1, pp. 243–246, Washington, DC.

* Friedman, J.H., 1991. "Adaptive spline networks." In *Advances in Neural Information Processing Systems 3* (R.P. Lippmann, J.E. Moody, and D.S. Touretzky, eds.), pp. 675–683. San Mateo, CA: Morgan Kaufmann.

* Fukunaga, K., 1990. *Statistical Pattern Recognition,* 2nd ed. San Diego, CA: Academic Press.

Fukushima, K., 1975. "Cognitron: A self-organizing multilayered neural network." *Biological Cybernetics* **20,** 121–136.

* Fukushima, K., 1980. "Neocognitron: A self-organizing neural network model for a mechanism of pattern recognition uneffected by shift in position." *Biological Cybernetics* **36,** 193–202.

Fukushima, K., 1988a. "A hierarchical neural network model for selective attention." In *Neural Computers* (R. Eckmiller and C. von der Malsburg, eds.), NATO ASI Series, pp. 81–90. New York: Springer-Verlag.

Fukushima, K., 1988b. "Neocognitron: A hierarchical neural network capable of visual pattern recognition." *Neural Networks* **1,** 119–130.

* Fukushima, K., S. Miyake, and T. Ito, 1983. "Neocognitron: A neural network model for a mechanism of visual pattern recognition." *IEEE Transactions on Systems, Man, and Cybernetics* **SMC-13,** 826–834.

Funahashi, K., 1989. "On the approximate realization of continuous mappings by neural networks." *Neural Networks* **2,** 183–192.

Gabor, D., 1954. "Communication theory and cybernetics." *IRE Transactions on Circuit Theory* **CT-1,** 19–31.

Gabor, D., W.P.L. Wilby, and R. Woodcock, 1960. "A universal nonlinear filter, predictor and simulator which optimizes itself by a learning process." *Proceedings of the Institution of Electrical Engineers (London)* **108,** 422–435.

* Gabriel, M., and J. Moore, ed., 1990. *Learning and Computational Neuroscience: Foundations of Adaptive Networks.* Cambridge, MA: MIT Press.

Galland, C.C., 1993. ''The limitations of deterministic Boltzmann machine learning.'' *Network* **4**, 355–379.

* Galland, C.C., and G.E. Hinton, 1990. ''Discovering higher order features with mean field modules.'' In *Advances in Neural Information Processing Systems 2* (D.S. Touretzky, ed.), pp. 509–515. San Mateo, CA: Morgan Kaufmann.

Gallant, A.R., and H. White, 1988. ''There exists a neural network that does not make avoidable mistakes.'' *IEEE International Conference on Neural Networks,* Vol. 1, pp. 657–664, San Diego, CA.

* Gallant, A.R., and H. White, 1992. ''On learning the derivatives of an unknown mapping with multilayer feedforward networks.'' *Neural Networks* **5,** 129–138.

Gallistel, C.R., 1990. *The Organization of Learning.* Cambridge, MA: MIT Press.

* Gardner, D., 1993a. ''Back-propagation and neuromorphic plausibility.'' *World Congress on Neural Networks,* Vol. 2, pp. 590–593, Portland, OR.

* Gardner, D., ed., 1993b. *The Neurobiology of Neural Networks.* Cambridge, MA: MIT Press.

Gardner, E., 1987. ''Maximum storage capacity in neural networks.'' *Electrophysics Letters* **4,** 481–485.

Gee, A.H., 1993. ''Problem Solving with Optimization Networks.'' Ph.D. dissertation, University of Cambridge, UK.

Gee, A.H., S.V.B. Aiyer, and R. Prager, 1993. ''An analytical framework for optimizing neural networks.'' *Neural Networks* **6,** 79–97.

Geman, S., and D. Geman, 1984. ''Stochastic relaxation, Gibbs distributions, and the Bayesian restoration of images.'' *IEEE Transactions on Pattern Analysis and Machine Intelligence* **PAMI-6,** 721–741.

Geman, S., E. Bienenstock, and R. Doursat, 1992. ''Neural networks and the bias/variance dilemma.'' *Neural Computation* **4,** 1–58.

Gersho, A., 1982. ''On the structure of vector quantizers.'' *IEEE Transactions on Information Theory* **IT-28,** 157–166.

* Gerstein, G.L., 1962. ''Mathematical models for the all-or-none activity of some neurons.'' *IRE Transactions on Information Theory* **IT-8,** S137–S143.

* Gerstein, G.L., and M.R. Turner, 1990. ''Neural assemblies as building blocks of cortical computation,'' In *Computational Neuroscience* (E.L. Schwartz, ed.), pp. 179–191. Cambridge, MA: MIT Press.

* Gerstein, G.L., P. Bedenbaugh, and A.M.H.J. Aersten, 1989. ''Neural assemblies.'' *IEEE Transactions on Biomedical Engineering* **36,** 4–14.

* Ghosh, J., and Y. Shin, 1991. ''The pi-sigma network: An efficient higher-order network for pattern classification and function approximation.'' *International Joint Conference on Neural Networks,* Vol. 1, pp. 13–18, Seattle, WA.

* Ghosh, J., S. Chakravarthy, Y. Shin, and C. Chu, 1991. ''Adaptive kernel classifiers for short-duration oceanic signals.'' *IEEE Conference on Neural Networks for Ocean Engineering,* pp. 41–48. Washington, DC.

Gibson, G.J., and C.F.N. Cowan, 1990. ''On the decision regions of multilayer perceptrons.'' *Proceedings of the IEEE* **78,** 1590–1599.

Gidas, B., 1985. ''Global optimization via the Langevin equation. *Proceedings of the 24th Conference on Decision and Control,* pp. 774–778, Ft. Lauderdale, FL.

Giles, C.L., D. Chen, C.B. Miller, H.H. Chen, G.Z. Sun, and Y.C. Lee, 1991. ''Second-order recurrent neural networks for grammatical inference.'' *International Joint Conference on Neural Networks,* Vol. 2, pp. 273–281, Seattle, WA.

* Girosi, F., and T. Poggio, 1989. ''Representative properties of networks: Kolmogorov's theorem is irrelevant.'' *Neural Computation* **1,** 465–469.

Girosi, F., and T. Poggio, 1990. ''Networks and the best approximation property.'' *Biological Cybernetics* **63,** 169–176.

Glauber, R.J., 1963. ''Time-dependent statistics of the Ising model.'' *Journal of Mathematical Physics* **4,** 294–307.

* Gluck, M.A., and D.E. Rumelhart, eds., 1990. *Neuroscience and Connectionist Theory.* Hillsdale, NJ: Erlbaum.

Goggin, S.D.D., K.M. Johnson, and K. Gustafson, 1989. ''Primary and recency effects due to momentum in back-propagation learning,'' OCS Technical Report 89-25. University of Colorado, Boulder.

Golden, R.M., 1986. ''The 'Brain-State-in-a-Box' neural model is a gradient descent algorithm.'' *Journal of Mathematical Psychology* **30,** 73–80.

Goles, E., 1986. ''Antisymmetrical neural networks.'' *Discrete Applied Mathematics.* **13,** 97–100.

Goles, E., and S. Martinez, 1990. *Neural and Automata Networks.* Dordrecht, The Netherlands: Kluwer.

Golomb, B.A., D.T. Lawrence, and T.J. Sejnowski, 1991. ''Sexnet: A neural network identifies sex from human faces.'' In *Advances in Neural Information Processing Systems 3* (R.P. Lippmann, J.E. Moody, and D.S. Touretzky, eds.), pp. 572–577. San Mateo, CA: Morgan Kaufmann.

Golomb, S.W., ed., 1964. *Digital Communications with Space Applications.* Englewood Cliffs, NJ: Prentice-Hall.

Golub, G.H., and C.F. Van Loan, 1989. *Matrix Computations,* 2nd ed., Baltimore, MD: Johns Hopkins University Press.

Goodman, R.M., C.M. Higgins, J.W. Miller, and P. Smyth, 1992. ''Rule-based neural networks for classification and probability estimation.'' *Neural Computation* **4,** 781–804.

Gori, M., and A. Tesi, 1992. ''On the problem of local minima in backpropagation.'' *IEEE Transactions on Pattern Analysis and Machine Intelligence* **14,** 76–86.

Gorin, A., 1992. ''Network structure, generalization and adaptive language acquisition.'' In *Proceedings of the Seventh Yale Workshop on Adaptive and Learning Systems,* pp. 155–160. Yale University, New Haven, CT.

* Gorman, R.P., 1991. ''Neural networks and the classification of complex sonar signals.'' *IEEE Conference on Neural Networks for Ocean Engineering,* pp. 283–290. Washington, DC.

* Grabec, I., 1991. ''Modeling of chaos by a self-organizing neural network.'' In *Artificial Neural Networks* (T. Kohonen, K. Mäkisara, O. Simula, and J. Kangas, eds.), Vol. 1, pp. 151–156. Amsterdam: North-Holland.

Granger, R., J. Whitson, J. Larson, and G. Lynch, 1994. ''Non-Hebbian properties of LTP enable high-capacity encoding of temporal sequences.'' *Proceedings of the National Academy of Sciences of the U.S.A.,* to appear.

* Graubard, S.R., ed., 1988. *The Artificial Intelligence Debate: False Starts, Real Foundations.* Cambridge, MA: MIT Press.

Gray, R.M., 1984. "Vector quantization." *IEEE ASSP Magazine* **1,** 4–29.

* Gray, R.M., 1988. *Probability, Random Processes, and Ergodic Properties.* New York: Springer-Verlag.

Gray, R.M., 1990. *Entropy and Information Theory.* New York: Springer-Verlag.

Gray, R.M., and L.D. Davisson, 1986. *Random Processes: A Mathematical Approach for Engineers.* Englewood Cliffs, NJ: Prentice-Hall.

Greenberg, H.J., 1988. "Equilibria of the brain-state-in-a-box (BSB) neural model." *Neural Networks* **1,** 323–324.

Grenander, U., 1983. *Tutorial in Pattern Theory.* Providence, RI: Brown University.

Grossberg, S., 1967. "Nonlinear difference—differential equations in prediction and learning theory." *Proceedings of the National Academy of Sciences of the U.S.A.* **58,** 1329–1334.

Grossberg, S., 1968. "A prediction theory for some nonlinear functional-difference equations." *Journal of Mathematical Analysis and Applications* **21,** 643–694.

Grossberg, S., 1969a. "A prediction theory for some nonlinear functional-difference equations." *Journal of Mathematial Analysis and Applications* **22,** 490–522.

Grossberg, S., 1969b. "On learning and energy-entropy dependence in recurrent and nonrecurrent signed networks." *Journal of Statistical Physics* **1,** 319–350.

Grossberg, S., 1972. "Neural expectation: Cerebellar and retinal analogs of cells fired by learnable or unlearned pattern classes." *Kybernetik* **10,** 49–57.

Grossberg, S., 1976a. "Adaptive pattern classification and universal recording: I. Parallel development and coding of neural detectors." *Biological Cybernetics* **23,** 121–134.

Grossberg, S., 1976b. "Adaptive pattern classification and universal recording: II. Feedback, expectation, olfaction, illusions." *Biological Cybernetics* **23,** 187–202.

Grossberg, S., 1977. "Pattern formation by the global limits of a nonlinear competitive interaction in n dimensions." *Journal of Mathematical Biology* **4,** 237–256.

Grossberg, S., 1978a. "Decision, patterns, and oscillations in the dynamics of competitive systems with application to Volterra–Lotka systems." *Journal of Theoretical Biology* **73,** pp. 101–130.

Grossberg, S., 1978b. "Competition, decision, and consensus." *Journal of Mathematical Analysis and Applications* **66,** 470–493.

* Grossberg, S., 1980. "How does a brain build a cognitive code?" *Psychological Review* **87,** 1–51.

Grossberg, S., 1982. *Studies of Mind and Brain.* Boston, MA: Reidel.

Grossberg, S., 1988a. "Competitive learning: From interactive activation to adaptive resonance." In *Neural Networks and Natural Intelligence* (S. Grossberg, ed.), pp. 213–250. Cambridge, MA: MIT Press.

Grossberg, S., ed., 1988b. *Neural Networks and Natural Intelligence.* Cambridge, MA: MIT Press.

Grossberg, S., 1988c. "Nonlinear neural networks: Principles, mechanisms, and architectures." *Neural Networks* **1,** 17–61.

Grossberg, S., 1990. "Content-addressable memory storage by neural networks: A general model and global Liapunov method." In *Computational Neuroscience* (E.L. Schwartz, ed.), pp. 56–65. Cambridge, MA: MIT Press.

Guckenheimer, J., and P. Holmes, 1983. *Nonlinear Oscillations, Dynamical Systems, and Bifurcations of Vector Fields.* New York: Springer-Verlag.

Guyon, I., 1990. *Neural Networks and Applications,* Computer Physics Reports. Amsterdam: Elsevier.

Guyon, I., 1991. ''Applications of neural networks to character recognition.'' *International Journal of Pattern Recognition and Artificial Intelligence* **5,** 353–382.

* Guyon, I., P. Albrecht, Y. LeCun, J. Denker, and W. Hubbard, 1991. ''Design of a neural network character recognizer for a touch terminal.'' *Pattern Recognition* **24,** 105–119.

Guyon, I., V. Vapnik, B. Boser, L. Bottou, and S.A. Solla, 1992. ''Structural risk minimization for character recognition.'' In *Advances in Neural Information Processing Systems 4* (J.E. Moody, S.J. Hanson, and R.P. Lippmann, eds.), pp. 471–479. San Mateo, CA: Morgan Kaufmann.

Hagiwara, M., 1992. ''Theoretical derivation of a momentum term in back-propagation.'' *International Joint Conference on Neural Networks,* Vol. 1, pp. 682–686, Baltimore, MD.

* Hajek, B., 1985. ''A tutorial survey of theory and applications of simulated annealing.'' *Proceedings of the 24th Conference on Decision and Control,* pp. 755–760, Ft. Lauderdale, FL.

Hamilton, A., A.F. Murray, D.J. Baxter, S. Churcher, H.M. Reekie, and L. Tarassenko, 1992. ''Integrated pulse stream neural networks: Results, issues, and pointers.'' *IEEE Transactions on Neural Networks* **3,** 385–393.

Hammerstrom, D., 1990. ''A VLSI architecture for high-performance, low-cost, or–chip learning.'' *International Joint Conference on Neural Networks,* Vol. 2, pp. 537–544, San Diego, CA.

Hammerstrom, D., 1992. ''Electronic neural network implementation,'' Tutorial No. 5. *International Joint Conference on Neural Networks,* Baltimore, MD.

Hammerstrom, D., 1993a. ''Neural networks at work.'' *IEEE Spectrum,* **30,** 26–32.

Hammerstrom, D., 1993b. ''Working with neural networks.'' *IEEE Spectrum* **30,** 46–53.

Hammerstrom, D., and S. Rahfuss, 1992. ''Neurocomputing hardware: Present and future.'' *Swedish National Conference on Connectionism,* September 9 and 10, Skövade, Sweden.

Hampshire, J.B., II, and B. Pearlmutter, 1990. ''Equivalence proofs for multi-layer perceptron classifiers and the Bayesian discriminant function.'' In *Proceedings of the 1990 Connectionist Models Summer School* (D.S. Touretzky, J.L. Elman, T.J. Sejnowski, and G.E. Hinton, eds.), pp. 159–172. San Mateo, CA: Morgan Kaufmann.

Hampson, S.E., 1990. *Connectionistic Problem Solving: Computational Aspects of Biological Learning.* Berlin: Birkhäuser.

* Hancock, P.J.B., R.J. Baddeley, and L.S. Smith, 1992. ''The principal components of natural images.'' *Network* **3,** 61–70.

Hanson, L.K., and P. Solamon, 1990. ''Neural network ensembles.'' *IEEE Transactions on Pattern Analysis and Machine Intelligence* **PAMI-12,** 993–1002.

Harel, D., 1987. *Algorithmics: The Spirit of Computing.* Reading, MA: Addison-Wesley.

Harrison, R., S. Marshall, and R. Kennedy, 1991. ''The early diagnosis of heart attacks: A neurocomputational approach.'' *International Joint Conference on Neural Networks,* Vol. 1, pp. 1–5, Seattle, WA.

Hartman, E., 1991. ''A high storage capacity neural network content-addressable memory.'' *Network* **2,** 315–334.

Hassibi, B., D.G. Stork, and G.J. Wolff, 1993. ''Optimal brain surgeon and general network pruning.'' *IEEE International Conference on Neural Networks,* Vol. 1, pp. 293–299, San Francisco, CA.

Haussler, D., 1988. ''Quantifying inductive bias: AI learning algorithms and Valiant's learning framework.'' *Artificial Intelligence* **36,** 177–221.

* Haussler, D., M. Kearns, M. Opper, and R. Schapire, 1992. ''Estimating average-case learning curves using Bayesian, statistical physics, and VC dimension methods.'' In *Advances in Neural Information Processing Systems 4* (J.E. Moody, S.J. Hanson, and R.P. Lippmann, eds.), pp. 855–862. San Mateo, CA: Morgan Kaufmann.

* Hawkins, R.D., and G.H. Bower, eds., 1989. *Computational Models of Learning in Simple Neural Systems.* San Diego, CA: Academic Press.

Haykin, S., 1983. *Communication Systems,* 2nd ed. New York: Wiley.

Haykin, S., 1991. *Adaptive Filter Theory,* 2nd ed. Englewood Cliffs, NJ: Prentice-Hall.

Haykin, S., 1992. ''Blind equalization formulated as a self-organized learning process,'' *Proceedings of the Twenty-Sixth Asilomar Conference on Signals, Systems, and Computers,* pp. 346–350, Pacific Grove, CA.

Haykin, S., and T.K. Bhattacharya, 1992. ''Adaptive radar detection using supervised learning networks.'' *Computational Neuroscience Symposium,* pp. 35–51, Indiana University–Purdue University at Indianapolis.

Haykin, S., and C. Deng, 1991. ''Classification of radar clutter using neural networks.'' *IEEE Transactions on Neural Networks* **2,** 589–600.

Haykin, S., and H. Leung, 1992. ''Model reconstruction of chaotic dynamics: First preliminary radar results.'' *IEEE International Conference on Acoustics, Speech, and Signal Processing,* Vol. 4, pp. 125–128, San Francisco, CA.

Haykin, S., and L. Li, 1993a. ''16 kb/s adaptive differential pulse code modulation of speech.'' In *Applications of Neural Networks to Telecommunications* (J. Alspector, R. Goodman, and T.X. Brown, eds.), pp. 132–137, Hillsdale, NJ: Lawrence Erlbaum.

Haykin, S., and L. Li, 1993b. ''Real-time nonlinear adaptive prediction of nonstationary signals.'' CRL Report No. 276, Communications Research Laboratory, McMaster University, Hamilton, Ontario.

Haykin, S., W. Stehwien, P. Weber, C. Deng, and R. Mann, 1991. ''Classification of radar clutter in air traffic control environment.'' *Proceedings of the IEEE* **79,** 741–772.

He, X., and A. Lapedes, 1991. ''Nonlinear modeling and prediction by successive approximation using radial basis functions,'' Technical Report LA-UR-91-1375. Los Alamos National Laboratory, Los Alamos, NM.

Hebb, D.O., 1949. *The Organization of Behavior: A Neuropsychological Theory.* New York: Wiley.

Hecht-Nielsen, R., 1987. ''Kolmogorov's mapping neural network existence theorem.'' *1st IEEE International Conference on Neural Networks,* Vol. 3, pp. 11–14, San Diego, CA.

Hecht-Nielsen, R., 1990. *Neurocomputing.* Reading, MA: Addison-Wesley.

Hertz, J., A. Krogh, and R.G. Palmer, 1991. *Introduction to the Theory of Neural Computation,* Reading, MA: Addison-Wesley.

Herz, A., B. Sulzer, R. Kühn, and J.L. van Hemme, 1988. ''The Hebb rule: Storing static and dynamic objects in an associative neural network.'' *Electrophysics Letters* **7,** 663–669.

Herz, A., B. Sulzer, R. Kühn, and J.L. van Hemme, 1989. ''Hebbian learning reconsidered: Representation of static and dynamic objects in associative neural nets.'' *Biological Cybernetics* **60,** 457–467.

* Heskes, T., and B. Kappen, 1991. ''Neural networks learning in a changing environ-

ment.'' *International Joint Conference on Neural Networks,* Vol. 1, pp. 823–828, Seattle, WA.

Hetherington, P.A., and M.L. Shapiro, 1993. ''Simulating Hebb cell assemblies: The necessity for partitioned dendritic trees and a post-not-pre LTD rule.'' *Network* **4,** 135–153.

Hillis, W.D., 1985. *The Connection Machine.* Cambridge, MA: MIT Press.

Hinton, G.E., 1981. ''Shape representation in parallel systems.'' *Proceedings of the 7th International Joint Conference on Artificial Intelligence,* Vancouver, British Columbia.

Hinton, G.E., 1987. ''Connectionist learning procedures,'' *Technical Report CMU-CS-87-115,* Carnegie-Mellon University, Pittsburgh, PA. This report is reproduced in J. Carbonell, ed., 1990, ''*Machine Learning: Paradigms and Methods.*'' pp. 185–234. Cambridge, MA: MIT Press; and 1989, *Artificial Intelligence* **40,** 185–234.

Hinton, G.E., 1989. ''Deterministic Boltzmann machine learning performs steepest descent in weight-space.'' *Neural Computation* **1,** 143–150.

* Hinton, G.E., ed., 1990a. *Connectionist Symbol Processing.* Cambridge, MA: MIT Press.

Hinton, G.E., 1990b. ''Using cross-validation to avoid overfitting.'' *Lecture presented at Workshop on Neural Networks,* Niagara-on-the-Lake, Ontario.

* Hinton, G.E., and J.A. Anderson, eds., 1989. *Parallel Models of Associative Memory,* Updated Edition. Hillsdale, NJ: Erlbaum.

Hinton, G.E., and S.J. Nowlan, 1987. ''How learning can guide evolution.'' *Complex Systems* **1,** 495–502.

Hinton, G.E., and S.J. Nowlan, 1990. ''The bootstrap Widrow-Hoff rule as a cluster-formation algorithm.'' *Neural Computation* **2,** 355–362.

Hinton, G.E., and T.J. Sejnowski, 1983. ''Optimal perceptual inference.'' *Proceedings of the IEEE Computer Society Conference on Computer Vision and Pattern Recognition,* pp. 448–453, Washington, DC.

Hinton, G.E., and T.J. Sejnowski, 1986. ''Learning and relearning in Boltzmann machines.'' In *Parallel Distributed Processing: Explorations in Microstructure of Cognition* (D.E. Rumelhart and J.L. McClelland, eds.), Cambridge, MA: MIT Press.

* Hirayama, M., E. Vatikiotis-Bateson, K. Honda, Y. Koike, and M. Kawato, 1993. ''Physiologically based speech synthesis.'' In *Advances in Neural Information Processing Systems* (S.J. Hanson, J.D. Cowan, and C.L. Giles, eds.), pp. 658–665. San Mateo, CA: Morgan Kaufmann.

* Hirsch, M.W., 1987. ''Convergence in neural nets.'' *1st IEEE International Conference on Neural Networks,* Vol. 2, pp. 115–125, San Diego, CA.

Hirsch, M.W., 1989. ''Convergent activation dynamics in continuous time networks.'' *Neural Networks* **2,** 331–349

Hirsch, M.W., and S. Smale, 1974. *Differential Equations, Dynamical Systems, and Linear Algebra.* New York: Academic Press.

* Hodgkin, A.L., and A.F. Huxley, 1952. ''A quantitative description of membrane current and its application to conduction and excitation in nerve.'' *Journal of Physiology* (*London*) **117,** 500–544.

Hoeneisen, B., and C.A. Mead, 1972. ''Fundamental limitations in microelectronics. I. MOS technology.'' *Solid-State Electronics* **15,** 819–829.

* Holden, S.B., and P.J.W. Rayner, 1992. ''Generalization and learning in Volterra and radial basis function networks: A theoretical analysis.'' *IEEE International Conference on Acoustics, Speech, and Signal Processing,* Vol. 2, pp. 273–276, San Fransico, CA.

Holland, J.H., 1975. *Adaptation in Natural and Artificial Systems.* Ann Arbor: University of Michigan Press.

Holland, J.H., 1992. *Adaptation in Natural and Artificial Systems.* Cambridge, MA: MIT Press.

* Holler, M.A., 1991. ''VLSI implementations of learning and memory systems: A review. In *Advances in Neural Information Processing Systems 3* (R.P. Lippmann, J.E. Moody, and D.S. Touretzky, eds.), pp. 993–1000. San Mateo, CA: Morgan Kaufmann.

Holler, M.A., S. Tam, H. Castro, and R. Benson, 1989. ''An electrically trainable artificial neural network (ETANN) with 10240 'floating gates' synapses.'' *International Joint Conference on Neural Networks,* Vol. 2, pp. 191–196, San Diego, CA.

Hopcroft, J., and J. Ullman, 1979. *Introduction to Automata Theory, Languages and Computation.* Reading, MA: Addison-Wesley.

Hopfield, J.J., 1982. ''Neural networks and physical systems with emergent collective computational abilities.'' *Proceedings of the National Academy of Sciences of the U.S.A.* **79,** 2554–2558.

Hopfield, J.J., 1984a. ''Neurons with graded response have collective computational properties like those of two-state neurons.'' *Proceedings of the National Academy of Sciences of the U.S.A.* **81,** 3088–3092.

Hopfield, J.J., 1984b. ''Collective processing and neural states.'' In *Modeling and Analysis in Biomedicine* (C. Nicollini, ed.), pp. 370–389. Singapore: World Scientific.

Hopfield, J.J., 1987a. ''Networks, computations, logic, and noise'' *1st IEEE International Conference on Neural Networks.* Vol. 1, pp. 107–141, San Diego, CA.

Hopfield, J.J., 1987b. ''Learning algorithms and probability distributions in feed-forward and feed-back networks.'' *Proceedings of the National Academy of Sciences of the U.S.A.* **84,** 8429–8433.

* Hopfield, J.J., 1990. ''The effectiveness of analogue 'neural network' hardware.'' *Network* **1,** 27–40.

Hopfield, J.J., and T.W. Tank, 1985. '' 'Neural' computation of decisions in optimization problems.'' *Biological Cybernetics* **52,** 141–152.

Hopfield, J.J., and D.W. Tank, 1986. ''Computing with neural circuits: A model.'' *Science* **233,** 625–633.

* Hopfield, J.J., D.I. Feinstein, and R.G. Palmer, 1983. '' 'Unlearning' has a stabilizing effect in collective memories.'' *Nature* (*London*) **304,** 158–159.

Hornik, K., M. Stinchcombe, and H. White, 1989. ''Multilayer feedforward network are universal approximators.'' *Neural Networks* **2,** 359–366.

Hornik, K., M. Stinchcombe, and H. White, 1990. ''Universal approximation of an unknown mapping and its derivatives using multilayer feedforward networks.'' *Neural Networks* **3,** 551–560.

Hotelling, H., 1933. ''Analysis of a complex of statistical variables into principal components.'' *Journal of Educational Psychology* **24,** 417–441, 498–520.

Houk, J.C., 1992. ''Learning in modular networks.'' In *Proceedings of the Seventh Yale Workshop on Adaptive and Learning Systems,* pp. 80–84. New Haven, CT: Yale University.

Houk, J.C., and A.G. Barto, 1992. ''Distributed sensorimotor learning.'' In *Tutorials in Motor Behavior II* (G.E. Stelmach and J. Requin, eds.), pp. 71–100. Amsterdam: Elsevier.

* Hrycej, T., 1990. ''A modular architecture for efficient learning.'' *International Joint Conference on Neural Networks,* Vol. 1, pp. 557–562, San Diego, CA.

* Hrycej, T., 1991. ''Back to single-layer learning principles.'' *International Joint Conference on Neural Networks,* Vol. 2, p. A-945, Seattle, WA.

* Hubel, D.H., 1988. *Eye, Brain, and Vision.* New York: Scientific American Library.

Hubel, D.H., and T.N. Wiesel, 1962. ''Reeceptive fields, binocular interaction and functional architecture in the cat's visual cortex.'' *Journal of Physiology (London)* **160,** 106–154.

Hubel, D.H., and T.N. Wiesel, 1977. ''Functional architecture of macaque visual cortex.'' *Proceedings of the Royal Society of London, Series B* **198,** 1–59.

Huber, P.J., 1985. ''Projection pursuit.'' *Annals of Statistics* **13,** 435–475.

Hush, D.R., and B.G. Horne, 1993. ''Progress in supervised neural networks: What's new since Lippmann?'' *IEEE Signal Processing Magazine* **10,** 8–39.

Hush, D.R., and J.M. Salas, 1988. ''Improving the learning rate of back-propagation with the gradient reuse algorithm.'' *IEEE International Conference on Neural Networks,* Vol. 1, pp. 441–447, San Diego, CA.

Illingsworth, V., E.L. Glaser, and I.C. Pyle, 1989. *Dictionary of Computing.* New York: Oxford University Press.

* Iltis, R., and P. Ting, 1991. ''Data association is multi-target tracking: A solution using a layered Boltzmann machine.'' *International Joint Conference on Neural Networks,* Vol. 1, pp. 31–36, Seattle, WA.

* Intrator, N., 1992. ''Feature extraction using an unsupervised neural network.'' *Neural Computation* **4,** 98–107.

* Jackel, L.D., B. Boser, J.S. Denker, H.P. Graf, Y. LeCun, I. Guyon, D. Henderson, R.E. Howard, W. Hubbard, and S.A. Solla, 1990. ''Hardware requirements for neural-net optical character recognition.'' *International Joint Conference on Neural Networks,* Vol. 2, pp. 855–861, San Diego, CA.

Jackson, E.A., 1989. *Perspectives of Nonlinear Dynamics,* Vol. 1. Cambridge, UK: Cambridge University Press.

Jackson, E.A., 1990. *Perspectives of Nonlinear Dynamics,* Vol. 2. Cambridge, UK: Cambridge University Press.

Jackson, I.R.H., 1989. ''An order of convergence for some radial basis functions.'' *IMA Journal of Numerical Analysis* **9,** 567–587.

Jackson, J.D., 1975. *Classical Electrodynamics,* 2nd ed. New York: Wiley.

Jacobs, R.A., 1988. ''Increased rates of convergence through learning rate adaptation. *Neural Networks* **1,** 295–307.

Jacobs, R.A., and M.I. Jordan, 1991. ''A competitive modular connectionist architecture.'' In *Advances in Neural Information Processing Systems 3* (R.P. Lippmann, J.E. Moody, and D.J. Touretzky, eds.), pp. 767–773. San Mateo, CA: Morgan Kaufmann.

Jacobs, R.A., and M.I. Jordan, 1993. ''Learning piecewise control strategies in a modular neural network architecture.'' *IEEE Trans. Systems, Man, and Cybernetics* **23,** 337–345.

Jacobs, R.A., M.I. Jordan, S.J. Nowlan, and G.E. Hinton, 1991a. ''Adaptive mixtures of local experts.'' *Neural Computation* **3,** 79–87.

Jacobs, R.A., M.I. Jordan, and A.G. Barto, 1991b. ''Task decomposition through competition in a modular connectionist architecture: The what and where vision tasks.'' *Cognitive Science* **15,** 219–250.

Janssen, P., P. Stoica, T. Söderström, and P. Eykhoff, 1988. ''Model structure selection for multivariable systems by cross-validation.'' *International Journal of Control* **47,** 1737–1758.

Jayant, N.S., and P. Noll, 1984. *Digital Coding of Waveforms.* Englewood Cliffs, NJ: Prentice-Hall.

Jelinek, F., 1976. ''Continuous speech recognition by statistical methods. *Proceedings of the IEEE* **64,** 532–536.

Jelonek, T.M., and J.P. Reilly, 1990. ''Maximum likelihood estimation for direction of arrival using a nonlinear optimizing neural network.'' *International Joint Conference on Neural Networks,* Vol. 1, pp. 253–258, San Diego, CA.

Johansson, E.M., F.U. Dowla, and D.M. Goodman, 1990. ''Back-propagation learning for multi-layer feed-foward neural networks using the conjugate gradient method,'' Report UCRL-JC-104850. Lawrence Livermore National Laboratory, Livermore, CA.

Jolliffe, I.T., 1986. *Principal Component Analysis.* New York: Springer-Verlag.

* Jones, J.P., and L.A. Palmer, 1987a. ''The two-dimensional spatial structure of simple receptive fields in cat striate cortex.'' *Journal of Neurophysiology* **58,** 1187–1211.

* Jones, J.P., and L.A. Palmer, 1987b. ''An evaluation of two-dimensional Gabor filter model of simple receptive fields in cat striate cortex.'' *Journal of Neurophysiology* **58,** 1233–1258.

* Jones, J.P., A. Steponski, and L.A. Palmer, 1987. ''The two-dimensional spectral structure of simple receptive fields in cat striate cortex.'' *Journal of Neurophysiology* **58,** 1212–1232.

Jordan, M.I., 1986. ''Attractor dynamics and parallelism in a connectionist sequential machuine.'' *8th Annual Conference of the Cognitive Science Society,* pp. 531–546. Amherst, MA.

* Jordan, M.I., 1988. ''Supervised learning and systems with excess degrees of freedom.'' In *Proceedings of the 1988 Connectionist Models Summer School* (D. Touretzky, G. Hinton, and T. Sejnowski, eds.), pp. 62–75. San Mateo, CA: Morgan Kaufmann.

Jordan, M.I., 1992. ''Recent developments in supervised learning,'' Tutorial Notes. *International Joint Conference on Neural Networks,* Baltimore, MD.

* Jordan, M.I., and R.A. Jacobs, 1990. ''Learning to control an unstable system with forward modeling.'' In *Advances in Neural Information Processing Systems 2* (D.S. Touretzky, ed.), pp. 324–331. San Mateo, CA: Morgan Kaufmann.

Jordan, M.I., and R.A. Jacobs, 1992. ''Hierarchies of adaptive experts.'' In *Advances in Neural Information Processing Systems 4* (J.E. Moody, S.J. Hanson, and R.P. Lippmann, eds.), pp. 985–992. San Mateo, CA: Morgan Kaufmann.

Jordan, M.I., and R.A. Jacobs, 1993. ''Hierarchical mixtures of experts and the EM algorithm.'' Technical Report 9203. MIT Computational Cognitive Science, MIT, Cambridge, MA.

Kaas, J.H., M.M. Merzenich, and H.P. Killackey, 1983. ''The reorganization of somatosensory cortex following peripheral nerve damage in adult and developing mammals.'' *Annual Review of Neurosciences* **6,** 325–356.

Kadirkamanathan, V., M. Niranjan, and F. Fallside, 1991. ''Sequential adaptation of radial basis function neural networks.'' In *Advances in Neural Information Processing Systems 3* (R.P. Lippmann, J.E. Moody, and D.S. Touretzky, eds.), pp. 721–727. San Mateo, CA: Morgan Kaufmann.

Kailath, T., 1968. ''An innovations approach to least-squares estimation: Part 1. Linear filtering in additive white noise.'' *IEEE Transactions of Automatic Control* **AC-13,** 646–655.

Kailath, T., 1971. ''RKHS approach to detection and estimation problems. Part I. Deterministic signals in Gaussian noise.'' *IEEE Tranactions on Information Theory* **IT-17,** 530–549.

Kailath, T., 1974. ''A view of three decades of linear filtering theory.'' *IEEE Transactions on Information Theory* **IT-20,** 146–181.

Kalman, R.E., 1960. ''A new approach to linear filtering and prediction problems.'' *Journal of Basic Engineering* **82,** 35–45.

* Kamgar-Parsi, B., and J.A. Gualtiri, 1990. ''Solving inversion problems with neural networks.'' *International Joint Conference on Neural Networks,* Vol. 3, pp. 955–960, San Diego, CA.

Kandel, E.R., and J.H. Schwartz, 1991. *Principles of Neural Science,* 3rd ed. New York: Elsevier.

Kangas, J., T. Kohonen, and J. Laaksonen, 1990. ''Variants of self-organizing maps,'' *IEEE Transactions on Neural Networks* **1,** 93–99.

Kanter, I., and H. Sompolinsky, 1987. ''Associative recall of memory without errors.'' *Physical Review A* **35,** 380–392.

Karhunen, K., 1947. ''Uber lineare methoden in der Wahrscheinlichkeitsrechnung.'' *Annales Academiae Scientiarum Fennicae, Series A1: Mathematica-Physica* **37,** 3–79 (Transl.: RAND Corp., Santa Monica, CA, Rep. T-131, 1960).

Kassam, S.A., and I. Cha, 1993. ''Radial basis function networks in nonlinear signal processing applications,'' *27th Annual Asilomar Conference on Signals, Systems, and Computers,* Pacific Grove, CA.

Katz, B., 1966. *Nerve, Muscle and Synapse.* New York: McGraw-Hill.

Kawamoto, A.H., and J.A. Anderson, 1985. ''A neural network model of multistable perception.'' *Acta Psychologica* **59,** 35–65.

* Kawato, M., 1990. ''Feedback-error learning neural network for supervised motor learning.'' In *Advanced Neural Computers* (R. Eckmiller, ed.), pp. 365–372. Amsterdam: North-Holland.

Kay, J., 1992. ''Feature discovery under contextual supervision using mutual information.'' *International Joint Conference on Neural Networks,* Vol. 4, pp. 79–84, Baltimore, MD.

Keeler, J.D., 1986. ''Basins of attraction of neural network models.'' In *Neural Networks for Computing* (J.S. Denker, ed.), pp. 259–264. New York: American Institute of Physics.

*Keesing, R., and D.G. Stork, 1991. ''Evolution and learning in neural networks: The number and distribution of learning trials affect the rate of evolution.'' In *Advances in Neural Information Processing Systems 3* (R.P. Lippmann, J.E. Moody, and D.S. Touretzky, eds.), pp. 804–810. San Mateo, CA: Morgan Kaufmann.

Kelso, S.R., A.H. Ganong, and T.H. Brown, 1986. ''Hebbian synapses in hippocampus.'' *Proceedings of the National Academy of Sciences of the U.S.A.* **83,** 5326–5330.

Keyes, R.W., 1987. *The Physics of VLSI Systems.* Reading, MA: Addison-Wesley.

Kirkpatrick, S., 1984. ''Optimization by simulated annealing: Quantitative studies.'' *Journal of Statistical Physics* **34,** 975–986.

Kirkpatrick, S., and D. Sherrington, 1978. ''Infinite-ranged models of spin-glasses.'' *Physical Review, Series B* **17,** 4384–4403.

Kirkpatrick, S., C.D. Gelatt, Jr., and M.P. Vecchi, 1983. ''Optimization by simulated annealing.'' *Science* **220,** 671–680.

* Kirschenbaum, S.S., and D.C. Regan, 1990. ''Facets of adaptability.'' *IEEE International Conference on Systems, Man, and Cybernetics,* pp. 800–801, Los Angeles, CA.

* Kleinfeld, D., 1986. ''Sequential state generation by model neural networks.'' *Proceedings of the National Academy of Sciences of the U.S.A.* **83,** 9469–9473.

* Klimasauskas, C.C., 1989. *The 1989 Neuro-Computing Bibliography.* Cambridge, MA: MIT Press.

Klopf, A.H., 1982. ''The Hedonistic Neuron: A Theory of Memory, Learning, and Intelligence.'' Washington, DC: Hemisphere.

* Klopf, A.H., and J.S. Morgan, 1990. ''The role of time in natural intelligence: Implications for neural network and artificial intelligence research.'' In *Advanced Neural Computers* (R. Eckmiller, ed.), pp. 201–207. Amsterdam: North-Holland.

Knudsen, E.I., S. duLac, and S.D. Esterly, 1987. ''Computational maps in the brain.'' *Annual Review of Neuroscience* **10,** 41–65.

Koch, C., and I. Segev, eds., 1989. *Methods in Neuronal Modeling: From Synapses to Networks.* Cambridge, MA: MIT Press.

Koch, C., T. Poggio, and V. Torre, 1983. ''Nonlinear interactions in a dendritic tree: Localization, timing, and role in information processing.'' *Proceedings of the National Academy of Sciences of the U.S.A.* **80,** 2799–2802.

Kohonen, T., 1972. ''Correlation matrix memories.'' *IEEE Transactions on Computers* **C-21,** 353–359.

Kohonen, T., 1982a. ''Self-organized formation of topologically correct feature maps.'' *Biological Cybernetics* **43,** 59–69.

Kohonen, T., 1982b. ''Clustering, taxonomy, and topological maps of patterns.'' *Proceedings of the 6th International Conference on Pattern Recognition,* pp. 114–128, Munich, Germany.

Kohonen, T., 1986. ''Learning vector quantization for pattern recognition,'' *Technical Report TKK-F-A601.* Helsinki University of Technology, Finland.

* Kohonen, T., 1987. ''State of the art in neural computing.'' *IEEE International Conference on Neural Networks* **1,** 77–89.

Kohonen, T., 1988a. ''An introduction to neural computing'' *Neural Networks* **1,** 3–16.

Kohonen, T., 1988b. *Self-Organization and Associative Memory,* 3rd ed. New York: Springer-Verlag.

Kohonen, T., 1988c. ''The 'neural' phonetic typewriter.'' *Computer* **21,** 11–22.

Kohonen, T., 1990a. ''The self-organizing map.'' *Proceedings of the IEEE* **78,** 1464–1480.

Kohonen, T., 1990b. ''Improved versions of learning vector quantization.'' *International Joint Conference on Neural Networks,* Vol. 1, pp. 545–550, San Diego, CA.

Kohonen, T., 1993. ''Physiological interpretation of the self-organizing map algorithm.'' *Neural Networks* **6,** 895–905.

Kohonen, T., and E. Oja, 1976. ''Fast adaptive formation of orthogonalizing filters and associative memory in recurrent networks for neuron-like elements.'' *Biological Cybernetics* **21,** 85–95.

Kohonen, T., E. Reuhkala, K. Mäkisara, and L. Vainio, 1976. ''Associative recall of images.'' *Biological Cybernetics* **22,** 159–168.

Kohonen, T., G. Barna, and R. Chrisley, 1988. ''Statistical pattern recognition with neural networks: Benchmarking studies.'' *International Conference on Neural Networks,* Vol. 1, pp. 61–68, San Diego, CA.

Kohonen, T., J. Kangas, J. Laaksonen, and K. Torkkola, 1992. ''LVQ-PAK: The learning vector quantization Program Package.'' Helsinki University of Technology, Finland.

* Kolen, J.F., and J.B. Pollack, 1990. ''Backpropagation is sensitive to initial conditions.'' *Complex Systems* **4,** 269–280.

Kolmogorov, A.N., 1942. ''Interpolation and extrapolation of stationary random sequences.'' Translated by the Rand Corporation, Santa Monica, CA., April 1962.

Kosko, B., 1992. *Neural Networks and Fuzzy Systems.* Englewood Cliffs, N.J.: Prentice-Hall.

* Kosowsky, J.J., and A.L. Yuille, 1991. ''Solving the assignment problem with statistical physics.'' *International Joint Conference on Neural Networks,* Vol. 1, pp. 159–164, Seattle, WA.

* Kraaijveld, M.A., and R.P.W. Duin, 1991. ''Generalization capabilities of minimal kernel-based networks.'' *International Joint Conference on Neural Networks,* Vol. 1, pp. 843–848, Seattle, WA.

Kramer, A.H., and A. Sangiovanni-Vincentelli, 1989. ''Efficient parallel learning algorithms for neural networks.'' In *Advances in Neural Information Processing Systems 1* (D.S. Touretzky, ed.), pp. 40–48. San Mateo, CA: Morgan Kaufmann.

Kreyszig, E., 1988. *Advanced Engineering Mathematics,* 6th ed. New York: Wiley.

Krishnamurthy, A.K., S.C. Ahalt, D.E. Melton, and P. Chen, 1990. ''Neural networks for vector quantization of speech and images.'' *IEEE Journal of Selected Areas in Communications* **8,** 1449–1457.

Kuan, C.-M., and K. Hornik, 1991. ''Convergence of learning algorithms with constant learning rates.'' *IEEE Transactions on Neural Networks* **2,** 484–489.

Kuffler, S.W., J.G. Nicholls, and A.R. Martin, 1984. *From Neuron to Brain: A Cellular Approach to the Function of the Nervous System,* 2nd ed. Sunderland, MA: Sinauer Associates.

Kullback, S., 1968. *Information Theory and Statistics.* New York: Dover.

Kung, H.T., and C.E. Leiserson, 1978. ''Systolic arrays (for VLSI)'' In *SPARSE Matrix Proceedings* (I.S. Duff and G.W. Stewart, eds.) pp. 256–282. Philadelphia, PA: SIAM. This paper is reproduced as Section 8.3 in C.A. Mead and L. Conway: *Introduction to VLSI Systems,* pp. 271–292, Reading, MA: Addison-Wesley.

Kung, S.Y., and C.I. Diamantaras, 1990. ''A neural network learning algorithm for adaptive principal component extraction (APEX).'' *International Conference on Acoustics, Speech, and Signal Processing,* Vol. 2, pp 861–864. Albuquerque, NM.

Kung, S.Y., and K.I. Diamantaras, 1991. ''Neural networks for extracting unsymmetrical principal components.'' *First IEEE Workshop on Neural Networks for Signal Processing,* pp. 50–59, Princeton University, Princeton, NJ.

Kushner, H.J., and D.S. Clark, 1978. *Stochastic Approximation Methods for Constrained and Unconstrained Systems:* New York: Springer-Verlag.

Lane, S.H., M.G. Flax, D.A. Handelman, and J.J. Gelfand, 1991. ''Multi-layer perceptrons with B-spline receptive field functions. In *Advances in Neural Information Processing Systems 3* (R.P. Lippmann, J. Moody, and D.S. Touretzky, eds.), pp. 684–692. San Mateo, CA: Morgan Kaufmann.

Lang, K.J., and G.E. Hinton, 1988. ''The development of the time-delay neural network architecture for speech recognition,'' Technical Report CMU-CS-88-152. Carnegie-Mellon University, Pittsburgh, PA.

Lapedes, A., and R. Farber, 1986a. ''A self-optimizing, nonsymmetrical neural net for content addressable memory and pattern recognition.'' *Physica* **22D,** 247–259.

Lapedes, A., and R. Farber, 1986b. ''Programming a massively parallel, computation universal system: Static behavior.'' In *Neural Networks for Computing* (J.S. Denker, ed.), pp. 283-298. New York: American Institute of Physics.

* Lapedes, A., and R. Farber, 1987. ''Nonlinear signal processing using neural networks: Prediction and system modeling,'' *LA-VR-87-2662.* Los Alamos National Laboratory, Los Alamos, NM.

* Lapedes, A., and R. Farber, 1988. ''How neural nets work.'' In *Neural Information Processing Systems* (D.Z. Anderson, ed.), pp. 442–456. New York: American Institute of Physics.

Larson, J., and G. Lynch, 1989. ''Theta pattern stimulation and the induction of LTP: The sequence in which synapses are stimulated determines the degree to which they potentiate.'' *Brain Research* **489,** 49–58.

LaSalle, J.P., and S. Lefschetz, 1961. *Stability by Liapunov's Direct Method, with Applications.* New York: Academic Press.

* LaVigna, A., 1989. ''Nonparateric classification using learning vector quantization.'' Ph.D. thesis, University of Maryland, College Park.

LeCun, Y., 1985. ''Une procedure d'apprentissage pour reseau a seuil assymetrique.'' *Cognitiva* **85,** 599–604.

LeCun, Y., 1988. ''A theoretical framework for back-propagation.'' In *Proceedings of the 1988 Connectionist Models Summer School* (D. Touretzky, G. Hinton and T. Sejnowski, ed.) pp. 21–28. San Mateo, CA: Morgan Kaufmann.

* LeCun, Y., 1989. ''Generalization and network design strategies. In *Connectionism in Perspective* (R. Pfeifer, Z. Schreter, F. Fogelman-Soulié, and L. Steels, eds.), pp. 143–155. Amsterdam: North-Holland.

LeCun, Y., B. Boser, J.S. Denker, D. Henderson, R.E. Howard, W. Hubbard, and L.D. Jackel, 1990a. ''Handwritten digit recognition with a back-propagation network. In *Advances in Neural Information Processing Systems 2* (D.S. Touretsky, ed.), pp. 396–404. San Mateo, CA: Morgan Kaufmann.

LeCun, Y., J.S. Denker, and S.A. Solla, 1990b. ''Optimal brain damage.'' In *Advances in Neural Information Processing Systems 2* (D.S. Touretzky, ed.), pp. 598–605. San Mateo, CA: Morgan Kaufmann.

Lee, C.C., 1990. ''Fuzzy logic in control systems: Fuzzy logic controller—Part I and Part II.'' *IEEE Transactions on Systems, Man, and Cybernetics* **20,** 404–418, 419–435.

Lee, J.-C., B.J. Sheu, W.-C. Fang, and R. Chellappa, 1993. ''VLSI neuroprocessors for video motion detection.'' *IEEE Transactions on Neural Networks* **4,** 178–191.

Lee, T.-C., A.M. Peterson, and J.-C. Tsai, 1990. ''A multi-layer feed-forward neural network with dynamically adjustable structures.'' *IEEE International Conference on Systems, Man, and Cybernetics,* pp. 367–369, Los Angeles, CA.

Lee, Y., and R.P. Lippmann, 1990. ''Practical characteristics of neural networks and conventional pattern classifiers on artificial and speech problems.'' In *Advances in Neural Information Processing Systems 2* (D.S. Touretzky, ed.), pp. 168–177. San Mateo, CA: Morgan Kaufmann.

Lee, Y., S. Oh, and M. Kim, 1991. ''The effect of initial weights on premature saturation in back-propagation learning.'' *International Joint Conference on Neural Networks,* Vol. 1, pp. 765–770, Seattle, WA.

Lee, Y.C., G. Doolen, H.H. Chan, G.Z. Sen, T. Maxwell, H.Y. Lee, and C.L. Giles, 1986. ''Machine learning using a higher order correlation network.'' *Physica* **D22,** 276–289.

* Leen, T.K., 1991. ''Dynamics of linear feature-discovery networks.'' *Network* **2,** 85–105.

Leen, T.K., and G.B. Orr, 1992. ''Weight-space probability densities and convergence times for stochastic learning.'' *International Joint Conference on Neural Networks,* Vol. 4, pp. 158–164, Baltimore, MD.

Leen, T.K., M. Rudnick, and D. Hammerstrom, 1990. ''Hebbian feature discovery improves classifier efficiency.'' *International Joint Conference on Neural Networks,* Vol. 1, pp. 51–56, San Diego, CA.

Leerink, L.R., and M.A. Jabri, 1993. ''Temporal difference learning applied to continuous speech recognition.'' In *Applications of Neural Networks to Telecommunications* (J. Alspector, R. Goodman, and T.X. Brown, eds.), pp. 252–258. Hillsdale, NJ: Lawrence Erlbaum.

Lefebvre, W.C., and J.C. Principe, 1993. ''Object oriented artificial neural network implementations.'' *World Congress on Neural Networks,* Vol. 4, pp. 436–439, Portland, OR.

Leung, H., and S. Haykin, 1990. ''Is there a radar clutter attractor.'' *Applied Physics Letters* **56,** 592–595.

Levi, I., 1983. *The Enterprise of Knowledge: An Essay on Knowledge, Credal Probability, and Chance.* Cambridge, MA: MIT Press.

Levin, E., N. Tishby, and S.A. Solla, 1990. ''A statistical approach to learning and generalization in layered neural networks.'' *Proceedings of the IEEE* **78,** 1568–1574.

* Levin, S.A., ed., 1978. *Studies in Mathematical Biology,* Parts 1 and 2. Washington, DC: The Mathematical Association of America.

* Levine, D.S., 1991. *Introduction to Neural and Cognitive Modeling.* Hillsdale, NJ: Lawrence Erlbaum.

Levine, M., 1985. *Man and Machine Vision.* New York: McGraw-Hill.

* Levy, W.B., and N.I. Desmond, 1985. ''The roles of elemental synaptic plasticity.'' In *Synaptic Modification, Neuron Selectivity, and Nervous System Organization* (W.B. Levy, J.A. Anderson, and S. Lehmkuhle, eds.), pp. 105–121. Hillsdale, NJ: Erlbaum.

Li, B.X., and S. Haykin, 1993.'' Chaotic detection of small target in sea clutter.'' *International Conference in Acoustics, Speech, and Signal Processing,* Vol. 1, pp. 237–240, Minneapolis, MN.

Li, L.K., 1992. ''Approximation theory and recurrent networks.'' *International Joint Conference on Neural Networks,* Vol. 2, pp. 266–271, Baltimore, MD.

Light, W.A., 1992. ''Some aspects of radial basis function approximation.'' In *Approximation Theory, Spline Functions and Applications* (S.P. Singh, ed.), NATO ASI Series, Vol. 256, pp. 163–190. Boston, MA: Kluwer Academic Publishers.

Lin, D.-T., J.E. Dayhoff, and P.A. Ligomenides, 1992.'' Adaptive time-delay neural network for temporal correlation and prediction. ''In *SPIE Intelligent Robots and Computer Vision XI: Biological, Neural Net, and 3-D Methods,* Vol. 1826, pp. 170–181. Boston, MA.

Lin, D.-T., P.A. Ligomenides, and J.E. Dayhoff, 1993. ''Learning spatiotemporal topology using an adaptive time-delay neural network.'' *World Congress on Neural Networks,* Vol. 1, pp. 291–294, Portland, OR.

Lin, S., 1965. ''Computer solutions of the traveling salesman problem.'' *Bell System Technical Journal* **44,** 2245–2269.

Linde, Y., A. Buzo, and R.M. Gray, 1980. ''An algorithm for vector quantizer design.'' *IEEE Transactions on Communications* **COM-28,** 84–95.

Linsker, R., 1986. ''From basic network principles to neural architecture'' (series). *Proceedings of the National Academy of Sciences of the U.S.A.* **83,** 7508–7512, 8390–8394, 8779–8783.

Linsker, R., 1987. ''Towards an organizing principle for perception: Hebbian synapses and the principle of optimal neural encoding,'' IBM Research Report RC12820. Yorktown Heights, NY, IBM Research.

Linsker, R., 1988a. ''Self-organization in a perceptual network.'' *Computer* **21,** 105–117.

Linsker, R., 1988b. ''Towards an organizing principle for a layered perceptual network.'' In *Neural Information Processing Systems* (D.Z. Anderson, ed.), pp. 485–494. New York: American Institute of Physics.

Linsker, R., 1989a. ''An application of the principle of maximum information preservation to linear systems.'' In *Advances in Neural Information Processing Systems 1* (D.S. Touretzky, ed.), pp. 186–194. San Mateo, CA: Morgan Kaufmann.

Linsker, R., 1989b. ''How to generate ordered maps by maximizing the mutual information between input and output signals.'' *Neural Computation* **1,** 402–411.

Linsker, R., 1990a. ''Designing a sensory processing system: What can be learned from principal components analysis?'' *International Joint Conference on Neural Networks,* Vol. 2, pp. 291–297, Washington, DC.

Linsker, R., 1990b. ''Self-organization in a perceptual system: How network models and information theory may shed light on neural organization.'' In *Connectionist Modeling and Brain Function: The Developing Interface* (S.J. Hanson and C.R. Olson, eds.), Chapter 10, pp. 351–392. Cambridge, MA: MIT Press.

Linsker, R., 1990c. ''Perceptual neural organization: Some approaches based on network models and information theory.'' *Annual Review of Neuroscience* **13,** 257–281.

Linsker, R., 1992. Private communication.

Linsker, R., 1993. ''Deriving receptive fields using an optimal encoding criterion.'' In *Advances in Neural Information Processing Systems 5* (S.J. Hanson, J.D. Cowan, and C.L. Giles, eds.), pp. 953–960, San Mateo, CA: Morgan Kaufmann.

Lippmann, R.P., 1987. ''An introduction to computing with neural nets.'' *IEEE ASSP Magazine* **4,** 4–22.

Lippmann, R.P., 1989a. ''Review of neural networks for speech recognition.'' *Neural Computation* **1,** 1–38.

Lippmann, R.P., 1989b. ''Pattern classification using neural networks.'' *IEEE Communications Magazine* **27,** 47–64.

* Lisberger, S.G., 1988. ''The neural basis for learning of simple motor skills.'' *Science* **242,** 728–735.

* Lisman, J., 1989. ''A mechanism for the Hebb and the anti-Hebb processes underlying learning and memory.'' *Proceedings of the National Academy of Sciences of the U.S.A.* **86,** 9574–9578.

Little, W.A., 1974. ''The existence of persistent states in the brain.'' *Mathematical Biosciences* **19,** 101–120.

Little, W.A., and G.L. Shaw, 1975. ''A statistical theory of short and long term memory.'' *Behavioral Biology* **14,** 115–133.

* Little, W.A., and G.L. Shaw, 1978. ''Analytical study of the memory storage capacity of a neural network.'' *Mathematical Biosciences* **39,** 281–290.

Littman, M., and J. Boyan, 1993. ''A distributed reinforcement learning scheme for network routing.'' In *Applications of Neural Networks to Telecommunications* (J. Alspector, R. Goodman, and T.X. Brown, eds.), pp. 45–51. Hillsdale, NJ: Lawrence Erlbaum.

* Liu, W., A.G. Andreou, and M.H. Goldstein, 1992. ''Voiced-speech representation by

an analog silicon model of the auditory periphery.'' *IEEE Transactions on Neural Networks* **3,** 477–487.

Livesey, M., 1991. ''Clamping in Boltzmann machines.'' *IEEE Transactions on Neural Networks* **2,** 143–148.

Ljung, L., 1977. ''Analysis of recursive stochastic algorithms.'' *IEEE Transactions on Automatic Control* **AC-22,** 551–575.

Lo, Z.-P., M. Fujita, and B. Bavarian, 1991. ''Analysis of neighborhood interaction in Kohonen neural networks.'' *6th International Parallel Processing Symposium Proceedings,* pp. 247–249. Los Alamitos, CA.

Lo, Z.-P., Y. Yu, and B. Bavarian, 1993. ''Analysis of the convergence properties of topology preserving neural networks.'' *IEEE Transactions on Neural Networks* **4,** 207–220.

Lockery, S.R., Y. Fang, and T.J. Sejnowski, 1990. ''A dynamical neural network model of sensorimotor transformations in the leech.'' *International Joint Conference on Neural Networks,* Vol. 1, pp. 183–188, San Diego, CA.

* Loève, M., 1963. *Probability Theory,* 3rd ed. New York: Van Nostrand.

* Lorentz, G.G., 1966. *Approximation of Functions.* Orlando, FL: Holt, Rinehart & Winston.

* Lorentz, G.G., 1976. ''The 13th problem of Hilbert.'' *Proceedings of Symposia in Pure Mathematics* **28,** 419–430.

Lorenz, E.N., 1963. ''Deterministic non-periodic flows.'' *Journal of the Atmospheric Sciences* **20,** 130–141.

Lowe, D., 1989. ''Adaptive radial basis function nonlinearities, and the problem of generalisation.'' *1st IEE International Conference on Artificial Neural Networks,* pp. 171–175, London, UK.

Lowe, D., 1991a. ''What have neural networks to offer statistical pattern processing?'' *Proceedings of the SPIE Conference on Adaptive Signal Processing,* pp. 460–471, San Diego, CA.

Lowe, D., 1991b. ''On the iterative inversion of RBF networks: A statistical interpretation.'' *2nd IEE International Conference on Artificial Neural Networks,* pp. 29–33, Bournemouth, UK.

Lowe, D., 1992. Private communication.

* Lowe, D., and A.R. Webb, 1989. ''Adaptive networks, dynamical systems, and the predictive analysis of time series.'' *1st IEE International Conference on Artificial Neural Networks,* pp. 95–99, London, UK.

Lowe, D., and A.R. Webb, 1990. ''Exploiting prior knowledge in network optimization: An illustration from medical prognosis.'' *Network* **1,** 299–323.

Lowe, D., and A.R. Webb, 1991a. ''Time series prediction by adaptive networks: A dynamical systems perspective.'' *IEE Proceedings (London), Part F* **138,** 17–24.

* Lowe, D., and A.R. Webb, 1991b. ''Optimized feature extraction and the Bayes decision in feed-forward classifier networks.'' *IEEE Transactions on Pattern Analysis and Machine Intelligence* **PAMI-13,** 355–364.

Lucky, R.W., 1965. ''Automatic equalization for digital communication.'' *Bell System Technical Journal* **44,** 547–588.

Lucky, R.W., 1966. ''Techniques for adaptive equalization of digital communication systems.'' *Bell System Technical Journal* **45,** 255–286.

Luenberger, D.G., 1969. *Optimization by Vector Space Methods.* New York: Wiley.

Lui, H.C., 1990. ''Analysis of decision contour of neural network with sigmoidal nonlinearity.'' *International Joint Conference on Neural Networks,* Vol. 1, pp. 655–659, Washington, DC.

Luo, Z., 1991. ''On the convergence of the LMS algorithm with adaptive learning rate for linear feedforward networks.'' *Neural Computation* **3,** 226–245.

Luttrell, S.P., 1989a. ''Hierarchical vector quantization.'' *IEE Proceedings* (*London*) **136** (Part I), 405–413

Luttrell, S.P., 1989b. ''Self-organization: A derivation from first principle of a class of learning algorithms.'' *IEEE Conference on Neural Networks,* pp. 495–498, Washington, DC.

Luttrell, S.P., 1991a. ''Code vector density in topographic mappings: Scalar case.'' *IEEE Transactions on Neural Networks* **2,** 427–436.

Luttrell, S.P., 1991b. ''Self-supervised training of hierarchical vector quantizers.'' *2nd IEE International Conference on Artificial Neural Networks,* pp. 5–9, Bournemouth, UK.

* Luttrell, S.P., 1991c. ''A hierarchical network for clutter and texture modelling.'' *SPIE Proceedings on Adaptive Signal Processing,* Vol. 1565, pp. 518–528, San Diego, CA.

Luttrell, S.P., 1992. Private communication.

* MacGregor, R.J., 1987. *Neural and Brain Modeling*. Orlando, FL: Academic Press.

* MacKay, D.J.C., and K.D. Miller, 1990. ''Analysis of Linsker's simulations of Hebbian rules.'' *Neural Computation* **2,** 173–187.

Macq, D., M. Verleysen, P. Jespers, and J.-D. Legat, 1993. ''Analog implementation of a Kohonen map with on-chip learning.'' *IEEE Transactions on Neural Networks* **4,** 456–461.

MacQueen, J., 1967. ''Some methods for classification and analysis of multivariate observation.'' In *Proceedings of the 5th Berkeley Symposium on Mathematical Statistics and Probability* (L.M. LeCun and J. Neyman, eds.), Vol. 1, pp. 281–297. Berkeley: University of California Press.

Mahowald, M.A., and C. Mead, 1989. ''Silicon retina.'' In *Analog VLSI and Neural Systems* (C. Mead), Chapter 15. Reading, MA: Addison-Wesley.

Makhoul, J., S. Roucos, and H. Gish, 1985. ''Vector quantization in speech coding.'' *Proceedings of the IEEE* **73,** 1551–1587.

Mandelbrot, B.B., 1982. *The Fractal Geometry of Nature.* San Francisco, CA: Freeman.

Mann, R., 1990. ''Application of the Kohonen self-organising feature map to radar signal classification.'' M. Eng. Thesis, McMaster Univerisity, Hamilton, Ontario.

* Marcus, C.M., and R.M. Westervelt, 1988. ''Basins of attractions for electronic neural networks.'' In *Neural Information Processing Systems* (D.Z. Anderson, ed.), pp. 524–533. New York: American Institute of Physics.

Marr, D., 1982. *Vision.* New York: Freeman.

Martinetz, T.M., H.J. Ritter, and K.J. Schulten, 1990. ''Three-dimensional neural net for learning visuomotor coordination of a robot arm.'' *IEEE Transactions on Neural Networks* **1,** 131–136.

Mason, S.J., 1953. ''Feedback theory—Some properties of signal-flow graphs.'' *Proceedings of the Institute of Radio Engineers* **41,** 1144–1156.

Mason, S.J., 1956. ''Feedback theory—Further properties of signal-flow graphs.'' *Proceedings of the Institute of Radio Engineers* **44,** 920–926.

Mazaika, P.K., 1987. "A mathematical model of the Boltzmann machine." *IEEE 1st International Conference on Neural Networks,* Vol. 3, pp. 157–163, San Diego, CA.

McBride, L.E., Jr., and K.S. Narendra, 1965. "Optimization of time-varying systems." *IEEE Transactions on Automatic Control* **AC-10,** 289–294.

* McCulloch, W.S., 1988. *Embodiments of Mind.* Cambridge, MA: MIT Press.

McCulloch, W.S., and W. Pitts, 1943. "A logical calculus of the ideas immanent in nervous activity." *Bulletin of Mathematical Biophysics* **5,** 115–133.

McEliece, R.J., E.C. Posner, E.R. Rodemich, and S.S. Vankatesh, 1987. "The capacity of the Hopfield associative memory." *IEEE Transactions on Information Theory* **IT-33,** 461–482.

McLachlan, G.J., and K.E. Basford, 1988. *Mixture Models: Inference and Applications to Clustering.* New York: Dekker.

Mead, C.A., 1987a. "Silicon models of neural computation." *1st IEEE International Conference on Neural Networks,* Vol. I, pp. 93–106, San Diego, CA.

* Mead, C.A., 1987b. "Neural hardware for vision." *Engineering and Science* 2–7.

Mead, C.A., 1989. *Analog VLSI and Neural Systems.* Reading, MA: Addison-Wesley.

Mead, C.A., 1990. "Neuromorphic electronic systems." *Proceedings of the IEEE* **78,** 1629–1636.

Mead, C.A., and L. Conway, 1980. *Introduction to VLSI Systems.* Reading, MA: Addison-Wesley.

* Mead, C.A., and M. Ismail, 1989. *Analog VLSI Implementation of Neural Systems.* Boston, MA: Kluwer.

Mead, C.A., and M.A. Mahowald, 1988. "A silicon model of early visual processing." *Neural Networks* **1,** 91–97.

* Mead, C.A., and M. Mahowald, 1990. "A silicon model of early visual processing." In *Computational Neuroscience* (E.L. Schwartz, ed.), pp. 331–339. Cambridge, MA: MIT Press.

Mead, C.A., X. Arreguit, and J. Lazzaro, 1991. "Analog VLSI model of binaural hearing." *IEEE Transactions on Neural Networks* **2,** 232–236.

* Mel, B.W., and C. Koch, 1990. "Sigma-pi learning: On radial basis functions and cortical associative learning." In *Advances in Neural Information Processing Systems 2* (D.S. Touretzky, ed.), pp. 474–481. San Mateo, CA: Morgan Kaufmann.

* Mel, B.W., and S.M. Omohundro, 1991. "How receptive field parameters affect neuronal learning." In *Advances in Neural Information Processing Systems 3* (R.P. Lippmann, J.E. Moody, and D.S. Touretzky, eds.), pp. 757–763. San Mateo, CA: Morgan Kaufmann.

Memmi, D., 1989. "Connectionism and artificial intelligence." *Neuro-Nimes '89 International Workshop on Neural Networks and Their Applications,* pp. 17–34, Nimes, France.

Mendel, J.M., 1973. *Discrete Techniques for Parameter Estimation: The Equation Error Formulation.* New York: Dekker.

* Mendel, J.M., and K.S. Fu, eds., 1970. *Adaptive, Learning, and Pattern Recognition Systems; Theory and Applications,* New York: Academic Press.

Mendel, J.M., and R.W. McLaren, 1970. "Reinforcement-learning control and pattern recognition systems." In *Adaptive, Learning, and Pattern Recognition Systems: Theory and Applications* (J.M. Mendel and K.S. Fu, eds.), pp. 287–318. New York: Academic Press.

Mesulam, M.M., 1985. ''Attention confusional states, and neglect.'' In *Principles of Behavioral Neurology* (M.M. Mesulam, ed.), Philadelphia, PA: Davis.

Metropolis, N., A. Rosenbluth, M. Rosenbluth, A. Teller, and E. Teller, 1953. ''Equations of state calculations by fast computing machines.'' *Journal of Chemical Physics* **21,** 1087–1092.

* Mézard, M., and J.-P. Nadal, 1989. ''Learning in feed-forward layered networks: The tiling algorithm.'' *Journal of Physics A* **22,** 2191–2203.

Mézard, M., G. Parisi, and M.A. Virasoro, 1987. *Spin-Glass Theory and Beyond.* Singapore: World Scientific.

Micchelli, C.A., 1986. Interpolation of scattered data: Distance matrices and conditionally positive definite functions.'' *Constructive Approximation* **2,** 11–22.

* Michel, A.N., J. Si, and G. Yen, 1991. ''Analysis and synthesis of a class of discrete-time networks described on hypercubes.'' *IEEE Transactions on Neural Networks,* **2,** 32–46.

Miller, K.D., J.B. Keller, and M.P. Stryker, 1989. ''Ocular dominance column development: Analysis and simulation.'' *Science* **245,** 605–615.

Miller, R., 1987. ''Representation of brief temporal patterns, Hebbian synapses, and the left-hemisphere dominance for phoneme recognition.'' *Psychobiology* **15,** 241–247.

Miller, W.T., III, R.S. Sutton, and P.J. Werbos, eds., 1990. *Neural Networks for Control.* Cambridge, MA: MIT Press.

Minai, A.A., and R.J. Williams, 1990. ''Back-propagation heuristics: A study of the extended delta-bar-delta algorithm.'' *International Joint Conference on Neural Networks,* Vol. 1, pp. 595–600, San Diego, CA.

Minsky, M.L., 1954. ''Theory of neural-analog reinforcement systems and its application to the brain-model problem.'' Ph.D. Thesis, Princeton University, Princeton, NJ.

Minsky, M.L., 1961. ''Steps towards artificial intelligence.'' *Proceedings of the Institute of Radio Engineers* **49,** 8–30.

* Minsky, M.L., 1986. *Society of Mind,* New York: Simon & Schuster.

Minsky, M.L., and S.A. Papert, 1969. *Perceptrons.* Cambridge, MA: MIT Press.

Minsky, M.L., and S.A. Papert, 1988. *Perceptrons.* Expanded Edition. Cambridge, MA: MIT Press.

Minsky, M.L., and O.G. Selfridge, 1961. ''Learning in random nets.'' *Information Theory, Fourth London Symposium.* London: Butterworth.

Mitchison, G., 1989. ''Learning algorithms and networks of neurons.'' In *The Computing Neuron* (R. Durbin, C. Miall, and G. Michison, eds.), pp. 35–53, Reading, MA: Addison-Wesley.

* Moody, J.E., 1992. ''The effective number of parameters: An analysis of generalization and regularization in nonlinear learning systems.'' In *Advances in Neural Information Processing Systems* (J.E. Moody, S.J. Hanson, and R.P. Lippmann, eds.), pp. 847–854. San Mateo, CA: Morgan Kaufmann.

Moody, J.E., and C.J. Darken, 1989. ''Fast learning in networks of locally-tuned processing units.'' *Neural Computation* **1,** 281–294.

Moon, G., M.E. Zaghloul, and R.W. Newcomb, 1992. ''VLSI implementation of synaptic weighting and summing in pulse coded neural-type cells.'' *IEEE Transactions on Neural Networks* **3,** 394–403.

Morgan, N., and H. Bourlard, 1990. ''Continuous speech rcognition using multilayer perceptrons with hidden Markov models.'' *International Conference on Acoustics, Speech, and Signal Processing,* pp. 413–416, Alburquerque, NM.

Morita, M., 1993. ''Associative memory with nonmonotonic dynamics.'' *Neural Networks* **6,** 115–126.

Morozov, V.A., 1993. *Regularization Methods for Ill-Posed Problems.* Boca Raton, FL: CRC Press.

Mpitsos, G.J., 1990. ''Chaos in brain function and the problem of nonstationarity: A commentary.'' In *Chaos in Brain Function* (E. Başar, ed.), pp. 162–176. New York: Springer-Verlag.

Müller, B., and J. Reinhardt, 1990. *Neural Networks: An Introduction.* New York: Springer-Verlag.

Muller, D., and G. Lynch, 1988. ''Long-term potentiation differentially affects two components of synaptic responses in hippocampus.'' *Proceedings of the National Academy of Sciences of the U.S.A.* **85,** 9346–9350.

* Murray, A.F., 1989. ''Silicon implementations of neural networks.'' *1st IEE International Conference on Artificial Neural Networks,* pp. 27–32, London, U.K.

Murray, A.F., D. Del Corso, and L. Tarassenko, 1991. ''Pulse-stream VLSI neural networks mixing analog and digital techniques.'' *IEEE Transactions on Neural Networks* **2,** 193–204.

* Najand, S., Z. Lo, and B. Bavarian, 1992. ''Using the Kohonen topology preserving mapping network for learning the minimal environment representation.'' *International Joint Conference on Neural Networks,* Vol. 2, pp. 87–93, Baltimore, MD.

Nakano, K., 1972. ''Association—a model of associative memory,'' *IEEE Transactions on Systems, Man, and Cybernetics* **SMC-2,** 380–388.

Naraghi-Pour, M., M. Hedge, and P. Bapat, 1993. ''Fault tolerance design of feedforward networks.'' *World Congress on Neural Networks,* Vol. 3, pp. 568–571, Portland, OR.

Narendra, K.S., and A.M. Annaswamy, 1989. *Stable Adaptive Systems,* Englewood Cliffs, NJ: Prentice-Hall.

Narendra, K.S., and K. Parthasarathy, 1990. ''Identification and control of dynamical systems using neural networks.'' *IEEE Transactions on Neural Networks* **1,** 4–27.

Narendra, K.S., and M.A.L. Thathachar, 1989. *Learning Automata: An Introduction.* Englewood Cliffs, NJ: Prentice-Hall.

* Nasrabadi, N.M., S. Dianat, and S. Venkatoraman, 1991. ''Non-linear prediction using a three-layer neural network.'' *International Joint Conference on Neural Networks,* Vol. 1, pp. 689–694, Seattle, WA.

Natarajan, B.K., 1991. *Machine Learning: A Theoretical Approach.* San Mateo, CA: Morgan Kaufmann.

* Nerrand, O., P. Roussel-Ragot, L. Personnaz, G. Dreyfus, S. Marcos, O. Macchi, and C. Vignat, 1991. ''Neural network training schemes for non-linear adaptive filtering and modelling.'' *International Joint Conference on Neural Networks,* Vol. 1, pp. 61–66, Seattle, WA.

Newell, A., and H.A. Simon, 1972. *Human Problem Solving.* Englewood Cliffs, NJ: Prentice-Hall.

Ney, H., 1984. ''The use of a one-stage dynamic programming algorithm for connected word recognition,'' *IEEE Transactions on Acoustics, Speech, and Signal Processing* **ASSP-32,** 263–271.

Ng, K., and R.P. Lippmann, 1991. "Practical characteristics of neural network and conventional pattern classifiers." In *Advances in Neural Information Processing Systems 3* (R.P. Lippman, J.E. Moody, and D.S. Touretzky, eds.), pp. 970–976. San Mateo, CA: Morgan Kaufmann.

Nguyen, D., and B. Widrow, 1989. "The truck backer-upper: An example of self-learning in neural networks." *International Joint Conference on Neural Networks,* Vol. 2, pp. 357–363, Washington, DC.

Nielson, G.M., and B. Shriver, eds., 1990. *Visualization in Scientific Computing.* Los Alamitos, CA: IEEE Computer Society Press.

Nilsson, N.J., 1965. *Learning Machines: Foundations of Trainable Pattern-Classifying Systems.* New York: McGraw-Hill.

Nilsson, N.J., 1980. *Principles of Artificial Intelligence.* New York: Springer-Verlag.

Niranjan, M., and F. Fallside, 1990. "Neural networks and radial basis functions in classifying static speech patterns." *Computer Speech and Language* **4,** 275–289.

Novikoff, A.B.J., 1962. "On convergence proofs for perceptrons." In *Proceedings of the Symposium on the Mathematical Theory of Automata*, pp. 615–622, Brooklyn, NY: Polytechnic Institute of Brooklyn.

* Nowlan, S.J., 1990. "Max likelihood competition in RBF networks," CRG Technical Report TR-90-2. Department of Computer Science, University of Toronto.

Nowlan, S.J., and G.E. Hinton, 1991. "Evaluation of adaptive mixtures of competing experts." In *Advances in Neural Information Processing Systems 3* (R.P. Lippmann, J.E. Moody, and D.S. Touretzky, eds.), pp. 774–780. San Mateo, CA: Morgan Kaufmann.

* Nowlan, S.J., and G.E. Hinton, 1992. "Adaptive soft weight tying using Gaussian mixtures." In *Advances in Neural Information Processing Systems 4* (J.E. Moody, S.J. Hanson, and R.P. Lippmann, eds.), pp. 993–1000. San Mateo, CA: Morgan Kaufmann.

Obermayer, K., H. Ritter, and K. Schulten, 1991. "Development and spatial structure of cortical feature maps: A model study." In *Advances in Neural Information Processing Systems 3* (R.P. Lippmann, J.E. Moody, and D.S. Touretzky, eds.), pp. 11–17. San Mateo, CA: Morgan Kaufmann.

* Oğuztöreli, M.N., and T.M. Caelli, 1986. "An inverse problem in neural processing." *Biological Cybernetics* **53,** 239–245.

Oja, E., 1982. "A simplified neuron model as a principal component analyzer." *Journal of Mathematical Biology* **15,** 267–273.

Oja, E., 1983. *Subspace Methods of Pattern Recognition.* Letchworth, UK: Research Studies Press.

Oja, E., 1989. "Neural networks, principal components, and subspaces." *International Journal of Neural Systems* **1,** 61–68.

Oja, E., 1991. "Data compression, feature extraction, and autoassociation in feedforward neural networks." In *Artificial Neural Networks* (T. Kohonen, K. Mäkisara, O. Simula, and J. Kangas, eds.), Vol. 1, pp. 737–746. Amsterdam: North-Holland.

Oja, E., 1992a. "Principal components, minor components, and linear neural networks." *Neural Networks* **5,** 927–936.

Oja, E., 1992b. "Self-organizing maps and computer vision." In *Neural Networks for Perception* (H. Wechsler, ed.), Vol. 1, pp. 368–385. San Diego, CA: Academic Press.

Oja, E., 1993. "Nonlinear PCA: Algorithms and applications." *World Congress on Neural Networks,* Vol. 2, p. 396, Portland, OR.

Oja, E., and J. Karhunen, 1985. "A stochastic approximation of the eigenvectors and eigenvalues of the expectation of a random matrix.'' *Journal of Mathematical Analysis and Applications* **106,** 69–84.

* Oja, E., and T. Kohonen, 1988. ''The subspace learning algorithm as formalism for pattern recognition and neural networks.'' *IEEE International Conference on Neural Networks,* Vol. 1, pp. 277–284, San Diego, CA.

Oja, E., H. Ogawa, and J. Wangviwattana, 1991. ''Learning in nonlinear constrained Hebbian networks.'' In *Artificial Neural Networks* (T. Kohonen, K. Mäkisara, O. Simula, and J. Kangas, eds.), pp. 385–390. Amsterdam: North-Holland.

Orlando, J., R. Mann, and S. Haykin, 1990. ''Classification of sea-ice using a dual-polarized radar.'' *IEEE Journal of Oceanic Engineering* **15,** 228–237.

Osherson, D.N., S. Weinstein, and M. Stoli, 1990. ''Modular learning,'' In *Computational Neuroscience* (E.L. Schwartz, ed.), pp. 369–377. Cambridge, MA: MIT Press.

* Ottaway, M.B., P.Y. Simard, and D.H. Ballard, 1989. ''Fixed point analysis for recurrent networks.'' In *Advances in Neural Information Processing Systems 1* (D.S. Touretzky, ed.), pp. 149–159. San Mateo, CA: Morgan Kaufmann.

* Pagels, H.R., 1989. *The Dreams of Reason.* New York: Bantam Books.

Palm, G., 1982. *Neural Assemblies: An Alternative Approach.* New York: Springer-Verlag.

Palmieri, F., 1993. ''Linear self-association for universal memory and approximation.'' *World Congress on Neural Networks,* Vol. 2, pp. 339–343, Portland, OR.

Palmieri, F., and S.A. Shah, 1990. ''Fast training of multilayer perceptrons using multilinear parameterization.'' *International Joint Conference on Neural Networks,* Vol. 1, pp. 696–699, Washington, DC.

Palmeri, F., and J. Zhu, 1993. ''Hebbian learning in linear neural networks: A review.'' Technical Report 5193, Department of Electrical and Systems Engineering, The University of Connecticut, Storrs, CT.

Palmieri, F., M. Datum, A. Shah, and A. Moiseff, 1991. ''Sound localization with a neural network trained with the multiple extended Kalman algorithm.'' *International Joint Conference on Neural Networks,* Vol. 1, pp. 125–131, Seattle, WA.

Palmieri, F., J. Zhu, and C. Chang, 1993. ''Anti-Hebbian learning in topologically constrained linear networks: A tutorial.'' *IEEE Transactions on Neural Networks* **5,** to appear.

Papoulis, A., 1984. *Probability, Random Variables, and Stochastic Processes,* 2nd ed. New York: McGraw-Hill.

* Parisi, G., 1986. ''A memory which forgets,'' *Journal of Physics A* **19,** L617–L620.

Park, J., and I.W. Sandberg, 1991. ''Universal approximation using radial-basis-function networks.'' *Neural Computation* **3,** 246–257.

Parker, D.B., 1985. ''Learning-logic: Casting the cortex of the human brain in silicon,'' Technical Report TR-47. Center for Computational Research in Economics and Management Science, MIT, Cambridge, MA.

Parker, D.B., 1987. ''Optimal algorithms for adaptive networks: Second order back propagation, second order direct propagation, and second order Hebbian learning.'' *IEEE 1st International Conference on Neural Networks,* Vol. 2, pp. 593–600, San Diego, CA.

Parker, T.S., and L.O. Chua, 1989. *Practical Numerical Algorithms for Chaotic Systems.* New York: Springer-Verlag.

Parthasarathy, K., and K.S. Narendra, 1991, ''Stable adaptive control of a class of discrete-time nonlinear systems using radial basis function networks.'' Technical Report No. 9103, Center for Systems Science, Yale University, New Haven, CT.

Parzen, E., 1962. ''On estimation of a probability density function and mode.'' *Annals of Mathematical Statistics* **33,** 1065–1076.

* Pearlmutter, B.A., 1989. ''Learning state-space trajectories in recurrent neural networks.'' *Neural Computation* **1,** 263–269.

* Pearlmutter, B.A., 1992. ''Gradient descent: Second order momentum and saturating error.'' In *Advances in Neural Information Processing Systems 4* (J.E. Moody, S.J. Hanson, and R.P. Lippmann, eds.), pp. 887–894. San Mateo, CA: Morgan Kaufmann.

Pearson, K., 1901. ''On lines and planes of closest fit to systems of points in space.'' *Philosophical Magazine* **2,** 559–572.

Peretto, P., 1984. ''Collective properties of neural networks: A statistical physics approach.'' *Biological Cybernetics* **50,** 51–62.

Peretto, P., and J.-J. Niez, 1986. ''Stochastic dynamics of neural networks.'' *IEEE Transactions on Systems, Man, and Cybernetics* **SMC-16,** 73–83.

Perrone, M.P., and L.N. Cooper, 1993. ''Learning from what's been learned: Supervised learning in multi-neural network systems.'' *World Congress on Neural Networks,* Vol. 3, pp. 354–357, Portland, OR.

Perry, J., 1990. ''Basins of attraction revisited.'' *International Joint Conference on Neural Networks,* Vol. 1, pp. 853–858, San Diego, CA.

Personnaz, L., I. Guyon, and G. Dreyfus, 1985. ''Information storage and retrieval in spin-glass like neural networks.'' *Journal de Physique, Lettres (Orsay, France)* **46,** L-359–L-365.

* Peterson, C., 1990. ''Parallel distributed approaches to combinatorial optimization: Benchmark studies on traveling salesman problem.'' *Neural Computation* **2,** 261–269.

Peterson, C., 1991. ''Mean field theory neural networks for feature recognition, content addressable memory and optimization.'' *Connection Science* **3,** 3–33.

Peterson, C., and J.R. Anderson, 1987. ''A mean field theory learning algorithm for neural networks.'' *Complex Systems* **1,** 995–1019.

Peterson, C., and E. Hartman, 1989. ''Explorations of the mean field theory learning algorithm.'' *Neural Networks* **2,** 475–494.

Peterson, C., and B. Söderberg, 1989. ''A new method of mapping optimization problems onto neural networks.'' *International Journal of Neural Systems* **1,** 3–22.

* Phatak, D.S., and I. Koren, 1992. ''Fault tolerance of feedforward neural nets for classification tasks.'' *International Joint Conference on Neural Networks,* Vol. 2, pp. 386–391, Baltimore, MD.

Pineda, F.J., 1987. ''Generalization of back-propagation to recurrent neural networks.'' *Physical Review Letters* **59,** 2229–2232.

Pineda, F.J., 1988a. ''Dynamics and architecture in neural computation.'' *Journal of Complexity* **4,** 216–245.

Pineda, F.J., 1988b. ''Generalization of backpropagation to recurrent and higher order neural networks.'' In *Neural Information Processing Systems* (D.Z. Anderson, ed.), pp. 602–611. New York: American Institute of Physics.

Pineda, F.J., 1989, ''Recurrent backpropagation and the dynamical approach to adaptive neural computation.'' *Neural Computation* **1,** 161–172.

* Pineda, F.J., 1990. ''Time-depenent adaptive neural networks.'' In *Advances in Neural*

Information Processing Systems 2 (D.S. Touretzky, ed.), pp. 710–718. San Mateo, CA: Morgan Kaufmann.

* Pinker, S., and J. Mehler, guest eds., 1984. Connectionism and symbol systems. *Special Issue of the International Journal of Cognitive Science* **28,** 1–246.

* Pinter, R.B., and B. Nabet, eds. 1992. *Nonlinear Vision: Determination of Receptive Fields, Function and Networks.* Boca Raton, FL: CRC Press.

Pitts, W., and W.S. McCulloch, 1947. "How we know universals: The perception of auditory and visual forms." *Bulletin of Mathematical Biophysics* **9,** 127–147.

* Platt, J.C., and F. Faggin, 1992. "Networks for the separation of sources that are superimposed and delayed." In *Advances in Neural Information Processing Systems 4* (J.E. Moody, S.J. Hanson, and R.P. Lippmann, eds.), pp. 730–737. San Mateo, CA: Morgan Kaufmann.

Plumbley, M.D., 1993. "A Hebbian/anti-Hebbian network which optimizes information capacity by orthonormalizing the principal subspace." *IEE Artificial Neural Networks Conference*, ANN-93, pp. 86–90, Brighton, UK.

Plumbley, M.D., and F. Fallside, 1988. "An information-theoretic approach to unsupervised connectionist models." In *Proceedings of the 1988 Connectionist Models Summer School* (D. Touretzky, G. Hinton, and T. Sejnowski, eds.), pp. 239–245. San Mateo, CA: Morgan Kaufmann.

Plumbley, M.D., and F. Fallside, 1989. "Sensory adaptation: An information-theoretic viewpoint." *International Joint Conference on Neural Networks,* Vol. 2, p. 598, Washington, DC.

* Poggio, T., 1990. "A theory of how the brain might work." *Cold Spring Harbor Symposium on Quantitative Biology* **55,** 899–910.

Poggio, T., and S. Edelman, 1990. "A network that learns to recognize three-dimensional objects." *Nature (London)* **343,** 263–266.

Poggio, T., and F. Girosi, 1990a. "Networks for approximation and learning." *Proceedings of the IEEE* **78,** 1481–1497.

Poggio, T., and F. Girosi, 1990b. "Regularization algorithms for learning that are equivalent to multilayer networks." *Science* **247,** 978–982.

* Poggio, T., and C. Koch, 1985. "Ill-posed problems in early vision: From computational theory to analogue networks." *Proceedings of the Royal Society of London, Series B* **226,** 303–323.

* Poggio, T., V. Torre, and C. Koch, 1985. "Computational vision and regularization theory." *Nature (London)* **317,** 314–319.

Polak, E., and G. Ribiére, 1969. "Note sur la convergence de methods de directions conjures." *Revue Francaise Information Recherche Operationnelle* **16,** 35–43.

Pomerleau, D.A., 1992. "Neural network perception for mobile robot guidance." Ph.D. Dissertation, School of Computer Science, Carnegie Mellon University, Pittsburgh, PA.

Pöppel, G., and U. Krey, 1987. "Dynamical learning process for recognition of correlated patterns in symmetric spin glass models." *Europhysics Letters* **4,** 979–985.

* Posner, M.I., ed., 1989. *Foundations of Cognitive Science.* Cambridge, MA: MIT Press.

* Posner, M.I., and S.E. Petersen, 1990. "The attention system of the human brain." *Annual Review of Neuroscience* **13,** 25–42.

* Powell, M.J.D., 1977. "Restart procedures for the conjugate gradient method." *Mathematical Programming* **12,** 241–254.

Powell, M.J.D., 1985. "Radial basis functions for multivariable interpolation: A review."

In *IMA Conference on Algorithms for the Approximation of Functions and Data.*, pp. 143–167, RMCS, Shrivenham, UK.

Powell, M.J.D., 1988. ''Radial basis function approximations to polynomials.'' *Numerical Analysis 1987 Proceedings,* pp. 223–241, Dundee, UK.

Preisendorfer, R.W., 1988. *Principal Component Analysis in Meteorology and Oceanography.* New York: Elsevier.

Priestley, M.B., 1981. *Spectral Analysis and Time Series,* Vol. 1: Univariate Series; Vol. 2: Multivariate Series, Prediction and Control. New York: Academic Press.

Priestley, M.B., 1988. *Non-linear and Non-stationary Time Series Analysis.* New York: Academic Press.

Quereshi, S., 1985. ''Adaptive equalization.'' *Proceedings of the IEEE* **73,** 1349–1387.

Rabiner, L.R., 1989. ''A tutorial on hidden Markov models and selected applications in speech recognition.'' *Proceedings of the IEEE* **77,** 257–286.

Rabiner, L.R., and B.H. Juang, 1986. ''An introduction to hidden Markov models.'' *IEEE ASSP Magazine* **3,** 4–16.

Rabiner, L.R., and R.W. Schafer, 1978. *Digital Processing of Speech Signals.* Englewood Cliffs, NJ: Prentice-Hall.

Radons, G., H.G. Schuster, and D. Werner, 1990. ''Fokker–Planck description of learning in back propagation networks.'' *International Neural Network Conference,* Vol. 2, pp. 993–996, Paris, France.

* Raghunath, K.J., and V. Cherkassky, 1992. ''Analysis of the noise performance of associative memories.'' *International Joint Conference on Neural Networks,* Vol. 2, pp. 184–189, Baltimore, MD.

Rall, W., 1989. ''Cable theory for dendritic neurons.'' In *Methods in Neuronal Modeling* (C. Koch and I. Segev, eds.), pp. 9–62. Cambridge, MA: MIT Press.

Rall, W., 1990. ''Some historical notes.'' In *Computational Neuroscience* (E.L. Schwartz, ed.), pp. 3–8. Cambridge, MA: MIT Press.

Ramacher, U., 1990. ''Hardware concepts of neural networks.'' In *Advanced Neurocomputers* (R. Echmiller, ed.), pp. 209–218. New York: Elsevier.

Ramacher, U., 1992. ''SYNAPSE—A neurocomputer that synthesizes neural algorithms on a parallel systolic engine.'' *Journal of Parallel and Distributed Computing* **14,** 306–318.

* Ramacher, U., and M. Wesseling, 1992. ''Treating weights as dynamical variables—A new approach to neurodynamics—.'' *International Joint Conference on Neural Networks,* Vol. 3, pp. 497–503, Baltimore, MD.

Ramacher, U., J. Beichter, and N. Bruls, 1991. ''Architecture of a general-purpose neural signal processor.'' *International Joint Conference on Neural Networks,* Vol. 1, pp. 443–446, Seattle, WA.

Ramón y Cajál, S., 1911. *Histologie du système nerveux de l'homme et des vertébrés.* Paris: Maloine; Edition Francaise Revue: Tome I, 1952; Tome II, 1955; Madrid: Consejo Superior de Investigaciones Cientificas.

Rao, C.R., 1973. *Linear Statistical Inference and Its Applications,* New York: Wiley.

Rashevsky, N., 1938. *Mathematical Biophysics.* Chicago, IL: University of Chicago Press.

Reeke, G.N., Jr., L.H. Finkel, and G.M. Edelman, 1990. ''Selective recognition automata.'' In *An Introduction to Neural and Electronic Networks* (S.F. Zornetzer, J.L. Davis, and C. Lau, eds.), pp. 203–226. New York: Academic Press.

Reif, F., 1967. *Fundamentals of Statistical and Thermal Physics.* New York: McGraw-Hill.

* Reilly, D.L., L.N. Cooper, and C. Elbaum, 1982. ''A neural model for category learning.'' *Biological Cybernetics* **45,** 35–41.

Renals, S., 1989. ''Radial basis function network for speech pattern classification.'' *Electronics Letters* **25,** 437–439.

* Renals, S., and R. Rohwer, 1989. ''Phoneme classification experiments using radial basis functions.'' *International Joint Conference on Neural Networks,* Vol. 1, pp. 461–467, Washington, DC.

Renals, S., N. Morgan, H. Bourlard, H. Franco, and M. Cohen, 1992a. ''Connectionist optimization of tied mixture hidden Markov models.'' In *Advances in Neural Information Processing Systems 4* (J.E. Moody, S.J. Hanson, and R.P. Lippmann, eds.), pp. 167–174. San Mateo, CA: Morgan Kaufmann.

Renals, S., N. Morgan, M. Cohen, H. Franco, and H. Bourlard, 1992b. ''Improving statistical speech recognition.'' *International Joint Conference on Neural Networks,* Vol. 2, pp. 302–307. Baltimore, MD.

Richard, M.D., and R.P. Lippmann, 1991. ''Neural network classifiers estimate Bayesian a posteriori probabilities.'' *Neural Computation* **3,** 461–483.

Ridgway, W.C. ''An Adaptive logic system with generalizing properties,'' *Technical Report 1556-1.* Stanford Electronics Laboratories, Stanford University, Stanford, CA.

Riesz, F., and B. Sz-Nagy, 1955. *Functional Analysis,* 2nd ed. New York: Frederick Ungar.

Risken, H., 1989. *The Fokker-Planck Equation.* New York: Springer-Verlag.

Rissanen, J., 1978. ''Modeling by shortest data description.'' *Automatica* **14,** 465–471.

Rissanen, J., 1989. *Stochastic Complexity in Statistical Inquiry.* Singapore: World Scientific.

Ritter, H., 1991a. ''Asymptotic level density for a class of vector quantization processes.'' *IEEE Transactions on Neural Networks* **2,** 173–175.

* Ritter, H., 1991b. ''Learning with the self-organizing map.'' In *Artificial Neural Networks* (T. Kohonen, K. Mäkisara, O. Simula, and J. Kangas, eds.), Vol. 1, pp. 379–384. Amsterdam: North Holland.

* Ritter, H.J., and K. Schulten, 1986. ''On the stationary state of Kohonen's self-organizing sensory mapping.'' *Biological Cybernetics* **54,** 99–106.

Ritter, H.J., and K. Schulten, 1988. ''Convergence properties of Kohonen's topology conserving maps: Fluctuations, stability, and dimension selection.'' *Biological Cybernetics* **60,** 59–71.

Ritter, H.J., T.M. Martinetz, and K.J. Schulten, 1989. ''Topology-conserving maps for learning visuo-motor-coordination.'' *Neural Networks* **2,** 159–168.

Ritter, H.J., T. Martinetz, and K. Schulten, 1992. *Neural Computation and Self-Organizing Maps: An Introduction.* Reading, MA: Addison-Wesley.

Robbins, H., and S. Monroe, 1951. ''A stochastic approximation method.'' *Annals of Mathematical Statistics* **22,** 400–407.

Robinson, A.J., and F. Fallside, 1991. ''A recurrent error propagation speech recognition system.'' *Computer Speech and Language* **5,** 259–274.

Robinson, D.A., 1992. ''Signal processing by neural networks in the control of eye movements.'' In *Computational Neuroscience Symposium,* pp. 73–78. Indiana University-Purdue University at Indianapolis.

Rochester, N., J.H. Holland, L.H. Haibt, and W.L. Duda, 1956. ''Tests on a cell assembly theory of the action of the brain, using a large digital computer.'' *IRE Transactions on Information Theory* **IT-2,** 80–93.

* Rohwer, R., 1990. ''The 'moving targets' training algorithm.'' In *Advances in Neural Information Processing Systems 2* (D.S. Touretzky, ed.), pp. 558–565. San Mateo, CA: Morgan Kaufmann.

Rohwer, R., and B. Forrest, 1987. ''Training time-dependence in neural networks.'' *1st IEEE International Conference on Neural Networks,* Vol. 2, pp. 701–708, San Diego, CA.

* Rolls, E.T., and A. Treves, 1990. ''Neural networks in the brain.'' *Physics World,* 3, 31–35.

Rosenblatt, F., 1958. ''The Perceptron: A probabilistic model for information storage and organization in the brain.'' *Psychological Review* **65,** 386–408.

Rosenblatt, F., 1960a. ''Perceptron simulation experiments.'' *Proceedings of the Institute of Radio Engineers* **48,** 301–309.

Rosenblatt, F., 1960b. ''On the convergence of reinforcement procedures in simple perceptrons,'' Report, VG-1196-G-4. Cornell Aeronautical Laboratory, Buffalo, NY.

Rosenblatt, F., 1962. *Principles of Neurodynamics.* Washington, DC: Spartan Books.

* Rosenbleuth, A., N. Wiener, W. Pitts, and J. Garcia Ramos, 1949. ''A statistical analysis of synaptic excitation.'' *Journal of Cellular and Comparative Physiology* **34,** 173–205.

Roy, S., and J.J. Shynk, 1990. ''Analysis of the momentum LMS algorithm.'' *IEEE Transactions on Acoustics, Speech, and Signal Processing* **ASSP-38,** 2088–2098.

Rubner, J., and P. Tavan, 1989. ''A self-organizing network for principal component analysis.'' *Europhysics Letters* **10,** 693–698.

Rueckl, J.G., K.R. Cave, and S.M. Kosslyn, 1989. ''Why are 'what' and 'where' processed by separate cortical visual systems? A computational investigation.'' *Journal of Cognitive Neuroscience* **1,** 171–186.

Ruelle, D., 1989. *Chaotic Evolution and Strange Attractors.* New York: Cambridge University Press.

Rumelhart, D.E., and J.L. McClelland, eds., 1986. *Parallel Distributed Processing: Explorations in the Microstructure of Cognition,* Vol. 1. Cambridge, MA: MIT Press.

Rumelhart, D.E., and D. Zipser, 1985. ''Feature discovery by competitive learning.'' *Cognitive Science* **9,** 75–112.

Rumelhart, D.E., G.E. Hinton, and R.J. Williams, 1986a. ''Learning representations by back-propagating errors.'' *Nature* (*London*), **323,** 533–536.

Rumelhart, D.E., G.E. Hinton, and R.J. Williams, 1986b. ''Learning internal representations by error propagation.'' In *Parallel Distributed Processing: Explorations in the Microstructure of Cognition* (D.E. Rumelhart and J.L. McClelland, eds.), Vol. 1, Chapter 8, Cambridge, MA: MIT Press.

* Ruoppila, V.T., T. Sorsa, and H.N. Koivo, 1993. ''Recursive least-squares approach to self-organizing maps.'' *IEEE International Conference on Neural Networks,* Vol. 3, pp. 1480–1485, San Francisco, CA.

Russo, A.P., 1991. Neural networks for sonar signal processing, Tutorial No. 8. *IEEE Conference on Neural Networks for Ocean Engineering,* Washington, DC.

Ruyck, D.W., S.K. Rogers, M. Kabrisky, M.E. Oxley, and B.W. Suter, 1990. ''The multilayer perceptron as an approximation to a Bayes optimal discriminant function.'' *IEEE Transactions on Neural Networks* **1,** 296–298.

Saarinen, S., R.B. Bramley, and G. Cybenko, 1991. "The numerical solution of neural network training problems," CRSD Report No. 1089. Center for Supercomputing Research and Development, University of Illinois, Urbana.

Saarinen, S., R.B. Bramley, and G. Cybenko, 1992. "Neural networks, backpropagation, and automatic differentiation." In *Automatic Differentiation of Algorithms: Theory, Implementation, and Application* (A. Griewank and G.F. Corliss, eds.), pp. 31–42. Philadelphia, PA: SIAM.

Säckinger, E., B.E. Boser, J. Bromley, Y. LeCun, and L.D. Jackel, 1992a. "Application of the ANNA neural network chip to high-speed character recognition." *IEEE Transactions on Neural Networks* **3,** 498–505.

Säckinger, E., B.E. Boser, and L.D. Jackel, 1992b. "A neurocomputer board based on the ANNA neural network chip." In *Advances in Neural Information Processing Systems 4* (J.E. Moody, S.J. Hanson, and R.P. Lippmann, eds.), pp. 773–780. San Mateo, CA: Morgan Kaufmann.

Sage, A.P., ed., 1990. *Concise Encyclopedia of Information Processing in Systems and Organizations.* New York: Pergamon.

* Saha, A., and J.D. Keeler, 1990. "Algorithms for better representation and faster learning in radial basis function networks." In *Advances in Neural Information Processing Systems 2* (D.S. Touretzky, ed.), pp. 482–489. San Mateo, CA: Morgan Kaufmann.

Saha, A., J. Christian, D.S. Tang, and C.-L. Wu, 1991. "Oriented non-radial basis functions for image coding and analysis." In *Advances in Neural Information Processing Systems 3,* (R.P. Lippmann, J.E. Moody, and D.S. Touretzky, eds.), pp. 728–734. San Mateo, CA: Morgan Kaufmann.

* Samad, T., 1990. "Backpropagation improvements based on heuristic arguments." *International Joint Conference on Neural Networks,* Vol. 1, pp. 565–568, Washington, DC.

Samuel, A.L., 1959. "Some studies in machine learning using the game of checkers." *IBM Journal of Research and Development* **3,** 211–229.

Sanger, T.D., 1989a. "An optimality principle for unsupervised learning." In *Advances in Neural Information Processing Systems 1* (D.S. Touretzky, ed.), pp. 11–19. San Mateo, CA: Morgan Kaufmann.

Sanger, T.D. 1989b. "Optimal unsupervised learning in a single-layer linear feedforward neural network." *Neural Networks* **12,** 459–473.

Sanger, T.D., 1990. "Analysis of the two-dimensional receptive fields learned by the Hebbian algorithm in response to random input." *Biological Cybernetics* **63,** 221–228.

Sanner, R.M., and J.-J.E. Slotine, 1992. "Gaussian networks for direct adaptive control." *IEEE Transactions on Neural Networks* **3,** pp. 837–863.

* Sasiela, R.S., 1986. "Forgetting as a way to improve neural-net behavior." In *Neural Networks for Computing* (J.S. Denker, ed.), pp. 386–391. New York: American Institute of Physics.

* Sauer, N., 1972. "On the density of families of sets." *Journal of Combinatorial Theory* **A13,** 145–147.

* Schneider, C.R., and H.C. Card, 1991. "Analog CMOS modelling of invertebrate learning." *2nd IEE International Conference on Artificial Neural Networks,* pp. 49–53. Bournemouth, UK.

Schrodinger, E., 1952. *Statistical Thermodynamics: A Course of Seminal Lectures,* 2nd ed., New York: Cambridge University Press.

Schumaker, L.L., 1981. *Spline Functions: Basic Theory.* New York: Wiley

Schuster, H.G., 1988. *Deterministic Chaos: An Introduction.* Weinheim, Germany: VCH.

* Schwartz, A., 1993. ''A reinforcement learning method for maximizing undiscounted rewards.'' *Machine Learning: Proceedings of the Tenth International Conference.* San Mateo, CA: Morgan Kaufmann.

Schwartz, E.L., ed., 1990. *Computational Neuroscience.* Cambridge, MA: MIT Press.

Schwartz, R., Y. Chow, O. Kimball, S. Roucos, M. Krasner, and J. Makhoul, 1985. ''Context-dependent modeling for acoustic-phonetic recognition of continuous speech.'' *International Conference on Acoustics, Speech, and Signal Processing,* pp. 1205–1208, Tampa, FL.

Scofield, C.L., and L.N. Cooper, 1985. ''Development and properties of neural networks.'' *Contemporary Physics* **26,** 125–145.

Scott, A.C., 1977. *Neurophysics.* New York: Wiley.

Segee, B.E., and M.J. Carter, 1991. ''Fault tolerance of pruned multilayer networks.'' *International Joint Conference on Neural Networks,* Vol. 2, pp. 447-452, Seattle, WA.

* Sejnowski, T.J., 1976. ''On global properties of neuronal interaction.'' *Biological Cybernetics* **22,** 85–95.

Sejnowski, T.J., 1977a. ''Strong covariance with nonlinearly interacting neurons.'' *Journal of Mathematical Biology* **4,** 303–321.

* Sejnowski, T.J., 1977b. ''Statistical constraints on synaptic plasticity.'' *Journal of Theoretical Biology* **69,** 385–389.

* Sejnowski, T.J., and P.S. Churchland, 1989. ''Brain and cognition.'' In *Foundations of Cognitive Science* (M.I. Posner, ed.), pp. 301–356. Cambridge, MA: MIT Press.

Sejnowkski, T.J., and C.R. Rosenberg, 1987. ''Parallel networks that learn to pronounce English text.'' *Complex Systems* **1,** 145–168.

Sejnowski, T.J., P.K. Kienker, and G.E. Hinton, 1986. ''Learning symmetry groups with hidden units: Beyond the perceptron.'' *Physica* **22D,** 260–275.

* Sejnowski, T.J., C. Koch, and P.S. Churchland, 1988. ''Computational neuroscience.'' *Science* **241,** 1299–1306.

Sejnowski, T.J., B.P. Yuhas, M.H. Goldstein, Jr., and R.E. Jenkins, 1990. ''Combining visual and acoustic speech signals with a neural network improves intelligibility.'' In *Advances in Neural Information Processing Systems 2* (D.S. Touretzky, ed.), pp. 232–239. San Mateo, CA: Morgan Kaufmann.

Selfridge, O.G., R.S. Sutton, and C.W. Anderson, 1988. ''Selected bibliography on connectionism.'' *Evolution, Learning, and Cognition* (Y.C. Lee, ed.), pp. 391–403. Singapore: World Scientific.

* Shadafan, R.S., and M. Niranjan, 1993. ''A dynamical neural network architecture by sequential partitioning of the input space.'' *IEEE International Conference on Neural Networks,* Vol. I, pp. 226–231. San Francisco, CA.

Shah, S., and F. Palmieri, 1990. ''MEKA—A fast, local algorithm for training feedforward neural networks.'' *International Joint Conference on Neural Networks,* Vol. 3, pp. 41–46, San Diego, CA.

Shamma, S.A., 1989a. ''Spatial and temporal processing in central auditory networks.'' In *Methods in Neural Modeling* (C. Koch and I. Segev, eds.), pp. 247–289. Cambridge, MA: MIT Press.

* Shamma, S.A., 1989b. ''Stereausis: Binaural processing without delays.'' *Journal of the Acoustical Society of America* **86,** 989–1006.

Shanno, D.F., 1978. ''Conjugate gradient methods with inexact line searches.'' *Mathematics of Operations Research* **3,** 244–256.

Shannon, C.E., 1948. ''A mathematical theory of communication.'' *Bell System Technical Journal* **27,** pp. 379–423, 623–656.

Shannon, C.E., and W. Weaver, 1949. *The Mathematical Theory of Communication.* Urbana: University of Illinois Press.

* Shavlik, J.W., and T.G. Dietterich, eds., 1990. *Readings in Machine Learning.* San Mateo, CA: Morgan Kaufmann.

* Shepard, R.N., 1987. ''Toward a universal law of generalization for psychological science.'' *Science* **237,** 1317–1323.

* Shepherd, G.M., 1978. ''Microcircuits in the nervous system.'' *Scientific American* **238**(2), 92–103.

* Shepherd, G.M., 1979. *The Synaptic Organization of the Brain,* 2nd ed. New York: Oxford University Press.

Shepherd, G.M., 1988. *Neurobiology,* 2nd ed. New York: Oxford University Press.

Shepherd, G.M., ed., 1990a. *The Synaptic Organization of the Brain,* 3rd ed. New York: Oxford University Press.

Shepherd, G.M., 1990b. ''The significance of real neuron architectures for neural network simulations.'' In *Computational Neuroscience* (E.L. Schwartz, ed.), pp. 82–96. Cambridge, MA: MIT Press.

Shepherd, G.M., and C. Koch, 1990. ''Introduction to synaptic circuits.'' In *The Synaptic Organization of the Brain* (G.M. Shepherd, ed.), pp. 3–31. New York: Oxford University Press.

Sherrington, C.S., 1933. *The Brain and Its Mechanism.* London: Cambridge University Press.

* Sherrington, D., 1989. ''Spin glasses and neural networks.'' In *New Developments in Neural Computing* (J.G. Taylor and C.L.T. Mannion, eds.), pp. 15–30. Bristol, UK: Adam Hilger.

Sherrington, D., and S. Kirkpatrick, 1975. ''Spin-glasses,'' *Physical Review Letters* **35,** 1972.

Shynk, J.J., 1990. ''Performance surfaces of a single-layer perceptron.'' *IEEE Transactions on Neural Networks* **1,** 268–274.

Shynk, J.J., and N.J. Bershad, 1991. ''Steady-state analysis of a single-layer perceptron based on a system identification model with bias terms.'' *IEEE Transactions on Circuits and Systems* **CAS-38,** 1030–1042.

Shynk, J.J., and N.J. Bershad, 1992. ''Stationary points and performance surfaces of a perceptron learning algorithm for a nonstationary data model.'' *International Joint Conference on Neural Networks,* Vol. 2, pp. 133–139, Baltimore, MD.

* Simard, P., and Y. LeCun, 1992. ''Reverse TDNN: An architecture for trajectory generation.'' In *Advances in Neural Information Processing Systems 4* (J.E. Moody, S.J. Hanson, and R.P. Lippmann, eds.), pp. 579–588. San Mateo, CA: Morgan Kaufmann.

Simard, P.Y., M.B. Ottaway, and D.H. Ballard, 1989. ''Fixed point analysis for recurrent networks.'' In *Advances in Neural Information Processing Systems 1* (D.S. Touretzky, ed.), pp. 149–159. San Mateo, CA: Morgan Kaufmann.

Simard, P., B. Victorri, Y. LeCun, and J. Denker, 1992. ''Tangent prop—A formalism for specifying selected invariances in an adaptive network.'' In *Advances in Neural*

Information Processing Systems 4 (J.E. Moody, S.J. Hanson, and R.P. Lippmann, eds.), pp. 895–903. San Mateo, CA: Morgan Kaufmann.

Simard, P., Y. LeCun, and J. Denker, 1993. ''Efficient pattern recognition using a new transformation distance.'' In *Advances in Neural Information Processing Systems 5* (S.J. Hanson, J.D. Cowan, and C.L. Giles, eds.), pp. 50–58. San Mateo, CA: Morgan Kaufmann.

* Simmons, J.A., 1989. ''A view of the world through the bat's ear: The formation of acoustic images in echolocation.'' *Cognition* **33,** 155–199.

Simmons, J.A., 1991. ''Time-frequency transforms and images of targets in the sonar of bats,'' *Princeton lectures on Biophysics.* NEC Research Institute, Princeton, NJ.

Simmons, J.A., and P.A. Saillant, 1992. ''Auditory deconvolution in echo processing by bats.'' *Computational Neuroscience Symposium,* pp. 15–32. Indiana University-Purdue University at Indianapolis.

Simmons, J.A., P.A. Saillant, and S.P. Dear, 1992. ''Through a bat's ear.'' *IEEE Spectrum* **29**(3), 46–48.

Singh, S.P., ed., 1992. *Approximation Theory, Spline Functions and Applications.* Dordrecht, The Netherlands: Kluwer.

Singhal, S., and L. Wu, 1989. ''Training feed-forward networks with the extended Kalman filter.'' *IEEE International Conference on Acoustics, Speech, and Signal Processing,* pp. 1187–1190, Glasgow, Scotland.

Singleton, R.C., 1962. ''A test for linear separability as applied to self, organizing machines.'' In *Self-Organizing Systems* (M.C. Yovits, G.T. Jacobi, and G.D. Goldstein, eds.), pp. 503–524. Washington, DC: Spartan Books.

* Sivilotti, M.A., M.A. Mahowald, and C.A. Mead, 1987. ''Real-time visual computations using analog CMOS processing arrays.'' In *Advanced Research in VLSI: Proceedings of the 1987 Stanford Conference* (P. Losleben, ed.), pp. 295–312. Cambridge, MA: MIT Press.

* Skarda, C.A., and W.J. Freeman, 1987. ''How brains make chaos in order to make sense of the world.'' *Behavioral and Brain Sciences* **10,** 161–173.

Slepian, D., 1973. *Key Papers in the Development of Information Theory.* New York: IEEE Press.

Smith, M., 1993. *Neural Networks for Statistical Modeling.* New York: Van Nostrand Reinhold.

* Smolensky, P., 1988. ''On the proper treatment of connectionism.'' *Behavioral and Brain Sciences* **11,** 1–74.

* Snyder, W., D. Nissman, D. Van den Bout, and G. Bilbro, 1991. ''Kohonen networks and clustering.'' In *Advances in Neural Information Processing Systems 3* (R.P. Lippmann, J.E. Moody, and D.S. Touretzky, eds.), pp. 984–990. San Mateo, CA: Morgan Kaufmann.

* Solla, S., E. Levine, and M. Fleisher, 1988. ''Accelerated learning in layered neural networks.'' *Complex Systems* **2,** 625–640.

* Sommerhoff, G., 1974. *The Logic of the Living Brain.* London: Wiley.

Sompolinksy, H., and I. Kanter, 1986. ''Temporal association in asymmetric neural networks.'' *Physical Review Letters* **57,** 2861–2864.

Sondhi, M.M., 1967. ''An adaptive echo canceller.'' *Bell System Technical Journal* **46,** 497–511.

Sondhi, M.M., and D.A. Berkley, 1980. ''Silencing echoes in the telephone network.'' *Proceedings of the IEEE* **68,** 948–963.

* Sontag, E.D., 1989. ''Sigmoids distinguish more efficiently than Heavisides.'' *Neural Computation* **1,** 470–472.

Sontag, E.D., 1992. ''Feedback stabilization using two-hidden-layer nets.'' *IEEE Transactions on Neural Networks* **3,** 981–990.

* Southwell, R.V., 1946. *Relaxation Methods in Theoretical Physics.* New York: Oxford University Press.

Specht, D.F., 1966. ''Generation of polynomial discriminant functions for pattern recognition,'' *Technical Report* No. 6764-5. Stanford Electronics Laboratories, Stanford University, Stanford, CA.

Speidel, S.L., 1991. ''Sonar scene analysis using neurobionic sound reverberation.'' *IEEE Conference on Neural Networks for Ocean Engineering,* pp. 77–90, Washington, DC.

Sprecher, D.A., 1965. ''On the structure of continuous functions of several variables.'' *Transactions of the American Mathematical Society* **115,** 340–355.

* Stanton, P.K., and T.J. Sejnowski, 1989. ''Associative long-term depression in the Hippocampus induced by Hebbian covariance.'' *Nature* (*London*) **339,** 215–218.

Steinbuch, K., 1961. ''Die Lernmatrix.'' *Kybernetik* **1,** 36–45.

* Steinbuch, K., 1990. ''Die Lernmatrix—The beginning of associative memories.'' In *Advanced Neural Computers* (R. Eckmiller, ed.), pp. 21–29. Amsterdam: North-Holland.

* Steinbuch, K., and U.A.W. Piske, 1963. ''Learning matrices and their applications.'' *IEEE Transactions on Electronic Computers* **EC-12,** 846–862.

Stent, G.S., 1973. ''A physiological mechanism for Hebb's postulate of learning.'' *Proceedings of the National Academy of Sciences of the U.S.A.* **70,** 997–1001.

Sterling, P., 1990. ''Retina.'' In *The Synaptic Organization of the Brain* (G.M. Shepherd, ed.), 3rd ed., pp. 170–213. New York: Oxford University Press.

* Sterzing, V., and B. Schürmann, 1993. ''Recurrent neural networks for temporal learning of time series.'' *IEEE International Conference on Neural Networks,* Vol. 2, pp. 843–846, San Francisco, CA.

Stevens, C.F., 1979. ''The neuron.'' *Scientific American* **241,** 54–65.

Stevenson, M., R. Winter, and B. Widrow, 1990. ''Sensitivity of layered neural networks to errors in the weights.'' *International Joint Conference on Neural Networks,* Vol. 1, pp. 337–340, Washington, DC.

* Stiles, G.S., and D-L. Deng, 1985. ''On the effect of noise on the Moore-Penrose generalized inverse associative memory.'' *IEEE Transactions on Pattern Analysis and Machine Intelligence* **PAMI-7,** 358–360.

Stone, M., 1974. ''Cross-validatory choice and assessment of statistical predictions.'' *Journal of the Royal Statistical Society* **B36,** 111–133.

Stone, M., 1978. ''Cross-validation: A review.'' *Mathematische Operationsforschung Statistischen, Serie Statistics* **9,** 127–139.

Stork, D., 1989. ''Is backpropagation biologically plausible.'' *International Joint Conference on Neural Networks,* Vol. 2, pp. 241–246, Washington, DC.

Strang, G., 1980. *Linear Algebra and Its Applications.* New York: Academic Press.

Suga, N., 1985. ''The extent to which bisonar information is represented in the bat auditory cortex.'' In *Dynamic Aspects of Neocortical Function* (G.M. Edelman, W.E. Gall, and W.M. Cowan, eds.), pp. 653–695. New York: Wiley (Interscience).

Suga, N., 1990a. ''Cortical computational maps for auditory imaging.'' *Neural Networks* **3,** 3–21.

Suga, N., 1990b. ''Computations of velocity and range in the bat auditory system for echo location.'' In *Computational Neuroscience* (E.L. Schwartz, ed.), pp. 213–231. Cambridge, MA: MIT Press.

* Suga, N., 1990c. ''Biosonar and neural computation in bats.'' *Scientific American* **262**(6), 60–68.

* Sun, G.C., and D.L. Chenoweth, 1991. ''Principal components applied to multi-layer perceptron learning.'' *2nd IEE International Conference on Artificial Neural Networks,* pp. 100–102, Bournemouth, UK.

* Sussman, H., 1989. ''The mathematical theory of learning algorithms for Boltzmann machines.'' *International Joint Conference on Neural Networks,* Vol. 2, pp. 431–457, Washington, DC.

Sutton, R.S., 1984. ''Temporal credit assignment in reinforcement learning.'' Ph.D. Dissertation, University of Massachusetts, Amherst, MA.

Sutton, R.S., 1986. ''Two problems with back-propagation and other steepest-descent learning procedures for networks.'' *Proceedings of the Eighth Annual Conference of the Cognitive Science Society,* pp. 823–831. Hillsdale, NJ: Lawrence Erlbaum.

Sutton, R.S., 1988. ''Learning to predict by the methods of temporal differences.'' *Machine Learning* **3,** 9–44.

Sutton, R.S., ed., 1992a. Special Issue on Reinforcement Learning. *Machine Learning* **8,** 1–395.

Sutton, R.S., 1992b. ''Gain adaptation beats least square?'' In *Proceedings of the Seventh Yale Workshop on Adaptive and Learning Systems,* pp. 161–166. New Haven, CT: Yale University.

* Sutton, R.S., and A.G. Barto, 1981. ''Toward a modern theory of adaptive networks: Expectation and prediction.'' *Psychological Review* **88,** 135–170.

Sutton, R.S., A.G. Barto, and R.J. Williams, 1991. ''Reinforcement learning is direct adaptive optimal control.'' *Proceedings of the American Control Conference,* pp. 2143–2146, Boston, MA.

* Szu, H., 1986. ''Fast simulated annealing.'' In *Neural Networks for Computing* (J.S. Denker, ed.), pp. 420–425. New York: American Institute of Physics.

Szymanski, P.T., and M.D. Lemmon, 1993. ''Adaptive mixtures of local experts are source coding solutions.'' *IEEE International Conference on Neural Networks,* Vol. 3, pp. 1391–1396, San Francisco, CA.

* Takagi, H., 1993. ''Neural network and genetic algorithm techniques for fuzzy systems.'' *World Congress on Neural Networks,* Vol. 2, pp. 631–634, Portland, OR.

Takahashi, Y., 1993. ''Generalization and approximation capabilities of multilayer networks.'' *Neural Computation* **5,** 132–139.

Tang, D.S., 1990. ''Analytic solutions to the formation of feature-analysing cells of a three-layer feedforward visual information processing neural net.'' In *Advances in Neural Information Processing Systems 2* (D.S. Touretzky, ed.), pp. 160–165. San Mateo, CA: Morgan Kaufmann.

Tang, D.S., 1991. ''Information theory and early visual information processing.'' In *Self-Organization, Emerging Properties, and Learning* (A. Babloyantz, ed.), pp. 113–125. New York: Plenum.

* Tank, D.W., and J.J. Hopfield, 1986. ''Simple 'neural' optimization networks: An A/D

convertor, signal decision circuit, and a linear programming circuit.'' *IEEE Transactions on Circuits and Systems* **CAS-33,** 533–541.

* Tank, D.W., and J.J. Hopfield, 1987. ''Neural computation by concentrating information in time.'' *Proceedings of the National Academy of Sciences of the U.S.A.* **84,** 1896–1900.

Tapia, R.A., and J.R. Thompson, 1978. *Nonparametric Probability Density Estimation.* Baltimore: The Johns Hopkins University Press.

Taylor, W.K., 1956. ''Electrical simulation of some nervous system functional activities.'' In *Information Theory* (E.C. Cherry, ed.), Vol. 3, pp. 314–328. London: Butterworth.

* Taylor, W.K., 1964. ''Cortico-thalamic organization and memory.'' *Proceedings of the Royal Society of London, Series B* **159,** 466–478.

Tesauro, G., 1992. ''Practical issues in temporal difference learning.'' *Machine Learning* **8,** 257–277.

Tesauro, G., 1994. ''TD-Gammon, A self-teaching Backgammon program, achieves master-level play,'' *Neural Computation* **6,** to appear.

Tesauro, G., and R. Janssens, 1988. ''Scaling relationships in back-propagation learning.'' *Complex Systems* **2,** 39–44.

Teyler, T.J., 1986. ''Memory: Electrophysiological analogs.'' In *Learning and Memory: A Biological View* (J.L. Martinez, Jr. and R.S. Kesner, eds.), pp. 237–265. Orlando, FL: Academic Press.

Theodoridis, S., C.M.S. See, and C.F.N. Cowan, 1992. ''Nonlinear channel equalization using clustering techniques.'' *IEEE International Conference on Communications* Vol. 3, pp. 1277–1279, Chicago, IL.

Thorndike, E.L., 1911. *Animal Intelligence.* Darien, CT: Hafner.

Thrun, S.B., 1992. ''The role of exploration in learning control.'' In *Handbook of Intelligent Control* (D.A. White and D.A. Sofge, eds.), pp. 527–559. New York: Van Nostrand-Reinhold.

Tikhonov, A.N., 1963. ''On solving incorrectly posed problems and method of regularization.'' *Doklady Akademii Nauk USSR* **151,** 501–504.

Tikhonov, A.N., 1973. ''On regularization of ill-posed problems,'' *Doklady Akademii Nauk USSR* **153,** 49–52.

Tikhonov, A.N., and V.Y. Arsenin, 1977. *Solutions of Ill-posed Problems.* Washington, DC: W.H. Winston.

* Todd, P.M., and D.G. Loy, eds., 1991. *Music and Connectionism.* Cambridge, MA: MIT Press.

* Tombs, J., and L. Tarassenko, 1991. ''A fast novel, cascadable design for multi-layer networks.'' *2nd IEE International Conference on Artificial Neural Networks,* pp. 64–68, Bournemouth, UK.

Tomlinson, M.S., Jr., D.J. Walker, and M.A. Sivilotti, 1990. ''A digital neural network architecture for VLSI.'' *International Joint Conference on Neural Networks,* Vol. 2, pp. 545–550, San Diego, CA.

* Toomarian, N., and J. Barhen, 1991. ''Fast temporal neural learning using teacher forcing.'' *International Joint Conference on Neural Networks,* Vol. 1, pp. 817–822, Seattle, WA.

Touretzky, D.S., and D.A. Pomerleau, 1989. ''What's hidden in the hidden layers?'' *Byte* **14,** 227–233.

* Townshend, B., 1991. ''Nonlinear prediction of speech.'' *International Conference on Acoustics, Speech, and Signal Processing,* pp. 425–428, Toronto, Canada.

* Tuckwell, H.C., 1989. *Stochastic Processes in the Neurosciences.* Philadelphia, PA: Society for Industrial and Applied Mathematics.

Turing, A.M., 1952. ''The chemical basis of morphogenesis.'' *Philosophical Transactions of the Royal Society, Series B* **237,** 5–72.

Udin, S.B., and J.W. Fawcett, 1988. ''Formation of topographic maps.'' *Annual Review of Neuroscience* **2,** 289–327.

Ukrainec, A., and S. Haykin, 1989. ''Adaptive interference canceller.'' Canadian Patent 603,935.

Ukrainec, A., and S. Haykin, 1992. ''Enhancement of radar images using mutual information based unsupervised neural network.'' *Canadian Conference on Electrical and Computer Engineering,* pp. MA6.9.1–MA6.9.4, Toronto, Canada.

* Urbanczik, R., 1991. ''Learning temporal structures by continuous backpropagation,'' *2nd IEE International Conference on Artificial Neural Networks,* pp. 124–128, Bournemouth, UK.

Uttley, A.M., 1956. ''A theory of the mechanism of learning based on the computation of conditional probabilities.'' *Proceedings of the 1st International Conference on Cybernetics,* Namur, Gauthier-Villars, Paris.

* Uttley, A.M., 1966. ''The transmission of information and the effect of local feedback in theoretical and neural networks.'' *Brain Research* **102,** 23–35.

Uttley, A.M., 1979. *Information Transmission in the Nervous System.* London: Academic Press.

Valiant, L.G., 1984. ''A theory of the learnable.'' *Communications of the ACM* **27,** 1134–1142.

Van Essen, D.C., 1985. ''Functional organization of the primate visual cortex.'' In *Cerebral Cortex* (A. Peters and E.G. Jones, eds.), pp. 259–329, New York: Plenum.

Van Essen, D.C., C.H. Anderson, and D.J. Felleman, 1992. ''Information processing in the primate visual system: An integrated systems perspective.'' *Science* **255,** 419–423.

van Laarhoven, P.J.M., and E.H.L. Aarts, 1988. *Simulated Annealing: Theory and Applications.* Boston, MA: Kluwer Academic Publishers.

Van Trees, H.L., 1968. *Detection, Estimation, and Modulation Theory,* Part I. New York: Wiley.

Vapnik, V.N., 1982. *Estimation of Dependences Based on Empirical Data.* New York: Springer-Verlag.

Vapnik, V.N., 1992. ''Principles of risk minimization for learning theory.'' In *Advances in Neural Information Processing Systems 4* (J.E. Moody, S.J. Hanson, and R.P. Lippmann, eds.), pp. 831–838. San Mateo, CA: Morgan Kaufmann.

Vapnik, V.N., and A.Y. Chervonenkis, 1971. ''On the uniform convergence of relative frequencies of events to their probabilities.'' *Theoretical Probability and Its Applications,* **17,** 264–280.

Venkatesh, S.S., 1986. ''Epsilon capacity of neural networks.'' In *Neural Networks for Computing* (J.S. Denker, ed.), pp. 440–445. New York: American Institute of Physics.

Venkatesh, S.S., G. Panche, D. Psaltis, and G. Sirat, 1990. ''Shaping attraction basins in neural networks.'' *Neural Networks* **3,** 613–623.

Viterbi, A.J., 1967. ''Error bounds for convolutional codes and an asymptotically optimum decoding algorithm.'' *IEEE Transactions on Information Theory* **IT-13,** 260–269.

von der Malsburg, C., 1973. ''Self-organization of orientation sensitive cells in the striate cortex.'' *Kybernetik* **14,** 85–100.

* von der Malsburg, C., 1981. ''The correlation theory of brain function,'' *Internal Report 82-2* Department of Neurobiology, Max-Planck-Institute for Biophysical Chemistry, Göttingen, Germany.

von der Malsburg, C., 1990a. ''Network self-organization.'' In *An Introduction to Neural and Electronic Networks* (S.F. Zornetzer, J.L. Davis, and C. Lau, eds.), pp. 421–432. San Diego, CA: Academic Press.

von der Malsburg, C., 1990b. ''Considerations for a visual architecture.'' In *Advanced Neural Computers* (R. Eckmiller, ed.), pp. 303–312. Amsterdam: North-Holland.

von der Malsburg, C., and W. Schneider, 1986. ''A neural cocktail party processor.'' *Biological Cybernetics* **54,** 29–40.

von Neumann, J., 1956. ''Probabilistic logics and the synthesis of reliable organisms from unreliable components.'' In *Automata Studies* (C.E. Shannon and J. McCarthy, eds.), pp. 43–98. Princeton, NJ: Princeton University Press.

von Neumann, J., 1958. *The Computer and the Brain.* New Haven, CT: Yale University Press.

von Neumann, J., 1986. *Papers of John von Neumann on Computing and Computer Theory* (W. Aspray and A. Burks, eds.). Cambridge, MA: MIT Press.

Waibel, A., and K. Lee, eds., 1990. *Readings in Speech Recognition,* pp. 1–5. San Mateo, CA: Morgan Kaufmann.

Waibel, A., T. Hanazawa, G. Hinton, K. Shikano, and K.J. Lang, 1989. ''Phoneme recognition using time-delay neural networks.'' *IEEE Transactions on Acoustics, Speech, and Signal Processing* **ASSP-37,** 328–339.

* Walter, J.A., and K.S. Schulten, 1993. ''Implementation of self-organizing neural networks for visuo-motor control of an industrial robot.'' *IEEE Transactions on Neural Networks,* **4,** 86–95.

Waltz, M.D., and K.S. Fu, 1965. ''A heuristic approach to reinforcement learning control systems.'' *IEEE Transactions on Automatic Control* **AC-10,** 390–398.

Wan, E.A., 1990a. ''Temporal backpropagation for FIR neural networks.'' *IEEE International Joint Conference on Neural Networks,* Vol. 1, pp. 575–580, San Diego, CA.

Wan, E.A., 1990b. ''Temporal backpropagation: An efficient algorithm for finite impulse response neural networks.'' In *Proceedings of the 1990 Connectionist Models Summer School* (D.S. Touretzky, J.L. Elman, T.J. Sejnowski, and G.E. Hinton, eds.), pp. 131–140. San Mateo, CA: Morgan Kaufmann.

Wan, E.A., 1994. ''Time series prediction by using a connectionist network with internal delay lines.'' In *Time Series Prediction: Forecasting the Future and Understanding the Past* (A.S. Weigend and N.A. Gershenfeld, eds.), pp. 195–217. Reading, MA: Addison-Wesley.

Wang, L.-X., and J.M. Mendel, 1992. ''Back-propagation fuzzy systems as nonlinear dynamic system identifiers.'' *IEEE International Conference on Fuzzy Systems,* pp. 1409–1418, San Diego, CA.

Watanabe, T., K. Kimura, M. Aoki, T. Sakata, and K. Ito, 1993. ''A single 1.5-V digital chip for a 10^6 synapse neural network.'' *IEEE Transactions on Neural Networks* **4,** 387–393.

Watkins, C.J.C.H., 1989. ''Learning from delayed rewards.'' Ph.D. Thesis, University of Cambridge, UK.

Watkins, C.J.C.H., and P. Dayan, 1992. ''Q-learning.'' *Machine Learning* **8,** 279–292.

Watrous, R.L., 1987. ''Learning algorithms for connectionist networks: Applied gradient methods of nonlinear optimization.'' *1st IEEE International Conference on Neural Networks,* Vol. 2, pp. 619–627, San Diego, CA.

Watts, L., D.A. Kerns, R.F. Lyon, and C.A. Mead, 1992. ''Improved implementation of the silicon cochlea.'' *IEEE Journal of Solid-State Circuits* **27,** 692–700.

Webb, A.R., 1993. ''Functional approximation by feed-forward networks: A least-squares approach to generalisation.'' *IEEE Transactions on Neural Networks* **5,** to appear.

* Wechsler, H., ed., 1992. *Neural Networks for Perception,* Vols. 1 and 2. San Diego, CA: Academic Press.

Weigend, A.S., and N.A. Gershenfeld, eds., 1994. *Time Series Prediction: Forecasting the Future and Understanding the Past,* Vol. 15, Santa Fe Institute Studies in the Sciences of Complexity. Reading, MA: Addison-Wesley.

Weigend, A.S., D.E. Rumelhart, and B.A. Huberman, 1991. ''Generalization by weight-elimination with application to forecasting.'' In *Advances in Neural Information Processing Systems 3* (R.P. Lippmann, J.E. Moody, and D.S. Touretzky, eds.), pp. 875–882. San Mateo, CA: Morgan Kaufmann.

Wieland, A., and R. Leighton, 1987. ''Geometric analysis of neural network capabilities.'' *1st IEEE International Conference on Neural Networks,* Vol. 3, pp. 385–392. San Diego, CA.

Wejchert, J., and G. Tesauro, 1991. ''Visualizing processes in neural networks.'' *IBM Journal of Research and Development* **35,** 244–253.

* Welstead, S.T., 1991. ''Multilayer feedforward networks can learn strange attractors.'' *International Joint Conference on Neural Networks,* Vol. 2, pp. 139–144. Seattle, WA.

* Werblin, F.S., 1973. ''The control of sensitivity in the retina.'' *Scientific American* **228**(1), 70–79.

Werbos, P.J., 1974. ''Beyond regression: New tools for prediction and analysis in the behavioral sciences.'' Ph.D. Thesis, Harvard University, Cambridge, MA.

Werbos, P.J., 1989. ''Backpropagation and neurocontrol: A review and prospectus.'' *International Joint Conference on Neural Networks,* Vol. 1, pp. 209–216, Washington, DC.

Werbos, P.J., 1990. ''Backpropagation through time: What it does and how to do it.'' *Proceedings of the IEEE* **78,** 1550–1560.

Werbos, P.J., 1992. ''Neural networks and the human mind: New mathematics fits humanistic insight,'' *IEEE International Conference on Systems, Man, and Cybernetics,* Vol. 1, pp. 78–83, Chicago, IL.

Werbos, P.J., E. Marsh, K. Baheti, M. Burka, and H. Moraff, 1992. ''Forward.'' In *Handbook of Intelligent Control: Neural, Fuzzy, and Adaptive Approaches* (D.A. White and D.A. Sofge, eds.), pp. xi–xv. New York: Van Nostrand-Reinhold.

Wettschereck, D., and T. Dietterich, 1992. ''Improving the performance of radial basis function networks by learning center locations.'' In *Advances in Neural Information Processing Systems 4* (J.E. Moody, S.J. Hanson, and R.P. Lippmann, eds.), pp. 1133–1140. San Mateo, CA: Morgan Kaufmann.

Wheddon, C., 1990. ''Speech communication.'' In *Speech and Language Processing* (C. Wheddon and R. Linggard, eds.), pp. 1–28. London: Chapman & Hall.

White, D.A., and D. A. Sofge, eds., 1992. *Handbook of Intelligent Control: Neural, Fuzzy, and Adaptive Approaches.* New York: Van Nostrand-Reinhold.

White, H., 1989a. ''Learning in artificial neural networks: A statistical perspective.'' *Neural Computation* **1,** 425–464.

White, H., 1989b. "Some asymptotic results for learning in single hidden-layer feedforward network models." *Journal of the American Statistical Society* **84,** 1003–1013.

* White, H., 1990. "Connectionist nonparametric regression: Multilayer feedforward networks can learn arbitrary mappings." *Neural Networks* **3,** 535–549.

White, H., 1992. *Artificial Neural Networks: Approximation and Learning Theory.* Cambridge, MA: Blackwell.

Widrow, B., 1962. "Generalization and information storage in networks of adaline 'neurons'." In *Self-Organizing Systems* (M.C. Yovitz, G.T. Jacobi, and G.D. Goldstein, eds.), pp. 435–461. Washington, D.C.: Sparta.

Widrow, B., and M.E. Hoff, Jr., 1960. "Adaptive switching circuits." *IRE WESCON Convention Record,* pp. 96–104.

Widrow, B., and M.A. Lehr, 1990. "30 years of adaptive neural networks: Perceptron, madaline, and backpropagation." *Proceedings of the IEEE* **78,** 1415–1442.

Widrow, B., and S.D. Stearns, 1985. *Adaptive Signal Processing.* Englewood Cliffs, NJ: Prentice-Hall.

Widrow, B., P.E. Mantey, L.J. Griffiths, and B.B. Goode, 1967. "Adaptive antenna systems." *Proceedings of the IEEE* **55,** 2143–2159.

Widrow, B., N.K. Gupta, and S. Maitra, 1973. "Punish/reward: Learning with a critic in adaptive threshold systems." *IEEE Transactions on Systems, Man, and Cybernetics* **SMC-3,** 455–465.

Widrow, B., J.R. Glover, Jr., J.M. McCool, J. Kaunitz, C.S. Williams, R.H. Hearn, J.R. Zeidler, J. Dong, Jr., and R.C. Goodlin, 1975. "Adaptive noise cancelling: Principles and applications." *Proceedings of the IEEE* **63,** 1692–1716.

Wiener, N., 1948. *Cybernetics: Or, Control and Communication in the Animal and the Machine.* New York: Wiley.

Wiener, N., 1949. *Extrapolation, Interpolation, and Smoothing of Stationary Time Series with Engineering Applications.* Cambridge, MA: MIT Press. (This was originally issued as a classified National Defense Research Report, February 1942.)

Wiener, N., 1958. *Nonlinear Problems in Random Theory.* New York: Wiley.

Wiener, N., 1961. *Cybernetics,* 2nd ed. New York, Wiley.

Wilks, S.S., 1962. *Mathematical Statistics.* New York: Wiley.

Williams, R.J., 1985. "Feature discovery through error-correction learning," *Technical Report* ICS-8501. University of California, San Diego.

Williams, R.J., 1988. "Toward a theory of reinforcement-learning connectionist systems," Technical Report NU-CCS-88-3. College of Computer Science, Northeastern University, Boston, MA.

Williams, R.J., 1992. "Simple statistical gradient-following algorithms for connectionist reinforcement learning." *Machine Learning* **8,** 229–256.

Williams, R.J., and J. Peng, 1990. "An efficient gradient-based algorithm for on-line training of recurrent network trajectories." *Neural Computation* **2,** 490–501.

Williams, R.J., and D. Zipser, 1989. "A learning algorithm for continually running fully recurrent neural networks." *Neural Computation* **1,** 270–280.

Williamson, D., R.A. Kennedy, and G.W. Pulford, 1992. "Block decision feedback equalization." *IEEE Transactions on Communications* **40,** 255–264.

Willshaw, D.J., and C. von der Malsburg, 1976. "How patterned neural connections can be set up by self-organization." *Proceedings of the Royal Society of London, Series B* **194,** 431–445.

Willshaw, D.J., O.P. Buneman, and H.C. Longuet-Higgins, 1969. ''Non-holographic associative memory.'' *Nature* (*London*) **222,** 960–962.

Wilson, G.V., and G.S. Pawley, 1988. ''On the stability of the travelling salesman problem algorithm of Hopfield and Tank.'' *Biological Cybernetics* **58,** 63–70.

Wilson, H.R., and J.D. Cowan, 1972. ''Excitatory and inhibitory interactions in localized populations of model neurons.'' *Journal of Biophysics* **12,** 1–24.

Winograd, S., and J.D. Cowan, 1963. *Reliable Computation in the Presence of Noise.* Cambridge, MA: MIT Press.

* Wolverton, C.T., and T.J. Wagner, 1969. ''Asymptotically optimal discriminant functions for pattern classifiers.'' *IEEE Transactions on Information Theory* **IT-15,** 258–265.

* Wong, Y., 1991. ''How Gaussian radial basis functions work.'' *International Joint Conference on Neural Networks,* Vol. 2, pp. 133–138, Seattle, WA.

Woods, W.A., 1986. ''Important issues in knowledge representation.'' *Proceedings of the IEEE* **74,** 1322–1334.

* Wright, W.A., 1989. ''Probabilistic learning on a neural network.'' *1st IEE International Conference on Artificial Neural Networks,* pp. 153–157, London, UK.

Xu, L., and M.I. Jordan, 1993a. ''EM learning on a generalized finite mixture model for combining multiple classifiers.'' *World Congress on Neural Networks,* Vol. 4, pp. 227–230, Portland, OR.

Xu, L., and M.I. Jordan, 1993b. ''Unsupervised learning by EM algorithm based on finite mixture of Gaussians.'' *World Congress on Neural Networks,* Vol. 2, pp. 431–434, Portland, OR.

Xu, L., and A. Yuille, 1992. ''Robust PCA learning rules based on statistical physics approach.'' *International Joint Conference on Neural Networks,* Vol. 1, pp. 812–817, Baltimore, MD.

Yang, H., and M. Palaniswami, 1992. ''Convergence of self-organizing nets with high dimensional neighborhood relation.'' *International Joint Conference on Neural Networks,* Vol. 3, pp. 347–351, Baltimore, MD.

Yang, J., and G.A. Dumont, 1991. ''Classification of acoustic emission signals via Hebbian feature extraction.'' *International Joint Conference on Neural Networks,* Vol. 1, pp. 113–118, Seattle, WA.

* Yao, Y., and W.J. Freeman, 1990. ''Models of biological pattern recognition with spatially chaotic dynamics.'' *Neural Networks* **3,** 153–170.

Yee, P., 1992. ''Classification experiments involving back propagation and radial basis function networks,'' Report No. 249. Communications Research Laboratory, McMaster University, Hamilton, Ontario.

Yee, P., and S. Haykin, 1993. ''Pattern classification as an ill-posed, inverse problem: A regularization approach.'' *International Conference on Acoustics, Speech, and Signal Processing,* Vol. 1, pp. 597–600, Minneapolis, MN.

Yockey, H.P., 1992. *Information Theory and Molecular Biology.* Cambridge, UK: Cambridge University Press.

Yoshizawa, S., M. Morita, and S.-I. Amari, 1993. ''Capacity of associative memory using a nonmonotonic neuron model.'' *Neural Networks* **6,** 167–176.

Yuh, J.-D., and R.W. Newcomb, 1993. ''A multilevel neural network for A/D conversion.'' *IEEE Transactions on Neural Networks* **4,** 470–483.

Yuille, A.L., D.M. Kammen, and D.S. Cohen, 1989. ''Quadratic and the development of orientation selective cortical cells by Hebb rules.'' *Biological Cybernetics* **61,** 183–194.

Zadeh, L.A., 1953. ''A contribution to the theory of nonlinear systems.'' *Journal of the Franklin Institute* **255,** 387–401.

Zadeh, L.A., 1965. ''Fuzzy sets.'' *Information and Control* **8,** 338–353.

Zadeh, L.A., 1973. ''Outline of a new approach to the analysis of complex systems and decision processes.'' *IEEE Transactions on Systems, Man, and Cybernetics* **SMC-3,** 28–44.

* Zador, A., C. Koch, and T.H. Brown, 1990. ''Biophysical model of a Hebbian synapse.'' *International Joint Conference on Neural Networks,* Vol. 1, pp. 138–141, San Diego, CA.

Zeidler, J.R., 1990. ''Performance analysis of LMS adaptive prediction filters.'' *Proceedings of the IEEE* **78,** 1781–1806.

* Zhang, J., 1991. ''Dynamics and formulation of self-organizing maps.'' *Neural Computation* **3,** 54–66.

* Zipser, D., 1990. ''Subgrouping reduces complexity and speeds up learning in recurrent networks.'' In *Advances in Neural Information Processing Systems 2* (D.S. Touretzky, ed.), pp. 638–641. San Mateo, CA: Morgan Kaufmann.

Zipser, D., and D.E. Rumelhart, 1990. ''The neurobiological significance of the new learning models.'' In *Computational Neuroscience* (E.L. Schwartz, ed.), pp. 192–200. Cambridge, MA: MIT Press.

Zornetzer, S.F., J.L. Davis, and C. Lau, eds., 1990. *An Introduction to Neural and Electronic Networks.* San Diego, CA: Academic Press.

Index

P

Q

R

S